STONEWALL JACKSON

Books by James I. Robertson, Jr.

The Stonewall Brigade
The Civil War Letters of General Robert McAllister
4th Virginia Infantry
Civil War Sites in Virginia: A Tour Guide
18th Virginia Infantry
Soldiers Blue and Gray
General A. P. Hill: The Story of a Confederate Warrior
Civil War Virginia: Battleground for a Nation
Civil War! America Becomes One Nation

STONEWALL JACKSON

THE MAN, THE SOLDIER, THE LEGEND

James I. Robertson, Jr.

MACMILLAN PUBLISHING USA

New York

Maps by George Skoch; Wartime Winchester based on a map by Wilbur S. Johnston

Macmillan Publishing USA
1633 Broadway
New York, New York 10019

Library of Congress Catalog Card Number: 96-17042

Printed in the United States of America

printing number

1 2 3 4 5 6 7 8 9 10—ppr.
     5 6 7 8 9 0—case

Library of Congress Cataloging-in-Publication Data

Robertson, James I.
    Stonewall Jackson—the man, the soldier, the legend / by James I. Robertson, Jr.
        p.   cm.
    Includes bibliographical references and index.
    ISBN 0-02-864685-1 (hardc) (alk. paper)
    ISBN 0-02-865064-6 (pbk)
        1. Jackson, Stonewall, 1824–1863.   2. Generals—Confederate States of America—
Biography.   3. Confederate States of America.   Army—Biography.   I. Title.
E467.1J15R63   1997
973.7′092—dc20   96-17042
[B]   CIP

This paper meets the requirements of ANSI/NISO Z39.48-1992 (Permanence of Paper)

To Libba
whose understanding and love made it all possible

CONTENTS

PREFACE

THOMAS JONATHAN JACKSON'S walnut bookcase at the Virginia Historical Society contains six shelves filled with the volumes he collected. Almost in the center of the case stand three works side by side. The one in the middle is John Gibbon's *The Artillerist's Manual;* on its left is the Holy Bible; on the other side is Philip Bennet Power's *"I Will": Being the Determination of the Man of God.* These three books, positioned as they are, epitomize the life of General "Stonewall" Jackson: a man of arms surrounded by tenets of faith.

In 1861–63, his fame flashed across his own Southern Confederacy, soared over the land of his enemies, and traveled even beyond the seas. Jackson more than anyone else personified the compelling and the virtuous in what subsequent generations would label the "Lost Cause." Thousands of Southerners (and no small number of Northerners as well) would say for generations that, had Jackson lived, the Confederate quest for independence would have come much closer to realization.

Death removed him from the scene at the apogee of a military fame enjoyed by no other Civil War figure. His passing at a high point in Confederate success was the greatest personal loss suffered by the wartime South.[1] Jackson became the first icon, the ultimate offering for the Southern cause. Death at the hour of his most spectacular victory led to more poems of praise than did any other single event of the war. Jackson was the only officer to be pictured on Confederate currency, and his likeness graced the most expensive note issued in Richmond: a $500 bill.

His fame went beyond the borders of the wartime South. The Confederacy christened two naval vessels as the *Stonewall.* The first, a pilot boat, fell into Union hands in February 1863 and was converted into a tender for the remainder of the war. Although Federals employed the boat for a different mission, out of courtesy they retained the name *Stonewall.*

The exciting hopes of the South in 1861 and the smashing victories "Old Jack" achieved in 1862 lost much of their brilliance with his death in the war's third spring. Yet his devotion to God, duty, and country remain treasured legacies of the American people, just as they are inspirations to people everywhere.

Lord Frederick Roberts, commander in chief of the British armies in the early twentieth century, remarked: "In my opinion Stonewall Jackson was one of the greatest natural military geniuses the world ever saw. I will go even further than that—as a campaigner in the field he never had a superior. In some respects I doubt whether he ever had an equal." Fifty years later, General Douglas MacArthur characterized Jackson as "one of the most remarkable soldiers we have ever known. His mastery of two of the greatest elements for victory in war—surprise and envelopment—never has been surpassed. His magnetic personal leadership, which so dominated and inspired his men, constituted only one of his many attributes of greatness."[2]

Dr. Moses D. Hoge, a pillar of Presbyterianism at the time of the Civil War, saw the Virginian in a quite different light. "To attempt to portray the life of Jackson," Hoge said, "while leaving out the religious element, would be like undertaking to describe Switzerland without making mention of the Alps." English clergyman S. Parkes Cadman gave a more detailed explanation of the impact religion made on Jackson's character. "His alliance with eternal realities; his foretaste of the powers of the world to come; his deep and genuine piety, his adherence to the Bible, the Church, and the Lord's day, his keeping of his own conscience before God and men, are the outstanding traits of a spiritual prince who was greater than anything he did, and whose deeds took rise in his being."[3]

Jackson's faith permeated every action of his adult life. He began each task by offering a blessing, and he completed every duty by returning thanks to God. To say merely that he kept the Sabbath holy would be an understatement. In the prewar years, he would not read a newspaper or discuss secular subjects on Sunday. Jackson even refused to write letters on "the Lord's day." Of the eighty-eight letters excerpted in the biography by his nephew, none bears a Sunday date. Thirty-one were written on Saturday and twenty-seven on Monday. Letters penned on Friday and Saturday were not posted until at least the following Monday.[4]

Divine love and personal self-discipline combined in Jackson to create absolute fearlessness. He could look forward to the next world because he was so constantly aware of its existence.

Military genius and religious devotion are not common traits among mankind. When one individual possesses both seemingly incompatible qualities, he stands alone on a high pedestal that is extraordinary to some, enigmatic to others.

Jackson may be difficult to understand because he was a fascinating mixture of contrasts: complexity and simplicity, harshness and softness, restlessness and repose, eccentricity and excellence, ambition and humility, wrathfulness and righteousness. His comments may have been perceptive, but they were sometimes unorthodox.

In battle, he often said "Good, good," or "Very commendable," whether he was praising Confederate gains or reacting to bad news. Once when asked why he had appointed a personally unpopular officer to an important post, Jackson answered, "As he has no friends, he will be impartial in his reports." On another occasion, he and an aide were riding in the Shenandoah Valley. Jackson had been silent for a long period. The two men stopped to water their horses. The general was remounting when he turned to his companion and asked innocently, "Did you ever think, sir, what an opportunity a battlefield affords liars?"[5]

Strange utterances, and equally strange actions, gave rise to a host of exaggerations, fabrications, and outright untruths about Jackson. Yes, he had many strange mannerisms, but some were honest attempts to combat ailments both real and imagined. He believed in physical fitness and aerobics decades before either became an art. Many of his behavior patterns were unusual; a few seemed unprecedented. However, a staff officer wrote shortly after the war, "It has been the fashion to dwell on his peculiarities till one who does not know something of him is apt to get a view of him almost grotesque which does him an injustice." A minister and close friend added: "In his ordinary course with men, there was nothing about him to attract special observation, or to call for remark of any kind. His manners, it is true, were not 'polished,' but neither were they constrained. . . . He was just a simple *gentleman*."[6]

Throughout his adult years he followed a strict diet in an effort to overcome the sharp pangs of dyspepsia. That in turn gave rise to one of the most persistent of the Jackson myths, and one totally without foundation: his supposed infatuation with lemons. Novelist John Esten Cooke was one of the first writers to concoct the story of Jackson gnawing feverishly on lemons. General Richard Taylor adorned it shortly by asserting that Jackson "was rarely without one." Taylor always had a tendency in his postwar writings to convert everyone into characters—especially his own superior, General Richard S. Ewell.[7]

No member of Jackson's staff, no friend, not even his wife ever mentioned Jackson having a particular penchant for lemons. His Virginia Military Institute colleague, Raleigh Colston, tried to put the story to rest by declaring that a lemon was "a rare treat" that Jackson "enjoyed greatly whenever it could be obtained from the enemy's camp." Yet that seemed only to give credence to the Jackson-and-lemons tale.[8]

The truth of the matter is that the general loved all fruit. Peaches were his favorite; but he enjoyed with relish lemons, oranges, watermelons, apples, grapes, berries, or whatever was available. Still, the lemon myth refuses to die.

Such odd habits merely heightened the mystique that swirled around Jackson the soldier. A Confederate chaplain wrote in wonder: "His appearance at any part of the line always and instantly roused . . . wild cheers [that] rent the air as long as he was in sight. . . . This popularity was all the more remarkable when it is remembered that he was very stern, very silent, very reserved, and by no means an ideal leader in appearance." A commissary in one of Jackson's brigades presented a widely accepted interpretation of the general: "Nobody seemed to understand him. But so it has been and ever will be: when we ordinary mortals can't comprehend a genius we get even with him by calling him crazy."[9]

In truth, however, Jackson's many facets formed a natural and acceptable blend in his makeup. Only modern writers have created the double-imaged figure of inconsistencies. Those who knew Jackson agreed with John T. L. Preston, one of the founders of the Virginia Military Institute. Jackson might have been "the object of pleasant jests for singularities and peculiarities," Preston declared, "but the confidence of his integrity, force of character, and soundness of mind was universal." Fifty years ago, the most noted historian of the Army of Northern Virginia admitted the modern difficulty of trying to capture the full depiction of Jackson. "The taste of our generation would tone down the pigments his contemporaries used. . . . He does not lend himself to portraiture. His features, his peculiarities and his subtler characteristics must be developed slowly, shade after shade, by verbal color printing."[10]

To understand Jackson, one must begin with a childhood so filled with loneliness that he would not discuss it in later years. He never knew his father, who died (along with an older sister) when Jackson was two. His mother died five years later after entrusting him to other members of the family. She was always an inspiration in his dreams, not in his memories.

A younger sister, Laura, was all that remained of Jackson's immediate kin. They were raised miles apart. Jackson's guardian was a bachelor uncle whose interests lay in material things. Cummins Jackson gave his nephew security. The lad interpreted that as love. In such surroundings, Thomas Jackson should have matured with strong attitudes of cynicism and connivance. Instead, and on his own, he developed an unwavering honesty, a powerful sense of integrity, and deep feelings of responsibility; and he did it all with a minimum of formal education as well as little or no religious training.

West Point was the greatest challenge of Jackson's formative years. He saw the military school as the one opportunity to improve his lot in life. Yet he was ill prepared for the classroom challenges of the academy. He struggled initially; he pursued studies falteringly but with an unbreakable determination expressed in one of his favorite axioms: "You may be what ever you resolve to be."

With no time for frivolities and little talent in making friends, his cadet years were solitary. Loneliness, awkwardness, obsessive uncertainty about his health, the hope somehow of restoring luster to a tarnished family name, all induced Jackson to mold his life into a rigid orderliness that struck many as eccentric. Surprises he did not understand; mistakes he would not tolerate.

The Mexican War brought him a hero's mantle, three brevet promotions, and the realization that the systematized regimen of a military environment was his natural milieu. When the same sense of duty that made him a good soldier threatened his career in 1851, Jackson left the army but not the military. For the next ten years he was a professor of optics and artillery tactics at the Virginia Military Institute. Lexington became the only permanent home Jackson ever knew. There he acquired social graces, two wives, and civic attainments that compensated in large part for his poor reputation as a teacher. The emptiness of childhood slowly receded into the past.

It was also in Lexington that the other factor so vital to Jackson's life emerged. He found the Presbyterian church and in it the God with whom he could be absolutely comfortable. From the moment of his alignment with the Presbyterian faith, Jackson gave his whole allegiance to living the Christian life.

James Power Smith, one of his faithful aides in war, observed in later years that "the religion of Jackson was the man himself. It was not only that he was a religious man, but that he was that rare man among men to whom religion was everlasting." Smith also made a prediction: "The religion of Stonewall Jackson will be the chief and most effective way into the secret spring of the character and career of this strong man."[11]

Buoyed by faith, Jackson came to understand that his youth and the deaths of his parents, siblings, first wife, and first two children were all part of a divine purpose. Turning to God because he had nowhere else to go, Jackson fervently absorbed the biblical assurance that "all things work together for good to them that love God."

He was thirty-four when he bought his first—and only—home. For a year and a half he knew its sanctuary and its pleasures. Then came civil war. Love of his birthright, Virginia, was one reason Jackson sided with the Southern cause. Defense of hearth and home was another. A third was more philosophical.

Like many men of the South in 1860, Jackson was convinced that Northerners had violated principles of both the Founding Fathers and Christianity by attempting to create a new society that lacked order as well as cohesiveness. The North seemed to be striving to alter basic American structures. Such activity flew in the face of God's preordained notion of what America should be. If the South did not resist, it would stand in failure of God's will and possibly become subservient to Northern domination. Thus, in the words of a recent writer, much of the Confederate ideology to which Jackson subscribed "transformed God himself into a nationalist and made war for political independence into a crusade."[12]

At the order of Virginia authorities, Jackson led the VMI cadets into service. When he departed Lexington that Sunday afternoon in April 1861, "the Major" had no way of knowing that he would never see his adopted hometown again.

Fame and an eternal nickname came to Jackson in the first major battle of the war. By the following spring, an irresolute Confederacy seemed tottering near the edge of defeat. Suddenly Jackson exploded into action in the Shenandoah Valley. Federal forces exuding high confidence one week were fleeing across the Potomac the next; Union confidence turned to concern; officials in Washington went into near panic and sounded the call for additional troops—all the result of an obscure, stern, and reticent Southern general who seemed to be everywhere and nowhere at the same time.

A North Carolina drillmaster remarked at the time: "It seems Jackson is to be the Napoleon of this war. . . . He resembles Bonaparte in his plan of beating the enemy in detail, in his rapidity of movement and execution, in the attachment of his troops and above all in his good fortune which has never deserted him. He has put an entirely new face upon the appearance of this War." By the end of spring 1862, Jackson was arguably the most famous field commander in the world. North and South alike viewed his aggressiveness with wonder. A leader of the U.S. Sanitary Commission in Washington conceded that Jackson "has evinced more genius & more real adequacy to military success than any body on either side."[13]

One of Jackson's classmates at West Point (and a Union officer in the Civil War) wrote in the 1880s:

His chief characteristics as a military leader were his quick perceptions of the weak points of the enemy, his ever readiness, the astounding rapidity of his movements, his sudden and unexpected onslaughts, and the persistency with which he followed them up. His ruling maxim was that war meant fighting, and fighting meant killing, and right loyally did he live up to it. Naturally taciturn, and by habit the keeper of his own designs, it was as difficult for his friends to penetrate them, as it was easy for him to deceive the enemy. . . .

In any other person this would have been taken as cunning and deceit; but with him it was the voice of the Lord piloting him to the tents of the Midianites.[14]

Unspoken throughout all this praise was the tacit understanding that Jackson's achievements came as a subaltern, not as the commander of a full army. His executive ability was perhaps unrivaled. Yet he lacked the administrative skills and the political tact to manage a major host while appeasing president, politicians, and the press. Jackson's no-nonsense approach to war served him well in the field. It would have brought him major problems as an army leader with a dozen armchair generals looking constantly over his shoulders.

In many ways, Jackson blended religion and war. When the sectional struggle began, for example, no list of regulations existed for the composition of a general's staff. Commanders were left in the main to amass and use whatever size staff they saw fit. Jackson put together a rather large inner family of aides, and in recommending staff appointments he attached overriding importance to a man's piety. His simple deduction was that a good Christian could serve well at any task.

Hence, his staff ranked among the most devout in the entire Civil War. An early chief of staff, Robert L. Dabney, was an esteemed Presbyterian cleric. Jackson's favorite staff officer, "Sandie" Pendleton, was the son of an Episcopal rector. Another aide, James Power Smith, left divinity studies to join the staff. R. Kidder Meade was the grandson of an Episcopal bishop. Kyd Douglas was the son of a Dutch Reformed minister. Joseph G. Morrison grew up in a Presbyterian manse.[15]

Jackson always believed in aggressive action: prompt, fierce, and decisive. Strike the foe before he can deliver a blow. If repulsed, fall back and be ready instantly to strike again if the opportunity arises. Seek ever to change a defeat into victory. If successful in the attack, pursue the enemy relentlessly and, by decisive assaults, destroy the force in front. This will end the war.

Such strategy worked brilliantly for Jackson. A widely circulated story throughout the Confederacy was of the devil sending Jackson a petition to stop sending him so many Yankees because he was running out of room![16]

Years after the war, a Manassas resident who as a lad saw Jackson several times summed up the general succinctly: "Wasn't much to look at, but you ought to have seen how his men would look at him. Just like he was God himself." Soldiers idolized him. A brigadier general (whom Jackson did not particularly like) explained in part why. "It was their common baptism of fire in the battles . . . and his absolute fearlessness, if not unconsciousness, of danger, which endeared him to his men; and gave rise to the saying, when a shout was heard on the march, or in camp, 'Pshaw! It is only Jackson or a rabbit!'"[17]

His calmness in battle was likewise inspirational. Only three times in the Civil War—at Winchester, Gaines' Mill, and Cedar Mountain—did Jackson evince great excitement. Then, one of his compatriots observed, his "fiery spirit fairly broke from his customary restraints and bore him away with a tempest of passion and triumph by which his face and person were literally transfigured."[18]

History remembers him as "Stonewall," a sobriquet that received mixed reactions from his soldiers. Aide James Power Smith explained: "Outwardly, Jackson was not a stone wall, for it was not in his nature to be stable and defensive, but vigorously active. He was an avalanche from an unexpected quarter. He was a thunderbolt from a clear sky. And yet he was in character and will more like a stone wall than any man I have known. . . . No one of his staff ever knew him to change his mind." Complete secretiveness marked the General's every move. Smith noted: "He mystified and deceived the enemy by concealment from his own generals and his own staff. We were led to believe things that were very far from his purpose." Jackson liked it that way. With compelling logic, he once asserted, "If I can keep my movements secret from my own people, I will have little difficulty in concealing them from the enemy."[19]

That extreme taciturn nature, combined with Jackson's belief in blind obedience to orders, often led to confusion both on the march and in battle. Jackson would have been more successful as a field commander if he had been more communicative—if he had followed the example of General John Sedgwick, for example. That Union officer placed a man of limited intelligence on his staff. The aide's major task was to read Sedgwick's orders and announce whether or not he understood them.

Seeking always to escape the limelight brought Jackson distinction as well as constant attention. His homeliness appealed to the common folk. Modesty was among his greatest attractions. "He would blush like a school-girl at a compliment," his brother-in-law noted. "He was easily confused by the presence of strangers, especially if they were ladies." Praise made Jackson genuinely uncomfortable. The same writer commented of hearing Jackson say that "the honor paid to himself, and Gen. Lee, filled him with alarm."[20]

The Confederate people believed that Jackson was oblivious to his own greatness. A number of Southern writers extolled "the magnificent plainness of 'Stonewall' Jackson." His natural shyness and devotion to duty were part of the explanation; but there was something more.

Victories came solely from God, who was alone entitled to the credit. Earthly ambition, as well as excess of love between all humans save inside families, was wrong. It tempted the wrath of a jealous God. To give too much attention to the world was to overlook part of the glory that lay in heaven.

Was Jackson ambitious? The answer is both yes and no. Surgeon Hunter McGuire came to know the general as well as anyone in the army. He thought that ambition was part of Jackson's makeup. "Under the grave and generally serious nature," McGuire stated, "there was intense earthly ambition. . . . Ambition! Yes, far beyond what ordinary men possess. And yet, he told me when talking in my tent one dreary winter night . . . that he would not exchange one moment of his life hereafter, for all the earthly glory he could win." The general's topographical engineer, "Jed" Hotchkiss, put Jackson's desire to succeed in a different light. "Of ambition in the ordinary sense of the term I do not think Jackson could be accused. He was brim full of a lofty earnestness or purpose to do his best in the sphere assigned to him and to accomplish results that might lead to the conclusion that he desired and that he prayed and believed to be desirable for his people. He never took credit for himself for any of his victories, and never spoke of them as personal matters."[21]

Jackson, in short, was an unaffected commander who cultivated humility as he sought success in the name of God. To many acquaintances, the motto of his life was, "Lord, what wilt Thou have me to do?"

As an instrument of "an all-wise Providence," therefore, Jackson fought with the zeal of a crusader and with the confidence that he was a military instrument of "an ever-kind Heavenly Father." That is why, after the battle of Fredericksburg, he could write a fellow officer: "Through God's blessing the enemy suffered severely."[22]

Jackson repeatedly told his soldiers, "Never take counsel of your fears." No place for fear existed if faith was strong. He demanded the impossible of his men for good reason: with God's abiding help, nothing was impossible. Jackson insisted on the same blind obedience to orders that he exhibited. For failure to do so, he would remove a general from command as swiftly as he court-martialed a private for violation of authority. Jackson's stern conception of duty was often an affront to human feelings. The latter, as far as he was concerned, were always subservient to the holy cause of the Confederacy.

He marched relentlessly, fought hard, and counseled with no one. He prayed often, in the solitude of his tent and in the chaos of battle. In preparation for combat, one of his brigadiers noted, Jackson "did not reach his conclusions hastily, but after mature deliberation and prayerful consideration; and when once definitely reached, he was like a meteor in executing." A Federal officer who termed Jackson "the sledgehammer of the war" was captured in battle. He was not prepared for the stern and un-prepossessing appearance of the Confederate commander. "The first time I saw his face, my heart sank within me."[23]

Margaret Junkin Preston, his sister-in-law and confidante, put Jackson's thinking in perfect context. "To serve his country, to do God's will, to make as short work as possible of the fearful struggle, to be ready for death if at any moment it should come to him—these were the uppermost ideals of his mind, and he would put aside, with an impatient expression, the words of confidence and praise that would be lavished upon him. 'Give God the glory' would be his curt reply."[24]

The Civil War was a contest in which both sides fought gallantly for the absolutes of freedom and independence. Yet Jackson constantly had a higher goal in mind. This servant of the Lord prayed intensely, led his forces with the hope that they might become "an army of the living God," and even found time in an hour of victory to send an overdue contribution to his home church. Such attitudes may have struck a few observers as unusual, but they were part of the magnetism that made good men want to serve under him.

By November 1862, a matron in the northern end of the Shenandoah Valley was writing: "No one would have thought one year ago that his fame would be spread the wide world over as one of the greatest of Captains. He may well be fearless, as he is ready to meet his God; his lamp is burning, and he waits for the bridegroom."[25]

The lamp flickered at Chancellorsville and went dark a week later. One reason Jackson's death struck the South so hard was the widespread belief that he had a charmed life and was immune from serious injury. In the eyes of Confederate soldiers, the general was indispensable. A Georgian acknowledged: "His fights were our fights, his victories were our victories. My individuality, with that of thousands of others, was represented in the power wielded by that great military chieftain." News of his death stunned the Army of Northern Virginia. "A greater sense of loss and deeper grief never followed the death of mortal man," a member of the Richmond Howitzers lamented. "Under him we had never suffered defeat. I don't believe we ever thought of it. We knew that he would provide for our needs to the full of his opportunities. We were the machine he needed to thresh his grain, and the machine must be in order. We knew he would not needlessly risk our lives, and we knew that when needful to accomplish an object, our lives were as nothing, success was all that counted. We had a confidence in him that knew no bounds, and he knew and appreciated it. He was a soldier, and a great one, to our cause; his loss was irreparable."[26]

Jackson's passing marked a line of demarcation in the annals of the Army of Northern Virginia. In the ten months that Lee and Jackson were together, delegation of authority had been so lenient—orders permitting a wide latitude in execution so regular—as to create one of history's greatest military partnerships. Thereafter, starting at Gettysburg, the system failed Lee. He had no executive officer of first-rate ability. He tried to do it all himself. It did not work.

Beyond Gettysburg, and without Jackson, lay something else about the Confederacy's premier army. Declining strength would naturally play a role; nevertheless, because there was no Jackson, Lee never again attempted the spectacular dividing of his army in the face of numerical superiority or the sweeping flank marches that he undertook when Jackson silently awaited his call. Jackson represented Lee's mobility, the prime ingredient the Southern army had to have for survival. Without it, the Civil War in the East became a slugging match that the Confederacy could not hope to win.

Judge George L. Christian expressed those thoughts in one of the countless eulogies to Jackson:

> A hero came among us, as we slept;
> At first he lowly knelt, then rose and wept,
> Then gathering up a thousand spears,
> He swept across the field of Mars,
> Then bowed farewell, and walked among the stars
> In the land where we were dreaming.[27]

Stonewall Jackson has been the subject of dozens of previous works. Too many are superficial studies based on a minimum of research into printed sources. Others are products of selective research done to "prove" preconceived notions. Several "biographies" concentrate on the battles rather than the leader, while others emphasize Jackson's alleged peculiarities and provide little enlightenment on the man. The genuinely good Jackson biographies number no more than a half-dozen and are unfortunately dated.

Intensive research eliminates most of the mystery surrounding Jackson. The answers to lingering questions about facets of his life and military career have lain for decades in manuscript sources previously overlooked. Valuable collections of papers bearing on the man exist in depositories from Massachusetts to California and from Michigan to Texas.

This study is not a biography of a great general; it is the life story of an extraordinary man who became a general. Because I have done research down every known path where Jackson material might exist, the thirty-nine years of his life can be told as completely as is possible at this time. No attempt has been made to explain in full detail the battles in which Jackson participated. It would be at the least redundant to present in-depth overviews when excellent book-length works are available on all of the major Civil War campaigns. The intent here is to see life as Jackson saw it, to hear his words, to read his thoughts, to walk beside him and know little more than he knew at a given time and place.

Quotations abound because of the need for (and the obvious value of) contemporary comments on Jackson and his activities. What the people of his age thought of him is the basis for the judgment of posterity. Those early opinions explain in large measure why Jackson's exploits and reputation have risen in esteem with the passage of time. Today he is an American hero. More than ever, Jackson embodies the famous observation made at his death by one of his former cadets: "He is not Virginia's alone: God gave him to the world."[28]

Another VMI student waited until 1886 to express his admiration. With the perspective of thirty years' reflection, Captain Thomas M. Boyd wrote of his commander: "His fame is as lasting as the solid stones of his native hills . . . and yet there is for him a purer, nobler record—his quiet Christian walk in life, his right words, his faithful, manly bearing, his victory over self, his known devotion to the word of truth. He was indeed a soldier of the cross."[29]

≈ ACKNOWLEDGMENTS ≈

Any writer who undertakes a full-length historical study should be aware that successful completion comes only with the help of others. Friends old and new encouraged me to produce a thoroughly researched biography of Stonewall Jackson, and their help at every step of the long journey was essential. It is not possible to thank everyone who contributed to this book.

This section was done last for fear that someone would be inadvertently omitted from the list of nice people to whom gratitude is openly expressed. To any helper who wrote or called and whose name does not appear here, please know that my apologies for the oversight are deeper than any disappointment you may feel.

Research is time consuming and expensive. A semester's leave from teaching granted by Virginia Tech enabled me to spend four uninterrupted months visiting depositories from New York to New Orleans. Travel expenses, motel bills, photocopies, microfilm, and other costs were absorbed by the Frank L. Curtis Memorial Fund, J. Ambler Johnston Research Fund for Virginia History, and James I. Robertson Endowment Fund, all part of the Virginia Tech Foundation.

A casual reading of the endnotes will give adequate proof that this book could not have been written without the assistance of many librarians, archivists, curators of manuscripts, and other custodians of unprinted materials. My special thanks go to the staffs of the depositories listed in the bibliography. Their cheerful assistance throughout the process of research made hard labor a pleasurable experience. To individuals who shared their private collections, and to curators and librarians who expressed regrets when queried at not being able to provide material, I am also deeply grateful.

For twenty-five years, Lowell Reidenbaugh has shared with me his incomparable knowledge of Jackson (as well as his damnation of writers who took liberties with facts about the general's life). His encouragement—as well as his participation—from start to end of this project were inestimable. Not only did he read each chapter twice; he never hesitated to make corrections, additions, and suggestions—every one of which enhanced the narrative. Lowell has been an ideal collaborator. I more than he am the better for it.

Michael Anne Lynn and Joanna L. Smith, Dennis E. Frye, Ted Alexander, and Frank A. O'Reilly read individual chapters that treated areas of their own expertise. I thank them all for catching the inevitable and little factual gremlins that plague a study of this scope.

Several people volunteered help above and beyond the call of duty by sending information regularly whenever they uncovered Jackson nuggets. Heartfelt appreciation goes to Peter Carmichael, Gregg S. Clemmer, Mary P. Coulling, William C. Davis, Guy Di Carlo, John E. Divine, Keith Gibson, Vicki Heilig, Michael P. Musick, T. Michael Parrish, Ben Ritter, Richard Selcer, Richard J. Sommers, Guy Swanson, and Gary Weiner.

Sincere thanks goes to the physicians who responded kindly and fully to queries about Jackson's health problems and death and about general medical treatment in the nineteenth and twentieth centuries. Dr. Richard E. Bullock worked closely with me on a number of matters in the first half of this biography. A principal regret will always be that Dick did not live to see the completion of this study. Yet memories still bloom of the many happy hours we spent together exchanging facts of history and medicine.

My indebtedness is likewise genuine to the other physicians who provided assistance: Robert F. Bondurant, Gaston de la Bretonne, Stuart Kent Cassell, Jr., Charles L. Cooke, Edwin J. Harvie, J. Stephen Hudgins, Michael E. Slayton, and Frank G. Turner.

Howard R. McManus, who was an outstanding graduate student, deserves a postgraduate award for discovering and presenting to me a *carte de visite* of Jackson from the original 1862 negative. This unretouched full-length likeness is published here for the first time.

In a variety of ways, other friends came forward with assistance that uniquely and significantly enhanced research on this book. Each knows what he or she contributed; to each, I express gratitude for your unselfish aid: M. William Adler, Alan C. Aimone, Rufus Barringer, Fred Barson, Hunter M. Bennett, Jr., Paul Bernabeo, Tom Broadfoot, Beth R. Brown, Rosine I. Bucher, Chris Calkins, Cortlandt P. Creech, Richard C. Datzman, Dorothy U. Davis, Hampton Dunn, A. Roger Ekirch, Stephen D. Engle, Philip Friedman, Robert B. Giles, William M. Grace, Edward Hahn, Megan Haley, Mary C. Herdegen, John M. Jackson, Edgar M. Jarrett, Jr., Wilbur S. Johnston, Roger D. Judd, Robert K. Krick, E. A. Livingston, William T. McColm, Buddy McCoy, Louis H. Manarin, Pat Perkinson, Donald C. Pfanz, Douglas Schanz, John C. Scully, John R. Sellers, Laurie Shea, Charles E. Smith, John Stewart, Rev. William E. Thompson, Donald C. Timberlake, Frank E. Vandiver, Gray Williams, Jr., Terry Winschel, James F. Wolfe, Don C. Wood, and Noble K. Wyatt.

To William C. Davis, Gary W. Gallagher, Joseph T. Glatthaar, Grady McWhiney, and Emory M. Thomas—colleagues who annually gather on the New River to dissect history and one another—I express deepest thanks most of all for their friendship.

A host of people contributed to the production of this book. The staff at Macmillan—especially editor Catherine Carter, managing editor Andrew Ambraziejus, and marketing director Clare Williams—worked conscientiously in the conversion of 2,200 pages of manuscript into an attractive book. Copyeditor David L. Severtson displayed a patience and a skill that is truly remarkable. George Skoch once again demonstrated why he is one of the nation's leading mapmakers. Wilbur S. Johnston was commendably unselfish in supplying a qualitative diagram of wartime Winchester. To the many others who molded and manufactured this study, I am eternally grateful.

When this project began seven years ago, my wife, Libba, shared my enthusiasm even though she knew from the start that relegation to the background as well as outright neglect might often be her lot. It was. Yet she never wavered in her support, whether it be on long, tiring research trips or during low periods in the writing stages. Like me, Libba came to have increased respect and admiration for the general. As he became a constant presence in our lives, she accepted him graciously into the family. I dedicate this book to her with my love. It is an inadequate gesture for all that she has given.

James I. Robertson, Jr.

Virginia Tech
Winter 1996

⌛ LIST OF MAPS ⌛

1

STRUGGLES OF AN ORPHAN

TO THE YOUNG OF HEART AND MIND, the West Fork River has a never-ending fascination. A series of creeks and springs starts somewhere in the mountains and foothills of northern West Virginia. The streams gain momentum as they tumble down the creases of the slopes. Once the waterways hit the broad valley that is the center of Lewis County, they intersect with each other and form the West Fork. The river twists and turns northward toward the Monongahela—and ultimately the Ohio and the Mississippi. The West Fork's swift current, plus its varying depth, result in an endless array of sparkles, ripples, and sounds. Especially is this the case as the river makes a sweeping horseshoe bend at a place called Jackson's Mill.

Young Tom Jackson lived there, and he loved the West Fork. It provided an escape for a small boy. Across the river, in a narrow flatland wedged between the water and a range of foothills, was a thick grove of white poplars near where an earlier sawmill had stood. This retreat was Tom's sanctuary. He often went there alone. In the protecting shadows of the trees, the boy could feel the cool breezes generated by the stream; he could stare at the reflections in the water and ponder the few nooks and crannies of his little world. Farm chores gave him but brief opportunities to enjoy these solitary times. Yet Jackson crossed the river whenever possible to rest and to wonder about his lot. His was a lonely existence, to be sure, but it was all that an orphan could remember. His past was but hearsay.

The lad never knew that the American branch of the Jackson family began in British criminal courts. John Jackson, Tom's great-grandfather, was born either in 1715 or 1719 near the village of Coleraine in Northern Ireland's County Londonderry.[1] His family appears to have been typically Scotch-Irish in background. When about the age of ten, John Jackson moved with his father and two older brothers to London. The father died shortly afterward. John eventually pursued a career in the building trade.

It was not a successful undertaking. By the time he had reached his early thirties, John Jackson was living in St. Giles and had descended to servant status in the home of a "near relation," Henry Jackson. The low situation proved too much to bear. On December 30, 1748, John Jackson told his kinsman of his determination to leave and seek employment elsewhere. He did so—after breaking into a cupboard and stealing 170 pounds in cash and nine remnants of gold lace.

His employer quickly apprehended John Jackson in a nearby town. The servant freely admitted his crime, even though larceny was then a capital offense. In mid-

January 1749, Jackson was prisoner 4 at the second session of court at Old Bailey in London. The judge found him guilty as charged and ordered Jackson held for transportation to America for a seven-year indenture.[2]

Three months later, prisoner 290 appeared before the fourth session of the Old Bailey court. Elizabeth Cummins (AKA Elizabeth Comings and Elizabeth Needles) stood likewise accused of theft. Born January 8, 1723, in either England or Ireland, Cummings grew to over six feet. She had blond hair, great strength and energy, plus an indomitable will that matched her muscular abilities. Writers traditionally liken her to a Viking or an amazon.

According to family legend, her widowed mother married a man with whom Elizabeth was constantly at odds. A heated argument ended when the fifteen-year-old stepdaughter hurled a water pitcher at her antagonist and then ran away from home. Early in 1749, Cummins was employed in the home of Thomas Holland in St. Catherine Coleman parish. She and an accomplice, Hannah Martin, stole nineteen pieces of silver, jewelry, and fine lace. The two women were apprehended and, on April 5, 1749, brought to trial. Martin testified against Cummins in exchange for clemency. A plea for mercy by Mrs. Holland may have saved Elizabeth Cummins from the gallows. In judging her guilty, the court directed that she be banished to America under a seven-year indenture.[3] Thus did John Jackson and Elizabeth Cummins involuntarily join at least 40,000 of England's unwanted who were dispatched in the eighteenth century supposedly to oblivion in the Maryland and Virginia colonies.

The prison ship *Litchfield*, commanded by Captain John Johnston, departed London in May 1749 with 150 convicts sentenced "to some of his Majesty's colonies and Plantations in America." Jackson and Cummins met on board and were in love by late July, when the *Litchfield* arrived at Annapolis, Maryland. The majority of the prisoners had been consigned to the Bladensburg estate of Dr. David Ross, a physician with extensive business interests throughout the Maryland colony.[4]

Whether Jackson or Cummins was part of the shipment to Ross cannot be determined. What is known is that Jackson's indenture sent him to Cecil County in northeastern Maryland, while Cummins served out her sentence in Baltimore. They were hardly alone in their low social status. In the period 1746–75, a leading authority on the subject has tabulated, the Maryland colony contained over 9,400 indentures and convicts—a figure representing no less than 35 percent of the colony's total population.[5]

Separation and servitude could not break the love they shared. Both were able to satisfy their indentures early. In July 1755, John Jackson and Elizabeth Cummins married. They faced the New World together as freedmen with no debts to society. Few American couples of humbler beginnings would rise to loftier heights.

At the same time, few American couples were more contrasting as individuals. A family acquaintance noted that Elizabeth "was a lady of remarkable strength of intellect, and her husband of moderate capacity. She [was] large, tall, & of great muscular development and he rather under size and not remarkable for physical strength." Another kinsman added that Elizabeth "was a lady of great business capacity, and perhaps the 'man of the house.'" Well educated, strong-minded, hard-working, and loving to family and friends, Elizabeth Jackson was without challenge the pillar of the family.[6]

In the spring of 1758, after the births of sons George and Edward, the Jacksons followed the paths of thousands of others and migrated west toward the Allegheny Mountains. They traversed the Blue Ridge, crossed the great valley of the Shenandoah, soon turned south along the South Branch of the Potomac River, and settled near the vicinity of Moorefield (sixty-five miles west of modern-day Winchester, Virginia). In 1770, the family pulled up stakes and moved farther west to the Tygart valley along a clear and broad river. The Jacksons began acquiring vast tracts of virgin farmland in the area encompassing the present-day town of Buckhannon. Elizabeth Jackson herself took patent on 3,000 acres—an uncommon action for a woman in that era.[7]

The family responded to the American Revolution with the same aggressiveness that would mark most Jackson undertakings. Father and mother had been away from their homeland less than thirty years, but they were among the first American patriots to step forth. John Jackson and his two teenage sons enlisted in the Continental forces. Their military service included furnishing supplies to the American armies, organizing defenses, and fighting hostile Indian bands in the rugged mountain territory. By war's end, John Jackson held a captain's commission and was regarded as one of the Revolutionary heroes in his home region. The bravery of his sons foreshadowed outstanding careers for both.[8]

Meanwhile, Elizabeth Jackson had been anything but idle. When the menfolk departed for the army, she took command of the homeplace, "Jackson's Fort," and converted it into a haven for refugees during frequent Indian raids. This remarkable woman demonstrated repeatedly that she had a cunning more than equal to that of the Indians. She was also a deadly marksman with a musket. Exactly how many Indians she personally killed during raids is a matter of local legend.

With American independence secured, the Jacksons expanded in both numbers and holdings. John Jackson gave primary attention to his family's well-being. He also served his community as justice of the peace, member of the county court, and county commissioner of revenue. Large tracts of choice land, numerous slaves, public positions of influence and power (including seats in the Virginia General Assembly and the U.S. Congress), all became part of the family domain. Jacksons were dominant in their economic pursuits and extraordinarily close in family associations.[9] Not one of the Jacksons was ever noted for strong religious convictions.

In fact, a certain ruthlessness became a family characteristic. Ambition, extending on occasion to the realm of brutality, marked some of the steps in the family's progress.Instrumental in settling northwestern Virginia, John Jackson and his sons proved energetic and skillful at acquiring wealth.

Advancing age led John and Elizabeth Jackson to move to Clarksburg to live with their children. On September 24, 1801, the former indentured servant who had built a family dynasty died in the arms of his wife at the age of eighty-six. "The long life of this good man," a granddaughter said in praise, "was spent in those noble & virtuous pursuits which endear men to their acquaintance and make their decease sincerely regretted by all the good and virtuous." Elizabeth Cummins Jackson lived in widowhood for twenty-seven years and reigned over four generations of the family. She died at the age of 105 and was buried beside her husband in Clarksburg.[10]

By then, Edward Jackson, the second son of John and Elizabeth, was enjoying high prosperity. Born March 1, 1759, Edward also fought Indians and gained officer's rank en route to adulthood. He acquired skills as a surveyor and civil engineer, and he became prominent in establishing county boundaries. His October 1783 marriage to Mary Hadden linked him with an extremely well-to-do family in Randolph County. This brought Jackson additional fame, fortune, and happiness. Mary Hadden Jackson bore her husband six children before her 1796 death.

Three years later Jackson moved to the Clarksburg settlement, became the town's first merchant, and married Elizabeth Wetherholt Brake of a nearby and prominent farming family. Nine children came from the second marriage. The father steadily rose to a man of considerable substance. Yet ambition created a restlessness for more success. Seeing great possibilities in the sparsely settled area south of Clarksburg, Edward Jackson in 1801 took his ever-increasing family to a permanent home in what became Lewis County.

The grandfather of the future Confederate general fell in love with the region. In time, he acquired at least 1500 acres in and around a bend in the West Fork River. A few miles to the south, Edward Jackson laid out the streets for a cluster of two dozen small houses that became known as Weston. Yet the settler's main concern was his own property.

While the Jackson holdings stretched through the valley and up into a range of foothills to the west, the center of the estate stood in the peninsula formed by the confluence of Freeman's Creek and the West Fork River. On a prominent knoll about 100 yards from the latter, Jackson built his home. It was a two-story log structure, twenty by forty feet, with a wing that ran perpendicular to the main house. The residence was qualitative and unadorned—a typical frontier home. In 1808, on the other (east) side of the river, Jackson constructed a sawmill and grist mill.

Once the settlement of Weston began, the Jackson mill ran day and night throughout the year in supplying the lumber for the frame houses of the town. In steady fashion, Edward Jackson became the area's most dominant businessman. An early Lewis County judge wrote of the family: "Col. Edward Jackson . . . was a stout sun burned man of great physical power, but of ordinary mental capacity, kind and generous to his friends but a determined enemy. . . . [He] was one of the first justices of the peace of the County & represented it in the General Assembly for several years. His second wife was rather a weak minded woman and her children were mostly so except her son Cummins E. Jackson."[11]

Some sources disagree over the exact date of Edward Jackson's passing, but the family Bible and his tombstone at Jackson's Mill clearly show that he died on Christmas Day, 1828, at the age of sixty-nine. His widow remained at Jackson's Mill until her death seven years later.[12]

All fifteen of Edward Jackson's children lived to at least middle age. The father was generous to each of his offspring. Such benevolence diluted the family fortune.

Worse, many of the children did not handle their inheritance with care. Jonathan Jackson, the third oldest child, was a tragic case in point.

Born September 25, 1790, in Randolph County, Jonathan received his education in a Clarksburg male academy before studying law under his kinsman, Judge John G. Jackson of Clarksburg.[13] Jonathan's admission to the bar in December 1810 elevated him from squire to law partner. Acquaintances thought him a "noble and highly promising young man."[14]

Jonathan Jackson was not overly impressive in appearance. Of short stature and ruddy complexion, he was a good-hearted man with an overly cheerful countenance that did not promote confidence in others. His intelligence was average, his disposition amiable. Although not a member of any church, he was instrumental in the June 20, 1814, establishment of the first Masonic lodge in Clarksburg. Jackson was loyal and loving to any man who called him a friend. That, unfortunately, proved his downfall.

The young attorney's career generally fluctuated between disappointing and disastrous. Perhaps it was frustration over living in the shadow and under the patronage of his illustrious cousin, John G. Jackson; or possibly Jonathan Jackson was simply a man of limited ability and knew it. When Judge Jackson went to Washington as a U.S. congressman, he left Jonathan in charge of the Clarksburg law firm. The cousin promptly demonstrated a deficiency in initiative. He had to be told what to do—and supervised closely while doing it. In 1812, Jackson helped raise a cavalry company for service against the British. He was elected lieutenant, but the unit never left Clarksburg.

During the period 1814–15, he served as collector of federal revenue for Harrison County (of which Clarksburg was county seat). It was a bad appointment; young Jackson combined irresponsibility with an inability to manage any large sum of money. On January 20, 1814, his benefactor, Judge Jackson, wrote his wife from Washington: "I anticipated your wishes as to Jonathan. I refused being his surety and wrote him by mail that if he did not behave well, I would have him removed from office."[15]

The warning fell on deaf ears. Within a year Jonathan Jackson's accounts were $3,500 in arrears. The judge not only gave him a tongue-lashing and had him removed as revenue collector; he also refused to cover his debts and save him from embarrassment.[16] Jonathan had to sell large inherited land holdings to cover his shortages; he took out at least one sizable loan from a friend. Those actions satisfied only part of his indebtedness. Jonathan Jackson was a defendant in two claims suits during this period.[17]

Publicly in ridicule, reduced to practicing law alone, Jonathan Jackson knew only minimal and occasional success. One reason for such lack of recovery, a Lewis County law clerk later recalled, was that Jonathan "was kind and amiable . . . but not above the average. He had a higher standing as chancery lawyer than as advocate." Another resident of Weston termed Jackson "a good counsellor but deficient as an advocate in speaking talent."[18]

Generosity likewise contributed to Jackson's undoing. The blue-eyed attorney had "a genial and affectionate disposition." In the frontier region of Clarksburg, where banks were few and business rested for the most part on credit, those needing advances often sought lawyers of good standing to endorse their notes. Every resident of the area was to Jonathan a neighbor or an ally. Moreover, and because he desperately needed the business, Jonathan Jackson was cosigner for dozens of notes. He eventually had to cover a large number of them out of his own pocket. "It has been said by some of the newspapers," a Weston attorney stated, that Jackson "was broken up by being security for others."[19]

Greater weaknesses crippled Jackson's legal career. He could not pay many of his debts because he was a compulsive gambler who loved a game of cards anywhere and at any time. Jonathan Jackson was no more lucky at poker than he was at law. Further, he possessed more than an occasional fondness for alcohol. A contemporary wrote succinctly: "Jonathan was fond of cards & drink, & ran through a valuable landed estate, dying poor."[20]

Early in 1817, Jackson made a surprise announcement of his intention to marry. A hopeful Judge Jackson told his wife: "In regard to the presumed marriage you referred to, I will not interfere. If the disposition to gaming were suppressed, and perhaps that connection will destroy it, I would say [marriage] is not objectionable."[21]

Julia Beckwith Neale lived in Parkersburg, eighty miles west of Clarksburg. She was born February 28, 1798, in Loudoun County on a farm near the present site of Little River Church. Julia was the third of eleven children of Irish settlers Thomas and Margaret Winn Neale. The father had served as a private in a Virginia regiment during the Revolutionary War. Around 1800, the family had moved to Wood County near the Parkersburg area. There Thomas Neale achieved high prosperity as a merchant and trader on the Ohio River.

The few extant descriptions of Julia Neale are glowing. One of her schoolteachers remembered that Julia "was rather a brunette, handsome face, and when at maturity of medium height and symmetrical form." She was "very intelligent" for that time and possessed of a "graceful and commanding presence" plus "a comely and engaging countenance." While one or two writers labeled her "a most devoted Christian," a universal sentiment reigned that she was "a belle in society and one of those gentle and yet positive characters everybody loves to love."[22]

When and how Jonathan Jackson and Julia Neale first met is regrettably unknown. On September 28, 1817, they were married in Parkersburg at the brick home of her parents. James McAboy, a Baptist minister, performed the ceremony. Jackson had just turned twenty-seven; his bride was nineteen.[23]

The couple moved to Clarksburg. Jackson purchased lot 5 on the north side of the road serving as Clarksburg's main street. This property was no more than 100 feet diagonally across the road from the county courthouse. On the large lot was an apple tree and a three-room brick cottage with inset porch and semi-attic. The home faced to the side rather than toward the main street. Jackson planned to live there until he could build a larger home. Then he intended to use the cottage for his law office.[24]

At the time of the Jackson wedding, Clarksburg was part of the settled area of "the northern strip" of what became West Virginia. A commercial town of diverse business, it was on a watershed where all the streams in the area flowed together. Around it, sharp-rising foothills crowded so close to one another that the narrow valleys in between emerged from somewhere and seemed to snake nowhere. On the straight main thoroughfare, which rose and fell as it paralleled the nearby ranges of hills, the Jacksons settled into married life and became town favorites because of their engaging personalities. Jonathan's prior indiscretions were momentarily forgotten as the family began to increase in number. The first child, Elizabeth, was born in 1819. A son, Warren, came two years later in January.

Even though "an affectionate and devoted husband and father," attorney Jonathan Jackson was soon struggling again. Court records show him borrowing not only against livestock but household furniture as well. Collateral for an 1823 loan even included the family bed and bedding.[25]

In that bleak atmosphere, and during a bitingly cold night, Dr. James McCally went to the Jackson home to deliver another baby. The longtime Clarksburg physician was positive that the third child, a son, arrived in the final minutes of January 20, 1824. However, the family was convinced that the birth occurred just after midnight on Saturday, January 21. That date has prevailed ever since. The child, with his mother's brown hair and his father's blue eyes, was christened Thomas in honor of his maternal grandfather.[26]

A seven-year marriage had produced three children. Financial woes continued to mount slowly and the young family of five struggled. Too soon Julia became pregnant again. She was approaching her time of delivery when dreaded typhoid fever struck six-year-old Elizabeth Jackson.

The mother was too incapacitated to provide much help to her daughter. While Dr. McCally called at least twice each day, Jonathan sat by the child's bed throughout the painful ordeal. On March 6, 1826, Elizabeth Jackson died. Before the parents could even begin to cope with their grief, Jonathan Jackson fell ill with the same disease. He had little strength with which to fight; he succumbed on March 26. The next day, Julia Jackson gave birth to a daughter, who was named Laura.

At the age of twenty-eight, Julia Jackson found herself a widow with two infants and a new baby. Her firstborn was gone; so was her husband, who left behind an accumulation of debts and pathetically few assets. Two-year-old Thomas experienced the emotional turmoil of two deaths in the family, but without the sense of personal loss. Recollections of his father thereafter were nonexistent. Rarely did he even mention his name. The one legacy that Jonathan Jackson bequeathed to his son was an eventual realization that the childhood miseries Thomas knew were the result of irresponsibility. It was a lesson Thomas never forgot.

After the father's death came family destitution. It took everything the widow had—including the sale of their home—to cover outstanding debts. Members of the Jackson and Neale families offered help, but Julia Jackson refused charity. Only when the family lost the home did she relent and accept from the local Masonic Order the use of a one-room house, "about 12 feet square on the back of a lot on an alley with only the ground it covered."[27]

To make ends meet, Mrs. Jackson did sewing regularly and taught school in three-month sessions. She fought self-pity. Occasionally she made brief trips to Parkersburg to be with members of the Neale family. There she maintained a joyful front. A friend who saw Julia Jackson a year after the loss of husband and firstborn observed: "She was looking as cheerful and animated as usual, her easy, graceful manners and pleasant conversation always making her a welcome guest." Yet the young widow was ailing, physically as well as mentally. What family members called "pulmonary trouble" was the first symptom of tuberculosis.[28]

A child grieves by seeing others grieve. Sorrow in infancy becomes unredeemed sorrow in adulthood. Little Thomas Jackson had a sweet face, everyone agreed, but few smiles ever graced it. As young as he was, he watched the mother he adored painfully trying to provide for all of them but finding little time to give attention and love to any one in particular. This had a deep effect on the boy during an impressionable period of his life. Julia Jackson could not always conceal her unhappiness, nor could Thomas fail to feel it.

Quiet, pensive, delicate, introspective, Thomas in many ways was never a child. No room existed in his young life for capriciousness and frivolities. With a mixture of love and sympathy, he looked on his mother as life itself. General Robert E. Lee would observe many years later of Jackson: "The early instructions of his mother, whom he seems never to have forgotten . . . had great influence in shaping his course through life."[29]

The Jackson children were familiar and—in their poverty—often pitiful sights in Clarksburg. Townspeople occasionally extended a helping hand. One hot day Thomas and his brother Warren ran into Ed McCullough's mercantile store. The two boys were shirtless, with only strings holding up their ragged linen pants. After learning that their mother had washed the only shirts the two boys had, and that the shirts were hanging on the line to dry, McCullough took Thomas and Warren to the back of his store. There the merchant gave the boys a large piece of shirting. Henceforth, he announced, they would have two shirts apiece instead of one.[30]

It was in his seventh year that Thomas Jackson's already shaky world began to crumble.

No one was quite sure what had brought Blake B. Woodson to Clarksburg in 1824. Descended from a prosperous Cumberland County family in central Virginia, he was a well-educated member of the bar with "social, popular manners." Woodson established a meager law practice in Clarksburg. Sometime in the late 1820s he began courting Julia Jackson. Members of the Jackson and Neale families reacted angrily. Woodson was fifteen years older than Mrs. Jackson; he had eight children scattered in every direction but under his care. A contemporary dismissed him as "a sort of decayed gentleman." To a Lewis County judge, Woodson was "fond of company & good living [but] always hard run for means." Such shortcomings were too apparent to be overlooked. Yet Julia Jackson went through a courtship and then accepted Woodson's proposal of marriage. Relatives threatened to take the children in order to ensure their well-being and education. Mrs. Jackson was undaunted. Some speculation had the widow blindly in love with this man old enough to be her father and of little fortune as well. But Julia Jackson was aware of her declining health; she may have been in desperate need of adult companionship and the hope of future security. On November 4, 1830, Julia Jackson married Blake Woodson in a private Clarksburg ceremony performed by the Reverend Daniel Limerick.[31]

Within six months the new family was again in critical financial condition. Julia Jackson Woodson tried hard to do good in all things. On May 17, 1831, she (but not her husband) joined the new Presbyterian church in Clarksburg. In spite of her efforts to mold a strong family, Woodson's paltry income proved inadequate for the basic needs of two adults and three children. Julia Woodson's health continued to deteriorate. All too soon she was pregnant. The stepfather, so engaging and outgoing in public, became a harsh and verbally abusive parent who blamed the youngsters for his economic straits. On occasion, he encouraged the children—as young as they were— to "seek homes elsewhere."[32]

Such oppression caused a despairing young Thomas to draw close to his mother. He could not understand why her protective hand was not stronger when he needed her so much more. In the spring of 1831, what appeared to be relief for the little boy became disaster.

That year the Virginia General Assembly created the new Fayette County in the untamed mountain wilderness over 125 miles south of Clarksburg. Edwin S. Duncan, a Clarksburg jurist and longtime friend of the Jackson family, became first presiding judge in the new county. Duncan named Woodson to be clerk of the court. It seemed like a good opportunity, but that view was only surface-deep.

Around June 1831, the family moved south into New River country and settled in the village of New Haven (shortly renamed Ansted). It was little more than a country crossroads, having a store, blacksmith shop, post office, and a dozen small houses. Woodson purchased fifty acres of all but worthless land two and a half miles east of New Haven. The home was spacious but dilapidated.[33]

Isolated, without friends, and falling deeper into debt, the Woodsons floundered in their new surroundings. Poor health practically incapacitated Julia Woodson. Some relief had to be secured. Warren, the oldest child at ten, went to Parkersburg to live with Uncle Alfred Neale. Mrs. Woodson tried earnestly to keep Thomas and Laura, but the strain was overbearing. Nothing remained but to send them to Jackson's Mill and the several relations there.

This announcement devastated seven-year-old Thomas. His mother was the only anchor in his life; he begged not to be sent away. It was no use. One day a Jackson uncle (in all likelihood Cummins E. Jackson) and a slave named Uncle Robinson arrived at the Woodson cottage. Five-year-old Laura was bewildered. Thomas ran terrified from the house and hid in the woods. Nightfall and much coaxing finally brought him back into the home. Throughout the following day, he listened as his uncle extolled the virtues of life at Jackson's Mill and offered inducements to Thomas and his sister. Aware that no alternative existed, the lad agreed to leave his mother and face the unknown.

Julia Woodson sobbed uncontrollably as she hugged her small son and tried to tell him goodbye. The child fought back tears while being placed on a horse. As the party of riders started away, the hysterical mother ran to her son and held him once more. Julia Woodson never recovered from that farewell. As for Jackson, his second wife observed many years later: "That parting he never forgot; nor could he speak of it in future years but with the utmost tenderness."[34]

The slow journey northward took a week. For the children, it was a mixture of excitement and uncertainty. Mountain ridges loomed on either side as the riders made their way down narrow valleys. Occasionally the group went up and over a long range. The view to Tom and Laura was breathtaking. Soon the two adults and two children were in a wider than usual valley. They passed through the Lewis County seat of Weston and continued for another four miles. There the West Fork River swerved to the east for a quarter-mile before bending back to the northwest. Bottomland swept out on either side of the river to distant foothills. Inside a giant wooded arc formed by the river was the center of the 1,500-acre tract known as Jackson's Mill.

A large conglomeration of family members poured from the two-story log home to greet Tom and Laura. The step-grandmother, Elizabeth Brake Jackson, then fifty-nine, was the second wife and widow of Edward Jackson. Indulgent and loving, she quickly embraced the two children as her own. Her daughters Catherine Jackson White, thirty-one, and Margaret (called Peggy), nineteen and engaged to be married, likewise showered affection on the new arrivals.

Then, one after another, six of Tom Jackson's bachelor uncles stepped forward awkwardly and gruffly to introduce themselves. Young Tom already knew the oldest, twenty-nine-year-old Cummins Edward Jackson. Next came James Madison Jackson; twenty-six; John Edward Jackson, twenty-one; Return Meigs Jackson, seventeen; Edward J. Jackson, fourteen; and Andrew Jackson, ten. Tom and Laura quickly felt the strong attachments that bound all Jacksons together in a mixture of tenderness to one another and defiance of unwanted intrusion. It gave a seven-year-old boy a steadying sense of safety.

How totally Tom Jackson came to need that security became apparent three months later. In November 1831, having barely settled in at Jackson's Mill, the lad and his little sister climbed back on horses for another trip to Fayette County. It was a long journey they did not want to make. Their mother was dying.

Julia Jackson Woodson had struggled until no strength remained. Wracked by tuberculosis, she nevertheless managed on October 7 to give birth to a son. Tom Jackson's half-brother was named William Wirt. The hard pregnancy proved more than the mother could endure. Lingering fever and chronic dysentery over the next six weeks exacerbated her condition. Knowing that the end was near, Julia Woodson summoned her children one last time.

From her bedside she gave each "her farewell and blessing." On December 4, 1831, the cares of the unhappy thirty-three-year-old mother ended. Blake Woodson informed the Jackson family: "No Christian on earth, no matter what evidence he might have had of a happy hereafter, could have died with more fortitude. Perfectly in her senses, calm and deliberate, she met her fate without a murmur or a struggle. . . . I have known few women of equal, none of superior, merit."[35]

Little Tom Jackson was not there when they buried his mother. Pallbearers bore the crude coffin in the rain up a mountainside near Ansted to a new seven-acre cemetery on the farm of George Hunter. The burial site was simply an open space in the forest. The Reverend John McElhenny, a local Presbyterian minister, conducted the brief service. A handful of mountain folk sang a hymn, listened to a homily, bowed their heads to the usual prayers, and then trudged home through the dripping woods.

Probably because of straitened circumstances, Blake Woodson did not erect a stone over his wife's grave. A year later, on December 27, 1832, he married Elizabeth Foster of Fayette County. Woodson died five months later. His worldly assets consisted of about fifty articles of household and kitchen furniture.[36]

At Woodson's death, a brief but bitter custody fight erupted over the children. Julia Jackson Woodson's family had little respect for the Jacksons and no respect at all for Cummins Jackson, leader of the clan. Thomas Neale, at whose Parkersburg home Warren Jackson was living, made a concerted effort to obtain his other two grandchildren. On June 6, 1833, Neale sent a heated letter to attorney Lewis Maxwell in Weston. The elder Neale left nothing to imagination as to how he felt about the uncle who had assumed control of two small children. "My daughter Julia Jackson, who married Mr. Blake B. Woodson, took Two of her Children to Layfaett County, Thomas and Laury Jackson. After her Death, Mr. Woodson still wish[ed] to keep the Children. As soon as Mr. Woodson Died, his son W. C. Woodson wrote on to me to Come after the Children or they would be Bound out." Neale quickly asked Benjamin Willard, a friend who had business in the Fayette County area, to collect the children and escort them to Parkersburg. When Willard arrived in Ansted, "he was inform'd that Coming Jackson had been after them about 10 days before."

> I have receiv'd a letter since from Mr. Woodson . . . that Jackson promised when he took the Children that he would give them up if I Demanded them. He would be the last man in the world if She [Julia Jackson Woodson] was living to have her Children, for she spoke of him in the most Contemptable terms. He had treated her Ill before her Children and I am inform'd they are a ruff roudy Set.
>
> I want [to] get in your favor to See if he will give them up. If not I want you to take Such Steps against him as will compel him. I want the Children to be brought up with Some breeding & manner. . . . I have the Legal right to the Children, and what he [Cummins Jackson] wants with them I am at a loss to no without he wants to make dredges of them. My daughter inform'd me he attempted to take them in her life time.[37]

Thomas Neale wrote this letter when he was elderly, perhaps ill, and certainly in a state of high agitation; some of his allegations doubtless were overstatements. Nevertheless, he raised the unanswered question of why Cummins Jackson was so anxious to have Thomas and Laura at Jackson's Mill. Still, Neale's efforts to reunite the three Jackson children under his care failed. The old widower died eight months later. Meanwhile, seven-year-old Thomas strove to adapt to the surroundings at Jackson's Mill, which would be his home for eleven years.

The West Fork River had carved a broad valley that stretched from Weston to Morgantown. Unbroken hills on either side isolated the valley, which was a combination of thick woods and the best farmland in the region. A single road wound alongside the river from Clarksburg, eighteen miles upstream. The Jackson's Mill estate was large and lucrative. Family holdings extended up and down the valley and in both directions across the bottomland and over the hills. On an open rise of ground amid apple trees and facing south stood the main residence. Five windows extending across the front of the second story indicated its large size. The home was so well constructed and furnished that it was a showpiece in the county.

Downstream from the home, grandfather Edward Jackson in 1806 had built the area's first sawmill. That operation was the core of the estate. Nearby woods thick with oak, maple, and white poplar provided a steady source of raw materials. The sawmill shed, a long one-story structure with sloping roof, ran night and day for most of the year. Lumber for a steadily growing Weston came from the primeval forests on the Jackson estate and was carried the four miles to town via paths on either side of the West Fork.

A grist mill had originally stood on the east side of the river. Yet the bend of the stream threw the current against the side, and the resultant erosion caused part of the building to collapse. Prior to Tom Jackson's arrival, the mill's foundation timbers and machinery were moved across the West Fork into a new grain mill. This second installation was forty feet square; it had a stone foundation and was two and a half stories high. An eight-foot dam harnessed the West Fork River's power with two horizontal water wheels built beneath the building's first floor.

In addition to the two mills, the Jackson property also contained a carpenter's shop, blacksmith forge, quarters for a dozen slaves, numerous barns and outbuildings, plus a general store. Being the largest millers in the area put the Jacksons in position to exert great influence on local politics. Jackson's Mill was the natural community center for all of Lewis County. Men gathered there to talk and catch up on news while waiting for grain to be ground or trees to be converted into building lumber.[38]

Presiding over this vast domain in 1831 was Cummins Jackson, the oldest of Edward Jackson's sons by his second wife. His name "was a household word in Lewis County," one resident stated. Certainly the gregarious Cummins Jackson was the most influential person in Tom Jackson's growing years. He provided a small orphan boy with a home and friendship. Uncle Cummins instructed the lad in all of the practical workings of the Jackson's Mill operation. The elder Jackson looked on Tom as being older than he was. Hence, the youngster enjoyed only glimpses of boyhood.

Many biographers portray Cummins as a father figure to his nephew. That is an exaggeration. The boisterous and brawling Cummins Jackson never inspired paternal love from his ward (or anyone else, for that matter). He was at best a big-brother companion to Jackson. The youth would refer to him as "Uncle" and once remarked that he "would stick to him through thick and thin."[39] Cummins Jackson had neither the time nor the desire to want more. Jackson's Mill and money were his twin loves.

He was a man of sharp extremes. Born July 25, 1802, at Jackson's Mill, Cummins was only twenty-six when his father died. He wasted no time in assuming control of the family enterprise. One had only to look at him to see his grandmother Elizabeth Jackson's build. Six feet, two and a half inches tall, Cummins Jackson weighed over 200 pounds and was extremely muscular. A clean-shaven face accentuated piercing blue-gray eyes. Cummins walked with a natural stoop because of the constant need to bend over when entering doorways. It was not unusual to see him carrying a barrel of flour under each arm. He set a brisk pace when work needed to be done.

Cummins Jackson had many good qualities. He made friends easily and was gracious to people he liked. A strong-minded, vigorous, and shrewd manager of affairs, the huge man became the idol of the laboring class because he gave employment to many persons at all times of the year. A kinsman remembered Cummins as "a man of remarkable intellect & energy, of temperate & industrious habits, skillful in business, generous & free-handed."[40]

There the traditional picture of Tom Jackson's guardian usually stops. However, an ominously dark side existed to Cummins Jackson. His many liabilities overrode his virtues. Unscrupulous and vindictive streaks coursed through his makeup. An unidentified acquaintance once termed him "a rascal" with good cause. After his father's death in 1828, Cummins "confiscated his father's estate and kept the rest of the heirs from coming into their rightful portion of it."[41] In 1835, his own mother brought suit in an effort to get the heirs of Edward Jackson their legal share of the estate. The case was never settled.

In this same period, Cummins arbitrarily constructed a six-foot-high dam stretching 150 feet across the West Fork. Additional water power was imperative, Cummins asserted, but in seeking it he displayed total disregard for the water needs of his neighbors downstream. They angrily sued in Lewis County Circuit Court over "the great damage and common nuisance" the illegal water barrier brought to "all the good Citizens of our said Commonwealth."[42]

Cummins Jackson thoroughly enjoyed this fracas (which he apparently won because the dam remained standing). He himself was absurdly litigious—bringing suits over delinquent accounts, fence lines, uncertain land claims, timber rights, late payments, alleged slanders, and any other points of law. Cummins Jackson's legal controversies not only involved much of his time; they also consumed a large share of the Jackson's Mill earnings. Moreover, quick to sue, Cummins was just as quick to overlook the law. "He omitted to pay his duties," one judge declared, "& put the law & its officers at defiance." Add to these shortcomings the uncle's lack of education, his apathy with religion, as well as a strong fondness for gambling, horse racing, and drinking, and it is apparent that Cummins Jackson was hardly a role model for the young boy supposedly under his moral tutelage.[43]

Greed and strapped finances were ultimately the doom of Cummins Jackson. Sometime in 1844, when the nephew was halfway through West Point, Jackson discovered a thin vein of silver near his property. He began counterfeiting half-dollar coins by using lead and coating them with silver. The scheme worked for several months before a federal grand jury indicted Cummins Jackson on one charge of forgery and twenty-six charges of counterfeiting in the backwoods of Jackson's Mill. Two kinsmen were accused of conspiracy in the operation.

Defense attorneys succeeded in delaying the cases for more than three years. Cummins Jackson sank more heavily in debt than ever during that interim. In 1848, the forgery trial began. One day, when it was obvious that the case was going against him, Jackson leaped through the courthouse window and fled into hiding at Jackson's Mill while a sheriff's posse combed the countryside. The uncle then fled to the California gold fields. He died there a few months after arriving.[44]

Tom Jackson's growing years at the mill were always full but not always fulfilling. Looking back on his childhood during the years of rigid discipline at West Point, Jackson observed: "Times are very different from what they were when I was at my adopted home. None to give their mandates; none for me to obey but as I chose; surrounded by my playmates and relatives, all apparently eager to promote my happiness." That backward view was wishful thinking. By adulthood, Jackson painstakingly avoided recollections of what a close friend called the "melancholy temperament" of his lonely orphan youth.[45]

To a small lad, Jackson's Mill was a beehive of activity; and under his uncle's constant guidance, Tom Jackson acquired skills in a wide variety of tasks. He felled trees, helped out at the mills, cared for the sheep and cattle, raised chickens, plowed and harvested crops, produced maple syrup with the help of Celia, a black servant in charge of household duties. In time, Jackson learned to transport wool to a carding firm two miles away in the hamlet of Jane Lew. He drove oxen, hitched to logs sometimes forty feet in length, to the sawmill. Although age and the constant presence of uncles prevented Jackson from exercising any leadership roll on the estate, he would carry an acquired love of farming and gardening into adulthood. At least once during the Civil War, he expressed the desire someday of returning to the Shenandoah Valley and becoming a gentleman-farmer.

On the east side of the river, Cummins Jackson had a four-mile racetrack and maintained a number of blooded horses. The nephew learned to race at an early age and became Cummins's favorite jockey in community races. Tom Jackson rarely fell from a horse, despite his extremely awkward appearance in the saddle. He rode with short stirrups and had a jockey's habit of leaning far forward in the saddle. Strangers watching Jackson in a gallop were convinced that he was going to topple over the horse's head or neck at every step. In maturity, Jackson employed unusually long stirrups, but he continued to ride with his head almost on the same plane with that of his mount.[46]

Such practical training throughout his youth instilled in Jackson a self-reliance that complemented his inherent honesty and dependability. In a sense, the child became father to the man. Tom Jackson was first attentive and then determined; and if on occasion he displayed a quiet independence of action more characteristic of an adult, that was expected of him. A neighbor would recall: "Tom was always an uncommonly well-behaved lad, a gentleman from the boy up, just and kind to every one, never controversial, but doing his duty right and left, in a devoted, dreamy sort of way."[47]

His childhood friends were few and somewhat slow in developing. Uncle Andrew Jackson was but three years older than Tom; a cousin, Sylvanus White, was three years younger. Sons of distant kinsmen in the Arnold and Hays families occasionally came to the mill to play, and Jackson may have visited them when riding with his uncle. The lad made few trips to Weston during his first years at Jackson's Mill.

At the top of Tom Jackson's small list of friends was his sister Laura. The two shared a deep love intensified by the bonds of orphanage. No secrets existed between them; they faced the world side by side. Until Laura moved to Parkersburg to live with her mother's relatives, the two children were comfortable only when each knew where the other was.

Tom and Laura initially explored every acre of Jackson's Mill, and they engaged in the normal enterprises of youth. Soon the lad had found his favorite spot on the farm. With the help of kindly Uncle Robinson, young Jackson built a crude but sturdy raft. Frequently, the brother rowed his sister across the West Fork to the solitude of the opposite shore and a thick stand of white poplars and sugar maples. There the two youngsters studied the wonders of nature and conversed about the minor things so important to children. More often, the introspective and pensive Tom Jackson crossed the river alone and sat quietly lost in thought amid the companionship of the trees.[48]

The West Fork River also provided young Jackson with occasional income. At that time, the stream brimmed with fish, notably pike. Jackson from an early age was an excellent fisherman. He was only eight or nine when he began supplying daily catches to gunsmith-merchant Conrad Kester in Weston. For every pike over a foot in length, Kester paid Jackson fifty cents. It was an arrangement satisfactory to both parties, and it led to an oft-told story about Jackson's integrity.

One day the lad was walking down Weston's main thoroughfare toward Kester's store. In his arms was a giant pike three feet in length. Colonel John Talbott, a local resident, saw Jackson and called out: "Hello, Tom, that's a fine fish you have. I will give you a dollar for it." Without halting, Jackson answered: "Sold to Mr. Kester." Talbott then offered a dollar and a quarter for the fish. Jackson looked back over his shoulder and replied: "If you get any of this pike, you will get it from Mr. Kester." Young Tom arrived at the store and laid the huge fish on the counter. Kester attempted to pay Jackson double the normal price. "No, sir," came the reply. "This is your pike at fifty cents, and I will not take more for it. Besides, you have bought a good many from me that were pretty short."[49]

Several writers have perpetuated the myth that in childhood Jackson "was extravagantly fond of the violin," owned an instrument, and had several favorite songs he enjoyed playing. As a matter of fact, Jackson was completely tone-deaf. If he experimented in his youth with a violin, it would have been as disastrous as his attempt after the Mexican War to learn to play the flute. That endeavor lasted through six months of frustration and indescribable sounds. Jackson simply found it impossible to distinguish one melody from another. This situation never improved. At a social gathering during the Civil War, he asked a young vocalist to sing "Dixie"—immediately after she had finished doing so.[50]

Tom and Laura were together for four years at Jackson's Mill. On August 19, 1835, step-grandmother Elizabeth Brake Jackson died at the home place. By then, the two maiden aunts had married and left. Only bachelor uncles and slaves remained on the estate. It was not a good environment in which to raise two children. For Tom and Laura, another move and a permanent separation then took place.

Laura, accompanied by Aunt Rebecca White, tearfully bade her brother farewell and went to Parkersburg to join the Neale family. Tom was sent to live with his Aunt Polly (his father's sister) and her husband, Isaac Brake, on a farm four miles from Clarksburg. Still shy of his twelfth birthday, the lad had faced the deaths of an infant sister, his father, his mother, and his stepfather—while at the same time being separated from his brother and remaining sister. A lonely and uncertain child traveled to his new home.

His stay with the Brakes was short and traumatic. Jackson always had a deep fondness for his Aunt Polly. She had four children at the time; all were close to Jackson's age. The setting was there for a happy time. Yet friction quickly developed between uncle and nephew. Isaac Brake was of German stock: solid, a hard worker, and demanding. He treated Jackson as the outsider that he was. Verbal abuse became part of the boy's new life, and he suffered at least one severe whipping. After about a year, it was more than Jackson was willing to endure. So he ran away.

Late one afternoon he appeared at the Clarksburg home of either his cousin, Mrs.

John G. Jackson, or her daughter, Mrs. John J. Allen. The small boy politely asked for food and a place to spend the night. He then informed his surprised relatives that because he and his uncle were in strong disagreement, he was not going back to the Brakes. Family members remonstrated with Tom, who was respectful but unpersuaded. When his cousin begged him a final time to return to Aunt Polly's, the youngster replied: "Mabe I ought to, ma'am, but I am not going to."[51]

The next day Jackson left Clarksburg and walked the eighteen miles through mountain wilderness to Jackson's Mill. When he explained the ordeal he had undergone at the Brakes, his uncles welcomed him warmly. Jacksons always looked after their own. The small boy settled anew in the only place he could call home. "Uncle was a father to me," he later said of Cummins Jackson.[52]

Only once in the next seven years was Jackson absent from the Lewis County area for any extended period. He had just turned twelve when his sixteen-year-old brother Warren visited the mill. Warren Jackson was already a successful schoolteacher in Upshur County, east of Weston. However, a gypsy spirit seemed to keep him restless. Warren was en route to visit Laura and the Neales in Parkersburg. He invited Tom to go with him. Looking up naturally to an older brother, and anxious to see his beloved Laura, Tom jumped at the opportunity. Cummins Jackson strangely voiced no objections, so the two youths trekked eighty miles through frontier country to the home of their aunt and uncle, Alfred and Clementine Neale.[53]

The 150-acre Neale farm was on James Island in the Ohio River near Parkersburg. Alfred Neale sold firewood and other wares to steamboats plying the river. Jackson was thrilled to see Laura again; but somewhat like his brother, the lure of the mighty Ohio cast a spell that sent imaginations soaring. Warren became certain that if he and Tom went downriver, they could make just as much money as Uncle Alfred selling wood for ship boilers. He convinced an impressionable brother to go south and seek their fortune. The boys traveled twenty miles to Belleville, where they visited their father's sister, Rebecca White, and her husband. Following a stay of several days, the two lads in the spring of 1836 resumed their journey.

Warren and Tom reached the mouth of the Ohio, then descended the Mississippi to an island near the southwestern corner of Kentucky. There they spent the summer and autumn alone in a deserted cabin while cutting wood for passing steamers. The work was hard, income small, food scarce, insects constant, cleanliness and amusements absent. For six months or more, Warren and Tom endured an existence that neither of them would ever reveal when asked. What determination remained deserted them when both boys contracted malaria.

Tom then resolved to get home somehow. Warren now agreed. Fortunately, a charitable steamboat captain offered them a ride northward. In February 1837, two travel-soiled, ragged, emaciated youths knocked at the door of the Neale home. Uncle Alfred and Aunt Clementine greeted them with relief and affection. Tom soon returned to Jackson's Mill, poorer but wiser for his experience. Warren never recuperated fully from the river trip. He went back to teaching in Upshur County with but a few years left to live.[54]

For the next three years, attempts at formal education dominated Tom Jackson's hopes. The early adversities of his life now inspired the young boy with the singular resolve to secure an education so as to improve his chances in life. Perhaps this could be called ambition; in all likelihood, Tom Jackson wanted to rise from the lowly position in which orphanage had placed him and to get out from under painful dependence on his relatives. "My mother and father died when I was very young," he once told a niece, "and I had to work for my living and education both."[55]

Pursuit of the latter was difficult. Uncle Cummins had no interest in educational matters, and he considered Tom the dullest of his brother's three children. Further, a rural school was small in size, primitive in facilities, plain in instruction, and confined largely to winter months in order not to interfere with farming activities. Teachers were usually young men seeking a better job, or they were boys with special proficiency in a single subject.

Tom Jackson's desire to learn soon convinced his uncle that the quest for knowledge could not be ignored. Cummins Jackson then prevailed upon Robert P. Rhea, a Lewis County citizen with more than average education, to establish a school for boys at the mill. (The school was later moved to nearby McCann's Run.) From the moment Jackson tasted learning, his thirst became unquenchable. Although mathematics seemed to come naturally to Jackson, every other field of endeavor was a challenge from which he never shied.

A childhood acquaintance noted that Jackson "was by no means . . . brilliant, but was one of those untiring, plain, matter-of-fact persons who would never give up . . . until he accomplished his object." He read rapidly but learned slowly. Sometimes he gained proficiency in one subject at the expense of another. Years later he remarked to a niece: "If a person commences reading before learning to spell well, he will not be apt to ever learn much about spelling, because reading is more pleasant than spelling. . . . Still I am mortified at my spelling words wrong."[56]

On the other hand, the habit of spending hours on a point until he had mastered it to his own satisfaction was a characteristic that Jackson always exhibited in acquiring knowledge, even though it sometimes made him appear ignorant in the subject.

One embarrassing incident occurred. Jackson struck a deal with one of the slave boys: if the lad would furnish him with pine knots to use for light in studying borrowed books, Jackson would teach the slave to write "just like Mr. Ray taught me." Jackson kept his word; but once the slave learned to write, he forged a pass and fled via the underground railroad to Canada. Happily, Uncle Cummins was more amused than angered by the episode.[57]

The quest for education soon took Jackson to Weston on a regular basis. By then the town contained thirty dwellings and some 200 residents. Log hauling had reduced the streets to lanes of mud holes where hogs wallowed undisturbed. The houses were poplar log structures over which weather-boarding had been nailed. Few of Weston's buildings had felt contact with a paint brush. Hence, to strangers the town had a dilapidated and neglected appearance.[58]

At Weston, in 1837, Jackson became one of six children being taught by prominent citizen Phillip Cox, Jr. Wintertime sessions convened in the Bailey House, the town's lone but imposing hotel. Enrollment was limited to poor children whose families lacked the means to pay tuition. By that time, the Jackson's Mill operation, under Cummins's clumsy management, was annually losing both profits and prestige. Yet putting Tom in a class of indigent children remains baffling.

Two years later, Jackson studied for several weeks in Lewis County's first courthouse building. His teacher was Weston's resident scholar, Colonel Alexander Scott Withers, an accomplished man of letters who became much attached to the quiet and serious student. So did Matthew Edmiston, a promising young lawyer who had recently settled in Weston. Edmiston had a small library of books. Not only did he freely lend volumes to Jackson, but he also helped him in his studies.[59]

Good conduct would always mark Jackson's educational career. William J. Bland of Weston remembered schoolboy Jackson well. "He was then sociable & kindly . . . fond of country frolics and dancing." However, "if he thought himself imposed on, inflexible; & although he might be pressed down by superior strength, would in his school boy fights never cry enough." Another contemporary added that Jackson "was always ready for play—not very swift of foot but excelling in jumping & climbing. When the school was divided into two companies for playing, he was sure to be chosen captain of one of them & his company was usually the one to win the game."[60]

Jackson's horizons slowly widened during these formative years. During the summer of 1837, Cummins got him a job as an engineering assistant for the long-awaited turnpike that was being constructed through Lewis County and would eventually connect Parkersburg and Staunton. This was young Jackson's introduction to surveying, a profession that his grandfather and great-grandfather both had pursued with success. Jackson also had opportunities to apply his facility with mathematics to practical problems. To his disappointment, the turnpike job ended with the passing of summer.

In 1838, Jackson acquired one of his closest teenage friends when the Benjamin Lightburn family moved from Pennsylvania to property on McCann's Run, an hour's walk downriver from Jackson's Mill. Joseph A. J. Lightburn was exactly eight months younger than Tom. His father, like Cummins Jackson, was a miller. Between Joe Lightburn and Tom Jackson, there developed a special bond—one that endured until civil war cast them as generals on opposite sides.

The Lightburns were a reading family with a sizable library. Jackson was always free to borrow books, which he did with relish. The two boys each came to have a favorite volume. Joe was especially fond of Parson Weems's exaggerated and exciting biography of Francis Marion, the "Swamp Fox" of the American Revolution. Lightburn was enthralled by the guerrilla strategy and hit-and-run tactics of a Revolutionary War hero. Tom Jackson had acquired from somewhere a copy of the Bible. For him, the Bible opened a whole new world.[61]

He scrutinized all of the major military campaigns narrated in the Old Testament and the Apocrypha. In the New Testament were promises of love and security he had never before encountered. It was a revelation. The boys spent many hours studying and discussing the two books. Joe Lightburn was extremely devout even at that early age; in 1859, he became a Baptist minister. Every reason exists to believe that he—as much as anyone—awakened the youthful Jackson to the wonders of religion.[62]

Jackson had spent most of his youth in a household where Christianity was rarely mentioned and where men drifted with the tide of events. Yet the lad's search for knowledge, plus a natural curiosity, produced inquisitive probes into religion. He began reading the Bible with genuine interest. Joe Lightburn added exegesis for passages that Jackson could not understand.

The Lightburns encouraged this newfound interest by inviting Jackson to attend Broad Run Baptist Church on a regular basis. The 800-square-foot log structure, on a hilltop overlooking the Lightburn farm, was the closest house of worship to Jackson's Mill. Occasionally, Jackson went to services at Harmony Methodist Church in Weston to hear its spellbinding preacher, the Reverend John Mitchell. The minister's daughter once noted that "Thomas Jackson, a shy, unobtrusive boy, sat with unabated interest in a long sermon, having walked three miles in order to attend."[63]

At an impressionable period of Jackson's life, religion entered his soul. He took it seriously (as he did all avenues of enlightenment). Sometime before 1841, he began praying nightly. In the years that followed, his letters to Laura contained increasing references to "Almighty God" and "an all-wise Providence."

During his teenage years, Jackson gave repeated thought to becoming a minister. But several things combined to steer him away from that career: he was not affiliated with a formal church, he had a limited education, and he was uncomfortable with public speaking. Jackson would subsequently state to Aunt Clementine Neale: "The subject of becoming a herald of the Cross has often seriously engaged my attention, and I regard it as the most noble of all professions."[64]

Not all of Jackson's religious "instruction" was serious. A stonemason employed at the mill remembered one day when Jackson and another youth, Joseph Bailey, hauled stones with teams of oxen. In time, Bailey became a local Baptist preacher of note, but that day he was leading his team with a mixture of spiritual sermon and layman's exhortation. "And the Lord spake unto Moses, saying—Whoa, haw there, Buck!— Speak unto the children of Israel—Gee, Berry!—And I tell you, my brethren—Gee, Berry, you old fool!" The mason added that Jackson calmly issued military commands to his team and got better results.[65]

Solid progress in his studies led to sixteen-year-old Tom Jackson's first experience as a schoolteacher. On November 25, 1840, he accepted the county's invitation to teach a three-month term in a log cabin near Freeman's Creek only a short distance from Jackson's Mill. To follow in his older brother's footsteps was both a privilege and a challenge. Jackson shared his knowledge of reading, writing, and spelling with three girls and two boys eleven and twelve years of age. A surviving axiom of the class, supposedly in Jackson's hand, declared: "A man of words and not of deeds is like a garden full of weeds."[66]

After the term ended on February 28, 1841, the county began processing a voucher for payment of $5.64 to "Thomas J. Jackson." This is the first recorded instance of Jackson using a middle initial. Whether it stood for his father Jonathan's name is not known.[67]

Despite a rugged childhood largely spent out of doors, Jackson had a delicate constitution. He was fifteen when he began to experience the intense gastrointestinal pains that recurred for almost twenty years. One of the first physicians to examine Jackson ventured the opinion that Tom would not survive to manhood. Jackson refused to surrender to such a death sentence. Not even a brief paralysis in 1841 could shake his determination "to conquer every physical, mental, and moral weakness of his nature."[68]

When pain once became almost unbearable, the youngster resorted to external treatment by putting a hot mustard plaster on his chest. Uncle Cummins then sent him on a long horseback ride so that Jackson would think less of the plaster but continue to wear it. Discomfort from the counterirritant became so intense that Jackson fainted and fell from the horse. Yet he resolved "not to yield to trials and difficulties." Jackson soon visited Dr. William J. Bland in Weston. This well-known physician thought Jackson's health "was much impaired by a vernicular & dyspeptic disease of the stomach. To improve his constitution by horseback exercise, & to make something for a liberal education (for which he *always* was *eager*), his friends had him appointed constable of half [of] Lewis County." Another early writer thought that the constabulary emanated from a higher authority. "There are some persons in this world to whom God gives natures and characters older and maturer than their years, and young Jackson was one of these."[69]

Neither poor health nor divine authority was the major reason Jackson became a constable. At seventeen he was approaching manhood. The independent spirit and self-control that would mark his later military career was by then very awake. Being an official of the court offered an avenue for a career, albeit a poor one. Yet it was better than a life with no future at Jackson's Mill.

Lewis County was then a huge domain. (Six counties would ultimately be carved from it.) A constable vacancy occurred in the West Fork district. Colonel Withers, Jackson's former teacher, and Major Minter Bailey, a lifelong friend, were serving as justices of the peace with considerable administrative authority. They were empowered to employ constables as "minor sheriffs" to serve court papers, hunt down debtors, obtain judgments, and perform other duties at the direction of the court.

Constable positions normally went to mature men of callous disposition. The job was not one for the quiet temperament of Tom Jackson. Still, the pay was good, the experience would be useful, and the training would prepare him for the vicissitudes of adulthood. Influential friends pushed for his appointment. Because Jackson was a minor, Cummins Jackson and Minter Bailey agreed to post the $2,000 required bond. On June 11, 1841, Jackson received the job. He appeared in court that day and took "the several oaths prescribed by Law, the Court being of the opinion that he is a man of honesty, probity and good demeanor."[70]

Jackson held the position of constable for ten months. It was not always a pleasant job: iron nerve, vigor, and persistence were constant requirements. He had to ride far afield through the half-settled region. The position thrust Jackson into the company of men who were unscrupulous and often prone to violence. Jackson regularly encountered a low, immoral element of society with which he had previously been unfamiliar. In 1863, the usually reliable Dr. Bland made the unsupported allegation that Jackson "became wild" as a constable and was "said to have had an illegitimate child (by a Miss Brown), still living as a Miss Racer & now reputable."[71]

On the positive side, Tom Jackson demonstrated ingenuity in the collection of one outstanding debt. For some time, a local preacher named Holt had owed ten dollars to a widow living downriver from Weston. The widow appealed to the court, and Jackson was assigned to collect the money. Jackson confronted Holt, who agreed to meet the constable in Weston on a certain day and settle the debt. The minister failed to appear as scheduled. Jackson paid the widow from his own pocket and said nothing more about the incident.

A few days later, Holt rode into the county seat and hitched his horse near the blacksmith shop. Jackson learned that the man was in town and went in search of him. Holt saw the constable approaching and leaped upon his horse for safety. In that age there prevailed a common law that a man could not be dismounted by force. Jackson had anticipated such a move. He quickly grabbed the reins and led the horse toward the doorway of the blacksmith's establishment. The entrance was not high enough for the mounted Holt; Jackson intended to "scrape off" the rider, if necessary. Holt jumped from the saddle and paid Jackson either in cash or with the horse.[72]

Extant records disclose Jackson collecting twenty-nine delinquent accounts for Weston merchant John H. Hays and receiving thirty cents each for serving warrants on six Lewis County residents. Court ledgers also show that many of the debtors Jackson hauled into court were men owing money to Cummins E. Jackson. A local miller who termed Jackson "Cummins' favorite nephew" added of the constable: "He was quick in his movements but nothing remarkable in his appearance. At supper he was a silent listener."[73]

The duties of constable fluctuated in volume. Jackson thus had periods of free time. Less than two months into the new job, he agreed to go to Parkersburg for Uncle Cummins and bring back a small piece of mill machinery that had arrived by boat from Pittsburgh. The trip would give Jackson a chance to see Laura and his favorite uncle, Alfred Neale. The journey would be long in both distance and time. Hence, when Jackson reached Clarksburg on the morning of August 1, 1841, he invited teenager Thaddeus Moore to accompany him. The two boys attended the Presbyterian church twice that Sunday to listen to the Reverend Ezekiel Quillan exhort. Moore, who kept a detailed journal of the trip, commented of Jackson that day: "He said he only hears the Presbyterian doctrine when he comes down to his home[town], and prefers it to the Baptist at Broad Run meeting house."[74]

Moore had to have a saddle strap repaired the next morning for one of the two horses that Jackson had brought with him. During the wait, Jackson walked up the street to see the brick cottage that had been his first home. The house looked as Jackson vaguely remembered it; after fourteen years the apple tree was noticeably larger. Memories were too few, familial ties too brief, for Jackson to feel profound loss. Moore soon rode up. Seeing Jackson standing alone at the gate to the property, the companion noted: "I felt genuine sorrow for the boy."

The travelers spent the night of August 2 at the Stone House at Pennsboro. There, by sheer luck, they met Samuel Houston. The future "Father of Texas" was en route home to Rockbridge County. He made a number of inquiries about members of Jackson's family. Resuming their journey at daybreak the next morning, Jackson and Moore reached Parkersburg two days later. As always, Uncle Alfred and Aunt Clementine received him warmly. Tom and Laura had a wealth of news and thoughts to exchange. Of the stay there, a detached Thad Moore observed that the Neales "are kind to Thom and he is grateful for their kindness. He does not forget at night to say his prayers. This good habit he gets from the Neales."

With the machinery in tow, the two boys began the return trip to Lewis County. One afternoon they rode past a Mr. Adams's farm. A slave funeral was in progress. "Thom seemed to be very sorry for the [black] race," Moore wrote, "and said that Joe Lightburn said they should be taught to read so they could read the Bible and he thought so too. I told him it would be better not to make known such views and if they were carried out we would have to black our own boots. He said with him that would be only on Sunday and not even in the winter."

Although the two lads were the same age, Moore considered Jackson older in wisdom and conduct. The youth parted in Clarksburg, with Jackson continuing upriver to the mill. "He is a first rate boy," Moore concluded, "and I am just getting to know him."[75]

Late in October, Jackson had to make another, much sadder journey. His brother Warren had never recovered from the Mississippi River excursion. Tuberculosis developed; as Warren lay dying, he sent for his brother and sister. Whether Laura made the long journey from Parkersburg to Upshur County is not known. Tom rode hard to reach his brother's bedside. He tarried with him into November, when Warren's suffering ended. The brother's "premature death" was a great blow to Tom. Yet a newfound strength enabled him to tell a friend that Warren had "died in the hope of a bright immortality at the right hand of the Redeemer."[76]

Of Jackson's immediate family, now only Laura remained. Frail, dark-haired, and somber, Laura resembled her brother markedly but had the advantage of years of love and contentment with the Neales.

January 1842 brought Jackson's eighteenth birthday. Not yet at his final height of almost six feet (five inches above the average for males of that day), he had brown hair kept short because it tended to curl, a bronzed complexion from outdoor life, high forehead, curved Indian nose, and thin lips. Large blue-gray eyes dominated his facial features. His natural expression was a combination of thoughtfulness and fatigue. Jackson's frame was solid and erect but marred by feet several sizes larger than normal. With that extreme reticence cultivated over a lifetime, Jackson could easily disappear in a crowd of three people.

In 1841, a Lewis County resident and kinsman by marriage, Samuel L. Hays, entered the U.S. Congress. The forty-six-year-old Hays was a highly respected attorney and staunch Democrat. He succeeded to the seat that two Jacksons had previously occupied. What attracted Jackson's attention, instantly and totally, was Congressman Hays's announcement that he would shortly interview candidates for an appointment to the U.S. Military Academy at West Point, New York.

Suddenly Jackson saw the single answer to a number of hopes. West Point could provide a free and qualitative education he deeply desired; the military might be the rewarding career he had long sought; he would march in the footprints of forebears who had been distinguished soldiers; the army would surely improve his health; personal ambition could be satisfied; prestige might return to the family name. Tom Jackson went after the appointment with an intensity he had never before exhibited. Going to West Point became the most important goal in his young life.

Four applicants emerged for the appointment: Johnson N. Camden, Joseph A. J. Lightburn, Gibson J. Butcher, and Jackson. The congressman asked Captain George Jackson, a professional soldier and veteran of the War of 1812, to do some preliminary screening of the candidates. At that examination, Camden turned out to be two years below the minimum age limit. The affable Joe Lightburn, Jackson's closest friend, fell by the wayside for unknown reasons. That left Butcher and Jackson as the competing candidates.

Gibson J. Butcher was Jackson's age, a deputy clerk in the Lewis County court, and supposedly the illegitimate son of a traveling attorney named Stringer. "Gip" Butcher and Tom Jackson were longtime acquaintances and schoolmates. Both youths had been dependent upon relatives for support since childhood. Because Butcher lived in Weston, he had had the benefit of more educational opportunities. In his court job, Butcher had obtained legal training, good penmanship, and a solid knowledge of the English language.

Congressman Hays personally came to Weston for the final examinations and selection. Jackson stood out in athletics and in mathematics, a subject that was the bedrock of the military academy's curriculum. Butcher excelled in all other areas of study. On April 19, 1842, official notification of appointment to West Point went to Gibson Butcher.[77] The disappointment Jackson felt was crushing. He had lost perhaps the first thing he had ever wanted with all his heart.

Jackson had survived his growing years because of three factors. One was an inborn temperament that separated those who rise above adversity from those who cannot adjust to setbacks. Next was the presence of helpful adults, such as Uncle Cummins and the Neales, who provided instruction and sentiments of caring. Third was a sense of self-esteem: a belief that, if but given the chance, he could succeed.

At an early age, Tom Jackson had concluded that what happened today was not important if something tomorrow held a greater meaning in life. Such an attitude would later make religion the very essence of his being; but in mid–April 1842, Jackson's present became bleak and the future looked empty.

Losing the appointment to West Point was the capstone of the temple of despair in which he had dwelled for so much of his existence. The effect was deep seated. "In his after years," Jackson's second wife would write, "he was not disposed to talk much of his childhood and youth, for the reason that it was the saddest period of his life."[78]

2

COMING OF AGE AT WEST POINT

O N JUNE 3, 1842, Gibson Butcher arrived at West Point. He immediately found the stern and demanding life completely unnerving. By June 4, Butcher was on his way back to Weston without even informing academy officials. He returned home with the casual air of one who had been on a vacation. To inquisitive neighbors, Butcher explained that at West Point "he was not pleased with things [and] disliked the climate, which he found very cold and unsuited to the summer clothing he had taken with him."[1]

Jackson's boyhood friend, gunsmith Conrad Kester, was one of the first Weston residents to learn of Butcher's return that Saturday evening. Kester saw a resurrected opportunity for Tom Jackson. By morning, Kester had enlisted several citizens to petition Congressman Hays to appoint Jackson to the military academy. Meanwhile, the lad himself could not be found.

A frantic search ensued. Finally, Dr. Evan Carmack discovered Jackson at a religious meeting "at Simmons' school-house." Carmack knew that Jackson was there more as a bystander than as a participant, so he barged into the service and pulled the youngster outside. Jackson's excitement at the news was controlled; after all, he was painfully familiar with disappointment.[2]

Time was of the essence. The school year at West Point began in less than three weeks. Jackson did not have an appointment. Endorsements had to be solicited; his constable duties and personal affairs needed to be put in order; and whenever a vacant hour or two existed, Jackson needed to "cram-study" for West Point's entrance examinations. To Jackson, it was a respite and a challenge he met with gritty determination.

First he sought out William E. Arnold, a lifelong acquaintance whose judgments Jackson respected. Arnold vividly recalled the meeting. "Knowing that he had no influential friends to urge his appointment, and that even if he secured it, he was poorly prepared to pass the preliminary examination, I at first discouraged him in his purpose." Jackson would not bend or quit in his resolve. "Seeing that his mind was made up," Arnold concluded, "I did all I could [thereafter] to advance his interests."[3]

Town merchants, leading farmers in the area, and Captain George Jackson, the previous chief examiner, all cast their support for Jackson. One powerful citizen remained to be convinced. On a dark afternoon, a rain-soaked Jackson appeared at the law office of Jonathan M. Bennett. The twenty-six-year-old attorney's connections were far-reaching and powerful. Jackson ignored the rainwater dripping from his clothes as he asked Bennett for a letter of introduction to Congressman Hays in

Washington. The attorney interrogated him thoroughly, then asked if the poorly prepared Jackson could stand up against the rigid demands of the U.S. Military Academy.

Jackson had been staring somewhat dejectedly at the floor while Bennett spoke. At this question, Jackson raised his head, stared straight at Bennett, and replied: "I know that I shall have the application necessary to succeed. I hope that I have the capacity. At least I am determined to try, and I wish you to help me to do this." Bennett thereupon agreed to help in every way.[4]

It took several days to settle the business of constable. After Jackson submitted his resignation, he still had to attend to small outstanding accounts that creditors had placed in his hands for collection. At one point, Cummins Jackson asked his nephew if he had sufficient funds to cover expenses for the trip he would have to make. Tom answered that he had plenty of money in his possession as a result of recent debt payments. Very little of it, however, was his own. Cummins Jackson rarely had available cash in hand, but he remained influential in the community. He convinced local storekeepers to let Tom have what funds he needed from the collections on Cummins Jackson's promise to make good on all claims.

The generosity of the merchants in this instance backfired. Tom's later absence, Cummins Jackson's failure to press the claims the nephew had entrusted to him, and some shrewd maneuvers by the debtors resulted in nonpayment and several lawsuits. Ten years later, after Jackson had moved to Lexington, he personally covered all of the debts.[5]

On occasion during those frantic days of June 1842, Matthew Edmiston put aside his law practice to help Jackson improve his skills in mathematics. Colonel Alexander S. Withers provided a "crash course" in grammar and spelling. Too soon there was no time for further academic pursuit. Jackson, armed with letters of recommendation, had to go to Washington and present his case personally to Congressman Hays. Leaving Jackson's Mill was akin to pulling anchor from a sea of uncertainty; yet the future held promise, and Jackson rode away with no backward glances of regret.

Every conceivable version of that trip to Washington has been offered—including an account that Jackson walked barefooted the 250 miles from Weston to Washington, thence continued on foot to West Point![6] In truth, the tall and awkward boy donned his best though ill-fitting homespun, his scuffed shoes, and a wagoner's hat. The rest of his skimpy wardrobe Jackson stuffed into a pair of travel-stained saddlebags. He mounted a horse and, accompanied by a slave who was to return the animal, rode through driving rain to Clarksburg to catch the eastbound stagecoach.

The two horsemen reached Clarksburg about an hour after the stage had departed. Jackson, with the servant striving to keep pace, galloped twenty miles through rain and mud until he caught up with the stage at Grafton. A weary Jackson climbed into the carriage and napped through a bouncing ride to Green Valley Depot, sixteen miles east of Cumberland, Maryland. There he boarded a Baltimore and Ohio train and experienced his first rail trip as he completed the last leg of his journey to the national capital.[7]

On June 17 (barely two weeks after Gibson Butcher abandoned West Point), a mud-splattered and rumpled Tom Jackson appeared unannounced at Samuel Hays's congressional office in Washington. The representative was not aware that Butcher had returned to Weston. Jackson presented Hays with Butcher's letter of resignation plus a small but impressive stack of recommendations in his own behalf. The letters praised Jackson as "a meritorious young man . . . quite a smart youth in every respect for his age and opportunity . . . a youth . . . with many noble facultys of soul and great moral worth . . . a fit and proper person . . . a young man of industry and perseverance."[8]

Aware that West Point had a habit of opening its doors more widely to young men lacking one or both parents, eighteen Lewis County petitioners collectively pointed out: "An orphan in early age, he has inspired by his conduct, confidence in his rectitude, and won the acclaim of the community. Descended from a family which has discovered much of the country, and with nothing but his individual exertions to advance him in life, we consider him as having a claim upon the country as great as that of any other young man." These friends of "Thomas J. Jackson" urged his immediate appointment.[9]

Congressman Hays needed no persuasion. He was from Lewis County and was familiar with Jackson's background. Further, his first appointment to the military academy had reneged. With Jackson presumably still in his office, Hays wrote Secretary of War John C. Spencer. He apologized for Butcher's hasty resignation. Hays assured the secretary that he had a worthy replacement ready to proceed at once to West Point. Hays was "personally and intimately acquainted" with Thomas J. Jackson. He praised the lad for his "fine athletic form . . . manly appearance . . . good moral character . . . improvable mind." Hays urged the secretary to act promptly and favorably on the application.[10]

Spencer did so. The appointment (conditional upon passing the entrance exams) was made the following day. With the acceptance certificate bearing the signature "Thomas J. Jackson," the new middle initial was now official. One small technicality remained. Because Jackson was an orphan, the law required him as a cadet to have a legal guardian. Cummins Jackson eventually granted parental consent by scratching through "son" at the bottom of the appointment form, inserting "ward," and signing his name.[11]

A relieved Hays invited Jackson to remain in Washington a few days and see the capital's many attractions. Jackson declined. Ambition and determination were his controlling motivations. The school year at the military academy was about to begin, and Jackson needed to proceed there at once. The eager appointee did consent to take a quick look at Washington from the roof of the unfinished Capitol. Thanking Hays as warmly as his shy nature allowed, Jackson caught a northbound afternoon train.

He rode all night to New York City. Wasting no time, Jackson made his way to the docks. There he paid the fifty-cent fare and boarded a Hudson River ferry. Near noon on Sunday, June 19, the solitary teenager stepped onto the boat landing at the base of the bluff on the west side of the river. At the top, on a flat plain, stood the U.S. Military Academy.

Jackson slung his saddlebags over his shoulder before walking slowly up the steep incline. He registered at the West Point Hotel and was given room 48 in the attic.[12]

Paying scant attention to the accommodations, he returned outside to get a long look at what he earnestly hoped would be his home for the next four years.

West Point had just entered its fourth decade of existence. Its forty acres of flat land provided a panoramic view of the Hudson River from the west. Farther to the west was another steep elevation on which were the remains of venerable Fort Putnam, which had guarded the river during the American Revolution. Dominating the West Point skyline were two stone barracks: the four-story North and the three-story South.

The heart of the campus was the academic building, a long stone structure on West Point's southern edge. It was 275 feet long, 75 feet wide, and two stories tall and was completed only a couple of years earlier (after its predecessor burned in 1838). A riding hall was on the ground floor of this structure, known simply as the Academy. Nearby were a long mess hall, cadet hospital, a six-year-old chapel, and brand-new library. Quarters for officers and staff clustered around the perimeter of the campus complex.

The academy had survived its growing pains and, in the process, become the leading school of engineering in the nation. By 1842, over 1000 West Point graduates were pursuing careers in construction, railroad engineering, exploration, teaching, and of course the military. West Point's reputation and heritage were firmly established.

On Monday morning, Jackson made his way to the adjutant's office to verify his identification and to sign the institution's register. He joined company with several other late arrivals and marched in irregular step to the post hospital. There three physicians ensured that each potential cadet was between the ages of sixteen and twenty-one, at least five feet tall, and neither deformed nor afflicted by any disease that would make him unfit for military service.

Hasty but professional examinations continued: a surgeon thumped the young man's chest, looked at teeth for excessive decay, and inspected feet. For eyesight, the physician went to one end of the room while the applicant stood at the other. The doctor held up a small coin; the cadet had to state whether he saw heads or tails.[13]

Room assignments in South Barracks were the next order of business. Four newcomers, all Virginians, were standing outside the dormitory when Jackson in company with a cadet sergeant approached the building. Dabney H. Maury of Fredericksburg stared at the ungainly new arrival. The stranger was almost six feet tall but seemed shorter because he kept his head downcast in thoughtful abstraction. Baggy homespun, weather-beaten hat, and oversize feet taking abnormally long strides added to the youth's strange appearance. Cold bright eyes and a firmly set jaw were a contrast to the rest of his appearance. Turning to his companions, Birkett D. Fry, A. P. Hill, and George E. Pickett, Maury declared: "That fellow looks as if he has come to stay." When the three asked the sergeant for the name of the new fellow, he replied: "Cadet Jackson, of Virginia."[14]

Jackson next reported to the quartermaster to draw all the supplies considered necessary for a new cadet: a pair of blankets, a chair, arithmetic text, slate, bucket, tin dipper and washbasin, cake of soap, candlestick, and a few sheets of stationery.[15] A little later, Jackson was assigned to a policing detail to remove trash from the campus. This duty brought him into contact with Cadet Maury, who sought "to show my interest in a fellow country-man in a strange land" by being humorous and feigning an air of authority. Jackson responded with a cold and wordless stare.[16]

Maury turned away; but after a moment's reflection, he concluded that he had unintentionally made Jackson angry. When the policing was finished, Maury sought out the victim of his jokes and said: "Mr. Jackson, I find that I made a mistake just now in speaking to you in a playful manner—not justified by our slight acquaintance. I regret that I did so." Back came another baleful, icy look, followed by a curt statement: "That is perfectly satisfactory, sir." Now it was Maury's turn to be indignant. He stalked back to his three friends and blurted: "Cadet Jackson, from Virginia, is a jackass!" Maury, Hill, Fry, and Pickett resolved to have little to do with Jackson thereafter. They proved true to their word.[17]

Maury's negative impression of Jackson was one ultimately shared by a large number of cadets, and for good reason. From interlocked backgrounds laced with social graces and congeniality, most of the young men at West Point did not understand the shy and withdrawn orphan from the mountains.

Jackson likewise found his new associates an odd if not alien lot. He was years in advance of most of them but in every other respect far behind them. Jackson knew nothing of conviviality and cared nothing for conversation. Childhood control had instilled in him an abhorrence of levity, trivia, and wasted time. At the academy, he would evince a laborious perseverance that Maury labeled a "terrible earnestness" to succeed.[18] It was almost natural that the humorless loner would withdraw into a shell when confronted with things he did not comprehend or value. No cadet at the academy had more to learn than Jackson; none was more eager to learn than he.

For the first week, and still without uniforms, four to five cadets were crowded into barracks rooms that had the aura of unfurnished jail cells. An individual cadet had about twelve square feet of living space. At night, the plebes slept on the floor with nothing but a blanket. During the day, screaming third classmen branded the appointees "animals," "beasts," "things," too worthless to deserve respect.

Bewildered aspirants were herded here and there in unexplained haste. They were subjected to hours of marching on the drillfield. John Tidball, who entered the academy two years after Jackson, recorded the scene of fourth classmen trying to master the art of drill: "As we marched or tried to march, there was a constant losing of step, occasioning the most ludicrous and to us the most vexatious, shuffling, stumbling and kicking of heels."[19]

Three days after Jackson's arrival came the admission examinations. The psychological pressure made them appear more difficult than they actually were. Each applicant had to be able to read distinctly and pronounce correctly, write a legible hand, and solve a mathematical problem at the blackboard. Jackson crammed his head with facts for this first hurdle, which almost was his last.

A fellow cadet identified only as "P" witnessed Jackson's performance. "His whole soul was bent upon passing. When he went to the blackboard the perspiration was streaming from his face, and during the whole examination his anxiety was painful to witness. While trying to work out his example in fractions, the cuffs of his coat, first the right and then the left, were brought into requisition to wipe off the perspiration." When told that he had solved the math problem satisfactorily, Jackson took his seat with a sublime look on his face, while "every member of the examining board turned away his head to hide the smile which could not be suppressed."[20]

On Friday afternoon, June 24, the roster of "duly qualified" cadets was posted. The last name on the list was "Tho. J. Jackson." He was a member of the "Immortals," as the weakest section of a class was called. Jackson admitted that he had passed "by the skin of his teeth," but he had passed; and for the moment, that was all that mattered.[21]

Jackson was part of the largest entering class that West Point had ever known. A total of 133 young men had been appointed from twenty-six states; 123 proceeded to West Point in June. The first exams rejected thirty of that number. A Massachusetts plebe was not impressed with the remainder. "I verily believe that not one half of those appointed can *possibly* graduate," George Derby stated. Presumably the writer placed himself in the positive bloc.[22]

Most of the new cadets were under eighteen years of age; one of them—George B. McClellan of Pennsylvania—was only fifteen years, seven months old when he received special permission to enter the academy. The ninety-three freshmen were no different from any other entering class except for their number. A Washington newspaperman wrote of plebes: "They constitute, in point of personal appearance and apparel, the type of every class in the community—from the well-dressed and carefully-tended darling of rich parents, to the scantily-clothed and hardly-used child of destitution. In actual rags do some appear . . . while few comparatively have the exterior that denotes wealth." Jackson was one of six orphans in his class; twenty-two of the plebes had only one living parent.[23]

By the first week of July, the "animals" moved from barracks onto the open plain for summer encampment. Three cadets lived in a single tent, an accommodation that made closeness even more pronounced. In fact, everything at "Camp Spencer" was purposefully designed to be uncomfortable and demanding as the weeding out of misfits continued.

Starting at 5:30 A.M. and lasting until sundown, Jackson's routine included hours of drilling, maneuvers, and long marches. Plebes received instructions in every arm of the military; the manual of arms was a daily ritual, as were guard duty, fatigue details, and parades. Equipment had to be inspection-ready around the clock. New uniforms consisting of gray coatee, white pantaloons, and majestic cylindrical cap with pompon and spread eagle were to be spotless at all times and in all kinds of weather.

Never absent from the new cadets was the servitude demanded by their masters, the wolflike third classmen who snarled and snapped constantly. Putting up their masters' tents, carrying their water, running their errands—such were the easy tasks for plebes. It was the hazing—the verbal abuse—that broke many beginners and sent then scurrying home. Hazing at that time was an integral part of West Point education because it accomplished a number of objectives simultaneously. Constant public ridicule quickly identified the weak, helped many plebes to remain alert and to forget any feelings of homesickness, forced new cadets to react blindly to command, and created a closer relationship among the victims: the class as a whole. Cadet John Tidball thought hazing "rather beneficial than otherwise; a weaning, as it were, of the new cadets from boyhood to manhood." Fellow West Pointer William E. Jones (whom cadets nicknamed "Grumble") saw the system in a darker light. "The rigid discipline, entirely new to many sent here . . . makes the change of life as sudden as it is disagreeable. . . . Vengeance on persecutors is out of the question, so the afflicted are left to the comfort misery draws from company."[24]

New cadet Jackson, with his gangling appearance and simpleminded diffidence, should have been a prime target for the derision of the upperclass oppressors. Such was not the case. Cadets deemed the mountain boy thoroughly unprepossessing, just as gregarious George McClellan was the opposite.

Of course, Jackson was older than the average plebe, a fact that may have made him unattractive to harassers seeking "fresh meat." (The sobriquet "Old Jack," by which his soldiers would know him in later years, first came to him at the academy.) Cadet Jones of Virginia felt that Jackson's "already extensive contact with the world foiled the boys in their fun. Among the more advanced cadets he soon made warm friends." In overdramatic fashion, Jackson's first major biographer attributed his escape from the usual hazing process to "his courage, his good temper, and the shrewdness and savoir-faire acquired during his diversified life in the country."[25]

The accumulation of 200 demerits in any academic year was grounds for dismissal from West Point. While that total seems large, demerits were liberally issued for any and all infractions. William Dutton, one of Jackson's classmates, wrote home after a month at Camp Spencer: "You can have no idea how easy it is to get 'demerits.' . . . Should anything be at all dirty or any of the brass mountings not perfectly bright we get demerits, [even] for not touching our hat to an officer."[26]

Good conduct and obedience to duty would always mark Jackson's years at the academy. He completed the summer camp with an accumulation of but six demerits: one for being late at morning parade; two for "inattention at morning drill"; two for "not dressing properly" for parade; and one for "coat torn at Company inspection."[27] The backwoods lad with the nonengaging personality had adapted surprisingly well to the initial demands of cadet life.

Summer encampment ended in late August. Jackson and his classmates in Company D moved into the first floor of North Barracks in preparation for the start of the 1842–43 school year. Two cadets normally shared a room. (When occasional crowding forced three youths into the same quarters, one slept on the floor.) Cadets had the rare luxury of being able to choose their own roommates—even upperclassmen, if the latter were so inclined.

Barracks life was Spartan. A typical room was twelve feet square with a bare pine floor "which from long use, presented a rough surface of knots and splinters." Iron bedsteads, plus desks and chairs as old as they were uncomfortable, stood against the wall opposite the door. Every accoutrement had its assigned place, each article of clothing its proper peg for hanging. Mattresses were rolled up when not in use. Blankets had to be folded perfectly; a hint of a wrinkle brought one or more demerits. No decorations were allowed on the whitewashed walls. Poor ventilation resulted in a room being hot in summer and frigid in winter. A drafty fireplace provided some warmth when needed. An old-fashioned well outside the barracks was the only source of water. Cadets carried water to their rooms in buckets.[28]

For six days each week, cadets went through an unvarying schedule that epitomized the regimentation of West Point. The drum beats of reveille sounded at dawn (5 A.M. in summer, 6 A.M. in winter). Roll call took place immediately upon awakening. Inspection of rooms and accoutrements came thirty minutes later. Study occupied the remainder of the time before 7:00 and a thirty-minute breakfast. Guard mounting and recreation preceded 8:00 and the start of the academic day.

Classes—"recitations"—occurred for five consecutive hours. Lunch from 1 to 2 P.M. offered a brief midday opportunity for relaxation. Two more hours of classes followed. The period from 4 P.M. until sunset was spent in drill, other maneuvers, and a parade. Cadets had an hour for supper, after which study in their rooms was a requirement. With 9:30 tattoo, cadets had a half-hour for next-day preparation and any final chores of that day. At 10 P.M., lights went out and all cadets were supposed to be in bed.

Thus ended a daily routine that included ten hours of classroom work and study, three hours of military exercises, two and a half hours of recreation, and two hours for meals.[29] Rarely was a cadet not under observation. Officers and upperclassmen conducted inspections at least once daily; they scrutinized cadets as they marched to and from barracks, meals, classes, and chapel on Sunday. Supervision was constant, privacy rare.

Regulations called for cadets to bathe once a week, presumably on Sunday. To do so more frequently required the permission of the superintendent.

No cadet in Jackson's time ever went hungry, but no one ever boasted of the food service either. The dining hall at times assumed the frenzy of a battleground. Silently the plebes entered the hall. Then came a shout: "Take seats!" Stillness exploded into a chaos of noise. Samuel Raymond of Jackson's class described the scene succinctly: "Such a 20 minutes of clawing jawing cursing calling masticating and hauling is rarely seen."[30]

Lunch was the largest meal of the day. Every meal was repetitious and bland: heavy on meat, potatoes, and bread while short on vegetables, fruit, and sweets. Cadet John Buford, a contemporary of Jackson's, once observed: "The fare of the mess hall is miserable . . . it would be quite a luxury to miss a meal." Farmboy Jackson never voiced any complaints. However, one cadet noted that Jackson "was always moderate and the sight of a fly in the food or other evidence of untidy negligence so common to the mess hall cooks always terminated the meal. He ate rapidly, usually finishing before others were half done."[31]

Jackson paid no attention to food, or to anything else not directly related to studies. He was facing one of the most demanding academic programs in America. A faculty member acknowledged: "Our course of studies is a difficult one to accomplish and requires great industry under the many restrictions and deprivations of military discipline—not at all agreeable to a young man not fond of study for its own sake."[32]

The West Point curriculum began with the pattern of the French military academy. Under the godfatherlike leadership of Sylvanus Thayer, who served as superintendent during the 1817–33 period, West Point's course of study came to stress much more than military subjects. Cadets in Jackson's day were required to do passing work in no fewer than ten fields of study.

Mathematics was the dominating subject, with cadets spending an hour and a half each day, six days a week, trying to master mathematical principles. Algebra, geometry, and the other forms of math accounted for 40 percent of cadet failures and discharges at West Point. French was a necessary part of the curriculum because so many military and technical works were in that language. Drawing consisted of a progression of sketch work from human figures through topography to landscape designs. Physics, mechanics, and astronomy were but one grouping in a catchall area known as natural and experimental philosophy. Horsemanship, geography, history, and the use of the sword were among the other subjects in the curriculum.[33]

Almost three-fourths of the West Point course work concentrated on mathematics, science, and engineering. What Thayer essentially created was a school of engineering. He ran it as such, and so did his successors for decades to come.

Thayer also initiated the method of West Point study. Every entering class of cadets was soon divided into small sections of twelve to fifteen students. Each section contained cadets of roughly the same ability. Low-numbered sections were those moving at a fast pace through a subject. Poorer cadets proceeding more slowly formed the high-numbered groups, with the "Immortals" being the last or poorest section.

Daily recitation was the basis for West Point education. In class, the instructor would explain an axiom or show how to solve a problem. That afternoon cadets returned to their dorms with facts from a half-dozen classes swirling in their heads. Trying to sort everything out consumed the evening hours. On the following day came the moment of judgment. The instructor would pick at random some cadet to review the solution to the problem under discussion the previous day. Said cadet went to the blackboard, took chalk and sponge eraser, then stood at attention until ordered to begin work. He wrote without interruption until finished, whereupon he again faced the professor for final questions or admonishment. While the cadet returned to his seat, the instructor recorded a grade.

To vary from either the lecture or the textbook was akin to heresy. Hence, memorization was always the basis of learning. Daily grades and two semiannual examinations determined each cadet's standing at the end of the year.

Authorities at West Point were as imperious as the curriculum was inflexible. From the academy's beginnings through 1866, the Corps of Engineers ran the school. Superintendents were officers from that branch of the army. In command at Jackson's arrival was Major Richard Delafield, who had led the West Point class of 1818. Delafield began a seven-year term in 1838 as the academy's chief executive officer (and he served another stint as superintendent just prior to the Civil War).

He was a pudgy man with thick hair and eyebrows, large nose, and seemingly boundless but undirected energy. One of the little-known but positive changes Delafield initiated in cadet life was to replace the side-button trousers with fly-fronts. Ladies on the post recoiled in horror. Cadets came to see the full advantage of the new style.

Because Delafield was a stickler for discipline at every level, he had few friends at the post. His habit of sardonic one-liners earned him the nickname "Dicky the

Punster." When he boarded the ship at his 1845 departure, an Irish janitor remarked that "there was many a dry eye at the dock."[34]

Some of the professors under whom Jackson studied were already on their way to becoming academic legends in the nineteenth century. Preeminent among the teachers was Dennis Hart Mahan, first in the class of 1824 and a mainstay at the academy until his 1871 accidental death from drowning. Mahan was thin and goateed, with piercing eyes and a sarcastic tongue. More than one cadet found his courses in engineering and the science of war an ordeal of survival. Mahan was an aloof scholar whose abrasive personality limited his friendships. Yet his name was the one most associated with the reputation and the quality of West Point.

Albert Ensign Church, number one in the class of 1828, became a professor in 1837 and presided over the academy's world of mathematics for forty-one years. Stocky, half-bald, with sleepy eyes and a head that seemed always to tilt to one side, Church was not a dynamic figure in the classroom. Cadets thought him "an old mathematical cinder" and "dry as dust." He conducted daily recitations with the intensity of military drill. Those students well prepared received Church's warm approval. In the case of those who lacked the necessary ability or desire, Church failed them quickly and gave his attention to others.

William Holmes Chambers Bartlett, professor of natural and experimental philosophy, was Mahan's closest rival in notability among the West Point faculty. In 1836, Bartlett began a career at the academy that spanned thirty-seven years. His lectures in acoustics, astronomy, physics, and associated topics often tended to reduce complicated scientific principles to simple mathematical formulas. Bartlett's textbook, *Elements of Analytical Mechanics*, was a standard manual at military schools for years. Darting eyes and a huge shock of unmanageable hair gave Bartlett an awesome appearance, but it was one tempered considerably by an engaging personality.

Jackson would study French under Claudius Berard, West Point's senior faculty member in length of service. Beginning in 1815, Berard wrote texts and taught language with a detachment that kept him unknown to cadets as a person. Jacob Whitman Bailey was a walking science department equally effective whether teaching chemistry, botany, mineralogy, or geology.

The Reverend Martin Philip Parks presided over courses in geography, history, and ethics. At chapel services on Sundays, he also presented heavy doses of Episcopalianism. Among the lower-ranked faculty that Jackson encountered either in horsemanship or in artillery class was Francis Taylor, whose spiritual influence on the young Virginian after West Point would be considerable.[35]

West Point was the challenge of Jackson's life. Within the corps of cadets were some of the brightest and most cultured young men in the nation. Jackson's scholastic preparations were poor, his social amenities undeveloped. One of his few West Point friends, "Grumble" Jones, remembered that Jackson began his cadetship "under great disadvantage—others were trained at the start but his mind was still the unbroken colt, shying here, tottering there, and blundering where his companions already knew the difficulties of the ground."[36]

Jackson would rely on cold impassivity as a shield in the new life of a cadet. Shyness, aloofness, silence became his behavioral characteristics. A grave, thoughtful expression was constant. He cared nothing of the opinions of others; he tolerated rather than cultivated associations with other cadets. Jackson's overly mature ways brought him two nicknames at West Point: "the General" and "Old Jack."

Although he professed to be content in his new surroundings, evidence is strong that Jackson was not happy in his first year at the academy. Absorbing an education under his many handicaps was deadly serious business. Rigid conformity left no room for levity.

The critical first semester began in September 1842 with all plebes still on probationary status until January and midterm examinations. Jackson was in academic hot water by the end of the first week. He had one course in French and three in mathematics. A product of the mountainous frontier, Jackson knew absolutely nothing about foreign languages. He had excelled as a youth in addition and division, but he had never encountered the likes of algebra, geometry, and trigonometry. Nor was he prepared for the presentations and assignments made by professors who appeared uninterested where an individual's comprehension—or lack of it—was concerned.

Jackson struggled valiantly to keep pace in class. Some help came from an unexpected quarter. Cadet W. H. Chase Whiting was the leader of the third class and in charge of the initial indoctrination of Jackson and his fellow plebes. Whiting was the last person who might have been expected to show compassion to newcomers, particularly since the Mississippian was on his way to compiling the highest academic ranking ever achieved at the academy to that point. Yet Jackson was desperate.

Hesitatingly, he asked Whiting for an explanation of some difficulties in the day's homework. "He seemed to me," Whiting stated, "far from quick of apprehension, & acquisition of knowledge was a labor." Nevertheless, Whiting added, "I was much attracted by his determination to get through, his application, & his modesty."[37]

Whiting assisted Jackson so regularly thereafter in fractions and mathematical systems that the Virginian became known as "Whiting's Plebe." Such tutorial sessions were momentary boosts rather than permanent elevation. John Gibbon of the class of 1847 never forgot that in math classes Jackson's "efforts at the blackboard were some times painful to watch. No matter what proposition was assigned to him to recite on, he would hang to it like a bull dog and in his mental efforts to overcome the difficulty great drops of perspiration would fall from his face, even in the coldest weather, so that it soon became a proverb with us that whenever 'Old Jack' . . . got a difficult proposition at the blackboard, he was certain to flood the entire room."[38]

Compounding Jackson's problems was his absolute refusal to skim over any arduous portion of the textbook. When one or more problems of a previous day's assignment remained vague or unsolved, Jackson would not move to the next lesson until, by constant mental hammering, the earlier problems were understood. On such occasions, he sometimes was called to the blackboard for recitation. Jackson would reply that since he had not mastered yesterday's work, he had not yet reached the lesson for the day. The professor was left with no choice but to grade Jackson as unprepared for that class.[39]

Homesickness further impaired his efforts. This is somewhat strange, given the fact that he was an orphan who had never known a strong immediate family. Perhaps his ailment was not so much homesickness as it was loneliness. He missed Jackson's Mill,

Laura, his friends in Lewis County; he felt outside the realm of life at West Point. One almost equates fourth classman Jackson with young student Ebenezer Scrooge in Dickens's *A Christmas Carol.*

Daily setbacks could not break Jackson's will. He *could* learn French, he *would* master mathematics. First classman Ulysses S. Grant is supposed to have remarked at one point during the year that Jackson "was the most honest human being I ever knew—painfully conscientious, very slow in acquiring information, but a hard, incessant student."[40]

The words "hard" and "incessant" are appropriate. Jackson devoted as much as sixteen hours a day to his studies. He made it a rule when reading to sit rigidly upright with his back to the door and to speak to no one who entered the room. He might stare at a blank wall for an hour while straining to memorize facts and figures. His first roommate, Tennessee native Parmenas Turnley, declared: "No one I have ever known could so perfectly withdraw his mind from surrounding objects or influences."

Cadet Jones knew that his friend "was always at his books and many times when others were asleep he was still at work." Cadet Maury put it more dramatically. Just before lights-out sounded each night, Jackson "would pile his grate high with anthracite coal, so that by the time the lamps were out, a ruddy glow came from his fire, by which, prone upon the bare floor, he would 'bone' his lessons for the next day, until it literally burned into his brain."[41]

He plodded, he persevered, but Jackson continued to struggle. On October 12, 1842, he was dropped to the fifth section in mathematics; the following month Jackson plunged to the tenth section in French. January dismissal loomed larger, and Jackson prepared a speech should this occur and he be forced to return to Weston. "If *they* had been there," he was going to say, "and found it as hard as [I] did, they would have failed too." Yet Jackson had no intention of giving up voluntarily. He "would go through or die," he exclaimed proudly.[42]

Semiannual examinations began on the first Monday in January and extended over a two-week period. They took place in the library. Blackboard and oral presentations were made before a faculty committee. An icy wind sliced across the snowy campus when, on Tuesday, January 3, 1843, Jackson had his rendezvous with destiny.

Sweating profusely, but with facial features firmly set, he strode in long and gangling steps to the blackboard. Furiously he wrote while chalk dust settled over everything in the immediate area. Oblivious to all else, Jackson unloosed all of the knowledge he had amassed over the past four months.

It was sufficient—barely so. Of the 101 cadets in his class, Jackson stood sixty-second in mathematics and eighty-eighth in French. Exemplary conduct helped his case: he had amassed but four demerits at that halfway point. In the first ranking of his class, Jackson was seventy-first with a general merit of 144.51 out of a possible 300 points. (The number one cadet, Charles S. Stewart, had a 298.45 general merit.)

Jackson doubtless could have expressed the same sentiments as those classmate Samuel Raymond sent to his mother a week after the examinations. "I might as well be contented with my standing in my class," Raymond exclaimed, "as it is not as bad as it might be, especially when I compare my condition with those who have been obliged to pack up and be off through lack of industry or talents. I pitied the poor fellows from the bottom of my heart, their hopes destroyed, their friends disappointed, themselves disgraced. Yesterday sixteen were sent away from causes mentioned above."[43]

On February 20, 1843, plebe Jackson's probationary period officially ended. He signed an oath of allegiance to the U.S. Army and received his warrant as a full-fledged cadet. The great first hurdle was behind him. West Point's curriculum would remain a constant challenge, but Jackson had learned to concentrate on his studies and to shut out completely the distractions of the world.

Academic demands continued to rank first in Jackson's priorities during the second semester. Meanwhile, he was learning the rudiments of social graces: the benefits of cleanliness (keeping one's hair trimmed and combed, fingernails clean and cut), how to dress, when to bow, proper table manners, and the like.

To help himself remember, as well as to expand his gentlemanly horizons, Jackson began keeping a book in which he penned moral and ethical maxims. He made his entries with care. The handwriting is large, meticulous, and correct, in contrast with the scrawling style of later years. The axioms related to morality, manners, the principal aims of life, and other avenues for self-improvement. These quotations were not original or especially profound, yet they reflected Jackson's determination to make the most of life's opportunities.

Dozens of entries by which Jackson modeled his adulthood ultimately made their way into the five-by eight-inch notebook. At the outset were such pronouncements as "Through life let your principal object be the discharge of duty. . . . Sacrifice your life rather than your word. . . . Let your conduct toward men have some uniformity." The most famous of the statements in this class was: "You can be whatever you resolve to be." Other maxims concerned social behavior. "Temperance: Eat not to fullness, drink not to elevation. . . . Silence: Speak but what may benefit others or yourself; avoid trifling conversation. . . . It is not desirable to have a large number of intimate friends. . . . Never weary your company by talking too long or too frequently. . . . Never try to appear more wise and learned than the rest of the company." Jackson adhered faithfully to these precepts.[44]

In the spring semester of 1843, Jackson began a slow rise up the academic ladder. There were numerous bumps along the way; but as William Jones correctly observed, "henceforth his was a gaining race. Every time he left scores behind—increased labor seeming only to increase his speed."[45]

End-of-year examinations came in June. Cadets went before the Academic Board as well as the Board of Visitors, which annually met at that time. A special guest was also in attendance. Fourth classmen in June 1843 got their first look at a giant of a legend: the army's commanding general, Winfield Scott. The term "larger than life" surely applied to the grand soldier, who stood six feet, five inches tall and whose girth matched his height. Cadets looked at him in awe; fellow officers viewed Scott with a respect bordering on worship. All were moved when the nation's premier warrior confessed: "Scarcely a day elapses without my having occasion sincerely to regret that I did not have the advantage of a West Point education."[46]

Jackson made noticeable improvement in the second semiannual testing period. He jumped from sixty-second to forty-fifth in mathematics and from eighty-eighth to seventieth in French. What raised his cadet standing solidly was good conduct. He ranked thirty-eighth among 223 cadets in behavior. Of the nine demerits Jackson received from September through June, half of them were the result of being late to roll calls. Long hours of study were not without penalty. "His military deportment & his general conduct were exemplary," upperclassman Chase Whiting observed, and they remained that way.[47]

In four years at West Point, Thomas Jackson never received a demerit for any form of misconduct. His infractions were minor violations of the academy's endless regulations. Jackson's accumulation of but fifteen demerits for the entire twelve-month plebe period stood in sharp contrast to 123 for Barnard E. Bee and 167 for George E. Pickett.[48]

With the beginning of July 1843, Jackson's class experienced a keen sense of advancement. William Jones summarized: "After a year of endurance the plebe becomes a third classman and changes from the persecuted to the persecutor. It is probably the proudest moment of his whole life. He enters on his new career with all the zest of disimprisoned youth, and all the skill of a doctor just out of the disease. The enjoyment is exquisite and in proportion to the perplexities inflicted."[49]

Third classman Jackson did not fit that mold. He forsook much in his quest for an education. No time was available for hazing or recreation of any form. Group swims in the Hudson, summer dances, hours with large groups of cadets for the inevitable "bull sessions," participation in sports, taking the lead in any campus activities—none of those outlets had appeal for Jackson.

He took no dancing courses at West Point, nor did he make any use of social betterment available to the cadets. Jackson never could even recall speaking to a woman at any time while at the academy. His half-dozen friendships were genuine and warm. He was kind and courteous to everyone, convivial from a distance, possessed of deep and outward sympathy for a cadet experiencing distress of any form.

Jackson's only known diversions consisted of solitary walks or strolls with a friend through the campus and nearby hills. He especially enjoyed tramping alone up the mountainside to the ruins of Fort Putnam. Pieces of stone wall jutted as high as thirty feet; rocky skeletons were all that remained of the buildings. Yet the ruins offered Jackson a sense of protection much like the white poplars across the West Fork River had shielded him in youth.

The view from Fort Putnam was also magnificent. Below were the tents on the West Point plain, the academic buildings surrounding the drillfield, and beyond the campus the majestic Hudson River twisting and turning its way toward the ocean. Such quiet solitude above the tempest of cadet life gave Jackson opportunity to meditate.[50]

Brisk walks were his opportunity for exercise. Only calisthenics interrupted the fast pace. Sometimes Jackson's attention to physical matters brought him close to danger. Once asked if he were ever guilty of a deliberate infringement of the rules at the academy, Jackson replied sheepishly: "Yes. I remember one overt act, but it was the only one in which I consciously did what I knew to be wrong. I stepped behind a tree to conceal myself from an officer, because I was beyond bounds without permit."[51]

More mathematics and French, plus English grammar and the first doses of some 650 hours of drawing, composed the curriculum for third classmen. Jackson began the 1843–44 term eagerly; his grasp of descriptive and analytical geometry and of calculus were now so firm that on September 30 he was transferred up to the third section. While French and English were alien enough to keep Jackson in a state of semi-perplexity, it was Robert Walker Weir's drawing classes that threatened to be Jackson's undoing.

Weir was a well-known artist whose painting *Embarkation of the Pilgrims* still hangs in the U.S. Capitol rotunda. He was a perfectionist who expected no less of his students. The West Point drawing courses included intensive work in lettering, sketches of human figures, topographical compositions, and paintings with oil and watercolors. Each one of the assignments provided a veritable crisis for young Jackson. The harder he tried to draw prescribed patterns, the worse it got. Bad from the outset, his performance went steadily downward.

Of seventy-nine cadets in his class at the January 1844 examinations, Jackson ranked twenty-first in mathematics, sixty-first in French, and fifty-eighth in grammar. As for drawing, he was seventy-fourth—one of the "Immortals."[52] Although Jackson bore down with his usual unflappable resolve, thoughts of home after a year and a half's absence continued to interrupt his concentration. This prompted the first letter in a seventeen-year correspondence Jackson would maintain with his sister Laura.

January 28, 1844, was the date of the initial communique. Jackson's rough grammar is occasionally apparent as he sought to be upbeat and self-confident when describing his situation. "My health is far better than it was when I parted with you, and indeed more flattering than it has been for the last two years. . . . The examinations closed a few days since, and rather to my advantage, as I rose considerably in mathematics, and a few files in the French language, though in the same time I fell a few files in ethics and in drawing. There was only one Virginian found deficient in my class. . . . I am also homesick, and expect to continue so until I can have a view of my native mountains, and receive the greetings of my friends and relatives. . . . It is the anticipation of one day realizing them that fills my heart with joy, and causes me to urge forward and grasp that prize which will qualify me for spending my life with them in peace and honor." Jackson then expressed optimism about his West Point training and pessimism on a career in the army. "I feel very confident that unless fortune frowns on me more than it has yet, I shall graduate in the upper half of my class, and high enough in it to enter the Dragoons. Be that as it may, I intend to remain in the army no longer than I can get rid of it with honor, and means to commence some professional business at home."[53]

It was as a third classman that Jackson presumably had the most disturbing altercation of his West Point career. William Jones, one of Jackson's few real friends at the academy, presented an impassioned summary of the incident.

Though [Jackson was] incredulous of vice in others, when conviction came there was no mercy to be expected. Once when his musket, always scrupulously clean, had been taken, and another in bad order left in its place, Jackson notified his cadet captain of the fact and of his private mark [on his weapon]. That evening at inspection his musket was found in the hands of Cadet McLean, usually called Old Bison. The prevarications of the latter when questioned convinced Jackson of malicious design, and his rage became almost uncontrollable. The petty theft, prompted only by laziness, seemed to show a moral depravity disgracing to humanity. He was determined West Point should no longer endure such a nuisance, and desisted from a prosecution of charges only at the instance of the commandant of cadets and other professors.[54]

This is a well-known and long-accepted story, but Thomas J. Jackson was not involved in the incident. Cadets Thomas K. Jackson of South Carolina and Nathaniel H. McLean of Ohio, both of the class of 1848, were the two principals in the affair. It was the South Carolina Jackson who got the dirty McLean musket and then sought to have the Ohioan expelled from the academy. Thomas Jackson of Virginia became part of the incident only because on November 3, 1844, the demerits intended for Thomas K. Jackson were inadvertently placed on his record. Once the mistaken identity became known, the demerits assigned to T. J. Jackson were deleted.[55]

The 1843–44 school year ended with Jackson on an upswing. He ranked eighteenth in mathematics, fifty-second in French, fifty-fifth in English grammar, and sixty-eighth in drawing. Strong in conduct and mathematics, weak in the other subjects, Jackson stood thirtieth among the seventy-eight cadets of his class. His general merit was 461.1 as compared to the high of 642.9 and the low of 269.

His conduct as a third classman should have been better. Unexplained laxity—including such offenses as "absent from muster," "tent walls not raised at inspection," "firing before the command," "inattention at drill," and "absent from relief parade"—brought him twenty-six demerits for the year. This would be the highest number of marks he would accrue in a twelve-month period. Yet Jackson ranked fifty-seventh in good conduct among 211 cadets. Darius N. Couch had no demerits that year, while Ambrose E. Burnside accumulated 198 (two demerits short of dismissal).[56]

The thrill of becoming second classmen in July 1844 was secondary to Jackson and his classmates, for with the start of the junior year came summer vacation. This was the only extended leave a cadet got during his four years at West Point. Jackson received furlough starting at 2 P.M., June 25, and extending to August 28 tattoo. The young Virginian was excited at the prospect of going home.

Jackson spent the first part of his vacation with Laura, who by then was living with relatives in Beverly, a thriving mountain community fifty miles east of Weston. Beverly boasted a courthouse, two hotels, and a half-dozen merchandise stores. Tri-weekly stagecoaches connected the town with the rest of western Virginia. Jackson arrived on one of the nine-passenger coaches. He brought with him his first gift to Laura: a silk dress he had purchased with funds saved at the academy.

Brother and sister enjoyed their first reunion in almost three years. Laura was eighteen; and with the same chiseled features, the resemblance with Thomas was obvious. Although the brother was but two years older, he "felt a fatherly, as well as a brotherly interest in his sister" and discussed every facet of life with her. This closeness was clearly evident throughout their two decades of correspondence.[57]

The time was pleasant in Beverly, a town Jackson would come to know well. Then it was on to Jackson's Mill for a reunion with uncles and slaves. "His meeting with them after an absence was not unlike an old time love feast," a family friend noted. "Such a shaking of hands and laughing loud enough to shake the house tops, was a sight worth seeing."[58] The home place had changed—as do all sites of yesteryear—

and Jackson had to be aware of the now-seedy appearance of the farm he had long called home.

On his first Sunday at the mill, Jackson set out to attend church at Broad Run. He was dressed in a new uniform and mounted on one of the Jacksons' fine horses. Accompanying him were his cousin Sylvanus White, Miss Caroline Norris, and several others. The group was crossing the West Fork at Withers' Ford when Jackson's mount stumbled and pitched its rider into the water. The river was three feet deep, and Jackson emerged thoroughly drenched.

His companions expressed concern as Jackson remounted. A proposal was made to return to the mill so that Jackson could change into dry clothes. No, he politely answered, "it will soon be church time, and we must not be late." To the amusement of many that Sabbath, a waterlogged West Pointer participated actively in the Baptist service.[59]

Later Jackson talked with White about the rigors of cadet life. "Oh, I tell you I had to work hard," Jackson admitted. He had but three weeks "to learn English grammar." A failing grade would have meant expulsion from the academy. "Would they send for you if you did not come back?" White asked. "Oh, I think not," came the reply. "But not for Lewis County would I fail to go back. I am going to make a man of myself if I live. What I will to do I can do."[60]

By August 28, 1844, Jackson was back at West Point. Although he did not know it, the next day a federal court in western Virginia indicted Cummins Jackson on counterfeiting charges. What Cadet Jackson did find waiting for him as a surprise was appointment as a sergeant in the corps. Jackson was not overly moved. "During my furlough I was made an officer," he wrote Laura, "consequently my duties are lighter than usual."[61]

His roommate in the junior year was George Stoneman, a New Yorker who would later gain fame as a Union cavalry general. Stoneman was the oldest of ten children, reticent and meditative by nature. Like Jackson, he preferred to think rather than to talk. In the adjacent barracks room lived Cadet John Tidball, who remembered: "These were such quiet neighbors I scarcely knew they were there." Tidball, a fellow Virginian, came to know (and to admire) Jackson well over the next two years. A little-known description of Jackson is unusually revealing.

In consequence of a somewhat shambling, awkward gait, and the habit of carrying his head down in a thoughtful attitude, he seemed less of stature than he really was. . . . Being an intense student, his mind appeared to be constantly pre-occupied, and he seldom spoke to anyone unless spoken to, and then his face lightened up with a blush, as that of a bashful person when complimented. His voice was thin and feminine—almost squeaky—while his utterances were quick, jerky and sententious, but when once made were there ended; there was . . . no hypothesis or observation to lead to further discussion. When a jocular remark occurred in his hearing he smiled as though he understood and enjoyed it, and never ventured comment to promote further mirth. . . .

There were occasions, as I observed, when his actions appeared strangely affected; as, for instance, a drenching shower caught sections returning from recitations, or the battalion from the mess-hall, and ranks were broken to allow the cadets to rush for shelter to the barracks, [but] Jackson would continue his march, solemnly, at the usual pace, deviating neither to the right nor to the left. This, and other things like it, I saw him do time and again, showing a design to it; but what the design was he alone appeared to know, for no one bothered themselves to discover it or did more than remark: "See old Jackson!"[62]

Such behavior always made Jackson a natural target for pranks by the cadets. A section fought back snickers one day when Jackson was called to the blackboard. On the back of his uniform coat someone had printed "General Jackson" in chalk. An exasperated professor forced the guilty party to make a public apology. Jackson, for his part, seemed rather unconcerned about the whole affair.[63]

As a second classman, Jackson now left the quicksand of mathematics for the morass of science. His courses in the 1844–45 year were chemistry, natural philosophy, and a continuation of drawing. This was the point at which Jackson came into direct contact with Professor William Bartlett, the brilliant scientist whose lectures in optics the Virginian never forgot. By this point, Jackson had learned to study and to absorb. An intellectual pursuit of any kind was no longer an Armageddon; it was a fascinating new avenue. Of all of Jackson's senior West Point instructors, the dwarflike and impatient Bartlett came to be his favorite.

After midterms in January 1845, Jackson ranked fourteenth of sixty-three classmates in philosophy, twenty-sixth in chemistry, and a still-embarrassing fifty-seventh in drawing.[64] He was rising in all three courses. More commendably, Jackson was on his way to leading the full corps of cadets in conduct. He would go through his junior year without accumulating a single demerit.

In February, Jackson learned that Laura four months earlier had married Jonathan Arnold of Beverly. He was twenty-four years her senior, a transplanted Pennsylvanian and prosperous attorney-landowner-cattle dealer in the Beverly area. She was his third wife. The inexplicable delay in Laura telling her brother the news did not bother Jackson.

"My sincere desire," he told his sister, "is that you may both enjoy all the blessings which a bountiful Providence can bestow. I think that if happiness exists in this world, matrimony is one of the principal factors." Jackson used that same letter to remind Laura to begin addressing him with his middle initial "J." The presence by then of another cadet, Thomas K. Jackson, made this necessary rather than desirable. Just before closing, Jackson made a passing remark: "I expect to commence taking exercises in riding in a day or two."[65]

The former child jockey proved to be totally unprepared for the rigors of cavalry training. It instantly became apparent. Dabney Maury thought Jackson "awkward and uncomfortable to look at upon a horse. . . . We used to watch him with anxiety when his turn came . . . he seemed in imminent danger of falling headlong from his horse." Another classmate observed: "In the riding hall I think his sufferings must have been very great. He had a rough horse and, though accustomed to horseback-riding, was awkward, and when the order came to cross stirrups and trot, 'old Jack' struggled hard to keep his horse. When he advanced to riding at the heads, leaping the bars, etc., his *balance* was truly fearful, but he persevered through the most perilous trials, and no man in the riding-house would take more risks than he, and certainly no one had our good wishes more than he."[66] Jackson's horsemanship would never reach the graceful level.

By mid-May, Jackson was able to tell Laura: "The annual examination will commence in about two weeks. . . . If fortune should favor me in a degree corresponding to the past, I will have a better standing in my class than I have formerly had." His prediction came true. Of sixty-two cadets remaining in his class, Jackson was eleventh in Professor Bartlett's natural philosophy, twenty-fifth in chemistry, and fifty-ninth in drawing. Jackson's perfect conduct among 204 cadets partially offset the low marks in Professor Weir's drawing laboratories. Jackson was now in the upper third of his class. His accumulated general merit of 474.9 was closer to leader Charles S. Stewart's 594.4 than to tail-ender George Pickett's 229.5.[67]

No cadet rank came to Jackson in his senior year. He had not demonstrated any aptitude for command. His record and personality seemed to be those of a follower, not a leader, so in 1845–46 Jackson held the meaningless title of "High Private." The final year at West Point began on a traumatic note. In July, the first classmen got their baptism into the intricacies of artillery practice. Military training for Jackson was never a snap. For one thing, a cadet once stated, "artillery and infantry tactics are disgusting. I would as soon commit to memory a table of logarithms as some of the lessons in these studies."[68] Moreover, Jackson had matured in every way at West Point save in coordination.

The professor in the theory and practice of artillery was Lieutenant Daniel Marsh Frost, a recent graduate of the academy. Frost never forgot his ordeal with Cadet Jackson.

It became my duty as artillery instructor to "set him up at the Gun"—a duty which I found it very difficult to perform, because he was saw-boned, still jointed, and totally devoid of all grace of motion. . . . I found it hard to make any kind of an artillery man out of him, much more a graceful one. . . . Placing him in position as "No. 1" to load the piece, "heel of the right foot in the hollow of, and at right angles with, the left"—at the word "Load" he was to extend the right foot straight forward, bending the right knee, straightening the left, etc. But at the word "Load" he would go all to pieces as it were. "Let us try it again, Mr. Jackson." Again he would be put in position and again the same result. Over and over this was repeated, until at last losing all patience I had learned to practice in drilling awkward cadets, I exclaimed, "d—n it, Mr. Jackson, how often must I show you this simple movement!"

Instantly regretting my improper exclamation I cast my eyes from his feet to his face and became filled with remorse. The face revealed the soul touching patience and suffering of the "Ecce-homo." No anger, no impatience, only sorrow and suffering. It was a hot July day and the sun was blazing down upon us. The perspiration was rolling down his face and dropped from his chin—a mosquito had fastened upon his nose, and yet his hands hung by his sides.

Frost apologized for the outburst and gently continued to help Jackson master the procedure. The lieutenant became impressed with "the patience and perseverance" displayed by Jackson throughout the class.[69]

Courses in the first half of the senior year included engineering (civil and military), ethics, and mineralogy. Engineering was "the capstone of the academic program" at West Point. First classmen marched daily into the section room to hear Dennis Hart Mahan expound on engineering sketches, fortifications, and the science of war.

Mahan had unabashed admiration for Napoleon Bonaparte, the foremost soldier in European history. All cadets in Mahan's classes became well versed in the exploits of the French legend. Jackson learned, for example, that Napoleon believed rapid marches and maneuver to be a larger factor in battle than numbers. In studying the great struggle at Austerlitz, the acme of Napoleon's brilliance in the field, Cadet Jackson absorbed the value of exploiting geography to one's advantage. The reticent and shy first classman also saw in Bonaparte that a convivial personality was not a requisite for military success.

Professor Mahan stressed other ideas of what a commander should do on the battlefield. Celerity (a favorite word with Mahan) and boldness, daring tempered with common sense, were the basic ingredients for military success. Jackson also embedded those principles deep in his mind.

As a student, Jackson was better at ingestion than recitation in Mahan's course. Like Napoleon, the Virginian would become a great executor of warfare—one who took other people's ideas and brilliantly put them into action. Jackson's moderate grades under Mahan did not reflect the insights and knowledge he gained there on the art of war.

His best classroom performance that year came in ethics. It was a subject that Jackson considered "preferable to any other" he studied at the academy.[70] This rather strange phenomenon seemed in keeping with Jackson's rather strange ways.

Cadet John Gibbon did not understand it. "That Jackson's mind possessed a certain peculiarity is evidenced by the fact that though he stood low in all his studies during three years, when he entered the first class & commenced the study of *logic* [ethics], that bug-bear to the root majority of others, he shot like a meteor from near the foot of class to very near its top. Certainly his future career demonstrated him to be in military matters naturally logical, though his love of the dry study had any thing to do with making him the best executive officer developed in our great war, it is difficult to say."[71]

Late in November, Laura informed Jackson of Uncle Cummins's many troubles with the law. Jackson expressed "remorse for the misfortunes of an uncle who has been to me a true friend." It is significant that any previous thoughts of the uncle as a "father" had now given way to "friend." Feelings of orphanhood were still acute in Jackson.[72]

Offsetting such pangs was the growing esteem that Jackson won in his last two years at the academy. His close friends were by choice few in number, but admiration for the quiet Virginian was widespread and surprisingly mutual. A former roommate, Parmenas Turnley, was convinced that "while there were many who seemed to surpass [Jackson] in intellect, in geniality, and in good-fellowship, there was no one of our class who more absolutely possessed the respect and confidence of all." Jackson in turn was saying at the same time: "It grieves me to think that in a short time I must be separated from amiable and meritorious friends whom an acquaintance of years has endeared to me by many ties."[73]

Turnley and Jackson spent much time together in their final West Point year. Another cadet wrote admiringly: "Whenever the regulations would allow it Jackson and his friend might be seen on their rounds. Scarcely an evening when both of them were off duty but they walked together around the promenade of the Point and every Saturday evening they explored the extreme limits of cadet bounds and some times ventured a little beyond. Their stride was long and quick, more like business than pleasure—passing rapidly all walkers in their way. During the leisure of Sunday evenings when the weather favored it they were usually seated on the granite rocks overhanging the Hudson, discussing either some religious or metaphysical subject."[74]

One reason for Jackson's long, forced walks was his attempt to improve what he regarded as failing health. His physical condition was a matter of constant apprehension. In his first letters to his sister, Jackson reported being blessed with good health;

yet sometime in the 1844–45 period, he became convinced that he was suffering from consumption and dyspepsia, among other ailments. "My constitution has received a severe shock," he told Laura at one point, "but I believe I am gradually recovering." He hoped that proper exercises would have "the desired effect of restoring me to perfect health." Dabney Maury thought him hypochondriacal; most cadets regarded his health concerns as eccentricity; William E. Jones believed that several of Jackson's organs were in fact malfunctioning. Relying on his own judgment, Jackson adopted a number of "therapeutic" measures for self-cure. He "complained that one arm and one leg were heavier than the other," an incredulous Maury wrote. Therefore, Jackson "would occasionally raise his arm straight up, as he said, to let the blood run back into his body, and so relieve the excessive weight."[75]

Long rapid walks were an integral part of his schedule. Jackson would not bend his body when studying, for fear that compression of some important organs might increase the chance of disease. He sat so straight and stiff that any chair he used might as well have been without a back. Obsessed as well with the notion that paralysis might strike his limbs at any time, Jackson was known to "pump his arm for many minutes, counting the strokes, and feeling annoyed beyond measure whenever his companions interrupted him in his count."[76]

In the January 1846 examination, Jackson was fourth of fifty-nine in ethics, forty-first in engineering, and tenth in mineralogy. He had already acquired the seven demerits he amassed during his senior year. Three of those demerits came at one time from missing artillery drill.[77] Eagerly he and his classmates entered the final grading period, which was a "catchall" semester involving small helpings in several courses.

Thoughts of graduation and furlough were remote among Jackson's class that spring. The United States and Mexico were in dispute over the Texas border; and while American expansionists were staring covetously at all of the Southwest lying between Texas and California, a strong anti-American regime led by General Santa Anna took control of the Mexican government. War clouds grew thicker and closer. Jackson reassured Laura: "Rumor appears to indicate a rupture between our government and the Mexican. If such should be the case the probability is that I will be ordered to join the army of occupation immediately . . . and the next letter you receive from me may be dated from Texas or Mexico. . . . I shall continue to love you with a brother's love."[78]

On May 27, 1846, the cadets learned that the United States had declared war on Mexico two weeks earlier. Most of the class of 1846 would go from graduation to combat, and Jackson hoped earnestly to be one of the fortunate ones sent. Final academy grades for the year came out in mid-June. They showed that Thomas Jackson had compiled one of the most amazing records in the history of West Point. Mired with the "Immortals" at the outset, he now ranked seventeenth among the fifty-nine graduating cadets. He stood eleventh in artillery, twelfth in engineering, fifth in ethics, twenty-first in military tactics, eleventh in mineralogy, and twenty-fourth among 213 cadets in conduct. His general merit of 1837.8 compared quite respectably with the 2236.5 high and 855.7 low in his class. More than one observer was convinced that had the West Point curriculum lasted another year, the pitifully prepared mountain boy of 1842 would have graduated at the top of his class.[79]

Jackson had hoped to win assignment to the artillery—an honored arm that Napoleon had also chosen at the outset of his military career. The Virginian got his wish. Graduates in the academic ranking from number nine to number twenty-seven were tabbed for artillery duty. Jackson's initial service would be in the First Artillery Regiment.

The pay for a brevet (provisional) second lieutenant was $300 annually—an amount established in 1812 and not changed until 1857. However, assignment to the artillery branch entitled Jackson to an allowance for a horse plus emoluments for subsistence. His total annual stipend would be in the $1,000 range.[80]

What thoughts went through Jackson's mind as he departed the academy can only be suggested. West Point had been his home for four years. It had repaired his sketchy educational background and given him one of the most outstanding courses of learning available. Instilled in Jackson as well was a dedication to duty, honor, and country. Four years of instruction had polished away his rough edges and strengthened his self-discipline. The Spartan cadet life, with its primitive living quarters, drill, military maneuvers, and lock-step regimentation, had toughened him physically (his own doubts notwithstanding). Long hours of study developed powers of intense concentration. That was not all good, for such devotion to education deepened Jackson's reserve and probably blocked many friendships that might otherwise have been made.

In return, Jackson's contributions to the school seemed minimal at most. His academic record was solid rather than brilliant; his conduct was excellent but not unexcelled. He had been a noncommissioned cadet officer in only one of the three years when he was eligible. No one would recall Jackson for hilarious pranks, youthful escapades, or even a memorable phrase uttered anytime during four years. He appeared, achieved, and disappeared. The one monument he did leave behind would be historical. Twenty graduates in 1846—fully a third of the class—would become Civil War generals. The easy-to-forget mountaineer from Virginia would be without question the most famous in the group.[81]

By custom, no graduation ceremonies took place at West Point. Nor were any diplomas presented. Chaplain Parks delivered a sermon to the class, their names appeared in orders announcing their satisfactory completion of all course work, and the new brevet second lieutenants headed in every direction on furlough while awaiting duty orders.

Jackson was part of a quintet that traveled southward toward Virginia. In the party were Dabney Maury, who had thought Jackson a humorless "jackass" four years earlier; Archibald B. Botts, a fun-loving Virginian who had matched George Pickett demerit for demerit all the way to graduation; C. J. L. "Dominie" Wilson, also of Virginia, number nine in the class and bound for the cavalry; and Tennessean Cadmus Wilcox, whose class ranking of fifty-fourth may have been due to his reputation of being a friend with every cadet at the academy.

The five young officers reached Washington and took a room on the top floor of Brown's Hotel. Wilcox went out for the evening. On his return around 1 A.M., the temperature rose at every landing as he made his way to the top floor. Wilcox discovered boisterous noise coming from behind the locked door of the room. He pounded furiously until a rather unsteady Maury finally opened the door.

Wilcox could not believe what he saw. "Archie" Botts had apparently passed out on a bed, which was not unusual; but Jackson and Wilson, each clad in a skimpy garment because of the heat, were dancing arm in arm around the room and shouting a popular drinking song of West Point cadets. Loud revelry continued until the inn-keeper threatened to evict them all. The next day, with most of the group the worst for wear, they warmly bade each other farewell and went their separate ways.[82]

Lieutenant Jackson admitted that he "burned with enthusiasm" to be one of those selected for duty in Mexico. Daily he reviewed all the factors he thought were in his favor. For the time being, however, he could only await orders and hope. He spent two weeks in Beverly visiting his sister and getting to know his new brother-in-law, Jonathan Arnold. Mutual affection grew. In the meantime, day after day passed without any orders from the War Department. Jackson began to despair. Another of life's disappointments seemed at hand.

On Monday, July 20, he arrived at Jackson's Mill to see his uncle and family. Jackson found the mill barely surviving on its own. Uncle Cummins seemed preoc-cupied. So the next day the young officer went to Weston to say hello to friends. "He attracted great attention and looked every inch a soldier," an admiring resident stated. "Many who knew him well spoke of the great change made by West Point in his appearance."[83]

That day, by coincidence, Colonel William McKinley was holding the annual muster of his 150th Virginia Militia Regiment. The aging McKinley asked Jackson to take command of the lead company. "No," Jackson replied, "I would probably not understand your orders." The colonel persisted. Jackson relented, went onto the parade ground, and took position in front of the small company of militiamen. The regiment started around the parade ground. McKinley became flustered and failed to give the proper command. Jackson's company continued marching, off the parade ground, up Main Street, and through Weston. Asked why he took such an illogical course, Jackson replied in a serious tone that he was simply obeying orders.[84]

It had been but a small taste of drilling strangers; but coupled with the excitement building with the Mexican War and the continuing absence of any communique from the army, Jackson's anguish at marking time was becoming unbearable. If he was not soon ordered to Mexico, he concluded to go there by enlisting as a volunteer in the ranks.[85] On Wednesday afternoon, July 22, the long-sought army orders arrived. Jackson was to proceed with all dispatch to Fort Columbus, Governor's Island, New York, and report to Captain Francis Taylor, commanding Company K of the First Artillery.[86]

Early on Thursday morning, the twenty-two-year-old said goodbye to the Jacksons. Now the hand of war was reaching out to test the mettle of the young soldier.

3

MEXICO AND A HERO'S MANTLE

TWENTY-TWO-YEAR-OLD Thomas Jackson proceeded under orders to Fort Columbus, New York, with all the enthusiasm expected of a brevet second lieutenant on his first military assignment. He reached Fort Columbus early in August, only to learn that Captain Taylor had departed and was at Fort Hamilton on nearby Long Island. Jackson rushed to that installation and found Taylor but not Company K. It had already departed for Mexico with its new guns; the captain had remained behind initially because of what a fellow officer termed "a sad domestic affliction."[1] Taylor was then directed to collect recruits and horses for his battery and to join it in Texas.

Herding horses and recruits was an inauspicious beginning for Jackson's military career. He was undeterred. On August 12, 1846, he appeared at a justice of the peace in New Utrecht, New York, and signed the usual oath of allegiance. "His sense of duty was the paramount feeling of his nature," a friend recalled Jackson saying, "and even at this time he would have died rather than violate it."[2] Thus, Jackson pursued his new tasks as junior second lieutenant and company quartermaster with earnestness. He looked on his first commanding officer as a teacher. Jackson was fortunate to have an excellent mentor.

Francis Taylor, the son of George Taylor, a merchant from Alexandria, Virginia, was barely sixteen at his 1821 appointment to the U.S. Military Academy. He graduated ninth in the class of 1825 and began his field career when Jackson was a year old. Active service in the 1836–37 Seminole wars in Florida had earned Taylor his promotion to captain. He saw duty as an artillery officer at a number of posts along the Atlantic seaboard, and in 1844–45 Taylor superintended publication of a new manual on artillery tactics. On June 3, 1846, he had requested transfer from garrison duty at Pensacola, Florida, to recruiting service in the Northeast. The War Department acceded and ordered him to New York. Reward for ten years of drab service in Florida was command of the First Artillery Regiment's "flying artillery," a highly mobile battery of guns much smaller than conventional cannon. Taylor was a serious and conscientious officer. Jackson admired his devotion to duty; the subaltern came in time to find Taylor's religious convictions infectious.[3]

On August 19, Taylor and Jackson left Fort Hamilton for Texas with thirty recruits and forty horses. They marched almost 400 miles overland to Pittsburgh. The remainder of the long journey was by boat. On September 6, aboard the *Swatara*, the contingent reached Newport, Kentucky, across the Ohio River from Cincinnati. Taylor reported to Washington that he still had forty horses but only twenty-two men. Two had fallen ill en route, another had received a discharge, and five had deserted. That all of the animals were in hand was seemingly of more concern to Taylor than the loss of 20 percent of his manpower in less than three weeks of travel.[4]

Down the Ohio and toward the Mississippi, the party proceeded on the ship *Hendrik Hudson,* which must have had the appearance and smell of a floating stable. Taylor was continually on the lookout for more recruits and additional mounts. Jackson was intrigued by the scenery. He searched the area where the Ohio joins the Mississippi for the island where he and his brother Warren had sought their fortunes. The memories of a fun-loving brother now dead were bittersweet.

Unknown to all at the outset of this war, American cannon were to be the vital element in every battle. Jackson's artillery wing of the U.S. Army was to come into its own in Mexico. As the ship bore Taylor's company with the current down the Mississippi, Jackson learned from the captain and others the background of the war to which he was going.

The struggle, U. S. Grant would later write, was "one of the most unjust ever waged by a stronger against a weaker nation."[5] In 1821, the Mexicans had wrested independence from the Spanish empire. Yet their twenty-five-year history as a nation had been an almost unbroken series of revolts as one faction after another vied for control of the unstable government. Meanwhile, trouble with the northern provinces had escalated. Texas battled successfully for its freedom; and when the United States in 1845 officially annexed Texas, Mexico became worried that this was but the first step in an American plan to seize California and all of the territory between it and Texas.

It was the annexation of Texas that cocked the hammer on war. Mexicans, nurtured for years on anti-American rhetoric, determined to recapture Texas and defend other threatened land interests. American authorities were riding a high wave of expansionist feeling. They were equally resolved to protect Texas and to absorb any other regions that stood in the way of the prevailing sentiment of Manifest Destiny.

In the early summer of 1846, President James Knox Polk had made an extraordinary albeit foolish move. Antonio Lopez de Santa Anna, a Mexican general and former president with powerful influence, was living in exile in Cuba. The one-legged commander somehow convinced the Polk administration that if restored to power, he could and would bring peace between the two countries—and at a profit to the United States. In August, an American naval vessel conveyed Santa Anna to Mexico. A month later, the Mexican leader had amassed a huge army and turned it against the Americans.

Polk dispatched a force into Texas to protect the area north of the Rio Grande River. Command of that army went to General Zachary Taylor, an officer junior to General Winfield Scott, whom Polk detested. Taylor was a common man in a general's uniform—a plainly dressed, tobacco-chewing general who rarely used the pronoun "I" in his conversation. He knew little about strategy but much about fighting.

After leading his men to victories at Palo Alto and Resaca de la Palma, Taylor advanced slowly toward the mountain fortress the Mexicans had created at the provincial capital of Monterrey. It was one of the largest cities in northern Mexico, and it guarded the main avenues leading south to the capital at Mexico City.

Meanwhile, Captain Francis Taylor's command had reached the army's main staging area at New Orleans and disembarked. While the twenty-seven men and eighty-four horses now in the party enjoyed the feel of land, Jackson took the opportunity to express his thoughts of the future in a quick letter to Uncle Alfred Neale in Parkersburg. The young officer's feelings were not bright. "In an action, if all the officers of the company should be well, I will have to carry dispatches, being unfortunately too low [in rank] to have a command." He could only be hopeful of getting into battle. Jackson closed the letter by voicing some concern about his physical well-being. "I am enjoying comparatively good health at present and I do not believe that I have the liver complaint but am under the impression that the disease is nuralgia."[6]

Following a couple of days in New Orleans, men and horses of Company K boarded the *James L. Daly* for the final leg of the trip. The vessel followed the winding Mississippi through marshy country out into the Gulf of Mexico and then hugged the coastline as it continued southward. On September 22, the month-long journey ended when the ship joined dozens of other boats anchored in front of Point Isabel, Texas, where an important road from Corpus Christi ended at the gulf. Mexican forces had earlier burned the small village at the point, yet the harbor remained the base of operations for General Taylor's expeditionary force.

The advance element of the First Artillery's Company K had already skirmished with the enemy at Camargo in the Mexican interior. Jackson was anxious to join his regiment and experience the thrill of combat. To his uncle in the first letter, he stated, "I expect to start up the Rio Grande by steamer for the purpose of joining the main body of the army as soon [as] possible."

This proved to be wishful thinking. On the day Company K reached Point Isabel, Mexican forces at Monterrey surrendered to General Taylor. The American commander allowed himself to be talked into an eight-week armistice. To many, the war was over. However, none of Taylor's successes had been decisive.

The Mexican army withdrew from Monterrey and remained defiant. Taylor was left with a useless town and the heart of a nation untouched by the American invaders. Almost 600 miles of broken and hostile country stood between Taylor's army and the enemy capital at Mexico City. Any disappointment Jackson may have felt about not seeing battle would be short-lived.

Captain Taylor and Jackson got their detachment onto crowded steamboats and started upriver from Point Isabel. On October 5, the party finally reached the staging area at Camargo, a town of 5,000 residents on the Mexican side of the Rio Grande. A month passed as Taylor and Jackson fought heat and insects while impatiently awaiting orders to move with the battery of siege guns they were to escort.

At last, the contingent started southwestward away from the river and toward Monterrey. The route zigzagged up into the mountains; heavy rains turned roads into passageways of mud. One of Jackson's West Point classmates, Dabney Maury, was serving as a cavalry lieutenant. Maury came upon Jackson trying to move the heavy field pieces forward. With "that terrible earnestness which was the characteristic of his conduct in battle or in work," Maury wrote, Jackson "worked at [the guns] in the muddy road as he used to do at West Point . . . and they had to move along."[7]

It was November 24 before Captain Taylor's party finally reached Monterrey.

There it joined the rest of Company K. Jackson was dismayed to hear new opinions that the war was about to end because the Mexicans had had enough fighting. He curbed pangs of frustration as he made introductions with the members of his unit. In command of the First Artillery was Colonel Ichabod B. Crane, who had joined the U.S. Marines in 1809. He was a career soldier with more seniority than ability, and he would soon be succeeded by Colonel Thomas Childs. Company K consisted of four guns, seventy-eight men, and eighty horses. Francis Taylor was captain, with William W. Mackall and Isaac S. K. Reeves as first lieutenants and James G. Martin and Joseph F. Irons as second lieutenants. Jackson, a brevet officer, was a sort of "swing" man to be used where needed.[8]

None of the officers in the First Artillery, or any other unit, had ever commanded bodies of troops of any size. Like Jackson, the great majority of American officers in Mexico were young and untried. At West Point, the cadets had been taught the art of war with squads. One of them, Richard S. Ewell, would confess later: "During my twenty years of service on the frontier, I learned all about commanding fifty United States dragoons and forgot everything else."[9]

Jackson spent four days in Monterrey. His duties were minimal and the new sights were delightful. He thought Monterrey "the most beautiful city which I have seen in the north of this distracted country." His quarters, Jackson informed Laura, were a brick adobe with adjoining orange orchard and swimming pool. He regarded the mountain community as an exception to northern Mexico, which Jackson dismissed as "a vast, barren waste."[10]

On November 29, Company K started west with Zachary Taylor's army in a new (and, for Jackson, welcomed) offensive. No gains had emerged from the eight-week armistice. Authorities in Washington were now anxious to press the war before the Mexican congress convened in December. A heavy show of force might convince the Mexicans to ask for peace. The American army made a general advance fifty miles west toward Saltillo, which guarded the main pass leading through the Sierra Madre Mountains and into the rich valley granaries beyond. Jackson felt exhilaration at the prospect of combat. However, when the Americans reached Saltillo on December 2, they found it deserted save for a sullen civilian populace.

Francis Taylor's company established camp near what became Fort Polk.[11] Another waiting period followed. In that interim, the Mexican legislature convened and belligerently reelected General Santa Anna as president. This ensured that the war would continue.

Jackson's low opinion of Mexicans did not improve at Saltillo. He was somewhat impressed by the homes sprinkled alongside the mountains and the dry air of the town's 2,000-foot altitude. Yet the central building provoked criticism:

The church is the most highly ornamented on the interior of any edifice which has ever come under my observation. On entering this magnificent structure we are struck with the gaudy appearance of every side but most especially the opposite end which appears to be gilded with gold. At the bottom is a magnificent silver altar and on each side are statues which can not fail to attract the attention of the astonished beholder. . . . The priests are robed in the most gaudy of apparel. The inhabitants take off their hats on approaching the church and do not replace them until past it. . . . One day . . . I saw a female looking at a statue and weeping like a child. Such is the superstition of this race.[12]

As weeks of inactivity drifted into 1847, a major change occurred at the command level of the American army. General in Chief Winfield Scott announced his intention to enter the field. The army's commander had thoroughly reviewed the military situation. Zachary Taylor's force was still 600 miles north of the major war objective, Mexico City, and moving barely at all. Scott proposed to take personal command of a new and larger force, then lead it on a joint army-navy operation. His troops would embark on ships, steam down the Mexican coast, and force their way onto the beaches at Veracruz, Mexico's principal port. From there, the Americans would push inland along the famous National Road.

By nineteenth-century military thinking, true victory meant occupying the enemy's capital. Scott's goal at the other end of the National Road, therefore, was Mexico City. The distance was only 260 miles; the natural obstacles in Scott's path were less forbidding than the desert regions hampering Taylor's movements. A short overland campaign seemed to be the easy path to winning the war.

President Polk opposed Scott's idea, in large part because Polk was a Democrat and Scott a Whig with growing influence. Polk urged Taylor to make a concerted drive south toward Mexico City. When Taylor pointed out the unsoundness of such an advance, Polk relented. The president ordered Taylor to hold his position, and Scott received a grudging green light to undertake his offensive.

Scott's strategy was not original. Three hundred years earlier, Hernando Cortez had followed the same route in the Spanish conquest of Mexico. The bold ingredient in Scott's thinking lay in developing and executing the largest amphibious operation in American history. Tremendous logistics were involved.

Two thoughts dominated Scott's actions as he prepared for the campaign. First, he wanted Regular Army troops, not volunteers, for the intricate movements. This meant drawing units away from Taylor's command. Much diplomacy was involved in effecting such a transfer, but Taylor accepted graciously what he essentially could not prevent. Second, Scott desired as many West Pointers as he could get for his army. The general had served a long stint as chairman of the Board of Visitors at the academy. He was convinced that those young graduates had better talent, education, and enthusiasm for battle than did most of the old regular officers.

The division of General William Worth, to which the First Artillery was attached, was the principal command transferred from Taylor in the northern interior to Scott along the Mexican coast. Jackson's unit departed Saltillo on January 9, 1847, but it took almost six weeks to make the relatively short journey to Scott's marshaling point at Lobos Island, 180 miles by sea from Veracruz. The problem lay in the buildup for the American invasion. Logistics kept going awry: transports not where they were supposed to be, troops delayed or momentarily lost, many supplies here and no supplies there, and so on.

Winfield Scott was then sixty years old. He had been a general for half of his life, and he looked the part. Almost six and a half feet tall, with a bulk to match, he possessed large helpings of ability, courage, and vanity. The general's insistence on discipline and procedure had earned him the nickname "Old Fuss and Feathers." Like Zachary Taylor, Scott had presidential aspirations. President Polk had ample reason to view him as a political threat.

As March approached, Scott became increasingly impatient. The reason was not simply the pursuit of personal glory. He had to get his army ashore, across the flat country, and into the highlands by the opening of spring. Otherwise, his troops would confront *el vomito*—yellow fever—which struck annually with deadly fury. (Ultimately in the war, the disease killed more American soldiers than did the Mexicans.)

On February 6, Jackson and Company K arrived at the mouth of the Rio Grande. The 107 men and ninety-five horses now swelling the command added to a massive logjam awaiting transportation southward to Scott's rendezvous for the Veracruz landing. Jackson begrudged leaving Taylor's army and then missing the February 23 battle of Buena Vista. As he wrote Laura: "It would have afforded one much pleasure to have been with the gallant and victorious General Taylor at the battle of Buenavista in which he has acquired laurels as imperishable as the history which shall record the invasion of Mexico by our victorious armies." Nevertheless, Jackson added with unconcealed anticipation, he was headed toward "the most important portion of the army and on the most important line of operations."[13]

Company K was marking time one afternoon at the coastal installation of Camp Page when Lieutenant D. Harvey Hill of the Fourth Artillery paid a courtesy call on his old friend, Captain Francis Taylor. The two officers were chatting when a young, serious-looking officer came walking toward them. His ungainly strides kicked a spray of sand along the beach. Taylor nodded toward him and asked Hill: "Do you know Lieutenant Jackson?" Hill replied that he did not. "Jackson will make his mark in this war," Taylor predicted. "I taught him at West Point. He came there badly prepared, but was rising all the time, and if the course had been two years longer, he would have graduated at the head of his class. He never gave up on anything and never passed over anything without understanding it."[14]

Taylor made the proper introductions and the three talked for a few minutes. Hill's curiosity was aroused by the young lieutenant's reticence. It bordered on shyness. To Hill's surprise, Jackson abruptly proposed a walk along the beach. Hill never forgot that, while they were strolling slowly, Jackson asked a series of questions about battle: the emotions it generated, how difficult it was to handle troops under fire, and the like. "I really envy you men who have been in action," Jackson exclaimed. Then, with "a bright and peculiar smile," Jackson said with feeling, "I want to be in one battle."[15]

Many personnel shifts were occurring at this time. In time one individual would have significant bearing on Jackson's army career. First Lieutenant William H. French, West Point class of 1837, joined Company K while it waited restlessly at the mouth of the Rio Grande.[16]

Not until February 25 did Jackson's company board the *Arkansas*, one of 200 ships in the American flotilla. The heavy-laden vessel lumbered down the coast through rainstorms toward Lobos Island. By March 5, the *Arkansas* had reached its destination at the naval anchorage. Scott had only half the men and munitions he had requisitioned, but he was eight weeks behind schedule and the dangers of spring were

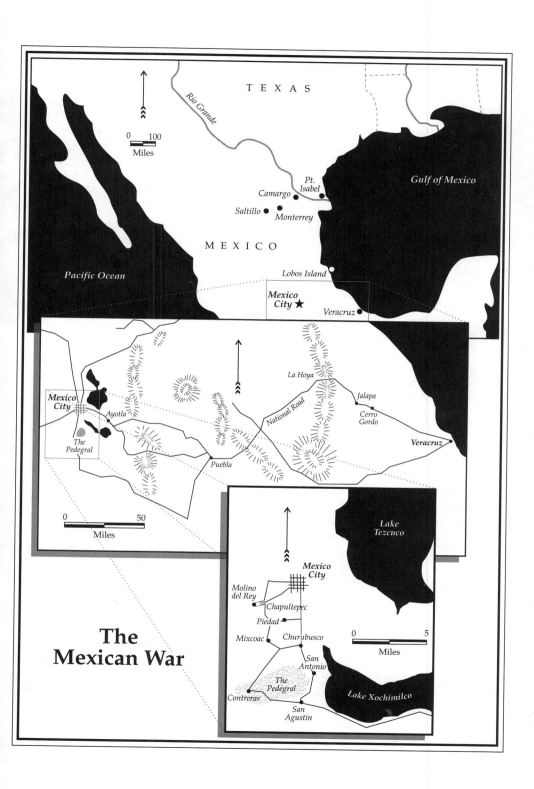

TEXAS

Rio Grande

Gulf of Mexico

Pt. Isabel

Camargo

Saltillo • Monterrey

MEXICO

Pacific Ocean

Lobos Island

Mexico City ★

Veracruz

Mexico City

Ayotla

La Hoya

Jalapa

National Road

Cerro Gordo

Veracruz

The Pedegral

Puebla

Lake Tezcuco

Molino del Rey

Mexico City

Chapultepec

Piedad

Mixcoac

Churubusco

San Antonio

The Pedegral

Contreras

San Agustin

Lake Xochimilco

The Mexican War

rapidly approaching. He could either move on Veracruz or watch disease shatter his command.

Scott gave the necessary orders; and in mid-afternoon of March 9, the first wave of his 13,500-man army bobbed ashore in surfboats. A second wave followed. Then Jackson, as part of the third contingent, climbed into the huge rowboats. The sight of large numbers of troops marching in order under a cloudless sky, with bands playing and flags rippling in the breeze, was a spectacle that Jackson never forgot.

For the landing, the First Artillery had been temporarily designated as infantry. Jackson got his first taste of leading foot soldiers. Scott's fourth and final wave of troops stepped ashore around 10 P.M. Intense resistance from the Mexicans had been expected but never materialized. The Americans suffered no casualties in establishing a beachhead in front of the fifteen-foot-high walls that protected Veracruz. Yet Scott appeared for the moment to have blundered into a spider's web of dangers.

The beach was narrow for accommodating all of the 13,000 American soldiers. Many deployed along sand hills behind the city. Veracruz's walls seemed too strong for scaling, and more than 100 Mexican cannon stared menacingly from gunports. A large number of Scott's men straddled the National Road. These dispositions virtually isolated Veracruz. In the days that followed, violent storms of rain and blowing sand pummeled the troops. When the elements calmed, voracious insects began their assaults in swarms.

Scott was anxious to move forward, but not at needless cost of life. He therefore determined to effect the surrender of Veracruz by siege and bombardment. After two weeks of digging trenches and gun emplacements, the Americans on March 22 began a cannonade against the fortress city. Mexican heavy guns held Scott's forces at bay for a time, but superior firepower soon began to have a psychological effect on the unsupported garrison of 3,360 Mexican soldiers.

Jackson had his first encounter with war at Veracruz. The operations of Company K, he wrote Laura, "consisted principally in bombarding and cannonading which continued until not only the city but the castle of San Juan Dulloas agreed to surrender." His behavior was that of a veteran as he moved from gun to gun and supervised the salvoes. His behavior under fire attracted notice throughout the siege. Jackson confided to his sister that while engaged in one artillery exchange, "a cannon ball came in about five steps of me." An academy classmate who watched Jackson at one point in the bombardment stated that "Old Jack" was "as calm in the midst of a hurricane of bullets as though he were on dress parade at West Point." The Virginian was with Harvey Hill during one stage of the siege. Legend has it that the two officers were asleep in their tent when an enormous shell from the Castle of San Juan de Ulua ripped through the shelter. Providentially, neither man was injured.[17]

By March 27, the Mexicans had endured enough. The white flag went up. Scott's capture of Veracruz, coming on the heels of Zachary Taylor's victory at Buena Vista, put the Americans squarely in control of the war. Jackson expressed understandably extravagant pleasure with most of the Veracruz operations. At the end of his March 30 letter to Laura, he said: "This capitulation has thrown into our hands the strong hold of this republic and being a regular siege in connexion with other circumstances must in my opinion excell any military operations known in the history of our country. I approve of all except allowing the enemy to retire; that I can not approve of in as much as we had them secure and could have taken them prisoners of war uncondi- tionally."[18] Even at this early stage, Jackson thought in terms of unrelenting offen- sives and complete victory.

He was confident that promotion would come in the wake of his conduct at Veracruz. Yet Jackson did not take the credit himself. Captain Taylor had been encouraging Jackson to seek the value of individual religion. According to a close friend, Jackson now "was finally convinced that it was a reasonable thing for him to do; and he made up his mind to do it, just as he would have made up his mind to undertake some new branch of study."[19] Jackson, slowly clothing himself with a new robe of faith, must have surprised Uncle Isaac Brake when he wrote, "I have seen many vicissitudes of fortune but in all the changing scenes the hand of an allwise God can be seen."[20]

Jackson did not expect any praise for his efforts, and he was sincere in not seeking any. As he explained to Laura: "I presume that you think my name ought to appear in the papers, but when you consider the composition of our army you will entertain different views. Its composition is such that those who have independent commands only are as a general rule spoken of; for instance Ridgely, May, Bragg, Duncan, Ringold, Smith all commanded companies. If an officer wishes to distinguish himself he must remain long in service until he obtains rank, then he obtains the praise not only for his efforts but for the efforts of the officers and men under him. That portion of praise which may be due me must of course go to those above me or be included in the praise given to the army." Meanwhile, Jackson admonished both his sister and his uncle, "you will take particular care that neither this nor any subsequent letter falls into the hands of an editor & consequently gets into a newspaper." The lieutenant also reassured family members that "my health is extremely good; I probably look better than I have for years."[21]

His participation in the Veracruz bombardment was sufficient for Jackson to ac- quire an unusual degree of confidence. On March 30, he wrote the quartermaster general of the U.S. Army. Extra compensation due him as company quartermaster while on the trip from New York to Mexico had not been made, and Jackson now requested the same. Americans might be celebrating a great victory at the moment; with Jackson, duty and reward were integral parts of a soldier's life and not affected by emotions of the hour.[22]

Like other American soldiers, the lieutenant was eager to see the interior of the great prize of Veracruz. He was surprised at what he found. The five-day bombard- ment had been loud and spectacular; it had breached the great wall, blown away gun positions, and destroyed the morale of the Mexican soldiers. Yet the cannonade had not been very destructive to the city itself.

Daniel Frost, an artillery lieutenant and one of Jackson's instructors at West Point, observed that "notwithstanding the rain of shells poured" night and day at Veracruz, "on examination after the surrender it was found that comparatively little damage had been done—a few houses had been shattered, a few had been burned, a few people had been killed, but as a whole the town stood intact."[23]

The crowded city possessed a degree of charm. Plazas were busy and attractive, churches numerous and impressive. Stout white walls overlooked a pleasant water-front. On the western side of Veracruz, jungles reached almost to the city ramparts. On the negative side, the seaport was now steaming in the sun, the season's first outbreak of *el vomito* had occurred, and word circulated that Santa Anna's army was moving to confront Scott's forces.

Leaving behind a sizable garrison to secure Veracruz, Scott early in April started his army west on the National Road. Progress was slow and painful. *Banditos* and guerrillas struck the American lines of communication regularly. The Mexican interior was almost as unforgiving. While the National Road was the country's best highway, it had seen better days.

Worse for Scott, the road snaked up through a number of mountain passes and towns en route to Mexico City. Santa Anna had several good places where he could make a stand. Keeping the Americans in the low hot country as long as possible would enable dreaded yellow fever to decimate the ranks of the invaders.

Scott had reorganized his army into two divisions commanded by Generals William J. Worth and David E. Twiggs. Each division contained two brigades of infantry. With Twiggs were two batteries, one of which was Company K of the First Artillery. Twiggs himself, a soldier recalled, was "a grand-looking old man, six feet two inches in stature, with long, flowing white hair, and a beard which hung over his broad breast like Aaron's."[24]

On April 8, "Old Davey's" division took the lead and marched from Veracruz. The initial destination was Jalapa, seventy-four miles distant and the first town of any size on the way to Mexico City. At an altitude of 4,000 feet, Jalapa was a much more healthy spot than the coastal area. Yet on April 12, some thirteen miles from Jalapa, Twiggs's cavalry encountered elements of Santa Anna's army. It soon appeared that at least 4,000 Mexican soldiers had entrenched atop commanding hills that hung over both sides of the narrow road as it began its climb upward. The pass and the nearby village were known as Cerro Gordo ("Big Hill") because of an enormous cone-shaped mountain that dominated the region.

Twiggs halted his column of 2,600 troops and awaited the arrival of Scott with the rest of the army. The commanding general and his contingent reached the Cerro Gordo vicinity on the 14th and increased the American strength to 8,500 men. Scott prepared for the first real battle of the campaign. Two probes against the Mexican line were repulsed handily. Scott became convinced that any direct attack against the mountain fastness would be suicidal. He then sent engineering officers fanning out in search of a way to flank the enemy position. It was Captain Robert E. Lee who found a hidden way through the steep ravines and tangled growth around the Mexican left flank.

Scott quickly formulated a battle plan. Twiggs's division would get behind Santa Anna's left and rear, fortify its position astride the National Road, and hold while Scott's troops assailed the Mexicans in front. Yet as Twiggs advanced on April 17, Mexicans spotted the movement and opened a concentrated fire. The Americans had no choice now but to attack under fire and strike for the enemy's first-line position. They did so successfully and were moving across a flat plateau toward Cerro Gordo when darkness halted the fighting.

At 7:00 the next morning—Sunday, April 18—Scott launched a two-pronged offensive against the Mexican left. The enemy line bent, then crumbled. As the Mexican left flank collapsed, the right gave way from lack of anchorage. By midmorning, 1,200 Mexicans had been killed or wounded, another 3,000 had been taken prisoner, and the remainder of Santa Anna's force was running pell-mell toward the capital. American casualties were 431 dead and wounded.

Jackson's role in the battle, like that of his company, seemed relatively minor. He summed up his participation at Cerro Gordo by telling Laura, "We followed close on the retreating column until night and came near enough to give the retreating enemy a few shots from the battery but they succeeded in effecting their escape for want of our dragoons."[25]

Actually, Jackson understated both his and the battery's activities. Captain Taylor reported that Company K was in advance of Scott's army and pursued the fleeing Mexicans for some twelve miles. Taylor added: "The second section of my battery, under Lieut. Irons, joined me in the advance as soon as it was possible for him to do so; and through the great exertions of Lieut. Jackson, the caissons were brought up early in the night. It may be proper for me to add that the difficulties of getting Artillery over the hills of the Cerro Gordo were great. Taking out the horses, the pieces were drawn up by men by means of picket ropes attached to the carriages."[26]

Cerro Gordo was a learning experience for Jackson. The ever-studious Virginian watched Scott's engineering skills in probing for the enemy's weak points. American success came from a flanking movement that neutralized an impregnable position. Scott had also employed a swift and hard pursuit to keep the crippled foe reeling in disorder. Jackson appreciated that kind of strategy because it resulted in smashing victory.

On the morning after the fight, Jackson rode over the battlefield. His first sight of a mangled and bloated corpse "filled me with as much sickening dismay as if I had been a woman." Cognizant of his low tolerance for pain, Jackson now realized as well that he could not stand to witness suffering. That obstacle he must somehow overcome in his quest to be a good army officer.[27]

Cerro Gordo taught the young lieutenant one other thing. Fame came to the daring leaders. The only artilleryman who gained real distinction in the battle was Captain John B. Magruder. Attempting to join other units of the First Artillery, Magruder and nine of his cannoneers "passed gallantly through a shower of bullets from the enemy's musketry."[28] Magruder came upon some abandoned Mexican cannon, turned them around, and delivered several parting shots at the enemy. Scott gave the captured guns to Magruder as a reward, and Jackson saw in him the type of commander who could be the means to acquiring a high reputation. For that reason, Jackson began thinking of the desirability of a transfer.[29]

American forces occupied Jalapa without a fight. Scott's soldiers were unanimous in praising this "lovely little town on the slope of the mountains." The city had delightful weather, fancy parks, winding streets, and fountains in the squares where the 2,000 residents gathered on a regular basis. One of Jackson's fellow artillerists said of Jalapa, "This ideal Mexican town . . . is free from the fevers and thorns and ticks and all other detestable plagues of the hot lands, and enjoys all the delights of the . . .

Temperate zone, including not only all the delicious fruits of the tropics but many of those of our own climate, such as pears, plums, cherries, etc."[30] The scenery was breathtaking, the citizens friendly. It was easy to forget that Jalapa was the birthplace of Santa Anna.

Late in April, the expected promotion from brevet (temporary) to regular second lieutenant reached Jackson. It was dated March 3 and it removed the disliked term "brevet" from his title. With elevation in rank came assignment to Company G of the First Artillery. However, Francis Taylor had enough influence to keep Jackson for the moment in Company K on "detached service."[31]

Jackson used part of the three-week lull at Jalapa to amble over the countryside and admire its beauties. He sent an unusually long and descriptive letter to Laura. The markets of "lovely Jalapa," he began, were filled with pineapples, bananas, tomatoes, oranges, green corn, peas, beans, and other delectables, he noted. "The surrounding country is fine & much resembles that of our own heaven favored Western Virginia with the exception of the lofty peak of Orizaba, covered with perpetual snow, which presents a beautiful view from my door on a clear day." Slipping next into a rare humorous vein, Jackson noted, "There are many pretty ladies here but you must not infer from this that you will have one of them for your sister-in-law, for such is not my intention at present and not theirs I hope."[32]

He informed his sister that he had begun a study of Spanish because of his "imperfect knollege" of what he considered a "liquid and beautiful" language. Uncharacteristically, Jackson then expressed strong opinions about the two American commanders in Mexico. In doing so, the young Virginian was voicing his own early beliefs in military fundamentals. General Scott, wrote Jackson,

is by far the most talented and scientific and at the same time the most vain and conceited. His comprehensive mind embraces not only different objects and ends but their general and combined bearings with regard to the ultimate objects. If you call on him for a past time, he may disgust you with his forthright and strong expressions, but if you call on him on business & military matters, then you may expect to call forth the mighty powers of his mighty mind, and upon information so obtained I would rather rely than on all the other officers in our armies in Mexico.

With reference to [Taylor], he is a plain . . . strait-forward, & undesiring man. If you knew him you would certainly admire him. General Taylor is as brave as a lion, and I believe that he by his own personal bravery saved the battle of Buenavista. . . . But he wants comprehensive views of means to an end. . . .

From what I have said you may imagine that I esteem General Scott more than General Taylor. But such is not the case. I esteem General Scott most only as a military [leader]. . . . General Taylor was deceaved at Monterey. He . . . did not prepare himself. . . . At Buenavista his army was again slaughtered and he [was] unable to follow up Santa Anna. But General Scott took Vera Cruz, a place stronger than Monterey, with but a slight loss and again he has beaten the enemy with comparatively a slight loss considering the strength and opposition with which he was opposed at Cerro Gordo.[33]

Jackson's first experience with court-martial duties occupied some of his time at Jalapa. On the morning of May 10, a regimental court-martial convened to hear charges against six men accused mostly of insubordinate conduct. The tribunal consisted of Captain Taylor, Lieutenant Jackson, and Lieutenant William H. French. Typical of the cases was that involving Private George A. Fish of the First Artillery.

Fish, it was charged, "did refuse, positively and with oaths, to groom a horse, when ordered to do so by 1st Sgt. Thomas Wilson . . . and when the same orders were repeated by Lieut. J. G. Martin, did waver to obey it in a surly and unsoldierlike manner, cursing and swearing in the presence of said Lieut. Martin." Fish pled guilty. Under the stern army punishments of that age, the court sentenced him "to forfeit seven dollars of his pay, and to walk eight hours a day, four in the morning and four in the afternoon, with a knapsack on his back, containing twenty-four pounds weight, for ten days."[34]

The court had just completed its work when Jackson's world seemed to collapse in sequential fashion. Even though under orders to do so, he did not want to transfer to Company G and its heavier, less mobile guns. Taylor made every effort to keep Jackson in Company K; "but to my regret," Jackson told Laura, "did not succeed in getting my application granted but it is understood that I will remain with him until the officer who is promoted to this company joins it." Jackson had heard rumors that his new command might be shifted from field service to garrison duty. He tried to be cheerful in the face of desperation. "In case I am ordered to join Company G," he noted in the same letter to Laura, "I shall apply for permission to go forward as a dragoon officer, or in some other capacity."[35]

That possibility evaporated quickly. Colonel Thomas Childs, commanding the First Artillery, received orders from Scott to assume the duties of military governor of Jalapa. Childs moved to get his regiment in proper order as a first step in his new command. Among other things, Childs wanted to ensure that all officers were where they were supposed to be.

On May 12, Jackson was directed to report forthwith to Captain John H. Winder's Company G.[36] He was transferring from a light battery to a cumbersome heavy artillery unit. That was not all bad, for many heavy artillery companies had been used as infantry for lack of guns. Commanding foot soldiers offered officers a better chance for battle and glory. However, before Jackson could fully rationalize the benefits of his new assignment, an even worse blow came.

The army was starting toward Perote, thirty miles to the west and the next stop en route to Mexico City and victory; but it was going without Company G. That battery was ordered to remain behind at Jalapa on garrison duty. The war was moving away from Jackson. "I have the mortification of being left to garrison the town of Jalapa," a crestfallen Jackson wrote Laura late in May.[37] Any other officer might have been delighted with the chance to languish in quietude, pleasant climate, and alluring señoritas. Not so with Jackson. He had come to Mexico to make his mark in the military.

Trying to appear content, and falling back on the newfound religious feelings he had acquired from Captain Taylor, Jackson looked for a brighter side to the situation. "I throw myself into the hands of an all wise God and hope that it may yet be for the better. It may have been one of his means of diminishing my excessive ambition and after having accomplished his purpose, what ever it may be, he then in his infinite wisdom may gratify my desire."[38]

Jackson spent the rest of the May 25 letter to Laura on personal matters. "I am in fine quarters and making rapid progress in the Spanish language and have an idea of making some female acquaintances shortly." Laura had recently given birth to a son whom she named for her brother. Jackson in time would grow exceedingly close to Thomas Jackson Arnold. "I see many things here of interest by the way of ornaments and fruits," he wrote. "Wish that I only had the opportunity of sending some to you and Thomas. I know well that he would like to have a ranchero (Mexican) on horse back followed by some large dogs."[39]

The lieutenant then expressed a wish to hear something from his ailing half-brother, Wirt Woodson, "poor fellow." Apparently, Laura had informed Thomas of some business troubles that Uncle Cummins and Edward Jackson seemed to have surmounted. Jackson expressed concern about the matter. He then closed the letter to his beloved sister by commenting: "Think of you often and my heart has more than once upbraided me for my neglect of you. But I feared to inform you of things as they were in this unholy land."[40]

Inactivity and impatience caused time to pass slowly at Jalapa. To while away the hours, Jackson became more absorbed in learning Spanish. Social outlets were unappealing. He resumed the old West Point habit of taking long, solitary walks.

On June 18, Jackson was immensely pleased to learn that Company G had been ordered forward to Scott's army. A portion of Captain Winder's battery started west toward the Sierra Madre range. Jackson was only a day or so out of Jalapa when his small detachment reached a narrow defile at La Hoya. A band of Mexican guerrillas attacked the Americans, and a hand-to-hand fight ensued, lasting several minutes. Then the Mexicans turned heel and galloped away with a loss of four killed and three captured. Jackson dismissed the affair as routine, except to express pleasure at capturing "a beautiful sabre and some other equipment."[41]

The American party slowly made its way the remaining ninety miles to Puebla. This second-largest city in Mexico had become the staging area for Scott's climactic offensive against Mexico City, seventy miles away. Jackson and his company reached Puebla on July 8 and marveled at the two-month buildup of American forces massed for the final drive.

No sooner had Jackson reached Puebla than his hopes jumped with a new development. General Scott had designated four artillery companies to become light and mobile units popularly known as "flying artillery." One of the units so rewarded was the First Regiment's Company I, under Captain John B. Magruder.[42] What stirred Jackson's eagerness was the fact that Magruder was badly in need of a second lieutenant, and young officers were not beating a path to Magruder's headquarters to apply for the position. The reason was the company commander.

Born in tidewater Virginia in 1807 and a graduate of the "undistinguished" West Point class of 1830, Magruder had been an artilleryman for sixteen years. He had proven himself able and audacious in combat but egotistical and ostentatious behind the lines. A childish love for pageantry had brought the handsome Magruder the nickname "Prince John." It was also said that he could drink and talk for twenty-four hours without interruption. Yet his men, especially his junior officers, saw a different Magruder: a severe disciplinarian with a hot temper and an unsettling commander who sought personal advancement through battle and at any cost.

Jackson was willing to overlook the negative aspect for the opportunity to serve under the fellow Virginian. He is said to have told a friend afterwards: "I wanted to see active service. I wished to be near the enemy and in the fight, and when I heard John Magruder had got his battery, I bent all my energies to be with him, for I knew if there was any fighting to be done, Magruder would be on hand."[43]

Magruder's battery would be an independent unit that would flow with the tide of battle. The captain's reputation as a fighter was already established; his company would receive attention wherever it was located. In short, Jackson saw the new Company I not merely as an outlet for leaving garrison duty but also as an avenue for distinction on the front line.

He promptly applied for the vacant lieutenancy. Once again Jackson failed in his quest. The appointment went to Lieutenant Truman Seymour. Jackson would not accept defeat this time. He met with Seymour, a West Point classmate who expressed no desire to serve under Magruder. The two lieutenants jointly petitioned regimental headquarters to reverse assignments. Jackson would go to Company I while Seymour replaced Jackson in Company G. Colonel Childs approved the request; and on July 13, a confident Jackson reported to his new command. He joined Captain Magruder, Lieutenants Seth Williams and John P. Johnstone, and seventy-one men of a new flying artillery unit.[44]

If one can believe the memoirs of West Point graduate (later academy superintendent and brevet major general) John C. Tidball—and no reasons exist to doubt them—Magruder took an immediate and strong dislike of Jackson. Tidball stated: "Prince John Magruder, as he was called because of his affected elegance, was in reality only a prince of humbugs. No greater difference could possibly exist between men than between Magruder and his lieutenant. The former was a dissolute, reckless braggart, whose chief aim in life was display and deceit. He despised Jackson because first, although the latter was from Virginia, he was not an F. F. V. and did not, like himself, pretend to be one and put on airs accordingly; and secondly, [Magruder] saw nothing in [Jackson] to admire except what he considered only 'stupid bravery.' In fact but few others saw much more at that time."[45]

A month of army inactivity at Puebla gave Jackson time to familiarize himself with Company I and its personnel. Jackson obeyed every order instantly and to the minutest degree. Magruder would have no reason for command criticism of his second lieutenant. When the day's duties were completed, Jackson pursued his usual habit of sightseeing on foot. Undoubtedly, his appraisal of life at Puebla coincided with that of a fellow artillery officer, Lieutenant Daniel Frost, who declared:

We found Puebla a beautiful well built City, with many fine churches and whose inhabitants received us with resignation if not cordiality. . . . Owing to its great elevation the climate of Puebla was very agreeable, even in the months of June and July, whilst the nights were always quite cool. We had abundance of delicious fruits and provisions of every kind and occupied comfortable quarters in the public buildings, but still got very tired of the uneventful sameness of our existence and longed for the order to move towards the 'Halls of Montezuma'—a term we always used to designate the City of Mexico.[46]

Those coveted orders came on August 7, when Scott's army resumed the march through the mountains. Over 10,700 troops moved out in four divisions under Generals Worth, Twiggs, Gideon J. Pillow, and John A. Quitman. Santa Anna, with an army estimated at 30,000 demoralized soldiers, was waiting somewhere in front. Magruder's battery was part of Pillow's division. It was third in the line of march; as such, it was August 10 before Jackson's command began its westward trek.

The uphill climb was difficult and performed in chilly weather. By the time Pillow's column breasted the continental divide and beheld the great fertile valley with the walled capital twenty miles in the distance, Scott with the lead elements of the army had advanced five miles farther to the village of Ayotla. The Americans halted. Between them and the enemy capital were three huge lakes, swamps formed by innumerable meandering streams, and a series of causeways that had become the framework of Santa Anna's defenses.

As if those obstacles were not forbidding enough, also in front of Scott was the Pedregal, a huge lava field two miles long, five miles wide, laced with ravines and without discernible roadways. One of Scott's men regarded the Pedregal as "a heap of Rocks allmost impassable for infantry and totally so for Artillery and Cavalry." Another soldier classified the region simply as "hell with the fires out."[47]

Scott again dispatched his engineering officers to determine the most feasible approach to the town of San Augustin, south of the capital and directly in front of the lava field. At the same time, and leaving Twiggs's division at Ayotla to convey the impression of an American movement on Mexico City from the north, Scott struck for San Augustin with the troops of Worth, Pillow, and Quitman. A two-day struggle through rain and deep mud brought Scott's forces in sight of San Augustin. Mexico City was less than nine miles to the north, but Santa Anna's huge army was closer than that.

The Mexican commander placed himself squarely between the Americans and Mexico City. His line of defense was impressive. The western flank was atop an insulated hill at Contreras. There Santa Anna had infantry and artillery in force. His eastern flank was at Churubusco, where the largest force of Mexicans waited behind strong field works. In terms of manpower, the Mexicans held a three-to-one advantage over their opponents. Yet Santa Anna had committed a fatal blunder. The key points in his position were the two flanks. They were too far apart to be of help to one another if help were needed.

Scott's army, at San Augustin, faced the center of the Mexican position. To get to Mexico City in a straight line meant that Scott had to drive through the towns of San Antonio and Churubusco. Both were heavily fortified. To Scott's right were swamps and Lake Xochimilco; on the left was the unearthly looking lava field. In skirmishing with Mexican cavalry on August 16 and 17, Jackson's old battery—Francis Taylor's command—more than held its own. What may have rankled Jackson a bit was that of the four lieutenants in Company K, William H. French came in for the highest praise from Taylor.[48]

Meanwhile, Scott was facing the prospect of delivering a frontal attack he did not want to make. He would be doing exactly what Santa Anna expected, and the casualties would be high. Scott sent Captain Robert E. Lee of his staff on one last search of the Pedregal for a flanking passage. Lee found a path that was little more than a mule trail; but if improved rapidly for artillery and wagons, Scott could circle westward around the Mexicans and assail them from the rear.

Early on August 19, some 500 of Pillow's infantrymen went to work with pickaxes and shovels. Soldiers sweated profusely as they carved a makeshift road through the Pedregal's rocky terrain. Lee supervised the project. Gunners of Magruder's light battery and Lieutenant Franklin Callender's quartet of howitzers dragged their weapons by hand through the rough country. In all likelihood, Jackson saw Robert E. Lee for the first time. He may have been part of a conference with Scott's engineering officer.

About noon, the work stopped. Shells from some of the Mexican heavy guns began ranging in on the site. Captain George McClellan rode up with orders from Pillow: the two American batteries were to move into position at the western edge of the lava field and some 1,000 yards from the enemy works. No cover existed; at 2 P.M., artillerists unlimbered in the road and began a heated return fire on the Mexicans. Magruder reported that the improvised trail ahead "was raked for nearly a mile by the enemy and intersected by natural & artificial obstacles of a serious nature, the latter being stone walls thrown across it to prevent our advance."[49]

The two light artillery units of Magruder and Callender were no match at all for the intensity of the Mexican bombardment. Jackson's friend, Harvey Hill of the Fourth Artillery, was a witness to the one-sided duel. Hill wrote with characteristic bluntness: "Certainly of all the absurd things that the ass Pillow has ever done this was the most silly. Human stupidity can go no farther than this."[50]

The only effect of the fire from the two batteries was to divert attention away from Pillow and Twiggs as the American infantry moved slowly to flank San Antonio. The countryside echoed with the deep roar of cannon fire. Now the sleepy community of Contreras had become the site of one of the war's major battles.

Magruder had divided his battery into two sections and placed them on each side of Callender's howitzers. Jackson's two guns were on the right. "Being in a subordinate position," a fellow officer wrote, Jackson "evinced no higher military trait than that of indomitable sticking qualities." His position was at a turn on the road. Enemy fire pelted his gun emplacements. "From the character of his position he could do little or nothing in reply, yet he stayed there without a thought of withdrawing. He had been ordered there, and his conception of duty as a lieutenant required him to stay. His men were falling around him, and he too, with the last, would have fallen, had not the phase of battle changed and relieved him from his dangerous predicament."[51]

The change came an hour into the unequal contest. Lieutenant Johnstone, in command of Magruder's other section, fell mortally wounded from a large shell. Magruder frantically searched for Jackson and the other guns. In the smoke, explosions, and confusion, Magruder suddenly feared that Jackson's section had been overrun and possibly its leader slain. Yet "in a few moments," Magruder stated, "Lieut. Jackson, commanding the second section of the battery, who had opened a fire upon the enemy's works from a position on the right, hearing our own fire further in front, advanced in handsome style, and being assigned by me to the post so gallantly filled by Lieut. Johnston[e], kept up the fire with great briskness and effect."[52]

The artillery battle at Contreras lasted almost three hours as Magruder's six-pounders and Callender's equally small howitzers battled valiantly against twenty-two

Mexican guns that included several eighteen-pounders and at least three eight-inch howitzers. Darkness and a heavy rainstorm ended the contest. Magruder withdrew his battered unit under the downpour. His casualties included one officer killed, four men wounded, and ten horses dead or crippled. Of his four guns, one was destroyed and two were damaged.

On the positive side, Magruder's opinion of his tall lieutenant had undergone an abrupt change. The captain considered Jackson's behavior "conspicuous throughout the whole day." Magruder added: "I cannot too highly commend him to the Major Genl's. favourable consideration."[53]

General Twiggs cited Jackson among a list of officers singled out for "coolness and determination . . . whilst under fire." In praising the batteries of Magruder and Callender, General Pillow emphasized "their great gallantry and daring, the proof of which is found in their losses, and in the fact that both of their batteries were much cut up by the terrible fire of the enemy's heavy guns."[54]

Promotion—both brevet and regular—would come to Jackson as a result of his bravery at Contreras. That was not as important to him as the opportunity to perform in battle and the courage he had felt under fire. Asked years later what feelings he had in his first major battle, Jackson responded: "Afraid the fire would not be hot enough for me to distinguish myself."[55]

On the following day, Scott attacked the Mexican force at Contreras from front and rear. The fighting lasted barely twenty minutes before the Mexicans broke and ran. Scott made a vigorous pursuit and clashed briefly with the enemy at San Antonio. This remnant of Santa Anna's army retreated northward to Churubusco. There the Mexicans took a new position behind strong works. Intense fighting continued through the afternoon. When the Mexicans began running out of ammunition, Santa Anna abandoned Churubusco. The fighting on August 20 cost Scott 1,000 casualties, including 133 killed. Santa Anna lost about a fourth of his command—some 4,000 killed or wounded, plus 3,000 captured.

Magruder's battery had no part in the engagements because he had no weapons to employ. The men of Company I spent much of the day appropriating Mexican cannon for their own use and becoming familiar with their workings. Jackson, from a vantage point overlooking the battles, became even more convinced of the strategic advantage of flanking movements.

An armistice did go into effect while peace commissioner Nicholas Trist sought to negotiate an end to hostilities. Scott was of the opinion that the devastating defeats suffered by the Mexicans on August 19–20 would bring a speedy move for peace, especially with the American army hovering at the outskirts of the capital. No time limit was placed on the armistice, but both sides agreed that the truce could be terminated on forty-eight hours' notice.

Two weeks passed; Trist made no progress and Scott ran out of patience. With negotiations at a stalemate, Scott on September 6 announced a resumption of military activities and started his forces toward the capital. The commander had no choice. A hostile 250 miles separated the Americans from their coastal base of supplies. Mexico City was the only major source of food within reach. Thus, for the first time since

Hernando Cortez two centuries earlier, the Mexicans found their capital seriously threatened.

Jackson and his company had spent the lull near Pillow's encampment at the settlement of Mixcoac. Cornfields and orchards, intersected by deep irrigation ditches, covered the flatland where they had paused. The battery moved forward with the American army in a September 8 dawn assault on Molino del Rey. This group of stone buildings stood on the western end of a walled park containing the great castle known as Chapultepec. Supposedly, the Mexicans had erected at Molino del Rey a foundry for melting church bells and recasting the metal as cannon. This report proved untrue.

Scott's attack at Molino del Rey was ill conceived and ill executed. It ultimately drove off the Mexicans but cost the Americans engaged a fourth of their strength. Magruder's guns took no active role beyond helping to blow apart a Mexican cavalry charge. That event reinforced Jackson's abhorrence of blind assaults against fortified positions.

On September 9, Worth's division and Magruder's battery moved forward and took possession of the village of Piedad. Jackson was now a first lieutenant and commanding one of the two sections of Company I. Magruder placed Jackson's two guns in the most exposed position in front of Piedad and close to the enemy lines. Jackson exchanged brief fire with Mexican gunners on September 11, but no damage occurred on either side.[56] This was but one of numerous skirmishes that preceded Scott's assault on Mexico City.

The last obstacle between the Americans and the enemy capital was the venerable castle atop a 200-foot-high hill that both overlooked and commanded the causeways approaching Mexico City from the south. No one was quite sure of Chapultepec's origins. The name meant "Grasshopper Hill," and the place had once been the resort of Aztec princes. If the phrase "Halls of Montezuma" had reality, this was it. Since 1833, the huge complex had been Mexico's military college. Hence, it had traditional as well as strategic value.

A quarter of a mile wide, the castle was three-quarters of a mile long. High stone walls frowned on the southern and eastern sides; two small gates were the only breaks in the masonry on those two faces. Behind, on the north side of the castle, were two causeways that led two to three miles into Mexico City. Scott was uncertain how many Mexican troops were inside the Chapultepec compound. However, the castle appeared much stronger than it really was. Some 2,000 soldiers were needed for an adequate defense. The commander at the moment, General Nicolas Bravo, had no more than 850 troops on hand—and that number included fifty teenage cadets.

At dawn on September 12, Scott began what became a fourteen-hour bombardment of the fortress. This steady pounding broke the morale of the small garrison. General Bravo begged Santa Anna for immediate assistance. Reinforcements came forward but at a snail's pace owing to the intensity of the American cannonade.

Scott used the artillery fire to cover final preparations for storming the castle. Scaling ladders were assembled, grappling hooks readied, other equipment brought to the front. Pillow and Quitman's divisions would make the attack on the southern and western walls. Soldiers under Worth and Persifor Smith would stand in support. Jackson, with Magruder's battery, was on the extreme left of the American line. That flank rested on the Anzures causeway, which ran along the northern side of the Chapultepec rectangle. The two sections of Magruder's company were part of a force that included the Eleventh and Fourteenth Infantry under Colonel William B. Trousdale. Its tasks were twofold: to block any reinforcements from Mexico City reaching Chapultepec and to prevent any Mexican retreat from the beleaguered castle.

General Gideon Pillow's order for Jackson to act independently with his section in the coming battle "excited my abiding gratitude," the young artillerist subsequently told a friend. Thereafter, Jackson always had respect for the widely disliked Pillow because the general had given him "an opportunity to win distinction," and Jackson intended to make the most of it.[57]

At 5:30 A.M. on Monday, September 13, Scott's batteries opened a concentrated fire. Around 8:00 the cannonade slackened to permit the American infantry to advance. Trousdale's force began moving eastward along the causeway on Chapultepec's northern face. American infantry had barely covered a quarter-mile when the soldiers stumbled headlong into the enemy.

Cannon fire came from a strong redoubt in front; a large force of Mexican infantry in support of the artillery were discharging muskets as quickly as they could load. At the same time, small arms fire from high above in the citadel rained down on the American column. This cross fire was heavy and accurate. Trousdale went down from a wound. The Americans could neither advance nor retreat.

At that point, Jackson rushed forward with his two little six-pounders. He tried to find a good position for a return fire, but the Mexicans were banging away in large force. Jackson later told Laura that his section was "in a road which was swept with grape and canister, and at the same time thousands of muskets from the Castle itself pouring down like hail."[58]

Jackson recalled those moments a few years later: "I was ordered to advance with a section of my battery upon a road swept by the fire of six or eight pieces of Mexican artillery at very short range. It was ticklish work, but there was nothing to be done but to obey orders. So I went on. As soon as [we] debouched into the main road, the Mexicans opened fire, and at the first discharge, killed or disabled every one of the twelve horses of my two guns. We unlimbered, however, and returned their fire."[59]

Precisely at that moment, Lieutenant George H. Gordon and a body of cavalry rode into the area. Gordon was another of Jackson's West Point classmates. "Never," he stated, "shall I forget the woe-begone appearance Jackson bore, as he stood gazing at the corpses of six horses in harness attached to the foremost piece of his section. As our squadron galloped by, I had just time to salute him with: 'Well, Old Jack, it seems to me you are in a bad way!' and, amid the clanging of sabres and clamor of hoofs, catch his reply of: 'Pears I am!'"[60]

One of Jackson's guns was damaged to the point where it could not be moved; most of the horses were dead or dying; demoralized gunners had fled for cover behind rocks and bushes. Everyone was on the edge of panic except Jackson. He paced back and forth in the road while bullets kicked up dirt and ricocheted off boulders. "There is no danger!" he kept shouting to his scattered men. "See? I am not hit!" The men were unconvinced. So was Jackson. Later in life, he admitted that the statement was the only lie he ever knowingly told.[61]

Jackson was standing with his legs wide apart when a cannon ball spun between them. This episode, occurring at a moment when Jackson was being reported as killed in action, was proof to many soldiers of the young officer's invulnerability. An old sergeant then stepped forward to help with the one usable gun. The two men strained until they got the piece across a ditch and into firing position.

Amid a storm of grapeshot and musketry, Jackson calmly aimed the weapon and began answering the fusillade. Later asked why he did not fall back in the face of such a one-sided contest, Jackson replied: "Oh, never, it would have been no disgrace to have died there, but to have failed to gain my point it would."[62]

In a moment, another gunner crawled from cover and made his way forward to Jackson. The lieutenant needed the help of more than a single individual. Pointing to the rear, Jackson shouted to the soldier above the battle's roar: "Go back yonder! Tell Colonel Trousdale to send men forward! Tell him we want experienced men! Tell him with fifty men we can overrun the battery ahead!"[63]

The private raced back toward the American lines—and ran past General Worth, who had ridden into the area close enough to witness Jackson dueling alone with a major part of the Mexican army. Worth directed Jackson to retire from the field. Instead of obeying the order instantly, Jackson responded that it was more dangerous to fall back than to remain in the forward position. The lieutenant was still aiming and firing his one cannon when Magruder galloped onto the field. His horse went down from a fatal bullet wound just before the captain reached Jackson's gun.

Magruder quickly picked himself up from the ground and dashed across the ditch to Jackson's side. Uppermost in Jackson's mind now was getting his other piece into the action. Magruder, with the help of two or three gunners, rushed to the disabled weapon and dragged it by hand into position. Soon Jackson was sighting his two six-pounders and firing furiously.[64]

This was the scene of which legends are made: a tall, young subaltern, in advance of the whole American army, contesting against insurmountable odds and showing no fear as he matched his small volleys against massive salvoes. He had even refused to retire, although ordered to do so. That refusal may well have turned the tide of the battle for Chapultepec.

The brigade that Worth rushed into the area was able to carry the redoubt at the very moment that the defenses at Chapultepec began to give way. Jackson's exploit would pass from mouth to mouth through the whole army. However, his day's work was not yet ended.

Chapultepec fell, but not Mexican resistance. Santa Anna frantically tried to rally the remnant of his army at the gates of Mexico City. Scott and the other American generals were anxious to press forward without delay before Santa Anna could get a coordinated resistance in place. With that end in mind, Scott ordered an attack through the San Cosme gate on the west side of the city.

Meanwhile, Jackson had acquired some wagon limbers. He attached his guns to them and wasted no time striking out on the road to the San Cosme entrance. In such haste, Jackson's section got far ahead of the main assaulting force. Jackson came up on two other officers whose ardor had exceeded their orders. Neither Lieutenant Harvey Hill nor Lieutenant Barnard E. Bee had heard the directive for the advance elements to fall back and concentrate. Between them, the two officers had no more than forty men; but they were pushing the Mexican army down the Tacumbaya causeway like cowboys driving a herd of cattle. Hill and Bee were a mile in advance of Scott's forces when they realized their error. They were about to retire when up rumbled Jackson and his two guns.

Jackson at once volunteered to provide artillery support for the little band of infantry, if Hill and Bee wished to resume the offensive. While the three were talking hastily, Magruder arrived on the scene. He promptly vetoed the idea of an advance by four dozen soldiers; the odds of losing half of his battery were too high. The three lieutenants begged for permission to drive the enemy.

Magruder, always with a flair for the dramatic, relented. The little force moved forward another half-mile and then found itself facing some 1500 Mexican lancers who suddenly came charging down the road toward them. The horsemen would easily have overrun the Americans but for the fact that they were galloping on the causeway. This forced the cavalry to ride in a tight formation.

The observant Jackson saw the situation in a flash and placed his guns in an almost ideal position. "I opened on them," he told a friend years later, "and [with] every fire we cut lanes through them. Whenever they got a little too far, we limbered up and pursued at full gallop until the bullets of their rear guns began to fall near the leaders, then we would unlimber and pour it into them—then limber up again and pursue. We kept it up for about a mile." At this point, the listener observed, Jackson's face was "kindling up, as with the light of battle, and with peculiar emphasis in the words," Jackson exclaimed, "It was splendid!"[65]

The fighting for Mexico City ended at nightfall. The city's defenses had been breached but not overrun. Scott had suffered 850 casualties, of whom 130 lay dead. Mexican losses exceeded 3,000 men. That figure included 820 soldiers and six generals captured. Under darkness, Santa Anna abandoned the capital with what was left of his shell-shocked forces.

By nightfall of September 13, Jackson's begrimed guns were on a hill and trained down on the San Cosme gate to Mexico City. The artillery company had taken a pounding that day but not a crippling one. Magruder fell wounded late in the action, two privates also suffered battle injuries, and twelve horses were dead or crippled. As Jackson rested in front of a campfire that evening, he was surprised to find his uniform coat torn by a bullet or shell fragment. The projectile had missed him.[66]

Little sleep came to Jackson that night. The best day of his life had occurred. He was a hero; he knew it, and so did everyone else familiar with the events of Chapultepec. Jackson had met crisis with courage. His behavior had seemed instinctive, as if something deep inside him had lain dormant until that sultry Monday in his twenty-fourth year.

Henceforth, Jackson would know that when combat became intense, he gained self-composure and control. The confusion of battle triggered in him the calmness of an officer who always expected ultimate success. This was an exhilarating revelation, and Jackson would savor it for a long while.

He fully expected to enter Mexico City with the first Americans on the morning of the 14th, but Jackson received orders to continue covering the western gate to the capital with his guns. An ugly incident occurred that morning. City residents had been alerted that the town would be shelled unless surrender took place by a certain time. Mexican authorities failed to give sufficient heed to the warning. When the hour came, the main thoroughfare remained filled with panic-stricken civilians.

Jackson was watching the mob scene when a directive arrived: he was to sweep the street with his guns at once. Without hesitation, Jackson sent several volleys through the San Cosme gate. When the gunsmoke slowly drifted away, a line of Mexicans lying dead in the street gave clear evidence of the paths of his shells. Jackson abhorred such action. Yet at the same time he felt no reason to question a directive from his superiors. "My duty is to obey orders!" he said then and always. It was an axiom he demanded just as absolutely from those serving under him.[67]

Scott's army filed into Mexico City throughout the day. It was a triumphant procession. Scott had every reason for elation. Never had an American general accomplished more, with fewer men, and with less support from his government. The Scott campaign in Mexico had been brilliant. No one knew that better than its architect.

The First Artillery that Tuesday found temporary quarters in the arsenal building. Amid the glow of victory, American commanders in the days that followed began preparing official reports of the Contreras-Churubusco-Chapultepec operations. Jackson's name was conspicuous in the reports that counted relative to Chapultepec.

Magruder concluded his extremely lengthy commentary with the following: "I beg leave to call the attention of the Major Genl. commanding the Division to the conduct of Lieut. Jackson of the 1st Artillery. If devotion, industry, tallent [sic] & gallantry are the highest qualities of a soldier, then he is entitled to the distinction which their possession confers. I have been ably seconded in all of the operations of the Battery by him, & upon this occasion when circumstances placed him in command for a short time of an independent action, he proved himself eminently worthy of it."[68]

General Pillow stated: "Captain Magruder's field battery, one section of which was served with great gallantry by himself, and the other by his brave Lieut. Jackson, in the face of a galling fire from the enemy's position, did invaluable service preparatory to the general assault." From General Worth came equally lavish praise for an officer who was not even under his command. "After advancing some four hundred yards we came to a battery which had been assailed by a portion of Magruder's field guns—particularly the section under the gallant Lieut. Jackson, who, although he had lost most of his horses and many of his men, continued chivalrously at his post combating with noble courage."[69]

The height of laudation in battle comes from being mentioned in the commanding general's report. Jackson was there. Scott wrote: "To the north . . . the 11th Inft. under Lt. Col. [Paul O.] Hebert, the 14th under Col. Trousdale, and Capt. Magruder's field battery, 1st Arty. one section, advanced under the command of Lieut. Jackson. All of Pillow's division had, at the same time, some spirited affairs against superior numbers. . . . In these, the officers and corps named gained merited praise."[70]

Promotion to brevet major was swift, if not inevitable. Jackson had been on active duty for only fifteen months; during six months in the field, he had won advancements to permanent first lieutenant and brevet major. The brevets carried no extra pay or privileges. They were badges of distinction to which every army officer aspired. A compatriot noted: "No other officer in the whole army in Mexico was promoted so often for meritorious conduct or made so great a stride in rank."[71]

The greatest compliment to Jackson came publicly and from the general in chief himself. Shortly after the occupation of Mexico City, General Scott hosted a reception for his officers. Jackson eagerly attended to get an up-close view of the living legend commanding the American forces. A fellow artillery officer considered Scott "the grandest physical man that I have ever beheld. He [was a] full portly figure without grossness, weighing perhaps near three hundred pounds. The expression of his face was full of gentleness approaching to sweetness, and yet peculiarly leonine. His manner was full of grace yet of a dignity that repelled any advance toward familiarity. He impressed me at the time as a demi-god."[72]

Jackson was moving dutifully through the receiving line at the levee as he waited his turn to be introduced to the commander. "Lieutenant Jackson," came the announcement. Whereupon Scott drew himself to full height and, placing his hands behind his back, proclaimed in a loud, commanding voice: "I don't know if I will shake hands with Mr. Jackson!" Silence swept over the hall as all eyes turned toward the young officer who, blushing and confused, stared at the floor as he stood uncertainly before his general. Scott, now with everyone's attention, then said to Jackson: "If you can forgive yourself for the way in which you slaughtered those poor Mexicans with your guns, I am not sure that I can!" Jackson felt a rush of humiliation course through him. Suddenly he beheld Scott's massive right hand extended toward him while a warm smile of affection and respect spread across the commanding general's face. Jackson shook Scott's hand as applause filled the room. An officer in attendance declared: "No greater compliment could have been paid a young officer for courage & zeal."[73]

Company I, along with Scott's army, settled down for a lengthy stay in Mexico City. The prize had been captured, but the war had not ended. For the next five months, with Santa Anna having resigned and out of the country, American emissaries searched for someone with whom to negotiate a peace.

The unstable Mexican government collapsed anew. Weeks would pass before the country could choose representatives to begin peace discussions. In the meantime, Scott's battle-worn and somewhat strapped forces would be an army of occupation. American troops must enforce laws while, through their presence, they apply pressure to end the war. Almost six months would elapse before a peace treaty became reality.

September's last days were a tense time for the American army. Scott had 6,000 soldiers to police a city of 180,000 dispirited residents. Strict disciplinary measures were necessary, and Scott announced them promptly. Occupation rules were akin to an eagle and a dove flying together: guerrilla bands, assassins, and terrorists received instant and harsh punishment; law-abiding citizens were treated with the utmost courtesy. In that atmosphere, order and peace drifted through the neighborhoods of Mexico's largest city.

Although the army had stopped fighting, the soldiers had not stopped suffering. Jackson demonstrated at this early stage in his career that he was never callous to the sight of pain. In an overdue letter to his sister, he confessed: "I have since my entry into this land seen sights that would melt the heart of the most inhuman of beings: my friends dying around me and my brave soldiers breathing their last on the bloody fields of battle, deprived of every human comfort, and even now I can hardly open my eyes after entering a hospital, the atmosphere of which is generally so vitiated as to make the healthy sick. I would not live in one a week, under the circumstances in which I have seen them, for the whole of Mexico. To die on the battlefield is relief when compared to the death in a contaminated hospital."[74]

The months ahead proved to be a pleasant time for Jackson. His frontier upbringing was now to give way to marked social and intellectual improvement. For awhile, military duties were light and routine. Jackson had quarters in the mammoth national palace and found it commodious and convenient. He quickly began adopting a number of local customs.

One of the first was growing a beard and mustache, which he kept closely trimmed. Jackson followed Mexican habit in the morning by having coffee and sweet rolls while still abed. He had to adjust to no lunch. Since the main meal of the day came after sundown, Jackson bridged the appetite gap by having afternoon tea and by consuming much fruit. This is the time when the Virginian developed a deep fondness for peaches, cherries, plums, lemons, and the full run of tropical delicacies. His love for fruit would remain strong for the rest of his life.

With greater zeal now, Jackson resumed his study of the Spanish language. Even though no grammar texts could be found in Mexico City, Jackson was determined to read and speak Spanish fluently. At least one Mexican gave him instruction. In an incredibly short time, he had so mastered the Mexican dialect that he spoke Spanish easily for as long as he lived. Years later his second wife observed: "His admiration for the language was great, and he always said that it was meant for lovers, the terms of endearment being so musical and abundant. He adopted them for his own use, and delighted in lavishing them upon those dearest to him."[75]

An immediate reason for Jackson's stronger interest in the Spanish language was social. For the first time in his life, he was encountering aristocracy, culture, and all of their by-products. Jackson was fascinated; and when his shy and always-courteous demeanor brought him invitations to dinners with some of Mexico's oldest and wealthiest families, he felt an obligation to be as prepared as possible. A logical starting point was to eliminate any language barrier.

Doing so brought Jackson, also for the first time, into the company of charming señoritas. He learned not only how to dance but how to do so in the proper tempo, remarkable achievements considering that Jackson was musically tone-deaf. Jackson became a regular attender at the Sunday night balls occasionally held in the capital. Asked in later years about such frivolous behavior, a stern Jackson responded, "Remember, I lived then up to all the light I had, and therefore I did not then, nor do I now, reproach myself."[76]

An oft-told story concerned the flute, for which the Virginian suddenly developed a liking. He acquired one, blew on it with his usual persistence, and in time managed to play one tune that was barely recognizable. This tale is entertaining but without any basis of fact.[77]

His correspondence at this time suggests that Jackson experienced his first true infatuations with women. Being a novice in romance, he naturally was swayed by the presence of beautiful women his age in Mexico City; being an orphan, he still had a base of loneliness in his makeup. After Chapultepec, Jackson was convinced that the American forces would remain in Mexico for a long period of occupation. The prospect of continuing to live alone was strongly unappealing. Thus, even though he had been in the capital barely a month, Jackson made a statement to Laura more serious in intent than previous writers have acknowledged. "I think that probably I shall spend many years here and may possibly conclude (though I have not yet) to make my life more natural by sharing it with some amiable Señorita."[78]

Jackson was tempted but never taken. One prominent family displayed unusually warm hospitality to the officer, and he remained ever grateful for the kindnesses. Yet he soon found it necessary to discontinue his visitations. Forced to give an explanation a decade later, Jackson blushed. The family contained "several charming daughters," he said, and he found that "the fascination of some of the female charms which he met there was likely to become too strong for his prudence, unless he escaped them in good time."[79]

For what he called "the mere delight of living," Jackson considered Mexico City "to surpass all others he had ever known." The country, he told Laura, "offers more inducements for me than the United States, inasmuch as there is more room for improvements in everything that is good and commendable." A decade after Jackson's death, his widow told a reporter that "my husband fell in love with Mexico during his campaigns there, and had there been any sort of stable government in that country, he would certainly have made it his home."[80]

Yet there was much about Mexico that Jackson did not like. "The term corruption expresses the state of this unfortunate people better than any other in the English language," he asserted. Mexicans possessed a "beautiful climate" and an "alluring" country but seemed incapable of doing anything about either. If the integrity of the people equaled the beauty and charm of the nation, Jackson would have been impressed. However, he was repelled by "a hollow and corrupt state of morals, and a debasing religion, with all [its] radical principles."[81]

Many of Jackson's brother officers felt in the same vein. A fellow Virginian, Henry Heth, who graduated from West Point in 1847 and fought Indians on the Plains after his Mexican War service, observed of Mexico City's residents: "The blankets they wear give them an opportunity to conceal their plunder. I never met but one other people who could steal as quickly and conceal their thefts as readily, as Mexicans. They were the Pawnee tribes of Indians."[82]

Always anxious to improve himself, Jackson began devoting a certain period of each day to intellectual study. He perused histories of Mexico written in both English and Spanish; enjoyment also came from reading the works of William Shakespeare and Lord Chesterfield. Manuals on good manners and the rules of society armed him with information to use at soirees and similar gatherings. All of this knowledge he absorbed by himself, without benefit of any exchange of ideas with a friend or acquaintance. Just as he read alone, Jackson rode alone. A day of good weather would all but guarantee his taking a horseback ride to some area on the outskirts of the capital.

Jackson's friend and future brother-in-law, Harvey Hill, asserted that Jackson in

Mexico "had no particular regard for religion" but relied instead on a "tenderness of conscience."[83] Hill wrote that statement after the Civil War, when his feelings for Jackson had undergone a rather negative shift. Hill was misinformed. During the Mexican period of self-improvement, Jackson slowly gravitated to a reawakened interest in Christian faith. This time he would pursue the subject with a new fervor.

Captain Francis Taylor, "an earnest Christian who labored for the spiritual welfare of his soldiers," had been the first person to speak seriously of religion to Jackson. At Taylor's urging, Jackson began a systematic reading of the Bible. He did so, his close friend Margaret Preston noted, with "a singular deliberateness" characteristic of the man. Jackson read Holy Scriptures "just as he would have taken up a mathematical problem to work it out." He read, he digested, and he initially did so "without one emotional feeling beyond the sense of duty."[84]

Jackson had little base on which to build a faith. His mother, he thought, was a Methodist, yet after her death Jackson had received little formal religious education. He did not even know if he had ever been baptized. At West Point he had come under the influence of the Episcopal church because most of the army chaplains were of that denomination. So was Francis Taylor, but the captain in no way tried to implant his form of worship in Jackson. As a result, Jackson began his religious studies in Mexico with a completely open mind. His only resolution was that he "would conscientiously satisfy himself with the most scriptured" denomination, and he wanted a faith he could pursue with "characteristic straightforwardness."[85]

He started with the oldest Christian form of worship. The Catholic church in Mexico intrigued Jackson, not only because of its ornate buildings and other outward manifestations but also because of the extremely close relations existing between clergy and laity. Early in the occupation of Mexico City, an acquaintance introduced Jackson to a community of monks. The inquisitive Virginian spent several days visiting the monastery. This was Jackson's real introduction to Catholicism. He next read extensively about the sect, plied his mind with facts and questions, and then requested an audience with no less than Juan Manuel Irisarri, the sixty-three-year-old archbishop of Mexico.

This most powerful of Catholic prelates in that country must have been bemused when a tall, young American army officer came before him in somewhat diffident fashion. Yet the earnestness of Jackson's queries and the depth of his thinking quickly gained the archbishop's attention and friendship. Several conferences took place between the two contrasting figures. Jackson had great respect for the cleric's friendship and candor, but he became convinced that the Catholic religion was not his road to salvation. Mrs. Jackson explained tactfully: "His preference for a simpler form of faith and worship led him to wait until he could have the opportunity of learning more of other churches." The Protestant minister who later became Jackson's pastor was blunt in his assessment: Jackson "made himself acquainted with the distinctive principles of that corrupt branch of the church, and was fully convinced of the unsoundness of those principles." That is not true. Thanks to the Mexican archbishop, Jackson modified his impressions of Catholicism. Thereafter, his Christian associate J. T. L. Preston declared, Jackson "had more tolerant views of popery than most zealous Protestants."[86]

The seeds of an active faith were now sown. Jackson read the Bible; he prayed; he meditated; he examined the nooks and crannies of scriptures and his own soul. In doing so, he began to undergo a change that would eventually create the very foundation of his being.

His letters to Laura, which he tried to pen twice a month to go out with the mail pouches, contained an increasing number of references to a living and ever-present God. Jackson became a devoted servant before he found the religious family he wanted. Also, at this time Jackson established a rule he never violated: he would neither write nor mail a letter on Sunday.[87] The Lord's day was holy, and Jackson intended to keep it so.

Jackson family members liked to recount one humorous story associated with the new interest in religion. When he arrived at the Mexican monastery for his visit, Jackson agreed to guard a chest containing a large sum of money. That night, before retiring, he placed the chest beneath his bed for safekeeping. Jackson had been asleep only a few minutes when he awakened with a jolt. The bed was moving.

He leaped up and grabbed his sword. He searched but found no one else in the room. He lay down again; soon the bed moved a second time. Out of the bed Jackson came, again prepared to do combat. Yet he was still alone. "This time," Jackson told a cousin, "I was scared indeed, till my attention was called to a shouting in the street, and then I found that it was an earthquake passing under the city of Mexico that had lifted my bed up and given me so much apprehension."[88]

By then, he and Captain Magruder had grown so close that Jackson agreed to carry a challenge for a duel from the captain to General Franklin Pierce. Magruder was convinced of an impugning of his honor by the affable New Englander.

Nothing came of the challenge in part because Magruder had to relinquish command for several months owing to disability. A physician testified that the captain was affected "with very serious irritation of the brain and the whole nervous system, accompanied with chronic torpidity of the liver" and an injured leg that needed surgery. Another contemporary had a vastly different opinion. Because Magruder was "a man of remarkably intemperate habits, it almost invariably happened" that he would become incapable of performing his duties.[89]

Whatever the nature of Magruder's indisposition, Jackson on October 19, 1847, assumed temporary command of Company I. He approached his new responsibilities with accustomed seriousness. On November 11, Jackson requested new troops for the battery. The 100-man battery was down to fewer than thirty soldiers, with several of the artillerists on a variety of detached assignments. Acquiring reinforcements, Jackson wrote, "is necessary to make the Battery as official as it should be. Even the drill cannot be executed with the present number for it is necessary to take the cannoneers as drivers in the maneuvers of the Battery." Jackson received the loan of some troops but no permanent replacements.[90]

Company leadership for Jackson was enjoyable but short-lived. On December 4, Lieutenant William H. French transferred to Company I with orders to succeed Jackson at the head of the battery. French had seniority of rank, which entitled him to command. French possibly flaunted his assignment; perhaps Jackson felt a natural human twinge of resentment at being replaced by an "outsider" of equal rank—especially French, with whom, by all indications, Jackson shared little cordiality.

Any tension between the two men was brief: on January 19, 1848, Jackson was directed to return to his first unit, Company K. Rejoining Captain Francis Taylor was genuinely pleasurable. Jackson reported for duty promptly. On his arrival, he greeted Lieutenant A. P. Hill, a fellow Virginian who had finished West Point a year behind Jackson. Powell Hill joined the company in the same orders that Jackson received. He and Jackson had little opportunity for association; in a matter of weeks, the former transferred to French's battery.[91]

It was in the early part of 1848 that Jackson became a second in another challenge to a duel. This time the disagreement ended on the field of honor.

Adjutant Daniel Smith Lee and Lieutenant Benjamin F. Hartley were both members of the Eleventh Infantry. Following the battle of Molino del Rey, an unsigned article in an American newspaper related how Lieutenant Colonel William M. Graham fell mortally wounded in the action and died in the arms of Lee. In reality, Hartley was embracing Graham when the colonel breathed his last. Hartley accused Lee of being the author of the news story and of perpetrating the lie. Soon, fellow officers were ostracizing Lee. The adjutant reacted by challenging Hartley to mortal combat. At the same time, Lee asked Jackson to serve as his principal second.

Hartley quickly accepted the challenge. He chose Jackson's fellow Virginia mountaineer, Lieutenant Birkett Fry, as his second. Hartley was a crack marksman; being the challenged, he chose muskets at thirty paces. Jackson "won the word," in dueling parlance, and became the judge in charge of the contest.

It took place on the roadside between Mexico City and the village of Lerma. The weapons were Mississippi smoothbores. Jackson stood at rigid attention in the broad space between the two antagonists. "In stentorian tones, audible over a forty-acre lot," he "instructed the principles as if he were drilling an awkward squad." He then backed out of the line of fire. "Are you ready?" he shouted. "Take aim . . . One . . . Two . . . Three . . . Fire!" Lee and Hartley shot simultaneously. Both missed. Lee stood silent in the field; Hartley angrily threw his musket to the ground and sent a member of his party to demand a second fire. Jackson "instantly and peremptorily refused to accede," an eyewitness reported, "stating that his principal had been accused of cowardice, which charge was absolutely disproved by the duel which had just occurred." Hartley cursed and stormed unreconciled from the area. The affair ended. But for Jackson's dominant role, the duel would have come to a more tragic conclusion.[92]

After his return to Company K, Jackson found his old unit much changed in personnel. The admired Captain Taylor was still in charge. First Lieutenant Isaac S. H. Reeves was a South Carolinian who had graduated from West Point in 1838 and taught artillery at the academy prior to the war with Mexico. He would receive promotion to captain in 1850 and die within a year thereafter.

The newest arrival in the battery was Second Lieutenant Otis H. Tillinghast, New York born and in the top third of his 1847 class at the academy. In the ranks of Company K were eighty-seven men and eighty horses. Within a month after Jackson's arrival, transfers would bring the battery to a swollen complement of 111 cannoneers. Jackson quietly resumed his duties as company quartermaster. With his usual precision, he not only submitted reports punctually; he also pointed out errors in previous summaries not of his composition.[93]

On the last Monday in February 1848, Jackson sent a long and loving message to his sister. Laura had mentioned in a previous letter that her health was precarious. "I may not live to receive your answer," she stated. This greatly upset Jackson. By the age of eleven, he had experienced the deaths of a six-year-old sister, his father, his mother, and his stepfather—while at the same time being separated from his brother and sister. Now only the sister remained.

In responding to Laura's feeling of possible death, Jackson vividly displayed some of the newfound faith that was becoming more and more dominant in his makeup. "I hope," he wrote, that Laura's words "imply nothing beyond what they literally state. This is the earnest prayer to God of your brother. But if He in His great wisdom had afflicted you with disease incurable, then may He in His infinite goodness receive you into His heavenly abode where, though I should be deprived of you here in this world of cares, yet I should hope to meet you in a land where care and sorrow are unknown; there with a mother, a brother, a sister and yourself, and, I hope, a father, to live in a state of felicity, uncontaminated by mortality."[94]

Jackson then sought to be cheerful by summarizing his current situation. "Do not allow my words about marrying in Mexico disturb you. I have sometimes thought of staying here, and again of going home. I have no tie in this country equal to you. . . . I dress as a gentleman who wishes to be received as such. I do not gamble, nor spend my money, as I think, foolishly. . . . My health, I think, is improving in this country, and at all events my knowledge of Spanish is."[95]

His need for the language was about to dissipate. On March 10, the U.S. Senate ratified the Treaty of Guadalupe Hidalgo. To secure peace, the Mexicans had ceded more than half of their territory to the United States. Many officers in Scott's army did not believe that the peace would hold: the Mexican people had been forced to relinquish too much of their land. Yet the beaten nation could resist no more. The one-sided contest made America a truly transcontinental nation, but it did so at the direct expense of Mexico.[96]

The subject of war's end did not come up in Jackson's next letter to Laura. He preferred to report on his schedule and habits in the Mexican capital.

I thought at one time of writing a journal but I can not find the time, as although I am usually up at six o'clock and retire to bed at ten or eleven, still the day is not long enough. The morning hours I occupy in studies & business and the evenings in a similar manner, and sometimes a ride on the Paseo or elsewhere in the evening. . . . When not on duty I generally pay a visit after supper or tea. Among those families which I visit are some of the first in the republic, as Don Licas Abeman, Martinez del Rio and I also have the acquaintances of others of some distinction. . . .

Owing to my knowledge of the language of the country and the acquaintances which I have made I think that I keep my time more agreeably than the greater portion of the officers of the army but if your company could also be had I would spend my hours still more agreeably.[97]

Jackson closed his letter by mentioning the several sharp rivalries that had erupted on the command level relative to battle plans and conduct, official report statements, and the like. It was not a good conclusion to an American victory. Jackson stated with an air of detachment: "General Scotts case has been investigated. The charges against

Col. Duncan were with drawn. Also General Worth withdrew his against General Scott. General Pillows case is now being investigated."[98]

Having heard nothing from Laura in six weeks, Jackson began his next communique by expressing concern over her well-being. "I do not know of any other reason but your health which could have prevented your writing to a brother who is interested in every thing that interests you. And I hope that if you have any regard for my peace of mind, that you will write at least once every fortnight. If your health forbids you writing at any time, then get some one to write for you, if it should be but a dozen lines. I do not think that a regular mail has left this city, without carrying a letter from me."[99]

Jackson then noted: "The treaty has arrived from Washington, with its amendments. Many think that it will receive the ratification of this [Mexican] government. But some think it will not. For my own part I hope it will."[100]

Amid the succeeding paragraphs of his letter, a theme of Jackson's desire to come home emerged. "The rain is quite abundant here at present and interferes somewhat with my evening visits. . . . We are told here that our people at home think that the army do not wish to return from Mexico, but if such is the truth they are much mistaken. . . . The general hospital is ordered to be moved to Jalapa, and General Patterson I believe will go down at the same time, to take command of that station. This movement appears to indicate an anticipation of leaving the country."[101]

On April 15, Jackson's months of temporary duty as Company K's quartermaster and commissary officer became official. Thereafter, he was directly responsible for all food and other supplies for his battery. The command level of Taylor's unit by then had undergone further changes. Jackson was the senior first lieutenant. Of similar rank was Vermont's Truman Seymour, who had graduated two notches behind Jackson in the academy's class of 1846. James B. Fry of Illinois, an 1847 West Point graduate (and future Civil War general), was the only second lieutenant on duty with the battery.[102]

By the end of May, the United States and Mexico had officially exchanged ratification documents. The Treaty of Guadalupe Hidalgo went into effect, and with it war ended. Scott's army began embarking for home in stages. Jackson was among the first contingent of artillerists to start for the Gulf coast. The eleven officers and 102 men of the First Artillery left Mexico City on June 5 and retraced the route to Jalapa. A two-week wait followed there. On July 5, the First Artillery segment departed Jalapa for the three-day march to Veracruz. Two more days of waiting ensued there before the men left Mexico aboard the *Mary Kingsland* for the week-long voyage to New Orleans.[103]

The journey was long enough and uneventful enough for Jackson to ponder the many things he had learned during his first twenty-three months as a soldier.

He had traveled hundreds of miles by horseback, boat, and on foot. He had mastered the responsibilities as an officer, quartermaster, and commissary with no apparent difficulty. Jackson had entered a foreign country for the first time; he could always boast of having been part of America's largest amphibious operation.

Fresh out of West Point, he had gained firsthand knowledge about functions of an army and strategy in action. He had seen the shortcomings of volunteers and half-trained troops, the compensatory effect of discipline over inexperience, the importance of drill in everything military. The filth and neglect ever present in the military hospitals of Mexico similarly made a lasting impression. No such medical conditions would ever be tolerated under his command, if it was possible to prevent them.

At the strategic level, Jackson learned the incalculable value of reconnaissance and logistical planning. He would henceforth be an outspoken advocate of flanking movements. Cerro Gordo, Contreras, the movement across the Pedregal, the march to San Augustin, the action at Chapultepec were all examples of how strongly fortified and seemingly impregnable works could be carried by turning movements.

The success of surprise attacks was something else indelibly etched in Jackson's mind. Campaigns against the Mexicans convinced Jackson that the bold commander triumphed over the timid one. It was the nature of war, he fervently believed.

Most of all, Jackson realized from the Mexican experience that the military was his true vocation and war his natural element. The army provided the orderliness, discipline, and sense of duty so consistent with his personal makeup. Battle was a stimulus—an opportunity for achievement that pushed bad health aside and sent nervousness into oblivion.

On July 17, Jackson and his battery went ashore at New Orleans. The city extended a hero's welcome to the soldiers. Jackson spent three days in an atmosphere of celebration. Whatever his activities were in New Orleans, only one incident was recorded: he posed for photographs. The likeness shows an officer of fairly slender build with a shock of hair and well-kept mustache and beard. Dominating the photograph are the eyes, which seem to reflect simultaneously the sternness of a professional soldier and the confidence of a proven fighter.

The innocence of youth had yielded to the experience of manhood, and Jackson felt proud.

4

HEALTH, BAPTISM, AND CONTROVERSY

O N THURSDAY, JULY 20, 1848, the paddle-wheeler *Arkansas* eased away from a pier at New Orleans and began struggling up the Mississippi River. On board was the First Artillery's Company K, bound for Fort Columbus, New York. Lieutenant Thomas J. Jackson watched sugar plantations, cotton fields, and shorelines pass slowly on this first leg of a long journey. He ruminated over the future as the battery proceeded by boat and horseback to the north and northeast. There was much to ponder but not unlimited time in which to do it. Jackson was in temporary command of the battery and remained so after its August 16 arrival at Fort Columbus.

Fortunately, the stay at Fort Columbus was brief; for in a word that installation was a mess. It was regimental headquarters for the First Artillery, a duty station, a depot for recruits, and a depository for both ordnance and quartermaster supplies. Fort Columbus was overcrowded. Worse, no place existed to store live ammunition that was lying anywhere space permitted. The sixty-three men of Company K were quickly shifted to more desirable Fort Hamilton.[1]

Jackson had planned to request a lengthy furlough as soon as the battery settled into new quarters. However, he was always sensitive to rank and to his future, and the situation in Company K caused him to reconsider applying for leave. "I had hopes of visiting you this fall, but I have not been able to arrange my affairs here for that purpose," he wrote Laura. "For instance, if I should leave, some other officer might be attached [to the company] during my absence who would rank me in case of his remaining with the company after my return." Jackson was certain that Captain Taylor would protect his position as much as he could, "but my absence might reduce the number of officers so much as to render another officer necessary to the company." All Jackson could do was hope to get extended leave the following summer. "If so I propose on visiting the springs at several places" to improve his health, which was "still getting better."[2]

Lack of time prohibited further contemplation. Three days after his letter to Laura, Jackson received orders to report to Carlisle Barracks, Pennsylvania, for court-martial duty. The work was dull, the environment rather drab, but Jackson found "many interesting ladies" and enjoyed himself at soirees held "almost every day since my arrival." Duty at Carlisle Barracks proved of short duration. From Beverly came word that his sister's health was not good. She wanted to see her brother before year's end.

Jackson appealed to Captain Taylor for intercession; and on September 5, Jackson sent Laura a combination of lecture and love letter. "I propose to see you in your own house on the 10th of October, which is earlier than you even requested. As I have already given you my reasons for not coming this fall, it is unnecessary to state what I may sacrifice in visiting you. But on reading your letter I concluded that I would use my influence to do that which I so desire to do—to visit you." In order to call on all of his relatives while he was in Virginia, Jackson asked for three months' furlough. He told Laura: "When I obtain my leave, should I get it, you must not expect me to stay with you more than a month. And I hope that your health will be much improved by that time." On September 14, Jackson began a three-month leave of absence. What eased his mind considerably as he started south from New York was the publication on the day of his departure of Company K's official roster. The three officers listed were Captain Taylor, First Lieutenants Jackson and Truman Seymour, plus Second Lieutenant James B. Fry.[3]

The war hero arrived in Beverly by stagecoach. He had not seen his beloved sister in two and a half years. Finding Laura much improved in health by then, Jackson had a long and pleasant visit with the Arnolds. They lived in an imposing two-story brick home on a corner in the center of town. On either side of the double portico in front were small one-story wings.[4]

Arnold had purchased the home when he married Laura. It was both comfortable and impressive. Jonathan Arnold had made it so starting with a lucrative law practice. He was so much older than Laura that Jackson always addressed him as "Mr. Arnold." The two men spent a number of hours in political discussions. Arnold was a staunch Whig while Jackson was a Democrat with an inquisitive mind.

Much of Jackson's attention went to his three-year-old nephew and namesake, Thomas Jackson Arnold. An unabashed love of children marked Jackson's entire life. To the impressionable Arnold lad, Jackson was a military hero with a fascinating array of war "trophies": sword, silver spoon, inkstand adorned with doves, and spurs worn by a Mexican officer.

Young Arnold later recalled that Jackson "walked & sat very erect & my Mother from that time forward made me do likewise. I was a delicate child & it was thought the erect position would be very beneficial for me." Arnold had no memory of his uncle on a horse. "He walked a great deal & I generally accompanied him on his walks; he walked fast, & I had to move pretty lively to keep up." These outings between man and boy did much to draw adult and child close together. In time, Jackson assumed an almost fatherly attitude toward "Little Tom," as he often called the lad.[5]

Laura was the only member of the Arnold family who gave Jackson concern. Her health was an issue, but the greater problem was that brother and sister seemed to be going in opposite directions in faith. She was sliding toward agnosticism while Jackson was adopting more and more the tenets of Christian religion. He would struggle hard in the months ahead to "recapture" his sister on behalf of the Almighty.

In November, with Laura physically unable to accompany him, Jackson left the Arnolds and journeyed alone to see friends and kinfolk at Clarksburg and in Lewis

County. His regional loyalties, instilled as a child, would always remain strong. Among his first stops was the Turkey Run home of his cousin, Isaac Newton Brake. The farmer later recalled of Jackson: "I can see him yet standing up before the fire in our home. . . . Although he wore civilian clothes on his furlough home, he maintained a natural military bearing." Brake was struck by the fact that Jackson "was not much to talk about his exploits but conversed freely about the war and the heroism of others in that conflict."[6]

The visit to Jackson's Mill was sad. Recollections of childhood flooded Jackson's mind. On the positive side were the cool waters and refreshing breezes of the West Fork River, whose opposite bank had so often been a refuge from the world's uncertainties. Yet the might-have-beens of his youth rekindled dormant frustrations.

To add to the unhappiness, Jackson discovered the family circle breaking apart. Uncle Edward Jackson had died the preceding October, his Aunt Elizabeth was terminally ill, and Uncle Cummins seemed to be in more legal entanglements than ever before. Even charges of counterfeiting were pending in federal court. The uncle was naturally distracted throughout what was the last time he ever saw his nephew.

Needless to say, Jackson spent much time during the Lewis County stop to visit friends in Weston. He met briefly with the man he considered his benefactor, Congressman Samuel Hays, and regretted that they did not have longer to talk. The citizens of Weston were anxious to give their soldier a hero's welcome. A public reception was held in the middle of town; and blushing with embarrassment, Jackson accepted from the citizens an ornate sword of honor. The young officer and his remaining kin thought the ceremony "a proud and memorable occasion."[7]

Later that day, or shortly thereafter, Jackson visited the law firm of Dexter Williams and William E. Arnold. The latter had been a trusted friend to Jackson during his teenage years. The three men engaged in a lengthy conversation, which both Arnold and a bystander recorded. Jackson began by describing the life of a soldier. Nothing seemed to please him more than to discuss army commanders, strategy, battles, and peace treaties—with particular emphasis on the recent contest in Mexico.

Arnold thought his friend "enamored with the pomp and circumstance of war." The attorney continued: "One of the marked characteristics of this extraordinary man was his extreme modesty. It was with the greatest difficulty that he could be induced to speak of any act, however meritorious, with which his name was associated. No young officer was ever more highly complimented by his superior than he in our war with Mexico; and yet, if that act had been left alone for him to have told, it would never have been known."

Williams and Arnold soon changed the subject. Jackson's army salary was barely equivalent to that of a college teacher. Promotion in service was strictly by seniority; ability had little or nothing to do with permanent advancement. Equally as bad, no provisions existed in the army for retirement. An officer remained on duty until resignation, dismissal, or death. Having pointed out these debits to Jackson, the two attorneys then asked if he would consider joining them in the field of law.

They would take him into their legal practice at once. He would receive a share of the profits while he studied for the bar. Material gain was obviously an object here, for

Williams and Arnold knew that Jackson's reputation would undoubtedly attract many new clients. Yet genuine friendship for an orphan of great promise underlay everything else.

Jackson politely declined. He knew now that the military was where he belonged. "Law is not my line," he told the two men. "If there is another war, I will soon be a general. If peace follows, I will never be anything but Tom Jackson." The subject of a law career never rose again.[8]

Late in November, Jackson returned to Beverly for a second, short stay with the Arnolds. For Jackson's return to Fort Hamilton, Mr. Arnold lent him his prize (and well-known) stallion for the first leg of the trip, to Hot Springs. From there, Jackson would catch the triweekly stage to Staunton, then proceed to Richmond. Jackson said goodbye to the Arnolds around noon, rode some twenty miles, and arrived after dark at the inn of Peter Conrad. Without informing Conrad who he was or where he was going, Jackson left orders for his horse to be fed and saddled at 3 A.M. He then went to bed.

Jackson was up and ready to go at the appointed hour. The horse was not. Innkeeper Conrad had recognized the animal; no stranger was leaving in the middle of the night with Mr. Arnold's most valuable mount, and that was that! Host and guest argued for hours. In the end, both won. It was daylight when Jackson finally was able to resume his trip. By then, he had missed the stage, and his journey was extended by two days.

On his first journey to the capital of Virginia, Jackson called on John S. Carlile. This distant kinsman was a native of Winchester, a former attorney in Beverly and Clarksburg, and then a state senator. The Richmond visit was short but pleasant. Carlile received him "in a very cordial manner," Jackson stated to Laura, "and during my stay there he allowed no opportunity to pass unimproved in which he could manifest his kindness."[9]

The return trip to New York was harsh because of bitterly cold weather and atrocious road conditions. On December 14, obeying his orders, Jackson returned to duty at Fort Hamilton. A severe attack of rheumatism would mar his first weeks on duty.[10]

Jackson's new assignment station was one of the prides of the U.S. Army. Fort Hamilton was on the eastern (or Brooklyn) side of the Narrows, the entrance to New York harbor. Nearby was the pleasant community of New Utrecht. As early as 1819, the army had begun planning a permanent installation at the Narrows to protect the great New York port. Construction did not get underway until June 1825; the site on the southwest extremity of Long Island was a hubbub of building activity for years. On October 31, 1831, the fort named for Alexander Hamilton officially opened.

It was an imposing rectangular structure, built of granite rather than of brick. Fort Hamilton contained fourteen casemates and twenty-six barbettes; it was capable of withstanding attack from both sea and land. Initially, the fort, where Robert E. Lee was stationed from 1841 to 1846, was a subpost for nearby Fort Columbus. When Jackson arrived there in December 1848, the 105 men from Companies G and K of the First Artillery were stationed in the garrison.[11]

Peacetime army routine was not overly time consuming. The army was gearing down from war. Tightening ranks, procedure, and discipline occupied most of an officer's time. While Jackson was on furlough, Colonel Ichabod Crane had issued a directive prohibiting officers and men in the First Artillery from wearing mustaches. Jackson dutifully shaved his upper lip but retained extended sideburns (or "jaw-whiskers") for the next ten years.[12]

Standard chores as company quartermaster and commissary filled the lieutenant's first days at Fort Hamilton. Six weeks of court-martial duty began in early February. To these responsibilities were occasionally added temporary roles as both company commander and post adjutant. Jackson pursued each assignment with the punctilious devotion to duty that was so fundamental to his makeup. No matter slid through channels; no detail escaped his attention. He became so inundated with paperwork at one point that he went two months without writing Laura.

Jackson had to submit monthly quartermaster reports and quarterly summaries of company activities. Seeking official answers to minor questions was time consuming but, in his estimation, necessary for the good of the service. He once drafted a long letter to the War Department on the subject of how regulations could be bypassed for the sake of supplying sufficient firewood for an ordnance sergeant's quarters. On another occasion, Jackson asked the quartermaster general of the army whether civilian mechanics were entitled to the whiskey ration distributed to soldiers. The answer was no. Jackson once inquired if officers could have their horses shod at public expense. The answer was yes.[13]

A crusade for knowledge begun in Mexico continued in New York. Jackson carefully set apart a period each day for study. He felt proud of the broadening of intelligence that he had undertaken. "I hope," he wrote Laura, "that when I shall have informed myself well that my letters will be more entertaining and useful."[14]

At this same time, Jackson was growing increasingly concerned about not receiving official notice of the brevet promotions he had been promised. He therefore decided to write to the man who had opened the doors to an army career for him. On February 2, 1849, he composed an unusually humble letter to Congressman Samuel L. Hays. "Having to a great extent recovered my strength, and I hope my health," Jackson began, "I take pleasure in returning you my most sincere thanks for your repeated kindness towards me, hoping at the same time, that some opportunity may present itself, of discharging my debt of gratitude, in some other way: though at present I must admit that I can not see very clearly in what way I can ever be serviceable to you."

Jackson then broached the subject of the Mexican War promotions.

I believe that the list of brevets is now being made out, and from what you intimated to me [in Weston], and from information received since, and the strong grounds on which I have been presented, I have but little or no doubt but that I shall be advanced, provided my claims should be presented to the Secretary of War; but I am afraid that the case may from forgetfulness not be brought to his consideration at this time, as the list is being filled up.

I would be glad to converse with you, as I know that my conversation would be directed to my best friend; but that pleasure I must forego for the present. My sense of gratitude for the interest which you have taken in my welfare is easier to be appreciated by the heart, than to be expressed by words.

At this point, Jackson wished to assure the congressman of the intensity with which he was seeking self-improvement of mind. "I propose with the blessings of Providence to be a hard student, and to make myself not only acquainted with military art and science but with politics, and of course [I] must be well versed in history. My historical studies I have arranged in the following order: first of general history, ancient and modern, and then, special histories of important events, countries, &s. I have commenced with Rollins ancient history, and have read about one fourth of it: reading about forty or fifty pages per day."

Jackson closed his long message to Hays by commenting on how California's "gold fever is running quite high here." Prompting this statement may have been the news Jackson had recently received that his uncle had become "infected" by the fever and had gone to California. What the nephew did not know was that Cummins Jackson had fled west as a fugitive from justice.[15]

The letter to Hays had not even reached Washington when Jackson received word of his promotion to brevet captain. Appropriately, he took command of the fifty-five-man Company K, for Captain Taylor had departed on an extended furlough. In the first week of March, another elevation in rank was officially announced. Jackson became "Major by Brevet" for "gallant and meritorious conduct in the battle of Chapultepec, promotion to date from Sept. 13, 1847."[16]

After a couple of months at Fort Hamilton, Jackson had his work day so organized as to have idle hours at his disposal. He promptly applied many of them to a favorite pastime of sightseeing. Eleven miles from the fort was New York City, which Jackson visited with increasing frequency. The huge metropolis offered endless attractions to a young man of rural if not isolated background. He once commented to Laura: "Yesterday, whilst walking through the city, I thought of the pleasure which I would derive from sharing the contemplation of its beauties and wonders with you. . . . In New York may be found almost anything which the inclination may desire but peaceful quiet. Everything is in motion, everything alive with animation."[17]

He knew little of art, so he made it a point to enlighten himself. Margaret Preston, who would be his closest friend, remembered Jackson saying that he "never came to New York City without finding time to step into one of the best galleries available."[18]

Jackson became enthralled as well by bookstores. He spent hours examining volumes on the shelves. Determined to become a soldier in every possible way, he began purchasing historical narratives and military biographies. Ancient history and treatises on the campaigns of Napoleon Bonaparte were his favorites. On occasion, Jackson would secure a contemporary periodical to feel the pulse of national events. Rarely did he read a newspaper.

Despite the varied and pleasurable activities occupying his time at Fort Hamilton, Jackson came more and more to worry about his health.[19] He was convinced that he possessed a weak constitution. Certainly, the Mississippi River trip he and his brother Warren took as youngsters had an adverse and lingering effect. Thomas had long pursued an informal program to improve his health. Yet after a few months at the New York post, something was wrong with the lieutenant. His weight slowly dropped from 164 to less than 140 pounds.

Naturally, physical condition soon dominated his thinking. It not only became habitual; at times it was obsessive, and the ailments directly affected his activities for the next decade. Health became a common theme in Jackson's letters to his sister. He was always getting better or getting worse. The timing and nature of Jackson's illnesses suggest that when he was active or preoccupied with important matters, he felt good; but when he was inactive, bored, or unproductive, his thoughts turned inward and physical problems seemed to materialize. Jackson always felt better in war than in peace.

This sharp concern about physical well-being first became noticeable in a New Year's Day 1849 letter Jackson sent to his sister. "I suppose that you begin to think it time that I should write, but I am not certain that my physician agrees with you about that . . . but at all events I shall venture to say that I am still living, and, with the blessing of God, hope to live for some years to come." Before closing the letter, Jackson declared: "My physician has pronounced my lungs and liver sound, and that the liver has only been sympathetically affected."[20]

A month later, Jackson gave another health report to Laura. "The cholera has entirely disappeared from this place (Quarantine). The weather is quite disagreeable. I caught the rheumatism in your salubrious mountain air, which is harassing me no little. I am gaining strength and flesh. . . . I am well fixed here, having my rooms both carpeted and decently furnished."[21]

The improvement would be only temporary. In this decade of his life, Jackson became convinced that every one of his organs was malfunctioning to some extent. He fretted about his vision, hearing, throat, digestion, liver, kidneys, blood circulation, nervous system, muscular structure, and joints. He began extensive reading on human anatomy.[22] Jackson employed self-care as a cure for his ailments. In many cases, he used irrational means to combat imagined illnesses.

Jackson dosed himself with a wide variety of medicines and compresses. He inhaled glycerine, silver nitrate, and the smoke of burning mullein. He ingested a number of ammonia preparations. If Jackson heard of some "sure-fire" cure, he was ready to try it. He moved from physician to physician, fad to fad, and theory to theory, sometimes with eagerness and sometimes with resignation. Eventually (through the powers of elimination, many thought), the major disabilities became a combination of rheumatism and neuralgia, weak eyesight, and dyspepsia. Rheumatism, contracted while returning from autumn furlough, persisted into the following spring. "It would be a source of gratification to write you every fortnight," he next told Laura, "but writing, as I may have told you, gives me pain in my right side, and which I am by no means free from at this moment."[23]

Early in April, Jackson reported a marked improvement in his rheumatic problem because he had gone "under the care of one of the finest medical men of New York City." The physician told Jackson to stop his confinement—to exercise and socialize more. Jackson, ever the good patient, did as told. He began a regimen of walking or riding five miles daily whenever possible, and he devised a series of calisthenics that included hopping and broad jumps. As for the second half of the prescription, he announced to Laura that he had lately commenced visiting acquaintances and colleagues more frequently. "Every few evenings," Jackson stated matter-of-factly, he received "an invitation to some social party."[24]

The rheumatoid-neuralgic condition remained with him in one form or another for years. Writing to one of his colonels in the second year of the Civil War, Jackson stated: "I regret to hear that you are a victim to neuralgia. I know what it is from good personal experience."[25]

A possible by-product of that muscular or nervous disorder was a strange habit Jackson exhibited thereafter. He once informed a group of fellow officers "of a peculiar malady which troubled him, and complained that one arm and one leg was heavier than the other, and [he] would occasionally raise his arm straight up, as he said, to let the blood run back into his body, and so relieve the excessive weight."[26]

Weak eyesight began to bother Jackson in the late spring of 1849 and, for the next two years, understandably created fearful moments. "Through the blessings of that all Ruling Being," he wrote Laura in early summer, "I'm allowed the privilege and pleasure of communicating with you. . . . My eyes were so weak for some months since that I could not look at objects through the window and to look out of doors was frequently painful, though but for a moment, and I was reduced to the necessity of masking my looking glass on account of its reflection. And could not look at a candle, not even for a second, without pain. I consulted my physician, and he told me not to use them, and at the same time to avoid spectacles. I do so and at present, I can read a letter of three or four pages, without feeling any inconvenience."[27]

Jackson's acute sensitivity to light (photophobia) was most likely the result of uveitis. This internal inflammation of the eye can develop from a number of different causes. In Jackson's case, the problem was chronic but not permanent. Physicians of that day did not regard spectacles as an always-good prescription for eye problems. Jackson never resorted to glasses. He preferred to read extensively on eye problems and eye care as preliminaries to self-treatment.[28]

Since Laura had mentioned having trouble with her own eyesight, Jackson proceeded to give her the benefit of his recently acquired knowledge on the subject. "Remember that the best Physicians are opposed to straining that important organ, and when it fails, or begins to fail, naturally they recommend spectacles. But this should be the last resort, and should only be used when necessary: for instance, some persons can walk about, out of doors and in doors without the light hurting their eyes, but most use the auxiliary in reading. The great objection to spectacles is, that when their use is once commenced, it must be generally continued through life. A person in purchasing a pair should select the lowest number, which will answer the proposed end, and then, as circumstances require, increase it. But I would advise you not to use them as long as you can do without them (at the same time avoiding pain)."[29]

The eye condition would come and go. On at least one occasion, Jackson was forced to dictate letters. The timing of many of these optical attacks would appear to be associated with stress. Jackson began wearing a shade whenever he did extensive reading. As with other ailments, he searched for a cure through a number of physicians, treatments, and medicines.

No illness bothered Jackson more, or spurred him to greater efforts in search of relief, than dyspepsia. It became his "arch-enemy," his wife stated. Dyspepsia was a catchall phrase in the nineteenth century usually denoting an indigestion problem or "nervous stomach." Jackson first experienced it at the age of seventeen when he became constable of Lewis County. He then followed local advice and sought a cure through extensive outdoor activity. In 1849, the mysterious ailment struck again, this time in full force. Dyspepsia robbed him of sleep. This in turn produced fatigue and strain, which had a direct effect on both appetite and digestion.[30]

By trial and error, Jackson worked out a rather elaborate defense against the intestinal attacks. He initiated new habits of exercise and became severely strict on himself in the matter of food. Early in July 1849, Jackson outlined the entire regimen to Laura.

I have so strictly adhered to my wholesome diet of stale bread and plainly dressed meat (having nothing on it but salt), that I prefer it now to any thing else. The other evening I tasted a piece of bread with butter on it, and then the bread without it, and rather gave my preference to the unbuttered bread, and hence I may never taste any more of this once relished seasoning. And I think that if you would adopt for your breakfast a cup of moderately strong black tea, stale wheat bread (wheat bread raised and not less than 24 hours old), fresh meat, broiled or roasted is best, the yolk of one or two eggs (the white is hardly worth eating as it requires digestion and affords but little nutrition). For dinner the same kind of bread & meat, one vegetable only, say peas, beans or this year's potatoes, and for drink, plain water. For tea the same kind of bread and drink as for breakfast, and nothing else, unless you choose a little butter. The great beauty of the foregoing is that it furnishes all the nutrition which food can give, and at the same time does not interfere in the digestive process like other substances such as salt meats, cabbage, lettuce, dessert (such as pies, preserves, nuts and all kinds of sweetmeats). Of what I have recommended, you can eat as much as your appetite craves, provided that you take regular meals and plenty of exercise, say not less than three hours per day. . . . I regard green tea & coffee so injurious to the nerves that you should always prefer water to either. But you must bear in mind that your meals must be at fixed hours. If you arise at five or six o'clock, and go to bed at nine or ten, then seven would be a good hour for breakfast, one for dinner, and seven for tea. And you ought always to retire to bed before eleven. . . . I think that a small quantity of fruit, eaten when ripe, and in the fore part of the day, is advantageous. . . . Remember that good wholesome food taken at proper times is one of the best of medicines. . . . If you commence on this diet, remember that it is like a man joining the temperance society: if he afterwards tastes liquor he is gone.[31]

Such odd behavior with food did not go unnoticed at Fort Hamilton. Lieutenant John Tidball commented on the "excentric traits" he began to notice in his acquaintance from academy days. "Becoming a hypochondriac," Jackson "had strange imaginings about his food and his mode of living, confining his diet almost exclusively to bread, which he procured fresh from the bakery. This he placed to season on a shelf above his door, and sat observing it, with watch in hand, until the proper moment arrived for him to partake of it." As an afterthought, Tidball observed that officers in close association with Jackson "began to think his mind a little shaky."[32]

Strange habits notwithstanding, Jackson's overall condition slowly took a turn for the better. Near the end of the year, he could report to Laura: "My disease is improving, for which I feel thankful to Omnipotent God, from whom every blessing cometh. I believe that my infirmity is Dyspepsia, but not of a dangerous character." By the following spring, his weight would be at 166 pounds, two pounds more than he had ever known.[33]

Jackson by then had become convinced that the greatest boon to his recovery was hydropathy. Earlier in the century, Vincent Priessnitz, a Silesian peasant, had pioneered a renaissance of water treatment for all illnesses. "Using the waters" became a national fad. Thousands of people with real or imagined infirmities regularly flocked to innumerable spas to obtain relief. Jackson went to one such "water cure establishment," felt better as a result of the experience, and was a faithful supporter of the baths thereafter. A visit to a mineral springs or a hydropathic institution always brought some restoration in body and mind. In time, summer vacation would be synonymous with a visit to one or more of the spas. Since exercise and diet were regarded as essential parts of hydropathic treatment, Jackson became even more convinced he was on the right track of treatment.

He might have surrendered to the maladies that beset him if something else had not also enlarged in scope at the same time. In Mexico, Jackson had acquired an inquisitiveness about religious faith. Since then, he had continued to read the Bible and study some theological writings, and he said prayers daily; but these pursuits were more routine than inspirational. The growing attention to religion was the most important change in Jackson's life. That pilgrimage had just begun.

No abrupt or startling transformation occurred. The search for a denomination that would bring Jackson in close and comfortable association with God was slow— but steady. Starting with his West Point letters to Laura, Jackson had always made reference here and there to a divine providence. A new, more active outlook began in 1849, when physical decline and religious stirring erupted simultaneously. Jackson quickly developed the tendency to mention sickness and God together. In time, he came to regard the two subjects as inseparable.

During Jackson's two years at Fort Hamilton, three men exerted strong religious influence on him. The first was Captain Taylor, now a brevet lieutenant colonel as a result of gallantry in the Mexican War. Taylor, who had planted the seeds of religious curiosity in Jackson, was always mindful of the temptations inherent in camp and barracks idleness. Hence, at Fort Hamilton he sought to get the officers involved with the Bible and some branch of the Christian church. Taylor played on Jackson's sense of duty by repeated suggestions that the pursuit of religion was an obligation every man had. Jackson recognized the logic of this assertion and, as was his custom, undertook a methodical investigation of the subject.

The next person who helped turn Jackson more strongly toward God was the Rev. Martin Philip Parks. A native of North Carolina and an 1826 graduate of West Point, Parks had been a Methodist minister before converting to the Episcopal church. He was chaplain at the academy during most of Jackson's cadet years; he was also founder of the Cadet Choir. In 1846, he became rector of Trinity Church in New York City. To maintain a connection with the military as well as to spread the Anglican faith, Parks also served as chaplain at Fort Hamilton. He was quick to see Jackson's inquisitive mind, so Parks began stimulating and steering it along an Episcopal avenue.[34]

Once Jackson seemed genuinely interested in that form of worship, Parks turned him over to the Rev. Michael Scofield. This priest was rector of St. John's Church. Established in 1834, the one-story wooden church, with the bell tower above the double-door entrance, was within walking distance of Fort Hamilton and was one of the first Episcopal parishes in that part of New York. Robert E. Lee had been a St. John's vestryman in the early 1840s. Scofield and Jackson formed an instant friendship. "I was very intimate with Jackson," the rector later stated, "meeting him, visiting him or walking with him almost daily, and was very much attached to him as a friend and companion. He was of fine person, diffident, truthful, devout. . . . I esteemed him as a man, and loved him as a brother."[35]

Jackson, on his part, "greatly admired and loved" Scofield and "to a great extent approved and embraced" the Episcopal doctrine. He felt comfortable enough with it to take the first step toward church affiliation. Reverend Scofield made the following notation in the parish register: "On Sunday, 29th day of April, 1849, I baptized Thomas Jefferson Jackson, Major in the United States Army. Sponsors Colonels Dimick and Taylor, also of the army. M. Scofield, Rector."[36]

A number of benefits came to Jackson from the baptism. First was the obvious satisfaction of official admission into the family of Christ. Jackson now had a "small, but neat and commodious" church he could attend near the fort and feel at least partially at home.[37] He participated in services of morning prayer, evening prayer, and holy communion. The rigid and formal services were not always to his liking. Hence, Jackson occasionally visited other churches in the area.

Due caution and consideration were still nurturing his religious journey. He therefore subjected the Episcopal church to the same scrutiny he had used with Catholicism in Mexico. His minister in later years would declare of Jackson: "No man was ever more honest or earnest to learn the truth."[38]

Either through gift or purchase, Jackson obtained his own copy of the Episcopal hymnal. He wrote his name on the flyleaf, and, judging from its well-worn condition, Jackson consulted it often in the months after his baptism. He also made a number of new friends in the St. John's parish. In or near the forefront of this group were Dr. Roland Houghton and his wife Marie Louise. Houghton was a gynecologist who often treated his patients with the water cure; Mrs. Houghton wrote essays regularly on the rewards of hydropathy. Their influence on Jackson was considerable.

How deep and enriched Jackson's faith had become was quite evident in a letter he sent to Laura two months before his baptism: "I regret to learn . . . that death has made such a havoc among your neighbors; yet all must pay the same final debt, and my sincere desire and thrice daily prayer is, that when your exit comes that your previous preparation will have been made. How glorious will it be in that august and heaven-ordained day to meet with mother, brother, sister and father around the shining throne of Omnipotence; there I wish and hope to meet you, with a joy that shall never be alloyed by separation."[39]

For the remainder of 1849, court-martial duties occupied much of Jackson's time. The first of such assignments was to Carlisle Barracks, Pennsylvania, where Jackson spent a month hearing seven cases. All but one were adjudged guilty. From Carlisle, Jackson proceeded to similar duty at Fort Columbus, New York. Five desertions were on the docket.

Private Henry Fihan of the First Artillery was one of the culprits. In March 1849, he deserted his company at Fort Washington, Maryland, but voluntarily surrendered to authorities a few weeks later at Frankfort Arsenal, Pennsylvania. As punishment, Fihan was required to forfeit all pay still due him, to receive a branding on the hip with a one-and-a-half-inch letter "D," and to be drummed out of service.[40]

More court-martial duty followed. In mid-October, Jackson was again at Fort

Columbus, where he, Captain Taylor, and Lieutenant Otis Tillinghast were a court-martial for twelve cases. Late in November, Jackson made a third court trip to Carlisle Barracks. By then he had a number of acquaintances at the Pennsylvania base, so he could write Laura that "I had a pleasant week among its amiable and I might say lovely ladies."[41]

Jackson was back at "rather dull" Fort Hamilton in time for Christmas. Major Levi Whiting was in command of the post. Company K consisted of sixty-six cannoneers. In addition to Captain Taylor and Lieutenant Jackson, the other officers were First Lieutenant Samuel K. Dawson and Second Lieutenant Otis H. Tillinghast. Dawson was an 1839 West Point graduate from Pennsylvania. He was en route to a distinguished army career. New Yorker Otis Tillinghast finished at the academy a year behind Jackson and spent his tragically brief service in the artillery.[42]

Personal matters occupied Jackson's thinking as the first months of 1850 passed. Health led the list. His first letter to Laura that year opened: "Again I am permitted by an Indulgent Providence to say that I am still among the living, and continue able to correspond with an endeared and only Sister. My health, I believe, is still improving. My strength certainly is. I can not take so much exercise as deservable, owing to a sore foot." However, Jackson added, "when I return home, I shall want to take much exercise, and expect that by combining it with the Mountain air, to receive much benefit."[43]

Jackson was soon able to report his weight at 166 pounds, the heaviest he had ever been. "When circumstances admit of it, my exercise partakes of the most active kind, such as running, leaping, swinging, &c." Such calisthenics became an integral part of his routine, for Jackson was convinced that exercise was the key to good health. "My muscles have become quite solid," he informed Laura. "My exercises are of a violent character, when the chilblains of my feet do not prevent it."[44]

Two developments brought Jackson anguish in the early part of that year.

First, he had become convinced that all illnesses were a punishment by God. "My afflictions," he told Laura, "I believe were decreed by Heaven's Sovereign, as a punishment for my offences against his Holy Laws: and have probably been the instrument of turning me from the path of eternal death to that of everlasting life."[45]

Laura Jackson Arnold had carried the family faith up to that point. Yet her poor health, the serious illness of an infant daughter, and possibly Jackson's newfound religious zeal combined to produce a negative reaction in Laura. She abandoned Christianity as he grasped it. This reversed the roles of brother and sister. Now Jackson felt a moral responsibility to bring Laura back into the fold. In a long remonstrance of late winter, he sought to guide his sister onto the path of salvation. "I do hope that my dear little niece has entirely recovered her health," he wrote.

But do you not think, my dear sister, that her illness has been the result of a Divine Decree. You remember that once you were a professed follower of Christ, and that subsequently you disavowed his cause. This, my dear sister, I do not believe will go unpunished unless you return to him. Will you not do it? . . . I remember that before the age of maturity, I too endeavored to lead a Godly life, but obstacles so great presented themselves as to cause me to return to the world, and its own. But within the past years, I have endeavored to live more nearly unto God. And now nothing earthly could induce me to return to the world again. . . .

And I fear that unless you again acknowledge obedience to his Divine Laws, that some great affliction will yet be your lot. Remember that you have children on whom you dote, and a brother whom you love. For my part, I am willing to go hence when it shall be his great will to terminate my earthly career. I should regret to leave you unconverted, but his will and not mine be done. . . . Yes my sister, rather than wilfully [sic] violate the known will of God, I would forfeit my life. It may seem strange to you, but nevertheless such a resolution I have taken, and I will by it abide.

Oh! Sister, do drop your Infidel Books. Come lead a happy life and die a happy death. And indeed I hope to see that day, when you will pour forth your soul in pure prayer. My daily prayers are for your salvation.[46]

The second personal blow Jackson had to endure at that time was belated news of the death of Uncle Cummins Jackson. In April 1849, the forty-six-year-old Cummins was on trial in federal court for counterfeiting. A guilty verdict was all but a foregone conclusion. Approaching the end of the case, Cummins one afternoon bolted from the courtroom and fled western Virginia with a nephew. In company with thirteen others, Cummins Jackson and his young kinsman traveled across the continent to California and its lure of gold.

Cummins Jackson apparently struck it rich and "took much money" from a mine near Mt. Shasta. Then he fell ill, either with pneumonia or typhoid fever. Cummins suffered for almost a month before his death on December 4, 1849, in Shasta County, California. He was buried in an unmarked grave. The nephew who had accompanied him west reportedly gambled away all of the gold and returned to Virginia penniless.[47]

Not until mid-March did Tom Jackson learn from a cousin of his uncle's death. Disbelief was his first reaction. The future of Jackson's Mill next entered his mind when another uncle, attorney James Madison Jackson, informed him that the family place would likely have to be sold. The young army officer was far from home and limited in what he could do. Nevertheless, Jackson sent a quick reply.

Though the rumor of Uncle Cummings' death may be true, yet I can not believe it, without further evidence. I shall write to California and try to ascertain. I hope that no decree will be obtained for selling his property; but should such authority be obtained, then will not some of his friends come forward and prevent its sacrifice. Certainly if he has a friend, now is the time for its manifestation. You spoke of giving assistance; but my pecuniary affairs are so arranged that I have not ten dollars in cash which I can call my own.

There is no man on earth, whom I would befriend, sooner than Uncle Cummins. Let me know who betrayed him, and in what he has been betrayed. Give me a full history of names and facts, as soon as possible; and strain every nerve to prevent the granting of the decree. I expect to return home in the Fall, when I will see what can be done, though I fear that I will not be able to do any thing.[48]

Cummins Jackson left no will. His nephew determined not to get involved in any property dispute. Jackson eventually inherited a few hundred dollars after the sale of what was left of the Jackson's Mill estate. He dutifully gave the money to a needy aunt, Mrs. Catherine White, in gratitude for her befriending him in his first weeks as an orphan.

Jackson's only reference to his uncle thereafter came almost three months later, when he told Laura: "Uncle Cummins is undoubtedly dead. This is news which goes to my heart. Uncle was a father to me."[49] On the surface, Jackson seemed to be lamenting a personal loss. In reality, he grieved that another close member of his dwindling family had passed away.

Acquaintances and neighbors in the Fort Hamilton area never saw beneath the surface of Jackson. To them, the young officer was an interesting person with odd ways. He took brisk walks through town and in the countryside. His stride was quick and unusually long. Jackson often strolled with a cane that took on the characteristics of a saber for anyone in his path. Chopping wood gave him great delight, for he considered such work a fundamental form of good exercise. His calisthenics were amusing rather than instructional to witnesses.

What some hostesses found anything but amusing was Jackson's rigid adherence to diet. One of his closest friends later wrote of him: "His delicacy of constitution required great care in order to maintain equable health. He studied his physical nature with a physician's scrutiny; and having once adopted a regimen which he believed perfectly suited to himself, nothing would ever tempt him to swerve in the slightest degree from it. . . . He ate, as he did everything else, from a sense of duty." Hence, whenever Jackson received an invitation to a dinner party, he dutifully accepted the invitation—but took his own food with him.[50]

On May 8, Jackson and Captain William H. French journeyed to Plattsburgh Barracks, New York, for six weeks of court-martial duty. Jackson praised the "charming scenery" of the Lake Champlain area. He told Laura, "I should like very much to visit Montreal and Quebec before returning south, but want of time and money will prevent it."[51] His repeated references to lack of adequate funds leads to the conclusion that Jackson was banking most of his army pay and guarding the deposit vigilantly.

Most of June and July found Jackson on court duty at Fort Columbus. Once, while briefly back at Fort Hamilton, he made an insurance payment for an Alabama friend and expressed kind remembrances of Judge Arthur F. Hopkins and his "estimable daughters." Early in August he reported to Fort Ontario, New York, for more court-martial service. There he had his first prolonged experience with hydropathy. He explained everything to Laura.

I am now about twelve hours' travel from Niagara Falls, and consequently intend visiting there before returning home. . . . Fort Ontario is situated on the lake of the same name and in view of the city of Oswego. . . . My health is still improving, but is as yet so delicate as to render much regularity necessary, and it is probable that I am more particular in my rules than any person of your acquaintance. . . . I am to commence starting at a water cure establishment this evening, where I expect to remain during my stay here. I have great faith in them for such infirmities as mine.[52]

September brought Jackson pleasant orders to report for court-martial duty at his alma mater. This was his first visit to West Point since graduation four years earlier. To Jackson, the intervening time was much longer. He renewed friendships with courtly Dabney Maury and congenial George McClellan, his classmates who were then on the faculty. One of Jackson's fellow Virginians, George H. Thomas, presided over the officers' mess.

Jackson enjoyed that time as much as his nature would allow. Writing in almost overly mature fashion, he told Laura: "I am again at my first military station, and a very pleasant visit it is. Here I see objects which recall many pleasant & agreeable associations of my youth; but it is my lot to meet but few of my comrades for those bygone days." Although his health was still not good, he reassured his sister that "had it not been for my judicious application of water, I can not say what would have been the consequences."[53]

The carefree months of army life in the East ended. Company E of the First Artillery was short an officer. Jackson was thereupon directed to report to that unit on October 1 for permanent duty. Leaving the command and friendship of Captain Francis Taylor was something Jackson deeply regretted. He was indebted to Taylor for more kindnesses than he could possibly repay. The new assignment contained little solace. Jackson's superior officer would be Captain (brevet Maj.) William H. French.[54]

A native of Baltimore and appointee to West Point from the District of Columbia, French graduated nine years ahead of Jackson in a class that included future generals John Sedgwick, Joseph Hooker, Braxton Bragg, Jubal A. Early, and Arnold Elzey. French's first service was in the Seminole War. His brevet promotions for gallantry in Mexico had come from some of the same engagements in which Jackson had won fame. Being on the staff of General Franklin Pierce for a time was no impediment to French's career.

The paths of Jackson and French had crossed several times in the three years they had known one another. They were acquaintances, not friends, and the two shared some characteristics. Both were anxious to promote their respective army careers; both were sticklers for discipline and duty; both were noted for less than outgoing personalities. While Jackson was courteous, French tended to be abrasive. In marked contrast to Jackson, French was an aggressive, sometimes witty man who enjoyed good food and fine wines. He was also married.

Company E of the First Artillery was, as Jackson knew, a reorganized unit whose rank and file had been together for less than a year. In addition to Jackson and Captain French, the company had two other officers. First Lieutenant John M. Brannan, a West Point graduate five years before Jackson, would soon move up to regimental adjutant. Second Lieutenant Absalom Baird was a recent graduate of the academy and destined to teach mathematics there for six years after a brief stint in the field.

The great majority of the enlisted men in Company E could be classified as recruits. Jackson continued serving as both company commissary and company quartermaster.[55]

When Jackson learned that his company was being sent to duty in Florida, he quickly made application for twenty days' furlough. He had no idea how long he would be at the new and distant post, but any stay at the southern tip of America would be too long without first visiting Laura and the Arnolds. What happened thereafter is somewhat hazy. Jackson's furlough request went through channels to regimental commander Colonel Ichabod Crane, who denied it on grounds that Jackson "was required with his company." By then, however, the lieutenant had somehow procured a furlough from some superior and was en route on what his nephew later termed "the expected visit" to Beverly.[56]

Jackson took his several artifacts from the Mexican War, including an artillery saber, cap, small brass cannon, and several other accoutrements for safekeeping at the

Arnolds. Little Tom Arnold assumed that the relics were a gift, not a loan. "He always brought us children beautiful & interesting presents," Arnold recalled.[57]

The Arnold family showered the army officer with love and attention during the short stay. Jackson then traveled alone to Florida. Sometime around the second week of December 1850, he joined a portion of his unit at Fort Harner. The remainder of Company E was not far away at Fort Casey, the basic rendezvous point for all American troops on the west coast of Florida.[58]

French's unit numbered fifty-two men. The officers were Captain French, Lieutenants Jackson and Baird, and Assistant Surgeon Jonathan Letterman. On December 11, Company E was put on alert for transfer to Fort Meade in the Florida interior.

Colonel Thomas Childs's subsequent directive to Jackson was complete and possessed of unintended humor. "You will without unnecessary delay repair to the post [Fort Brooke] with the detachment under your command by the steamer Col. Clay. You will bring with you the wagons, mules & boards; if there is any other public property you will put it on board. I do not mean that you will remove any of the buildings."[59]

From December 16 to 18, the artillerists marched east forty-six miles through a jungle to Fort Meade. There Jackson's unit relieved Company H of the First Artillery. The "public property" of the fort became the responsibility of Assistant Quartermaster T. J. Jackson.[60]

The surroundings were new to Jackson in every respect. Doubtless, several people had to explain Florida's history and geography to the ever-inquisitive lieutenant. At first, the only thing Jackson knew was that twenty years of intermittent and bloody conflict with the Seminole Indians was coming to a close.

Andrew Jackson's efforts to suppress the Indians in Spanish Florida had led in 1817–18 to the first Seminole war. Occasional outbursts flared thereafter. In May 1832, the Seminoles signed the Treaty of Payne's Landing, by which they agreed to move to lands specifically designed for them west of the Mississippi River. The Indians supposedly had the right to inspect and approve the reservations beforehand. A year later, a delegation of Seminoles signed the Treaty of Fort Gibson. Now the western transfer seemed complete and binding. Yet only portions of the Seminole nation had accepted the treaties.

Pressures for removal soon encountered pressures of resistance. A great deal of physical pushing ensued; verbal accusations went back and forth. In 1835, hostilities exploded anew in Florida. Fighting lasted for the next seven years as Seminoles struck isolated settlements and American troops gave pursuit.

By the time this second Seminole war ran its course in 1842, the U.S. Army was embarrassed and bloody. Some $20 million in expenditures had gone to curtail the small, marauding bands of Indians, and American casualties had climbed to over 1,500 men. A forced migration westward followed, but some 300 Seminoles managed to avoid exile by hiding in the Florida jungles and swamps. Most of them simply wanted to live in peace, but local politicians found it advantageous "to wave the bloody shirt" from time to time in order to compress further what little claims the Indians had to anything. Their presence was an ongoing threat to every American homestead. Fear kept army detachments posted all over the state.

Jackson and the other artillerists found Florida climate a welcome relief from the frigid winds of New York. However, the southern state was for the most part still a wilderness. Its 87,000 inhabitants (half of whom were slaves) either lived in the cotton country along the Alabama and Georgia borders or clustered along the undulating coastline. Of the thirty-eight million acres in Florida, only two-thirds of them had even been surveyed. The interior could be as dangerous as it was uncharted.

That situation, coupled with an 1840 outburst of violence, had led the army to establish the Western Division of Florida. Headquarters were at Fort Brooke at Tampa Bay. The garrison, which could accommodate up to 3,000 soldiers, was the port of embarkation for Seminoles going west and the principal arrival point on Florida's west coast for incoming soldiers. Commanding the division was Colonel Thomas Childs, a venerable officer whose 1814 graduation from West Point was too long ago for most men to remember.

What Jackson saw at Tampa was a community of eighty buildings and about 200 residents. An 1848 hurricane had torn the settlement to pieces. The town's small Methodist congregation was in the process of erecting a new church when Jackson arrived. He attended at least one Sunday service and donated five dollars to the building fund.[61]

Whatever Jackson expected of Fort Meade, he had to be disappointed at what he saw on his December 18 arrival. It was but a link in a chain of small strongholds along a military road that extended from Tampa and the Gulf Coast to Fort Pierce on the Atlantic seaboard. The post was barely a year old. Lieutenant George G. Meade, an engineering officer, had selected the site. It was several miles north of the Indian boundary and thus no threat to peace. A "swamp and hammock" known as Kendrick Branch ran south through the jungle and then turned east into the Peace River. Kendrick Branch enclosed a half-mile square of firm ground on which were scattered pine and oak trees that provided shade, winter protection, and some firewood. The riverbank at that point was firm and high.

Work on the post, which the departmental commander named in honor of his engineering officer, was sporadic. When Company E arrived in mid-December, Fort Meade was neither stockade nor blockhouse. It was a collection of rough wooden buildings huddled along the west bank of Peace River and astride the military trail snaking through the tangled growth.

The beef pens were to the south on Kendrick Branch. Stables stood between the branch and the river. North of them were a few storehouses. Enlisted men's barracks were on the north side of the road. Farther north was a cabin for the commanding officer. A few hundred yards along the trail to the west and close to the river were officers' quarters. Two hundred yards from there was a crude hospital that would be hopelessly inadequate during the summer epidemics of malaria and yellow fever.

It was not an easy environment for the men of Company E. No other settlement existed within ten miles. One risked his life in venturing too far into dense bushes, nearby swamps, and grassy fields. An occasional scouting expedition was the primary means of relieving boredom. Only officers were allowed to have families with them. None did, except Captain French. His vivacious wife, Caroline Read French, became the garrison's only hostess.

On the day of his arrival, Captain French took a hard look at the post. Nothing he saw pleased him. He immediately formed a board, chaired by Jackson and consisting of Surgeon Letterman and Lieutenants Thornley S. Everett and Absalom Baird. This investigating committee was "to examine upon the superior eligibility for a permanent military site, of the ridge . . . about half a mile from this post. The board will give the reasons which would compel a change, should such be recommended, from the present site."[62]

Jackson and the other officers told French what he wanted to hear. Three days later, the captain wrote Colonel Childs and requested permission to shift Fort Meade to the commanding ridge in question. It was comfortably above the swampy lowland, looked out for miles to the west, and had sloping sides for good natural protection. Childs gave his approval. The old site, in existence for only twelve months, was in the process of being abandoned throughout Jackson's brief period there.[63]

Ten days after arriving at Fort Meade, French proudly informed headquarters: "My command is actively engaged erecting quarters, and learning to ride and take care of horses. Every man is employed from reveille to sunset." Company duties were minimal, but French ensured that they spanned the full day.[64]

Reveille was thirty minutes before sunrise. Following roll call on the "parade ground," each man groomed his horse for a full twenty minutes. Then came breakfast, followed at 8:30 with sick call and the first guard mount at 9 A.M. Lunch was at noon. The second guard mount began at 4:30 P.M. Retreat was at sunset, lights out at 8:45.[65]

French quickly demonstrated that he was exacting to the point of being picky. On December 30, he named Jackson and Baird as an administrative council "for the purpose of transacting the business prescribed by the Gen[eral] regulations of the Army." The very next day, the two officers were directed to report why a musket belonging to one of the privates was broken. A quick investigation ensued; French then received a formal statement "that the musket alluded to was broken by falling from the rack on which it was kept and that no blame is to be attached to the private in whose possession it was."[66]

No incident escaped French's fastidious eye. He complained about liquor being smuggled into Fort Meade. "It is believed," Colonel Childs replied, "that the butchers are the purchasers from the teamsters, and whenever the [wagon] train arrived they avail themselves of that opportunity to sell, that suspicions may rest on persons with the train." Early in January 1851, French sent a detail of men to help deactivate Fort Casey. One of the privates got intoxicated and tried to pose as a sergeant, whereupon Lieutenant Samuel F. Chalfin "knocked him down and gave him a good beating." The private was in the hospital for two weeks. French promptly filed assault charges against the lieutenant but withdrew them under pressure from headquarters.[67]

French's intolerance of alcohol seemed at this time to be more rigid than Jackson's. In the second week of January, Jackson presided over the case of Corporal Martin Holden. The defendant stood accused of drunkenness on duty and unsoldierly conduct. A guilty verdict and recommendation of punishment went to French, who rejected the punishment as too lenient. Jackson reconvened the court. It proposed that Holden be reduced to the rank of private and fined five dollars. This was more to French's liking.[68]

Jackson respected such meticulous adherence to the military code. His similarity of feeling with French at first produced a degree of congeniality between the two officers. French, being nine years senior, enjoyed the role of a mentor; Jackson was comfortable being the student.

After Mrs. French and the family arrived at Fort Meade, Jackson was a frequent guest at their quarters through late February. It was a pleasant place to go, thanks largely to Mrs. Caroline French. The great-great-granddaughter of Delaware statesman and Declaration of Independence signer George Read, Mrs. French was gracious and captivating. She was only four years older than Jackson; being well read and interesting, as well as interested in the lieutenant, she and Jackson developed a healthy friendship.[69]

Those happy moments could not offset the unpleasant hours that Jackson increasingly experienced in a number of areas. The swampy climate at once had an adverse effect on his health. In particular, his vision began to bother him. No nearby church existed to guide the religious fervor then coursing through his being. Jackson also found himself the busiest man in Fort Meade. As commissary and quartermaster, he had to ensure that the post was well fed and equipped. The construction of the new fort required all but constant attention. Being one of a few commissioned officers at Fort Meade, Jackson was obliged to take his turn in leading an occasional scouting expedition into the surrounding wilderness. While such activity offered an escape from boredom, the quest for action always came up empty-handed.

Jackson was also aware that a bright future for him was not likely in the army. This made garrison life all the more unappealing. He later told a friend that while campaigning was extremely congenial to his tastes, the life of a military post in times of peace was just as repulsive. To Jackson, army officers usually neglected self-improvement. They "rusted, in trivial amusements," at isolated posts. If war occurred, the military men who had left service for civilian pursuits "might expect even more promotion in the army than those who had remained in the dull tread-mill of the garrison."[70]

Many of the army's best officers were leaving the service rather than vegetate in peacetime lethargy. Jackson could now understand such resignations. The dazzling exploits in Mexico five years earlier had left Jackson still a first lieutenant in permanent grade. Ten other officers of the same rank were ahead of him in the First Artillery alone. In view of the seniority obstacles, Jackson requested influential friends in Lewis County to send letters of recommendation to Washington on his behalf for a captaincy in one of the new regiments then being formed. He asked Captain French to assist him in using the correct terminology in his petitions. French stated: "I not only gave him the advice but at his request wrote the letter of application for him, in order that it might be properly made and most strongly expressed." All of those efforts would come to naught.[71]

Jackson went on his first scout near the end of January. Colonel Childs was anxious to learn if any Indians were threatening the scattered settlements around Lake Tohopekaliga, forty miles northeast of Fort Meade. Childs ordered French to send out a detachment. The colonel displayed a mixture of contempt and respect by adding: "You will caution & charge the officer in command that his utmost vigilance will be required night and day if he takes any Indian prisoners or they will get away from him. . . . In fact he will have to guard them and even be present himself. He ought to carry with him irons for the feet. You cannot iron an Indian by the wrist. He will ever slip his hands out."[72]

On January 27, with fourteen men, a guide of limited intelligence, and no map, Jackson embarked on his reconnaissance. The party struggled through the tangled jungle, inspected the lake country, and returned to Fort Meade. Not only were no Indians found; Jackson was not even certain he reached Lake Tohopekaliga. Still, he moved ninety miles in six days, covering thirty-three miles through wilderness on one day.

Jackson's efforts were not appreciated at this time, however. French could not understand a ninety-mile expedition yielding no prisoners and little information: every scouting party ought to achieve its goals. Hence, he dispatched a second expedition only a day or so after Jackson's return.

Most of February passed with routine duties for Jackson. The men continued work on the buildings at the new site of the fort. French was reasonably satisfied: he termed discipline "subordinate" and equipment "serviceable." On February 7, a court-martial consisting of Jackson, Letterman, and Baird met to try two soldiers on charges of intoxication. Both men were found guilty and fined three dollars.[73]

In the middle of the month, with scouting expeditions continuing to be unproductive in French's estimation, the post commander sent Jackson again to find Lake Tohopekaliga. Jackson was to proceed via Forts Fraser and Gentry to the lake's southern point, then scout along the eastern shore as far as practicable. French closed the order to Jackson with the terse statement: "Seven days rations, forage, &c. for men and horses will be taken and a wagon is to transport them a days march after which you will order it to return to the post."[74]

Jackson led his party from the fort on the 18th and rode into a prolonged rainstorm. "Owing to deep water, and the miry condition of the country in the vicinity of the lake," he later reported to French, "I was unable to pass it at its Southern point. I scouted along the West & North of the lake until I arrived at Everett's Boat-Yard. . . . During the scout, I found no Indians or recent signs of them. I conversed with several citizens, but could obtain no information to induce me to believe that there are any Indians north of their territory."[75]

On February 25, Jackson led his waterlogged and bone-weary troops back into Fort Meade. He overlooked his appearance, and his mail, in order to prepare a report of his trip and to hand carry it to the post commander. French was furious. Jackson had not carried out his instructions; no enemy had been encountered.

The day after Jackson's return, French informed headquarters in Tampa that he would lead a scout himself "and endeavor to turn the southern & eastern points of the Lake." He personally would ensure that no Indians were "on the other side at this season which is corn planting time."[76]

The captain delayed his excursion, but his announcement caused considerable damage to morale and post relationships. French's intention to do the job himself either inferred a belief that his subordinates were incompetent or reflected ambition to succeed at anyone's expense. French then compounded the error by issuing the following order on March 7:

> Hereafter whenever an Officer or non-commissioned Officer is placed in charge of a scouting or other party for military purposes, he will keep such party together and remain with it until it returns to the post.
>
> The Commanding Officer regrets that the deviation from such an important military principle, in two recent instances, renders an order upon the subject necessary.[77]

Meanwhile, after Jackson had given French a report of his second expedition into the interior, the Virginian had started through an accumulation of mail. One letter immediately captured his attention. Dated February 4, 1851, and written by Colonel Francis H. Smith, superintendent of the Virginia Military Institute in Lexington, it stated:

> Dear Sir, The Board of Visitors of this Institution will elect a Prof. of Nat. and Expr. Phil. in June next and your name has been mentioned among others for the appointment. Would such a situation be agreeable to you. You are perhaps aware that the V M Institute is an Institution of the State organized upon the model of the U. S. M. Academy. It has always enjoyed a large share of favor from the State, and as an evidence of its popularity we are soon reconstructing our Barracks at an expense to the State of $41,000. The salary allowed is $1200 and quarters. Should you desire such a situation I would be pleased to present your name to the Board.
>
> I have no authority to pledge the Board in support of any candidate, & am only authorized to make those inquiries which will enable them to act understandingly.

Jackson drafted a reply the same day he opened Smith's letter.

> Dear Sir, I have just received your communication of the 4th inst. containing the kind proposition of bringing my name before the Board of Visitors of the V. M. Institution as a candidate for the Professorship of Nat & Exp. Phil.
>
> Though strong ties bind me to the army, yet I can not consent to decline so flattering an offer. Please present my name to the Board and accept my thanks for your kindness.[78]

Although Jackson did not concentrate on the VMI opening, he occasionally gave it long and careful thought. The military school was barely eleven years old and, by any standard, was small. The position carried little excitement and no chance for military advancement. Jackson would be a teacher; and unless he had honest talents in that regard as well as a love for students, success would elude him.

On the other hand, the institute was located in and funded by Jackson's native state. What little he knew of it was favorable. Should he be offered a professorship, he would in effect still be in the military community without all of the uncertainties of army life. He would also be in a position that would not harm his chances of high rank should America become involved in another war. Further, teaching at a military academy offered greater stimulus for the mind than years of stagnation at isolated army garrisons. Living in Lexington would give him a permanent opening into civilian society. VMI's location at the southern end of the beautiful Shenandoah Valley gave it an added attraction. The position would leave him free in the summers to study and travel. Jackson had just turned twenty-seven. Many years of productive service lay before him.

The advantages associated with the professorship clearly outweighed the disadvantages. Yet Jackson felt an obligation to wait for positive developments before asking friends to intercede in his behalf. During the waiting period, he had more than enough things to keep his mind occupied at Fort Meade.

No hint of dissatisfaction with his lot was evident in a March 1 letter Jackson addressed to his sister. He began, as was becoming almost natural by then, with the subject of religion. "You must not suppose that I would like you to profess religion without possessing it. A hypocrite is in my opinion one of the most detestable of beings. My opinion is, that every one should honestly and carefully investigate the Bible; and if he can believe it to be the word of God, to follow its teachings."[79]

Jackson next turned to his personal situation. "My pay is seventy dollars per month, but as I receive 14 dollars for extra duties, it amounts to 84 dollars per month. You are very kind in offering me assistance in case that I should enter civil life. It is doubtful whether I shall relinquish the military profession; as I am very partial to it."[80]

The new surroundings was a topic that Jackson thought would interest Laura.

Florida, so far as I have seen it, is a vast plain, with occasional slight elevations. It is covered with beautiful forests of pine; the yellow pine growing on the elevations, and the pitch pine growing on the lowlands. The country is filled with lakes and swamps. The soil is very sandy and generally very thin. It produces corn and most northern productions, with the exception of wheat, rye, oats and barley. . . . But the most profitable occupation here is raising cattle. Here a cow and calf will cost ten dollars. . . .

I have just returned from an 8 days scout, in which I saw about 20 deer in one forenoon. I could find no Indians. I traveled more than 100 miles without seeing a house. I like scouting very much; as it gives me a relish for every thing, but it would be still more desirable if I could have an occasional encounter with Indian parties.[81]

Jackson's efforts at getting a transfer to a new unit having failed, he applied on March 3 for a nine-month furlough with permission to leave the country. His eyesight was becoming progressively weaker; if it improved, he hoped to visit Europe. Of a more immediate nature, Jackson desired to get away from Captain French and to do it in quiet fashion. The leave application began its snail-like progression through channels to the departmental commander.[82]

The March monthly return for Company E listed Jackson without comment as sick. Eyestrain may have worsened, or possibly some other ailment had struck the lieutenant. Illness did nothing to improve relations with the post commander. In fact, growing friction between French and Jackson exploded into the open that month.

As post commander as well as the officer who had suggested the change of the fort's location, French naturally felt supreme authority over anything and everything pertaining to both the old and the new fort. Jackson was second in command and chairman of the committee recommending a location move. He was also the post quartermaster and, as such, in charge of the construction of any new buildings. French was a brevet major, and so was Jackson. One writer summarized the situation well. "French, anxious to command a garrison successfully, could not tolerate a subordinate who resented subordination. Jackson, at the same time, could not bear a commanding officer who so insisted on commanding."[83]

Jackson and a single artificer had been directing most of the construction, with French always looking over their shoulders and making numerous changes. Soon Jackson's patience gave way to anger. He began to "cut" French, a military term meaning that Jackson ignored the captain when they passed on the post or whenever informal conversation occurred. The lieutenant spoke to the captain only when required to do so. French did likewise. Tension soon descended like a pall over the small garrison.

French always insisted that he sought to calm the situation but to no avail. Jackson, the captain freely acknowledged, actually made the first move toward conciliation by stopping French one day, explaining how he felt, and seeking the reasons why the post commander did not like him. French tried to reassure Jackson of his high regard for the subaltern. Then French claimed that he expressed a willingness to submit the whole matter of the post construction to divisional headquarters for a judgment and that Jackson eagerly accepted the invitation. In view of the angry statements made subsequently by both officers, French's account of this first showdown is a wondrous exercise in fiction.[84]

On March 23, 1851, Jackson fired off a letter to Colonel Childs's adjutant at Tampa headquarters.

Sir: In my opinion paragraph 927 of the army Regulations of 1841, gives me the right of superintending the construction of the Public buildings on the ridge at this Post. And also, that paragraph 93a of the same Regulations places the Artificer at this Post under my direction. These rights Captain and Bt. Maj. Wm. H. French, 1st Artillery, has denied me informing me that I had not controll whatever, over the construction of the buildings above referred to, and in the construction of which the Artificer of Company E, 1st Artillery, is employed.

I respectfully request that if my views as above expressed are correct, that I may be restored to my proper position. Please bring the above to the early consideration of the General commanding the Troops in Florida.[85]

French penned a strong endorsement to the back of Jackson's letter. "I would briefly remark that my entire Command has been employed erecting cantonments on the new site at the Ridge, out of Material drawn from the resources of the Country, that personally I have given superintendence to the entire work. Under these circumstances it can hardly be considered that a Subaltern or Company Officer is to assume to himself more importance than the commandant of the post."[86]

The more French pondered Jackson's statements thereafter, the more concerned he became that headquarters might take the lieutenant's side in this argument. Three days after sending Jackson's letter forward, French composed a blistering indictment of his subordinate and rushed it by courier to Tampa.

The pretensions of Brevet Major Jackson, acting asst. Qr. Master at this post, to exercise an independent position as far as his duties as Quarter Master are involved, are of long standing and he has continued to urge them with a pertinacity so constantly increasing that finally I informed him that any communication he might desire to forward upon the subject of what he styles his 'rights' would be transmitted by me to higher authority.

Hence this letter.—On account of this official misunderstanding Bt. Major Jackson has for some time carried it into his private relations with me to such an extent that I was obliged to call his attention to paragraph No. 418, Gen. Reg. 1847.

This unpleasant state of things has grown out of a mistaken view which Bt. Maj. Jackson has taken in reference to his relation to his commanding officer, and as this anxiety manifested itself in minor ways with officers junior to him, I am impressed with the belief that the opinion and decision of the General commanding will do much to restore a better feeling at this post.[87]

Brevet Brigadier General Childs's response to both Jackson and French came quickly and was unmistakably clear on the subject of military responsibilities.

Paragraphs 927 & 930 [of army regulations] give the Quartermaster superintendence & control under such instructions as he may receive from time to time from the Comdg. Officer. They give the Quartermaster no discretion independent of the Comdg. Officer. The Quartermaster is to put up the buildings as ordered, and to make purchases & expenditures as ordered; for all of which the Commanding Officer, and not the Quartermaster, is responsible. . . . The only credit due to the Quartermaster is the zeal with which he carries out the views of the Commanding Officer and keeping the public property with which he is charged in the best possible order, and furnishing supplies, when required, promptly.

The Genl. Comdg. knows of no state of military affairs where the Comdg. Officer can divide responsibility with a junior, if his orders have been promptly obeyed. . . .

It is not strange the young officers should make claims of this kind, from the fact that older ones have asserted their independence in many matters relating to their official duties, which, if sanctioned, would reverse an established military principle, that the Senior Officer, when eligible, shall command & give all necessary orders.

A difference of opinion amongst Officers may honestly occur on points of duty. It ought never to degenerate into personalities, or be considered a just cause for withholding the common courtesies of life so essential in an Officer & to the happiness & quiet of garrison life.[88]

The rebuke from headquarters stung Jackson. Moreover, the references to "personalities" and "the common courtesies of life" persuaded Jackson that French had written the general about matters other than the simple issue of who was in charge of construction. To Jackson, French was taking advantage of his position—again. That was Jackson's original complaint.

Events now tumbled forward to a dark climax. On April 1, French departed Fort Meade on the scouting mission he had announced earlier. Jackson assumed command of the garrison in the captain's seven-day absence.[89] He had time to reflect on his future, especially on the opportunity at VMI.

By then he very much wanted the professorship; and with his candidacy still alive, Jackson was optimistic about his chances. Even though Laura was his closest confidante, Jackson waited almost two months before informing her of a possible career change. On the day after French left on his scout, Jackson wrote his sister: "I have hopes of being able to live near you for a while. I received a letter from Colonel Smith . . . in which he kindly offers to present my name to the Board of Visitors, in June next, as a candidate for the Professorship in Natural and Experimental Philosophy in the Institute. I have accepted his offer, but am unable to say whether I shall be elected. If I knew who would compose the Board, then I could form a better idea. . . . I consider the position both conspicuous and desirable. I will be in about 150 or 160 miles from you, will have quarters, and receive twelve hundred dollars per year. Philosophy is my favorite subject. I hope through the blessings of Providence to succeed in securing the post."[90] What Jackson did not know until a few days later was that he had already been elected to the professorship.

The little academy at Lexington had enjoyed remarkable growth in the dozen years of its existence. Much of the success was due to its "principal professor and commandant" (a title later changed to superintendent), Francis Henney Smith. Ranked number five in the West Point class of 1833, the Virginia-born Smith had taught mathematics on the college level before agreeing to take the reins at VMI. By 1850, climbing student enrollment made the hiring of an additional faculty member imperative. Especially did Major William Gilham need help. Gilham taught all of the physical sciences; he was also developing courses in chemistry, mineralogy, and geology. He conducted classes in the mornings, he was infantry instructor in the afternoons, and he served as commandant of cadets around the clock.

Colonel Smith recommended that a new faculty member be named to teach natural and experimental philosophy and to instruct in artillery. This would free Gilham of many of his duties. The Board of Visitors concurred and directed Smith to make suitable inquiries. Among those recommended to him were George B. McClellan of the Engineers branch of the army, Jesse L. Reno of Ordnance, and William S. Rosecrans of the Engineers—all destined to become Union generals in the Civil War. Early in September the search committee voted four to one to give the professorship to Robert E. Rodes, a distinguished graduate of VMI.

Smith opposed such a move: he wanted a West Point graduate to fill the position. The board thereupon rescinded its vote and soon made an offer to Alexander P. Stewart, an 1842 graduate of West Point and then a professor of mathematics and philosophy at Cumberland University in Tennessee. Smith's pleasure turned to near panic early in 1851 when Stewart surprisingly declined the professorship.

At this point, providentially, D. Harvey Hill entered the scene. Jackson's Mexican War friend had resigned from the army in 1849 to accept a job as professor of mathematics at Washington College in Lexington. Hill and Smith, with shared military background, academic credentials, and deep religious convictions, had become close friends. Hill knew that Smith was agonizing over the vacant professorship and caught in the middle of a debate whether to hire a West Pointer or a native Virginian.

One afternoon early in February 1851, Hill paid a courtesy call to Smith's office and found the colonel "in a good deal of trouble" relative to the faculty position. Smith asked Hill to look through the army register and propose "an officer of talent & character." The Carolinian began thumbing through the register; suddenly, at the top of page 278, appeared Jackson's name and resume. Hill remembered Captain Taylor's remark in Mexico: "Jackson will make his mark in this war," and Jackson had done precisely that. So strongly did Hill push his Virginia friend that Smith promptly wrote Jackson to see if he would be interested in the job.

Harvey Hill later claimed that Jackson "was elected upon my testimonial alone," but more than one man worked hard to get the VMI post for the beleaguered officer. After Colonel Smith received Jackson's February 25 letter, he made a quick trip to Richmond. His purpose was to confer with John S. Carlile, the state senator from the Lewis County area and a distant relative of Jackson. As luck would have it, Carlile had also just been appointed by the governor to the VMI Board of Visitors. Now Carlile took the lead on Jackson's behalf.

On March 28, at Smith's summons, the eleven-man board met at the capital. Colonel Philip St. George Cocke, president of the board, called the meeting to order and asked the clerk to read the list of names of those nominated for the faculty position. The moment that was done, Senator Carlile nominated Jackson. He presented a strong case. Jackson was a native Virginian, West Point graduate, and recognized hero in the Mexican War. Having Jackson on the faculty would strengthen the standing of the institute in Jackson's home country, the northwestern quadrant of the state. Carlile's nomination received a hearty second, and Jackson was selected by acclamation.[91]

Smith mailed the letter of offer immediately after the meeting adjourned. The $1200 per annum in salary and $120 yearly housing allowance was roughly $220 more than Jackson was making in the army. July 1, 1851, would be Jackson's reporting date.[92]

The timing of the appointment may have had a significant bearing on Jackson's unusual actions a week later. The sequence of events in Florida now became as important to Jackson's story as his own mental and physical condition at the time.

It was on the day after Smith sent the notification letter that Jackson received the sharp rebuke from division headquarters. In the second week of April, the French-Jackson feud reached a hemorrhaging climax. Jackson was suddenly confronted with the specter of gross immorality from the man who was his superior officer.

At the time, the French family consisted of at least two small children. Mrs. French was not well and spent much of this period in bed. Also in the household was a dark-skinned servant girl named Julia. She had been with Captain and Mrs. French for nine years and was treated as a member of the family. Yet the sight of French and the young girl occasionally taking late afternoon and evening walks together between the old and new Fort Meade gave rise to gossip of the two having an ongoing, illicit affair. The enlisted men began to joke that any man wishing to call on Julia had better think twice because French "had taken her himself."

Jackson heard the rumors just before or just after the arrival of the offer from VMI (precisely when is irrelevant). Possessed of an overwhelming sense of personal integrity, he could not sit idly and ignore such blatant conduct by the base commander. Jackson's reaction was unexpectedly violent.[93]

From morning to mid-afternoon on Saturday, April 12, Jackson summoned to his office a steady procession of enlisted men: Sergeants Henry Newman and George Lytle, Corporal Henry Bruning, Privates Henry Barrows, Joseph Brown, Edward Cooney, William Hendricks, and at least five others. Jackson reassured each soldier that he had nothing to fear, then questioned each closely about "Major French" (Jackson always used brevet ranks in referring to officers because he desired the same courtesy). Had the man seen the post commander and the servant together? Was the soldier aware of any imprudent conduct between French and Julia? Had he heard reports on the post of misbehavior by the couple? When one soldier recalled passing French's quarters one evening and seeing a foot inside the window, Jackson wanted to know if the foot was a man's or a woman's and whether it was bare or covered.

The enlisted men had sense enough not to provide evidence that one officer could use against another. All were fearful of their own positions in this duel between their superiors. Hence, and as a group, they went to the first sergeant late that day and told him what had happened. With no intention of being caught in the middle of the dispute, the first sergeant quickly reported the events to French.

His response was predictable. Early on Sunday morning the 13th, French placed Jackson under arrest, relieved him of his duties, and ordered him to confine his movements to the limits of Fort Meade.[94] Yet this was only the first round.

Surgeon Jonathan Letterman seemed sympathetic to Jackson's feelings but steered a course outside the controversy because of his long friendship with the French family. The surgeon's concern was the pain this matter would bring to Mrs. French if it were made public. Letterman appealed to Jackson to forget the whole episode and not bring shame to the wife because "of her husband's unfaithfulness."

Jackson's eyes filled with tears. The thought of hurting Mrs. French "was agony" to him, he replied, but "conscience compels me to prosecute the case." Here was a hint of the future general: a kindhearted man but a soldier with an unbending will to do what was right.[95]

Hours later, Jackson violated his rule of not writing letters on Sunday and fired his first salvo to headquarters.

Sir: On being informed that Capt. and Bt. Maj. Wm. H. French, 1st Artillery, was guilty of conduct unbecoming an officer and a gentleman, I considered that it was my duty as the next officer in rank to him, to investigate the subject, and for such investigation he has placed me under arrest. I Respectfully request that I may be released from arrest as I was actuated by a sense of duty in the course which I pursued. I am of the opinion that the interest of the service loudly calls for a Court of Inquiry on the conduct of the commanding officer of this Post, as I believe that it would elicit facts which can not be otherwise elicited.

Later that same day, French did some investigating of his own. He listened closely, and interjected often, as the post adjutant, Lieutenant Absalom Baird, questioned each of the enlisted men about Jackson's queries. French knew he was fighting for his life in this latest debacle with Jackson. Accusations of immorality, unless disproved, could destroy an army career. So French struck back with full force. Yet he made a tactical error in arresting Jackson, for this gave the subordinate ample time to prepare his case.

The following day—April 14—each side bombarded the other with paperwork. Jackson filed formal charges against French. The four specifications accused the captain of intimate relations with his servant inside the post on or about March 7, improper strolls by the couple on or about March 9 in nearby woods, a long walk by the two on the night of March 14 outside the fort, and common knowledge among the troops that French "had cut them out" in regards to any attention toward the girl. All of this, Jackson asserted, constituted both unbecoming conduct by an officer and conduct to the prejudice of good order and military discipline in the army.

While Jackson was compiling his charges, French was also writing headquarters. His long letter, bristling with attacks on his disrespectful subordinate, accompanied Jackson's allegations. All of the enlisted men had pled ignorance of any impropriety by the base commander, French stated, "yet in order that the truth may keep an even pace with so malicious a slander and falsehood" as embodied in Jackson's charges, he was reluctantly demanding judicial proceedings against "the malevolent Bt. Major Jackson."

French gave a summary of his family situation: the ongoing process of moving into new quarters, Mrs. French's delicate health, and the like. "On two or three occasions, through the forgetfulness of servants, essential articles were found wanting in the afternoon, which would not permit of a delay until the next day." Not wishing a woman to move alone around the fort, French had escorted his servant girl on such errands. He described Julia as "a respectable white woman" to whom the family had long been attached. "I know of nothing," French declared emotionally, "which should or shall prevent me from appearing in public as in private what I am, and ought to be, her friend and her protector."

Jackson had fabricated the entire case, the base commander wrote.

Some suspicion may be thrown upon the purity of Bt. Major Jacksons motives when it is stated that some time previous to these alleged occurrences Brevet Major Jackson adopted the system of non-intercourse, vulgarly styled 'cutting' on the ground that he was deprived of his official rights. . . .

Foiled thus in his last attempt to have my official conduct reprehended, he altered his course, and descending into the purloins of the camp he has changed his attacks to a charge upon me and my family, but so blindly and upon ground so absolutely untenable that finding himself without a support in proof, he wishes to escape from the consequences of his act and be allowed to retire unscathed upon the plea of "a sense of duty."

French would not hear of it. Jackson had publicly raised the issue; a public resolution was now in order.

In the middle of the paper cross-fire that day came official notification from headquarters that Jackson's request for a nine-month leave of absence had been approved. French dutifully acknowledged receipt of the communique but bluntly told division headquarters: "I withhold this order . . . in consequence of his arrest until I can receive information as to what action will be had on my charges." French was going to keep Jackson on the hook for however long it took to decide the controversy in French's favor.

April 15 brought the most amazing document in this entire affair. It was a letter from prosecutor Jackson to defendant French.

Sir: I have been on the sick report for about a month, and some time back my eyes have been weak, and so much so since writing the accusations against you on the 13th inst. as in my opinion to render it unsafe to use them either in forwarding or writing. I am desirous that additional accusations against you should be forwarded by the Steamer which leaves Tampa Bay for N. Orleans on Thursday next. . . . About twenty specifications which are for Conduct unbecoming an Officer & a Gentleman have been made out for some time, but owing to ill health have not been copied, and in their present condition ought not to be forwarded.

In Jackson's view, military courtesy was above and beyond the current controversy. He therefore asked French to assign one of the soldiers to Jackson to help in composing the final charges being levied against the post commander! Equally amazing, French honored the request and assigned Corporal Bruning—one of the enlisted men originally involved in the matter—to act as Jackson's secretary. Jackson thereupon drew up twenty-two breaches of conduct against French.

Overnight the quarrel widened on both sides. Jackson likely concluded that his case was weak; he thereupon asked for a formal investigation of the whole Fort Meade operation. In an April 15 letter to Captain John M. Brannan at New Orleans, Jackson stated of French: "There are other accusations against him which as they effect myself I feel a delicacy in preferring. It might be inferred that I was actuated by vindictive Matters, & consequently [I] prefer that they should result from the investigation of a Court of Inquiry."

French wanted no such court of inquiry. He demanded a court-martial of Jackson. He wanted his lieutenant tried at Fort Meade rather than Tampa to ensure that Jackson could not plead ill health and request a travel delay. Moreover, a court-martial could inspect French's post firsthand and see how well it was functioning. Jackson opposed Fort Meade as the site of any tribunal. French's dominating influence there would override everything else.

Both men were under heavy pressure by this time. It was French who began to disintegrate. On April 16, he officially accused young Lieutenant Baird of conspiring with Jackson to undermine French's authority. Baird was placed under arrest. This left only two officers on duty at the fort.

On the same day, French filed eight court-martial charges against Jackson. The fundamental offense was Jackson's "attempt to injure the private reputation" of his superior officer. "When Major Jackson is brought to trial for his outrageous conduct," French asserted, "the evidence which I will bring before the court will cover him with the infamy he deserves." Someone had planted in Jackson's ear a reprehensible lie about French's personal conduct. "I cannot yet trace the informant. . . . The villain yet lurks undiscovered." Nevertheless, French added, the "frivalous & false" charges concocted by Jackson were "scandalous and infamous, conceived in malice and found-ed on suspicion."

By April 21, a nonchalant attitude in higher channels gave French an inkling that his case was slipping away. He then expressed a willingness even for a court of inquiry. Jackson, he informed division command, still "employed himself trumping up charges against me sometimes on suspicion, sometimes on imperfect remembrances of official transactions in which he has been mortified by being obliged by me to keep within the strict line of his duties." A full investigation, French assured headquarters, "will exhibit to the Colonel commanding the very vague and indefinite meaning that [Jackson] has of the term Subordination."

Neither French nor Jackson knew it at the time, but their mutually damaging contest ended at this point. All of the pertinent paperwork had been submitted; and as the flow of charges and countercharges moved through channels, authorities be-came more bored in its presence. General David Twiggs, the new departmental commander, was a man with many duties and little patience. He promptly rejected both sets of presentations and told the two feuding officers to forget the matter because he planned to do so.

Jackson had performed his duty. Ordered now to cease and desist, he did so without hesitation. French, who had no intention of letting the issue drop, simply paused for second wind before resuming the dispute.

Meanwhile, on the day following French's last installment in the series of accusa-tions, Jackson gave his attention to a more pleasant subject. He wrote two letters in that atmosphere of uncertainty. The first was to Francis H. Smith:

Col.: Your letter of the 28th, informing me that I have been elected Prof. of Natural and Experimental Philosophy and Artillery Tactics, in the Virginia Military Institute, has been received.

The high honor, conferred by the Board of Visitors, in selecting me unanimously, to fill such a Professorship, gratified me exceedingly.

I hope to be able to meet the Board on the 25th of June next, but fear that circumstances, over which I have no control, will prevent my doing so before that time. For your kindness in endeavoring to procure me a leave of absence [from the army] for six months, as well as for the interest you have otherwise manifested in my behalf, I feel more strong and lasting obligations.

Should I desire a furlough of more than one month commencing on the 1st of July next, it would be for the purpose of visiting Europe.

I regret that recent illness has prevented my giving you an earlier answer.

Unsure of the length of his furlough or exactly what the near future held for him at Fort Meade, Jackson concluded the letter with the statement, "Any communication you may have to make previous to the 1st of June please direct to this place."[96]

Jackson then addressed a quick note to his sister. "Good news. I have been elected Professor of Natural & Experimental Philosophy in the Virginia Military Institute, and you may expect me home in the latter part of June. Your Bro. P.S. I am recovering from a recent attack of sickness and owing to the weakness of my eyes do not like to write myself."[97]

Weak vision and aggravated dyspepsia would be the public reasons given for Jackson's departure from the army. (Physical maladies over which he had no control seemed to Jackson better excuses for leaving the army than taking another job for personal gain.) A friend subsequently asked him if he did not think it presumptuous to accept the VMI post with such incapacitation. "Not at all," came the reply. "The appointment came unsought, and was therefore providential; and I knew that if Providence set me a task, He would give me the power to perform it. So I resolved to get well, and you see I have. As to the rest, I knew that what I willed to do, I could do."[98]

It was May 16 when French reluctantly ordered Jackson released from arrest and informed him that his furlough had been granted. Jackson gave no hint of his thirty-eight-day confinement in a quick note to Laura later that day. "My Dear Sister, I expect to leave for home next week or the week after. My health is better than it has been for years except my eyes, which are still weak."[99]

Four days later, Lieutenant Amos Beckwith received orders to assume all of Jackson's duties at Fort Meade. Beckwith, a Vermont native and 1850 graduate of West Point, would spend his career on staff assignments. He was to get an early and rude awakening while serving under French. Jackson happily relinquished all files and records to Beckwith's care. On May 21, 1851, Jackson left Fort Meade—and the army. Officially he was on furlough for nine months. That was only a formality. Jackson was about to begin a new phase in his life.[100]

His departure did not calm the storm at the Florida post. Quite the contrary. French was alone. The dispute had no resolution. He was now the one on the hook because of allegations made but not removed. The commander could not be appeased. Convinced that his honor had been severely damaged, French continued his case against Jackson. He became paranoid in the process. No one escaped his wrath.

Lieutenant Baird requested (and ultimately received) a transfer to another company of the First Artillery. On the day Jackson left Fort Meade, French ordered Baird and Beckwith to examine all of Jackson's records in search of expected irregularities. French then sent a long summary of grievances directly to the adjutant general in Washington. He next accused Jackson of gross dereliction of duty in not having all accounts and records in order at the time of his departure from Fort Meade.[101]

Time could not heal French's anger. Lack of redress only increased his wrath. When General Twiggs forwarded another set of French's complaints to General Winfield Scott in Washington, the departmental commander added an endorsement: "I [do] not think an investigation of 'the cases' necessary. I can see nothing to change my opinion & trust the Genl.-in-Chief may not sustain Bt. Major French's application."[102]

The Fort Meade commander was undeterred. Late in June he ordered a court-martial for Sergeant Newman, one of the soldiers involved in Jackson's investigation of French and his servant. On July 22, French preferred the first of two different sets of charges against Surgeon Letterman. A month later, he formally accused Letterman and Lieutenant Beckwith of improper conduct. French repeatedly asked higher authorities to prosecute Jackson for any of his many offenses. Of the four officers—Jackson, Baird, Letterman, and Beckwith—whom French indicted, not one was ever arraigned on any charges.[103]

Finally, Department of Florida authorities could take no more of French's complaints. On October 1, he was relieved from command of the outlying Fort Meade post and ordered to more established Fort Myers, Florida. The change of scenery did nothing to improve French's disposition.

On March 6, 1852, he appealed for redress to no less than the Secretary of War. That was enough for Twiggs. The general dispatched another officer to take command at Fort Myers and relegated French to a subordinate role. Twiggs's written reaction to French's latest letter of grievances was all but a career-killer. Major French, the general stated, "has preferred charges successively against all the officers serving under his orders, and has shown himself incapable of conducting the service harmoniously at a detached post." With that censure, the French-Jackson debacle officially ended.[104]

Throughout most of the long quarrel, Caroline French had endured another pregnancy. In 1852, she gave birth to a daughter, Emma Read, who in time married John L. Clem, the Civil War's most famous drummer boy and a soldier known more by his nickname, "Johnny Shiloh."[105]

Both Jackson and French were losers in the Fort Meade debacle, and both men had a burden of guilt to bear. Unquestionably, the whole episode drifted through army gossip channels and did nothing positive for the reputation of either officer. Jackson displayed incredibly bad judgment in initiating a probe, especially a personal investigation, of his superior's conduct. Nothing in army regulations gave him such latitude. French should have known better than to give the appearance of improper conduct with a servant girl.

Jackson became blinded by a sense of duty; French by a determination to free his character from reproach in every way possible. Each officer overreacted. Neither displayed any willingness to resolve the controversy quietly and for the good of the service. Jackson's uncompromising insistence on military obedience would be one of his most positive attributes, but it did not serve him well in this instance.

It is impossible to know his thoughts on the dispute as he headed toward his native state. In all likelihood, Jackson gave no further thought to the matter. He had done what he considered right. Now a new life lay before him.

5

ESTABLISHING ROOTS IN LEXINGTON

THE HORSEBACK RIDE FROM FORT MEADE to Tampa took the better part of three days. Next came a long boat trip south around the Florida keys and north up the Atlantic coast to New York. The first item on Jackson's agenda was a visit to kinfolk and home place. He made straight for Beverly to see his sister and her family. As always, the Arnolds heaped attention and affection upon him.

No doubt, Jackson spent much time in counseling Laura on her sagging faith. Whether his revelation that he had begun tithing and was giving a tenth of his army pay to charities had any effect on the sister is not known.

Jackson took daily walks in Beverly. His young nephew, Thomas Jackson Arnold, usually accompanied him. On one such stroll, they were passing the home of the Reverend Thomas Collett when the minister's ferocious dog bounded toward them with teeth bared. Jackson told his nephew to stand perfectly still, as he was doing. The animal got to within thirty feet, then suddenly stopped. Jackson had his head cocked a little forward; he stared intently at the dog with eyes that seemed to have become hot coals. After a few seconds with no motion by any of the participants, the dog turned and ran, frightened, back to the house. Tom Arnold never forgot the drama of the incident, especially the power of Jackson's gaze.

A side trip to Jackson's Mill proved more nostalgic than enjoyable. Jackson met Sylvanus White, the cousin and boyhood friend who had been with Cummins Jackson in California. For two days, the kinsmen called on relatives in the Clarksburg-Weston area. They spent one night at Jackson's Mill. The West Fork's clear water still beckoned, the river's sound was still a blanket of comfort; but the property was neglected and dilapidated, inhabited only by former black servants. Beholding the sights of childhood ravaged by the indifferent hand of time hurt Jackson, but not as much as it would have had Jackson's Mill been his natural home and the residence of his parents.

White eagerly brought Jackson up to date on family matters. He described the search for gold in the far west and Uncle Cummins's last days. Jackson related the bravery of several fellow officers in the Mexican War. White then asked his cousin to narrate his own acts of heroism. Jackson replied: "Oh, if I have to blow my own horn, it will be a long time before it is blown." White persisted and finally elicited from Jackson some incidents of battles in Mexico.[1]

It was now late June. Jackson had grown lukewarm to the idea of a European vacation, and he prepared to report for duty at VMI in August. Natural curiosity induced him to visit Lexington for the first time and inspect the school that would be his new home. He arrived in Lexington by stagecoach late one day and quietly secured a hotel room. The next morning he made his way up a gradual slope to the eighty-foot promontory a half-mile north of Lexington. A castellated new barracks building stood on the edge of the plateau and overlooked both the North River and the town. That huge structure, then undergoing renovation, was the Virginia Military Institute.

Final exams were in progress as Jackson proceeded to the superintendent's quarters in the old arsenal building. Bookcases and many pictures of military scenes reflected the power and influence of Colonel Francis H. Smith. Yet the man himself radiated friendliness and gave undivided attention to every visitor. Tall, thin, lithe, the thirty-eight-year-old Smith wore a blue uniform and bore himself as a high-ranking officer. Gold spectacles emphasized the naturally inquisitive expression on his face. At that time, it was difficult to tell where the blond hair changed into gray. Smith's life and that of the institute were one and the same. A masterful politician in Virginia, he had an extraordinary talent for enlisting legislative support for his school. The superintendent also knew the minutest detail in every department at VMI. The personal interest he took in each cadet entrusted to his care was "at once a warning and stimulus to the boy."[2]

Smith gave Jackson a quick tour of the facilities, then asked him to postpone his plans for a sightseeing trip to Europe. The new faculty member was sorely needed for the school year. Jackson showed no disappointment in agreeing to the delay.[3] Duty always took precedence over recreation. Besides, he was anxious to begin work at the military school.

Raleigh E. Colston was one of the instructors on the faculty, and he was eager to meet his new colleague. His first impression of Jackson was anything but positive. Jackson was five feet, eleven inches in height; he seemed taller because he carried himself ramrod straight. Side whiskers extended from the ears down the jaws but stopped short of the chin. The hair was brown; its tendency to curl led Jackson to keep it short. Compressed lips and a ruddy complexion marked the lower part of Jackson's face. When Jackson removed his cap, a high, white forehead became conspicuous. The eyes, his most striking facial feature, were dark blue and seemed to change tint with his mood.

Colston noted of Jackson that

there was nothing striking about his exterior. . . . His figure was large-boned, angular and even ungainly for his hands & especially his feet were very large. He had a heavy, ungraceful & lumbering walk, altogether different from the springy regular & soldier-like gait which is produced by early military training. . . .

He wore at that time the old style military side-whiskers 'not lower than the corner of the mouth' as prescribed by army regulations. This gave to his countenance a stiff and formal expression which his conversation by no means tended to remove, for he had but little to say, spoke in brief sentences & curt tones & was somewhat constrained in his manners, as was natural with one who had mingled but little in general society.[4]

Barely six weeks remained of Jackson's vacation. Jackson then went to New York City. Motivations for the trip are obscure, but two probabilities exist. One was a desire to straighten out some affairs at a New York bank. During the Fort Hamilton duty,

Jackson had established a savings account at a nearby financial institution. Jackson needed to make a change in the nature of the funds. This he did, to his betterment. By 1859, the account showed $1520 on deposit.[5]

The ongoing search for better health is the reason most commonly given for the New York journey.[6] Jackson was convinced that someone somewhere had a cure for his dyspepsia. Once in New York City, he went to 47 Bond Street to call on his old acquaintances, Dr. and Mrs. Roland Houghton. They had introduced him to the potential wonders of hydropathy; they were also prominent socialites who counted Edgar Allan Poe among their legion of friends.

Jackson attended a dinner party given by the Houghtons. His refusal to eat more than a minimum of the plainest offerings caught Mrs. Houghton's sympathetic eye. Her first husband was a widely respected hydropathic practitioner; she herself was the author of *Water Cure for Ladies* (1844). More important for Jackson, Marie Houghton's father, Dr. Lowry Barney, was in attendance that evening and also became especially interested in Jackson.

Barney was a well-known and highly respected physician–investigator. He had built a solid reputation on the belief that proper diet and exercise could conquer any illness. Patients flocked to his clinic at Belleville, in the far northwest part of New York near Lake Ontario.

In the course of the evening, Barney queried Jackson about his digestive problems. The Virginian described his symptoms at length. Barney immediately offered to help. "Why don't you come up to my home for a few weeks?" he asked. "I think I could help you. We haven't any conveniences there such as you would find in a city, and fewer luxuries; but I can offer you rest and quiet and a pleasant, bracing climate and plenty of good, wholesome food."[7]

Jackson liked the idea and accepted the invitation. He spent the next six weeks at the doctor's farm, located in a quiet countryside, with bracing air. Jackson received treatments from Barney and meals from Mrs. Barney. The prescribed diet was buttermilk and cornbread. Jackson took a two-mile walk each day and considered the drinking water from Lake Ontario to be likewise beneficial. He became close friends with the Barney family, especially with Andrew Jackson Barney, the twenty-two-year-old son of his host.

The physician, in time satisfied with Jackson's progress, then gave him long-range advice. Diet and regular exercise were mandatory. Yet Jackson must learn to overcome stress. Recreation would help; so would marriage. He would be the master of his own fate.[8]

Dutifully obeying the physician's suggestions, Jackson experienced steady improvement in health. His friend Harvey Hill exaggerated a bit when he recalled that when Jackson arrived at VMI to start his new career, "he was a dyspeptic and something of a hypochondriac. His health was bad, but he imagined that he had more ailments than he really did have. . . . The prescription had been given him to live on stale bread and buttermilk, and to wear a wet shirt next to his body. He followed these directions for more than a year after coming to Lexington. . . . These peculiarities attracted much attention, and he was much laughed at by the rude and coarse. But he bore all their jests with patience, and pursued his plan unmoved by their laughter."[9]

Two years later, Jackson would write Barney: "I have derived so much benefit from your wholesome and wise instructions that gratitude to you will accompany me to the grave."[10]

Improved health made Jackson all the more eager to begin his new job at VMI. The trip from upstate New York to Lexington took the better part of a week. He arrived at Lexington in time to make a close inspection of the institute and its history before officially reporting for duty. Jackson liked what he learned and saw.

In February 1816, the Virginia General Assembly had authorized the construction of three arsenals in the state. One was to be in Richmond, another in the mountains of far western Virginia, and the third in Lexington at the southern (upper) end of the Shenandoah Valley. Each arsenal would be a storehouse for 20,000 arms and have a thirty-man military garrison. The Lexington site was above Jordan's Point on a highly defensible ridge that dominated the northern approach to the town.

The years passed and the threats of Indian attacks vanished. Soon, wrote a future cadet, "the soldiers, having nothing else to do beyond a little guard duty, fell into bad habits, committed petty depredations, and became drunken and worthless." The "staid, orderly Scotch-Irish" citizens of Lexington frowned on such behavior. In December 1834, local attorney John T. L. Preston and several other townspeople initiated steps to disband the arsenal and replace it with "a military and scientific school" modeled after the U.S. Military Academy.[11]

Soon after the first of the following year, the General Assembly created a five-man board of visitors. Its first president was Claudius Crozet, a former French soldier under Napoleon and an engineer of exceptional skill. (Crozet built one of the most noted railroad tunnels in America.) The board then sought out Professor Francis Smith at Hampden-Sydney College and asked him to become superintendent of the proposed academy. Smith would preside over the school for a half-century. He more than any other individual would shape the development of VMI.

On November 11, 1839, the Lexington academy opened for business. It was the second governmental military school in the nation. Of twenty-eight students that first year, twenty were "State cadets" from Virginia's senatorial districts. They received free tuition in return for performing such soldierly duties as guarding the governmental supplies still on deposit. The next year brought twice the number of new cadets. The class that entered VMI the year Jackson arrived numbered 117 students, six more than Jackson's entering class at West Point.

Less than a decade after VMI welcomed its first cadet, expansion of facilities became necessary. Requests for new construction led to a protracted debate in 1848–49 over moving the academy to another location. The Lexington faction won.[12] When Jackson arrived, a new barracks was being built around the original 1816 structure. Jackson's quarters during his first month at VMI were of necessity a second-floor room at the Lexington Hotel.

His academic home at the institute was in the stylish neo-Gothic design popular in that era. Designed by architect Alexander Jackson Davis of New York, the structure was U-shaped, with the base being longer than the arms. The front section (or main building) was then under construction. It overlooked the town and the Valley Turnpike. Its limestone foundation, octagonal towers, crenelated parapets, and Gothic style made it the most conspicuous landmark in that area.

The barracks faced east across the northern front of Lexington. A local newspaper stated in the spring of 1851: "The new building for this flourishing school is being rapidly constructed. The brick work of the main building is nearly finished . . . and will greatly adorn the appearance of our town." One of the students later boasted of the new edifice: "The cadet barracks was a handsome four-storied building, occupying three sides of a quadrangle, with towers at the corners and a sally-port with central arch. On the inner side were three broad stoops running all around the building, reached by stairways upon the stoops."[13] The 1854 dedication of a statue of George Washington in front of the sally port led to the name Washington Arch for the main entrance.

Cadets wore uniforms, and so did the officers who taught them. A military atmosphere permeated every facet of the school except the curriculum. The course of study was heavy in mathematics, with some instruction in infantry and artillery tactics in the upper classes as well as course work in engineering and mechanics during the final year. Undergraduates did not study for a military career. Only West Pointers could obtain army commissions upon graduation. Those at VMI who completed their studies satisfactorily might secure militia appointments, but these came as adjuncts to civilian careers.

Colonel Smith interpreted the principal goal of VMI to be that of training young men to become teachers across Virginia in the fields of mathematics and science. He came to view VMI's mission as threefold: to supply teachers through the Commonwealth, to elevate the standards of scientific education in the state, and, after John Brown's raid in 1859, to provide for the defense of Virginia.

Smith was also determined to instill deep and abiding faith in every cadet. Church attendance on Sunday was compulsory; prayer meetings were a regular part of cadet life; Smith conducted informal Bible classes in his office; he established the tradition of presenting each graduating senior with not only a degree but a Bible as well.

Military service may not have been the primary goal of the curriculum. Nevertheless, one observer pointed out, "in all essential respects the Military Institute was little behind West Point. The discipline was strict, the drill was but little less precise. . . . No pains were spared by either the State or the faculty to maintain the peculiar character of the School; and the little battalion, although the members were unlikely to see service, was as carefully trained as if each private was someday destined to become an officer."[14]

Discipline was fundamental to life at VMI. The Board of Visitors stated in its first report to the governor of Virginia: "At an age when passions are yet unmitigated by the lessons of experience, it is generally imprudent to trust to the self-government of a young man. Habits of unrestrained indulgence have frequently laid the foundation of ruin of youths. . . . The wise and prudent parent will choose for his son that education which will impart to him habits of order and regularity."[15]

A cadet who had been at VMI for two years before Jackson arrived insisted a half-century later that the 1850s were "the most brilliant" in the school's history. He stated to a fellow classmate: "For the greater part of that period the patronage was restricted to Virginians and the finest families of Virginia. The military and civil records of the Institute will also show that the men educated in that time made the most profound impression in military and industrial life. . . . I have never seen together a hundred and fifty young men equal to the corps in your time and mine."[16]

Jackson officially reported for duty at VMI on Wednesday, August 13, 1851, and it was a less-than-anticipated beginning.[17] Confusion was the order of the day. Although the corps was on summer vacation, a sizable contingent remained on campus to guard the arsenal. Construction of the new barracks compelled the cadets to live in tents at one end of the parade ground. The new building would not be ready on schedule, so the start of the 1851–52 school year was delayed. With Major William Gilham out of town, now Major Jackson found himself entering his new duties as temporary commandant of cadets.

If he had any reservations about the assignment, he kept them to himself. The next morning, the cadets assembled for parade and drill. A larger-than-usual crowd assembled to watch the activities. It was Jackson's first appearance; for one of the few times in his ten-year association with VMI, he dressed with care: dark blue, double-breasted frock coat with shoulder straps, white pantaloons, white gloves, new kepi cap perched strangely on his head, enormous feet encased in worn but well-blacked artillery boots. Nothing seemed to fit quite right, but Jackson was resplendent from head to toe. He joined the audience on the edge of the parade ground and tried to appear inconspicuous.

After the small VMI band played a short military air, Adjutant Thomas T. Munford of Richmond, the ranking cadet at the time, was just about to order the column forward when from the ranks a youthful voice shrilled: "Come out of them boots! They are not allowed in this camp!"[18]

Munford turned and swept the bystanders with his eyes. To his horror, he saw that the object of derision was a VMI officer. The man was rather handsome; blue-gray eyes flashed to and fro from an unsmiling face; sideburns began at the ears and extended almost to the chin; the officer's entire countenance was one of absolute seriousness. He had to be the new man—the acting commandant, Munford concluded.

The adjutant turned command over to the officer of the day, rushed to the crowd, gave his best salute, and apologized to Jackson for not seeing him when the cadets assembled. (Munford felt doubly remiss because Major Gilham had asked him to help the new officer get acclimated to life at VMI.) Jackson kindly dismissed the slight. He had visited the barracks, he said, and merely stopped by the parade ground to observe the contingent of cadets at drill.

Munford escorted Jackson to corps headquarters and began explaining to Jackson what was expected in planning and announcing daily schedules. As Munford spoke, Jackson pored over the order book in seeming indifference to the cadet's oral presentation. The major then requested a copy of cadet regulations. When Munford handed over the small volume, Jackson gave a hint of a smile and stated: "This is our *chart.*"[19]

It was many years later when Munford recalled these events, but he insisted that Jackson next sat down, looked at him rather balefully, and declared: "Adjutant, I am here amid new men, strange faces, other minds, companionless. I shall have to rely upon you for much assistance until I can familiarize myself with the routine duties, and the facilities for executing them. There is a great similarity I see to West Point, where I was educated. I trust ere long to master all difficulties."[20]

This made an instant friend of Tom Munford. The young Richmonder learned quickly that discipline was Jackson's byword. He was "painfully exacting in details,"

Munford wrote. "Yet there was an earnestness in his manner and precision in his commands that indicated unmistakably what was meant." The cadet went out of his way to assist Jackson in every undertaking until his graduation the following year. Munford would exhibit that same pride a decade later when he became Jackson's cavalry chief.[21]

In spite of makeshift accommodations that first month, Jackson pursued his new duties with determination and the singleness of mind that marked any endeavor he undertook. He left the Lexington Hotel before dawn each morning. With long and rapid strides he proceeded to the institute and attacked his duties with unflagging energy. It was usually far into the night before Jackson returned to his hotel room for a few hours of sleep.

More than enough was in Lexington to keep him busy. There were colleagues, cadets, and townspeople to meet plus new locales to explore. "Summer vacation" at VMI was hardly that. A school year ended near the Fourth of July holiday and a new one began near the end of August. Jackson presided over a cadet court-martial in his first week at the institute. Before August ended, he directed a twenty-one-gun salute by cadets in honor of a brief visit by President Millard Fillmore.

All of Jackson's first impressions about his professorship were favorable. "I am very much pleased with my situation," he stated in his first letter from Lexington to his sister. "I have commenced my military duties and am reviewing one of my text books. My health has much improved since you heard me say good bye." His delight extended as well to the countryside. "From my present room which is in the 2d story of the Lexington Hotel I have a lovely view of the mountain scenery."[22]

The new barracks remained uncompleted at the beginning of September, when all cadets reported to the school. Colonel Smith therefore directed Jackson to take the corps on a two-and-a-half-week "practice march" to some of the several spas in the area. The major received full authority to determine the line of march and the length of stay at each resort. His only restriction was to be back in Lexington with the cadets by the 27th of the month.

Smith no doubt selected the springs as stopping points because they were within marching distance and offered recreational outlets. Jackson, of course, was delighted at the prospect of testing Virginia's mineral waters.

On September 9, with Major Jackson mounted and at the head, the corps marched west from Lexington. Two days and thirteen miles later, the column reached Rockbridge Alum Springs. It was widely regarded as second in elegance and benefits only to White Sulphur Springs. As many as 500 guests might be there at any given time.

A thirty-eight-mile march to the northwest brought Jackson and the cadets next to Bath Alum Springs. "Decidedly the nicest place in the mountains," as one newspaper adjudged it, Bath Alum was a complex of ten small buildings backed up to a long ridge. The cadets' stay was brief because of limited accommodations. A five-mile hike farther to the west led to Warm Springs, whose sprawling rows of cottages and 98-degree waters attracted scores of guests during the season—even though, as one visitor concluded, the drinking water was "rather hard to take."[23]

Jackson thoroughly enjoyed the daily morning and evening baths at each of the spas. This outing also provided him with the opportunity to become better acquainted with VMI cadet life. While the youngsters gave no indication of being enamored of Jackson's leadership on the long marches, Jackson's attitude toward the cadets was positive. He sent a quick note from Warm Springs to Uncle Alfred Neale. "I have reported at Lexington and am delighted with my duties, the place and the people." Jackson then apologized for not visiting Parkersburg earlier in the summer, "but I am anxious to devote myself to study until I shall become master of my profession."[24]

Punctual to a fault, Jackson led the corps from Warm Springs on the forty-five-mile hike to Lexington and arrived at VMI three days ahead of schedule. At 4 P.M. on Wednesday, September 24, 1851, four faculty and 117 cadets began moving into the new barracks.[25] The bottom segment of the U-shaped building was the academic wing. Its entrance way faced to the south. Jackson and Major William Gilham shared living quarters 22–24 on the third floor in the tower on the eastern side of the entrance. Immediately below their windows was the Valley Turnpike; in the distance lay the rolling country on the northern outskirts of Lexington.

It was appropriate that Jackson should have as a first roommate the man whose workload he had been hired to relieve. Just as Francis Smith was VMI's administrative star in the institute's developing years, William Gilham was its academic star. The tall, straight, clean-shaven Gilham, with dark hair and intense eyes, was born in 1818 in Vincennes, Indiana. In the West Point class of 1840, he ranked fifth among forty-two cadets—one notch above William T. Sherman. Three years as an assistant under the famous Professor Bartlett at West Point preceded Gilham's brief duty in the Mexican War. He served in the Third Artillery and won citations for gallantry at Palo Alto and Resaca. In October 1846, Gilham had resigned from the army to become professor of sciences as well as commandant of cadets at VMI.

Colonel Smith came to the opinion that Gilham "had no superior" as a commandant. "Quick, accurate, and self-possessed, he had a magnetic power on the drill [field] which made the corps of cadets superior even to the cadets at West Point." Cadet Munford thought that Gilham "was the brightest professor we had in his day—scientifically—and was a superb drill master, the best I ever saw."[26]

James T. Murfee of the class of 1853 wrote in later years: "I thought then, as the cadets thought, that [Major] Gilham exerted more influence upon the characters of the young men than any other officer or professor there. 'Old Gill,' as we all called him, was our beau-ideal of an educator, gentleman, and drillmaster; he commanded our profound respect, admiration, and love. To us he was almost the whole institution."[27] In personality, Jackson and Gilham were a far cry from one another, but their sense of duty and love for VMI pulled them together into a working team that lasted into civil war.

Getting to know the other VMI faculty was not difficult; they were few in number. Colonel Smith ("Old Spex" to the cadets) taught mathematics. "Old Parlez" was the student name for Raleigh Colston, who taught French, so important in military schools of that period. John Preston ("Old Bald"), who would become one of Jackson's closest friends, was in charge of modern languages and English literature. Another Virginian, Thomas H. Williamson ("Old Tom"), had been in the same West Point class (1833) with Francis H. Smith but did not graduate. He joined the VMI faculty as instructor in tactics and drawing. When Jackson arrived in 1851, Williamson switched to a professorship in engineering. Within a decade, he gained the reputation of being "undoubtedly the most accomplished Engineer of the State."[28]

Four young instructors completed the staff. Daniel Trueheart, who shared Jackson's faith in water cures, and William D. Stuart assisted in tactics and engineering; Robert E. Rodes helped Gilham with basic chemistry courses; James W. Massie was an instructor in mathematics. All of these junior faculty were VMI graduates.

For six days each week, the schedule at the institute was the same. Reveille came at daybreak; breakfast at 7 A.M.; guard mount at 8; class recitations from 8 to 1 P.M. dinner; recitations again from 2 until 4 P.M.; a period of recreation before dress parade; supper, followed by study, until the signal for lights out. Cadets "recited" by solving problems each day at the blackboard. Daily grades played a prominent part in a student's final standing. General examinations occurred biannually on the first Monday in January and on an appointed day late in June.

Jackson learned his class schedule on the day before the 1851–52 academic year began. His first course met from 8 until 9:30 A.M.; the second ran from 9:30 to 11 A.M. Artillery tactics and drill filled the 2–4 P.M. period. Jackson's classroom (the section room, it was called) was on the southwest corner of the second floor of the barracks. A line of whitewashed pillars extended perpendicular to the rows of desks. Two windows behind Jackson's desk were angled because they were on the side walls of a stairwell leading up from ground level. The section room was spacious in spite of the choppy appearance created by its triangular shape.[29]

A week after classes began, Jackson happily informed Laura, "My health has through the blessing of Providence been so much improved as to enable me to enter on my duties, with which I am delighted."[30] That statement would be unbelievable except for Jackson's rigid honesty. If he felt "delighted" in his new duties, it was because he was accustomed to deriving simple pleasure from intense pain.

In many respects, Jackson's talents were ill suited for a professor's responsibilities. Only that unbreakable determination enabled him to stay academically afloat. He undoubtedly was aware of all the classroom obstacles he faced; but as deeply private as he was, Jackson found a measure of strength in concealing his anxieties. From preparation to performance, from appearance to attitude, the role of a teacher was basically unnatural for Jackson's talents. Had he been more realistic and less determined, he would have recognized the unsound situation for what it was.

The first explanation for his limited competence as a teacher lay with Jackson himself. A member of the VMI Board of Visitors met Jackson that autumn and observed: "The impression he produced upon me was that he was a man of peculiarities, distinctly marked from the ordinary man of note, reserved yet polite, reticent of opinion, but fixed in the ideas he had formed, sensitively averse to obtruding them upon others, but determined and inflexible in their advocacy. . . . The striking characteristic [of the man] was his strict sense of duty. This with an abrupt manner and a crisp but not brusque form of expression did not tend to render him popular with the young men under his charge."[31]

Jackson had a direct manner of walking, never looking left or right but staring straight ahead. Still, he always greeted an acquaintance or a woman by lifting his cap. Cadets voiced the belief that Jackson had eyes all around his head. At meals, Jackson sat stiffly upright. He had "a curious way of holding up his head very straight, whilst his chin would appear as if it were trying to get up to the top of his head."[32]

Some cadets needed more than instruction. A large percentage of the students were in military school to receive discipline, no doubt because many sons of affluent Southern families had experienced no restraints at home. Consigned to a military academy for education, these cadets still retained an independence of spirit that rebelled at any abridgement of what was deemed freedom of action. Jackson was more demanding than most professors. Hence, some cadets were less cooperative in class. As one stated belligerently: "He does not seem to realize that we are the sons of gentlemen, and [he] is disposed to treat us as officers do the common soldiers in the regular army."[33]

It might have been better if the major had taught history at VMI. He was an avid reader who enjoyed military narratives, especially volumes on the wars of Napoleon Bonaparte. Jackson would surely have imparted more ardor in teaching the glories of Napoleon and Frederick the Great than in wading through the dull, inanimate subjects assigned to him.

The natural and experimental philosophy course for which Jackson was responsible was one of the most difficult offerings at a military school because of both the content and the learning process. Popularly considered now as the study of physics, the course was a loose conglomerate of physics, astronomy, mechanics, and sprinklings of other sciences. Subjects included electricity, magnetics, acoustics, the science of heavenly bodies, and the properties of light (optics). Professors lectured during part of each class period; cadet recitations filled the remainder of the assigned time. While some work was done with barometers, telescopes, and other basic instruments, course grades resulted from cadet performance at the blackboard, which required not only much memorization but near-total recall of mathematical techniques.

Jackson certainly subscribed to the principles of the subject because an orderly universe conformed to his own sense of organization and discipline. However, his knowledge of natural and experimental philosophy proved positive while his efforts to teach it were negative. Rote memorization and unquestioning obedience to authority were the basic commandments in the section room. Jackson never learned how to put life into a subject or how to convey material in a fashion that bred understanding and fostered absorption. The old-fashioned, stern approach to teaching had marked his own instruction at West Point. Doubtless, Jackson believed that was the acceptable method.

One of Jackson's first students noted mildly that he "went in to Major Jackson & was not remarkably well entertained the hour & [a] half that he kept us." The major's lecture notes attested to that. The discussion for one session began: "In order to explain the physical constitution of bodies we shall adopt the views of Boscovich so far as may be necessary for understanding the subjects which may come under our consideration. According to his theory an atom is an indivisible and unextended element of matter. When two atoms are in sensible contact the forces they exert on each other are called atomic or molecular forces."[34]

Many cadets were simply not ready for such heavy doses of knowledge. On the flyleaf of a copy of Bartlett's text used in Jackson's class, a cadet wrote despairingly:

'Tis said that Optics treats of light,
But oh! believe it not, my lark;
I've studied it with all my might,
And still it's left me in the dark.

Jackson knew little about the subjects and was "strangely out of place in expounding their formula." For the first year at VMI, he was barely able to stay a lecture or two in advance of the students. Yet he was convinced that he could "add to his knowledge" and "keep ahead of any class" because "he could always do what he willed to do."[35]

A limitation in vision was another of the impediments besetting Jackson. After suffering eye problems in 1848, he became convinced that only the most meticulous care would prevent him from going blind. Jackson therefore formed study habits that would provide the least strain on his eyes. This included doing no reading by artificial light, especially after dark. As a result, in the afternoon he would commit the next day's class material to memory. Following supper, the major would faithfully devote at least two hours sitting bolt upright, or standing rigidly with his face to a wall, while he reviewed the material he was to present. His power of concentration and a photographic memory—both acquired at West Point—served Jackson well in retaining facts and figures. Yet it made him a totally uninspiring teacher.

Granted, optics and higher mathematics did not lend themselves to any form of excitement. Even if they had, Jackson's classroom performance would have squashed all levity. His thinking was too strict, his approach to learning too dutybound. Cadet James McCabe voiced criticism and admiration with the comment: "In the section room he would sit perfectly erect and motionless, listening with grave attention and exhibiting the great powers of his wonderful memory, which was, I think, the most remarkable that ever came under my observation."[36]

Whenever Jackson attempted anything like an original question, it was the closest thing to humor that the class ever witnessed. He once asked "why a telegram could not be sent from Lexington to Staunton." Cadets offered various scientific theories, each of which was pronounced incorrect. One of the last cadets so queried replied in exasperation: "I do not know, unless it is because there is no telegraph wire between the two places." That elicited from Jackson an excited, "Yes, sir, that is right!"[37]

According to a popular phrase, Jackson became "exact as a multiplication table and full of things military as an arsenal." Paraphrasing the textbook line for line, he always pursued a single avenue of logic. If cadets did not understand the presentation, Jackson could only repeat it—word for word. Analogies or parallel explanations were beyond his perception, for he had no gift of elucidation.

On those few occasions when he attempted an ironic or metaphorical remark, Jackson would modify his statement by adding: "Not meaning exactly what I say."[38] Cadets quickly picked up the phrase and used it as a tag for everything in life.

The peculiarities in Jackson's lifestyle provided much ammunition for student ridicule. At the same time, cadets derided his insistence on rigid discipline, taunted him as an unreasonable advocate of military etiquette, and sought to ignore his beliefs in institutional system and orderliness. Jackson maintained always that because a military school could not survive without such ideals, no relaxation from those foundations would be tolerated. To younger cadets, that became a challenge to frivolous rebellion.

Cadet James C. Hiden, who later became a Baptist minister, stated in matter-of-fact terms: "Jackson's life, as a teacher, was singularly monotonous. He seldom opened his mouth except from absolute necessity. . . . He had his text-books, and he prescribed the lessons—fearfully long and desperately hard lessons they were—and at the appointed time he 'heard' them, and this was about all of it. Discussions in the classroom were unknown, and even explanations were infrequent, and when they did occur they usually left the matter where they found it."[39]

The major was precise to a fault in small details. "What are the three simple machines?" he once asked a cadet. "The inclined plane, the lever, and the wheel," the student replied proudly. "No, sir," Jackson snapped. "The lever, the wheel, and the inclined plane." They were listed in that order in the textbook, and that was the way they were supposed to be identified.[40]

Single-mindedness is a great asset in an army commander but deadly in a college professor. Jackson never descended to the students' level of understanding. Rather, he pointed toward answers that cadets themselves were expected to find. Because his own boyhood had been shaped by concentration and high ambition, Jackson thought that all other youths should follow the same course. Hard work was the key to success. Time was too valuable to be wasted, even amid the thoughtlessness of youth.

Brighter and more conscientious students were able to struggle successfully through Jackson's course; weaker cadets floundered. J. T. L. Preston correctly saw that Jackson "made good scholars of better students, but failed to work up the laggarts."[41] While the major gave every student the benefit of the doubt when it came to grades, he had no tolerance whatsoever for laziness. Slipshod performance at daily recitations brought low marks. Hence, frustrations were common reactions to the major's classes.

Reaction took the forms of verbal criticisms, written putdowns, mocking, pranks, and the like. A colleague noted, "The ungainly form and awkward gait, his large feet, his accent & pronunciation derived from his West Va. birth, certain gestures & expressions habitual to him in the class-room, were the source of much juvenile wit & merriment, and the black-board offered the cadets a fine field for the perpetuation of their jokes."[42] Blackboard drawings of a figure with grotesquely large feet often greeted Jackson when he entered the section room for a class.

Marginal notes in textbooks and letters from cadets to relatives and friends contained much doggerel regarding the ineffectual Jackson. "The Major skinned me this morning by asking me extra questions on Venus," Cadet Thomas Robinson wrote. "I wish he would let me and Venus be."[43]

Young Charles M. Barton complained that optics was "so difficult & taught by such a *hell of a fool*." Barton further expressed his scorn in verse:

The V.M.I. O what a spot
In winter cold, in summer hot
Great Lord Al—— What a wonder
Major Jackson Hell & Thunder[44]

Big feet brought him the nickname "Square Box." (The man who made his oversize boots insisted that Jackson would buy a pair only if they squeaked. The bootmaker solved this demand by inserting split quills in the soles.) To most cadets, Jackson was "Old Jack," "Tom Fool," and "Old Hickory." The last sobriquet likened the major to the serious-minded Andrew Jackson.

In view of his stern and humorless demeanor, it is strange that Jackson was a poor section-room disciplinarian. Cadets sat at desks arranged in a horseshoe curve around the professor's lectern table. When Jackson had his back turned to watch intently as one student performed at the blackboard, other cadets threw spitballs of paper and created other "wanton disorder" that bordered (wrote one student) on "downright disrespect." Yet Jackson "was imperturbable throughout the cross fire of youthful witticism," and he "passed on unmoved and generally unconscious" of it all.[45]

One day, for example, cadets Giles Cooke and Hays Otey became especially rambunctious. Otey began caterwauling. Jackson sought in vain to locate the sound. Soon Cooke started imitating a barking dog. Jackson peered sternly at the class, then said, "I perceive there is a puppy in the room." The sounds stopped.[46]

Muskets and projectiles were the subjects of another day's class period. A cadet asked straight-faced if a gun could not be constructed so that it would shoot around a corner. Jackson thought for a moment, then replied that he would take the question under consideration and give the young man an answer the following day. The next morning, the major called on the cadet, who rose and stood at attention. Jackson then gravely informed him that in his measured opinion no gun could be manufactured with the capacity of shooting around a corner. The cadet bowed, Jackson saluted, and the student returned to his desk with "a sickly grin" on his face while the rest of the class strained to maintain somber expressions.

Randolph Barton, another cadet, reflected on Jackson in later years: "No one recalls a smile, a humorous speech, anything from him while at [VMI]. He was not sullen, or gloomy, or particularly dull. He was simply a silent, unobtrusive man, doing his duty in an unentertaining way—merely an automaton. And yet the cadets held him in high estimation. There was no enthusiasm felt for him. The feeling was one which no one could well describe. He was not praised; he was abused. He was the butt of boyish pranks, but not the victim of malevolence."[47]

That is not quite correct. On one occasion, a cadet dropped a brick on Jackson from a barracks window. The block missed him by inches. Jackson gave no indication of its existence. Many of the cadets condemned such loathsome conduct by one of their number, but the culprit could not be identified. One of the professors asked Jackson why he did not try to ascertain the cadet's name. The major responded: "The truth is, I do not want to know that we have such a coward in the corps of cadets."[48]

For the most part, Jackson did not dwell on such misbehavior. He brought to the section room the same dedication to duty as he took to the battlefield. Students watched every movement of the strange professor. Cadet James H. Lane, for example, stated: "When questioning the cadets, he had a peculiar way of grasping his lead pencil, with his thumb on the end towards the cadets, and when a mistake was made, he would say, 'Rather the reverse,' and slip his thumb back on the pencil. We believed that this was from a desire to do justice, that he used his pencil as the Indian his stick, to notch down the mistakes, that he might know how much to 'skin' us" when posting daily grades.[49]

Classroom image did little to assuage negative opinions about Jackson. Lane noted: "Jackson was remarkably stiff and officially polite in his section room. He always mistered the cadets, and saluted them when they had completed their demonstrations at the blackboard, or he had finished questioning them. He was grave, dignified, and rarely smiled."[50]

Jackson delivered his material in a polite but slow monotone and with a high-pitched drawl characteristic of mountain folk. Always lacking in the finer points of coordination, Jackson was clumsy and often unsuccessful in trying to conduct experiments. "His fingers were all thumbs," Professor Colston recalled. "He announced one day to his class that he would that night take the telescope on the parade ground & show them the satellites of Jupiter, & asked me & several others to be present. We found Jackson and his class assembled about seven o'clock. For nearly two hours, he worked & fumbled at the instrument, trying in vain to get it in working order. Meanwhile the Cadets had become impatient and amused themselves with . . . crowing & barking, and pinning papers to Jackson's coat tails. Finally he gave it up & sent a messenger to . . . Maj. Gilham, [who] was as quick as Jackson was slow, and in five minutes the telescope was adjusted in perfect order. After that, Jackson never attempted to exhibit any but the simplest experiments & the greater part of the apparatus remained unused."[51]

In his afternoon artillery classes, Jackson displayed more animation because this instruction gave him the greatest satisfaction. He was an artilleryman by experience; that arm of service was always his favorite. Colonel Smith was convinced in the beginning that Jackson would be most successful as a teacher of artillery. The superintendent told a friend a month after the school year began: "I have no doubt the Major will make a most effective [artillery] drill. He has the reputation of being one of the best artillerists of his rank in the service."[52]

Since 1845, a battery of six guns had been at the institute for instructional purposes. The four six-pounder bronze cannon and two twelve-pounder howitzers had been stripped down for cadet use and weighed less than 600 pounds each. Jackson "loved his guns," one observer commented, "and for the little brass pieces . . . he seemed to have the affection and pride of a mother who launched upon society her young and blushing daughters."[53]

A member of the class of 1861 wrote two years later: "As soon as the sound of the guns would fall upon his ears, a change would come over Major Jackson. He would grow more erect; the grasp upon his sabre would tighten; the quiet eyes would flash; the large nostrils would dilate, and the calm, grave face would glow with the proud spirit of the warrior."[54]

Cadets in the third and fourth classes did not share his enthusiasm. With no horses available to move the guns, lower classmen had to act as horses during each drill. The parade ground, carved from the hilltop, contained numerous ruts and gullies. Jackson stood in the middle of the field in order to direct all gun crews easily. His shouted commands were loud and precise, except that Jackson had the military habit of drawing out the last syllable of each order: "Un-lim-be-e-e-r!" "Cease fir-i-i-i-ng!" The major was unable to infuse his own ardor into every student. One youngster who later became a brigade commander under Jackson remembered: "His long, drawling commands were in striking contrast with the sharp, quick ones of Major Gilham, who had charge of us in infantry drill. In our ignorance of the importance of this difference in giving commands in artillery and infantry, Major Jackson amused us not a little; and several cadets soon learned to mimic him to perfection."[55]

Nonchalance marked more than one cadet's behavior in the artillery class. Young Joseph Hambrick once had to perform the troublesome duty of pulling one of the cannon. Across the field came Jackson's loud directive: "Limbers and caissons, pass your pieces, trot, march-h-h-h!" Hambrick failed to move promptly and Jackson put him on report for "not trotting at artillery drill." When asked for an excuse, Hambrick wrote: "I am a natural pacer."[56]

Students also performed the same pranks semester after semester. A bell hidden somewhere on the caisson would tinkle merrily during the drill. On other occasions, mischievous cadets would draw the linchpins from the cannon wheels. When the guns made the turn near the parapet, the wheels fell off and the pieces tumbled over the slope. The first time this occurred, Jackson looked ruefully over the edge and remarked: "There must be something defective in the construction of these linchpins. They seem to fly off whenever the pieces in rapid motion change direction." Eventually, he realized the trick being played. The major gazed long and silently at the gun crew; "in a brief space," one of the cadets noted, "we were placed under arrest—officers, cannoneers, horses, and all." That particular episode did not happen again.[57]

Nothing, however, ever caused Jackson to waver from duty. One afternoon artillery drill was proceeding with more than usual difficulty. Cadets were growing weary of dragging cannon all over the parade ground. Suddenly, a black cloud overhead unleashed a torrent of rain. The major was indifferent to the storm. Drill continued. As the battery maneuvered into proximity to the barracks, cadets with one accord ducked inside for cover. From the doorway and the windows they watched as "Old Tom Fool" Jackson stood at rigid attention, sword drawn, until 4 o'clock adjournment time. He then marched from the field, alone and with rain still pouring.[58]

Practical jokes and disrespect were common occurrences on the drill field, but the fact remained that Jackson taught several hundred cadets in the study of artillery. Those who heeded his instructions received the best artillery training the prewar South had to offer. Many cadets later became outstanding Confederate cannoneers, thanks solely to the sometimes odd major who introduced them to the wonder of big guns.

To Jackson, VMI was the Southern equivalent of West Point; as such, duty and orders were to be obeyed at all levels at all times. Because a teaching career ran so counter to his nature, Jackson pursued it doggedly under the dual proposition that teaching improved his knowledge as well as gave him the opportunity to prove that he could succeed at a task when he set his mind to it.

On balance, however, Jackson did not possess the classroom talents that give life and ease to education. Colonel Smith quickly came to the same conclusion. "As a Professor of Natural and Experimental Philosophy," Smith wrote, "Major Jackson was not a success. He had not the qualifications needed for so important a chair. He was no *teacher*, and he lacked the tact required in getting along with his classes. Every officer and every cadet respected him for his many sterling qualities. He was a brave man, a conscientious man, and a good man, but he was no professor. His *genius* was in the Science and Art of War."[59]

James Henderson Smith, the superintendent's son, reached the same conclusion. "Major Jackson was as indifferent a teacher as one could easily find. . . . A thorough soldier . . . he had as little in common with the scholarly academician as Gustave Adolphus and Erasmus. . . . He was awkward, peculiar, bizarre. . . . He would endeavor to administer his department on principles applicable to a garrison of regulars . . . [yet] Major Jackson held his own place in the respect of the cadets."[60]

A student at nearby Washington College was more picturesque and blunt. "'Old Jack' . . . was so plain in manner and attire, there was so little effort at show, his feet were so large and his arms and hands fastened to his body in such awkward shape, that the cadets didn't take much pride in him as a professor. They feared him in the lecture room, they paid the strictest deference to him on parade, but in showing a stranger the sights about the Institute, a cadet was never known to point out 'Old Jack' as one of the ornaments of the institution."[61]

That Jackson had peculiarities is uncontestable. VMI cadets were aware of his strange ways long before they encountered him in class. They expected a queer fellow in optics; and when they encountered him, they nurtured—and often expanded—the image (possibly as a rationale for the low grades so many of them received in Jackson's courses).

Three overlooked considerations need to be inserted at this point. First, Jackson entered a new and alien world at VMI. The military was all he knew. The complexities of simple society were beyond his knowledge. Teaching was something he had done briefly and informally ten years earlier, and it had occurred in a borrowed room inside a mountain town rather than at a military academy. In many ways, Jackson had more to learn than did the cadets; and learning for him was still a slow process.

Second, the overwhelming majority of stories, allegations, and anecdotes relative to Jackson came from fourth and third classmen: youngsters prone to exaggerate. The tales were also first impressions that lingered until the rudiments of leadership Jackson sought to instill in them finally took root. As often as not, those young cadets who most ridiculed Jackson became officers who begged to serve under his command in war. They laughed at him in one decade; they died for him in the next.

Last, and contrary to popular legend, not all VMI cadets viewed Jackson as a character; and many of those who did were quick to put ability above eccentricity. Cadet Thomas M. Boyd thought Jackson's classroom manner stern. He "sat erect with his coat buttoned to the chin." Boyd added: "Owing to his rigid adherence to duty and the extreme care he took to fulfill the rules and regulations to the very letter, the cadets and sometimes the professors would say he was crazy . . . but I always felt assured that he was a great and good man."[62]

Thirty years after graduating from the institute, Thomas T. Munford clearly remembered his artillery drillmaster. "One stride of his would equal two of Gilham's; his foot occupied double the space, the tone of his voice was entirely upon a different key. He measured distance with his eye slowly, and was painfully exacting in details. . . . When he would give the command to the cannoneers to Fire! the ring of that voice [gave] life and nerve to the holder of the lanyard."[63]

Cadet Legh W. Reid watched Major Jackson in action for four years. Just before his graduation, Reid composed poems about four of his professors. Three of the works were decidedly derogatory. The fourth, pertaining to Jackson, read:

> Like some rough brute that ranged the forest wild
> So rude—uncouth, so purely Nature's child
> Is Hickory, and yet methinks I see
> The stamp of genius on his brow and he
> With his wild glance and keen but quiet eye
> Can draw forth from the secret sources where they lie
> Those thoughts & feelings of the human heart
> Most virtuous, good & free from guilty art
> There is something in his very mode of life
> So accurate, steady, void of care or strife
> That fills my heart with love of him who bears
> His honors meekly & who wears
> The laurels of a hero—This in fact
> So here's a heart & hand of mine for Jack.[64]

Jackson's relations with Colonel Smith became strained in time, but with fellow faculty he cultivated and gained a close camaraderie. Raleigh Colston was a case in point. Born in 1825 of wealthy Virginia parents residing in France, Colston came to America at the age of seventeen to enter VMI. He graduated third in the class of 1846 and remained at the institute to teach French, history, and (after 1854) military strategy. Clear blue eyes and dark, swept-back hair gave Colston a handsomeness that complemented an engaging personality.

Of his first contacts with Jackson, "Old Parlez" wrote:

It was not long before, through the appearance of coldness & reserve, which was habitual to him, but which arose mainly from his own diffidence, we perceived in him the sterling qualities & the kindly disposition which marked his character. Almost the first words he addressed to me were that he felt like a stranger among the Faculty but that he expected to look upon them soon as friends and brothers. . . .

There never occurred the least unpleasant word or feeling to mar the friendship that arose between us from the beginning of our acquaintance. Nor is it to be wondered at, for there was never a man with whom it was easier to keep on friendly terms than with him. He was not demonstrative, but he was one of the most obliging of men, ever willing to do any favor that might be asked of him, without any regard to his personal convenience.

Nobody was ever more ready than he to sit up all night with a sick friend or even with a stranger if he thought he could be of any service. . . . He was punctiliously courteous and never failed to return the salutation of even the most humble servants with as much formality as that of his equals. In fact, his politeness was carried to an excess which sometimes made it appear almost ludicrous, but every one that knew him felt that his courtesy was not a mere outside warmth but was that of a true gentleman, coming from his honest heart.

Colston admitted that Jackson did have several personal oddities. He would endure only so much humor at their expense, Colston added. "At one time he fancied that one side of him was wasting away—and to remedy this evil he resorted to the pump [motion] every morning to exercise the arm & leg whose energies he thought were failing. This gave rise to much merriment & fun among his young brother officers, who assailed him with numerous jokes. For a while he stood it patiently, but at last he said to them with that peculiar look & expression . . . that they had gone far enough—and that if any thing more was said on the subject, he would hold the speaker personally responsible. No more jokes were uttered about the pump."[65]

It was important for Jackson to put behind him the emotional experiences of Fort Meade and to start a new life unencumbered by the past. The VMI position offered an opportunity, but it presented a hurdle as well. For the first time in his adult life, Jackson had a hometown in which he had to face—and at least to handle—the many intricacies of civilian society. To date he had only sampled that way of life. Now he was part of it.

Fortunately, Jackson became enamored with Lexington from the beginning. The fondness grew deeper as the months passed. On his arrival there in mid-August 1851, he had told Laura: "Lexington is the most beautiful place that I remember of having ever seen in connexion with the surrounding country." In November, he wrote his sister: "I admire the citizens of this place very much." At the end of his first year at the institute, Jackson was unusually laudatory about his new home. "I have for months back admired Lexington; but now for the first time, have I truly and fully appreciated it. Of all places which have come under my observation in the U. States, this little village is the most beautiful."[66]

One of his favorite pastimes was to explore on horseback or on foot the country he had adopted. Lexington itself is in the James River watershed, but immediately north is the famed Shenandoah Valley, formed by the two easternmost ranges of the Allegheny Mountains. It was one of the most bountiful agricultural regions in the eastern part of the nation. Grain of all kinds, beef cattle, horses, hogs, poultry, apples, and garden crops came in profusion from its farms. Valley communities were small market towns whose slow growth never affected their quaint character.

By the middle of the nineteenth century, the Shenandoah Valley was emerging from being an isolated region of limited commercialism. Yet the process was slow. Jackson found that many of the valley's inhabitants practiced a democracy familiar to his frontier background and quite in contrast to the aristocratic demeanor of eastern Virginia. Settled in the main by proud, individualistic Scotch-Irish and German immigrants, the valley was often called "dissenter territory."[67]

The wealthy were few and so were the poor. A comfortable middle class comprised the overwhelming majority of citizens. Valley towns, one resident stated, "were noted for three things: churches, academies of learning and distilleries. The latter flourished in spite of the former, and among a less sturdy, intelligent and godly race of people, would have led to utter demoralization."[68]

At the southern end of the valley was Rockbridge County. The name came from the great Natural Bridge, whose ninety-three-foot height and 215-foot width makes it one of the wonders of the world. By 1850, Rockbridge County boasted 11,476 whites, 4,196 slaves, and 368 freedmen. In the same 1778 act establishing the county was a provision for a county seat to be founded fourteen miles north of Natural Bridge as a site for regular court sessions. The town was to be called Lexington in honor of the Massachusetts village so conspicuous at the start of the American Revolution.

With the exception of Main Street, the hilly thoroughfares of Lexington were named for distinguished Virginia statesmen: Henry, Jefferson, Nelson, Randolph, and Washington. The community had only 766 citizens in 1840; but thanks in part to the establishment of VMI and the natural growth of businesses and educational institutions such as Washington College, the population in 1850 was 1,105 whites and 638 blacks. Those figures would grow by only 400 in the next decade.

Lexington was always small enough so that everyone knew when a stranger was in town. Roads fanned out from the community in every direction. A stagecoach arrived each day near sundown.[69]

Lexington had its critics. One observer pointed out that in Lexington "there were eight groggeries and court day was no time for a self-respecting woman to be seen on the streets." A visitor looked critically on the large Scotch-Irish element in town. "Their impress was upon everything in the place. The blue limestone streets looked hard. The red brick houses, with severe stone trimmings and plain white pillars and finishings, were stiff and formal. The grim portals of the Presbyterian church looked cold as a dog's nose."[70]

Strong differences of opinion also prevailed among the townspeople. The local newspaper, for example, gave little attention to affairs at VMI during the school's first two decades. The *Gazette* gave a strange editorial explanation. "Like physicians increase sickness; lawyers litigation; merchants, extravagances, &c., so military men increase the chances of war, and the number of wars. We regard schools for their instruction therefore as evils which . . . we hope at some time may be entirely suppressed."[71]

Jackson never wasted time on such negative thoughts. He had found a home, and he sought to enjoy its pleasures whenever and wherever possible. His progress toward that end was always slow and sometimes painful. Being unmarried, at first affiliated with no church, and with but a few acquaintances in town, Jackson had to labor hard to ingratiate himself with Lexington society. He had neither the personality nor the experience to accomplish the task easily.

Despite its small size, Lexington had an unusually large ruling elite of professionals. Giving an intellectual aura to the town was Washington College, which its namesake had helped to endow. The Reverend Dr. George Junkin, learned and generally loved, was its president. He had a charming wife, vivacious daughters Margaret, Elinor, and Julia, plus a number of sons. On the college faculty was Major D. Harvey Hill, who had been Jackson's early benefactor.

The Ann Smith Academy was an excellent finishing school for young ladies. Four unmarried daughters of retired Washington College president George Baxter were local schoolteachers. VMI faculty were included in most social affairs. The paternal and soft-spoken Colonel Smith was a salon favorite. Major Gilham had a scholarly manner, which gave way delightfully to moments of quick wit.

Major John Preston was one of the founders of the institute as well as among Lexington's most influential citizens. Ex-Governor and Mrs. James McDowell and their daughters were social pillars. John Letcher was moving steadily up the political ladder toward the governorship. Dr. William S. White, the Presbyterian minister, gave and received affection in abundance.

Two men became Jackson's confidants in the first, somewhat uncertain months in Lexington. The first was Harvey Hill, a South Carolinian two-and-a-half years older than Jackson. Hill had graduated from West Point the year Jackson entered the academy. He received two brevet promotions in the Mexican War, where he first met Jackson, then left the army to become professor of mathematics at Washington College. Hill's Calvinistic tenets and his patient wife, the former Isabella Morrison, kept his personality generally positive, yet dyspepsia and a spinal ailment sharpened a sarcastic tongue.

Hill could be stubborn; he was always opinionated. In 1851, he was one of three Washington College professors who submitted their resignations over some academic matter. The college accepted two but refused to give Hill his release. Thin, of medium height, with darting eyes and a naturally stern expression, Hill proved to be somewhat unpredictable. That his judgments of men ran to extremes was certainly true in the case of Jackson. Hill greatly admired the Virginian at first, and Jackson called on him often for companionship and advice.[72]

John Blair Lyle was a much more sincere and generous friend. Born in 1807 on the family farm north of Lexington, Lyle attended Washington College and became inseparable friends with John Preston. The two courted the same woman, Sally Caruthers. When Preston won her hand, Lyle left town for a period. He returned and opened a bookstore on the west side of Main Street.

In the years that followed, the "courteous, jolly, and lovable old bachelor" developed his store until it became—in the words of one patron—"a sort of clubhouse in which assembled frequently the professional men of the town, the professors and officers of the College and Institute, and every genteel young man of the community." Lyle's business was an "automatic bookstore" because with the proprietor so much engaged with friends, customers were left to browse alone through the stacks and at departure to deposit money on the counter if they purchased anything.[73]

Lyle was a dedicated member of the Lexington Presbyterian Church: faithful attender, elder, Sunday school teacher, member (and sometimes director) of the choir. He became one of the first Lexingtonians to befriend Jackson, whose initial ventures into local society consisted of enjoyable hours pursuing knowledge and new acquaintances in the bookshop. Lyle would play a leading role in helping Jackson find a religious sanctuary.[74]

To one of his new comrades, Jackson made this statement regarding friendships: "The kind of friends to whom I am most attached are those with whom I feel at home, and to whom I can go at all proper times and informally tell them the object of my call, with the assurance that, if practicable, they will join me in carrying out my plans, whether they are an evening promenade, a musical soiree, or whatever they may be;

and all this, without the marred pleasure resulting from a conviction that afterwards all my conduct must undergo a judicial investigation before 'Judge Etiquette,' and that for every violation of his code, I must be censured, if not socially ostracised."[75]

John G. Gittings was a distant relative as well as a plebe from Jackson's home area. He was disappointed after his first meeting with the major. "Though entertaining, he appeared ill at ease, and this, I noticed afterward, was characteristic of him when conversing in the presence of strangers. . . . He wore side whiskers, and one noting his fair complexion and reserved manner might have mistaken him for an English-man. . . . As I sat in his presence and observed his diffidence, this thought passed through my mind: Can this modest man be the one who fought so bravely in Mexico?"[76]

Modest and shy by nature, Jackson had to work painfully to gain behavioral experience in society. Proper manners had not been an important item in his early years. A learning process began in Mexico. In the spring of 1848, Jackson told Laura that "my studies are not principally directed to the formation of my manners and the rules of society and a more thorough knowledge of human nature. . . . I doubt not but that the former two objects will [be] very important to a mans success in life."[77]

The first years in Lexington were a challenge to Jackson to "better" himself through scrupulous attention to correct behavior in public gatherings. He saw good manners as the means to social acceptance and advancement; and while group behavior at times might clash with private convictions on such matters as health, the major pursued all goals with diligence.

Jackson never became a genuine "society man," his wife stated. "He was so honest and conscientious that he could not indulge in the little meaningless flatteries with which young people are so prone to amuse themselves." The major accepted almost every invitation tendered, but he did so "from a sense of duty than from inclination;" and his attendance had several self-imposed restrictions.[78]

No evening affair interfered with his rigid schedule. If invited to dinner, Jackson had his usual frugal supper beforehand and then consumed only water at the formal meal. He accepted no refreshments, not even the simplest appetizer, after sundown. Convinced that rich foods provoked attacks of dyspepsia, Jackson still adhered to a bland diet. His self-control over food amounted to stoicism. He never used tobacco in any form; he avoided whiskey fanatically because he liked the taste. Jackson once told an astonished hostess: "The moment a grain of black pepper touches my tongue, I lose all strength in my right leg."[79]

The Reverend Dr. Dabney noted: "Amidst the clatter of china and conversation, and the sparkle of wine and ices, the tall form of the Major stood firm; polite, yet constrained; in the gay throng, but not of it." Jackson arrived at a social gathering promptly at the stated hour; and since he retired to bed at 10 P.M. (to prevent drowsiness from triggering dyspepsia), he was always the first to leave a party—and usually when it was just approaching peak enjoyment for everyone else."[80]

There was more. Because of his inherent shyness and reticence, Jackson could never relax at a social function. Always he fell back on military discipline. He was precise, intent, and dutiful from start to end of a gathering. A college student who went to a party expressly to see Lexington's Mexican War hero was stunned at Jackson's demeanor. "There was so little animation, no grace, no enthusiasm. All was stiffness and awkwardness. He sat perfectly erect, his back touching the back of the chair nowhere; the large hands were spread out, one on each knee, while the large feet, sticking out at an exact right angle to the leg (the angle seeming to have been determined with mathematical precision), occupied an unwarranted space. The figure recalled to my boyish mind what I had once seen—a rude Egyptian-carved figure intended to represent one of the Pharaohs."[81]

He spoke in short sentences with a melodious voice that never rose in anger. Yet informal conversation was beyond Jackson. Talking at random was alien to him. He took every word at its literal meaning. A person who used "you know" in casual conversation would be regularly greeted by Jackson with "No, I do not know." One evening a British visitor to Lexington was chatting with Jackson. The subject was history. The Englishman began: "You remember, Major, that at this period Lord Burleigh was Queen Elizabeth's great counselor." Jackson interrupted: "No, I don't remember, for I did not know it."[82]

Honesty was almost an obsession with Jackson. Cadet John Gittings, a distant cousin, recalled the major borrowing the key to the library of one of the local literary societies and promising the secretary to return it within the hour. However, Gittings wrote, "becoming absorbed in his book, he put the key into his pocket and did not think of it again until he reached his boarding-house in the town, nearly a mile away. Then, although a hard storm had sprung up in the meantime, he turned about and marched all the way back through the rain to deliver the key as he had promised, though he knew the library would not be used, and the key would not be needed on that day."[83]

Too often at social functions, Jackson gave the impression that he had come to perform a duty and was determined to do it. However, young Clement Fishburne observed, "he seldom allowed conversation to flag, although he certainly could not be said to be a great talker. He was at least a good listener."[84]

That was especially true in the case of women. Jackson once told Mrs. John H. Moore, "I feel that all ladies are angels." No man, his wife commented, "was more respectful and chivalrous in his bearing towards the gentler sex." A "Southern lady" after meeting Jackson for the first time murmured admiringly: "The expression of his soft eyes was gentle yet commanding, giving you a delightful feeling of the sweetness, purity, and strength of his character. His dress . . . was always in good taste, and faultlessly neat."[85]

At a party, Jackson felt a compulsion to give primary attention to the young lady he thought was the most neglected among the guests. "This became so well known," said his friend and colleague, John Preston, "that to be singled out by Jackson was the mark of a wallflower in other young people's eyes."[86]

His odd ways struck many as an endless series of eccentricities. The Lexington years have traditionally been regarded as the time when Jackson's behavior was the most ambiguous. Generations of writers have gone to lengths to strengthen the legend of "Tom Fool" Jackson at VMI, because popular appeal always surrounds a subject who personifies the adage, "Genius comes wrapped in strange packages."

But Lexington itself played a contributing role. It had two colleges and an unusually high degree of intellectual attainment and culture for a town of its small size. The homogeneity of its society and the same general patterns of life among the residents combined to produce a more unified mindset than normally found in other urban areas. Consequently, a new professor with a hero's reputation instantly became the center of attention in that community devoted largely to education. When his personality and habits did not fit the standard patterns, gossip began. Different conduct soon became extraordinary conduct, which quickly became eccentricities. Seeds of peculiarity, nurtured by anecdotes and exaggerations, grew into myths.

Furthermore, any detailed study of the writings of VMI cadets and Lexington residents will show that many of Jackson's idiosyncrasies were attributed from first impressions. His reputation as a strange professor began in the early Lexington years, not the later ones, just as stories of his oddities as a Civil War commander originated in the first year of the war, not subsequently.

Testimony abounds in substantiation of the admiration that developed for Professor Jackson. Fellow faculty member Raleigh Colston asserted:

At the outset of his academic career he was not popular with the cadets. Fresh from the army and accustomed to command regulars with whom the sternest discipline was a necessity, he could not at once tone down his peremptory manner and abrupt ways; yet though he excited the dislike of some who did not look beneath the surface, I never knew one who did not entertain a deep respect for the honesty of his intention. . . . After he became more accustomed to his duties & appreciated better the material upon which he had to work, he abated much of the abruptness & rigidity of his intercourse with the Cadets.[87]

Cadet James H. Lane was one of Jackson's first students. He found the professor "wonderfully eccentric," but he quickly added, "Jackson soon impressed the cadets as being a man of great bravery, conscientious and fearless in the discharge of every duty, strictly honest and just in his intentions." James T. Murfee, who graduated from VMI a year ahead of Lane, viewed Jackson more philosophically. "We respected [his] fidelity and moral courage . . . but as boys we were not able to comprehend the military genius that was within him. . . . Not only did we not understand him, but I think that no one at that time understood him; for genius is incomprehensible until displayed in action."[88]

James L. Hubard was another cadet who saw through the strange exterior of the physics professor and artillery drillmaster. Jackson, Hubard observed, "knew perhaps as well as any man how to wear the dignity and reserve of a Teacher, but when off duty he was always the familiar friend of his old pupils, and accessible to them all. He ranked high with all of us at the Institute, particularly for firmness and strength of character, and there was a universal feeling amongst us, that if 'Old Hickory' . . . undertook to do anything, nothing under the sun could stop him."[89]

Similar sentiments to an even greater degree materialized in Lexington circles. "He was voted eccentric in our little professional society," Margaret Preston said of Jackson. "It was only when we came to know him with the intimacy of hourly converse that we found that much that passed under the name of eccentricity was the result of the deepest underlying principle, and compelled a respect which we dared not withhold." Maggie's husband, John Preston, was more succinct but just as emphatic. Jackson "was the object of pleasant jests for singularities and peculiarities, but the confidence in his integrity, force of character, and soundness of mind was universal."[90]

6

GOD AND "DEAREST ELLIE"

A S SOON AS JACKSON SETTLED into the physical environs of
Lexington, he turned his military precision to a search for a religious home.
From the time of his baptism two years earlier, he had participated actively in
the Episcopal church until he was transferred to Florida. He was now twenty-seven
and in a settled life. It was time to ally himself formally with God through church
membership.

Lexington in 1851 boasted five churches in close proximity to one another. In the
square block bounded by Randolph, Nelson, and Main Streets were the sanctuaries of
Lexington Presbyterian (established in 1797), Randolph Street Methodist (1816), and
Lexington Baptist (1841). On the southern edge of the Washington College campus
was Grace Episcopal (1840). A schismatic group of Methodists had been meeting in
the county courthouse since 1847; in 1853, these believers would move into their own
building. A small frame church for blacks stood on the outskirts of town near the
North River.[1]

Grace Church doubtless attracted Jackson first. Colonel Smith had been instrumental in its founding. The majority of its communicants were VMI faculty, adminis-
trators, and cadets. The church was then without a rector. By no coincidence, the
"supply preacher," the Reverend Lewis P. Clover, was also unofficial chaplain at the
institute. Jackson attended one or more services there during his first weeks in
Lexington, but he also followed a pattern and made the rounds of all local churches.[2]

Several persuasions began to draw Jackson to the Presbyterian faith. It was the
oldest, largest, and most influential church in Rockbridge County. The Lexington
congregation numbered 250 worshipers from every walk of life, including two doctors
of divinity and five Presbyterian ministers, "only two of whom had any stated professional engagement." Townspeople occupied the main floor pews; cadets and Washington College students sat in the balcony.[3]

The shepherd of this huge flock was fifty-one-year-old William Spottswood White.
Born in Hanover County, Virginia, White had graduated from Hampden-Sydney
College and Virginia's Union Theological Seminary. He held a D.D. degree from
Princeton. White had served two years as chaplain at the University of Virginia prior
to his 1848 appointment as pastor of Lexington Presbyterian. His influence in church
circles was such that he already served on Washington College's Board of Visitors.

White's intellectual credentials were solid, yet he was best known as "a devout and
earnest man of God, whose kindness and affability made him very winning to the
young and to strangers." Of medium height and size, with long graying hair swept

over a round head and large eyes always expressive, White presided over a family of
five sons and three daughters. Overwork continued to impair his health and doubtless
contributed to a slight limp.[4]

Congenial bookseller and churchman John B. Lyle first aroused Jackson's interest
in the Presbyterian denomination. The major knew little of its tenets, but he was
willing to learn. He began conversing with Lyle, who, it was said, "could speak to
anyone on personal religion in a way so affable and gentle as never to give offence, and
yet so pointed as to learn just what he wanted to know."[5]

Jackson pursued the subject further with his confidants, Harvey and Isabella Hill.
She was a Presbyterian minister's daughter, and Hill was a man of strong Calvinist
beliefs. One afternoon Hill read Jackson some statements from the *Shorter Catechism*
of Presbyterianism. Jackson borrowed the small volume, kept it a week, and returned
it with a whetted appetite. Hill then lent him the larger Confession of Faith. Jackson
read it carefully and compared its statements with biblical teachings. According to
Hill, Jackson "professed himself pleased with everything except predestination and
infant baptism. His scruples about the latter did not last long . . . but his repugnance
to predestination was long and determined."[6]

The next step was to start attending services at the church. Jackson later confessed
that "the simplicity of the Presbyterian form of worshipping and the preaching of her
well-educated ministry impressed him most favorably." What Jackson especially liked
in the Presbyterian service was its plainness and democratic overtones. Dignity prevailed only in the ritual. By mid-autumn, Jackson was ready to begin conversations
with Dr. White. John Lyle made the proper introductions.[7]

White was a wise and patient man, accustomed to groping questions from the
insufficiently informed. He was not prepared for the earnestness and pressing seriousness with which Jackson pursued every facet of Presbyterianism. The major "strongly
objected" to some beliefs, White declared, and he stated "with the utmost clearness
and frankness"—to White as well as to prominent laymen in Lexington—how he felt
about other tenets. Jackson voiced his inquiries "honestly, persistently and prayerfully," White noted.[8]

When the pastor succeeded in convincing Jackson that a good Presbyterian did not
have to give blind allegiance to all church doctrine, the major was content. He was
ready to be admitted to the faith. On November 22, 1851, three applicants—Jackson,
Edward Leyburn, and Theodore Perry—were each examined and accepted to full
membership in Lexington Presbyterian.[9]

With church affiliation, Jackson underwent an instant and remarkable change. No
other single event in his life equaled the impact on mind, soul, and action as did the
acceptance of God through Presbyterianism. Indeed, Jackson did not accept this
religion: he absorbed it—hungrily, constantly, totally. Harvey Hill, an extraordinary
believer himself, stated of Jackson: "The striking characteristic of his mind [became]
his profound reverence for divine . . . authority. I never knew any one whose reverence for Deity was so all pervading, and who felt so completely his entire dependence
upon God." Colonel Smith added that Jackson's new faith was "as simple as a child's
in taking the word of God as his guide, and unhesitatingly accepting all therein
revealed."[10]

If a letter attributed to Jackson can be accepted as authentic, an imaginative sentiment lay beneath the stern and humorless exterior. Writing once to a friend, Jackson supposedly stated:

I love to stroll abroad after the labours of the day are over, and indulge feelings of gratitude to God for all the sources of natural beauty with which He has adorned the earth. Some time since, my morning walks were rendered very delightful by the singing of the birds. The morning caroling of the birds, and their notes in the evening, awaken in me devotional feelings of praise and gratitude, though very different in their nature. In the morning all animated nature (man excepted) appears to join in active expressions of gratitude to God; in the evening, all is hushing into silent slumber, and thus disposes the mind to meditation.[11]

Presbyterian doctrine in the antebellum South stressed personal salvation and individual morality. The faithful viewed efforts to improve society, to join in national causes, and the like as outside the purview of church members because such activity challenged God's preordained conceptions of earthly existence. Beginning in the autumn of 1851, Jackson's primary desire in life was twofold: he wanted to love God fully, and he wanted God to love him in return. The first resolution Jackson made regarding these goals was never to "violate the known will of God." He kept his word—at times to the discomfort of members of the congregation. Jackson's practice of faith became so intense that even some of the most devout seemed in comparison to be weak Christians.

One of his first purchases after the open profession of faith was a copy of the New Testament. It became the family Bible, replete with birth and death dates. Jackson read the volume daily and underlined a number of passages. Two appear to have become his favorites. He found consolation for personal tragedies in Revelation 21:4: "And God shall wipe away all tears from their eyes; and there shall be no more death, neither sorrow, nor crying, neither shall there be any more pain: for the former things are passed away." However, the verse that most inspired him was Romans 8:28: "And we know that all things work together for good to them that love God, to them who are the called according to *his* purpose."[12]

To obtain the Almighty's favor, Jackson altered many aspects of his behavior. He felt it a duty to adopt a strict code of moral conduct in order to live his religion every waking hour of the day. A starting point was systematic reading of the Bible and religious books. He took a pledge (unnecessary though it was) not to drink, smoke, or gamble.

Commensurate with church membership, he adopted the ancient Hebrew practice of tithing. He contributed 10 percent of his income to the church every remaining year of his life. Jackson gave up dancing, theatergoing, and all amusements that he felt might distract his thoughts from holy things. If a person asked him about the good or evil of a certain indulgence, Jackson would usually smile and reply, "Well, I know it is not wrong not to do it, so I'm going to be on the safe side."[13]

He also relied on a number of printed guides for devout behavior. George Winfred Hervey's *The Principles of Courtesy*, written "to illustrate and enforce the duty of Christian courtesy," appeared in print just after Jackson's conversion. It became one of the most consulted books in his small library. Jackson pored through the endless series of dos-and-don'ts; he underlined scores of one-sentence pronouncements. Yet a passage on the Sabbath got his complete attention: "It is especially for the benefit of weary enslaved souls that this day is ordained to be hallowed. If we examine Isaiah's exposition of this command, we shall find it requires us to abstain from every thought, word, and action which affords gratification to a worldly mind."[14]

Amen! Jackson concluded. Since the fourth commandment instructed Christians to "remember that thou keep holy the Sabbath-day," and since Hervey reinforced that directive, Jackson obeyed it beyond reproach. Henceforth, he would not read a newspaper or discuss secular matters on Sunday. He would not mail a letter late in the week if he thought it might still be in transit on the Lord's Day. That entire day belonged to God, and Jackson regarded it as such both in church and in private meditation.

The Presbyterian church became his home, his fortress, his refuge. Dr. White (like all ministers for Jackson) was the intermediary with the Heavenly Father; White could greatly strengthen Jackson in doing God's will. Jackson consulted with his pastor often and regularly. He looked on White as a father. On the other hand, and by then thoroughly imbued with military protocol, Jackson regarded White as a superior officer in the great campaign for salvation. It took White awhile to become accustomed to Jackson's constant reports to him of religious activities and theological views. White also learned that any request he made to Jackson was treated as an official order.

In time, all preachers of the gospel received attention if not allegiance from Jackson. The major had been a Presbyterian only a few weeks when he met the Reverend B. Tucker Lacy, who was five years older than Jackson, a graduate of Washington College, and then pastor of a church forty miles south of Lexington. Lacy gave a sermon on the value of missionary work in the mountainous southwestern region of the state. Jackson lingered after the service in order to meet Lacy. Dr. White introduced them, and Jackson came straight to the point. "Sir, the cause you presented has interested me much. It is a worthy and noble cause, and as you may fail to meet me tomorrow, I wish to hand you my contribution today." Jackson thereupon presented Lacy with a check for fifty dollars; he wished he could give more, Jackson added, but he expected to make annual donations to the program. The new convert proved as good as his word. Each time they met thereafter, Lacy stated, it was always "with great cordiality and constant reference to the state of religion in southwestern Virginia."[15]

He came to treat clergymen with reverence in great part because he had an underlying wish to be one of them. Several times in the years thereafter, Jackson commented that if he had possessed a more appropriate education and greater gifts as a speaker, he would have entered the ministry. He once told an aunt: "The subject of becoming a herald of the cross has often seriously engaged my attention, and I regard it as the most noble of all professions. It was the profession of our divine Redeemer, and I should not be surprised were I to die upon a foreign field, clad in ministerial armor, fighting under the banner of Jesus. What could be more glorious? But my conviction is that I am doing good here, and that for the present I am where God would have me be."[16]

Jackson's faith, Dr. White noted, "not only made him brave, but gave form, order, direction and power to his whole life." Once Jackson concluded that God did indeed love him, that belief became central to every part of his existence. He reaffirmed that love with constant prayer. A cadet who came to know Jackson well concluded, "He laid every plan, purpose, and desire before his Great Master, implored his direction, and when assured what the will of God was, he never deviated one hair's breadth from the path of duty."[17]

Countless times each day, Jackson looked upward in thanksgiving and for guidance. He prayed for major hopes and minor wishes. A few years after joining the church, Jackson told his sister-in-law: "I have so fixed the habit in my own mind that I never raise a glass of water to my lips without a moment's asking of God's blessing. I never seal a letter without putting a word of prayer under the seal. I never take a letter from the post without a brief sending of my thoughts heavenward. I never change my classes in the section room without a minute's petition on the cadets who go out and those who come in."

"And don't you sometimes forget to do this?" the sister-in-law asked.

"I think I scarcely can say that I do," Jackson responded. "The habit has become as fixed almost as breathing."[18]

Praying silently came easily and in time naturally to Jackson. Offering prayers in public, on the other hand, was a traumatic ordeal that required practice and supreme determination.

Lexington Presbyterian normally held two services on Sunday and a Tuesday evening prayer meeting. One Sunday shortly after Jackson joined the church, Dr. White admonished the congregation for not attending prayer services with more regularity. Further, White underscored in his sermon, every good Presbyterian male should offer prayer at such meetings. Jackson quickly sought out his friend John Preston, one of the church elders. Was the pastor sincere in such a statement? Preston assured him that Dr. White always meant what he said. Jackson immediately took White's admonition as a personal, direct order. He hastened to the manse to discuss the matter further.

White listened as the major explained his predicament. Lacking any experience in public speaking, Jackson was afraid that his efforts at praying openly would fall short of success. Then looking earnestly at White, Jackson declared: "If you, as my pastor, think it is my duty, call on me whenever you think proper. My personal comfort is not to be consulted in the matter."[19]

The minister assured Jackson that the effort was what mattered. Yet White waited a couple of weeks to give his new church member adequate time to prepare. Accordingly, one Tuesday evening White called on Jackson to pray. The major arose, lips pressed together and presenting an expression of stern intensity. Jackson shut his eyes tightly and began speaking. Yet his voice was so halting, his manner so diffident, that words and sentences tumbled forth in utter confusion. The harder he tried, the worse it became. The total effort, Preston recalled, "was painful to all hearers."[20]

Jackson dutifully attended subsequent prayer meetings. White did not ask him to participate. One day Jackson met his pastor on the street. "Are you trying to save me pain?" he asked. The minister replied as tactfully as he could. "My comfort or discomfort is not the question," Jackson stated forcefully. "If it is my duty to lead in prayer, then I must persevere in it until I learn to do it aright; and I wish you to discard all consideration for my feelings." When next White looked to the major for prayer, Jackson performed surprisingly well. He improved steadily with each opportunity. White was joyful that Jackson "soon attained to a leadership of utterance in prayer which made his participation in our services eminently acceptable and useful." John Preston agreed. "Ultimately his prayers were exceedingly edifying, his tones most supplicatory, in perfect contrast with his curt manner of speech." Jackson's spontaneous prayers became fluent and moving.[21]

"The name of fanatic will probably stick to Jackson," his sister-in-law correctly predicted, "but a fanatic, a visionary, an enthusiast he was not." Jackson never attempted to force his views of God on others. Nor did he offer rules to society for the good life. He acted his faith but kept his beliefs to himself. "His fanaticism," said Margaret Preston, "consisted in the intensity of his own religious convictions." Given the nature of nineteenth-century Protestantism, a good case can be made that Jackson was simply "a mainstream southern evangelical."[22]

One clear refutation of the claim that Jackson was a religious fanatic could always be found in his demeanor at church services. At Lexington Presbyterian Church, two aisles led into the sanctuary from the vestibule. Jackson habitually sat on the left-hand side of the left aisle, near the wall adjacent to Nelson Street. He occupied the same seat, and he slept during every service.

Jackson attributed the drowsiness to weakness caused by dyspepsia. That is open to question; what is not is his inability to stay awake regardless of how moving the service was. He might hear Dr. White's opening sentences, "but after that all was lost."[23] His sitting posture consisted of two 90-degree angles on the front edge of the pew (which was conspicuous in itself), and his head early in the sermon simply fell on his chest. Fellow worshipers whispered to him, poked or nudged him, all to no avail. One incensed matron jabbed him with a hat pin. Jackson never moved.

Nobody was more embarrassed by the sleeping than Jackson. A friend once discussed the matter with him. "If you can't help it, pray don't sit bolt upright and nod, for it attracts all the more attention." Back came the reply: "I will do nothing to superinduce sleep by putting myself at ease, or making myself more comfortable; but if in spite of my resistance I yield to my infirmity, then I accept as punishment the mortification I feel, because I deserve it."[24]

A popular story that circulated in Lexington for years concerned a noted hypnotist who came to town. Faculty from both Washington College and VMI received invitations to the lecture. Townspeople packed the auditorium. At one point, the mesmerist called for a volunteer on whom he could demonstrate the wonders of hypnotic unconsciousness. Jackson stepped onto the stage.

The lecturer began his procedure. Yet no matter how arduously he tried, he could not get inside his subject. Jackson stared unblinkingly at the hypnotist and showed no reaction. The audience began to snicker. One of the McDowell girls then spoke loudly: "No one can put Major Jackson to sleep but the Reverend Doctor White!" The hall exploded in laughter.[25]

It is regrettable that any correspondence Jackson had with his sister during his gravitation to Presbyterianism is lost. At that time, Jackson opened his soul only to Laura Arnold. She alone would have known the intensity of his feelings. Laura, who had been Jackson's spiritual guide during the West Point period, had for some reason undergone a radical change. As mentioned earlier, she was abandoning her faith. In contrast, Jackson had found his God. He now had both an exhilarating sense of strength and the usual zeal found in a recent convert. To spread God's word, Jackson determined to begin with Laura's backsliding.

His early attempts were overkills. Only two months after joining the church, Jackson wrote Laura what amounted to a weighty sermon.

The best plan that I can conceive for an unbeliever in *God*, as presented to us in the Bible, is to first consider things with reference merely to expediency. Now considering the subject with reference to expediency only, let us examine whether it is safer to be a Christian or an infidel. Suppose the two persons, one a Christian, and the other an infidel, to be closing their earthly existence. And suppose that the infidel is right, and the Christian is wrong; they will then after death be upon an equality. But instead of the infidel being right, suppose him to be wrong, and the Christian right; then will the state of the latter after death be inestimably superior to that of the other. And if you will examine the history of mankind, it will be plain that Christianity contributes much more to happiness in this life than that of infidelity. Now having briefly glanced at this subject, to what decision are we forced on the mere ground of expediency; certainly it is the adoption of Christianity; the next point is to consider whether we can believe the teachings of the *sacred* volume; if so, then its adoption should of necessity follow. I have examined the subject maturely, and the evidence is very conclusive; and if we do not receive the Bible as being authentic and credible, we must reject every other ancient work, as there is no other in favor of which so much evidence can be adduced.[26]

One can hardly imagine the sister being constructively affected by such a discourse. Yet Laura surely reflected on thoughts sent to her a month later by her brother. "We are all children of suffering and sorrow in this world. . . . Amid affliction let us hope for happiness. . . . However dark the night, I am cheered with an anticipated glorious and luminous morrow. . . . No earthly calamity can shake my hope in the future so long as God is my friend."[27]

Almost every letter to Laura thereafter would contain a combination of instructions and entreaties for the path of righteousness. Jackson was just starting to build momentum on behalf of the Lord's work. That was only one outlet for Jackson's newly acquired faith. Harvey Hill was superintendent of Sunday school at the Presbyterian church. Whether Hill asked or Jackson volunteered is unknown, but on February 1, 1852, Jackson began teaching one of the Sunday school classes.[28]

Meanwhile, his first year at VMI proceeded well enough so that on February 20, 1852, Jackson officially resigned from the U.S. Army. At the same time, he requested a court of inquiry to investigate fully the whole affair in Florida with Major French. Jackson wanted to leave the army "with an unblemished character." No such court ever convened.[29]

Although health was always a concern to Jackson, for the most part it remained good during this period. In February 1852, he reported a "delicate" condition owing largely to cold weather. By mid-May he could inform Laura: "Though my manner of living is very abstemious, yet health has not returned with all its blessing. However, I am much better than when I last bid you good-bye." He attributed much of his improved condition to daily walks of five or six miles. Two weeks later, with spring in the air, Jackson was upbeat about his condition. "I am enjoying myself more than I have done for some years, but still my health requires much care and rigid regard to diet."[30]

Jackson's inquisitive mind was active and, to some of his colleagues, amusing. French professor Colston recalled:

When he joined our Faculty, his acquirements were limited almost entirely to the scientific training he had received at West Point—to which he had added professional experience and a knowledge of Spanish. . . . He sought to extend his knowledge by conversation upon subjects in which he felt himself deficient & which he would sometimes introduce at the most unexpected time and place. I well remember his suddenly asking me once as we were walking from the Institute to town, 'What is poetry?' and desiring a full discussion of the subject to utilize the few minutes of our walk.[31]

In that first year at VMI, Jackson was president of one student court-martial and member of another. Neither of the convicted cadets remained in school. Young James Lane noted that Jackson "made but few reports against cadets, but when he did make them, he made them 'stick.'" Once Jackson turned in a cadet with the notation: "Tobacco . . . saw him spit."[32]

On rare occasions, Jackson could display a fiery temper. The first known instance came when he reported a cadet for drunkenness. With expulsion facing him, the young man came in a rage to see Jackson. "You would not have reported me," the cadet shouted, "if your faculty position did not shelter you from personal consequences."

Jackson leaped to his feet; with cheeks red and eyes blazing, he exclaimed: "I'll fight you, sir, if you think so! I'll fight you, sir!" Instantly he remembered who he was. In a calm voice he declared: "No, sir, I can't fight you. I am a professor and you are a cadet. I can't fight you even if you are dismissed. I won't do it, sir!"

A "transient gleam" in Jackson's eyes, and the stern expression on his face, convinced the cadet that "it would not be safe to try him too far, and he was glad enough to drop the matter."[33]

The most famous confrontation Jackson ever had at VMI occurred in the spring of 1852 in his class. At issue was the proper method for solving a problem. The defendant was hot-tempered and argumentative Cadet James A. Walker, who was a senior due to graduate in two months.

One morning late in April, Jackson sent Walker to the blackboard to perform daily recitation. Walker wrote out the problem. Jackson, dissatisfied with the steps to the answer, interrupted Walker and told him to return to his seat. In a rude tone, Walker challenged Jackson on the correct answer. The major ignored the outburst and ordered another cadet to go to the blackboard.

As the second cadet worked, Jackson looked over his papers and discovered that Walker had been using an edition of the textbook that employed a different procedure for solving the problem in question. The professor sent Walker back to the board; but as Walker repeated the previous day's work, Jackson began explaining the correct sequence. Walker objected to the interruptions, and after class he sought to continue the debate. Jackson refused to do so.

The next morning, Jackson again called on Walker to go to the board and solve the problem. Walker muttered that he did not know how to work it. When Jackson observed that he had demonstrated the correct steps to Walker the previous day, the cadet snapped that Jackson had failed to make himself understood. The professor termed that answer improper. Walker, now uncontrollably angry, began shouting at Jackson. When he refused to obey Jackson's directive to sit down and be quiet, the major had no choice but to place him under arrest.

At 9 A.M. on May 2, the court-martial began. Major John Preston was president of the court, with Major Gilham and Cadet Marcellus P. Christian as the other judges. Testimony ran to more than sixty pages. Walker's sole defense was an accusation of prejudice on Jackson's part. The cadet was found guilty on all charges and ordered expelled from the institute.[34]

Walker immediately challenged Jackson to a duel. In an accompanying note, he swore that if "the professor failed to give him satisfaction in that way, he would kill him on sight." Walker even specified the time of day and the place where the assault would take place.

Jackson sought out his friend, Harvey Hill, and discussed the propriety of getting a restraining order against Walker. Hill opposed such an action; nevertheless, Jackson went to the courthouse and tried to secure a peace warrant. All of Lexington was so alarmed at Walker's threat, however, that (according to Hill) the magistrate would not deliver the order.

The more plausible story is that Hill urged Jackson to seek civil protection but Jackson refused. Such a move implied that he cowered under the threat of an angry youth. "I will not do it," he told Hill, "for it would be false. I do not fear him. I fear no man."[35]

Superintendent Smith thereupon obtained a restraining order. The colonel also wrote Walker's father: "I would advise you to come up and take him home as I have reason to believe he may involve himself in serious difficulty." Walker left VMI and returned to his home in nearby Augusta County.[36]

A more damaging and lasting disagreement took place at this time between Jackson and his superior, Colonel Smith. At artillery drill one afternoon, cadets had committed the popular prank of pulling the linchpins from one of the cannon. The gun had gone bounding off in three different directions, to the shouts and laughter of the students. Smith, walking across the parade ground at the moment, saw the incident. He instructed Jackson to hold cadet officers responsible and to report them for allowing disorder. When the drill ended, Jackson went to his quarters and wrote Smith a note requesting that the superintendent "put his severe reprimand in writing."[37]

For a considerable period thereafter, Jackson evinced a sharp coolness toward Smith. He would have nothing to do with the colonel outside official boundaries. Professors were required to submit weekly reports to the superintendent at 4 P.M. each Friday. Jackson would arrive early in front of Smith's office. Regardless of the weather, he would march back and forth until the clock struck four. Then, with military precision, Jackson entered the office, saluted, placed his report on the table, saluted again, and left the room without uttering a word. Only Smith's tolerance and patience kept such behavior from becoming a crisis.[38]

One complaint against Jackson appeared near the end of the school year. On June 16, 1852, the father of Cadet Charles T. Mason voiced a protest with Colonel Smith.

The son had "expressed more apprehension from Maj. Jackson's rigid aversion towards him in his recitations than any one else. . . . He has concluded by attributing his fears upon Natural Philosophy to his own defects and apprehensions as much as to the harshness of Professor J————."[39]

Smith defended his new faculty member. "The Major," he wrote Mason, "has charge of the most difficult department in the class but he carries the regulations into operation with the most punctilious care. . . . When he is better known to the classes he will be better liked, for they will discover that the highest toned principles actuate him."[40]

Jackson had been looking forward eagerly to summer vacation. When the three-month recess began in July, he wasted no time in taking advantage of it. On July 11, he checked into a crowded Rockbridge Alum Springs resort. Room and board was ten dollars weekly; his reservation called for a three-week stay. The spa was designed for 300 people, but 500 visitors were on hand. Such crowding did not bother Jackson.

"I arrived," he informed Laura, "in as good health as usual, and am delighted with the waters so far. . . . I succeeded in procuring half a bed. . . . This water I consider is the water of waters. . . . My appetite and digestion have already improved, and I indulge rather freely. My dinner was principally bread, which was rather fresh, potatoes and green corn, which is by no means digestible; my supper rich corn bread, and the same for breakfast, using butter freely at every meal." Jackson was convinced that his health began a steady improvement less than twenty-four hours after his arrival at Rockbridge Alum.[41]

From the spa, Jackson traveled to Beverly to visit his sister and her family. Brother and sister had an affectionate reunion. By then, they bore a striking resemblance to one another. Laura had Jackson's high forehead, large Indian nose, and wide, thin mouth. Her eyes were as round as her gaze was piercing. Laura wore her hair parted in the middle and pinned tightly on the sides. A look of determination was her natural expression.

At Jackson's request, the two of them journeyed farther west to visit family and partake of the waters of at least one spa. At Parkersburg, they spent time with the Alfred Neales and other family members. During a short visit at nearby Mineral Springs, Jackson and Laura met several Weston friends, including Major Minter Bailey. Brother and sister returned to Beverly via a short stopover in Weston. No record exists that the two visited Jackson's Mill.

Back at Laura's home, Jackson continued his crusade to restore Laura firmly to the Christian fold. He must have been at least temporarily successful because a missionary zeal thereupon struck the major. Jackson became "grieved to find that infidelity prevailed" among so many Beverly-area citizens. "I was anxious to do something to remedy this evil," Jackson proclaimed.[42]

He conducted a number of one-on-one conversations, and he distributed a quantity of tracts. Something larger was needed. With some trepidation, Jackson offered a series of lectures on "Evidences of Christianity." Speaking to an alien audience was one of the greatest trials he ever faced, Jackson subsequently told Dr. White, but "my success greatly exceeded my expectations."[43]

Upon his return to Lexington, Jackson sought out his pastor: he wanted to organize a Sunday school class of young boys. White gave enthusiastic approval to the idea, and the class soon came into being. Over the years, Jackson taught God's blessings to many of Lexington's youth—an unusually large number of whom later served under him in the army.[44]

Jackson had new living quarters for the 1852–53 session at VMI. Renovations to the barracks were finished. The major moved into a tower room on the fourth floor. His roommate for the year was Lieutenant Thomas A. Harris. An 1851 VMI graduate, Harris served a brief time as a subprofessor at the institute before pursuing a career in medicine.[45]

The long visit with Laura had strengthened ties between the two. Jackson's letters increased in frequency. For the first time, Jackson spoke romantically of a specific individual. His summer trip through western Virginia brought him into contact for the first time with a distant cousin. Little is known of Harriet Murdock, who lived in Parkersburg, but Jackson's thoughts dwelled on her long after his return to Lexington. "She is a lovely lady," he confided to Laura, "and if she were not my cousin, I might cordially desire her to be my wife."[46]

Six weeks later, Jackson stated: "Cousin Harriet I regard as being one of the sweetest ladies with whom I have ever met. I wish we could be together frequently. I hope that she will make a visit next summer to this most beautiful of all places." Jackson sent at least two letters to Miss Murdock. She did not respond. When he learned a year later that the lady was engaged to be married, Jackson did not mention her again.[47]

Good health attended Jackson that autumn. He weighed 172 pounds, "six more pounds than any former weight," he boasted. "I hope that through the blessings of *God* I will ultimately enjoy perfect health." Toward that end, and to combat "nervousness" and cold feet, Jackson later reported: "My dishes are very plain; generally brown bread is the principal article for breakfast and tea; and sometimes I probably do not taste meat for more than a month; and I have not to my recollection used any other drink than cold water since my return home."[48]

On October 9, Jackson happily wrote Laura that he had purchased several bushels of apples and peaches. This was not an odd statement. Although he rigidly maintained an ascetic diet, he coveted and enjoyed any kind of fruit. Jackson relished everything from pears and plums to lemons and persimmons. In time, myths would arise about his so-called preference for lemons. He rarely ate them. Peaches were his favorite fruit, with strawberries and cherries not far behind in preference.[49]

Later that month, Jackson acquired another outlet for expressions of his faith. The Rockbridge County Bible Society held an organizational meeting at the Presbyterian church. Jackson was among the first enlistees, and he became one of thirteen members of the Board of Managers. He rarely missed a monthly meeting. Over the ensuing six-and-a-half years, Jackson contributed $79.50 to the society's work.[50]

The major gave more than money to the organization. He once received a list of people from whom he was to solicit funds for the society. He returned with an unexpectedly large sum of money, and his list contained many names added in pencil at the bottom. Society officials asked Jackson who those unfamiliar persons were. Jackson replied characteristically: "They are the militia. As the Bible Society is not a

Presbyterian but a Christian cause, I deemed it best to go beyond the limits of our own church." Most of the contributors whose names he had added were black freedmen in the community.[51]

With Jackson's faith slowly becoming all consuming and expressing itself through a number of channels, he became better acquainted with the Reverend Dr. George Junkin. The president of Washington College was an old-school conservative Presbyterian, energetic and indefatigable, with a commanding presence that stood him well in the pulpit and in various crusades. Junkin willingly offered the hand of friendship to Jackson, who accepted it eagerly. The two men talked often about life in general and theology in particular.

In late autumn 1852, Jackson's visits to the campus home of the Junkins started becoming more frequent. Dr. Junkin stimulated Jackson's religious and intellectual thinking, but the family offered attractions, too. Mrs. Julia Miller Junkin, a product of Philadelphia high society, was a model of quiet grace and charm. She struck Jackson as an ideal mother. That she had to be; for in addition to Dr. and Mrs. Junkin, three to five children plus two nephews were residents on a regular basis. This was Jackson's introduction to the atmosphere of a large family. It was novel and gay; it was wonderful.

The oldest and most talented of the Junkin daughters was Margaret. Four years older than Jackson, she was redheaded and shy, accomplished at poetry and essays, introspective but intense in her thinking. "Maggie" also shared an inseparable relationship with her sister Elinor. This second daughter, born March 6, 1825, was prettier, more self-assured, and possessed of a stronger faith than her sister.

Some acquaintances thought "Ellie" to be the older of the two; others concluded that Maggie overshadowed her younger sibling. Actually, the two complemented one another comfortably. They were childhood roommates who dressed alike, rode horseback regularly, performed chores side by side, and socialized together. Both had gentleman callers, but neither to date had displayed much interest in marriage.

Maggie was fiercely protective of Ellie for a reason other than the fact that she was older. In 1830, at the age of five, Ellie suffered a disfiguring injury. She was holding straw for her brother George to cut with an axe. Young George swung, the instrument slipped, and the blade severed portions of two fingers from Ellie's right hand. A self-consciousness over the maimed fingers lived with Ellie thereafter. Yet she had a vivaciousness that people found engaging.[52]

Jackson met Ellie shortly after his arrival in Lexington. Undoubtedly, he was struck by her natural beauty: chestnut hair parted in the middle and combed tightly on the sides in the fashion of the day, girlish complexion, bright and expressive eyes, and lips that smiled easily. They became closer friends in February 1852, when each began teaching Sunday school at the church. They shared biblical passages and thoughts about religion and were mutually convinced that they were children of God.[53]

When Jackson first came courting Ellie, the Junkins were a little surprised. Ellie had received callers in the past, but none so stiff, serious, and formal as the professor. It took awhile for most of the family to adjust to him. Jackson did little to push his own cause with the Junkins. For many months, the family knew nothing of his distinguished career in the Mexican War.[54]

One evening, Jackson went to see his confidants, the Hills. The Washington College mathematician expected the usual conversation from Jackson about religion or academics. Instead, Jackson kept bringing up the subject of Miss Ellie Junkin. "I don't know what has changed me," he finally said in a perplexed manner. "I used to think her plain, but her face now seems to me all sweetness." Harvey Hill burst out laughing. "You are in love! That's what's the matter!" Jackson, unfamiliar with the emotion of romantic love, blushed deeply. He subsequently gave the matter serious thought. Once he had concluded that he indeed must be in love, he pursued Ellie with matrimony in mind. Mrs. Isabella Hill, who reveled in playing the role of local matchmaker, encouraged Ellie and Jackson at every turn.[55]

By the first weeks of 1853, a Junkin cousin reported that "Elinor is in love with Major Jackson . . . and Margaret wont let him come to the house as she is afraid Elinor will marry him and go away." As love blossomed between Jackson and Ellie, dislike for Jackson grew with Maggie. Even after the couple announced their engagement, Maggie was unreconciled.[56]

Suddenly, to Jackson's chagrin, Ellie broke the engagement. In all likelihood, the younger sister could not cope with Maggie's persistent opposition to both Jackson and a wedding. Ellie made the announcement to Jackson one evening. At midnight, he awakened the Hills and begged Isabella to visit Ellie at once in an attempt to repair the situation.

Mrs. Hill went to see Ellie the following day, but the rift continued. Harvey Hill wrote of his professorial friend: "I don't think I ever saw any one suffer as much as he did during the two or three months of estrangement. He was excessively miserable, and said to me one day: 'I think it probable that I shall become a missionary and die in a foreign land.'"[57]

As usual now in times of despair, Jackson sought solace in the church. He looked to Dr. White for guidance. One day, the pastor observed that "in our country the man who can speak multiplies himself by five." Jackson took that thought immediately to heart. He determined to become proficient at public speaking, no matter how difficult it might be.

The best forum for that new aspiration was the remarkable Franklin Literary Society. Chartered in 1816 and one of the oldest social groups in Lexington, it met in a building at the corner of Jefferson and Nelson Streets almost every Saturday evening. Local businessmen and institutional faculties traditionally composed its leadership. Public debates over popular issues filled the agenda. The audience was always large and usually vocal. On March 19, 1853, Jackson gained election to membership. He rarely missed a meeting during the next six years.

His first efforts at participating in a discussion were pitiful, Raleigh Colston observed. "It was with difficulty that he found words to express his ideas, and more than once he broke down before the end of his speech. His delivery was indistinct and his gestures ungraceful; but he persevered in the face of difficulties. . . . He spoke frequently for he was determined to learn to speak. . . . By degrees he improved in his style and expression, his manner becoming more pleasing and even his gestures less awkward."[58]

Ellie soon discovered that her love for Jackson was greater than her concern for

Maggie's feelings. At springtime, the couple resumed their engagement, yet they did so in secret. Ellie wanted no one but her immediate family to be aware of the contemplated marriage, a common practice at the time.[59]

Jackson honored Ellie's request to the fullest. His sister never knew of the engagement until after the wedding—a situation that brought a short but sharp break in their relationship. Yet had Laura paid closer attention to Jackson's letters that spring and early summer, she would have seen several hints that something unusual was afloat. Jackson in a rare display included cheerful, light messages. "I am invited to a large party tonight," he once stated, "and among the scramble, expect to come in for my share of fun." References to his health became minimal. On April 1, he informed Laura that "with my present views the future is holding richer stores in reserve." Two weeks later, he asked Laura to return the smiling photograph made of him in New Orleans on his return from the Mexican War. No explanations were forthcoming. His beloved had asked him to be closemouthed. That behavior came easily.[60]

The Lexington social season that spring found Jackson an extraordinarily active participant. He envisioned a joyful future; he felt alive; he was genuinely happy. The major even took increased delight in his teaching—to the extent of volunteering to broaden the curriculum. In his end-of-the-year report to Colonel Smith, Jackson wrote: "With a view to making this Department more efficient, I respectfully recommend that instruction be given in Pyrotechny and Mortar firing. For this purpose an Assistant would be necessary."[61]

In late May, Isabella Hill's two younger sisters arrived in town for a prolonged visit. Mary Anna and Eugenia Morrison were North Carolina belles delighted at being away for a spell from home life in a parsonage. Jackson was the first gentleman to call on the sisters. Although Eugenia was more attractive and outgoing, Anna seemed to occupy the greater part of Jackson's attentions.

The major offered to escort the two wherever they wished to go; and to their amusement, he insisted that they look upon him as if he were a brother. Jackson knocked on the Hill door almost every day during their six-week stay in Lexington. Exploiting town gossip, the two young women teased Jackson about his alleged engagement with Ellie Junkin. Jackson blushed, smiled, and admitted nothing. He and Ellie were rarely seen together in public.[62]

With the end of the school year, Jackson began in earnest to make wedding preparations. Among the first things on the list, perhaps unintentionally, was a showdown with Maggie Junkin. In July, a family member noted: "Maggie still looks with gloomy fore-boding to the future; though she does not object to Ellie's marrying nor to the Major; but still she cannot divest herself of the idea that Ellie cannot be . . . the same companion & confidante she has so long been." Maggie's dolefulness soon brought a confrontation with Jackson. Later, the older sister wrote Ellie: "I deserved the reproof. Instead of letting *you* go, I will try & add *him*."[63]

Jackson then made a quick trip to Beverly to see his ailing sister, who was suffering from a pregnancy. The subject of a wedding was never mentioned. From Beverly, Jackson went to Rockbridge Alum Springs for a day's enjoyment.

The plot thickened on Wednesday, August 3. Jackson sent a quick note to Laura: he wanted her to tell a mutual friend "that she must be on the lookout for something in relation to me, and in reference to which she called my attention." Laura did not pursue the mystery.[64]

That afternoon he borrowed an empty trunk and induced the VMI quartermaster, Richard H. Catlett (who was to be a groomsman at the wedding), to ride with him in a buggy the seventeen miles to Rockbridge Alum Springs. Whoever wanted to return to Lexington first, Jackson said, could use the buggy. The two men departed town, giving the impression to all that they were embarking on a protracted journey. After supper that evening at the springs, Jackson suddenly announced that he was going back to Lexington; and before Catlett had time to reply, Jackson was in the buggy and speeding away. He returned to Lexington in the middle of the night for a special mission a few hours later.[65]

Early Thursday morning, August 4, Jackson secured a marriage license as quickly as the clerk could unlock the courthouse door and fill out the form. An hour or so later, his secret deed accomplished, Jackson appeared at the Hill home for a courtesy call on the Morrison sisters. He seemed relaxed and attentive as they sang duets, and he easily parried their mischievous questions about his engagement to Ellie.

A more difficult task emerged in early afternoon, when the well-laid plans came close to collapsing. A frantic Jackson appeared at the home of Harvey and Isabella Hill. The black washerwoman who cleaned Jackson's uniform trousers had mistakenly ironed them so that the creases were on the sides rather than in front and rear. Jackson could not find the maid, and he had but one pair of dress white trousers. "Greatly to the Major's relief," Isabella Hill ironed the trousers properly.[66]

Near sundown, in the parlor of the Washington College president's home, Dr. Junkin performed the wedding ceremony joining together twenty-nine-year-old Thomas Jackson and twenty-eight-year-old Ellie Junkin. One of the handful of witnesses in attendance remarked of the couple: "She was fair as a lily. Clothed in her bridal robes, her graceful bearing and bright intellectual face contrasted strongly with her tall, dark, reticent husband."[67]

By the time surprised townspeople heard of the marriage, Major and Mrs. Jackson had embarked on their honeymoon. A shock of almost equal force was that they were not alone. Maggie Junkin was accompanying the couple. From a modern-day perspective, such an arrangement seems bizarre. Yet in the mid-nineteenth century, it was not unusual for relatives or even friends to accompany the bride and groom on their wedding trip. Ladies could assist one another in dressing and keep each other company when the husband needed to make travel arrangements or wished to pursue a masculine pastime such as viewing military scenes. The strangeness in this honeymoon was that the one who had most opposed the marriage was with the couple in their first happy hours together.

The thinking of the three individuals seems clear enough. Maggie still wanted to be with her sister under any circumstances. Ellie saw Maggie's presence as a facilitation in the transfer of primary affection from sister to husband. Jackson doubtless thought that having his sister-in-law on the trip could only improve relations between the three of them. All three deduced correctly to some extent.[68]

The trio traveled by stagecoaches to Philadelphia for three days of sightseeing. Then it was on to West Point. Jackson "was delighted" to meet some of his old army colleagues at the academy and to point out to his bride the beauties of his alma mater. As he later wrote: "The beautiful plain, the frowning ruins of Fort Putnam, the majestic river, and magnificent scenery, all conspired to enhance my happiness which had already been of a high order. The Ladies were also much pleased with it."[69]

Next came a fatiguing trip across New York State to Niagara Falls. Jackson secured rooms at the Cataract House on the American side. He could not visit the falls often enough. "This of all natural curiosities is the most sublime and imposing which has ever come under my observation," he exclaimed. "When looking at this wonder of nature, I desired to be left to my own uninterrupted thoughts."[70]

A long but scenic boat ride down the St. Lawrence River brought the Jackson party to Montreal. The women were dressing for church on Sunday morning when Jackson announced that he was going to watch a Highland regiment perform its intricate drill. Ellie and Maggie expressed surprise and disappointment at Jackson's failure to observe the Sabbath more appropriately. He replied that he did not regard his decision as a violation of the Lord's day. "If anything is right and good in itself," Jackson asserted, "and circumstances are such that [a man] cannot avail himself of it any time but Sunday, it is not wrong for him to do so, inasmuch as it thus becomes a matter of necessity."

The two sisters scoffed at such a rationale. Maggie added: "It was curious to see to what odd conclusions such a conscientious man as he could come to when arguing from insufficient data."

Jackson was adamant. He witnessed the drill, accidentally met some West Point friends thereafter, and spent the entire afternoon "in hilarious conversation" with them. Ellie and Maggie remonstrated with him that evening for forgetting what day of the week it was. Ellie was especially outspoken. In a scolding manner, she told her bridegroom: "This is a very sophisticated way of secularizing sacred time."

She then gave several examples of a parallel nature. To Maggie's surprise (she had not expected Jackson to be so open-minded), he thought for awhile and then told Ellie: "It is possible my premises are wrong. When I get home, I will go carefully over all this ground and decide the matter for myself." (He kept his resolve and, after making a thorough investigation of the Sabbath and his actions, concluded that he had been in error. Thereafter, Jackson became unbendable in his spiritual observance of Sundays.)[71]

Quebec was the next stop on the tour. For the first time to either Ellie or Maggie, Jackson exhibited a "military enthusiasm." He was anxious to visit the Plains of Abraham, where the British had won a spectacular 1759 victory over the French. Jackson hired a carriage, and the threesome rode to the plains one sunny afternoon.

Maggie was somewhat taken back by Jackson's behavior at a memorial to British General James Wolfe, mortally wounded in the battle. As her brother-in-law approached the monument, "he took off his cap, as if he were in the presence of some sacred shrine. I never shall forget the dilating enthusiasm that seemed to take possession of the whole man; he stood a-tiptoe, his tall figure appearing much taller than usual . . . his clear blue eyes flashing . . . his thin, sensitive nostrils quivering with emotion, and his lips parting with a rush of excited utterance, as he turned his face towards the setting sun, swept his arm with a passionate movement around the plain, and exclaimed, quoting Wolfe's dying words—'I die content!'" Then Jackson added in a trembling voice: "To die as *he* died, who would not die content!"[72]

A hope in Jackson's mind at the beginning of the honeymoon was to visit his therapist and friend, Dr. Lowry Barney, in western New York. By the time the Canadian trip ended and the Jacksons reached Boston, he knew that seeing the physician was not possible. Jackson then sent a warm letter to Barney from Boston's Revere House. Remembering the doctor's suggestion that he improve his health by seeking a lifelong companion, Jackson stated: "I was married on the 4th inst. to an intellectual, pure and lovely lady. . . . So you observe that I continued to carry out your advice."[73]

Late in August, the "wedding party" returned to Lexington. Jackson and Ellie had enjoyed their travels. Maggie had not. "That trip was a disappointing affair to me in many respects," she confessed. Nor had she accepted the fact that she was no longer Ellie's first love. The word "marriage," she told a friend, "*jars* my ears to hear it. It took from me my only bosom companion, the only one perhaps I shall ever have— and put between us a stranger."[74]

Neither Jackson nor Ellie had time to dwell on Maggie's unhappiness. The new school year was imminent, and the couple had to settle into living quarters. Fortunately, a solution to the latter problem materialized during the honeymoon. A combination bedroom and study had been added to the northern wing of the first floor of the Junkin home. Space was severely limited, but it offered privacy and the semblance of a home to the Jacksons.[75]

Married life brought no change in Jackson's daily preparations for class. Ellie learned quickly to leave the major alone for his periods of memorization and review. Indeed, the new Mrs. Jackson possessed an orderliness grounded in love and faith that gave her a tranquility he had never had without laboring for it. It was Ellie who drew him from his shell of shyness. She joked with him, took him to new places, substituted affectionate companionship for the lonely evenings he had endured. Jackson became more relaxed and more open. With Ellie, he let down the wall of reserve that a lifetime had constructed.

Lexington society wanted the couple at every social function. Jackson went, with more frequency and less hesitation. Most joyful of all was something that went deeper. Jackson had spent his life—especially the impressionable years of youth— longing for a home, for a family atmosphere, for the collective love that such an association fosters. Now, at long last, he had it. Jackson was happier than he had ever been.

He and Ellie resumed teaching Sunday school. Maggie joined them in November, during a large revival at the Presbyterian church.[76] Jackson attended Franklin Literary Society meetings as often as possible, and his friendships with the leaders of Lexington strengthened. He debated several times in favor of a national prohibition. Reluctance to speak in public had all but disappeared. Jackson displayed pride with his extended arm as he escorted Ellie to church services (even though she too was helpless in keeping him awake during the sermon). Cadets continued to tease him, but Jackson was winning their admiration through perseverance.

Another sentiment he had to win was Laura's affection. Jackson seemed unaware of how hurt his sister was by not being told of Jackson's engagement and marriage. Her closeness with her brother extended far beyond the feelings of a sister. In many respects, he was a father-figure to her. Once Laura learned of the wedding, added fears arose that marriage to Ellie would lessen the love between brother and sister. Laura became both resentful and moody. She refused to write.

Jackson sought to ameliorate the situation by sending a stream of cheery letters to Laura. He gave her a careful description of his honeymoon. In mid-October, he wrote: "The weather here is beautiful, and I am enjoying life. To me my wife is a great source of happiness." By late November, Jackson was pleading. "I hope that upon the receipt of this you will be induced to break your long silence. Do not think that because I am married that I would not be glad to receive a letter from you."[77]

Not until February 1854 did Laura respond, primarily to announce that she had given birth some weeks earlier to a daughter—the fourth child by Jonathan Arnold. Jackson replied at once. "Your long looked for letter arrived at last. I am much pleased at having another niece and hope that she may prove as pretty and interesting as Grace [the oldest child]." The loving brother enclosed a gift and made a request, both common practices of that day. "I send you a lock of Ellie's hair, which she reluctantly parts with because of its color, which she hopes may prove more acceptable to your taste than it has ever been to hers. My message to you is that you must prize it very highly as being the token of a sister's love and from a brother's wife. Send us a lock of your hair and also one from Grace."[78]

What at first appeared to be a strange event in Jackson's life started in the last weeks of 1853 when he began seeking a position elsewhere. On the surface, Jackson seemed ready to forsake the contentment of Lexington. Yet a number of factors came into play simultaneously.

The situation began with the death that autumn of Professor Edward Henry Courtenay at the University of Virginia. The Maryland-born Courtenay had graduated at the top of the West Point class of 1821; he had taught natural and experimental philosophy at the academy until his 1842 appointment as professor of mathematics at Virginia. Courtenay introduced there the West Point system of mathematics. Jackson was not merely familiar with it; he still regarded the science of numbers as his best subject. That was the first reason prompting Jackson to apply for the Virginia position.

Even though it was only fourteen years older than VMI, the university had 400 students and was the state's largest school. Its educational attractions over a small military academy were many. One of them was the salary: the mathematics professorship paid $3000 annually—twice Jackson's current stipend. Charlottesville was a bustling metropolis in comparison to the little community beyond the upper end of the Shenandoah Valley.[79]

To at least one friend, Jackson's interest in the Charlottesville position seemed to mark a change in earthly goals. The major previously had regarded being a member of a military school faculty as "the purpose of his life" because war was his proper avocation. Closer ties with God had changed his mind, Jackson admitted; he would no longer enter a war blindly. The morality of the struggle would be a major determinant in his actions. Only if he felt that divine approval was behind one side in a contest would he be a part of that contest. Meanwhile, "he regarded it as every man's duty to seek the highest cultivation of his powers, and the widest sphere of activity within his reach."[80]

Other considerations doubtless came into play with the university opening. Jackson's relations with Colonel Smith may still have been strained. The superintendent and Dr. Junkin often differed over matters of theology and education—a situation that literally left Jackson in the middle of the disputes. Jackson also may have had the natural desire to obtain a home of his own a respectable distance from in-laws. Ellie Jackson apparently pushed her husband toward the Charlottesville professorship. Perhaps she wished to get away from the Junkins, the dominant Episcopalians at VMI, or both.

On January 2, 1854, Jackson dispatched a letter to the University of Virginia Board of Visitors:

> The object of this communication is to present my name as a candidate for the vacant mathematical chair at the University of Va.
> I graduated at West Point in 1846 and served as an officer in the U.S. Army until 1851, when I was elected Professor of Natural and Experimental Philosophy at the Va. Military Institute, and in the discharge of the duties of this office I have continued to the present time.
> My recommendations are herewith enclosed.

With that rather bland application came endorsements from Professors Hill and John Lyle Campbell of Washington College. Hill asserted that Jackson was "*eminently* qualified to discharge the duties of the Chair to which he aspires and [I] think that his appointment would reflect credit upon the University." Campbell added as a postscript: "From an acquaintance of more than two years with the character & attainments of Maj. Jackson, I feel free to express a full concurrence in the opinion above given."[81]

Jackson solicited letters of recommendation from his kinsman by marriage, Judge John J. Allen. Colonel Smith, West Point and VMI Professors Dennis Mahan, J. W. Massie, William Gilham, and Henry Coppee, plus Captain Francis Taylor all submitted letters in Jackson's behalf. So did Robert E. Lee. Yet far too much has been made of that recommendation.

Lee was then superintendent at West Point; his letter in support of Jackson was little more than a summary of Jackson's military record and probably came from a military registry at West Point. Six weeks later, Lee sent a similar recommendation on William Nelson Pendleton for the same position.[82]

From the beginning, Jackson was aware that his candidacy would be an uphill contest because the University of Virginia desired to fill the mathematics position with one of its own graduates. In June, the university named Albert T. Bledsoe to the post. Bledsoe was a West Point product, with no ties to the Virginia university, but he was also an older and more experienced teacher well versed in the field of mathematics. Jackson took the defeat in stride and expressed pleasure that "my friends have acted nobly in my cause."[83]

What might have happened if Jackson had received the University of Virginia professorship is food for thought. He would have risen in academic standing, but the new position would have removed him from the military community that was his natural habitat.

As events proved, the eight additional years at VMI gave Jackson more training as an artillery instructor and direct participation in the military preliminaries to the Civil War. That period also brought him into tutorial and personal relationship with scores of young men who later became his subordinate officers in the field. If Jackson turned from the lost position at Virginia with his firm belief that "the Lord's will be done," developments thereafter gave him reason to feel the belief justified.

The eccentricities so much in evidence in Jackson's first year in Lexington seemed to have dispersed by the time 1854 began. One illustration of this change was Jackson's emergence as a respected businessman. He had come to Lexington with no financial means except what he had been able to save during five years in the army. Yet he learned more about being frugal and how to make the right investments. The result of such fiscal responsibility was his January 1854 appointment to the Board of Directors of the Lexington Savings Institution. His associates on the board were the town's most prosperous business leaders, who appreciated the professor's economic acumen.[84]

VMI cadets were beginning to learn that beneath the major's cold exterior was a kind and tender heart. Some days in class, when recitations were satisfactory to all, a cadet would take his cue from the major's slight smile of accomplishment and raise the subject of Jackson's experiences in the Mexican War. The professor could no longer keep his military reputation under wraps, any more than he could suppress his fondness for battle. So he would often describe events and scenes south of the border. On those occasions, one student recalled with affection, "the cadets' tyrant of the class-room had become the chum of the stoop."[85]

Jackson even grew a bit more tolerant of cadet misbehavior. One afternoon at artillery drill, a prankish cadet threw a clod of dirt at the preoccupied professor. Jackson saw the last second of the action and ordered the young man placed under arrest. Around 11 o'clock that rainy night, the cadet officer of the day received word to report to Major Jackson at the barracks entrance way. The professor returned the cadet's salute and came directly to the point. "I arrested Mr. Blank today. I believe it was he who threw the clod, but I don't feel absolutely certain, and I would rather a guilty man should escape than an innocent one should suffer. Tell him he is released from arrest."

"Very well," the officer of the day responded. "He is asleep now. I will tell him in the morning."

"No," Jackson stated in a firm voice. "His being under arrest may disturb his mind and deprive him of rest. I came expressly to let him know he is released, and you will please inform him *now.*" The cadet officer hastened to do as he was told.[86]

Jackson's new happiness and contentment showed forth most in late winter, when hints turned to certainty that Ellie was pregnant. Jackson rejoiced. He had always had an unusual fondness for children. Now he was to have one of his own. Like all expectant fathers, he became impatient for delivery time in the fall.

Within the first month of Ellie's pregnancy, however, the whole Junkin family had to combat grief. Dr. Junkin was the patriarch, to be sure, but Mrs. Julia Junkin ran the household and held the family together. She had been suffering from what was thought to be chronic rheumatism. On February 23, she died. Jackson honored her memory. In a lengthy letter to Laura about his mother-in-law, he noted that "hers was a Christian life and hers was a Christian death." Mrs. Junkin's passing "was no leaping in the dark. She died in the bright hope of an unending immortality of happiness."[87]

Maggie collapsed in anguish at the loss of her mother. Ellie, to Jackson's pride, proclaimed God's will at work and accepted the loss quietly. Father, sons, sisters, and in-laws were all together at the Junkin home one evening not long after the funeral. Earthly sorrow became the topic of discussion. Family members, aware of Jackson's new and abiding faith, began to quiz him on how great a calamity he could absorb as long as he knew it was the will of God. Could he endure blindness without remorse? Jackson thought a moment, then answered: "Yes, even such a misfortune could not make me doubt the love of God." Would he feel the same if he also had to endure painful confinement in bed? Yes, came the reply. Suppose, in addition to everything else, he was so destitute that he had to accept charity. Would that shake his faith? Jackson pondered the question for several moments; then in a low and sincere tone he responded, "If it was God's will, I think I could lie there content a hundred years."[88]

As winter gave way to spring, Jackson attended to a number of personal matters. Two of Laura's infant children went through long illnesses. As their suffering lingered, the mother's faith again deserted her. Jackson sought through letters to boost her spiritual strength, but without success.[89] Correspondence with Uncle John White about heavily indebted Jackson's Mill spread over a month's time. Jackson relinquished all claim to what paltry sum resulted from the sale of the farm. The last ties with the home of his youth were now severed.[90]

Jackson also lost two treasured friends late that spring. The Hills had become increasingly disenchanted with life in Lexington. "Dyspepsia and college drudgery" plagued Harvey Hill. His Washington College salary was low, he considered the college inferior in many ways to adjacent VMI, and Lexington citizenry struck him as "Presbyterians of the old school, remarkable for their piety, bigotry, hospitality and intolerance."[91]

When his father-in-law, a founder and trustee of Davidson College in North Carolina, asked Hill to join the faculty there and lend both his mathematical knowledge and his disciplinary skills to the student body, Hill accepted. He and his wife departed Lexington in early summer. Jackson never forgot their kindnesses and counseling at a time when he urgently needed friends.

Ellie's pregnancy advanced with no problems beyond the anxieties of bearing a first child. Of more concern was a facial neuralgia that kept her in gnawing pain through the spring months.[92]

Jackson spent much of that period in expanding and polishing the book of maxims he began keeping at West Point. Most of the entries were made in the early years at VMI, when Jackson was seeking to improve himself socially, intellectually, and spiritually. He maintained running lists of sayings and proverbs under three headings: choice of friends, rules of conversation, and general principles or personal maxims. In the first category, he developed the following reminders for accumulating friends:

1. A man is known by the company he keeps.
2. Be cautious in your selection.
3. There is danger of catching the habits of your associates.
4. Seek those who are intelligent & virtuous & if possible those who are a little above you, especially in moral excellence.
5. It is not desirable to have a large no. of intimate friends. You may have many acquaintants but few intimate friends. If you have one who is what he should be, you are comparatively happy.

   That friendship may be at once fond and lasting, there must not only be equal virtue in each party, but virtue of the same kind: not only the same end must be proposed but the same means must be approved.

Because Jackson had such difficulty in social conversation, the list of sayings under that topic was longer.

1. Ascertain in your conversation as well as you can wherein the skill & excellence of the individual lies & put him upon his favorite subject. Every person will of his own accord fall to talking on his favorite subject or topic if you will follow and not attempt to lead him.
2. If you seek to improve in the greatest degree from the conversation of another, allow him to take his own course. If called upon, converse in turn upon your favorite topic.
3. Never interrupt another but hear him out. There are certain individuals from whom little information is to be desired such as use [of] wanton, obscene or profane language.
4. If you speak in company, speak late.
5. Let your words be as few as will express the sense you wish to convey & above all let what you say be true.
6. Do not suffer your feelings to betray you into too much vehemence or earnestness or to being overbearing.
7. Avoid triumphing over an antagonist.
8. Never engross the whole conversation to yourself.
9. Sit or stand still while another is speaking to you—[do] not dig in the earth with your foot nor take your knife from your pocket & pare your nales or other such actions.
10. Never anticipate for another to help him out. It is time enough for you to make corrections after he has concluded, if any are necessary. It is impolite to interrupt another in his remarks.
11. Say as little of yourself & friends as possible.
12. Make it a rule never to accuse without due consideration any body or association of men.
13. Never try to appear more wise or learned than the rest of the company. Not that you should affect ignorance, but endeavor to remain within your own proper sphere. Let ease & gracefulness be the standard by which you form your estimation (taken from etiquett).

The longest of the lists in Jackson's book of maxims consisted of guides for good behavior. He obviously considered these to be the most important axioms that he could follow.

1. Through life let your principal object be the discharge of duty: if anything conflicts with it, adhere to the former and sacrifice the latter.

   Be sociable—speak to all who speak to you and those whose acquaintance you do not wish to avoid, hesitate not to notice them first.

   When in company, do not endeavor to monopolize all the conversation unless such monopolization appears necessary, but be content with listening and gaining information, yet converse rather than suffer conversation to draw to a close unnecessarily.
2. Disregard public opinion when it interfears with your duty.

   After you have formed an acquaintance with an individual, never allow it to draw to a close without a cause.

3. Endeavor to be at peace with all men.
   Never speak disrespectfully of any one without a cause.
4. Endeavor to do well every thing which you undertake through preference.
5. Spare no effort to suppress selfishness unless that effort would entail sorrow.
6. Sacrifice your life rather than your word.
   Be temperate. Eat too little rather than too much.
7. Let your conduct towards men have some uniformity.
   "Temperance—Eat not to dullness, drink not to elevation.
   Silence—speak not but what may benefit others or yourself: avoid trifling conversation.
   Order—Let all things have their places: let each part of your business have its time.
8. Resolution—Resolve to perform what you ought: perform without fail what you resolve.
   Frugality—Make no expinse but to do good to others or yourself: i.e., waste nothing.
   Industry—Lose no time; be always employed in something usefull; cut off all unnecessary actions.
   Sincerity—Use no hurtfull deceit: think innocently and justly, and if you speak, speak accordingly.
   Justice—Wrong none by doing injuries or omitting the benefits that are your duty.
   Moderation—Avoid extremes: forbear resenting injuries so much as you think they deserve.
   Cleanliness—Tolerate no uncleanliness in body clothes or habitation.
   Tranquility—Be not disturbed at trifles nor at accidents common or unavoidable.
   Chastity
   Humility"
   "You may be what ever you will resolve to be."

Motives to action (Viz)
1. Regard to your own happiness.
2. Regard for the family to which you belong.
3. Strive to attain a very great elevation of character.
4. Fix upon a high standard of character.
5. ' ' ' ' ' action.
   It is man's highest interest not to violate or attempt to violate the rules which infinite wisdom has laid down.
   The means by which men are to attain great elevation may be classed in three great divisions: physical, mental & moral.
   Whatever relates to health belongs to the first.
   ' ' ' improvement of the mind belongs to the second.
   The formation of good manners & virtuous habits constitutes [the] third.

Politeness & good-breeding
   Good breeding or true politeness is the art of showing men by external signs the internal regard we have for them.
   It arises from good sense improved by good company.
   It must be acquired by practice and not by books.
   Be kind, condescending & affable.
   Any one who has any thing to say to a fellow human being to say it with a kind feeling & sincere desire to please & this when ever it is done will atone for much awkwardness in the manner of expression.
   Forced complaisance is fopping [sic] & affected easiness is ridiculous.
   Good breeding is opposed to selfishness, vanity or pride.
   Endeavor to please with out hardly allowing it to be perceived.
   Plain rules for attaining the character of a well bred man:
1. Never weary your company by talking too long or too frequently.
2. Always look people in the face when addressing them & generally when they address you.

3. Attend to a person who is addressing you.
4. Do not interrupt the person who is speaking by saying yes or no & such at every sentence. An occasional assent by word or action *may* be well enough.[93]

Some of Jackson's idolaters credit him with conceiving most or all of the quotations in his book of maxims. Conversely, his critics accuse him of plagiarism. Both views are unfair. Jackson was neither a philosopher nor a phraseologist. He lacked both the training and the aptitude to be a wordsmith. Over a period of years he simply jotted down thoughts or phrases that influenced his thinking. Not once did he ever presume authorship for any of the statements listed; and in the case of the most famous of the sayings—"You may be whatever you resolve to be"—Jackson isolated it with quotation marks. Such an action absolves him of any charge of taking someone else's words and phrases and passing them off as his own.[94]

A tragic chain of events began in late spring. First, Jackson learned that his youngest niece had died after a protracted illness. "Your loss is one which I have never been called upon to bear up under," he wrote Laura. "I can well conceive of the tender union which is thus sundered. You have my sympathy." Jackson had not planned to visit Beverly that summer, but Laura's grief started him thinking otherwise.[95]

Ellie's condition remained positive. When her two brothers and younger sister Julia invited her to accompany them on a week's vacation to Natural Bridge, Jackson urged his wife to go. She did so while Jackson attended to duties associated with the end of the school year at VMI.

Marring that pleasant period was another rift with Colonel Smith. The Episcopal rector, William Nelson Pendleton, was also involved. At issue were procedures for the Rockbridge County Bible Society. The disagreement could not be resolved, so Jackson resigned from the Board of Directors and played only a small role thereafter in society affairs.[96]

By the end of the school term, Jackson was suffering from a number of physical ailments. All of them could be improved by visits to one or more of the mineral springs to the west, he thought. "The Major's nervous system is out of order," young Julia Junkin wrote a friend, "or he imagines so at least; but to see him you would not think him sick at all."[97]

Jackson felt an almost paternal need to go to Laura in her hour of sadness. The cooler mountainous climate of Beverly offered an additional enticement when hot weather came early that year to the Shenandoah Valley. Coupled with these thoughts of Jackson's was the anticipated thrill of having his sister and his wife meet and become friends. He concluded at the end of June that the time was opportune for an extended visit to the Arnolds.

In a quick note to Laura on July 1, Jackson stated that he and Ellie hoped to be in Beverly the following week. Ellie filled the remainder of the sheet with her first and only message to her sister-in-law: "The Major is so busy with his duties at the Institute that he has commissioned me to finish this letter for him; indeed I have scarcely seen him to-day. He wishes me to say to you that he hopes you will not exert yourself by making any preparations to receive us; he does not want you to weary yourself or injure your health on our account."[98]

Had Jackson been knowledgeable about pregnancy, he would have been far more concerned about his wife than about his sister. Ellie was six months into bearing a child, and she had fears about the torturous stage rides to and from Beverly. Yet she voiced no hesitations. Jackson obviously had none.

The stage journey over rough and twisting mountain roads was an ordeal. The Jacksons survived its rigors and spent the better part of a month with the Arnolds. Young Tom Arnold was quite taken with "Aunt Ellie." She "was of medium stature," he recalled, "of rather slight build, auburn hair, erect, pleasing features, good looking & charming; cordial & winning in her manners."[99]

Laura and Ellie became instant friends. They found they had much in common, including a deep affection for Thomas Jackson. He must have considered the Beverly visit worth every bump and inconvenience. The return trip was just as arduous. Ellie was exhausted by the time she reached home. Nevertheless, her pregnancy was strong. She spent the ensuing weeks in Lexington busily making plans for her baby's arrival. Jackson became immersed in the start of another school year.

Childbirth in the nineteenth century was a dangerous event under the most ideal of circumstances. Few physicians possessed special training in the field of obstetrics. For the most part, they were midwives with little understanding about prolonged labor, hemorrhaging, convulsions, or breach births. In the rural South at that time, about one of every six white mothers died while giving birth. It was not unusual for a mother to lose a third or even half of her children in the birthing process.[100]

Ellie displayed calm anticipation about her approaching labor. She had not experienced any problems of note during the pregnancy. Her mother had borne nine children successfully. A local physician was monitoring her progress. Her sisters Maggie and Julia would be at her side when the time came, and her beloved husband would see to her every wish.

The catastrophe seemed to occur in a flash. On Sunday afternoon, October 22, 1854, Ellie went into labor. Jackson himself described what followed: "The Doctor said that all was well. The womb closed apparently healthfully, though the child (a son) was dead. The Doctor left the house for a few minutes, and I was admitted into the room and upon observing her agonizing pain I desired the Doctor to return. He soon after entered, but a sudden change had taken place: the womb had relaxed, and in a short time her spirit took its flight."[101]

Simply stated, Ellie gave birth to a stillborn son but appeared to come safely through the ordeal. An hour or so later, however, an uncontrollable hemorrhage began and quickly proved fatal.

Jackson was devastated. The twin blow was unexpected and crushing. He tried to think, but grief obliterated reasoning. Death had once again shattered his small world. With the exception of Laura, everyone to whom Jackson had turned for affection had been wrenched from him. When Ellie entered his life, she became his deepest love. She was his hope for future happiness, the port where his sometimes floundering ship could find a haven. Now she—and the child he never knew—were gone. Utter despair coursed through Jackson's being. Yet he refused to show it.

One of the first townspeople to hear of the tragedy was Jackson's colleague, Professor Raleigh Colston. He rushed to the Junkin home to extend his sympathy and services. "Sadly but calmly," Colston stated, Jackson "led me to the chamber of death, and with unfaltering hand, removed the veil which covered the dead infant resting upon its dead mother's breast. Then as quietly [he] replaced it. There were no tears, no quivering of the lips, only a few whispered words, and a casual observer would hardly have perceived the powerful emotions of his soul—kept down only by his indomitable will."[102]

Jackson could have cried out in anger at God. It would have been easy, if not natural, for him to denounce religion with its promises of the good life. Yet faith was the only place to which Jackson could turn. He looked to God's merciful care for protection and strength.

On the day after the death of Ellie and the baby, Jackson told Laura of the dual tragedy. "I have been called to pass through the deep waters of affliction, but all has been satisfied," he wrote. "The Lord giveth and the Lord taketh away, blessed be the name of the Lord. It is his will that my Dearest wife & child should not longer abide with me, and as it is His holy will, I am perfectly reconciled to the sad bereavement, though I deeply mourn my loss. My Dearest Ellie breathed her last on Sunday evening, the same day on which the child was born dead. Oh! the consolations of religion! I can willingly submit to anything if God strengthens me. Oh! my Sister would that you could have Him for your God! Though all nature to me is eclipsed, yet I have joy in knowing that God withholds no good things from them that love & keep his commandments. And he will overrule this *Sad, Sad* bereavement for good."[103] As Jackson was to find, the washing away of tears would require a long expanse of time.

At 10 A.M. on Tuesday, October 24, funeral services were conducted at the Presbyterian church. A single coffin held the remains of mother and child. The VMI corps of cadets marched in the procession the few blocks up Main Street to what was then the Lexington Presbyterian Cemetery. Snow flurries were in the air; a fierce wind sliced through the large gathering of mourners.[104]

Ellie and her child were buried in the Junkin family plot. Jackson stood alone over the open grave, holding his VMI cap in his hand and appearing drained. Cadet Thomas M. Boyd thought the major "extremely pale but calm and resigned. He did not shed a tear, yet everyone who saw him was impressed with the intense agony he was enduring."[105]

At the conclusion of the service, everyone but Jackson dispersed for the warmth of fireplaces. He continued to stand at the grave until Dr. White walked back into the cemetery and gently led him away.[106]

By week's end, Jackson had returned to the section room and drillfield. He was paler and quieter; beyond that, and the black crepe he wore on his cap and sword handle, no one would have known the heartache through which he was passing. Jackson visited Ellie's grave daily, regardless of the weather. He later told Harvey Hill that he often felt "irresistibly inclined" to open the grave and "look once more upon the loved ashes of his dear wife."[107]

Friends soon began to fear that Jackson was losing his mind. His vision became weak as eye problems struck anew. Laura offered to come and stay with him, but Jackson did not wish her to make the hard journey in the uncertain weather of autumn. To his sister and friends, Jackson made it clear that he had no regrets at Ellie's passing. God had unloosed the heavy blow for his own good.

In subsequent weeks, Jackson's thoughts centered on when he would again be with his wife. "She has now gone on a glorious visit through a gloomy portal," he told Laura. "I look forward with delight to the day when I shall join *her*. Religion is all that I desire it to be. I am reconciled to my loss and have joy in hope of a future reunion when the wicked cease from trembling and the weary are at rest."[108]

One evening, in the solitude of his room at the Junkin home, thirty-year-old Jackson added an even more personal touch to his book of maxims. On the front page he wrote:

Objects to be affected by Ellie's Death:
To eradicate ambition
'   '   resentment
' produce humility
If you desire to be more heavenly minded, think more of the things of Heaven and less of the things of Earth.

7

THE SEARCH FOR ONESELF

"I DO NOT SEE THE PURPOSE of God in this, the most bitter, trying affliction of my life, but I will try to be submissive though it breaks my heart." Jackson confessed those thoughts to a friend.[1] In the weeks and months following Ellie's death, he bared his soul to many people. Sympathy was not what he was seeking; Jackson simply needed to share his thoughts with someone.

The Junkins insisted that he remain at their home. After all, he was family. A brokenhearted Jackson agreed to stay. He had nowhere else to go and could not think with any depth. The once-crowded and lively Junkin home had a tomblike quietness to it now. Mother Junkin and Ellie had died within eight months of one another. Margaret was so stunned by grief that she could not bear to visit Ellie's grave. With her health failing, she left in December on an extended visit with her brother George in Philadelphia. The only members at the family home in Lexington were Dr. Junkin, his youngest daughter Julia, and Jackson.

Shock and grief were so heavy that for weeks Jackson wrote no letters and did no more than was necessary. Dr. Junkin noted that his son-in-law was "growing heavenward faster than I ever knew any person to do. He seems only to think of E[llie] and heaven." More than once in the weeks after his wife's death, Jackson would exclaim, "Ah, if it might only please God to let me go now!"[2]

Jackson shut himself from the world as much as circumstance would permit. In the solitude of heartache, he took a long dirge composed by Margaret, made a few alterations to underscore his own pain, and produced a new copy in his own handwriting. The stanzas more than compensate with pathos what they lack in style.

To my sister
A cloud is on my heart, Ellie
A shade is on my brow
And the still current of my thought
Glides often sadly now
The careless smile comes seldomer
Than once it used to come
And when the *playful* jest goes round
My lips are strangely dumb.

I meet your lifted eyes, Ellie
Yet while their gleam is gay
The beaded tears are on my cheeks

160

And I must turn away
And often when you speak to me
With softness in your tone
Tis silence only that can hide
The faltering of my own.

You do not know how fond, Ellie
Are all the thoughts you share
You cannot think how sobbingly
I breathe your name in prayer
And plead that God may teach me how
I sweetly may resign
That deepest sympathy of soul
So long I've claimed as mine.

From very childhood years, Ellie,
We've known *no separate joy*
Whatever grieved *your* heart, could bring
To *mine* a like annoy
Together o'er one page we bent
In sunshine and in shade
Together thro' life's summer walks
Our kindred feet have strayed.

But now our paths diverge, Ellie
A thought I may not share
Has severed your spirit's sovereignty
And claims to govern there
Yet while as if discrowned of love
I feel an exile's pain
Believe me that I question not
His sacred right to reign.

And when I know how kind, Ellie
How faith and how true
The life-pulse of that firm strong heart
Is throbbing now for you
A secret and unselfish joy
Thro' all my own should thrill
To think how many dreams of bliss
Your future shall fulfil.

But yet the tears will come, Ellie
Soft-dropping, sad and slow
You are so very—very dear
How can I let you go
For never seemed your silent kiss
So warm upon my brow

And never clung my soul to you
So yearningly as now.

You are too rich in Love, Ellie
To feel a sense of *need*
If *mine* should lessen to you *now*
But I were poor indeed
If from the hoarded stores of home
You take your rich supply
And leave me with a yearning want
I cannot satisfy.

Ah! home must lose its charms, Ellie
As fast the years come on
And one by one the cherished hearts
Will go—till all are gone!
'Tis but the common work of Time
To mar our household so
And I must learn to choke the sob
And smile to see them go.
Forgive these saddened strains, Ellie

Forgive these eyes so dim!
I must—*must* love whom *you* have loved
So I will turn to him,
And clasping with a silent touch
Whose tenderness endears
Your hand and his between my own
I bless them with my tears.[3]

A week before Christmas, to Jackson's surprise, he received a warm and touching letter from an unexpected source: his sister-in-law Margaret, who had heretofore been sparing in affection if not in courtesy. Now Maggie was asking for commiseration and help in the wake of their common loss.

"My dear Brother," she began, "I feel an irresistible desire to write you today—for my heart has been so exceedingly oppressed in dwelling upon our loss, that perhaps to write to you may be some relief. It may seem selfish to go to you to pour out some of my sorrow—you have more than enough of your own to bear." Maggie asked Jackson to write her in Philadelphia, "but I shall know why [if] you don't." Should he choose not to reply, Maggie concluded, she hoped he would at least "remember *me* in your prayers, and believe me, always, your most affectionate and sympathizing sister."[4]

Jackson could not respond immediately. It was too difficult even to write Laura. When in late December he received a letter of condolence from Ellie's favorite uncle, David X. Junkin in Washington, Jackson sent back his thanks. "You not only have mine, but my dear departed Ellie also, if she looked back with her human feelings, and saw you thus endeavoring to wipe away my tears for her loss; and pointing me upward to the house not made with hands where she awaits me in happiness inexpressible, must have been alike thankful." Jackson then stated: "This world Dear Uncle to me is eclipsed; the sun of my Earthly happiness has set. . . . But what is life, it is but a span, it will soon be over, and I welcome its close."[5]

At times, Jackson seemed momentarily to wrestle with his faith. To George Junkin he wrote early in February 1855: "I cannot realize that Ellie is gone; that my wife will no more cheer the rugged and dark way of life. The thought rushes in upon me that it is insupportable—insupportable! But one upward glance of the eye of faith, gives a return that all is well, and that I can do all things through Christ that strengthens me." The phrase "the eye of faith" may have been an oblique reference to the serious vision problems he was still having in this period of sorrow. "I have suffered so much with my eyes lately," he told Aunt Clementine Neale, "that I have had great fears that I might lose them entirely, but all things are in the hands of a merciful Father, and to His will I hope ever cheerfully to submit."[6]

On Wednesday, February 14, Jackson finally wrote to Maggie:

Your kind and affectionate letters have remained too long unanswered. Often I have wished to reply to them, but you well know the reason why I have not done so. . . . You and I were certainly the dearest objects which [Ellie] left on Earth. And if her emancipated spirit comes back to Earth, and sees how we are bound together, and how we have a mutual [bond] of strong affection for *her*, do you not suppose that it thrills her with delight? . . .

When I stood by her grave, and that of Mother last Saturday, they were both covered with snow; though their bodies rested beneath the cold covering, yet was it not in color emblematic of their spiritual robes of white?

Jackson apologized near the end for describing his own feelings so much. "Though I have not said much about you here, yet I have thought of you much, and prayed for you much, and your best interests are at my heart. I am very anxious to see you."[7]

Thus began an exchange of correspondence between these two relatives who were quite opposite from one another: Jackson was almost six feet tall, of dark complexion and silent demeanor; Maggie was barely five feet tall, red-haired, and quite emotional. Now the two lived under the shadow of Ellie's spirit. They had been the "dearest things" to Ellie; Jackson was Maggie's only "brother" at home in Lexington; he could understand her heartache because he was similarly afflicted.[8] So the number of letters increased, and a warm and mutual affection began to bloom.

"When you tell me of your sorrows and joys," Jackson wrote on March 1, "it makes me feel that we are nearer to each other: such was the case with the now sainted *Sister* and *wife*. . . . I am very glad to see that your eyes and health have both so much improved, and I hope and pray that there is yet much happiness in store for you, even in this world. But I am afraid that you are coming home too soon. Glad as I would be to see you, I would rather forego that pleasure, than that you should leave Phila-delphia until it meets with your Physicians approval." Jackson closed by stating: "You don't know the pleasure which your letters have given me, and you must not neglect to write to me when leisure will permit." He signed the letter, "Your very affectionate brother Thomas."[9]

A few days later, Jackson felt compelled to write his "sister" again. "I can sympathise with you, dear Maggie, and can appreciate your desire to comfort me. This you have much contributed to by your prayers, your conversation, your letters, and by the various other means by which your interest in me has been manifested."[10]

Maggie did not completely restore Jackson's feelings, however. By the middle of March, he still saw little of value in earthly life. Jackson responded to a letter of condolence from his West Point friend, "Grumble" Jones, by confessing that although Ellie's presence "would make this world a happy one for me, I desire no more days on the Earth. Of all the moments, of this life, none are looked forward to by me with so much pleasure as the one which will emancipate me from this body. I with patience abide my time, knowing that it is not too distant when I expect to enter into the joy of *my Lord*."[11]

In April 1855, Maggie returned to Lexington. Yet her delicate health—especially nagging back pains—kept her in seclusion and somewhat disconsolate.[12] Jackson more than anyone gave her regular attention. They became as solicitous of one another as any loving brother and sister. In that setting, both began to emerge from the depths of despair.

Jackson still maintained his rigid evening schedule of reviewing the memorized presentation for the next day's classroom lectures. Maggie watched him quietly several times, then wrote: "His habits of study were very peculiar, and never relaxed, save from illness. He would rise in the midst of the most enlivening conversation—if the appointed hour had struck, and go to his study. He would, during the day, run superficially over large portions of French mathematical works, and then at night, with his green silk eye shade over his eyes, and standing at his upright desk, neither paper nor book before him, he would spend hours in mentally digesting what he had taken in during the afternoon, in a mere mechanical way. His power of concentration was so great, that he was able wholly to abstract himself from whatever was extraneous to the subject in hand."[13]

When Jackson had finished this daily regimen, Maggie would come to his room for what she called "an hour or two of relaxation and chat." She later elaborated: "I came to know the man as never before. His early life, his lonely orphanage, his struggle with disease, his West Point life, his campaigning in Mexico . . . all these furnished materials for endless reminiscence." On a rare occasion, she stated, Jackson would let his reserve fall and relate amusing stories. He would get "so carried away with them himself, as almost to roll from his chair in laughter."[14]

Maggie in turn talked about the difficulties of a woman writer making progress in a man's world. She discussed literary projects she had in mind. Jackson and Maggie studied Spanish together; and since both loved the language, it became a regular part of their communication. If they went to church together, it was always with other members of the family. Maggie once surprised her father and sister by observing that Jackson was "the very stuff out of which to make a stirring hero." To the other Junkins he was more a "dear son and brother."[15]

Meanwhile, Jackson's eyesight was little improved that spring. When Laura wrote that she too was having vision problems, Jackson responded with a suggested treatment: "I would recommend you to fill a basin full of water, and put your face under the water, and hold your eyes open in it as long as you can hold your breath. Just do this whenever your eyes are very painful. . . . I do it about six times a day in cold water, & the water should be as cold as when just drawn from the well or taken from the river. My eyes are quite bad at present."[16]

The uveitis that struck Jackson in 1848 had returned again. By 1855, he was having the additional problem of "floaters" in his vision. In all likelihood, Jackson had contracted vitritis, an inflammation of the vitreous humor oftentimes associated with uveitis. Jackson's prescription of submerging the face in cold water is similar to the modern-day practice of using cold-water compresses for various eye inflammations. The treatment Jackson adopted was proper, but his optical problems continued for the remainder of the year.[17]

In the aftermath of the death of a loved one, it is natural to start reflecting on the past and on other members of one's family. Few relatives existed to warrant Jackson's concerns. One who did was his half-brother (his mother's last child), Wirt Woodson. He was then twenty-four, seven years Jackson's junior, and had been raised in Parkersburg by the Neales.

Woodson acquired little education and wanted little. The life of a farmer was all that appealed to him. Jackson offered him money, and once he volunteered to purchase a farm for Woodson. Large sections of Jackson's letters in this period dwelled on Woodson's limited ability and unknown future. The half-brother ignored advice and soon migrated first to Missouri and then to California. "It looks like almost a hopeless case to be of any service to him," Jackson conceded.[18]

On June 1, Jackson informed Laura that the metal railing for Ellie's grave had arrived and been installed. A tombstone was on order from a Philadelphia manufacturer. It was of Italian marble, with "a full blown rose and a rosebud on top." Still in the pit of loneliness, Jackson declared, "Had I one request on earth to ask in accordance with my own feelings and apart from duty, it would be that I might join her before the close of another day after this."[19]

Motivated by grief to retrieve the past, Jackson spent his summer vacation on an extended trip to the sites of his youth. He departed Lexington around July 5, underwent an "exceedingly tiresome" stage ride through the mountains, and spent a few days in the baths at Healing Springs before proceeding to the Arnold home in Beverly. His loss was readily apparent to his sister and her family. "He was more serious in manner than I had ever known him," young Tom Arnold stated.[20]

Laura was not much help in raising the spirits of her brother. Nor was his beloved nephew, Tom, although he did remember one amusing incident during Jackson's visit. He accompanied the major to a service at the local Methodist church. "When the minister announced that we would unite in prayer, the congregation turned & knelt in their seats, I with the others. It was in those days customary in the Presbyterian Church to stand in prayer. Major Jackson stood up. It occurred to me that he was not thinking of his being in a Methodist church & that his standing would be remarked on; so I reached around & caught the tail of his coat & gave a slight pull; as he did not seem to notice this, I gave a harder tug—this I repeated 2 or 3 times, each time still harder, until he turned his head & looked at me. I then let him alone."[21]

The lonely widower then rode to Weston and Jackson's Mill. Cool water from the West Fork River and the soothing sounds of pastoral surroundings embraced his soul.

Yet the area had changed in so many respects that Jackson had difficulty keeping memories in focus. He left those scenes of childhood with little thought of seeing them again, and he never did.

Next was a stop in Clarksburg, where he got a cousin to show him the graves of his father and older sister. They lacked headstones and were in dilapidated condition. Jackson made arrangements with Aunt Katy Williams to have the graves filled and contoured. He resolved to erect grave markers at a later date.[22]

In gypsy-like fashion, Jackson made his way to Parkersburg. There he received a warm welcome from Uncle Alfred and Aunt Clementine Neale. During his stay at Neale's Island, Jackson made at least one visit to Mineral Springs in search of beneficial hydrotherapy. The waters were of little help. A family acquaintance chanced upon him there. "His spirits were visibly depressed," the man noted, "and his manner and speech more or less absent and dreamy. . . . He very frequently was seen on a rustic bench, all by himself, perusing his paper with profound attention, seldom looking up or around until he was through." In grief, Jackson may have pretended to read to discourage interruptions from well-meaning people.[23]

The lonely Jackson sent Maggie a chatty letter from Parkersburg. In the middle of it, he opened his heart: "Though far from you, yet in my solitude you are with me. Though you are far from me, yet it is a pleasure to be holding converse with you, as though distance did not separate us. To sum it up, Dear Maggie, I want to see you again. I desire to mingle in the society of one with whom I have so many endearing associations. Your kindness to me and your affection for me, Dear Maggie, has no little influence in lightening up the gloom which for months has so much enveloped me." Jackson closed by inviting Maggie to "come to me with every joy, and every sorrow, and let me share them with you."[24]

Then began the most painful quest of Jackson's summer trip. From Parkersburg he traveled by steamboat down the Ohio River to Point Pleasant and then up the sparsely settled Kanawha Valley to Hawks Nest and the hamlet of Ansted. Jackson was searching for his mother's grave. Frustration marked his effort. "The gentleman with whom I put up," he told his aunt, "was at my mother's burial and accompanied me to the cemetery for the purpose of pointing out her grave, but I am not certain that he found it. There was no stone to mark the spot. Another gentleman, who had the kindness to go with us, stated that a wooden head or foot board with her name on it had been put up, but it was no longer there."[25] The hope of seeing at last where his mother slept had failed. Jackson would never know exactly where she was buried.

He returned by stage to Lexington. In spite of persistent pain in his eyes, Jackson threw himself into the start of another academic year. Some motivation energized him in business matters. Jackson purchased a sizable lot of shares in the new Lexington Building Fund Association and eventually acquired government bonds, stock in the Bank of the Commonwealth of Virginia, and part ownership in a Lexington tannery.

For a time, Jackson toyed with the idea of purchasing land in Illinois and Kansas. In both instances, he changed his mind. The reason was that at this early date he envisioned a possible civil war. After learning that Wirt Woodson was somewhere west of the Mississippi River, Jackson stated to Laura: "I do not want him to go into a free state if it can be avoided, for he would probably become an abolitionist; and then in the event of trouble between North and South he would stand on one side, and we on the opposite."[26] At this point, Jackson assumed that Laura's beliefs in states' rights were as strong as his own.

Throughout the latter part of 1855, with the sad memories of the summer journey so painfully fresh, Jackson turned more and more to the church for new life. A meeting of the state synod in Lexington was "a delightful assembly." Dr. White's congregation had grown to 307 whites and eleven black members. Sunday school was getting proportionally larger. Jackson immersed himself in the class of college students and cadets that he had been teaching for some time. This new effort brought him more in contact with the assistant superintendent of Sunday school classes. He was an acquaintance and associate of Jackson's; now a deepening friendship began.[27]

John T. L. Preston was not a Lexington individual as much as he was a regional institution. Born April 28, 1811, in Lexington of highly affluent parents (his grandfather was Edmund Randolph, America's first attorney general), Preston received a superb education at Washington College and Yale. Foreign travel coupled with intellectual pursuits occupied his early adulthood. Preston then became an enterprising attorney and businessman with extensive land holdings in Rockbridge County. He was a leader in the Presbyterian church and in any other endeavor that interested him. His oratorical skills earned him the sobriquet "Lexington's Demosthenes."

In 1836, Preston had originated the idea of converting the Western Arsenal in Lexington into a military and scientific college. When the Virginia Military Institute became a reality, he accepted appointment as professor of Latin and English—a position he held for thirty-seven years.

Preston stood a full six feet tall. He was clean-shaven, with piercing blue eyes, prematurely gray hair, and the ruddy complexion of an outdoorsman. His wife, the former Sally Caruthers, bore him eight children in eighteen years. A figure whose presence in Lexington was constant and widespread, Preston was known to most people as imaginative, dignified, fluent, and masterful. Yet no man is universally loved. Being conspicuous, Preston had critics. One cadet thought him "like some huge porpoise rolling in the sea." A business associate charged that Preston "cared but little for anybody but his family—and his friend John Lyle." That last assessment is incorrect. Preston was genuinely fond of his colleague and fellow churchman, Major Jackson.[28]

Indeed, it was a joint effort of Preston and Jackson that got a famous black Sunday school class underway. Whites had taught the tenets of Christianity to slaves and freedmen as early as 1843, when Colonel Smith organized a Sunday school for slaves in Lexington. Two years later, St. John's Episcopal Church in Richmond began such a Sunday school. Lexington Presbyterians undertook a similar project at the same time. Local opposition and lack of participation doomed all three of these initial experiments.[29]

One early source claimed that Jackson first began teaching the scriptures to slaves in his room at the Junkin home; and when the room "became filled to overflowing with eager pupils," he then decided to organize a class at the church. The facts tell a different story. Jackson became concerned about the lack of spiritual guidance among Lexington's black population. A Washington College student who later assisted Jackson in the black Sunday school believed that the "neglected condition" of the slaves "excited [Jackson's] sympathy, and a sense of duty impelled him to make an effort to redeem them from the slavery of sin." Anna Jackson gave a more succinct explanation: "His interest in that race was simply because they had souls to save."[30]

Jackson studied the earlier failure of the Sunday school for slaves and freedmen. He then conferred at length with Dr. White and church school superintendent Preston about making another try at a black class. White was all for the idea, of course, and Preston volunteered to use his influence and persuasion wherever needed to make the venture a success. Hence, in the autumn of 1855, a new Sunday school class for blacks began in the church building adjacent to the main Presbyterian sanctuary. Jackson, Dr. White observed, "threw himself into this work with all of his characteristic energy and wisdom."[31]

The Presbyterian church gave Jackson every encouragement and aid, but the initial stages of the project were stormy for all concerned. Many blacks were reluctant to engage in yet another attempt at a Sunday school. Several residents openly laughed at the experiment. Apparently, a small but vocal group of whites opposed what Jackson was trying to do.

A staple of Old South philosophy was that the more uninformed a slave was about everything, the more docile he tended to be. Further, while chapter 198, sections 35–36, of the Virginia Code permitted "negroes" to gather in daylight for religious services, the laws forbade whites to teach blacks to read and write about any subject. Jackson was therefore on the perimeter of the law by leading a service on Sunday afternoons.

"Some of the Bourbon aristocracy" of Lexington, one resident declared, criticized Jackson's activity "and even went so far as to threaten prosecution." An individual named J. Cleveland Cady even alleged that Jackson had to tolerate "taunts and scorns for the sake of those poor people that nobody cared for." The truth of such statements is questionable; still, Jackson had to toil long and dutifully to get the black class organized and meeting regularly. Once the starting pains had alleviated, progress surpassed everyone's anticipations—except Jackson's.[32]

He organized and managed, educated and monitored, encouraged and rewarded. The class, consisting of blacks of all ages, was conducted like a military operation with a benevolent hand in control. Black enrollment ultimately ranged from eighty to over 100 people if Jackson was there. When the major was on summer vacation, attendance dropped to about fifty students. Jackson used twelve teaching assistants "recruited from among the educated ladies and gentlemen" in town. One such aristocrat was Jessie Hainning, who taught at the Ann Smith Academy until her 1858 appointment as principal of the New Market Female Academy.

Each Sunday afternoon at 2:45, the church bell called the faithful to worship. Precisely at 3:00, Jackson closed and bolted the classroom door. Latecomers were not tolerated. He called the school to order with a prayer usually so "earnest and full of feeling," one assistant exclaimed, that it "went straight to the hearts of all who heard it."[33]

The major had neither ear nor voice for music, but he was especially fond of the hymn "Amazing Grace." The service therefore began with Jackson croaking the first notes and the blacks singing the first stanza or two with fervor: "Amazing grace, how sweet the sound / That saved a wretch like me."

Bible readings followed, always accompanied by Jackson's simple explanations. One of the white teachers observed: "His way of stating old truths was charming in its freshness and simplicity." Next was prayer, usually offered by Jackson. The assemblage then broke into small study groups for rudimentary instruction in the Bible, in Brown's *Child Catechism*, or "some other suitable formula of truth."[34]

An oral examination of two of the catechisms or two small sections of scripture completed the instruction. On the first Sunday of each month, Testaments and Bibles were awarded to those who had displayed outstanding progress. The school adjourned promptly at 3:45 with the singing of the remaining stanzas of "Amazing Grace."

Jackson issued monthly reports to owners on the attendance, attitude, and progress of each slave. If pupils had been absent, he delivered the summaries in person. Dr. White noted that Jackson usually "conferred with the family about all matters connected with the behavior or misbehavior of the pupils."[35]

Even after Jackson left for the army and war, one of his first inquiries often made to Lexington friends who visited him in camp was, "How is the colored Sunday school progressing?" If the report was favorable (and it almost always was), "he never failed to respond with a strong expression of gratitude."[36]

The Sunday school was of benefit to Jackson in three ways. It gave him a new and challenging outlet at a time when he needed to get his mind more occupied with earthly things. The school also deepened Jackson's own faith; for in teaching others the blessings of Christianity, Jackson absorbed anew many of his own postulates. Finally, working weekly with blacks provided an insight into the institution of slavery.

In Jackson's mind, slaves were children of God placed in subordinate situations for reasons only the Creator could explain. Helping them was a missionary effort for Jackson. Their souls had to be saved. Although Jackson could not alter the social status of slaves, he could and did display Christian decency to those whose lot it was to be in bondage. He learned and used the name of each of his students. They in turn referred to him affectionately as "Marse Major."

Maggie Junkin noted that "it was pleasant to walk about the town, and see the veneration with which the negroes saluted him, and his unfailing courtesy towards them. To the old gray-haired negro who bowed before him he would lift his cap as courteously as to his commander-in-chief." Dr. White later stated of the relationship between Jackson and his Sunday afternoon students: "In their religious instruction he succeeded wonderfully. His discipline was systematic and firm, but very kind. . . . His servants reverenced and loved him, as they would have done a brother or father. . . . He was emphatically the black man's friend."[37]

The first half of 1856 passed rather quietly for Jackson. He and John Preston became closer because of common sorrow. On January 4 of that year, Sally Preston died. She was the second VMI faculty wife to perish in fifteen months. Because of Preston's influence at the academy, final exams were suspended so that cadets could attend one of the largest funerals ever held in Lexington.

Jackson's personal activities in the spring months were basically twofold. He wrote Laura, Aunt Clementine, and several business people about erecting tombstones over the graves of members of his family. Early in April, Jackson began participating fully in a great interdenominational revival that occupied Lexington's attention for several weeks.[38] "We have such an outpouring of the *Spirit of God* in our churches here as I never remember of having seen elsewhere," Jackson exclaimed, "I feel very thankful to *God* for such divine blessings."[39]

Maggie Junkin departed for Philadelphia on May 10 in search of relief for her ailing back. She had been gone three weeks when Jackson sent her a letter in Spanish. "My dearest Sister," he stated, "although I have not had the advantage of your conversation, I had instead the hope of improvement in your health, which to you is of the greatest value." Jackson closed the letter with reference to his black class. "Our afternoon Sunday school Our Lord blessed very much last Sunday. I had about one hundred Students. Pray much for it."[40]

Unknown to Jackson, he was the center of a controversy that marked the end of the 1855–56 VMI school year. Complaints about his classroom performance and the difficulty of his final examinations (which always consumed the full four-hour allotment) had persisted throughout his years at the institute. By June 1856, outcries were numerous enough to be serious. Some graduates felt that Jackson was a failure as a teacher, would always remain so, and that VMI would suffer from his presence.

Superintendent Smith sought outside referees in the matter. One person he contacted was James Murfee, who had graduated first in the class of 1853 and was teaching mathematics at a college in nearby Lynchburg. Murfee straddled the line in his response to Smith's query. The ex-cadet did not wish to hurt Jackson's feelings, but he felt compelled to be truthful. "I wish to be understood as having the greatest regard for Maj. Jackson as a man," Murfee began. On the other hand, "I know that he did not, nor has not done as far as I know, anything like justice to his department, and from the same opinion on the part of many, it seems that the Institute is suffering much." Jackson's failure to make better use of instruments in class was particularly irksome to Murfee. "I would about as soon study watch-making without a watch and instruments, as I would study, as I did at the V. M. I. Nat. Phil. without an apparatus." He considered the professorship of natural philosophy and chemistry to be the most vital in a school with VMI's goals. Only half of that foundation existed, in Murfee's judgment.[41]

The Society of the Alumni appointed John B. Strange (class of 1842) to present to the Board of Visitors a resolution abhorring the mismanagement of the "Department of Natural and Experimental Philosophy." Jackson lacked "capacity adequate to the duties of his chair," the petition stated.[42]

Members of the Board of Visitors could not ignore the complaints, but they did the next best thing. They unanimously approved General William H. Richardson's motion to table the resolution. In later years, Anna Jackson was of the opinion that Superintendent Smith "never appreciated" Jackson's efforts and gave him little support in this crisis. The opposite was true. Smith defended his colleague and even paved the way for Jackson to be given a larger and better-equipped classroom.[43]

It was a year later before Jackson learned of the campaign against him. In typical fashion, he asked for a formal investigation of every charge. The Board of Visitors had more important things to do. It promptly tabled that motion as well.[44]

Jackson had intended that summer to make his first trip to the West. He was going to Washington, D.C., to ascertain the location of available land, and then strike out across the continent in search of about 3000 acres of the "best land" he could find. He planned to acquire only half of that acreage in Northern states, he told Laura. "I am a little afraid to put much there for fear that in the event of a dissolution of the Union that the property of Southerners may be confiscated."[45]

This second early reference to a possible civil war is rather startling; for although national passions were heating in 1856, the ideas of a fragmented union or a fratricidal war were not commonplace at that period. Jackson also felt more strongly on the issue than his letter hinted. Sometime in June he abandoned plans to go west. Instead, he asked Colonel Smith for a leave of absence to make a trip he had postponed five years earlier. Smith readily assented. On July 10, the local newspaper announced that "Maj. Thos. J. Jackson, the accomplished Professor who fills the chair of Natural Philosophy and Astronomy" at VMI, "left on Saturday last for a European tour."[46]

In addition to fulfilling a longtime dream and spending the summer in novel surroundings, Jackson had another reason for going abroad. While en route across the Atlantic on the steamship *Asia*, Jackson wrote Laura that "even with you [this summer] I would be reminded of the loss of that happiness which I once enjoyed with *My Ellie.* So I have to some extent torn myself away from that state of mind which I feared, should my summer have been passed at home or in the U. States."[47]

Jackson's tour of Europe was like anything else he undertook: energetic and complete. He visited England, Scotland, Belgium, France, Germany, Switzerland, and Italy; he then returned to Paris, crossed the channel to England, and sailed for home. Jackson told Maggie that the summer "was full of enjoyment and profit."

Surprisingly, Jackson paid little attention to battlefields and other military sites. What he sought on the summer journey was a broadening of knowledge through things cultural. He had an undeveloped love of art. Now was the time to nurture it. Jackson organized his visits with a rigid schedule that permitted no deviation. Guidebooks prepared him for each day's outing. For sixteen hours daily—from 5 A.M. to 9 P.M.—he was touring, sightseeing, inspecting. The objects of his attention were churches, public buildings, paintings, sculpture, remains of once-stately architecture, large cities, mountains, harbors, and local customs.

An English acquaintance observed that Jackson "seemed never weary of dwelling on the magnificence of our lofty cathedrals, and other public buildings, which must have impressed him as a wonderful contrast to the modest little wooden churches and Court-houses of his native mountains."[48]

The major later wrote rapturously of "the romantic lakes and mountains of Scotland, the imposing abbeys and cathedrals of England; the Rhine, with its castellated banks and luxuriant vineyards; the sublime scenery of Switzerland, with her lofty Mont Blanc and massive Mer-de-Glace; the vestiges of Venetian beauty; the sculpture and paintings of Italy; the ruins of Rome; the beautiful Bay of Naples, illuminated by Vesuvius; and lovely France, with her gay capital."[49]

At each stop, Jackson made copious notes; he filled small notebooks with telescopic phrases and hastily scribbled memoranda, most of which made sense only to him. Jackson concluded that "Roman Catholics laundry their churches." He was not impressed by a black-robed minister who preached extemporaneously for two hours. Florence had "more ostentatious display than I have yet met with." After attending services in one European church, Jackson commented dryly: "If they have enough children they could have a sabbath school."[50]

One military site Jackson did visit was the great battlefield at Waterloo. Years later Jackson discussed the pivotal engagement with his army physician, Dr. Hunter McGuire. When McGuire asked whose troop dispositions were the wisest, Napoleon's or Wellington's, Jackson leaped up from a camp stool and replied with much enthusiasm, "Napoleon's, by all odds!" McGuire then asked, "Well, why was he whipped then?" Jackson answered without hesitation, "I can only explain it by telling you that I think God intended him to stop right there."[51]

The oceanic voyage home gave Jackson much time to recall all the wonders he had beheld and to establish their relevance in his life. It had been an incalculable experience. "I would advise you," Jackson told a friend, "never to mention my European trip to me unless you are possessed with a super-abundance of patience, as the very mention of it is calculated to bring up an almost inexhaustible assemblage of proud and beautiful associations."[52]

Jackson saw the hand of God in every phase of his trip. He informed his aunt: "It appeared to me that Providence had opened the way for my long-contemplated visit, and I am much gratified at having gone." He also declared: "Passing over the works of the Creator, which are far the most impressive, it is difficult to conceive of the influences which even the works of His creatures exercise over the mind until one loiters amidst their master productions."[53]

Three months in Europe wrought a marked change in Jackson's thinking. Never before had he seen God's artistry so abundantly and magnificently. The world was limitless in beauty, thanks to an all-loving Creator. Every painting, every segment of scenery, every revelation, strengthened Jackson's faith.

He now could put the loss of Ellie in proper perspective. She was gone, but so much of life remained. It was time to forget the past and to look to the future. Jackson returned to Lexington a changed man. The grief had passed away. He was seeking happiness—and a new wife. God, he was convinced, would help him in both quests.

Jackson was late by a fortnight in reaching Lexington. The fault was not his. He arrived on time at the port of embarkation, but "the steamer was delayed by the act of Providence." VMI was already in session by the time he arrived home.

Since the major was painstakingly punctual, he had to undergo several gibes about his tardiness. To each he responded with what was for him a full explanation: "I did all that lay in the compass of human power and foresight to be here at the appointed time, but when those over whom I had no control occasioned the delay, my responsibility was at an end."[54]

Some sunshine had returned to the Junkin home while Jackson was in Europe. On August 22, Julia married Washington College professor Junius M. Fishburn. He was in his mid-twenties, a highly educated, accomplished, and pious man who with his bride (and a new Jackson) instilled life again in the rooms of the president's home.

With another school term in session, Jackson again became a familiar sight on campus and in town. His classes were as academically challenging as ever. "He had by

far the most difficult branches included in the course of instruction," one upperclassman observed, "that is, the application of mathematics to natural philosophy. Bartlett's Mechanics was our special dread. [Jackson] was, however, thoroughly conversant
with every principle, and had the elaborate equations at his finger's end."[55]

This did not keep youngsters in the lower classes from pranks at Jackson's expense.
The major's section room was surrounded by the sleeping rooms of cadets. Many of
them could indulge in disruptive antics and then "scurry to their holes like so many
rats, with little or no chance of detection." Cadet W. N. Mercer Otey recalled being in
one of Jackson's sections and seeing "some mischievous cadet from the stoop shooting
water at the Professor by means of a syringe through a knot hole in the door."[56]

Florence McCarthy, the new pastor of the Baptist church, met Jackson at this
period. A number of the major's features struck McCarthy as interesting. "When he
walked it was with a long, methodical stride, and accompanied with a leisurely,
pendulum-like swaying of the arms." Commenting on Jackson's face, McCarthy
stated: "The mouth is usually a great index of character; but any one would search
Jackson's mouth in vain for any signs of greatness. His lips were thin and red . . . and
the corners of his mouth slightly upturned; the whole mouth expressing in a most
unmistakable way a vast amount of sweetness and gentleness, but giving no hint of
courage . . . or any sort of genius. Jackson's voice was like his mouth, very soft, kindly
and inarticulate, sometimes like a faint jabber."[57]

He resumed his social obligations in Lexington alone and only from a sense of duty.
For example, Jessie Hainning, the young teacher who had assisted Jackson with the
black Sunday school, was studying Sanskrit under Dr. Junkin in the evenings. The
major walked the young woman home each night after her lesson.

After Jackson's longtime friend, bookseller John Lyle, suffered an incapacitating
stroke on November 2, he visited Lyle regularly at his room in the John Preston
home. Conversations with Preston were a natural and regular part of the visits.
Doubtless, the highly influential Preston helped accelerate Jackson's business ventures over the succeeding months.

Since Jackson customarily paid cash for what he bought, it is difficult to follow his
finances closely. However, and in spite of an erroneous conclusion by one of Jackson's
leading biographers, the major invested widely and wisely.[58] In the spring of 1857, he
bought $2000 worth of stock in the newly formed Bank of Rockbridge, opened a
checking account (which he used for large purchases), and became a member of the
bank's board of directors. Within four years, that one investment had grown to
$4000—a sum equivalent to at least twenty times that amount in the late twentieth
century.[59]

The major acquired holdings in all three of Lexington's banking institutions. His
investment of $600 in Bank of the Commonwealth shares first doubled and then
tripled in value over the space of a few years. In addition, a private banker known only
as "Blair" handled some of Jackson's money. Jackson undoubtedly used him because
of a high-interest yield.[60]

During this same period, he entered into a partnership with John Preston and
William Gilham on a number of business enterprises. They included purchases of a
lot on Randolph Street and a 320-acre tract of land in the Blue Ridge Mountains

eight miles east of Lexington. Jackson unobtrusively put his money to maximum good use, and he accumulated a very comfortable income as a result.[61]

But Jackson was seeking more than business success at this time; he was seeking happiness and permanent companionship. The search could not follow a logical path. Sadly, Jackson knew that the one who then held his heart would never be his wife. Maggie Junkin remained single far into adulthood. She never gave a full reason why, although she once hinted that "an unfortunate episode in very early life closed her heart."[62] Then Jackson intruded into her life. The resentment Maggie felt toward him vanished in the numbness created by Ellie's death. Amid their common loss, Maggie and Jackson drew closer and closer together.

Granted, she was four years older and better educated; he was maturer in action and more demanding. Yet they were so much alike: deeply religious, shy in public, plagued by maladies both real and imagined. Indications are strong that by the autumn of 1856 each was in love with the other.

Because they were such good Presbyterians, they could never be man and wife. A canon in the church of that day expressly forbade a man marrying his deceased wife's sister.[63] Jackson and Maggie knew church law; they lived in the home of a leading Presbyterian cleric. Church doctrine and family ties could not be disregarded. To do so would be to live in sin and disgrace. In spite of the depth of their mutual affection, Jackson and Maggie were forever brother and sister.

He had to look elsewhere. Methodically recalling the young women he had met in recent years, Jackson found his thoughts returning again and again to Mary Anna Morrison, who with her sister Eugenia had visited the Harvey Hills just before Jackson's marriage to Ellie. In retrospect, the major envisioned even more attraction in Anna's soft brown eyes, her dark brown hair, the calm and sunny disposition she seemed always to possess.

The Morrison girls were aware of Ellie's death. Yet Anna—six years Ellie's junior and seven-and-a-half years younger than Jackson—was not prepared for his romantic overtures. One day that autumn, Anna received a letter. It was the first correspondence with Jackson. The professor, Anna later stated, expressed "such blissful memories over reminiscences of the summer we had been together in Lexington that my sister Eugenia laughed most heartily over it, and predicted an early visit from the major."[64]

A few days before Christmas, Professor and Mrs. Harvey Hill were having breakfast at their North Carolina home. He was head of the mathematics department at Davidson College; she was the oldest of the six Morrison girls. One of the Morrison servants arrived to tell Mrs. Hill the latest family news. Isabella Hill inquired at one point if her sister Anna "had had any beaux lately." The mammy replied that as a matter of fact a gentleman was then calling on Miss Anna. She described him as a tall man, with brass buttons on his cap, and wearing very large boots. Harvey Hill chuckled. "That must be Jackson!" he stated. Hill was correct. A day or so earlier, Anna was peering out the parlor window when she saw "a tall form, in military dress, walking up from my father's gate [and] I could scarcely believe my senses."[65]

Jackson had taken a few days' leave in the middle of the school year for a quick trip to the Morrison home in North Carolina. This get-acquainted visit was pleasurable for all concerned—especially Jackson, who wanted a wife and who always enjoyed a large, close-knit family.

The patriarch of the household was Robert Hall Morrison. Born in 1798 near Concord, North Carolina, he had graduated third in a University of North Carolina class that included future president James Knox Polk. Morrison studied theology at Princeton Seminary and received ordination to the Presbyterian ministry. For many years, he organized and served a number of churches in the Charlotte-Fayetteville area. He married Mary Graham, the daughter of General Joseph Graham of Revolutionary War fame. She was also the sister of William A. Graham, who became North Carolina governor, U.S. senator, and Secretary of the Navy in the Fillmore administration. Mrs. Morrison spent most of her time bearing and caring for six daughters and four sons.

In 1835, Morrison began pushing for the establishment of a Presbyterian college in North Carolina. Once the idea gained official approval, he raised the first funds and oversaw construction of the first buildings. Davidson College opened its doors in 1837, with Robert Morrison as president. He led the school for only three-and-a-half years. "A serious throat trouble interfered with his teaching," a family member wrote, and this forced Morrison to relinquish his college duties.

He retired to his home sixteen miles away and continued as a member of the college's board of trustees for a quarter-century. A contemporary thought him "an exceedingly interesting character. Tall, straight, with a flashing black eye, and black hair that never turned gray, he always presented a picturesque appearance."[66]

Morrison had bought a 200-acre tract with a small home on it some twenty miles northeast of Charlotte. He called the place Cottage Home. Sometime later, when Morrison built a much larger house several hundred yards back from the original home place, he gave the new structure the same name. Cottage Home was actually a two-story, twelve-room mansion situated on a knoll and nestled in a grove of hardwood trees.[67]

Anna, born July 21, 1831, was the third of the Morrison daughters. She attended Salem Academy in Winston-Salem, North Carolina, but did not graduate. Small in stature and well-rounded in form, Anna was modest but cheerful, cordial but considerate. The Reverend James R. Graham, who came to know Jackson and his second wife intimately, stated of Anna: "Fair in person, and beautiful in character—amiable and loving by nature—intelligent, cultivated, refined and pious. She possessed all the qualities that could attract the love" of a man like Jackson.[68]

The Morrisons liked Jackson from the start. Robert Morrison was impressed with the lofty principles of the major's faith; the mother's heart went out to this man who exuded a combination of shyness and courtesy; for the Morrison boys, Jackson's experience and status as a soldier was fascinating; to the Morrison daughters, there was magnetism in this man who gave them attention by preferring to listen rather than to talk. As for Anna, she already enjoyed friendship with the Virginian. His short visit was the first step in molding amity into love.

Jackson made his intentions known to the family during the brief sojourn. The Morrison response was positive. His visit, Anna stated, "was one of mutual congeniality and enjoyment."[69] Jackson appears to have returned to Lexington an engaged man.

For weeks, he kept the betrothal a secret from everyone. Laura and Maggie were doubtless aware that he was very interested in Anna Morrison. The first open hint of a serious romance came in late February 1857 when, writing to his sister about his summer plans, Jackson declared, "I am unable to say whether I will visit Beverly or North Carolina."[70]

Another love affair suddenly took shape that winter. Maggie and Jackson's VMI colleague, John Preston, became a twosome at social affairs. When Preston, whose wife had been dead barely a year, proposed marriage, Maggie shocked many people by accepting. Preston was nine years her senior, with seven children ranging in age from five to twenty-two.

Meanwhile, Jackson was sending a regular flow of letters to his fiancée. One that was not cheery and romantic came in the wake of the death of Anna's infant nephew, Morrison Hill. Jackson was all too familiar with earthly loss. To Anna, he wrote philosophically and almost with an undertone of bluntness: "I was not surprised that little Morrison was taken away, as I have long regarded his father's attachment to him as too strong; that is, so strong that he would be unwilling to give him up, though God should call for his own. I am not one of those who believe that absolute attachment ever is, or ever can be too strong, for any object of our affection, but our love for God may not be strong enough. We may not love Him so intensely as to have no will but His."[71]

Prudence dictated that with his engagement to Anna, Jackson should relinquish his quarters at the Junkin home. He moved to the Lexington Hotel on Main Street. From there, he poured out his heart to Anna. It is abundantly clear in every one of his letters that he viewed the forthcoming marriage as that between three beings: himself, Anna, and God.

"It is a great comfort to me," he wrote, "to know that although I am not with you, yet you are in the hands of One who will not permit any evil to come nigh [to] you. . . . In my daily walks I think much of you. I love to stroll abroad after the labors of the day are over, & indulge feelings of gratitude to God for all the sources of natural beauty which he has adorned the earth. . . . And as my mind dwells on you, I love to give it a devotional turn, by thinking of you as a gift from our Heavenly Father."[72]

Early in May, Jackson told his beloved: "I take special pleasure . . . that the *glory of God* may be the controling & absorbing thought of our lives in our new relations. It is to me a great satisfaction to feel that God has manifestly ordered *our union*." A week later, Jackson confessed: "When in prayer for you last Sabbath, the tears came to my eyes, & I realized an unusual degree of emotional tenderness." Searching for an explanation, Jackson was "disposed to think that it consisted in the idea of the intimate relation, existing between you, as the object of my tender affection, & God, who I looked up to as my Heavenly Father. I felt that day as though it were a Communion day for myself."[73]

As much as Jackson looked forward to letters from Anna, he had two unbroken rules about reading them. He would not open a letter at night for fear of aggravating his sensitive eyesight; and in honor of the Sabbath he would wait until Monday morning to read a letter received late Saturday. Jackson and a friend were walking to church one Sunday. The friend, knowing that a letter from Anna had arrived the previous evening, asked Jackson if he had digested its contents. "Assuredly not," came the reply. "What obstinacy!" the acquaintance exclaimed. "Don't you know that your curiosity to learn its contents will distract your attention from divine service far more than if you read it? Surely, in this case, to depart from your rule would promote a true Sabbath observance, instead of injuring it." Jackson shook his head. "No. I shall make the most faithful effort I can to govern my thoughts and guard them from unnecessary distraction; and as I do this from a sense of duty, I expect the divine blessing upon it."[74]

Before the coming of spring, both Jackson and Maggie were reconciled to one another's weddings. Maggie journeyed to Philadelphia to obtain her trousseau. She also agreed to purchase Jackson's wedding gifts for Anna. He gave her $150 in advance for a watch, string of pearls, chain, and ring. In a May 25 letter to Maggie, Jackson spelled out precisely what he wanted each item to be.[75]

That same day, Jackson asked Clement Fishburne, a member of the Davidson College faculty and brother of Lexington's Junius Fishburn, to be one of the groomsmen at the wedding (although brothers, the two men spelled their surnames differently). Fishburne accepted, although his acquaintance with Jackson was slight.[76]

About this same time, Jackson sent a teasing message to his sister. Jackson wrote: "I will begin by stating that I have an invitation for you; and what do you think it is? and whom from? For it is not often that I am authorized to send you invitations, and especially pressing ones. And I suppose you begin to think, or may think, Well what does he mean? Why doesn't he tell me at once and be done with it?" Rambling for another half-page, Jackson finally got to the point: "Well, now, having cultivated your patience a little, as all women are said to have curiosity, I will tell you that Miss Mary Anna Morrison, friend of mine . . . is engaged to be married to an acquaintance of yours living in this village, and she has requested me to urge you to attend her wedding in July next. . . . The wedding is not to be large."[77]

Nor was it leisurely. Anna had chosen the evening of July 16 for the ceremony. That was also commencement day at Davidson College. Jackson left Lexington in the second week of July and traveled to Davidson. For several days he was a guest of his old friends, the Harvey Hills. Jackson met several faculty members and attended at least one final examination.

Thursday, July 16, 1857, was uncomfortably hot, humid, and too full of activity. The major attended Davidson's commencement in the morning. Jackson was accorded a seat of honor on the rostrum. The school president, Dr. Drury Lacy, proved long-winded for Jackson's attention span. To the chagrin of the bride's family, he went to sleep during Lacy's opening remarks.

It was early afternoon before the sixteen-mile journey to Cottage Home began. In Jackson's party were Dr. Lacy (who was to perform the wedding rite because Dr. Morrison did not feel emotionally up to the task), the Harvey Hill family, Clem Fishburne, and Thomas P. Cocke (substituting for his ill cousin, Tom Preston). The carriages bounced through thick dust and heat before reaching the Morrison home around 4 P.M.

Chaos prevailed when they arrived there. Anna's trousseau, shipped from New York City, had arrived only two hours before the wedding. Some technicality then arose over the marriage license. One of the groomsmen had to gallop to the county seat at Lincolnton to unravel that snag. With the wedding scheduled for "early candlelighting," the hubbub of preparations seemed to increase. Fishburne related the next stage for Jackson:

> The room into which we were put to prepare for the ceremony was upstairs and had been heated by the western sun so that dressing was hot business. The Major undertook to put on a new collar, a 'stand up,' such as there were then worn, and he called on me to help him adjust it. By the time I got it buttoned it was limp. I told him it would not do, we must try another. He produced another somewhat different in shape and by cutting the buttonholes before we began the adjustment we managed to get him rigged out in a dry stiff collar which stood the heat very well. He wore the uniform of the Professors at the Institute . . . and in due time the ceremony of dressing being completed, we marched down to the parlour.[78]

Anna was still flustered from the last-minute arrival of her gown. Jackson looked awkward and uncomfortable. He stood at rigid attention, the long side whiskers curling toward lips pressed tightly together. Fishburne and Cocke were the grooms-men; two of Anna's younger sisters and two first cousins served as bridesmaids. The Morrison and Hill families were the other witnesses at the ceremony.

A loquacious Dr. Lacy went slowly through the service. Even Anna was led to comment: "Whether or not it was his usual formula, or whether he was impressed by the very determined and unbending look of the military bridegroom, Dr. Lacy made him promise to be an 'indulgent husband,' laying special stress upon the adjective; but he was equally emphatic in exacting obedience on the part of the bride."[79]

The last prayer finally ended; Lacy pronounced the couple man and wife. Anna Morrison, who had once said that she would never marry a Democrat, a widower, or a soldier, had pledged her troth to all three.[80]

After spending the night with the Morrisons at Cottage Home, the newlyweds departed for Charlotte and the start of a northern honeymoon. The itinerary was parallel to much of Jackson's wedding trip with Ellie (and Maggie). However, following stops at Richmond and Baltimore, Anna developed a painful enlargement of one of the glands in her throat.

Jackson took her quickly to Philadelphia and its renowned medical school. The physician who examined her could not make a diagnosis. Providentially, Jackson bumped into Dr. Archibald Graham, a Lexington physician who was visiting in Philadelphia. Graham—like all of Lexington's physicians—was a firm believer in hydropathy. He recommended that Anna partake of the waters of Rockbridge Alum Springs at the end of the honeymoon.[81]

With Anna insistent that the trip continue, the Jacksons proceeded to New York City, West Point, Niagara Falls, and Saratoga. Sightseeing filled the hours in New York. Jackson's "delight was unbounded" during the brief stop at his alma mater. Anna shared his wonder at the magnificence of Niagara Falls. The couple shunned the social festivities at Saratoga in order to take walks together into the beautiful country-side. Anna also remembered that her husband "found a delightful recreation in rowing me over the lovely lake, where placid waters were, at that time, covered with water lilies." By the time they started south toward Lexington, Anna was pregnant.[82]

On August 5, the couple arrived at Rockbridge Alum Springs for a three-week stay.

Jackson eagerly introduced Anna to water treatments. When not seeking therapy in the baths, they took walks, read, and "spent the time enjoying themselves and their surroundings." The swelling in Anna's throat dissipated. "I regret that we have been unable to visit you this summer," Jackson wrote Laura from the springs, "but I felt under the circumstances it was my duty to make Anna's health the first object of concern."[83]

Jackson and his bride reached Lexington just before the start of the academic year. They took rooms at the Lexington Hotel. Favorite evening pastimes for the couple were reading and memorizing the *Shorter Catechism* of the Presbyterian church. After a few months at the hotel, Jackson obtained larger and less expensive accommodations at a boardinghouse near the VMI campus.

He was still dissatisfied with the arrangements. "I shall never be content until I am at the head of an establishment in which my friends can feel at home in Lexington," he proclaimed. "I have taken the first important step by securing a wife capable of making a happy home, and the next thing is to give her an opportunity."[84]

The first person to whom Jackson introduced his wife in Lexington was his bookseller friend, John Lyle. Although partially paralyzed by a stroke, Lyle warmly greeted the couple. "His smiling and hearty welcome," Anna stated, "went directly to the heart of the stranger."[85]

Anna knew a few people in Lexington, but no one well. Her first months in an unfamiliar society would have been lonely indeed but for the selfless assistance of Maggie Junkin Preston. Now, as mistress of a large family, a three-storied mansion, and most of Lexington society, Maggie Preston stepped forward to make Anna feel at home. At their first meeting, she embraced Jackson's new wife and declared, "You are taking the place that my sister had, and so you shall be a sister to me." Although Maggie was inundated with new responsibilities, she saw to it that the Jacksons were never excluded from any social function of note.[86]

High among Anna's initial obligations was to write Laura Arnold, who felt slighted that she had been omitted from a visit during the honeymoon or in the immediate months thereafter. The first letter Anna sent reflected the great tact and capacity for affection that she possessed. "No apology is necessary for writing to you, as I feel that my husbands only sister ought to be very near and dear to me. . . . It was quite a disappointment to both Mr. Jackson and myself that we could not carry out our intention of visiting you and we have felt very sorry to learn from your letters that you feel so hurt at being disappointed by us."

Anna then explained her throat problem, at the same time reminding Laura of Jackson's rigid sense of duty;

I was reluctant to forego the pleasure of visiting you (for I was really anxious to see you dear sister), but my husband thought it was his duty to follow the physicians advice and you know he always makes every pleasure give way to duty. . . .

Mr. Jackson has improved very much in health this summer and is now looking better than I have ever seen him. He has been very busy since his return and is rather more studious than I would like him to be as I see nothing of him in his study hours.[87]

The statement on Jackson's health was premature. While he himself thought in late autumn that his physical condition was improving, the winter of 1857–58 would be one of the worst periods of his life. Disorders had begun by November 1, when he told Laura: "At present I suffer more with cold feet than anything else. I have been accustomed to bathing them in cold water, but they have cracked open so much as to render the discontinuance of it necessary."[88]

In mid-December, Jackson apologized to his sister for not writing sooner. "Owing to an inflamation of the tube leading to the ear and also inflamation of the throat (chronic), and very painful nuralgia, I have been constrained to give up my correspondence for a while. I never remember having suffered so much as with pain the last three weeks, and now I am compelled to use a vial of chloroform liniment per day externally, and am also using internally a preparation of amonia. The hearing of my right ear is impaired; but I trust not permanently. I have continued to attend to my recitations, notwithstanding my sufferings. In a few days I hope to be free from pain. The eye medicine helped me for a while I think; but I can't say that I have been permanently benefitted."[89]

Jackson had never before acknowledged pain and openly fought discouragement. Things got progressively worse. Early in February 1858, he wrote Laura, "I have nearly, if not entirely, lost the use of one ear, and my throat has to be cauterized about twice a week." A month later, no improvement had occurred. "My throat, to which I alluded, has been inflamed, and I have lost the use of one ear, or nearly so, in consequence of the inflamation . . . and the other ear is also affected. But we know that all things work together for good. This is my great consolation."[90]

By May, Jackson was still experimenting with cures. "My eyes have been troubling me much lately. . . . I am now using glycerine which is the essence of oil. I take it through the nostrils for the purpose of curing the inflamation at the entrance of the nasal tubes into the mouth and I find it of great service. God has blest its use to me very much. I tried caustic or nitrate of silver, but with much less effect."[91]

Jackson was correct in one supposition: the 1858 chronic middle-ear infection left the hearing in his right ear permanently impaired.

Naturally, as his infirmities mounted, Jackson threw himself into the work of the Lord. "His zeal and activity in the cause of religion were always among his most striking characteristics," a cadet at the time noted. "Yet while he labored constantly, he did so quietly and modestly."[92]

Jackson had read the Bible cover to cover many times since his alliance with the Lexington Presbyterian Church. By the time of his second marriage, he was hard at work on a concordant grouping of scores of biblical passages. The blank pages of a copy of *Mitchell's Ancient Atlas, Classical and Sacred* became his notebook. Dozens of biblical verses that appealed to Jackson went under such headings as "Purification thro' the righteousness of Christ," "Love of God in Christ, as displayed in the work of Redemption," and "Humility—Its necessity & importance." The well-worn hinge of the book is evidence that it received regular use.[93]

Sunday was his busiest day of the week. He attended both church services, taught a young men's Bible class in the morning, and directed his black school in the afternoon. Anna agreed to help with the Sunday school. She was touched by Jackson's tenderness toward his black pupils. Later she confessed that she "never saw her husband look more earnest than when telling those poor people the story of the cross." Mrs. Jackson also learned to avoid any reference to secular topics on the

Sabbath. If one arose, Jackson would smile kindly and reply: "We will talk about that tomorrow."[94]

Another church duty came to Jackson late that year. Earlier in 1857, the state Presbyterian synod urged member churches to reactivate the office of deacon. The Lexington church moved to comply. On December 26, the congregation unanimously elected three men to serve in that capacity; and when Jackson, John W. Barclay, and Alexander L. Nelson held their first meeting of deacons, Jackson was selected chairman.[95]

The primary roles of the deacons were to look "to the general interests of the poor, and to collections for purposes in which the Session may desire their cooperation." Jackson and the two other deacons divided Lexington into three districts for collecting funds for the needy. His area "lay to the south and east of the 'old boat yard road' at the upper end of town."[96]

Deacon Jackson took his new position very seriously. "He rendered efficient service," Dr. White was quick to acknowledge. "His punctuality in attending the stated meetings of the Board of Deacons, in calling on the Pastor to report what he had done in his district, and to get instructions—or as he always said 'orders' for the ensuing month, were very characteristic. Regarding his Pastor as his superior in command, his course was precisely that of an inferior to his superior officer in the army."[97]

The major ran the diaconate with a firm grip. A brother deacon was not at one of the monthly meetings. Jackson met him on the street the next day. "We missed you last night," Jackson said casually.

"I had another engagement," the man answered.

A now-indignant Jackson snapped: "How could you have another engagement when you were already engaged at that hour to attend to the Lord's business?" Nothing the deacon offered thereafter as an excuse was acceptable.[98]

Within a few weeks, and in the face of his health problems, Jackson also submitted a resolution to expand the size of the sanctuary. Greater room was needed, especially for black worshipers. The motion to add thirty-seven pews downstairs and sixteen in the upstairs gallery passed easily. Jackson was the first person to make a pledge to the building fund. His $200 donation represented fifteen percent of his annual salary and was twice the amount pledged by any other member of the Lexington congregation.[99]

In February, Jackson had to leave Anna for a few days. The annual George Washington grand parade was to occur in Richmond. It was Jackson's turn to escort the VMI corps of cadets. The review went smoothly. That evening, Governor Henry A. Wise hosted a reception. The governor's son (and later a student at VMI) commented, "Major Jackson was plainly dressed, wore coarse shoes, had a weary look in his blue eyes, took very little part in conversation, seemed bored by the entertainment, neither ate nor drank, and, after paying his respects to the governor, and to General Winfield Scott . . . quietly disappeared."[100]

That observation was incorrect in one respect. Jackson would have been immaculately dressed. Cadet John Gittings wrote emphatically: "It was the custom . . . to fire salutes of artillery on the Fourth of July and Washington's birthday. In honor of such occasions Major Jackson would always don his best uniform and wear his finest sword."[101]

The school year at VMI proceeded without major incident. Jackson's personality was now ingrained at the institute. His colleague, Raleigh Colston, observed of

Jackson at this time: "He was one of the most straight-forward and single-minded men I ever knew. Outside of his family circle, he was serious and even grave in his deportment, and his countenance bore a rather melancholy expression. His smile was one of remarkable and peculiar sweetness, though not unmixed with a tinge of sadness, and I cannot remember that I ever knew him to give way to a hearty burst of laughter. In fact, it was a settled opinion with us that Jackson never could see a joke and was utterly incapable of appreciating a pun."[102]

One exception existed to this axiom, Colston stated, and it was a story that Jackson thoroughly enjoyed. Captain Israel Vogdes served a long tenure as mathematics professor at West Point before entering field duty. One day in Florida, Vogdes was supervising the excavation of tree stumps from a road. A brother officer appeared. "Hello, Vogdes," he shouted, "what are you doing?"

The former professor replied: "Well, I am at my old trade, extracting roots."

Colston added: "This Jackson evidently considered an excellent joke, for he related it to me repeatedly, certainly not less than once a year during the ten years that we were colleagues."[103]

On those occasions when Jackson engaged in informal conversation with cadets, few forgot the experience. He was warm and tolerant where the young men were concerned. Sometime that year he met with a group of first classmen. Cadets had long heard that at the battle of Chapultepec Jackson and a sergeant had behaved "as cooly as if they had only been at artillery practice." Now one of the cadets asked the major if the story were true. Jackson smiled and replied that it was.

"That was a hot place, wasn't it, Major?" another asked.

"Yes, sir, very hot," the professor answered.

A third cadet asked abruptly: "Why didn't you run, Major?" The group giggled, somewhat in embarrassment. Jackson saw nothing humorous in the question.

"I was not ordered to do so," he said. "If I had been ordered to run, I would have done so; but I was directed to hold my position, and I had no right to abandon it." This statement of resolve and of devotion to duty made a strong impression on the listeners.[104]

On March 26, 1858, Jackson's brother-in-law, Professor Junius Fishburn, died at the Junkin home following an attack of measles. He was twenty-eight. The Junkins again were "under the shadow of unspeakable grief."[105] The Jacksons expressed appropriate condolences. Yet they were too happy to be overly affected by Fishburn's passing. Anna was nearing the end of her pregnancy. All had gone blessedly well. The couple had the natural excitement of expectant parents awaiting their firstborn.

It came on Friday, April 30, at the boardinghouse. Mother and child came through the ordeal of delivery in fine fashion. The next day an elated Jackson mailed at least three letters of announcement. He stated to his mother-in-law, Mrs. Mary Morrison: "Dear mother, We have in our home circle a darling little namesake of yours, and she is a bright little one, her father being the judge. . . . I hope it will not be many years before our little Mary Graham will be able to send sweet messages to you all."[106]

To Rufus Barringer, the husband of Anna's favorite sister, Jackson wrote: "My dear brother, We have a little prodigy one day old this afternoon. She calls herself Mary Graham Jackson. Anna is doing very well, & joins me in love to yourself & Sister Eugenia."[107]

The third letter, of course, went to Laura. "I am very much pressed with business," Jackson told his sister, "but I must drop you a line to say that yesterday God blessed us with a charming little daughter, and we have named her after Mrs. Morrison. . . . Anna & the little one are both doing very well for which we are thankful to our Heavenly Father."[108]

Everything was not all right, however. The baby was lethargic, at times comatose. Quickly the skin acquired a yellowish hue. Three weeks of anxiety passed. Jackson informed Laura that "our little daughter [is] very ill of jaundice; and she may at any hour take her place among the redeemed in Paradise." On May 12, Jackson had purchased a $3.25 crib and $3.30 hair mattress from local merchant Milton Key. A few lines farther down the business ledger is a May 26 entry that $9.00 had been received from Jackson for "1 fine cloth coffin & box." Infant Mary Jackson had quietly died on May 25 from liver disorder.[109]

Jackson quickly signed a deed for a burial plot in the Presbyterian cemetery. Mary Graham became the first Jackson interred in the family square. The plot cost $20, which the major for unknown reasons did not remit until the middle of September.[110]

Anna understandably took the loss hard. The child's death, she also saw, "was a great, very great sorrow" to Jackson. However, he exhibited no outward signs of grief. After all, he and death had come face to face many times in the past. They were overly familiar with one another. Jackson naturally concluded that God had a specific reason for this latest calamity. He accepted divine judgment with complete obedience. With no fanfare or formal gathering, he buried his second child and gave every possible attention to his grieving wife. "He was the most tender, affectionate and demonstrative man at home that I ever saw," Anna stated. "His heart was as soft as a woman's; he was full of love and gentleness."[111]

Mary Graham's birth and illness had aroused Jackson's passions, but not always to the good. On the afternoon after the child's birth, Jackson got into a heated conversation in front of the courthouse with clerk of the court Samuel Reid and attorney William McLaughlin. Both men, convinced that the black Sunday school was in defiance of Virginia law, were arguing with Jackson. Soon, James D. Davidson, among the most prominent of the town's lawyers, joined the group.

"Major," he said to Jackson at the first opportunity, "whilst I lament that we have such a statute in our code, I am satisfied that your Sunday school is an unlawful assembly, and probably the grand jury will take it up and test it."

Jackson had become angry before Davidson's arrival. Now, with his temper barely in check, he looked sternly at Davidson and snarled, "Sir, if you were, as you should be, a Christian man, you would not think or say so."

An angry Davidson snapped a retort and walked hastily away. En route home, the attorney realized that he had been too forward and too outspoken in a conversation that he had not even initiated. He determined to make an apology. After supper, Davidson returned to his downtown office and had just started writing an expression of regret when a tap sounded on the door. It was Jackson. The major came straight to the point. "Mr. Davidson, I am afraid I wounded your feelings this evening. I have called to apologize to you."

"No, Major," came an instant response. "No apology from you to me. I am now writing my apology to you." The two talked for a half-hour. As Jackson departed, he grasped Davidson's hand warmly and exclaimed: "Mr. Davidson, these are the things that bring men together and make them know each other better."[112]

By a sad coincidence, Jackson became embroiled in a brief dispute with Superintendent Smith on the day Mary Graham died. Three days later, Jackson sent a note to Smith: "Colonel, Feeling that your verbal reprimand of me on Tuesday last was unmerited, I respectfully request that you will communicate the same to me in writing." Smith responded immediately: "Major—In reply to your note of this date I would say that I had no design of giving you a reprimand in the conversation which took place between us on Tuesday last."[113] This was but another instance of the superintendent's extraordinary patience in his dealings with the always dutiful, ever-alert Jackson.

The loss of his second child soon after birth had one noticeable effect on Jackson. He seemed to become even more aware of and affectionate toward children. Two weeks after Mary Graham's burial, an empty-handed father sent a letter to his ten-year-old niece in Beverly, Virginia. "Your very interesting letter reached me a short time before your sweet little cousin & my little daughter was called from this world of sin, to enjoy the Heavenly happiness of Paradise. . . . Jesus says, 'Suffer little children to come unto me, and forbid them not, for of such is the kingdom of Heaven.' Did you ever think, my dear Grace, that the most persons who have died and gone to heaven are little children?" The letter closed with "Your affectionate uncle, Thomas."[114]

Following Mary Graham's death, Jackson's health worsened. He made plans to visit a specialist in New York after making his annual visit to Laura and her family. Yet in mid-June he abandoned the idea of a trip to Beverly. "My disease is not understood by my physician here," he wrote disappointingly, "and I have nearly, if not entirely, lost my hearing in my right ear, and my left ear is diseased, and my nose is also internally affected." Jackson added that he was probably going to New York at the end of the school year. A Beverly trip might have to wait.[115]

Only a week later, family tragedy struck again. Anna's sister, Eugenia Morrison Barringer, died in North Carolina of typhoid fever. Anna was not even aware that the sister was ill until the arrival of the message announcing her death. The loss of a child and a sister who was almost as close as a twin—both occurring in the space of five weeks—sorely taxed Anna's emotions. Jackson was more determined than ever to get his wife out of town. As soon as the VMI commencement ended, he and Anna started on their second northern trip.[116]

The journey was a combination of pleasure, business, and health. Their route took the Jacksons first to Fort Monroe, where Jackson made an inspection of every nook and cranny in the Virginia coastal installation. A steamer voyage to Cape May, New Jersey, and several days of ocean bathing followed. Then a short boat ride brought the couple to New York City. Jackson secured an appointment with the highly respected Dr. John Murray Carnochan, professor of surgery at New York Medical College.

While waiting for the appointment date, the Jacksons passed the time in sightseeing and shopping. In the morning, Jackson would go through the city and note possible attractions. He then returned to the hotel, got Anna, and took her to the sites he thought she would like. In the evening, they remained in their room. Anna would read to Jackson—a practice begun in Lexington. On this trip, he acquired a greater interest in the works of William Shakespeare.

The couple devoted a good part of their New York visit searching for furnishings for the home they hoped to have. No doubt, Jackson was trying to turn Anna's mind from grief to pleasure. He also proved to be a careful shopper. Neither a miser nor a bargain hunter, Jackson bought high-quality products at the best available price. They purchased much in New York because the goods were more economical than those in Lexington's stores. Shipped home that summer were three stoves, a tub, a piano, nineteen boxes of roofing tin, thirteen boxes of furniture, plus other goods that filled a barrel, a keg, a bale, and four boxes.[117]

Appointments with Dr. Carnochan began around July 21, Anna's twenty-seventh birthday. Several examinations and tests led the surgeon to conclude that Jackson's right tonsil was inflamed and extending down the throat. Apparently the gland was too swollen for safe removal. "Paring off" part of the affected tissue was Carnochan's recommendation. The operation, performed August 19, at first appeared successful. As soon as Jackson recovered from the minor surgery, he and Anna returned to Lexington by way of a stopover at Rockbridge Alum Springs. Jackson may have thought he was in better physical condition. His friends were not so sure. Quartermaster Catlett wrote Superintendent Smith, then in Europe, that Jackson was back at the institute "not improved in health but worse [for] the new system of treatment."[118]

When Jackson and Anna returned to Lexington, the boardinghouse rooms seemed painfully lonely. Anna's heartache began anew. Jackson displayed none of his own inner feelings, but his instant and strong attention to children of other families added to the anguish that Anna felt. Whether Laura thought of the idea, or whether Jackson proposed it, Thomas Jackson Arnold came to Lexington in October to live for awhile with his uncle and aunt.

The reason given for the thirteen-year-old's appearance was to get a better education at the Reverend William McFarland's school. For the next eight months, Tom Arnold was a member of the Jackson family. The nephew was the closest thing to a son that Jackson ever had, and the major enjoyed not only the companionship but the opportunity to superintend the lad's education. Jackson determined that Arnold should take only one or two courses at a time in heavy doses rather than a full curriculum of small offerings. This approach seemed to work well.

Young Arnold had only one vice that annoyed Jackson: an insatiable appetite. The boy consumed anything within reach. To a man like Jackson who pursued diet with fanatical care and selectivity, such excessiveness was dangerous. Jackson sought in vain to curb Tom's food consumption; he even asked Laura not to send her son any boxes of food.

Beyond that, Tom Arnold was polite, obedient, and pleasant. The Jacksons enjoyed his presence. He especially coveted any time he had with his uncle. Arnold gave a vivid description of his namesake at this period. Jackson

was about 5 feet 11 1/2 inches in stature, in his boots. He was very erect—not sparely built, nor heavy. I would judge his weight to approximate 165 or 170 pounds; his complexion would be termed blond, though his hair & whiskers were dark, hair might be called black & was slightly inclined to curl. Eyes large, blue, good figure, good features of a good looking man: sufficiently striking to cause one in passing to turn the second time for a better look.

He was a modest, quiet, reserved man—didn't talk much about West Point, or Mexico. Would of course answer any questions that were asked, but he talked very little about himself. I asked him if he ever got hit by a bullet. He told me after one engagement [in Mexico] . . . he discovered the front of his coat cut & torn & he supposed it was by a bullet. He was rather a solemn, serious looking man, very dignified.

Arnold later observed:

While I was there I was with him more or less daily, frequently reciting my lessons to him, often accompanying him in his walks, almost always with him for Saturday and other holiday outings covering several miles, going with him to his farm and elsewhere. . . . I invariably went with him to church. . . . During our walks Major Jackson's conversation was interesting and in-structive, the instruction being imparted in an entertaining and attractive manner. His attitude might be aptly compared to that of a careful and painstaking tutor.[119]

October found Jackson's health little improved. A combination of concern and despair led him to submit letters of resignation as both superintendent of the black Sunday school class and deacon in the Presbyterian church. These actions were considered so serious that on October 11 the entire congregation met to discuss the matters.

No one wanted to lose Jackson's services, yet he did not feel able to continue satisfactorily in either position. A compromise was effected: Jackson was released from his duties with the Sunday school class, and he agreed to take only temporary leave from the office of deacon. Jackson would have been even more despondent had he known that the following day—October 12—his close army friend and counselor, Major Francis Taylor, died at Fort Brown, Texas.[120]

VMI cadets, of course, had no inkling of Jackson's personal life. They saw him from afar as the well-known and odd professor who presided over one of the insti-tute's most notorious courses. Students still looked at him with contrasting views—the number of opinions equal to the number who expressed them. By this stage, however, positive judgments were many.

R. Preston Chew entered VMI that year. To him, Jackson appeared "a calm and determined man, giving his whole thought and attention to the matter before him. He was not what you would call a graceful man, but he was a very good looking person. He was too intense a man to be what is called genial, though I [saw] him often with a delightful smile on his face."[121]

Another cadet, getting his baptism in Jackson's philosophy class, stated in wonder: "In the section room he would sit perfectly erect and motionless, holding his pencil in one hand and his class book in the other, listening with grave attention and exhibiting the great powers of his wonderful memory, which was, I think, the most remarkable that ever came under my observation. . . . In listening to a recitation he very rarely used a book. He was ready at any moment to refer to any page or line in any of the books and then to repeat with perfect accuracy the most difficult passages that could be referred to."[122]

As autumn descended over the valley and the trees shook loose their leaves in salute, Thomas and Anna Jackson shared the most happiness they had known since the birth of Mary Graham. A year-long search for a home ended. On the north side of Washington Street, sandwiched between the lots of Samuel M. Dold and Andrew Withrow, and across the street from the courthouse, was a house and lot owned by Dr. Archibald Graham. Jackson had been his patient since arriving in Lexington; and since Dr. Graham was a firm believer in the power of hydropathy, Jackson esteemed him as a friend.

The quarter-acre property in question—half of lot 13 in the original 1778 Lexington town plan—had a frontage of sixty-four feet on Washington Street and a depth of 195 feet to an alley in the rear. Schoolmaster William Tidd was the first owner of the land and in 1801 sold the property to Cornelius Dorman, the county jailor. Dorman evidently used the stone foundation of an earlier building as a starting point. In 1802, he constructed at the front of the lot a brick, two-story, four-bay Federal townhouse. Dorman and his son Charles inhabited the place until 1845, when it was purchased by Mr. and Mrs. Samuel Campbell, who sold the house and lot in April 1852 to Dr. Graham. He made a number of alterations. A stone addition to the rear of the home doubled the length of the structure. Graham also added a separate entrance in the front for patients who came to his office. On November 4, 1858, Graham accepted a $3000 offer from Jackson for the long-unoccupied property.[123]

For the Jacksons, the place had both assets and liabilities. It was located only a half-block from Main Street and slightly more than a block from the Presbyterian church. The VMI post was but a short walk away. However, the house was old, large, and badly in need of repairs.

An exposed English basement elevated the principal floor to what appeared to be the second story. The narrow and uncovered porch stretched across the middle half of the front to accommodate two half-light doors. Stairs parallel to the sidewalk went up from the left or west side.

The main door opened into a "passage" or large entry hall with doorways to four rooms. To the right of the entrance was a small (ten feet by seventeen feet) "study," which had been Dr. Graham's medical office. The partially glass door on the south front plus a window on the east wall provided adequate illumination. On the other side of the house front was a spacious parlor. Its one window faced the street. The sixteen-by-sixteen room served as a reception area for visitors as well as the Jacksons' sitting room.

Immediately behind it, across a hallway perpendicular to the main hall, was the master bedroom. It was eighteen by seventeen feet, with a small window on the side and a larger window in the rear. The dining room in the northeast quadrant of the house was the same size as the bedroom. On its north wall, a door and window opened onto a covered back porch.[124]

In the exposed basement, immediately below the dining room, was the kitchen. Storage rooms were also on that level and perhaps a small room for making butter and cream. On the third floor were probably furnished bedrooms and space for more storage.

Jackson bought the place for its availability and with the later intention of moving into a more desirable home when and if it materialized. The major began at once making some repairs; he brought in workmen for larger and more intricate tasks. Up to that point, Jackson's purchases from J. Compton & Sons, Dry Goods, in town had averaged $4 to $5 monthly. In November, he bought $103.46 worth of goods for the restoration of the house.[125]

The more attention Jackson gave to the house, the more enamored he became with it. For the first time in his life, he would be living in his home rather than a house. He "labored to make it comfortable and attractive," Anna stated, for "it was truly his castle."[126] It became a family center as well as Jackson's sanctuary. The couple made plans to take occupancy early in 1859—a year, Jackson anticipated, of peace and love for himself and those around him.

8

HOME LIFE GIVES WAY TO WAR

I N MID-JANUARY 1859, just before his thirty-fifth birthday, Jackson moved Anna and his nephew into the first house he had ever owned. Now he could pursue such personal recreation as gardening and home improvements. Moreover, with a wife who shared his ardent faith in God, Jackson could participate fully in the affairs of his church. His only fear was that death might claim Anna before it did him. The couple would occupy the Washington Street home for twenty-seven months, yet the two of them would have the place to themselves for barely a third of that time. Jackson and Anna were frequently absent for medical treatment and hydropathy; and with a steady stream of houseguests, the Jacksons had little time to pay heed to furnishings.

Although Jackson bought the best when he shopped, his tastes were basic. Hence, the furniture was high quality but spare. "Simplicity marked every article," Anna noted. Much of the furniture came from the couple's trip to New York City the previous summer; the sofa and other pieces of the parlor set, according to family tradition, came from Philadelphia. At a public sale of John Lyle's estate, Jackson obtained a bed and table. It surprised no one that Jackson liked every article of furniture in perfect position and order. He reminded Anna that there was "a place for everything, and everything in its place." The home remained a middle-class residence, plain, comfortable, and always eligible for improvements.[1]

Perfect system and regularity marked Jackson's daily habits once he settled into the home. He arose each morning at 6:00 and knelt for private prayers. Next came a cold bath, regardless of the outside temperature. A brisk half-hour walk followed. If the weather was inclement, he wore a pair of India-rubber cavalry boots and a cumbersome army overcoat. Jackson also acquired some gymnastic equipment and "greatly invigorated himself by their use."[2] He was firmly convinced that a well-ordered, steady dose of exercise would ease his ever-present dyspepsia.

At precisely 7 A.M., family prayers took place. The servants were required to be present and got stern remonstration for any tardiness. Breakfast followed. Jackson "said grace at every meal, with both hands uplifted," and with "childlike simplicity and earnestness." He still subsisted on plain fare, with brown bread and cold water being staples. Jackson left home at the same time each morning in order to make the half-mile walk to VMI and his eight o'clock class.[3]

He was now averaging fifteen cadets in each of his two sections. The second class ended at 11:00; and unless Jackson was conducting the springtime afternoon instruction in artillery practice or had some faculty committee meeting, his campus obligations were ended for the day. He would then return home and, except for a brief greeting with Anna, proceed straight to his study.

First attention went to the Bible, which he read daily with the same intensity as he prepared for his classes. Often he underlined passages and made marginal notations. Jackson next pored through his textbooks as he got ready for the next day's recitations. "During these hours of study," Anna noted with a hint of annoyance, "he would not permit any interruption, and stood all that time in front of a high desk, which he had made to order, and upon which he kept his books and stationery."[4]

Lunch was served precisely at 1 P.M. That was the time when Jackson forgot his duties and thought only of home life. His nephew remembered: "Following the blessing, the ordinary conversation of the family was indulged in while the repast was in progress. Major Jackson took part in the usual conversation in the home, as much so as any one ordinarily would. When there was company, which was not infrequent, he talked freely, and was entertaining in conversation, and seemed perfectly at ease."[5]

Between 1:30 and 2:00 was Anna's time. Jackson thoroughly enjoyed this "leisure and conversation" with his wife. She regarded it as "one of the brightest periods of the home life." Physical activity then occupied Jackson's attention for most of the afternoon. He had long desired to have a garden, and the huge backyard gave him abundant space for planting various vegetables and fruits. When not occupied in the yard, Jackson often performed manual labor on the house.

Late in the afternoon, Jackson and Anna went for a ride or walk or else engaged in conversation in the parlor. A light supper followed. Thinking it "injurious to health to go to work immediately," Jackson would relax with Anna for a few minutes. Then he would review his lessons for the following day. Since Jackson refused to use his eyes in such artificial light as candles, he relied in the evening on his powers of mental retention. He often sat with his face to the wall, his wife stated, "as silent and as dumb as the sphinx," remaining "in perfect abstraction" until he was satisfied with the organization and memorization. Then Jackson would turn to Anna with a "bright and cheerful face." They might then engage in a favorite pastime: Anna reading aloud for them both. Bedtime came at 10:00 and not a minute later.[6]

Jackson liked to read. His library was large and wide ranging. By 1861, he owned 122 volumes. History and biography dominated the collection. The twenty-six books in those subjects included classical studies of Xerxes, Mohammed, a history of the Jews, *Plutarch's Lives*, military treatises on Caesar, Washington, and Napoleon, national histories, plus popular biographies of Cromwell, Andrew Jackson, and Henry Clay.

Religious commentaries were next in number with twenty-four. Specific subjects varied from exegeses on the gospels and John Bunyan's *Pilgrim's Progress* to self-improvement guides for better morality. Eighteen volumes on science and mathematics reflected Jackson's academic responsibilities.

The remaining books treated of health, gardening, travel, manners, and poetry. Works of fiction were confined largely to a six-volume set of William Shakespeare's writings. Five Bibles (one each in French, Spanish, and Greek), plus appropriate foreign-language dictionaries, completed the library. Jackson made marginal notes or line markings in half of his books. This was especially the case with his historical and religious titles.[7]

A vastly different, if not astounding, Jackson emerged when he and Anna had moments of privacy. Anna later admitted that her husband's friends "would have found it hard to believe that there could be such a transformation as he exhibited in his domestic life. He luxuriated in the freedom and liberty of his home, and his buoyancy and joyousness of nature often ran into a playfulness and *abandon* that would have been incredible to those who saw him only when he put on his official dignity."[8]

In an unpublished letter, Anna became more specific. "No man could be more demonstrative, & he was almost invariably playful & cheerful & as confiding as possible. He commenced educating me (if I may so speak) to be demonstrative as soon as we were married, thought it added quality to happiness, & we rarely ever met alone without caresses & endearing epithets. I almost always met him on his return from the Institute, & his face would beam with happiness, & he would spend a few moments in petting me, as he called it, & then go to his duties."[9]

Playing pranks on Anna was a constant enjoyment for Jackson. One of his favorite tricks was to hide behind a door, spring out as she entered the room, and smother her with affection. By 1859, he had abandoned the prominent side whiskers and was wearing a full beard and mustache. One evening, Jackson began brandishing a sword over Anna's head with a look as ferocious "as a veritable Bluebeard." When Jackson saw that his wife was genuinely frightened, he threw down the weapon "and in a perfect outburst of glee," Anna stated, "speedily transformed himself into the very anti-pode of a wife-killer."[10]

Behind closed doors, Jackson reverted to Mexican War joys and strenuously danced the polka with Anna. This would have been shocking to straitlaced Lexingtonians, but Jackson was prepared to explain that he viewed such dancing as beneficial exercise.

Starved for abiding love, Jackson opened his heart to Anna in complete trust and gentle tenderness. He worshiped happiness; a long face from Anna cut to the soul; he addressed her with affectionate diminutives or pet words and phrases. "My Sunshine" was one of his early addresses. Foremost among the Spanish words Jackson employed with Anna was "esposita"—his "little wife."[11]

Jackson's family at this time was larger than generally believed, for slaves were included. Misunderstanding and inaccuracies have long surrounded Jackson's black servants and his relations with them. Jackson neither apologized for nor spoke in favor of the practice of slavery. He probably opposed the institution. Yet in his mind the Creator had sanctioned slavery, and man had no moral right to challenge its existence. The good Christian slaveholder was one who treated his servants fairly and humanely at all times.

During the late 1850s, six blacks were part of the Jackson household. Albert was the first. He had come to Jackson and begged to be purchased. In return, Albert promised to get a job and obtain his freedom through reimbursement to Jackson. The major agreed. For awhile, Albert was a waiter in one of the Lexington hotels. He also worked occasionally at Rockbridge Alum Springs. Jackson checked on him regularly to ensure that all was going well. During the 1858–60 period, Jackson rented Albert to VMI for $120 annually.

The second slave Jackson acquired was Amy, who was closest to Jackson's heart. Around 1855, the forty-year-old woman was on the verge of being sold at public auction when she too pled with Jackson to become his property. Jackson bought the servant and found her a position "in a good Christian family." There she remained until the Jacksons acquired their home. Amy thereupon came to work at the Jackson residence. "She proved her gratitude by serving him faithfully," Anna declared. "She was one of the best of colored cooks, and was a real treasure to me in my new experience as a housekeeper."[12]

Three of the slaves were a wedding gift from Dr. Morrison. Hetty had been Anna's nurse from infancy. She came to Lexington from North Carolina to assist Anna in the birth of her first child. After Mary Graham's death, Hetty remained with her mistress. Anna described her as "an energetic, impulsive, quick-tempered woman, with some fine traits, but inclined to self-assertion." The slave quickly found her superior in Major Jackson. Hetty then toned down "into a well-mannered, useful domestic, and indeed she became a factotum in the household, rendering valuable services."[13]

Cyrus and George, teenaged sons of Hetty, accompanied their mother to Lexington. Jackson at first did not trust them. He stated on one occasion that "if these boys were left to themselves they would be sure to go back to barbarism." On the other hand, Jackson later made arrangements for one of the boys to drive his carriage several days to Beverly in order to meet Jackson and Anna when they arrived at the train depot for a visit to Laura Arnold. The slave then returned to Lexington alone by train and stage. At Jackson's urging, Anna taught the two lads to read. The major saw to it that both Cyrus and George were unfailing attendants at church.[14]

Sometime in the 1859–60 period, while Anna was out of town, Jackson accepted from an aged widow in Lexington a black girl named Emma. He presented her to Anna as a welcome-home gift. Emma was a four-year-old orphan with some degree of learning disability. Anna thought her "troublesome" at first; and although Emma in time became useful, she was in Mrs. Jackson's eyes "never a treasure." Emma was "not bright," Anna recalled with a mixture of feelings, but Jackson "persevered in drilling her into memorizing a child's catechism, and it was a most amusing picture to see her standing before him with fixed attention, as if she were straining every nerve, and reciting her answers with the drop of a courtesy at each word." To all of the servants, Jackson was a strict but kind master. He willingly gave "that which is just and equal," and he expected prompt obedience in return.[15]

Springtime 1859 found a large garden flourishing in Jackson's backyard. Gardening became his favorite recreation. Naturally, he cultivated plants in an orderly and scientific manner. He worked much of the garden with his own hands, and eventually he was raising more foodstuffs than the family could consume. This meticulous care with his plant bed was in sharp contrast to his lack of concern over appearance in public. Love of the land also led Jackson that year to purchase a farm. It was an irregularly shaped tract of eighteen acres on the eastern edge of Lexington and a mile from the Jackson home. The major paid schoolmaster Jacob Fuller $500 for the property, which covered the top of a knoll. There Jackson would raise crops of wheat, corn, and vegetables.[16]

As was his habit in any undertaking, Jackson amassed all the information he could about the subject. He purchased a number of gardening books; he especially followed the information contained in Robert Buist's *The Family Kitchen Gardener: Containing Plain and Accurate Descriptions of All the Different Species and Varieties of Culinary Vegetables.* Marginal reminders abounded in Jackson's copy. Beside summaries of such foods as tomatoes, asparagus, watermelon, spinach, and turnips was the simple notation, "plant."

One minor irritation came from the gardening. In an undated letter to the editor of a periodical entitled *Planter,* Jackson stated: "Inclosed is a check for three dollars & seventy five cents. I have lost your bill; if the above is not the amount, please so inform me. While I strongly condemn your course in persisting in sending the Planter longer than I subscribed for, & after the Post Master notified you that it was not taken out of the office. Yet rather than have even an unjust suspicion of my being unwilling to pay a debt, I forward the check."[17]

With the coming of spring, Anna confessed to feeling unwell. An incredible coincidence had occurred. Like Ellie, Anna had contracted facial neuralgia. Jackson insisted on the best treatment available. He quickly secured a few days' leave from the institute and took his wife to New York.

Some hints have surfaced that Anna also sought medical treatment to heighten the chances of another pregnancy because she was so painfully aware of how much Jackson loved children. (A gentleman and his four-year-old daughter had recently been overnight guests. The father awakened during the night to find Jackson lovingly adjusting the bed covers around the sleeping child.) However, the pain of Anna's neuralgia and its ongoing presence for months thereafter negate the idea that she was likewise seeking consultation about bearing another child.[18]

It was necessary that Anna remain in New York several weeks for treatment. Classroom duties forced Jackson to return alone to Lexington. This was their first separation since marriage. Jackson wrote Anna every day except when he thought a letter might be in transit on Sunday. His letters reveal not only loneliness and love but also surprisingly affectionate thoughts that he freely committed to paper. Of all the major figures of the Civil War whose letters to home survive, the stern VMI professor sent the most intimate, emotional, and sentimental messages. Always they were sprinkled with words and phrases of endearment.

The first installment in this correspondence with Anna, written in March, began: "I got home last night in as good health as when I gave my darling the last kiss. Hetty and Amy came to the door when I rang, but would not open until I gave my name. . . . Your husband has a sad heart. Our house looks so deserted without my *esposa.*"[19]

Jackson liked to use the word "your" when writing to Anna. He said "your husband" rather than "I," and he referred to "your house," "your garden," and the like. At this time, he adopted the expression "your queridissimo," a Spanish word meaning "the dearest possible."

The garden and Anna's health were the topics on which he most expounded during her stay in New York. "I was mistaken about your large garden fruit being peaches," he confessed. "It turns out to be apricots & I enclose one which I found on the ground today, & just think, my little Dove has a tree full of them."[20]

In another letter, Jackson mentioned the appropriateness of a sermon he had just heard from Dr. Junkin. The theme was: "No affliction for the present seemeth to be joyous, but grievous, nevertheless afterward, it yieldeth to the peaceable fruits of righteousness to them who are exercised thereby."[21]

By mid-April, Jackson was writing: "Our potatoes are coming up & I shall send you a sample of the leaf. . . . Your garden has been thirsting for water until last evening." Jackson's loneliness and concern for his wife continued to increase. Early in May he confessed to Anna: "My little pet, your husband was made very happy at receiving two letters from you and learning that you were improving so rapidly. I have more than once bowed down on my knees, and thanked our kind and merciful Heavenly Father for the prospect of restoring you to health again."[22]

He wrote Laura that Anna "is learning to take things more philosophically; she says that the doctor still finds some inflammation. She is to remain there until the inflammation entirely subsides." A few days later, anticipating Anna's return to Lexington, Jackson stated: "Take care of my little dove. . . . When you come home, I want to meet you at Goshen in a private conveyance, and bring my little one gently over the rough roads."[23]

Anna returned home late that month and feeling only a little better. She had no time for quiet recuperation. In June, Jackson's sister arrived with her two younger children, eleven-year-old Grace and eight-year-old Stark. This was Laura Arnold's first visit to Lexington. The Jacksons greeted sister, niece, and nephew warmly. For a month, the major sought to entertain his kinfolk. Yet Laura was in ill health for much of the visit. Tom Arnold returned to Beverly with his mother and siblings. The Jackson home became quiet again.

July 4, 1859, was commencement day at VMI. It produced the largest crowd ever seen in Lexington. Jackson proceeded home after the ceremonies. In the afternoon, Thomas M. Boyd and a fellow graduate called on Jackson to say goodbye. Boyd never forgot those few moments. "He received us with his usual kindness. Very few words were spoken; he brought Mrs. Jackson to join him in wishing us God-speed. As my hand rested in his warm grasp I noticed a tear glisten in his large and peculiarly expressive gray eyes."[24]

The Jacksons attended a Lexington wedding in the first part of the summer. It was at the event that James Power Smith, later a member of Jackson's staff, first met the couple. Smith described Jackson as "a tall, square-shouldered man, not much over thirty years of age. . . . The first impression of him was that he was a neighboring farmer who had come to the wedding in the uniform of his militia rank. . . . He was scrupulously neat, with large hands and feet, a broad face, well bearded, and blue eyes that were both serious and gentle." Anna was "to all appearances her husband's opposite, for she was small, and not angular, very fair, and a most charming and graceful woman."[25]

Midsummer found both Jacksons ailing once again. His throat had become inflamed, and Anna still was struggling with her long illness. The major concluded that water treatment was the cure. He considered the stagecoach ride to White Sulphur Springs too fatiguing for his wife. Jackson therefore sent her to nearby Rockbridge Alum while he spent a fortnight at White Sulphur. By the time Jackson reached the springs, he was convinced that his liver was also infected.[26]

He experienced loneliness before improvement. "I am tired of this place," he wrote, "and wouldn't give my little pet for all the people here. I want to go and stay with my little woman. As yet I am not certain whether the waters are beneficial to me." Within a week, however, and thanks to the waters, applications of "smoking" muslin to his chest, and "the blessing of Providence," Jackson felt much improved. Sulphur water, he informed his sister, "appears to suit my disease better than any other remedy which I have met with."[27]

One evening at White Sulphur Springs, Jackson got into a conversation with VMI graduate James L. Hubard. The young man welcomed the opportunity to talk with his old professor. In the course of the conversation, the Mexican War surfaced as a topic for discussion. Hubard was intrigued at the fact that battle affects the minds and actions of men so differently. Jackson replied "that a battle always had the effect of brightening his faculties, and that he had always thought more clearly, rapidly, and with more satisfaction to himself in the heat of an engagement than at any other time."[28]

After the Jacksons returned home, it was obvious that Anna's health was still impaired. On September 9, 1859, Jackson sent her to Hampden-Sydney College to go under the care of a well-respected physician, Dr. Francis B. Watkins. Anna recovered sufficiently within three weeks to travel from southside Virginia to Cottage Home in North Carolina for a visit with her father.

A cheery letter from her husband reached the Morrison home when Anna arrived. "I watered your flowers this morning, and hoed another row of turnips, and expect to hill some of the celery this evening," Jackson reported. "Your old man at home is taking good care of one somebody's flower-slips. . . . I hope that my little somebody is feeling as lively as a lark!"[29]

Anna's original plan was to return to Lexington in November. One of her younger sisters, either Laura or Susan, would accompany her. But unknown factors delayed travel plans. As a result, Anna would not see her husband until dramatic events occurred and December came.[30]

Throughout this interim, Jackson was in his ninth year as a VMI professor. Cadet opinion over time had become slowly but markedly more positive. A young student, eager to meet him, experienced mixed feelings when the occasion arrived. "Instead of the handsome polished gentleman I had pictured, I found him awkward in appearance, severely plain in dress, and stiff and constrained in bearing, but when he began to talk my disappointment passed away. . . . Listening to his terse, well-rounded sentences, always instructive and full of meaning . . . I felt that he possessed power, which, in stirring times, would make him a leader among his fellows."[31]

Cadet James McCabe of the class of 1861 struck a fine balance in assessing the major. "He was always accessible and ever ready to render assistance to those who needed it. He would take any amount of trouble to aid his pupils. . . . But no one could ever be familiar with him. His reserve, which many people called coldness, prevented that." Yet, McCabe concluded, "a kinder, more generous and nobler spirit was never placed within a human breast than that which glowed with the heart of Major Jackson."[32]

The image of Jackson the man had also improved among Lexington residents. George H. Moffett, then a VMI cadet, vividly recalled that although Jackson "was reserved and austere in his bearing, he was one of the most popular men in Lexington. . . . Everyone, sooner or later, came to regard him as a remarkable man, and even if they did not claim him as a friend, they respected him sincerely, and were prompt to show that they did." John Preston agreed. "As a citizen and church member, he was the object of pleasant jests for singularities and peculiarities, but the confidence in his integrity, force of character, and soundness of mind was universal."[33]

Naturally, some negative opinion existed. Graham Ellzey, a member of the class of 1860, gave a unique combination of good and bad when he observed that Jackson's "deafness certainly impaired his usefulness as a teacher, and at times rendered him very irritable in the class room. . . . The fact is that this man had a kind heart, and a diffidence, which made him awkward and abrupt in what he said and did." Randolph Barton, another cadet described Jackson walking across the campus with those unusually long strides. "The stiff, stolid-looking man would pass on, turning his head neither to the right nor left, but a single touch of his cap was the silent recognition given of the deferential respect shown by the boys."[34]

In October, Jackson felt well enough to resume his duties as Presbyterian deacon and Sunday school teacher. He did so with his usual devotion to duty. The monthly meetings of deacons were held thenceforth in the Jackson home. Commitments to the church kept Jackson busy; otherwise, tranquility descended over the lazy days.[35]

On October 17, Jackson wrote his beloved: "I have been wishing that you could see our beautiful forests in their autumnal glory. I have been greatly enjoying their beauty, but my pleasure would be much enhanced if you were with me. I have just been thinking how happy you must be in your old home, and it makes my heart happy too to think of the happiness of my little darling."[36]

Unknown to anyone in Lexington, on the previous evening a militant abolitionist named John Brown had led a group of eighteen followers in a raid on a federal arsenal. The site was Harpers Ferry, only 150 miles down the Shenandoah Valley from Lexington. Brown's object was to confiscate weapons, arm thousands of slaves, and lead his black army down a bloody trail to freedom. The raiders killed three townspeople (including a black man) before a contingent of U.S. Marines under army Colonel Robert E. Lee arrived from Washington. The soldiers stormed the fire-engine house where part of Brown's band was barricaded. In a matter of minutes the invasion was over. Ten of the nineteen raiders had been killed; the leader and his survivors would go on trial for murder, treason, and insurrection. Not one slave enlisted in John Brown's cause.

It was October 20 before the first published reports of the Harpers Ferry action appeared in Lexington. One rumor had Brown at the head of a mini-army of 300 men. A week later, the *Lexington Gazette* reprinted stories and bulletins from the Baltimore newspapers. Those accounts were detailed but secondhand versions of the invasion by terrorists. Rumors and unconfirmed assertions produced frenzied reactions.

VMI cadets, observed one of their number, "magnified the dangers a thousand-fold. . . . The papers from the North gave long accounts of the sympathetic feeling for Brown and his band of assassins in that quarter, and the cadets fully believed that any day they might be ordered out to assist in repelling" another invasion of Virginia. On the Washington College campus, a sophomore noted that "the military fever broke out among the student body . . . like measles."[37]

Jackson's fellow Virginian and West Point friend, John C. Tidball, later saw the John Brown Raid for what it really was. "Although the enterprise failed so signally, it carried consternation through the South and deep excitement in the North. More than any other event which had up to this time happened, this intensified the bad feeling then existing between the two sections."[38]

The fact that Brown on November 2 was sentenced to die a month later did nothing to assuage passions of the hour. A Rockbridge County newspaper called on every community in the state to organize volunteer companies in order to combat future abolitionist raids. Overnight the "Rockbridge Rifles," fifty-three strong, came into existence.[39] It was the same throughout the South in general and Virginia in particular.

None of Jackson's correspondence for this period survives. In all likelihood, he paid little attention to the excitement. Since abandoning a plan three years earlier to purchase western lands, Jackson was aware of the growing schism between North and South. He was a Democrat with inherent respect for states' rights. Politicians of that bent were in control of the federal system.

That is probably as much thought as Jackson gave to the national picture. Marriage, the loss of another child, a new home, persistent illnesses, business ventures, renewed church activities—these were the matters of greater concern to the major. Besides, the course of the nation would be what God in His wisdom decreed. Worrying about it ran against Christian principles.

As the days moved steadily toward John Brown's hanging, Virginia seemed in ferment. Rumors equaled the hours of each day: attempts would be made to rescue Brown, another band of armed abolitionists were heading toward the Old Dominion, insurrection was imminent. The state had no military force save some militia units and the VMI cadets. On November 19, Governor Wise put the corps on notice for a possible trip to Charles Town "to preserve the peace and dignity of the common-wealth in the execution of John Brown."[40]

Colonel Smith conferred with his faculty and selected upperclassmen to stand by for duty. Sixty-four cadets would form two companies of infantry under Major Gilham, assisted by Lieutenants John McCausland, W. Hays Otey, and Scott Shipp. Twenty-one other cadets would man two howitzers under the direction of Major Jackson and his assistant, Lieutenant Daniel Trueheart. Gilham was in overall command of the detachment. Smith, by directive of the governor, left at once for Charles Town to take charge of the execution itself.[41]

Around 8 P.M. on November 25, orders arrived for the VMI contingent to proceed at once to Charles Town. Jackson probably dashed off a note to Anna before giving final instructions to the servants. At 10 P.M., cadets and faculty were on the move. A Staunton firm of brothers known as Harman and Company provided free stagecoach rides to Staunton. Railroads then bore the detachment and its equipment to Richmond, Washington, and Charles Town in the lower Shenandoah Valley. "We were a merry crowd," one of the cadets admitted, "and enjoyed [the trip] as youngsters naturally would under the circumstances." A Richmond newspaperman wrote of the passage of the VMI group through the capital: "The cadets were the lions yesterday, and they certainly deserve it for they are drilled to a marvelous degree of perfection. I do not think older persons could be taught the exercises as they are."[42]

Enjoyment coursed through Jackson on arrival at Charles Town. This was his first field service in eight years. His little artillery section had elicited praise for its appearance from the governor and other officials. The Brown execution had an aura of excitement and suspense to it. At the same time, and to most residents of the Old Dominion, justice was about to be served and crimes against Virginia avenged.

On November 28, Jackson's satisfaction was evident in a short letter he sent Anna: "I reached here last night in good health and spirits. Seven of us slept in the same room. I am much more pleased than I expected to be; the people appear to be very kind. There are about one thousand troops here, and everything is quiet so far. We don't expect any trouble. The excitement is confined to more distant points." Jackson was correct in his estimate of the number of troops. Over 650 soldiers of various designations had assembled in Charles Town for the execution. Another 300 armed men were in the immediate area, with 300 more in nearby towns and ready to move if needed. State officials had called on all citizens in the region to remain at home and guard their possessions against possible violence. As a result, Colonel Smith stated, only "a very small crowd" assembled for the hanging. The military far outnumbered civilians in attendance.[43]

December 2, 1859, was a clear and warm Friday. "Everything," one man observed, "was conducted under the strictest military discipline, as if [Charles Town] were in a state of siege."[44] By 9 A.M., military units had taken position at the site in two "hollow squares" or U-shaped formations. (The condemned man and execution party would proceed to the gallows through the open end of the lines.) That day, the VMI cadets were clad in gray trousers and red flannel shirts crossed by two white belts.

Jackson's artillery section was in front of the execution scaffold, a howitzer on either side of the pathway and about forty yards from the gallows. Nothing was left to chance. Lieutenant Shipp commented: "Major Jackson gave Lieutenant Trueheart the most detailed instructions as to what kind of ammunition to use under various contingencies, even directing how the fuses should be cut, should the enemy advance in this or in that direction! . . . The explicit nature of his preparations shows he was unwilling to be surprised, or found unprepared, in the most remote contingency."[45]

At 11 A.M., guards led John Brown from the county jail. The procession made its way slowly from the courthouse jail one block north, then four blocks east to the knoll of open ground that was the site of execution. Silence hung over the land. A young Charles Town boy stated: "Everything was done quietly. It was as tho' it were a funeral of one of our own people—quiet and awesome."[46]

Jackson's feelings during those moments are easy to define. Brown had committed murder. This was a violation of both man and the Heavenly Father. He must pay the penalty to satisfy civil code as well as the Old Testament principle of "an eye for an eye." Jackson's assigned duty was to ensure that justice was done. He considered Brown a godless man. Therefore, when he first saw the tall, thin, white-bearded figure approaching the gallows, Jackson offered a silent prayer for his salvation.[47]

Like everyone else in attendance, Jackson absorbed the details of Brown's last moments, his death, and the transfer of his remains northward. Jackson described it all later that day in a long letter to Anna.

John Brown was hung today at about 11 1/2 A.M. He behaved with unflinching firmness. The arrangements were well made under the direction of Col. Smith. Brown's wife visited him last evening. The body is to be delivered to her. The gibbet was south east of the town in a large field. Brown rode on the head of his coffin, from his prison to the place of execution. The coffin was of black walnut, enclosed in a poplar box of the same shape as the coffin. He was dressed in carpet slippers of predominating red, white socks, black pants, black frock coat, black vest, & black slouch hat. Nothing around his neck beside his shirt collar. The open wagon in which he rode was strongly guarded on all sides. Capt. Williams, formerly [one] of the assistants of the Institute, marched immediately in front of the wagon. The jailer & high sheriff & several others rode in the wagon with the prisoner. Brown had his arms tied behind him, & ascended the scaffold with apparent cheerfulness. After reaching the top of the platform, he shook hands with several who were standing around him. The sheriff placed the rope around his neck, threw a white cap over his head, & asked him if he wished a signal when all should be ready—to which he replied that it made no difference, provided he was not kept waiting too long. In this condition he stood on the trap door, which was supported on one side by hinges, & on the other (south side) by a rope, for about 10 minutes, until Col. S. told the Sheriff 'all is ready,' which apparently was not comprehended by the Sheriff, & the Col. had to repeat the order, when the rope was cut by a single blow, & Brown fell through about 25 inches, so as to bring his knees on a level with the position occupied by his feet before the rope was cut. With the fall his arms below the elbow flew up, hands clenched, & his arms gradually fell by spasmodic motions— there was very little motion of his person for several minutes, after which the wind blew his lifeless body to & fro.

After detailing where the cadets had stood throughout the ceremony, Jackson stated:

I was much impressed with the thought that before me stood a man, in the full vigor of health, who must in a few minutes be in eternity. I sent up a petition that he might be saved. Awful was the thought that he might in a few moments receive the sentence 'Depart ye wicked into everlasting fire.' I hope that he was prepared to die, but I am very doubtful—he wouldn't have a minister with him.

His body was taken back to the jail, & at 6 P.M. was sent to his wife at Harper's Ferry. When it reached Harper's Ferry the coffin was opened & his wife saw the body—the coffin was again opened at the depot, before leaving for Baltimore, lest there should be an imposition.[48]

As a lifelong Democrat who favored some form of compromise over the issue of slavery, Jackson was in total disagreement with Brown's thoughts and actions. Still, the man had waged war for what he thought was a sin against God. Jackson could admire that, as well as the intrepid way in which Brown met death. That is why Jackson openly confessed to watching the man dangle from a rope and offering a prayer for his soul.

Jackson's own conduct at the execution elicited praise. Major Raleigh Colston was the adjutant general of the VMI detachment. His duties required him to be in regular contact with Jackson. "I was struck at once with the change in his appearance" on the Charles Town assignment, Colston stated. "He seemed to be aroused—his movements were quick and his whole nature was changed for the time. . . . His orders were given with such perfect clearness and precision as left nothing doubtful to his subordinates. Nothing was forgotten—nothing was left to be inferred. . . . From that time my estimate of him as an officer became very high."[49]

The cadets remained three days in Charles Town for security reasons. A grateful and relieved Governor Wise then directed the VMI contingent to come to Richmond to be reviewed and applauded. At mid-morning on December 6, the contingent departed from Harpers Ferry by train and journeyed to Washington. There it spent the night, and the legend began of one of Jackson's most embarrassing moments.

Fellow faculty member Scott Shipp first related the alleged incident. According to Shipp, Jackson "placed his money in his stockings, which in turn he concealed beneath his pillow upon retiring at the hotel. The next morning he was unable to find his stockings, so donned a fresh pair. It was not until on the way to the depot, at the head of the battery, that he missed his money. Halting his command in the middle of Pennsylvania Avenue, he returned to the hotel where he recovered both his money and his stockings."[50]

It is difficult to believe that Jackson would have left twenty-one cadets and two cannon standing in the middle of the national capital's busiest thoroughfare while he returned to the hotel to retrieve personal belongings. It is easier to conclude, and more natural to accept, the idea that with the John Brown execution behind them, cadets relaxed and resumed normal habits—including a tall tale about "Tom Fool" Jackson.

On a freezing December 8, the cadet corps drilled on Capitol Square to a large and appreciative Richmond audience. At least one bystander was an exception. A Virginia politician of some status was not impressed by all he saw.

The only thing about this fine body that struck me as in any way lacking in soldierly appearance was the Commandant of the battery. He was not my ideal of a soldier, either in military bearing, or in the manner in which he gave his commands. His uniform was not new; his old blue forage cap sat on the back of his head; and he stood like a horse 'sprung' in the knees. His commands were given in a piping, whining tone, and he appeared to be deeply intent on his business, without paying much regard to the onlookers.[51]

The cadet detachment reached Lexington at 3 A.M. the next day. Jackson wrote his sister within the week. "Anna is an invalid still, but I trust that better health is in store for her. My throat has been troubling me again in consequence of a cold contracted during my military excursion." Jackson did not mention the Harpers Ferry raid or John Brown's execution.[52]

He took little or no part in the discussions of the day. The less said, the better, he was convinced. The majority of Virginia citizens thought otherwise. Words, passion, and excitement flashed across the state. Public debates and open forums were daily occurrences. Home guard and new militia companies mobilized in urban and rural areas alike.

In Lexington, the atmosphere was especially tense. The arsenal contained 30,000 stands of arms plus 500 barrels of gunpowder. Such an inventory surely would make

Lexington the likely target of the next raid. Rumors and fears collaborated; soon sentries were patrolling the state buildings as patrols scoured the nearby countryside. On Christmas Eve, Colonel Smith opened his heart to an Episcopal bishop. "Alas. Has it come to this? Preparing for war? Civil War? War against our brethren & friends. And yet wicked men are driving the country to such an issue. May God in his mercy avert such a calamity."[53]

Adding to this tension as 1860 began was a sudden eruption of smallpox in Lexington. Jackson had deep concern but not for his own safety. Anna's health was precarious. She was somewhat better but far from well. The dreaded pox struck hardest in the poorer section of town. Infected families had to burn clothes and bedding in an effort to contain the epidemic. Aiding the downtrodden was the primary function of Presbyterian deacons. Jackson and his colleagues did everything they could to alleviate the suffering. By month's end, providentially, the smallpox had run its course.[54]

Jackson meanwhile had been giving serious thought to the national situation. Just before his thirty-sixth birthday, Jackson wrote his beloved aunt: "What do you think about the state of the country? Viewing things at Washington from human appearance, I think we have great reason for alarm, but my trust is in God; and I cannot think that he will permit the madness of men to interfere so materially with the Christian labors of this country at home and abroad."[55]

The whole state of Virginia shuddered with apprehension following Brown's raid on Harpers Ferry. Jackson was not unduly alarmed. God would surely bring to the right—and the righteous—the proper solution to the sectional differences dividing North and South. Hence, he gave most of his attention during the winter and spring months to personal matters. In February, he sent a paternalistic letter of instruction to his young niece, Laura's daughter. In cautioning Grace Arnold about her current academic deficiencies, Jackson revealed much about himself.

First of all I want you to learn to spell well. Give particular attention to spelling, for I don't care how much you know about other things, if you don't spell well, you will be laughed at by educated people. . . . When I was young, I committed the blunder of learning to read before I had learnt to spell well, and though I am now 36 years old, yet still I am mortified at my spelling words wrong. In writing this letter I have had to look in the Dictionary to see how a word was spelt, and so I expect it will be all my life. . . . As your memory is better now than it may ever be, you can learn to spell more easily than when you become larger. When we are young we can recollect much better than when we are grown up. . . .

My Father and Mother died when I was very young, and I had to work for my living and education both; but your parents are both living, and have given you a kind hearth, and I trust that you will show them how thankful you are to them by studying hard.[56]

In March, with public meetings frequently being held on the value of the Union and the Constitution, the Presbyterian congregation approved a proposal for pew rentals at the church. Jackson quickly paid his $18 fee to retain the seat to which he was so accustomed. Two months later, he joined a partnership with VMI professor William Gilham and schoolmaster Jacob Fuller to purchase the Lexington Tannery on Randolph Street. Fuller served thereafter as financial agent, and Gilham did the traveling for company business. Jackson's leadership in (and purchases from) the tannery were minimal. His local investments over the years had been varied and wise.

The 1860 census listed Jackson as having $3800 in real estate and $5200 in personal property—quite tidy sums in those days.[57]

That spring young John Kyd Berkenbaugh, a law student in Lexington, heard much about the strange VMI professor named Jackson. After seeing him, Berkenbaugh said to his friend, former VMI cadet James B. Terrill, "Tell me something about Major Jackson, he's such an oddity!" Terrill smiled and replied: "Old Jack is a character, either a genius, or just a little crazy. He lives quietly and don't meddle. He's as systematic as a multiplication table, and as full of military as an arsenal. Stiff as you see, never laughs, but as kind-hearted as a woman; and by Jupiter, he teaches a nigger Sunday school. But, mind what I say, if this John Brown business leads to war, he'll be heard from!"[58]

State officials were already acting as if war was imminent. The General Assembly appropriated $500,000 for the manufacture and purchase of weapons. The governor appointed a three-man Commission for the Public Defense. One of its members was VMI Superintendent Smith. The commission took its charge seriously and sought to prepare the Old Dominion for any military contingency.

In the spring of 1860, it made an inspection tour of all Virginia-based arsenals. While at Harpers Ferry, the officials conferred at length with Captain Robert P. Parrott. He was a proprietor of the Harpers Ferry installation and a personal friend of Smith. Parrott had developed a rifled cannon with twice the range of the twelve-pounder Napoleon howitzer, then the standard cannon in use. The commission was so impressed with the effectiveness of the new cannon it asked Parrott to send a gun and 100 rounds of ammunition to VMI for testing by its artillery officer, Major Jackson. Parrott complied with the request, although the prototype did not arrive at VMI until after summer vacation had begun.

Upon Jackson's return to the institute in late summer, testing of the weapon began in earnest. Jackson had some tent flies set up as targets along a ridge across the North River from Lexington. He put the cannon through extensive trials. The major found the piece more than worthy of its advance billing. He recommended it so strongly that the state placed an order for twelve Parrott guns and accoutrements.[59]

In the midst of affairs relating to the gun, the health of both Jackson and Anna deteriorated anew. It had been a long, fatiguing school year for the major. By June, he and his wife were worn out and suffering. Anna's affliction was such that she had difficulty in walking. Jackson explained his own condition to Laura: "My eyes have improved greatly, through the blessing of *Him* who withholds no good thing from me, but in some respects my health is more impaired than it has been for some years." The pangs of dyspepsia had led Jackson to conclude that his kidneys were malfunctioning. If no improvement came soon, he told Laura, he was going north immediately after commencement and seek relief at "a Hydropathic establishment." The Jacksons hoped to visit Laura and her family in late summer, yet everything hinged on how well Jackson and Anna responded to water treatments. The kidney disease, Jackson noted, "gives me pain every day. I experience unusual pain whilst riding in a carriage."[60]

He enjoyed the 1860 graduation ceremonies at VMI primarily because one of his West Point mentors, the renowned Dennis Hart Mahan, was in attendance. The next day the Jacksons departed for Brattleboro, Vermont, and a highly recommended spa. Two weeks there brought no amelioration to either sufferer. Rather, Jackson came down with what he called "a bilious attack attended with high fever." Hence, on Anna's twenty-ninth birthday, the couple proceeded to Northampton, Massachusetts, and the facilities of the Round Hill Water Cure.[61] Round Hill was among the most popular water-cure establishments in New England. People from every sector of the East gathered there for hydrotherapy with its attendant fellowship.

Physical relief came almost at once. "A skillful water cure physician, through the blessing of a kind Providence," brought Jackson's fever under control. Anna was pleased that "the baths with the exercise gave increased fulness as well as vigor to his manly frame." As for the previously hobbling Mrs. Jackson, by the time she left the spa she was walking five miles a day.[62]

The Jacksons tended to stay by themselves and to become intimate with none of the other guests. Although most visitors to the spas shunned religious duties, Jackson and Anna faithfully attended every Sunday service and weeknight church meeting. A writer who claimed to have been at Round Hill penned a somewhat inaccurate picture of the Virginia professor: "Dwarfed to medium height by a planter's black broad-brimmed hat, clad in black broadcloth with a single-breasted coat buttoned up to the throat; dark-haired, dark-eyed, with dark whiskers of an inch or two in length, overhung by a cornice of dark mustache, he marched around the quiet streets of Norwood, nor did its people dream of the wild dark fate that the silent, quiet man was to send to many a brave, blue-eyed New England boy."[63]

While at Round Hill, the Jacksons found it impossible to escape from the political heat building up between North and South. That summer the Democratic party fractured into three parts trying to select a presidential nominee. Sectional bitterness became more pronounced. The Southern couple sensed "inhospitable elements" among the guests at the New England spa. According to Anna, Jackson "heard and saw enough to awaken his fears that it might portend civil war; but he had no dispute with those who differed from him, treating all politely, and [making] some pleasant acquaintances."[64]

During the first week of August, the physician treating the Jacksons informed them that Anna would need to continue her therapy until the first of October before a complete cure would be effected. Jackson's basic ailment was "a slight distortion of the spine," correctable with a minimum of six months' treatment. The major sought to get an extension of his summer vacation to undergo full therapy. Unsuccessful in delaying his return to VMI duties, Jackson determined to leave Anna in Northampton and return home alone. Separation from Anna was extremely painful; but "satisfied with the sweet assurance that all things work together for my good," he headed south alone for Lexington and the new school year.[65]

A different atmosphere permeated both town and school by late summer. The once-dominant Democratic party now had three presidential candidates in the field. The new Republican party was making a second run at the White House. While not all Republicans were abolitionists, Southerners were convinced that all abolitionists were Republicans. The party's nominee for president, a Midwestern unknown named Abraham Lincoln, offered no reassurances to citizens south of the Potomac River.

Growing discontent existed in Virginia, with the centers of excitement being college campuses. The 230 young men at VMI followed events and speculations closely. Cadets took a more serious interest in the military aspects of their training. Meanwhile, the Lexington newspaper warned: "The simple and single issue, before the people of the United States, in the present canvas, is UNION or DISUNION. Man may make whatever professions they please of attachment or adherence to the Union; but if their acts do not conform to their professions, it will make no difference what their professions are."[66]

Jackson paid close attention now to current events. It was impossible to remain immune to passions that seemed to be heating by the day. Moreover, he was one of the few Lexington residents who had experienced the strong sentiments in North and South. Yet his primary concern throughout September was to have his "little esposita" back home. "The house is very lonesome without Anna," Jackson admitted to his sister. "It hardly appears like home. Anna is well, so the doctor says, and she will come home so soon as her strength and health have been a little more tested and confirmed." The next day, in anticipation of his wife's return, Jackson sent her a long letter of instructions on how best to travel back to Lexington. He closed with tender thoughts: "Your husband feels bright, and the light of his approaching little sunshine makes him still brighter. Whenever you write or telegram for him, you may expect him to come to you in double-quick time."[67] Anna reached Lexington in good health and buoyant spirits. Jackson was delighted to have her home.

However, tensions steadily mounted as the national presidential election drew closer. Lieutenant Joseph Chenoweth, a native of Weston and member of the VMI faculty, expressed prevailing apprehensions when he wrote: "The only thing that breaks away the clouds of dullness that usually hover over Lexington is talk of the coming election. I do most sincerely hope that 'Lincoln' will not be elected. . . . If the 'Black Republicans' are victorious, God save the 'Union, the Constitution, and the Enforcement of the Laws.' Our homes will be the prey of the spoiler."[68]

Everyone voiced an opinion, and many did so often—with the exception of Jackson. He listened and remained silent. Firm allegiance to the Union was still one of his basic tenets. At the same time, however, Jackson was a states' rights adherent who did not think that the federal government had the authority to hold a state in the Union by force. "He never was a secessionist," Mrs. Jackson asserted, "and [he] maintained that it was better for the South to fight for her rights *in the Union than out of it*." Rockbridge County was overwhelmingly Whig in politics, but the major upheld the Jackson family allegiance to the Democratic party. In October, he quietly endorsed then-Vice President John C. Breckinridge, the "Southern" Democratic nominee for president.[69]

One evening just before the election, Breckinridge supporters held a rally at the courthouse. Professor Massie of VMI and noted local attorney E. Franklin Paxton presided over the meeting. The usual political speeches gushed forth, with appropriate resolutions proposed, seconded, and adopted. Interest ran its course, and in the dimly lit room men began to nod. Suddenly, from the back of the room, came a firm voice: "Mr. Chairman!" It was Jackson. A young man in attendance observed that Jackson's action in rising and requesting the floor took the audience by surprise.

Upturned faces listened to Jackson, whose earnest words obscured his awkward gestures. The major's fifteen-minute speech "made a more lasting impression than all the others." Jackson went straight to the point, "touching upon the dangers which threatened our common country and the need of every citizen making a decided stand for the right as he saw it. . . . When he had finished he turned abruptly and marched out with the quick firm step which was part of the man."[70]

November 6, 1860, was election day, and a sense of foreboding was heavy in the air as Virginians filed to the polls. John Bell, the so-called compromise Democrat whom opponents regarded as a peace-at-any-price candidate, polled 1,214 votes in Rockbridge County. Illinois Senator Stephen A. Douglas, representing the regular or Northern wing of Democrats, garnered 630 votes. Breckinridge came in a poor third with only 352 supporters. Republican candidate Lincoln received no votes in the county. Bell also carried Virginia, but by a slim margin over Breckinridge. Lincoln, with the Democrats fatally divided, won the presidency, albeit with barely 40 percent of the nationwide popular vote.[71]

For Jackson, Lincoln's election meant that, barring divine intervention, the days of the Union were numbered. Now was the time for serious discussion and meditation. He joined with eleven other Lexington gentlemen in issuing a call for a town meeting to consider the state of the Union. "By expression of our opinion," the group stated, residents could band together and "contribute our mite [*sic*] to arrest, if possible, the impending calamity—and if that is impossible, then to consult together as to what is the safest course for us to pursue in the event of a dissolution of the Federal government." Several gatherings took place, and a number of study committees came into being. Each produced much rhetoric but little resolution. As meetings became more inflammatory, Jackson's support dwindled. He soon stopped attending the sessions.[72]

Within a few days, Jackson relaxed. He had decided, as was his custom, to put his trust in God. Deacon Jackson would await further developments. Meanwhile, and as a deacon, Jackson had the responsibility for securing accommodations for visiting Presbyterian clergy. Jackson usually found it expedient to extend to such guests the hospitality of his own home.

The Reverend J. B. Ramsey of Lynchburg was at that time staying with the Jacksons. One morning the family had just risen from family prayers. Ramsey expressed lamentations over the state of the country. Jackson listened patiently, then gave the preacher a mini-sermon. "Why should Christians be disturbed about the dissolution of the Union? It can come only by God's permission, and will only be permitted if for His people's good; for does He not say, 'All things work together for good to them that love God?' I cannot see how *we* should be distressed about such things, whatever be their consequences."[73]

Still, Jackson could not alleviate his concerns about the future. The only hope lay with an all-wise Providence, but should not man seek his mercy? Jackson went to see his pastor. To Dr. White he exclaimed: "If the general government should persist in the measures now threatened, there must be war. It is painful to discover with what unconcern they speak of war, and threaten it. They seem not to know what its horrors are. I have had an opportunity of knowing enough on the subject to make me fear war as the sum of all evils." Then Jackson asked: "But do you not think that all the Christian people of the land could be induced to unite in a concert of prayer to avert so great an evil? It seems to me that if they would thus unite in prayer, war might be prevented and peace preserved." White immediately agreed and set aside Friday, January 4, 1861, as the date of the first prayer meeting.[74]

A rather tense letter from Jackson then went to Laura. "I am looking forward with great interest to the 4th of Jany. when the Christian people of this land will lift their united prayers as incense to the Throne of God in supplication for our unhappy country. What is the feeling about Beverly respecting secession? I am anxious to hear from the native part of my state. I am strong for the Union at present, and if things become worse I hope to continue so. I think that the majority in this country are for the union; but in counties bordering on us there is strong secession feeling."[75]

The next day, December 20, South Carolina left the Union. A public meeting quickly convened in Lexington to share opinions over this first secession. According to one participant, "a number of speeches were made in which Union sentiment predominated and found sympathetic response from the audience. Frank Paxton left the platform as the meeting closed and shocked the sentiments by raising his hat and proposing three cheers for South Carolina."[76]

Paxton was then thirty-two, heavy-set, bearded, and bullish. He had graduated from Washington College and Yale College and was at the top of his law school class at the University of Virginia. Failing eyesight in 1860 had brought an end to a highly promising legal practice in Lexington. That did not stop Paxton from active involvement in political matters. His son noted that "he was a man of ardent temperament and strong convictions such as did not permit him to remain an indifferent spectator of the exciting political occurrences of that period."[77]

Jackson and Paxton had been reasonably good friends until the secession crisis. At a Franklin Literary Society meeting, Paxton's blunt and outspoken views on behalf of secession took the form of a personal attack on Jackson's first father-in-law, Unionist Dr. George Junkin. Paxton's remarks incurred Jackson's displeasure. The two men did not speak thereafter until the outbreak of war brought them together in defense of Virginia.[78]

Secession deeply split the Lexington community. The great majority of citizens in and around town had a strong, inherited attachment for the Union. They were convinced that an adjustment could be reached and all dangers circumscribed. In contrast, VMI cadets and Washington College students had the rudderless ardor of youth and saw secession as a wonderful pathway to patriotism. Only a few citizens perceived that a breakup of the Union meant bloody civil war. Robert Morrison was one of those farsighted residents. He cautioned an overzealous son in Lexington, "To all human appearance your Hotheaded rash Fanatical southerners are about to bring upon themselves a sivel war that god only knows when & where it will end."[79]

Late in January, Jackson responded to a letter from his fifteen-year-old nephew and namesake. Thomas Arnold felt a special closeness to Jackson after living in his home for almost a year, especially since Jackson treated him as more adult than teenager. "I was glad to learn your Father's views respecting the state of the country," Jackson wrote.

I agree very much with him. In this Country there is a strong Union feeling. . . . I am in favor of making a thorough trial for peace, and if we fail in this and the state is invaded to defend it with terrific resistance—even to taking no prisoners. I desire to see the state use every influence she may possess in order to procure an honorable adjustment of our troubles; but if after having done so, the free states instead of permitting us to enjoy the rights guaranteed to us, by the Constitution of our Country, should endeavor to subjugate us, and thus excite our slaves to servile insurrection in which our Families will be murdered without quarter or mercy, it becomes us to wage such a war as will bring hostilities to a speedy close. People who are anxious to bring on war don't know what they are bargaining for; they don't see all the horrors that must accompany such an event.

For myself I have never as yet been induced to believe that Virginia will ever have to leave the Union. I feel pretty well satisfied that the Northern peoples love the Union more than they do their peculiar notions of slavery, and that they will prove it to us when satisfied that we are in earnest about leaving the [Union] unless they do us justice.[80]

Early February found seven Southern states out of the Union and banded together as the Confederate States of America. The president was Mississippi's Jefferson Davis; the capital was Montgomery, Alabama. Meanwhile, two political movements were underway in Virginia.

The state had summoned a Peace Conference to convene in Washington in an eleventh-hour attempt to stop the national landslide. Delegates from all states, with venerable statesman John Tyler in the chair, would study all options to avoid further division and future war. At the same time, Virginians were invited to go to the polls and select representatives for a Secession Convention. It would hold regular sessions in Richmond, monitor day-by-day affairs, and make a recommendation when events warranted.

In that setting, Jackson sent another letter to Laura. He began with a health report. "I have had a very severe cold and for the last two or three weeks have been suffering from neuralgia about the temples and forehead, but am much better at present. Anna's health is tolerable good." Then Jackson turned to the political climate.

I am much gratified to see a strong Union feeling in my portion of the state, but it may go a little further than I think it ought, though I hope not. For my own part I intend to vote for the Union candidates for the convention and I desire to see every honorable means used for peace, and I believe that Providence will bless such means with the fruits of peace. I hope that the majority of the votes will be in favor of referring the action of the Convention to the people for their final decision of the question involved, as this will not only be an additional safeguard to our own liberties but will give time for an amicable adjustment of our difficulties. But if after we have done all that we can do for an honorable preservation of the Union, there shall be a determination on the part of the Free States to deprive us of our right which the fair interpretation of the Constitution, as already decided by the Federal Court, guarantees to us, I am in favor of secession.[81]

VMI professors were hardly immune from the temper of the times. Smith, Colston, Preston, Gilham, John DeHart Ross, and others discussed little else outside the section rooms. The heat of the issue ameliorated much of the coldness of the winter. One snowy evening, Jackson attended a debate at Washington College. At issue was the topic, "Was South Carolina Justified in Seceding?" The meeting room was packed, with excitement high. When everyone expected to speak had done so, a cry went up for Major Jackson to say something. The request became a chorus. Jackson slowly rose to his feet; the audience grew quiet.

"Mr. President," he stated, "I have learned from Old Hickory, when I made up my mind not to do a thing, never to do it. I made up my mind, before coming here, not to make a speech, and I don't intend to do so." Jackson sat down to a mixture of laughter, disappointment, and applause.[82]

On February 18, Anna left for North Carolina to attend the wedding of her younger sister Susan to promising attorney Alphonso Calhoun Avery. Jackson started the first letter to his wife almost before she got out of sight. "My precious little darling, your husband has returned from the Institute, had his dinner all alone, and feels sad enough this afternoon; but I trust that my little pet has had a pleasant day's travel, and that the kind providence of God has kept her from all accident and danger, and has spread out before her many enjoyments." Another letter went into the mail the following day. "My darling pet, your husband feels a loneliness for which he can hardly account, but he knows if his darling were here he wouldn't feel thus. . . . I follow you in mind and heart, and think of you at the different points of your route."[83]

With the Secession Convention in daily session at Richmond—and its proceedings carried faithfully on the front page of the *Lexington Gazette,* many of the VMI cadets grew fidgety and a bit impulsive. "We were ourselves more impatient at the delay than we would acknowledge," one cadet admitted.[84]

George Washington's birthday seemed an appropriate time to make feelings known. It was customary on February 22 to suspend all academic duties and to begin the day with a thirteen-gun salute. Major Jackson arrived punctually on the parade ground to supervise the artillery firing. He immediately noticed a strange cloth waving from the Barracks tower where the Stars and Stripes usually hung. What Jackson saw was a crudely fashioned secession flag made from a bed sheet. Shoe blacking had been used to create the Goddess of Liberty and Virginia's state motto. Above those letters were the words: "Hurrah for South Carolina." Jackson sternly ordered the emblem removed. Yet the two cadets responsible for the banner managed to retrieve and hide it for use at another time.[85]

Secession flags popped out all over Virginia during the winter months. In Richmond, the senior class of the Baptist Female Institute ran up such a standard on top of the cupola of the school's main building. The college president angrily removed it and gave the students a verbal lashing on the demure conduct Southern ladies should always exhibit. One morning a large black flag of mourning suddenly appeared stretched across the main thoroughfare in Fredericksburg. It "bore a suitable inscription" and was put there to mourn the delay of Virginia in leaving the Union.[86]

Pro-Confederate emblems continued to appear on the campuses of VMI and Washington College. Secession became the dominant topic at every public gathering. In the middle of many debates was Jackson's first father-in-law. The outspoken Dr. Junkin not only rigidly adhered to a unionist view; he lambasted opponents for having idiotic enthusiasm for secession and independence. "I would not dissolve this union," he once thundered, "if the people should make the devil President!"[87]

Young law apprentice George Hundley went to several public discussions where "old Dr. George Junkin . . . with his squeaking voice frequently addressed these meetings and managed to make his shrill shouts of 'Union,' 'Union,' heard above the cackling of the obstreperous students." Among the hecklers was John H. Gilmer, Jr., of Richmond. As one unionist speaker was reaching the climax of his presentation, Gilmer hooted from the audience: "Come to my arms, you greasy fritter!"[88]

Jackson tried to steer clear of the emotionalism. On Saturday, April 6, he wrote a long letter to Laura—a letter he naturally did not mail until the Sabbath had passed. It was to be Jackson's last written communique with his cherished sister. Appropriately, Jackson's thoughts were of the devotion to God he felt and yet wanted to instill in his sister. His sentiments were a portent of what his actions were to be. He stated in part:

God withdraws his sensible presence from us to try our faith. When a cloud comes between you and the sun, do you fear that the sun will never appear again? I am well satisfied that you are a child of God, and that you will be saved in heaven. . . . So you must not doubt. . . . There is one very essential thing to the child of God who would enjoy the comforts of religion, and that is he or she must live in accordance with the law of God, must have no will but His; knowing the path of duty must not hesitate for a moment, but at once walk in it . . . [and] we should always seek by prayer to be taught our duty.[89]

As emotionalism for war built up in April, order at VMI melted. On April 12, Jackson submitted a weekly grade report for the seventeen first classmen in one of his sections. It took all of the space allotted to cite instances of misconduct. "Bray disorderly in Sec. room on the 11th. The same on the 12th. Heath leaving section room on the 9th. Coltrane disorder on the 12th. Hart using tobacco on the 12th. Lawson disorder on the 9th. The same on the 11th. The same not keeping his proper seat on the 10th."[90]

Local incidents had been minor, with heat confined to verbal jousting, until April 13. That was the day a beleaguered and battered Union garrison at Fort Sumter, South Carolina, surrendered to Confederate forces, thus setting the stage for civil war. Those developments were unknown far away in Lexington, yet only a spark was needed there to convert smoke into fire. On that warm Saturday, with many cadets on liberty and the town full of shoppers and starers, the inevitable confrontation materialized.

Unionists and secessionists—basically in the form of Captain Samuel Letcher's militia company and VMI cadets, respectively—got the idea at the same time to raise a flag of loyalty near the county courthouse. The cadets acted first, marching into the middle of town where a pro-Union crowd four times their number stood in open hostility. Some individual threats went back and forth, a one-on-one altercation flared here and there, but the situation remained in an uneasy calm.

Secessionists hoisted their flag, gave and listened to a few speeches, then began to disperse. Unionists then moved to raise their banner. Somehow, cadets the previous night had gained access to the unionist flagpole and bored a number of holes in it. As a result, when the Stars and Stripes caught the stiff breeze, the staff snapped. Several onlookers were slightly injured by the falling pole. Cadets gave a loud cheer of derision and sauntered back to campus for supper.

Near the end of the meal, a cadet who had remained at the courthouse rushed into the dining hall. "House Mountain men have fallen on some of the cadets uptown and killed them!" he shouted. Without a word, cadets dashed to their rooms and procured muskets, bayonets, and cartridge boxes. Some 180 angry young men poured out of the barracks. "Firing our guns in the air as we went," Cadet Charles Wight stated, the corps dashed in mob fashion toward the downtown.[91]

Colonel Smith was at home recovering from pneumonia. He had no idea what had caused the disturbance, but the seriousness of it was readily apparent. The superintendent intercepted the lead elements of the cadets. His weak appeals to reason were unconvincing. The students continued onto Main Street, where Cadet Captain Thomas S. Galloway shouted, "Form battalion!"[92]

Cadets promptly made the directed alignment. They loaded muskets, fixed bayonets, and stood ready to assault the mob of unionists who, gathered in the street several blocks away, had no intention of being intimidated by a bunch of uniformed boys. The rumor that one or more cadets had been murdered was unfounded, but no one bothered to seek verification. Smith again appeared before his students. He demanded that they return to barracks. Few made any move to do so.

The situation was extremely tense. At one end of Main Street, almost 200 eager cadets stood poised to attack local civilians. A few blocks away stood a large crowd of Virginia citizens, armed with a variety of weapons, defiantly prepared to assail cadets of the state's military academy. Professors Massie and Colston pled with the young men to retire from the scene. Irate cadets paid no heed to either officer.

At that moment, Major Jackson strode briskly to the front of the battalion. He had seemingly come from nowhere. Shoulders slightly stooped, lips compressed tightly, chin up and eyes blazing, he paced back and forth before the assembled ranks. No words came forth; none were needed as he glared sternly at the VMI contingent. At the same time, a delegation of moderates up the street were cooling the passions of the unionists. In a few minutes, the cadets tucked their heads, turned around, and slowly made their way back to the campus.

Colonel Smith summoned the corps at once to assembly. As the cadets entered the hall and took their seats, Smith stood at the rostrum. Massie, Preston, and Jackson sat behind him. In the words of one cadet, Smith dispensed with pleasantries and began "to excoriate the corps for its insubordinate conduct." Another cadet observed that the superintendent "made us an address to show how unwise and unsoldierly it was to attempt to rectify any fancied evils ourselves and in such a way."[93]

Preston and Massie in turn stepped forward and applied more gentle criticism. Smith then turned to Jackson and said: "I have driven the nail, but it needs clinching. Speak with them."[94]

No one gave thought to "Tom Fool" Jackson or to the eccentric who had long been the butt of campus jokes. What the cadets saw that night was a ramrod straight, inflexible soldier standing before them. Jackson remained erect and silent for several moments. What the cadets then heard was an authoritative voice of a quality never before perceived in the major. "Military men make short speeches," he stated in measured terms, "and as for myself I am no hand at speaking anyhow. The time for war has not yet come, but it will come and that soon, and when it does come, my advice is to draw the sword and throw away the scabbard."[95]

Jackson returned to his seat as the hall exploded in loud cheers of approval. After the assembly, and far into the night, shouts of "Hurra for Old Jack! He is the right stripe!" echoed across the campus. Cadet Randolph Barton stated fifty years later: "The thrilling effect of those words is felt by the writer to this day."[96]

On the preceding Wednesday, April 10, the spring meeting of the Presbytery of Lexington had been in session at the church. Deacon Jackson had hoped to participate actively in the deliberations and ceremonies. Several members were staying at his home. Fortunately, Anna was there to act as hostess while Jackson was attending to the crisis in town. He was unable to attend the climactic session on Saturday afternoon.[97]

A chain reaction of events toward war moved swiftly thereafter. As steady rain fell on Monday, April 15, President Abraham Lincoln sought to block any further activities of the Confederate States. He invoked a 1795 act and called on the states to furnish 75,000 troops "to execute the laws of the Union, suppress rebellions, repel invasions." Virginia's quota was three regiments totaling 2340 men, the units to rendezvous at Gordonsville, Staunton, and Wheeling.

John Letcher of Lexington had been governor for sixteen months. Letcher was a moderate, law-and-order executive who had done everything he could to keep secessionist hysteria under control and the Old Dominion in the Union. Lincoln's call for soldiers to make war against the South clearly drew the battle line. Neutrality could exist no longer; moderation was out of the question.

Rain was still falling on the 16th when Letcher sent a telegram in response to the Northern summons. "In reply to this communication I have only to say, that the militia of Virginia will not be furnished to the powers at Washington for any such use or purposes as they have in view. Your object is to subjugate the Southern States, and a requisition made upon me for such an object . . . will not be complied with. You have chosen to inaugurate civil war, and having done so, we will meet it in a spirit as determined as the Administration has exhibited towards the South."[98]

The sun broke through the clouds on Wednesday, April 17, and Virginians saw that as a divine omen for the Secession Convention. It had been in almost constant session since news of the fall of Fort Sumter reached Richmond. Discussions and debates fluctuated between hateful and tearful. By midweek, the only question seemed to be whether to make war on sister states with whom Virginia had traditional ties or to join the Southern move for independence.

Back on April 4, the convention had rejected secession by a firm majority. This time, with crowds filling the streets and clamoring enthusiastically for the Confederacy, popular appeal added weight to what was considered Northern oppression. The delegates thereupon voted 88 to 55 for Virginia to abandon the Union.

A Richmond newspaper expressed the sentiments of the majority: "The old Union, for which our fathers fought and bled, has been wilfully sacrificed by a Black Republican despot. . . . Virginia, which led the van in the war of '76, now meets him on the threshold. She has been slow to act, but she will be slower still to retrace her steps. The Union has lost its brightest planet, but it will henceforth become a star of the first magnitude in the purer, brighter and grander constellation of the Southern Cross."[99]

Rockbridge County, largely unionist on April 13, had become rabidly secessionist four days later. One citizen remarked that "the divided spirits on Saturday were one on Wednesday." The Lexington newspaper agreed, but more dramatically. "When the olive branch of peace, fairness and equality was rejected, and in place thereof the usurper's proclamation for her submission or subjugation was issued, then did the sovereign people of Virginia rise . . . and throw defiance in the faces of those who sought her oppression and declare that she was and of right ought to be free. It was her second declaration of independence and she will make it good."[100]

On the day after Virginia's withdrawal from the Union, a young resident was shocked at the overnight change at the seat of Rockbridge County. "The steady-going old town of Lexington had suddenly been metamorphosed into a bustling military camp. Volunteer companies were being organized, and every preparation being made for a horrible war." Captain Letcher's Rockbridge Rifles and a company of totally unarmed cavalry departed Lexington to help in the seizure of the vital armory at Harpers Ferry. A Washington College contingent of students began drilling under the direction of their Greek professor, James J. White.[101]

The Virginia Military Institute was doubtless the center of bustle and speculation in the county. "Great excitement prevails here since the reception of the secession ordinance (on which fifteen guns were fired in a salute of honor)," one cadet wrote his sister. Colonel Smith wired his neighbor and friend, Governor Letcher, "to tender the services of the officers and cadets of this institution for any duty to which the necessities of the State may call us." Smith boasted of having 250 "well armed and disciplined men" ready to march at an instant's notice.[102]

Superintendent Smith then journeyed to Richmond to become part of a three-man committee to advise the governor and legislature on military appointments and policies. Major Gilham soon followed to take command of the camp for volunteers being established at the Richmond fairgrounds.[103]

In Smith's absence, Major Preston took charge of VMI and immediately put the school on a war footing. All academic work not relative to military matters was discontinued. Artillery practice occupied the mornings, infantry tactics filled the afternoons, and battalion drill completed every day's activities. "Military instruction constitutes the order of the day," Cadet Stevenson muttered. "We drill from five in the morning until dark with slight intermissions."[104]

Major Jackson repeatedly urged Preston during those frantic days to arrange to have cannon balls cast and requisitioned arms delivered before the cadets had to leave on military assignments. A Lexington correspondent assured readers in Richmond that patriotism abounded in the upper Shenandoah Valley. "The late news has inflamed our people to an extent never before known. All are now united to defend the honor and interests of our beloved State. . . . The whole military force of the county, also the corps of Cadets, are waiting to receive marching orders."[105]

In the panorama of civil war, even in the detail of Virginia's preparation for action, Jackson was an insignificant figure. He was a teacher in a village segregated by mountains from the mainstream of the Old Dominion. Jackson was not even a good teacher, except in the categories of persistence and classroom discipline. Maturity had come to him quickly, but a broadened vista of society had developed tardily and oftentimes painfully. Jackson was a veteran of war and extensive travels; yet while a decade at VMI had brought some improvement in his means, it had produced no major alterations in his personality. His quiet and modest ways hardly foreshadowed any outstanding role in the conflict then enveloping states that had little knowledge of what "union" really entailed.

Jackson had no hesitation, no indecision, as to his proper course of action. A few years later, his wife commented: "He deplored the collision most earnestly. He believed that patriotic statesmanship might have averted it. He loved the Union as only one who had fought under the flag could love it. He would have died to have saved it in its purity and its just relations. But he believed that the constitutional rights of the States had been invaded, and he never had a doubt as to where his allegiance was due. His sword belonged to his State."[106]

As Jackson was a VMI faculty member, subject to the military regulations of the Commonwealth of Virginia, his status in the crisis was already determined (unless, of course, he resigned his post). However, much more was involved in Jackson's mind than a mere sense of duty. Faith, tinged by the ambition to do God's will, were his impulses. An all-wise Providence had placed a malediction on the land. That curse must be washed away by the bloodshed of war.

Victory would come to the side most heedful of God's teachings. The Confederate States existed because the Creator deemed it so. Its constitution made repeated appeals to a divine being. As far as Jackson was concerned, God clearly intended for the Southern nation to flourish in carrying out his purposes.

The Confederacy as Jackson envisioned it was the next step in the history of Christian people. He would serve it and, by doing so, glorify God. To Jackson, this war was a call to wage both a political battle and a religious crusade. Never did he make a differentiation between the two; never did he look back to reconsider. He would ride forward to do the Lord's work in the best way he could: as a soldier.

Jackson's first father-in-law adopted an opposite and impassioned course. President Junkin of Washington College had watched events with a growing anger as well as a loud voice of protest. His unflinching unionism caused students to brand him an abolitionist and to call him "Lincoln Junkin." The Presbyterian cleric was not deterred. Junkin damned secession as "the essence of all immorality"; and when the Old Dominion left the Union, Junkin scornfully called the action "a rebellion without cause."[107]

When students hoisted another flag over the main building of the college, and the faculty unanimously rejected the president's demand that it vote to have the banner lowered, Junkin angrily resigned. "I will not stay where the students dishonor their country's flag!" he thundered. The next day (April 19) Junkin climbed into his carriage with a widowed daughter and niece. He was heading back to Pennsylvania whence he had come, even though his daughter Margaret and three sons were remaining in the South.

After the carriage crossed the Potomac River, Junkin reined in his horses on the northern side and wiped the mud from the wheels. "Thus purified," he "journeyed north, never to return." Junkin continued to loathe all things secessionist—with the lone exception of his son-in-law. For Jackson, he always voiced a special affection.[108]

It was sad to break relations with a father-by-marriage, counselor, pastor, and friend. Jackson might have dwelled more on the loss had he not been so busy with institute and personal preparations. He more than doubled the usual time he spent at

VMI each day. At home, he began methodically packing for a quick departure. He had been a regular customer at Compton's dry goods store since bringing Anna to Lexington. On Friday, April 19, Jackson purchased two pairs of socks. That was the last time his name appeared in the store's ledger.[109]

Saturday was a day of expectation. State newspapers had stepped up the intensity of zeal in Virginia for the Confederate cause. One daily suggested that the Old Dominion's battle cry should be, "If I stand, support me; if I run, shoot me; if I fall, avenge me!"[110]

Jackson silently went about clearing his outstanding accounts. Anna just as calmly worked with needle and thread to get her husband's clothing in order. At supper, she made reference to Jackson's expected departure. He smiled, then replied: "My dear, tomorrow is the blessed Sabbath day. It is also the regular communion season at our church. I hope I shall not be called to leave until Monday. Let us then dismiss from our conversation and our thoughts pertaining to the war, and have together one more quiet evening of preparation for our loved Sabbath duties." The couple moved to the parlor. Jackson read aloud from a religious magazine—an unusual action in view of his strong policy against using his eyes at night. Husband and wife reviewed Bible lessons for the next afternoon's black Sunday school class, then went to bed.[111]

Sometime near dawn a telegram arrived at the institute. Governor Letcher wanted the corps of cadets to report to Richmond with all dispatch to serve as drillmasters for the flood of recruits gathering there. Jackson's doorbell rang shortly after sunrise that April 21 sabbath. It was a messenger from Acting Superintendent Preston. The corps (less forty-seven cadets, who would remain at VMI for various reasons) would be inspected at 10 A.M., fed, and "formed to march" at 12:30 P.M. Jackson was to lead the contingent. Once at the capital he would receive his own assignment to duty.

The major did not wait for the morning meal. He rushed to the institute and spent at least four hours ensuring that every detail of the forthcoming movement was in order. At some point in the final preparations, Jackson sent a request to Dr. White: he would like the pastor to make an "appropriate address of Christian counsel, and to lead in a fervent prayer" just before the cadets left for war.[112]

Near 11 A.M., Jackson returned home. He ate a hurried breakfast and cleared away the last sheet of paperwork. Hastily he packed what few items he would need. Then Jackson donned his best faculty uniform: blue double-breasted coat with twin rows of brass buttons and the epaulets of a major on the shoulders, blue trousers with thin gold piping down the legs, sash, sword, and forage cap.

Lovingly taking his wife by the hand, he went into the privacy of their parlor. Jackson opened his Bible and read aloud the fifth chapter of 2 Corinthians, which concludes: "And all things are of God, who hath reconciled us to himself. . . . Now then we are ambassadors of Christ, as though God did beseech you by us: we pray you in Christ's stead, be ye reconciled to God. For he hath made him to be sin for us, who knew no sin, that we might be made the righteousness of God in him."

Jackson then knelt on the floor and prayerfully begged that "if consistent with His will, God would still avert the threatening danger and grant us peace." He then committed himself and his family to the protecting love of the Almighty. Anna never forgot that moment. "His voice was so choked with emotion that he could scarcely utter the words."[113]

Taking his wife in his arms, Jackson kissed her tenderly and repeatedly. Quickly he turned and walked from the house he would never see again. He mounted an ordinary-looking horse and galloped the short distance to the VMI campus.

The day was warm and sunny. It was a few minutes before noon when Jackson arrived at the large arch that was the east entrance to the barracks. The statue of George Washington seemed more conspicuous that morning, the famous Virginian's facial expression more determined and proud. Excitement filled the air, except for the institute clock atop the barracks. The minute hand, oblivious to it all, moved with agonizing slowness. All was in readiness when Jackson appeared. Baggage and camp equipment were packed in wagons, the horses were hitched, and teamsters sat in place.

Four small companies of cadets, each company in two lines, stood at attention facing the barracks. The youths were excited as they sought to display a maturity they had never felt. All wore small kepis, shell jackets, and trousers stuffed into socks. Marching equipment was minimal.

An onlooker remarked that the 176 cadets "were in line, their cheeks aglow, and their eyes sparkling with the expectation of military glory awaiting them." The words in Colonel Preston's marching orders were one reason. "When the muster is held for men who have souls to defend their native soil from violation, insult and subjugation, the heart of every true Virginian responds to the voice as with stern delight he answers: Here! . . . The Corps of Cadets will prove their birth and breeding and exhibit to Virginia the worth of her favorite Institute. The Cadets will not fail to manifest the advantage which the military education gives to him over those not less brave than himself. The Corps will go forth [with] the pride of its friends, the hope of the state and the terror of her foes. May the blessing of the God of Hosts rest upon every one who is battling in this holy cause."[114]

The eight officers accompanying the corps looked now to Jackson for leadership. "Then again," Raleigh Colston stated, "I noticed at once but more evident than before the total change in his demeanor that I had observed at Charles Town. His speech quickened, his eyes glittered, his drowsy manner had left him, and his whole nature seemed to wake up."[115]

Departure time was a half-hour away. The institute's acting commandant, Lieutenant John Ropes, read the order for departure. With Dr. White "in clerical cloth" and standing in front of the archway, Jackson wanted to give his friend all of the time he needed. The major removed the floppy forage cap. "Let us pray!" he called out. White stepped forward and offered a moving plea for God to watch over and bless the young men about to go forth to battle and to bring success to the cause they espoused. The clergyman pronounced "Amen" and stepped aside. It was 12:10; twenty minutes still remained before the official time to start the journey.[116]

Jackson paced back and forth in front of the ranks for several minutes. He then sent to the mess hall for a stool and sat down near the Washington statue. Youthful impatience swelled up from the assembled cadets. "Let us go! Let us go!" they shouted. Except for occasionally looking at his watch, Jackson sat in unusually rigid fashion. He seemed lost in thought. One would have thought him asleep had his eyes not been open.

Major Colston, the second in command, was aware that the cadets had thirty-six miles to travel before stopping. Every mile of daylight was valuable. Colston edged up to Jackson. "Everything is ready, sir. Shall I give the command forward?" "No," came the curt reply. "When the clock strikes the hour, we will march, and not until then."[117]

Finally, almost like a clap of thunder, the clock announced the half-hour; its echo drifted across a Lexington that was soundless even of a bird's call. Jackson rose deliberately, mounted his horse, and rode some ten yards to the right end of the eight rows of cadets. His eyes again glowed brightly; the slightly flushed features seemed chiseled with intensity. "Attention Battalion!" he shouted without looking back at the column. "Right face! By the file left, march!"

Cadets two abreast in Company A stepped forward in cadence. The other three companies joined the line of march in sequence; and as a drum and fife set the tempo, the narrow little column started down the hill toward the North River. In front, behind Jackson, was a three-man color guard bearing the white VMI flag with blue and gray Virginia seal in the middle. One of the younger cadets left behind later exclaimed: "I don't believe a finer body of youths were ever together at college than the two hundred and fifty who were cadets . . . in 1860 and 61. They represented many of the best and most famous families of Virginia and of the Southern States."[118]

Townspeople tried to give one last goodbye, but many choked on the words. Everyone in the column was following Jackson, who was hardly an inspirational sight. A young observer noted that the major's arms were "flopping to the motion of his horse, over whose head, good rider as he was, it seemed he would certainly go."[119]

Down the hill from the campus the procession wound. It crossed the covered bridge over the North River, made a ninety-degree turn at the base of the hill, and disappeared around a bend. At least one source claimed that at some point in the first moments of the march, Jackson turned and waved his hat to the spectators still watching the departure.[120]

It is far more likely that Jackson never looked back at his adopted hometown. Any sentimentality in his makeup at the time was subservient to a sense of duty. He had been a servant all of his adult life—as soldier, professor, husband, Sunday school teacher, and church deacon. His ten years in a civilian environment were at an end. The summons of war had called him to the battlefield. Now was the time to aid Virginia and to fight for God. Raleigh Colston, who rode beside him that Sunday, later commented: "I have no doubt that after Jackson took the field, all the powers of his mind were concentrated upon two subjects alone to the almost entire exclusion of all others—religion & strategy."[121]

9

VIRGINIA DRILLMASTER

IT IS THE STUFF OF WHICH legends are made: 175 eager VMI cadets marching to war over thirty-six miles of miserable roads; a battery of four guns plus baggage wagons rumbling slowly behind them, unable to keep pace with the fast-stepping youngsters, who covered the distance in less than nine hours; all of this under the all-seeing and guiding eye of a professor soon to be famous for rapid movements. Both cadets and subsequent writers have described the trip from Lexington to Staunton in that fashion.[1]

Unfortunately for tradition, it did not happen that way at all. A mile or so out of Lexington, the cadet column found a veritable convoy of stagecoaches, wagons, and carriages awaiting them. Most of the vehicles were from the Staunton stage line of the Harman brothers. Cadets clambered into the conveyances for the journey to the Virginia Central Railroad depot at Staunton. Most of the officers continued the trip on horseback with the guns and wagons.

Major Colston remembered that he and Jackson rode side by side. The taciturn professor, Colston stated, "talked more than I had ever heard him before. . . . Jackson was eager for vigorous operations without delay. He was full of fire and eagerness. He cast his eye repeatedly along the artillery column with evident predilection and alluded to his marches in Mexico which the present scene brought back to his memory." Colston added: "I have no doubt that if it had been left to his choice he would have selected for himself the post of chief of artillery in the first organized division of Confederate troops."[2]

The cadets' 10 P.M. arrival in Staunton created no excitement. For the previous four days, military detachments had been embarking from there on the Virginia Central Railroad. The cadet corps managed to secure enough food to calm appetites before heading for bed in Staunton hotels. Sore but excited boys were up at dawn on April 22 because the four cannon had to be loaded on railroad cars. Once that chore was completed, the uniformed youngsters spent three hours or more in chatting with young ladies who came to the station to see what VMI cadets were like. At 10:15 A.M., Jackson and his young contingent left by train for Richmond. Officers and cadets were in passenger cars, cannon and baggage strapped onto flat cars.[3]

The troop train snaked eastward, then slowed more as the locomotive strained to make the climb up through the Blue Ridge Mountains. All was going well until the engine derailed inside the long tunnel near the mountaintop. It required two hours to get the locomotive back on the tracks. The train eased down the mountain and stopped to refuel at Mechum's River Station, a point Jackson would come to know well.

From there he dashed off a quick note to Anna. "We are now stopping for a short time on the eastern slope of the Blue Ridge. The train will hardly reach Richmond before night." Jackson was somewhat surprised at the reception they had received during the first part of the rail journey. "Here, as well as at other points of the line, the War spirit is intense. The cars had scarcely stopped here, before a request was made that I would leave a cadet to drill a company."[4]

Whistle screaming periodically, the train moved across the rolling Virginia piedmont and past stations—such as Gordonsville and Fredericks Hall—soon to be familiar sites to Jackson. Darkness had fallen when the cadets saw the lights of the capital and the state's largest city.[5] If the VMI cadets expected some kind of welcoming committee, they were disappointed. The 40,000 residents of Richmond were caught in the excitement of war; thousands of recruits had streamed into the city every hour of the day since secession. The Lexington group at first was merely part of the crowd.

This did not dampen the ardor of the cadets. Under the command of Colston (Jackson disdaining such pomp), the corps marched to Capitol Square. Gas lights and torches illuminated the area. The uniformed youngsters, a local newspaper reported admiringly, created "the most unbounded enthusiasm among the spectators. . . . The Cadets came prepared for war, fully armed and equipped. . . . These young men do not flinch from any duty, and herein they set a noble example."[6]

After being reviewed and complimented by an obviously proud Governor Letcher of Lexington, the corps marched to the major troop installation at Camp Lee (named for Revolutionary War hero Gen. "Light Horse Harry" Lee). Most of the youngsters went immediately to bed. Colston and Jackson spent the night together. Before retiring, Jackson sent his first impressions to Anna of the atmosphere in Richmond. The letter began with what, for Jackson, was unusually high praise of an individual.

> Col. [Robert E.] Lee of the Army is here & has been made Maj.-General. This I regard as of more value to us than Gen. Scott could render as Commander. It is understood that Gen. Lee is to be our Commander in Chief, & I regard him as a better officer than Gen. Scott. The Cadets are encamped in the Fair Grounds, which is about 1 1/2 miles west of the City. We have excellent quarters. So far as we can hear, God is crowning our cause with success, but I don't wish to send rumors to you. I will try & give facts, as they become known, though I may not have time to write but a line or two.

Colston disagreed with Jackson about the "excellent quarters." The foreign-languages professor noted: "He and I occupied a small room without any furniture . . . and he wrapped himself in a single blanket over his uniform, put his saddle under his head, and lay down on the floor as if he had never slept any other way in all his life."[7]

On Wednesday, April 24, a government clerk in Richmond wrote with some exuberance: "The cadets of the Military Institute are rendering good service now, and Professor Jackson is truly a benefactor. I hope he will take the field himself; and if he does, I predict for him a successful career." Jackson hoped the same; but after turning over the cadets to Virginia authorities, his job was done. No new orders were waiting for him. Jackson thereupon volunteered to serve as an artillery drillmaster at Camp

Lee. He joined former army officers Joseph E. Johnston and John C. Pemberton, along with VMI colleagues Gilham and Preston. Their job was to convert civilians into soldiers by overseeing the organization and instruction of the eager mobs flocking to Virginia's defense.[8]

All was bustle, expectancy, and controlled chaos. Most of the arriving companies, one cadet observed, were "undrilled and undisciplined, raw and without arms, except in instances where the individual had given play to his own imagination as to what would be useful in battle, and pursuant thereto had brought the squirrel gun, the shotgun [and] the butcher's knife."[9]

For the better part of two days, Jackson with twelve VMI cadets taught basic rudiments at the artillery training ground on the Richmond College campus near Camp Lee. His immediate superior was his former Mexican War battery captain, the flamboyant John B. Magruder. He, Jackson, and the cadets gave the first basic instructions to such future batteries of note as the Richmond Howitzers, Richmond Fayette Artillery, and Hampden Artillery. One of the new officers Jackson met on the drillfields was Dr. Robert E. Withers, who was about to take command of a Southside Virginia regiment. Withers found Jackson "very quiet and reticent, having little to say to any one." A major reason for Jackson's silence was the April 25 order appointing him a major in Virginia's topographical engineers.[10]

Jackson could not conceal the letdown he felt at this assignment. (His wife said he found it "distasteful.") What little Jackson knew about engineering he disliked. Drawing had been his worst subject at West Point; he barely passed the course work. The rank he had now been given was the same he had obtained by brevet fourteen years earlier in the army—and the same he had held at VMI for the past decade. Other men with less experience than he were receiving higher appointments as well as field duty. Last, and of most importance, an engineering job would put Jackson at a desk in some government building, not in command of troops in some battle arena.[11]

He sought to conceal his feelings in another and upbeat letter to Anna that day. "The scene here, my darling pet, looks quite animated. Troops are continually arriving. . . . I received your precious letter, in which you speak of coming here in the event of my remaining. I would like very much to see my sweet little face, but my darling had better remain at her own home, as my continuance here is very uncertain."[12]

The last statement was perhaps a hope for something better; or possibly Jackson knew that influential friends saw his placement in the engineers as a waste of talent and were taking action on his behalf. Jonathan M. Bennett, an old friend from Weston, was in Richmond as state auditor. When Bennett learned of Jackson's assignment, he promptly got an audience with another Jackson friend, Governor Letcher. The executive, who could not be expected to know the duties given every Virginia officer, agreed wholeheartedly that Jackson belonged in the field. On April 26, Letcher issued him a commission as colonel of Virginia volunteers. The Advisory Council endorsed it the following day.

When Jackson's name came before the State Convention for confirmation, one of the members asked, "Who is this Major Jackson?" Samuel McDowell Moore, the Rockbridge County delegate, rose to his feet and instantly responded: "I will tell you who Major Jackson is. He is a man who, if you order him to hold a post, will never leave it alive to be occupied by the enemy." Jackson's new appointment received unanimous approval.[13]

Jonathan Bennett was not through with his recommendations on behalf of Jackson. In a lengthy letter to Advisory Council president John J. Allen, Bennett urged that Jackson be sent to field service in the mountains of his home area. "Maj. Thomas J. Jackson is by all odds the best man we can procure for chief command in Northwestern Virginia," Bennett asserted. "Almost every second man is his kinsman, and in that country they have no one of experience to lead them on." Such an appointment "would be popular with the people, and a high position is deserved by him. N. West Va. should be defended. It contains one-fourth of the white population of the state."[14]

Whether Jackson's appointment to such a command could have blocked the northwestern part of the state from pulling out of the Old Dominion is conjectural at best. Jackson himself would always manifest a deep interest in affairs in the Clarksburg-Weston-Beverly region. Yet primarily because of distance from intervening Confederate territory that first had to be firmly secured, Jackson did not go to duty in his home area.

On the afternoon of April 27, Letcher summoned Jackson to the governor's mansion and informed him that within a few hours he would receive orders to take command at Harpers Ferry. Jackson made arrangements to leave that night for his new post of duty. Somewhere en route, he received his official directive from General Lee at headquarters. "You will proceed without delay to Harpers Ferry, Va., in execution of the order of the Governor of the state and assume command of that Post. After mustering into the service of the state such Companies as may be accepted under your instructions, you will organize them into Regiments or Battalions, uniting as far as possible, Companies from the same section of the state. These will be placed under the senior Captains until field officers can be appointed by the Governor."

Not mentioned in Lee's orders was a pertinent statement in Governor Letcher's memorandum to Lee about Jackson's assignment. "Direct him to make diligent inquiry as to the state of feeling in the northwestern portion of the State; if necessary appoint a confidential agent for that purpose, but great confidence is placed in personal knowledge of Colonel Jackson in this regard. If deemed best, he can assemble the volunteer forces of the northwest at such points as he may deem best, giving prompt information of the same."[15]

John Preston was delighted with the assignment of his friend and VMI colleague. "Jackson, with the rank of colonel, goes to supersede General Harper at Harper's Ferry," Preston wrote his wife, Maggie. "It is most flattering to him. Say to his wife that it is the command of all orders which he would most prefer. He is a noble fellow, and I rejoice in his success."[16]

At first, however, Jackson had to endure travel on Virginia's limited railroad system. On April 28, the Virginia Central Railroad carried him west toward the Shenandoah Valley. It was the Sabbath, and Jackson felt guilty about secular activity on the Lord's day. At Gordonsville, he detrained long enough to visit the local Presbyterian clergyman, Daniel B. Ewing, whom Jackson had met several years earlier at a presbytery in Lexington. Jackson's calmness in the first thunder claps of war surprised

Ewing. "His salutations were in his usually cordial manner. He did not seem to me to form any different estimates of the protracted and fearful character of this war from others." Ewing then contradicted himself somewhat by concluding that Jackson "was prepared to serve his country with his whole strength, in any capacity."[17]

From Gordonsville, Jackson continued by rail north to Manassas Junction, then west again on the Manassas Gap line to Strasburg. A ride of eighteen miles brought him in late morning to Winchester. This historic town of 4500 inhabitants had roots stretching back to the mid 18th century plus a bustling economy that made it one of the community centers of western Virginia. The many roads leading from Winchester resembled spokes fanning out from a wheel hub.

Jackson spent the forenoon of April 29 attending to a few military matters in Winchester and to bringing Anna up to date on his activities. "I came from Richmond yesterday, and I expect to leave here about 2:30 P.M. today for Harper's Ferry. I am thankful to say, that an ever kind Providence, who causes 'all things to work together for good to them that love him,' has given me the post which I prefer above all others, & has given me an independent command. To His name be all the praise." The new colonel warned his wife not to anticipate letters on a regular basis. "I expect to have more work than I have ever had in the same length of time before, but don't be concerned about me, as an ever kind Heavenly Father will give every needful aid." Jackson closed the letter by announcing that he was "in tolerable health, probably a little better than usual, if I had enough sleep."[18]

Within hours, Jackson discovered that he was in need of all the aid he could get from any source. He had expected some confusion to prevail in the Harpers Ferry area; he was not prepared for the chaos he encountered. It began with the trip from Winchester.

The colonel boarded cars of the Winchester and Potomac Railroad on Market Street in downtown Winchester. What followed was a slow and bumpy thirty-one-mile ride. The line could accommodate only light traffic; the rails were wooden, the bridges weak, the locomotives small and of limited power. Yet such travel was more predictable and easier than battling muddy roads and unpredictable weather. Later that day Jackson sent a succinct telegram to the governor: "Recommend construction of a railroad from Strasburg to Winchester for strategic purposes."[19]

Jackson's first sight of Harpers Ferry was anything but reassuring. Eighteen months earlier, John Brown had put Harpers Ferry on the front page of every newspaper in America. No community so small had enjoyed a notoriety so great. To one soldier, "the village is peopled of several hundred inhabitants and is built in a very irregular, rambling style, the houses rather rudely constructed, many of them of stone, and with a view more to comfort than ornament."[20]

The result of the 1859 abolitionist raid was to give the place a symbolic value far in excess of its actual military importance. Harpers Ferry was the site of one of the largest armories in the South. However, when Virginia forces swarmed down on the installation late on April 18, 1861, the forty-four-man Union garrison set fire to munitions and a number of buildings. Virginia troops managed to save most of the structures and 5,000 muskets, but 10,000 weapons had been destroyed in the Federal evacuation.

Again, the Ferry was at the confluence of the Potomac and Shenandoah rivers. Those large streams cut through the extension of the Blue Ridge Mountains to make a natural pass for both the Baltimore and Ohio Railroad and the Chesapeake and Ohio Canal. The former was the nation's largest rail network; the latter was a 154-mile engineering feat. The railroad bridge across the Potomac at Harpers Ferry was 900 feet in length. It rested on five heavy piers and was covered by a strong wooden roof.

Both railroad and canal were major lifelines between Washington and the west. Confederate control of them and the territory in and around the valley would force the Federals to make a looping trip through Pennsylvania and Ohio in order to get from one sector to another.

While many authorities considered Harpers Ferry the geographical key to the Valley of Virginia, that distinction belonged to Winchester. Harpers Ferry had the psychological advantage of being the northernmost point of the Confederacy. The village was the gateway to northwestern Virginia, which the Old Dominion was trying to maintain, and across the river from Maryland, which the Confederacy wanted to adopt.

Although rivers, roads, and railroads led to and from Harpers Ferry, the mountain setting gave it an air of remoteness. It also had an alluring beauty. A young sergeant in the 27th Virginia wrote: "Harpers ferry is one of the most Romantic places I ever saw. it looks like nature has carved it out for some great tragedy."[21]

Both sides seemed to become infatuated by the fact that Harpers Ferry was actually northwest of the Union capital. It protruded into enemy territory like a spear—but without support. Further, as a good field officer would discern immediately, the village snuggled in a hollow formed by mountains on three sides. Artillery placed on the surrounding heights could blast Harpers Ferry and everything in it to pieces. Virginia officials overlooked such basic weaknesses and fortified the place in the expectation that the first Federal invasion of the Old Dominion would come there.

The physical vulnerability of Harpers Ferry was bad enough. Had Jackson been an ordinary man, he would have blanched at what he found defending the post. The units were no army in any sense of the word. In reality, 2500 males ranging in age from young boys to old men had assembled. Some belonged to the expanding volunteer force being organized; others were in the state's antiquated militia. All were attired in every conceivable outfit and, when armed, sporting every impractical weapon.

On April 27, Governor Letcher had informed garrisons throughout the state that all militia officers above the rank of captain were relieved from duty upon the arrival of a duly designated army officer. Most of these militia commissions were issued years earlier, when Virginia's military system existed in name rather than in fact. Letcher's directive bore down especially hard on the Harpers Ferry officers. A young lieutenant after arriving there informed the homefolk: "Our General Officers are from the Militia and that is all I will say, you can imagine the rest."[22]

In command was Major General Kenton Harper, sixty years old, mayor of Staunton, and editor of its newspaper. Assisting him were three militia brigadiers, William H. Harman of Augusta County, Gilbert S. Meem of Shenandoah County, and James H. Carson of Frederick County. They and their entourage were a sight to behold.

Charles Grattan, a University of Virginia law student who had volunteered for quartermaster duty, reached Harpers Ferry a day or so before Jackson. Grattan later commented: "When it is remembered that each one of these four generals had the regulation staff and as many additional aids, adjutants and inspector generals as he had friends . . . and that each one of these was ornamented according to his taste and ability to acquire, with spurs, cocked hats, feathers, epaulets, sashes, &c. and armed with pistols, swords, sabres, and what not, it is easily conceived what an incongruous mass it was. . . . If there was a divinity that shaped their ends the rough hewing had been badly done."[23]

For eager recruits, the two-week period before Jackson arrived at Harpers Ferry had been the pleasant state of excitement at a carnival. Parades were a regular late-afternoon occurrence (even though no one knew much about the rudiments of drill). Male and female civilians visited regularly to see how loved ones were faring. Trains ran and canal traffic continued, all with extreme politeness exhibited on both sides.

Organization did not exist beyond the 100-man companies; hence, small groups operated independently. Many gentleman-soldiers had brought servants with them. Guard details were a farce, despite daily false alarms. There was little equipment, less ammunition, and deep shortages of supplies. No hospital existed; neither did ordnance, commissary, and quartermaster departments. Hundreds of volunteers wanting to be soldiers packed the village and waited for some sense of direction while B&O trains rumbled through town regularly loaded with coal and other raw materials for Union mobilization.

One youth met instant disappointment when he arrived to join a contingent from his home area. "I found the company quartered in one of the work shops of the army, anything but comfortable or desirable as quarters, for the room was filled with machinery and there was not an inch of space on the floor or benches but what was saturated with oil . . . our new uniforms and blankets soon became very much defaced." An assistant quartermaster confessed: "We did not have a single copy of the Army regulations in our office and if an officer had come to me with a requisition I should have thought he was putting on airs and wanted taking down." Beneath all of this unreality lay the conviction that peace was imminent: there was not going to be a war; Northerners would see the errors of their ways before any further damage occurred.[24]

Into this tangle of crowded personnel and widespread inertia rode Colonel Jackson the last Monday in April. After debarking from the train, he started walking up the hill toward headquarters. A number of VMI cadets recognized him afar and came running pell-mell to meet him. Jackson smiled warmly at them, grasped each by the hand, and said, "I am glad to see you and will take special interest in you." Having the professor as their superior gave the cadets "a feeling of greater security," one declared.[25]

On the other hand, Colonel Jackson appeared a sorry substitute for the brilliantly clad figures he was succeeding. A group of young militia officers, seeing Jackson for the first time, felt cheated. "There must be some mistake about him," one said. "If he was an able man he showed it less than any of us had ever seen." Wearing the plain blue uniform of a VMI faculty member, with neither insignia nor gold lace on the faded coat, Jackson walked up the main street of Harpers Ferry with those long, ungainly strides and with the faded cadet cap tilted over his eyes and seemingly blocking all vision save what was at his feet.[26] A newspaper correspondent spent a few minutes in Jackson's presence and concluded: "The Old Dominion must be sadly deficient in military men, if this is the best she can do. He is nothing like a commanding officer. There is a painful want in him of the pride, pomp and circumstance of glorious war. . . . His air is abstracted, his bearing is stiff and awkward . . . and [he] says little to any one."[27]

Others viewed Jackson's arrival in a positive light. Quartermaster Captain David Hopkins, in a misdated letter to his wife in Lexington, wrote: "I have this moment learned that Major Jackson of V.M.I. has arrived and is to take command of this place. we are pleased to hear it as a man of experience & military skill is much needed here. he will proceed at once to put matters in the best possible shape for defence."[28]

Jackson moved quickly to do precisely that. He and Major Preston took rooms in a small hotel near the railroad bridge. Most of the troops were quartered in government buildings alongside the Potomac River. The armory superintendent's home became headquarters.[29]

The small staff that had accompanied Jackson was VMI-bred and likewise clad in blue. Major Preston was assistant adjutant general (which corresponded to being chief of staff); Major James W. Massie, a tactical officer at the institute, was inspector general; Captain Marshall McDowell was Massie's assistant; Captain Edward Cunningham served as engineering officer; Dr. Edward L. Graham was post surgeon.

Ten cadets also came down from VMI to serve as drillmasters. Among them were R. Preston Chew and Milton Rouss, both from Kabletown. Their homes were barely fifteen miles away, and they anticipated numerous opportunities to visit loved ones. Jackson said no and refused to issue passes. Chew and Rouss were too young to accept undesirable orders. They went home the first weekend of their duty. Upon their return the following Monday, orders were waiting for them: they were to return at once to cadet duties at the institute. For Chew, who in time became an outstanding artillerist, it was the low point in his military career.[30]

The staff would grow slowly in number and quality as Jackson handpicked men who possessed high moral character, strict punctuality, and exactitude to duty. Among the first additions was Major John A. Harman, a month younger than Jackson, Mexican War veteran, and one of several prominent brothers from Staunton. Men came to call Harman "the old Major," and most people gave him wide berth. Big-bodied, big-voiced, short-tempered and incredibly profane, Harman was not afraid of anything. He became Jackson's first and only quartermaster. Harman worked tirelessly at his job; he would have ordered Jackson himself out of the way if necessary to obey Jackson's orders. Perhaps that is why Jackson drove him so hard. Repeatedly during the war, Harman would resign in anger, only to be talked into reconsideration by the man he sometimes termed "crack-brained." Behind Harman's gruff exterior, however, was a devoted family man who adored his wife and thirteen children.[31]

For the first time in his career, Jackson was to command a large force of infantry.

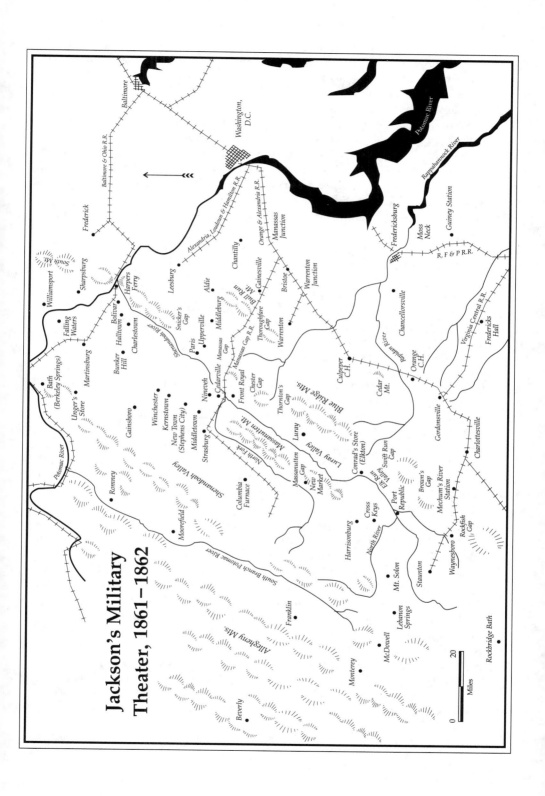

Jackson's Military Theater, 1861–1862

His knowledge of the training and tactics of foot soldiers was limited because of his long service as an artillerist. Yet he could learn; and while doing so, he had every intention of carrying out his responsibilities to defend Harpers Ferry, to prevent enemy crossings of the Potomac in that region, and to harass traffic on both the railroad and the canal.

His initial efforts concerned ever-increasing manpower. While recruits individually and in groups arrived daily at Harpers Ferry, Jackson also summoned all militia units in the valley to report to him for duty. Next he had to weave organization from confusion and to mold this force into some semblance of a unified command. All of this would begin in an atmosphere of hostility. Most militia field officers had departed in anger, many heading to Richmond to plead their individual cases before government officials. Some militiamen not subject to state regulations were returning home.

Jackson had little use for local defense troops, but he did ask several of the militia officers to remain and help in the buildup of a concentrated force. This act not only brought Jackson a number of able assistants; it also endeared him at once to a number of men faced with the humiliation of being stripped of all command.

One individual who came to his aid was Captain William S. H. Baylor. Born in Staunton in 1831, Baylor graduated with honors from Washington College and the University of Virginia law school. In 1857, he became commonwealth attorney for Staunton. Baylor was untutored in military affairs, but John Brown's raid and Southern patriotism led Baylor to organize a local company known as the West Augusta Guards. He became its captain, and in April 1861 he took it to Harpers Ferry to help in protecting Virginia territory.

The Staunton unit found itself cut adrift when all the militia field officers were relieved from command. Jackson then noted: "In consequence of the Volunteers being deprived of officers under whom they expected to serve, there was great dissatisfaction. To aid me in suppressing insubordination [Capt.] Baylor, instead of going to Richmond for the purpose of advancing his present interest, patriotically remained as long as I desired and was of great assistance in reestablishing order and subordination." Thereafter, Jackson held the Staunton officer in high esteem. Within a week, many of the former militia officers of field rank were back and ready for duty at lower levels in the Virginia forces. Former General Kenton Harper of the militia, for example, became colonel of the 5th Virginia Volunteers from his home area.[32]

Jackson kept an active but low profile in his first week of command. He made no speeches, held no reviews. Subordinates reported to him at daybreak for orders. One soldier remembered: "When thrown with him on duty he was uniformly courteous to all. He always kept his eyes half closed as if thinking, which he invariably did before answering; but his replies were short and to the point." He dispatched business promptly, for he knew what ought to be done and how to do it. Jackson was "much more in his element" than at VMI, a former cadet saw. "It seemed that the sights and sound of war had aroused his energies." A Winchester recruit was fascinated by the new commander. "Our senior colonel was a man who never spoke unless spoken to; never seemed to sleep. . . . He walked about alone, the projecting visor of his blue cap concealing his features; a bad-fitting, single-breasted blue coat, and high boots covering the largest feet ever seen, completed the picture."[33]

Appearance was deceiving. Within two days after Jackson's arrival, a visiting minister stated, "every man felt that some military mind was at work, making its impress on the material there, reducing the chaotic mass to order, and causing the crude elements to assume the aspect of dim-visaged war."[34]

Small wonder that this was so. To top off the first full day of duties, Jackson ordered the men on the night of May 2–3 to sleep on their arms. At 1:30 A.M., a full inspection and muster took place.[35]

White tents in increasing numbers studded the green mountainsides all around the village. Campfires kept the Harpers Ferry area shrouded in a veil of smoke. The babble of voices never seemed to cease. Through it all, companies slowly became regiments, senior captains on hand temporarily led the units. Discipline was ever present. An immense log guardhouse existed for those who shirked or paid no attention to duty.

Obtaining sufficient food for the thousands of troops was a problem at first. Jackson had no funds with which to purchase rations, Richmond officials seemed in no haste to supply money, and Virginia farmers were understandably reluctant to honor credit vouchers from a state authority 170 miles away. Fortunately, as it turned out, Jackson's quartermaster officers were local men with sound reputations. Some of them extended personal credit chits, which kept the Harpers Ferry garrison from getting hungry more often than it did. John Preston, now a lieutenant colonel, gave the principal credit to Quartermaster Harman. "I am amazed to see with what success" Harman has gathered supplies, Preston wrote to Colonel Smith in Lexington. "The same activity, shrewdness, common sense, and foresight that have made the Harman brothers successful in private matters have been brought together here."[36]

Harpers Ferry was an exposed post. Federals in strength might move on it at any time. Jackson quickly displayed the stern military manner that became his benchmark. Volunteers must become soldiers at once. The road to that end lay in drill.

Reveille broke the predawn stillness at 5 A.M. For the next seventeen hours of the day, recruits went through an arduous routine of instruction. Nine VMI cadets arrived from Richmond and taught new officers the fundamentals of command. (Ten more would join Jackson's "faculty" within a week.) Recently commissioned men needed help as badly as the troops they were supposed to lead. Lieutenant John N. Lyle of Lexington commented: "The field officers were from civil life and not up in tactics. The tangles they would get the regiment into on battalion drill were as intricate as a sailor's knot. The fun their performances afforded compensated us in a measure for the outrage that was being perpetrated on our stomachs."[37]

Seven hours of drill were part of the daily schedule. The area had few level places for marching, but Jackson took advantage of every clearing and sent the troops daily through every routine, including occasional cross-country tramps. The state of the weather was irrelevant. Early May was unusually wet and cool. One detachment marched twenty-four miles through a steady downpour and returned to camp "thoroughly drenched and disgruntled."[38]

An Augusta County company, responding to reports of a Federal raid on nearby Shepherdstown, also got caught in a severe rainstorm. "It fairly beat us to the ground," a recruit swore. "We were about like a parcel of affrightened sheep, endeavoring to gain some sort of protection." Discomfort changed to anger when the men learned why they had been ordered into the storm. "It is now supposed that the alarm of the trooper originated in heavy thunder, which he imagined was the abolitionists firing on the town."[39]

Those recruits unknowingly were making the painful transition from nonchalant civilian to regulated soldier. Enthusiasm is always highest with the young. Most of the units arriving at Harpers Ferry that spring contained a majority of volunteers in their teens and early twenties. One company affixed a member in his late twenties with the title "Uncle." The oldest member of a Frederick County unit was forty-one. Hence, the troops were highly impressionable. Rough order was nevertheless taking place under the ever-watching eyes of Colonel Jackson. Camp gossip had it that "Old Jack" was hard as nails where his orders were concerned; yet he always seemed courteous to his officers, and he showed an amazing tolerance of young recruits trying to absorb military intricacies to which they had never before been subjected.[40]

The colonel let it be known that men were supposed to make mistakes while learning. Mental lapses were tolerated, neglect of duty and insubordination were not. Jackson reminded his officers that patience and understanding—rather than harsh demands—produced the best soldiers. He also left instructions that his rations were to be the same in quantity and quality as those issued to the soldiers.

Such attitudes brought Jackson genuine respect inside the ranks. Captain John D. Imboden, commanding the Staunton Artillery, returned to Harpers Ferry after a quick trip to Richmond. "What a revolution three or four days have wrought!" he exclaimed. "I could scarcely realize the change."[41]

Most of the machinery at Harpers Ferry armory was partially dismantled and started on its way to the arsenals at Richmond. Meanwhile, the colonel viewed the surrounding mountains with growing uneasiness. Maryland was, at the moment, a neutral state. Confederates hoped that Maryland would join them; meanwhile, nothing must be done to incur the anger of Maryland authorities.

Jackson did not see the situation in a diplomatic light. He had a post to defend; and if Federal troops moved in his direction, he told Richmond officials, "I shall no longer stand on ceremony." Maryland Heights dominated everything around Harpers Ferry. That eminence must accordingly be controlled. So Jackson sent two companies across the river. One encamped near the farmhouse from which John Brown launched his 1859 attack; the other clawed its way to the top of Maryland Heights, erected some crude shelters, and began living a spartan existence.

The post commander sought to infuse his men with his degree of determination. Daily rumors of Federals poised to attack helped create a degree of serious attention to duty. A recruit in what became the 10th Virginia told the home folk: "Thar was a grate accitment in this place this evening the news wer that the enemy was cuming and the trups wer ordered out. . . . our boys were all as livly as crickets non of them wer scared I dont believe."[42]

Zeal was present in everyone seemingly except Jackson. Early in May, one of his former faculty colleagues, John DeHart Ross, arrived to assist in engineering duties. Jackson's first words to the young officer were: "Are you fresh or broken down?" "I am as fresh as a May morning," Hart exclaimed. "Good," Jackson replied. "I've work for you." That was the end of the conversation. Charles Wight, another drillmaster, looked over the post and noted: "All was new bustle and expectation. We were in the full enjoyment of the excitement & novelty of war, without any of its hardship or suffering." Most of the recruits "were crazy for an opportunity to use their guns."[43]

Inspections of the outposts were part of Jackson's daily routine; but to confuse the enemy, he never visited a spot at the same time. He usually had but a single officer with him. The two men would check locales on the perimeter and ride away without the guards knowing that the commander was even in the area. Nothing about Jackson was dashing. He came and went unnoticed, voiced few opinions, and sought to keep in the background. The volunteers were unfamiliar with—but impressed by—a soldier who was duty personified.[44]

Visitors to the Ferry got the same impression. One day a group of Maryland legislators came to the Ferry. Jackson received them cordially, for he was aware of their potential importance to the Southern cause. He was also aware of the overriding need for security at his post. One of the legislators casually asked how many troops were on duty there. Jackson quickly replied: "I'd be glad if Lincoln thought I had 15,000 men," then changed the subject.[45]

The most intriguing anecdote in the first weeks of the war concerned Jackson and the Baltimore and Ohio Railroad. John D. Imboden manufactured it, Jackson biographer G. F. R. Henderson gave it credence, and writers over the past century have delighted in recounting it in detail. Supposedly, Jackson dreamed up a way to bring operations on the very busy B&O line to a halt. Harpers Ferry lay roughly midway between Martinsburg and Point of Rocks. That twenty-five-mile stretch of line was double-tracked. The colonel complained that the never-ending train noise was disturbing his camps and must stop or else. Helpless railroad officials quickly agreed to funnel all traffic through the Ferry between 11 A.M. and 1 P.M. Trains were running both ways, cowcatcher to caboose, during that two-hour period when Jackson struck. He blocked the eastbound tracks at Point of Rocks, then shut down the westbound line at Martinsburg. The result was the capture of fifty-six locomotives and 300 cars. Jackson then leisurely destroyed the double-track section of line.

Delightful as the story is, it is totally fictional. Jackson could not have committed these actions on his own, and he had no orders to disrupt the B&O completely. The Confederate government would not have issued such a directive while making overtures of cooperation with Maryland. If such destruction had occurred, the Union government would have screamed in protest and initiated retribution. No such reactions are recorded.

For Jackson to have severed the B&O would have been a large and direct act of war against civilian commerce. The struggle between North and South had not yet reached that stage. Jackson was under strict orders not to interrupt civilian life. Further, it is inconceivable that the B&O's brilliant and hard-working president, John W. Garrett, or its indefatigable master of transportation, William Prescott Smith, would not have immediately seen through such a transparent ploy as constricting the traffic schedule. Certainly neither official would have compromised his devotion to the B&O by agreeing to jam trains together for the benefit of the Confederates and to the detriment of the Union.

The capstone in dismantling this myth is a May 21 letter from General Lee. He informed a friend that because all previous measures for limiting traffic on the B&O had "in part failed," other options were under consideration.[46]

Jackson did give much attention to artillery needs, for that branch of service was always closest to his heart. He discerned at once that artillery was the crucial element for control of the Ferry. Only sixteen guns ultimately became available for defending the site. Fortunately, Colonel Benjamin Huger, recently of the U.S. Army's ordnance bureau, was there to help. Jackson assigned him the task of placing the various types of guns in position while Jackson himself kept a steady stream of requests going to Richmond for more cannon.[47]

Next he set blacksmiths and carpenters to work converting the frames of carts and wagons into caissons. Unwilling to wait for Richmond authorities to authorize horses for a distant post on the Potomac, Jackson told Quartermaster Harman to go into nearby, horse-rich Loudoun County and purchase or impress as many animals as he needed. Harman carried out his assignment with a thoroughness that increased his usefulness to Jackson.

Harman was also responsible for acquiring Jackson's favorite mount in the Civil War. The colonel had been at Harpers Ferry only a few days when his men seized an eastbound livestock train in order to obtain fresh meat. Four cars were loaded with beefs, the other car with horses. Jackson at the time had no regular mount. He decided to purchase one of the horses from the Confederate government (to whom he had consigned the train and its contents). Harman volunteered to help him in the selection.

After inspecting most of the animals, Jackson settled on a large and powerful gelding. Then he saw another horse: a smaller, well-rounded sorrel gelding. Jackson decided to buy it as well and make it a present to Anna. Within a day, however, he discovered that the "big sorrel" was skittish and had too hard a gait. The smaller horse showed a smooth pace, even temper, and, in time, extraordinary endurance. Jackson kept both mounts, though he usually rode the smaller one.

Because he had acquired the animal for his wife, Jackson initially named it Fancy, and he used that name thereafter. To everyone else, the horse was Little Sorrel. It stood no more than fifteen hands high. More than one Confederate likened the gaunt, raw-boned sorrel to Don Quixote's little mount, Rosinante. The lineage of Jackson's horse was unknown. Kyd Douglas of Jackson's staff praised it as "a remarkable little horse. Such endurance I have never seen in horse flesh. We had no horse at Hd. Qrs. that could match him. I never saw him show a sign of fatigue." Lieutenant John Lyle seconded those opinions. "Old Sorrel did up the steeds of the staff," he wrote. "There was joy in the hearts" of Jackson's aides when someone stole Little Sorrel for a short period. "His recovery gave them no joy."[48]

The quiet professor wrought major changes in army life at the Ferry. Yet he was no miracle worker, and more than one recruit displayed reluctance in adapting to his ways. Jackson learned that some of the men had a cache of whiskey hidden in town and that a Mississippi soldier "took a drink of liquor and immediately fell dead." At that, the commander ordered all alcoholic spirits seized and spilled down the gullies of a street. Troops quickly gathered at the foot of the street and scooped up as much as they could. An irritated Jackson then directed that the remainder be poured over a bluff into the river. Again, fast-thinking men congregated at the riverbank and caught the liquor in buckets as it rained down upon them.

That led Jackson to go to the root of the problem. Pointing to "increasing irregularities occasioned by the sale of ardent spirits to soldiers," he directed all storekeepers to cease distributing whiskey to his men. "Upon proof of the violation of this order," Jackson warned, "the establishment of any one so violating it will be immediately closed and his stock of liquor taken possession of and turned over to each officer of the day for safekeeping."[49]

Fatigue from drill and an increasing awareness of army responsibilities made a deep impression upon many of the volunteers. A recruit in the 27th Virginia solemnly informed his mother, "I have not drank a drop of whiskey or Brandy since I left [home] and I do not intend to do so untill I get back."[50]

By May 11, the Harpers Ferry garrison numbered 4500 recruits, almost double the force Jackson had found there at his arrival two weeks earlier. The overnight transformation of the large encampment aroused even greater curiosity in the man responsible for it. Few soldiers got a closeup look at Jackson. One who did was Quartermaster Sergeant Grattan, who took his meals with the staff in one of the government buildings on the village hill. Grattan humorously recalled those first gatherings around a dinner table:

> The only moments of relaxation we enjoyed were those we spent at meal times, but here we were met by the grave, solemn countenance of our Commanding Colonel; all were afraid of him, for none knew how kindly and genial a heart beat in his bosom. . . . We regarded him with something of the awe of those who beheld the fingers write upon the wall of Balshazzers banquet. . . . We ate silent as mutes, ever and anon casting a healthy eye upon the Colonel to see if he ate like other men, or bolted raw meat and gnawed bloody bones. . . . The Surgeon, the Adjutant, the Aid and all others sat like oysters, they ate but spoke not.

Grattan soon wearied of the deathly silence at mealtimes. At dinner the next day, he made "a very diluted and mild joke." Everyone immediately looked at Jackson for his reaction. "I suppose it was sometime since the Colonel had had a joke poked at him, for he evidently did not seem to know exactly what to do, had a half-startled appearance, then subsided into a smile, then all those long faced Jeremiahs laughed, the ice was broken, we were saved from dyspepsia and learned to esteem the genial qualities of our great Commander."[51]

Within days, the staff underwent an overhaul. Major Massie departed to become second in command of the 51st Virginia, Captains McDowell and Cunningham left for Richmond to work in the C.S. Engineering Department, and Dr. Edward Graham transferred to service in the Virginia cavalry. On May 4, Governor Letcher moved to fill one of the vacancies by appointing Assistant Surgeon Hunter H. McGuire as medical director of the Harpers Ferry post. Born in 1835 in Winchester, the slender and mustached McGuire had graduated from medical school at the age of twenty, then taught anatomy and general medicine for the next five years. He had enlisted as a private in the 2d Virginia when it was organized but was quickly named a regimental surgeon.

When McGuire reported to Jackson, the commander was talking with one of his volunteer aides, venerable Colonel Angus W. McDonald. Jackson was surprised and obviously displeased at McGuire's appearance. He stared at the physician for a moment, then stated: "You look like a very young man." The proud McGuire retorted: "I am a young man." McDonald quickly pointed out McGuire's high regard in medical schools from Richmond to Philadelphia. Jackson motioned McGuire to a chair. For an hour, the two had what McGuire thought was an amiable conversation. It ended with Jackson stating, "You can go back to your quarters and wait there until you hear from me." A week passed. Then McGuire's appointment was announced at an evening dress parade. Months later, after he and Jackson had become fast friends, McGuire asked the reason for the delay. Jackson responded with a straight face: "You looked so young that I sent to Richmond to see if there wasn't some mistake."[52]

On Monday, May 6, Lee wrote Jackson to express a number of concerns. Perhaps reflecting anxieties on Governor Letcher's part, Lee warned Jackson about a possible Federal thrust at Harpers Ferry. Jackson should be especially vigilant of movements on the railroad and the canal. Be ready to burn the long railroad trestle spanning the Potomac and to do extensive damage to the canal, should the enemy assume the offensive. Lee also hinted that Jackson might spread out his force by sending a detachment as far as Martinsburg, eighteen miles to the west.[53]

Similar expectations of battle pervaded Jackson's encampment. Private John T. Anderson of the 13th Virginia wrote his sister on that same Monday: "some think we shall have an attack soon. we dont know and dont care much, we have as live fight or not. we heard that old Capt. [Winfield] Scott says he intended to have this place if it takes the last man he has and Major Jackson says he will kill the last man before he gets it so you may listen for the report of my musket if an attack is made."[54]

Jackson responded to Lee the same day. It was his first letter in what would be a regular two-year correspondence. "I have been busily occupied, organizing the command and mustering the troops into service," Jackson wrote. He had secured both Loudoun Heights and Maryland Heights, placing a sizable contingent of troops on the former but only a couple of companies on the Maryland mountain "by a desire to avoid giving offense to the latter State." Jackson requested four additional field pieces and informed Lee that he had ordered 1000 "flint-lock rifles" from the Lexington arsenal.[55]

The following day Jackson sent a more emphatic message to the commander of all Virginia forces. He had made up his mind to fortify Maryland Heights and hold the position, "be the cost what it may." Jackson expressed the need for more arms to fulfil his purpose, and he asked for reinforcements to bring his strength up to 10,000 men—a figure that undoubtedly stunned Lee, who had no garrison in Virginia of such a size.[56]

In justifying these requests, Jackson expressed his deep feelings about the strategic importance of Harpers Ferry. "I would be more than gratified could you spare the time for a short visit here, to give me the benefit of your wisdom and experience in laying out the different works, especially those on the heights. I am of the opinion that this place should be defended with the spirit that actuated the defenders of Thermopylae, and, if left to myself, such is my determination. The fall of this place would, I fear, result in the loss of the northwestern part of the State."[57]

Affairs in his home area were constantly on Jackson's mind. At one point early in May, Jackson proposed to Lee that part of the force at Harpers Ferry be rushed to the northwestern sector as soon as Virginia's vote on secession was official. Such an advance, Jackson reasoned, would remain in the mountainous country only until local units could be raised and armed. Lee rejected the idea. The state did not have the men to spare, and he was unwilling to risk Harpers Ferry by weakening its manpower.[58]

Judge Gideon Camden, a lifelong friend from Clarksburg, paid Jackson a visit shortly thereafter. Jackson "advised with me about the measures properly to be adopted in our section," Camden wrote. "I think he was looking to an occupancy there. He was particularly anxious to know the sentiments of the prominent citizens, and especially his relations and particular friends in that region. . . . No doubt if he (Jackson) had been charged with the defence of that region, as was expected by his friends, that he could have successfully defended it and the sentiments there would have been very different among the people."[59]

Unquestionably, Jackson had a highly personal reason behind his inquiries. Reports had come to him that Laura Arnold was an outspoken Unionist in Beverly. If Jackson wrote her following Virginia's secession, he never mentioned it; and if she sent any letters to him, they have vanished. No further correspondence would pass between brother and sister. Jackson "regretted that his sister entertained Union sentiments," Judge Camden recalled, "but his expressions about her were kind but brief." The last member of Jackson's immediate family now drifted away into the heat of war.[60]

The same could be said of some of his in-laws. In mid-May, the Reverend David X. Junkin visited Jackson. Nephew of Jackson's first father-in-law, Junkin had traveled from Pennsylvania in an effort to convince his son George, a member of the 4th Virginia, as well as Jackson, of the errors of their ways in supporting the Confederacy. The Presbyterian clergyman dismissed secession as "inexcusable"; Southerners and Northerners could still work together; slavery would eventually die of natural causes; the breakup of the Union would inaugurate "wars of a hundred generations in America and repeat the bloody history of Europe."[61]

Jackson listened without interruption. When Junkin finished speaking, the colonel was ready with an answer. Junkin had Jackson reply: "As a Christian man, my first allegiance is to my State, the State of Virginia; and every other State has a primal claim to the fealty of her citizens, and they may justly control their allegiance. If Virginia adheres to the United States, I adhere. Her determination must control mine." Private Junkin echoed his cousin's sentiments.[62]

Reverend Junkin realized that his mission had failed. As he prepared to depart, he extended his hand. Jackson took it warmly. "Farewell, Colonel," Junkin began. "May we meet under happier circumstances; if not in this troubled world may we meet in . . . " Junkin's voice broke. Jackson pointed upward with his gloved hand and finished the sentence with "in heaven." He then mounted and left father and son to a private farewell.[63]

In the second week of May, Jackson assured Anna that all was well in his own situation. "I am living in an elegant mansion, with Maj. Preston in my room. . . . I am strengthening my position, & if attacked, shall with the blessing of that God, who has always been with me, & who I firmly believe will never forsake, repel the enemy. I am in great health, considering the great labor that devolves on me, & the loss of sleep to which I am subjected."[64]

Lee wrote on May 9 that the cannon and muskets Jackson had sought would be sent as soon as possible. The general then informed Jackson: "In your preparation for the defense of your position it is considered advisable not to intrude upon the soil of Maryland unless compelled by the necessities of war. The aid of its citizens might be obtained in that quarter." Jackson already felt "compelled by the necessities of war." On that same day, he wired Lee: "There are about 2,200 Federal troops at the Relay House, others beyond Baltimore, and about 4,000 near Chambersburg, Pa. I have occupied the Maryland Heights with the Kentuckians and one company of infantry from Augusta County, making about 500 in all." Back came a prompt reply from Lee. "I fear you have been premature in occupying the heights of Maryland with so strong a force near you. The true policy is to act on the defensive, and not to invite an attack. If not too late you might withdraw until the proper time."[65]

It was "too late," as far as Jackson was concerned. His troops would stay on Maryland Heights. In that brief exchange of letters with Lee, a fundamental difference in thinking between the two men surfaced. One might say that in this early period of the war Jackson saw the future more clearly than did Confederate authorities, both military and civilian. This emerging warrior was not concerned with the historical principles underlying the sectional conflict. Southern "rights" occupied none of his attention, nor did thoughts of future relationships between Union and Confederacy. Jackson's simple perspective was that Virginia and the South were fighting to maintain an independence against an enemy determined to take it away. In Jackson's mind, that made the Civil War different from other contests. Freedom was the fundamental stake, not diplomacy, commercial advantages, a boundary line, or some minute point of honor. The existence of the South was the issue.

Therefore, Jackson felt, the Southern forces should take the offensive at once. Federal troops across the Potomac were as green as the Confederates; but if his men were properly drilled and disciplined (as Jackson hoped to make them), they would be the better fighters. Richmond authorities paid no heed to Jackson's reference to "the spirit which actuated the defenders of Thermopylae." They should have, for Jackson again was raising the desirability of a "black flag" policy. Such a fight to the death would be the most humane course, he thought, not only because it would shorten the war and produce fewer casualties but also because it was the best course for the weaker South to pursue in the name of justice. Jackson made his feelings quite clear a year later when he told Anna's brother-in-law:

> I myself see in this war, if the North triumph, a dissolution of the bonds of all society. It is not alone the destruction of our property (which both the nation and the States are bound to protect), but it is the prelude to anarchy, infidelity, and the ultimate loss of free responsible government on this continent. With these convictions, I always thought we ought to meet the Federal invaders on the outer verge of just right and defence, and raise at once the black flag, viz., "No quarter to the violators of our homes and firesides!"

The greatest authority Jackson knew supported such an approach. "The Bible is full of such wars," he declared, "and it is the only policy that would bring the North to its senses."[66]

Confederate officials, especially in the first months of hostilities, recoiled at the thought of a no-prisoners contest. A few months, one battle, and the Southern cause would be triumphant. Preserve as many niceties as possible in the meantime. Jackson never "cheerfully acquiesced" in that decision, as one early biographer stated; he quietly maintained his stern beliefs throughout his field service. As for the Harpers Ferry situation, he vowed that if the Federals did advance on the post, "we will give them a warm reception."[67]

Garrison defenses grew stronger with each passing day. "Colonel Jackson seems to think that the pick and shovel are great weapons of warfare," a Richmond correspondent stated. "In every direction redoubts and breast-works are being thrown up, and block houses and fortifications constructed. Men unaccustomed to toil and physical labor work with zeal and industry by the side of the stout and sturdy mechanic. What a leveller is war."[68]

Careless handling of the firearms produced one or more accidents daily. Jackson finally had to issue an order prohibiting soldiers not on guard duty from having loaded weapons in their possession. A newspaperman observed that this directive "has created considerable excitement among the pistol gentry."[69]

Only partially because of the soldiers' carelessness with loaded weapons, Jackson stepped up training in a unique area. The commander was new to the ways of infantry. He became one of the few field officers in the Civil War to believe in the usefulness of the bayonet. Soldiers just learning to march, and still trying to remember the steps in loading and firing a musket, now found themselves performing exercises with the long, thin bayonets that were never popular on either side.

The first major personnel problem came on May 10, when Lieutenant Colonel J. E. B. Stuart reported to Jackson for duty. He was nine years younger than Jackson and a native of southwestern Virginia. In the West Point class of 1854, Stuart had ranked thirteenth among forty-six cadets. His short army career had been solely with cavalry, the arm of service most suited for his dash and energy. Harpers Ferry was familiar ground to Stuart, for in 1859 he had served as an aide to Colonel Robert E. Lee in extinguishing John Brown's insurrection.

Stuart had received an infantryman's commission in the spring of 1861 because no mounted posts were available at the moment. A powerful man measuring five feet, eleven inches tall and weighing about 180 pounds, he had coarse features partially obscured by a full, red beard. An irrepressible spirit often became vanity—not always a vice with a cavalry leader. Stuart and Jackson were an unlikely pair: one outgoing, the other introverted; one flashily uniformed, the other plainly dressed; one Prince Rupert and the other Cromwell. Yet Stuart's self-confidence, penchant for action, deep love of Virginia, and total abstinence from such vices as alcohol, tobacco, and pessimism endeared him to Jackson.

The two soldiers would form a personal attachment and a mutual admiration of one another. Stuart was the only man in the Confederacy who could make Jackson laugh—and who dared to do so. Their association now began. Jackson, unconcerned about available openings for officers, forthwith placed young Stuart in charge of all cavalry in the Harpers Ferry district.[70]

That did not sit well with Captain Turner Ashby or his mounted volunteers. Ashby was then thirty-two, midway in age between Jackson and Stuart. He and his brothers ran a large farm in northern Virginia's Fauquier County. Lacking any formal military training, but sensing war in 1859, Ashby had organized a cavalry company and was with the Virginia forces that seized Harpers Ferry on the day after Virginia's secession.

He was small in stature, swarthy, with a dark beard flowing to his chest. Black eyes could be gentle one minute, beacons of death the next. Men would write of Ashby's splendid horsemanship, his love of combat, the inspiration he sparked in his troops. One of those soldiers thought Ashby "fearless as a lion, and like the lion of the forest he never stopped to count the enemies he was to encounter." The basic weakness with this otherwise splendid figure lay in his perception of leadership. Ashby was a small-group officer. He regarded personal direction as a substitute for the discipline he seemed unwilling or incapable of exerting. To him, patriotism would more than compensate for any disorganization in the ranks. Good fighters were always preferable to good formations. Jackson admired that quality, but only to a point.[71]

When Stuart reported to Harpers Ferry, Ashby was in charge of the few companies of mounted soldiers. Yet Stuart had cavalry experience and higher rank. It could have been an either-or situation had not Jackson resorted to compromise. The colonel assigned Ashby to lead two companies of scouts familiar with the area; the other cavalry units went to Stuart. This gave the two officers nonconflicting areas of responsibility. Thereafter, both justified that trust on a daily basis. Indeed, a chaplain under Ashby wrote of the post commander: "Never did man bend himself more unremittingly to the work of organizing and disciplining the troops under his command than did Col. Jackson."[72]

At this early point in the war, Jackson was but one of many post commanders who requested more arms than they had troops to whom to give them. On May 11, Jackson asked Lee for an additional 5000 shoulder weapons. Lee responded with an arithmetic lesson. "Over 2000 arms have already been sent you," he told Jackson the next day, "and 1000 more have been ordered this wk. If you only expect to receive sufficient volunteers to swell your force to 4500 men, I do not see how you can require 5000 arms, as you must now have nearly 3000 armed, beside the 3000 arms above mentioned ordered to you."[73]

Actually, Jackson's garrison had swelled to over 7000 men as hundreds of new recruits steadily congregated at the northwestern rendezvous. On the night of May 19, thirty-six hours of rain began; and in the middle of the downpour, a Confederate inspector general arrived to investigate facilities and defenses. His subsequent report was a mixture of commendation and criticism, with no fault levied against Jackson himself.[74]

Thursday, May 23, was the date when Virginians went to the polls to ratify the state's withdrawal from the Union. Although the outcome of the vote was not in doubt, the lopsided margin caught some people by surprise. The statewide tally was a four-to-one margin in favor of secession (with most of the opposition coming from the mountainous regions in western Virginia). Residents of the Shenandoah Valley went for the Confederacy in overwhelming numbers. In Augusta County, the secessionists prevailed, 3130–10; while in next-door Rockbridge County where Jackson lived, only one person voted against leaving the Union.

Those figures were somewhat deceiving. Untold numbers of Virginians marked their ballots with the same heavy heart as did one of Jackson's clerical friends, the Reverend Francis McFarland. "This is the most painful vote I ever gave," McFarland stated. "The course of the administration . . . seemed to leave me no alternative. I mourn in bitterness over the state of things, but Va. did all she could for peace."[75]

In the meantime, Jackson was unaware that he had officially been removed from command. Back on May 2, during his first week at Harpers Ferry, Virginia officials had given approval to the Confederate Constitution. The Old Dominion had become part of the new nation. Military affairs inside the state thereupon became the domain of the Confederate War Department, which on May 15 assigned one of its highest-ranking officers, Brigadier General Joseph E. Johnston, to take command of the Harpers Ferry installation. This seemed logical. The forward location of the post, its importance to that sector of the country, its brigade-size garrison containing units from Alabama, Kentucky, and Mississippi as well as Virginia—all required the attention of an experienced general rather than an untested colonel.

On May 18, while en route through southwestern Virginia to the Ferry, Johnston had informed Lee of his assignment. The commander of Virginia forces somehow neglected to tell Jackson of the forthcoming change.[76] The colonel was busily attending to affairs at his desk on the afternoon of the 23d when he received three visitors: the flawlessly uniformed Johnston and two of his staff members, Majors Eugene McLean and Chase Whiting.

Jackson recognized two of them. A month earlier, he had served briefly under Johnston at the Richmond instruction camps. Whiting was a fellow West Point cadet who had voluntarily tutored Jackson in the latter's first hectic weeks at the academy. After an exchange of pleasantries, Johnston informed Jackson that he was there to take charge of the Harpers Ferry garrison. Apparently the matter rested there for the night.

The next morning Johnston asked Jackson to announce the change of command as well as the appointments of McLean as quartermaster and Whiting as post engineer. The colonel surprised the Johnston party by politely declining to do so. He had received no written directive from either Governor Letcher or General Lee to relinquish his Virginia command, Jackson stated in careful tones. Since Johnston had inadvertently forgotten to bring a copy of his May 15 Confederate appointment, no written evidence existed that he was entitled to assume the duties of post commander.

Colonel Jackson added that he would be honored to take the brigadier on a tour of the Harpers Ferry defenses, but no change in command structure could occur until a written communique was at hand. For Jackson, the issue was not debatable: authority was clear-cut and spelled out; command was never relinquished on a verbal reassurance.

Johnston knew of the earlier friendship between Jackson and Whiting, so he sent his engineer to try and reason with the colonel. Whiting was probably not a good choice. He possessed a pomposity and an abruptness that would cripple his subsequent career. The South Carolinian "remonstrated" with his West Point friend, but to no avail. Whiting then warned Jackson that he might be arrested for his obstinacy in this matter. "I consider my duty clear," Jackson responded. No personal consideration could influence him. Whiting huffily concluded: "He was always very firm & in the military part of his life had no compromise in him."[77]

At this point, the situation was becoming uncomfortably embarrassing for Johnston. On the other hand, he recognized the military protocol involved here. His own sensitivity to command would prove to be even stronger than Jackson's and was part of his ultimate undoing as a field leader. Yet no one ever accused Johnston of being unsoldierlike. Born near Farmville, Virginia, in 1807, he was in the same West Point class as Robert E. Lee. Five wounds in the Mexican War brought Johnston a hero's mantle. He was Quartermaster General of the U.S. Army when he resigned in 1861 to defend his native state.

Johnston looked like a general. Somewhat below medium height, he was erect to the point of stuffiness. His close-fitting uniform was buttoned to the chin. Dominating a ruddy face were short side whiskers and a sharply pointed goatee. A naturally stern expression could give way to a pleasant smile. In this early period of the war, Johnston was popularly compared to a gamecock—small in size but eager for battle.[78]

If Johnston was deeply offended by Jackson's rigid adherence to orders (or lack of them), he displayed no indication of it. A telegram to Richmond would straighten out the misunderstanding. Before resorting to an embarrassing request for verification of assignment, Johnston rummaged through the papers he had with him. He found an endorsement from Lee to an application: "Referred to J. E. Johnston, commanding officer at Harper's Ferry. By order of Major-General Lee." That proved to be sufficient. Jackson read the lines and promptly stepped aside.[79]

"We are sorry to lose Col. Jackson, as he has proved himself a true soldier," a Confederate private wrote. Prominent civilians felt the same. Following a mid-May visit to the Ferry, the respected James M. Mason had reassured Lee that "even my limited observation there confirmed the general tone of all around [Jackson], that all were in good hands under his command."[80]

In retrospect, Jackson had nothing to regret during his almost four weeks of command. Lee was undoubtedly pleased with his performance at the Confederacy's northern outpost. Jackson's administration had been decisive, thorough, and somewhat surprising in view of his inexperience with recruits in all three arms of service at a forward garrison. He had managed to reduce chaos to simple confusion with organization and discipline. The persistence of confusion was the result of unbounded enthusiasm in the war's first weeks, plus a too-cautious approach on the part of authorities at Richmond.

Never hesitant when the proper course seemed obvious, Jackson had fortified the heights of a neutral state, advocated a military advance into the northwestern mountains in order to maintain that sector as part of Virginia, and voiced a determination to hold Harpers Ferry to the last man. Such viewpoints from a VMI professor with limited background and strange ways struck many Southern officials as being over-eager and dangerous. Jackson's real accomplishment—the building of a powerful garrison at Harpers Ferry—gave the Confederacy the opportunity to entrust the post to someone more experienced if not more reliable. General sentiment in Richmond seemed to be that Jackson was a good man so long as he had a competent superior to think for him and keep him under control.

Troops at the Ferry were not wise enough to the ways of war to have strong feelings on the transfer of command. On that same May 24, Private Andis of the 4th Virginia informed the family that all was well in camp save for bad colds and diarrhea. "We sleep ruff, and live tuff, and we hardly get enough of Scotch Snuff, but we must be satisfied and hope for the better."[81]

Jackson felt precisely the same way. When Colonel Smith, still serving on Governor Letcher's advisory council, sent a congratulatory letter on the performance at Harpers Ferry, Jackson responded in hearty fashion. "Your very kind letter expressing the entire approval of the Governor and Council of my conduct while in command of this post . . . is a source of great gratification. I hope that making the success of our Cause the great and controlling motive, I shall under the blessing of Providence continue to merit their approval, and give them no cause to blush for the confidence which has or may be reposed in me."[82]

He waited until Monday, May 27, to write Anna. Always cheerful and conversational in his letters, Jackson delivered no treatises except of a religious nature. He had never written complaints of superior officers, and he did not do so in discussing the Harpers Ferry situation. Jackson told his wife not to be concerned at the change of command. "Colonel Preston will explain it all to you. I hope to have more time, as long as I am not in command of a post, to write longer letters to my darling pet." Anna had wanted to come to Winchester to visit her husband. He now advised against it because of probable troop movements.[83]

Since her husband's departure for war, Anna had lived in Lexington with Mr. and Mrs. William N. Page. He was principal of the Ann Smith Academy and she had befriended Anna from the moment of her arrival in town. Anna wanted badly to see her husband, but the unpredictable nature of the northern Virginia situation made that impractical. She therefore closed the Washington Street home and sent the family servants to "good homes among the permanent residents" of Lexington. Accompanied by her brother Joseph, Anna traveled to Cottage Home in North Carolina to live with her father until Jackson summoned her.[84]

What to do with the replaced Jackson was only a momentary issue. Lee thought he would be excellent as chief of artillery at the Ferry. Johnston considered him more valuable in another role. On May 27, Jackson received orders to take command of all Virginia regiments at the post. This assignment essentially meant that Jackson, now commanding most of the infantry, was to be Johnston's principal lieutenant.[85]

One of Johnston's first directives was to create a stronger organization of the troops under his command. He left the 300 cavalry in detachments but formed the 4800 infantry and artillery into three undersized brigades. These Johnston positioned at points along the Potomac in order to put up a stronger show of force. Maintaining Harpers Ferry from atop Bolivar Heights in the rear of the village, and within cooperating distance of any unit that needed help, were Colonel Jackson and his First Virginia Brigade.

Initially, this unit consisted of four regiments and an artillery battery. All components were from the general vicinity of the Shenandoah Valley. (This was done purposefully by the Confederate War Department for the sake of giving the brigade a sense of neighborhood allegiance.) The 2d Virginia originated in the Winchester-Martinsburg-Charles Town region. Its colonel was James W. Allen, an 1849 graduate of VMI and a Bedford County farmer. A female admirer described Allen, who was six feet, three inches tall, as "a glorious man" whose troops were devoted to him. Allen had a booming voice that, when giving orders, reputedly could be heard half a mile away.[86]

Men in the 4th Virginia came from a line of rural counties extending southward from Rockbridge to Grayson. James Francis Preston was in command; but owing to poor health at the time, he had temporarily turned over the regiment to Lieutenant Colonel Lewis T. Moore. Winchester attorney (as well as part owner of the Taylor Hotel) and a prewar militia colonel, Moore was in his mid-forties and had a maturity his men needed.

The 5th Virginia was organized in large part with companies from the Staunton area. Sixty-year-old Kenton Harper, Staunton Spectator editor and former militia general, led the regiment during the first months of the war. Rounding out the infantry regiments in Jackson's brigade was the 27th Virginia. Its companies were from the regions south and west of Lexington. In command of the regiment was Lynchburg-born John Echols, a year older than Jackson and a graduate of both Washington College and the Harvard law school.[87]

If a "showcase" component existed in Jackson's brigade, it was the Rockbridge Artillery. It was organized in Lexington at the time of Virginia's secession. John McCausland, a junior member of the VMI faculty, was the first captain. He quickly left to become colonel of the 36th Virginia, whereupon the battery members turned to the Reverend William Nelson Pendleton, fifty-two years old. An 1830 graduate of West Point and later Episcopal rector in Lexington, "Old Penn" took his duties seriously and led his unit proudly. The membership consisted "principally of agreeable & intelligent men—many of them being young & from college." Its weapons were three small six-pounders and a twelve-pounder howitzer. In deference to their clergyman-captain, the artillerists christened the guns Matthew, Mark, Luke, and John.[88]

One of the line officers in Jackson's brigade insisted that "a finer body of men were never mustered" than existed in the ranks of the valley regiments. "Among them were to be found men of culture, men of gentle training, men of intellect, men of social position, men of character at home, men endeared to domestic circles of refinement and elegance, men of wealth . . . and men who for conscience sake made a living sacrifice of property, home and comfort and were ready to add crimson life to the holy offering."[89]

Probably no brigade in the Civil War contained more educated men. The unit also had the characteristic of a "cousinwealth." So many families sent fathers, sons, brothers, cousins, and nephews into the army that company muster rolls often resembled genealogical tables. When men were not related, they probably were neighbors. One soldier stated in bewilderment of camp life: "I never saw so many persons I knew in my life, every third person speaks to me."[90]

Jackson was pleased to be away from the endless paperwork associated with post command. As he organized, drilled, and came to know better the officers and men under him, his satisfaction increased. His staff underwent further improvement. Major Frank Jones of the 2d Virginia became his adjutant for the moment. Surgeon McGuire was brigade medical director. Major Harman continued as Jackson's quartermaster, while Major Wells J. Hawks of the 2d Virginia was brigade commissary. Lieutenant Colonel Massie still served as an aide, and young Lieutenant Alexander "Sandie" Pendleton joined the staff as ordnance officer.[91]

The important thing for Jackson was that he was in the field and preparing troops for battle. That was what he wanted; that was where he belonged. One new recruit scoffed at Jackson's sleepy look and uninspiring appearance in the saddle. Yet, the man admitted, "he was a strict disciplinarian, and ultimately went to work to prepare his brigade for the great work before it."[92]

In a good frame of mind, Jackson took advantage of a steady rain on June 4 to write Anna. Throughout his career as a Confederate officer, Jackson loved receiving letters from Anna. He would thoroughly digest one of Anna's communiques, then destroy it. Jackson considered the epistles too sacred to have them fall into other hands. Of late, however, Anna's letters had been somewhat fretful because Jackson's messages to her were so brief. "Little one," Jackson stated, "you wrote me that you wanted longer letters, and now just prepare yourself to have your wish gratified. You say that your husband never writes you any news. I suppose you meant military news, for I have written a great deal about your esposo and how much he loves you. What do you want with military news? Don't you know that it is unmilitary and unlike an officer to write news respecting one's post?" Jackson then described his new quarters: an elegant mansion with beautiful roses growing up the wall to his second-floor bedroom, plus a large green yard in front. He closed the letter as was his habit by giving thanks to God for all of his blessings.[93]

While Jackson's feelings grew happier, those of "Uncle Joe" Johnston plunged in the opposite direction. The more he saw of the Harpers Ferry post, the less he liked it. First there were the eager but unproven volunteers who composed the garrison. Johnston was a Regular Army man who greatly preferred professional soldiers. He had been in command only a couple of days when the 2d Virginia marched past. Dr. McGuire, standing beside Johnston, turned and commented that those men from his home county would demonstrate their fighting prowess in the first battle. Johnston snorted: "I would not give one company of regulars for the whole regiment!" Feelings hurt, McGuire repeated Johnston's words to Jackson. The brigade commander replied: "Did he say that? And of those splendid men?" Jackson paused for a moment, perhaps thinking of Old Testament armies, then with a stern voice added, "The patriotic volunteer, fighting for country and his rights, makes the most reliable soldier on earth."[94]

Volunteer soldiers were just the first point of Johnston's dissatisfaction. Firearm accidents climbed in number once the general allowed the men to resume carrying loaded weapons. Moreover, Harpers Ferry itself was beginning to show the wear and tear of an overcrowded military post. A newspaperman wrote of its physical shape: "The dust of the place is really a terror. When we have rain, the mud is knee deep; when dry, the dust fills the air. The transition from wet to dry is made in about an hour and vice versa."[95]

The basics of life also left something to be desired. A cavalryman told his father: "I cannot eat any thing hardly that is brought to us by the Quartermaster for we have Beef here now in our tents that has been lying here for several days without any salt on it and you may depend upon it: it dont smell like ripe peaches." Moreover, in the judgment of a visiting missionary, Harpers Ferry was "a dreadful place for religion."[96]

Beyond those drawbacks, in Johnston's opinion, was something even more fundamentally wrong. He regarded Harpers Ferry as indefensible. "The position is easily turned by crossing the river above or below," he stated in his first communique to Richmond. "The present force is not sufficient for defense against a superior one. . . . Considered as a position, I regard Harper's Ferry as untenable by us at present against a strong enemy." Johnston felt strongly that "the occupation of Harper's Ferry by our Army perfectly suited the enemy's views. We were bound to a fixed point; his movements were unrestricted." He urged that the installation be abandoned.[97]

Confederate authorities still saw the Ferry as an indispensable point of defense and a symbol of resistance. For days, Johnston's pleas to be allowed to fall back were denied. Like Jackson, Lee did not want to surrender Harpers Ferry. Such a move would be widely interpreted as a defeat; it would literally and figuratively place Maryland farther away from the Confederacy.

Lee believed that holding the Ferry would impair Union communications with the west and, at the same time, be a salient for a Confederate force to use in striking the flank of an enemy army moving into northern Virginia. Jackson and Lee were thinking alike in this early stage of the contest. Johnston's conclusions about Harpers Ferry were sound; but his reluctance from the beginning to confront the burdens of command, plus his refusal to accept decisions not to his liking, were dark portents for Johnston's future usefulness as a commander.[98]

To protect his flanks somewhat, Johnston began destroying bridges on the Potomac. He ordered Jackson to burn the span some twelve miles upriver at Shepherdstown. Jackson determined that a night march to the target offered the best avenue for surprise and success. Although the end result was successful, the surprise ingredient disappeared at the outset. Carriages filled with mothers and sisters, escorted by portly fathers on horseback, followed the westward trek of 4500 soldiers.

A Winchester recruit described the next stage. "As darkness fell apace, all were left behind but the soldiers. It was our first night-march, and by two o'clock we were 'dead beat!' Many fell asleep by the roadside, and were only aroused by the rattling of the muskets, as the foremost regiment fired a volley without orders, and swept across the bridge, only to be sternly ordered back by 'Old Jack, the sleepless,' who reprimanded its colonel then personally superintended the firing of the wooden structure."[99]

From the beginning, the thirty-seven-year-old Jackson was "Old Jack" to his soldiers. They never adopted any other nickname. The origins of "Old Jack" lay in affection and in the fact that the great majority of his "men" were youths. "The truth is," one of them stated, "we were soldier boys, and the boys were sometimes more in evidence than the soldier." That is why, a former cadet wrote, Jackson "preserved the most rigid discipline among them, and this was in a great measure the cause of their wonderful success."[100]

Jackson was continuing to mold a fighting force with his regiments when he received a letter from his influential friend, Jonathan M. Bennett. The state auditor and Weston native wanted to have Jackson promoted to brigadier general and transferred to command of the Clarksburg-Weston region, where unionists were steadily gaining the upper hand. That area was dear to Jackson's heart. He responded quickly. "Your very kind letter . . . meets with my grateful approbation. The sooner it is done the better. Have me ordered at once, that country is bleeding at every pore, and I feel a deep interest in it, and have never appealed to its people in vain."[101]

The prospect of a generalship had a certain degree of appeal to Jackson, but it is obvious that defending his homeland was the overriding factor. Duty in the remote mountainous country of the northwest offered little opportunity for glory and less for further advancement. Personal ambition played no role in Jackson's feelings. He had wanted to go into northwestern Virginia from the start of the war. His motivation was the ageless stimulus of fighting for one's home. This assignment, which Jackson coveted, never materialized.

Johnston, meanwhile, persisted with his appeals to be allowed to retire from what he termed the Harpers Ferry deathtrap. He had 7000 men by his reckoning, while one Federal column was at Williamsport, a day's march away, and another 2000 enemy troops had advanced to Romney, sixty miles to the west. The presence of these two forces threatened both Johnston's flank and Winchester. Johnston stepped up his policy of severing transportation lines along the Potomac; he also took the liberty of loading wagons with baggage for a speedy retirement toward Winchester. The long-sought green light came on June 13, when Adjutant General Samuel Cooper at Richmond wired Johnston: "You will consider yourself authorized, whenever the position of the enemy shall convince you that he is about to turn your position . . . to destroy everything at Harper's Ferry . . . and retire upon the [Winchester and Potomac] railroad towards Winchester."[102]

Moments after reading the dispatch, Johnston ordered Jackson's brigade to see to the evacuation of the Ferry. Everything movable of military value would be taken to Winchester. What could not be removed would be destroyed. Jackson spent the hectic day arranging for wagons to transport baggage and for trains to carry off the sick, records, and staff personnel.

Members of the Virginia regiments placed charges under or inside installations marked for demolition. A quiet night ended on June 14 at 5 A.M., when a huge explosion echoed through the valley of the Potomac. The splendid 900-foot metal B&O railroad bridge was blown into rubble. However, it was but the first of nine times in the Civil War that the bridge was destroyed and later rebuilt.[103]

In the course of the day, Jackson's troops systematically razed the lower part of Harpers Ferry. Put to the torch were armory buildings, the depot, telegraph office, trestles, and machine shops. A powder charge sent the Shenandoah River bridge collapsing into the water. Heat from the flames became so intense that many of the Confederates were forced to scamper onto Bolivar Heights. One of the few structures to escape destruction was the engine house where John Brown had made his final stand. Soldiers on both sides saw an omen in this.[104]

Billows of black smoke still rolled skyward as Johnston's force moved along the Charles Town road for Winchester, some thirty miles to the southwest. Confederates marched briskly, receiving food and encouragement from farmers along the way.

Johnston urged on the column, for he wanted to get as many miles as possible between himself and the Federals.

His aim was to move to Bunker Hill, ten miles north of Winchester, and make a new stand there. Although only a hamlet, Bunker Hill lay midway between Winchester and Martinsburg; it was the intersection of the Valley Turnpike with the road to Charles Town and Harpers Ferry. Abundant springs existed around Bunker Hill, and it was close to the strategic Potomac River.

Jackson saw the village as the spot for a battle. He was always convinced that the sooner combat took place, the earlier the accursed struggle would end.

The Confederates reached Charles Town, turned west toward the famous Valley Turnpike, and marched another four miles before bivouacking for the night in a clump of woods. It was then that Jackson's commissary got an abrupt introduction into his commander's secret nature. Wells J. Hawks was a forty-three-year-old native of Massachusetts. A poor boy with little education, Hawks came to Winchester in 1839 and became an apprentice in a carriage business. He soon established his own factory in Charles Town. By 1861, Hawks had served a term as mayor, three terms in the state legislature, and was Charles Town's foremost businessman. Everyone in camp near Berryville that night was anxious to learn where the column would be moving the next day. (A soldier in the 27th Virginia complained at this time: "We never know where we are going until we get there.") Hawks agreed to find out. The gray-bearded, mild-looking commissary left his huge wagon train parked in a field and dismounted at Jackson's tent. He saluted Jackson, then said, "As we are going to make an early start tomorrow morning, I would like to know how to head the train."

"Arrange the wagon train with the heads of the horses toward the pike," came the reply.

Hawks was perplexed. "But shall I head it up the pike or down the pike?"

Jackson flashed the officer a hard look and snapped, "I said toward the pike, sir." The commissary left the tent with the resolve never again to ask Jackson about future movements.[105]

Johnston was optimistic as he moved toward Winchester. The town controlled all of the major roads into the Shenandoah Valley, and the one railroad to northern Virginia would be at his disposal. Rumors were afield that 18,000 Union soldiers under aged General Robert Patterson were also advancing on Winchester. Prospects seemed good for a long-awaited fight.

The van of the Confederate column was Jackson's brigade. He drove his men hard to get to the Valley Turnpike and across the path of the enemy invaders. The Virginians "were so inspirited," Jackson boasted, "as to apparently forget the fatigue of the march, & tho' some of them were suffering from hunger, this & all other privations appeared to be forgotten, & the march continued at the rate of about 3 miles per hour."[106]

Instead of offering battle, however, Johnston turned south after reaching the turnpike and "made some disposition for receiving the enemy, if they should attack us." The valley regiments moved toward the defense "in snail-like pace."[107] Whether it was Johnston's arrival in the Winchester area or some other factor, the Federals quickly withdrew across the Potomac.

Johnston's reluctance to have a showdown with Patterson's force left Jackson baffled and somewhat angry. In a rare display of annoyance, he told Anna: "I hope the General will do something soon. Since we have left Harper's Ferry, something of an active movement towards repelling the enemy of course is expected. I trust that through the blessing of God, we will soon be given an opportunity of driving the invaders from this region."[108]

Johnston carefully prepared his defenses along the Bunker Hill line north of Winchester. During the process, he also completed the organization of what he styled the "Army of the Shenandoah." He formed his 9000 troops into four brigades. Jackson, being the senior colonel, led the first. South Carolinian Barnard E. Bee, who graduated from West Point a year ahead of Jackson, took charge of four regiments from Mississippi, Tennessee, and Alabama. Arnold Elzey (West Point, 1837), a Marylander, led the third brigade with its mixture of Virginia, Maryland, and Tennessee units. Francis S. Bartow, Georgia planter and Yale graduate, had resigned his seat in the Confederate Congress to accept a colonel's commission. His brigade consisted of three Georgia regiments and two Kentucky battalions.

On June 19, Jackson got an opportunity for action. It was not exactly what he wanted, but it was better than vegetating at Bunker Hill. Colonel "Jeb" Stuart and his 330 Confederate horsemen were at Martinsburg, some twenty miles north of Winchester. Federals were thought to be moving on it from the river town of Williamsport, Maryland. Johnston wanted the extensive B&O railroad shops at Martinsburg destroyed to prevent their future use by the enemy.

Jackson was not pleased with the assignment: the equipment could be saved, transported on the same-gauge Winchester and Potomac line to the safety of the Confederacy, where it could be put to good use. Yet orders were orders. Jackson never hesitated at a directive.

The valley regiments got on the road at 5 P.M. on the 19th and marched half the night before Jackson permitted them to rest. Moving again at dawn, the column filed into Martinsburg in mid-morning. Jackson established a line of couriers to maintain contact with Johnston in Winchester. Cautious Federals showed no sign of contesting Jackson's presence. However, the Confederates found themselves in obviously hostile country. Private Ted Barclay of the 4th Virginia thought Berkeley County "the meanest Abolition hole on the face of the earth, Martinsburg especially."[109]

Pursuant to orders, but against his better judgment that railroad equipment should always be saved, Jackson began a systematic destruction of the Martinsburg yards. Details ripped up track and burned cross-ties; other groups of soldiers set fire to the round houses and machine shops. Some fifty-six locomotives and tenders, as well as at least 305 coal cars, were either set afire, heaved into the Opequon River, or dismantled to the point of uselessness.

"The fires were great," Lexington's John Lyle stated, "and the work looked like vandalism." One elderly and indignant matron shouted repeatedly to the Confederates that she hoped General Winfield Scott would hang the last man of them.[110]

A conflict between military destruction and military confiscation of railroad equipment persisted in Jackson's mind. Within a few days, he developed a plan for accomplishing both ends. Two railroad engineers, Hugh Longust and Thomas R. Sharp, arrived in Martinsburg from Richmond. They selected the thirteen least damaged locomotives. Mechanics dismantled the engines, then entrusted the pieces to teamsters, who used forty-horse teams and hauled the iron loads thirty-eight miles to Strasburg. Each trip required three days of hard labor.

At Strasburg, the Manassas Gap Railroad became the next leg of a journey that ultimately took the locomotive parts to Richmond. There they were reassembled, and the old B&O locomotives returned to their normal ways on rails after traveling in part and in pieces over roads. The practice of sending railroad rolling stock overland to points elsewhere originated with Jackson and became fairly common thereafter.

Jackson's men were completing their work on June 22, when Stuart reported a Union column across the Potomac and heading toward Martinsburg. Positive action at last! Jackson thought. He sent word of the approaching enemy to Johnston with a call for support while he unleashed the 5th Virginia and Pendleton's battery to move forward and offer battle. "We will have an engagement soon with the cowardly ruffians," a member of the 4th Virginia eagerly stated. "The troops have great confidence in the coolness, the bravery and the military skill of Col. Jackson."[111]

Johnston was not ready for such a confrontation.[112] In his eyes, Jackson seemed too anxious for battle, too inclined to strike without proper reconnaissance, too likely to pursue a retreating foe into Maryland. Such actions Johnston viewed as militarily and politically unwise. "It is not yet time for us to invade," he told Jackson in the predawn hours of June 23, and the rest of his instructions were implicit. Jackson was to hold his position, unless the enemy appeared in his front in force. Then, screened by Stuart's cavalry, Jackson would fall back toward Winchester. Above all, a general engagement was to be avoided.[113]

If Jackson was not furious at this directive, he had to be extremely frustrated. Johnston had abandoned Harpers Ferry; now he backed off from a fight even the men in the ranks wanted. The commander did not understand this war, Jackson concluded. The South must attack and carry destruction into Union territory. Only in that way could victory come quickly and with minimum pain. A waiting game meant ultimate defeat. Other considerations were involved in Johnston's decisions, of course; Jackson was either unaware of them or did not care about them.

Hat pulled down over forehead, and ungracefully rocking on the back of Little Sorrel, Jackson silently led his troops back toward their encampment four miles northeast of Martinsburg. His men were more fatigued than dispirited. Lieutenant Langhorne wrote home: "Ma, we dont know one hour where we may be the next. Col. Jackson never lets anyone know his intentions." Another soldier termed Jackson "some peripatetic philosophical madman, whose forte was pedestrianism." He might be a good commander, the man added, "but I should admire him much more in a state of rest than continually seeing him moving in the front."[114]

Letter writing for Jackson was usually on Monday. Hence, on June 24, he spent several hours writing at his desk. One letter was to Anna, who had been hearing pessimistic reports in North Carolina on the future of the Confederacy. Jackson responded in part: "You spoke of the cause of the South being gloomy—it is not so here. I am well satisfied that the enemy are afraid to meet us, & our troops are anxious for an engagement." Jackson then spoke with envy of Colonel A. P. Hill's 13th Virginia and how it captured two cannon and a regimental flag in a sweep on Romney.[115]

Another letter reflected Jackson's dissatisfaction at serving under Johnston as well as his continuing wish to see duty in the northwest. Jonathan Bennett had reassured Jackson that efforts were still being made on his behalf in the capital. Jackson was now anxious to assist in those efforts. "Knowing your success in carrying your measures [and] the energy with which you press them," he told Bennett, "the thought struck me, that there might be some obstacle in the way which, if made known to me, I might be able to remove. I am in command of a promising Brigade, and I would be greatly gratified, if you could secure me a Brigadier Generalcy, and if I can not be ordered to North Western Va., of course I would be continued in my present command, and as I am so far west, an opportunity might soon offer of having me with my command ordered into that region. Providence has greatly blessed me in securing good staff officers. . . . I feel deeply for my own section of the state." But unknown to Jackson, his words and actions since entering the field had given him the reputation of a fanatic. Doubts existed in Richmond about entrusting a general's responsibilities to this rather unpredictable and volatile VMI professor. Among those highly suspicious of his abilities was President Jefferson Davis.[116]

The valley regiments spent about two weeks encamped in a clover field and grove of trees north of Martinsburg. Jackson established his headquarters in the front yard of a house alongside the turnpike and near the tents of the 4th Virginia. The colonel refused the comfort of a room, preferring instead to spread his blanket at night on the ground along with his staff.

In spite of an epidemic of measles, rigorous training marked the period at "Camp Stephens." Drill occurred six times daily, interrupted only by roll calls and camp duties. A recruit in the 2d Virginia complained that Jackson "marched us back and forth every day, and at least half of every night." Discipline was as intense as the training. Heat and dust added to the discomfort. Grumbling began to mark camp life; some prominent citizens in the area from which the 2d Virginia originated pronounced Jackson "unfit to command gentlemen." James J. White, former Greek professor at Washington College and now captain of the "Liberty Hall Volunteers," commented in a letter, "Jackson is considered rigid to the borders of tyranny by the men here, and some of them have been greatly surprised to get an insight into his character as a Christian man."[117]

Morale inside the ranks increased almost in spite of it all. One of Jackson's men announced that they "were in perfect trim" and "felt like soldiers." Another reason for high spirits was the simple fact that Jackson seemed to go out of his way to care for his men. Captain White felt that Jackson enjoyed "the entire confidence of his command." A recruit from the southern extension of the valley declared: "There is not a man in the Southern army who does not in his heart believe he can whip three Yankees. He would consider it beneath his manhood to count upon whipping a less number, in any sort of fight." Although Jackson's brigade numbered only 2300 troops and four guns, its spirit was a factor in Federal General Patterson estimating its strength at 16,000 men and twenty-two guns.[118]

Tuesday, July 2, was the day Jackson got his first taste of battle in the Civil War.[119] At 7:30 A.M., after a nighttime rainstorm, one of Stuart's couriers galloped into the yard where Jackson had his headquarters. Federal troops had crossed the Potomac and were less than five miles away in a strong column moving on Martinsburg. Jackson did not react noticeably to the news. He had been up and on duty for hours—and waiting days for such news. His men were as trained as he could make them and as eager as their colonel for the meeting with Federals.

The first order of business was movement. Jackson was quite aware of Johnston's directive of June 23: retire if the enemy approaches your front in force. But was the enemy now in force? The only way to determine that was to advance and make contact.

Jackson's orders were as quick as they were precise. Harper's 5th Virginia and Pendleton's battery again would make the reconnaissance; the 27th Virginia was to get all baggage loaded into wagons, while the 2d and 4th Regiments stood in readiness at Camp Stephens for a possible summons. Within thirty minutes, Jackson, one of the few men in the brigade who had ever been under fire, was leading the column northward.

It moved a mile on a muddy road toward Falling Waters, a natural defensive point on a bend in the Potomac. The country was like the rest of the valley: undulating and cultivated wherever land was unencumbered by thick timber and rock outcroppings. Halfway to the destination, Jackson got a glimpse of Federal cavalry in the distance. To prevent risking too much, he directed three of Pendleton's four guns to take position on either side of the road to protect against a mounted approach in strength. At 9:15 A.M. the Confederate force—380 infantry and a six-pounder—advanced to do battle.

Jackson's detachment had proceeded another mile and was nearing Hoke's Creek. Skirmishers sighted blueclad troops in woods to the right of the road on the Porterfield farm. An eager Colonel Harper, more active than his sixty years might indicate, halted the advance and asked Jackson if he was to move straight ahead toward the enemy. "No," came the reply. "Detach a company to make explorations of the woods on the right."

Captain James H. Waters's "West Augusta Guard" plunged into the timber. Finding nothing, the young soldiers rushed out into a clearing and promptly came under musket fire from Federals "concealed in the rye and grass." Harper now sent forward five more companies. They advanced on either side of the road and delivered a fire "with such effect," stated Jackson, "as to force those of the enemy back on their reserve."[120]

Two companies of the 5th Virginia took possession of the Porterfield barn and nearby home. From such cover, they increased their fire on the irregular Union lines 100 or so yards away. However, Union artillery now became a factor. After firing several shells toward the rear of Jackson's force (ostensibly to determine if more Confederates were behind the party that was visible), the Union guns turned on the Porterfield buildings and other Southern positions.

A line of Federals two regiments wide came into view. The 5th Virginia, spread out in loose files but firing bravely, was in danger of having both flanks overlapped. Jackson ordered his men to fall back. As they slowly did so, Jackson sent Captain Pendleton with his gun to find a favorable spot in the rear where he would have command of the road. If the enemy "sufficiently crowded the road in front," Jackson told the captain, Pendleton was to open fire with solid shot.

Within minutes, a column of Union cavalry came around the bend some 800 yards in the distance. Pendleton waited behind his concealed gun until the range was point blank. Then the cleric looked heavenward and intoned loudly: "May the Lord have mercy on their souls! Fire!" According to Jackson, that ball "entirely cleared the road in front." Pendleton fired seven more shots, but none had the telling effect of the unexpected first blast.[121]

It was more than evident now that Union troops greatly outnumbered Jackson's small band. He was under strict orders to retire in such a situation. Jackson began a slow withdrawal from the field, "checking the enemy whenever it became necessary, so as to give time for any wagons to get in column at [Camp Stephens], before I should arrive there." Jeb Stuart helped greatly at this point. He further delayed Union movements by swooping around the enemy's right flank and capturing half a company from the 15th Pennsylvania Cavalry.[122]

Jackson slowly fell back three miles under fire—a difficult tactical procedure even for veterans. Yet the colonel's calm reassurances and total self-possession made young men feel like seasoned soldiers. One of them said proudly that Jackson under fire was "stolid, imperturbable, undisturbed, as he was watched by every eye, and his example was quieting and of decided moral effect."[123]

The detachment reached Camp Stephens around noon. A dispatch came from an obviously concerned Johnston: "Genl. Bee has been ordered to prepare to move to your support in case your next report indicates the necessity. The other troops will be ready to follow if we find that you are pressed. Don't commit yourself, however. Caution & prudence are the qualities your position requires. I have confidence in you."

Jackson paused to scribble a quick reply. It was necessary for Johnston to know that the Confederates had committed themselves—and gained success for the effort. Corporal William M. Brown of the Rockbridge Artillery watched his colonel. "Seating himself on a large, loose, round stone on the north side of the road, he commenced to write an answer. . . . A shot from a Federal battery struck centrally, ten feet from the ground, a large white oak that stood in the fence corner close to Jackson and knocked a mass of bark, splinters and trash all over him and the paper on which he was writing. He brushed away the trash with the back of his hand, finished the dispatch without a sign that he knew anything unusual was going on, folded it, handed it to the courier and dismissed him courteously: 'Carry this to General Johnston with my compliments, and see that you lose no time on the way.'"

Still prepared to fight again, Jackson drew his full brigade up in a new line on the northern edge of Martinsburg. Federals soon could be seen on the flanks. Jackson withdrew through town and moved two-and-a-half miles farther south to Darkesville. The enemy was content to stop at Camp Stephens. Jackson's blows, Lieutenant Lyle chortled, had made the Yankees "step pussy-footed."[124]

The Union expedition consisted of a brigade of 3000 troops under General John J. Abercrombie, General Patterson's son-in-law. Union losses were six to ten killed, eighteen wounded, and fifty captured in the two-hour affair. Patterson reported that his troops had encountered 3500 Southerners (ten times Jackson's actual number), whom his men "hotly pursued for four miles" after a twenty-five-minute contest. Patterson's additional claim of inflicting sixty casualties is overblown. Jackson reported twelve wounded and thirteen missing, while Harper put the 5th Virginia losses at eleven wounded and nine missing.[125]

From the Darkesville bivouac, on July 4, Jackson proudly recounted details of Falling Waters to Anna. He was as convinced as ever that he was doing the Lord's work. "I am very thankful that an ever kind Providence made me an instrument in carrying out General Johnston's orders so successfully," he wrote. "When the battle does come, I expect that God will give us the victory. My officers & men behaved beautifully, in this skirmish, & are anxious for a battle." Jackson also praised Jeb Stuart's role in the short contest.[126]

In his first action as a brigade commander, Jackson performed well in a number of ways. He handled untested men in a calm and patient manner, with the result that they became soldiers smoothly and proudly. Jackson moved promptly to thwart the Union advance; in what would become one of his trademarks, he sent a flanking column to turn the enemy position as he unhesitatingly accepted the challenge of combat. When the high numerical superiority of the enemy became apparent, the Virginian dutifully obeyed his instructions and withdrew. He did so with rear-guard actions, blunting Union probes as he contested the ground all the way back to Martinsburg.

No great risks had been taken, no foolish moves made. The reticent colonel from VMI had faced enormous odds in manpower; but he had given more than he received and, with the same cool leadership, taken his men from danger. Of equal importance, and at a time when caution and uncertainty seemed to be the foundations of Confederate war policy, Jackson had lashed out at the enemy and won a success in spite of all the disadvantages. The news of this feat was inspiriting to every corner of the state. At Winchester, one soldier listened to accounts of the skirmish and then wrote in his diary, "Saw the cause then right for the first time."[127]

A vastly relieved Johnston read Jackson's message at sunset on July 2 and ordered his forces northward in support. Soon after daybreak the next morning, Johnston's main body joined Jackson's men at Darkesville—"not a village," a soldier noted, "only a farm-house near a fine spring." In that position, six miles south of Martinsburg, Johnston shook loose his brigades in battle array in full anticipation of a Federal attack. The Confederates waited four days. Nothing happened. One of Jackson's men commented: "Our troops were frequently drawn up in order of battle, and always 'fell in' as joyfully as the bridegroom hastens to the wedding; but each alarm proved false. . . . Our troops were eager to attack them, uncaring for odds; but Gen. Johnston held them back." The two opposing commanders had no intentions of risking anything by an assault.[128]

Jackson's troops got their first view of Johnston at Darkesville. "All were favorably impressed with his handsome and martial appearance," Lieutenant Lyle recalled. "He was built as trim as a game cock, dressed well and had a courtly and affable bearing that was very winning. The greenest civilian could have picked him out as the commander of the host." The Virginia regiments were so curious to see "Uncle Joe"

Johnston that they forgot to cheer him as he rode past. One of the general's staff sneered, "That brigade don't seem to be aware that other officers besides Jackson are around."[129]

"Uncle Joe" was not offended. In fact, Johnston spent part of the Darkesville stay praising Jackson and urging his promotion. The strict discipline that Jackson maintained had first attracted Johnston's approval. Jackson's "admirable courage & conduct" at Falling Waters convinced Johnston that his senior colonel—and Stuart as well—deserved advancement in rank. Johnston sent recommendations to that effect to Richmond on July 4—a couple of days too late to have any impact. Jackson's conduct at Falling Waters was the final leverage in a change-of-mind evolving inside the Confederate government. On July 3, Lee sent Jackson a brief message: "My dear general, I have the pleasure of sending you a commission of brigadier-general in the Provisional Army, and to feel that you merit it. May your advancement increase your usefulness to the State."[130]

The news did not reach Jackson until July 8, when Johnston abandoned his position in Patterson's front and returned to the greater security of Winchester. Jackson chafed at another retreat. The war was not going to end until battle settled the issues. Turning your back on an enemy who was in a forward and exposed position, and then retiring to a town full of idle soldiers, measles, mumps, and typhoid fever, was not Jackson's idea of tactics. "I want my brigade to feel that it can itself whip Patterson's whole army," he stated, "and I believe we can do it."[131]

As soon as he reluctantly settled in camp near the town that he would come to know so well, Jackson sent a letter to his wife. He concealed his disappointment at Johnston's lack of military initiative and wrote in tones both cheerful and spiritual. "I have been officially informed of my promotion to a Brigadier Generalcy of the Provisional Army of the Southern Confederacy. . . . My promotion is beyond what I anticipated, as I only expected it to be in the volunteer forces of the State. One of my greatest desires for advancement is the gratification it will give my darling, & of serving my country more efficiently. . . . I should be very ungrateful if I were not contented, and exceedingly thankful to our kind Heavenly Father. May his blessing ever rest on you is my fervent prayer."[132]

As evidence of his faith, Jackson always donated one tenth of his army pay to the church. At times during the war, his contribution exceeded the tithing level. His only comment on the matter was: "I do not want to come out of the war a richer man than when I entered it."[133]

Jackson's regiments camped on hills northeast of Winchester. Orders forbade the men from entering the town. Monotony descended heavily on the encampment. One officer in the brigade was convinced that the campsite had formerly been a "rendezvous for hogs from the number of fleas that exhibit themselves." Sickness—notably measles and typhoid fever—were also playing havoc inside the ranks of Jackson's brigade. In an Augusta County company that numbered fewer than 100 men when it entered service, twenty-one were in Winchester hospitals.

The new brigadier had his headquarters in Winchester. "The people here are very kind," he told Anna, "so much so that I have to decline many invitations to accept their hospitality. At present I am in a very comfortable building, but we are destitute of furniture, except such things as we have been able to gather together. I am very thankful to our Heavenly Father for having given me such a fine brigade."[134]

Jackson could also be thankful for divine protection. John Lyle described an incident that could have had fatal consequences. The general "reviewed the brigade one afternoon and came down the lines at top speed as if he were riding [in] a race. The command looked on in open-mouthed wonder at his seeming recklessness, and, when he passed the left regiment kept on over the hill, his Christian character was all that saved him from a suspicion that he had been 'imbibing' too frequently. His horse, we learned afterwards, was running away with him, altho, judging from his quiet demeanor whilst in front of us, one would not have suspected such to be the case. Jackson was not a graceful rider except when leading a charge, but, as the boys said, 'he stuck to the horse like a tick.'"[135]

On July 15, the 33d Virginia under Colonel Arthur C. Cummings became part of Jackson's brigade. Only eight companies of the regiment had been mustered, and one of them was armed with ancient flintlock muskets. Yet the 450 men were badly needed. Sickness and disease had ravaged the army so severely that the average regiment was at 500 men, or half-strength. Jackson was optimistic. "God will, I am satisfied, in His own good time and way, give us the victory."[136]

He told Anna of sleeping regularly outdoors and how agreeable it was to his health. "My table is rather poor," he noted, "but I usually get corn-bread. All things considered, however, I am doing well." When Mrs. Jackson later published this letter, she omitted a passage where Jackson addressed her complaint that he did not write often enough. Jackson reminded Anna of his habit of not writing, or having letters in transit, on the Sabbath. In a sermonic tone he added: "I have, through the blessing of God, never had occasion, after years of experience, to regret our system. Look how kind our Heavenly Father has prospered us. I feel well assured that in following our rule, which is Biblical, I am in the path of duty, & that no evil can come nigh [unto] me."[137]

10

EMERGENCE OF "STONEWALL"

THE CONFLICT OF THE 1860s has aptly been called the first complete railroad war. So vital a role did the "Iron Horse" play on both sides that one writer later entitled a book *Victory Rode the Rails*. In Virginia, the principal north-south railroad was the Orange and Alexandria. It stretched 148 miles from the Potomac River to Lynchburg in the center of the state. Thirty-four miles out of Alexandria, the O&A met the eastern end of the Manassas Gap Railroad. That line twisted through the Blue Ridge Mountains and curled up the Shenandoah Valley as far as Mt. Jackson. It was only seventy-seven miles in length, but the Manassas Gap connected all of the lower valley with all of northern Virginia. The two lines linked at Manassas Junction.

By July 1861, for Confederacy and Union alike, this was the most important military site north of Richmond. Some 22,000 Southern recruits were in a rough defensive line around the junction. In command of this untested aggregation was General P. G. T. Beauregard. A mercurial little Frenchman from Louisiana, Beauregard had much ambition and some ability. His ideas of war were always grandiose. Winfield Scott once described him as "a bulldog with his ears pinned back." Yet at this time, because of his successful direction of the Fort Sumter bombardment, Beauregard was the South's hero of the hour. He would have basked in the glory of his newly won reputation had he not been convinced that the Bull Run area was "absolutely unfavorable" for a defensive position.[1]

Optimism was equally lacking in Beauregard's adversary. Irvin McDowell was an 1838 West Point graduate who had never commanded in the field. At the outbreak of civil war, an admiring General Scott jumped McDowell from major to brigadier general and put him in command of the forces gathering at Washington. McDowell now had a mob of 33,000 recruits under his wing. They were not an army, and McDowell was not a leader; but when ordered by an impatient Federal government to take the field, McDowell had learned enough to know that he had to advance on Richmond. Victory, he was also aware, had to be via Manassas Junction in order to control the railroads on his flank and in his rear.

On July 16, McDowell started his armed crowd on the thirty-mile march from Washington toward Bull Run. Beauregard's 22,000 Confederates were waiting at the stream. Simple arithmetic told McDowell that if General Robert Patterson's Federals could hold Johnston's 11,000 Southerners in the valley, McDowell could confront Beauregard with superior numbers. Patterson's duty was clear and simple—to everyone but Patterson.

A sixty-nine-year-old Irishman who had worked himself up through the ranks of the army, Patterson had been Winfield Scott's second in command in Mexico. It was a useless position behind the dynamic Scott. By 1861, Patterson should have been in retirement, not in the field. Lacking any experience with an independent command, seeing pitfalls in every move, Patterson became a combination of bewilderment and vacillation in the lower Shenandoah Valley.

His first in a series of tactical errors came on the day that McDowell started his advance. Patterson's presence at Bunker Hill, only ten miles from Winchester, held Joseph E. Johnston firmly inside the town. Suddenly, the uneasy Union commander sidled to Charles Town in order to be a little closer to his Washington line of communication. That "adjustment" put Patterson twenty-three miles from Winchester, and it gave Johnston some breathing room.

That was the situation when, at 1 A.M. on Thursday, July 18, Johnston received a wire from the Confederate War Department. It informed him of McDowell's offensive and directed Johnston, "if practicable," to move as quickly as possible to Beauregard's assistance at Bull Run. An urgent call for help from Beauregard came an hour later. Johnston met with his brigade commanders in the darkness of early morning. The brigades were to prepare for an immediate move; Johnston arranged for the care of 1700 sick soldiers at Winchester, and he assigned two militia units to protect the town as much as they could.

Jeb Stuart's horsemen galloped off shortly after sunrise. They headed toward Charles Town to create dust and confusion while sealing off any avenues of reconnaissance that Patterson might think of exploiting. The ruse by Johnston's chief of cavalry worked perfectly. The entire day—and most of the next—passed with Federals unaware that Johnston's army was disappearing from their front.[2]

Jackson wasted no time implementing his orders. His brigade of 2611 men would be the van of Johnston's column. The fifty-seven-mile journey over the Blue Ridge to Manassas was to begin sometime around noon. Although Jackson had his men packed and ready in short order, he was not pleased at going to confront McDowell's force. For weeks, in the face of Johnston's caution, the new brigadier had displayed what Surgeon McGuire termed "impatience and anguish" that was "simply remarkable."[3] Now Johnston was abandoning Winchester, the valley, the northwest. Jackson's home country was being left to its own fate.

Near 1 P.M., Jackson's brigade took the lead and began marching down Market Street. "A proud sight it was," a Winchester matron wrote, "with the Confederate banners waving, the bands playing and the bayonets gleaming. . . . Many of the companies were made up of mere boys, but their earnest and joyous faces were fully as reassuring as the martial music was inspiriting."[4]

A stern-looking Jackson had ridden only a couple of blocks when Robert Y. Conrad and several other businessmen stopped him. The group was upset at Winchester being deserted. "General Jackson," Conrad stated, "are you going to take these Virginia boys away from here, and leave us to the horde of Yankees who are coming down upon us? Let the other people go and you stay here!" Jackson answered abruptly: "I am a soldier and obey orders." Yet, a member of his staff noted, "his face was more full of mental anguish and grief than I had ever seen it before."[5]

The long line of Confederates wound slowly on the Millwood Pike south and east toward the Blue Ridge. Troops marched at a leisurely pace because the men had no idea where they were going. Some thought that the army was moving to block a Federal thrust from Charles Town; others concluded that the brigades were shifting position to areas where the water was better.[6] By the time Jackson's Virginians had advanced five miles, it was mid-afternoon and the rear of the Confederate force had cleared Winchester. Johnston halted the column. Regimental adjutants then read to their respective units a communique:

> The Commanding General directs the Regiments to be informed, immediately after they have left the city, that General Beauregard is being attacked by overwhelming forces. He has been ordered by the Government to his assistance, and is now marching across the Blue Ridge upon the enemy.
>
> General Patterson and his command have gone out of the way to Harper's Ferry and are not in reach. Every moment now is precious, and the General hopes that his soldiers will step out and keep closed, for this march is a forced march to save the country.

After hearing "this stirring appeal," Jackson observed, "the soldiers rent the air with shouts of joy, and all was eagerness and animation where before there had been only lagging and uninterested obedience." Lexington's John Lyle put it more enthusiastically: "As to stepping out like men as the general asked them to do, they hit the road at a pace that would have landed them that night at Manassas, fifty miles away."[7]

Johnston did not agree with Lyle's assessment. "The discouragement of that day's march to one accustomed, like myself, to the steady gait of regular soldiers, is indescribable." He began to "despair of joining General Beauregard in time to aid him." When it took over nine hours to cover the thirteen miles to the Shenandoah River, the general's patience vanished. He sent Major Whiting ahead to Piedmont Station, the nearest depot on the Manassas Gap Railroad, to arrange for one or more trains to carry the infantry the remaining thirty-four miles of the trip.[8]

Interestingly, and for an officer who thrived on alacrity, Jackson displayed no concern over the alleged slow pace. He halted his men for an hour at Millwood, where water was abundant and food from "the ladies of the surrounding country" was bountiful. The march then resumed. Two miles beyond Millwood, the Virginians reached Berry's Ferry at the Shenandoah River. "The water was waist deep," Jackson noted, "but the men gallantly waded the river." Actually, troops happily entered the water to wash away layers of dust and perspiration. As for the Shenandoah being waist-deep, Lieutenant Lyle commented: "That depended on the height of the man. It struck Henry Myers and Jack McCaughtry about the neck." Surgeon Daniel B. Conrad of the 2d Virginia stated, "I did not see my mare for two days; nearly a dozen cousins and brothers and other relatives had to use her in the crossing."[9]

Ashby's Gap in the Blue Ridge loomed straight ahead. Weary troops who had already tramped thirteen miles to cross the Shenandoah River now ascended the Blue Ridge on a dry but hard road. They stumbled in the dark over the crest and eased down the eastern slope. The column leveled out into the rolling Piedmont country.

Near 2 A.M., Jackson led the head of his column into the village of Paris. Many were all but out on their feet. Jackson called a halt and directed the soldiers to get a few hours' rest.

What occurred thereafter in the night became one of the early and adored fables of Confederate literature. It is known as the "lone sentry" story. Part of its origin was Jackson himself. In a subsequent letter to Anna, he declared: "My men were so exhausted that I let them sleep while I kept watch myself." He did not mean that he remained awake all night to stand guard over them. This made his statement only partially true and strongly misleading. Mrs. Jackson sought to correct it, but largely to no avail. A number of early biographers—Robert L. Dabney and G. F. R. Henderson, for example—adorned the quotation by Jackson and presented it at the least out of context. Other writers, including veterans whose memories had been "refreshed," joined in the chorus. One wrote a commemorative poem about Jackson the lone sentry; another went so far as to assert: "All night he rode round that lonely camp, a lonesome sentinel for that brave but weary . . . body. . . . And when glorious morning broke the soldiers woke fresh and ready for action, all unconscious of the noble vigil kept over their slumbers."[10]

Surviving evidence, plus common sense, prove otherwise. Overlooked in Mrs. Jackson's narrative is what she added after the Jackson statement. Once the troops bedded down, she wrote, her husband walked at least once around the camp, then leaned watchfully against a fence until an unnamed member of his staff volunteered to maintain the vigil in his stead. Whereupon Jackson "threw his own wearied form down upon a bed of leaves in a fence corner" and slept soundly for an hour or two. Harvey Hill, Jackson's brother-in-law, challenged even that version. The whole "lone sentry" incident, Hill snarled, was "monstrously absurd, and reflects but little credit on Jackson as a soldier."[11]

For once, the outspoken Hill was correct. With Jackson's brigade isolated from the rest of Johnston's army by a mountain and a river, and with the likelihood strong that enemy troops were somewhere in the Piedmont region, Jackson would not have posted a single guard—even himself—to provide safety for over 2600 men. The bivouac was well patrolled that night and every night. Further, the previously unidentified staff member was Surgeon Hunter McGuire. He and Jackson propped against a fence while the infantry filed into the hamlet and found resting places. Jackson insisted on sitting up until Captain Pendleton and his artillery caught up with the column. The minutes became an hour. Seeing how fatigued Jackson was, McGuire volunteered to wait for the guns while he urged the general to lie down and rest. Jackson finally agreed and slept until the predawn hour.[12]

Jackson had his men on the road by the time the sun climbed over the horizon. Several exaggerated reports of a fight at Manassas the previous day circulated through the ranks. By 8 A.M., Confederates had covered the six miles to Piedmont Station. There, while undergoing "vexacious delays" waiting for trains to arrive, famished soldiers gobbled down the first food they had received since breakfast the previous morning.

Many were still eating as they boarded a line of Manassas Gap freight and cattle cars. "We packed ourselves like so many pins and needles," Surgeon Conrad stated, "and, as safety for engine and cars was more essential than speed, for we had one engine only . . . we slowly jolted the entire day."[13]

The thirty-four-mile trip took eight hours, "without much suffering to my men or to myself," Jackson told his wife. A more observant member of the 2d Virginia commented: "All along the road the people greeted us with shouts of joy. The ladies waved their handkerchiefs and bid us 'God speed' at every station. Eatables were offered us in abundance."[14] Completely lost on the recruits was the fact that for one of the first times in history, they were part of a large-scale movement of troops to battle by means of a railroad.

Late-afternoon storm clouds were gathering when the men reached the end of the line and detrained in farm country broken by pine woods. Manassas Junction consisted of a half-dozen nondescript frame houses and a rudely constructed building that served as a depot. The place gave no hint of having any strategic importance whatsoever.

Jackson was there only long enough to obtain directions to army headquarters. He then rode off to get orders. Beauregard had summoned his six brigade commanders for a conference at the Wilmer McLean farmhouse, and they were in earnest conversation when Jackson entered the room and reported the arrival of his 2600 soldiers.

Beauregard was shocked. He had expected the valley forces to come in on the Federal right flank, not join the main army. Could the bulk of Johnston's forces strike McDowell's flank? Beauregard asked.

The newly arrived brigadier was somewhat uncomfortable in the presence of high-ranking officers he did not know. At times like that, reticence became Jackson's armor. He replied simply that a flank movement was unlikely because Johnston was coming east by train. Beauregard thought Jackson mistaken about Johnston's route, while at least one of the other officers in the room found Jackson's answer as curt as his manner was unimpressive. The commanding general dismissed Jackson with instructions where to place his brigade.

Unperturbed by the reception, Jackson led his tired men three miles due north from the junction through a downpour to a pine thicket alongside the road. A mile ahead was Blackburn's Ford, the center of Beauregard's overextended defense line along Bull Run and the scene on the previous day of a Federal probe. That sharp fight had convinced Federal General McDowell of the bloody cost of trying to force his way directly across the stream. Jackson's men found what shelter they could from the rain and quickly bedded down for the night.[15]

Saturday, July 20, was hot and humid. Late in the morning, some of the valley recruits walked up toward Blackburn's Ford to inspect the site of the heavy skirmish two days earlier. "A line of fresh dug graves was rather depressing," one of Jackson's men stated. "The trees were lopped and mangled by shot and perforated by minnie balls. The short, dry grass showed in many spots a dark, chocolate hue, spreading irregularly like a map, which the next day became a too familiar sight."[16]

Beauregard made his rounds at some point in the morning. He halted to greet Jackson; but seeing the brigadier stretched out on the ground, sound asleep, Beauregard refused to allow soldiers to awaken him. Later in the day, while the men were "lying on our arms, living on ship biscuit [hardtack] which have about as much substance in them as so much shavings," Jackson inspected the unfamiliar country.[17]

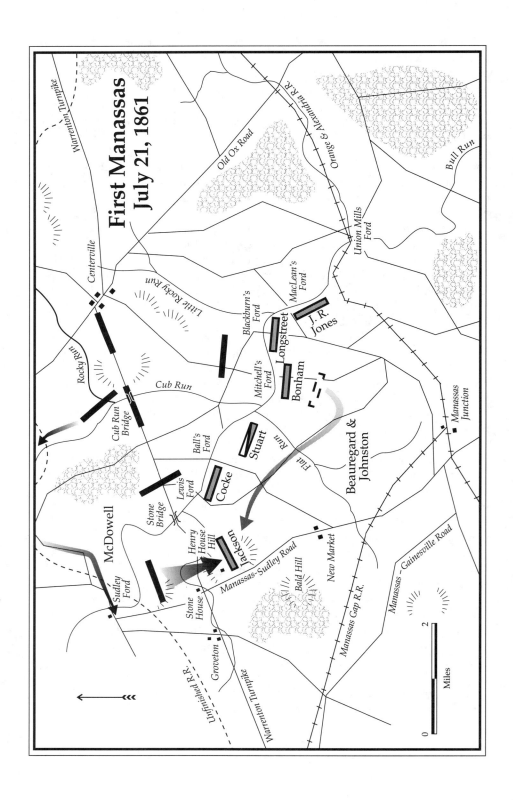

The dominant stream in the area offered no enticement to the valley troops. Charles Wight of the 27th Virginia complained, "The water we use is from Bull Run and is so gritty and muddy that it is as hard to take as a dose of oil."[18]

Bull Run meandered basically west to east and in places resembled a huge moat. Both banks, but especially the southern side, were steep and provided a good defense. The eight-mile front established by Beauregard followed the convolutions of Bull Run and blocked no fewer than ten long-used fords across the stream.

To the south behind the Southern line was a plateau on which stood Manassas Junction and Beauregard's main supply base. Several small creeks sliced the high ground into a series of hills and gentle slopes. The most important of those streams was Young's Branch. It was four to five miles west of Jackson's position, and it wrapped around two sides of the commanding eminence known as Henry House Hill.

At midday, Johnston arrived at Manassas with the brigades of Barnard E. Bee and Francis S. Bartow. Arnold Elzey's regiments were en route from the valley, along with the new brigade of Colonel Jubal A. Early. Johnston's additions gave Beauregard 32,000 men, only 1000 fewer than his Union opponent. While Beauregard thought in offensive terms, Johnston habitually argued the value of defense. By late Saturday evening, both sides knew that McDowell was poised to attack the next day. Beauregard concluded to relieve the pressure on his line by assaulting the Federal left (or eastern) flank near Centreville. He was confident that such a strike would throw the enemy off balance and bring victory to the South by noon. The major weakness in Beauregard's elaborate scheme was the assumption that McDowell would stand still while the Confederate attack unfolded.[19]

Meanwhile, McDowell's search for an undefended crossing of Bull Run had finally brought reward. Sudley Ford, to the north of the Confederate left flank, was unguarded. The Union commander resolved to make a feint against Beauregard's right while some 13,000 Federals made a nighttime march in the opposite direction to Sudley Ford. They would cross Bull Run, sweep around Beauregard's left, and turn the Southern dream of independence into history.

As a result of such planning on the two sides, daylight on July 21 found Confederate and Union forces alike leaning heavily toward their right, preparing to deliver flank attacks. The nature of the battle became established when McDowell unleashed his offensive first.

Jackson was awake and on his knees hours before dawn. Many things merited his prayers. This was Sunday, the Lord's day, the acme of every week; thanksgiving must be offered for all the gifts of life that Jackson enjoyed. The day was also Anna's thirtieth birthday. Praise of her being and of her love, and pleas for her continued protection, must be sent heavenward. The prevailing concern, however, was over a battle that was imminent. Now, at last, Jackson would wield the sword of God against the infidel who would desecrate his sacred homeland. Now he could begin the long but holy task of lifting the Almighty's scourge from the country and obtaining God's blessing on the most faithful side. It was fitting that the day was the Sabbath. Fighting for the Father on His day seemed righteous as well as sublime.

Jackson roused his men sometime after 3 A.M. and permitted them a hasty breakfast. Then came what most of the troops regarded as strange preparations for battle.

First they received white cotton strips to tie around hats and arms so that in the melee they could be recognized by friends. "We presented the appearance of so many lunatics," a Staunton infantryman complained. Next came a watchword and signal to be used throughout the day. When encountering an unidentified soldier, the Virginian was to strike his left breast with his right hand and shout: "Our homes!" This order produced guffaws in the ranks. Who was going to remember all of that in the heat of battle? How often were the men supposed to stop fighting and go through the procedure? One 5th Virginia recruit added, "They did not tell us that while we were going through this Masonic performance, we thus gave the other fellow an opportunity to blow our brains out."[20]

Cynical remarks to the contrary, Old Jack had ordered the procedures. Young enlistees seeking to become mature soldiers did as they were told.

To add to the confusion of that day, the First Brigade was wearing gray while its commander was attired still in the VMI blue faculty member's uniform. The only difference in the garb since Jackson's departure from Lexington was that the epaulets denoted a brigadier general rather than a major.

At 4 A.M., Jackson received a request from General James Longstreet for two regiments to reinforce the main line at Blackburn's Ford.[21] They were sent forward at once through the quiet woods. Gunfire off to the west shattered the stillness at 5 A.M., followed thereafter by an order from Beauregard for Jackson's brigade to move in support of General Milledge L. Bonham's Carolina brigade at Mitchell's Ford. Yet it was soon apparent that Beauregard had been traumatized by the Federal offensive in advance of his own.

He began issuing orders and counter-orders with almost reckless abandon. Units were soon rushing here, there, and back to here. Jackson had difficulty in unravelling successive directives to support Bonham in the center, to support Colonel P. St. George Cocke's brigade on the far left, and to support both Bonham and Cocke simultaneously. Beauregard's aide, Colonel Alexander Chisholm, had the embarrassing task of alerting Jackson of each desired movement. Jackson glossed over it in his official report. His only comment was, "These instructions were executed in the order in which they were given."[22]

Around 9:30 an urgent dispatch reached Jackson from Cocke (whom he had known in the prewar years). Federals were pressing in on the Confederate left; Jackson was needed quickly in that sector to guard the stone bridge over which the Warrenton Turnpike crossed Bull Run. Jackson wasted no time putting his regiments on a narrow road leading west. The trail passed through a wide belt of scrub oak and pine before breaking into open country.

Jackson quickened the pace. "At the time," a member of the 4th Virginia stated, "there was cannon firing all along our line, but the heaviest was on our left, where the sharp rattle of musketry plainly told us that there the work had begun." A soldier from the upper valley sprinkled his account of the march with a liberal dose of drama. "Our brigade was ordered to double-quick for about five miles to the extreme left . . . running that distance like panting dogs with flopping tongues, with our mouths and throats full of the impalpable red dust of that red clay country, thirsting for water almost unto death, and worn and weary indescribably."[23]

Confederate apprehensions about the left flank were more than justified. Throughout the morning, thousands of Federals had been pressing hard against some 900 Southerners under General Nathan G. "Shanks" Evans. The grossly outnumbered force waged a desperate defense north of the Warrenton Turnpike. Evans soon got help from 2800 men under General Bee and Colonel Bartow of Johnston's contingent. In woods and along fences, the battle raged.

Seemingly endless numbers of blueclad troops began lapping around both Confederate flanks. The Southerners fell back in the direction of Henry Hill. Union soldiers stopped to rest on Matthews Hill, on the north side of the turnpike across from the end of the Confederate line. That delay gave Jackson time to get into position.[24]

Jackson's regiments arrived in the stone bridge area before 11 A.M. The noise of battle to the immediate west was deafening. "I had reason to believe that General Bee was hard pressed by the enemy," Jackson stated. Without orders, and without seeking any, "I marched to his assistance, notifying him at the same time that I was advancing to his support."[25]

One more time the valley units shifted position. This move brought no muttering from within the ranks. Combat was near, and help was needed. Jackson's column, four men abreast, emerged from some woods onto the eastern edge of Henry Hill and found itself in the midst of a mass of disorganized troops withdrawing rapidly. Bee's regiments were falling apart.

A 4th Virginia soldier observed that "the wounded commenced passing us, some with the blood streaming down their faces, some with legs broken and hobbling along assisted by a comrade, and some seriously wounded and borne on stretchers. Those who could talk told us that their commands were cut all to pieces and the day lost. Such talk was very inspiriting to raw troops. It was calculated to make a boy wish himself a thousand miles away and in the trundle bed at his mother's house."[26]

After halting his men in order to keep his lines intact, Jackson encountered Captain John Imboden. He had been helpful in organizing the artillery at Harpers Ferry, but now he was angrily leading three guns of his Staunton Artillery to the rear. Imboden had attempted to provide cover from Henry Hill but instead had taken a beating from Union batteries. He proceeded to give Jackson a long and profane account of the one-sided contest. Jackson waited politely for the first open moment, then said: "I'll support your battery. Unlimber right here."

Imboden had but three rounds of ammunition left. He suggested going to the rear to fill his caissons and then returning. "No, not now," Jackson replied. A new defense line had to be established to give at least the appearance of strength. "Wait till the other guns get here." Imboden turned his three cannon around at a point 300 yards from the Henry House.[27]

Jackson rode slowly up onto the hill. His eyes swept over the terrain in search of the strongest defensive position he could find. The importunity of the moment was critically clear: unless Henry Hill remained in Confederate hands, the enemy would fatally turn the flank. Jackson saw that the hilltop was a gently rolling and expansive plateau. Henry House was on the northwestern shoulder; open ground provided unobstructed vision save for small clumps of thickets on the eastern and southeastern edges. Behind Jackson, to the south, was a line of young pines that merged into a denser woodland near a secondary road between Warrenton and Alexandria.

Had Jackson been the flighty, battle-prone commander as many officials in Richmond considered him, he would have marched his men forward straight into the enemy ranks—or at least far enough to provide close support to the retreating troops of Evans and Bee. He did neither. Stabilization and surprise were the elements Jackson saw to gaining the upper hand. Therefore, rather than place his line on the northwestern face of Henry Hill, nearest to and in full view of the enemy, Jackson selected the back side or "reverse slope" to make his stand.

Several reasons prompted this decision. Inside the pines behind the hilltop, his line would be invisible to Federals massing on Matthews Hill for a renewal of the attack. The woodland offered some protection from Union artillery fire beginning to rake the area. Further, artillery professor Jackson saw that he could fire his guns from the crest, load in safety after recoil sent the pieces behind the crest, then push the cannon forward for the next volley.

From the edge of the woods, Jackson would have an open field of fire some 300 yards deep. All the while, Young's Branch protected his right flank while thick timber covered his left. Finally, from his stationary position, Jackson would not become entangled with Confederates still falling back up and over the hill.[28]

The temperature was approaching the low eighties, with no breeze and but a hint of clouds in the sky. For an hour, amid exploding enemy shells, drifting gunsmoke, and the confusion of a broken Confederate line streaming past, Jackson carefully put his force into position. He recalled Imboden's three cannon to the front, and brought up Pendleton's Rockbridge Artillery and two guns of Captain Philip B. Stanard's Thomas Artillery from Richmond. The nine guns formed an unbroken and formidable line.[29]

Jackson next ensured that infantry support fully enveloped the guns. The battle line he established faced northwestward and extended for 700 yards. Kenton Harper's 5th Virginia took position on the right and deflected inward to maximize protection of the guns. James Preston's 4th and John Echols's 27th Virginia formed into four lines behind the batteries. James Allen's 2d Virginia was to the immediate left of the guns, while the newest addition to the brigade—Colonel Arthur Cummings's undersized 33d Virginia—occupied the extreme left of Jackson's line.

This 400-man regiment (only eight of the ten companies were present) was new to the ways of the army. Its line stretched into pine trees. The left flank was neither refused nor anchored on good defensible ground. Jackson had enough concern over this weakness to request Jeb Stuart's cavalry as a buttress on the left flank.[30]

Beauregard and Johnston rode into the area at noon. Within the next two hours, they would rush additional men and guns in support of Jackson. The two Confederate commanders doubtless knew that they no longer had direct control over the action. The First Virginia Brigade and its leader were the key to how this contest would turn.

For two hours and forty minutes, Jackson's men lay at the edge of the woods while opposing artillery kept up an uninterrupted roar. For awhile, it was a one-sided contest. Jackson had eight old six-pounders trying to maintain a contest with twenty-four Federal pieces, mostly rifled guns.[31] The sun was hot, the men thirsty. Exploding shells made the earth tremble, sent trees splintering, and filled the air with more noise than any man had ever heard.

The Union bombardment also produced casualties. At least twenty-seven members of the 4th Virginia behind Jackson's batteries were killed or wounded by shell fire. Many of the Confederates felt like Lieutenant Lyle. "In strict confidence, I tell you, I was scared. I said all the prayers I knew, even 'Now I lay me down to sleep,' and threw in some shorter catechisms and Scripture for good measure." What steadied those civilian soldiers was Jackson. He rode slowly back and forth along the line—moving "about in that shower of death as calmly as a farmer about his farm when the seasons are good," one soldier stated in admiration. A young member of the 33d Virginia watched Jackson and concluded that all former VMI cadets in the ranks that day "saw the warrior and forgot the eccentric man."[32]

Still another soldier saw at once the essence of Jackson. "A closer glance easily penetrated his apparent tranquility and carelessness. The trust in God, and utter reliance on His will was surely there—but no apathetic calmness. The blaze of the eye . . . was unmistakable—there plainly was a soul on fire with deep feeling, and the ardor of battle. A slumbering volcano clearly burned beneath that face so calm and collected." While his face seemed somewhat pale, Jackson's whole being reflected a brutal resolve. An aura of confidence seemed to surround him. So did Jackson's quiet words: "Steady, men, steady! All's well!"[33] He offered those reassurances despite the fact that he had been painfully wounded.

At Manassas, Jackson displayed a gesture he would repeat in many engagements. In unannounced fashion he would thrust his left arm toward the sky with the palm facing forward. Many soldiers dismissed the action as just another of Jackson's eccentricities; others were convinced he was offering an oblation for victory to the Commanding Father. At some point during the bitter exchange of artillery fire, Jackson was talking to Captain Imboden and threw up his arm. He instantly jerked it down. Blood was pouring from his hand. "General," Imboden said with alarm, "you are wounded." A bullet or piece of shrapnel had fractured the middle finger. "Only a scratch, a mere scratch," Jackson answered as he wrapped a handkerchief around his hand and resumed the close watch of his lines.[34]

The broken regiments of Evans, Bee, and Bartow had crossed the bottom land of the Warrenton Turnpike, cut obliquely across part of Jackson's front, and taken cover in a ravine near Young's Branch on Jackson's right. Across the way, dust rolling skyward to signal the movement, Federals were descending Matthews Hill in a resumption of the attack. "The enemy were as thick as wheat in the field," a 2d Virginia soldier observed, "and the long lines of blue could not be counted." A newspaper correspondent looked over the field and concluded that "the fortunes of the day were dark. The remnants of the regiments . . . gave gloomy pictures of the scene and as up to this time . . . no point had been gained, the event was doubtful . . . hope seemed almost gone."[35]

Over on the right of Jackson's line, a solitary horseman came up from the bottom of

Henry Hill. The man was fully six feet tall, and he sat in the saddle with the mature bearing of a soldier. Jet-black eyes, dark mustache and goatee, long hair, and a general's uniform "made him the cynosure of all," one of Jackson's men commented. The officer reined to a halt inside the lines and inquired what troops they were. A surgeon identified the valley brigade and pointed to Jackson giving instructions. As the rider approached, Jackson instantly recognized his West Point friend and comrade-in-arms, Barnard Bee. The South Carolinian saluted quickly and, with understandable agitation, gave a quick report of the collapse of his lines. He suddenly exclaimed, "General, they are driving us!" Jackson looked to the northwest with brutal determination etched in his face. His reply was just as stern: "Sir, we will give them the bayonet."[36]

Now occurred one of those dramatic moments in history when legend is born. Bee had no high regard for the bayonet, but Jackson's resolve filled him with new confidence. The Carolinian galloped back to the ravine where officers were trying to untangle bits and pieces of units and establish a defensive line. Bee rode into the middle of the throng; pointing his sword toward the crest of Henry Hill, he shouted in a booming voice: "Look, men, there is Jackson standing like a stone wall! Let us determine to die here, and we will conquer! Follow me!" Bee would die there later in the day.[37] He gave to the Southern cause not only his life but also the most famous nickname in American military history.

Beauregard and Johnston were working furiously to get every available unit into line on the Confederate left. The Southern position slowly stiffened, then began to broaden. Reinforcements from fords to the south double-timed into the area. As units arrived, they went into line to the left and right of Jackson. His brigade had become the centerpiece of the Southern army.

Early in the afternoon, McDowell sought to apply more artillery pressure on the Confederates by ordering forward two regular batteries of eleven rifled guns under Captains James B. Ricketts and Charles Griffin. Ricketts had graduated from West Point in 1839 and was a victim of slow promotion in the army. Griffin finished at the academy a year behind Jackson. Both artillerymen were Union generals by the end of the Civil War. Advancing up Henry Hill with the Union guns were the 11th New York ("Ellsworth's Zouaves") and the 14th New York ("Red-legged Devils" from Brooklyn).

The two Union batteries moved bravely to an exposed position just south of Henry House and only 330 yards from Jackson's left flank. Seconds after unlimbering, the Union pieces were in a furious duel with Jackson's guns. A member of the 4th Virginia declared, "And then the strife was fiercest, and the thunder of the battle was loudest."[38]

Griffin shortly made a fatal mistake. He moved his guns forward 130 yards in order to gain a better enfilade fire. The 11th New York, in support of the battery, likewise advanced on the flank toward the pines where Jackson's left was located. A large contingent of Jeb Stuart's 1st Virginia Cavalry was also in the woods now, and the troopers had been fidgeting for action. Stuart sent his adjutant, Lieutenant William W. Blackford, to inform Jackson of the approaching enemy soldiers and of the readiness of the cavalry to do battle.

When Blackford gave Jackson the message, the general's stern visage gave way momentarily to a smile. Even though he was holding up his hand to minimize the pain, Jackson replied with a favorite expression: "That's good! That's good!" Blackford returned to Stuart with orders to strike the approaching Federals.[39]

Some 150 Southern horsemen charged up the Manassas-Sudley road on Jackson's left and slammed first into and then through the red-trousered Federals. The 11th New York "broke and fled" the field. In the meantime, with Jackson's batteries in defilade on the far edge of the hill, they were delivering far more damage than they were receiving. Simultaneous with the disintegration of the New York regiment, the 33d Virginia on the far left went into action on its own volition. Put more simply, the colonel of the 33d Virginia got tired of waiting.

Arthur C. Cummings was an 1845 VMI graduate and an attorney and farmer in Abingdon, Virginia. Like Jackson, he had won brevet promotions to major in the Mexican War. Cummings was aware that his little regiment consisted of "undrilled and undisciplined" youths who were little more than "raw recruits." Jackson earlier that day had warned the colonel to beware of Federals on his flank. If any arrived, Cummings was to wait until they "were within thirty paces, and then to fire and charge bayonets." Soon, in spite of the dissolution of the 11th New York on the far left, the two Federal batteries plus the 14th New York and the 1st Michigan were all firing at Cummings's Virginians. This, he said, "caused considerable confusion in a part of the regiment." Concluding that his inexperienced command was close to falling apart, and not concerned about any thirty-yard firing distance, Cummings jumped out in front of his line and shouted for the men to charge the closest enemy battery. Jackson would afterwards understate in his official report that "one of [the enemy's] Batteries was thrown so near to Col. Cummings, that it fell into his hands in consequence of his having made a gallant charge on it with his regiment."[40] Yet there was a good deal more to the story.

At this opening stage of the war, neither side had fully adopted one color for its uniforms. The 33d Virginia that day was wearing blue. In the smoke and confusion of battle, Union gunners mistook the advancing Virginians as more Federals moving up in support of the guns. The men of the 33d Regiment scaled a snake-rail fence, got to within seventy yards of Griffin's battery, then knelt and delivered a murderous volley that left artillerists and horses around the guns sprawled amidst the cannon.

Ricketts went down with multiple wounds, but Griffin managed to draw off four of the guns. With a shout, Cummings's men raced forward and took possession of the other rifled pieces. This act marked the first real Confederate success of the day.

Celebration over the capture left the 33d Virginia somewhat disorganized. The regiment was also far in advance of the line and all by itself. At that moment, Union infantry appeared in a rough battle line. It was the 14th New York, its red trousers, trimmed jackets, and red kepis startling contrasts in the smoke of battle. The Brooklyn soldiers quickly overlapped the left of Cummings's line, then delivered a concentrated volley of musketry into the Confederates—"cutting us to pieces," the 33d Virginia's John Casler stated.[41] A third of Cummings's regiment was killed or wounded around the guns.

No alternative remained for the Virginians but to fall back. Some did so with such alacrity that they dashed through the ranks of the 2d Virginia and sent much of that unit into confusion. Colonel James W. Allen quickly ordered his three left-most companies to draw back at an angle to present a more solid front. The colonel's directive was misunderstood: the entire regiment began falling back with the 33d Virginia. Allen had lost his right eye in a teenage accident; now a wood fragment struck him in the good eye. For a time Allen was blind, a situation that made for still greater confusion on Jackson's left.

An obviously excited junior officer in the 33d Virginia rushed up to Jackson. "General! The day is going against us!" he shouted. Jackson gave the man a cold stare and replied in a low tone: "If you think so, sir, you had better not say anything about it."[42]

Federal infantry were advancing up Henry Hill and past the neutralized batteries of Ricketts and Griffin. No feints or flanking movements this time—McDowell was making a pure frontal assault, and in numbers that gave the Federals two-to-one superiority on the field. Jackson watched their progress for only a moment, then rode quickly to the 4th and 27th Virginia behind his batteries. According to Private John B. Jones of the 4th, Jackson's shouted instructions to both regiments were the same: "Reserve your fire until they come within fifty yards! Then fire and give them the bayonet! And when you charge, yell like furies!"[43]

The Federals closed. Only shouting distance separated the two sides. Suddenly Jackson's line—infantry and artillery together—poured an intense fire into the Union ranks. Scores of enemy soldiers fell to the ground dead or badly wounded; the others sought to reform for another try. Again a blast of balls and shells from Jackson's position drove them back. Stunned, the Federals reeled momentarily before surging forward a third time. They got to within feet of the Virginians. More concentrated fire caused the Union line to waver, then break. New York survivors stumbled back down Henry Hill.

This was the moment for counterattack! Beauregard concluded. The order went to Jackson, who stated: "The advance of the enemy having reached a position which called for the use of the bayonet, I gave the command."[44]

It was 3:30 when the five Virginia regiments sprang forward. One soldier who had been crouching in the woods for hours exclaimed: "Believe me, it was a relief for our boys to get up from their dangerous position and dash forward in the charge."[45]

Now the men could charge the enemy and, in Jackson's words, "yell like furies!" They did both, and at that moment the world heard for the first time the screams of what became known as the "Rebel yell." A Confederate who later became an Episcopal priest perhaps gave the fullest description: "There was in that sound something of the shrill horror of the boy's fierce play of Indian warfare; something of the exultant shout to hounds when the deer breaks cover; something of the wild laughter of reckless youth that mocks at death; something of the growl of hunted beast whose lair has been invaded; and then the deeper tones of that wordless rage of the strong man as he leaps to guard the threshold of his home." Another soldier gave a succinct comparison: The Federals "all cheer as one man. . . . The Rebels cheer like a lot of school boys, every man for himself."[46]

For the next thirty minutes, bitter fighting surged back and forth across the Henry farm. Three times Confederates captured and recaptured the batteries of Ricketts and Griffin. Musket balls filled the air and mingled with the explosions of artillery shells. Bayonets and clubbed muskets were in use everywhere. Jackson's whole line was sweeping slowly downhill, the men leaning forward as if they were confronting a strong wind. Bartow died in battle; Bee went down, mortally wounded. So did Captain Otis H. Tillinghast, a Union quartermaster who had served with Jackson back in 1849 at Fort Hamilton. He fell while voluntarily helping Griffin's guns get back into action.

The momentum was now with the Confederates. Beauregard and Johnston were hurling regiments into battle as fast as they could find them. McDowell was doing the same. The battle began to resemble a crowd throwing logs onto a huge bonfire. It was past mid-afternoon, Beauregard noted, when Jackson's brigade "pierced the enemy's center with the determination of veterans and the spirit of men who fight for a sacred cause." Jackson undoubtedly appreciated that thought.[47]

His brigade and other units swept across the level ground almost to the Warrenton Turnpike. In rushing forward so quickly, however, the Confederates left their own flanks unprotected. McDowell frantically sent four brigades forward in a new counterattack, and within fifteen minutes the Federals reclaimed much of the lost ground. The din of battle continued unabated while a July sun baked both sides unmercifully.

At one point, Jackson rode down toward the Young's Branch ravine to round up a sizable number of stragglers and get them back into the fight. He got them in reasonable order and assigned officers to lead the way. Those troops needed some sort of impetus. "Now if you see any Yankees coming out of those pines up there," he shouted in a high-pitched voice while pointing to the front, "give them . . . pepper!" The men hooted good-naturedly over Jackson's attempt at profanity. Turning in his saddle as he rode back toward his lines, the general added, "And salt too!" This brought another outburst of laughter from the soldiers, one of whom shouted after Jackson, "That fellow is not much at cussin,' but something in a fight!"[48]

Clem Fishburne, who had been a groomsman at Jackson's second wedding and was now in the Rockbridge Artillery, was moved by Jackson's appearance a few minutes later. As the battle seemed to be building to a climax, Fishburne saw the general ride slowly toward the inferno of combat, "his chin cocked up as if he was expecting a rain." Jackson had his hand raised again—not in prayer but to ease the pain, Fishburne thought. Jackson's bay horse was limping from a thigh wound; one or more bullet holes had torn the bottom of the general's uniform coat.[49]

Shortly after 4 P.M., as McDowell braced to launch still another attack, two fresh brigades from Johnston's valley army rushed obliquely into battle. Their commanders, Jubal Early and E. Kirby Smith (soon wounded and succeeded by Arnold Elzey), led the men in separate and sweeping marches that brought them in on McDowell's unprotected right flank. These surprise onslaughts sent the Union army reeling backward.

It was now 4:40, and McDowell's great effort to end the Civil War at Manassas had failed. Union recruits that morning were now exhausted soldiers. They had fought as hard as they knew how; no fight was left in them. McDowell ordered a retreat. The problem was that the Union soldiers had no experience in making an orderly withdrawal under fire after losing a battle. It required an orderliness and steadiness lacking in the beaten Union army. What had been styled a Union army turned into a disorganized crowd of individuals with the single thought of getting back to Washington as quickly as possible. They collided with hundreds of civilians who had come out with picnic baskets to see the Civil War end, and they too were trying to get back to the Northern capital on the same road.

A massive traffic jam was developing. Parting artillery fire from Confederates blew up a wagon in the middle of Stone Bridge and blocked it to traffic. Then more fire knocked down another bridge farther up the road. Chaos replaced confusion among the Federal host. The retreating army became a wild mob several miles long and a hundred yards wide as soldiers and civilians raced each other for whatever safety the Northern capital offered.

Jackson and his men took no part in the brief pursuit of the Union army. They had made their stand on Henry Hill and successfully defended the height. Fittingly, the newly christened Stonewall Brigade took responsibility for securing the hill. Storm clouds rumbled overhead; with approaching darkness came a steady rain to calm a countryside transformed that day into a battlefield.

The last sounds of combat were drifting away to the east when Johnston rode onto the hill to congratulate Jackson for his conduct throughout the day. The commanding general noticed the bandaged hand and insisted that Jackson go at once for medical treatment. Jackson started to the rear. By then, throbbing pain was so intense that he stopped at the first field hospital he passed. Surgeons concluded that the finger must be amputated. As they went to get their instruments, Jackson silently mounted his horse and rode off in search of Dr. McGuire.

In a few minutes, Jackson found his brigade's first aid station beside Young's Branch at the northeastern foot of Henry Hill. Surgeon McGuire stopped ministering to an injured soldier and started toward the general. Jackson waved his good hand. "No, no, don't leave your patients for me. I am not much hurt. Attend to them first." McGuire assured Jackson that sufficient surgeons were present to handle all of the injuries. "Then you may dress mine," Jackson stated, "as I wish to go back to the field."

The surgeon's diagnosis was precise. "The middle finger of the hand was struck just below the articulation between the first and second phalanges. The ball struck the finger a little to one side, broke it, and carried off a small piece of the bone." Jackson watched McGuire's expressions.

He then said to the surgeon: "I expect you had better have it cut off, as those gentlemen advise. But what do you think of it?"

"Why, I think it can be saved," came the reply.

Obviously relieved, Jackson stated, "Then do what you think best." McGuire placed a splint on the palm side of the finger, covered the hand with lint, and put the arm in a sling. He told Jackson to soak the bandage regularly in cold water—a hydropathic treatment that met with Jackson's instant approval.[50]

A few minutes later, President Jefferson Davis rode into the hospital area. He had rushed from Richmond to Manassas to be near the battle. All the way from the train station, Davis had encountered stragglers who told him that the Confederate army was defeated. Davis galloped to Henry Hill, saw the mass of soldiers at the field hospital below, and hastened to that spot. Face pallid but eyes flashing, the former soldier stood up in the stirrups and shouted: "I am President Davis! All of you who are able follow me back to the field!"

Jackson did not recognize Davis, nor, with his hearing impairment, did he understand what the president said. McGuire told him who the rider was. According to the surgeon, Jackson immediately stood up, removed his cap, and shouted enthusiastically, "Three cheers for the President!" Then he exclaimed: "We have whipped them! They ran like dogs! Give me ten thousand men and I will take Washington tomorrow!"[51]

At least part of this incident is somewhat suspect where truth is concerned. This is the only time in Jackson's career when he supposedly led cheers for anyone, even Robert E. Lee. Moreover, Jackson rarely expressed personal opinion in the company of strangers, and he never made public boasts. Either Jefferson Davis failed to hear Jackson's offer, or he chose to overlook it in all of his writings. Yet the basic circumstances have a ring of authenticity.[52]

Two points in the story are indisputable. Jackson—perhaps alone among all Confederate leaders—had a full appreciation of the extent of the Southern victory at Manassas, and he afterwards spoke of the Confederate failure to follow up the success as one of the greatest mistakes of the war.[53]

The South should concentrate its forces for a massive offensive strike, Jackson always maintained. "We must give them [the enemy] no time to think," he once said to Anna. "We must bewilder them and keep them bewildered. Our fighting must be sharp, impetuous, continuous. We cannot stand a long war." Jackson repeated these thoughts in personal letters. His wife commented: "Nothing was so certain to him as that a protracted struggle would wear the South out. He believed that we had but one hope, and that was to press the Federals at every point, blindly, furiously, madly."[54]

Controversy would swirl for generations over why the Confederate army did not capitalize on its triumph and push toward the capture of Washington. Davis, Beauregard, and Johnston all went to their graves accusing one another of blocking a potentially successful pursuit. In truth, Confederate transportation and supply problems at the moment were acute, and the trauma of the nine-hour battle had surpassed all expectations. Despite Jackson's eagerness to launch a major counteroffensive, the Confederates were as disorganized in victory as the Federals were in defeat.

The South's failure to take military advantage of its success made the battle's casualties all the more painful to Jackson. McDowell's force had suffered 1575 men killed and wounded, plus another 1200 captured. Confederate losses approximated 2000 soldiers.

Jackson initially reported brigade losses at 111 killed, 368 wounded, and five missing. A day later, he added another five men to the missing list. This brought his total casualties to 489 men, roughly 16% percent of his strength. The 33d Virginia had lost one of every three men; in the 4th Virginia, both Colonel James Preston and Lieutenant Colonel Lewis Moore sustained career-ending wounds.

Soldiers always managed to find some levity amid the bloodshed of battle. A popular story in Jackson's brigade thereafter concerned the jackets of some Confederate artillerists. In the heated artillery duel on Henry Hill, sweating gunners removed their coats and hurled them into a pile. A Federal shell exploded on the spot and sent the jackets high into the air. One soldier kept looking up into the sky after pieces of coats drifted earthward. "What are you staring at?" a comrade asked. The soldier, continuing to gaze upward, replied: "I'm looking for the men that were blown out of those jackets!"[55]

Praise of Jackson inside the army was widespread. "The conduct of General Jackson," Beauregard was quick to announce, "requires mention as eminently that of an able, fearless soldier and sagacious commander, one fit to lead his efficient brigade. His prompt timely arrival before the plateau of the Henry house, and his judicious disposition of his troops, contributed much to the success of the day."[56]

Brigade pride abounded inside the valley regiments. Major Edwin "Ned" Lee of Jackson's staff informed his wife, "Our Brigade is almost immortalized; but for us the day would have been lost." Lieutenant Frank Paxton, one of Jackson's Lexington neighbors and a member of the 27th Virginia, solemnly informed his wife: "We spent Sunday last in the sacred work of achieving our nationality and independence. The work was nobly done, and it was the happiest day of my life, our wedding-day not excepted."[57]

Jackson felt expansive too, but he was quick to give credit where he thought credit was due. He told Jonathan Bennett: "You will find, when my report is published, that the First Brigade was to our army what the Imperial Guard was to the First Napoleon—that, through the blessing of God, it met the thus far victorious enemy and turned the fortunes of the day." In a letter to Anna, Jackson emphasized the divine assistance he received in the contest. "Yesterday we fought a great battle, & gained a great victory, for which all the glory is due to God alone. . . . My preservation was entirely due, as was the glorious victory, to our God, to whom be all the glory, honor & praise. Whilst great credit is due to other parts of our gallant army, God made my brigade more instrumental than any other in repulsing the main attack." His innate modesty then surfaced. "This is for your information only. Say nothing about it. Let others speak praise, not myself."[58]

Commendations in the press, however, went to Beauregard, Bee, Bartow, and South Carolina units. References to Jackson were limited and garbled. The Richmond newspapers made no mention of Jackson for a week after the battle. Then a Dispatch writer reported that in the action Jackson had a horse shot from under him and a finger blown off. Yet he remained "cool as a cucumber" as his men "butchered" Federal units right and left. It was August before his troops received this praise: "If Virginia does nothing more than was done by this Brigade on the field of Manassas, she has repelled the imputation of degeneracy, and proved that she is equal to her best days."[59]

At Manassas, Jackson had exhibited no greater heroism than any other Southern officer on the field. What made him stand out in the action was a grim determination covered by an outward display of calmness. He was not swept along by the rising tide of battle; the near panic that seized some generals at various points never entered Jackson's makeup.

In the intangibles of war, Jackson's brigade found itself the keystone of the entire Confederate line. It held fast when needed, and it assaulted victoriously when requested. The firmness and the performance of the valley soldiers were a reflection of the man who led them. Jackson's stonewall-like determination lay in small part to his being a soldier; the dominant factor came from his complete belief in the guidance of the Almighty. Conquering for God, Jackson was confident in battle. His faith permitted nothing less.

Jackson's regiments sought cover from the rain that Sunday night in nearby woods. Despite weariness and his wound, the general would not rest until he personally saw that rations had been distributed to all the units under his command. Men who were on or near the battlefield never forgot the post-battle hell that came late in the day. Surgeon John A. Hunter of Jackson's brigade called it "the most heart rending scene ever witnessed—men wounded in every conceivable form, some cursing, some praying, and some begging for help, some screaming at the top of their voices."[60]

Rain continued to pour well into Monday the 22d. Details went out into the storm and buried comrades in the mud. Jackson let neither victory nor weather compromise his disciplinary standards. Early in the day he issued an order prohibiting the discharge of firearms anywhere near the encampment, allowing no one to leave camp without written permission, and promising arrest to all violators.[61]

Not all was sternness with Jackson that day. He found time to send a quick note to his pastor back in Lexington. A crowd eager for news of the battle thronged the town post office when the mail arrived. Dr. William S. White immediately recognized Jackson's scrawl on the letter handed him. The minister cried out, "Now we shall know all the facts!" A hush settled over the townspeople. White then read the letter. "My dear pastor, in my tent last night, after a fatiguing day's service, I remembered that I had failed to send you my contribution for our colored Sunday school. Enclosed you will find a check for that object, which please acknowledge at your earliest convenience, and oblige yours faithfully, T. J. Jackson."[62]

Camp routine followed for a couple of days. Jackson insisted on daily periods of drill, for he knew that one battle did not make permanent soldiers. At the same time, as his men learned appreciatively, he had a genuine concern for their welfare. Johnston shifted the brigade back to an encampment near Mitchell's Ford.

Within hours, the men dubbed it "Camp Maggot" and "Camp Mud Hole." Sickening odors from the battleground became intolerable. ("Wee will Hav to burry the Yankeys today to keep them from stinking us to death," one Confederate noted.)[63] Drinking water, from creeks flowing through that area, had become polluted from bloated corpses in and along streams.

When sickness—notably typhoid fever—erupted, Jackson fired off a strong letter to Johnston. "I am apprehensive that unless the Brigade is changed to a more healthy location, especially so that it can get better water, many who ought to be preparing for hard campaign service will be unable to attend to any military duty by reason of sickness. I have not as yet succeeded in finding any suitable encampment, except that near Centreville to which I called the General's attention a few days since."[64]

Not surprisingly amid such filth, Jackson's wound became infected. He had followed McGuire's instructions painstakingly: Jackson spent hours at a time pouring cups of water over the hand. The contaminated water brought inflammation. Lieutenant Lyle paid him a visit and marveled at his power of endurance. "He wouldn't give any sign in public that his finger hurt him, keeping his face as serene as a May morning. . . . As I drew near I saw him sitting just inside the flap of his tent. He had the sore hand grasped in the other, and was nursing it and making wry faces as if in agony. When he became aware of my approach he took a Spartan grip on his nerves and muscles, and his reply, 'Better, thank you,' to my inquiry . . . was accompanied by a winning smile." All Jackson would say to Anna was, "My finger troubles me considerably, and renders it very difficult for me to write, as the wind blows my paper, and I can only use my right hand." He kept his left hand raised as much as possible in an effort to ease the pain. Jackson never completely broke the habit thereafter. Because he wrote so slowly, he more than once had to request an aide to hold the sheet of paper while he wrote.[65]

The only pleasant thing the soldiers remembered about Camp Maggot was the July 28 service of thanksgiving. Practically the entire brigade attended. Jackson sat in the front row as Chaplain Charles Miller preached from Psalms 34: "O, taste and see that the Lord is good." The congregation was very solemn throughout the service, one member of the brigade noted.[66]

On August 2, Jackson led the brigade through rain to a new campsite. It was eight miles north of Manassas and a mile east of Centreville. Indefatigable quartermaster John Harman had picked the site, so the encampment was named in his honor. Moving to a new camp, Captain James J. White of the 4th Virginia told his wife, was like going "from Hell to Heaven." A compatriot added that Camp Harman was ideally located "in a field, nearly surrounded by woods, within a step to the main road, well drained and sandy," with an abundance of uncontaminated springs nearby.[67]

Jackson established his headquarters less than a half-mile away on the estate of Philip Utterback. The staff pitched tents in the front yard of a spacious home atop a rise on the west side of the Warrenton Turnpike. "The place is elevated," young Sandie Pendleton of Jackson's staff noted, "& the air . . . as pure as our mountain air, and as soft & balmy as possible."[68]

Camp Harman would be the brigade's home for the next six weeks. The only major interruptions to camp routine were three false alarms that sent the men on forced marches to Fairfax Courthouse, six miles away. Army life became rather tranquil. Cleon Moore of the 2d Virginia noted that the soldiers amused themselves largely by reading and playing cards. "In the evening [we] would sit around the trees talking and smoking. Most of us got to be inveterate smokers." The 4th Virginia's John Lyle speculated that from Jackson's vantage point up at the Utterback house, "he must have witnessed some of the laziest company maneuvers ever performed this side of Mexico."[69]

Taskmaster Jackson did not allow an abundance of such laxity. Nor was it all quiet for the general. Throughout the move to Camp Harman and the constant pain from a hand that slowly recovered from infection, Jackson found it necessary to calm a very irritated wife. Anna was still at her family home near Charlotte. Local newspapers were extolling the battle deeds of South Carolina officers at Manassas and giving scant attention to the Virginian who, she was convinced, was most responsible for the victory. Jackson sought to appease Anna by writing: "You must not be concerned at seeing other parts of the army lauded, & my Brigade not mentioned. Truth is powerful & will prevail. When the reports are published, if not before, I expect to see justice done the noble body of patriots."[70]

Anna remained indignant in her letters. That led to an even longer plea for patience from her husband. "You think that the newspapers ought to say more about me," he wrote.

My Brigade is not a brigade of newspaper correspondents. I know that the 1st Brigade was the first to meet & pass the retreating forces, to push on with no other aid than the smiles of God. . . . I am well satisfied with what it did, & so are my Genls., Johnston & Beauregard.

It is not to be expected that I should receive the credit that Gen. Beauregard or Johnston would, because I am under them, but I am thankful to an ever kind Heavenly Father that He makes me content to await His own good time & pleasure for commendation, knowing that 'all things work together for any good.' Never distrust our God, who doeth all things well. In due time, He will make manifest all His pleasure, which is all His people should ever desire.

If my Brigade can always play an important & useful a part as in the last battle, I shall always be very grateful, I trust.[71]

By coincidence, and within a week after Jackson's last letter, Richmond newspapers published stories about his "distinguished participation" in the recent battle. One account concluded: "In person, General Jackson is nearly six feet high, with an erect, muscular, well knit frame. He has a fine eye, brown hair, and a full beard. His whole bearing indicates a man of iron will and stern courage, and marks him as one peculiarly 'fitted to command.'"[72]

The "iron will" that relaxed during the move to Camp Harman soon reappeared. Captain White told his wife that there was "nothing to do but drill, drill, drill, & obey orders. There is nothing of a man's individuality left." Another Lexington soldier commented, "The mounting of the guard resembled the parade of a regiment, so great was the number . . . detailed for such duty." Discipline was tight. "The guard house—two log pens without roofs—was always full of petty offenders."[73]

Sickness, shortages, weather, and complaints all went hand in hand in an army encampment. Greenbrier County's Andrew Cook wrote home from a field hospital: "I pitty the Soldier who has to be Sick in camp. the Sick Bed is a terror at home But there is no more comparison Between the 2 than there is Between Paradise and Purgatory."[74]

Jacob Click told his sweetheart back in Rockingham County: "thare are som whers in a bout a hunderd and thirty sick in our regiment. . . . this is the pores cuntry that I ever saw in my life and the pores peple too." Ted Barclay of Lexington seconded those thoughts. "They say the country is so poor that the rabbits and foxes carry haversacks between blackberry bushes."[75]

Persistent rain throughout August dampened everything, including spirits. One soldier had to hold a spade over his small fire while he tried to boil coffee. A member of the 4th Virginia told the homefolk, "The inclemency of the weather cuts short our foraging expeditions, and nothing is left but to loll about in our tents and kill flies." Former Montgomery County farmer William Switzer was not alone in his opinion about the present situation. "I tell you I am pintedly tired of this thing playing the

Soldier, for it is not the thing it is cracked up to be." One of Switzer's superiors, Lieutenant Jonathan Evans, added his voice to the chorus: "Cous, it is no place for a sick man. I never saw a set of fellows want to leave a place so bad in my life."[76]

Furloughs became commonplace in parts of the Confederate army, but not in Jackson's brigade. The general expected his men to share his rigid devotion to duty. He neither took leave nor granted it.

Late in August, Colonel Kenton Harper of the 5th Virginia learned that his wife had fallen ill in Staunton and was not expected to live. Harper submitted an application for an emergency furlough. Jackson denied the request. The agitated subordinate made a personal appeal. When it was obvious that Jackson was not going to bend, Harper cried out emotionally: "General, General, my wife is dying! I must see her!" A look of sadness swept over the general's face; then he said earnestly, "Man, do you love your wife more than your country?" Jackson turned away, ending the conversation.

The colonel promptly resigned his commission. In the same mail that brought acceptance of the resignation, came a note informing Harper of the death of his wife. Harboring deep and permanent bitterness, Harper returned to an empty home in Staunton.

Such opinions did not bother Jackson. He found a new commander for the 5th Virginia and turned his attention elsewhere. "The success of our cause," he told Anna, "is the earthly object near my heart, and if I know myself, all I am and have is at the service of my country."[77]

During the Camp Harman stay, several people saw Jackson from varying perspectives. Joseph Packard was a minister and teacher in Fairfax County. He came to camp to visit his son, a member of the Rockbridge Artillery. Captain Pendleton introduced the cleric to Jackson, who promptly invited the two men to dine at his table. Even though Jackson's arm was in a sling, Packard stated, "he stood by us while we ate our dinner of bacon and corn bread, spread out of doors." Jackson was not merely a gracious host, Packard added. "He asked me to sketch for him all the roads to Washington."[78]

A number of clergymen visited the general at the Utterback home. Dr. William Brown, a kinsman of the Morrisons and editor of the periodical *The Central Presbyterian*, made at least one trip to the camp from Richmond. Jackson's Hampden-Sydney College acquaintance, Professor Robert L. Dabney, stayed long enough to conduct a worship service at headquarters. An Augusta County friend, the Reverend Francis McFarland, also shared Jackson's tent on at least one occasion.[79] Most enjoyable of all was a five-day visit from his pastor, Dr. William White.

The minister brought all of the news from Lexington about Jackson's friends, white and black. White was surprised to discover Jackson continuing his practice of morning and evening prayers. At the general's insistence, White led the worship for a couple of days. Then White asked Jackson late one afternoon to give the prayer. "Never while life lasts can I forget that prayer," White confessed. "He thanked God for sending his Pastor to visit the army and prayed that He would own & bless his ministrations both to officers and privates so that many souls might be saved. He gave thanks for what it had pleased God to do for the church at Lexington. . . . He then pled with much tenderness & fervor that God would baptize the whole army with His Holy Spirit, until my own hard heart was melted with penitence, gratitude and praise."[80]

After the two rose to their feet, Jackson asked White to teach him more about faith. The two men, both soldiers of the cross, talked until long past midnight. White freely admitted that "the Pastor received more instruction than he imparted."[81]

One cleric thought Jackson insane. He had come upon the general in the woods, walking back and forth, muttering incoherently to himself. When Dr. William Brown visited Jackson at the Centreville encampment, he inadvertently learned the reason for his fellow minister's conclusion. Jackson was in the midst of another, long conversation about faith when he suddenly told Brown, "I find that it greatly helps me in fixing my mind and quickening my devotions to give articulate utterance to my prayers, and hence I am in the habit of going off into the woods, where I can be alone and speak audibly to myself the prayers I would pour out to my God." He then added with unintended humor, "I was at first annoyed that I was compelled to keep my eyes open to avoid running against the trees and stumps; but upon investigating the matter I do not find that the Scriptures require us to close our eyes in prayer, and the exercise has proven to me very delightful and profitable."[82]

At least once a week, Jackson reported in person to his superior, General Johnston. The commander's headquarters was a former hotel in Centreville. Members of Johnston's staff were not impressed by the man being called "Stonewall." One aide sneered that when Jackson arrived at headquarters, he "would go at once to Gen. Johnston's room and when he came out go straight to his horse, never stopping to talk to anyone." The same officer thought Jackson "rather stiff and awkward in his movements, both on foot and on horseback, always rather shabby in his appearance and badly mounted, at a time when fine horses and stylish uniforms were the rule. He was always courteous, but beyond a salute he rarely had anything to say."[83]

The last statement was not exactly so. On occasion, Jackson would engage in random conversation; and while he talked little, he said much. One rainy evening, he and his staff got into a discussion of military maneuvers preparatory to battle. Major Harman began to give his civilian views on how to advance an army to the point of attack. Jackson listened quietly, then interjected: "Mystery, mystery, Major, is the secret of success. Napoleon marched his men fifty miles in twenty-four hours and fought and won pitched battles, and ours can do the same."[84] Mystery and speed were the elements that Jackson would utilize to the fullest in the months ahead.

Of course, there was one person with whom he conversed whenever possible. Jackson's letters to Anna are remarkable for quantity as well as variety and depth of emotion. Once her irritation cooled over the initial lack of praise for her husband, he stripped away his reserve and wrote what he felt. "I am glad that the battle [Manassas] was fought on your birthday," he joked, "so you can never tell me any more that I forget your birthday. See if I don't always remember it, though I do not my own."[85]

When Jackson learned that General Robert E. Lee had gone into the western Virginia mountains to aid in the military effort there, he declared: "I hope that we will soon hear that our God has again crowned our arms with victory. If Gen. Lee remains in the N.W., I would like to go there & give my feeble aid, as an humble instrument in the hand of Providence, in relieving the downtrodden loyalty of that part of my native state. But I desire to be wherever those over me may decide."[86]

To Anna's pleas that he take leave and visit her, Jackson was adamant. "My darling, I can't be absent from my command, as my attention is necessary in preparing my troops for hard fighting should it be required; and as my officers and soldiers are not permitted to go and see their wives and families, I ought not to see my esposito, as it might make the troops feel that they were badly treated."[87]

Jackson, like Anna, heard the rumors of a long period of inactivity ahead. He discounted them all. "Don't put any faith in there being no more fighting till Oct. It may not be till then, & God grant, that if consistent with His glory, it may never be. Sure I desire no more, if our country's independence can be secured without it. . . . If I fight for my country, it is from a sense of duty, a hope that thro' the blessing of Providence, I may be enabled to serve her, & not because I merely prefer the strife of Battle to the peaceful enjoyment of Home."[88]

A late August false alarm sent the brigade hurrying to Fairfax Courthouse, supposedly under threat of attack. Jackson summarized the trip succinctly: "I had a ride of twelve miles for nothing; and my wounded finger suffered from it, but I trust, with the blessing of an ever-kind Providence, it will soon be well." In the same letter, Jackson confided: "This morning I had a kind of longing to see our lot—not our house, for I did not want to enter its desolate chambers, as it would be too sad not to find my little sunshine there." He closed another letter by stating: "I know not one day what will take place the next, but I do know that I am your doting esposo."[89]

With the war seeming to become more of a stalemate, Jackson's longing for Anna multiplied. He decided that the opportunity was available and safe for Anna to come for a visit. She eagerly journeyed to Richmond. On September 8, accompanied by Captain J. Harvey White (who was going to Fairfax to see a sick brother), Anna managed to board a crowded northbound train. She wired Jackson to meet her at Manassas Junction.

He did not get the telegram until after dark. By then, Anna was vainly searching the empty train platform at Manassas. A distraught wife saw no alternative but to remain under Captain White's protection, reboard the train, and continue to Fairfax. Jackson returned empty-handed to Camp Harman, while Anna spent the night at Fairfax in the railroad car because no hotel accommodations were available in the overcrowded town.

Sunday morning, September 9, found a lonely, hungry, and tired Anna sitting in the passenger car. Suddenly, a team pulling a military wagon came galloping up beside the tracks. Out bounded Jackson. The couple had not seen one another in five months. They exchanged embraces and conversation all the way to the brigade encampment.

Episcopal Bishop John Johns was conducting a service from the porch of the Utterback home when Jackson arrived with his wife. Worship momentarily stopped as soldiers—many of them old Lexington acquaintances—swarmed around the wagon to greet the general's lady. Jackson and Anna then took seats in the yard and the worship service resumed.

For a couple of days, Jackson was able to rent a room for Anna in the Utterback home. The accommodations were cramped, but Anna happily took most of her meals with the staff at a table beneath the large trees in the front yard. During the ten days the Jacksons were together, a loving husband sought to show his wife all the nearby sights. Jackson even insisted on taking Anna to the Manassas battlefield, still reeking with death. In the meantime, Anna found her husband more handsome and healthy than ever before. The broken finger remained sore, but he voiced no complaints.

What impressed Anna most was the deep and mutual attachment between the general and his soldiers. She recalled: "General Jackson was justly proud of his brigade, and their affection for him was beautiful to behold. They all felt so inspirited by the great victory they had just gained, and their general's part in it was rehearsed with pride by every one who called upon his wife, while he, with his characteristic modesty, gave all the credit to his noble men."[90]

This was not solely a wife's biased opinion. Captain James J. White, who previously had chafed under Jackson's demanding ways, wrote his wife at this time: "Gen. Jackson is gaining very fast in the high opinion of his men—those who know nothing of his private character as we Lexington men do. . . . It gives me great pleasure to attest his elevated Christian character in the hearing of those who know nothing of it. I believe that his men would follow him any where—such is their confidence both in his courage & his capacity."[91]

During Anna's visit, Jackson searched the entire neighborhood in vain for adequate quarters. Philip Utterback could not be of help: his home was already full of family refugees when the general's wife arrived. According to James Edmondson of the 27th Virginia, Jackson "said that this was no place for a lady any how (it smells of sour grapes)."[92]

Orders then came for the Confederate army to shift closer to Washington. With that, Anna stated, "I was sent back sorrowfully to North Carolina."[93]

On September 17, Jackson and his regiments moved northeastward and went into a new camp on widow Mary A. Burke's farm three miles from Fairfax Courthouse. The Southern picket line extended to Mason's and Munson's hills commanding the approaches to Alexandria and overlooking Washington itself. At the new Fairfax encampment, water was less plentiful but the area initially was cleaner.

Sickness continued to be a problem for the Confederate army—but not as much in Jackson's brigade. Many attributed the better health to Jackson. "He is said to exercise great vigilance in having his camp clean," a civilian heard. "The soldiers are required to strike their tents so many times a week, to bury all refuse, pieces of meat & suchlike precautions which tend to preserve health."[94]

Jackson was not a man to let time pass uselessly. Those idle days of autumn were but the lull before the storm. The North was showing every intention of pressing the war. In Washington, thousands of uniformed recruits were marshaling for a mighty army. At its head was the Union's new general in chief, Major General George B. McClellan. He had been a West Point classmate of Jackson's and a longtime friend of Johnston's. A brilliant organizer and dynamic leader, McClellan gave far greater promise as a field commander than did the hapless McDowell.

So Jackson ignored the lethargy that settled over the Confederate army and prepared his own troops for a long war. Drill and discipline were the ingredients for military success, he was convinced, and he ensured that they received paramount attention from the troops. Four times daily his men underwent ninety-minute periods of drill. Inspections, police duty, and picket assignments filled the other hours to such an extent that some soldiers grumbled about not having enough time to eat.

In the process of becoming a seasoned infantry leader, Jackson also developed a somewhat different idea about the use of musketry in battle. His tactics required more patience and courage because they stressed independent and minimum firing over rapid, concentrated volleys. Jackson explained: "I rather think that fire by file is best on the whole, for it gives the enemy an idea that the fire is heavier than if it was by company or battalion (volley firing)." Circumstances might occasionally dictate otherwise; "but my opinion is . . . to reserve your fire till the enemy get—or you get to them—to close quarters. Then deliver one deadly, deliberate fire—and charge!"[95]

The weather began to turn cold and wet with the approach of autumn. In his first letter to Anna after her return to North Carolina, Jackson gave proper thanks for a break in the rainy season. "This is a beautiful & lovely morning, beautiful emblem of the morning of Eternity in Heaven. I greatly enjoy it, after our cold chilly weather, which has made one feel doubtful of any capacity, humanly speaking, to endure the campaign, should we remain long in tents. But God, our God, will, & does all things well, & if it is His pleasure that I should remain in the field, He will give me the ability to endure all the fatigues."[96]

Weariness was not Jackson's problem; frustration was. No one in authority seemed to be doing anything in the quest for victory; no one seemed to think that anything needed to be done. Jackson despaired for the Confederate cause. On the last day of September, President Jefferson Davis arrived by train at Fairfax to review the army. The president received much attention and many cheers, as expected.

One morning Jackson and several of his officers called on the chief executive. The brigadier and the head of state greeted one another stiffly. Jackson was immediately disappointed. "I saw no exhibition of that fire which I supposed him to possess." Davis somehow knew of Jackson's background in northwestern Virginia. He alluded to Federal troops overrunning the area and to much of the population declaring openly for the Union. Jackson replied in agitated fashion. The majority of northwestern citizens were not pro-Union, he asserted. A vigorous military campaign into the region would restore Confederate strength. Jackson expressed "a very deep interest" in participating in such an offensive. Yet, to his disappointment, the president "did not even so much as intimate that he designed sending me there." Davis spoke hopefully of the northwest, then changed the subject.

By then, Davis likely was aware that on the night of the Manassas victory, Jackson had jumped up at a field hospital and excitedly asked to take part of the army and make a headlong assault on the Northern capital. Now the president was hearing the same officer advocate an immediate campaign in force away from the Federal army at Washington and far into the isolated and Union-dominated mountainous region of northwestern Virginia. Davis concluded that Jackson was some kind of fanatic. His having independent command was, for the moment, out of the question.[97]

Camp reports of Jackson's appeal to Davis led to the rumor that the general had been ordered to the northwest. "I doubt the truth of it," an officer in the 27th Virginia stated, "but if it is so, I shall feel very much inclined somehow or other and in some capacity to go with him if I can. If the General was to leave us, I do not know what we would do; it would be like breaking us up."98

To Jackson's surprise, he received promotion rather than transfer. Johnston correctly believed that the thirteen brigades under his command would function more efficiently if they were grouped in four divisions. President Davis and the War Department concurred; and on October 7, Jackson (along with Earl Van Dorn, Gustavus W. Smith, and James Longstreet) each became a major general and division commander in the Provisional Army. Yet Jackson was not content with high rank just in the provisional forces. He wanted command rank in the Confederate Army.

Accordingly, he responded to promotion by firing a letter to the War Department. It was his first communique with Secretary of War Judah P. Benjamin, but certainly not his last. Jackson summarized his military career and underscored that at his 1851 resignation from the U.S. Army, "my brevet rank was superior to that of any other West Point graduate who did not enter the Academy previous to myself." He cited his ten years at VMI but added only one sentence about his Confederate career to date.

The War Department's response seemed condescending. On October 31, Jackson was additionally appointed a major of artillery in the Confederate forces. He viewed that as neither promotion nor recognition.99

As usual, Jackson masked his military feelings to Anna. His next letter was a chatty communique ranging over a number of subjects. "My finger has been healed over for some time, and I am blest by an ever-kind Providence with the use of it, though it is still partially stiff. . . . If I get into winter-quarters, will little ex-Anna Morrison come and keep house for me, and stay with me till the opening of the campaign of 1862?" Jackson then told Anna of the promotion in a humble way. "I am very thankful to that God who withholds no good thing from me (though I am so utterly unworthy and ungrateful) for making me a major-general in the Provisional Army of the Confederate States." The actual assignments of brigades to Jackson's division never materialized.100

By mid-October, Johnston's army was in a semicircular position near the Potomac. The Southern commander began to worry about the vulnerability of his flanks, should McClellan advance his Union forces across the river. Orders therefore came forth for the Confederate army to fall back to Centreville. Jackson's brigade was designated as the reserve. It found an encampment on a farm two miles west of Centreville alongside the Warrenton Turnpike. Jackson established his headquarters at the home of A. S. Grigsby.101

The retrograde march caused Jackson to fidget more with impatience and frustration. With each passing day, McClellan's army increased in size and Confederate opportunities dwindled. Victory was slipping away because of inactivity. Jackson had to talk to somebody. He finally went to see General Gustavus W. Smith, a fellow division commander.

Smith had graduated with honors at West Point, served with distinction as an engineer in the Mexican War, and taught at the academy. McClellan had only an army of recruits, Jackson said. "We are ready at the present moment for active operations in the field, while they are not."[102] He was all in favor of carrying the struggle into the North—of invading enemy territory. As Smith listened, Jackson unloaded his thoughts with increasing fervor.

Crossing the upper Potomac, occupying Baltimore, and taking possession of Maryland, we could cut off the communications of Washington, force the Federal government to abandon the capital, beat McClellan's army if it came out against us in open country, destroy industrial establishments wherever we found them, break up the lines of interior commercial intercourse, close the coal mines, seize and, if necessary, destroy the manufactories and commerce of Philadelphia, and of other large cities within our reach; take and hold the narrow neck of country between Pittsburgh and Lake Erie; subsist mainly on the country we traverse, and making unrelenting war amidst their homes, force the people of the North to understand what it will cost them to hold the South in the Union at bayonet's point.[103]

Smith was taken back by the boldness of Jackson's proposals. He then shook his head helplessly. President Davis, Smith replied, is bent on a defensive posture while the Confederacy waits for European intervention on behalf of King Cotton. That will produce a longer war but a less bloody victory.

Jackson rose from his seat. He took Smith's hand warmly. "I am sorry, very sorry," Jackson said dejectedly. He then walked to his horse, mounted, and rode slowly back to his encampment.[104]

One formal letter Jackson mailed at this time was to VMI officials. The Board of Visitors was trying to assemble faculty in order to reopen the school. Letters of inquiry went out to existing faculty, most of whom were in the army. Jackson promptly responded. "I only took the field from a sense of duty; and that the obligation that brought me into active service still retains me in it, and will probably continue to do so, as long as the war shall last. At the close of hostilities, I desire to reassume the duties of my chair, and accordingly respectfully request that if consistent with the interests of the Institute, that the action of the Board of Visitors may be such as to admit of my return upon the restoration of peace."[105]

As Jackson wrote this letter, he was unaware that his career was in the process of taking a sharp turn in another direction.

Early in October, a prominent citizen of Jefferson County—part of the lower face of the Shenandoah Valley—informed Secretary of War Benjamin that Union forces were massing across the Potomac. Only Virginia militia stood in their path, and they were sadly lacking in leadership. The resident declared: "I beg leave to submit whether it be not practical and expedient to send here . . . some competent regular or experienced officer of the army to take charge of and direct the whole military operations in this quarter."[106]

A few days later, Alexander Boteler lent his voice to the chorus of pleas from the valley. Boteler was in his early forties, but his voice carried great weight. The Shenandoah Valley native had served in the U.S. Congress and was then a member of the Confederate legislature. The usually affable statesman wrote Secretary of State Robert M. T. Hunter: "The condition of our border is becoming more alarming every day. No night passes without some infamous outrage upon our loyal citizens."[107]

Meanwhile, primarily to ease personal tensions between Davis, Johnston, and Beauregard, a reorganization of the Confederate army was taking place. The War

Department followed presidential direction and established the Department of Northern Virginia, under Johnston's command. Inside the department were to be the Valley, Potomac, and Aquia districts. Beauregard would have the Potomac theater, General Theophilus H. Holmes the Aquia.

Around October 23, Jackson learned who was to be in command of the Valley of Virginia. He received a long letter from the secretary of war. Judah Benjamin was a consummate politician who combined shrewdness, diplomacy, and a smiling aplomb into a mixture that was not always palatable. Yet the secretary now told Jackson what the general wanted to hear. The "exposed condition" of the Virginia frontier between the Blue Ridge and Allegheny mountains, plus constant appeals from inhabitants therein to have "a perfectly reliable officer for their protection," had led to the formation of the Valley District. "In selecting an officer for this command, the choice of the Government has fallen on you." The appointment was the result of Jackson's high abilities, his intimate knowledge of the country, and the many appeals from residents that he be the one selected.[108]

Benjamin then sidled closer to Jackson. "The administration shares the regret which you will no doubt feel at being separated from your present command, when there is a probability of early engagement between the opposing armies, but it feels confident that you will cheerfully yield your private wishes to your country's service in the sphere where you can be rendered most available." Having said that, the secretary then relayed bad news disguised in patriotic wrappings. "Altho' your forces will for the present be small, they will be increased as rapidly as our means can possibly admit, whilst the people will themselves rally eagerly to your standard as soon as it is known that you are in command. . . . I will be glad to receive any suggestions you may make to render effective your measures of defence."[109]

Benjamin omitted several points in his letter. Jackson's assignment came more from valley requests than from governmental confidence. Having him across the Blue Ridge Mountains removed from the major theater in the Piedmont a man whose thinking was radical. Jackson would have enough logistical problems to keep him occupied, according to standard military thinking. Benjamin also omitted the hope in Richmond that Jackson could somehow do what other commanders had failed to accomplish: pull the northwestern part of the state back into the fold of Virginia.

Presbyterian clerics William White and Francis McFarland were visiting Jackson at the time. (The general was sleeping on the ground so that the sickly McFarland could use his cot at night.) Jackson read Benjamin's letter carefully. Then he handed it to Dr. White. As the cleric finished digesting its contents, Jackson said with simplicity and candor: "Such a degree of public confidence and respect, as puts it in one's power to serve his country, should be accepted and prized; but apart from that, promotion among men is only a temptation and a trouble. Had this communication not come as an order, I should instantly have declined it and continued in command of my brave old brigade."[110]

Giving up command of the regiments he had molded into the image of himself hurt Jackson the most. He had regarded the bond with the valley soldiers as unbreakable. Further, any luster attached to this semi-independent command faded in the reality of what was involved. Jackson had a vast area to protect, no troops of any size, the necessity of starting from scratch to put together some kind of army—all on the western fringe of Confederate Virginia.[111]

Former militia cavalryman Angus McDonald heard of Jackson's assignment and immediately rode from the valley to Centreville. He wanted to help Jackson as much as he could. Colonel McDonald congratulated the general, then asked what force he was bringing with him to the valley. Jackson looked at McDonald and replied calmly, "No force, Colonel, except my staff."[112]

The orders sending Jackson to the valley, with headquarters at Winchester, came on October 28, but Johnston held them back while he made a last effort to keep Jackson under his immediate command at Centreville. Johnston quickly came to see the increasing danger to the Shenandoah. Further, the valley was the flank of the whole Confederate army. It must be secured. Early on Monday morning, November 4, Johnston ordered the new major general to Winchester.[113]

Jackson had been packed for several days. The only thing left to do before departure that overcast, cool day was to say goodbye to the Stonewall Brigade. His sternness could not repel all the pain. The regimental colonels came first in a group. To their compliments Jackson replied that they could not feel more regrets at his leaving than he did. He shook hands with the colonels and said, "May the richest blessing of God ever attend you and your commands, and may victory such as you gained on the Plains of Manassas ever be perched upon your banners."[114]

An hour later, the line officers of the various regiments came in progression to Jackson's tent. The general expressed to each group the earnest hope that the valley regiments would soon join him and become part of his division. Again he grasped each officer's hand warmly. "The scene was very effecting indeed," the 27th Virginia's Captain James Edmondson admitted.[115]

It was 1 P.M. when Jackson rode out onto the field where his brigade stood at attention in close regimental file. Jackson was mounted on "Little Sorrel," with the staff behind him. He looked slowly along the ranks. It was obvious that he was having a problem with his emotions. Jackson removed his hat; then in a sharp but earnest voice he began.

"Officers and men of the First Brigade! You do not expect a speech from me. I come to bid you a heartfelt goodbye.

"This brigade was formed at Harper's Ferry and the command of it assigned to me. You have endured hard marches, the exposure and privations of the bivouac, like men and patriots. You are the brigade which turned the tide of battle on Manassas Plains and there gained for yourself imperishable honor, and your names will be handed down with honor attached in future history."

Jackson paused, his eyes continuing to sweep the silent ranks. Some soldiers had begun to weep; a few in the front ranks thought that Jackson's steel lips were quivering. Now he rose in the stirrups, let loose the reins of his horse, raised his arms, and exclaimed in an even louder voice:

"You were the First Brigade in the Army of the Shenandoah, the First Brigade in the Army of the Potomac, the First Brigade in the Second Corps, and are the First Brigade in the hearts of your generals. I hope that you will be the First Brigade in this, our second struggle for independence, and in the future, on the fields on which the Stonewall Brigade are engaged, I expect to hear of crowning deeds of valor and of victories gloriously achieved! May God bless you all! Farewell!"[116]

Tears welling in his eyes, Jackson wheeled his horse and galloped off to hide his emotions. The men, "many left weeping," unloosed a deafening roar of cheers in Jackson's wake.[117]

Chief of staff John T. L. Preston and aide "Sandie" Pendleton accompanied Jackson to the Manassas Junction depot. The three men filed into a passenger car on a westbound train. Jackson said little to his staff officers. It is doubtful if he was thinking of anything save the future. Yet much had happened to Jackson in a short space of time.

Barely six months earlier he was a major on the faculty of a military school hidden in the mountains of western Virginia. Now he was a major general about to take command of a vast and vital area of the Confederacy. In the spring, he had been a nondescript professor from whom little was expected. By autumn, he was known throughout much of the South as the resolute "Stonewall" Jackson, whose ideas were sometimes radical but whose determination was unconquerable. A train was bearing him west. He was moving up to a new and challenging plateau of command—one that would test every fiber of his ability.

The slow swaying of the cars soon had Jackson dozing. In late afternoon, as the train rounded a curve, Jackson looked up. The Blue Ridge Mountains loomed ahead like a waiting sentry line. Behind the rounded peaks was the great valley he had been ordered to defend as best he could.

Anna needed to be told of his destination. Jackson secured paper and then began writing carefully. "I have received orders to proceed to Winchester," he announced. "I don't expect to sleep much to-night, as my desire is to travel all night, if necessary, for the purpose of reaching Winchester before day to-morrow. My trust is in God for the defense of that country. I shall have great labor to perform; but through the blessing of an ever kind Heavenly Father, I hope He will enable me, and other instrumentalities, to accomplish it. Continue to pray for me, that I may live to glorify God more and more, by serving Him and my country."[118]

11

STORMY ROAD TO A RESIGNATION

IXED OPINIONS FOLLOWED JACKSON westward to the valley. Robert Kean, head of the Bureau of War in Richmond, asserted, "The general opinion of his friends and old pupils was that a separate command might cause the loss of the laurels he had won as a subordinate." Yet state newspapers chortled: "We learn with great pleasure that the command of our troops in Northwestern Virginia has been given to Gen. Thomas Jackson—him of the 'Stone Wall Brigade'—who is a native citizen of that country. . . . He will prove himself an instance of 'the right man in the right place.'"[1]

Public reaction was inconsequential to Jackson. His sole concern on November 4 was to get to Winchester as expeditiously as possible. The train ride was familiar: over the rolling Piedmont country, up the Blue Ridge range and through Thoroughfare Gap, down the mountain, through a quiet Front Royal, and across the Shenandoah River on a 450-foot trestle. It was dark when the train screeched to a halt at Strasburg. There the line turned south, so Jackson, along with his aides John Preston and Sandie Pendleton, disembarked and secured horses. The three men were weary, but the general was insistent on reaching Winchester that night.

The eighteen-mile ride down the Valley Turnpike was long, cold, and fatiguing. Near midnight, a sleeping Winchester came into view. The officers continued on the turnpike, which became Loudoun Street and the town's central roadway. On the left-hand side of the street in the center of town was the historic Taylor Hotel. It was a three-story structure with porches extending across the front on all three levels. Among its earlier guests were Senators Henry Clay and Daniel Webster. All was quiet in town as Jackson, Preston, and Pendleton entered the lobby. The three officers were assigned room 23 and promptly went to bed.[2]

Townspeople flocked to the hotel the next morning to greet the new military commander. Some had met Jackson during the organizational days of springtime; others had natural curiosity to see the warrior known as Stonewall. The general established his headquarters at the hotel for the time being. He politely declined invitations and audiences because the Shenandoah Valley demanded his immediate and complete attention.

Jackson was aware that the Confederacy was not going to take the offensive to the north. His posture must be defensive. Everything he found at Winchester toward that end was anything but reassuring. The starting point for Jackson was to familiarize himself more thoroughly with geography: the area's relative position, defensive potentialities, and pathways.

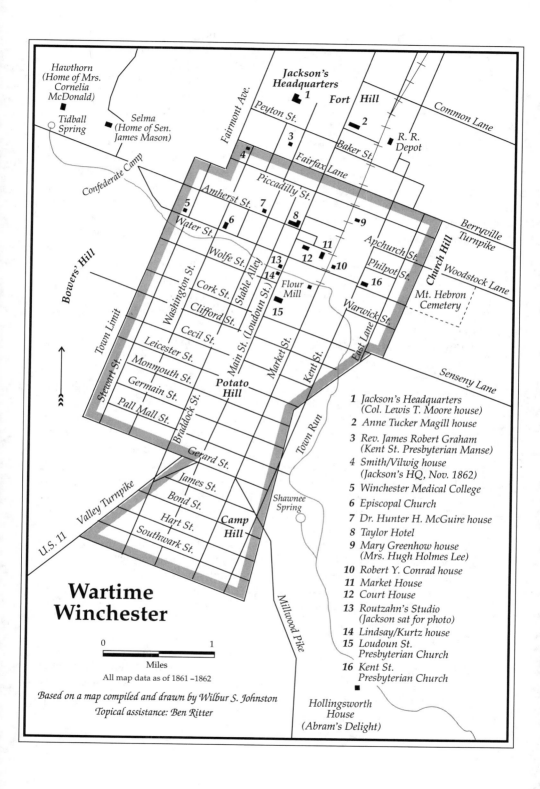

Wartime Winchester

Hawthorn
(Home of Mrs. Cornelia McDonald)

Tidball Spring

Selma
(Home of Sen. James Mason)

Jackson's Headquarters
1

Fort Hill
2

Common Lane

R. R. Depot

Fairmont Ave.

Peyton St.

3

Baker St.

Fairfax Lane

4

Confederate Camp

Amherst St.

Piccadilly St.

7

8

9

Berryville Turnpike

Bowers' Hill

5

Water St.

6

Wolfe St.

13

11

12

10

Apchurch St.

Woodstock Lane

Church Hill

Washington St.

Cork St.

Stable Alley

14

Flour Mill

Philpot St.

16

Mt. Hebron Cemetery

Town Limit

Clifford St.

Cecil St.

Main St. (Loudoun St.)

15

Warwick St.

Leicester St.

Market St.

Kent St.

East Lane

Stewart St.

Monmouth St.

Germain St.

Braddock St.

Potato Hill

Senseny Lane

Pall Mall St.

Gerard St.

Town Run

Valley Turnpike

James St.

Bond St.

Shawnee Spring

Hart St.

Camp Hill

U.S. 11

Southwark St.

Millwood Pike

1 Jackson's Headquarters
   (Col. Lewis T. Moore house)
2 Anne Tucker Magill house
3 Rev. James Robert Graham
   (Kent St. Presbyterian Manse)
4 Smith/Vilwig house
   (Jackson's HQ, Nov. 1862)
5 Winchester Medical College
6 Episcopal Church
7 Dr. Hunter H. McGuire house
8 Taylor Hotel
9 Mary Greenhow house
   (Mrs. Hugh Holmes Lee)
10 Robert Y. Conrad house
11 Market House
12 Court House
13 Routzahn's Studio
   (Jackson sat for photo)
14 Lindsay/Kurtz house
15 Loudoun St.
   Presbyterian Church
16 Kent St.
   Presbyterian Church

Hollingsworth House
(Abram's Delight)

0   Miles   1

All map data as of 1861–1862

Based on a map compiled and drawn by Wilbur S. Johnston
Topical assistance: Ben Ritter

From Winchester, it was eighty miles by telegraph to his superior, Johnston, at Centreville. The Confederate front extended from Fredericksburg to Winchester. Jackson's district, of course, was the extreme left of the line. It was connected with Johnston's main army by a 2700-man detachment across the Blue Ridge at Leesburg. In command of it was Jackson's cantankerous brother-in-law, General Harvey Hill.

"Daughter of the Stars," the Shawnee Indians had called the great valley, and the "Shenandoah" it remained. From Lexington, the valley stretched 150 miles to the Potomac River. Its width varied between twenty and thirty-five miles. The Shenandoah River and its tributaries drained the valley. That river began with two branches: the North Fork west of the huge Massanutten Mountain, which bisected much of the Shenandoah, and the South Fork on the east side of the Massanutten. The forks came together three miles north of Front Royal, with the full Shenandoah River hugging the Blue Ridge as it flowed northeastward into the Potomac at Harpers Ferry.

Prior to 1861, the valley was often called the "Garden of Virginia"; during the Civil War, it became the "Breadbasket of the Confederacy." The agricultural yields there were unrivaled. Wheat production averaged fifteen and a half bushels per resident; annual corn production was twenty bushels for every inhabitant. The valley was the source for a third of all the hay in the state, plus enormous quantities of rye, oats, barley, and potatoes. Large orchards and huge herds of cattle, sheep, and hogs were veritable landmarks.[3]

Forming the western wall of the valley were the thick and rugged Allegheny Mountains. Most of that area was in Federal control. On the east side of the valley was the line of the picturesque Blue Ridge Mountains and Confederate territory. Eleven passes broke the Blue Ridge; every one was of strategic importance. The valley was the buffer between Confederacy and Union in the eastern theater.

Four railroads existed in parts of the Shenandoah. The Baltimore and Ohio traversed the northern face of the valley at Harpers Ferry and continued west beyond Cumberland, Maryland. In 1835–36, a branch of the B&O was laid between Harpers Ferry and Winchester. The Manassas Gap line ran from Manassas west to Strasburg and then south to Mt. Jackson, where in 1859 construction had ended forty miles short of its Staunton destination. At the southern end of the valley was the Virginia Central Railroad, which meandered 115 miles from Jackson's River through Staunton, Waynesboro, and Charlottesville to Richmond.

Railroads were at extreme ends of the great valley. The Shenandoah River was not navigable. Those factors made the Valley Turnpike the major artery for the long Shenandoah corridor. Begun in 1834, the road stretched from Winchester to Staunton. It was a two-lane macadamized pike, paved eighteen feet wide with pulverized limestone packed tightly to make the roadbed impervious to rain. Road shoulders were two feet wide on each side.

No grade on the pike exceeded three degrees. In marked contrast to other roads built in that day east of the Mississippi River, the Valley Turnpike was as straight as possible. At many points, the turnpike ran unbent for two or three miles. The section between New Market and Mauzy was seven miles long and contained a single curve. Opened for traffic in 1840, the Valley Turnpike had been regarded since then as an engineering wonder.[4]

Jedediah Hotchkiss, who became Jackson's great cartographer, once responded to a question about the general's familiarity with the area. "Jackson of course had a very good knowledge of the Shenandoah Valley from passing up and down in the stage coach which furnished the only way of getting to the great cities, but I do not think he had much accurate knowledge of the valley from his own observations" in the early stages of the Civil War.[5]

The Virginia Central Railroad made Staunton the principal city at the southern end of the Shenandoah. Its counterpart at the northern end was Winchester, Jackson's headquarters. It lay in the midst of open country, it could be easily attacked from any direction, but it had to be protected.

Founded in 1743 by English pioneers, Winchester was the first community of note in the valley. Its street names—Loudoun, Piccadilly, Cork, and the like—reflected the British influence. George Washington had spent time there first as a surveyor and then in command of Virginia troops defending the frontier against the French and Indians. The crossroads village came to life after the American Revolution as the market for goods traveling in every direction in the lower valley.

By 1860, it had 701 families and a population of 4400 people, which made it three times larger than Lexington.[6] The town contained 708 slaves and 655 freedmen. It was both a county seat and a commercial center. A handsome courthouse, market place, fifty mercantile stores, two banks, a dozen churches, and several taverns all stood along paved streets. The town had more than an average number of schools. It even possessed a medical college.

Nine roads and turnpikes converged on the place. A railroad, whose depot was in the center of downtown, carried goods and passengers the thirty-odd miles to Harpers Ferry for a linkup with the mighty Baltimore and Ohio rail system. Winchester was not merely the largest town on the west side of the Blue Ridge; its location made it the commercial, military, and psychological key to the entire valley.

On November 5, 1861, Jackson found himself a commander without a command— a general in charge of a 6000-square-mile district with few defenses and few defenders. He was happy to be in the valley, but he would have preferred going farther west, deep into the mountains, to expel Federal troops from the home of his childhood. That would have been strategically sound, though militarily difficult. Yet Jackson never relinquished the idea of such a campaign. He always felt that the best defense of the Shenandoah was to control the Alleghenies to the west; and in the months that followed, he regularly eyed the Alleghenies as a desired area for decisive military action.

Jackson did not keep those thoughts a secret. Less than a week after he arrived at Winchester, one of his officers wrote home: "I do not know how long we may stay here. I think however not long. I think the General will move on to Romney in a short time."[7]

The Shenandoah Valley was Jackson's jurisdiction, but large parts of it were under direct threat by the Federals. For example, 4000 Union troops were firmly established at Romney, forty-three miles west of Winchester and the town controlling the fertile valley of the South Fork of the Potomac River. Some 6000 other enemy soldiers were at various stations in the lower valley itself. Jackson quickly learned their locations, and he saw cause for alarm. If one Federal column drove east from Romney and another came south through Martinsburg, the two could converge on Winchester in enough strength to force Jackson's retreat. Fortunately for the Confederates, the Union commands were divided. Troops to the west were in the Department of Western Virginia and disconnected from the mainstream of Union activity. Federals to the north were still part of the Army of the Potomac. Little cooperation existed between the two forces.

Jackson's task was simple but exacting. He had to defend an extremely long frontier against superior enemy numbers on two fronts. The best (if not the only) hope Jackson had was to keep the two threats separated and off balance.

To do this, Jackson had for starters three widely dispersed militia brigades. Some of the men were armed with antiquated flintlock muskets; others were armed with nothing. Their ranks had thinned as members enlisted in volunteer regiments. Hence, colonels led company-size units while captains were in command of handfuls of men. A negative attitude prevailed among most of the officers, a Winchester resident observed. "The Militia generally have but little confidence in those who are placed over them & make all manner of fun about them."[8]

The cavalry at Jackson's disposal were barely 500 men under Colonel Turner Ashby, whose independence had been such that he previously answered directly to the adjutant general in Richmond. His horsemen were "a band of brothers" full of fire and fight but lacking in basic organization and discipline. The only other cavalry field officer besides Ashby was Major Oliver Funsten. He was a good recruiter but an inexperienced field leader. Many of the mounted companies had no officers. This bothered no one in particular. As a trooper commented, "every private was a general and needed no guidance or direction from his officers." That had to change. Jackson met with Ashby within forty-eight hours after reaching Winchester. Exactly what was said is unknown; yet one of Ashby's men reported that the cavalryman "returned from the interview in excellent spirits . . . much pleased with his new General." As for artillery, Jackson had a few guns but no gunners to operate them.[9]

This added up to 1700 men available for the defense of the Shenandoah Valley. Rumors abounded of an imminent Federal advance. Jackson immediately issued a call for the remainder of the state militia in the area to rally at Winchester. The result was surprisingly good. Within three weeks the militia aggregate reached 3000 men. Yet untutored militia were no match for well-trained Union soldiers.

So Jackson dispatched Colonel Preston to Richmond with an urgent request for more troops. All Confederate units to the south and west should be ordered to Winchester. That specifically would include the troops of General William W. Loring at Huntersville and Colonel Edward Johnson's smaller detachment guarding mountain passes. Jackson declared, "It is very important that disciplined troops of not only infantry, but also of artillery and cavalry be ordered here" to buttress "the defenseless condition of this place."[10]

First on the list of the general's personnel desires was what Anna Jackson termed "his chief reliance in battle, his invincible Stonewall Brigade." That was not easily accomplished. When Jackson departed for the valley, according to a semiliterate member of the 27th Virginia, "he told General Johnson that he thought he dadent treat him wright for taking his brigaid away from him and he thouh he warent a doing wright by leaving us. He said he a go to write to the Adjt General to get him to assign this Brigaid to his command in the valley."11

Apparently, Jackson did make a prompt move to get the Stonewall Brigade transferred to Winchester, for on November 5 the War Department ordered the unit to proceed to the valley "with the least practicable delay." Johnston angrily protested. Because Jackson "will be opposed to raw troops, me to the enemy's best," the most experienced Confederate units should remain under his command. Secretary of War Benjamin promised to send Johnston twice the number of men he was losing with the brigade.

"Uncle Joe" remained irritated. He sarcastically told one of his officers, "The Secretary of War will probably establish his headquarters within this department soon." The situation for Johnston became worse when President Davis got into the dispute and criticized Johnston for saying that he was left with "raw" troops. "The success of the army requires harmonious co-operation," Davis told Johnston in a condescending manner that widened an already dangerous gap between the two proud men.12

Five infantry regiments and the Rockbridge Artillery were in high spirits over returning to Jackson and the valley. Many of the men got into high quantities of spirits en route. An incredibly large number of the artillerists and infantrymen were thoroughly intoxicated by the time they reached the Shenandoah River. Lieutenant William Poague wrote disgustingly: "We had a wagonload of drunken men—dead drunk. I never saw the like before or since." Sergeant Andrew Cook of the 27th Virginia confessed to a friend: "however firm the Stone wall may stand a gainst the thundering storm of yankee cannon I tell you king alcohol has thrown many a one of them since they came to the valley. the morning we left centreville I thought the 27th looked large enough for a little army. But when we reached [Winchester] I dont believe we had over 200 men, other Regiments looking in proportion." A sober James Langhorne of the 4th Virginia told his father, "We will have some hard fighting in the Valley, I expect, but with Old Jack at the head of this Brigade I fear no reverses." Yet jubilation turned to grumbling when the units reached the Winchester area in a pouring rain.13

Instead of allowing the men to take quarters among hospitable townspeople, Jackson closed Winchester to the soldiers and ordered them into an open encampment south of town near the hamlet of Kernstown. The troops had no field equipment with them. "Being entirely without those things which can make a soldier comfortable," a member of the 5th Virginia muttered, "both officers and men were highly incensed."14

More manpower had to be found for the valley's defense. Jackson now leaned on the Confederate statesman who became his close friend, confidante, and chief liaison in Richmond: Alexander R. Boteler. Born in Jefferson County in 1815, Boteler was a descendant of the famous patriot and artist Charles Willson Peale and the son of a prominent physician. Boteler had graduated from Princeton before settling into the life of a gentleman-farmer on the family estate ("Fountain Rock") near Shepherdstown. Twice he ran for Congress; twice he was defeated by Charles James Faulkner.

The two political aspirants—both of whom would serve on Jackson's staff—almost fought a duel at one point.

In 1859 Boteler won election to the Congress. He received the highly unusual honor for a newcomer by being nominated for Speaker of the House of Representatives. Boteler withdrew his name. At Virginia's secession he resigned from Congress with a widely quoted speech. Quick elections followed, first to the Virginia General Assembly, and then to the Confederate Congress. Boteler and Jackson gravitated to one another through the abiding love they shared for northwestern Virginia.[15]

When Boteler called on Jackson shortly after the latter's arrival in Winchester, the general dispatched him at once to gain an audience with Governor Letcher in Richmond. Reinforcements were imperative for the valley's safety. Jackson was convinced that at least 40,000 Federals were threatening him from north and west. He had only 4000 ill-organized Confederates under his command. The valley was essential to Virginia; its defenders were willing to make any sacrifice for its safekeeping. Jackson emphasized that the valley "ought to be and, if possible, must be defended." Union authorities involuntarily helped the Confederate situation by exaggerating the size of Jackson's force. One Federal report had 26,000 Southern soldiers poised for action at Winchester.[16]

Jackson found some moments in those first days of command to attend to personal matters. Maggie Preston had informed him of the death in Lexington of Amy, his faithful cook and housekeeper. Jackson made no effort to conceal his grief. He told Maggie: "More than once your kind and touching letter . . . brought tears to my eyes." Yet, he informed Anna, he was convinced that Amy "has gone to a better world." Periodically, Jackson checked on the other servants who had been subcontracted to Lexington friends. The general always asked that the slaves be required to attend Sunday school for the betterment of their "spiritual interests."[17]

It was shortly after Jackson arrived in Winchester that Jim Lewis became his camp servant. Of the people intimately associated with the general, less is known of this figure than any other person. Lewis was black and a Lexington resident. Beyond that, facts are few and confusing. Most sources refer to Lewis merely as Jackson's "servant." Some writers have classified Lewis as a freedman who volunteered to become Jackson's valet.[18] A good case can be made that Lewis was a slave whom Jackson hired from his owner.

During the war, Jackson made sporadic entries in a pocket account book. It contains a number of references to Lewis. On November 7, 1861, Jackson gave $10 to the servant. Early the following month, Jackson paid Lewis $30 preparatory to sending the man on a brief trip to Lexington. (Colonel Preston wrote his wife, Maggie, at the time: "Jim lewis is going home on furlough. . . . White people have no chance of getting a furlough; it is only our colored friends who can escape for a time the evils of war.")[19]

This would seem to infer that Lewis was a freedman receiving payment for his services. Yet other entries in the little account book point to a different conclusion. On Christmas Day, 1861, Jackson sent "W. C. Lewis" in Lexington a check "for hire"—presumably of a servant. A year later, Jackson paid the same W. C. Lewis $150 for "hire of Jim." The 1860 slave census for Rockbridge County listed William C.

Lewis, a sixty-three-year-old commissioner, as owning seven slaves. Two appeared to be man and wife; four were children all under the age of eleven; the seventh was a fifty-year-old male. At least one source referred to Lewis during the war as "Uncle Jim." Since Lewis died shortly after the conflict, he was in all likelihood in an advanced age at the time of the conflict.

There the search for identity ends. Whatever his status or his age, Lewis became a beloved figure around Jackson's headquarters. "Faithful, brave, big-hearted Jim, God bless him!" Dr. McGuire exclaimed after the war. Although Kyd Douglas accused Lewis of being "fond of liquor" and "addicted to cards," Alexander Boteler gave a sharply contrasting opinion. The congressman saw unique similarities between Jackson's servant and Jackson's favorite mount: "The servant and 'Old Sorrel' being about the same color—each having the hue of gingerbread without any of its spiciness—their respective characters were in a concatenation accordingly. For they were equally obedient, patient, easy-going and reliable; not given to devious courses nor designing tricks; more serviceable than showy and, altogether, as sober-sided a pair of subordinates as any Presbyterian elder with plain tastes and a practical turn, need desire to have about him. Both man and horse seemed to understand their master thoroughly and rarely failed to come up fully to all his requirements."[20]

On his first Sunday in Winchester, Jackson attended services at Kent Street Presbyterian Church. He probably had met its minister, the Reverend James Graham, earlier in the year. A strong bond of affection would develop between the two men. This was a natural thing for Jackson, who always looked to ministers as sincere friends and spiritual counselors. On Graham's part, his admiration for both Jackson and the Confederacy certainly took a giant step as a result of the Confederacy declaring Friday, November 15, as a day of "humiliation and prayer." Jackson had acknowledged that declaration in an announcement of his own. "With adoring gratitude to God for having disposed the President of the Confederate States to issue the foregoing proclamation . . . all drills will be suspended, in order that the Army of the Valley may gratefully respond . . . and thus devote the day to the service of *Almighty God* to whom we are indebted for not only every victory that has crowned our arms but for every other blessing."[21]

Graham scheduled a church service that day with some apprehension. Anti-Northern feelings were heated and often blasphemous; the town was full of recuperating soldiers who would attend the service; everything could get out of hand. When the worship hour came, the church was full. Graham thought he had picked an even-tempered member of the congregation to start the prayer service; yet with the soldiers loudly vocal in their exhortations, and to Graham's horror, the man offering the prayer soon "was telling the Lord, with singular distinctness, what sort of people were making war upon us, and how He ought to let our armies deal with them."[22]

By then, Graham was in despair. The service was on the verge of disintegrating into a profane rally on behalf of the Confederacy. The congregation was singing the first hymn when the minister saw Jackson enter the sanctuary and take a seat offered by a soldier near the door. At the end of the hymn, in desperation but with "some misgiving," Graham called on the general to lead in prayer. The request caught Jackson by surprise. A long moment of silence followed, then Jackson stood and closed his eyes. According to Graham, "he led us at once into the presence of God, and to the throne of grace." Jackson confessed the unworthiness of everyone as sinners and their absolute dependence on divine mercy. He begged God to help their afflicted country and to bring success to the armies defending it. Graham suddenly beheld not a stern soldier but a humble disciple. "Not a single word did he utter inconsistent with the command to love your enemies. Not once did he venture to tell God what He ought to be in that great crisis." The remainder of the service passed in an air of newfound reverence.[23]

It took Jackson only a few days to decide on a change of headquarters. The Taylor Hotel in the center of Winchester was always crowded, and everyone, it seemed, flocked there to meet the hero of Manassas. Jackson needed a quieter, less public place to oversee his command. A subaltern, Lieutenant Colonel Lewis T. Moore, came forward with near-perfect accommodations.

Moore was a Winchester bachelor, second-in-command of the 4th Virginia in the Stonewall Brigade, and incapacitated by a leg wound suffered at Manassas. He was hospitalized at the moment. No one was occupying his home, "Alta Vista," near the top of Braddock Street. Moore happily offered the place to Jackson as a combination headquarters and home. Jackson as happily accepted.

The residence was on the west side of Braddock (initially called Upper) Street, a block to the west of the main thoroughfare. Braddock was a level street downtown, but its northernmost half-dozen blocks climbed to the top of a ridge. Moore's home was two doors beyond the Presbyterian manse and at a point where Braddock Street became little more than a trail to the top of the hill. The house actually faced on Peyton Street, with a circular driveway leading on and off the side street. Of added importance to Jackson, the location was close to the fairgrounds and the largest of the Confederate encampments around Winchester.

Alta Vista was more an elegant cottage than a stately mansion. Built in 1854 by dentist William M. Fuller, it was a two-storied structure with three rooms on each floor. The entrance to the T-shaped home was a bank of steps that led a half-story up to the main floor. Jackson's office was immediately to the right of the front door, the staff's office was on the left, with the dining room and kitchen to the rear. Upstairs were two bedrooms and a storage room. Jackson's bed chamber was directly above his office.

Across the hall was the bedroom for members of the staff. It was always crowded. Jackson often invited Colonel John Preston to share his sleeping quarters. The Lexington friend declined; he was aware that several times daily Jackson retired to his bedroom for prayers.

The home was off the beaten path and detached from the hubbub of downtown activity. However, it was only a six-block walk to the Presbyterian church. "If I only had my little woman here," Jackson wrote wishfully. Yet, he added, "through the blessing of an ever-kind Heavenly Father, I am quite comfortable."[24]

Shifts of three soldiers guarded the home around the clock. For most of the November–December period, Washington College students in the 4th Virginia's Liberty Hall Volunteers had that assignment. Jackson and his aides—the regal Preston, young Sandie Pendleton, kinsmen Alfred Jackson, and George Junkin—were together constantly. The staff members were full of gaiety, Preston noted, but Jackson was "grave as a signpost, till something chances to overcome him, and then he breaks out into a laugh so awkward that it is manifest he has never laughed enough to learn how."[25]

Cold winds were already signaling the approach of winter as Jackson settled into his new quarters. In surroundings more conducive for work, he continued to strengthen his command. The Stonewall Brigade was at Nill's Dam south of town because it had a large water supply. Yet the men quickly found the lowlands to be uncomfortable and isolated. Jackson shifted the brigade to the north side of Winchester on Widow Carter's farm, where many of the units had encamped back in the spring.

Few details inside his brigade escaped Jackson's attention. When Joseph Carpenter moved up to captain of Company A of the 27th Virginia, Jackson remembered what a splendid artillery student he had been at VMI. The general thereupon converted the infantry company into an artillery unit. Carpenter's Battery soon took its place beside the Rockbridge Artillery as the Stonewall Brigade's major big-gun support.

Relations between commander and subordinate officers were not always upbeat, however. A week after the Stonewall Brigade arrived in the valley, Jackson was in dispute with the regimental field officers. Weather undoubtedly was a factor. Major Frank Paxton told his wife Elizabeth, "The wind is perhaps more severe than the rain, as it makes our outdoor fires very uncomfortable, it being doubtful whether it is best to stand the cold or the smoke." This situation led the troops to seek shelter in the nearby confines of Winchester. Jackson had already issued strict orders making the town off limits to enlisted men. He then expanded the directive to include officers. His colonels and majors reacted with indignation. In a joint communique to Jackson, nine of them alleged that his directive was "an unwarranted assumption of authority . . . an improper inquiry into their private matters . . . [an] abuse of the privileges accorded in every other department of the army . . . [that] it disparages the dignity of the offices which they have the honor to hold, and, in consequence, detracts from that respect of the force under their command which is necessary to maintain their authority and enforce obedience."[26]

Jackson responded instantly, sternly, and pointedly. He informed the complainants that since the brigade's arrival, "either from incompetency to control their commands or from neglect of duty," Colonels Allen of the 2d Virginia and Harper of the 5th had "so permitted their commands to become disorganized and their officers and men to enter Winchester without permission, as to render several arrests necessary." Jackson then sent a broadside against them all: "If officers desire to have control over their commands, they must remain habitually with them, and industriously attend to their instructions and comfort, and in battle lead them well, and in such manner as to command their admiration."[27]

The field officers were anything but appeased. Nor did Jackson sympathize at all with the collective complaint—especially since one of the major offenders, Colonel Allen, was temporarily in command of the brigade. The district commander began searching for a brigadier general who could give his complete attention to the valley brigade.[28]

Late in November, Jackson had to wrestle with an even graver disciplinary matter:

the first execution of a soldier in his command. The crime and ensuing court-martial had already taken place when Jackson arrived in the valley; but as commanding officer he could amend the sentence. The Reverend Graham never forgot Jackson's "firmness of principle" in the matter.

When the war began, James A. Miller lived in Harpers Ferry and had a wife and three children. He joined a Jefferson County mounted unit under Captain John Henderson. One evening, sometime in the early autumn, Miller and several of his comrades got roaring drunk. An altercation with Henderson ensued. In a moment of anger, Miller shot the captain. The ball pierced the shoulder and permanently paralyzed the right arm. Miller went before a military tribunal and was sentenced to death by firing squad on November 26 in Winchester.[29]

As that Tuesday approached, a number of pleas came forth in Miller's behalf. John Preston contacted Presbyterian cleric Graham and asked him to intercede. Graham talked to a contrite Miller, then went with Winchester resident William L. Trent to see Jackson and plead for mercy. Tears swelled in Jackson's eyes as he listened silently to Graham's entreaties. The general suggested several last-minute actions that might be taken.

Graham and Trent felt hopeful as they stood to leave. Jackson then warned them against being optimistic. "A pardon might work greater hardships," he said. "Our soldiers are brave, but undisciplined; and discipline is essential to success. In an army, resistance to lawful authority is a grave offense. To pardon it would be to encourage insubordination, and ruin our cause. Still, I will review the whole case; and no man will be happier than myself if I can reach the same conclusion with you." Jackson could not; and with what Graham characterized as "inexpressible pain," a firing party from the 2d Virginia carried out the sentence as scheduled.[30]

The Miller case was but an emotional distraction for Jackson. What was dominating his thoughts was the bigger picture of war. He continued to drill his men and construct earthworks in front of Winchester. His troops ensured that the B&O Railroad remained inoperable by tearing up the double tracks between Harpers Ferry and Martinsburg and wrecking another seven-and-a-half miles of the line west of Martinsburg. Yet after two weeks of marking time at Winchester, Jackson was increasingly restless.

Waiting to see what would happen ran counter to his military philosophy. The battle should be carried at once to the enemy. Jackson was greatly outnumbered, but the Federals were dispersed here and there throughout the lower valley and from the Ohio River to the Shenandoah. Once they came together and advanced in concert, Jackson's little force would be no match. The best way to keep the enemy on the defensive was to attack. That seemed elementary to Jackson.

Of course, personal considerations also affected his thinking. The land to the northwest was home. Federal occupation there had been harsh in locales, with citizens calling pitifully for help. Jackson heard them, and he wanted to react forcibly to their appeals.[31]

By November 20, he had a plan. He outlined it to Secretary of War Judah Benjamin. It is an extremely important letter because it marked the first time that Jackson offered a proposal for an independent and offensive operation. He began by requesting that William W. Loring's three brigades of more than 5000 troops be ordered at once to Winchester from the mountains to the southwest. Once reinforced, Jackson would launch a strike forty-three miles to the west and capture the strategically located town of Romney. It had been under Federal occupation since June and was like a dagger pointed at Winchester's flank. At the moment, several thousand Union soldiers were encamped in the vicinity. Their commander was General Benjamin F. Kelley, a fifty-four-year-old western Virginian whose primary responsibility was to guard the sections of the B&O Railroad that Jackson had not rendered inoperable. "The attack on Romney," Jackson explained to Benjamin, "would probably induce McClelland [*sic*] to believe that the [Confederate] army of the Potomac had been so weakened as to justify him in making an advance on Centreville, but should this not induce him to advance I do not believe that anything will during the present Winter." If McClellan started forward, Jackson would rush to Centreville with his and Loring's men. That would crush the enemy and allow Jackson to return to the conquest of the Northwest. He would

move rapidly Westward to the waters of the Monogarhela [*sic*] and Little Kanawha. Should General Kelley be defeated and especially should he be captured I believe that by a judicious disposition of the militia, a few Cavalry and a small number of Field pieces no additional forces would for sometime be required in this District. I deem it of great importance that North Western Virginia be occupied by Confederate Troops this Winter.

At present it is to be presumed that the enemy are not expecting an attack there and the Army supplying resources to that region (necessary for the subsistence of ours) are in greater abundance than at almost any other season of the year. Postpone the occupation of that section of the state until spring and we may expect to find the enemy prepared for us & the resources to which I have referred greatly exhausted.

Jackson conceded that such a campaign would be "an arduous undertaking" and a sacrificing "of much personal comfort" for the soldiers. Yet Confederate victory and personal pride would be far greater compensations. As for the possibility of winter or hidden factors hampering the offensive, such problems would be handled "through the blessing of *God* who has thus far so wonderfully prospered our cause."[32]

The plan had to go through channels. First to study it was General Joseph Johnston at Centreville. He was ambivalent: Johnston admired Jackson's sagacity but felt the proposal overly ambitious in mountainous terrain and unpredictable weather. Yet it posed few risks and was worth the try. Johnston gave a favorable endorsement to Jackson's letter. "I submit that the troops under General Loring might render valuable service by taking the field with General Jackson, instead of going into winter quarters, as now proposed." Secretary Benjamin also liked the idea, but it was his habit to move along a politician's path. Loring had already made clear his desire to spend the winter guarding the Staunton-Parkersburg Turnpike. General Lee seemed of a like mind. Benjamin therefore took the middle road. He sent Loring a copy of Jackson's plan and urged lightly that it be implemented. However, the secretary told Loring, "if, upon full consideration, you think the proposed movement objectionable and too hazardous, you will decline to make it, and so inform the Department."[33]

Loring was lukewarm to the plan yet agreed reluctantly to cooperate. He expressed some reservations, one of which would have dark consequences in future weeks. "I consider a winter campaign practicable if the means of transportation sufficient to move this army can be obtained. . . . With warm clothing, good tents, and proper attention by the regimental and company officers there need be no suffering from the climate in that region." More immediately irritating, the meticulous Loring announced that he would move his command in stages while ensuring that all wagon trains accompanied their respective units. That would take awhile, and Jackson considered time of the essence. Neither he nor Benjamin was encouraged by Loring's statement that he would join the valley army "with a spirit to succeed."[34]

Jackson's impatience with a general whom he had never met led him to the extraordinary action of making an appeal directly to Governor Letcher. Should the Confederacy not be able to send troops promptly, he hoped that the governor would dispatch Virginia soldiers. "Let not the idea of Federal Forces wintering in Romney be tolerated for one moment," Jackson asserted. He needed men, and his militia needed up-to-date weapons. "If you do not hear of strong reinforcements coming here, then please send me eight good field pieces . . . and with the forces here, aided by the Militia coming in, let us drive the Invader from the Valley." A touch of diplomacy marked the end of Jackson's letter to Letcher. "You must not misunderstand me by supposing that I am complaining of the Confederate States government; on the contrary it is to be presumed that the Confederate Government will do all that it can; but if it is unable to relieve Romney, I ask that the State give assistance to our people."[35]

Letcher was sympathetic. The governor dispatched 1550 percussion muskets to replace the flintlocks with which the militia were struggling as well as an artillery battery of five guns with full equipment.[36]

Secretary Benjamin gave official approval to the plan for a winter offensive. Jackson determined to get underway as quickly as all of Loring's brigades reached Winchester. He urged the War Department to prod Loring into swift movement. "If General Loring's command were here I would, with God's blessing, soon expect to see General Kelley's army, or a large portion of it, in our possession; but if General Loring is not here speedily my command may be a retreating instead of a victorious one."[37]

While waiting for Loring, Jackson asked Boteler to try to have the government pay militia members. They had received no stipend since the previous summer. Then Jackson turned his attention anew to his Stonewall Brigade. It was encamped four miles northeast of Winchester on the farm of James W. Stephenson. The troops had christened their new home "Camp Stephenson." By and large the accommodations were comfortable, although Colonel Preston commented to his wife: "Perfume is scarce in this service, I can assure you. A crane would hold up his neck high, and step along in daily disgust at our doings here."[38]

Jackson was always concerned about the brigade's well-being. Yet he stumbled in the process of getting it a new commander. He did not feel that any of the regimental colonels in the unit were deserving of promotion. He regarded lax discipline as a common weakness among them all. Entitled to that opinion, he nevertheless erred in not spelling out what sort of brigadier he wanted and in not recommending a specific individual for the post. That left the War Department free to assign whom it wished.

Richard B. Garnett, the man who reported for duty on December 7 never measured up to Jackson's standards, even though he was far more capable than one had a right to expect.[39]

Garnett was seven years older than his new commander and a product of Virginia tidewater aristocracy. He finished West Point five years ahead of Jackson. (Of forty graduates in his class alive in 1861, twenty-one became generals.) Garnett had seen twenty years of frontier duty that included fighting both Indians and land squatters.

Such a life left him a bachelor in spite of his handsomeness. Of medium height, with light blue eyes, blonde hair, and clean-shaven, Garnett seemed "quite military in appearance and gentlemanly." Jackson expected Garnett to be a stern taskmaster for troops who sometimes needed much control. The valley commander was unaware of an appraisal of Garnett by one of his friends: "He is as sensitive and proud as he is fearless and sweet-spirited."[40]

Garnett's short tenure had a stormy beginning. Succeeding Jackson, everything he did was measured against "Old Jack's" ability. Resentment in the ranks over an "outsider" taking command of the Stonewall Brigade hampered Garnett's initial efforts. Most unsettling of all, Jackson did not like him.

Perhaps it was the aristocratic background, or handing over a prized brigade to an unknown. Jackson was not impressed with Garnett's background; according to one source, Jackson considered Garnett a political appointee with little military experience. Moreover, in quick time, the commander would discover that Garnett was not the stern and demanding brigadier that Jackson liked at the head of brigades.[41]

Jackson's Romney offensive was predicated on speed and strength. He got neither as the days continued to pass. Three-fourths of Loring's command was moving leisurely toward Winchester, while the Federal garrison at Romney had been reinforced to a reported 7000 soldiers. A combination of balmy weather, a wish to provide his green troops more military experience, and a desire to occupy his mind with something else, all led Jackson to launch a small diversionary offensive.

On December 7, he sent a detachment under Major Frank Paxton to break the Chesapeake and Ohio Canal due north of Martinsburg. The waterway ran parallel to the Potomac River for better than 150 miles. Since the destruction of the B&O Railroad, it was the only commercial link of note between Washington, Cumberland, Maryland, and the west. Confederates had previously damaged the canal, but it had been repaired and was handling boat traffic again.

The specific target of the Confederates was Dam No. 5, originally constructed in 1832–34 of rubble and a wooden crib. In 1857, replacement work had begun on an eighteen-foot masonry barrier. Construction was near completion when the Civil War began. The dam was unusually long, and the lake behind it extended for almost a mile before the river channel reappeared. It watered twenty-two miles of the C&O Canal. Demolition of that particular barrier would sever one of the Union's most important arteries.

Paxton's men reached the area in mid-afternoon that Saturday. From high ground 200 yards downstream on the south bank, Confederate artillery easily drove Federals away from the opposite side. Two companies of infantry plunged into the icy, waist-deep water and laboriously made a small breach before Union sharpshooters drove them from the river. Darkness brought a halt in the operations. Early the next morning, Paxton opened again with artillery. This time the Federals were better sheltered and could not be dislodged. Paxton abandoned the project and retired to Martinsburg.

Publicly, Jackson attributed the setback to "the enemy's resistance and for want of adequate means." Privately, he was convinced that the second day's action had been a violation of the Sabbath and thus doomed to failure.[42]

The general would not accept defeat. To be closer to the target, he shifted his headquarters on December 10 to Martinsburg. He was leading his men northward when he came to a persimmon tree loaded with its green plums. Jackson relished any kind of fruit, and the sight of the persimmons was too tempting to ignore. Quickly dismounting, he scampered into the tree and ate for awhile with the enjoyment of a child. Soon Jackson had become so entangled among the limbs that he could not get down from the tree. Staff members, laughing heartily, brought up some fence rails and improvised a ladder. Jackson remounted his horse as casually as if nothing unusual had occurred and resumed his ride up the road. John Lyle of the 4th Virginia could not understand what the general wanted in the first place with the half-green fruit. Unripe persimmons, he pointed out, "will pucker the mouth till you can't tell if you are whistling or singing."[43]

Martinsburg became field headquarters for ten days. Meanwhile, the first contingent of Loring's command reached Winchester.[44] It was a mixed brigade of Virginia, Georgia, and Arkansas regiments under Colonel William B. Taliaferro, another Virginia blue blood. Jackson knew Taliaferro personally as well as by reputation. The aristocrat was head of the VMI Board of Visitors during part of Jackson's tenure at the institute. Cantankerous and self-righteous, Taliaferro would bear watching closely.

Whether it was threats of secession by western Virginia counties, the Dam No. 5 operations, or other stimuli, Richmond newspapers began paying attention to the land beyond the Blue Ridge and issuing reassurances about the northwest. "There can be no Virginia unless it includes both Eastern *and* Western Virginia," the *Daily Dispatch* editorialized. "If we cannot hold Western Virginia . . . we cannot hold Virginia [and] we can hardly defend the South." The *Enquirer* told its readers: "Let us sympathise with our brethren. . . . We will carry them help and deliverance! We will remove the incubus that weighs them down, and, side by side, assist in chasing the foul foe across the Ohio."[45]

A week after the abortive raid on Dam No. 5, Jackson tried again. This time he personally led the full Stonewall Brigade, several regiments of militia, and part of Ashby's cavalry—just in case Federals were waiting in force. Jackson also took a second precaution. Colonel Preston had been unable to procure enough blasting powder on Saturday. He obtained a sufficient quantity the following day and got even more before the raiding party set out on Monday. One of Jackson's last acts before departing was to summon Preston. In strong tones Jackson said, "Colonel, I desire that you will see that the powder which is used for this expedition *is not the powder that was procured on Sunday!*"[46]

This second advance began on December 17 with a demonstration by General James H. Carson's militia on Falling Waters and Williamsport. Jackson and the main column marched rapidly to Dam No. 5 and resumed work. Several dozen Confederates entered the water with crowbars, axes, picks, and shovels. Their intent was to make several holes at the base of the dam. The pressure of the water from both behind and above would then shatter the entire barrier. While the rest of Jackson's force blazed away at Federals on the opposite bank, the Union infantrymen tried to fire at both Jackson and the wrecking party.[47]

For four days the contest over the dam continued. The demolition party consisted in the main of troops from the 5th Virginia and thirty Irishmen of the 27th Virginia. Jackson had erected a crude stone fortification between the workers in the water and Federals across the river. The only danger to the men was going to and from the dam. The rest of the time they slashed at the wooden cribs until a large hole sent water gushing downstream as the lake upstream began to drain.

Nights were cold. The troops had left their tents behind, and nearness to the enemy prevented campfires. One evening Jackson was shivering in the darkness. Surgeon McGuire insisted that he take a drink of whiskey as a stimulant. The general swallowed the liquid and made a wry face. "Isn't the whiskey good?" the physician asked. "Yes, very," Jackson replied. "I like it, and that's the reason I don't drink it."[48]

On December 21, Jackson led his band through wind and sleet back to Camp Stephenson. He had neutralized Dam No. 5—but only for the few days it took Federals to repair the damage. The expedition cost one man killed and four wounded. Jackson himself continued on to Winchester. There he received doubly bad news: Loring's command was still not at hand, and the Federal garrison at Romney was rumored to have increased to 11,000 soldiers.[49]

Those reports were not as disturbing to Jackson as they might have been. A wonderful distraction gripped his mind: his beloved Anna was due to arrive in Winchester at any time. For weeks she had been begging to join her husband. When he seemed agreeable in mid-November, Anna packed quickly for the trip. She refused to wait for the aide Jackson promised to send as an escort. Friends accompanied her to Richmond; "a kind-hearted but absent-minded old clergyman" traveled with her the rest of the way—even though he managed to lose Anna's trunk in the process.

The final stagecoach ride brought Anna to Winchester late at night. She disembarked in front of the Taylor Hotel without baggage and with no one to greet her. With uncertainty she started up the hotel steps. A heavily bearded soldier stepped away from a group of people on the sidewalk and slowly walked up behind her. Powerful arms swung Anna around; kisses rained on her face. It was Jackson. He had ridden down to the hotel with the hope that the midnight stage might bring his wife.

Jackson took Anna to his headquarters-home. The next morning, Lexington soldiers in the guard mount "were as glad to see her as if their mothers had visited them." For a few days the Jacksons ate their meals in the dining room behind the general's office in the Moore home. This proved so unsatisfactory that Jackson soon accepted the invitation of the Reverend and Mrs. James Graham that they eat two doors down the street at the Presbyterian manse.

Anna blended into Winchester society at once. Jackson attended an occasional function now that his wife was there. He became especially fond of Mrs. Anne Tucker Magill, Mrs. Graham's mother and a descendent of the famous statesman John

Randolph of Roanoke. On one occasion, Jackson made the extraordinary statement to Anna that he hoped she would be like Mrs. Magill in her advanced years.[50]

An Augusta County soldier in early December had written the local newspaper to praise Jackson. "We do not look upon him merely as our commander—do not regard him as a severe disciplinarian . . . but as a Christian, a brave man, possessing moral courage . . . " That soldier may have changed his mind by Christmas week. Many of the men understandably applied for holiday furloughs. Jackson refused them all. The requests were not "consistent with the good of the Public service." A campaign was imminent; everyone was needed in the ranks. "I think it hard but we must submit," one Stonewall Brigade member concluded. Kyd Douglas of the 2d Virginia responded in adolescent fashion. "Man (or rather soldier) proposes, Maj. Genl. Jackson disposes," he wrote a female friend three days before Christmas. "I shall endeavor to pass the present week, secretly determined that if ever Genl. Jackson & I change places, I will send him to do duty in the summer time in Mississippi positively forbidding him to visit his wife (which after all might not be much of a banishment)."[51]

Parts of Loring's command were still drifting into Winchester. The 1st Tennessee arrived amid galelike winds. One of the first officers the men saw was Jackson, "riding upon his old sorrel horse, his feet drawn up as if his stirrups were too short for him, and his old dingy military cap hanging well forward over his head, and his nose erected in the air."[52]

Not even Anna's presence could curb for long Jackson's growing testiness over inactivity. He tightened the picket guard around Winchester and repeatedly told Ashby to remain especially vigilant. On Christmas Eve morning, Jackson sent a lengthy report of his frustrations to his immediate superior. Loring had not arrived, he told Johnston; the size of Loring's total force was unknown; those troops had been on duty in the mountains and were not well drilled; Federal forces in his front were building up faster than Jackson could counter. He asked Johnston for an additional 5000 volunteers, a regiment of cavalry, and another artillery battery. Knowing Johnston, Jackson added: "It may be thought that I am applying for too many troops; but it is a miserable policy to merely base the estimate for troops on one side for future operations upon the enemy's present strength when he is continually receiving reinforcements." Once Loring's men were at hand, inspected, and supplied, Jackson planned "to march on the enemy, unless I receive orders to the contrary."[53]

Just as Jackson was finishing the letter, General William W. Loring rode into Winchester. He would be the first—but not the last—general officer with whom Jackson would clash bitterly.

Born December 4, 1818, in Wilmington, North Carolina, Loring had given his life to the military. He fought Seminole Indians at the age of fourteen and got his first officer's commission at eighteen. A stint in the Florida legislature preceded service in the Mexican War. He lost an arm at Chapultepec but returned to the states a brevet colonel. In 1856, the brevet was removed from that rank. When Loring resigned from the army in 1861, he was the youngest line colonel on duty. Promotion to Confederate brigadier general was instant.

Loring was an experienced officer but never an inspiring one. He possessed little aptitude for high command and seemed incapable of maintaining tight organization among his troops. He could be brusque and belligerent.

The incisive Jed Hotchkiss once gave this analysis of the man: "General Loring always struck me as lacking in nearly all the qualities necessary for command of an army designed to carry on an offensive campaign in a difficult region. He was always hesitating [in] what to do, was always suggesting difficulties in the way of active operations, and worse than all in my mind, he was always filling himself with brandy and thus incapacitating himself for his duties."[54]

Christmas Day was cold and cloudy. Duties were suspended, church services well attended. The Jacksons and the general's staff were invited to dinner at the McGuire home, two blocks down Braddock Street from headquarters. Conviviality and a family atmosphere marked the occasion. Old friend John Preston kept Anna in conversation; young and animated Sandie Pendleton was engaging to all; Major Alfred H. Jackson, a distant relative of the general, proved a good listener; Dr. McGuire supplied humor that more than offset Quartermaster Harman's gruff demeanor; aide George Junkin, dear Ellie's cousin, was eager to please; Commissary Hawks was preoccupied with the food demands of the army about to take the field. The dining table sagged with food. The ever-frugal Jackson dined on cornbread, butter, and buttermilk.[55]

The day after Christmas, a fifty-six-year-old statesman offered his services to Jackson. Charles J. Faulkner of Martinsburg was a graduate of Georgetown College, former state legislator, four-term congressman, and ambassador to France. On returning to America after Virginia seceded, Faulkner was arrested and imprisoned for several months. Federal authorities released him in exchange for New York congressman Alfred Ely, captured in the postbattle confusion at Manassas. Faulkner would accompany Jackson through the first stages of the Romney campaign as a lieutenant colonel and volunteer aide. A breakdown of his health would force him home, but Faulkner would rejoin Jackson a year later.[56]

On December 27, the last element of Loring's "Army of the Northwest" had arrived. In that contingent was the 21st Virginia. A Richmond soldier in the unit wrote: "As we filed to the left at one of the cross streets, we saw standing in the crowd on the sidewalk a man with full dark whiskers and hair . . . and wearing a long blue overcoat with a large cape. His coat reached to his boots, which were worn outside of his pants in regular military style. . . . His head was covered by a faded gray cap, pulled down so far over his face that between cap and whiskers was very little to see. Yet as we passed we caught a glimpse of a pair of dark flashing eyes from beneath the brim of his cap. That man was Stonewall Jackson."[57]

Jackson received calls that night from two officers in Loring's command. Colonel William Gilham, his VMI colleague, paid a courtesy visit and brought with him the 21st Virginia's Lieutenant Colonel John M. Patton. Jackson warmly greeted the slightly built and heavily bearded Gilham. Patton, a Culpeper County neighbor and five years younger than Jackson, had graduated in 1846 from VMI and then achieved success as a Richmond attorney.

The suave Patton lost no time in letting Jackson know the strain of the recent, long march. "General, "he said, "both my regiment and myself are ready to execute your orders, but I feel it my duty to say to you that my men are so foot sore and weary that they could just crawl up barely and if they have any double-quicking to do from the character of your orders, I suppose they will." An impatient Jackson replied: "Colonel, if that is the condition of your men, I will not send them on this expedition. Take them back and report to your brigadier." Patton quickly softened his opinion of the 21st Virginia's condition. Jackson changed the subject.[58]

Loring's three brigades (under William B. Taliaferro, Samuel R. Anderson, and Jackson's VMI colleague William Gilham) were not in the best of shape, but they swelled Jackson's numbers to 11,000 men and twenty-six guns. He still wished for more men. When the War Department suggested that a regiment of Choctaw Indians might be available, Jackson eagerly agreed to take them.[59] In the meantime, he would launch the offensive with what soldiers he had. Jackson dispatched two local cavalrymen to reconnoiter the Romney area while he attended to final details at Winchester.[60]

The major objective of Jackson's offensive was a village of about 500 inhabitants. Yet Romney's size had nothing to do with its military importance. A number of valleys paralleled the great Shenandoah. Three mountain ranges to the west of Winchester was the most extensive and strategic valley. Formed by the South Branch of the Potomac River, it was the "garden" of three counties and stretched for a full 100 miles. Wide meadows on either side of the South Branch made it extremely bountiful in corn and hay as well as near-ideal pasture land for livestock. Romney, the seat of Hampshire County, was the principal community in the South Branch valley. Founded by Lord Fairfax, it was one of the oldest settlements in the region. Hills and mountains surrounding Romney on all sides made it a natural fortress. Whoever controlled the town controlled the whole valley.

Jackson believed that every mile he could open between the Federal troops and his own was an advantage. As long as Romney was in Federal hands, Winchester faced a serious threat. Union depredations had already been widespread. In one seventeen-mile area, forty-one homes had been burned.[61] Such destruction could be a portent of Winchester's fate.

Federals had been steadily strengthening the Potomac region upriver from Washington. However, they adopted a policy of dispersing defense by placing garrisons everywhere. Jackson accurately concluded that no single Union force would attack him, nor would an enemy so accustomed to a defensive posture unite to strike into the Shenandoah Valley. Hence, the Confederate general would employ a divide-and-conquer premise.

West of Martinsburg, the towns of Bath (now Berkeley Springs) and Hancock faced each other on the Potomac near its confluence with the Big Cacapon River. Jackson's plan was to march northwest from Winchester, capture Bath, and disperse the enemy at Hancock. That would secure his rear and flank, thus enabling Jackson to turn southwest and make for Romney.

Virginia regiments had just been awarded new state flags from the governor. On New Year's Eve came orders from Jackson. The men were to draw five days' food, prepare one day's rations, arise at 3 A.M., and begin a march three hours later. Lieutenant Langhorne of the 4th Virginia was not excited. Instead of being at home celebrating New Year's "with those I love so dearly," he informed his family, "I will be

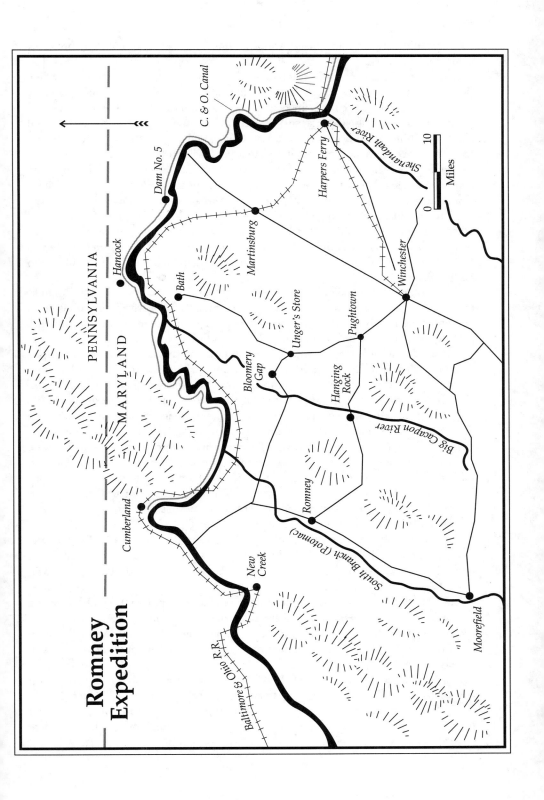

Romney Expedition

PENNSYLVANIA

MARYLAND

Hancock

Cumberland

New Creek

Baltimore & Ohio R.R.

Dam No. 5

C. & O. Canal

Bath

Bloomery Gap

Unger's Store

Martinsburg

Harpers Ferry

Shenandoah River

Winchester

Pughtown

Hanging Rock

Big Cacapon River

Romney

South Branch (Potomac)

Moorefield

Miles

0

10

on a hostile march against those whom at this time last year I called 'brothers, countrymen & friends.'"[62]

January 1, 1862, was a deceivingly smiling Wednesday, an April-like sun sending the temperature into the fifties. Jackson's first offensive in force was unexplainably tardy. It was 9 A.M. before the army began filing out of town and heading northwest on a dusty road.[63] Young soldiers inexperienced in the ways of war left overcoats and blankets behind for the wagons to carry. Guides led the first stage of the march. Jackson tarried in Winchester to attend to a personal matter.

Around noon he walked two doors down Braddock Street to the Presbyterian manse. It was another of those narrow homes in which the main floor was a half-story above the ground. The front door and hallway were on the left side of the house, the main rooms off to the right. Jackson greeted his friend, the Reverend Graham, and asked a large favor. Would the Grahams care for Anna during his absence? She was a stranger in town; but as a minister's daughter, she would fit naturally into the Graham family's routine. Jackson emphasized the kindness that such hospitality would be to both Anna and himself.

The Grahams were delighted to have the company. Near 2 P.M., Jackson brought his wife to the door. They embraced a final time. Jackson asked the minister to remember him daily in prayers. The general then mounted his horse and, with a parting wave to those on the porch, galloped off to join his army.[64]

It needed him badly that afternoon. Everything about the movement had developed a chaotic atmosphere. The units had left from various encampments all around Winchester. Traffic snarls were inevitable in that early period of service under Jackson. Columns of men were advancing in lurches rather than in a smooth march. No one knew where they were going. Rumor had it that the objective was Romney. Yet the line of march was north toward the Potomac, not west into Hampshire County.

Jackson was leading four brigades. Three of them were Loring's and therefore unfamiliar entities to Jackson. In addition, he had five artillery batteries and General Gilbert S. Meem's "brigade" of 545 militia. A dozen different ideas prevailed on how far and how fast the men were to march. To make matters worse, Quartermaster Harman was forced to remain in Winchester because of tonsillitis. He would not be in the march to "cuss" the supply wagons into a tight formation.[65]

Soldiers in the ranks had little inkling of such logistical problems. Most of the troops, a captain reported, "were in fine spirits and seemed anxious to proceed." One regiment even began singing a popular song: "So let the wide world wag as it will, we'll be gay and happy still."[66]

Initially, the route from Winchester was across flat terrain, then up and over Little North Mountain. Broken country thereafter made the advance more difficult. What cooled the enthusiasm of the men, however, came in late afternoon. A northwestern wind rapidly sent the temperature plummeting. Troops lacking outer clothing began shivering.

Near sundown the column halted at Pughtown (now Gainesboro). A half-dozen houses huddled close together in a small valley. Jackson's men had covered eight miles. Wagon trains that were supposed to accompany each brigade were strung out far to the rear, with traffic jams commonplace. In the Pughtown hollow, soldiers utilized whatever shelter they could find. It was useless to build campfires; the wind scattered them at once. Most of the men spent the night without cover on the frozen ground—an exposure that opened the way for much sickness in the days to come. Jackson and his staff huddled through the night in an abandoned log hut.[67]

The rear units were marching under Jackson's orders at dawn the next morning. By 11 A.M. they had caught up with the Stonewall Brigade in the van. Jackson's whole force now resumed the march, except for wagons still bogged down miles away. Without blankets during the night, the soldiers were without food during the day. Jackson rode in silence. The temperature did not get above twenty-seven degrees, but it felt colder because winds sent blinding snow swirling around the columns.

Even Jackson began to suffer from the chill. Prior to the army's departure from Winchester, Robert Y. Conrad gave his fellow townsman, Hunter McGuire, a bottle of very smooth—and very powerful—brandy. Jackson and his staff were shivering over a meager lunch. Knowing that Jackson was cold, Dr. McGuire pointed to the bottle that he had placed on the table. "General," he said, "you had better take some of this. It will be good for you."

"Do you think so, sir?" Jackson replied. "If you tell me I need it, of course I will take some." With that, and while the staff watched in wonder, the unsuspecting Jackson filled a large tumbler to the brim and drank it down without removing the glass from his lips. He resumed his meal and, as was his custom, said little.[68]

General and staff then walked outside into the freezing weather to remount and continue the journey. However, Jackson almost immediately took out a handkerchief and began wiping perspiration from his forehead. The party rode in silence a short distance. Jackson then turned to an aide and commented, "Lieutenant, I am glad to see that it is moderating rapidly. The troops will not suffer much." With that, Jackson unbuttoned his overcoat. The staff member, painfully aware that no rise in temperature had occurred, merely answered: "Yes, sir." A few more miles passed in silence. Jackson then opened his coat and loosened his collar. "Lieutenant," he stated to the aide, "I don't think that I ever noticed such a remarkable change in temperature in such a short time." Again the young aide simply acknowledged Jackson's statement. The remainder of the staff, on the other hand, could hardly suppress their laughter at the sight of their stern, Calvinistic leader undergoing the strange throes of inebriation.[69]

Snow muffled the sounds of Jackson's men straining to keep moving forward. The earth had turned white; ice bent tree limbs and heavy snow caused evergreens to sag. Jackson's objective that day was Unger's Store, the point where the road to Winchester crossed the graded road leading from Martinsburg to Romney.

Now highways already frozen to rocklike hardness grew treacherous from ice and snow. Soldiers began slipping and falling along the rutted path. In addition, Colonel Gilham later stated, Jackson had a choice of several roads to Unger's Store but inexplicably "chose the worst one."[70]

Somehow the Confederates made seven miles before dark. No wagons were yet in sight. Men had been a day and a half without rations and warm clothing. The army had barely covered fifteen miles in two days, and it was losing all effectiveness in the bone-numbing cold.

The general established headquarters on Washington Unger's large estate. He refused an offer to stay in the home and opted instead for a log cabin missing most of its roof. While Jackson penned a note advising Johnston of his intention to attack the Bath garrison the next day, the staff succeeded in getting a small fire started in the half-destroyed fireplace. That was the only comfort for the party except in the case of Jackson. He ate several lemons that Quartermaster Harman had managed to send up to him from Winchester.[71]

Later that night, with teamsters cursing and whipping horses that were having difficulty maintaining their balance, some 160 wagons rumbled into the bivouacs. The arrival of food and supplies elicited from Jackson a simple comment: "That's good." Carson's brigade of militia and a handful of cavalry, which had been advancing on a parallel route, joined the main force during the dark hours. This brought Jackson's force up to 8500 men.

Such was the good news. Then came word that Loring had arbitrarily sent his men into bivouac a few miles short of Unger's Store. He even told them to prepare what food they had while he reported to Jackson. The commander gruffly ordered Loring to bring up his regiments immediately. An assault on Bath would begin at sunrise.

Loring was furious. He returned to his troops and bellowed: "By God, sir, this is the damnedest outrage ever perpetrated in the annals of history, keeping my men out here in the cold without food!" Yet Loring led them unfed through the night. His troops shared their general's anger. Soldiers "got rebellious—almost mutinous," a Tennessean wrote. "They called him 'Tom Fool Jackson.' They blamed him for the cold weather; they blamed him for everything."[72]

On a partly sunny Friday, January 3, the thermometer did not climb above eighteen degrees. Jackson was unconcerned about weather. The work of the Lord and of the Confederacy was paramount. Yet hungry men did not share such feelings of devotion. Members of the Stonewall Brigade dug out of snow that morning to see the welcome sight of supply wagons. Men wanted food; Jackson was anxious to press ahead. The general made a concession: grab what rations you can and get on the road with all dispatch.

General Garnett disagreed. His men had not eaten for over thirty hours. They would march better with appetites curbed. Garnett directed his regiments to fall out. Soon roaring fires were sending the smell of bacon drifting over the countryside. Jackson rode up and heatedly demanded an explanation. "I have halted to let the men cook their rations," Garnett began calmly. Jackson interrupted: "There is no time for that!" Garnett persisted. "But it is impossible for the men to march farther without them." During a moment's silence, Jackson glanced at the troops who were gathering to listen to the exchange between the two generals. Then he gave Garnett a sharp look and snarled, "*I* never found anything impossible with this brigade."[73]

A few minutes later, the troops were plodding northward while Jackson sought to understand how soldiers could want to eat when an opportunity to strike the infidel lay a few miles away. However, sometime around midday, the general stopped at the home of the Reverend John Shockley for lunch. He spent most of the brief period obtaining information on all the roads leading to Bath. By the middle of the afternoon, the Confederates had marched some eleven miles. They were moving through a long valley occasionally interrupted by a foothill. The 870 militia under Carson and Meem soon veered to the left to swing around and approach Bath from the Cacapon Mountain to the west. This would give Jackson a two-pronged attack and cut off the major escape route for the Union garrison inside the resort. Jackson then put Loring's command in the lead of the main column—doubtless so that he could keep an eye on its progress.

Strenuous marching was to be in order for the remainder of the day. Such exertion never occurred. First, the militia moved with extreme caution. It was painfully clear that Jackson had entrusted green troops with too much responsibility. And they were green: one regiment, on active duty only two weeks, had not fired a musket.

The main advance fared no better. Three miles from Bath, Jackson's skirmishers made contact with a Union picket of about sixty men. A brisk exchange of fire netted eight Federals captured and four Confederates wounded. The element of secrecy in Jackson's march was now gone.

Colonel Gilham, whose brigade was in the van, deployed hesitatingly. Jackson quickly discerned that only a thin sheath of enemy resistance stood in the way. He ordered his former VMI colleague to sweep the Federals aside. Gilham was preparing to do so when Loring countermanded the directive and told Gilham to put his men in bivouac.

Jackson had planned to overwhelm the 1400-man garrison (mostly inexperienced recruits in the 39th Illinois and 84th Pennsylvania) and then enter Bath before nightfall. Gilham's unauthorized halt broke the timetable. Jackson stormed with anger. He sought out Loring, and unpleasant words passed between the two. Loring used the opportunity to complain about being kept in the dark about Jackson's intentions and especially his plans. "If you should be killed," Loring almost shouted, "I would find myself in command of an army of the object of whose movement I know nothing!" Nor was he going to learn anything from the distrusting Jackson, who turned without a word and rode away.[74]

Nightfall found the two wings of the Confederate force poised for the attack on Bath. Snow flurries broke through the darkness and heralded a three-inch blanket of white. The next morning—Saturday, January 4—revealed ermine mounds that gave bivouac areas the appearance of large cemeteries buried in snow. With daylight, Lieutenant Lyle observed, "these mounds were burst asunder and live men popped out of them, as if a resurrection was in progress."[75]

Jackson had laid careful plans for the capture of the Federal garrison. Success should have been easy. Mountain ranges close to the east and west squeezed Bath into a long, slender, and vulnerable north-south axis. Yet whatever hopes Jackson had for success that day were dashed early and often.

The militia tried to resume its march. It encountered road obstacles, stepped around them, and bumped into Federals trying to withdraw. "Each fired a volley," a chaplain wrote disgustingly, "and fled as fast as legs would carry them, in opposite directions." One of Jackson's two wings had fallen apart.[76]

Gilham's men, still leading Loring's advance, slipped and slid to within a half-mile of Bath when fire from another Union rear guard rained down from a ridge a mile and a half from town. Gilham sat down again rather than push through the thin enemy line. For most of the day he appears to have done little more than stare at the country. Even worse, Gilham did not even tell Jackson of his inactivity. Loring, meanwhile, managed to scatter the rest of his command all over the countryside—except toward the front.[77]

An exasperated Jackson galloped into this mess and was almost trampled by Southern horsemen fleeing from an ambush down the road. The general got them calmed down. His inspector general, Colonel William S. H. Baylor of Staunton, took command of the cavalrymen and led them charging into town. At one point, they ran into more concealed fire, whereupon Jackson brought up two cannon and blasted a clear passage ahead.

In mid-afternoon, Jackson dashed into Bath in advance of his own skirmishers and Loring's now-moving ranks. The general rode out of town and up to the bluffs overlooking the Potomac River and Maryland. From a full 100 feet above river level, he watched with disappointment as the enemy "was rapidly pursued by ours, but could not be overtaken."[78] Had the militia to the west closed the escape route, the fruits of victory would have been greater.

Confederates bagged two dozen prisoners, secured Bath, and began enjoying captured supplies. Jackson then reported: "As the U.S. troops had repeatedly shelled Shepherdstown, and had even done so when there were no troops in the place and it was not used as a means of defense, I determined to intimate to the enemy that such outrages must not be repeated and directed a few rounds from McLaughlin's [Rockbridge] battery to be fired at Hancock" across the river. The "few rounds" consisted of a bombardment almost three hours in duration.[79]

Bad roads, freezing weather, inexperienced commanders, plus a lack of close coordination on Jackson's part made the day one of limited success. Jackson established his headquarters that night at Strother's health resort in Bath. The buildings were large enough to quarter most of the Stonewall Brigade. Those men were fortunate, for they got to plunder abandoned Union supplies. Nighttime temperature plunged to eight degrees, causing shoe soles to freeze to the ground. Blazing fires throughout the little valley told of where Loring's men were trying to keep warm. Surely, a cavalryman observed, "no man on the continent ever encountered worse weather."[80]

January 5 was the Sabbath, but Jackson could not release the pressure of his drive for the Lord's Day. Snow fell silently for most of the daylight hours. The first positive accomplishment of the campaign came on this fifth day of operations, and Jackson saw the hand of God at work. The 3d Arkansas burned the recently rebuilt bridge over the Big Cacapon River and destroyed a large chunk of B&O Railroad track. Other Confederates stripped a railroad warehouse of ordnance and commissary stores before setting fire to the building. The railroad had run eastward forty-five miles from Cumberland to Hancock. Now the line went only to Patterson's Creek, eight miles east of Cumberland.

Colonel Ashby arrived in Bath later in the day. Jackson sent him across the river under a flag of truce to demand the surrender of the garrison and thus spare any injury to women and children in the town. The Federal commander, General Frederick W. Lander, had just arrived in Hancock and refused Jackson's overture. On receiving Ashby's report, Jackson ordered his guns to open fire from the commanding heights along the south bank of the river.

Union soldiers a mile away in Hancock took cover principally behind two churches. Federal cannon responded for a time. "The enemy literally snowballed us," Colonel Taliaferro stated, "for the missiles from their guns scattered the hard snow, and hurled the fragments upon us, almost as uncomfortable to us as the splinters from their shells." Jackson kept up the bombardment for an hour. No casualties on either side resulted.[81]

Six inches of snow blanketed the ground by the following day. The arrival of Union reinforcements at Hancock, plus ice clogging the river, convinced Jackson to abandon efforts to take the town. It could still be accomplished, but at heavier casualties than Jackson cared to pay. After all, Romney was still the primary object of the expedition. Having disrupted the telegraph, destroyed more of the railroad plus an important trestle, "thus throwing material obstacles in the way not only of transmitting intelligence from Romney to Hancock, but also of receiving reinforcements from the East," Jackson turned his attention to Romney.[82]

The Confederate army spent part of the afternoon and half the night of Tuesday, January 7, traveling back to Unger's Store. The region by then was in the throes of a major snowstorm. That day was the worst of the campaign for the troops. Although the temperature was only in the twenties, the wind-chill factor made it feel like zero.

A regimental band sought to cheer up the marchers by playing "Listen to the Mockingbird," but it was to no avail. John Lyle of the 4th Virginia asserted that the march was reminiscent of Napoleon crossing the Alps. The 2d Virginia's Kyd Douglas related: "The road was almost an uninterrupted sheet of ice, rendering it almost impossible for man or beast to travel, while by moonlight the beards of the men (not mine), matted with ice & glistening like crystals, presented a very peculiar yet ludicrous appearance. I have not been able to find a man in the 2nd Reg. who did not fall down at least twice. . . . 3 men in our Brig. broke their arms by falling, several rendered their guns useless. Several horses were killed & many wagons were compelled to go into night quarters along the road, being unable to get along at all."[83]

Because of an oversight, the horses were without winter shoes. The animals were of but limited use in pulling wagons and cannon. Icicles of blood hung from the horses. Loring was badly bruised when his mount slipped and caused the general to fall to the ground. On at least two occasions, Jackson dismounted and put his shoulder to the wheel of a wagon to keep it from slipping back on a hill. Straggling was rampant. Men stopped anywhere they thought there was an opportunity to obtain warmth, food, or rest.[84]

Jackson arrived at Unger's Store to equally chilling news: some 2000 Federals had surprised and overwhelmed the 700 militia and cavalry at Hanging Rock. That was the only Confederate outpost on the Romney-Winchester road. The troops there were taken by surprise and attacked from two directions. In fleeing to safety, Confederates abandoned almost everything—including, to Jackson's chagrin, two pieces of artillery. The main avenue to Winchester was now unobstructed for the Federals, whose strength at Romney was thought to be 18,000 men. Jackson rushed a force to

Hanging Rock to keep an eye on movements. However, for reasons still unclear, the Federals abandoned the post and returned to Romney.[85]

For the better part of four frustrating days, Jackson fought impatience at Unger's Store. His headquarters again was the imposing Washington Unger home, which stared down in every direction from a commanding knoll. Jackson wanted to advance toward Romney because the Federals might be doing the same in the direction of Winchester. Yet the horses still alive needed to be "ice-calked," which consisted of adding naillike iron wedges to the hooves for sturdier footing.

Jackson reported having 8300 troops on hand at Unger's Store. In truth, he probably had no more than two-thirds of that number. Sick and injured men were hobbling back to Winchester in a steady procession. A six-room frame house just down the road from the country store became a crude and hopelessly overcrowded hospital. Young James Langhorne of the 4th Virginia wrote home: "Ma, I have *witnessed* and *experienced* all of a winters campaign that I desire. . . . I have endured & seen others endure that if a man had told me 12 months ago that men could stand such hardships, I would have called him a fool."[86]

Misery characterized the bivouacs at Unger's Store. The troops encamped in the wet bottomland on either side of Unger's Creek. Food was as scarce as exposure was ever-present. The 5th Virginia named its first site "Camp Mud." Ordered a day or so later to a new location, the men christened it "Camp No Better." Clem Fishburne told of fellow gunners in the Rockbridge Artillery eagerly tearing down fences for firewood in the face of strict orders against such actions. "Sleep was impossible, but men sat about the fires nodding, faces begrimed with smoke, and with freezing backs. Many shoes were burnt out."[87]

While getting his forces ready for a resumption of the campaign, a thoroughly irked Jackson made some changes in command and troop dispositions. He also was awaiting action on a strongly worded recommendation to Richmond. That document was a startling request that Lieutenant Colonel Seth M. Barton of the 3d Arkansas be jumped two notches in rank to brigadier general and assigned to command the Stonewall Brigade. Jackson was completely disenchanted with Garnett at this early point, and he made it painfully clear in his letter to the secretary of war.

> Whilst I am much attached to Genl. Garnett as a gentleman possessing high social qualities, yet my duty to our country requires me to say to you that General G. is not qualified to command a Brigade. Having myself been in command of his Brigade up to the time of my assignment to this District, I feel justified in expressing the belief that it has no superior in our service in proportion to its numbers. And yet I do not feel safe in bringing it into actions under the present commander; as he has satisfied me that he is not able to meet emergencies even in the proper management of his Brigade in camp and on the march. Such being the case he can not be expected to make proper dispositions of his command under fire, where unforeseen emergencies continually arise.

Jackson did not know how accurate that last statement would prove to be two months later. He then praised Colonel Barton, an 1849 graduate of West Point, as a soldier "acquainted with the principles of his profession" and one who "understands the art of their application." The letter closed in typical Jackson fashion, "I am aware that in recommending that Genl. Garnett be thus superseded, my conduct may be condemned; but I believe it to be my duty to report to the Department every change which in my opinion the interest of the Public Service requires." Garnett's ties with Virginia aristocracy, public awareness that his cousin, Robert Selden Garnett, had been the first general officer killed in the Civil War, and the fact that Dick Garnett had led the Stonewall Brigade for barely a month, led Confederate authorities to ignore Jackson's request.[88]

While at Unger's Store, Jackson also issued a number of "furloughs" to officers such as Colonel Gilham and Lieutenant Colonel Scott Shipp, who went back to VMI to resume faculty duties. Meem's militia brigade left for Moorefield, twenty-four miles south of Romney. It would guard Jackson's left on the drive. Similarly, Carson's militia returned to Bath to protect Jackson's right. Ashby's cavalry moved forward to scout the area around Romney.

Preparations for the advance were almost completed when Jackson received unexpected news from Ashby: the Federals had abandoned Romney! They had fled in a near panic, leaving tents where they had been erected, unopened crates of supplies piled in the streets, and hastily set fires licking skyward but doing little damage. Two companies of Ashby's cavalry were already in the town.

Jackson considered this development nothing short of a miracle from God. Some of the men thought it more likely that Federal numbers at Romney had been exaggerated from the start. The reality was that Union officials had overestimated Jackson's force as grossly as he had theirs. Rumors estimating Confederate strength had increased daily. Hence, with reports that Jackson was approaching, Federals hastily evacuated Romney.[89]

With a thaw changing ice to slush, Jackson on January 13 led his army toward Romney. The Stonewall Brigade was in the lead. Nothing about the march could be termed exhilarating. A valley soldier stated: "Muddy roads and many streams to cross. At every step some one cursing 'old Jackson' for taking us on such a march at such a time and in such weather. In the midst of the cursing and grumbling, along rides our general on Old Sorrel. Immediately the cursing stops, and all with one accord begin to cheer. He gallops by, his cap in hand and eyes to the front, his staff following him as best they can. . . . Though the march was hard and toilsome, we felt that he knew what he was doing and that it was for the best."[90]

Morning sunshine gave way to overcast skies and falling temperatures in the afternoon. Two inches of fresh snow fell during the night while the army bivouacked at Slanesville. On January 14, Jackson marched into Romney with his old brigade. It was hardly a triumphant entry. Major Jones of the 2d Virginia wrote, "We reached Romney in the evening of Wednesday cold & wet for we had been exposed to a sleeting rain, it was strange to see the men encased in ice & icicles hanging from the visors of their caps." Loring's men, floundering badly, stumbled into town two days later.

An artilleryman near the end of the long column voiced displeasure in his journal: "That little old faded cap that General Jackson wears may shelter a brain that is filled with . . . war maps, and battle-field plans, but if he thinks we are Indian-rubber and keep on courting Death with impunity . . . he will find that by the time the robins sing again half of his command will be in the hospital or answering roll call in some other clime." On the other hand, a soldier enjoying some of the captured spoils in town commented, "We forgot much of our annoyance with Jackson on this trip, and all began to think 'he had method in his madness.'"[91]

Romney belonged to Jackson, along with some $60,000 worth of stores. The campaign had cost only four dead and twenty-eight wounded. Some 18 percent of his force was on the sick list; yet that was "the usual average of armies," staff officer Sandie Pendleton noted, and included "a large number playing old soldier to shirk hard duty."[92]

Jackson was not content with what had been accomplished. The enemy was in retreat. More might be achieved if pressure were renewed. From his headquarters in John Baker White's comfortable brick home a couple of blocks east of the courthouse, the general drafted a victory announcement to the War Department. "Through the blessing of God I regard this district as essentially in our possession. There is reason to believe that there are medical and other stores in Cumberland, which would, if in our possession, be of great value to our Government." Toward that end, Jackson added that, with another 4000 infantry and 350 cavalry, he was prepared to push immediately another twenty-five miles to Cumberland and seize its railroad bridges, vast stores, and east-west communications links.[93]

When Benjamin could not dispatch the soldiers Jackson desired, the valley commander on January 17 devised new strategy. The brigades of Garnett and Taliaferro would move rapidly the next day due west to New Creek (now Keyser). Destroying the railroad bridge there would isolate Cumberland to the north and enable Jackson to launch an offensive at some future point without danger to his left flank or fear of Union reinforcements.

It was a good plan, but it never came to pass. "The extent of demoralization" in Taliaferro's regiments was too widespread. George Harlow of the 23d Virginia, for example, sent his misery tumbling forth in a letter home. "Part of the time I was verry wet and had to stop at night and build up a fire in the woods and Dry our selves the best we could and do our cooking ready to start the next morning and some of us verry near bear footed at that. I tell you I never knew what hard times were before. . . . Half of our men are sick now."[94]

A daring offensive has little potential for success when the soldiers are untrustworthy. The Stonewall Brigade could not accomplish the task by itself. Hence, Jackson reluctantly abandoned thoughts of a new advance.

Preparations now went forward to go into winter quarters and defend what had been won. Spies such as "Catholic priests in Martinsburg" would keep Jackson apprised of any serious Federal movements. In two letters to his superior, General Johnston, Jackson outlined his winter dispositions. He was dividing his forces but keeping the segments close enough to one another to provide quick support if needed.

Loring's three brigades had "become very much demoralized," Jackson stated. They were broken down because the men had no experience with hard marches. Hence, Loring's command would continue to occupy Romney and the South Branch valley. Carson's militia would remain at Bath; Meem's militia would shift to Martinsburg; the Stonewall Brigade, Jackson announced, "will return to Winchester, and nearer Centreville should you so direct; but in my opinion it should not go farther than Winchester, if the enemy are to be kept out of this district." In another report, Jackson added, "The position assigned to [Garnett's] brigade as a reserve would enable it promptly to move towards any threatened point as circumstances might require." Jackson would direct all operations from district headquarters at Winchester.[95]

Two points stand out in Jackson's orders for the winter. He made it clear from the beginning that the Stonewall Brigade would make the long march back to Winchester, after which it might well be ordered to march again—and possibly into action. North of Winchester, on the Maryland side of the Potomac, a major Union force under General Nathaniel P. Banks stood poised. If it advanced, Garnett's brigade would have to be the first line of defense.

Loring's command (which constituted two-thirds of Jackson's strength) would remain encamped at Romney in order to catch its breath and reorganize. Jackson was aware of the drawbacks. The South Branch area was an advanced position and somewhat exposed. It contained several routes that enemy troops could use to maneuver around Romney. Those enemy troops were at Cumberland, only twenty-five miles away. Romney by then had little appeal of its own. "Of all the miserable holes in creation," one soldier wrote, "Romney takes the lead." He dismissed the place as nothing more than a "hog pen."[96]

If favoritism was involved in Jackson's troop placements, however, Loring's men would seem to be the recipients. To give added security to three full brigades occupying a relatively small valley, Jackson also assigned James Boggs's Hampshire County militia and two companies of locally recruited cavalry to patrol the region. Every man in those units was intimately acquainted with the region and its people. Loring also had thirteen pieces of artillery. In addition, Jackson planned to establish squads of relay couriers while he constructed a telegraph line between Romney and Winchester. Loring would be anything but isolated and alone in the valley of the South Branch.

Rain fell steadily for three days as Jackson completed the winter arrangements. On January 19, he attended Sunday service in a local church and heard a Tennessee chaplain in Loring's command preach on Numbers 32:23: "And be sure your sin will find you out."

It was still cold and wet on Thursday, January 23, when Jackson and the Stonewall Brigade filed out of Romney. A number of fistfights had occurred between the Virginians and Loring's men because, Lieutenant Lyle said, "the Stonewall Brigade reserved to itself the exclusive right to cuss 'Old Jack.'" On the day of departure, Garnett's soldiers cheered as they marched away. Loring's troops watched with sullen anger.[97]

The gains of the Romney campaign are too often shrouded by the stormy aftermath. Jackson had seized his objective, Romney, thereby blocking an almost certain Federal advance against him. In two weeks, the Confederate general had driven the enemy from most of three counties and brought protection to Winchester's western flank as well as liberation to scores of residents suffering under unwanted Federal control. Union garrisons were farther apart than they had been—a situation that kept their commanders more on edge.

Jackson's men had destroyed close to 100 miles of main line and side tracks of the

B&O Railroad. The amount of stores confiscated exceeded what Jackson had at hand at the outset of the campaign. Total casualties in the undertaking were fewer than thirty-five men. Although the expedition had filled hospitals to overflowing in Winchester, Berryville, and other nearby communities, the great majority of soldiers would be returning to duty in as steady a stream as they got away from duty. Jackson had accomplished all that he set out to do, in spite of miserable weather and a second in command whose vanity overrode his sense of responsibility.

All of Jackson's contemporaries voiced complaints about the movements. Later, in their memoirs, many veterans became more positive about the dividends of the Romney offensive. Certainly the campaign revealed in Jackson two characteristics as controversial as they were persistent. First was his unfaltering resolution to push ahead in spite of any and all obstacles. Jackson allowed no distraction to keep him from his objective.

On a more negative note, his uncommunicative nature did not serve him well. Officers could have performed better had they known their destinations and goals. Revealing a few plans to Loring would have partially cooled a heated situation. Had Jackson explained why he thought it necessary to guard Romney, soldiers might have reacted differently. Yet Jackson never thought it necessary for men to understand his orders. He wanted the same blind obedience from them as he gave to his superior, his Heavenly Father.[98]

So anxious was Jackson to see his beloved wife that he rode forty-three miles through the mountains to Winchester in the course of one day. General and staff were nearing Winchester in the mud and slush, Little Sorrel still pounding forward, when one of the aides shouted: "Well, General, *I* am not anxious to see Mrs. Jackson as to break my neck keeping up with you! With your permission, I shall fall back and take it more leisurely!"[99]

The general reined to a halt at the Taylor Hotel. There he removed his mud-coated uniform, cleaned up as best he could, and then hastened to the Graham home a few blocks away. He bounded into the sitting-room "as joyous and fresh as a schoolboy" and embraced his surprised wife. His face, Anna recalled, was "all aglow with delight." At one point that evening, by then a victim of fatigue, Jackson exclaimed, "Oh! This is the very essence of comfort!" In that brief mood of invigoration, Jackson celebrated his thirty-eighth birthday.[100]

Garnett's brigade halted the next afternoon four miles from Winchester on the Pughtown road and began constructing winter quarters. Jackson moved in with Anna at the Graham's after the Reverend convinced him that "it would be cruel to turn Mrs. Jackson out of *her home.*"[101] Headquarters continued to be a few feet up Braddock Street at the Moore home.

The general expressed pleasure at the recent campaign. Yet he found himself in an air of hostility throughout Winchester. The presence of hundreds of sick soldiers appeared to repudiate Jackson as an able field commander; his secrecy and zeal no longer seemed assets; his seeming partiality to his old brigade brought them the unkind nicknames of "Mud Fence Brigade" and "Jackson's Pet Lambs."

Aggravating the displeasure further was Jackson's refusal to grant blanket leaves of absence. He considered the military situation too unstable to weaken his command through furloughs. Jackson made no exceptions. Captain William F. Harrison of the 23d Virginia learned that his infant daughter Julia was seriously ill. Naturally, the father wanted to rush home. He told his wife, "I made an application for a leave of absence but was refused by Genl. Jackson which I think is too hard & also a great injury to the service." The angry captain added, "If Julia is still sick write me immediately & I think I will just come home & they may help themselves."[102]

If Jackson heard criticisms—and he would have had to be totally deaf to have missed all of them—he displayed no reaction. A guard at headquarters stated that the general led "a hermit life in his office" but often went "riding alone about the country, looking grand, gloomy, and peculiar."[103]

That quiet tension exploded all too soon with a series of communiques out of Romney. From the moment Jackson departed the outpost, a roar of dissatisfaction gushed forth. Rain, sleet, and snow falling created a stormy environment in more ways than one.

Loring convinced himself that he was in a perilous situation. In truth, no danger existed. The Potomac River was near flood stage; any crossing was dangerous. Federal detachments were scattered, indifferently disciplined, and of no mind to tangle with Jackson's forces. Union General Lander likened his whole command to "more like an armed mob than an army."[104]

Romney, under Loring's supervision, continued to deteriorate. The courthouse was full of rotten meat, and the streets oozed with raw sewage. A once-proud Army of the Northwest was thoroughly broken down mentally as well as physically. It seemed inclined to wallow in its misery rather than seek improvement. The 1st Georgia and 1st Tennessee claimed to have less than 50 percent of their numbers able to perform any duty.

Sentiment was unanimous throughout Loring's ranks that the campaign to Romney had accomplished nothing but to bring men to the verge of death. The blame for all the misfortunes lay with the "crazy general from Lexington" who was "a maniac for dragging his command" through the snow and frigid temperatures to no good purpose.[105]

The problem with such large claims of sickness has to do with where truth lies. After the war, Surgeon Hunter McGuire asserted sternly: "I went back from Unger's Store to Winchester with five or six surgeons, organized a guard and a guard-house, arrested hundreds of Loring's men who claimed to be sick, had them examined by the surgeons and returned to duty unless they were sick enough to stay in the hospital. In this way in a very few days I sent back to Loring's camp fully 1000 men."[106]

Many of Loring's officers paid no attention to reality. They convinced themselves that prompt and sweeping remedial action had to be taken. Colonel Samuel V. Fulkerson of the 37th Virginia took the lead. A Mexican War veteran and respected jurist from southwestern Virginia, Fulkerson was a good soldier—up to a level of obedience. What Loring's command was having to endure was inhuman, Fulkerson concluded. So he fired off a letter outside military channels to two friends, Confederate congressmen Walter Preston and Waller Staples. The soldiers, Fulkerson charged, had been subjected to an unnecessary and nonproductive winter campaign of indescribable hardship. Now the men were struggling against additional deprivations at

Romney for no sensible reason. Morale was so low, Fulkerson asserted, he probably could not get a single man in his regiment to reenlist as long as the soldiers continued to suffer in Romney.[107]

Colonel William Taliaferro, influential and delighting in it, quickly got into the act. He endorsed Fulkerson's letter with a ringing plea: "It is ridiculous to hold this place. For Heaven's sake urge the withdrawal of the troops, or we will not [have] a man of this army for the spring campaign."[108]

Next in the paper bombardment was an extraordinary petition signed by eleven of Loring's officers—all of the infantry officers in two of Loring's three brigades. (The Tennessee brigade and the artillery units stayed away from the public dispute.) The circular was addressed to Loring, and the first two signers were Taliaferro and Fulkerson. It repeated the same complaints and demanded the kind of relief that only retirement to Winchester would bring.[109] Before Jackson could affix his disapproval at the bottom, however, news of the situation was making governmental rounds in Richmond.

The principal source was Taliaferro, who enjoyed machinations whether in military circles or political arenas. Loring displayed no caution in allowing Taliaferro, Fulkerson, and possibly others to bypass channels and take their case directly to the capital. There Taliaferro began a heavy lobbying among his political friends to get Loring's command recalled to Winchester. With black hair and beard surrounding eyes peering out below heavy brows, Taliaferro roamed the legislative halls in search of those who would lend a sympathetic ear to his stories.

An audience with Confederate Vice President Alexander H. Stephens was fruitful. "He was exceedingly indignant," Taliaferro happily informed Loring, "and said some very hard things against the Secy of War, denounced the Romney expedition in the severest terms, and talked about fools and knaves, etc." On the following day, Taliaferro managed to gain President Davis's ear. It was a gross error of protocol on the commander-in-chief's part to spend time listening to the resentments of a colonel. It was even worse to react to them, and Davis did. The president expressed shock and surprise at what Jackson had done to Loring's brave soldiers. Taliaferro felt comfortable in telling Loring after the conference: "Jackson's prestige is gone, public sentiment is against him. The leading men of the N.W. have asked me if he was not deficient in mind."[110]

That was blatantly untrue. Alexander Boteler and Walter Preston were not fooled by Loring's minions. Sometime that week one of Loring's dissatisfied officers remarked in Preston's hearing that Jackson was unquestionably insane. The congressman quickly stated, "It's a great pity, sir, that General Jackson has not bitten some of his subordinates on furlough and affected them with the same sort of craziness that he has himself!"[111]

Bureaucratic wheels nevertheless were turning. On January 26, Secretary of War Benjamin wrote General Johnston at Centreville that accounts from the Valley District "fill us with apprehension." The president wished Johnston to look at once into the true state of affairs. Johnston was perplexed (he knew nothing of the Loring-Taliaferro machinations); and not being on the best of personal terms with Davis or

Benjamin, Johnston replied somewhat stiffly that he would send his acting inspector general to the valley.[112]

Meanwhile, another "report" was heading east from Romney. Loring directed his acting chief engineer, Lieutenant Colonel Seth M. Barton—whom Jackson had recommended for promotion to brigadier general—to make a survey of the roads and defenses around Romney. Within hours, Barton concluded that "for a small force this point is indefensible." Apparently everyone there regarded Loring's three infantry brigades, plus militia, plus two batteries of artillery, plus at least three companies of cavalry together a small force. Loring added some sharp intimations of potential doom to the report, sent it forward, and congratulated Barton on a job well done.

Colonel George W. Lay made his inspection for Johnston during the same period. He submitted his findings on the last day of January. Lay considered all accounts of hardships and sufferings at Romney to be greatly fabricated, and he closed with thinly veiled criticisms of Loring's conduct as a field commander.[113]

Barton's survey and Loring's endorsement were inconsequential to the chain of events. A decision had already been made in Richmond. For over a century and a quarter, the hapless Benjamin has borne the brunt of guilt for what transpired. Blame should be placed where blame originated: at the feet of Jefferson Davis. It was "at the President's instance," Benjamin let slip days later, that he sent a message to the commander of the Valley District.

On a snowy Friday morning, January 31, Jackson went earlier than usual to headquarters for his before-breakfast check of things. A stack of messages awaited his attention. One telegram caused Jackson to become rigid. It was explosively short. "General T. J. Jackson, Winchester, Va.: Our news indicates that a movement is being made to cut off General Loring's command. Order him back to Winchester immediately. J. P. Benjamin, Secretary of War."[114]

Jackson was stunned. Three months of planning, organization, and hard work had all been for naught. There was no enemy "movement" of any kind underway toward Romney; the secretary's telegram had not gone through channels first for Johnston's perusal and reaction; no explanation for the order was there or seemed forthcoming; what new adjustments Jackson was supposed to make in troops dispositions after the abandonment of Romney were not mentioned.

Benjamin's telegram was the last straw. While some earlier writers believed that Jackson may have waited the better part of a day to acknowledge Benjamin's directive, his reply came forth within the hour. It was as much to the point as the War Department's communique to him.

Hon. J.P. Benjamin, Secretary of War, Sir:
Your order requiring me to direct General Loring to return with his command to Winchester immediately has been received and promptly complied with.
With such interference in my command I cannot expect to be of much service in the field; and accordingly respectfully request to be ordered to report for duty to the Superintendent of the Virginia Military Institute at Lexington; as has been done in the case of other Professors. Should this application not be granted, I respectfully request that the President will accept my resignation from the Army.
I am, sir, very respectfully, your obedient servant, T. J. Jackson.[115]

A courier bearing the letter galloped out of Winchester toward Johnston's headquarters at Centreville. Jackson checked to ensure that Loring's command would be alerted that morning to abandon Romney. Then he returned to his room at the Graham's. A few minutes later, Jackson for the first time came downstairs alone to breakfast. His quiet demeanor gave no reason for concern.

Anna soon appeared, obviously distressed. Mrs. Graham asked conversationally how she was feeling. Anna tried to reply, burst into tears, and rushed from the room. Jackson, voice calm, apologized. "Mrs. Jackson is a good deal disconcerted by the change we have decided upon. We expect soon to return to our home in Lexington." The general casually mentioned that Loring's command had been recalled to Winchester. Pressed by Graham, he explained the situation. "My indignation was aroused even to fierceness," the Presbyterian cleric confessed. He expressed outrage at the actions of Confederate officials. Jackson raised a hand to stop Graham's explosion, then remarked: "The [War] Department has made a serious mistake; but no doubt it has been made through inadvertence, and with the best intentions. They have to consider the interests of the whole Confederacy, and no man shall be allowed to stand in the way of its safety. If they have not confidence in my ability to administer wisely the affairs of this district, it is their duty to repair the damage they believe I am doing."[116]

Perhaps Jackson was trying to convince himself as much as his clerical friend. He returned to headquarters in mid-morning. The snow had stopped and the temperature was climbing. Jackson was angry, without question. Resentment coursed through his being. He tried to see God's hand at work; perhaps it was time for Jackson to return to VMI and shape the minds of young men; perhaps his work as a Southern soldier was meant to be two campaigns. No question exists but that Jackson prayed for guidance several times during the day.

Knowing that it would take time for his resignation to go through channels and get to Richmond, he sat at his desk and wrote a long, personal letter to John Letcher. The governor was a friend; he would be the one to order him back to VMI. It was important to Jackson that Letcher know exactly what was at issue. Benjamin's order, he stated, "was given without consulting me, and is abandoning to the enemy what has cost much preparation, expense and exposure to secure, and is in direct conflict with my military plans, and implies a want of confidence in my capacity to judge when Genl. Loring's troops have to fall back, and is an attempt to control military operations in detail from the Secretary's desk at a distance." Jackson was not seeking either reconsideration or redress. "I ask as special favor, that you will have me ordered back to the Institute." He was certain that Benjamin's order would "destroy the entire fruits" of the recent campaign. "A sense of duty brought me into the field, and has thus far kept me. It now appears to be my duty to return to the Institute, and I hope that you will leave no stone unturned to get me there." Whatever effectiveness over the soldiers Jackson had developed came "through the blessing of Providence" and had now been undone by Benjamin's directive. "I desire to say nothing against the Secretary of War," Jackson concluded. "I take it for granted that he has done what he believed to be best but I regard such a policy as ruinous."[117]

By sunset, all of Winchester's citizenry knew of Jackson's resignation. Distress and anger permeated the town. Everyone displayed agitation except Jackson. "So far as I knew," Graham observed, "he was the *only* calm and unexcited man among us." Dr. McGuire added that every Confederate soldier in the town was "mad and excited."[118]

Johnston held Jackson's letter for a couple of days while he sought to reason with his principal lieutenant. That was difficult to do, especially since Johnston himself was livid at Davis's interference as well as his lack of military courtesy. Johnston's endorsement of the resignation was pointed: "I don't know how the loss of this officer can be supplied." He forwarded another dispatch to Richmond with the curt comment: "Respectfully referred to the Secretary of War, whose orders I cannot countermand."[119]

In an open and conciliatory vein, Johnston sent a letter to Jackson. "My Dear Friend," he began, "The dangers in which our very existence as an independent people lies, requires sacrifice from us all who have been educated as soldiers. I have taken the liberty to detain your letter to make this appeal to your patriotism—not merely for warm feelings of personal regard, but for the official opinion which makes me regard you as necessary to the service of the country in your present position."[120]

Even stronger reactions came from two of Jackson's political friends, Alexander Boteler and John Letcher. On the morning of February 1, Boteler—who somehow had a copy of Jackson's letter of resignation—arrived at the War Department at the same time as Benjamin. The secretary, as was his wont, tried to open the conversation with pleasantries. Boteler was in no mood. Are you aware, he snapped as he placed the letter in front of the secretary, that General Jackson has resigned from the army because of your order? The secretary read the letter and blanched. He then returned the sheet to Boteler. "You had better take this letter to the President," Benjamin mumbled.[121]

Boteler stalked from the War Department. A few minutes later, he sat across from Davis in the Confederate White House. The President read Jackson's communique. "I'll not accept it, sir!" Davis exclaimed. Boteler informed him in an icy tone that he might not have any choice in the matter. While Davis pondered what to do next, Boteler went to the governor's mansion. The bespectacled and usually mild-mannered John Letcher went into a rage at the news. With "a miscellaneous assortment of oaths," he stormed down the street and into Benjamin's office. Controlling his anger, Letcher asked the secretary not to take any action on Jackson's resignation for the time being. Benjamin was delighted to agree with the Virginia statesman.[122]

What else passed between the two men is unknown, but two things are clear: Benjamin realized that he had blundered into a hornet's nest trying to be the president's messenger boy, and Letcher was irate. The governor was stomping from the War Department's general office when he overheard a clerk say, "Jackson is a crazy man." In a voice easily heard by everyone in the room, Letcher shouted: "Crazy! Crazy! It's a damned pity that Jackson's character or insanity does not attack some in this department!"[123]

A couple of days later, Letcher told VMI's Colonel Smith that the War Department was "falling into disrepute . . . with the people. Complaints are loud." Yet Letcher and others suspected strongly that Davis was behind the no-confidence action with Jackson. Popular condemnation, however, centered on Benjamin.[124]

Letcher solicited letters to Jackson from Jonathan M. Bennett and Boteler; he himself wrote a long and personal appeal. These petitions were but large drops in a flood of correspondence that poured into Winchester headquarters. Friends, slight acquaintances, admirers all pled with the general not to leave the field. Colonel S. Bassett French of Davis's staff exclaimed of Jackson's resignation, "No heavier blow has yet befallen us or likely to befall us." A Harrisonburg citizen told Jackson of the "universal regret which the people of our County feel at the thought" of losing his services. Even an Englishman visiting in the valley felt compelled to tell President Davis that Jackson was "a brave Soldier & a truly Christian man" whose very name "appears to be a tower of strength."[125]

Presbyterian cleric Francis McFarland made a deep impression on Jackson when he wrote, "I think God has raised you up to serve your Country in this day of her greatest calamity & she cannot afford to dispense with your services." A captain in the Stonewall Brigade made a sweeping judgment: "No man in the Confederacy can ever gain the confidence of the people so entirely as Jackson has. Hence, no one can fill his place."[126]

On February 4, with four inches of fresh snow on the ground, Letcher sent a personal letter via Colonel Boteler to Jackson. The governor was convinced that Jackson must not leave the army. Boteler had dinner with the Jacksons, after which the two men repaired to Jackson's office in the Moore home. Boteler marveled at how calm and courteous Jackson appeared in the midst of what had become almost a national crisis.

With Jackson seated and Boteler standing, the congressman made it clear that he was there to try to talk Jackson out of resigning. Jackson expressed a willingness to reconsider the matter, "if I can do so consistently with my sense of duty." He made it clear, though, that he could not manage his military district or a campaign and continue to be subject to the whims of someone "sitting at a desk three hundred miles away."[127]

Boteler agreed; yet, he said, Jackson was overreacting. Pro-Jackson sentiment was running at high speed in Richmond. Such a mistake as Benjamin's directive would not happen again. More to the present, Boteler stated, the Confederacy would be grievously wounded if Jackson left it now. Surely, the statesman added, "you will not permit yourself to be an exception to those who are dedicating themselves, their time, talents, energies, and all that they owned besides, to the love and service of Virginia."[128]

That was the wrong thing to say, and Boteler realized it at once. Jackson leaped to his feet; standing rigidly, eyes flashing, lips compressed, he began pacing back and forth in the room. Then he stopped in front of his congressional friend. In a loud but courteous voice he exclaimed:

Sacrifices! Have I not made them? What is my life here but a daily sacrifice? War has no charms for me; I've seen too many of its horrors. Preferment has no allurements to compensate me for its trials and temptations. My only ambition is to be useful.

The hope of being serviceable as a soldier brought me here. I gave up the peaceful pursuits of a congenial occupation for the cares, discomforts, and responsibilities of the camp. I left a very happy home, Colonel, at the call of duty, and duty now not only permits but commands me to return to it.

A pause, and Jackson added in a more composed tone: "I shall, of course, seek other opportunities to serve our State. I will serve her anywhere, and in any way, in which I am permitted to do it with effect, even if it be as a private in the ranks. Sacrifices, do you say, Colonel? You know not what a sacrifice it is for me to leave my old command, now that I have learned to love them and that I know how much they are attached to me!" He stared at Boteler for a moment, then made what became a famous comment, "If the Valley is lost, Virginia is lost." Jackson then sat down, his case presented in sum and his opinions expressed in full.[129]

Boteler understood and sympathized. Yet Jackson must remain in a command position. The Shepherdstown resident resumed his appeals. Virginia needed all of her sons, Jackson must not quit in the middle of a fight, the whole Confederacy would be demoralized if he turned his back on the cause. The general's indignation was obviously melting. Finally, Boteler stood to leave. "Well," he asked, "what message am I to take back to our good friend, the Governor, in answer to his letter?" Jackson stared out the window into the night for what seemed several minutes. Then, pausing between phrases, he replied: "Tell him . . . that . . . he'll have to do . . . what he thinks . . . is best . . . for the State."[130]

Two days later, Jackson asked Letcher to withdraw his resignation. A happy Lieutenant Douglas told one of his female friends: "It's tolerably well established now that Genl. Jack's resignation will not be accepted. It better not be if Sect. Benjamin would die in peace."[131]

Now back in full command, Jackson wasted no time in correcting what he considered the delinquencies of others. A week earlier, Quartermaster Harman had observed, "Loring is like a scared turkey, and so is his command." Cause for alarm was real. The day after withdrawing his resignation, Jackson preferred charges against Loring. The seven specifications ranged from dereliction of duty to insubordination. Johnston concurred with Jackson's wish to court-martial Loring. His regiments were "in a state of discontent little removed from insubordination." By then, President Davis and Secretary Benjamin just wanted to forget the whole episode. Airing dirty laundry with a lengthy court-martial was not the answer. Reorganization would accomplish the same thing in quieter fashion.[132]

The Army of the Northwest ceased to exist. Loring received promotion to major general and banishment to southwestern Virginia. His units were ordered dispersed to a number of posts. Davis was convinced that "the good of the service requires that no part of General Loring's command be left with General Jackson." The reshuffling, however, did not turn out that way—perhaps as a gesture of atonement by the secretary of war. Jackson retained all of Loring's Virginia units: the 21st, 42d, and 48th Regiments plus the 1st (Irish) Battalion of infantry, plus the Fredericksburg and Danville batteries of artillery.[133]

When the smoke of the Romney controversy cleared, Jackson had won a personal battle. He did not gloat because such was not part of his nature. Any "exoneration" was meaningless to him. Soldiers had balked at his style of leadership; civilians had openly questioned his capacity to command. A threatened resignation certainly did not endear him to the Confederate high command. His court-martial preferments were ignored. So were his pleas for more troops. If Jackson were triumphant in the early months of 1862, it was a hollow triumph indeed.

Even worse, his gains of icy January became the president's disasters in muddy February. Jackson had staked his career on the Romney expedition, which ultimately became a failure. Once Loring abandoned the South Branch valley, Federal soldiers reoccupied Romney and Moorefield. The Confederate outpost at Bloomery Gap, only twenty-one miles from Winchester, fell to surprise Union assault. Sixteen officers and at least thirty-five men were captured in the rout. Winchester was again vulnerable to attack.

Federals rebuilt the railroad bridge over the Big Cacapon above Bath. By February 23, the Baltimore and Ohio Railroad was repaired and open as far west as Hancock. Loring's machinations undid all the work of Jackson's toilsome marches. Moreover, in Loring's haste to get back to Winchester, his men even burned most of the Confederate supply wagons to keep them from falling into enemy hands. Small wonder that Federal General Nathaniel P. Banks, gathering this information on the other side of the Potomac, advised McClellan, "The enemy was never in a feebler condition than at this time."[134]

No long-range achievements came from Jackson's expedition. He severed and battered Union communication lines for a month. Federals had to engage in a winter campaign not of their liking. Jackson drove the enemy from three Virginia-minded counties, but Federal forces came back and reoccupied the areas. All of the gains had been Jackson's; all of the losses came from the interference of Davis.

Jackson deserves high marks for strategic planning and for persistence in the face of many adversities. Low marks are equally glaring. He never untangled supply lines— and never seemed too concerned to do so. Jackson expected too much from Loring's brigades, which he should have known were not up to the quality of his own troops. The confidence Jackson repeatedly placed in militia, who consistently came up short, is another characteristic of Jackson.[135]

Loring departed in February, but the Federal army remained. Its misconduct after recapturing Romney elicited unusually harsh language from Jackson in his official summary of the campaign: "I do not feel at liberty to close this report without alluding to the reprobate Federal Commanders, who in Hampshire County have not only burnt valuable mill property, but also many private houses. Their track from Romney to Hanging Rock, a distance of fifteen miles, was one of desolation. The number of dead animals lying along the roadside, where they had been shot by the enemy, exemplified the spirit of that part of the Northern Army."[136]

Jackson would not forget. It is ironic that at precisely this time Jackson's former West Point classmate and now Federal general in chief, George B. McClellan, sent a warning to General Frederick Lander: "If you gain Romney look out for [the] return of Jackson, whom I know to be a man of vigor & nerve, as well as a good soldier."[137]

12

THE LESSONS OF KERNSTOWN

CONDITIONS IN WINCHESTER by mid-February 1862 could scarcely have been more propitious for Stonewall Jackson. Elements both military and conjugal had united to create an atmosphere that was almost euphoric. It revived the general's longing for a child to fill the void caused by the short life of infant Mary Graham four years earlier. Anna Jackson became pregnant that month.

Jackson had emerged triumphantly from a crisis that could have terminated his military career. He had withdrawn his resignation from the Confederate army amid acclaim from one end of Virginia to the other. "Everyone is rejoicing over it, as he is beloved by all," a soldier in the 27th Virginia wrote home. "Whenever Genl. Jackson comes in sight of his old brigade they yell out as if they had gained a victory."[1]

Elevating Jackson's spirits even more was the presence of Anna in Winchester that entire winter. This was the first—and only—time in the war when the couple had an extended period together. Reverend Graham quickly discovered how Anna "seemed to be the greatest alleviation to [Jackson's] trials. . . . His devotion to her was unbounded & he lavished upon her every attention & expression of tenderness."[2]

The Graham home and family provided the kind of atmosphere that intensified feelings of love in both Jackson and his wife. It was a warm, Christian, happy home with three small children—a place possessed of all the ingredients needed to bring out maximum tenderness from the general. While the Jacksons occupied the upstairs bedroom on the northeast corner of the house, the whole manse became their home.

James and Fanny Graham were perfect hosts. The Presbyterian clergyman was six months younger than Jackson and a native of Montgomery, New York. After completing ministerial studies in 1850, Graham had served a series of small churches in western Virginia. On October 9, 1851, he had become pastor of the Kent Street Presbyterian Church in Winchester. He would hold that post for the next forty-eight years.

In October 1853, Graham had married Fanny Bland Tucker Magill of Winchester. A son later described her as "a red hot Southerner on both sides of her house." When the Jacksons moved in with them, the Grahams had three children: a daughter who was five, a son three, and another son eighteen months old. The middle child, Alfred, became Jackson's favorite.[3]

Graham came quickly to consider Jackson "really a member of my family. He ate every day at my table, slept every night under my roof and bowed with us morning and evening at our family altar. He called my house his home." The cleric scoffed at all those who regarded Jackson as an eccentric. "In my intercourse with him during all that period, I cannot recall a single act or word, which I would have wished were different, or which the most censorious could construe to his disadvantage. His demeanor and conversation were those of a dignified and refined gentleman . . . and while carefully observing all the amenities and courtesies which true politeness exacts, he largely contributed, by his uniform cheerfulness and thoughtful consideration, to the happiness and comfort of all about him."[4]

To the Grahams, Jackson was *"strictly methodical"* in his habits. He arose at the same early hour and went straight to his headquarters. There he attended to mail and issued orders for the day. A few minutes before 8 A.M., he returned to the manse so that at precisely on the hour he could escort his wife downstairs to breakfast. Anna's health was not good at the time—she had "quite a severe attack" of some ailment in mid-February, according to Lieutenant Pendleton—so Jackson was particularly solicitous of her comfort.

The general refused to conduct any official business at the parsonage. If a courier arrived with a dispatch, or an officer required a word, Jackson escorted him a few doors up the street to the Moore home-headquarters and attended to the matter there. Similarly, Jackson would not discuss military matters inside the Graham home except to the minister in private. A lady dinner guest who pressed Jackson for some specific information finally dropped the subject when he looked at her intently and stated: "I'll have to say to you, as the schoolboys sometimes say, 'Ask me no questions and I'll tell you no lies.'"[5]

Beneath Jackson's grave earnestness, Reverend Graham noticed, were "expressions of warm affection, and of the value of friendship, and the charms of home." This was especially the case with the Graham children. It took them a few days to warm up to the dark, bearded man in mud-splattered uniform. Yet he continued to make a fuss over them and to cultivate their friendship. "His fondness for children was remarkable," Graham stated. "He would seize them with eagerness, hug & kiss & fondle & try to amuse them." When Jackson could make one laugh, it "seemed to please & tickle him very much." Often at mealtimes Jackson would come into the dining room on his hands and knees, making loud horselike sounds while little Alfred Graham sat on his back like a rider and squealed with delight.[6]

One evening a group of young artillery officers called to pay their respects to Mrs. Jackson. Fun-loving by nature, the Confederates were soon using the chairs as cannon and waging an artillery fight with the Graham children. The antics in the parlor were robust and loud. Soon the door opened. The noise had drawn Jackson downstairs. Everyone in the room became still with embarrassment. Yet Jackson caught the gist of what was taking place. With mock authority, he said: "Captain Marye, report this engagement tomorrow—along with the casualties." He then took a seat and enjoyed the revelry.

Jackson looked on James Graham as the same spiritual authority and commanding officer as he had viewed Dr. White in Lexington. Graham was familiar with both military affairs and the situation of the war. Hence, Jackson felt quite at ease in discussing war philosophies with the minister. When Graham once asked him for a candid opinion of his West Point classmate and now Union general in chief, George

B. McClellan, Jackson expressed a high estimate of his talents as an organizer and strategist. "If he can handle his troops in the field with the same ability with which he organizes them in camp," Jackson added, "he will be simply invincible."[7]

In another evening discussion, Jackson became expansive. "War means fighting," he declared forcefully. "The business of a soldier is to fight. Armies are not called out to dig trenches, to throw up breastworks, and live in camps, but to find the enemy, and strike him; to invade his country, and do him all possible damage in the shortest possible time." Graham was somewhat taken back. "This would involve great destruction of both life and property," he commented. Jackson nodded. "Yes, while it lasted; but such a war would of necessity be of brief continuance, and so would be an economy of prosperity and life in the end. To move swiftly, strike vigorously, and secure all the fruits of victory, is the secret of successful war."[8]

As military commander of that district, Jackson had to endure much adoration and curiosity. Gifts began to arrive in what would be an increasing stream. Two sisters-in-law from Jefferson County were among the first donors. They sent several bottles of wine as a "small testimonial of our approbation of your well earned fame & heart-felt gratitude for the '*Stone Wall*' defence of our frontier."[9]

Participation in religious services almost always subjected Jackson to unwanted attention. On a rainy Sunday afternoon, February 23, he attended a prayer service at the Episcopal church. The rector, J. B. T. Reed, was also mayor of Winchester. Reed was so struck by Jackson's presence that, at the close of a hymn, he asked: "Will General Jackson lead us in prayer?" Jackson rose, closed his eyes tightly, and crossed his arms over his chest. His voice reached every corner of the packed sanctuary. "O Lord, God of Hosts, prevent, we beseech thee, the effusion of blood; but if we *must* fight, give us the victory. Amen." Methodist minister Benjamin Brooke, also at the service, declared: "I shall never forget the emphasis he put on the words 'if we must fight.' He felt that we were on the defensive." Another worshiper used Jackson's prayer as a lead-in for her own exultation. A teenager in attendance described what happened next: "The church was crowded and by way of enlivening the crowd and for the special edification of said crowd, a young lady, by name of Josephine Singleton, concluded to have a *fit*, which she had, creating much excitement." Everyone in the church turned to the sound of the woman's screams—except for Jackson. Brooke stated that the general "kept his eyes steadfastly fixed on the altar, nor changed a muscle of his face. I have never witnessed such respect for the house of God." The clergyman added: "If he fights as he prays—short and to the point—he will be apt to do some execution."[10]

Jackson moved precisely in February to put the whole Loring episode behind him. He filed charges against Loring in the first week of the month and forwarded other charges against Colonel William Gilham two weeks later. No military tribunal ever convened to hear the cases, much to Jackson's disappointment. According to Kyd Douglas, Jackson gave vent to his anger in a February 12 note to his congressional friend and liaison, Alexander Boteler. "An official dispatch received this morning informs me that the enemy are in possession [again] of Moorefield. Such is the fruit of evacuating Romney. Genl. Loring should be cashiered for his course."[11]

Other concerns of a more immediate nature pressed upon Jackson. With the dispersement of much of Loring's force, the valley army shrunk in both numbers and potential. Quartermaster John Harman informed his brother in Staunton: "If we are not reinforced we will certainly have to leave Winchester. Don't speak of this; it is too bad. Loring's advent into the valley broke up the efficiency of the whole army, and this encouraged the enemy to press upon us, but still, I hope for the best."[12]

Jackson's units remained part of Joseph E. Johnston's Confederate army. Yet Jackson was virtually isolated in the Shenandoah Valley. Even worse, he was operating separately against two opponents, each of whom greatly outnumbered the valley defenders.

Federal General Nathaniel Banks was in the same situation as Jackson in that he was commanding in the lower valley but officially remained part of the main Union army concentrated in the Washington area. In the Alleghanies west of the valley was a second Union force. Its presence was a constant threat to Jackson's flank and rear. To add to Jackson's troubles, he was trying to defend the northern end of the Shenandoah, but the most strategic site was at the other end of the valley. The town of Staunton could not be lost; it was the western railhead of the Virginia Central Railroad, the major communication link between the upper Shenandoah Valley and Richmond.

To offset his numerical shortcomings, Jackson employed a combination of hard work, drill, discipline, and preparedness. He was at his desk six days a week. Staff members made morning reports and received daily assignments before departure. Jackson oversaw paperwork so meticulously that little of note escaped his attention. He reviewed his official report of the Romney campaign several times prior to its February 21 submission.

In foul weather and fair, he rode out to examine troop positions. Mary Katharine McVicar, a young teenager, got her first glimpse of the general as he went to inspect the lines. "He rode rapidly to the front and returned more slowly in a short time," she noted. "I must have looked my youthful enthusiasm for he bowed courteously as he passed, and no monarch on earth could have seemed so grand to me."[13]

Jackson did not construct any system of earthworks for the defense of Winchester. Three reasons lay behind that decision. He did not believe that soldiers should lose their fighting edge by spending a lot of time as "laborers and ditchers." Jackson was convinced that his Winchester position could be turned from any direction—a situation that rendered a defensive line potentially fatal for those locked in it. Further, as one of Jackson's aides said, the general preferred "to hear the lark sing rather than the rat squeak." The officer's metaphor testified that Jackson chose to fight in the open where he had room to maneuver.[14]

Still more details occupied Jackson's daytime moments in the military lull and the wet days of late winter. While he freely acknowledged the Stonewall Brigade to be the best-armed unit in the Confederate army, he sought better weapons for the other components of his army, especially the cavalry.[15]

A more immediate question for Jackson was manpower. The valley army had a paper strength of 13,759 men. Yet because of sickness, recruitment furloughs, and desertion, no more than 5000 men were present for duty. That was the equivalent of a good-sized brigade. Federal General Nathaniel Banks was no military leader, but he had better than 38,000 soldiers behind him. Eight-to-one odds were formidable under any circumstances. For Jackson, securing more troops at the moment was a touchy issue.

The Confederacy was born in chaos and never fully outgrew it. Obtaining men for the armies was a typical case in point. The Confederate Congress's first series of acts regarding terms of service for soldiers was hasty and confusing. By the end of 1861, men were in service for six months, a year, three years, or for unspecified lengths of time. The first remedial step came in January 1862, when Congress enacted a law whereby all state militia and volunteers enlisting thereafter would serve for three years or the duration of the war. Such a long-term obligation did not sit well with men possessing short-term patriotism.[16]

On February 8, the Virginia General Assembly also moved to strengthen Old Dominion regiments. The one-year enlistments of most Virginia troops was steadily approaching expiration; no great rush at reenlistment was taking place. This prompted the February bill under which all males between the ages of eighteen and forty-five not then in service would be put in a military pool. From it they were subject to being conscripted to fill the ranks of "volunteer" units. To many, freedom of choice seemed to be in peril.[17]

While both recruitment measures rested on good intentions, the results were too often disastrous. Men reenlisted, took the furlough that accompanied it, and disappeared. Jackson limited those recruitment furloughs to no more than a third of any command at one time. Units such as the Stonewall Brigade reenlisted "encouragingly." Dissatisfaction and desertion were widespread in other segments of the valley army, especially on the heels of the Romney ordeal. Much of the discontent among volunteers concerned militia. Although Jackson had frozen their terms of service on January 4, the militia characteristically gave the appearance of dwelling in the lap of peaceful luxury.[18]

Another sore subject with Jackson was the statewide practice of allowing units that reenlisted to elect their officers. He had strong opinions against the policy—so strong, in fact, that he took it upon himself to urge Governor Letcher to intervene in having the practice curtailed. "Do that as far as practicable, that lax discipline, resulting from electioneering for office, may be avoided. . . . We may expect an inefficient set of officers from such a system; and inefficient officers must have inefficient commands." Jackson reminded the governor: "We must make our cause superior to every temporal consideration."[19]

To Jackson's pleasure, the soldiers who remained on duty exhibited high morale. By the end of the month, a member of the Stonewall Brigade reported, "Our troops, under the lead of the gallant Jackson, are in fine spirits, and although the enemy may outnumber them, are eager for the fray and sanguine of success."[20]

Keeping civilians of suspected loyalty either in custody or under surveillance was an unsolvable problem for Jackson. "With regard to putting the female Tories in the Winchester jail," he stated, "I think it would be impolitic; as the Lawyers have even annoyed me about my disloyal male prisoners."[21]

The closest Southern force to Jackson was Harvey Hill's command at Leesburg, roughly midway between Jackson and Johnston. Hill's force consisted of four Mississippi regiments, the Richmond Howitzers, and a few companies of cavalry. The two brothers-in-law were in agreement that they needed to strengthen their lines of communication. While Hill kept a strong patrol in the Blue Ridge at Snicker's Gap, through which curled the main Winchester-Leesburg road, Jackson set about to construct a raft bridge for the road across the Shenandoah River at Castleman's Ferry.[22]

Despite a strict regimen of drill and discipline, Jackson was never completely able to keep liquor away from his soldiers. The failure was not from want of trying. He banned all troops, except those under special authorization, from visiting Winchester. Because wagons were traveling down the valley with whiskey in crates labeled as food, Jackson directed all brigade commanders to examine every wagon coming to camp. "If liquor is found in them, spill it out and turn the wagons and horses over to the Chf. Quartermaster," he ordered. Jackson even asked for a national prohibition act of sorts. To Boteler he wrote: "I have recently been much concerned about so many distilleries in our country. Cannot Congress take steps for stopping them? I would like, if practicable, to have the copper thus used taken possession of, and turned into Ordnance Departments for the purpose of making cannon. Copper is very scarce."[23]

In that same last week of February, an engineering officer whom Jackson had requested weeks earlier finally reported for duty. James Keith Boswell would become one of Jackson's most reliable staff members. Born November 18, 1838, the son of a Virginia physician, Keith Boswell was a civil engineer who worked at railroad construction first in Missouri and then in Alabama. He returned to Virginia at the outbreak of civil war and served on the staff of General John B. Magruder before joining Jackson. The young aide was both an outstanding engineer and a congenial companion. Another member of Jackson's staff regarded him as "an excellent, good-natured, honest Presbyterian . . . is well off, has a sweetheart in Fauquier [County], where the Yankees are, and he talks much about her."[24]

Boswell's arrival coincided with the long-anticipated Federal advance in force across the Potomac. The lead elements of Banks's army moved in slow and uninspired fashion to Harpers Ferry. They secured the town, its nearby heights, and several miles of riverbank stretching in both directions.

Jackson warned Harvey Hill of the enemy offensive and put his own forces on alert status. "If I fall back, it will be in the direction of Strasburg," Jackson told Hill, "but I trust that *God in all his wise providence* will render such a movement unnecessary."[25]

Meanwhile, Boswell had made a quick inspection of the Winchester defenses and pronounced them "almost worthless." This judgment caused Jackson to take the unusual action of asking Johnston's advice about fortifying the town at that late stage.

Even though Johnston failed to reply, he was not in favor of Jackson making a stand in the lower valley. So often Johnston's movements followed the premise of "when in doubt, retreat." He was unaware at this time that McClellan was planning to transfer his huge army by boat to the Virginia peninsula and approach Richmond from the east. Johnston, expecting the Army of the Potomac to march to Manassas, planned to retire in front of it toward the capital.

In that eventuality, Johnston expected Jackson to fall back on line with the main army's withdrawal. Such a parallel rearward movement by Jackson would protect Johnston's left flank, secure the passes through the Blue Ridge, and impede enemy progress up the valley. Above all else, Johnston wanted his lieutenant in the Shenandoah to forestall Banks from reinforcing McClellan, who already substantially outnumbered all the forces Johnston could bring to bear.[26]

What Johnston actually expected of Jackson early that March was vague and somewhat contradictory. "After it had become evident that the valley was to be invaded by an army too strong to be encountered by Jackson's division," the departmental commander wrote, Jackson "was instructed to endeavor to employ the invaders of the valley, but without exposing himself to the danger of defeat, by keeping so near the enemy as to prevent him from making any considerable detachment to reenforce McClellan, but not so near that he might be compelled to fight."[27]

Jackson interpreted that order differently from the way Johnston intended it. Both generals were cognizant of a steady series of Confederate defeats that winter. Union forces had gained a toehold on the Atlantic coast at Roanoke Island, North Carolina. Federals there seized 2500 prisoners and thirty guns. In the West the situation was worse. Following a Confederate rout at Mill Springs, Kentucky, came the losses of Forts Henry and Donelson in Tennessee. Another 14,000 men and a dozen heavy guns fell into Union hands. Nashville had become the first Southern capital to surrender. Across the Mississippi River, Southern efforts came to naught at Pea Ridge, Arkansas.

Perhaps Johnston was unconcerned about such developments, but to Jackson they imparted a stern sense of urgency to the military picture in Virginia. That is why he gave secondary consideration to retreat and thought primarily of attack. This was typical Jackson. The Southern government was hard pressed on all fronts. Units were falling back in both major theaters. Yet Jackson, at the most northern point of the Confederacy, wanted to launch an offensive "if practicable" (one of his favorite expressions).

Jackson dispatched Turner Ashby's cavalry to ascertain if the Harpers Ferry defenses had a weak point that could be assaulted. The general also forgot his aversion to soldiers shoveling and put everyone to work converting Winchester into as much of a fortress as was possible. Such a move might cause the Federals to hold back any further advance while Jackson collected reinforcements from unspecified sources. If Banks should decide to send out a probing party, Jackson would be ready to pounce upon it.

He knew that Johnston did not agree with such strategy. Jackson covered himself with his superior by explaining the impracticability of retiring in tandem with Johnston's army. The valley was a military theater unto itself, he explained. Jackson could not be a buffer and protect Johnston's flank as long as retreat was the order of the day. He planned to strike at any opportunity. Keeping the enemy off balance would be the best safeguard for Johnston's soldiers.

Jackson seemed oblivious to his precarious geographical position in all of this planning. It was sixty miles to Culpeper and the nearest linkup with any of Johnston's forces. The only support available to Jackson was General Edward Johnson's little command, which was ninety miles away in the mountains to the southwest. Undeterred, Jackson stood firm at Winchester. "If we cannot be successful in defeating the enemy should he advance," he told Johnston, "a kind Providence may enable us to inflict a terrible wound and effect a safe retreat in the event of having to fall back." In another letter that same day to Congressman Boteler, Jackson was more forceful. "What I desire is to hold the country as far as practicable until we are in a condition to advance, and then with *God's* blessing, let us make thorough work of it." It must be done that way, Jackson insisted. "I have only to say that if this valley is lost Virginia is lost." That was the essence of Jackson's thinking then and in the weeks to come. It was the strategy he would pursue—the military activity that would catapult him into the front rank of generals in the second spring of the Civil War.[28]

By early March, Winchester was no place for his beloved Anna. She must head south to safety. Jackson put her on a stage to Strasburg, where she could board a train bound for Richmond. Telling his wife goodbye in the midst of great uncertainty was a chore for the general. Yet he had to appear happy in seeing to the well-being of the one person he idolized. Anna remembered: "In the midst of all this terrible mental strain my husband maintained the most perfect self-control and cheerfulness. . . . To the last moment he lingered at the door of the coach in which I left with bright smiles, and not a cloud upon his peaceful brow."[29]

They parted, neither knowing that it would be thirteen months before they would see each other again. Anna made her way first to Hampden-Sydney College in southside Virginia. For the next three months, she alternated her time in the college homes of two second cousins. One was Mrs. Benjamin M. Smith, whose husband was a theology professor at the seminary. The other was Lavinia Morrison Dabney, the wife of another cleric-professor, the Reverend Robert L. Dabney. Anna's prolonged temporary home at Hampden-Sydney College turned Jackson's mind repeatedly toward the Presbyterian church and his friends in the clergy. Before the end of the month, Jackson would draw Dabney into field service.[30]

Weather fluctuated in the first days of March between rain and snow. A combination of mud and caution slowed the Union army as it edged toward Winchester. Jackson toiled even longer hours, especially after Anna's departure. If he had to abandon Winchester, he would leave behind nothing of military value. Jackson's way, one of his men observed, "was to save everything already on hand and never destroy anything there was a chance to save. It was a saying in the command that he would carry off a wheelbarrow load rather than let it fall into the hands of the enemy." Now he worked diligently "getting everything out of reach of the enemy, in case he should be compelled to leave" the town.[31]

Jackson was undoubtedly proud of the accomplishments of his profane but equally hard-working quartermaster. Major John Harman, convinced that the evacuation of Winchester was inevitable, started early in removing the vast accumulation of supplies from Winchester to Strasburg, eighteen miles away. Establishing 250 teams with cooking and feeding stations at the two ends of the route, Harman kept wagon trains moving on a schedule that called for a round trip every twelve hours. Mules strained and wagons creaked day and night. Harman got all the supplies removed to Strasburg at the rate of 500 loads every twenty-four hours.

Jackson's commissary, Major Wells J. Hawks, was equally efficient. For the previous six weeks, Hawks had kept the army abundantly provisioned with food gathered from the agricultural coffers of the valley. The commissary now began diverting shipments for Winchester to Strasburg. By the second week of March, and to give more protection to foodstuffs, Hawks set up a new depot farther up the valley at Mt. Jackson.[32]

On March 7, Johnston began withdrawing from the Manassas line. The likelihood of giving up Winchester became more certain. Yet on the west side of the Blue Ridge that day, Jackson offered battle to Banks. The Union commander did not know how to respond for one simple reason. Even though he was the fourth ranking general in the Union armies at the time, Nathaniel P. Banks was not a soldier. He was one of those prominent politicians appointed a general because of his influence in his home state, in this case Massachusetts. Nearly everyone in 1861 thought the war would be over in a few months, so a number of appointments as general went to political leaders for obvious reasons. Banks was then in his mid-forties; he had spent his adult life climbing the political ladders through Congress to the governor's office. He was slight, short, with an absurdly large mustache that seemed to conceal everything below his nose. Throughout his bland military career, Banks always treated the Southern people leniently. On occasion, he would display surprising military audacity, but not at this early stage of the war.

On Friday the 7th, Banks shuffled forward to within five miles of Winchester and bumped into Ashby's horsemen. A brief firefight ensued. Jackson promptly moved his infantry into a battle line two miles north of town and waited for combat. Banks refused to take the bait. For the next three days the Federal general was content to extend his lines into a ninety-degree arc and to inch carefully toward Winchester. Confederates grew anxious as reports of enemy movements multiplied. A member of the Rockbridge Artillery expressed the prevailing sentiment: "I know not what we are going to do; rumors are as numerous as 'persimmons in the state of Fluvanna,' but Old Jack keeps his counsel and *says nothing.*"[33]

Jackson's boldness and Ashby's cavalry activities convinced Federal officers that a large force was inside heavily fortified Winchester. A brigade commander informed Banks that Jackson "is being considerably re-enforced, some say very strongly; that the slopes of the hills west of Winchester are strongly entrenched with rifle-pits and several earthworks with heavy guns. . . . One man recently in Winchester reports Jackson as saying that he left Winchester once to whip us at Manassas, and now he is going to do the same for us here." Another Northern officer, who should have known better, stated disgustingly of Jackson's defenses at Winchester, "One could have jumped over them as easily as Remus over the walls of Rome." Young Sandie Pendleton of Jackson's staff agreed. The lieutenant informed his father that Jackson had "in all not over 5500 men 'for duty'—rather a small force considering they have certainly over 12000 with[in] 25 miles of us." Pendleton conjectured, "The plan seems to be to hold those points until they amass a large force in front of us, and force us to retire."[34]

Whatever Jackson had in mind, he had few troops with which to do it. His "army" was a gross misnomer, for it consisted of no more than 3600 soldiers. The First or Stonewall Brigade, under Richard Garnett, included the 2d, 4th, 5th, 27th, and 33d Virginia. Each regiment was supposed to number 1000 men. The 4th Virginia mustered barely 300, and a third of them were without weapons.

Colonel Jesse Burks commanded the Second Brigade, which contained the 21st, 42d, 48th Virginia, and 1st Virginia Battalions. Burks was a year older than Jackson, a VMI graduate, Bedford County farmer, and former state legislator. The Third Brigade, under "Judge" Samuel Fulkerson, contained only the 23d and 37th Virginia. Jackson's six batteries had a total of twenty-seven guns of small caliber. Ashby commanded roughly 600 cavalrymen.

On the positive side, Jackson was leading an all-Virginia force in which half of the regimental colonels and a third of the battery captains were VMI alumni. On the negative side, the 3000 badly needed muskets that Jackson had requested were nowhere in sight. The general, who believed in the value of the bayonet, was now considering the use of pikes for lack of anything better.

Johnston and the main body of the Confederate army were now behind the Rappahannock River. McClellan had advanced to the abandoned Manassas works. Banks sought to keep pace with McClellan. His left moved cautiously and, early in the afternoon of March 10, occupied Berryville to the east of Winchester. About 40,000 Federals—ten times Jackson's force—now threatened Winchester from three directions.

The general masked his concerns that day in a cheerful letter to Anna. "The troops are in excellent spirits," he began. Then Jackson commented on the state of his own physical being. "I am very thankful for the measure of health with which He blesses me. I do not remember having been in such good health for years." Other than expected fatigue, Jackson's physical condition would remain amazingly good throughout his field service. No eye problems beset him further; his constitution suffered no malfunctions; complaints of dyspepsia were nonexistent. This seemed to confirm anew that when Jackson was active, especially with military matters, his health was excellent. Having reassured Anna of his well-being, he concluded his letter with the announcement: "My heart is just overflowing with love for my little darling wife."[35]

Jackson continued the forlorn hope that Johnston would release Harvey Hill's force at Leesburg so that it could unite with the Winchester army. To his brother-in-law, Jackson stated: "I have reason to believe that a kind Providence would give us a rich military harvest. As yet, the enemy have not come within nearer than five miles of me; but may do so at any time, if not prevented by God."[36]

The next day Jackson decided to become God's instrument. Early in the afternoon the Union host came into view: "an immense force steadily advancing on the Martinsburg road . . . with waving banners winding along the hillsides west of the pike, like some huge shiny snake in a coat of mail, reflecting the bright afternoon sunlight that flashed with shattered splendor from thousands of glittering muskets and burnished trappings."[37] Winchester must not be abandoned without a fight, Jackson determined. The Federals were superior in numbers but inferior in spirit. He would meet Banks's slow advance with a fierce assault of his own during the hours of darkness.

On the afternoon of Tuesday, March 11, Jackson summoned Garnett and the regimental colonels from the Stonewall Brigade. He presented to them plans for a surprise attack to be made sometime in the night. The men would march to the southern end of Winchester, secure food from the quartermaster wagons, and rest for a few hours. Then the soldiers would slip back through Winchester and proceed four miles north of town to be in position to assail the enemy in the darkness.[38]

Exhilarated at the prospect of smiting a sinful invader, Jackson walked down Braddock Street that mild afternoon to partake of food and prayers with the Reverend Graham. The general "was really joyous in spirit," Graham noted, "speaking with *glee* & delight at the conduct & eagerness of his men to engage the enemy." Jackson ate a light meal, prayed fervently with his pastor, and left "full of spirits & completely relieving us of all our fears" as to the safety of Winchester.[39]

Near sundown, Jackson reconvened the council at the already stripped-down headquarters. Almost instantly his affable disposition changed to angry exasperation. Supply wagons, which were to be parked just south of Winchester, had mistakenly been taken eight miles farther south to Newtown. The soldiers had tramped there to obtain rations. It would require an all-night march of twelve miles to bring them back into battle position. The troops were too weary for such a move. Furthermore, every one of Jackson's senior officers expressed opposition to the idea of a surprise attack. The general abruptly broke off the meeting.

Within the hour, Jackson was back at the Graham home. "A sadder, more dejected countenance I never saw," the clergyman stated of the general. Jackson informed Graham that he would have to evacuate Winchester without a battle. "This I grieve to do! I must fight!" Jackson exclaimed with flashing eyes as he drew his sword halfway from the scabbard.[40]

He stood motionless in meditation for a moment, then his shoulders slumped. "No, it will cost the lives of too many brave men. I must retreat." He thrust the sword back in place. "I am compelled to say goodbye," he told the Grahams. "Nothing but necessity and the conviction that it will be for the best induces me to leave." Jackson added that if he "survived the war" (which Graham said was one of the general's favorite expressions), he hoped "that a good Providence will permit me to return and bring deliverance to the town." With that, Jackson left the parsonage with bowed head and depressed spirits.[41]

A full moon lit the sky when the Confederate army filed slowly out of Winchester. Citizens lined the sidewalks. Some wept; others watched silently. One small lad kept shouting forlornly: "Jackson's gone! Jackson's gone!"[42]

Even in the dark of night, the sadness permeating the ranks was detectable. Many of the soldiers had family and friends in the lower Shenandoah Valley; others had grown to consider Winchester a second home. To march away without a fight, and with an enemy host moving in the wake, was demoralizing.

Jackson and Surgeon Hunter McGuire left Winchester together. The two rode to a high point overlooking the town, stopped, and looked back. McGuire, realizing that he was abandoning his family, Winchester home, and everything dear to him, momentarily lost his composure and began to weep quietly.

Then he looked at Jackson, whose face "was fairly blazing with the fire that was burning in him." His facial muscles twitched, his lips were pressed firmly together as he gazed at the lights of the town and then at his retreating soldiers. Jackson broke the silence by snarling in a loud voice, "That is the last council of war I will ever hold!"[43]

Wheeling his horse around, Jackson started toward the head of his column. Lieutenant John Lyle stared in wonder at the general. "He came riding furiously like the driving of Jehu, and looked as if the thunderbolts of Jupiter were pent up in him, and [Jackson] would like to hurl them on Banks and his army." A short distance from Newtown, Jackson finally reined to a halt. He dismounted and went to sleep in a fence corner.[44]

Ashby's cavalry hovered in Winchester until 8 A.M. the next day before retiring defiantly. A deathlike stillness pervaded the town for a half-hour, Mrs. Hugh Lee noted in her diary. "Then music and some cheering announced their approach; the Yankees came in on different streets, more quietly than I had anticipated." An Ohio surgeon thought the march of the Union army into Winchester to be a wondrous sight. "Regiment after regiment with colors flying and music filling the air! One's heart could almost be caught in the teeth as it bounded with patriotism." However, most Union soldiers quickly pronounced Winchester to be anything but hospitable.[45]

By sunrise on March 12, the Confederate army had resumed its march up the valley. Jackson, on foot leading his horse, brought up the rear for part of the journey. His force halted at Strasburg, eighteen miles from Winchester. The old Byers tavern alongside the Valley Turnpike became headquarters for the next couple of days. Jackson appeared to be "in good spirits" as he watched for any Federal pursuit and weighed his options. "Will we continue our retreat or fight?" Major Frank Paxton asked rhetorically in a letter to his wife. "No one knows. Jackson always shows fight, and hence we never know what he means."[46]

The short stay at Strasburg did not pass idly. Jackson collected supplies and consolidated his forces. Thanks to recent state decrees, he also began increasing the size of his army. On March 8 the Old Dominion had called up 40,000 militia from the male population. Some 12,000 of them were to go to the defense of the valley.

Jackson knew that he was not likely to receive anywhere near that number. However, on March 12, Governor Letcher issued an executive order empowering departmental and district commanders to enroll on active duty all militiamen in their area. Jackson promptly ordered the militia in the valley to join him "as soon as practicable." Although the response was good, acceptance into the ranks was slow and sometimes traumatic. "The volunteers were disposed to sneer at them," John Lyle of the 4th Virginia stated after viewing one militia regiment. "The companies were not in uniform and each man was wearing the style of dress that suited his taste and his purse. The colonel of the regiment was an amicable, intelligent and patriotic old farmer, who did not know, or pretend to know, anything about military matters."[47]

Many of the militia used umbrellas on the march as a shield against the sun. "Some of the men carried shot guns and others squirrel rifles, and others had no guns of any kind. These latter would 'fight'm with gate hinges.'" Such units seemed totally unworthy of being part of Old Jack's force.[48]

Jackson was not ready for any open battle. In his estimation, the men were insufficiently drilled and the situation too unstable at the moment. The ranks must be strengthened and morale elevated; equipment was ragged and in short supply. Reports that Banks was sending General James Shields's division of 9500 Midwesterners up the valley convinced Jackson on March 15 to shift his forces to the Woodstock-Mt. Jackson region.[49]

Like residents of Winchester, townspeople of Strasburg watched helplessly as the Confederates abandoned the area. The 5th Virginia's James McCutchan admitted: "I had to cry myself when I came through Strawsburg. The doors & pavements were filled with Ladies old & young & even the little children some weeping, [led] to do so by the tears of their Mothers & Sisters."[50] The withdrawal was unhurried. It could not be called a retreat. The Virginia Central Railroad was the only rail link now available to the Confederates, making the Staunton terminus Jackson's main base of supplies. Falling back toward it was sound tactics.

A regular letter writer to one of Richmond's newspapers gave a valid overview of feelings inside Jackson's ranks. "It is hard, indeed, to give up this beautiful and fertile country, the Valley of Virginia; but it is policy to curtail our line of defence, and fall back where we can concentrate all our forces. Perhaps we will make Staunton our permanent rendezvous; but Gen. Jackson will take his time getting there, and all the troops in Yankeedom will scarcely make him swifter in his movements."[51]

Turner Ashby and his horsemen covered Jackson's rear and skirmished daily with Federals who ventured too close. In spite of steady rainfall, the Confederates made a leisurely twenty-seven-mile march southward on the double-laned, macadamized surface of the Valley Turnpike. Troops set their own pace, while the long wagon trains moved as smoothly as railroad cars. Locomotives on the Manassas Gap line pulled all rolling stock to the railhead at Mt. Jackson.

As the long column moved along the turnpike, Jackson rode in front and gave sharp attention to an unusual feature of the Shenandoah Valley. Starting at Strasburg, a large and interlocking system of high ridges obscured the Blue Ridge as it stretched fifty miles up the valley before descending into the valley floor east of Harrisonburg. This chain was called the Massanutten Mountain; it was a veritable stone and forested wall imposing enough to split the Shenandoah corridor into two separate passageways. On the west side of the Massanutten was the wider, open ground of the great valley, more adaptable to troop maneuvers. To the east of the imposing ridge was the smaller Luray corridor with its single, rough road.

Figuratively speaking, the Shenandoah Valley from Strasburg to Harrisonburg resembled a capital "H." The lefthand arm was the main valley; the righthand arm was the Luray valley; between the two corridors stood the Massanutten. The crossbar in the "H" was the sole road over the Massanutten in the entire fifty-mile span. That route went through a pass at the halfway point and connected New Market with Luray. Jackson could see that he was vulnerable to an enemy turning movement unless both valleys were adequately defended. He was also aware of another fact: he could use both valleys as avenues for his own offensives.

The general halted his force at Rude's Hill, three miles south of Mt. Jackson but still north of the vital Massanutten Gap crossing. By nature, Rude's Hill was one of the strongest defensive points in the area. The ridge was more than 100 feet above the valley floor. Between it and Mt. Jackson, a spur of the Massanutten jutted westward and caused the North Fork of the Shenandoah River to make two ninety-degree angles in curling around the hilly intrusion. This left a moatlike expanse of lowland directly in front of Rude's Hill. Such "lay of the land" would discourage any attack from the enemy. Further, a single wooden bridge crossed the low ground. It was usable enough for Confederates to protect and combustible enough to prevent Federals from securing it.

Hideous climatic conditions during the Romney campaign had taught Jackson several things about logistics, and he never forgot the lessons of those winter marches. Now the general selected good campsites for his troops, ensured that they had sufficient food, occupied their time to good advantage with drill, worked arduously at filling ranks, and enforced discipline as every good commander should.

Jackson established his headquarters on March 19 at the home of Israel Allen in the settlement of Hawkinstown, three miles north of Mt. Jackson. First-floor rooms became quarters for the staff; Jackson's bedroom was on the second level. The general did not pause to rest, however. "He daily found something to do to improve the character of his command," Jed Hotchkiss observed. "He was always interviewing subordinates in reference to one thing or another in this direction. . . . He frequently called the heads of staff departments to him for daily reports as to the condition of their supplies, the wants of the army, the condition of transportation, etc. Especially was he very active in looking after the artillery arm of his service . . . he had but little time left for social intercourse." Yet the soldiers saw him regularly.[52]

At least once a day Jackson rode through "Camp Buchanan." He chatted here and there with individuals; and by doing so he cultivated a sense of acquaintance between general and enlisted men. The optimism that resulted in the ranks showed forth in a letter from Sergeant George Peterkin of the 21st Virginia to his mother. "Surely our retreat has been conducted in the most masterly manner. We have now more men than we had when we left Winchester, owing to recruits and re-enlisted men coming in, and our army is in better spirits, and better organized and prepared in every way."[53]

Federals applied no pressure to the Confederate encampment. In order to disrupt enemy pursuit, Jackson set Ashby to work burning every bridge between Strasburg and Mt. Jackson. Meanwhile, Shields's division, which had halted at Strasburg, showed no inclination to pursue farther—particularly since "reliable" estimates put Jackson at New Market with 35,000 men. Moreover, winter still lingered persistently, with blustering winds and low temperatures. It was not a good climate in which to fight.[54]

A raw wind added to the discomforts of March 20 as 500 Augusta County militia reported for duty at Rude's Hill. Attached to the group was an engineer who proceeded to headquarters and announced the militia's arrival to Jackson. The staff officer was thirty-three-year-old Jedediah Hotchkiss. At seventeen he had left his home in southern New York State to make his place in the world. A self-made man with a love of learning, he was accustomed to success. Hotchkiss had settled near

Staunton, become principal of Mossy Creek Academy at twenty-one, and by the outbreak of civil war was a leading geologist in Virginia. Cartography was one of Hotchkiss's favorite pastimes.

Schoolmaster and scientist, almost six feet in height, he had sleepy eyes and a scraggly beard. Hotchkiss was not an exciting figure, but serious in disposition, spurning both alcohol and tobacco. His only major vice was an occasional tendency toward long discourses. Devotion to duty and God were Hotchkiss's hallmarks.

These were the precise qualities that Jackson most admired in a man. Hotchkiss and Jackson were not total strangers. They had become acquainted in the 1850s when Hotchkiss was a house guest of the Junkin family in Lexington and Jackson was still living with his in-laws. Now the highly versatile Hotchkiss was anxious to serve under Jackson in the field.

The adopted Virginian found Jackson busy, careworn, but pleasant. "He had many questions to ask," Hotchkiss stated. Jackson "was much pleased to hear of the good condition of our men—enquired especially if we had Dunkers with us, & if they were opposed to fighting."[55]

No man had deeper respect for religious beliefs than did Jackson. However, three large valley denominations—Mennonites, German Baptists ("Dunkers"), and Quakers—were ardently pacifistic. While their young men could be forced into the Confederate army, Jackson was aware that they refused to fire a gun in anger and were prone to desert at the first opportunity. How to blend war needs and religious tenets occupied part of Jackson's attention at Rude's Hill.

He came up with what he regarded as a workable arrangement. Male members of pacifistic sects would enter the army, be organized into units, and learn the rudiments of drill short of the point of firing weapons. They would then serve as teamsters and in other support roles for soldiers on the front lines. "If these men are, as represented to me, faithful laborers, and careful of property," Jackson stated to authorities in Richmond, "this arrangement will not only enable many volunteers to return to the ranks, but will also save many valuable horses and other public property, in addition to arms." Jackson closed with an afterthought: "It may be that officers for these companies would be a useless expense."[56]

A rude awakening came to the militia field officers the next day. Jackson ordered all of the regimental officers into the ranks as company leaders. "There were some very much put out because they were cut down," Hotchkiss declared, but they kept quiet when Jackson rode out at noon "and *looked* at the Militia."[57]

Meanwhile, the wheels of activity on the Northern side had picked up speed. General-in-Chief George McClellan was transferring his large Army of the Potomac to the Virginia peninsula to strike at Richmond from the less strongly defended eastern side. President Lincoln had reluctantly approved the wide-swinging, mass-and-maneuver offensive, but he insisted that enough Federal troops be left in the Washington area to keep the Union capital "entirely secure." Among the forces McClellan consented to leave behind was the Federal corps on the upper Potomac with headquarters at Frederick, Maryland. That was the corps of General Nathaniel Banks.

In a few days, however, McClellan concluded that 4600 Confederates under a college professor with a reputation for eccentricities posed no threat to the North in general and Washington in particular. On March 16, the Union commander ordered Banks to "post your command in the vicinity of Manassas" and leave four regiments and two batteries to guard the Manassas Gap Railroad bridge over the Shenandoah River. "Something like two regiments of cavalry," McClellan felt, should be enough "to occupy Winchester and thoroughly scour the country . . . up the Shenandoah Valley."[58]

Banks carried out his instructions in deliberate fashion. As far as he was concerned, his operations in the valley had been a complete success. The first order of business now was to pull James Shields's division back from Strasburg to Winchester so that the Federal force could start en masse across the mountains.

Friday, March 21, was another raw day. Rain was blowing in sheets early in the afternoon when Jackson received a hasty note from his cavalry chief, Turner Ashby. Shields was retiring northward, while a long procession of loaded Federal wagons was moving east from Winchester toward the Blue Ridge Mountains. Ashby rather nonchalantly informed Jackson that he was giving pursuit of Shields's full division with three companies of cavalry and Preston Chew's battery of horse artillery.

Jackson at once deduced the meaning of the Union movements. Banks's whole corps was leaving the valley to join McClellan for a drive on Richmond that could end the war. It was up to Jackson, and Jackson alone, to block the enemy consolidation. "Apprehensive that the Federals would leave this military District," Jackson reported later, "I determined to follow them with all my available forces."[59]

Major General Thomas J. "Stonewall" Jackson was not a familiar figure in the Civil War at this moment. It had been nine months since he had done anything extraordinary. Now he was embarking on a campaign that would make his name a household word. Operations for the next three months were the product of his imagination and daring alone. The military network in Richmond had comparatively little involvement. One of Jackson's staff officers was adamant on that point. "Lee left it to Jackson's discretion as to what he should do with Banks and his associates, and Jackson then acted on his own judgment."[60]

At dawn on March 22, Jackson's command was tramping northward. How the men marched that day was how they always marched. It was "route step"—in other words, walk as you please so long as you keep up with the column. Soldiers proceeded four abreast; many units found it easier to march in a semblance of step so as to keep the ranks moving steadily without men stumbling over the heels of one another. Each man carried his gun and equipment any way that was comfortable. Whatever rations a soldier had consisted of what he had prepared in the early-morning darkness before the day's march began.

Jackson would occasionally leave the head of the march and ride the length of the column to check on progress. "Press on, press on," is all he said, but he did so with urgency. The files moved steadily forward; men by the scores soon dropped along the way from exhaustion; wagons fell miles behind the infantry, who soon and proudly would call themselves "Jackson's foot cavalry." Cleon Moore of the 2d Virginia remembered the events of that Saturday. "The head of the column moved towards Winchester. We were in high spirits. Suffice it to say, we made a forced march . . . that resulted in aching limbs, sore feet, empty stomachs. . . . For one day and half we marched as only Jackson's men could march."[61]

Despite cold winds and deep mud, most units covered twenty-one miles that day. The rear regiments trudged twenty-seven miles before bivouacking in the vicinity of Cedar Creek. Jackson made his headquarters in Strasburg, close to the advance elements. He counseled that night with no one but God, and the general doubtless spent a good part of the nighttime hours on his knees.[62]

He had reason to be thankful. His command, in spite of heavy straggling, was within a day's march of Winchester and the enemy. That afternoon Ashby's little band of horsemen had embarrassed the Federals in Winchester in an action as dramatic as it was daring. Surgeon Samuel Sexton of the 8th Ohio reported that Ashby's cavalry "came up Saturday evening, drove in our pickets, captured a few wagons, and almost took the town! Indeed many of us were not certain at one time but what we were prisoners. (Our troops were all encamped 3 or 4 miles on the opposite or Martinsburg side of town.) But in less than an hour troops were pouring in front of the [Confederates] on the hill, for battle. A brisk cannonading was kept up until dark."[63]

Ashby inflicted more than confusion in the fight. One of Chew's artillery shells exploded near Shields; a fragment struck and broke the general's arm just above the elbow. False rumors spread on both sides that the limb had to be amputated. Shields fainted twice from the pain; he was furious at being severely wounded in nothing but a skirmish. A doughty Irish immigrant, he had commanded infantry in the Mexican War and had three scars to show for it. Of equal importance on that March 22, Shields kept his composure and soon rebuffed Ashby's probe. He did so with a small detachment while keeping the bulk of his division on the Martinsburg road north of town—and out of Ashby's view.[64]

Ashby never learned the full strength of the Federals. Hence, he relayed to Jackson dangerous misinformation on Shields's numbers at Winchester. Accounts differ as to why this happened. One of Ashby's cavalrymen had Winchester ladies saying that only a skeleton force of the enemy was still in town. Another reliable source stated that several of Ashby's scouts disguised themselves, entered Winchester, and made troop tabulations themselves. In other quarters, reports circulated of a Confederate traitor misrepresenting the number and locality of the Federals. In time, some valley residents came to believe that Jackson received a forged message from General Johnston to enter an abandoned Winchester. Still another report was that the Union army rapidly fell back en masse to put down a citizens' uprising in Maryland. In any event, Ashby informed Jackson that only four Union regiments and a battery or two of artillery were still in town, and they were hastily preparing to withdraw to Harpers Ferry.[65]

The weather changed for the better during the night. March 23 dawned bright and warm. At 6:50 A.M., Jackson informed Johnston, "With the blessing of an ever kind Providence I hope to be in the vicinity of Winchester this evening."[66] Jackson accelerated the rate of march that morning. Men already fatigued from the strain of the previous day could not keep up. Stragglers soon lined the roadside as the Confederates made a second forced march, this one of about fourteen miles.

Around 2 P.M., Jackson's three brigades wearily drew to a halt near the southern outskirts of the hamlet of Kernstown. Winchester was four miles away. Yet the two-day advance had stripped Jackson's force to 2700 infantry, 290 cavalry, and thirty guns. At least one of his companies was unarmed. The general was aware of the fatigue of his men. It was also the Sabbath. He ordered the troops to bivouack. The enemy could be destroyed tomorrow; the peace of the Lord would not be violated.[67]

Military necessity soon changed his mind. On the east side of the Valley Turnpike was open ground that Union guns could dominate. The west side of the pike was different. About a mile from the turnpike was a high ridge that began just to the west of Winchester and extended southwest without interruption for six miles. It was called Sandy Ridge, even though thick oak and cedar covered the height from one end to the other.

Immediately to the west of Kernstown, and between the turnpike and Sandy Ridge, was a prominent elevation known as Pritchard's Hill. From its crest a Union battery (evidently part of Shields's rear guard, Jackson concluded) was shelling Ashby's advanced position and probing for the range of Jackson's main force spread out now along the turnpike.

Pritchard's Hill gave the Federals a clear view of the size of the Confederate force. Any delay now on Jackson's part would give the Federals the opportunity to bring up reinforcements, entrench, or threaten Jackson's left flank. As he rode through a portion of his command, Jackson mistook—intentionally or otherwise—the jubilation of the soldiers at the command to bivouack to mean "good spirits at the prospect of meeting the enemy."[68]

It was the Lord's Day, Jackson freely acknowledged, but promising circumstances were at hand for doing the Lord's work. The God of battle would be the ultimate judge. As Jackson later told Anna, who also raised the question of fighting on Sunday, "I was greatly concerned, too; but I felt it my duty to do it, in consideration of the ruinous effects that might result from postponing the battle until the morning." Jackson admitted that his decision was "very distasteful to my feelings." Yet "I believed that as far as our troops were concerned, necessity and mercy both called for the battle."[69]

Accepting Ashby's judgment that little more than a brigade of Federals remained in Winchester, Jackson quickly formulated his strategy. Pritchard's Hill, adjacent to the turnpike, was obviously the western anchor of the Union position as well as the key to the whole arena. West Point textbooks and Mexican War experience had taught Jackson the elementary value of seizing high ground, especially on the flank. He would gain control of Sandy Ridge a mile and half west of the turnpike, turn the enemy line, and seize the main Kernstown-Winchester road in the Federals' rear. This would allow him to rout the enemy and march unhindered into Winchester.

The first strike at the wooded ridge would come from Fulkerson's two regiments. Garnett and his four regiments would be on the right, slightly behind, and in support. The battery of Captain Joseph Carpenter (one of Jackson's former VMI cadets) would go forward with the infantry to provide covering fire.

Dispositions were simple because Jackson's force was small, the battle zone was narrow, and the movements were elementary. Ashby and half of his cavalry would

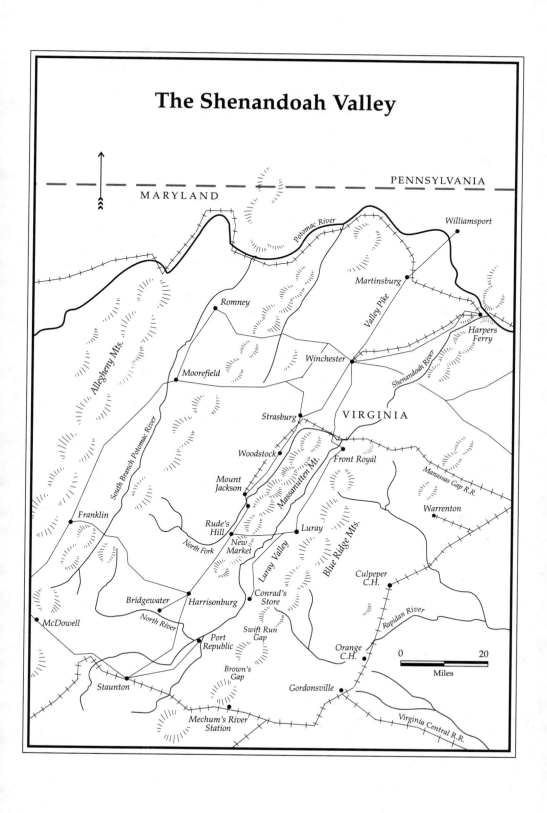

The Shenandoah Valley

PENNSYLVANIA

MARYLAND

Potomac River

Williamsport

Romney

Martinsburg

Valley Pike

Harpers Ferry

Allegheny Mts.

Moorefield

Winchester

Shenandoah River

South Branch Potomac River

Strasburg

VIRGINIA

Woodstock

Massanutten Mt.

Front Royal

Manassas Gap R.R.

Mount Jackson

Warrenton

Franklin

Rude's Hill

Luray

Blue Ridge Mts.

North Fork

New Market

Luray Valley

Culpeper C.H.

Bridgewater

Harrisonburg

Conrad's Store

McDowell

North River

Swift Run Gap

Rapidan River

Port Republic

Orange C.H.

0   20

Brown's Gap

Miles

Staunton

Gordonsville

Mechum's River Station

Virginia Central R.R.

guard Jackson's right flank east of the turnpike. The other half, under Major Oliver Funsten, would protect the Confederate left. Colonel Jesse Burks's little brigade, strengthened by the 5th Virginia from the Stonewall Brigade, would remain in the rear as a reserve.

At least 100 recruits in the 5th Virginia had no weapons. Jackson quickly resolved their dilemma. They were ordered to form in the rear close to compatriots in line of battle. As one of the armed men fell dead or wounded, a recruit was to take his musket and join in the battle.[70]

At 4 P.M. Jackson unleashed his attack. The hour was late, but he expected no major hindrance to the advance. Jackson rode over to the left just as one of Carpenter's guns sent a shell tearing into a barn filled with Union sharpshooters. "Good! Good!" shouted the artillery professor in praise of his former student.

By then, Jackson's face was twitching convulsively, as it usually did at the outset of a battle. Writers disagree whether the spasms were nervousness or resolve. His troops had a different idea; they would come to say that "Old Jack is making faces at the Yankees."[71]

Command mistakes occurred from the first. Kernstown would demonstrate Jackson's penchant to try to maintain personal control over every facet of an action. He sent aides scurrying with orders to this regiment and that battery. The directives were not always clear or timely.

Jackson paid no heed to military channels below him. Just as he did with Loring on the Romney expedition, Jackson left his second in command, Richard Garnett, completely in the dark as to intentions and movements. Adhering to blind obedience himself, Jackson expected the same in others. This worship of secrecy boded Jackson well on many occasions. Kernstown was not one of them.

Fulkerson's 23d and 37th Virginia swept up Sandy Ridge to the west of both the turnpike and Pritchard's Hill. Behind them (somewhat tardily, Jackson felt) was Garnett's Stonewall Brigade. The 27th Virginia, moving with the skirmishers, caught the brunt of Federal infantry fire from the top of the ridge and reeled back. Moments later, the 21st Virginia rushed to its assistance and restored the broken line.

Meanwhile, Fulkerson's regiments dashed to a stone wall that Union soldiers were also trying to reach. The Virginians won the race and "opened a destructive fire which drove back the Northern forces in great disorder after sustaining a heavy loss, and leaving the colors of one of their Regts. upon the field," Jackson stated admiringly.[72] The battle had now become general.

Jackson watched the action carefully from a rise of ground on the west side of the turnpike. He sat quietly on his horse, Lieutenant Lyle of the 4th Virginia noticed. "His expression was that of anxiety, and his face was pale. There was a set to his jaws that boded no good to the enemy." Animation at the moment was more visible in General Dick Garnett, who was "riding gallantly" amid his troops and cheering them forward.[73]

The fighting on the ridge swelled for an hour and a half, then seemed to slacken. Jackson inferred that his men were sweeping over the Union position. He confidently ordered his reserves forward into position on Garnett's right to finish the contest.

Suddenly, gunfire exploded on Jackson's left-center; dirty white smoke shrouded the broken country. Federal artillery fire rumbled louder than the two batteries Jackson thought the enemy had. The Stonewall Brigade, in the center of the line, found itself in a fight for survival. Colonel Charles Ronald of the 4th Virginia confessed, "The firing was so heavy at this point that my horse became unmanageable and ran away with me, hurting me very much."[74]

Something was drastically wrong. Jackson saw it and dispatched Sandie Pendleton of his staff to ascertain why Federal resistance remained so strong. The young aide rode in front of the hard-pressed Southern batteries, took a long look, and galloped back to Jackson. The Federals did not have four regiments, he reported; they had at least triple that number, and all were moving into the action. "Say nothing about it," Old Jack cautioned Pendleton, but "we are in for it."[75]

Jackson's flank attack had been a surprise. It probably would have been a smashing success had not Colonel Erastus B. Tyler, an Ohio fur merchant, rushed his brigade into action to meet the threat. The stiff resistance of those Ohio regiments gave enough time for Colonel Nathan Kimball, commanding Federal forces in place of the wounded Shields, to send two additional brigades in support. For another hour the stubborn contest raged. Neither side would give way. "It was the most desperate time I ever was in," a young soldier in the 23d Virginia admitted. "Our boys behaved bravely."[76]

Fulkerson's regiments on the far left and Burks's equally small brigade on the right maintained a steady fire while Garnett's men bore the brunt of the Union volleys. The intensity of the battle there is clear from the official report of the 5th Ohio: "Five times were our colors shot down, and as quickly did they arise again. The national flag received forty-eight bullet-holes and the regimental flag ten; even the flagstaffs were broken in several places."[77]

Jackson rode up close to give quick orders when needed. He was "intense and magnetic, directing and energizing his soldiers," a member of the Rockbridge Artillery stated. Private Cleon Moore of the 2d Virginia was more laudatory. Jackson "showed great personal courage in the battle, exposing himself constantly on the front lines. His bravery amounted to almost recklessness."[78]

Confederates along Sandy Ridge hurled back attacks and in some places managed to advance several yards, but fresh lines of Federals kept moving into position. Soon the volume of gunfire began to slacken. The Southerners were running out of ammunition.

Soldiers in a growing stream began drifting toward the rear. Jackson's stern expression deepened. He stopped one Confederate and demanded to know where he was going. The soldier explained that his cartridge box was empty and he did not know where to get more ammunition. "Then go back and give them the bayonet!" an angry Jackson shouted as he galloped toward the front.[79]

Three strong Federal brigades were in the action against Jackson's small force. Union troops were pounding the Stonewall Brigade in the center of Jackson's line. Garnett's position was becoming shaky, his flanks were weakening, and his soldiers one by one were shooting away their last rounds. The forty-one-year-old Garnett was an experienced soldier. Although unaware of the overall state of the engagement, he knew that the battle in his front was lost. Garnett saw two choices: he could continue to stand and take more casualties while he awaited instructions from Jackson, or he could abandon the field under his own decision and save his regiments.

Garnett opted for the latter course. "Had I not done so," he later declared, "we would have run imminent risk of being routed by superiority of numbers, which would have resulted probably in the loss of part of our artillery and also endangered our transportation."[80]

That may have been true; but when Garnett at 6:30 P.M. ordered his men away from the front line, the move uncovered Fulkerson's regiments in good position behind a stone wall on the left. Jackson's entire line began to withdraw. Federals in large numbers rushed forward to secure the victory. As soldiers retired in the face of the enemy, some bolted to the rear in panic. The Confederate retreat began to disintegrate into a rout. Off the ridge, across open bottomland, through woods and clouds of battle smoke, Southerners dashed rearward in disorder. Massed Northerners pursued with equal disorder.

Jackson had been watching the progress of the battle. While victory was taking longer than he had anticipated, he remained confident that the Lord would intercede at the proper moment. Suddenly, to Jackson's astonishment and wrath, he saw the lines of his old brigade giving way. Men were breaking to the rear. Jackson's entire battle line was teetering on the verge of collapse.

Angrily he made his way forward. Jackson found Garnett, who was shouting himself hoarse in a vain effort to effect an orderly withdrawal. "Why have you not rallied your men?" Jackson sternly demanded. "Halt and rally!"

Garnett could only offer excuses. Jackson, his temper almost out of control, seized a young drummer by the shoulder. "Beat the rally!" he shouted. "Beat the rally!"[81]

The efforts of the frightened drummer boy were drowned in the uproar of battle. With his hand still grasping the lad's shoulder, and oblivious to the musket balls whizzing about him, Jackson tried desperately to check the flight of his men. He was aware that the 5th and 42d Virginia were coming up—600 fresh troops who might be able to turn the tide. Yet not known to Jackson, their advance had stopped.

Garnett had galloped up to Colonel William Harman, whose 5th Virginia was moving through the woods to the left, and directed the regiment to a defensive position on the crest of a small hill. The 5th Virginia must stand fast, Garnett exclaimed, and buy time for the retiring infantry and artillery to gain a rallying point in the rear.

When Jackson finally discovered that the 5th Virginia was involved in a defensive fight, he knew it was too late to alter the situation. Nothing else could be done but to abandon the field and lead his battered brigades to safety. Accomplishing that was not easy. Harman's regiment was squarely athwart the Union advance and hopelessly outnumbered.

For at least ten minutes, the 5th Virginia stood alone and resolute. Then the 42d Virginia of Burks's brigade aligned on Harman's right. The two units fired desperate volleys into the enemy ranks and were raked by musketry in return. Somehow the Confederate line held until nightfall. Under darkness, the infantry fell back behind Ashby's screen of cavalry.[82]

Jackson exhibited no haste in leaving the Kernstown field. Fuming with anger, frustrated by a setback that had occurred at the height of what seemed to be a successful battle, he slowly and sullenly rode southward.

Legend has it that Jackson announced his determination to stay on the field until every wounded man and every discarded weapon had been collected. That was not true. Such a stand, in the face of overwhelming numbers, would have been foolhardy. Jackson had already lost a fourth of his command. Most of his wounded, as well as his dead, were left behind where they fell. Two pieces of artillery were also lost.[83]

Confederates were baffled, overpowered, and bone-tired as they slowly retraced their path for six miles to Bartonsville. "I did not see but one regiment in any kind of order," a soldier noted.[84] Under trees, around wagons, in fields along the turnpike, men too weary to eat collapsed into exhaustive sleep. Jackson was among the last to leave Kernstown. Head down, obviously depressed, he rode alone from the field at dark.

On the Valley Turnpike, he met his commissary, Major Wells Hawks. The general directed Hawks to distribute rations to the men as quickly as possible. Hawks hesitatingly told Jackson that the supply wagons had already proceeded to Newtown several miles farther south. That news did not sit well with Jackson. He dispatched the commissary to Newtown to bring sixty-five wagons of food back to the army.

Jackson then wearily dismounted and stood silently in front of a campfire alongside the road. A long cloak was draped over his shoulders. One of Ashby's horsemen walked up to the fire. When he recognized his commanding general, the cavalryman sought to make conversation. "The Yankees don't seem willing to quit Winchester, General." A pause followed before Jackson responded: "Winchester is a very pleasant place to stay in, sir." The young soldier continued to the point of boldness. "It was reported that they were retreating, but I guess they're retreating after us." Jackson, eyes still fixed on the campfire, snapped back: "I think I may say I am satisfied, sir!" That ended the exchange. The cavalryman departed as quickly as politeness allowed.[85]

Jackson then sat down before the fire. That is where Hawks found him when the commissary returned from his errand. No word passed between the two men for several minutes. Jackson then arose and asked Hawks to accompany him. The two rode a distance up the pike. Jackson turned off into an orchard and dismounted in a fence corner. "Could you make a fire?" he asked Hawks. Then, as if about to commit a felony, the general who ordinarily forbade such action added, "We will have to burn rails tonight." Hawks soon had a large blaze cracking. The commissary next gathered some long fence rails and began laying them neatly on the ground.

When Jackson asked what he was doing, Hawks replied: "Fixing beds for a place to sleep."

"You seem determined to make yourself and those around you comfortable," Jackson said in a stern but transparent tone.

Hawks was not finished with his chores. He was aware that Jackson had not eaten since daybreak. The major rode over to a nearby bivouac and returned with meat and bread. Jackson ate with obvious hunger. Then he committed himself and his soldiers "to the care of our Heavenly Father." It was near midnight. The general lay down on the rails without any blanket. Within minutes he was in a deep sleep that lasted until almost dawn.[86]

During those same nighttime hours, a bubbling Shields was extolling his division's accomplishments to the Union War Department. The battle had "raged" for eight hours; Jackson's army was double the size of the Federal force; Confederate losses were in the same proportion. Shields assured Washington authorities that at daylight on the following day "I will renew the attack as soon as we have sufficient light to point our guns, and feel confident the enemy cannot escape."[87]

Sunrise on March 24 found still-weary Southerners trudging up the valley. By then, one infantryman stated, "the stragglers had come together, discipline was renewed and everything and everybody was ready to meet the enemy, if he advanced."[88]

Although Sergeant George Peterkin of the 21st Virginia thought Jackson "crazy on the subject of fighting" and blind to the fact that "two thousand men cannot whip ten thousand," a Rockbridge gunner spoke for the majority when he observed: "I have a great deal of confidence in Genl. Jackson & think any order from him is all right. He is . . . a humble Christian. When danger is to be faced our Genl. is *always* in the lead."[89]

Jackson rode alone at the head of the column. "Little Sorrel" navigated without any pull on the reins for its rider was lost in thought. Jackson's battle plan had been flawless, its execution good. Faulty reconnaissance had put the Confederate offensive in jeopardy from the start.

The mistaken estimate of Shields's strength led to a costly tactical defeat. That Jackson also had overtaxed his men by a long march before the battle opened did not appear to enter his mind. His army needed more training. Drill and more drill would make the troops efficient marchers and eliminate straggling.

In Jackson's mind, however, those things were not the critical points in the battle. Obedience was the issue. "Though our troops were fighting under great disadvantages," he wrote in his after-action report, "I regret that Gen. Garnett should have given the order [for his brigade] to fall back, as otherwise, the enemy's advance would at least have been retarded, and the remaining part of my Infantry reserve have had a better opportunity for coming up, and taking part in the engagement, if the enemy continued to press forward."[90]

Jackson had never been comfortable with Garnett leading his Stonewall Brigade. The brigadier's unauthorized movement at Kernstown proved his incompetence. In Jackson's eyes, Garnett's behavior was inexcusable. Three regiments were in reserve, including Garnett's own 5th Virginia. The bayonet could have been used when all ammunition was expended. Almighty God might have interceded if the situation truly merited it. In Jackson's view, Garnett never considered divine intervention.

His precipitate withdrawal had lost the battle. Jackson's casualties—eighty killed, 375 wounded, 263 captured—were meaningless sacrifices. As a personal embarrassment, the missing included Jackson's young aide, Lieutenant George G. Junkin, a cousin of the general's first wife. He fell into Union hands near the end of the battle.[91]

Subsequent writers credited Jackson with divine powers and with the ability to see immediately what he had really accomplished over the long run, but at the time the general had to grope for positive observations about Kernstown. His disappointment in the first couple of days after the action was profound. Time would show that

Jackson's tactical "defeat" on March 23 was a strategic victory. Kernstown unhinged the entire Union offensive in Virginia that spring. Jackson had underestimated Federal numbers before the battle. His swift, bold assault and the ferocity of the fighting caused Union officers to overestimate Confederate numbers after the battle. Suddenly, the little pocket of Southern resistance in the Shenandoah Valley had materialized into a full-blown military theater.

Jackson's sheer audacity had immediate and important results on Union movements. The departure of Banks's two divisions from the valley was canceled. Those Federal brigades already across the Blue Ridge Mountains turned around and retraced their steps westward as angry muttering coursed through the ranks. Union authorities shelved a planned pincer movement on Richmond by McClellan from the peninsula to the east and General Irvin McDowell from Fredericksburg to the north. Lincoln created a new Department of the Rappahannock, with McDowell in charge, and ordered his large command to remain in northern Virginia as a safeguard for Washington. Further, and near the end of March, General Louis Blenker's division of 10,000 Federals received orders to leave McClellan's army and reinforce General John C. Fremont's command in the mountains west of the valley.

When Jackson completed his after-action report in the second week of April, what he had achieved was visible. Thus he could say of his efforts at Kernstown: "Though Winchester was not recovered, yet the more important object, for the present, that of calling back troops that were leaving the valley, and thus preventing a junction of Banks' command with other forces was accomplished, in addition to his heavy loss in killed and wounded." Reflecting several days later, Jackson exclaimed: "I am well satisfied with the result. . . . Time has shown that while the field is in possession of the enemy, the most essential fruits of the battle are ours. For this and all of our Heavenly Father's blessings, I wish I could be ten thousand times more thankful."[92]

The Monday after Kernstown was raw and overcast. Jackson was "very stubborn in retreating" that day. Not intimidated, the Confederate column wound slowly along the Valley Turnpike. On reaching Woodstock, Jackson made his headquarters at Shaeffer's Hotel. There he sent a reassuring note to Anna. "Yesterday important considerations, in my opinion, rendered it necessary to attack the enemy near Winchester. . . . Our men fought bravely, but the superior numbers of the enemy repulsed me. Many valuable lives were lost. Our God has been our shield. His protecting care is an additional cause for gratitude."[93]

On the following day, when Federals advanced to within three miles of Woodstock, Jackson moved on to Narrow Passage. There the North Fork of the Shenandoah River makes a great ox-bow curve and Narrow Passage Creek flows into the North Fork on the right shoulder of the 180-degree bend. The site was strategic because of the ease with which it could be defended. Jackson paused there to do battle, if the Federals offered it. They did not. The Confederates then continued south toward the final destination at Rude's Hill.

It was a leisurely march. Jackson pulled back only from necessity, and he rotated fresh troops to the skirmish line in order to maintain a strong front. Federal units following in his wake inched forward. Despite Shields's declarations of imminent triumph, the Federals were constantly apprehensive that Ashby's horsemen would strike in the rear and sever supply lines. "I can't catch them, sir," one Union cavalry officer told his colonel. "They leap the fences and walls like deer. Neither our men nor our horses are so trained."[94]

Union infantry advanced with even less enthusiasm. A Massachusetts officer wrote home: "This may seem a silly fancy but I often find myself indulging in it—that Genl. Jackson is a perfect nuisance. We made two winter marches to Hancock after him and still we are chasing him without success."[95]

Near the end of his march, Jackson asserted, "We must resolutely defend this Valley." He told a friend that "our army is in fine spirits, and when the tug of war comes I expect it, through Divine blessing, to nobly do its duty."[96]

Pausing at Israel Allen's home near Hawkinstown, Jackson sent an optimistic letter to his wife. "My little army is in excellent spirits," he stated. "This is a beautiful country. . . . After God, our God, again blesses us with peace, I hope to visit this country with my darling, and enjoy its beauty and loveliness."[97]

Personnel matters occupied much of Jackson's attention during the march up the valley. Possibly the capture at Kernstown of George Junkin underscored the need for additional staff officers. Jackson moved to increase his military family and on March 27 summoned volunteer engineer Jedediah Hotchkiss to his headquarters. The two briefly discussed Hotchkiss's topographical work the previous autumn in northwestern Virginia. Jackson abruptly cut to the present. "I want you to make me a map of the Valley, from Harpers Ferry to Lexington, showing all the points of offence and defence in those places. Mr. Pendleton will give you orders for whatever outfit you want. Good morning, sir."[98]

Such apparent gruffness from the preoccupied Jackson did not bother Hotchkiss. He promptly began his work as mapmaker for a general who still had some difficulty in understanding topography and the intricacies of drawing. Hotchkiss would serve Jackson well.

The need to have clergymen close at hand had persisted for a good while. Jackson wrote Robert L. Dabney at Hampden-Sydney College. The forty-two-year-old Presbyterian minister, nationally known for theological scholarship and inspiring sermons, had served briefly as chaplain of the 18th Virginia until "camp disease" forced his return to civilian life. Anna was still visiting the Dabneys. By then, she was convinced that next to her father, her cousin's husband was the most brilliant theologian alive. She conveyed to Jackson the wish of the minister to see field service. No doubt Anna added strong endorsements of her own. Jackson expressed the hope that Dabney might enter the chaplaincy service; on the other hand, should Dabney want to become involved in military matters, Jackson offered him a staff position. With that tender, however, Jackson made it clear that Dabney would be expected to remain close to him until the end of the war.[99]

Staff officers were expected to be organized, energetic, and quick to obey orders, Jackson stressed. Lieutenant Junkin had been captured, the general pointed out sternly, because he wandered too slowly and too far to deliver orders. "Examples must be made of Staff officers as well as others who disregard orders," Jackson declared. He then closed the letter (as he especially did to a member of the cloth) on a spiritual level. "I am thankful to God for sending so many of His children into this army and my prayer is, that He will continue to send them, and that He will bless them and those with whom they cast their lot.[100]

Three miles south of Mt. Jackson, the valley army went into camp in the midst of a sleet storm. The site was Rude's Hill, a range of highlands overlooking the North Branch of the Shenandoah River and five miles from New Market. A single bridge was the only access to the wide expanse of fertile meadowland bordering the stream. The Valley Turnpike passed through the bottomland and was within easy artillery range of the dominant hill to the south.

Safe from any sudden attack, Jackson established his headquarters at the base of the hill in the home of Lutheran minister Anders R. Rude. Sandie Pendleton described the owner as a "Danish Lutheran preacher" who was "a true Christian, and a thoroughly refined, educated and polished gentleman." In a single room containing a bed, two chairs, a table, a lamp, and no adornments, Jackson began energetically to reorganize and enlarge his army.[101]

A command change had first to be made. The move was probably the most controversial personnel action in Jackson's Civil War career. His outward mood in the days after Kernstown had been, if not cheerful, at least positive. Yet Jackson seethed over the climax of the engagement south of Winchester. Back in January, he had warned the War Department that Richard Garnett was "unable to meet emergencies" of any kind and could "not be expected to make proper dispositions of his command under fire."[102] Kernstown had proven Jackson right. Garnett had broken off the battle without orders; his retirement had forced the entire Southern army to withdraw from the field; his excuses were superficial; an able officer had no need to make excuses.[103]

On March 28, Jackson personally requested that Johnston send a new brigadier to the valley. Four days later, Jackson relieved Garnett from command of the Stonewall Brigade and placed him under arrest pending formal charges before a court-martial. "I regard Gen. Garnett as so incompetent a Brigade commander," Jackson had stated earlier, "that, instead of building up a Brigade, a good one, if turned over to him, would actually deteriorate under his command."[104]

The announcement of Garnett's dismissal, coming as it did without any warning, ripped through the valley army like a tornado. Usually modest and unassuming, Dick Garnett had acquired an affection from his soldiers second only to that which they felt for Jackson. Perhaps Garnett at Kernstown had committed an "unfortunate blunder," as one officer termed it. Every person was entitled to a mistake and a second chance. Jackson obviously did not subscribe to such mortal thinking.[105]

Confederates fighting thereafter under Jackson would experience other engagements as desperate as Kernstown, but the general was ensuring early in this campaign that no one thenceforth would even think of retreat without being ordered to do so. Strict discipline was imperative to success, the youthful soldiers and officers must learn. Obedience to commands would be instant and unbroken. Anything less were grounds for expulsion with attendant humiliation. The Almighty might have instilled in men the tendency to give way in the face of hopelessness; yet it was clear from this point forward that Jackson expected true servants of God to rise above such human weakness.

Garnett reacted to his dismissal with cold fury. He demanded an immediate trial. To friends he was uncharacteristically intemperate in his remarks. Mrs. William N. Pendleton in Lexington told her husband: "Gen. Garnett, I am afraid, has the tendency of his family to free speech. He uses no measured language about Jackson's 'Winchester Folly' and says nothing but the timidity of the enemy prevented a total defeat."[106]

The five regimental colonels in the Stonewall Brigade felt Garnett's actions at Kernstown to have been justified. Deep resentment coursed through the ranks of Jackson's old brigade. Major Frank Jones of the 2d Virginia was especially outspoken. He told his wife that "our Brigade is astounded at the order & had it not been that our cause was too sacred to jeopardize there would have been considerable commotion made amongst us."[107]

For a good while, the brigade refused to cheer Jackson when he rode through their encampment. Not one of the regimental commanders made any effort to conceal his anger. Sandie Pendleton of the staff summed up the situation in a letter to his mother. "The brigade is in a very loud humour at [Garnett's arrest] for he was a pleasant man and exceedingly popular. . . . I am sorry for him for he can get no trial and is virtually ruined for the war. The arrest was, however, necessary, and I now see why Napoleon considered a blunder worse than a fault. Genl. G's fault was a blunder."[108]

To add insult to injury, Jackson bypassed all of the regimental colonels in his command and imported a total stranger to lead the Stonewall Brigade. If morale and sunlight were the same, dark days indeed had descended.

Sidney Winder did not deserve the open hostility that greeted his arrival, nor did he cower under it. He was a professional soldier who shared Jackson's strong devotion to discipline. It would take time for his men to see another, more benevolent side to the man. Born October 7, 1829, to a prominent Maryland family, Charles Sidney Winder was imbued with the military. His uncle, John H. Winder, had taught at West Point and was a Confederate brigadier general. A brother had died in action in the Mexican War. Sidney Winder (he preferred to be called by his middle name) entered West Point the year Jackson departed and graduated in the middle of his 1850 class.

He was just another young infantry officer until 1854, when he sailed to Panama on a troop ship. A hurricane wrecked the vessel, but Winder's heroism in the crisis brought him promotion in the 9th Infantry. He became the youngest captain then on duty. Winder enhanced his reputation with a solid record in campaigns against the Indians in the Washington Territory.

Two weeks before Fort Sumter, he resigned from the army and offered his services to the Confederacy. A brief stint in the artillery preceded his July 1861 appointment as colonel of the 6th South Carolina. Winder was still awaiting his first action as an infantry commander when General Joseph Johnston recommended him for promotion to brigadier. He had been confirmed as a general less than a month when he received assignment to Jackson's forces.

Sidney Winder was an impressive figure. Tall, lean, and polished, he took pains to be immaculately dressed and well mounted. He had wavy hair combed straight back, a high forehead, deep-set eyes, and a long, curling beard. Winder was competent in large part because he was strict. The troops would come to view him as a tyrannical general who put on airs and cared little for human feelings.

Winder's unpublished diary, on the other hand, reveals a loving family man who saw war and everything therein as an evil. In the summer of 1861 he wrote: "Oh that I was with my own precious darling wife & children as happy as one year ago." A month later his love for home still persisted. "Up early, thinking of my own darling pets, longing so sadly to be with them. . . . God grant this war may soon end and we be restored to each other. In God is my trust."[109]

The thirty-two-year-old brigadier was "sorry to relieve" his friend Dick Garnett. He understood the resentment in the Stonewall Brigade. Yet to the colonels, whom Winder summoned after hissing greeted him in camp, he made it pointedly clear that discipline was to prevail over personal feelings. Initially, the regimental commanders went to brigade headquarters only when ordered there. In time, the cool relationship melted.[110]

Jackson spent two busy weeks at Rude's Hill. The men needed rest from long marches, and he gave it to them. Yet he himself toiled from dawn to late night. "Jackson does not say much," new staff member Hotchkiss observed. "He is quite deaf; spends most of his time in his room, by himself, except when in the saddle." Some of the solitary hours initially went into the official report of Kernstown. Jackson sat at two ninety-degree angles on the edge of a chair in front of a table and personally wrote the account rather than dictated it. As was his custom, he heavily revised his first draft.[111]

Each day he rode out to watch his men drill in camp and to check on outposts. "He had his eyes everywhere," a recruit in the Rockbridge Artillery declared. "Silent, inscrutable, and exacting he was, but we were fast learning to trust him."[112]

A contingent of Rockingham County militiamen were of a different sentiment. Militia units always seemed to be in a condition somewhere between disorganized and chaotic. Recent legislation had disbanded militia forces and ordered their members into volunteer units in the field. To about sixty of those part-time soldiers, such conscription was tantamount to illegal coercion. They fled en masse toward remote homes near Swift Run Gap in the Blue Ridge. Jackson could have ignored this small display of disloyalty—but he would not have been Jackson if he had. On hearing of the rebellion, he promptly dispatched four companies of infantry, a company of cavalry, and two pieces of artillery to end the resistance by whatever means necessary.

Lieutenant Colonel John R. Jones, a Harrisonburg native who was familiar with the region, took command of the "posse." It marched quickly into the mountains where Jones suspected the fugitives to be hiding. Encountering them in a thick woodland, Jones unlimbered his guns on high ground and began shelling the entire hillside. One man was killed, while two dozen panicky mountaineers dashed forward to surrender.

For days thereafter, Jackson kept Jones's force combing the neighborhood in search of the remainder. They were to be placed in arrest and charged with the capital offense of desertion. Jackson threatened even worse punishment a few weeks later on a small group of mutineers.[113]

In the middle of April, the Confederate Congress enacted America's first conscription law. Quartermaster Harman supposedly brought Jackson word of the new law. "Jackson was so elated," a mutual friend stated, "that he slapped the Major on the shoulder—a very unusual thing for him to do—and fairly shouted: 'Now, Major, we'll have war in earnest! Virginia has waked up!'"[114]

The new law would bring in heavy reinforcements. Within a month, the size of Jackson's army increased 50 percent to 6000 men. Another section of the conscription bill directed that all soldiers over the age of thirty-five be discharged. Jackson's army therefore became bigger and younger, and in time it would get tougher.

Two reasons the general was able to give so much attention at Rude's Hill to internal matters were his understanding of the Union force in front of him and its misunderstanding of him. What acquaintance Jackson had with Banks and McClellan led him to feel no threat from the enemy. Banks, he told Longstreet, "is very cautious. As he belongs to McClellan's army I suppose that McCl. is at the helm, and that he would not even if B. so desired, permit him to advance much further until other parts of his army are further advanced." It would take "hard fighting to rout Banks, if attacked only in front," Jackson stated. By his observation, at least 17,000 more men and twelve additional guns would be necessary for such an offensive.[115]

While Jackson felt no pressure from Union presence halfway up the valley, Federal soldiers were convinced that the Confederate army had disintegrated into turmoil. One of Banks's staff officers accepted fully the testimony of a deserter from a Virginia militia unit. "He says Jackson's principal force lies between Rude's Hill and New Market without heavy guns and is ready for flight. The force is much disorganized, drinking whiskey furiously." A private in the 66th Ohio felt even more confident. "Our men has got Jackson hemmed so that he will have to fight or give up or climb a hard range of mountains or drown in the Shenandoah River."[116]

Snow was falling on Monday, April 7, when Jackson paused in his duties to send a quick letter to Anna. She was still with her cousins at Hampden-Sydney College. Of concern to Jackson were some problems his wife was undergoing because of her pregnancy. He had already buried two babies, yet he told his wife to seek the same strength on which he relied. "My precious pet, your sickness gives me great concern; but so live that it, and your trials, may be sanctified to you, remembering that 'our light afflictions, which are but for a moment, work out for us a far more exceeding and eternal weight of glory.'" Anna's discomfort soon passed, to the gratification of both wife and husband.[117]

Jackson followed his letter to Anna with an invitation to the Reverend Dabney to become his assistant adjutant general. According to Dabney's biographer, men and women believed the clergyman "possessed of a many-sided capacity." Jackson "saw in this minister of the gospel . . . the materials, although in somewhat unformed condition, for a capital chief of staff." If Dabney were interested, Jackson would make the necessary recommendation to Confederate authorities. "Your rank will be Major," Jackson stated; but, he warned, "your duties will require early rising and industry." That appealed to the self-assured Dabney, especially since he had recently received a less-than-cordial response from General D. Harvey Hill on entering the army again as a chaplain. "Our Regimental Chaplains, as a general thing," the caustic Hill had exclaimed, "are as trifling as the Regimental Surgeons, which is the strongest denunciation I can make."[118]

Snow became rain, and steady downpours in the days that followed turned the countryside into a swamp. "Our encampment is worse than any barnyard," the 2d Virginia's Frank Jones observed, "for in many places there seems no bottom."[119]

In the midst of one storm, Jackson received from Johnston a letter that combined bad news and good news. The main Confederate army was abandoning Virginia's northern piedmont, Johnston wrote, and reconcentrating in front of McClellan's army on the lower peninsula. Only General Richard S. Ewell's division would remain behind to cover the Rapidan River line near Orange. Jackson must continue to impede Banks's advance in order to protect the Virginia Central Railroad and Staunton. Should Banks push hard, Jackson was to fall back the thirty-odd miles to Swift Run Gap in the Blue Ridge east of Harrisonburg. Then came the good news. Johnston authorized Jackson to call Ewell's division to his assistance in case of necessity; and Ewell "was instructed to comply with such a call." Johnston repeated that in the event Jackson had to retire farther southward, Ewell was to march via Madison Courthouse to Fisher's Gap or Swift Run Gap. There he and Jackson would unite and fight Banks's army near the crest of the Blue Ridge.[120]

Defense was not the paramount thought in Jackson's mind at this new development. Ewell's four infantry brigades and five artillery batteries represented a larger force than Jackson commanded. Adding it to the valley army opened the door for a number of offensive possibilities!

Ewell apparently made the first contact with an April 11 note to Jackson. Eagerly and almost daily came Jackson's responses. "Should I fall back in consequence of the enemy's advancing, I will let you know immediately." The next day Jackson told Ewell: "All is quiet in front. . . . We will have a strong position this side of Fisher's Gap and at the Gap. But I do not much expect that Banks will follow me." Yet should he do so, Jackson stated in tough terms, "you will have time enough to join me before he reaches the top of the mountain, as he will be retarded in his march. I wish he would pursue & let us with our united force meet him on the mountain." However, "I hope that Banks will be deterred from advancing much further towards Staunton by the apprehension of my returning to New Market and thus getting in his rear." While sending this stream of correspondence, Jackson felt so joyful at prospects of success that on Sunday, April 13, he went through part of his encampment and distributed religious tracts to any soldiers who would accept them.[121]

Two personality matters quickly erased some of the euphoria of having Ewell's division available just over the mountains. Jackson still needed brigade commanders. Colonel Jesse Burks, leading the Second Brigade, was on indefinite sick leave. Colonel Sam Fulkerson still commanded the Third Brigade, but Jackson had some reservations about his loyalty following Fulkerson's involvement against Jackson in the Loring dispute during the winter.

Johnston ironically picked this moment to return William B. Taliaferro to Jackson. The politically influential tidewater officer who had led the anti-Jackson movement in the Romney campaign now sported a brigadier general's rank. He was to reassume command of the 23d and 37th Virginia, with the 10th Virginia added to the brigade. Taliaferro was not particularly happy at his assignment. As a new brigade commander, working under an old nemesis (Jackson), he was under a severe handicap.

It was now Jackson's turn to protest, and he did so. The language of his letter to the War Department was unusually strong. "Through God's blessing my command though small is efficient, and I respectfully request that its efficiency may not be impaired by assigning it to inefficient officers. Last winter Genl. Taliaferro had charge of a Brigade and he permitted it to become so demoralized that I had to abandon an important enterprise. . . . Notwithstanding the demoralized condition of his brigade, he left it, and visited Richmond, thus making a second visit there within two months. His brigade since he left it has under other hands become efficient and it, as well as the others, bid fair to render good service, if not placed under incompetent officers."[122]

Voicing complaints directly to Richmond rather than through channels was precisely what Loring's mutinous officers had done. Confederate authorities ignored Jackson's appeal. He and the brigade commander had no confrontations that spring, but a chill descended over army headquarters whenever Taliaferro appeared.

Among the many developments that took place during Jackson's stay at Rude's Hill was yet another example of his devotion to duty. Quartermaster John Harman received word that all five of his children in Staunton were critically ill with scarlet fever. Jackson gave him a forty-eight-hour emergency leave to go home. By the time Harman arrived, two children had already died and a third was sinking rapidly. Harman requested an extension of his furlough. Jackson refused. "My Dear Major," he wrote his quartermaster. "Your sad letter has been received and I wish that I could relieve your sorrowing heart, but *human aid* cannot heal the wound. From me you have a friend's sympathy, and I wish my duty to our suffering country permitted me to show it. But we must look to the living, and those who come after us, and see that with *God's* blessing, the freedom which we have enjoyed is transmitted to them. What is life without honor? Degradation is worse than death. The interest of the service requires that you should be at your post this morning. Join me as soon as possible. Your sympathising friend, T. J. Jackson."[123]

A sorrow-filled Harman returned to the army. A few days later came word that the third child had succumbed. Harman's request for leave to attend the funeral was denied. "Poor fellow," Hotchkiss noted, "he is completely unmanned."[124]

Somehow the quartermaster was able to write to his heartbroken wife: "Do not judge the General too harshly. I thought he might spare me for a few hours under such trying circumstances, but he thought otherwise, and I had to obey his command and pour out my grief apart from your loving and consoling sympathy."[125]

John Harman was not permanently vindictive toward Jackson, as previous writers have charged. "Some must suffer and why not I?" he said to a brother.[126] On the other hand, his subsequent relations with Jackson were a mixture of cold resentment and guarded respect. Jackson, accustomed to the sorrows of life, never wavered from his belief that all human feelings were subservient to duty—especially when soldier life and the work of the Lord were one and the same.

By April 15, the weather had cleared. Road conditions were improving, although snow still covered the landscape in the upper elevations. Jackson now anticipated a renewal of the slow Federal push into the upper valley. He pulled back his advanced infantry to Rude's Hill and told Ashby to abandon his forward position if he were hard pressed. Major Harman was preparing the railroad property at Mt. Jackson for destruction. Ashby would ensure that nothing of value remained at the railhead for enemy capture.

What transpired next would be a clear indication to Jackson that while Ashby had no superior where personal courage was concerned, his cavalry command was falling apart from external pressures and internal weaknesses. At daybreak on the 16th, Union horsemen galloped into Columbia Furnace, only seven miles from Mt. Jackson. The Federals discovered no pickets posted; an entire company of Ashby's cavalry was asleep in a church. Some sixty men, with all of their horses and baggage, were captured.

In the predawn hours of the next morning, Northern infantry and artillery stormed Ashby's main line at Mt. Jackson. Surprised, almost overwhelmed, the Southern horsemen galloped toward Rude's Hill after making a halfhearted attempt to set fire to the supplies and equipment in town. Union cavalry moved in quickly and saved a large amount of stores, including several locomotives. Ashby sought unsuccessfully to burn the single bridge over the North Fork. The colonel's horse received mortal wounds but jumped over two fences and bore its rider to Rude's Hill before falling dead.[127]

Jackson was not impressed; far from it. He watched with disbelief as his cavalry for the first time scattered in flight. Elements of a Federal brigade had seized the vital river crossing and were arching around the Confederate flanks. (Unknown to Jackson, the enemy troops were under the command of Colonel George H. Gordon, one of his West Point classmates.) Mt. Jackson was lost. So in the middle of the afternoon of April 17, Jackson ordered the valley army to retire southward. He alerted Ewell to prepare to head for a rendezvous at Swift Run Gap.

The hope of making a stand at New Market vanished when Federals again began to flank the column to the west. Jackson continued on to heights at Big Spring, midway between New Market and Harrisonburg. Informed that the enemy was no longer pushing toward him, Jackson sent his men into bivouac. He established headquarters at the Lincoln home to the west of the turnpike. A descendant of that family had gone to Kentucky at the turn of the century, and one of his grandsons was now the Northern president.

At supper that night, aged Mrs. Jacob Lincoln sat at the head of the table. She kept peering at Jackson over her spectacles. Finally she asked: "Gineral, are you any kin to *Old* Gineral Jackson? You look mighty like him." Jackson gravely replied: "Not that I know of."[128]

Rain followed the Confederates up the valley as the long column wound its way twenty miles to Harrisonburg. Jackson and his staff left the midway point of the march and galloped ahead to the town. As the general passed the ranks, men cheered him heartily—the first time they had made such an expression since Kernstown.

Jackson dined at the Reverend William Henry Ruffner's home on the southern edge of Harrisonburg.

That afternoon the commander directed all unnecessary baggage to Staunton, while the remaining wagons turned east with the infantry and moved slowly through the rainstorm six miles to Peale's Cross Roads. There the army halted for the night.

Captain J. Samuel Harnsberger had been in charge of Jackson's couriers during the two-day march. Harnsberger was at Jackson's side the whole time. Near the end of the second evening, Jackson turned and asked: "Have the troops water and wood?" "Yes, General," Harnsberger replied. That was the extent of two days' conversation.[129]

April 19 was yet another wet day; and for Jackson it was a day of disappointment and accomplishment. Three bridges over the South Fork needed to be destroyed to keep Federals from any movements in the Luray Valley. For the first time, cavalry orders went not to Ashby but to a staff officer. Jackson deemed the razing of the three spans—White House Bridge, Columbia Bridge, Red Bridge—so important that he directed Hotchkiss to take charge of the mission of demolition. First, however, the mapmaker would have to find the cavalrymen. Jackson had no idea where they were.

Hotchkiss searched until he located two companies inside an old foundry. Most of the men were in various stages of intoxication from applejack. Before any of the spans could be burned, Union horsemen arrived. A brief fight ensued, with a large number of Ashby's men skedaddling drunkenly from the field. Hotchkiss was not a part of what he called "a perfect stampede" and a "disgraceful affair." He managed to set fire to one of the bridges en route back to Jackson's army.[130]

Meanwhile, starting at dawn, Jackson had led his force another fourteen miles to its final destination in the Elk Run Valley. Who selected the site is unknown. Jackson had not been there previously. (He had to ask Hotchkiss to make a map of the area for him.) Hotchkiss might have had a familiarity with the region, or one of the regimental colonels might have suggested the place. One fact was certain: although Jackson's force had retreated 100 miles the past month, it was now in a near-ideal location.

Several peaks formed the northern face of the Massanutten range at Strasburg. A single hill formed the southern end, and it dropped abruptly to valley level east of Harrisonburg. Dense forests of oak and pine covered the ridges and ravines of the Massanutten and made it more foreboding. Jackson marched around the southern tip and disappeared from view. His men crossed the South Fork at Conrad's Store and went into camp in Elk Run Valley.

This flat land, timbered and well watered, extended six miles from the river to the Blue Ridge. The South Fork protected Jackson's front, and at the time it was swollen from spring rains. Pathless spurs of the Blue Ridge jutted westward toward the river and provided almost impregnable positions for defense to north and south. Immediately behind Jackson's encampment was Swift Run Gap, a popular crossing traditionally thought to have been where Alexander Spotswood in 1716 led his Knights of the Golden Horseshoe through the Blue Ridge to explore the great valley and western lands beyond. The road through the pass was solid, and it was to be Jackson's primary communication link with all Confederate forces east of the mountains.

Other considerations made the Conrad's Store location a strong haven for Jackson's army. Swift Run Gap was as strategically important to Harrisonburg as Luray

Gap was to New Market. By placing his troops at the base of the pass, Jackson
controlled it and the Luray Valley as well.

South of Harrisonburg and the Massanutten, the valley widened to about twenty-
five miles. No strong position existed for confronting Union soldiers advancing on
Staunton. Even if a natural defense had been there, Jackson could not afford to use it.
He would be facing a stronger opponent with limited freedom of action.

On the other hand, at Conrad's Store Jackson was an unseen but dangerous threat
to the Federals. Should Banks push south through Harrisonburg and move on Staunton, Jackson could nimbly pounce on the Union flank and rear. The Elk Run Valley
area thus became an entrenched camp from which the Confederate general could
launch a number of surprise offensives on the enemy. However, for the first days in
the new position, Jackson had friend and foe alike off balance.

Ewell began on April 17 "hourly expecting a summons to Jackson's aid." The
summons came, but in both profusion and confusion. On the 17th, Jackson directed
Ewell to march his division to Swift Run Gap. The next morning Jackson changed the
destination to Fisher's Gap farther north. Later in the day, Jackson told Ewell to alter
his course toward Harrisonburg via Swift Run Gap. Yet two days afterward, Jackson
directed Ewell to halt east of the Blue Ridge at some intersection from which he could
proceed through the mountains by way of either gap.[131]

Dutifully, Ewell made all of the starts and stops, and he voiced no complaints in
writing. Still, he must have thought at this early point that the new general to whom
he was soon to report was a bit unstable.

If Ewell was perplexed by Jackson at this time, Banks was bamboozled. The Union
general had moved up the valley in casual fashion. He encamped at New Market, sent
scouts toward Harrisonburg, and put a covering force atop the Massanutten at Luray
Pass. Contrary to statements by G. F. R. Henderson and earlier Jackson biographers,
Banks did not halt for fear of a counterattack by Jackson. The Federal commander
thought that his Confederate opponent had left the valley.

Beginning on April 19 and extending over a twelve-day period, Banks successively
reported Jackson out of the valley, en route to Gordonsville in the piedmont, at
Stanardsville east of the Blue Ridge, and bound for Richmond. Federal General
James Shields informed the War Department that Jackson was "flying from the
department." Banks agreed. Jackson's army, he told his superiors, was retreating,
"reduced, demoralized, on half rations."[132]

One Union officer who came to see the situation more clearly was Major Wilder
Dwight of the 2d Massachusetts. Writing from New Market in the third week of
April, the former Roxbury attorney commented: "Jackson was ready to run, and
began to do so as soon as we begun to move. But perhaps we hastened him a little.
Here we are, eighty miles from our supplies, all our wagons on the road, our tents
and baggage behind, our rations precarious, and following a mirage into the desert."[133]

That is precisely the position and the disposition that Jackson wanted his enemy to
have. Many of his own men were ignorant of where they were and what they were
going to do. Quartermaster Harman wrote his brother in Staunton: "Here we are
after a hard march. . . . The place seems to be out of the world. . . . I feel dreadfully

depressed." Harvey Black of the 4th Virginia could only tell his homefolk: "Direct your letter to Valley District. I dont know where we will go."[134]

Jackson was his usual reticent self at the Conrad's Store encampment. He made his headquarters in the two-storied Kite home at the base of Swift Run Gap. From there he confessed to Anna, "I do so much want to see my darling, but fear such a privilege will not be enjoyed for some time to come." Nevertheless, he could exclaim, "our gallant little army is increasing in numbers, and my prayer is that it may be an army of the living God as well as of its country."[135]

Rain was falling steadily on April 20, but that could not stop a grateful Jackson from attending church service. It was Easter Sunday.

13

"A CRAZY FOOL"

PRING 1862 CAME LATE. Weather in the last ten days of April fluctuated between cold rain, sleet, and snow. As Jackson had sent all tents to Staunton, his men huddled in the woods or along the mountainside in a vain effort to get protection from the elements. Members of the 21st Virginia burned some fence railing during a snowstorm to try to keep warm. An unsympathetic Jackson ordered the men to maul rails and rebuild the fence. Regimental punishment, he warned, would follow another such violation of orders.

Everyone complained, including Surgeon Harvey Black of the 4th Virginia. "You ought to have seen me last night shovelling away the rocks to put down my bed," Black told his wife. "Dont you think I will appreciate the comforts of our humble home when I get there." Quartermaster Harman was equally discontent. "I think Gen'l. Jackson is entirely too close about everything. We are here in a small valley away from everything and everybody."[1]

With weather curtailing any movements on either side, Jackson gave attention to the reorganization of his army. He started with his staff. One of four additions made at the time was Richard K. Meade, a Clarke County youth who was attending Washington College when war began. Meade enlisted in the 2d Virginia as a private and lost his right arm at Manassas. Jackson admired his bravery, but he appointed him a lieutenant on his staff largely because of his eagerness to serve in the ranks, even in the face of his inability to do so. Hotchkiss termed Meade "a good negative sort of man, kindly disposed and willing to do all he can." That proved to be not good enough. The short and somnolent Meade never displayed the alacrity Jackson demanded of his inner family. Later in the year, Meade transferred to Taliaferro's staff as an engineering officer.[2]

Colonel Thomas H. Williamson, hailed as "the most accomplished Engineer of the State," joined the staff to assist young Keith Boswell with engineering matters. Williamson had taught at VMI for twenty years, pausing only to serve as an aide to Joseph Johnston in the Manassas campaign. Williamson would be with Jackson only ten days, yet his knowledge and suggestions helped pave the way for Jackson's explosive renewal of the campaign in the Shenandoah.[3]

Later that month, Jackson acquired the youngest staff member he ever had. Henry Kyd Douglas was born in the autumn of 1840 at Shepherdstown. That his father was a minister no doubt influenced Jackson's confidence in the judgment of the youth. Douglas was seventeen when he graduated from Franklin and Marshall College in Pennsylvania (the only out-of-stater in his class). He then went to Lexington, Virginia, to study law under Judge John Brockenbrough. There he became friends with Sandie Pendleton. Douglas was practicing law before his twenty-first birthday.

The Old Dominion had been out of the Union a week when the medium-sized, clean-shaven Douglas enlisted in the 2d Virginia. Promotion to lieutenant came in the summer. Douglas's service to Jackson as a volunteer courier, as well as his enthusiasm and drive on behalf of the Southern cause, further attracted the General's attention and led to Douglas's appointment to the staff as acting assistant adjutant general.

He had an immature, cocky air that some associates found irritating. Out of Jackson's sight, Douglas often smoked a cigar or held one jauntily in the corner of his mouth. Yet he made a positive first impression on the staff. Douglas "is one of your wide awake smart young men," Hotchkiss stated after their initial meeting. "I like him too."[4]

Perhaps the poorest appointment Jackson ever made was that of Robert L. Dabney as adjutant general. Born three years before Jackson in Louisa County, the well-educated Dabney had enjoyed a distinguished theological career. In 1860, he declined an offer to be minister at New York City's prestigious Fifth Avenue Presbyterian Church. He also turned down a professorial chair at Princeton Seminary—both times because of his love for Virginia and the South.

Jackson's appointment of Dabney to head the staff was an amazing piece of short-sightedness. The theologian was a misfit from the start. That was evident from his first meeting with Jackson at Swift Run Gap. "I am glad you have come," Jackson stated sincerely. Dabney replied that he had made the trip from southside Virginia to show his physical unfitness for the task. Jackson dismissed the argument. "Providence will preserve your health, if He designs to use you." The minister then pled ignorance of weapons and all military science. "You can learn," said Jackson.

"When would you have me assume my office?"

"Rest today, study the Articles of War, and begin tomorrow," came the simple reply.

"But I have neither outfit, nor arms, nor horse, for immediate service."

"My quartermaster shall lend them, until you can procure your own."[5]

Dabney continued pessimistic. The Confederacy was languishing, he asserted. The thought that he was needed was what had brought him into the field—reversing, he told Jackson, the way of rats when they left a sinking ship. Jackson missed the humor in the remark. "If the rats will only run this way," he snapped as an end to the conversation, "the ship will not sink."[6]

The next day Dabney—unofficially Jackson's chief of staff—appeared wearing a Prince Albert coat and large beaver hat. As he rode with the general and his staff, the newly commissioned major raised an umbrella over his head as a shade from the sun. Troops began jeering; staff members smiled derisively. Jackson saw the painful situation. "Gentlemen! Let us ride!" he shouted as he turned from the road and galloped into a thick forest. For half a mile Jackson led his staff dashing through brush and tree limbs. By the time the party emerged back into the open, Dabney was holding onto the pommel for dear life, his coat was torn, the hat misshapen, his umbrella in shreds. Later in the day, an unconcerned Major Harman found Dabney an ill-fitting uniform and military cap while the cleric struggled with the rudiments of the myriad details associated with an army.[7]

The thoroughly pious Jackson seemed always to feel that a man of the cloth was able to perform outstanding service on any plane. Not even the brief and disappointing tenure of Major Dabney could shake that resolve.

As Jackson filled his staff, he also turned to one of the most serious problems he faced: his cavalry. Colonel Turner Ashby's command seemed to be breaking apart. In the first weeks under Jackson, Ashby's cavalry had performed well. Even a Union officer conceded that the Confederate horsemen "scale the fences most beautifully and show themselves very fearless," while Union cavalry "is good for kicking up a dust, doing foraging, capturing horses and stealing them, and for not much else."[8]

With added responsibilities, however, the performance of the Southern cavalry began to deteriorate. On April 16, at Columbia Furnace, at least fifty horsemen had been captured while asleep. Three days later, another detachment was too drunk to carry out a simple assignment. So disorganized was Ashby's command by late April that precisely how many companies he had is unknown. It was somewhere between twenty-one and twenty-six.

The only officers above the rank of captain amid all of those horsemen were Ashby and Major Oliver Funsten. In short, two field officers existed for the equivalent of two cavalry regiments. Ashby himself was bold, fearless, always eager to engage the enemy. Yet discipline and organization were almost nonexistent among the troopers he led. "The cavalry is in . . . perfectly disorganized and inefficient conditions and Col. Ashby rather a humbug," Lieutenant Colonel E. T. H. Warren of the 10th Virginia wrote home. Ashby could not see—or would not see—that his command had grown beyond his ability to control it.[9]

Ashby had been effective as a jousting cavalier. While Jackson operated under a system of rigid discipline, the two commanders operated in separate orbits. Why the unsatisfactory cavalry situation persisted for so long was because of Jackson's obedience to orders—orders that should never have been issued. Late in February, in the wake of the Romney controversy and with Ashby's fame well publicized throughout Virginia, either a distrustful President Davis or a bumbling Secretary of War Benjamin had stumbled again. The secretary had sent a letter (via Alexander R. Boteler) giving Ashby independent authority to raise and command his own cavalry force. Ashby was empowered to muster as many companies into service as he could secure. Of course, the War Department expected him to band the companies into regiments and battalions "as may be expedient." Ashby thereafter carried out all but the last step in the directive.[10]

What convinced Jackson at Conrad's Store that something had to be done were two April 16 letters from Richmond. In the first, Lee expressed concern over the poor organization of Ashby's cavalry and suggested that the creation of two regiments with appropriate officers would greatly improve its efficiency. The second letter was from Governor Letcher's military aide, Colonel S. Bassett French. He informed Jackson that Ashby had bypassed military channels and sent directly to the governor's office a requisition for arms and equipment. Governor Letcher refused to consider it.[11]

Such usurpation of military policy by Ashby could not be tolerated, Jackson concluded. Lee's communique was all the ammunition he needed. On April 24, Jackson took action. Secretary Benjamin's authorization notwithstanding, the general ordered eleven cavalry companies to report to General Taliaferro and to be attached to his brigade. The remaining mounted units were assigned as part of Winder's brigade. Ashby would henceforth command the advance and rear guards, "with authority to call for portions of his command as necessity required."[12] Jackson's orders in effect stripped Turner Ashby of his command.

Ashby reacted expectedly. As Major Harman wrote the next morning: "We are in a great danger from our cracked-brained Genl. . . . A great calamity has befallen us: that is a rupture between Ashby and Jackson. The Col. has tendered his resignation. . . . Do not speak of it. It will hurt us bad enough anyway."[13]

The letter of resignation, sent through Congressman Boteler, was lengthy and heated. "This indignity" by Jackson, "without any apparent failure to do my duty, leaves me in utter astonishment" Ashby exclaimed. "I feel bold to announce the fact, without a fear of being considered vain, that for the last Two Months I have saved the Army of the Valley from being utterly destroyed. . . . This I have done without the aid of Gen. Jacksons command and embarrassed by the want of such information from him which I considered myself entitled to, as not knowing his movements has made my dutys much more arduous." If his men lacked discipline, Ashby continued, they were not alone. "I deem Gen. Jacksons Army in the worst condition it has been in since it came into the Valley." The colonel then closed by stating: "I have asked Gen. Jackson for a specification or charge or some reason for this seducing and partitioning my command. I believe he thinks it is for the best, but am sorry to say that he cannot appreciate the condition of his Army and its daily demoralisation."[14]

Sidney Winder averted what could have been a crisis in command structure. The new leader of the Stonewall Brigade had become close friends with Ashby. On hearing of Jackson's directive, Winder visited Ashby and talked with him at length. The brigadier next went boldly to Jackson with a plea that the general discuss the matter with Ashby for the good of the service.

Jackson agreed to a meeting that rainy night. He had not expected Ashby to resign (even though he himself had pursued an identical course after a major command disagreement). To lose Ashby would be a catastrophe to morale as well as to the fighting qualities of the Confederate force. The two officers talked long and openly. Both men were incapable of any other conversation.

Later, Jackson explained the action he agreed to take. "Such was Col. Ashby's influence over his command that I became well satisfied that if I persisted in my attempt to increase the efficiency of the Cavalry [by dividing it], that it would produce the contrary effect, as Col. Ashby's influence, who is very popular with his men, would be thrown against me. Under the circumstances, I refrained from taking further action in the matter (as I was in the face of the enemy) until the War Dept. should have an opportunity of acting in the case."[15]

Although Quartermaster Harman accused Jackson of "backing square down" in the dispute, the general effected a loose compromise. He "detailed" the cavalry companies to Ashby, who agreed to tighten discipline. Ashby would lead the companies but not have direct command over them. The colonel was satisfied; he and Major Funsten withdrew their resignations. Jackson, although not as pleased, had at least managed to avoid the risk of losing his cavalry in the early stages of what he intended to be a major campaign.[16]

He hinted at such an offensive in a thank-you note to a Winchester admirer. "I hope that our God in his providence will soon permit me to return to your town of which I have so many pleasant recollections, and see it again under that government to which it has shown so much loyalty."[17]

Much preparation had to be made toward that end. Under Jackson's command now, and within easy reach, were three Confederate forces. His own army numbered about 6000 troops. A third of the men were either unarmed or poorly armed. Jackson's cavalry chief enjoyed near adoration from his men, and that was at the least unsettling. Ewell's larger and better-equipped contingent of 8000 soldiers was just over the Blue Ridge. General Edward Johnson, with whom Jackson conferred at some length on April 19, had an isolated detachment of about 3000 men guarding the western approaches to the key city of Staunton.

Jackson's force was the largest he had ever led. Most of the troops were Virginians, many of whom (such as soldiers from Rockingham and Shenandoah Counties in the 10th Virginia) were returning to home country. All of the soldiers knew of Jackson's discipline and methods of warfare—as well as his dubious track record at Romney and Kernstown. They would wait before passing judgment.

That was fine with Jackson, who would initiate the soldiers to his system and pass judgment himself. "We are getting our army reorganized and will soon have order out of chaos I suppose," Jed Hotchkiss told his wife. One of the major problems, the bearded cartographer added, was that "no one knows what Jackson intends to do."[18]

Excitement would have shattered the languor of the Conrad's Store encampment had anyone in Jackson's army been privy to the high-level developments taking place between Richmond officials and valley headquarters. Ideas were evolving into strategy; a slight acquaintance was on the verge of maturing into a confident partnership.

With Johnston and the main Confederate army confronting McClellan's massive host on the peninsula east of the capital, General Robert E. Lee became more active in the direction of the war in the Old Dominion. Lee was the president's military advisor; with Davis's approval, he began acting with all the authority of a chief of staff. The highly respected Virginian was aware that the most immediate and dangerous threat posed by enemy forces swarming in the state was an advance southward on Richmond from Fredericksburg by General Irvin McDowell's corps. That could put the Confederacy's capital and industrial center in peril on two fronts. Moreover, Banks might leave the valley and strengthen further the Union drive. Such pressures would diminish the odds of holding Richmond and maintaining the war. The one Confederate weapon that might prevent an overwhelming concentration of Federal soldiers was the unimposing little force and its strange former professor way out in the Shenandoah Valley.

Johnston was too busy and too removed to give adequate attention to the motley contingent of Confederates near Harrisonburg.[19] Yet Lee had watched Jackson's movements for the past weeks and had recognized a soldier who thought with Lee's own sense of aggressiveness. Hence, and certainly with the backing of the president, Lee assumed de facto command of affairs in the valley.

No formal orders or official change of command emerged. Johnston was not even told that he was being bypassed. Lee and Jackson simply began filling a command vacuum with direct correspondence. From the start, this was a sensitive arrangement, for Johnston was ever touchy about the scope of his authority. Lee skirted quicksand: he was between Davis, who insisted on exercising control, and Johnston, who was supposedly in control.

On April 21, Lee began the one-on-one exchange by sending Jackson an unusually open and candid letter. It became one of the most historic communiques of the Civil War. Not only did Lee suggest a grand strategy—with options—for Jackson to take; the president's military advisor also displayed an audacity that would make him one of America's foremost field generals.

Lee explained to Jackson the dangers of a linkup between McDowell north of Richmond and McClellan east of the capital. Then he outlined three offensive possibilities for the valley commander. First and foremost, if Jackson thought that with Ewell's assistance he could drive Banks's legions down the valley, he was authorized to do so. This, Lee emphasized, "will prove a great relief to the pressure on Fredericksburg." Should Jackson think Banks too strong to be attacked, Ewell could fall back in a supporting capacity. He would take a position on or near the Virginia Central Railroad to assist Jackson, Johnston, General Charles Fields's small force twelve miles below Fredericksburg, or whomever might need reinforcements. Last, if Jackson felt confident of being able to hold Banks in check with his own force, Ewell could march east to assist in the defense of Richmond.

Jackson did not conceal his excitement when he replied two days later (April 23) to Lee's suggestions. He would assail the enemy then advancing on Harrisonburg at the first expedient moment. "My object," Jackson stated, "has been to get in his rear at New Market or Harrisonburg if he gives me an opportunity. . . . It appears to me that if I remain quiet a few more days he will probably make a move in some direction . . . and thus enable me, with the blessing of Providence, to successfully attack his advance." Should Banks prove too strong and then attempt a pursuit of Jackson through Swift Run Gap, "our forces would have greatly the advantage."[20]

Lee responded by return mail. He called Jackson's attention to the wide dispersal of Confederate units in the valley. "A more rapid concentration of our troops" could wreck Union strategy in the Shenandoah, if not throughout Virginia. Lee then closed with a thought to which Jackson fully subscribed: "The blow wherever struck, must, to be successful, be sudden and heavy."[21]

From the number of times Lee mentioned the subject thereafter, he obviously favored Jackson and Ewell assailing Banks in the lower valley. If victory were not possible, Lee hoped that Jackson would at least sweep around Banks's eastern flank and strike Union communication lines at Warrenton or another point in northern Virginia. Jackson could help the most, Lee was saying, by lashing out at the enemy.

This the valley commander had every intention of doing. Lee had significantly lengthened Jackson's leash. Instructions from Johnston had always been to protect supply lines, retard Banks's advance, but to give battle only when the chances of victory were heavily in Jackson's favor. Now Lee was urging Jackson to strike, and to do so when and wherever he thought it advantageous for the good of the valley and for the defense of Richmond. Jackson could act now and explain later.[22]

Meanwhile, Banks gave Jackson all the time he needed by moving slowly and poking ineffectually. The only harassment of the Confederate forces came from the 2d

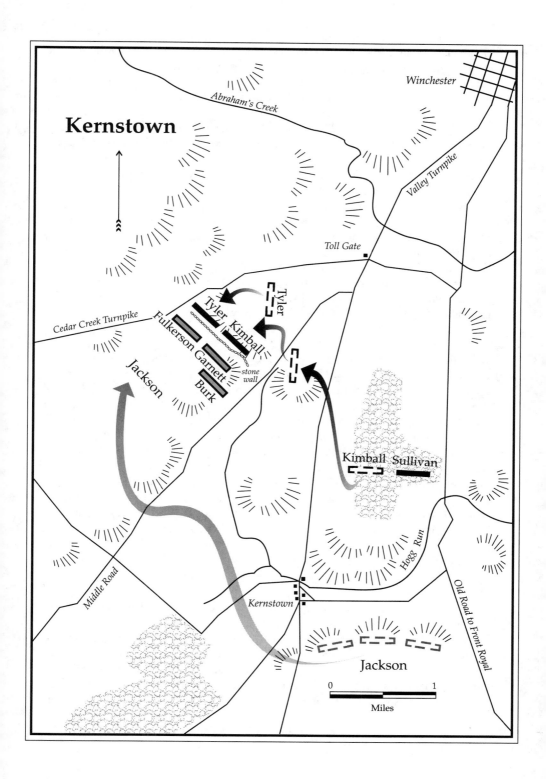

Kernstown

Winchester

Abraham's Creek

Valley Turnpike

Toll Gate

Cedar Creek Turnpike

Tyler

Tyler

Kimball

Fulkerson Garnett

Burk

stone wall

Jackson

Kimball

Sullivan

Hogg Run

Middle Road

Kernstown

Old Road to Front Royal

Jackson

0   1

Miles

Massachusetts and 1st Michigan Cavalry. They were under the command of Colonel George H. Gordon, a West Point classmate of Jackson. Not until April 24 did the lead elements of Banks's army—two infantry brigades and 600 cavalry—reach Harrisonburg. Colonel Francis Smith at VMI became so alarmed at the proximity of the Federals that he tendered the corps of cadets to Jackson.

The general politely declined the offer because they were not needed at the moment. It had taken Banks thirty days to cover the sixty-seven miles from Winchester to Harrisonburg. The two miles that the enemy was averaging daily was a distance Jackson's men could cover in less than an hour. Nor did Jackson share Richmond's concern about McClellan's advance up the peninsula. "He lacks nerve," Jackson said in dismissing his former West Point classmate.[23]

With Banks's main force of 19,000 troops at Harrisonburg, Jackson moved to offset the threat. On April 26, he told Ewell to advance on Stanardsville for better protection of Jackson's 6000 men. When Banks did nothing the next day, Jackson directed Ewell to slow his march and to bring his soldiers leisurely on the 28th as close to Swift Run Gap as possible. Jackson did not want the support troops to struggle through mud and over rough country and then arrive too exhausted to be of help.

Although Lee had suggested a diversionary attack on Warrenton as an offensive possibility, Jackson never took the idea seriously. He wanted Banks. The sprawling Union columns, he told Lee, provided "the golden opportunity for striking a blow." First, however, Jackson had to blunt an enemy thrust at Staunton.[24]

To the west, deeper in the Alleghanies, was the 20,000-man Federal army of General John C. Fremont. It was only thirty-five miles from Harrisonburg and seventy-five miles from Staunton. Fremont separated his force by starting General Robert H. Milroy and 6000 troops toward the vital railhead at Staunton. In front of the town to oppose the enemy advance were General Edward Johnson and his relatively untested band of fewer than 3000 Confederates. The Warm Springs turnpike afforded Banks a chance to link with Fremont, or Banks could assail the Confederate rear while Johnson grappled with Milroy in his front. Either way, Staunton was in imminent danger. Jackson had to make some kind of move.

His plan was simple but daring. Success depended on secret marches and sudden strikes. Ewell would cross the Blue Ridge to Conrad's Store and replace Jackson poised on Banks's flank. Jackson would march to Johnson's aid with the intention of striking Milroy before Fremont could bring his full force to bear. A quick pursuit and slashing at the remainder of Fremont's brigades would neutralize that enemy threat. Then Jackson would march back into the Shenandoah Valley, pick up Ewell, and go after Banks.

Jackson doubtless cleared the operation with Lee, who must have felt some unspoken doubts. The politician-soldier Banks and the adventurer Fremont were moving on Jackson from opposite directions and with superior numbers. At the moment, in high Confederate circles in Richmond, Jackson had a shaky reputation if he had a reputation at all. His personal appearance was unimpressive; his performance of late—especially at Romney and Kernstown—had done nothing to improve his image. However, Lee was willing to gamble with Jackson, and Jackson was willing to take the risks.

April 27 was Sunday. Jackson attended a camp religious service that afternoon. He heard Major Dabney preach appropriately from the text: "Boast not thyself of to-morrow; for thou knowest not what a day may bring forth." Jackson, one bystander noted, "stood with head uncovered through the whole exercise, whilst the soldiers formed a circle and sat on the ground."[25]

The general offered fervent oblations that day. "My prayer," he wrote Colonel Smith at VMI, "is that the proposed undertaking will receive *God's blessing*, for without it I can do nothing."[26] Jackson said nothing to Smith about precisely what he had in mind.

Next in Jackson's preparations was to meet with Ewell. "My dear General," he wrote early on Monday in typically guarded language, "please let me see you as early as practicable, as I wish to consult with you upon important business." A few hours later, Major General Richard S. Ewell dismounted at Jackson's headquarters for his first meeting with the man called "Stonewall." Ewell had heard so many negative reports on Jackson, and his directives from the valley commander had been so muted and at times contradictory, that Ewell was even then seeking assignment to any other command.[27]

Ewell himself was hardly an impressive figure in appearance or in manners. He was really one of nature's characters. Although seven years older than Jackson (whom he nevertheless called "Old Jack" behind his back), Dick Ewell was five feet, seven inches tall, with gray eyes and light complexion. What hair he had was brown. "Old Baldhead" had bulging eyes that stared balefully, thin mustachio, and the movements of a startled bird. He barked commands in a high, piping voice, and his heated temper was something over which he had no control. Ewell shared Jackson's affliction with dyspepsia. That often caused him to pass the night curled around a camp stool—which "was enough to dislocate an ordinary person's joints," one soldier insisted. This awesome exterior covered the inner toughness of a mule driver.

Ewell was a solid soldier without ambition for high command. Aggressive and devoted to the Confederate cause, he always served well—as long as he was told precisely what to do. His imagination was as limited as his profanity was endless.[28]

The conference between Jackson and Ewell lasted several hours. Ewell returned to his division with instructions to cross the mountains at Swift Run Gap and occupy Jackson's encampment at the western base. That Jackson did not tell the division commander the full battle plan would be evident in Ewell's growing exasperation in the days ahead.

Naturally, Ewell's men had no idea what strategy their new and reportedly strange commander had in mind. The 1st Maryland was part of the van of Ewell's division. Shortly after sundown on April 29, it reached the top of the Blue Ridge. Below them, Jackson's campfires were clearly visible.

One of the Marylanders stated: "At the first sound of reveille next morning, every man sprang nimbly to his feet. They wanted to see Jackson, to talk with his troops . . . but, to our utter amazement, when we turned our faces to where we had passed his army the evening previous, nothing met our gaze but the smouldering embers of his deserted camp-fires. We rubbed our eyes and looked again. . . . But gone he was, and whither for what no one could tell. Quietly, in the dead of night, he had arisen from his blanket, and calling his troops around him, with them had disappeared."[29]

Banks had convinced himself that Jackson was incapable of further resistance.

From Harrisonburg on April 28, the Federal general informed his war department: "Our force is entirely secure here. The enemy is in no condition for offensive movements. . . . I think we are now just in condition to do all you can desire of us in the valley—clear the enemy out permanently." Two days later, Banks confidently reported: "Jackson is bound for Richmond. This is the fact, I have no doubt."[30]

Jackson started eastward, to be sure. He alone understood what was taking place. "Heaven only knows where he is bound for now," a member of Chew's Battery wrote in his diary. "I know that ninety-nine out of a hundred of his men have no more idea of where they will turn up next than the buttons in their coats." Another of Jackson's men observed, "We were retiring and advancing at the same time, a condition an army never undertook before."[31]

At 3 A.M. on April 30, the march began and quickly went from bad to worse. Some 8500 infantry, with Ashby's 1000 horsemen leading the way, followed the South Fork of the Shenandoah upstream toward the village of Port Republic. Rains had turned the roads into quagmires; the fields on either side varied in appearance from morasses to lakes.

The 10th Virginia's Joseph Kaufman confided in his journal: "Old Jack is a hard master from the way he is putting us through. My feet have given out but still I have to travel on. Oh, I wish peace would be declared." Sandie Pendleton of the staff had more faith in his general. "I firmly believe we shall be victorious wherever we fight them here," he told his father, "for I believe that God will ever, as he has hitherto, bless a cause with so Godly and upright a man as our Genl. at its head."[32]

With the wagon trains in front of the infantry, progress went at a snail's pace. Wheels sank to their hubs. Soldiers used muskets to help move their feet as they slogged forward through the mud. Other troops lent hands and shoulders in an attempt to get imbedded rolling stock moving again.

Rain commenced anew in the middle of the afternoon. The downpour had become steady when Jackson rode through the troops to get to the front of the column. "Let us make Old Jack get his head wet!" a couple of soldiers shouted. The men began cheering lustily in spite of the elements. Jackson removed his hat in acknowledgement. A degree of comedy then ensued for the troops. A bareheaded Jackson on Little Sorrel came splashing by at a full gallop. The staff, on less spirited mounts, followed in what could only be called a ludicrous race. Major Dabney, Hotchkiss recalled, cut "a sorry figure in his clerical outfit of leggings, umbrella, sober old horse, &c."[33]

Men spent the night huddled and crouched in the mud as rain continued unabated. Jackson took refuge in the spacious home of John F. Lewis east of Port Republic. His command had advanced that day a grand total of five miles. Unknown to Jackson, this was the first of sixty-three consecutive days in which he would be engaged in nonstop activities. The strain would show with time.[34]

Rain fell the next day too. Streams were out of their banks; the mountains were barely visible through the dreary rainfall. Men, horses, and equipment floundered almost hopelessly in soil completely water-logged. Jackson urged on soldiers who were straining to keep wagons and cannon moving. At least once that day, the general dismounted and helped collect rails and stones to give greater traction for the vehicles.

While so engaged, Jackson walked up to a soldier also collecting stones from the mud. The man was intent at his work and cursing Jackson for subjecting troops to such hardships. "It is for your own good, sir," a voice behind him said. The soldier turned and saw Jackson likewise toiling in the mud.[35]

The following day brought no improvement. Jackson's force struggled up the Blue Ridge toward little-used Brown's Gap. "Many dead horses that had succumbed to deep mud and the hard pulling were strewn along the road," one man noted. Surgeon Harvey Black of the 4th Virginia added, "My horse fell in a mud hole and I thought was gone, but after lying for a little time sprang out."[36]

On Saturday, May 3, the clouds broke. Sunshine bathed the drenched country as the Confederate column wound down the east face of the Blue Ridge. Then the men struck a hard road over relatively flat country. It was a welcome relief after the agonies of the previous three days.

By nightfall, Jackson's force was in bivouac on the hills and in the meadows around Mechum's River Station on the Virginia Central Railroad connecting Staunton with Richmond. Five or six short trains stood idle on the main line and siding. Their presence was a silent indication that the journey for the Confederates was not yet done.

Some of the men washed away mud and perspiration in the nearby streams. A pleased Jackson dashed off a note to Ewell: "The bad roads here greatly impeded my progress, but my opinion is, that the roads have been so repaired by my command that they are in a better condition than before I left you." To Colonel Smith, who had volunteered the VMI Corps of Cadets for duty, Jackson warned: "It is very important to keep our movements concealed from the enemy, and, to this end, our people should say nothing about our Army. With you I am assured our God will prosper our cause."[37]

May 4 was supposed to be a day of rest out of respect for the Sabbath. Yet early in the morning came orders for the regiments to move to the train station. There Jackson helped to sort out the sick and the lame. They were packed into the dilapidated railroad cars, most of them too dispirited at leaving the valley to care about comfort.

Soon the first train began moving, followed by the second, with a third close behind. Pained and feverish troops on board perked up, looked at one another, then began cheering wildly. The trains were not heading east toward Richmond but westward for the climb up the Blue Ridge and back into the valley! Jackson next collected the able-bodied men, his guns and his wagons, then led the force by road toward Staunton.

A few of the soldiers may have discerned what was happening. No announcement came from Jackson, who as always kept his own counsel. Before dawn that day had come urgent news from General Edward Johnson in the mountains west of Staunton. Fremont's advance guard was pushing toward him faster than anticipated. Jackson had planned to combine with Johnson in due course and eliminate this Federal menace.

Now he had to move at once; and as Jackson bobbed in the saddle, leaning almost over Little Sorrel's head, he read again a May 1 dispatch from Lee. "If you can strike an effective blow against the enemy west of Staunton, it will be very advantageous. You might then avail yourself of your success, to bring with you Genl. Johnson's command . . . and move your army thus reinforced back to the Blue Ridge. Should your combined forces, with those of Genl. Ewell prove strong enough to warrant an attack on Genl. Banks, it might then be made."[38]

As Jackson led part of his command through the Blue Ridge, trains—some with two locomotives in front, others with pusher engines at the rear—strained to get over the mountain at Waynesboro. In Staunton, meanwhile, rumors of Jackson's abandonment of the valley and alarms over approaching Federals had residents on edge. The faithful streamed into church services that morning.

In the middle of the afternoon, the long wail of a train whistle sounded down the line. A second whistle could be heard in the distance. Crowds rushed to the depot. It was Jackson's men! Muddy, barefooted, ragged soldiers found themselves hailed as conquering heroes.[39]

Jackson and his staff reached Staunton around 5 P.M. The carnival-like atmosphere then sweeping through the town gave him immediate concern. A need for secrecy and security was imperative. Jackson promptly directed Ashby's cavalry to seal off Staunton. No one was allowed out or in. The general established his headquarters at the Virginia Hotel while the Stonewall Brigade encamped two miles to the east and the rest of the army fanned out as it arrived to the west of Staunton.

Good news greeted Jackson on Monday morning. Federal sources reported him en route to Richmond, Waynesboro, Staunton, Port Republic, Gordonsville, even back to Harrisonburg.[40] More welcome was confirmation that Banks had withdrawn his forces from Harrisonburg and was retiring northward down the valley. The Federal commander deemed Harrisonburg an unimportant and overly exposed point. Since Jackson was no longer considered a threat, Washington officials had directed Banks to establish a new command post at New Market.

With his spirits already elevated by developments on May 5, Jackson derived additional pleasure as the VMI cadets—some 200 strong—marched into Staunton in uniformed splendor.[41] Not even a cold rain on the first day's march spoiled the nattiness of their dress. Perhaps seeing the meticulously outfitted cadets made Jackson aware of his seedy appearance. When the cadets asked to pass in review for their general the following day, Jackson took pains to be presentable.

First he got a haircut. He then laid aside the blue U.S. Army uniform that he had worn for a decade at VMI and had acquired the shabbiness of reduced gentility. In its place—momentarily—he donned a full gray uniform with the insignia of a Confederate general on the collar. (Jackson would fall back to his blue coat often thereafter simply because, one staff member explained, "he was too absorbed to give thought or time to the subject.")[42]

Soon a party of young girls appeared at the hotel to get a look at the general. They walked back and forth in the street until he appeared. "When he saw our eager faces," one said, "he took off his hat, smiled, and passed on." It was also in Staunton that he received from a grateful valley matron a letter addressed to "Stone W. Jackson."

On that same May 5, Jackson's old friend, the Reverend Francis McFarland, conducted a morning church service for the troops. In the afternoon, the Presbyterian cleric twice visited Jackson's room and was treated, he noted, "very kindly."[43]

Hours later, reports reached Johnson's Confederates in the mountains to the west that Jackson and his forces were in Staunton and coming to their aid. Adjutant Charles Wight of the 58th Virginia observed: "Some of us laugh at the idea; others busy themselves planning a campaign. . . . Now we knew we were to have war in earnest, for Gen. Jackson was known to be an active, daring officer."[44]

Jackson's mood turned sour the next day. His troops spent that May 6 resting and making arrangements for a tedious march into the Allegheny Mountains. While the staff continued to gather information about the Union advance on Staunton, Jackson concentrated on personnel matters, none of which he found positive.

Ashby and Funsten, the only two cavalry officers of field-grade rank, were sick. The Confederate horsemen were showing even less cohesiveness than normal. In a revealing, personal letter to his congressional liaison, Alexander Boteler, Jackson expressed uncharacteristically strong opinions about some of his subalterns. "With regard to Col. Ashby's promotion, I would gladly favor it, if he were a good disciplinarian, but he has such bad discipline and attaches so little importance to drill, that I would regard it as a calamity to see him promoted."[45]

Jackson displayed inflexibility in his belief that commanding generals should have right of approval over any colonel elevated by the War Department. "Brig. Genls. Taliaferro and [John] Echols have both been promoted from colonelcies when neither of them should have been." Then Jackson lashed out at all political appointments. When will they cease? he asked. "The great interests of the country are being sacrificed by appointing incompetent officers. I wish that if such appointments are continued, that the President would come in the field and command them, and not throw the responsibility upon me of defending the District when he throws such obstacles in my way." Garnett and Taliaferro were two such bad examples, Jackson stated; and while he and Echols were "warm personal friends," Jackson did not think him sufficiently professional at the moment to be a brigadier in field service.[46]

Jackson also disapproved of the commander in chief's desire to defend every inch of the Confederacy at all times. As a cadet at West Point, Jackson had learned—and strongly endorsed—the axiom of Frederick the Great that "he who attempts to defend everything ends up defending nothing."

The one bright light in the military hierarchy, Jackson observed, was Lee. "I have great confidence in Genl. Lee, and believe that he has done all that he consistently could for the valley, though I would like to see adopted the policy of abandoning for the moment one section of the country, in order to concentrate forces and sweep the enemy from another, and then return and crush him in the locality which had been abandoned, and thus keep our troops continually employed in successful work." Jackson quickly added: "But Genl. Lee sees things from a higher stand point than I do. I know but little comparatively outside my District."[47]

With that admission, Jackson turned his attention to the military situation in his front. Before 6:30 A.M. on May 7, his soldiers were moving west from Staunton. Taliaferro's brigade was in the lead. Jackson was obviously not expecting battle that morning or he would have assigned a more reliable commander to be on the point.

As a final attempt to keep his destination secret, Jackson himself practiced a little deception. He mounted his horse without notice. While staff members struggled to catch up, Jackson galloped south for several miles as if heading for Lexington. Then he turned to the right on a byroad and joined the marching column on the Staunton and Parkersburg turnpike. Staff members ignorant of the movements of the army muttered to themselves about the unnecessary amount of riding that day.[48]

The twenty-mile march entailed crossing four ridges of Shenandoah Mountain. Part of the Southern column was either climbing or easing its way downhill. "This is the meanest country I ever saw," Sandie Pendleton observed, "but still it is old Virginia and we must have it."[49]

Jackson planned to confront the Federals somewhere in Highland County, a miniature Switzerland in terrain. Approaching the Confederates was the van of Fremont's army: five regiments from Ohio and two from western Virginia. A bold but inexperienced Hoosier named Robert H. Milroy was at their head. Unfortunately, the column, like Fremont's entire command, was beset "by every imaginable difficulty, and from every imaginable cause." Soldiers were a mixture of all nationalities; the force, isolated in the mountains, had been all but forgotten by the Union War Department; many of the troops were without shoes; their arms were for the most part antiques.[50]

Edward Johnson's Confederates were far in front of Jackson and driving to engage the Federals. On that May 7, Johnson overpowered an enemy garrison near Rogers' Toll-gate, twenty-three miles from Staunton and on the eastern slope of Shenandoah Mountain. Most of the Federals managed to escape. Johnson threw out skirmishers left and right as he led his troops up the mountain.

Later that day, Union artillery got even by surprising Jackson's column with a sudden barrage. Jackson halted his troops, thereby widening the distance between himself and Johnson to a march of about five hours. Jackson considered that by simple arithmetic to be critical. If he could unite with Johnson, the two would bring 10,000 soldiers to bear against Milroy's 6000 troops. Should Johnson have to fight by himself, Milroy would have a two-to-one advantage.

At 5:10 A.M. on Thursday the 8th, Jackson sent a long dispatch to Ewell. Banks was then at New Market, Jackson stated. Ewell must keep his division within striking distance of the Federals and not let them cross the Blue Ridge without a contest. "This morning," Jackson added, "we move forward, and I pray that *God* will bless us with success."[51]

Jackson and Hotchkiss rode rapidly ahead to establish personal contact with Johnson's force. As he passed the rear units, Jackson recognized the vestige of Loring's old Army of the Northwest. It consisted in the main of six untested regiments—the 12th Georgia and the 25th, 31st, 44th, 52d, and 58th Virginia—plus three batteries of artillery. The regiments were organized into two small brigades under Colonel John A. Campbell, a prominent southwest Virginian and former member of the state's Secession Convention, and Colonel William C. Scott, a Powhatan attorney who had been a brigadier general of militia at war's outset.

The Virginia units were delighted to have Jackson in their midst. Duty up to that point had basically consisted of fighting boredom in the isolated mountainous country. "I hope our Regiment will follow Jackson," Major John Ross of the 52d Virginia wrote his wife, "as it is better to be marching around in search of adventures as did the doughty Don Quixote then to be seated on top of the Shenandoah in vain-glorious ease."[52]

When Jackson and Hotchkiss reached the crest of Bull Pasture Mountain, the village of McDowell—and Milroy's contingent—were three miles away. General and aide started down the western slope on the turnpike, which, at that point, was wedged between Bull Pasture Mountain on the left and Hull's Ridge on the right. The road passed through a narrow, boulder-lined gorge that could be a certain death trap.

Hotchkiss was familiar with the area. He soon turned left off the main road and led Jackson over to a rocky spur of Bull Pasture Mountain. It was known as Sitlington's Hill; and while it commanded a clear view of the valley below, numerous ravines and seams partially concealed by thick timber gave it a certain vulnerability.

Heavy skirmishing had begun. Captain Edward Alfriend and a detachment of the 44th Virginia were driving in a Federal outpost when Jackson rode into the area. The general seemed oblivious to musketry tearing through the woods and ricocheting off boulders. A concerned Alfriend broke away from the fight. He raced up to Jackson, raised his hat in salute, and said, "General, allow me most respectfully to remonstrate with you against this most unnecessary exposure of your life." Jackson flashed a quizzical look at Alfriend. It vanished instantly. With a subdued voice, Jackson replied, "I wish to look forward here." Alfriend and his men quickly cleared the area of enemy soldiers.[53]

On top of Sitlington's Hill, Jackson found the officer he was seeking busily deploying the lead units of his force. Jackson returned a salute and studied the man closely. Forty-six-year-old General Edward Johnson was a character in a war that produced many characters. A sometimes uncouth man, Johnson boasted a strong personality and loud voice that commanded attention where physical good looks did not. Born in Chesterfield County near Richmond, raised in Kentucky, educated at West Point, he had fought Seminole Indians and Mexicans with equal ferocity.

Johnson entered the Civil War as colonel of the 12th Georgia. A brigadier's rank came months later. Disdaining sword and pistol, Johnson customarily carried a large thick club into battle. "He is a Stirring old Coon allways on the alert," one of his Georgia soldiers wrote admiringly.[54]

A huge body, bushy goatee, and natural frown gave Johnson a rough-looking image. Unfortunately, too, an affliction in one eye caused him to wink incessantly—a habit that ladies found offensive. One socialite maintained that Johnson's head "is strangely shaped, like a cone or an old-fashioned beehive . . . there are three tiers on it."[55] When angry, both of Johnson's ears wiggled.

Soldiers under "Allegheny" or "Old Clubby," as he was variously called, regarded him as a brave and good officer. His gruff, no-nonsense approach to war attracted Jackson's respect early. Johnson's "high qualities as a soldier," Jackson stated, "admirably fitted him" to be at the head of the Confederate advance into the mountains.[56]

Jackson, Johnson, and an escort of about thirty men moved to the western face of Sitlington's Hill to reconnoiter and discuss terrain. So large a group caught Milroy's attention. He sent skirmishers through the woods at the base of the height, while at the same time opening fire with a section of artillery from the western edge of Bull

Pasture Valley. The elevation was too high for cannon range, and the riders with Jackson and Johnson held off the Union advance with comparative ease.

From the hilltop, enemy camps were visible a mile away around McDowell. A thin Federal line also existed on Hull's Ridge to the north of the turnpike but proved of no consequence in subsequent movements. A Federal line of march from the north gave quick proof that Milroy was being reinforced. General Robert C. Schenck's brigade was arriving after a forced march of thirty-four miles in twenty-four hours. Schenck was a Dayton, Ohio, attorney, four-term congressman, and possessed of a courtly manner that contrasted with Milroy's strange combination of snow-white hair and jet-black beard.

Jackson stared long and silently at the Union host as he began eliminating options. He quickly discarded any idea of delivering a frontal assault on the Federals in the village. The Confederates would have to funnel down the turnpike, in the face of a concentrated fire, and ford rain-swollen Bull Pasture River before striking the enemy lines. It was now afternoon and Jackson's three valley brigades were still struggling to get through the mountains. The day was too far spent to unleash a heavy attack.

With his artillerist's eye, Jackson considered a more logical move. Sitlington's Hill dominated the surrounding country. From there Southern guns could tear apart Milroy's camps. Yet hauling artillery pieces up the precipitous ridges would be both time consuming and difficult. Milroy could easily escape bombardment by pulling his men out of range. Further, and if Jackson for some reason had to make a hasty withdrawal, he would stand in danger either of losing one or more guns or being slowed by cannon in descending the mountain.[57]

A better course, Jackson concluded, was a flanking movement. He dispatched Hotchkiss to explore the mountains for a road by which Jackson could get men and guns in Milroy's rear in order to strike a blow the next day. Concluding that no fighting would occur until then, Jackson sent most of his staff back to headquarters at John Wilson's Hotel on the eastern base of Bull Pasture Mountain. Johnson remained in command at the front.

Milroy was aware that his force of 3500 infantry was no match against Jackson's 9000 men. Still, he was eager to make some kind of attack. Near 3 P.M., Milroy received word that Confederates were about to post artillery atop Sitlington's Hill. The report was false, but Milroy did not know it and he ordered an immediate assault against Jackson's line.

Around 4:30, Ohio and western Virginia regiments under Cincinnati attorney Nathaniel McLean passed through the valley, entered woods, and started up the steep incline. Neither side knew the other's strength. As it turned out, the Federals were at a sharp disadvantage. Five Union regiments totaling 2300 troops were attacking six entrenched Confederate regiments of 2800 soldiers. Despite the numerical advantage, the defensive position had worried Johnson from the start.

The summit of Sitlington's Hill was a salient-shaped curve pointing toward the Union forces. On the flanks in good defensive position were the 52d and 44th Virginia. The 58th Virginia moved behind the 52d as support; the 31st Virginia moved below the hill to protect the turnpike. The 12th Georgia formed a sharp apex to Johnson's line and was dangerously exposed on three sides.

Jackson described the initial assault: "Milroy . . . was determined to carry the Hill if possible by direct attack. Advancing in force along its western slope, protected in his advance by the character of the ground, and the wood interposed in our front, and driving our skirmishers before him, he emerged from the wood & poured a galling fire into our right, which was returned, and a brisk and animated contest was kept up for some time." Johnson rushed his remaining troops into line. "The fire was now rapid and well sustained on both sides," Jackson stated, "and the conflict fierce & sanguinary."[58]

He did not know that at the time. Jackson had started somewhat nonchalantly over Bull Pasture Mountain to join his staff for supper. When sporadic gunfire erupted, Jackson was not unduly alarmed. Protocol dictated that Johnson should be allowed to perform his duty without a superior looking over his shoulder. Yet as the noise of battle escalated quickly, Jackson reined in his horse in the mountain gap and began looking for reinforcements.

Taliaferro's brigade was nearby. Jackson ordered it forward to Johnson's aid. The commanding general "was evidently in a bad humor," a soldier in the 10th Virginia noted. Jackson "told us to hurry up."[59]

Ascending the winding country road, three regiments under Taliaferro reached the crest of Sitlington's Hill just as the 12th Georgia began to give way after intense hand-to-hand fighting. The Virginians moved straight into action. Meanwhile, still alone on the mountainside, Jackson summoned Lieutenant Colonel Richard H. Cunningham and ordered him to advance his brigade of Virginians to the right of Johnson's position so as to strengthen the flank as well as protect the turnpike. As Cunningham wheeled to rejoin his men, Jackson shouted in his sharp way: "Tell your men they must hold that road!"[60]

The roar of musketry, somewhat strange without overtones of artillery, echoed through the mountains. Men fought at unusually close range. Federals grappled stubbornly to break Jackson's position.[61] Confederates in increasing numbers beat back assaults or held the enemy at bay.

Jackson's staff was eating a mile or more away when the contest began. The terrain muffled all sound of the battle. By the time the aides learned what was happening, it was near sundown. Staff members galloped up the mountain until they found the solitary figure of Jackson still standing in the road. The general promptly sent one aide to find the Stonewall Brigade and bring it up quickly. He "was very anxious for it to arrive," Hotchkiss noted.[62] Jackson then instructed Hotchkiss to ride forward and determine the situation on the battlefield.

The mapmaker had gone only a short distance when he met Quartermaster Harman riding by the side of a wagon. On the bed of the wagon was General Ed Johnson. He had been in the thick of the action, cursing loudly as he waved his big club back and forth, when a bullet shattered the bones in his ankle, producing a wound that would knock the colorful leader from action for a year.

Hotchkiss led the wagon to Jackson, who spoke briefly with Johnson and then turned back to Hotchkiss. "Go to General Taliaferro and tell him I am coming, in person, with the Stonewall Brigade, and must hold the position until I come." By then it was so dark that Hotchkiss had to make his way over the rough country on foot. He arrived at Sitlington's Hill shortly before 9 P.M. "We had repulsed the enemy," Hotchkiss wrote, "and our troops were mingled together in the greatest confusion imaginable, calling for comrades, commands, &c. like a swarm of bees, no one able to distinguish another in the darkness." Hotchkiss finally located Taliaferro, who appeared to have little control over the situation.[63]

Jackson arrived on the field a few minutes later with the lead regiment of the Stonewall Brigade. One of its soldiers thought Jackson "cold—collected—impenetrable—saying but little—watchful—thoughtful." The general actually had pangs of anxiety as he rushed his favorite battle unit up to high ground. However, after four hours of fighting, the Federals had fallen back under cover of darkness.

Immediate pursuit was out of the question. Although Jackson's force was numerically superior, it was in disarray. The cavalry was of no use on the steep and broken ground. Jackson may well have put Winder in charge of the sector, for he conferred at length with the commander of the Stonewall Brigade before starting down to his headquarters.

A bright moon in a cloudless sky provided light for the general and his staff. The night was cold: frost and fog blanketed the countryside. Jackson was so weary that he dismounted and walked in order to stay awake. When the party reached Wilson's around 2 A.M., house and yard were filled with wounded men. Jackson politely refused Jim Lewis's offer of food. The general stretched out on the ground to get a few hours' sleep before seeing what additional gain he could make from the battle.[64]

It had not been a major engagement by later standards of the Civil War. For once, Jackson had been caught napping; and the contest had fairly well run its course by the time he reached the battlefield. Jackson had won at McDowell by refusing to lose—by stubbornly maintaining a strong defensive position against a smaller attacking force.[65]

Union casualties were thirty-four killed, 220 wounded, and five missing, for a total of 259 men. Confederate losses, on the other hand, were 116 killed, 300 wounded, and four missing, a total of 416 men.[66] That the defensive side would lose 60 percent more men beclouded the victory.

Milroy had attacked in the belief that he needed to do so to save his own force. In hurling back the Federal assaults, Jackson had not only protected Staunton and the Virginia Central Railroad; he undoubtedly deflated some of Fremont's bluster about what he planned to achieve in the Virginia mountains.

At 5 A.M. on May 9, Jackson learned that the Federals had abandoned McDowell and fallen back toward Franklin and Fremont's main column. A short time later, Old Jack shifted his headquarters to the brick home of Mrs. Felix Hull in the village. John D. Imboden came to see him early that morning. The captain was preparing to leave for Staunton to check on new companies reporting for duty. If Jackson had any dispatches to send by telegraph to Richmond or elsewhere, Imboden would be happy to take them.

Jackson asked him to wait. He needed to report to Richmond about yesterday's action. Seated at a table, the general wrote a short message. Then he rose and stood before the fireplace for a moment before tearing up the paper. He wrote a shorter communique, read it, and tore it to pieces. Jackson began pacing the room. Finally, he took a seat again and wrote a couple of lines. He handed the message to Imboden. "Send that off as soon as you reach Staunton," he said. Later that day, Adjutant

General Samuel Cooper read Jackson's report: "God blessed our arms with victory at McDowell yesterday." One of Jackson's less-than-devout generals reacted to the wording of the message by snorting, "I suppose it is true, but we would have had no victory if we hadn't fought like the devil!" While the cryptic dispatch was typical of Jackson's reliance on few words, it also and easily gave the mistaken conclusion that he had initiated and won a decisive victory. Neither was the case.[67]

Few officials in Richmond even knew where McDowell was. Precisely what Jackson had done remained a mystery. By then Jackson had a reputation (largely outside the Shenandoah Valley) of being dangerously impetuous. In Richmond, the matronly Judith McGuire later wrote, "The croakers roll their gloomy eyes, and say, 'Ah, General Jackson is so rash!' and a lady even assured me that he was known to be crazy when under excitement, and that we had every thing to fear from the campaign he was now beginning in the Valley."[68]

On the other hand, Jackson's success came at a time when the Confederacy was trying to recover from the loss of Fort Henry and Fort Donelson in Tennessee, Roanoke Island, Port Royal, and Fort Pulaski on the Atlantic coast, and New Orleans. Major defeats in battle had occurred at Pea Ridge, Arkansas, and Shiloh in Tennessee. McClellan's massive Union army was now firmly planted on the peninsula east of Richmond. Gloom was growing.

Jackson's accomplishment, however limited it might have been, was the one ray of sunshine amid dark clouds over the Confederacy. Southerners turned to it with a combination of joy and hope. The *Lynchburg Virginian* exulted: "Who can doubt when Jackson speaks? Like a Christian hero, as he is, he ascribes the victory to the Lord of hosts. Long live Jackson! May an overruling Providence shield him in the day of battle, and preserve him to drive our enemies out of the fair land they have despoiled."[69]

Jackson was working at his McDowell headquarters on the morning of the 9th when a sergeant brought in a "plain, simple minded old man." The soldier informed Jackson that the man had freely taken an oath of loyalty to the United States. Is that so? Jackson asked.

The man answered: "Why, you see, Mister, the Yankees came to my house."

"I don't wish to know about the Yankees," Jackson interrupted. "Have you taken the oath?"

The man persisted. "Why, you see, Mister, the Yankees came to my house and made my wife get a rope and . . . " Again Jackson broke the conversation.

"I do not wish to know anything about your wife or the rope. Did you or did you not take the oath?"

"Well, Mister, I spose I did."

Jackson snapped: "You have no business being on this side of the Potomac River." Several of the man's neighbors were present. They were quick to tell Jackson that the Federals had threatened to hang the man if he did not sign the loyalty pledge. In addition, the farmer had two sons then in Confederate service

A pause, then Jackson asked, "Will you take the oath of allegiance to the Confederate States?"

Back came the quick reply, "Why, Mister, I'll take *two* or *three* of them!" Jackson smiled and sent the man home.[70]

It was almost noon before Jackson was able to put his army in motion. Rations were late in arriving, and the command had to be fed. Jackson left Colonel John Preston and the cadets to guard the prisoners and stores at McDowell. (The VMI contingent, Hotchkiss explained, was "pretty much used up by the hard marches, guard duty, &c., mere boys that most of them were.")[71] By the time the main column started north in pursuit of Milroy and Schenck, the Federals had a commanding head start.

Confederates made about six miles that day, the men being "all tired and exhausted" by the time they bivouacked at the turnpike junction with the road leading to Franklin.[72] It was not until 11 P.M. that Harman's supply wagons caught up with the main force. Jackson had increased concern that Fremont might try to effect a linkup with Banks in the valley.

To block such a move, Jackson took Hotchkiss aside for a private conference. The staff member was directed to round up some cavalry and block the three mountain passes leading into the Shenandoah Valley. "Take couriers along," Jackson instructed, "and send one back every hour telling me where you are." Jackson then gave his aide a parting thought: "Now don't take counsel of your fears."[73] Hotchkiss galloped off on a fifty-mile errand. He found a handful of riders and also enlisted the aid of sympathetic citizens along the way. They rolled boulders on the roads, felled trees, and burned bridges. One after another, the possible routes between Fremont and Banks were closed.

Strenuous marches over the next two days brought Jackson closer to the enemy. Yet full contact never came. Schenck slowed down the Confederates by the unique expedient of setting fire to the woods along the road. Heavy smoke literally stifled Jackson's men. Occasional ambushes further retarded the Confederate advance.

Frustrations led to a number of exaggerated statements by Jackson's soldiers. William Montgomery of the 33d Virginia described the first impediments in the chase to catch Milroy: "but the most horrible they do on the retreat was that they hid some 50 odd boddies on or near the field covered them over with brush & leaves set the woods on fire burned the dead & some that was not dead when the fire got to them."[74]

In addition, little enthusiasm prevailed on the command level of the pursuers. Jackson preferred to have a staff officer lead a column rather than a brigade commander knowing where he was to go. Resentment resulted. On one occasion, after Hotchkiss's return from blocking the Federals' passage through mountain passes, the mapmaker was directing Taliaferro's movements. In telling that general which road to take, Hotchkiss was privy to "an invariable exposition of wrath at each cross road we came to."[75]

Jackson's chase proceeded slowly. Under the best of circumstances, no one could move very fast on those atrocious mountain roads. Yet Jackson was optimistic of a successful maneuver. On May 10, he wrote Ewell: "I desire to follow the enemy as far as practicable today. My troops are in advance. Should circumstances justify it I will try through *Gods blessing* to get in Banks rear, and if I succeede in this, I desire you to press him as far as may [be] consistent with your own safety should he fall back."[76]

Ewell was bewildered. Although Jackson had kept him reasonably informed, the division commander had no idea what Jackson was doing or what he intended to undertake later. Jackson's "meandering," while Ewell sat immobile and stared in the direction of Banks, put the subordinate's temper on edge.

Around May 11, Turner Ashby rode into Ewell's camp. He saluted and asked Ewell how he was. "I've been in hell for three days! Been in hell for three days, Colonel Ashby! What's the news from Jackson?" Ashby replied, "General Jackson says the Lord has blessed our arms with another glorious victory." With that, Ewell's spirits brightened, albeit temporarily.[77]

Jackson's relations with General Sidney Winder by then had also become strained because of a series of misunderstandings. On May 10, the Stonewall Brigade was in the lead on the march toward Franklin. About seven miles northwest of McDowell, the troops came to a fork in the road. The Staunton-Parkersburg Turnpike went off to the left; the right fork headed north but lacked any sign of identification. No one was there to give Winder directions. He therefore halted the column, told the men to stack arms, and sent back for instructions from Jackson. Soon Major G. Douglas Mercer, Winder's quartermaster, rejoined the column. He had just returned from Staunton, where, he stated, a report was circulating that Jackson had ordered Winder's arrest for not having his brigade in line promptly at McDowell. Winder was seething over the rumor when a battery came down the narrow road. This forced the troops to unstack arms in order to let the guns pass. At that point, Jackson rode into the area. Winder, face red from anger, saluted and demanded to know if Jackson had authorized his arrest. "I have always obeyed your orders," he exclaimed.

Jackson interrupted: "But General Winder, you are not obeying my orders now. My order is that whenever there is a halt, the men shall stack arms."

"I did obey your orders," Winder snapped, "but had to break the stacks to let a battery pass." Winder added that as the second in command in Jackson's army, he wanted his rank respected by everyone. At that moment, a courier arrived with a dispatch from Richmond. Jackson read it, handed it to Winder, and briefly discussed its contents before riding off on the northbound road. The entire incident at the fork was not mentioned again, but Winder was slow in forgetting it.[78]

May 12 found Jackson's army drawn up before Franklin. Milroy and Schenck had heavily fortified a hill that dominated the country around the village. The valley through which the Confederates were passing extended in width no more than a quarter-mile, with high peaks staring menacingly on both sides. Jackson could not advance farther without making a full assault. He had no intention of doing that. Banks, not Fremont, was his primary target.

A proclamation came from headquarters early that Monday. Jackson had wanted merely "to render thanks to Almighty God for having crowned our arms with success and to implore His continued favor." However, Major Dabney, who had been struggling arduously with military matters since becoming chief of staff, now had a chance to write a call to worship. He made the most of the opportunity. The announcement was issued over Jackson's name. "Soldiers of the Army of the Valley and the North West: I congratulate you on your victory at McDowell. I request you to unite with me, this morning, in thanksgiving to Almighty God, for thus having crowned your arms with success; and in prayer that He will continue to lead you from victory to victory until our independence shall be established, and make you that people whose God is the Lord. The Chaplains will hold Divine service at 10 o'clock A.M. this day, in their respective Regiments."[79]

Most of the prayer meetings occurred near the meadow where Jackson had his headquarters. Hence, he attended at least two of them. His first stop was with Lexington-area friends in the Rockbridge Artillery. A cavalryman who joined the service noticed Jackson, "cap in hand and with bowed head," standing in the midst of about fifty men "while some soldier was engaged in earnest prayer." One of the gunners unfamiliar with the general's religious habits concluded that Jackson stood through the meeting because "he was afraid he would go to sleep" if he were seated.[80]

From there, Jackson rode to the camp of the 44th Virginia. Its Presbyterian chaplain, Richard McIlwaine (who later served twenty-one years as president of Hampden-Sydney College), was considered an inspiring preacher. Captain Edward Alfriend of the 44th was standing in the road and smoking a pipe when a lone rider came into view. It was Jackson. Alfriend jerked to attention and removed his hat.

"Good morning, General," he said.

Jackson reined his horse, lifted his hat, and asked: "Captain, is divine service going on in your camp?" An uncomfortable Alfriend confessed that he did not know.

"Where is your colonel's headquarters?" came the next question. The captain quickly volunteered to lead the way. Soon Jackson spied the church service taking place in a clump of woods.

He stopped for a moment, looked Alfriend sternly in the eye, but asked in a kindly way: "Captain, the next time I order divine service to be held, won't you promise me to attend?"

"Yes, sir," the embarrassed officer replied instantly.[81]

Alfriend watched Jackson throughout the prayer meeting. By the time Chaplain McIwaine reached the benediction, rain was falling. Yet Jackson stood "with his head uncovered, his arms crossed on his chest, and his form bowed." To Alfriend, it was "a sublime exhibition of his noble religious character."[82]

Unknown to Jackson, Banks's army at this time was in motion. What Confederate officials in Richmond had feared had become a reality. Banks issued orders dividing his command. With two infantry brigades and a brigade of cavalry, he left New Market for Strasburg. Shields's division crossed the Massanutten Mountain at New Market and proceeded north toward Manassas Gap and the road to Fredericksburg and McDowell's corps.

Back at Swift Run Gap, while Jackson gave thanks to God, General "Baldy Dick" Ewell watched developments and gave vent to anger. Two recorded instances exist when his temper exploded. Colonel James A. Walker of the 13th Virginia—the same Walker whom Jackson had expelled from VMI in a stormy incident a decade earlier—visited Ewell on regimental business. He found the general in a "towering rage." Walker decided to forgo mentioning the reason for his call. He was trying tactfully to leave Ewell's tent when the commander, in his high-pitched voice, asked loudly: "Colonel Walker, did it ever occur to you that General Jackson is crazy?"

"I don't know, General," Walker replied diplomatically. "We used to call him Tom Fool Jackson at the Virginia Military Institute, but I don't suppose he is really crazy."

Ewell was not appeased. Anger mounting, he roared: "I tell you, sir, he is as crazy as a March hare! He has gone away, I don't know where, and left me here with some instructions to stay until he returns, but Banks's whole army is advancing on me and I haven't the most remote idea where to communicate with General Jackson! I tell you, sir, he is crazy and I will just march my division away from here! I do not mean to have it cut to pieces at the behest of a crazy man!"[83]

Walker then rode to brigade headquarters to confer with General Arnold Elzey. He found the brigadier in an angry state of mind over an order just received from Ewell. After listening to a second tirade, Walker stated: "I don't know what to do. I was up to see General Ewell just now, and he said that General Jackson was crazy; I come down to see you, and you say that General Ewell is crazy." Walker shook his head. "It seems I have fallen into evil hands."[84]

A night or so later, Ewell's trusted cavalry chief, Captain Thomas T. Munford, awakened the general. It is now confirmed, Munford reported: Shields and his full division were leaving the valley for a linkup with McDowell at Fredericksburg. Ewell bounded from bed wearing only a nightshirt. Taking a map and crude lantern, he dropped to his knees and spread the chart on the bare ground. "His bones fairly rattled," Munford observed, "his bald head and long beard made him look more like a witch than a Major-General." The longer Ewell studied the map, the angrier he grew at Jackson. Finally, with an oath, Ewell yelled: "This great wagon hunter is after a Dutchman, an old fool! General Lee at Richmond will have little use for wagons if all these people close in around him! We are left out here in the cold! Why, I could crush Shields before night if I could move from here!" Drawing a quick breath, Ewell added, "This man Jackson is certainly a crazy fool, an idiot!"[85]

Unknown to Ewell, Jackson was done with the first stage of his campaign. Milroy had fallen back to Fremont's main body. Jackson was in no condition to attack Fremont without Ewell's division at hand. Fremont had relinquished any idea of trying to effect a junction with Banks. Some 20,000 or more Federal soldiers had been kept busy in the valley region when they might otherwise have been moving on Richmond.

These were the positives. Arrayed against them were a like number of negatives. McDowell was twenty-three miles west of Staunton. Franklin was thirty-four miles north of McDowell. That put Jackson sixty-seven miles from anything akin to a base of supplies. Moreover, time was growing valuable. A crisis at Fredericksburg or in front of Richmond could lead to Ewell's recall—a development that would prevent Jackson from assailing Banks. Jackson needed now to get back into the open country of the Shenandoah Valley. Communiques from Johnston and Lee said as much.[86]

On May 13, Jackson's army began retracing its steps toward Staunton. The VMI cadets under Colonel Francis Smith were still at McDowell. They had performed well the duties of guarding prisoners, burying the dead, and gathering supplies. Now it was time for the youths to return to the institute and resume their studies. Jackson directed Colonel Smith to take them home. The youths were ready to go. Major John Ross, a former VMI faculty member, noted: "They will not be sorry to get back. I think they are heartedly tired of soldiering."[87]

Jackson's order for the cadets to return to Lexington with their superintendent contained personal and affectionate overtones. "In thus parting with this patriotic officer, and those who had for a time left their scientific and literary pursuits for the purpose of co-operating in repelling the danger which threatened the Virginia Military Institute (which has by its graduates contributed so efficiently to the success of this war), the Major-General commanding tenders his thanks . . . for the promptitude and efficiency with which they have assisted in the recent expedition."[88]

Jackson's regular troops meanwhile found themselves encased in a marching procedure that had been sent to every regimental commander prior to departure from Franklin. The schedule overlooked nothing and became Jackson's hallmark in subsequent campaigns. Such orders in time would give Jackson's infantry the proud nickname of "foot cavalry."

Appropriately, the top of the orders read, "Headquarters, Valley District, Camp on the Road." The order of march first instructed troops to leave camp in cadence for the first 200–300 yards, then break into a comfortable "route step." The column would march fifty minutes, rest ten minutes, march fifty, rest ten, and so forth for however many hours Jackson kept them moving. A one-hour halt would be made for lunch. "Nothing will be carried in the baggage wagon except entrenching tools, cooking utensils and Officer's baggage," the directive continued. "No man unless he is too unwell to keep up with his Company will be permitted to leave ranks, except in case of necessity, and then only for a few minutes, and during this time he will not be permitted to take his musket with him—but it will be carried by another man whom the Company Commander will detail for that purpose." Roll call would take place at regular intervals through the day. Brigade commanders and members of their staffs would make periodic inspections of the marching column. Above all, Jackson emphasized, "men will be required not only to keep in ranks, but the proper distance must be preserved as far as practicable, and thus convert a march, as it should be, into an important drill, that of habituating the men to keep in ranks."[89]

Such rigid discipline was needed in the days ahead, for few marches of the war occurred under more adverse conditions. Torrential rains that began on May 12 continued with few interruptions for the next five days. The entire countryside turned to mud. Wagons broke down or overturned, spilling contents into the mire. Every piece of clothing became water-logged. Piecemeal shoes either were held together with twine or became no shoes at all. Hundreds of men sloshed barefooted through ankle-deep mud. Food ran low; drinking water became scarce. Everyone suffered. A soldier in the 31st Virginia noted in the middle of the trip: "Marched about 15 miles and encamped somewhere—has no name, nor never should have—on the road leading to Harrisonburg."[90]

Jackson continued to push his troops at least fifteen miles daily. The strain began to take a heavy toll. "Jackson is killing up all my men," a company commander in the 10th Virginia asserted. "Only half of them are fit for duty." George Harlow of the 23d Virginia regiment told his father: "I am living and am well except a verry bad cold from so much exposure and fatigue. . . . I have not had time to wash my clothes for a month." Yet, Harlow stated with resignation, "the Lords will be done."[91]

Soon, however, the unimpressive line of soldiers was back in the Shenandoah and approaching Harrisonburg. A Rockbridge Artillery private commented, "After bleak mountains with their leafless trees, the Old Valley looked like Paradise."[92]

In the meantime, Ewell had found his lack of activity intolerable. He unloaded his frustrations on the 13th to a niece. "I have spent two weeks of the most unhappy I ever remember. I was ordered here to support Genl. Jackson pressed by Banks. But the former immediately upon my arrival started in a long chase after a body of the enemy far above Staunton & I have been keeping one eye on Banks & one on Jackson & all the time quizzed up from Richmond until I am sick and worn down. . . . I am compelled to remain [here] untill that enthusiastic fanatic comes to some conclusion. . . . I have a bad headache. . . . I have never suffered so much from dyspepsia in my life."93

Late in the day came a green light from Jackson. "If Banks goes down the valley I wish you to follow him; so that he may feel that if he leaves the Valley, that not only will we occupy it, but that he will also be liable to be attacked so soon as he shall have sufficiently weakened his forces on this side [of] the Shenandoah." Ewell was delighted at the opportunity to do something. Fearful lest Jackson might change his mind at any moment, he determined to march down the Luray Valley on the east side of the Massanutten Mountains and protect the passes as he made for Thornton's Gap. Part of his division (Gen. Lawrence Branch's brigade) was still at Gordonsville. It would come into the valley through Fisher's Gap. Ewell told the brigade commander to proceed rapidly and with little encumbrance. Possibly borrowing from Jackson, Ewell warned, "The road to glory cannot be followed with too much baggage."94

He had been fussing and cursing, complaining and badmouthing, but Ewell had stood firm at Swift Run Gap like the good soldier that he was. His problems were petty compared to the issues pressing on Jackson as he led his men through the mud back into the valley. At the head of the list was how to smash Banks's forces. Keeping Ewell in the valley under his command was equally as important—and as uncertain.

Then came a veritable list of personnel matters. Jackson needed a replacement at the head of Edward Johnson's brigade. He was also keeping his eye on Sidney Winder. The Stonewall Brigade had at last warmed up to the Marylander; but Jackson, who always looked on his old brigade as a solicitous father, still harbored some doubts about Winder's command abilities. A new disagreement with Quartermaster Harman had also materialized. When Jackson pointed out to the sensitive major that he seemed to lack his former "driving disposition" and was interfering too much in military matters not of his responsibility, Harman asked to be relieved. Jackson would not honor the request.95

Next was a deeper crisis over the position of chief of artillery. Daniel Trueheart, a friend with whom Jackson had vacationed in New York before the war, had been Jackson's artillery commander for several months. Back in January, Jackson had filed charges against Trueheart for "drunkenness on duty and extreme insubordination."96 Confederate officials ignored the charges, and Jackson strangely forgot the matter until March, when a court-martial went into session. Then Jackson ordered Trueheart under arrest and appointed Lieutenant W. E. Cutshaw as temporary successor.

Since an officer of higher rank and experience was needed, Jackson in mid-May named Lieutenant Colonel Stapleton Crutchfield as chief of artillery. Commanding the guns of a general experienced not only in handling artillery but in teaching its theories was an ominous task. Yet the twenty-six-year-old Crutchfield had studied under Jackson at VMI, graduated first in his class, taught at the institute for six years, and enjoyed a relationship of mutual respect with his former professor and colleague.

Crutchfield would have little time to learn his duties before becoming a key player in a battle. Although future events would show the tall, thin artillery officer to be a man of only average talents, Jackson nevertheless held him in high esteem. He even overlooked the fact that Crutchfield liked to sleep late. In time, Jackson would try to have him promoted to brigadier general.[97]

Another officer of questionable talent added to the command at this time was Brigadier General George H. Steuart. He was to organize all Maryland soldiers into a single legion to be known as the "Maryland Line." Chief of Staff Dabney announced "Maryland" Steuart's appointment in grandiose terms. Steuart was a West Pointer with long service with the Dragoons against the Indians.

The cavalryman took charge of the 1st Maryland as the nucleus for his command, and he became controversial at once. Some soldiers liked Steuart (he "had no superior as a camp officer," one said). Yet Steuart's insistence on enforcing discipline to the strictest letter of the old army regulations made him extremely unpopular with the rank and file. Hotchkiss thought him "considerably puffed up with his own importance." The mapmaker later avowed that Steuart was "a coarse, beefy sort of fellow and always decidedly stupid."[98]

In the midst of problems with individuals, Jackson also had to cope with an uprising in the Stonewall Brigade. Seventeen Irishmen of the 27th Virginia became aware of the expiration of their twelve-month enlistments. The rigors of the campaign through which they had passed convinced the "Hibernians" that the new conscript law just enacted by the Confederate Congress—and which froze in service those regiments already in the field—was a violation of human rights. The malcontents thereupon stacked their arms and demanded discharges. Lieutenant Colonel Andrew J. Grigsby was a bit unsure what action to take, so he forwarded a report of the situation to Jackson.

The general began reading Grigsby's statement with furrowed brow. Jackson's eyes began flashing. He turned to Dabney and almost shouted: "What is this but mutiny? Why does Colonel Grigsby refer to me to know what to do with a mutiny? He should shoot them where they stand!"[99]

A succinct reply went to the colonel. Being himself an officer with little patience where insubordination was concerned, Grigsby moved at once. He ordered the full 27th Virginia formed in an open field; each man carried a loaded musket. After seventeen mutineers had been marched in front of the regiment, Grigsby gave the men a choice: return to duty at once, or be shot on the spot. All of the men meekly went back into the ranks. Thereafter, stated a member of the 27th, the Irishmen could not "be distinguished from the rest of the regiment in their soldierly behavior."[100]

In the meantime, General Joseph Johnston hinted that he wanted Ewell, and possibly Jackson as well, with him on the peninsula. Simultaneously, Lee urged Jackson to consider an offensive in the valley. Banks was not moving south, which was the reason Ewell had been left at Swift Run Gap. Rather, he was falling back to Strasburg and giving indication of quitting the valley altogether—a possibility that must be prevented, Jackson was convinced.

After studying Hotchkiss's detailed maps, Jackson came to a decision. He would hasten to Harrisonburg and unite with Ewell. "I am on my way," Jackson told Ewell.[101]

Such reassurance was necessary, for everything depended now on Ewell. If he were ordered elsewhere, Jackson—even with Edward Johnson's brigade now marching with him—was not sufficiently strong to attack Banks. Jackson and Ewell together produced an entirely different situation. "It may be that a kind Providence will enable us to strike a successful blow," Jackson stated with earnestness.[102]

Propitiously, Lee felt the same way. The military predicament in Virginia was escalating. McClellan's army was closing in on the capital. On May 15, Confederate forces had beaten back a Union naval thrust at Drewry's Bluff on the James River, barely seven miles from downtown Richmond. Lee's concern for the welfare of the city was evident in a letter to Jackson the next day. "Whatever may be Banks's intention it is very desirable to prevent him from going either to Fredericksburg or to the Peninsula. . . . A successful blow struck at him would delay, if it does not prevent, his moving to either place."[103]

It might become necessary "for you to come to the support of General Johnston," Lee told Jackson. The valley commander should "hold yourself in readiness to do so if required." Meanwhile, Lee concluded in pointed terms, a heavy diversion in the Shenandoah could accomplish significant results. "Whatever movements you make against Banks, do it speedily, and if successful, drive him towards the Potomac, and create the impression as far as practicable that you design threatening that line."[104]

Lee had given Jackson even more leeway than he had sought. He had a green light for attack; and if he could exact a smashing victory, he was free to sweep down the valley all the way to the Potomac River—and possibly beyond. Jackson had the potential of changing the whole war picture.

By May 17, his army was in the Mount Solon-Bridgewater area. Harrisonburg and the Valley Turnpike were only ten miles away. Jackson instructed Ewell to start northward from his encampment and head for Luray. Should Banks move from Strasburg toward the Blue Ridge, Ewell was to give pursuit. "But this cannot be determined upon," Jackson stressed, "until we know what the enemy is doing."[105]

Ewell knew precisely what the Yankees were doing. That is what had him in a stew and what had produced a crisis in command. The hapless Ewell had been sitting at Swift Run Gap for two weeks while a rising tide of communiques from Jackson and Johnston flooded his desk. At least twenty-seven messages arrived in the space of fourteen days.

Typical of the communiques was a May 17 confidential letter from Jackson that Ewell must have read at least twice to understand fully. "I desire you to encamp beyond New Market on next Wednesday night. If any of the troops at Gordonsville can not join you for want of transportation please direct them to send their cooking utensils and entrenching tools by the R. R. to Staunton, and with four days cooked rations in their haversacks to march at dawn on next Monday morning via Fisher's Gap for New Market. Let us, relying upon God for success, prepare for attacking Banks."[106]

The other messages were similarly confusing, except for one whose wording was quite clear. Early on May 17, Ewell received from Johnston—and immediately forwarded to Jackson—a letter written four days earlier. The communique carried new and enormous weight in light of the fact that Shields and possibly as many as 6000 Federals had left Banks's army and started across the Blue Ridge. It also dashed cold water on everything that Jackson intended to do. Johnston started by vetoing Jackson's desire to assault the Union army. "If Banks is fortifying near Strasburg the attack would be too hazardous." Jackson can keep an eye on Banks; Ewell should start eastward to rejoin the main army below Richmond. To make his point emphatic, Johnston added: "We want troops here; none, therefore, must keep away, unless employing a greatly superior force of the men."[107]

That directive brought Confederate movements in the valley to an abrupt halt. Jackson agreed that Ewell must obey orders. Yet with Shields gone, Banks was weak. His 9000 soldiers were rapidly throwing up earthworks at Strasburg. He must be attacked promptly.

Jackson felt helpless as he sent an almost pleading message to Johnston. "I have been moving down the Valley for the purpose of striking Banks; but the withdrawal of Genl. Ewell's command will prevent my purpose being executed. I will move on toward Harrisonburg and if you desire me to cross the Blue Ridge please let me know by telegraph. My design was to try and defeat Banks, and then by threatening Fremonts rear, prevent him from advancing up the South Branch. . . . If I do not hear from you soon I will continue my march until I get within striking distance of him."[108]

To his credit on May 17, Dick Ewell hesitated. Jackson was preparing some kind of action, he knew, although he was uninformed of any details. Something was pending; before he made a move in any direction, Ewell wanted to be apprised of the whole situation. Therefore, and without orders, he left his division on the night of the 17th and rode thirty miles through the darkness to confer with the crazy man who was his immediate superior.

Shortly after sunrise on May 18, Ewell reached Jackson's headquarters at Mount Solon.[109] Jackson did not like surprises, but he was pleased at the opportunity to talk in person with his division commander. On Ewell's part, what he beheld upon his arrival only increased his doubts about Jackson's military prowess. He expected to see Jackson's army either on the road or prepared to march. Yet it was Sunday, Ewell was told. Jackson had ordered his troops to obey the commandment.

The two generals then repaired to an old mill nearby and began serious discussions. Foremost among the topics was Johnston's order for Ewell to leave the valley. Jackson told Ewell of the letter he had sent the previous day to Johnston. He expressed the hope that his superior would reconsider.

Ewell agreed, yet he reminded Jackson of his duty to obey orders. Major Dabney embellished Jackson's response with too many adjectives, but the general in essence replied: "Then Providence denies me the privilege of striking a decisive blow for my country, and I must be satisfied with the humble task of hiding my little army about these mountains, to watch a superior force."[110]

In midmorning Jackson halted the conversation. He insisted that Ewell accompany him to religious services that Major Dabney was conducting in the camp of the 12th Georgia. Ewell complied but without enthusiasm. Nevertheless, he found the biblical text for Dabney's sermon highly appropriate: "Come unto me, all ye that labor and are heavy laden, and I will give you rest."

By the time the two men resumed their talks, Ewell had developed a bold plan— one quite out of keeping with his nature as a follower rather than a leader. What Ewell proposed could be termed courageous insubordination. His division was officially part of Johnston's army. At the same time, it was in the valley under Jackson's authority. Ewell suggested the possibility of disregarding Johnston's order until such time as Jackson received a response to his May 17 telegram to Johnston.

Such usurpation caused Jackson to wrestle with his conscience. No man in any Civil War army was more obedient to authority than he; but to throw away the chance for victory over Banks because of orders from one who admittedly was unfamiliar with the situation in the valley might be the greater crime. Jackson weighed another factor. Johnston's May 13 order to Ewell seemed outdated in the face of Lee's May 16 recommendation that Jackson assume the offensive. Further, Lee was military advisor to the commander in chief. Jackson placed more stock in Lee's position and judgment than those of a field commander in another theater 150 miles away.

He accepted Ewell's strategy. The two men agreed to rendezvous with their commands at Luray. Ewell rode away, weary in body but refreshed in mind. That "crazy fool" had good qualities after all. Ewell's deep admiration for Jackson took root that Sunday. A rise in Jackson's spirits also occurred that afternoon. Major Harman was not sure why, but he took it personally. "The Gen'l. is quite friendly," he wrote. Thinking of their recent altercation, the quartermaster added, "I do not know but in the future he will be more upon his guard."[111]

To present an appearance of innocence in this bit of conspiracy, Jackson sent a message to Ewell. He reminded the subaltern that he was still in the Valley District and part of Jackson's command. Jackson gave Ewell bogus instructions to encamp between New Market and Mount Jackson—unless, Jackson added pointedly, "you receive orders from a superior officer and of a date subsequent to the 16th instant."[112]

Ewell split his division for the march. Two of his three brigades would move north down the Luray Valley on the east side of the Massanutten Mountain. The Louisiana brigade, under dapper General Richard Taylor, was to swing around the southern face of the Massanutten, move into the main region of the valley, and link up with Jackson somewhere near New Market. Why one of Ewell's brigades made an oblique march to Jackson has never been explained. A likely reason was Jackson's attempt to impress any enemy observers in the area that Ewell's entire division was with Jackson.

At 3 A.M. on May 19, Jackson began his pursuit of Banks. The Confederates passed over the rain-swollen North River at Bridgewater on an engineering wonder. Black pioneers under Captain C. R. Mason had pushed wagons into the river one after another, then placed planks that extended from the top of one wagon bed to the next. Ashby's cavalry, ranging far afield, swept back Federal scouts and gathered up-to-date information.

Jackson pitched his tent that day near a stream just south of Harrisonburg. Time allowed a quick letter to Anna. "How I do desire to see our country free and at peace!" he wrote. "It appears to me that I would appreciate home more than I have ever done before. Here I am sitting in the open air, writing on my knee for want of a table."[113]

At the same time, a Confederate soldier far to the east near Richmond was writing his wife: "We do not know where our noble & pious Jackson is. But in him I have the most unbounded confidence. If the yankees are to be driven from the Valley, I believe that Jackson will be the one instrument by whom it will be done."[114]

The army swept through Harrisonburg early the next morning. Jackson directed the soldiers to leave all unnecessary equipment in the Rockingham County court-house. "We knew there was some game on hand then," John Casler of the 33d Virginia commented, "for when General Jackson ordered knapsacks to be left behind he meant business." A Georgia captain gave a different and strange interpretation of the order. "Our tents were sent to the rear. Jackson did not believe in tents. They were breeding places of typhoid fever."[115]

By Jackson's decree the rate of march quickened. The army was on familiar ground. Spread out before them in all of its spring richness was the beloved Shenan-doah Valley, with the green barrier of the Massanutten a couple of miles off to their right. Jackson was intent on joining Ewell's command in the vicinity of New Market, but the long daily marches (fifteen miles that day) in home territory were taking a heavy toll of the soldiers. Private James Hall of the 31st Virginia noted in his diary, "A night's rest appears to do us no good—just as sleepy and languid in the morning as when we stop in the evening."[116]

Fifteen miles north of Harrisonburg, the column went into bivouac at Tenth Legion. The gap in the Massanutten east of New Market was already visible. Jackson summoned Ashby and gave him instructions for the next two days. The cavalry leader was to draw Banks's attention by riding down the Valley Turnpike toward Strasburg. Ashby should watch for any movements by the enemy; then, on the morning of May 22, he was to leave a strong detachment as a screen in front of Strasburg, sever communication lines in the valley, and follow Jackson's path to wherever it led.[117]

Jackson was pleased. Everything was going well, and the prospects looked bright. At dawn on May 20, he arose refreshed and energetic. Suddenly all of his plans collapsed.

A courier arrived from Ewell. Johnston had ordered General Lawrence Branch's brigade east of the Blue Ridge to move at once to Richmond. Ewell was to follow with the remainder of his division. Jackson's force, Johnston asserted, was sufficient for monitoring any activity by Banks. This time Johnston's orders were not discretionary; there was no room for maneuvering.

Agonizing moments followed. Jackson's duty, of course, was to release Ewell, but he simply did not have the will to do it. Johnston's directives continued to be days old and out of touch with the real situation. In the valley, time was of the essence. Any offensive must begin immediately. Yet Jackson could not embark on his own authority and in the face of contrary orders. He had one hope left: Lee.

A rider soon sped to the telegraph office at Staunton. He bore a simple message from Jackson to the president's military advisor. "I am of the opinion that an attack should be made to defeat Banks, but under instructions just received from General Johnston I do not feel at liberty to make an attack. Please answer by telegraph."[118]

Having dragged his feet, ignored past directives, and gone over Johnston's head, Jackson now committed open insubordination. He scribbled a quick command to Ewell: "Suspend the execution of the order for returning to the east until I receive an answer to my telegram [to Lee]."[119]

Jackson retained an outward calm in the hours that followed. Apprehension doubt-less triggered acute dyspepsia. All he could do was wait, and pray. The course of events that transpired when Jackson's telegram reached Richmond is unknown. Lee was the only high-ranking military official there who appreciated the situation in the valley. He apparently did not consult with Johnston but went straight to the president. Davis may still have harbored some misgivings about Jackson's potential as a field commander, but Lee made a convincing case. The telegram that Jackson received in reply was approval to move forward with his and Ewell's brigades.

The arrival of a communication later in the day showed that all of the anxieties and machinations by Jackson, Ewell, and Lee had been unnecessary. Johnston was neither close-minded nor nearsighted in this matter; quite to the contrary. Sometime around midday, from halfway down the peninsula, he had written Ewell. His message again was delayed; this one did not arrive in the valley until late on the 20th. In it Johnston relinquished control of events in the valley by imparting discretionary powers to Jackson. He informed Ewell: "The whole question is, whether or not General Jackson & yourself are too late to attack Banks. If so the march eastward should be made. If not (supposing your strength be sufficient) then attack."[120]

The welcome dispatches from Lee and Johnston arrived in the afternoon. As Jackson's men settled in for food and rest late in the day, a line of troops came marching down the turnpike. It was the Louisiana brigade of Ewell's division, one of the most colorful outfits in the entire Virginia theater. The personnel in the 6th, 7th, 8th, 9th Louisiana and Rob Wheat's battalion embraced just about every social class in the Pelican State.

One of the regiments in that 3000-man unit was an unruly mob of dock workers from New Orleans; another consisted of yeomen who held their own against any foe; a third were fun-loving Acadians from the bayous; the fourth in the main contained wealthy planters and sons from the plantation region of northern Louisiana. However, the center of attention in the brigade was the battalion of "Louisiana Tigers."

For the most part adventurers, cutthroats, and rowdies from the river towns, they were intractable in camp and fierce in combat. "They every now and then get out and steal something," one civilian noted angrily. Rumor had it that at the battle of Manassas, the "Tigers" threw away their muskets and happily charged the Union lines brandishing knives. The only officer who seemed able to control them was a six-feet-four, 240-pounder, Major Roberdeau Wheat. Son of an Episcopal priest and international soldier of fortune, Wheat was as exceptional as the men he led.[121]

At the head of the Louisiana brigade was thirty-six-year-old Richard Taylor: Yale graduate, son of a U.S. president, brother-in-law of the Confederate president. Dick Taylor was a sugar planter whose only military experience had been as secretary to his father when Zachary Taylor was a general. The son was widely read, including the science of war; he had the intelligence and personal qualities to become a superior soldier.

Taylor spoke French like a native and cursed like a sailor. His commissary officer thought him "genial, full of humor, and witty," brown eyes sparkling as a melodious voice held an audience enraptured. On the other hand, Taylor had a knack then—and a habit in his postwar memoirs—of manufacturing facts for the sake of a good story. At least one fellow officer disliked Taylor for his "total irreverence for any man's opinion." While Taylor and Ewell got along well throughout their association, each thought the other strange.[122]

One of the more charming accounts in Confederate history is Taylor's version of his first meeting with Jackson. Unfortunately, everything about the narrative has dubious overtones. According to Taylor, his men had marched over twenty-five miles that warm May day, but on reaching Jackson's bivouac they were "neat in fresh clothing of gray with white gaiters, bands playing at the head of their regiments, not a straggler, but every man in his place, stepping jauntily as if on parade."[123]

Always portraying Jackson as an eccentric who spent most of his life on his knees, alternately praying and sucking lemons, Taylor next described his initial encounter with the commanding general. Jackson was sitting on a fence, appearance disheveled, his attention given completely to the battered remnants of a lemon. Taylor dismounted, saluted smartly, and waited. Finally, Jackson asked in a low voice which road he had taken and how far he had marched that day. "Keezletown road, six and twenty miles," came the reply.

"You seem to have no stragglers," Jackson observed.

"Never allow straggling," Taylor answered cockily.

Jackson replied: "You must teach my people. They straggle badly." At that moment, one of the Louisiana bands purportedly struck up a light tune. Soldiers began singing and doing an impromptu dance. Kepi slanted down over his eyebrows, Jackson stared for a moment at the scene. Then he grunted, "Thoughtless fellows for serious work." That was the end of the conversation as presented by Taylor.[124]

Rain fell during the night, and May 21 dawned cloudy. Ewell summoned Lieutenant Frank Myers of the 35th Virginia Cavalry Battalion and gave him a bundle of dispatches to deliver to Jackson. Myers galloped to New Market and turned south on the main valley road. He soon met a heavy column of infantry coming toward him. Spying a group of mounted officers, Myers selected the shabbiest-looking of the lot as a courier and asked him to point out General Jackson among the nicely dressed group. The rider snapped: "I am General Jackson. Where are you from, sir?" Myers stammered an identification and gave the dispatches to Jackson. The general read them hastily, asked the lieutenant a couple of questions, then sent him back to Ewell with the simple reply: "I will see you at Luray tomorrow."[125]

Sunshine had begun to bake Jackson's army as it moved into New Market. Abruptly the long line turned east toward the mountains. Only a few murmurs came from the ranks. "We were getting used to Jackson's divergences from the straight road ahead," one officer stated without feeling.[126]

The campaign for control of the Shenandoah Valley was now to be centered on the Massanutten Mountains, which rise precipitately within the valley like a rectangular-shaped island. The range stretched north for roughly fifty miles between the Blue Ridge and the Valley Turnpike. At the north end, the Massanutten split in two like a "Y." Bleak and uninhabited, the imposing ridge could be crossed at only one place: a winding mountain road extending from New Market to Luray.

Hour after hour, troops wound up and through the pass. Robert Barton of the Rockbridge Artillery never forgot the view from the top. "The rising sun greeted us as we reached the tip of the mountain, whence looking down its western slope a long line of rifles on the winding road glistened in its rays. The army in the far off curves of the road looked like a great snake with a shining back, twisting its sinuous path."[127]

Jackson led the way. Periodically he received a dispatch or sent one. Richard Taylor, riding part of the way with the commander, did not know how to handle his reticence. "I began to think that Jackson was an unconscious poet, and, as an ardent lover of nature, desired to give strangers an opportunity to admire the beauties of his Valley."

In truth, Jackson was unusually communicative that day. He had a lengthy chat riding over the mountain with Confederate Congressman John Brockenbrough, who had come for a brief visit with his three soldier-sons.[128]

Late in the day Jackson halted at a church just to the east of White House Bridge and the South Fork of the Shenandoah River. There he learned that the other two brigades of Ewell's division, having marched from the southern end of the Massanutten, were in bivouac a few miles ahead. Jackson prayed long and hard that night. He sought to curb excitement with expressions of faith.

Now that he had Ewell's full division with him, 16,000 soldiers and twenty-seven guns were at his disposal. He had crossed the Massanutten undetected and was in the Luray (or Page) Valley, completely hidden from enemy eyes. "We know little of Gen. Jackson's movements," the Lexington newspaper would state the following day, "but we are expecting to hear of him creating a *stir*, somewhere between Harrisonburg and the Potomac before many days."[129] That was precisely what Jackson had in mind.

Federal General Banks was giving his attention at the moment to Strasburg. The town was not as strong a military position as he had thought at first. It was the spot where the Manassas Gap Railroad made its first contact with the Valley Turnpike, and it had some defensive features. On the other hand, Banks's command was dangerously scattered. A contingent of 1000 Federals was on duty at Front Royal; Banks had 4476 infantry, 1600 cavalry, and sixteen guns at Strasburg; some 1450 soldiers guarded supplies at Winchester; 800 other men were protecting the twelve-mile stretch of the Manassas Gap Railroad from Strasburg to Front Royal. Within a day, Banks would begin begging the War Department to send additional troops to the valley.[130]

May 22 was a cloudy Thursday. By 6 A.M., Jackson's army was in motion. Ewell's brigades took the lead, with Taylor's Louisianians and Colonel Thomas Flournoy's 2d and 6th Virginia Cavalry fanned out as the advanced guard. Weary troops of Jackson's division formed the rear of the column. The route was northward down the Luray Valley, which was much narrower and contained less farm land than the big valley to the west. The road undulated more strikingly than did the Valley Turnpike.

Sometime early in the day, Jackson informed his principal lieutenants where they were going and why. Their position in the Luray Valley was squarely between Banks and the piedmont. No additional brigades from Banks's army could reinforce McDowell or McClellan. Being on the eastern side of the Massanutten put Jackson out of sight and allowed him to move in an unmolested manner to the merger of the Luray and Shenandoah Valleys at Front Royal.

There Jackson would be on Banks's flank. The Federal commander had constructed strong entrenchments at Strasburg, but they faced south. Jackson was to the east. Yet that would make no difference if the Confederates did not drive through Front Royal quickly. Doing that would enable Jackson to sever Banks's communications with the main Union armies to the east; the Confederates could also get in Banks's rear and either trap him at Strasburg or force the Federals to abandon the valley.

In the first stage of the day's march, Jackson remained in the rear of his line with his own troops. Then he rode forward to get a view of progress. Doing so gave him his first sight of Ewell's regiments. It also provided them with the first glimpse of their commander.

A soldier in the 13th Virginia, near the front of Ewell's column, was caught up in the excitement. "Hearing loud cheering in the rear, which came nearer and nearer, we soon saw that it was Stonewall himself, mounted on that old sorrel." Clad in a rumpled gray uniform, dark beard glistening with perspiration, and head uncovered, Jackson galloped swiftly past the line. As usual, his stirrups were unusually short and he leaned forward almost over the neck of his horse while keeping his chin high and head up. Jackson looked odd and inspiring all in one. "We took up the shout," the Virginia soldier continued, "and gave a hearty greeting to the great captain, who had come to lead us to victory, and the mountains echoed and re-echoed with the great acclaim."[131]

At the same time that Jackson was receiving shouted praise, Abraham Lincoln was with McDowell's large corps eight miles south of Fredericksburg. The Union leader gave approval for McDowell to start the thirty-mile journey to link up with McClellan at the gates of Richmond. Unknown to both sides, what happened now in the valley assumed enormous importance.

Jackson bivouacked that night at Bentonville, a hamlet only ten miles from Front Royal. The Confederate movement remained shrouded in secrecy, as it had for the previous ten days when Jackson led his troops 120 miles. Now they were poised and ready for action. Before starting his evening prayers, the general again studied his maps.

Front Royal had a strategic importance far in excess of its half-dozen blocks of stores. A mile and a half north of town (in 1862), the Shenandoah River became one stream. There the North Fork, following a course roughly parallel to the Valley Turnpike, twists around the face of the Massanutten and meets the South Fork, which drains the Luray Valley.

Also a short distance north of Front Royal, the Manassas Gap Railroad passed over the South Fork on a 450-foot wooden trestle. Jackson had burned the bridge in March, but Federals made complete repairs by May. The railroad flattened out from a mountainous descent to Front Royal and continued twelve miles west to Strasburg and Banks's main supply base. It was imperative that Jackson capture the railroad trestle and nearby bridge before they could be destroyed again. Otherwise, the Confederates would have difficulty coming speedily to grips with Banks.

What Jackson knew, and what Banks never seemed to realize, was that Front Royal was indefensible. High peaks loomed to the west, southwest, and east. Unless a large force controlled all of the mountain passes around the town, Front Royal could not withstand attack. The town was also vulnerable to flank movements by other mountain valleys from Strasburg to the west and Chester Gap to the east. The problem was not in taking Front Royal, Jackson knew, but in seizing it so quickly that he could trap the garrison and move toward Banks's rear before any Federal reaction occurred from Strasburg.

As the army got much-needed rest that night, Jackson contemplated the geographical triangle in his immediate front. Just down the road was Front Royal. Twelve miles to its left was Strasburg. Twenty-one miles beyond Front Royal lay the key to the Shenandoah Valley and Jackson's other Virginia residence: Winchester.

≋ 14 ≋
ENCOURAGING HOPE

T HE SUN ROSE INTO a clear sky shortly after 5 A.M. on Friday. Jackson's men were already marching by that hour. The temperature climbed swiftly on May 23 as the Confederates advanced on Front Royal. Unknown to anyone, Jackson was about to unleash a two-week campaign that would settle affairs in the Shenandoah Valley.

A direct march on Front Royal down the Luray Road was logical but potentially costly. The army might be detected before it got into attack mode, and Union artillery doubtless had the road well covered. Jackson did not know that he outnumbered the Federals by seventeen-to-one odds. Unsure what enemy strength he would encounter, Jackson characteristically resorted to his favorite tactic: a flank movement.

His battle plan was simple. Ashby's cavalry would strike out from Spangler's Crossroads to the northwest. The horsemen would cross the South Fork and, at Buckton or some other point between Front Royal and Strasburg, cut telegraph and rail lines. Ashby was to hold his position to impede either a retreat from Front Royal or reinforcements from Strasburg.

Ewell's division, with the 1st Maryland in front, would move northeast along the Luray Road. It would advance to Asbury Chapel, four and a half miles from Front Royal. The column would then turn right and proceed up a steep and narrow country lane to Gooney Manor Road. That highway ran north along the crest of a ridge and offered a safer, back-trail approach on high ground to Front Royal. Winder's Stonewall Brigade and the artillery in Jackson's division were to remain at Asbury Chapel until notified further.

Confederate strategy on the one hand was daring but on the other left little to chance. The Federal garrison could not go west because Ashby's troopers would be waiting for it; it could not go east through Manassas Gap (the lowest of the openings through the Blue Ridge) or south into the Luray Valley because Jackson would be attacking in that sector. If forced from Front Royal, the enemy had to go north. That is when the rivers would become a factor. A railroad trestle and a single wagon-pedestrian bridge crossed the South Fork; only one bridge existed for the smaller North Fork. It was imperative that Jackson seize those spans before the Federals could set them afire.

The army turned east at Asbury Chapel as ordered and started climbing a third of the way into the Blue Ridge. Thick pines on both sides of the road stifled breezes. The ascent was torturous: over 400 feet within a mile and a half. Men perspired

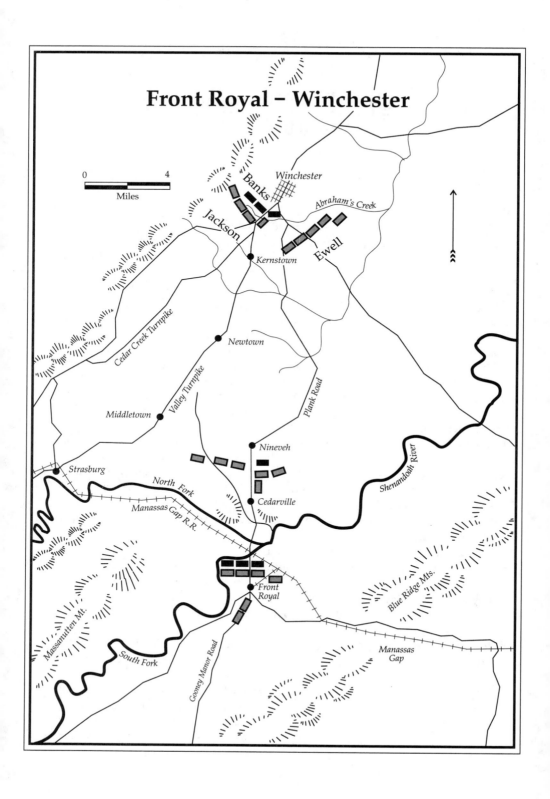

Front Royal – Winchester

0   4
Miles

Winchester

Banks

Jackson

Abraham's Creek

Ewell

Kernstown

Cedar Creek Turnpike

Newtown

Valley Turnpike

Plank Road

Middletown

Nineveh

Shenandoah River

Strasburg

North Fork

Manassas Gap R.R.

Cedarville

Massanutten Mt.

Front Royal

Blue Ridge Mts.

South Fork

Gooney Manor Road

Manassas Gap

heavily; leg cramps became common; more than one soldier staggered from the march to empty his stomach; straggling increased.

The element of secrecy, however, held throughout the morning. Jackson pushed his troops to within a mile and a half of Front Royal before he halted. He and Ewell rode forward with their staffs to the top of a rise overlooking the town. There they could easily see the Union defenses and the small force of soldiers manning them.

Living with an aunt at the time on the edge of Front Royal was eighteen-year-old Belle Boyd. Energetic and overly enthusiastic, the Martinsburg native had a hatred of Yankees matched only by her zeal to supply military information to Confederate leaders.[1] Boyd became obsessed that Jackson did not know of the weakness of the Front Royal garrison.

Captain G. Campbell Brown of Ewell's staff was in the general's party on the hilltop. "All of a sudden," he wrote in 1868, "Henry K. Douglas called my attention to a woman running like mad down the hill to our right, keeping a fence between her and the town and gesticulating wildly to us. Douglas rode up & showed her to Jackson, who sent him to speak to her. She talked excitedly for a minute; Douglas came up in great excitement. It was Belle Boyd & she told him there was only one Reg. in the town—the Fedl. 1st Maryland & 2 Cos. of a Penna. regt. He got Genl. J. to ride to her. She repeated to him her news, begged him to push on & he could take them all & then ran back to town."[2]

Regrettably, every account of what Belle Boyd supposedly did in the Civil War is a victim of exaggeration. The Front Royal episode is illustrative.[3] Boyd no doubt got some kind of message to Jackson, and she may have been the one who told of the Federal 1st Maryland being the only force of note in town. In any event, Jackson reacted with Old Testament anger. If Maryland infidels were going to invade Virginia, Maryland faithful would smite them. He promptly ordered the Confederate 1st Maryland to move to the front immediately.

Less-than-heroic behavior was then occurring in that Maryland regiment. The twelve-month enlistments of some members had expired, and they were anxious to join the cavalry. Colonel Bradley T. Johnson, the regimental commander, was a thirty-three-year-old Baltimore attorney with a soul-deep allegiance to the Confederacy. He ordered the loyal portion of the regiment to disarm the malcontents and hold them under guard. Johnson was reading the riot act to the group when Jackson's order arrived. The colonel thereupon gave a rousing speech laced with repeated calls to patriotism. The mutineers—many of them still teenagers—rushed back into ranks to take part in the action.[4]

"There was no token of the impending storm," a Union officer observed that day. Sentinels dawdled at their posts; officers passed the time doing nothing. "Trees of richest verdure were bathed in the morning sun, and fields sparkled with dew-drops shining amidst luxuriant grasses. Everything seemed more in harmony with life and peace than with bloodshed and death."[5]

When all appeared to be ready, Jackson gave the signal at 2 P.M. A long line of gray skirmishers broke down a hill and cheers echoed through the woods. Then the 1st Maryland and Wheat's battalion, with the rest of Taylor's Louisiana brigade supporting the flanks, swept forward in the afternoon heat. The Southerners easily overran the picket line south of Front Royal. Other Federals began to dash northward to the rear. A young friend rushed into the home of Lucy Buck. "Oh my God!" she screamed. "The Southern army is upon them! The hill above town is black with our boys!" Union soldiers took momentary cover inside buildings. Yet, Miss Buck stated, "some scattered parties of Confederate infantry came up and charged their ranks, when firing one volley [the Federals] wheeled about—every man for himself they scampered out of town like a flock of sheep—such an undignified exodus was never witnessed before." One of Jackson's soldiers wrote gratefully: "When we entered Front Royal, the women and children met us with shouts of the liveliest joy. As we passed through the place in double quick, we could not stop to partake of the hospitality so generously and profusely tendered on all hands."[6]

Federal Colonel John R. Kenly made as gallant a stand as his 1063 Maryland Federals and an artillery section would permit. He was woefully overmatched. Realizing instantly that he had no hope of making a stand in Front Royal, Kenly ordered his force north of town toward Richardson's Hill just east of the Winchester plank road. Confederates, Jackson reported, "pushed forward in gallant style, charging the Federals, who made a spirited resistance, driving them through the town and taking some prisoners."[7]

Two rifled Union guns began raking the advancing Southern lines at long range. Jackson dispatched a courier to bring up Winder's brigade and the guns of his own division. Colonel Crutchfield ordered up Ewell's artillery to blast the enemy from Richardson's Hill.

What the colonel beheld next made his enthusiasm vanish. A collection of six-pounder smoothbores and twelve-pounder howitzers comprised most of Ewell's guns. They lacked the range to duel with the Union pieces. Crutchfield, new to his post as Jackson's chief of artillery, finally managed to find three rifled guns in Ewell's command.[8]

Much time was lost while Crutchfield searched for cannon. The infantry ended up waging battle alone. Bradley Johnson's Marylanders surged straight ahead; raucous dock workers in the 6th Louisiana eased around the Union left via the railroad bridge; Taylor's other regiments slammed into the Federal right. Meanwhile, Confederate horsemen dashed over the fields west of the South Fork. If they could reach Pike Bridge at the North Fork first, Kenly would be trapped.

A veteran soldier who viewed affairs calmly and incisively, the Baltimore-born Kenly discerned his predicament. He set fire to his camp, quickly limbered his two guns, and raced through dust and gunsmoke toward the nearby bridge over the South Fork. Confederates followed in hot pursuit.

The Federals won the contest. They furiously began packing hay on the railroad and wagon bridges. Setting the spans afire would impede additional movements by Jackson. However, recent rains had saturated the wooden beams and planking. The hay burned, but Jackson's soldiers minimized the danger by throwing bundles of already burning hay off the bridges. Yet all of that consumed valuable minutes.

Jackson had been with the lead elements of his army since the attack began. On occasion, he even rode out in front of his skirmishers. To Confederates, it was obvious that their general "manifested the greatest impatience to press forward."[9]

Eyes ablaze, Jackson now galloped up to the bridges. Excitement was apparent throughout his being. He rode to the river's edge, looked upstream, and saw the enemy column moving rapidly northward. The destruction of the Federals was so close. "Oh, what an opportunity for artillery!" Jackson shouted. "Oh, that my guns were here!" Looking around quickly, Jackson beckoned one of his staff officers. "Hurry to the rear!" he exclaimed. "Order up every rifled gun and every brigade in the army!"[10]

That was easier said than done. Jackson and Crutchfield were mutually guilty of a blunder at Front Royal. The Stonewall Brigade and Jackson's own batteries had remained at Asbury Chapel, four miles south of town. Jackson intended for them to drive into Front Royal on the main road once the fighting got underway. Yet no one gave Winder specific instructions, and the youthful cavalryman that Jackson dispatched to bring up the reserves succumbed to panic in what was his first battle and fled the area.

As events materialized, the young rider's cowardice made no difference. Winder was unclear about what he was supposed to do, but he was still second in command of Jackson's division. His place was where the action was. Winder therefore had taken the Stonewall Brigade and the remaining half of Jackson's guns and dutifully fallen in behind the column making its way up the Gooney Manor Road. Still, this put them hours behind schedule and useless to Jackson that day.[11]

Ignoring the absence of his best brigade and the batteries that had previously served him well, Jackson resumed the chase. Federals had just started fires on Pike Bridge over the North Fork when Southern troops crowded into the area. Jackson personally supervised the fire fighting. The flames were extinguished, but the bridge was so heavily damaged that the cavalry were hesitant to make a dash across it. Jackson summoned Major Thomas S. Flournoy, in command of the 6th Virginia Cavalry and that portion of the 2d Virginia Cavalry west of the Blue Ridge. The men in those units were green and part of an army wing noted for its lack of strong organization. Jackson now determined to test their mettle in battle.

A good man was at the head of that mounted detachment. Flournoy was fifty-one, a native of Prince Edward County, and a graduate of Hampden-Sydney College. Former congressman, former friend of Abraham Lincoln, unsuccessful candidate for governor, and a political moderate, Flournoy also was as dedicated a soldier as his limited military knowledge permitted.

Jackson's directive to the major was straightforward. The cavalry were to cross the river at once and give rapid pursuit of the Federals. Strike the enemy before he makes a strong stand. Flournoy asked no questions. He took four cavalry companies, eased them across the North Fork bridge in single file, and then in a gallop disappeared behind a hill. Jackson rode after them to continue his personal command of the day's action.[12]

The horsemen raced two and a half miles north of Pike Bridge. They brought the enemy to bay at a cluster of houses known as Cedarville. Kenly had no choice but to turn and fight. As Flournoy formed his 250 cavalry for an attack, Jackson rode onto the open ground. No time must be lost, he told Flournoy. Strike at once.

A bugle shrilled above the late afternoon noise. Confederate horsemen who had been poised in line gave a wild cheer as they spurred their mounts into a gallop right at the Union center. Kenly's infantry fired one volley which emptied some saddles, yet the Confederates dashed ahead. Within seconds the Federal line broke.

Billy Yanks scampered to an orchard by the roadside. Jackson, watching intently, directed Flournoy to charge again. Mounted Confederates raced headlong at the Union position. They broke over the hastily improvised Federal works, wheeled right and left as they slashed with sabers, and fired revolvers at point-blank range. The Union line was shredded in minutes.

Lieutenant Charles A. Atwell, commanding the section of Pennsylvania artillery under Kenly, wrote of Flournoy's second assault: "The rebels, having advanced on our flanks under cover of the woods, succeeded in surrounding us, and I was unable to use my pieces, as the two forces were mixed up together, and my cannoneers, having no side-arms, were cut to pieces by the rebel cavalry. . . . The fighting here was terrible, as we were shown no mercy." Jackson noted that with the second charge, "the enemy's cavalry was put to flight, the artillery abandoned, and the infantry, now thrown into great confusion, surrendered."[13]

Confederate attackers had captured three times their numbers in a fight that took but minutes. For a rare moment, Jackson was overjoyed. Never in all his experience of warfare, he told his staff, had he seen a cavalry charge performed with such efficiency and gallantry. Then the general slid naturally back into stony silence.[14]

By nightfall, Jackson had cause for satisfaction. His army had pounced upon an unsuspecting enemy and punched a fatal hole in the Union line protecting the Manassas Gap Railroad. Jackson had also routed a force of over 1000 Federals and captured 700 of that number, including twenty officers. Two enemy ten-pounder Parrott guns were now in his possession, as well as a Union supply train, a long line of needed wagons, two locomotives (seized by Ashby), plus an estimated $300,000 worth of quartermaster and commissary stores.

All of this had been accomplished with a loss of fewer than 100 men. "The fruits of this movement were not restricted to the stores and prisoners captured," Jackson added. His men had marched twenty-four miles that day. "The enemy's flank was turned and the road opened to Winchester.[15] Equally as important to Jackson, he was in a position to threaten the main avenue of retreat for Banks.

Jackson was deeply fatigued at that point. He rode wearily and alone through the darkness to the Louisiana soldiers' bivouac near Cedarville. Dismounting, he sat down in front of General Taylor's campfire. Other than a muttered greeting, Jackson said nothing. For several hours, part of which was marked by a rain shower, the general sat motionless. His eyes never left the fire. Taylor "took up the idea that he was inwardly praying."[16]

Surely, oblations went to God several times that night. For most of the time, however, Jackson was thinking. Over and over he weighed the choices available to both Banks and to himself. What the Union general might do and what Jackson could do to thwart him were critical at that lull in the campaign.

Caution was essential for Jackson. Although Banks had been surprised and flanked, the Federal commander had four available options. Banks could have mistaken the Front Royal engagement as a mere raid. He then would be likely to remain at

Strasburg and await reinforcements from Fremont, from the piedmont, or both. Yet Fremont was never known for alacrity, and Confederates in the passes of the Blue Ridge could block or delay Union troops coming from the east. No, said Banks, "to remain at Strasburg was to be surrounded."[17] He dismissed that possibility almost at once.

The Union commander could retreat westward and unite with Fremont in the Alleghanies. That choice too was full of negatives. The roads were bad, a retreat would cost dearly in lost supplies, and Banks would be giving the clear impression of skedaddling to safety in the mountains. Moreover, all of that was predicated on Jackson not catching him en route.

A third alternative would be for Banks to fight his way eastward, turn Jackson's flank, and escape over the Blue Ridge. Yet the size of Jackson's army was unknown to the Federals. Banks had estimated Jackson as having 5000 men early on the 23d; by sundown that day, the Confederate army had grown in Banks's eyes to 20,000 soldiers. Still, a drive east by the Federals had positive considerations.

The fourth option, of course, was to dash eighteen miles down the Valley Turnpike to the supply base at Winchester and the roads leading from there to the Potomac River and safety. Such a move would give Jackson maximum room in which to maneuver.

Having pondered Banks's selections, Jackson carefully weighed the imponderables facing his own army. Exactly how many Federals were at Strasburg was not known. Rumors of Union strength ran as high as 15,000 men. Banks could therefore not be taken lightly. Second, Banks had the means and the route to escape if he moved rapidly.

Further, even Jackson had to concede that his soldiers and horses were exhausted. Over the past four days the men had marched at least eighty miles. The advance had been over roads either rock-strewn or muddy. Confederates were as footsore as they were bushed. A large segment of the army was strung out to the rear as useless stragglers. Banks's soldiers, one assumed, were rested, well equipped, and ready for battle.[18]

Jackson then reviewed the road system radiating from his present position. His men occupied the base line of a triangle that extended twelve miles from Front Royal to Strasburg. The Valley Turnpike ran northeast from Strasburg eighteen miles to the apex at Winchester. The other leg of the triangle was the good but curvy road that stretched twenty-one miles northwest from Front Royal to Winchester. The Confederate advance guard at Cedarville was actually closer to Winchester than was Banks at Strasburg. However, the Federals would have the advantage of a double-lane, macadamized highway. Jackson's soldiers were at the mercy of narrower and less compact roads.

Sometime in the middle of the night, Jackson devised a strategy to thwart any of Banks's probable moves. Ewell's cavalry, which Jackson had now placed under the senior and more experienced General George "Maryland" Steuart, would gallop north to Ninevah and then west to Newtown, nine miles south of Winchester on the Turnpike. Ashby's horsemen, skirmishers from Taylor's brigade, Chew's battery, and two Parrott guns from the Rockbridge Artillery would proceed seven miles due west of Cedarville. They would strike the turnpike at Middletown and remain alert for any movement Banks might make to the south. Jackson, with Ewell's division (his own was still at Front Royal), would advance along the plank road toward Winchester.

Should Banks lunge eastward in an attempt to reach the Blue Ridge, the Stonewall Brigade and rear elements of Ewell's force could contest the move. The 12th Georgia—conspicuous for its gallantry at McDowell—would remain at Front Royal to guard prisoners and, it was assumed, deter any Federal movement long enough for reinforcements to arrive.

Jackson mounted Little Sorrel at 4 A.M. that Saturday. For the next thirty-five hours, he would be continually marching, fighting, and pursuing the enemy.[19]

Meantime, Banks had spent the night at Strasburg beset by confusion and indecision. As late as May 22, he remained convinced that any attack from Jackson would come from the south. Banks never contemplated a major threat from the east. Late-afternoon news of the loss of Front Royal and its garrison put him in a stupor. He appeared listless to his staff as he kept saying monotonously: "I must develop the force of the enemy."

Officers urged Banks through the night to withdraw at once to the safety of nearby Winchester. At one point, the commander lost his temper. He jumped from his chair and shouted at an aide: "By God, sir, I will not retreat! We have more to fear, sir, from the opinions of our friends than the bayonets of our enemies!"[20]

Reason finally came to Banks with the May 24 sunrise. He ordered a retreat. The army would take the quickest available route: to Winchester. At 10 A.M. Union regiments began moving out of Strasburg amid immense fires from burning stores. Banks tarried long enough to send to Washington the first in a series of dispatches rationalizing what had gone wrong. He and his staff then rode slowly amid the crowd of soldiers and wagons northward down the turnpike. All the general seemed capable of saying were the emotionless words: "It seems we were mistaken in our calculations."[21]

Most of Jackson's army was dispersed well before sunrise. On paper, his plan was excellent. In execution, it would leave much to be desired. The farther north the general rode with Ewell's division, the more concerned he became at what Banks might do far in his rear. Shortly after 8 A.M. that May 24, Jackson halted Ewell's men. They were at the hamlet of Ninevah after marching only three miles.

There they would wait for news and a clearer picture of the situation. Jackson reined his horse at the Mason farmhouse and humbly requested some breakfast, which he promptly received. Ewell soon arrived to confer with Jackson. Ashby had left at dawn for the seven-mile ride to Middletown. Yet as the hours passed, no word came.

Jackson finally turned to Hotchkiss. The mapmaker and sixteen cavalrymen were to leave at once, reconnoiter near Middletown, and send back reports every half-hour. Occasional rain, with some hail, had begun falling. The day was unusually cool.[22]

For three hours, Jackson waited impatiently at Ninevah. What movements, if any, was Banks making? Jackson wanted to drive for Winchester, but he could not do so until he knew where his opponent was and what he was doing. Then a courier came pounding into the yard of the Mason farm. He brought a message from Steuart.

Confederate horsemen had struck the turnpike at Newtown and found the road packed with Federal wagon trains and soldiers. Steuart's men had dashed through the procession and, with a fusillade of shots, thrown everything into confusion. Yet Steuart needed help as soon as possible.

This was the information Jackson wanted! Now he knew that Banks was abandoning Strasburg and marching northeast on the turnpike. Now the Confederates were able to fight Banks in the open. Orders went out quickly. Ewell would resume his advance to Winchester. Jackson would backtrack to Cedarville and, with his own division, strike for Middletown.[23]

From Cedarville to Middletown was a wretched seven-mile march in every respect. The terrain was broken country and heavily forested. Several meandering streams bisected the area. Rain fell intermittently; the roads became more slippery by the hour. A casual walk would have been laborious under normal circumstances. Marching to battle was a toilsome effort. Colonel John Patton of the 21st Virginia later stated: "As the men limped along with weary limbs and feet throbbing with pain, on what seem[ed] to them an aimless march, I heard them denouncing Jackson in unmeasured terms to 'marching them to death for no good.' It was my duty no doubt to have rebuked these manifestations of insubordination, but, feeling that their sufferings in some measure condoned their offence, I took no notice of the breach of discipline."[24]

Another shower had just ended in the middle of the afternoon when Jackson reached high ground overlooking Middletown. Federal wagons, ambulances, and cavalry were inching along the turnpike. Stone walls on either side of the road kept the Federals wedged in a tight funnel. This was the situation an artillerist loved. Jackson ordered the batteries of Chew and William T. Poague onto rising ground. Crutchfield advanced some pieces to within canister range. The cannon opened fire, and the turnpike became a ribbon of death and debris.

It was "a most appalling spectacle of carnage and destruction," Jackson reported. "The road was literally obstructed with the mangled and confused mass of struggling and dying horses and riders. The Federal column was pierced, but what proportion of its strength had passed north toward Winchester I had then no means of knowing. Among the surviving cavalry the wildest confusion ensued, and they scattered in disorder in various directions, leaving, however, some 200 prisoners, with their equipments, in our hands."[25]

Kyd Douglas of Jackson's staff considered the artillery bombardment little short of murder. "I mildly suggested as much" to Jackson, he wrote. The general quietly replied, "Let them alone." Later in the day Jackson remarked to Hotchkiss, "It looks too bad to see so many of them disposed at once."[26]

Federal wagons could be seen racing wildly to the north. Jackson the "wagon hunter" was not going to pass up such a tempting feast. After them! he yelled to Ashby. His cavalry chief gathered several companies and sped in pursuit. Unsure of the whereabouts of the major portion of Banks's army, Jackson ordered most of his regiments south to confront anything approaching from Strasburg. He then entered Middletown and began conferring with townspeople. How long have the Federals been moving through town? he asked. Since early morning, came the replies.

This convinced Jackson that the bulk of Banks's command was between Middletown and Winchester. He recalled the Confederate units marching south. At 4 P.M., Major Dabney sent a message to Ewell: "The enemy has retreated en masse toward Winchester. Major-General Jackson requests that you will move on Winchester with all the force you have left as promptly as possible. He will follow in force in the enemy's rear. Please report hourly your advance and circumstances."[27]

Southern regiments backtracked to Middletown. Though footsore and hungry, most of them were in high spirits. They were heading for Winchester, the pearl of the lower valley! Robert Barton of the Rockbridge Artillery proudly recalled that everyone in the town "turned out to greet us, men, women, girls, children, dogs, cats and chickens." The 27th Virginia's Watkins Kearns deemed the march "a continual triumph. The ladies cheer and we bawl ourselves hoarse."[28]

Jackson put the Stonewall Brigade in front to set the pace and, at 5:30, pushed forward with his weary army to catch Banks. Confidence and understandable excitement engulfed Jackson. "From the attack at Front Royal," he noted, "every opposition had been borne down, and there was reason to believe, if Banks reached Winchester, it would be without a train, if not without an army."[29]

The Confederates tramped through Newtown to cheers from happy residents. One elderly and portly woman stood on her front porch, spread her arms widely, and called out several times: "All of you run here and kiss me!"[30]

A short distance beyond Newtown, Jackson came upon a disgusting sight. Federal wreckage and discarded equipment—some left inadvertently and some purposefully—were now buying time for Banks. Southerners giving chase had stopped in order to loot and hunt for much-needed equipment. Most of Ashby's companies had disintegrated into a plundering mob. Some men even detached horses from wrecked wagons and casually took them to nearby homes for safekeeping. Jackson was furious. "Forgetful of their high trust as the advance of a pursuing army," Ashby's men "deserted their colors and abandoned themselves to pillage to such an extent as to make it necessary for that gallant officer to discontinue further pursuit."[31]

Crutchfield's guns, left with no more than fifty cavalrymen as support, had no alternative but to retire south of Newtown. In that two-hour breakdown, Federals put four pieces of artillery in good position north of town. Their fire kept Jackson pinned down until the only light remaining was the glow of burning Federal wagons and supplies.[32]

The iron will of Stonewall Jackson now surfaced. He was eleven miles from Winchester. Having fought two months earlier at Kernstown, he was familiar with the dominating ridges south of Winchester. It was imperative that he be on those hills by dawn, in order to force Banks to make some sort of stand at his major supply base. Otherwise, Banks could fall back to Harpers Ferry or to the lifeline of the Baltimore and Ohio Railroad at the Potomac.

No meal stops, no hourly rests, no explanations, no human concern, came forth now from Jackson. A small cluster of horsemen—the general, his staff, and a squad of cavalry—silently led the Southern army along the turnpike and through the darkness. Jackson spoke only when necessary.

He was angry that his cavalry had deserted him at a critical time. He also considered the moves he would make at sunrise. So he rode head down, kepi cap concealing his face, while Little Sorrel maintained a leisurely pace. The general was surely in no mood to discuss the women of Winchester, as Douglas alleged later.[33]

On through the night the march continued. Many of the men, who now proudly called themselves "foot cavalry," nevertheless remembered the night of May 24–25 as the worst they ever endured. Discarded rolling stock and equipment formed an unbroken train six miles in length. It cluttered the road and precluded a unified advance. Burning wagons all along the way were eerie road markers.[34]

Soldiers by then were so exhausted that many "actually slept as we marched," wrote one.[35] Men bumped into each other or staggered in fatigue off the road. While the march that night was only four miles, no one believed it. The stop-and-go pace, added to everything else, made the journey seem endless.

Occasional ambushes, especially around the village of Bartonsville, impeded the Confederate advance and kept all nerves on edge—all, that is, except Jackson's. He rode in front and paid no attention to the bullets that several times whipped by him in the darkness. A sudden volley sent his cavalry escort bolting to the rear in such panic that gunners in Poague's battery scurried beneath their caissons to keep from being trampled. An enraged Jackson told his chief of staff: "Shameful! Did you see anybody struck, sir? Did you see anybody struck? Surely they need not have run, at least until they were hurt!"[36]

The 33d Virginia tried to move into the van but Ashby's stampeding men scattered the ranks. Winder quickly brought up three other regiments of the Stonewall Brigade. Gunfire died down and a semblance of order returned momentarily. Winder sent two companies from that area of the valley to take the point and feel their way through the blackness of night.

Bullets continued to whistle through the air or ricochet off trees. General Taylor, who rode with Jackson for awhile, became awed by the commander's fearlessness. "I quite remember thinking at the time that Jackson was invulnerable, and that persons near him shared that quality."[37]

By 2 A.M., the last elements of Banks's army had filed into Winchester. Jackson passed the high ground on the left where he had waged the battle of Kernstown. Fatigue was now so deep through the ranks that it could be sensed even in the darkness. Colonel Samuel Fulkerson then rode up to Jackson on the Turnpike. The commander of Jackson's Third Brigade reported his soldiers completely spent. They had marched fifteen miles that day and not eaten since early morning. "My men are falling by the roadside," Fulkerson stated. "Unless they are rested, I shall be able to present but a thin line tomorrow."

Jackson listened quietly to the Abingdon judge and respected friend. Then he replied: "Colonel, I yield to no man in my sympathy for the gallant men under my command; but I am obliged to sweat them tonight, that I may save their blood tomorrow. The line of hills southwest of Winchester must not be occupied by the enemy's artillery. My own must be there and in position by daylight. You shall, however, have two hours' rest."[38]

Men dropped in the road where they halted. Few cared that the southern outskirts of Winchester were only two miles away. No record exists of Jackson getting any sleep that night. He issued instructions to skirmishers and cavalry patrols, then carefully screened reports.

Major Harman, out of breath and obviously fatigued, rode out of the darkness. The quartermaster's announcement was not good: muddy roads in the Luray Valley had bogged down the supply wagons. It would be hours before food could arrive for the men. Jackson looked hard at the major. "The ammunition wagons?" Harman had anticipated the question.

"All right, sir. They were in advance, and I doubled teams on them and brought them through."

"Ah," said Jackson. Nothing more, yet in that single syllable Harman recognized genuine pleasure.[39]

The minutes crept by. Virginia infantryman J. William Jones believed that Jackson disdained any sleep and "stood sentinel at the head of the column." Another soldier reported Jackson and Ashby pacing back and forth on the turnpike in order to keep awake.[40]

Jackson certainly was aware that his achievements on May 24 had been limited. Utilizing always-perfect hindsight, one might conclude that the accomplishments were disappointing. Critics assert that Jackson "wasted" three hours at Cedarville when he could have been driving on Middletown to intercept the main body of Banks's army. Such a charge presumes that Jackson at 8 A.M. knew the whereabouts of the Federal army. He did not.

Another criticism pertains to the march and countermarch south of Middletown and the further delay it brought to Confederate movements. The fault was not Jackson's but the limited information he was getting from his cavalry. Had anyone confirmed the exact location of Banks's army at midday, no southward push would have been necessary. A final factor came into play that Saturday. Banks demonstrated that he could do in retreat what he could not do in advance: move quickly.

In spite of such Confederate disappointments, Jackson still had Banks where he wanted him. Sizable Federal forces remained in the lower valley region. Yet Banks and a force roughly the size of two brigades were locked at Winchester. Jackson was coming at him with twice as many Confederates, and he was picking both the direction and the manner of attack. The cruel march through the night had made all of this possible.

Jackson aroused his men before 4 A.M. ("early dawn," as he liked to call that time of day). The advance began in darkness. It was the Sabbath. Jackson on the previous day had hoped that hard marching might prevent the necessity of doing battle on the holy day. No matter. The Lord's work would be done with the bayonet rather than the Bible.

Skirmishers moved out in the gray light. Drenched in dew, they advanced cautiously over ditches and through fields of clover and wheat. Soon they could vaguely discern the forms of Union soldiers on the high ground south of Winchester.

Those heights, Major Dabney wrote, commanded both the town and the roads approaching it. Fences of wood and stone enclosed portions of the ridges. "Why the enemy did not post their powerful artillery upon the foremost of those heights . . . can only be explained by that infatuation which possessed them, by the will of God, throughout these events."[41]

Federal General George H. Gordon, who read those postwar lines, retorted heatedly that the will of God had nothing to do with it. "It was due rather to the will of the War Department, which deprived us of the requisite number of troops to hold any position against the overwhelming force in our front."[42]

Fog hung over the landscape and held back sunlight. Jackson, always conscious of his flanks, dispatched a courier with a simple message for Ewell: "Attack at daylight."[43] The eccentric soldier had been chafing at the bit for just such a directive.

Ewell sent his troops forward in spirited fashion against Winchester's southeastern corner. Similarly, Ashby's cavalry rode off to the left to provide protection for Jackson's other flank. Gunfire between skirmishers and the occasional bark of a cannon told Jackson that Banks planned to make a fight of it at Winchester. Not to do so would be to surrender control of the entire lower Shenandoah Valley.

Banks had about 6500 men. Although Jackson's army numbered 15,000, straggling had reduced the total by at least a third. Yet Banks remained convinced that 25,000 Confederates were bearing down on him.[44]

Neither the disorderly nature of the Union retreat on May 24 nor the shortage of time after reaching Winchester prevented Banks from having reasonably strong defenses. The town was a supply base, and Federals had toiled off and on for two months in constructing field works. Banks placed 1000 troops east of the turnpike and in front of Ewell. The main Union force (as Jackson expected) was on the hills southwest of town.

There the Federal line extended about a half-mile to the northwest. Banks positioned his men on the second line of hills, with some 400 yards separating it from the first expanse of high ground. However, near its western end, the Federal line curved toward the south. It formed an enfilade that looked down upon the ground toward which Jackson was moving. Along the Union line Banks had posted 4000 soldiers and a dozen cannon.

Jackson sought out Sidney Winder and ordered the Stonewall Brigade to advance with all dispatch to the high ground immediately west of the turnpike. Old Jack followed the advance to get a better look at the terrain ahead and to the left. The Stonewall Brigade, Jackson wrote with admiration, advanced "in handsome style" and secured the hilltop, "although the enemy made a resolute but unsuccessful effort to dislodge our troops from so commanding a position."[45]

It was around 6 A.M. when Jackson ordered up three batteries, posted them in the open behind the crest of the first ridge, and directed them to open fire. Union cannon responded promptly and accurately from ranges as close as 500 yards. This exchange touched off a fierce artillery duel. Federal sharpshooters to the left of the Southern artillery also began a deadly enfilade fire. Jackson's exposed batteries took a severe pounding. In one of Poague's sections, seven men and nine horses went down. All of the officers in Cutshaw's battery were casualties.

The fight of big guns lasted an hour before the Federal guns, also battered, fell back to a more secure position. Jackson the artilleryman had not done well in this predawn contest. He ordered three batteries into an open position when he should have positioned his superior firepower to better advantage. Perhaps fatigue still numbed his mind at the first stage of the battle, or possibly Jackson was convinced of the superiority of his cannoneers in a gun-to-gun exchange with the enemy. Whatever the cause, Jackson should have done better.[46]

Battle now roared as the Stonewall Brigade continued advancing along the turnpike. The valley soldiers moved forward bravely in the face of crippling cannon and musketry fire. Soon Winder's advance stalled. Jackson was about to summon additional troops into the area when, amid the dense smoke of combat, he saw a Union regiment moving to his left. Its destination was a stone wall almost at right angles with the line of Winder's brigade. A flank fire from there could shatter the main Confederate assault.

Jackson galloped back on the field in search of Winder. He found the brigadier directing the fire of his support batteries. Jackson asked how the battle was progressing. Winder pointed to the wall; an attack should be made there on the enemy's right. Jackson nodded. "Very well, I will send you up Taylor."[47]

Winder had thrown out the 5th Virginia as skirmishers, with three other regiments in battle formation and one in reserve. Colonel John Campbell's Second Brigade was on his left now, extending the Southern line. Jackson watched the units start forward, then rode over to confer with Campbell. The two started forward on horseback; Colonels John Patton and Andrew Grigsby followed on foot. Steadily the party moved into a storm of musket balls and shell fragments. Campbell fell wounded; Grigsby had a hole shot in his coat sleeve and, as was his wont, said some ugly words to the Yankees. Jackson sat motionless on his horse until satisfied of the Federal position and strength.[48]

As Jackson rode back through the Stonewall Brigade, he came upon the 33d Virginia in position on the western side of the battle-pocked ridge. Here were men literally defending their homes in the lower valley. In command of the regiment was twenty-eight-year-old John F. Neff, a well-mannered and beloved Dunkard who had briefly studied under Jackson at VMI. Neff was the youngest of the colonels in the Stonewall Brigade, and some of the troops thought him the strictest. He saluted and gave the general a brief report of where his troops were posted.

"What are your orders?" Jackson asked.

"To support that battery," Neff answered, pointing to two guns of W. E. Cutshaw's West Augusta Artillery then unlimbering.

Jackson gave Neff a piercing stare before shaking his fist in the air and exclaiming: "I expect the enemy to bring artillery to this hill. They must not do it! Do you understand me, sir? They must not do it! Keep a good lookout, and your men well in hand; and if they attempt to come, charge them with the bayonet, and seize the guns! Clamp them, sir, on the spot!"

"Very well, General," Neff replied calmly, "but my regiment is rather small."

Jackson pointed to the hill. "Take it!" he repeated. Fortunately, Neff and his men would not have to make any charge with the detested bayonet.[49]

Federals continued to move farther to Jackson's left. It was time to bring up reinforcements. Jackson started toward the rear. Soldiers in the 33d Virginia saw him riding down their line. Ordered not to cheer, they silently raised their hats as he passed. Jackson removed his cap in acknowledgement.

A moment later, he met Dick Taylor's Louisiana brigade. Broken down by heat, fatigue, and the loss of a hundred stragglers, it filed slowly onto the battlefield. Jackson directed Taylor to move at once and attack the guns blasting the Confederate left. The general pointed toward the distant ridge. "You must carry it," he told Taylor sternly. Then he wheeled Little Sorrel and started again toward the rear.[50]

Taylor led his men toward the high ground. He saw at once that he would have to flank the enemy's position in order to take it. To do so, Taylor turned his column farther to the west and parallel to the enemy lines. Suddenly, amid the noise, smoke, and flying bullets, he noticed Jackson riding silently alongside the troops. Union cannoneers by then had spied the flanking move and opened a telling fire that quickly blew gaps in the Confederate column.

In the face of the bombardment, and despite Jackson's presence, the Louisianians began to waver. An embarrassed and angry Taylor shouted above the din: "What the hell are you dodging for? If there is any more of it, you will be halted under this fire for an hour!" The soldiers regained their composure; and as they resumed the advance, Taylor felt a hand on his shoulder. He turned and looked straight into Jackson's face. It bore an expression of "reproachful surprise." The general said in a low tone: "I am afraid you are a wicked fellow." With that, and as Taylor watched red-faced, Jackson rode off to another sector.[51]

Any displeasure Jackson may have felt at Taylor's expletive vanished with the gallantry displayed by his soldiers. The Louisianians bravely marched across a field as if on parade. Not a man fired a shot as they started up the incline. At the top, behind a stone wall, a line of Federals unloaded concentrated musketry. Some of Taylor's men began to fall; the wall now seemed to be a wide fireplace spouting flame from one end to the other. Still the Louisianians held their muskets at the ready. Halfway up the hill, Taylor rose in his stirrups and shouted a command as loudly as he could. The brigade rushed up the now-steep grade in a massive sweep and poured over the wall into the outmanned Union ranks. Enemy soldiers broke frantically and fled down the back slopes toward Winchester.

Meanwhile, on Jackson's right, Ewell had been battling the enemy with what Jackson called "skill and spirit." Just as Taylor made his charge, Ewell launched a major attack with his full division. Jackson observed: "This simultaneous movement on both [Federal] flanks, by which his retreat might soon have been cut off, may account for the suddenness with which the entire army gave way. . . . The Federal forces were now in full retreat."[52]

At that moment of victory—about 8:30 A.M.—the brigades of Taylor, Campbell, and Winder moved steadily along Bowers' Hill and took possession of the high ground previously held by Union troops. Hotchkiss joined Jackson. "He was in front of the line," the cartographer stated, "had been holding up his hand, Pendleton said in prayer, and as the enemy wavered & then broke & fled, he swung his old gray cap & shouted: 'Now let's holler!'" Southerners obeyed the command with gusto. "For the first time in the Valley," Maryland soldier Randolph McKim stated, "'the Rebel yell,' that strange, fierce cry which heralded the Southern charge, rang high above the storm of battle." Federal soldiers also caught the sound of the disjointed screams. A Union drummer boy who remarked that "we could hear that infernal Rebel Yell" then added, "We had business toward the Potomac about that time."[53]

The cold warrior, the unflappable tactician, now became the joyful victor. Jackson, with Hotchkiss at his side, dashed forward in advance of his forces. Hotchkiss could see the Federals just ahead. He suggested to Jackson that they pause and wait for the army. It was difficult for Jackson to stop, but he did.[54]

Some of Ashby's men had taken possession of the Berryville road, the main eastern exit from Winchester. Banks was now beaten on both flanks; his line of retreat was endangered. Winchester was untenable. The Union forces must make a dash for the Potomac River. That was obvious to both sides; and with the fear that Banks might burn the town as he withdrew, the Confederates pursued with all speed.

At first it was an orderly Federal retreat. Then everything began to fall apart. As Jackson's men pressed forward into town, on their right appeared another mass of Confederates. Leading them was Dick Ewell, "galloping along the lines," one of his men wrote, "his head bare and bald, with dark, piercing eye and hooked nose, ugly, but oh! splendid."[55]

Jackson's full army was now pushing Banks's force. Then the Federals got hopelessly entangled in Winchester's narrow streets. Townspeople either tumbled from their homes in joy—which added to the growing traffic jam—or they angrily hurled a variety of missiles from their upstairs windows. The Union withdrawal rapidly broke into fragments. In less than forty-five minutes, Banks's brigades debouched on the other side of Winchester and reeled northward. The enemy, Jackson noted, had become "a mass of disordered fugitives."[56]

Few moments of the Civil War contained the drama that attended Jackson's entry into downtown Winchester. The Federal yoke had been lifted from the city. Its adored protector had returned. Captain James Edmondson of the 27th Virginia wrote home to Lexington: "I never saw such a demonstration as was made by the citizens, the ladies especially as we passed through—every window was crowded and every door was filled with them and all enthusiastically preparing for our Generals and soldiers, waving handkerchiefs and flags and others were engaged in supplying the soldiers as they passed with food and water."[57]

A North Carolina infantryman observed: "As we passed through Winchester, the whole town seemed mad with delight, cheering us at every stop." The soldier concluded, "My estimate of Jackson's generalship has risen a hundred degrees."[58]

He *was* the center of attention. Smiling as scores of residents crowded around him, Jackson bowed repeatedly and humbly from the saddle. A teenager remembered that "his face was alight with the glow of his triumphant pursuit." Writing to Anna the following day, Jackson looked back on the moment with feelings of pure happiness. "The people seemed nearly frantic with joy; indeed it would be almost impossible to describe their manifestations of rejoicing and gratitude. Our entrance into Winchester was one of the most stirring scenes of my life."[59]

No time could be spared to relish the reoccupation of Winchester that Sunday morning. Banks was beaten, but he must be destroyed. Jackson grew more impatient when he learned that the Union forces were not retiring toward Harpers Ferry and the protection of its garrison. They were on the Valley Turnpike, heading for Martinsburg. Banks was alone. He could be crushed if the Southerners drove hard. "Order the whole army to press on to the Potomac!" the aroused Jackson told Hotchkiss.[60]

Now his command failed him. Confederate infantry were scattered inside and around Winchester. The batteries were caught in the downtown traffic jam. Organization had cracked with success and elation.

Around 10 A.M., Jackson emerged from the north end of Winchester. He looked down on the open pastures through which the turnpike ran. Abandoned wagons and discarded equipment lined the roadway. Teamsters were fleeing in every direction. Some Union officers were trying to rally their men, but it was to no avail. "They would not have stopped if the angel Gabriel had been winding his trumpet," an eyewitness declared. The country was covered with crowds of blueclad fugitives. "Never have I seen an opportunity when it was more in the power of cavalry to reap a richer harvest of the fruits of victory," Jackson exclaimed. Nothing caused a demoralized army to disintegrate faster than mounted enemy soldiers galloping through the ranks. Eagerly Jackson turned and looked behind him. From the head of every Winchester street, columns of Southern infantry were emerging in a steady stream. Jackson's eyes darted back and forth. Yet not one of Ashby's twenty-seven companies was in sight. No one even knew where Ashby was. "Oh, that my cavalry were in place!" Jackson shouted in frustration.[61]

Then he remembered that in Ewell's division were the two regiments of Virginia cavalry under "Maryland" Steuart. Jackson dispatched his aide, Lieutenant Sandie Pendleton, to find Steuart and bring up his cavalry "in order that the enemy might be pressed with vigour."[62]

It took Pendleton the better part of an hour to locate Steuart and his command. They were lounging in a clover field two and a half miles out on the Berryville road. Even worse, the vain and haughty Steuart refused to obey any directive from a young staff officer. He was under Ewell's command, the brigadier asserted. "An order from General Jackson is peremptory and immediate!" an angry Pendleton shouted. Steuart would not budge.

Pendleton then made a two-mile search before locating Ewell. Naturally, the general immediately directed Steuart to go to Jackson with his troopers. Steuart did so with limited enthusiasm. Two hours had been lost in an entanglement of childish protocol.[63]

While Jackson waited for cavalry, the Federals gained a full head start. For two hours, Jackson made an impulsive pursuit. The turnpike was strewn with abandoned wagons, coats, blankets, knapsacks, and other accoutrements. Confederates grabbed what they wanted, and citizens picked over what was left. Some Federal stragglers were captured. The number would have been larger except for the knowledge inside the Union ranks that "Stonewall" Jackson was after them.

Southern soldiers marched as rapidly as they could before fatigue enveloped them in an ever-tightening noose. The men had already tramped 100 miles in the past seven days; they had been engaged in combat for the last thirty hours; now they were at the limit of endurance. Only one thing could make them forget their weariness. That was Jackson, who was "the greatest of warriors to them and the idol of the hour's affection."[64]

This was apparent when he rode up the line of his army to reach the forward point. A member of the Danville Artillery in Ewell's division wrote: "Yonder, in a faded gray coat, on Old Sorrel, came Stonewall himself, his cap in hand, his eye bright with victory, his hair fluttering in the wind, the very cyclone of battle, followed by his panting staff." Another artilleryman commented that "as he came the men pressed in shoals to the road-side and waved their hats enthusiastically. It was deafening. . . . I never saw a more thrilling scene. . . . General Jackson himself seemed much affected as he rode uncovered, bowing constantly."[65]

As the minutes passed, the interval between Confederates and Federals increased. Jackson's men were bushed. At one point, the general sought to improvise a cavalry force by ordering artillerymen to unhitch their horses and ride them in pursuit. That was unworkable. Worn-out horses, barely able to pull guns, were incapable of running.

It was too late. Jackson's shoulders slumped. He had maintained the chase for six miles. By then, his own army was disintegrating. Stragglers lined the road like fences from Stephenson's Depot three miles back into Winchester.

Steuart's cavalry and a small contingent under the shamefaced Ashby caught up with Jackson at Bunker Hill. Jackson brusquely demanded to know where Ashby had been. The excuses were not convincing. Jackson reported later in damning fashion: "There is good reason for believing that, had the cavalry played its part in this pursuit as well as the four companies had done under Colonel Flournoy two days before in the pursuit from Front Royal, but a small portion of Banks's army would have made its escape to the Potomac." That Banks's army was ripe for destruction is evident from the Federal general's own admission days later: "There were never more grateful hearts in the same number of men than when at midday of the 26th we stood on the opposite shore" of the Potomac River.[66]

A disappointed Jackson halted his army. The destruction of Banks would have to wait for another time. Jackson left logistics and mop-up operations to the staff and rode back into Winchester to enjoy the rare pleasure of visiting friends.

First on the list were the Grahams. The Presbyterian manse had been home for Jackson and Anna the previous winter. Putting military cares, frustrations, and successes behind him, Jackson climbed the front steps to the Graham home with the feelings of a member of the family.

He spent an hour accepting congratulations and passing along bits of personal news. Jackson said nothing at all about the memorable events of the day. "The general's little visit to us was a perfect sunbeam," Fanny Graham wrote Anna. "I never saw him look so fat and hearty, and he was as bright and happy as possible. . . . The evening he arrived here (which was Sunday) he came around, and said he did not think it was wrong to come home on Sunday. This was very gratifying to us. . . . The children were so delighted to see him."[67]

Leaving the Grahams, Jackson rode the few blocks to his headquarters at the Taylor Hotel. There he climbed the stairs to one of the rooms, fell face down on the bed still booted and spurred, and went instantly to sleep. His army encamped in the Stephenson's Depot area north of town. Late that night the wagons caught up with the soldiers, who received their first rations in forty-eight hours.[68]

Tribulations among the "foot cavalry" were many, but the rewards were far greater. Jackson had in truth driven the Union army from the Shenandoah Valley. Following the battle of McDowell, and including the few days of rest, Jackson had led his army 177 miles in seventeen days without any deviation from his overall plan. It had taken him but forty-eight hours to send Banks reeling fifty-three miles from Strasburg to the Potomac. "Our victory is complete," the 21st Virginia's Alfred Kelley exulted. "The Yanks are scattered if not to the four winds of heaven certainly to every point on the compass." A Connecticut drummer boy wrote home at the same time: "We were just two months going down [sic] the Valley after Stonewall Jackson. It was just 20 days getting back with Stonewall after us."[69]

The May 23–25 losses for the Confederates were only 400 men killed and wounded. Banks dashed to safety across the Potomac. He had suffered 3500 casualties—half of his command. Some 3000 of those men were prisoners.

Stores captured at Winchester were so voluminous that it required days to compile a complete inventory. Among the seizures at the Federal supply depot were 9354 small arms, 500,000 rounds of ammunition, two rifled cannon, 103 head of cattle, 14,600 pounds of bacon, 6000 pounds of hardtack, 1315 pounds of salt pork, 2400 pounds of sugar, and 350 bushels of salt.[70]

There was more. The medical supplies found in Winchester, Lieutenant Pendleton noted, were greater than those "in the whole Confederacy." One surgeon estimated the combined value of medicines and instruments at a quarter-million dollars. Two well-furnished military hospitals contained about 700 patients, plus attendants and nurses.

Eight Union surgeons chose to remain behind with the sick and infirm. Jackson could easily have sent them with the other captured Federals to Libby Prison or some other prisoner-of-war compound. Instead, and after conferring with Dr. McGuire, the general directed that the surgeons continue their ministrations under immunity. A few days later, Jackson granted them paroles and allowed them to return to their own lines.[71]

Unknown to Jackson, he had suddenly become the man of the hour. Soldiers looked at him in wonder. One of the Louisianians asserted that he had rather be a private under Jackson than an officer in another army. General Jeb Stuart, the Army of Northern Virginia's cavalry leader, wrote his wife from the peninsula, "Jackson's victories are glorious & when we hear from him again he will be in Md."[72]

Virginia newspapers began issuing blanket praise while reporting Jackson's activities and speculating on his next campaign. For example, the *Richmond Daily Dispatch* had given scant attention in the past to the Confederate commander in the valley. Now it gushed: "In all the transactions of this year, Jackson has proved himself to be a man of high military genius. He is very daring, but always upon calculation. The acts of his which appear rashest, are sure to be found the safest that could have been done. . . . Above all, Jackson has shown what a bold heart and ready wit can do with the most inadequate means. Men will follow such a leader anywhere. . . . He is the man for revolutionary times."[73]

Jackson's accomplishments in the May 23–25 period had been stunning. He had pushed his men with remorseless fury; and when a large part of his army had fallen by the wayside from simple inability to walk farther, Jackson had continued to press forward with the remainder. Unfortunately, he at times displayed more stern determination than tight organization. His artillery failed him at Front Royal; his cavalry failed him on the turnpike and at Winchester. Still, Jackson struck Banks before the latter was consolidated at Winchester. This event sent the Union army speeding northward in near disaster. Jackson's prayers of thanksgiving for the Front Royal-

Winchester victories were undoubtedly many. One suspects that he also asked for a little help with troop discipline.[74]

Union authorities in Washington were not aware of any such weaknesses inside Jackson's army; far from it. The sudden appearance of Jackson in the lower valley, followed by the rout of Banks's command, shocked the Federal government. On the night of May 25, Lincoln wired McClellan: "The enemy is moving north in a sufficient force to drive Banks before him. . . . I think the time is near when you must either attack Richmond or give up the job and come to the defence of Washington."[75]

For the next couple of days, alarm replaced shock in the Northern capital. The Lincoln administration overreacted. In a forty-eight-hour period, the War Department seized all Northern railroads for military purposes, called on Northern governors to dispatch any available troops to Washington, revoked a May 17 order permitting McDowell to start for Richmond with his corps, ordered him instead to stay at Fredericksburg and to start 20,000 soldiers to the valley, and put every Union commander in Virginia on alert for a possible attack from Jackson. Such fear was short-lived, but it altered strategy in the Virginia theater and abruptly brought Stonewall Jackson's name to the forefront of Northern military and civilian attention.[76]

Jackson, the soldier on the Sabbath, became Jackson the Christian the following day. He designated May 26 "for the purpose of rendering thanks to God for the success with which He has blessed our arms." He set an example by attending religious services in the camp of the 37th Virginia one day and in Taliaferro's brigade the next. Major Dabney went to work on a congratulatory order that in finished form read like a sermon Joshua might have delivered after the fall of Jericho.[77]

That afternoon Jackson sent a brief letter to Anna. "My precious darling, an ever-kind Providence blest us with success at Front Royal on Friday, between Strasburg and Winchester on Saturday, and here with a successful engagement on yesterday." Jackson ended the message on a personal note: "Time forbids a longer letter, but it does not forbid my loving my *esposita*."[78]

The man's compassion came into private view during this lull. Captain George Sheetz of Ashby's command had been killed in a May 23 cavalry action. Jackson took time to send a note to his father in Winchester. "The loss of your noble son is deeply felt by me. Tears come to my eyes when I think of his death. In imagination I see him before me, still you have my sympathy and prayers. In his death not only you and I, but also his country, has sustained a loss."[79]

In military matters, however, the general displayed his customary sternness. He warned his ragged men that anyone wearing captured Union clothing would be treated as a prisoner of war. No soldier was permitted inside Winchester without a duly authorized pass. Jackson also made public his disgust with Ashby's undisciplined cavalrymen as a result of the actions around Winchester. "Such troops cannot be depended on to secure brilliant results," he announced, "and hence they will not be placed in the advance of this army until satisfactory evidence shall be given that their disgraceful conduct will not be repeated." To keep everyone occupied on a positive enterprise, Jackson reinstated four hours of drill daily. His army might have been successful, but in his judgment it still needed improvement.[80]

After occupying Winchester, Jackson had informed Richmond of events. He probably offered suggestions for future movements as well. A response came on May 27 with the arrival of Jackson's "unconditional friend," Alexander Boteler. The Confederate Congress was in spring adjournment, so the forty-seven-year-old politician was available to serve another brief stint on Jackson's staff. Boteler brought with him instructions from the War Department.[81]

Jackson was ordered to demonstrate against Harpers Ferry while threatening both an invasion into Maryland and an attack on Washington. Such diversions hopefully would keep McDowell from reinforcing McClellan with his 40,000-man corps, and it might also draw part of McClellan's command away from the outskirts of Richmond. The orders coincided with Jackson's own sentiments. He felt it imperative to press his advantage while his opponent was off balance.

Moreover, keeping the Federals occupied would give Major Harman time to get the immense quantity of captured stores and baggage away from Winchester. Harman was not one to procrastinate at such a task. Within twenty-four hours, he had every carriage and wagon that could be either hired or impressed filled to the ceiling and wending its way up the Valley Turnpike toward Staunton. It would take Harman a week to haul away the bulk of the captured stores.[82]

On Wednesday, May 28, Jackson put his hard-marched soldiers back on the road. They headed east. Three reasons lay behind the move. Jackson wanted to press his advantage while he had a little time, he wished to keep the Federals preoccupied while Major Harman got the captured supplies away from Winchester, and Jackson wanted to create the impression that the Confederates intended threatening not only Harpers Ferry but the whole Potomac line as well.

The general gave serious thought to assaulting Harpers Ferry. Its 7000-man garrison and eighteen guns were tempting targets. Another victory over the Federals at this time could have major consequences for the war effort on both sides. How long it would take to invest the place was the big question.

Confederates spent most of May 28 making their way toward Charles Town in search of scattered fragments of Banks's army. As the main element of Jackson's command advanced through rain showers, Colonel Thomas T. Munford's 2d Virginia Cavalry galloped north to burn the Potomac bridges near Martinsburg. Another Confederate contingent occupied Martinsburg, which Banks had used as a supply base and then abandoned.

One of the gunners in the Rockbridge Artillery summarized the Martinsburg expedition by stating that Confederates "put the Yanks there to flight, captured & burned a considerable quantity of stores, & brought off with captured wagons, some of the most valuable stores, & several thousand stands of improved small arms. But still more important, burnt several large bridges on the main artery of supply to the Yankee capitol and army. Well might Lincoln & his minions quake in their boots at the near thunderings of old 'Stonewall' and his veteran Legion!"[83]

At Charles Town, the Stonewall Brigade encountered 1500 Federals arrayed in a defensive line. Sidney Winder did not wait for permission to do the obvious. He unfolded his regiments in battle formation and swept forward—a move that won him open admiration from proud valley soldiers and higher confidence from Jackson. Carpenter's battery, with the 33d Virginia in support, advanced and began firing into the enemy position. The already-demoralized Federals put up little fight. After twenty minutes of action, a pleased Jackson stated, "the enemy retired in great disorder, throwing away arms, blankets, haversacks, &c."[84]

Winder continued the pursuit to the hamlet of Halltown, three miles west of Harpers Ferry. He demonstrated in front of Bolivar Heights, discovered a stronger Union force, and pulled the Stonewall Brigade back to Charles Town. From his headquarters at Halltown, Jackson dispatched the 2d Virginia across the Shenandoah River to occupy Loudoun Heights "with the hope of being able to drive the enemy from Harper's Ferry, across the Potomac."[85]

Such a view was unrealistic. A single regiment, without artillery support, hardly constituted a threat to a garrison of 7000 soldiers with eighteen cannon. Moreover, on higher Maryland Heights were several Federal heavy guns that commanded the entire area, including Loudoun Heights.

Confederates were making camp when Commissary Wells J. Hawks returned from a brief visit to his family in Charles Town. Jackson asked the major if many residents had taken the Union oath of allegiance during the long occupation by enemy troops. "The people of Charles Town are true," Hawks replied. "I don't think any of them have taken the oath."

Jackson smiled. "That is a *jewel* of a place."[86]

Whatever Jackson's ultimate objectives were in this advance, the whole forward movement was hazardous: more dangerous to his own forces than to the Federals. Jackson was now twenty miles from the haven of Winchester. Ashby would inform him on the 29th that Fremont's army was coming east through the mountains toward Strasburg. The Confederate army numbered no more than 13,000 men. Jackson had put weary troops in a pocket that a concentrated superior force could close on all sides with a rapid movement. Worst of all, deep fatigue combined with growing anxiety over the Federals' next moves were chipping away at Jackson's usually unflappable countenance.

On the Union side, meanwhile, the sense of panic that had gripped Washington in the immediate aftermath of the Winchester loss had subsided. Calmer heads were prevailing in the Northern capital. One of them belonged to Abraham Lincoln. He knew that Banks's whole army had not been destroyed, as early reports indicated. Two other Federal hosts were available for service in the valley. Lincoln also demonstrated that he could read a map well and likewise act with dispatch. He had carefully followed Jackson's movements down the valley in the latter half of May, and he came to a correct conclusion.

If Jackson was driving through the lower valley, the upper valley was defenseless. Jackson's rear was unprotected. On May 24, therefore, while Banks's brigades were racing northward from Strasburg, Lincoln had ordered Fremont's mountain army to advance southward on Harrisonburg. At the same time, the War Department instructed McDowell at Fredericksburg to transfer two of his four divisions to the valley.

McDowell protested bitterly. In one communique, he showed uncharacteristic foresight in arguing against concentrating Union might against Jackson. "If the enemy can succeed so readily in disconcerting our plans by alarming us first at one point, then at another, he will paralyze a large force with a very small one."[87]

Neither Lincoln nor Secretary of War Edwin Stanton was swayed. Jackson must be stopped, for psychological as well as military reasons. With Fremont swinging up from the south, Shields with two more divisions coming in from the east, and Banks possibly able to initiate a second southward push, Federal pressure would be like a giant pincer on Jackson's outnumbered band. The initiative was suddenly passing to the Union side.

May 30 dawned overcast and sultry. Early in the day Jackson seemed almost nonchalant. He received a delegation of ladies who came to pay respects. After that, he rode out beyond Halltown to check on Winder's demonstrations against Harpers Ferry. Jackson watched an exchange of artillery fire between one of his batteries and Union guns near Bolivar Heights. Possibly one or more of the messages Jackson received at the time told him of the Union buildups on three sides.[88] Whatever the case, Jackson became more intense.

He was sitting on Little Sorrel monitoring the cannon fire when Winder joined him, along with General Arnold Elzey. Eight years older than Jackson, the Maryland-born Elzey was a West Point graduate and seasoned army officer. The first Maryland regiment contributed to the Confederate cause was under his command. At Manassas, Elzey's gallant conduct led Beauregard to proclaim him the "Blucher of the day."[89] President Davis reportedly promoted him to brigadier general on the spot. Elzey was courageous and proud; it was also widely known—and Jackson must have been aware—that he had a fondness for the bottle.

Elzey said little as Winder told Jackson of heavy Union reinforcements arriving at Harpers Ferry. The news did not sit well with the Southern commander. At that point, Elzey added that some long-range Federal guns were also in position atop Maryland Heights. Jackson swung angrily in the saddle. "General Elzey," he snapped, "are you afraid of heavy guns?" Elzey flushed with anger but said nothing. An awkward silence followed until a courier galloped up with an urgent dispatch. Jackson read it hurriedly, wheeled without a word, and dashed away. The note was confirmation that Fremont and Shields were closing behind him.[90]

That was of far more concern to Jackson than the fact that he had committed a gross breach of conduct by humiliating one general in the presence of another. Jackson now saw that he had done as much as he could along the Potomac line. It was time to move his army back into the safe interior of the Shenandoah Valley.

Colonel Boteler was not privy to the exchange between Elzey and Jackson, but he did witness another unusual action by the commander on the field in front of Bolivar Heights. Jackson rode back to resume monitoring the artillery duel. He suddenly dismounted and sat down with his back to a tree. After crossing his legs, he folded his arms over his chest, turned his head to one side, and fell asleep amid the din of cannon fire.

Boteler was the great grandson of noted artist Charles Willson Peale. He must have inherited some drawing talent because the congressman had early displayed skill at sketching scenes and people. The congressman could not let this opportunity pass. He began sketching the warrior. He had been drawing intently for awhile when he looked up from his pad and met Jackson's eyes fixed on him. With a disarming smile, Jackson extended his hand and said: "Let me see what you have been doing there." The aide passed him the sketch. Jackson gazed at it for a moment, then looked up at

Boteler. "My hardest tasks at West Point were the drawing lessons," he confessed. "I never could do anything in that line to satisfy myself—or indeed," he added with a chuckle, "anyone else." A long pause followed. Jackson then spoke again. "Colonel, I have some harder work than this for you to do. If you will sit down here now, I will tell you what it is."[91]

Jackson wanted the congressman to go forthwith to Richmond and try to obtain reinforcements that would bring the valley army to a strength of 40,000 men. Boteler replied that he would leave at once but that it would help if he knew the reason for the urgency and the need for so many additional soldiers. Asking Jackson for explanations was something no man usually did. Yet Boteler was a close friend who had been Jackson's champion in the Confederate capital for much of the war. He could be trusted implicitly. In uncustomary fashion, therefore, Jackson gave Boteler as full a report of the situation as he knew it.

"McDowell and Fremont are probably aiming to effect a junction at Strasburg, so as to head us off from the upper Valley, and they are both nearer to it now than we are. Consequently, no time is to be lost. You can say to them in Richmond that I will send on the prisoners, secure most, if not all of the captured property, and, with God's blessing, will be able to baffle the enemy's plans here with my present force, but that it will have to be increased as soon thereafter as possible." Banks's resurrected army, padded with part of General Rufus Saxton's garrison at Harpers Ferry, might hound the Confederates as they moved southward. With an enlarged force of 40,000, Jackson conjectured, "a movement may be made beyond the Potomac, which will soon raise the siege of Richmond and transfer this campaign from the banks of the James to those of the Susquehanna."[92]

Jackson had a number of papers to prepare for delivery to Richmond. He gave Boteler a couple of hours to visit his family nearby. Then Boteler was to proceed to Charles Town, where a Winchester and Potomac train was waiting at the station. Once he reached Winchester, Major Harman would arrange transportation to Staunton and thence to Richmond. Boteler departed on his mission.

Clouds were getting thicker overhead, and it was beginning to smell of rain, when Jackson ordered the bulk of his army to start back to Winchester. Winder and the Stonewall Brigade would make one final stab at Harpers Ferry and guard the rear during the withdrawal. Jackson rode in silence with his staff to Charles Town. Troops and wagons filled the road for a dozen miles, all heading south.

A cavalry lieutenant, seeing the procession, made his way to Jackson. "General," he asked unthinkingly, "are the troops going back?" Jackson gave the man an annoyed look and answered: "Don't you see them going?" The lieutenant persisted. "Are they all going?" At the second question, Jackson turned to Abner Smead, his inspector general. "Colonel, arrest that man as a spy." The frightened cavalryman was loudly protesting his innocence and offering apologies when Colonel Ashby arrived on the scene. Jackson retracted the arrest order after Ashby convinced him that the man was a devoted officer but not possessed of uncommonly good sense.[93]

In spite of the withdrawal and the reasons behind it, Jackson displayed little sense of urgency that afternoon. He regarded Banks as no longer a threat. Before departing Winchester, Jackson had sent Ashby and artillery support to command the one road by which Fremont could come across North Mountain and reach Strasburg.

At the same time, and to impair any advance by Shields on Strasburg, Jackson had put one of his best regiments at the Confederate supply base in Front Royal. The 12th Georgia, under Colonel Zephanier T. Conner, was to hold Front Royal as long as possible in case Jackson chose to use the Luray Valley as a line of retreat. Under no circumstances, Jackson emphasized to Conner, were the Federals to secure the bridges at Front Royal. If Conner had to fall back, the spans were to be destroyed in order to protect Jackson's flank and rear.

Rain was falling steadily when Jackson and some of his staff ate a midday meal at the home of Major Hawks. The downpour grew heavier when the general resumed the withdrawal. Colonel Boteler was just arriving at the Charles Town railroad station when up galloped Jackson and assistant adjutant Sandie Pendleton. Jackson had changed his mind: he was going to get ahead of his forces by taking the train and gaining shelter from the wet weather.

The Winchester and Potomac line was in sad disrepair and had a notoriously poor roadbed. (A Union chaplain termed the line a "miserable railway" that would "give out once a day or so.")[94] Nevertheless, Jackson boarded the one-car train and, after taking a seat, put his arm on the back of the seat in front of him as a headrest and went instantly to sleep. The bouncing and jerking of the train had no effect on his slumber.

Boteler and Pendleton stayed glued to the windows of the passenger car as lookouts for possible Union cavalry who might be attracted to the train. Near Summit Point, Boteler spotted a lone rider galloping hard through the rain toward the railroad. The congressman awakened Jackson, who ordered the train stopped. Quickly the man identified himself as a courier. He handed a note through the window. Jackson read it, tore it up, and calmly said to the conductor, "Go on, sir, if you please." Then he went immediately back to sleep.[95]

Before the train lurched to a stop in the middle of downtown Winchester, Jackson had shared with Boteler the worst news he had received in the valley campaign. Federals had swooped down on Front Royal in late morning and routed the Confederate defenders more decisively than Jackson's men on May 23 had done to Kenly's Union regiment. In panic, the 12th Georgia had broken and fled the town.

Federals would have seized all of the $300,000 worth of stores if an assistant quartermaster on his own volition had not set fire to most of it. Six officers and 150 men in Conner's regiment had been captured. Conner had raced to Winchester without a second glance at the plight of the regiment. Front Royal was back in Federal hands.[96]

Jackson and his army were now in a critical situation. Shields's division was only twelve miles from Strasburg, the Valley Turnpike, and a possible linkup with Fremont. Not a single Confederate force of any size was within twenty-five miles of Strasburg. The Stonewall Brigade was twice that distance maneuvering in front of Harpers Ferry. By the next morning, Shields could have 10,000 Federals blocking the turnpike. Another 10,000 were moving into Front Royal. Fremont's 15,000 soldiers could press hard from the west.

In other words, enemy forces double the number of Jackson's men could close the escape route easily and completely on the 31st. Further, Banks appeared to be sorting out his command. Along with the bulk of Saxton's command at Harpers Ferry, Banks formed a third peril for Jackson.

Confederate chances of escaping the trap were poor. Jackson could not wait at Winchester for the Stonewall Brigade. The army must head south to face a threatened pincer by Shields and Fremont. Wagon trains loaded with goods captured at Martinsburg and Charles Town were massing with the army inside Winchester. Some 2300 Union prisoners were also there. Jackson had no intention of relinquishing any of the booty for the sake of speed. Everything would go with the army.

Feverish activity and rain marked the night hours at Winchester. Jackson oversaw all preparations for the march. Yet a disciplinary matter needed prompt attention. He summoned Colonel Zephanier Conner to his headquarters at the Taylor Hotel. The 12th Georgia colonel saluted and began a dramatic account of what had happened at Front Royal. Jackson listened impatiently, in no mood for excuses. Conner finished his report. Jackson asked brusquely: "Colonel, how many men did you have killed, sir?" Since Conner had raced to Winchester and left his regiment to fend for itself, he was unaware of its casualties.

"None," he replied.

"How many wounded?"

"None, sir."

"Colonel Conner, do you call that much of a fight?" Jackson snapped as he dismissed the officer.

Conner left the room with Commissary Hawks. "Major," Conner stated, "I believe General Jackson is crazy."

A moment later, Lieutenant Pendleton came out the door. "Colonel Conner," he announced, "you are to consider yourself under arrest." With that, the colonel turned to Major Hawks. "Now I *know* he is crazy!"[97] As Conner also learned, his military career had ended. Jackson had him cashiered for dereliction of duty.

Around 10 P.M., Alexander Boteler came to the hotel. Aware that he had to make a ninety-mile horseback ride in the rain, he ordered two whiskey toddies to be delivered to Jackson's room. Boteler was talking with the general when the drinks arrived. The congressman offered one to Jackson, who drew back. "No, no, Colonel, you must excuse me. I never drink intoxicating liquors."

"I know that, General," Boteler responded, "but though you habitually abstain, as I do myself, from everything of that sort, there are occasions, and this is one of them, when a stimulant will do us both good. Otherwise I would neither take it myself or offer it to you. So you must make an exception to your general rule and join me in a toddy tonight."

Jackson shook his head again, but he took the tumbler and slowly began sipping its contents. A few minutes later, when he had consumed half of the drink, Jackson set the cup on a table and abruptly shifted the subject from military matters. A few moments later, he stared at Boteler. "Colonel," he said, "do you know why I habitually abstain from intoxicating liquors?"

Boteler shook his head. The general then answered his own question: "Why, sir, because I like the taste of them. When I discovered this to be the case, I made up my mind at once to do without them altogether."

With that, Jackson gave Boteler the documents to be delivered to Richmond and sent him on his way.[98]

Far into the night, preparations for departure continued. At 3 A.M. on Saturday the

31st, Jackson (who had had little if any sleep) awakened Hotchkiss. Winchester had to be abandoned; the army in all likelihood would go into battle somewhere to the south that day. Hotchkiss was to ride to Charles Town and bring back Winder's brigade with all speed. "I will stay in Winchester until you get here, if I can," Jackson told the aide, "but if I cannot, and the enemy gets here first, you must bring it around through the mountains."[99]

As Hotchkiss embarked into the darkness on his mission, he was struck by the "fine spirits" that Jackson exhibited. Yet, the mapmaker wrote later, the general "manifested more anxiety about getting the Stonewall Brigade back to his command in safety than I ever saw him do at any other time."[100]

After Hotchkiss left, Jackson started the main column of infantry, wagons, artillery, and prisoners southward. Rain was falling heavily. For hours men and rolling stock filed through the beloved town the Confederates had reoccupied only six days earlier. The only troops to remain were Ashby's horsemen. They were entrusted with keeping the road open for Winder's brigade if possible.

The combined forces of Banks and Saxton could have created havoc had they pushed south from the Potomac line. Yet the former stated that his 6000 men were still not up to field service, and the latter claimed that his garrison was not sufficient to do battle with Jackson.[101]

Jackson rode from town in midmorning. Lieutenant Douglas wrote: "We left our friends in Winchester trembling for our fate & more than we trembled ourselves. Everybody felt the great danger, but everybody also looked at Old Jack & seeing him calm & cool as if nothing was the matter, they came to the conclusion that their destruction could not be as inevitable as they supposed & endeavored to take things calmly too."[102]

Fortunately, the day was clear and not too warm. Wagon trains consisted of 200 vehicles ranging from large Conestogas to squat drays. The trains moved in a double column eight miles long. (Harman had to count wagons by the mile.) Then came Federal prisoners, followed by the headquarters command, infantry, artillery, and the usual congregation of stragglers at the rear. Ashby's men ranged far afield in front, principally west of the turnpike to persuade Federal cavalry not to venture too close.

Much of the long line had cleared Winchester when Jackson departed with his staff. As he made his way forward to the van, he superintended the march as closely as a shepherd tending his flock of sheep. Hurry! Keep up! Move along! Steadily the army proceeded southward. Fifty minutes of marching filled every hour. Rest periods never exceeded ten minutes, for rumors were circulating that Federals occupied Strasburg up ahead and were arrayed in full battle formation.

No time existed with general and staff to dwell on unfounded reports. Hotchkiss was guiding Winder's men somewhere to the north; Harman was driving the wagon trains to the south; Hawks was scouring the countryside for food; Pendleton, Douglas, Boswell, William L. Jackson, and other staff members were riding here and there with verbal orders or written instructions; Crutchfield was struggling—but successfully so—to keep the artillery covering the army's rear and flanks. At one point, the scholarly artillery chief shook his head and muttered: "Quem Deus vult perdere, prius dementat" (The one whom God wants to destroy, he first makes mad).[103]

Confederate men and materiel stretched fifteen miles along the turnpike. The head of the column was approaching Strasburg when the last elements were leaving Winchester. It was as inviting a target as appeared in the valley during the entire war. Fremont or Shields should have sliced Jackson's columns into pieces. "The whole country is looking with anxiety and hope," Federal General McDowell stated.[104] Yet not one Federal hampered the procession.

Jackson had no way of knowing that the Union "celerity of movement" necessary for his entrapment had turned into a comedy of errors. It began with Fremont's ineptitude on May 24, the day before Jackson seized Winchester. Lincoln had ordered Fremont to take Harrisonburg, forty miles away, and seal off the upper valley from Jackson. Fremont started forward but found the mountain passes blocked (the result of Jackson's precautionary efforts following the battle of McDowell). Instead of clearing the unmanned obstacles and advancing straight ahead, Fremont detoured on a 120-mile circuitous march to get to Harrisonburg.

At that point, Secretary of War Stanton interceded. With Jackson's movements unpredictable, Fremont was told to fall upon Jackson wherever he found him. The Union general changed course again and made for Strasburg—but at a pace that varied from no miles to ten miles per day.

Fremont used every known excuse for his delays. On May 31, while Jackson's army was strung out in the valley, Fremont reached a point four miles from the turnpike. He halted, made no final push, took no action. He seemed content to dally while a great opportunity slipped away.

General James Shields in similar fashion snatched defeat from the jaws of victory. Like Fremont, he correctly believed that alone he was outnumbered by Jackson's army. Shields was at Front Royal by May 31; but because a supporting division was a full day's march behind him, he paused to consider the whole matter. Shields was not sure of Jackson's location. The fog of war engulfed him as much as it did Jackson at the time.

If Shields remained at Front Royal, Jackson might fight his way past Fremont on the turnpike. If Shields advanced to Strasburg, the possibility existed of Jackson slipping into the Luray Valley ahead of the second Union division en route from Fredericksburg and getting behind him. Dividing his forces between Front Royal and Strasburg would make each wing an easy prey for Jackson.

As Shields pondered his options, Ashby's cavalry staged a noisy raid on the Union outposts north of Front Royal. That convinced Shields, who seemed to be searching for justification, to remain at Front Royal rather than make for the real objective along the Valley Turnpike.[105]

Jackson, of course, was unaware of this indecisiveness by the two Federal generals. He knew first that he had to get to Strasburg ahead of the enemy. Concern over the Stonewall Brigade also created deep worry. Throughout the afternoon, as his army moved quietly on the turnpike, Jackson's face "was as pale and firm as marble, his thin lips shut, his brow thoughtful and hard."[106]

Naturally, concern mounted as the long column approached Strasburg. If there was to be a fight, Strasburg would be the site. No sound of gunfire could be heard from that direction. Finally, Strasburg came in sight. The town was void of Federals. Jackson had won the first critical leg of the race. "Thanks to God our army is safe," was all a surgeon could say.[107]

Inside the weary Confederate ranks was a spirit of relaxation as tensions eased. Men shook their heads silently to acknowledge a bloodless success. All would have concurred with Captain Campbell Brown of Ewell's staff. "Our old chief, Jackson," Brown wrote home, "is the very man to be put in the Valley of Virginia, for he believes altogether in its importance, & it would be hard to convince him that the axis of the world does not stick somewhere between Winchester & Lexington."[108]

The Confederates bivouacked in a shallow semicircle north of Strasburg. Jackson established his headquarters at the George Hupp farm. Now squarely between the two enemy hosts, Jackson made it clear that he planned to stay there until the Stonewall Brigade, somewhere down the road, joined the column. Quick orders came forth. Major Harman and the supply trains were to continue south toward New Market; Ewell's division, in the rear of the army, would turn west to assist Ashby in confronting any pressure exerted by Fremont; Jackson would handle Shields's force, if necessary.

Boteler wrote admiringly of the moment: "Standing there like a hunted stag at bay defying his pursuers, [Jackson] presented so bold a front to them that Fremont paused in his advance near Wardensville, and Shields came no further than Front Royal. . . . Both were puzzled by the celerity of Jackson's movements, and, apparently, deterred by his audacity."[109]

Sunday, June 1, heralded what was probably the rainiest week of the war. The Stonewall Brigade was nowhere in sight. Shortly after dawn, Chaplain James Avirett of Ashby's command arrived at the Hupp house. Major Hawks informed him that the general was at his devotionals and would see him shortly.

Avirett began wandering around the house. He walked down the hall, looked through a partly open door, and saw Jackson kneeling in prayer. Soon the general emerged from the room and greeted the cleric. Avirett asked if troop movements that day would prevent divine services in camp.

"Is this Sunday?" Jackson asked. "It had escaped me. I have been very busy lately."[110]

While Avirett left headquarters knowing that no field services were going to be held on that particular Sabbath, Jackson expedited the movement of his wagons to the south. Then he rode out to watch Ewell's division wage a long-distance contest of artillery and musketry with elements of Fremont's command.

That Union general made a weak probe on the turnpike near Cedar Creek, but Ewell and Ashby made such a counterdemonstration that the Federals quickly retired. Fremont rationalized: "I was entirely ignorant of what had taken place in the Valley beyond, and it was now evident that Jackson, in superior force, was at or near Strasburg."[111]

All the while, Jackson kept glancing anxiously toward Winchester. Early in the afternoon, a line of men four abreast came through the rainy mist up the turnpike. Jackson stared intently, then breathed a sigh of relief. It was Winder with the Stonewall Brigade!

The valley regiments had fully sustained their sobriquet of "foot cavalry." On the previous day, in drenching rain and through a mud flow that once was a road, four regiments had tramped thirty-five miles. The other regiment, the 2d Virginia, had left

Loudoun Heights and marched forty-two miles in the same period. None of the men had eaten for two days.

Winder had reached Newtown on the 31st around 10 P.M. Stragglers outnumbered the men still in ranks. The brigadier turned the remnant of the brigade into a field on the left of the turnpike and ordered the soldiers to get some rest. Jackson wanted the brigade at Strasburg no later than 7 A.M. the next day. For once, Winder ignored orders. He was angry at the hard march imposed on his men. To an aide he declared that he had rather lose his men in a battle than on a march. Those in the Stonewall Brigade who had not fallen behind the pace could get a few hours' sleep. That would also allow some stragglers to catch up with their units.

At 5:30 A.M. June 1, Winder had his strapped men back on the road. They shuffled along in gloomy silence. Sometime after 8 o'clock, Confederates heard the booming of artillery in their front. No one in Jackson's old brigade spoke, but the same thoughts were on everyone's mind: Federals had blocked the turnpike; the Stonewall Brigade was trapped. Soon, however, word flashed through the ranks. The guns were Jackson's. He had taken enormous risks to hold the road open for them at Strasburg. Shouts rent the air: "Old Jack knows what he's about! He'll take care of us, you bet!" An older soldier added: "From that hour we never doubted him." The Stonewall Brigade reached Strasburg after one of the most extraordinary physical feats in the Civil War; and when it halted, scores of men threw themselves onto the muddy turnpike and went instantly to sleep.[112]

The valley army was together again, having slipped the noose of nearly 50,000 Federals. However, the enemy still remained on two fronts. To avoid being wedged between them, Jackson started up the valley as soon as darkness fell. He had the advantage of the macadamized turnpike. His adversaries were struggling on far muddier roads. Most of the Confederates were reeling from fatigue as sheets of rain lashed the winding column, but safety overrode weariness. "Better to lose one man from hard marching than five in battle," Jackson liked to say.[113]

A popular story developed in the ranks on this march. Some wag turned to a comrade and commented that Old Jack was a better leader than Moses. When asked why, the weary private answered, "It took Moses forty years to lead the Israelites through the Wilderness, while Jackson would have double-quicked them through in three days."[114]

As the Southerners cleared Strasburg, devotion to their general plus faith in themselves elevated spirits. The column moved in slow, deliberate, and confident fashion. Corporal Neese of Chew's battery wrote gleefully that Jackson's army "slipped through the jaws of the closing vice like a greased rat." Sandie Pendleton of the staff was more restrained. "Where we are to go I do not know," he told his mother. "Our force is too small and too much broken down by constant marching to do much good work for some time against an overwhelming force. But come when they may, they will find us ready for them, trusting in God and our righteous cause."[115]

Although Jackson appeared calm that night, his mind dwelled at length on every contingency the immediate future might hold. That Fremont and Shields had failed to unite at Strasburg raised a suspicion. Shields might be moving with his division up the Luray Valley to ambush Jackson at New Market. The road ran along the east side of the heavily swollen South Fork of the Shenandoah River. Only three bridges crossed the stream south of Front Royal and east of the Massanutten Mountains. Two of them (at White House and Columbia) were opposite New Market; the third was at Conrad's Store.

In order to neutralize Shields for the time being, Jackson sent a cavalry detachment to burn the two spans near New Market Pass.[116] That was done. Shields had no pontoon bridges at hand. Hence, a raging river and the Massanutten range separated the two Federal armies pursuing Jackson—and gave the Confederate commander adequate protection on his eastern flank. Jackson was free to fall back in moderate stages and to concentrate on what Fremont might do.

While Jackson established headquarters that night in the Walton law office at Woodstock, Turner Ashby gained a measure of redemption as a cavalry leader. Fremont was pressing Jackson with 1600 mounted troops and two batteries. At sundown, Union cavalry dashed into the Confederate rear guard with deceiving shouts of "We're Ashby's cavalry! Ashby's cavalry!" The Federals got close enough to fire a volley into Colonel Steuart's 6th Virginia Cavalry, which stampeded through the 2d Virginia Cavalry of Colonel Tom Munford.

According to Hotchkiss, Jackson had relieved Ashby from command for his May 24–25 derelictions at Winchester. Now the cavalry colonel was riding alone, somewhat in disgrace, at the tail end of the army when the Federals attacked. He galloped into a roadside thicket and, after the Yankees passed, rallied a group of straggling infantrymen into a fighting force. The Federals soon galloped back—straight into a withering fire that emptied a number of saddles.

Ashby mounted his stragglers on the captured horses and rode at their head to Jackson's headquarters in Woodstock. The general complimented Ashby on his gallant action and restored him to command not only of his own troopers but of the 2d and 6th Virginia Cavalry as well. All of Jackson's cavalry was now under the dark-complexioned and tireless Ashby.[117]

The Federals had wasted another day in trying to isolate Jackson. The Confederate army was still free and loose. From Front Royal on May 23 to Strasburg on June 1, Jackson had created havoc among the enemy, routed an army, captured enormous quantities of stores, and made his escape from converging Federal forces. Jackson had done all of that at a cost of about 500 men—a small loss in view of what had been gained. On the other side, one of Banks's staff officers considered Jackson's escape "the most disgraceful [affair] to the Federal armies that has occurred during the whole war. I am utterly humiliated to have been mixed up in it."[118]

Hail alternated with rain through the night. The march resumed on June 2 with rain still falling. Jackson had slept no more than three hours, which had become standard over the past week. Nevertheless, he was high-spirited in a letter to Anna. "I am again retiring before the enemy. They endeavored to get in my rear by moving on both flanks of my gallant army, but our God has been my guide and saved me from their grasp. You must not expect long letters from me in such busy times as these, but always believe that your husband never forgets his little darling."[119]

Weather, fatigue, and occasional salvos from Federal artillery soon reduced the moving column to gridlock. Many of the soldiers were so tired that they had thrown away their arms to get the weight off their shoulders. Wagon trains became bogged in the mud. By noon, a massive traffic jam existed.

An irritated Jackson, in front with his staff, galloped back to try to untangle the mess. He came first upon an officer whose brigade was ensnared in its own disarray. "Colonel," Jackson said gruffly, "why do you not get your brigade together, keep it together, and move on?"

The man responded: "It is impossible, General, I can't do it."

Back came an angry retort: "Do not say it is impossible! Turn your command over to the next officer. If he cannot do it, I will find someone who can, if I have to take him from the ranks!"[120]

Jackson gave the colonel no second chance. Old Jack straightened out the confusion and got his army moving again. That night he stopped at Israel Allen's home near Hawkinstown. The general normally did not impose upon civilians; but Allen was an old friend, rain was still falling, and Jackson was exhausted. Yet he had to feel somewhat relieved by nightfall. He continued to elude a Federal trap with the help of speed and heavy rains. In wet weather, the advantage lay with the defense. Jackson had made a fairly good march that day without a major encounter with the enemy.

Colonel John M. Patton of the 21st Virginia arrived at Allen's after dark and reported on a rear guard skirmish with Federal cavalry. In the course of his statement, Patton expressed regret that his men had killed three Union horsemen who bravely charged into the regiment. After the colonel finished his report, Jackson asked a couple of routine questions. Suddenly he looked hard at Patton. "Colonel, why wouldn't you have shot them?"

"I should have spared them, General," Patton answered, "because they were men who had gotten into a desperate situation."

"No, Colonel," Jackson replied sternly. "Shoot them all. I don't want them to be brave."[121]

Far into the night, ignoring weariness, Jackson wrote a long report of his situation to General Joseph Johnston at Richmond. "I did not fall back too soon," Jackson stated, "as the enemy's object was obviously to get in my rear, and had I not been in Strasburg yesterday the Federals would have been. We have brought off a large amount of medical, ordnance and other stores, but many have been destroyed for want of transportation, but the most valuable have been saved. I will hold myself in readiness to cross the Blue Ridge should you need me." Jackson realized, of course, that several days would pass before Johnston digested his letter. More fighting lay ahead before the campaign in the valley reached a resolution and Jackson could leave for Richmond. What Jackson did not know was that Johnston had been seriously wounded two days earlier in fighting at Seven Pines and was no longer in command of the Army of Northern Virginia.[122]

The rain continued. On June 3, a revitalized Ashby went into action again. He had just received word of his promotion to brigadier, and he wasted no time proving his mettle as a fighting general. Day and night his horsemen galloped along the pike, through woods, over stone walls, and across open expanses. The indefatigable Ashby seemed everywhere as he used all known means to delay Fremont's pursuit.

Jackson's forces crossed the North Fork of the Shenandoah at Meem's Bottom.

Ashby covered the Confederate rear, then burned the bridge in the face of the Federals as he retired. In a brief but spirited fight, Ashby's horse was killed and he narrowly escaped with his own life. Fremont sought to replace the bridge with a pontoon. Yet the stream rose ten feet in four hours and washed away the wagon span. That gave Jackson a full day's lead over Fremont.

Meanwhile, Shields was exactly where Jackson wanted him. Heavy rains had turned the countryside into endless mud. Shields's division was strung out for twenty miles in the Luray Valley; his supply trains were mired far to the rear; the swollen South Fork had him condemned from any junction with Fremont. Shields daily voiced both displeasure over his plight and frustrations at the great successes he could be reaping otherwise.[123]

It was even worse on the Confederate side. Jackson's march now defied description. Major Harman had shoved and cursed the wagon trains far into the advance, which meant no food for the marching soldiers. For them, day and night blurred into an unbroken ordeal. Men struggled in the mud; officers sought in vain to maintain a semblance of order in their units; straggling seemed to have gripped fully half of Jackson's command.

James Dinwiddie of the Charlottesville Artillery painted a dismal picture to his mother. "We have been on a retreat for five days and an awful time it has been. . . . It is still raining hard & has been all night. . . . I never saw so many barefooted men with their feet all swollen and bleeding. Hundreds & hundreds drag along the road." Captain James Edmondson of the 27th Virginia looked with dismay at the proud Stonewall Brigade, now more completely broken down than it had ever been. The 27th Virginia, which numbered 418 men a month ago, now contained 150 staggering soldiers.[124]

Good health and high morale were not on Jackson's mind at the moment. He was as bone-tired as any soldier, but he could not rest. Two Union armies, each larger than his own force, were in pursuit by separate routes. The Confederates were falling back closer and closer to the vital supply station and railhead at Staunton. Jackson had to find ground of his own choosing to do battle with the enemy.

Lack of sleep and personal fatigue with Jackson were so overwhelming that members of his staff became concerned for his health. Long rest was out of the question. Hotchkiss noted that on the night of June 3–4, Jackson "was almost afloat" when rain flooded his tent. He spent the rain-soaked days riding back and forth along his lines to keep them moving.

A June 4 message from President Davis explained not only the urgency of the crisis but also the new importance of Jackson to Confederate dreams. "I return to you my congratulations for the brilliant campaign you have conducted against the enemy in the valley of Virginia. Were it practicable to send you reinforcements it should be done. . . . It is on your skill and daring that reliance is to be placed. The army under your command encourages us to hope for all which men can achieve."[125]

15

VICTORY IN THE VALLEY

RAIN PELTED THE WINDOWS of John Strayer's hotel in New Market on Wednesday, June 4, as Jackson pored over maps and considered options for the days ahead. Twice he summoned Hotchkiss to inquire about topographical details. Initially, the mapmaker was puzzled by the focal point of Jackson's interest: the village of Port Republic. In time, Hotchkiss would understand clearly the brilliance of Jackson's thinking.

At Harrisonburg, Fremont and Shields would reach the southern end of the Massanutten Mountain. The only major barrier thereafter to uniting against Jackson was the South Fork of the Shenandoah River. A bridge at Conrad's Store, east of Harrisonburg, would enable Shields to cross into the main avenue of the valley. Destroying that bridge would continue to keep Shields and Fremont separated.

Fifteen miles south of Conrad's Store was the cluster of homes known as Port Republic. There the North and South rivers came together to form the South Fork. There Jackson must stop. Beyond that point the stream was no longer a barrier in Jackson's rear. South of Port Republic, its headwaters were easily fordable.

The South River was the smaller of the two converging branches. It could be crossed at a number of points. The North River, on the other hand, was wide and deep enough to require bridging. The one span south of Conrad's Store was at Port Republic. There Jackson would be able to cross from one side to the other as threats dictated. Further, Brown's Gap lay to the southeast of Port Republic and afforded a good exit from the valley to both the Virginia Central Railroad and the piedmont region.

On the afternoon of the 4th, under leaden clouds but without rain, twelve of Ashby's men left New Market with orders to destroy the South Fork bridge at Conrad's Store. That would force Shields to do one of two things. He could backtrack to Luray, rebuild the bridge there, and cross the Massanutten at New Market to join Fremont; or Shields could continue advancing south along the South Fork, cross it at one of the lower fords, and then strike for the bridge at Port Republic.

Perhaps interpreting the hand of God in the heavy rains and flooded streams, Jackson had determined to make his stand at Port Republic. In addition to the other advantages, the place was close enough to the base of the Massanutten to enable Jackson to assail Shields in a narrow corridor if his division turned west. Should Shields maintain his southward advance, he would march straight into Jackson's army. From Port Republic, Jackson would also be on Fremont's flank should that general press on toward Staunton. In short, at Port Republic, Jackson would control the upper Shenandoah Valley.

The care of sick and wounded was always of primary concern to Jackson. He therefore dispatched his engineering officer, Lieutenant Keith Boswell, to Mount Crawford to see if a bridge there could be used to transport the infirm across the North Fork and on a straight route to Staunton. Boswell found the original structure gone and the river higher than it had been for twenty years. Yet the enterprising Boswell was not deterred. He, Captain C. R. Mason, and the pioneers collected lumber at Bridgewater, built two boats, and succeeded in ferrying most of the incapacitated men across the river.

Jackson's last directive on June 4 was a 10 P.M. order for Hotchkiss and a signalman to ascend Peaked Mountain, the southwest end of the Massanutten range. From its crest, they were to watch Shields's movements in the Luray Valley and report regularly to headquarters—wherever it might be.[1]

On the sixth day of the march from Halltown, Confederates tramped through Harrisonburg. Before noon, the army had turned east toward Port Republic. A member of the Stonewall Brigade noted, "The road is in miserable condition and the troops all break down."[2] When Harman's wagons became hopelessly mired in a one-lane morass, Jackson detached fifty men from each brigade to help extricate the vehicles. Progress continued to be snail-like.

By then, Harman was in a rage at the weather, at the wagons, and at Jackson. "The yankees are all around us," he said in a quick note to his brother, "and if we do not succeed in crossing the river some time to-night, I fear the worst for our trains. If I get through this safely Genl. Jackson must either relieve me or reduce the train. I will not be worked so any longer through this trip."[3]

Harman had reason to feel exhausted. Keeping the scores of wagons together and moving at the same time taxed not merely the army's quartermaster but the most stalwart members of his command. Captain Alexander M. Garber, one of Harman's chief assistants, stated that on this march "every nerve was strained. . . . it was march day and night, the horses were fed, hitched up, the teamsters changed their clothes on horseback or on the march, washing was unknown and done in hours snatched from sleep, and Major Harman lived almost all the time on his horse, Dixie, with a piece of dried beef and a cracker doing for a meal."[4]

By nightfall, rain was falling again. Jackson's force floundered to a halt in the mud. The head of the column was near Port Republic. Yet the line of men and wagons stretched more than eleven miles back to Harrisonburg, to which Fremont was moving rapidly on the Valley Turnpike. Jackson pitched his headquarters tent alongside the Port Republic road.

While rain drummed against the canvas that night, the general received two encouraging bits of news. Ashby's men had demolished the bridge at Conrad's Store; and from Hotchkiss came word that Shields's division was bivouacked in the mud two miles north of Conrad's Store. Jackson would reach Port Republic well in advance of the Federals. He would not have to face the combined forces of Shields and Fremont if he chose to give battle.

The weather notwithstanding, Jackson appeared "confident and determined" that evening. His troops did not share such optimism, however. The men were jaded almost beyond measure. From May 30 through June 5, they had slogged 104 miles in mud and without a day's rest. Fully 20 percent of Jackson's army was missing. Some were sick, and many were straggling, but the majority of those 3000 absentees had simply given out. Even the usually reticent Sidney Winder was losing his patience. "Jackson is insane on these rapid marches," asserted the commander of the Stonewall Brigade.[5]

Madness was not Jackson's problem. Physical and mental fatigue were corroding his aggressiveness. Disappointments also added to the weight of weariness. The attention he was receiving in the press bothered him. Southern newspapers were singing his praises while Northern dailies reminded readers of his feats. Jackson resented this. Glory for his achievements belonged to God. Jackson resolved to stop reading newspapers altogether.[6]

On June 6—a sunny Friday after days of incessant rain, Jackson moved the last few miles to Port Republic. Harman got his wagon trains to the safety of the east bank of the North River. The staff established Jackson's headquarters at "Madison Hall," the home of Dr. George W. Kemper. Not only was the two-story residence spacious and fashionable; it also overlooked the village and the two streams that made Port Republic strategically desirable. Major Harman felt better. "I believe we can whip both Shields and Fremont if our men are allowed to rest," he exclaimed. "I would not have given one cent for our train if the yankees had been vigilant, though now I think it is safe."[7]

Jackson was not so upbeat. Exhaustion and frustration thwarted his offensive spirit. At Kemper's, he received President Davis's June 4 message. Amid its congratulatory phrases was the statement that no reinforcements could be sent for the grand Northern offensive Jackson contemplated. With Davis's announcement, Jackson probably felt that the valley campaign was over. In the middle of a long letter to General Joseph Johnston that day, Jackson declared, "At present I do not see that I can do much more than rest my command and devote its time to drilling."[8]

Such a statement leads naturally to the conclusion that Jackson did not expect to fight again anytime soon. That hardly coincided with the military situation at the moment. It also creates the strong suspicion that exhaustion was occasionally sapping Jackson's mental prowess. Robert E. Lee was certainly uneasy when he read the communique in which Jackson anticipated no further action. The new commander of the Army of Northern Virginia urged that some reinforcements be sent to the valley. "We must aid a gallant man if we perish," Lee declared.[9]

As the day passed quietly, Jackson's old division moved into positions opposite Port Republic. Ewell's division drew up at Cross Keys, roughly midway between Harrisonburg and Port Republic. Ashby, with a rear guard of cavalry and infantry, remained on the eastern outskirts of Harrisonburg.

Sometime after 2 P.M., Federal cavalry rode into the town and turned left to follow Jackson's trail. The 1st New Jersey Cavalry, in the lead, galloped into a Confederate ambush in woods southeast of Harrisonburg. Twenty-three troopers, the colors, and the regimental colonel, Sir Percy Wyndham, were captured. Wyndham was a British soldier of fortune who had fought in the French navy and the Italian and Austrian armies before migrating to America for a taste of the Civil War. Through his friend, General George McClellan, Wyndham had secured command of a cavalry regiment.

The colonel was handsome, dashing, with luxuriant mustache and natty uniform. Convinced that the cowardice of his men was responsible for his capture, and bleeding from a slight wound in the head, he voiced loud disgust as he was taken to Jackson's headquarters.[10]

Around 9 P.M., Jackson and his prisoner were chatting quietly at the Kemper home when an officer entered the room and asked Jackson to step out into the hallway. There the general received the most shocking report of the entire valley campaign. After the initial cavalry engagement, more Union horsemen had set out from Harrisonburg. A half-mile from town, on Chestnut Hill, they attacked Ashby's command. The new brigadier called for infantry support. His horse fell dead, whereupon Ashby led a counterattack on foot with the 1st Maryland and 58th Virginia. "Charge, men! For God's sake, charge!" he shouted as he led a battle line uphill through thick woods. Success marked the Confederate effort, but in the fighting Ashby had been killed instantly by a bullet that passed through his right forearm and out his left breast.[11]

Jackson was stunned. Exactly a month earlier, on May 6, he had told Boteler that Ashby's poor discipline would make it a calamity if he were promoted. The War Department had promoted him anyway. Jackson had taken heart from Ashby's recent performance, but now the cavalry leader was dead. Old Jack had always accepted without hesitation the Christian tenet that the Lord giveth and the Lord taketh away. Sometimes that affirmation was painfully difficult to accept, and this was one of those moments. A staff member hustled Wyndham from Jackson's office. The general returned to the room alone, locked the door, and paced the floor as he wrestled with the news of Ashby's death.

The next morning Ashby's remains arrived in Port Republic and were placed in the front parlor of the Frank Kemper home in the center of the village. A brief funeral service followed. Jackson then entered the room alone. The thirty-three-year-old Ashby lay in a pine box; no mark of death was visible. According to Major Dabney, Jackson "remained for a time in silent communion with the dead, and then left him, with a solemn and elevated countenance."[12]

His grief over the passing of Ashby was deep and long lasting. Ten months later, when he completed his report of the campaign, he wrote in unusually laudatory terms: "An official report is not an appropriate place for more than a passing notice of the distinguished dead; but the close relationship which General Ashby bore to my command for most of the previous twelve months will justify me in saying that as a partizan officer I never knew his superior. His daring was proverbial. His powers of endurance incredible. His tone of character heroic, and his sagacity almost intuitive in divining the purposes of the enemy."[13]

Forced now to rely on bands of scouts to keep him informed of enemy movements, Jackson spent most of June 7 grappling with an extremely difficult terrain problem and weighing options if Shields and Fremont continued to converge on his position. His focal points were two rivers with the confusing names and unusual direction of flow. The North River came in from the west—the main avenue of the valley. It merged with the northward flowing South River just to the northeast of Port Republic. In fact, the village lay in the angle formed by the confluence of the two streams. Behind Port Republic was a high ridge along which a road meandered the sixteen miles to Staunton.

A more commanding line of bluffs looked down on Port Republic from the south bank (or village side) of the North River. From there, all the ground east and southeast rolled away in gentle meadows and cultivated fields that extended almost two miles to the woods at the base of the Blue Ridge Mountains. Artillery from that high ground could sweep the whole area with unobstructed fire.

Of equal importance too were the river crossings. A long covered wooden bridge spanned the North River at the northern end of the village's main street. No bridges existed over the South River in that area. However, at either end of the village and no more than a half-mile apart were two fords. High, swift water at the time limited their accessibility and use. The road over the lower or northernmost crossing forked east of Port Republic. One lane led to Swift Run Gap, the other to Brown's Gap.

While Jackson was in a good defensive position, it was also a situation that could easily be turned against him. Holding back Fremont might permit Shields to move up the South River and get to that dominating ridge hugging the North River. Should Shields reach Port Republic, Jackson was in a dilemma. If he crossed the South River to confront Shields, Fremont might then be able to seize the high ground and use his artillery to sweep Jackson's position. Further, if Jackson moved to the east side to contest Shields, he would have to burn the North River bridge. That would prevent him from recrossing to face Fremont. The possibility always existed as well that while Jackson was battling one force, the other would continue to Staunton. Jackson's hope, therefore, was to draw Fremont into battle north of Port Republic. Fremont was closer to the village on June 7 than was Shields.

The resultant troop dispositions reflected Jackson's thinking in the face of all the possibilities. Ewell with three brigades of 5000 men prepared a defensive position at Cross Keys. Jackson put his division, Edward Johnson's regiments, and sufficient artillery on the commanding ridge north of Port Republic. Taylor's brigade of Ewell's division would join Jackson the next morning and give him about 8000 soldiers. Confederate cavalry were ranging to the west, north, and south of Port Republic.

In the afternoon of June 7, Jackson rode over to Cross Keys with the hope that Fremont might take some bait and attack. Yet only a single Union brigade appeared in reconnaissance. It quickly retired after an exchange of gunfire. The general returned to Port Republic at sundown. His manner was curt, his orders issued like rifle shots. General Sidney Winder, not privy to Jackson's inner feelings, was reaching the end of his patience with Old Jack's aloofness. "Growing disgusted with Jackson," Winder noted in his diary. At the same moment, Lieutenant Sandie Pendleton of the staff was writing home, "Gen. Jackson is completely broke down."[14]

Whether Jackson assumed that nothing would happen at Port Republic until he made it happen, or whether growing lassitude clouded his judgment on small but vital points, the general got sloppy that evening with final details over his position. Equally strange, not one of his officers—field or staff—recognized any of the several dangers he created or overlooked.

For example, all of Jackson's men were on the north side of the North River.

Headquarters was a half-mile away on the south bank. At the lower and more important of the two fords on the South River, Jackson placed a guard that he called "a small cavalry force." In fact, it was an undersized company led by Captain Emanuel Sipe. At the upper ford, he assigned Captain Samuel J. C. Moore and a dozen infantrymen from the 2d Virginia. No troops protected headquarters at the Kemper home.

In perhaps the most glaring fault of all, Jackson had permitted Harman's huge wagon train to park on the Staunton road and in the adjacent fields behind headquarters. The ammunition, food, and other needed supplies for the army stood on high ground, plainly visible and without sentries. The whole setup at Port Republic was a prescription for disaster if any Federals acted boldly. It also demonstrated all too quickly how much Turner Ashby was missed when it came to outpost functions such as reconnaissance and screening, for no one saw a Union raiding party bearing down rapidly on Port Republic.[15]

That movement had begun on June 2, when Shields dispatched a strike force to cut off Jackson's presumed retreat. The Union general believed that Jackson would continue in the valley proper and then turn left at Harrisonburg and head for Swift Run Gap or Brown's Gap. To block the movement, Shields organized a rather strange flying column.

In command of the attackers was thirty-year-old Colonel Samuel S. Carroll. His force included 150 troopers from the 1st Virginia (U.S.) Cavalry, four guns of Battery L of the 1st Ohio Artillery, and a picked contingent of infantrymen. The cannon were without caissons; the infantry carried nothing but essential equipment. Carroll's target was the South Fork bridge at Conrad's Store. "Everything depends on speed," Shields told Carroll; and to make the mission personally enticing, he added: "You will earn your star if you do all this."[16]

The Ohio colonel with muttonchop whiskers pushed southward with enthusiasm and speed. He reached the White House and Columbia bridges at Luray, only to discover them burned. He continued on to Conrad's Store where, on June 4, Carroll found that span also destroyed. While contemplating his next move, he learned of the bridge at Port Republic. Carroll apparently decided on his own to strike for that village. Since Jackson was not there at the time, the Union commander anticipated no opposition.

Shortly after midnight, a Confederate patrol spotted the vanguard of Shields's army six miles northeast of Port Republic. Jackson dispatched two companies of cavalry to investigate its strength and numbers. The general then went to bed for some desperately needed sleep.

Sunday, June 8, dawned bright, warm, and quiet. Jackson had been unable to observe the Sabbath for the past three weeks. Perhaps this day would remain quiet.

Major Dabney called on Jackson early that morning. "I suppose, General, divine service is out of the question today," he said. "Oh, by no means," Jackson replied. "I hope you will preach in the Stonewall Brigade, and I shall attend myself—that is, if we are not disturbed by the enemy."[17]

At that moment, Captain Emanuel Sipe rode into the front yard of the Kemper home. He announced almost breathlessly that twenty Federal troopers had been spotted near the North River bridge, and a mounted regiment had been seen at the Lewiston mansion two miles away on the Conrad's Store road. Jackson alerted Ewell and ordered him not to initiate an engagement at Cross Keys until the Port Republic situation was resolved.

It was about 9 A.M. Jackson and the staff were waiting in the yard for their mounts when two cannon shots broke the silence. As the reverberations faded, cavalryman Henry D. Kerfoot galloped up in obvious excitement. Federal troopers and artillery had crossed the lower ford of the South River! he shouted. They were already inside Port Republic!

An enemy force of some size stood squarely between Jackson and his army. It threatened the vital bridge over the North River, and it put the Confederate wagon train in imminent jeopardy. "Go back and fight them," were the general's only words to Kerfoot.

Seconds later, gunfire erupted in the direction of the village. The staff members with Jackson scattered. Hotchkiss instinctively headed for the wagons to spur the teamsters into action. Another aide rushed into the home to alert Dabney and two late sleepers, Colonel Crutchfield and Lieutenant Edward Willis.

Oblivious to personal safety, Jackson started downhill toward the action in long and awkward strides. Members of the staff followed also on foot. Confederate cavalry could be seen racing in every direction except to the point of danger. It was "disgraceful disorder," Jackson sneered. Jim Lewis rushed up with Jackson's horse while aides hastily scurried for their mounts. The general quickly climbed on Little Sorrel and galloped toward the North River bridge.[18]

Accompanied by Pendleton, Boswell, Harman, William L. Jackson, and Douglas, Jackson raced down the main street as bullets whistled close by. That Jackson was wearing his old blue VMI officer's coat may have kept Federals from delivering even heavier volleys. The little band of riders dashed over the North River bridge and up the hill to the safety of the Confederate lines. Miraculously, no one had been hit. It was Jackson's narrowest escape in the Civil War.[19]

Even though Jackson did not learn until later what occurred around the Kemper house, the events there determined the outcome of the morning action.

Federal cavalry started southward through the village following the passage of Jackson and his staff. Crutchfield and Willis, tardy in departing headquarters, were captured.[20] At the upper ford of the South River, Captain Moore and his twelve-man picket left their post at the first sound of musketry and raced to the Kemper home. They found the place deserted.

Worse, from the high ground, Moore could look north and see Union cavalry bearing down on him. To the south, Jackson's loaded wagon trains gleamed in the sun with their new white canvas tops. A dozen Confederates from the 2d Virginia seemed to be all that stood between the enemy and the wagons.

When the main street of Port Republic reached the Kemper property, it turned ninety degrees to the right (west). Moore posted his men behind a white picket fence next to the road. The large party of Union cavalry reached the Kemper estate and sped to the right toward the Staunton road and the wagon trains.

Suddenly, at a distance of 100 yards, Moore's little band delivered a volley of musketry. The mounted column staggered, at which point the handful of Confederates charged down the hill, yelling and firing as they ran. Confused Union riders dashed back into the village.

Meanwhile, behind the Kemper home and close to the wagons, Captain James M. Carrington's Charlottesville Artillery lounged in a field. The battery had reported for duty only two weeks earlier. Crutchfield had found the six-gun unit so poorly equipped that he had detailed it to the rear to obtain supplies, guard the wagon train, and stay out of the way. The gunners were mostly teenagers. Not one had ever fired a shell in anger. Seeing Jackson's cavalry galloping pell-mell had unnerved the youths; now the sound of gunfire nearby and the sight of Union cavalry moving toward them sent a number of the untested artillerists bolting to the rear.

Federal cavalry regrouped in the village and started forward again. Moore retired with his men back to their original position behind the Kemper fence. There he found one gun of Carrington's battery unlimbering. Federal skirmishers were advancing steadily now, enemy soldiers darting from one bit of cover to another.

Excited and inexperienced, the Charlottesville gunners could not find a canister shell and they forgot the fence immediately in their front. The youths rammed in a charge of black powder, slammed a round solid shell in front of the charge, and stood aside. A gunner jerked the lanyard and the cannon fired. The shell demolished the fence and sailed past the village, but wooden splinters went cartwheeling and whirring toward the Federals, who halted in sheer astonishment.[21]

When the Union attack began, Major Dabney had been lying in bed working on a sermon he planned to deliver that day as Jackson had suggested. The noise sent him dashing toward the wagons. On his way, Dabney collected two more of Carrington's guns and ordered everyone to the front of the Kemper estate. Moore's detachment continued a steady fire of musketry while the Charlottesville guns sent shells into the streets of the village. The combined action stopped the Federal drive south.[22]

Jackson knew nothing of these events at the time. He was on the other side of the North River trying to restore order—and, for several minutes, having difficulty doing so. From his spot on top of the commanding hill, Jackson knew that whatever the strength of the Federals, they could trap him on the same side of the river occupied by Fremont's army.

Captain William T. Poague of the Rockbridge Artillery had known his commander since prewar days in Lexington. "I never saw Jackson as much stirred up at any other time," Poague stated. "He had just made a narrow escape from capture personally and he did not know what force Shields was pushing in his rear. His first and only words, as he reached our battery, which was the nearest force to the bridge, were: 'Have the guns hitched up! Have the guns hitched up!'"[23]

Artillery professor Jackson watched the Rockbridge Artillery move its guns toward the crest of the hill. Then, while he hastened to fetch the Stonewall Brigade, one of his couriers rode off to accelerate the march of Taylor's Louisianians to the Port Republic area.[24]

Those dispositions made, Jackson rode to the edge of the hill overlooking the river and the village. He was an easy target silhouetted against the sky, a danger that never entered his mind. A hundred yards or so in front of him, a blueclad crew was unlimbering a cannon on the far side of the North River bridge. When the first piece of Poague's battery arrived, Jackson placed it in position. "Fire on that gun!" Jackson shouted as he pointed toward the bridge below. Gunners protested: they were Confederates, not Yankees. Poague rode up and added his voice of dissent. He was convinced that the crew at the bridge was part of the Charlottesville Artillery, which had left for war in blue uniforms. "Fire on that gun!" Jackson shouted again. Still the Rockbridge artillerists hesitated.

The general himself began to have qualms of doubt about the artillery piece. He rode forward and a little to the left until he was looking directly at the bridge. He yelled to the gun crew on the other side of the structure: "Bring that gun up here!" Getting no response, Jackson rose in his stirrups and called out again: "Bring that gun up here, I say!" An answer came with a shot from the cannon that buried in the side of the hill just below Jackson. The general turned to Poague impatiently. "Let them have it," he said sternly. Rockbridge gunners needed no further convincing. Their first shot tore into the Ohio section, whose responding fire sailed harmlessly overhead. Within minutes, Poague's guns were laying a blanket of fire around the south end of the bridge.[25]

Jackson then rode back to align infantry for a stand along the river. His men, already under arms, felt that Jackson would rather fight on the Lord's day than at any other time; and it was Sunday. The general had not ridden far when he encountered Colonel Sam Fulkerson and his 37th Virginia double-quicking toward the bluff. The southwest Virginians had been on parade that morning when the action began. They had moved toward the sound of fire from instinct rather than orders. Jackson was so pleased to see the judge and his regiment that he waved his cap above his head and exclaimed, "Charge right through, Colonel, charge right through!"[26]

That burst of emotion was momentary. William B. Taliaferro came onto the field shortly with the other two regiments of his brigade. He noted: "I met Gen. Jackson, minus his hat and part of his Staff, spurring up the road. He was not excited—he never was."[27]

Now Confederate artillery fire from the heights north of the river and the high ground of the Kemper estate south of the stream were slamming into the Union raiders. Fulkerson took his regiment in a straight-in assault with fixed bayonets.[28] The two Union cannon ripped away the front rows of Confederates, but the remainder rushed through the gunsmoke, made their way over the sagging bridge, and seized the two cannon. The Virginians quickly swung the guns around and opened fire on the Federals.

Surgeon Harvey Black of the 4th Virginia watched from the hilltop. "The cavalry that had made a dash upon Port Republic left in utter confusion, leaving everything behind, evidently glad enough to escape with a sound body—some did not, riderless horses scampered across the field. When the enemy broke, our boys sent a most glorious shout."[29]

Crutchfield, Willis, and other captured officers made their escape during the confusion. Cheers to the south told the main Confederate body that Moore and Carrington had held their ground. The wagon trains were safe. As Federals scurried across the river bottom, Jackson dropped the reins of his horse. With raised hands, he looked upward, closed his eyes, and engaged in silent prayer for an unusually long period.[30]

Echoes from the last guns were drifting over the countryside when up the road from the northeast appeared a long line of Union infantry. It was the support that Federal Colonel Carroll had expected to back up his attack. Jackson calmly oversaw the placement of ten guns to meet the new threat. No Union artillery protected the infantry line.

Hence, wrote Robert Barton of the Rockbridge Artillery, Jackson's guns "had their own way and we did tremendous execution. So fast was our firing that we had to cool our guns by pouring water down them from canteens. Gen. Jackson sat like a Statue immediately by the gun I was assisting to work, and he seemed quite to enjoy the firing." Federals soon fell back three miles to safety.[31]

No sooner had the area grown quiet again than the sound of cannon fire could be heard to the northwest. Jackson knew at once what was happening: Ewell and Fremont were locked in battle at Cross Keys. By later standards of the war, it was not much of a contest. Yet the fighting was serious enough to occupy Jackson's attention. Ewell had bivouacked the previous night some two miles southeast of the Cross Keys hamlet. He placed the 15th Alabama a mile in advance at Union Church. At 10 A.M. on June 8, Fremont took the offensive—gingerly so because he thought that he was facing Jackson's entire army.[32] Federal skirmishers eased forward toward the enemy. They, like their general, were unaware that they outnumbered their opponents by two-to-one odds.

Ewell had selected a good defensive position. His 4500 infantry were spread along a ridge, with Steuart's brigade on the left, Arnold Elzey's in the center, and Isaac Trimble's on the right. Timber protected each flank.

In front of the line was a small branch. Open ground lay beyond. A road passed through the center of the Southern line. Ewell considered the middle to be the weak point, so he posted four batteries there to command the road. No Confederate cavalry were at Cross Keys; as events showed, none were needed.

By 10:30, a protracted but unproductive artillery duel was underway. Signs became evident that Fremont intended to assail Ewell's right, commanded by an officer Jackson had met but did not know. Brigadier General Isaac R. Trimble was a Culpeper County, Virginia, native who had graduated from West Point two years before Jackson was born. Later he had become a successful Baltimore railroad executive. Trimble was now sixty years old, white-haired, fussy and feisty. He was a field commander who genuinely loved to fight.

That is why he watched approaching Union infantry with relish. His men were in good position behind a bushy fence and looking into a sloping wheatfield. Trimble told his brigade of Alabama, Georgia, Mississippi, and North Carolina soldiers not to fire until the Yankees came within fifty yards.

Federals marched up the incline as if on parade. At Trimble's signal, a sheet of flame erupted from the fence line. The Federal lines reeled; then another volley ripped through the ranks. Bluecoats stumbled and ran back to the cover of woods.

Fighting in Trimble's front and the artillery duel soon dwindled to occasional exchanges. Trimble's appetite for battle remained unsatisfied. When he spotted a Union battery unlimbering a half-mile away, the old man took it upon himself to launch a counteroffensive. Federal gunners took one look at a full Confederate brigade coming toward them and fled. Trimble did not halt his regiments until he had occupied ground a full mile in advance of his original position.

He then begged Ewell for reinforcements to rout Fremont completely. Ewell refused, and wisely so. He was unsure of Jackson's status at Port Republic; two of his brigade commanders, Arnold Elzey and "Maryland" Steuart, had been wounded.[33] Trimble persisted in his desire to continue driving forward. Finally, he asked permission to appeal directly to Jackson. Ewell was relieved to approve the request and remove the brigadier from sight for awhile.

Self-confident and assertive, Trimble rode to Port Republic. Jackson, listening to the general, was impressed. Men of audacity always gained his admiration. Yet in this instance an army chain of command had to be observed. "Consult General Ewell and be guided by him," Jackson told Trimble.[34]

Back to Cross Keys the subordinate rode for another appeal to Ewell. The division commander shook his head. "You have done well enough for one day, and even a partial reverse would interfere with General Jackson's plans for the next day."[35] Trimble continued to argue, but to no avail.

"Isaac R. Trimble was a West Pointer and a good soldier," in the opinion of Jed Hotchkiss,

but neither he nor his superior commander, Ewell, understood Jackson at the time; and for that matter very few of them did. Many of the West Pointers were older than Jackson and had continued in the regular service, and so thought they were entitled to more consideration than he gave to them; especially were they out of humor with him because he did not communicate to them his plans or counsel with them; and this must always be taken into account in reading the reports of any of the old West Pointers.[36]

The forces of Ewell and Fremont sparred for the remainder of that Sunday. By nightfall, Confederates held the ground from which Fremont had launched his probe. Ewell had demonstrated first-rate mettle in independent battle operations. His 300 losses were fewer than half those suffered by the enemy.[37]

Jackson's activities on June 8 following the action at Port Republic are difficult to catalogue. After the gunfire ceased, he stationed Taliaferro's brigade inside the village, posted the Stonewall Brigade on the ridge where it could observe an enemy approach, and put the remainder of his units in reserve to assist Ewell if necessary.

Sometime that morning he rode to Winder's position. For several hours, despite the sound of battle at Cross Keys, Jackson remained with the Stonewall Brigade. He expected Shields to attack momentarily in order to take advantage of Jackson's divided forces. Such concern over possible battle led Jackson to dismiss out of hand a written request from Winder for a transfer from Jackson's command.[38]

The behavior of Jackson in the forenoon or early afternoon struck some observers as odd. While engaged in military conversation with a group of officers, Jackson commented to a Winder aide how much he liked having Marylanders in his command. A short time later, Jackson suddenly turned to Dabney. "Major," he said, "wouldn't it be a blessed thing if God would give us a glorious victory today?" The officer who overheard the remark added, "I saw his face with an expression like that of a child hoping to receive some favor."[39]

Dabney chronicled a long and personal conversation he claimed to have had with Jackson as they rode to a "religious service" that hardly would have been held that day. It is more probable that Jackson went to Cross Keys during the afternoon to confer with Ewell. Dabney reported Jackson going to see Ewell "shortly after midday, when the battle was at its height."[40]

Surgeon Black of the 4th Virginia saw the general ride "rapidly down the road leading to Harrisonburg" (although Black put Jackson's departure at the unlikely moment when the artillery was blasting Union infantry approaching Port Republic). Lieutenant James Wood of the 37th Virginia also recalled Jackson galloping off in the direction of Ewell's position.

Adding credence to Jackson being at Cross Keys is an order he gave in the afternoon to Sandie Pendleton of his staff. "Write a note to General Ewell. Say that the enemy are defeated at all points, and to press them with cavalry, and, if necessary, with artillery and Wheat's Battalion."[41]

Perhaps Jackson learned these details from Trimble when the brigadier made his personal appeal. It is more likely that Jackson gained the information from a personal inspection of Ewell's position.

Jackson spent most of the day at Port Republic because he expected Shields to renew his attack. The general double checked artillery positions on the bluff commanding the bridge and village. When someone pointed to the possible danger of Shields advancing while Ewell was still engaged with Fremont, Jackson pointed to the cannon staring over the countryside and replied vigorously: "No, sir, no! He cannot do it! I should tear him to pieces!"[42]

In late afternoon, the general dismounted atop the Port Republic ridge. He stood alone and silent. The sharp angle of the kepi concealed most of his face as he stared at the ground. He was stationary, but thoughts tumbled through his mind. A battle plan was evolving.

Darkness came. Near midnight, the moon would rise in a chilly sky. Staff members awaited orders for the army to slip away in the darkness. Those orders never came. Instead, Jackson directed Harman to bring the wagons over the river so the men could have rations. Campfires soon dotted the landscape and told the Federals precisely where Jackson's army was located.

Douglas and other aides were astonished by Jackson's lack of anxiety. In fact, the general was abandoning secrecy for the moment. "As no movement was made by Gen. Shields to resume the action that day," Jackson reported later, "I determined to take the initiative & attack him the following morning."[43]

When asked months later why he chose to do battle with Shields instead of the seemingly more aggressive Fremont, Jackson replied that several reasons were involved. "First I was nearer to [Shields], second he had the [smaller] army, then I was nearer my base of supplies, had a good way of retreat if beaten—and Fremont had a good way to retreat if I had beaten him, while I knew Shields had a bad road to go over."[44]

Jackson's plan from the beginning was to divide and conquer. Fremont had been checked at Cross Keys and was unlikely to attack again the next day. Troops under Jackson would therefore cross the North River and assail Shields, who was advancing up a narrow, muddy lane between the South Fork River and the foothills of the Blue Ridge. Such an approach would restrict Federal maneuvers and require a smaller battle front from the Confederates.

If Jackson should defeat Shields quickly, he would be free to recross the river and assist Ewell in finishing off Fremont. In the event that things did not go well with Jackson, Ewell's division would reinforce him and burn the North River bridge behind it. That would block Fremont from a similar merger with Shields.

Intense activity in the Confederate camps and a series of conferences at Jackson's headquarters marked the late hours of June 8. Jackson never liked written communiques to subordinates. He insisted instead on meeting personally with a general, thereby ensuring through eye-to-eye contact that the officer understood exactly what was expected of him.

It was after 10 P.M. when Jackson summoned Ewell and cavalryman Thomas T. Munford to headquarters. The division commander brought Jackson up to date on Fremont's location and strength. Then Jackson outlined the next day's strategy.

Ewell was to obtain food and ammunition from his wagons that night and then send the train toward Brown's Gap via Port Republic. Munford was to take his 2d Virginia Cavalry and ensure that the road to Brown's Gap remained open at all costs. At daylight, the general continued, Ewell would start with most of his units to join Jackson. Trimble was anxious to tangle with Fremont, so his reinforced brigade would remain at Cross Keys and bluff the Federals as long as possible. Taliaferro—still not on Jackson's preferred list of brigadiers—could hold Port Republic and its heights. Jackson himself would take the four remaining brigades under his command and attack Shields.

This strategy was both daring and dangerous. Jackson's army lay to the north and west of Port Republic, Shields's army to the north and east. To attack Shields, Jackson had first to cross the North River bridge, which had been heavily damaged in the morning fight, and then ford the South River. Both streams were swollen and running fast. It would be a remarkable feat for the Confederates just to get into position for battle.

Around 11 P.M., Ewell and Munford left headquarters. As the two officers prepared to mount their horses, Ewell glanced at his cavalry chief. "Look here, Munford," he said in that familiar high-pitched voice, "do you remember my conversation with you at Conrad's Store when I called this old man an old woman? Well, I take it all back! I will never prejudge another man. Old Jackson's no fool." Ewell added: "He has a method in his madness."[45]

Taliaferro "remembered" a conference with Jackson around midnight. His details are so faulty that the truthfulness of the whole incident is suspect. According to the brigadier, he found Jackson pacing the floor in his small bedroom. Jackson greeted Taliaferro warmly (which would have been hypocritical on the part of the commander) and instructed him to attack with his brigade at early dawn (which was a direct contradiction of Jackson's own battle plan).

The Taliaferro story grows more improbable. Jackson then stated that he wanted to

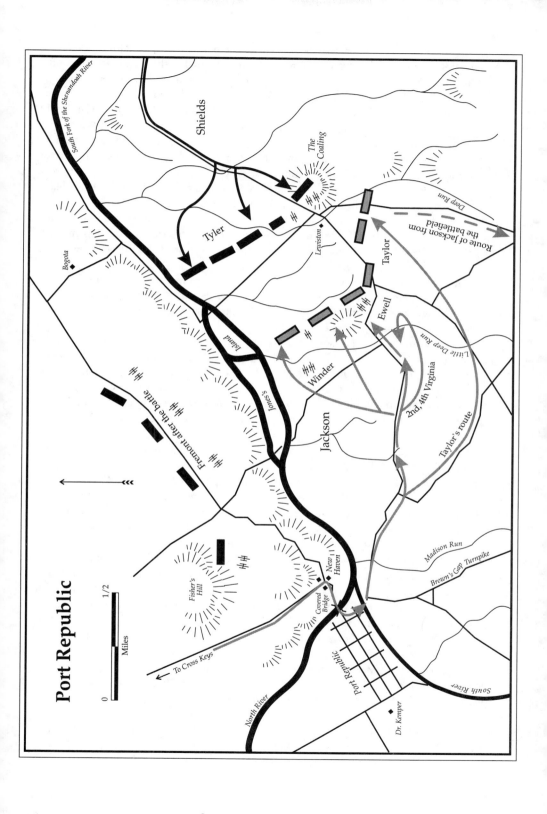

Port Republic

take a stroll in the Kemper garden adjacent to the home. The general told Taliaferro to lie down on the bed and get some rest until he returned. Taliaferro wrote solemnly: "His object in seeking the seclusion of the garden was to engage in prayer, unseen by any eye." Had Taliaferro been better informed, he would have realized that too many preparations were on Jackson's mind for the general to break off and take a midnight stroll in a garden.[46]

It is shocking rather than surprising that Jackson waited until so late an hour to give attention to how his attacking force of four brigades was to cross the South River some five hours later. Yet Major Dabney was specific in recalling the hour. The work party was to toil by moonlight. Jackson directed Captain C. R. Mason and his black pioneers to construct a bridge over the breast-high South River.

The resultant span consisted of wagons placed in the stream and planks laid across the tops of the beds to allow several men walking abreast to cross. Jackson spent most of the night watching the construction and offering suggestions to the workmen. The shaky structure was completed by 5 A.M.[47]

During the bridge building, Jackson had some lingering concern about the rear-guard action planned at Cross Keys. At 2 A.M., he sent for Colonel John M. Patton. The VMI graduate commanded the 21st Virginia, part of Trimble's rear guard that would be entrusted with holding off Fremont.

When Patton entered Jackson's room, the general promptly started a lecture on the colonel's role the next day. The withdrawal toward Port Republic must be deliberate and well protected, Jackson emphasized. "I wish you to throw out all your men, if necessary, as skirmishers, and to make a great show, so as to cause the enemy to think the whole army are behind you. Hold your position as well as you can, then fall back when obliged. Take a new position, hold it in the same way, and I will be back to join you in the morning."[48]

Patton was startled by Jackson's comment that he would be heading toward Cross Keys before noon. The colonel remarked that his troops were few in number and the country between Cross Keys and Port Republic open for a variety of Federal movements. How long should I be expected to hold the enemy in check? Patton asked. "By the blessing of Providence," Jackson answered, "I hope to be back by ten o'clock."[49]

The general then went to his room. Too tired to think further, with little time left before dawn, Jackson stretched out on the bed in full uniform without even removing his sword. At once he descended into a deep doze of an hour's duration.

Although friend and enemy alike believed that Jackson rarely slept, he actually required as much sleep as any normal person. He was a man of naps—one who slept when others talked, one who could get maximum rest from minimum opportunity. Now he was in desperate need of a full night's rest. Yet little of night remained. The sun was just behind the horizon. A day of battle was imminent. The Lord's will must be done.[50]

Shortly after 3 A.M. on a foggy June 9, Jackson was up and issuing orders.[51] His body ached from weariness; he wished that he was more clear-headed. Yet much work had to be done before the sun climbed into view. Supply wagons had yet to catch up with many brigades. Ewell's train was still crawling through Port Republic.

As usual, secrecy shrouded Jackson's intentions. A courier awakened Sidney Winder at 3:45 with instructions to bring the Stonewall Brigade to Port Republic within an hour. Winder's Virginia regiments were in the village and at the bank of South River on time. What was he to do next? the perplexed and angry brigadier wondered. He was nearing the end of his patience with Jackson's callous and uncommunicative leadership.

At the river, the first of two major early-morning snags occurred. The improvised bridge proved less than sturdy from the outset. Army wagons placed as crude pontoons in the swollen stream were of different heights. A two-foot step quickly developed halfway across the river. The plank boarding being used as footway slanted up as well as down; at some junctures, gaps of two feet or more added to the instability. With the South River over two feet above normal and flowing rapidly, the usually serviceable wagon-type bridge quickly began coming apart. Soldiers were forced to cross in single file. Some of the men lost their footing and toppled into the water. The bridge soon became so rickety that half of Jackson's strike force had to wade the river. Thick fog added to the confusion. Jackson's hope for a prompt march to meet the enemy vanished with the time it took the soldiers to reach the east bank.[52]

Sunlight burned away the haze as Jackson led a comparatively small column northeastward from the wagon-bridge. Major Dabney remained at the bridge to superintend—as best he could—the passage of the larger portion of Jackson's army. Whatever orders Jackson had issued were lost in the slow collapse of the makeshift span.

For an hour, the advance was slow and silent. Winder's skirmishers fanned out and moved forward cautiously. Jackson was in front, wrapped in frustration and lost in thought. It was near 7 A.M. and the men had marched a mile and a half when a cavalryman rode up with word that Federal pickets were just ahead. Winder, riding with Jackson, looked to the commander for instructions.

Jackson reined his horse and studied the terrain. It was not an ideal place for an attacker. Confederates faced to the northeast. On the left was the South Fork of the Shenandoah. A mile or so of open ground, mostly wheatfield, stood in the center. From the right a beautiful spur laden with mountain laurel jutted westward from the Blue Ridge Mountains. This shoulder rose some fifty feet above the river bottom land and commanded the plain. The crest of the height was a "coaling," a flat open expanse used for the production of charcoal. Federal cannon were there and beginning to send shells a mile across the plain toward the Confederates.

From the coaling across the dew-covered field to the river meandered a spongy branch. Parallel to its northern bank was a worm fence. Union infantry waited behind it. Little room existed for maneuver in the narrow valley.

Now came the second breakdown of the day for Jackson. Impatient from fatigue, he was in no mood for further delays. To wait until all five brigades he planned to use in the attack were up and in position would not only nullify what remained of surprise; it would as well negate results obtainable from an early assault. If Jackson were going to be finished with Shields in time to attack Fremont in midmorning at Cross Keys, the first stage had to be executed immediately. The tested Stonewall Brigade was at hand, along with the dependable valley batteries of Poague and Carpenter. God would take care of everything else. Jackson turned to Winder. Drive in the pickets and attack the enemy, he told the brigadier. Other brigades would give support as they arrived.

Jackson had done an inadequate job of reconnaissance. He did not have a sufficient striking force to face two Union brigades numbering 3000 men and having sixteen pieces of artillery.[53] The Federal field commander was General Erastus B. Tyler, a bearded Ohioan and former fur trader who had shown promise in the early stages of the war. Tyler placed his center on the Port Republic road and his right stretching to—and anchored on—the South Fork. Six guns on top of the coaling made the Union left the strongest point of Tyler's line. Against this line Jackson committed regiments piecemeal.

The 2d Virginia, 4th Virginia, and Carpenter's battery—a force comprising no more than 500 men—moved to the wooded base of the Blue Ridge with the hope of gaining control of the coaling. In the meantime, Poague's Rockbridge Artillery anchored Jackson's center and occupied the attention of the Federal guns. Winder deployed the remainder of the Stonewall Brigade for an assault across the open ground between the river and the road.

A Union soldier who was more dramatic than accurate in his writing described the opening of the battle: "Jackson hoped that a grand dash at the Federal center would break it. The ground from mountain to river was then a wheat-field, with nothing to obstruct a charge. The great Confederate fighter picked out five regiments of his best troops and hurled them against that wheat-field with a shock which made the earth tremble. As sudden as a thunder-peal, artillery boomed, musketry crashed and ten thousand men shouted and cheered. Over the rolling ground—over a barren strip—into the waving wheat marched the . . . men in gray with ranks unbroken. A double line of battle waited their coming with never a tremor. Then sheets of flame leaped over the wheat."[54]

Winder tried desperately to succeed. Two of Poague's Parrott guns drove Tyler's pickets to cover. Carpenter's battery, unable to ascend the steep side of the coaling, returned and joined Poague in the middle of the line. Suddenly, the Union guns at the coaling replied. This fire tore gaps in the ranks of the Stonewall Brigade as an unequal contest developed. Southern cannon might have done good work, except that most of the long-range pieces ran out of ammunition. While Colonel Crutchfield scoured the rear for shells, Confederate gunners could only watch helplessly as Federal guns (in the words of one of Jackson's officers) "swept the plain like the hot lava from an erupting volcano."[55]

From his position behind the center of the line, Jackson's trained artillery eye told him that the enemy cannon on the elevated position would likely blow his assault to pieces. Those guns had to be silenced.

The situation quickly grew worse. Canister ripped through the ranks of the 2d and 4th Virginia. Confederates staggered backward from the base of the spur. The 5th and 27th Virginia, advancing alone across the wheatfield, were brought to a halt by concentrated gunfire. Winder's fifth regiment, the 33d Virginia, had been on picket duty the previous night and was still trying to free itself from a horrendous traffic jam in the rear and get to the battlefield. By then the wagon-bridge at Port Republic had collapsed, artillery and cavalry were pushing through tangled knots of infantry, and the whole mass was stumbling in the general direction of the field of battle.

As Winder looked for the 33d Virginia, Jackson searched for Richard Taylor and his brigade. The general was now aware that his original plan of beating Shields swiftly and turning on Fremont before noon was unworkable. Jackson would be fortunate to beat Shields, unless something changed for the better.

Now a flurry of new activity erupted near where Jackson sat on his horse. To try to equalize the contest, the general ordered Taliaferro's brigade to the front. Crutchfield dashed to the rear to bring up Taylor's Louisianians. As Union fire continued to rake Winder's thin lines, Jackson sent a courier—and soon another—to Trimble. Forget the delaying action at Cross Keys. Come quickly to Port Republic, and burn the North River bridge behind you.

Dick Taylor's men had bivouacked the night before a little east of Port Republic. They came double-timing onto the field with battle raging. Taylor wrote of galloping up to Jackson, who raised his hand and shouted gleefully: "Delightful excitement!" Such language, totally out of character with Jackson, is another fabrication from the Taylor memoirs. An Alabama officer also provided a three-way conversation that allegedly took place among Jackson, Taylor, and the Louisianians.

In truth, Major Hotchkiss attested, Taylor did not even meet Jackson on the Port Republic battlefield. When Jackson saw Taylor's brigade approaching, he turned to Hotchkiss, swept his hand toward the coaling to the east, and shouted firmly: "Take General Taylor around and take that battery!" Hotchkiss met Taylor several hundred yards distant from Jackson and led the Louisianians toward the high ground.[56]

Jackson was oblivious to heavy musket fire as he rode forward for a closer look at the situation in his center. He discerned at once that Tyler was preparing to counter-attack. If the Federals did so before Taylor got to the coaling, Jackson's steadily dwindling line would collapse.

Before the general could determine his contingencies, Sidney Winder took the initiative. The Marylander ordered his battered lines forward—a movement that momentarily knocked the enemy off guard. Jackson observed proudly that Winder "advanced with great boldness for some distance." Confederates fought their way almost to the fence that shielded the enemy. There they "encountered such a heavy fire of arty. & small arms as greatly to disorganize [Winder's] command which fell back in disorder. The enemy advanced across the field & by a heavy musketry fire forced back our Infantry supports, in consequence of which our guns had to retire. The enemy's advance was checked by a spirited attack upon their flank by the 58th & 44th Va. regts. led by Col. [W. C.] Scott, although his command was afterwards driven back to the woods with severe loss." Although those two Virginia units (part of Colonel John Patton's brigade) had not eaten for twenty-four hours, they dashed onto the field following a rapid march from Cross Keys.[57]

Winder by then needed both men and ammunition. His line was disintegrating, and the infantry were shooting away their last cartridges. For Jackson, the specter of Kernstown loomed again. Sidney Winder noted in his diary in his usually cryptic style: "The musketry was tremendous. Loss great. My horse was shot three times. Obliged to dismount. Thanks to our Heavenly Father I escaped unhurt."[58]

The only direction to which Jackson could look for help was toward Ewell's division. It was on the way to Port Republic but in disjointed sections. For Jackson, the battle was on the verge of being lost.[59]

At this point in the battle, Captain John B. Brockenbrough and his Baltimore Artillery from Ewell's division rumbled onto the field. Brockenbrough ordered Private Joshua Davis of the battery to find Jackson and ascertain where the guns were to be placed. After searching hither and yon in the midst of the action, Davis came "to a rather secluded spot, where I found the General alone, seated on his horse, the bridle rein loose on the horse's neck, his cap held in his left hand, and his right hand extended toward heaven in the attitude of prayer." Davis waited quietly until the general finished. Jackson turned to him in an abrupt way. "Well, sir, what is it?" "General," Davis replied, words rapidly tumbling forth. "Captain Brockenbrough of the Baltimore Battery would like your permission to enter the fight, and if permitted what position should he take?" Jackson answered promptly. "Tell him to come into line immediately and take any position he thinks best."[60]

A few moments later, the Union cannon at the coaling ceased firing. Jackson (or more likely his adjutant) summarized with uncharacteristic drama what happened. In "gallant & successful" fashion, Taylor and his men moved "to the right along the mountain acclivity through a rough & tangled forest—& much disordered by the rapidity & obstruction of the march, Taylor emerged with his command from the wood just as the loud cheers of the enemy had proclaimed their success in front. And although assailed by a superior force in front & flank, with their guns in position within point-blank range, the charge was gallantly made & the battery consisting of six guns fell into our hands. Three times was this battery lost & won in the desperate & determined efforts to capture & recapture it."[61]

Taylor's seizure of the enemy guns in desperate hand-to-hand fighting held Federal attention and stopped the planned counterstroke against Jackson's center. Winder scraped together all available troops, including pieces of Taliaferro's brigade, several regiments from Ewell's division, and the fragments of the Stonewall Brigade. This mass swept forward in the first concerted effort by Jackson's army that day.

The Union line wavered for several minutes, then broke. At 11 A.M., Tyler ordered a retreat. Jackson came riding down the road at that climactic moment. "His head was bowed and his right hand, gauntleted, was pointing upward," a Virginia captain reported. "He was alone and seemed oblivious to all around him and presented the appearance of being in supplication or rendering thanks."[62]

Jackson undertook a prompt pursuit. Batteries followed infantry; and whenever the gunners had a field of fire or a good target, they unlimbered and opened on the retreating column.[63] Jackson led the chase for three or four miles, when the woods became too thick on both sides of the road to maintain any speed. The short pursuit was nevertheless profitable: Confederates seized 450 prisoners, 800 muskets, one field gun, and a wagon.[64] The victorious commander collected his booty and retraced his steps to Port Republic. Heavy rain was falling as the components of Jackson's army reunited and headed southeast away from the village toward Brown's Gap.

Fremont had advanced slowly from Cross Keys to Port Republic during the battle. Trimble's men crossed the North River and, per instructions, set fire to the bridge. Union troops from Cross Keys could only stand on the hills across the river and stare at the heavy smoke swirling skyward. Yet Fremont was determined to get in the last shots. In his words, "a parting salvo of carefully aimed rifled guns duly charged with shell hastened the departure of the rebels." Jackson did not see it that way. He reported sternly that Fremont "opened his Art. upon our ambulances & parties engaged in the humane labors of attending to our dead & wounded & to the dead & wounded of the enemy." How many of the helpless fell victim to Fremont's barrage is unknown.[65]

A soldier in Taliaferro's brigade observed of Shields and the battle: "We whiped him and took all his artillery and a great many Prisnors. we lost a right smart men ourselves." That was so. Jackson's casualties at Port Republic were about 800 men—heavy losses, in reality, because most of them came from the already-small brigades of Winder, Taylor, and Scott. Tyler lost 1018 men: sixty-seven killed, 393 wounded, and 558 missing.[66] Those statistics do not speak well for Jackson's performance.

Federals on the field numbered no more than 3000 men. Jackson had almost 8000 troops close at hand. It had taken him over four hours to dislodge the much smaller enemy, and, in the process, it cost him far more men than it should have.

Still, the end result is what is important. Late on June 9, Jackson sent a hasty and succinct message to Richmond: "Through God's blessing the Enemy near Port Republic was this day routed with the loss of Six (6) pieces of his artillery." To Anna, Jackson sent an even shorter note that day: "God greatly blessed our arms near Port Republican [sic] yesterday & today."[67] Headquarters on the night of June 9 was the home of John F. Lewis at Mt. Vernon Furnace near Brown's Gap. Jackson went to bed early, for obvious reasons. Before retiring, however, he attended to one small detail that underscored the importance he attached to artillery. Taliaferro mixed humor and anger in telling what happened.

> Late at night, Jackson sent an Officer to inquire if I had brought off the captured Artillery [after pursuing Tyler's force]. The reply was 'Every thing except an unserviceable caisson, and that only for the want of horses.' The weather was wretched, the roads intolerable; but the order came back, post haste, that if it took every horse in the command, that caisson must be brought up before daylight.
>
> It was ten miles off. The Officer who had to fetch it was very much of the opinion of the soldier who, when his Company was ordered to bring in a gun which had been left outside the skirmish line, proposed to his Captain to 'take up a subscription to pay for the durn thing, and let it be;' but he hardly ventured to make the suggestion to Jackson.

The caisson was in the Confederate encampment "on time."[68]

Jackson arose on June 10 hours before the sun. Though Shields's lead elements had been repulsed the previous day, Fremont remained a threat. Confederates prepared for battle until it became apparent that the two-pronged Union advance that had started up the valley late in May was at an end. Shields and Fremont had withdrawn from Jackson's front.

The former wanted out of the narrow Luray Valley as quickly as possible. Fremont, ordered to Harrisonburg, was so unnerved at being in an exposed position that he took his men instead twenty-five miles farther north to Mt. Jackson. With the retirement of the two Union hosts, the valley campaign ended. A Confederate line officer exclaimed proudly: "Gallant Jackson is again Master of the Glorious Valley."[69]

Frustrations and disgust permeated the Federal ranks. An Ohio surgeon snorted: "We have too many Maj. Genls.—too little brains. For instance, in the Deptmt [of] the Shenandoah we have Maj. Genl. McDowell, Shields, Freemont [sic], Sigel and Banks (5!). All equal in rank and envious of each other's reputation. Neither will do anything which would reflect credit on the other. Each one desires all the glory himself."[70]

The Lincoln government now agreed with the basic premise and made some changes. Banks, wearing the stigma of a loser, would mark time while other generals moved past him up the military ladder. Shields quickly faded from view as a Union commander. A few weeks later, when a junior officer was given command of a new Union army, Fremont angrily resigned his commission—"carrying with him everything but our regrets," one colonel wrote.[71]

In a phrase, what Jackson had done in the valley of Virginia changed the whole face of the Civil War in the state. His overall operations had been a strategic masterpiece. He alone had engineered the operations.[72] With never more than 17,000 men, Jackson had defeated forces totaling more than three times that number. He had inflicted close to 5000 casualties, captured 9000 small arms and tons of supplies, all at a cost of about 3100 soldiers (half of whom were captured). In the process, Jackson had routed the enemy from the major part of the vital Shenandoah Valley.

There was more. Jackson's movements isolated at Fredericksburg 40,000 potential reinforcements for McClellan's army advancing on Richmond. Captain William Lyman of the 31st Virginia asserted that "the dread of 'Jackson in the rear' seemed to paralyze whole divisions of the enemy and make cowards of them all." Even a New York newspaper gave grudging recognition. "Jackson is equally eminent as a strategist and tactician," it stated. "He handles his army like a whip, making it crack in out of the way corners where you scarcely thought the lash would reach."[73]

So effectively had Jackson utilized his comparatively small force that Union authorities had to alter their major plans for the capture of Richmond. McClellan stopped his advance with the May 31–June 1 fighting at Seven Pines. Confederate General Joseph Johnston fell wounded in the action. The first news of this loss doubtless pained Jackson. Johnston, in his own way and in the main, had supported the semi-independent operations in the valley. Jackson would always remember Johnston with respect.

With Johnston to be out of command for months, President Davis named Robert E. Lee commander of the Confederacy's major army. Lee's audacity would now come forth, and Jackson would come with it. In that regard, the valley campaign controlled the subsequent plan and execution of military operations by the contending armies in Virginia.

From the autumn of 1861 into the early spring of 1862, the Confederacy had suffered one battlefield loss after another. Attacks had gained little. Defensive fights had been at the least costly and at the most disastrous. Losses had occurred in the western theater at Mill Springs, Fort Donelson, Fort Henry, Pea Ridge, Shiloh, and New Orleans. The North's principal army had advanced up the Virginia peninsula and stood poised at the gates of the Confederate capital. Federal naval conquests along the Atlantic coast had occurred in unbroken fashion.

Pessimism had coursed through the South. The specter of surrender loomed on the horizon when suddenly, from the relatively obscure region of western Virginia,

Stonewall Jackson brought good news and a flash of hope. His feat was the first Southern success of any significance since his gallantry at Manassas eleven months earlier.

The advantage of hindsight and thirteen decades for reflection makes it easy to fault some of Jackson's actions in the valley. Impetuosity marked both the opening and the closing battles. At Port Republic, as at Kernstown, Jackson ignored reconnaissance and logistics for the sake of an immediate attack. The battle of McDowell, some writers have charged, required little more of Jackson than maintaining a stonewall-like position. Winchester was a case of an aggressive force maintaining momentum in flanking and overwhelming an enemy already at the point of demoralization. At Cross Keys, the Confederate position was so strong, the Federal assault so weak, that the action qualifies more as a skirmish than as a battle.

The same detractors do not stop with those analyses. Some of them accuse Jackson, the former artilleryman, of stumbling here and there in the process of learning to command an army primarily of infantry. The general displayed little control over his cavalry—the most valid of the charges—but this criticism ignores the powerful influence at the time of Turner Ashby. Artillery chief Stapleton Crutchfield was given enough latitude to commit more than one mistake, and he did.

Undeniably, and throughout the valley campaign, Jackson left in his wake a steadily growing number of personal confrontations. Garnett and Conner had been summarily removed from command; indispensable officers such as Ashby and Harman had submitted resignations; Ewell, Winder, and Taylor had sought transfers; several officers were under arrest; a larger number were unhappy. Jackson did not hide his distrust of Taliaferro, and he had publicly insulted Arnold Elzey.

Things were just as unsettled in the ranks. Unfounded rumor circulated through the Stonewall Brigade that Winder had appealed to the secretary of war for a thirty-day rest period to enable his men to catch their breath and nurse sore limbs—and that the request had been made in the face of Jackson's stern opposition.[74]

While Jackson's relations with subordinates have often been termed clumsy and the result of overriding ambition,[75] it is closer to the truth that discipline was the major reason for the clashes. Jackson equated serving God and fighting for the Confederacy. Because patriotism and religion were one and the same in his eyes, he was unbending in his dedication to both. There could be no laxity when fighting for the Lord.

Unquestionably, Jackson's overall performance in the valley was brilliant. He combined initiative, secrecy, audacity, rapid marches, flashing strikes at unexpected places, unrelenting assaults, and pursuits in quest of total victory. Familiarity with terrain, the ability to isolate segments of the enemy, turning a strategic withdrawal into a tactical offensive—these were Jackson's attributes. They were the ingredients that emerged in the valley and would mark the remainder of his career.

In the preceding spring, while talking with John D. Imboden, Jackson gave his own formula for success in battle. "Always mystify, mislead, and surprise the enemy, if possible; and when you strike and overcome him, never let up in the pursuit so long as your men have strength to follow; for an army routed, if hotly pursued, becomes panic-stricken, and can then be destroyed by half their number. The other rule is, never fight against heavy odds, if by any possible maneuvering you can hurl your own force on only a part, and that the weakest part, of your enemy and crush it. Such tactics will win every time, and a small army may thus destroy a large one in detail, and repeated victory will make it invincible."[76]

This method of warfare, borrowed in part from Napoleon, was precisely what Jackson had employed in the valley. The results rank among the most spectacular military achievements of the nineteenth century. General E. Porter Alexander, who would bitterly criticize Jackson's conduct on the peninsula, was laudatory in his summary of the campaign in the Shenandoah. The little-known Jackson, Alexander wrote, "suddenly broke loose up in the Valley of Virginia & not only astonished the weak minds of the enemy almost into paralysis, but dazzled the eyes of military men all over the world by an aggressive campaign which I believe to be unsurpassed in all military history for brilliancy & daring." Viscount Wolseley, later to become commander in chief of the British army, considered Jackson's operations in the valley an extraordinary campaign that "stamped him as a military genius of a very high order."[77]

Writers quickly began comparing Jackson with Napoleon. The Virginian's performance in the Shenandoah Valley certainly matched the Frenchman's campaign in Italy, especially when one kept in mind that while Napoleon led an army of professional soldiers, Jackson was at the head of volunteers.[78]

Grumbles arose from the weary ranks of the Southern army in the days immediately after Port Republic—and before those troops realized the full extent of their achievements. Thomas Wade of the Rockbridge Artillery told his sister: "I am still in the land of the living but dont know how long I will be if 'Old Jack' keeps us running about as much as he has done lately." Lieutenant George Peterkin of Ewell's division observed wryly: "I never saw a trench. General Jackson had no time to dig trenches, and he would have had no time to stay in them if somebody had dug them for him." These opinions paled in the face of the Georgia officer who confessed his inability to describe his experiences. "Dear," he informed his wife, "I cant write you [a] history of what weev been through for the last month. iv been so worn out that I hardly had time to think."[79]

Of far greater impact was the unbounded optimism that Jackson's campaign had created in the ranks and throughout Virginia. John M. Brown of the Rockbridge Artillery summarized prevailing sentiment after June 9 among the members of the Stonewall Brigade. "They had entered the campaign with lots of grit, with plenty of enthusiasm, but with no experience; they had emerged with rich experience, perhaps not so enthusiastic, but with a courage born of good leadership and pride of achievement. They might not shine on dress parade, but their country knew, and the world knew, they were soldiers. They had learned to understand and trust their General. . . . They knew how to interpret and to value his military genius, although it appeared sometimes in eccentric form. They had unconsciously adopted some of the General's ways; they were terse and laconic with strangers, and the answer, 'I don't know,' was often all they had to say. But their devotion was superb and their courage sublime."[80]

Captain Cooper Nisbet of the 21st Georgia now idolized Jackson. "His soldiers all love the old fighting cock." John Casler of the 33d Virginia echoed that sentiment. "Every time he would pass our brigade we would all commence cheering him. . . . It got to be a common saying in the army, when any cheering was heard in camp, or on the march, that it was either 'Jackson or a rabbit.'"[81]

The 23d Virginia's Valentine Southall was optimistic in spite of negative talk by his brigade commander. "Genl. Taliaferro thinks Jackson's Army will not be able to fight for a month—thinks the same of the Enemy—but I reckon Genl. Jack thinks contrary. This army is much worn out but six days will rest them."[82]

Jackson was now "the idol of the army" and "emphatically the hero of the war."[83] Yet the only kind of praise the general would have liked came from one of his devout gunners. "It is such a comfort and a great cause for thanksgiving to have such a Christian as Jackson as our general. No wonder the blessing of God attends his army in such a signal way."[84]

Similar exuberance prevailed behind the lines. One of Taylor's Louisianians observed that valley residents possessed a "love and faith" in Jackson "akin to idolatry." Another Confederate, stationed in Richmond, remarked to his father: "All eyes now seem to be centered on General T. J. Jackson. He has used his army as Hercules would his club in hurling it irresistibly against the enemy. . . . I am fully convinced that he is the only General on either side in this War who shows any of that Genius which is necessary to the managing of armies."[85]

A Richmond newspaper pronounced Jackson and his army "chief in the hearts of the nation," and it added: "Strange as it may appear, news from the armies within five miles of [this city] is of secondary importance. Invariably the crowds which daily flock around the bulletin boards ask first, 'What news from Jackson?'"[86]

Perhaps the greatest accomplishment in the Shenandoah Valley was the victory Jackson gained over the minds of people North and South. The speed with which he bolted to the forefront was startling to all. Three months earlier, the quiet, humorless professor-turned-general was barely known throughout his native Virginia. Now he was arguably the most famous commander in America. Only one person was unaffected by it all. Jackson did not have any reason to feel self-esteem. After all, he was but an instrument of his heavenly father.

June 10 was no day of celebration for the Confederates. Northern Virginia was littered with fragments of once-dapper Union armies, to be sure, but the Old Dominion bore mute and pitiful testimony to the ravages of war. A citizen of the valley observed: "It rather moves me to sympathy to see the trail of devastation that the two armies have left after them. Meadows of clover are trodden into mud; the tossing plumes of the wheat-fields along the line of march are trodden down, as though a thousand reaping-machines have passed over and through them. Dead horses lie along the road, entirely overpowering the sweet scent of the clover-blossoms. . . . Fences are not, landmarks have vanished, and all is one common waste."[87]

The victorious Southern army looked anything but successful. After Port Republic, an officer in the 13th Virginia recalled: "we encamped on the side of the mountain where it was so steep we had to pile rocks and build a wall to keep from rolling down when asleep, and to add to our discomfort the inevitable rain began to fall . . . and the men were wet to the skin. . . . The army had passed through terrible scenes and looked rough and dirty, as well as ragged. Jackson, himself, was not an exception to the rule."[88]

If Jackson looked like he felt, no one appeared in worse shape. The general was physically exhausted by the end of the valley campaign. Scuffed boots, mud-flecked uniform, soiled kepi, unkempt beard, and sagging shoulders reflected the activities of the past three months. The blue eyes were dull from fatigue. In a letter to Anna, he exulted, "God has been our shield, and to His name be all the glory." Then the mixed feelings of exhaustion emerged. "How I do wish for peace, but only upon the condition of our national independence."[89]

As scores of stragglers and men who had been ill made their way in the rain back to the ranks, Jackson dispatched scouts to monitor enemy movements while he attended to small details. Burial details from each brigade went out on the afternoon of the 10th to inter the bodies of their comrades. Shields requested permission to send Federals through the lines to gather their wounded and dead. Jackson tartly refused. The wounded were already receiving care, he stated, and the dead were being buried.

Jackson then considered it proper to follow with a strong reprimand. "Your wounded were permitted to lay on the field longer than they otherwise would have been had not General Fremont's Artillery, hours after the termination of the engagement, not only so fired upon the ambulances and their parties as to drive them from the field. The hospital was also fired upon, notwithstanding it as well as the ambulances were marked by hospital flags."[90]

Meanwhile, Jackson had become aware that Major Dabney was not making a smooth transition from theologian to chief of staff. Using the excuse that the adjutant's duties in his department were "too heavy for one officer," Jackson asked Richmond to promote Sandie Pendleton to assistant adjutant general. This was done at once. No small request from the hero of the hour met opposition at the War Department.[91]

Later on June 10, Jackson found time to visit some of his wounded men. He came upon a Virginia private who had suffered a disfiguring face injury. "I thank you for your gallantry on that day," Jackson said with feeling. To the maimed soldier, his captain observed, Jackson's remark "was a decoration—indeed, a scroll of fame."[92]

Reports of Federal forces in full retreat down the valley led Jackson to send out his mounted troops. "The only true rule for cavalry," he told Colonel Tom Munford, "is to follow as long as the enemy retreats." The VMI graduate proved tireless as a temporary replacement for the fallen Ashby. Munford occupied Harrisonburg on June 12 and sent patrols as far north as New Market. In Harrisonburg, the Confederates seized 200 Belgian muskets, plus wagons, medical stores, and equipment. Also captured were 200 sick and wounded enemy soldiers. "The Federal surgeons attending them were released," Jackson stated, "and those under their care paroled."[93]

Rain clouds finally dissipated on June 11; hence, before dawn the next day, Jackson led his men down from the cramped confines of the Blue Ridge because Federals no longer posed any threat. Jackson crossed the South River, proceeded a few miles southwest of Port Republic, and encamped in the grassy plains between Weyers Cave and Mt. Meridian.

The Middle River to the west offered both another water source and an additional line of defense. Harman got his supply wagons running to and from the railhead at Staunton. Jackson established headquarters for the next five days at the Gibbons home, a boxlike, two-story brick structure on a bluff near Mt. Meridian.

Unfamiliar and needed relaxation marked most of those days. The troops washed away dirt, napped contentedly, joked about all the luxuries they lacked, and bragged about their successes under Old Jack. The general regained a little strength, but he never compromised a sense of duty. A bit of daily drill went into effect so that the soldiers would remember that they were soldiers still. He also announced—on the same day—a religious service for the faithful and a resumption of courts-martial for the malefactors.[94]

During this period, the father of one of Jackson's young officers came to camp to request a furlough for his son. Jackson took the man into his tent and listened attentively to his petition. He then explained the patriotic need for the son to remain on duty, couching it in such moving terms that the old gentleman wept. As the man departed, he grasped Jackson's hand and exclaimed: "May God bless you, General Jackson! If it only pleased Him that the weight of fewer years were resting on these old shoulders, I should be with you myself, to aid in fighting this quarrel through, under your banner!"[95]

A bit of levity occasionally broke the solemnity of headquarters life. Commissary Hawks was at Jackson's tent one morning when Dabney appeared in his shirt sleeves with a wash basin in his hand and an exasperated look on his face. "Major," he said to Hawks, "I think General Jackson has fewer comforts than any man in camp. Look at this," Dabney said, raising the wash basin. "The General came home late last night and instead of calling a servant, he took care of the horse himself and fed him in this tin wash-basin. The consequence is that the horse put his foot through it and we have nothing to wash in!"[96]

Federal rumors now placed Jackson at Charlottesville, at Staunton, at Front Royal, and en route to Richmond. He was also said to have a reinforced army of up to 35,000 men. Meanwhile, the general quietly sought to relax in the middle of his beloved valley. Weyers Cave recalled memories of a visit he and Anna had made there. He mentioned that at the start of a long letter to his *esposita*.

Expectedly, Jackson wrote: "Our God has again thrown His shield over me in the various apparent dangers to which I have been exposed. This evening we have religious service in the army for the purpose of rendering thanks to the Most High for the victories with which He has crowned our arms, and to offer earnest prayer that He will continue to give us success, until, through His divine blessing, our independence shall be established." Having made his profession of faith, Jackson the Christian then became Jackson the loving husband. "Wouldn't you like to get home again?" he asked in longing fashion.[97]

While Jackson was writing to the beloved woman carrying his child, Colonel Sam Fulkerson of the 37th Virginia used a letter to analyze his commander.

Our General will certainly not give us much time while there is an enemy to meet. He is a singular man and has some most striking military traits of character, and some that are not so good. A more fearless man never lived and he is remarkable for his industry and energy. He is strictly temperate in his habits and sleeps very little. Often while near the enemy, and while everybody except the guards are asleep, he is on his horse and gone, nobody knows where. I often fear that he will be killed or taken.

Our men curse him for the hard marching he makes them do, but still the privates of the whole army have the most unbounded confidence in him. They say that he can take them into harder places and get them out better than any other living man. . . . He is an ardent Christian.[98]

Deep-seated weariness still crippled Jackson's effectiveness. It emerged during this time of inactivity in two abrasive incidents with subordinates.

The first encounter was but another chapter in the ongoing dispute with Quartermaster John Harman. Jackson had started the latest feud on the day after Port Republic. He ordered Harman to collect all small arms left on the field. When Harman commented later that many of the weapons looked like Confederate arms, Jackson "went into a towering rage" and told Harman he wanted to hear no further insinuations that Southern soldiers had abandoned their arms.[99]

The Staunton quartermaster had a temper of his own. He stormed from Jackson's tent and returned shortly thereafter with a letter of resignation. "Jackson's mysterious ways are unbearable," Harman told his brother. "He is a hard master to serve and nothing but a mean spirited man can remain long with him. God be with us all." Within twenty-four hours, just as he had done before, Jackson apologized for the unintended offense. This mollified Harman for the time being and he continued serving under Jackson.[100] Harman felt sorry for himself on many occasions, but he cursed his teams and commanded both performance and respect from his teamsters. Harman was a good quartermaster. Both he and Jackson knew it.

A rather glaring gap in the Sidney Winder diary during June 12–14 hints at a major breach with Jackson. Rancor at Jackson ignoring his transfer request, and ignorance over troop movements on June 9—when his Stonewall Brigade was the centerpiece of the attack—and the heavy losses incurred in the fighting at Port Republic combined to make Winder's disposition akin to that of a cocked pistol. In the lull at Mt. Meridian, Winder politely requested a short furlough to go to Richmond on personal business. Jackson's refusal was swift and blunt. Winder's anger exploded. He resigned from the army.

Just as Winder had previously interceded with Jackson on behalf of a miffed Ashby, now Dick Taylor stepped forward on behalf of Winder. The Louisianian had a long conference with Jackson, in which he emphasized the heroic and valuable service that Winder had performed throughout the valley campaign. Taylor urged Jackson to rise above petty differences. That night the commander rode to Winder's headquarters and patched the rift with the man in charge of his old brigade.[101]

Meanwhile, Jackson and Lee had established steady communication. Each was beginning to learn much about the other, and both liked what they saw. Lee's confidence in Jackson was such that even before the valley campaign ended, he had a new and cooperative offensive in mind.

On June 5, as Jackson was retiring through Harrisonburg toward Port Republic, and only four days after assuming command of all Confederate forces in Virginia, Lee sent a letter to President Davis. He wanted Jackson to join him soon in front of Richmond. Yet "after much reflection," Lee wrote, "I think that if it was possible to reinforce Jackson strongly" at this time, "it would change the character of the war."

Lee even speculated that with Federal forces reeling in defeat in the valley, Jackson might be able to strike across the Potomac and invade Pennsylvania.

Davis hesitated but finally concurred. Three days later, Lee addressed a carefully worded letter to Jackson. "Should there be nothing requiring your attention in the Valley, so as to prevent your leaving it in a few days, & you can make arrangements to deceive the enemy & impress him with the idea of your presence, please let me know, that you might unite at the decisive moment with the army near Richmond. Make your arrangements accordingly, but should an opportunity occur for striking the enemy a successful blow do not let it escape you."[102]

As rain fell on June 10 and further dampened any offensive ideas McClellan had for his army east of Richmond, Lee formulated his strategy for a counteroffensive. He simply could not send Jackson enough troops to launch an invasion of the North. Such a movement would be premature. However, Washington officials were quite concerned about the safety of the Northern capital. Any Southern offensive would likely bring a recall of McDowell's corps to protect Washington.

Perhaps with some reinforcements, Lee thought, Jackson could undertake a short but sharp campaign that would finish off the enemy in the valley. Jackson's entire force "can then be directed to move rapidly to Ashland, where I will re-enforce him with fresh troops, with directions to sweep down north of the Chickahominy [River], cut up McClellan's communications and rear, while I attack in front."[103]

Jackson's victories at Cross Keys and Port Republic further convinced Lee that with additional men Jackson "could take the offensive again" to quick and good effect. Lee had already ordered General Alexander R. Lawton's 3500-man Georgia brigade and a North Carolina battalion to the valley. With Davis's approval, Lee on June 11 directed General Chase Whiting to take two more brigades and join Jackson. That would bolster the valley army by 8000 men. The object of the reinforcements, Lee made clear to Jackson, "is to enable you to crush the forces opposed to you."[104]

Lee dispatched Whiting's brigades from Richmond with all the fanfare he could muster. Whiting's eight regiments paraded through town to the accompaniment of band music and cheers. Federal prisoners about to be paroled were allowed to "over-hear" reports of thousands of Confederates heading to the valley. This added further credence to the report. One of Lee's staff officers went to a railroad station and loudly spread the "news" of Jackson launching a new offensive as soon as reinforcements reached him. In order to make everything appear genuine, Lee then appealed in a halfhearted manner to Richmond newspapers to keep the movements secret. That all but guaranteed their publication.[105]

Contrary to the beliefs of some earlier historians, the transfer of Whiting's two brigades was not a ruse to mislead the Federals.[106] Lee's communiques of June 5, 8, and 11 (cited above) made it clear that the supreme commander hoped for a new offensive by Jackson in order to "crush" the enemy still in the Shenandoah and threaten Washington itself. Jackson should have been pleased at such open instructions: this was the kind of unrestricted fighting he considered necessary for ultimate victory. Yet he balked.

The troops of Fremont and Shields were scattered from New Market to the

Potomac River. For Jackson to disperse his own forces in an effort to gobble up the enemy fragments would leave him vulnerable everywhere. "My opinion is that we should not attempt another march down the Valley to Winchester," Jackson declared to Lee, "until we are in a condition under the blessing of Providence to hold the country."[107]

He had to have more men for a major new offensive. On June 13, he asked his unofficial envoy, Alexander Boteler, to make another trip to Richmond. With 40,000 reinforcements, Boteler was to tell authorities, the Confederates would drive down the valley and plunge into the North. "By that means, Richmond can be relieved and the campaign transferred to Pennsylvania," Jackson asserted.[108]

Boteler arrived in Richmond late the following day and gained an audience with Lee. Jackson's request for 40,000 men was out of the question at the moment, Lee stated. He then opened a conversation with Jackson's liaison.

"Colonel," Lee began, "don't you think General Jackson had better come down here first and help me to drive these troublesome people away from Richmond?"

Boteler hesitated, then replied: "I think that it would be very presumptuous of me, General, to answer the question, as it would be hazarding an opinion upon an important military movement which I don't feel competent to give."

"Nevertheless, I would like to know your opinion," Lee said.

"Well," Boteler began, "if I answer your question at all, it must be in the negative."

"Why so?"

"Because if you bring our valley boys down here at this season among the pestilential swamps of the Chickahominy, the change from their pure mountain air to the miasmatic atmosphere will kill them off faster than the Federals have been doing."

"That would depend upon the time they would have to stay here," Lee countered. "Have you any other reason to offer?"

"Yes," Boteler replied with growing confidence in the commanding general's presence. "It is that Jackson has been doing so well with an independent command that it seems a pity not to let him have his own way; and then, too, bringing him here, General, will be—to use a homely phrase—putting all your eggs in one basket."

Lee chuckled. "I see that you appreciate General Jackson as highly as I myself do, and it is because of my appreciation of him that I wish to have him here."[109]

Boteler's June 16 return to Jackson's headquarters coincided with the arrival in Staunton of the brigades of Whiting and Lawton. Apparently, Lee instructed Boteler to inform Jackson verbally that a Pennsylvania invasion required more troop support than could be supplied. Later that day, Jackson received from Lee written thoughts that appeared more like a personal request than a military directive.

If Jackson concurred, Lee wrote, he should start for Richmond as quickly as possible. Speed was imperative. "Unless McClellan can be driven out of his entrenchments he will move by positions under cover of his heavy guns within shelling distance of Richmond. I know of no surer way of thwarting him than that proposed. I should like to have the advantage of your views and be able to confer with you. Will meet you at some point on your approach to the Chickahominy." Lee warned Jackson to mask his movements as much as possible.[110]

Secrecy and deception, of course, were Jackson's strong suits. He was now ready to join Lee. Concentration at a threatened point was militarily sound, especially when diversion could accomplish nothing more. In addition, if Jackson began the march to Richmond at once, he could utilize inner lines of defense and get there well in advance of McDowell reuniting his scattered command and heading south from Fredericksburg.

Jackson now turned to young Tom Munford. His former VMI cadet had not only adapted better than Ashby to Jackson's stern demands; he also seemed to control the wayward valley horsemen with a firmer hand. Jackson ordered Munford to throw out a cavalry screen that would effectively block all outside awareness of Confederate preparations and movements. The only information to be passed to the countryside were rumors that Jackson wanted planted. The ruse worked perfectly. On June 17, Union reports had Jackson about to strike again down the valley with 20,000 fresh troops.[111]

Similarly, Jackson played a game of mystery with his own officers. One who immediately bristled at being kept in the dark was stuffy General Chase Whiting, who had just arrived at Staunton with two veteran and ably led brigades. One was under John B. Hood, a huge Kentuckian who now led Texas troops and whose powerful physique reflected a penchant for fighting. The other brigade was a mixed unit with regiments from three states. Its commander was Colonel Evander M. Law, a thin and scholarly Citadel graduate who bore a battle scar from Manassas.

Command of this small division unfortunately accentuated Whiting's feelings of grandeur. The South Carolinian and Jackson were the same age. Whiting was a showy intellectual who had graduated a year ahead of Jackson at West Point with the highest scholastic record ever attained up to that time. During Jackson's traumatic first term at the academy, Whiting had tutored the flustered Virginia mountaineer. He retained that feeling of superiority toward the lower classman.

Whiting was a brilliant engineer, endowed as well with piercing eyes and drooping mustache. Yet he was always a poor leader of men. The Carolinian was an even worse follower, for he tended to be intolerant of those he considered less gifted intellectually—and that was most of humankind.

On reaching Staunton, Whiting received a cordial written welcome from Jackson, who added, "Let me see you at my headquarters." Whiting promptly rode twenty miles to Weyers Cave. He returned to Staunton after midnight "in a towering passion." Whiting told his host, John Imboden, that Jackson had treated him "outrageously" by telling him nothing but to return to Staunton and await orders the following day. Whiting angrily told Imboden: "I believe he hasn't more sense than my horse!"[112]

At sunrise the next morning, a courier arrived with unexplained orders for Whiting to entrain his two brigades and travel to Gordonsville. Whiting exploded anew. "Didn't I tell you he was a fool?" Whiting screamed at Imboden. "Doesn't this prove it? Why, I came through Gordonsville day before yesterday!"[113]

Whiting's introduction to now-General Jackson produced an instant and growing resentment. Some of Whiting's men had serious reservations about their new superior. A North Carolina soldier wrote home that "we are under a hot head and long head old fellow for fighting for there is hardly a week passes without he gets in two or three fights."[114]

Throughout a hot June 17, Jackson seemed to be everywhere—and nowhere. Ewell's division was placed in readiness for a march over the Blue Ridge to Charlottesville. Jackson's brigades would follow. The troops of Whiting and Lawton would come later by train. (One of Lawton's Georgians commented, "Stonewall Jackson put his own soldiers that were used to marching and fighting in the front, for they could get along better than we could.")[115] Staff members were to oversee the movements of each component of the army.

Munford would cover the withdrawal and protect Jackson's rear by a series of loud demonstrations through the valley. Jackson gave Munford a quick postgraduate lecture on cavalry leadership. "Do all you can to cut off communications across the lines between us and the enemy," Jackson directed. "Also let there be as little communication as practicable between your command and that of our Infantry. Let your couriers be men whom you can trust, and caution them against carrying news forward if it may thereby reach the enemy."[116]

Jackson's entire army pulled a shroud of secrecy about itself as preparations continued through the day. Jackson rode out in the afternoon to check on a number of details. He came upon a lone soldier heading across a field toward an inviting cherry orchard. The general would not tolerate straggling when he could prevent it. He galloped up to the man. "What division do you belong to?" he sternly inquired.

"Don't know," came the reply.

"What brigade?"

"Don't know."

Jackson, thinking that the man would certainly be knowledgeable about the unit that gave a soldier the most pride, asked: "Well, what regiment?"

"Don't know."

The angry general then snapped: "What do you know, sir?"

Back came a quick answer: "I know that old Stonewall ordered me not to know anything, and damned if I ain't going to stick to it!"[117]

Jackson employed the same secrecy with respect in his June 17 movements. Late in the day he called Hotchkiss to his tent and asked for maps of the country between Port Republic and Lexington. Jackson quizzed his aide for an hour about roads, streams, and points of defense in that area. "Good, very good," he would say at intervals.

A half-hour after his departure, Hotchkiss received another summons from Jackson. Some fighting had taken place east of Richmond, the general said in matter-of-fact tones. He would like to see maps of that field of operations. Hotchkiss got the charts, which Jackson studied intently for two hours. The usual "Good, very good," comment punctuated the conversation. Hotchkiss left headquarters the second time convinced that the army was bound for Richmond.

At 10 P.M., accompanied only by his kinsman and aide, Colonel William L. Jackson, the general left camp and rode to Staunton. Shortly after midnight the army was awakened. Men were soon marching toward Waynesboro and Rockfish Gap looming above it. No one knew the whereabouts of Jackson. Even staff members were unacquainted with the general's plans. They were left to point direction and distance to the various commands.

Jackson evidently spent the night giving careful attention to logistical matters in Staunton. He momentarily forgot how tired he was. Personal concerns were secondary to military expediency. On the morning of the 18th, he left Staunton by rail and in late afternoon caught up with his forces at Waynesboro.[118]

The army's march that day through mud, dust, and ascending altitude had been wearisome. It had also been an awesome spectacle for those soldiers who observed the scaling of the Blue Ridge Mountains. For example, William McClendon of the 15th Alabama would write in later years: "The road was broad, and was likened to a flight of winding stairs. . . . When about halfway to the top I could look up a mile ahead and see the boys in grey marching four abreast, filing around the rugged clifts . . . and looking backward and downward, there as far as the eye could reach, I could see the balance of Jackson's corps advancing. The long line of troops . . . stepping in quick time, with their bright muskets and bayonets glittering in the sun, made an everlasting impression upon my mind, the sublimity and grandeur of which I will never forget."[119]

Many of those men would never see the valley again. For Jackson, it was his final departure from the upper Shenandoah.

Hotchkiss rejoined Jackson at Waynesboro and, at the general's request, dispatched a number of telegrams. When those duties were completed, the army commander and the mapmaker commenced their climb toward Rockfish Gap. For three miles, winking campfires faintly illuminated the western face of the mountain. Approaching darkness made it even more difficult for Hotchkiss to locate army headquarters. At length, the aide returned to Jackson. "General," Hotchkiss stated, "I fear we will not find our wagons tonight." For a moment, Jackson stared at Hotchkiss. Then he replied in a soft but earnest tone, "Never take counsel of your fears."[120] Of all of Jackson's axioms, this was one that became most embedded in Hotchkiss' mind.

Nightfall came with Jackson still attending to details. The hour grew late. One more message needed to be issued before he engaged in his final devotions of the day. It took longer than usual, Hotchkiss noted. Jackson sent a personal letter to his pastor, Dr. White, in Lexington. Two thoughts were on the general's mind. One was the hope that more chaplains could be found for the army. Next, embarrassingly aware of the fame that had come to him in the campaign for the Shenandoah Valley, Jackson begged Dr. White's assistance. "I am afraid that our people are looking to the wrong source for help, and ascribing our success to those to whom they are not due. If we fail to trust in God & give Him all the glory, our cause is ruined. Give to our friends at home due warning on this subject."[121]

FATIGUE

ROM ROCKFISH GAP, the view to the east is breathtaking. The Blue
Ridge Mountains drop away sharply, and on a clear day the rolling hill
country of the Virginia Piedmont extends as far as the eye can see. Ninety-five
miles across that undulating land of fields and woods and myriad waterways lay
Richmond, the heart of the Southern Confederacy. In June 1862, Union General
George B. McClellan's massive Army of the Potomac sprawled in a rough battle line
nine miles east of the city. Between McClellan and Richmond stood Robert E. Lee
with his heavily outnumbered Army of Northern Virginia.

Suddenly, the key figure in the operations of either side during those final spring
days of 1862 was "Stonewall" Jackson. His presence at the Confederate capital could
be the difference between success or failure for the South. That point was not visible
to many at the time, but Jackson was certainly the central figure in Lee's plans for a
counteroffensive against the invading Federal host.

A rare good night's sleep put Jackson on the morning of June 19 in an unusually
pleasant mood. He made a nine-mile ride down the mountain to Mechum's River
Station. Hotchkiss and perhaps one or two other staff members accompanied him.
Jackson was in a talkative mood. The subject of conversation soon turned to fortifications. At one point the general commented, "I have found that our men would rather
fight and march than dig."[1]

Jackson's strategy was to entrain his army and move it to Gordonsville, Fredericks
Hall, or some point closer to Richmond on the Virginia Central line. To prepare for
the transfer, he personally would take a train from Mechum's Station to Charlottesville. Before departing, however, it was necessary to meet with Major Dabney,
the chief of staff, and give him some idea of the march route. At the moment, not even
Quartermaster Harman knew where the wagons were to go. In a move that Jackson
would later regret, he sent Hotchkiss home to Staunton to prepare maps of the recent
campaigns in the valley.

The 18,500 Confederate infantry were still filing through the pass that morning
when Jackson arrived in front of the small hotel at Mechum's River Station. He took
Dabney to one of the rooms, locked the door, and then revealed in a low voice that he
was heading to Richmond to meet with General Lee. During his absence, Dabney was
to lead the army toward the capital. The troops would follow the Virginia Central
Railroad as closely as roads would permit. Ewell's division was to continue in the lead.
The utmost secrecy must be maintained. Jackson outlined what those precautions
were.

A somewhat perplexed clergyman-turned-adjutant listened silently. Perhaps Dabney did not understand enough about his assignment to have questions. He then watched as Jackson climbed into a postal car behind the locomotive of a long troop train. Soldiers from Whiting's command not only filled the other cars; they clambered onto the roofs so thickly that they seemed to one observer to "cover them all over like a cluster of bees."[2]

Later in the day, Colonel Boteler was returning from another trip to Richmond and was at Charlottesville quietly awaiting westbound transportation when an unexpected eastbound troop train thundered into the station. The locomotive wheezed to a stop; a startled Boteler saw Jackson seated in the postal car. When he approached the train, Jackson looked out the side door and recognized his trusted friend. The general shouted happily: "Glad to see you! Jump in!" Boteler grabbed the extended hand and climbed aboard. Jackson asked if he had pencil and paper. Yes, came the reply. "Then sit down, please, and write as I shall dictate to you."[3]

Jackson carefully outlined how he wished the troop transfer to be made, telegrams that needed to be sent, a signal detachment to be organized, eighteen additional battle flags made, and so on. When he had finished, the general escorted Boteler to the doorway and shook his hand. The colonel departed in search of a conveyance heading west. Jackson attended to a couple of other matters, and then his train left the station in a cloud of steam.[4]

A contingent of troops from the 4th North Carolina had been lounging on uneventful guard duty in Gordonsville, the rail junction northeast of Charlottesville. The sudden appearance of an eastbound train carrying perhaps upwards of 2000 soldiers sent Tarheels racing to the station. "This arrival came upon us like a clap of thunder," one of them wrote. "There is some important movement on hand but no one can even surmise what it is." In a moment, the soldier caught a glimpse of the officer in charge. "Gen. Jackson is a very ordinary looking man, a little and but a very little above the medium height. He is very shabbily dressed and has a short, shaggy beard, very prominent chin and a mouth indicating firmness and decision."[5]

The weather was good for the next two days as Jackson's army proceeded east in a hop-scotch movement novel to the ways of war. While at Charlottesville, Jackson conferred with Virginia Central Superintendent Henry D. Whitcomb. Alerted earlier to what was needed, Whitcomb had assembled all the rolling stock he could collect west of the South Anna River break in the line. The result was ten trains, each consisting of an assortment of eighteen to twenty freight, passenger, and flat cars.

By Jackson's orders, a single four-horse wagon was to be used for each 100 men. Only wagons in good condition were to make the trip east. They, along with cavalry, some guns, and artillery mounts, were to move by the roads near the track. Other cannon, plus stores and baggage, would go by train. Not enough passenger cars and locomotives existed to transport Jackson's entire force at one time, so an innovative system went into play.

Trains backed up the track and loaded one or two brigades in the rear of the marching column. A ride of a couple of hours carried the men the distance of a full day's march. The trains disembarked their loads, which resumed marching. Then the locomotives went in reverse with empty cars to the rear of the army, loaded up again, and repeated the procedure. The back-and-forth movements continued for two days.[6]

It was neither a smooth nor an efficient operation. The roads were none too good; rolling equipment moved slowly when it moved at all; a general lack of vigilance produced breakdowns in the advancing processions. The tail end of the infantry, knowing that it would soon be riding on trains, made little effort to maintain the pace with the rest of the army. Straggling—by those genuinely too footsore to continue and those who made a habit of breaking ranks to search for food—left a great wake of manpower.

Heat and the red dust of the Piedmont compounded all of the discomforts. A chorus of profanity sometimes echoed across the countryside. Usually, conversation was minimal. "Orders were issued," a Virginia soldier explained, "that we were not to know or tell anything until the next battle."[7]

By Saturday, June 21, most of the army had covered thirty miles and was filing into Gordonsville. A haggard Major Dabney was surprised to find Jackson there instead of at Richmond. The general had stopped at the village to investigate a report that Federals in force were on the Rapidan River sixteen miles to the north. Jackson postponed any thoughts of continuing eastward until a local citizen who knew the country could verify that the rumor was unfounded.[8]

Headquarters during this brief stop was at the large white home of Mrs. Mary E. Barbour on the northern outskirts of Gordonsville. She was the mother-in-law of the Reverend Daniel B. Ewing, the local Presbyterian minister. He and Jackson renewed an old friendship. Ewing was as impressed by Jackson's piety as fellow clergymen William White in Lexington and James Graham in Winchester had been. The Gordonsville pastor also found Jackson "simple and unsophisticated in his manners. He did not seem to think himself a great man. In conversation he did not aspire to be a leader [and] contributed his part with unaffected modesty."[9]

Jackson held Ewell's and his own divisions at Gordonsville. With Whiting's division and Lawton's brigade continuing toward Richmond, complete bewilderment existed in the ranks as to the army's destination. From the rail junction at Gordonsville, the Confederates could go in any direction. Jackson said nothing. Late in the afternoon the general asked Dabney to take a train ride with him. The major eagerly accepted. General and adjutant climbed into a postal car connected to a locomotive, and the short train rocked eastward. Jackson lay down on the mail clerk's bunk and was soon sound asleep. Dabney gazed out the window in perplexity.

Early on Sunday morning, the 22d, the train halted nineteen miles down the line at Fredericks Hall. There the troops of Whiting and Lawton were in bivouac. Open country lay in every direction; a half-dozen homes hugged a mile-long stretch of straight track. Jackson was now only fifty-two miles northwest of Richmond.

He took temporary quarters in the home of the village's most prominent resident, Nathaniel W. Harris. There he spent a quiet and meditative Sabbath amid heavy rain showers. Jackson attended an afternoon "camp preaching" in Hood's Texas brigade but transacted very little military business in the course of the day. He did, however, arrange for a guide to take him through the unfamiliar country ahead. Major Dabney summoned his brother, Captain Charles W. Dabney, a former commonwealth's attorney for Hanover County and quite knowledgeable about the major roads in the area.

Not wishing to travel farther by train for fear of being recognized, Jackson asked that an impressed horse be well rested and fed that evening. His mania for secrecy extended another step: he had General Whiting write out a pass for an unidentified colonel to proceed through the lines. Jackson, wearing no insignia of rank, was to be the officer.

Jackson made it clear that Dabney would continue to lead the army forward. The valley forces then stretched out along roads and railroad for some fifteen miles. Dabney, like his commander, was a strict Sabbatarian. He made no effort to consolidate the scattered forces that Sunday.

The clergyman was an intellectual with some administrative talents. Commanding a tired army in strange country exceeded his ability. Fellow staff members were of limited assistance. Dabney disliked their high spirits, and they viewed him as a civilian misfit.[10]

Further, Dabney was almost as much in the dark on what Jackson precisely had in mind as everyone else. Move the army toward Richmond, he had been told. Nothing else. This secrecy or noncommunication on Jackson's part would have adverse effect on the Confederate march eastward in the days to come.

In the evening, Mrs. Harris politely inquired what time the general wanted his breakfast. "Have it at your usual hour," he replied courteously, "and send for me when breakfast is ready." The lady went to Jackson's bedroom around 7 o'clock the next morning. Jim Lewis opened the door. "Lord," he said to the hostess, "you surely didn't spec to find the General here at this hour, did you? You don't know him, then. Why he left here at one o'clock this morning and I spec he is whipping the Yankees in the Valley again by now."[11]

With little if any sleep that night, Jackson had quietly ridden from Fredericks Hall. Accompanying him were Major Harman, Captain Charles Harris of the Quartermaster Department, and the guide, Captain Dabney. These companions were under strict orders to address Jackson as "Colonel." Although a number of stories exist of sentinels stopping the party en route, Jackson met no impediment during the long ride in humid and overcast weather.[12]

A Confederate officer recuperating in Richmond at the time did not know how close he was to the truth when he stated: "I have been looking on Gen. Stonewall Jacksons movements with great interest. . . . from his former character we are forsed to put him down as a bold, venturesome, energetick and skillful leader and will verry soon employ his forces somewhere that will pay. he has a peculiarity that I admire to a certain extent. he keeps his contemplated movements to himself."[13]

By using relays of commandeered horses, Jackson covered the fifty-two miles in less than fourteen hours. At 3 P.M. on that sultry Monday, Jackson and his three aides turned off Nine-Mile Road into the yard of the Widow Dabbs house. The two-story, rectangular mansion, set back from the road, was a mile and a half northeast of the Richmond city limits. It was also the field headquarters of General Robert E. Lee. There one of the most important councils of the war was about to convene.

Jackson dismounted stiffly. Dusty, travel stained, and obviously tired from a half-day's horseback ride, he still walked with those typical long strides that were an integral part of his makeup. An aide informed the visitor that Lee was at work. Jackson refused to disturb the commander and shyly walked back into the yard to wait. He slouched against a fence, with head bowed and cap pulled down over his face.

A few minutes later, Major General D. Harvey Hill rode into the yard. He looked at the man propped wearily against the yard-paling, then looked again. It was his brother-in-law, Jackson! He was supposed to be in the valley! Hill rushed over and the two were greeting each other warmly when Lee's aide appeared on the porch and beckoned to them.

Jackson and Hill entered the home and went to Lee's office, a rear room on the first floor. Lee cordially welcomed them and tendered refreshments. Harvey Hill accepted; Jackson requested only a glass of milk. Hill engaged in small talk while Jackson sipped on his milk and studied the man whom he had so long admired from a distance.

Lee was then fifty-five, the son of a Revolutionary War hero, and an exemplary soldier who had given three decades of service to the military. He had gone through West Point with a spotless record in conduct—an achievement "rare but not unheard of."[14]

At the outbreak of civil war, Lee had declined an offer to command all of the Union forces because he could not find it in his conscience to draw his sword against his native state and his birthright. Lee had taken command of Virginia's mobilization in the chaotic spring of 1861; it was he who put enough of an army together to meet and defeat the first Federal thrust into the state at Manassas.

Thereafter, Lee had served with sadly inadequate authority as a military adviser to Jefferson Davis. The president then displayed high confidence in Lee by naming him to succeed the wounded Joe Johnston as commander of the South's principal army. It was a courageous move by Davis, for Lee had only minimum field experience when placed at the head of the Army of Northern Virginia. Many generals in that force viewed the appointment with reactions ranging from unenthusiastic to hostile.

Such negative thoughts proved short-lived. Lee was stately, heavy set for that day, yet modest and quiet by nature. He combined boldness with skill, ingenuity, and common sense. A roving reporter for the *London Times* described Lee as having a "manner calm and stately, his presence impressive and imposing, his dark brown eyes remarkably direct and honest as they meet you fully and firmly." Lee was so courteous and gentle, the newspaperman added, that "a child thrown among a knot of strangers would inevitably be drawn to him . . . and would run to claim his protection."[15]

A young staff officer seeing Lee at this time felt the same admiration. "He is a splendid looking fellow, very tall and handsome. His hair is silvery gray and his beard, which is short, covers his face. He inspires the confidence of all."[16]

Lee was more than a soldier of the first magnitude; he was also a good and pious man. Those ingredients were enough to win Jackson's high regard.

Harvey Hill was a known quantity to Jackson, of course. Like Jackson, he had left the army after the Mexican War to pursue a career in higher education. Hill was married to Isabella Morrison, Anna Jackson's older sister. Jackson's senior by three years, he was small, rather bent, sharp tongued, but brave under fire. "Old Rawhide" his men called him, for good reason. Harvey Hill loved his God as fiercely as he hated Yankees.

Within a few minutes after Jackson and Hill entered Lee's headquarters, two other major generals arrived. At forty-one, James Longstreet was three years older than Jackson. A low graduate in the West Point class of 1842, he had languished in the army as an infantry officer and paymaster. The Civil War awakened the energies of "Old Pete" Longstreet. He was a powerful figure, nearly six feet tall, with broad shoulders, gray-blue eyes, and heavy beard that concealed an unsmiling mouth.

Only five months earlier, a scarlet fever epidemic had swept through Richmond and claimed three of Longstreet's children. A prior penchant for gaiety disappeared in the father; he became an uncommunicative soldier until he concluded that he had few if any superiors in military strategy. His performance to date in the field had been spotty. In time, Longstreet would demonstrate a slowness that would breed generations of postwar controversy. At this stage of the war, he was dogged, opinionated, and unbreakable.

The remaining subaltern in Lee's office had been one of Jackson's classmates at the academy, and he would be his principal nemesis in the months ahead. Ambrose Powell Hill personified the spirit of a Virginia cavalier. Born a year after Jackson into landed gentry, he had made fun of Jackson during the West Point sojourn. An embarrassing illness had delayed Hill's graduation by a year.[17]

Powell Hill's prewar army service had been routine. It took the Civil War to bring out his military qualities: hard fighter, sometimes impetuous, more tactician than strategist. Known as "Little Powell" because of his slimness, he was above medium height and wore his chestnut hair unusually long. Hill was a first-rate combat officer; yet he was sensitive and proud, quick to flash a temper at any perceived slight. Indifferent to popularity, Powell Hill never was a close friend to anyone but the men who proudly served under his command.

This was the first time in the war that these four major generals had been together. The visitor from the valley initially occupied the focus of attention. He was both the hero of the hour and a curious unknown. Monosyllabic replies to comments and questions heightened the enigma.[18]

Light conversation quickly ended as Lee turned to the matter that had brought them together. Few commanders had borne a heavier responsibility than that which now pressed down upon Lee. Yet his head was clear, his energy high, as he laid out plans for his first attack on McClellan's army. In the usual sense, this was not a council of war. Lee had already determined his basic strategy. The purpose of what would become a four-hour session was to discuss the details and work out the final points. First, however, Lee explained to his lieutenants the bold offensive he wished to unleash.

The Union army was east of Richmond in a north-south line two-thirds of the way across the peninsula formed by the York and James rivers. The Chickahominy River ran roughly midway between the two streams. All three rivers coursed from northwest to southeast. The average distance from the York to the Chickahominy was seven miles, and from the Chickahominy to the James was nine miles. The country was flat—swampy when it rained. Much of the land was covered in pine woods. Scores of roads and watercourses meandered aimlessly through the region.

Central to Lee's plan of operation was maneuver. He wanted to mount a successful attack against McClellan's right flank in the area north of the Chickahominy. Driving the Federal wing eastward would force McClellan to abandon his works in front of Richmond and cross the Chickahominy in order to protect the York River Railroad and his supply base at White House on the Pamunkey. This would enable Lee, having the initiative, to defeat the Union army in the open while the latter was falling back toward his supplies.

Jackson would approach to the east, curling around the upper reaches of the Chickahominy and around the reported Union right flank. That would take the valley forces deep into the Union rear near the headwaters of Beaver Dam Creek. The three other divisions—those of Longstreet and the two Hills—would cross to the north side of the river after Jackson passed. While Jeb Stuart's cavalry protected Jackson's left, the valley troops would uncover the crossings of the Chickahominy. Lee's other divisions would not have to make a forced passage of the stream.

The Confederate movement would be a huge wheeling motion toward the southeast, with some 56,000 soldiers turning *en echelon* from the outside in toward the center. On Jackson's arrival in the area, he would still be at least seven miles from Lee's army. Therefore, General Lawrence O. Branch's brigade from Powell Hill's division would advance up the Chickahominy to the river crossing at Half Sink. Branch would establish contact with Jackson, move down the river on a parallel route with the valley army, and brush aside any threat to Jackson's right flank.

Other units in Powell Hill's so-called Light Division (with six brigades, it was the largest division in the Confederate armies) would pivot as Jackson passed. Harvey Hill and Longstreet would press in from behind and follow the two forces in their front. Thus would the Federals on the flank—30,000 soldiers under General Fitz John Porter—have to abandon their position to avoid encirclement and annihilation.

Implicit throughout this strategy was one key point: no fighting would occur until the enemy had been flushed from his entrenchments. All four commands should be in a coordinated line. Thereupon, Lee's army would sweep down the Chickahominy and attempt to get between McClellan and his base on the Pamunkey River, one of the York's principal tributaries.

This proposal was extremely bold. It was also extremely risky. About three-fourths of the Southern army would secretly move away from McClellan's front and take position on the Union army's northern flank. If the Federal commander learned of the movement, little more than an armed nuisance stood between the Army of the Potomac and its goal: Richmond.

Lee was also basing his strategy on a complicated schedule in which everyone would wait until that component (Jackson) with the farthest distance to cover made the first strike. Timing was all important; and unless all parts of the Confederate host acted in complete liaison, critical problems would arise instantly. Further, the Union line was on good ground at Beaver Dam Creek. It was a strong position and might not crumble even in the face of a surprise attack.

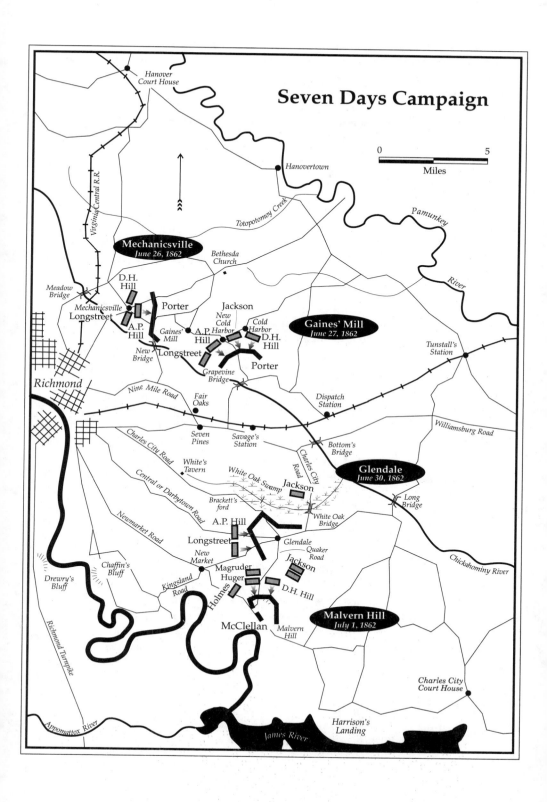

Seven Days Campaign

Mechanicsville
June 26, 1862

Gaines' Mill
June 27, 1862

Glendale
June 30, 1862

Malvern Hill
July 1, 1862

Hanover
Court House

Hanovertown

0   5
Miles

Virginia Central R.R.

Totopotomoy Creek

Pamunkey

River

Bethesda
Church

Meadow
Bridge

D.H.
Hill

Mechanicsville

Longstreet

Porter

A.P.
Hill

Gaines'
Mill

New
Bridge

Jackson

New
Cold
Harbor

A.P.
Hill

Cold
Harbor

D.H.
Hill

Longstreet

Porter

Grapevine
Bridge

Tunstall's
Station

Richmond

Nine Mile Road

Fair
Oaks

Dispatch
Station

Williamsburg Road

Seven
Pines

Savage's
Station

Bottom's
Bridge

Charles City Road

White's
Tavern

White Oak Swamp

Jackson

Charles City Road

Long
Bridge

Central or Darbytown Road

Brackett's
ford

White Oak
Bridge

Newmarket Road

A.P. Hill

Longstreet

Glendale

Jackson

Chickahominy River

Chaffin's
Bluff

New
Market

Quaker
Road

Drewry's
Bluff

Kingsland
Road

Magruder
Huger

Holmes

D.H. Hill

Richmond Turnpike

McClellan

Malvern
Hill

Malvern Hill

Charles City
Court House

Appomattox River

James River

Harrison's
Landing

In addition, the linkup with the Confederate segment left south of the Chickahominy would occur at New Bridge, the last Federal obstacle far down the peninsula. While Lee drove east, there was little to prevent McClellan from sidling around Lee's southern flank and advancing on the Confederate capital.

All things considered and as Lee saw the situation, nevertheless, the stakes were too high to dwell on negative possibilities. Lee knew McClellan to be slow to act or react. Momentum would be with the Confederates. So would success, if all went according to plan.

The army commander then did a curious thing. He told his four generals that he had some paperwork requiring his attention in the next room. The subalterns could work out the final points for the counteroffensive. With that, Lee departed.

The door had barely closed when discussion began. These four senior commanders knew little of one another's strengths and weaknesses. Yet they had to refine a battle plan in which each would be very dependent on the other. Regrettably, none of the four left a creditable record of what was said. Only bits and pieces of the conference exist.

Harvey Hill preferred a less dangerous operation altogether. Yet Lee had already announced what was to be done. The objection quickly passed. Longstreet then took control of the meeting. The top soldier remaining from the Joe Johnston regime, he assumed seniority without asking for it.

Jackson was the key. He would initiate the action with 18,500 soldiers, the largest segment in Lee's reinforced army. Yet the man who should have been asking the most questions was the least talkative. Everything Jackson had heard at the meeting was news to him. He had fought fatigue while trying to absorb all that had been said.

Certainly he needed to know more than he had been told, for he had never been part of such a large operation. At the moment, only two thoughts were firmly planted in Jackson's mind: Lee had ordered him to lead a major offensive, and he was more physically and mentally exhausted than he had ever been in his life.

The critical time element hinged on when Jackson could get on McClellan's flank. Jackson had ridden fifty-two miles in fourteen hours to attend this meeting. He would be spending another night in the saddle returning to his troops. Then the troops had to march basically over the same route to get into position. As Jackson pondered the elements of marching and time, someone asked when he could launch his strike in the Beaver Dam Creek area.

Controversy reigns on who posed the question and how Jackson replied. Harvey Hill recalled that Jackson set three days hence—June 26—for his appearance. That does not fit the known facts. The popular story is that Jackson mumbled his intention to return with his army on June 25, whereupon Longstreet suggested that he allow himself more time.

On the other hand, and in a little-known postwar conversation, Lee remembered coming back into the room, hearing the tentative timetable for a June 25 movement, and enjoining Jackson to move the date back by twenty-four hours for his own benefit. Jackson seemed surprisingly unconcerned about the starting time. In any event, the Confederate grand offensive was set for June 26 at 3 P.M.[19]

When the conference ended near sundown, Jackson started quickly to rejoin his army. Darkness enveloped the riders; rain began pouring. On through the wet night the horsemen galloped in a northwesterly direction. Jackson napped in the saddle in spite of the elements. It was not a good sleep, but it took the edge off exhaustion.

Around 10 A.M. on June 24, the general reached Beaver Dam Station in Hanover County. (This depot was some thirty miles from the creek of the same name.) He had ridden forty miles nonstop—and over ninety miles without rest during the past thirty-three hours. Two consecutive nights without sleep had further dulled his already crippled mental processes.

If Jackson could have been more alert, what he discovered at Beaver Dam Station would have aroused his anger and his energy. Only the van of the army was there. The rest of his force was strung out a full fifteen miles to the west on muddy roads broken by swollen streams. Confederates had gotten a late start that day and, Winder added, they were "having a very disagreeable time."[20]

Jackson had less than forty-eight hours to get his divisions into position more than thirty miles away. Yet he displayed no sense of urgency. Perhaps he felt that marching fifteen miles a day for the next two days was no hardship for his well-trained "foot cavalry." Jackson would wait for the rear units of his army to catch up with the main body.

That would put him behind schedule—badly so—but it seemed to matter little. Jackson was incapable now of thinking about more than one problem at a time. His men needed a strong controlling hand, yet their commander saw the situation through the blur of fatigue. In the middle of his thirty-eighth year, a man who needed rest as much as any other human, Jackson was simply not up to this kind of exertion without true sleep in forty-eight hours.

A few orders went out to members of the staff. Then Jackson rode to the nearby plantation of Henry Carter. There he hung out his wet and mud-caked uniform to dry. Jackson sat down and, for one of the few times in his life, picked up a novel and began reading it to pass the time. After awhile he struggled to his feet and went silently to bed.[21]

What had happened to Jackson's army during his absence was inexcusable even in the face of several explanations. Major Dabney, the stimulating preacher and brilliant professor of theology, had proved to be a misfit at army supervision. The overmatched cleric became increasingly strained by the responsibility of trying to keep the divisions moving in orderly fashion toward Richmond. The harder he tried, the worse it became. Lax marching discipline created confusion. Commissary wagons bogged down in mud miles to the rear. Dabney then fell ill with diarrhea, and the officers to whom he entrusted the march performed at an even lower standard.[22]

The highly individualistic command style that Jackson had utilized to extraordinary success in the valley had now failed him. It failed him because he was not there to oversee matters with his all-seeing perception; and Hotchkiss was not there to point out the best and most direct routes. Soldiers consequently straggled badly.

At one point, Sidney Winder assumed command of all brigades in Jackson's old division. Some order began to evolve with those men, but the rest of the army stumbled along the road in confusion. On one long, open-country stretch, water was so scarce that artillerymen gave horses water from the canteens. Most of Jackson's "foot cavalry" covered barely twelve miles that Monday, and officers were relieved that they traveled that far.[23]

In truth, the problem was not entirely of Dabney's doing. Jackson was moving the largest aggregate in his career. Yet there had been no corresponding increase in staff members, who customarily were shepherds on a march. Jackson may also have over-rated how valuable the Virginia Central Railroad would be to him. As for the valley fighters, they were in flat, marshy country and moving on poor roads that have been likened to disjointed connections of short lines built by farmers in colonial days. These troops had marched twenty-five miles a day in the Shenandoah, but that had been on the macadamized Valley Turnpike. In short, every ingredient existed to impede the advance toward the enemy army pushing on Richmond.

After nightfall on the 24th, Jackson received a copy of General Orders 75, Lee's battle plan. By now he was alert enough to discern the important points in the directive. Jackson was to spend the next night at "some convenient point west of the Central Railroad," then move at 3 A.M. on June 26 down the road toward Pole Green Church, northeast of Richmond.

At that juncture, Jackson would communicate his presence to Branch's brigade poised on the upper Chickahominy. Once contact with the other elements of Lee's army took place, the sweep down the river would begin. Nowhere in Lee's orders was there any mention of anticipated battle.

Wednesday, June 25, was uncomfortably hot. The sun blazed down fiercely on dusty roads. Dense woods on either side of the country lanes shut off air currents. Jackson's normal fifty-minute march per hour was impossible to maintain. Putting the army back together had consumed most of the night. It was after sunrise before the long and weary columns began moving anew to the southeast.

What sleep Jackson had obtained the previous night only teased his system for more. He was in a stupor most of the morning as he rode alongside his men. His usual encouragements, "Press on, press on," lacked persuasion. Most of the streams along the way were still out of their banks; roadways were mud lanes; missing bridges had to be replaced with makeshift spans.

By sundown, the bone-tired troops were just to the west of Ashland. That day they had covered twenty miles—an amazing feat amid all the adverse conditions. Yet Jackson was six miles short of Slash Church, the planned stopping point. He could not make it that night. The men were too fatigued.

The general's patience and his temper were short because he was so jaded. Early in the evening he told Winder to have his men fed and ready to move by "early dawn." Winder, himself worn down, replied, "That is impossible because of the position of my baggage-train." Jackson's head jerked in obvious anger. "General Winder, it *must* be done!" he snapped and then brusquely dismissed his most trusted brigade commander.[24]

To compensate for the six-mile shortage, Jackson informed Lee in a quick note, the troops would be back on the road a half-hour earlier at 2:30 A.M. Jackson called it "early dawn." His men snarled that it meant "the night before."

Unknown to Jackson or Lee, the element of secrecy surrounding Jackson's march was gone. McClellan by then was fully aware that his old West Point classmate was bearing down on his right flank.[25] Yet the Federals chose to brace rather than to relocate their lines.

Jackson's courier to Lee may have passed a rider going from Lee to Jackson. Historians have long suspected that the supreme army commander sent a detailed message to Jackson on the eve of battle, but no such communique could be found.[26] However, a letter does exist.

Never before published, it was Lee's detailed suggestion that Jackson send his army into action on two separate roads. Lacking Hotchkiss and good maps, Jackson became increasingly bewildered as he tried to digest what Lee had written from army head-quarters.

In your march tomorrow on reaching the Merry Oaks, the roads divide. By the map before me the right hand, called the Ash Cake road, intersects, near Mrs. McKenzies, a road leading by Shady Grove Church to Mechanicsville. If one of your columns followed the road to Shady Grove Church, it would there unite with Branch's brigade from 'Atlees,' and the rest of Genl. A. P. Hills division from the Meadow Bridge road. If a second column continued on the Ash Cake road to J. Overton, & thence on the road to Pole Green Church, it would strike the road from Shady Grove Church to Old Raleigh, a mile & three quarters east of the Shady Grove Church. Your two columns would there be in close communication, and north of Beaver Dam Creek. You would then be in a position either to take the road across Beaver Dam Creek by Walnut Grove Church and Gains' Mill to Cole Harbour; or to pursue the road by Old Raleigh, & Bethesda Church, to Cole Harbour; either of the latter routes would entirely turn Beaver Dam Creek. Perhaps it would be better for one of your columns to take the road by Walnut Grove Church, and the other the road by Bethesda Church, or Old Raleigh, which ever you find most advantageous.

These routes are suggested for your consideration.[27]

Jackson was studying a map with Lee's communique in hand when soldiers' cheers announced a welcomed visitor. General "Jeb" Stuart, Lee's cavalry chief, had arrived with 2000 horsemen and a three-gun battery to screen Jackson's left on the next day's march. Jackson and Stuart had first become acquainted during the latter's brief period of service at Harpers Ferry in the first weeks of the war. Stuart had been of inestimable aid to Jackson at the Manassas fight. Now, thanks to Stuart's recent reconnaissance around McClellan's army, he had acquired a fame approaching that of Jackson.

The two men were similarly tall and well built. Both had abiding religious faith, deep patriotism, and a combative spirit. Stuart was a dashing extrovert who enjoyed gaiety, jokes, and colorful uniforms—all of which Jackson disdained. The striking differences between the dour Puritan and the animated Cavalier had produced a friendship that would now escalate. However, their conversation that night was brief. Stuart gave Jackson what information he had and then led his command toward Ashland to begin his duties. Jackson was too tired to engage in a lengthy conversation.

Around midnight, Generals Whiting and Ewell called on Jackson. The commander had established headquarters at a farmhouse between Ashland and the Virginia Central Railroad. Jackson was still up and dressed. Not privy to Lee's most recent message, Ewell suggested that Jackson's marching column be shortened by having the men advance on parallel roads. The army could advance to their objective in half the time and at half the risk. Jackson listened and replied politely that he would consider the idea and let them know later.

Ewell and Whiting left headquarters and were walking across the yard when Ewell turned to Whiting. "Don't you know why Old Jack would not decide at once?" Ewell then answered his own question. "He is going to pray over it first!"[28]

The generals proceeded a bit farther when Ewell discovered that he had left his sword in Jackson's room. He walked back into the house and found Jackson's door ajar. The general was on his knees in prayer. Dabney was close to the truth when he stated: "His ardent soul, on fire with the grandeur of the operations before him, and with delight in their boldness and wisdom . . . forbade rest or sleep for him on this important night. He deliberately devoted the whole of it to the review of his preparations, and to prayer."[29]

By dawn on Thursday, June 26, Jackson had absorbed a total of eight hours' sleep in the previous three and a half days. He bore little resemblance in action to the proficient tactician in the valley.

Sidney Winder was up early that morning. While waiting to start what was surely going to be an ominous march, the brigadier made a diary entry that was both prayerful and prophetic: "God give us the victory & spare us from the dangers of battle."[30]

Guides for the day's march were Captain Charles W. Dabney (the chief of staff's brother) and Major Jasper Whiting, who had served on the staff of General Gustavus W. Smith in the first stage of the peninsula campaign and, like Captain Dabney, was familiar with the country. Those were the pluses.

The minuses began in getting the march underway. Jackson had intended his men to be on the road at 2:30 A.M. Still, nothing was going right for the weary general. Dabney later complained that the brigade commanders "would not or could not get rations cooked, their own breakfasts, and their men under orders earlier than an hour after sunrise, probably because their supply-trains were rarely in place, by reason of the indolence and carelessness of julep-drinking officers." Such an indictment did not go unchallenged. Kyd Douglas undoubtedly voiced the feelings of many of Jackson's officers when he countered that Dabney, with "no experience to fit him for the demands of his position," was "not equal to this occasion in the field."[31]

Whiting's division, with Hood's Texas brigade fanned out in front as skirmishers, actually got underway on time. Yet it was 8 A.M. before the army—seven brigades of infantry and nine batteries of artillery—started in force. The commissary wagons were late. A scarcity of drinking water in the Ashland area forced soldiers to range over the countryside in search of wells and springs. By sunup Jackson was irritated and snappish. He could not understand the delays, the vacillation of officers, the general breakdown of his proud army.

Once the Confederates were on the road, Jackson pushed the men along as rapidly as possible. The troops had just cleared Ashland when Stuart and his adjutant, Captain William W. Blackford, met the head of Jackson's column. The two generals conferred by the side of the road as the foot soldiers passed. Blackford was struck by the marked contrast between the two commanders.

Stuart rode an imposing stallion and was impeccably clad in gray uniform, yellow sash, polished boots, and the like. Jackson, on the other hand, "was mounted upon a dun cob of very sorry appearance, though substantial in build, and was dressed in a threadbare, faded, semi-military suit, with a disreputable old Virginia Military Institute cap drawn down over his eyes."[32]

Appearance notwithstanding, it was encouraging to most of Stuart's men to have Jackson at hand. A South Carolina cavalryman observed: "It was a great inspiration to feel the presence of this solemn and powerful man with high cheek bones and reddish brown beard. . . . The hero of the Shenandoah rode all day on his chestnut sorrel directly in front of our division with six cavalryman couriers, whom he would send quietly around to capture the enemy's pickets."[33]

One delay after another materialized in the course of the day. The soldiers, four abreast, crept forward warily over roads winding through tangled thickets and unknown woods. Alarms brought occasional halts. A report reached Major Dabney in the middle of the column that Federals were thought to be on the left. Dabney could not get word to Jackson at the head of the army, so he took it upon himself to halt his segment and check out the report. It proved false. Meanwhile, in the lead, Jackson had stopped the march until the ranks could close up.

The Confederates wound down Ashcake Road, passed Slash Church, and reached Peake's Turnout on the Virginia Central Railroad at 9 A.M. Jackson had been due at the crossing six hours earlier. He dutifully informed General Branch—his connecting link with Lee's army—of his whereabouts. Jackson then stopped for a quick breakfast at the home of Hector Bowe before resuming a march that continued to stall.[34]

Jackson was familiar with Branch's brigade. In time, it would become one of his most dependable fighting units. He had confidence in its North Carolina troops but some reservations about its present and inexperienced commander. The question proved well founded. After receiving word from Jackson, Branch seemingly disappeared with the message and his men into the woods.[35] That left Jackson and Ewell, proceeding on separate roads as the latter had urged the previous night, groping southward.

By 10 A.M. the railroad was behind Jackson's army. Ewell turned to the right three-quarters of a mile beyond the tracks. He marched south toward Shady Grove Church while protecting the right flank of the main column. Jackson continued for another three-quarters of a mile and turned in the same direction toward Pole Green Church. The roads were tracks more akin to channels serving as drains for adjacent thick forests. Turgid streams like the Chickahominy and its tributaries wound snail-like through jungles of underbrush and produced a rank odor as oppressive as it was obstructive.

Burned bridges, road barricades, volleys from small groups of concealed Federals, an occasional artillery shot, all opposed Jackson's progress. Stuart's men on his left roamed far afield and sent Jackson a steady stream of messages. Yet Jackson missed Turner Ashby; he was not accustomed to the energy of Stuart and his mounted troopers. At 11:20 that morning, Jackson reported a skirmish to Stuart in matter-of-fact terms: "I am engaged with the enemy. I trust that God will give our army a glorious victory."[36]

The sky was cloudless following two days of showers. While it was cool and pleasant in the morning, heat climbed with the sun. By noon soldiers were sweltering. The column slowed, despite Jackson's urging that the men press forward. He was doing so with an ignorance of where—and to what—they were moving.[37]

Extreme weariness in the ranks was one reason for some of the day's slow advance. Federal General Porter was also prompt in placing obstructions in the roads, because he had seen reports estimating Jackson's force at somewhere between 30,000 and 60,000 men. Beneath those excuses is a more fundamental fact for Jackson's seeming failure of alacrity. His official report makes it clear that he did not understand his mission.[38]

Lee had failed to give precise instructions; in his fatigue, Jackson had failed to ask for clarification. He simply obeyed orders without hesitation. Jackson moved along the directed line of march and notified Branch when he crossed the railroad. At 10 A.M., he sent Branch another note, advising him that the valley army was two miles beyond the Virginia Central and advancing toward Mechanicsville.[39] That was the sum total of all communication on June 26 between Jackson and anyone in the Army of Northern Virginia.

Nowhere in Jackson's orders was he required to be at a particular place at a specific time. He was unaware of how critical Lee and others thought it was to turn Porter's flank that afternoon. Hearing nothing from Lee, Jackson naturally concluded that nothing was pressing. Fighting would not take place until he got there.

This explains Jackson's lack of concern, which several officers noted that Thursday. Colonel Evander Law at one point came upon Jackson leaning carelessly against a fence, with General Chase Whiting standing beside him. Law wrote, "They were both perfectly silent, not a word passing between them, and, so far as I could judge from their attitudes, had been so from the time I came in sight."[40]

Around 4:30 P.M., having advanced sixteen hard miles, Jackson had passed Pole Green Church and reached the road junction of Hundley's Corner. There the lead elements of Ewell's division rejoined the main column. No one else was at Hundley's Corner. Something was wrong.

Ewell told Jackson of encountering Branch with his brigade ambling down a parallel road and knowing nothing about the movements of the rest of the Confederate army. Jackson and Ewell stared at each other in silent apprehension. They had more than one reason to do so. The sound of gunfire three miles beyond obscuring woods to the south gave unmistakable evidence that an engagement was underway.

What it meant was unknown. No word had come from Lee. Jackson had been directed to advance to Pole Green Church, communicate with Powell Hill, contact Harvey Hill on his right, and lead a combined movement down the Chickahominy toward Cold Harbor.

Lee's assumption was that Jackson's approach would be such a threat to Porter that the Federal general would retire without offering battle. Yet Lee based Jackson's movements on a faulty map that showed Pole Green Church a short distance beyond the headwaters of Beaver Dam Creek.

Pole Green Church was almost three miles from the headwaters of the stream. Even at Hundley's Corner, Jackson was in no position to turn Porter out of his entrenchments. Although Jackson had followed orders to the letter, he was not in the

An artist's conception of Jackson's Mill in 1843, the year after Jackson left for West Point. *Cook,* Family and Early Life

Laura Jackson Arnold, the only immediate family member Jackson had for most of his life. Civil war brought a permanent estrangement between brother and sister.
Courtesy of Stonewall Jackson Foundation, Lexington, Va.

This engraving of the earliest known likeness of Jackson shows the twenty-two-year-old officer at the time of his arrival in Mexico. *Author's Collection*

A painting from a daguerreotype made in New Orleans in July 1848, when Jackson returned from the Mexican War. *Author's Collection*

Maj. William H. French (who ultimately rose to the rank of major-general) was Jackson's superior officer in Florida, and was instrumental in the Virginian's leaving the army.   *National Archives*

An 1851 daguerreotype of Brevet Major Jackson, apparently made during a brief visit to New York. *Courtesy of Stonewall Jackson Foundation, Lexington, Va.*

This portrait of Elinor Junkin Jackson, the only one surviving, was taken by J. E. McClure in Philadelphia, date unknown. *Courtesy of Stonewall Jackson Foundation, Lexington, Va.*

Margaret Junkin Preston, redheaded sister of Jackson's first wife, became one of the closest friends he ever had. *Courtesy of Stonewall Jackson Foundation, Lexington, Va.*

The Virginia Military Institute as it appeared during Jackson's tenure there as a professor. *Virginia Military Institute*

Professor Jackson in 1857, from an ambrotype attributed to Samuel Pettigrew, Lexington, Va. *Courtesy of Stonewall Jackson Foundation, Lexington, Va.*

Photograph of a carte de visite of Mary Anna Morrison Jackson, the general's second wife and mother of his only child to reach adulthood. *Courtesy of Stonewall Jackson Foundation, Lexington, Va.*

The only home Jackson owned underwent a number of alterations in the decades following the Civil War. It has been meticulously restored to its appearance as it was in 1859-1861, when the Jacksons lived there. *Courtesy of Stonewall Jackson Foundation, Lexington, Va.*

In November 1862, Jackson posed for the first of two series of wartime images. The "Winchester Photograph" is the most popular image of the general. The famous misplaced button is on the outside row, third from the bottom.
National Archives

This previously unpublished carte de visite from one of the Winchester negatives presents a three-fourths view of Jackson and shows the badly wrinkled condition of his uniform coat.
Howard R. McManus

Jackson surrounded by several members of his staff. Starting with the two figures at the top and moving clockwise, the aides are Wells J. Hawks, Robert L. Dabney, William Allan, "Sandie" Pendleton, Joseph G. Morrison, D. B. Bridgford, H. Kyd Douglas, James Power Smith, Hunter McGuire, and Jedediah Hotchkiss.
U.S. Army Military History Institute

The "Chancellorsville Photograph," the last picture taken of Jackson, was made near Fredericksburg, Virginia, less than two weeks before the general received his mortal wounds.
National Archives

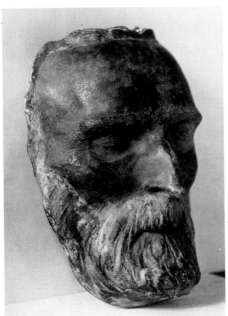

Death mask of the general, made on May 11, 1863, after the body arrived in Richmond, Virginia.
Valentine Museum

position necessary to execute the Confederate battle plan. He might as well have remained in the valley for all the good he was doing.

There was still another misunderstanding. The battle reports of Lee and Jackson point to different objectives that Thursday. Lee's expectation that Jackson would flank Porter's position is plain enough from what he wrote. Jackson, in two different statements, seemed to underscore his real destination as the vital road junction at Cold Harbor far in McClellan's rear.

Meanwhile, the noise of distant gunfire swelled. Combat was growing intense. Yet Jackson had no orders regarding any battle. He could not initiate any action on his own. It was unrealistic to expect Jackson's men to advance another three miles over unfamiliar roads in order to reinforce an attack that was not part of Lee's stated battle plan. To press forward would leave Jackson's force unsupported and vulnerable in front and on both flanks.

Moreover, Jackson's force was strung out on two different roads. The rear guard was at least five miles away. (This is why none of the field officers in Jackson's division near the end of the line of march mentioned hearing any sound of battle to the south.)

At sundown, Jackson ordered his men to bivouack in a state of semi-readiness. At that moment, Dabney observed, Jackson "appeared to me anxious and perplexed. . . . My surmise was and is that he was every moment hoping and waiting for some definite signal from Genl. Lee; and that having reached Hundley's Corner . . . and still no definite instructions, he concluded the risk was too much to go further."[41]

Only later would Jackson learn what happened that afternoon at Mechanicsville. Lack of communication, impetuosity, and inexperience all played a role in the first major Confederate offensive on the peninsula. Powell Hill was supposed to spearhead Lee's wing in the movement against the Union right flank. He was to do so in concert with Jackson's arrival.

As the daylight hours of June 26 passed, "Little Powell" grew increasingly anxious about Jackson's tardiness, the exposed position of Lee's army, and the failing odds against success. In midafternoon, Hill went ahead without Jackson. He crossed the Chickahominy with his division, drove east through the village of Mechanicsville, drew up his brigades in a long battle line facing Porter's elevated position behind Beaver Dam Creek, and without any further hesitation opened an attack. Apparently Hill expected Jackson to arrive on the field momentarily. Lee, caught off guard by Hill's action, had no choice but to send other units in support.

It was a lopsided contest from the start. The Union position was simply too strong, a point Hill did not comprehend until hours of assaults brought him heavy casualties—close to 1500 men, compared to Union losses of barely a fourth of that number. The complete Union victory would later in some quarters be attributed to Jackson___ ___ence on the field.

S___ ___usation of guilt was inaccurate as well as unfair. In Lee's General ___ ___hkiss r___inded one of Jackson's biographers, "A. P. Hill was *not* to ___ non___ ___ he discovered the movement of the columns of Jackson. ___ ___ve at 3 o'clock on the morning of the 26th, there was ___ ___, as [Fitzhugh] Lee states in his history, Hill grew ___ck."[42]

One can perhaps argue that if Jackson had been where he was supposed to have been, and on time, Powell Hill's assault would have struck empty earthworks. Yet no "attack" in a battle sense was in the master plan. Jackson's leadership in the June 24–26 period was ineffective because his physical and mental strength were exhausted. The one indictment with relevance against Jackson on June 26 is tardiness in his advance. That seems a minor failing when viewed against other breakdowns in the Confederate high command during those first hours of the Seven Days Campaign.

Lee had formulated an offensive in which unfamiliar pieces in a complicated framework were supposed to fall into place easily and punctually. The commander then showed no predilection to assume control of the situation once it developed. He was three miles away from the point where Powell Hill struck across the Chickahominy.

Some previous writers are wrong in asserting that Lee's staff work was poor. It was nonexistent. Mechanicsville was therefore a shakedown action by a new army seeking experience as an offensive machine.

Afterwards, Lee pointed no finger of blame in his official report. In fact, he painstakingly removed all hints of controversy with regard to his actions or those of his lieutenants. "In consequence of unavoidable delays," he stated, "the whole of Genl Jackson's command did not arrive at Ashland in time to enable him to reach the point designated on the 25th. His march on the 26th was consequently longer than had been anticipated, and his progress being also retarded by the enemy, A. P. Hill did not begin his movement until 3 P.M."[43]

Near sundown, a very welcomed face arrived at Jackson's headquarters. Alexander Boteler had returned from establishing a line of couriers from Louisa Court House to Charlottesville—another of Jackson's typical contingencies. The congressman and the general talked far into the night. When they sought to get some sleep, Boteler stated, it was impossible "amid the angry muttering of the storm of the coming of the battle." Artillery fire kept both men awake.

That night Jeb Stuart assigned cavalry pickets around Jackson's camp. John Esten Cooke, a novelist of repute, was a member of Stuart's staff. Cooke put his vivid imagination to work that evening by claiming to be sent with a message addressed to "Gen. T. J. Jackson, Somewhere."[44]

June 27 for the Confederates was another day of fumbling and missed opportunities. Federals had learned during the night of Jackson's proximity to the Beaver Dam Creek line. Porter conveyed the report to McClellan, who was convinced that he was facing at least 200,000 Southern troops and that they were far more familiar with the terrain than he.[45] As a result, he ordered Porter to withdraw from Beaver Dam Creek. Jackson's presence that night, not Powell Hill's attacks the preceding afternoon, caused this retirement.

Porter detached a brigade and two batteries as a rear guard, then withdrew his command with both skill and stealth. By daylight, the Federals who had stopped Hill's advance in its tracks were gone.[46] Jackson aroused his men early that steaming day. Cannon fire to the south built in crescendo and told that battle had resumed. Jackson voiced no eagerness to join the fray. His assignment remained to turn Mc-

Clellan's flank. Maneuver rather than fighting would be the order of the day as he headed for the road junction with the inapplicable name Cold Harbor.

Ewell's division took the lead and moved south to ensure that the enemy position at Beaver Dam Creek was flanked. The Confederates were approaching the intersection with an east-west road when Ewell's scouts spotted Federals. As Southerners deployed for action, General Chase Whiting made a fool of himself.

For several days, the little general had presumed upon his old West Point superiority to instruct Jackson on how to fight a war. His division was second in line that morning, but Whiting had ridden ahead of the entire column. Suddenly, he came galloping up the road. "General Jackson!" he shouted excitedly. "There is a heavy body of infantry yonder, less than a mile distant, to the northeast! I saw them myself across this wide open farm! They must be a body of enemy!"

Jackson said nothing but rode slowly to the crest of a small incline. For a full minute he eyed the distant movement from beneath the visor of his kepi. Whiting, fidgeting in the saddle next to Jackson, kept exclaiming: "There they are, General! They must be the enemy!" The head of Jackson's column had halted by that time. Jackson, paying no heed to Whiting, rode back and said to the officer in front: "Forward your column, Colonel."

Only then did a red-faced Whiting learn that the infantry he had seen were the predominantly Alabama and North Carolina brigades of Harvey Hill. That division had been sent from Mechanicsville to make contact with Jackson. As Jackson requested his brother-in-law to act as trailblazer east on the road to Bethesda Church, Whiting galloped off embarrassed and angry.[47]

A march of three miles brought Jackson's main column across Old Church Road and close to Walnut Grove Church. Gunfire could still be heard in the distance; but lacking maps and in a strange country, Jackson continued forward. No obstacles stood in his way.

As was his custom, Jackson ranged ahead of the column, oblivious to any danger from snipers. Soon he met a lone horseman. It was Major Walter H. Taylor, one of Lee's aides. The army commander had sent Taylor to find Jackson and lead the valley force to a junction with the rest of the army.

Had this been done the night before, Jackson would have had his men in motion before dawn and surely would have struck Porter's men as they sought to fall back from Beaver Dam Creek. Soon Walnut Grove Church came into sight. It was a one-story frame structure on the north side of Old Cold Harbor Road and near its intersection with the Telegraph Road. Jackson was now in mostly open and rolling country, dotted with patches of woods. Beaver Dam Creek lay two miles to the west.

Jackson rode up to the church and spied the thin figure of General Powell Hill. Finally! Here was someone who could tell him what was transpiring. The two officers saluted and began talking. In answer to one of Jackson's questions, Hill pointed south and east toward Gaines' Mill. The enemy had retired to that area. Powell Hill's division would presumably be on Jackson's right as it moved toward the Federals and another battle.

It was about 9:30 A.M. when a large body of horsemen came galloping up the road from Mechanicsville. In front was Lee, who had ridden from his headquarters to ascertain affairs first hand. Hill touched his hat in salute, made a comment or two, and withdrew to join his command. Lee and Jackson dismounted. They led their horses through the churchyard and halted. Lee, resplendent and impressive in a full uniform, sat on a cedar stump. Jackson stood in front of him with the seedy appearance of a farmer who had been plowing all day.

At one point, Jackson removed his battered cap. His forehead was startlingly white in contrast to the weather-beaten hue of the rest of his face. Jackson was in no mood to be cordial. He was too much of a soldier to be abrasive. He listened as Lee did most of the talking, and he replied to questions in clipped tones. No one was in earshot as the two conferred quietly but earnestly.

Lee seemed to have expected to find the Union army in line, facing west, behind Powhite Creek a mile east of Walnut Grove Church. It supposedly was the only stream where the Federals could make a stand while maintaining contact with forces south of the Chickahominy. Lee then directed Jackson to take charge of all Confederate units north of the river. This meant that Harvey Hill's division and Jeb Stuart's cavalry would be directly under his leadership. Jackson would be at the head of fourteen of the army's twenty-six brigades. The general with whom Lee was seemingly the most unfamiliar on a personal basis would command over half of the Army of Northern Virginia.

By Lee's directive, Jackson would continue to advance rapidly to Cold Harbor. This march of about eight miles would force McClellan from his strong north-south line to the east of Powhite Creek. A Federal retreat would be inevitable. When it occurred, Jackson could cut the York River Railroad and take a strong defensive position on the right and rear of the enemy. The troops of Longstreet and Powell Hill would drive the Federals eastward straight into Jackson's guns.

Jackson liked the plan. It was logical but daring, and potentially destructive to the enemy. When Lee finished the conference in the churchyard, it was 11 A.M. and uncomfortably warm. Jackson nodded in approval at Lee's final statement, mounted Little Sorrel, and rode eastward down the road. Nine hours of daylight remained to isolate and defeat McClellan's forces north of the Chickahominy.

Unfortunately, and for the second consecutive day, Lee had predicated his strategy on erroneous assumptions. The enemy was not where he thought it was. Further, defending the Pamunkey River supply line was no longer vital to McClellan's plans.

The Union commander had already determined to establish a new base at the other end of the line on the James River. Porter would not be racing eastward to rejoin any main force. His task on June 27 was to defend the north side of the Chickahominy long enough for McClellan to get the bulk of his army—particularly the heavily loaded wagon trains—moving southward across the peninsula.

Toward that end, Porter had not placed any troops behind Powhite Creek. Rather, he had led them farther to the east and onto the south bank of a sluggish waterway called Boatswain's Swamp. The Union position was a large semicircle curling from northeast to southwest. Swampy land for the most part protected the Union left to the Chickahominy, a half-mile away.

Porter gossiped too much to rise high in the top echelon of Federal generals; but he knew how to set up a defensive line, and he demonstrated that he could fight. His

35,000 troops were on high ground behind the swamp; the artillery positions were near perfect. At some points along Porter's line, Federals stood waiting in ranks six deep.

Near noon, Powell Hill's division, the van of Lee's army, made contact with Porter. Heavy skirmishing ensued until 2 P.M., when Lee sent Hill and Longstreet forward in an attack. Fierce battle exploded at once. Although the Federals were not where Lee expected, and despite the fact that the Confederates barely equaled Porter in numbers, Lee was optimistic. "The arrival of Jackson on our left was momentarily expected, and it was supposed that his approach would cause the extension of the enemy's line in that direction."[48] Lee's statement clearly and sadly shows that he expected Jackson to move toward battle—when, in fact, Jackson was marching away from it.

Two hours of intense combat produced heavy casualties, especially on the Southern side, but no tangible results. Soon Longstreet was fought out; Powell Hill's men were in a death trap at the bottom of a watery ravine. Lee now realized his mistake. Only a general assault by the entire Confederate army would bring victory. Yet Jackson's whereabouts were a complete unknown.

Again, Jackson had merely obeyed orders as he understood them. After his conference with Lee, he rode back toward his troops. Jackson came upon a company of the 4th Virginia Cavalry and asked if it contained any local men. Several troopers replied in the affirmative. Jackson selected Private John Henry Timberlake, whose family farm was midway between Ashland and Gaines' Mill. The twenty-six-year-old Timberlake had been part of Stuart's "Ride around McClellan" feat. He certainly had to know the country well.

Jackson told the cavalryman in low voice and with few words that he wanted him to lead the way to Cold Harbor. No explanation was given of the strategic designs Jackson had in mind. A number of roads went in that direction, so Timberlake led the divisions down the larger and more direct road. For an hour the column moved in silence. Then the route turned east. The sound of gunfire became heavier. "Where is that firing?" a startled Jackson asked while standing in the saddle. "From over at Gaines' Mill," Timberlake replied. "Does this road lead there?" the general quickly asked. "Yes, it passes the mill en route to Cold Harbor." A now-angry Jackson growled: "But I do not wish to go to Gaines' Mill. I wish to go to Cold Harbor, leaving that place on the right." Timberlake resented the tone of this rumpled and uncommunicative general. "Then the left hand road was the one you should have taken," he stated icily. "Had you let me know what you desired, I could have directed you in the right direction at first."[49]

The confusion resulted from two crossroads bearing virtually the same name. Timberlake had taken Jackson's force to New Cold Harbor; the general's destination was Old Cold Harbor. They were nearly two miles apart on the Old Church Road.

No choice remained but to reverse the column and backtrack for at least a mile and a half to Walnut Grove Church, then proceed to Old Cold Harbor. This would put Jackson's advance two hours behind expectations. Staff members grew edgy at the prospects of Jackson's disposition on the return march. However, he appeared outwardly calm. When Dabney asked if the delay might be fatal, the general answered in an even tone, "No, let us trust that the providence of our God will so overrule it, that no mischief shall result."[50]

Harvey Hill had encountered no such deviation on his eastward advance. By a separate route, he led his division via Bethesda Church to Old Cold Harbor. Hill made contact with Federals across the east-west extension of Boatswain's Swamp. Around 3 P.M., Jackson and his lead elements arrived at the crossroads area.

It was oppressively hot, with grimy smoke and the pungent odor of gunpowder hanging over the land. Jackson was both very tired and very ill humored. A lethargic air surrounded him as he gazed at the strange country to which he had been moving all day. He said nothing.

Jackson still anticipated Longstreet and Powell Hill driving Porter's corps toward him. Yet Jackson was apprehensive that his soldiers and those of Harvey Hill might be mistaken for the enemy and subjected to friendly fire. To avoid such an event, Jackson placed his brother-in-law's brigades in a position to trap any Federals forced eastward by the other segments of Lee's army. As far as Jackson was concerned, all of this was consistent with Lee's stated plan that morning.

Unknown to Jackson, the plan had changed. Lee now wanted to make a full-scale assault with his whole army. Again Major Taylor went in search of Jackson with orders from Lee. Jackson was to move into action from Cold Harbor. Ewell and his three brigades would depart at once to reinforce Powell Hill's hard-pressed lines. Jackson ordered Harvey Hill to advance with his troops, which now formed the left of the entire Confederate line. Ewell's brigades drove ahead on Hill's right.

The battle had increased in volume when Ewell arrived on the field. His ranks quickly took heavy losses, notably in the Louisiana brigade. Major Roberdeau Wheat fell dead at the head of his "Tigers"; and for the first time in the war, Taylor's Louisianians broke and had to be withdrawn from action. Isaac Trimble's brigade moved into the action, his men shouting at the retreating fragments: "Get out of our way! We will show you how to do it!" They did, but at a severe cost of life.[51]

Jackson's experienced ear by then told him that Powell Hill's men were not driving the enemy—that the Confederates had gotten the worst of it and were falling back. Ewell had been rushed into the contest. These developments began for the first time to confuse Jackson's concept of the situation.

Obviously, all Confederate assumptions had been wrong. The enemy was not where it was supposed to be, and it was putting up a stiff fight rather than withdrawing from the field. If Powell Hill had fallen back and Ewell had moved to his aid, a huge gap must exist between Harvey Hill's division and the rest of the Southern army. Whiting and Winder must fill that gap, and promptly.

That Jackson did not send a courier to Lee, a mile away, for clarification and instructions is strange. Jackson was completely unaware of the true situation. He made no initiative to learn the facts. Major Taylor's two visits were Jackson's only long-range contact with Lee.

Nevertheless, the roar of battle told Jackson that his presence was critically needed. Unlike a somewhat similar circumstance the previous day, Jackson could not ignore an obvious battle close at hand. Thereupon, Jackson stated, "I ordered a general advance of my entire corps."[52] Yet it would take almost two hours for his troops to move toward the fighting.

The divisions of Chase Whiting and Sidney Winder were stretched out for miles on the road to the north. They needed to be brought up before Jackson could enter the contest. The general turned to Major Dabney but remembered that his chief of staff was still debilitated from the effects of chronic diarrhea. Jackson then beckoned to Major John Harman. He had abiding faith in his quartermaster "because of the energetic way in which he managed the great wagon train that ever hung as an incubus upon army movements." Be that as it may, Hotchkiss sadly conceded, Harman "was always blundering when he had anything to do with matters strictly military."[53]

Jackson's instructions to Harman were anything but simple. A close approximation of what the general said was:

The troops are standing at ease along our line of march. Ride back rapidly along the line and tell the commanders to advance instantly *en echelon* from the left. Each brigade is to follow as a guide the right regiment of the brigade on the left, and to keep within supporting distance. Tell the commanders that if this formation fails at any point, to form line of battle and move to the front, pressing to the sound of the heaviest firing and attack the enemy vigorously wherever found. As to artillery, each commander must use his discretion. If the ground will at all permit, tell them to take in their field batteries and use them. If not, post them in the rear.

Harman had never before carried an order on a battlefield. Jackson should have had an aide put the orders in writing. Regardless, as Dabney continued to protest that he could handle the important assignment, Harman galloped off to the north. Dabney had watched Harman closely during Jackson's instructions, and the chief of staff felt even greater anxiety. "I saw by the man's face and manner that he was confused, but Jackson was so engrossed with his cares he did not stop to examine his countenance."[54]

The quartermaster found Whiting first because his division was in front of Winder's. The Carolinian, still smarting from Jackson's rebuff that morning, was in no mood to absorb the mumbling of an aide who obviously had no conception of the situation. Whiting snapped at Harman, asked pointed questions, and raised doubts about one point after another.

Under such pressure, Harman not only garbled Jackson's message; he told Whiting and Winder the exact opposite of what Jackson wanted. Thus, the two divisions of 12,000 soldiers remained where they were on the Old Cold Harbor Road.

An hour passed. The roar of war on the Longstreet-Powell Hill front grew louder than it had been all day. Jackson, in the corner of a field near the Cold Harbor crossroads, impatiently rode back and forth while waiting for his two divisions. A blanketing fatigue limited his range and depth of thinking. Staff members sat silently in their saddles.

Dabney now feared the worst from Harman. The cleric sneaked away from Jackson and rode as fast as he could to the two divisions. He found Whiting, who, to Dabney's disgust, "was in liquor." Whiting berated Harman, expressed resentment at the whole situation, and predicted doom.

Dabney finally interrupted him and said in pointed terms that the order was for him to advance without delay. When Whiting began to argue, Dabney pleaded expediency and hastily rode off in search of Winder. Soon the troops were in motion, but hours had been lost by the foul up.[55]

Other encumbrances now faced Jackson as his forces headed southward toward the battle. There was no time for any reconnaissance. The troops were marching through an intricate country where woodlands obscured vision and no elevated points existed to provide a clear view. Pine thickets and roads winding back and forth as they snaked up and down ravines combined to conceal portions of Jackson's own army. An advance of 400 yards hid one brigade from another. Heat was oppressive. Wool uniforms turned black from perspiration.

Jackson's advance, lacking both guides and instructions, was haphazard. His units gravitated toward the conflict at Gaines' Mill. The Confederates would engage the enemy where he was found. A march of two miles brought the van of Jackson's column to the battlefield. None of the brigades knew where they were supposed to go. Daylight was beginning to fade. Time remained for one more major attack.

The Union position behind Boatswain's Swamp was one of the strongest created in the Civil War. A member of Lee's staff described Porter's lines as being on

a plateau bounded on the north-west side by a bluff eighty or ninety feet in elevation, which, curving to the north and east, gradually diminished into a gentle slope. The plateau was bounded on its north side by a stream flowing along its base, whose banks gradually widened and deepened until, when reaching the bluff, they had gained the width of eight or ten and the depth of five or six feet, thus forming a natural ditch. Three lines of breastworks, rising one above the other, had been constructed upon the base of the bluff, and one line extended along the north-east crest for more than a mile, and batteries of artillery were in position in rear of the infantry.[56]

Jackson's men went into disconcerted action as they arrived on the field. Lee had already placed Ewell's division between those of the two Hills. Lawton's 3500 troops marched steadily into position behind Ewell just as the latter began to take a pounding. "Hurrah for Georgia!" Ewell shouted with relief. The last two divisions to arrive—Whiting and Winder—drifted farther to the right in support of Powell Hill. Jackson had lost personal contact with most of his soldiers.

His men were filing into various positions when Jackson himself galloped into the area. Word swept down the embattled Confederate position. A private in Longstreet's command far on the right wrote exuberantly: "Could it be true? A deafening shout burst from our men; thousands of throats took it up and rent the very air; it died away only to be repeated in greater emphasis and volume. The news ran along the lines like an electric flash. . . . Stonewall Jackson here!"[57]

The general had no such enthusiasm. Jackson had spent a long and frustrating day in alien country. He was near exhaustion again. Reaching into his haversack, Old Jack extracted a lemon and began sucking it as he rode toward the center of the Confederate line. He looked in no direction, spoke to no one. In another environment, Jackson could have passed for a nodding circuit rider.

At that moment, one of Stuart's men saw him for the first time and was disappointed. Jackson's uniform coat

was positively scorched by the sun—had that dingy hue, the product of sun and rain. . . . The cap of the general matched the coat—if anything was more faded. The sun had turned it quite yellow indeed, and it tilted over the wearer's forehead, so far as to make it necessary for him to raise his chin, in looking at you. He rode in his peculiar forward-leaning fashion, his old rawboned sorrel, gaunt and grim—but like his master, careless of balls and tranquil in the loudest hourly burly of battle.

Moving about slowly and sucking a lemon (Yankee spoil, no doubt) the celebrated General Stonewall looked as little like a general as possible. . . . He had the air rather of a spectator.[58]

Lee had been anxiously awaiting the arrival of Jackson. Hours of pounding against the enemy works had left the Federals unshaken and defiant. Their powerful artillery was firing fast as well as effectively. If the battle was to be won, every component of Lee's army must drive simultaneously against the enemy. Jackson's presence with over half of the Confederate force was crucial.

Impatiently, Lee rode in the direction from which Jackson was expected. The two generals met on the Telegraph Road to tumultuous cheering. Lee clasped his lieutenant's hand warmly and exclaimed: "Ah, General, I am glad to see you! I had hoped to be with you before!"

Jackson made a twitching motion with his head, as if trying to decipher Lee's meaning, and then mumbled something unintelligible to bystanders. Lee turned and listened for a few moments to the noise of battle.

"That fire is very heavy," he said to Jackson. "Do you think your men can stand it?"

Again Jackson was silent and contemplative. Then he exclaimed: "They can stand almost anything! They can stand that!" New instructions came from Lee. Jackson listened, saying little. He then saluted and galloped back toward his lines.[59]

Whatever Lee said, the brief meeting galvanized Jackson. Now he was caught up in the excitement of combat. He was at last on the field of battle after twenty-four hours of frustration. Sleepless eyes ablaze, he rejoined his full staff and began issuing orders like cracks of a whip.

Jackson sent for Stuart and suggested an immediate and concentrated cavalry charge on the Gaines' Mill position. Stuart shook his head. "Too many cannon." Jackson quickly realized the impracticality and shifted his thinking to other possibilities.[60]

Riding back and forth, he had become more animated than anyone had seen him since the campaign in the valley. Major Dabney recalled three times in the war when Jackson's "fiery spirit fairly broke from his customary restraints and bore him away with a tempest of passion and triumph by which his face and person were literally transfigured." This was one of those times.[61]

Jackson watched the Confederate lines hastily form into battle position. An hour of daylight remained. He dispatched staff members to all division commanders. "Tell them this affair must hang in suspense no longer! Sweep the field with the bayonet!"[62]

This was the old Jackson again, but it was also an expression of impatience. Aligning all units into position took time and care. Although the fighting had continued fiercely in Powell Hill's sector in the center of the line, it was 7 P.M. before Lee had his full army in battle formation. It had taken five hours to get everyone in place—five hours of fighting and heavy losses. The sun was setting when the entire Confederate line surged forward with a roar of gunfire and cheers.

Whiting moved forward with Hood's Texas troops. Ewell's division was down in the swampland, their commander urging the men forward. Aged Isaac Trimble, black plumed hat and all, was galloping up and down his line while exhorting his men to charge. Lawton's Georgia regiments advanced steadily. Pendleton rode up to announce that Winder had led the Stonewall Brigade into action. Jackson withdrew the lemon from his mouth. "We shall soon have good news from that charge!" he exulted. "Yes, they are driving the enemy!" With that, Jackson raised the mangled lemon aloft as if hoisting a victory standard.[63]

Pleasure was premature. The Stonewall Brigade rushed forward so eagerly that the 2d and 5th Virginia on the flanks got ahead of the other three regiments. The brigade took a frightful beating for several moments. William S. H. Baylor, former commonwealth attorney in Staunton and now colonel of the 5th Virginia, described the action that followed: "For three quarters of a mile a shower of shell fell around us but our boys kept up gallantly through the thick woods and miry swamps until we reached an open and wide field, which gradually ascended into a commanding hill, where the enemy was posted. . . . Our lines were thinned by many having fallen by exhaustion in the terrible effort to keep up at the rate we were going, and I do not think the brigade numbered over 800 now."[64]

The line stopped once, when Colonel James W. Allen and Major Frank Jones of the 2d Virginia were killed. Colonel John Neff of the 33d Virginia considered the action the "hottest fight" he had ever seen. "I was twice struck with spent balls but was not much hurt. I had some thirty odd men killed or wounded, out of one hundred that I took into the fight."[65]

For thirty agonizing minutes, men struggled like animals for control of the swampy country. Thinking was nonexistent; survival through victory was the major instinct as Johnny Rebs and Billy Yanks fought for life over death. Even the noise had an unbearable overtone. A private in the 10th Virginia later stated: "If you can form an idea of a hundred or more cannon and one hundred thousand or more small arms, and sometimes thousands of men—yelling at the top of their voice—then you can begin to understand the raging terror and the roaring, lumbering noise of this big battle that was going on."[66]

Jackson watched the action intently. Colonel Bradley T. Johnson and his 1st Maryland were near the commander. Johnson could not take his eyes off the general. "His teeth were clenched, his lips clamped closer than ever, and the blaze of his eye alone betrayed excitement. Straight in the saddle, straighter than usual . . . he sat, his head raised up, catching every sound." Suddenly, Jackson jerked in the saddle and raised his right arm. Johnson thought he was beckoning for the colonel and his men. He galloped forward for instructions. Jackson, looking down, said nothing. Then Johnson realized that the general was praying. "Abstracted, dead to the strife, and blind to all around, his soul communed alone with his God." In a moment, Jackson looked up at Johnson. His voice was hoarse from shouting. The general croaked loudly: "Colonel, send all the infantry in except a hundred to each battery. You cover them!"[67]

The climax of the battle of Gaines' Mill occurred when General John B. Hood led his brigade straight up into the Federal works and broke the line. One of the Texans recalled the charge in unique style.

A strange circumstance took place here when we were advanceing on the Enemies works, when we were within a hundred yards or so of the Enemies Lines every one Seemed to falter. Fireing almost ceased. An order was passed down the line to ceace fireing, that we were Shooting our own men. Our boys lay quiet for a few Minutes, when Some Keen eyed fellow discovered and Said they are Yankees Shure I can See the Blue uniform and the U.S. Buckles on their Shoulder Straps. Then the order to Charge was given. You ought to have seen those Texans go forward over gulies, ditches, Through and over a dence Mass of fallen timber, Onward Now into the Enemies works. McClellans line is now broken and his troops are on the Skedaddle as fast as their Legs Could Carry them across a large rolling Open field, to be Shot down like Varmits.[68]

When Jackson rode through the battle area and saw where Hood's Texans and supporting units had bravely fought their way up to and over Porter's entrenchments, the general could not conceal his admiration. "The men who carried this position are soldiers indeed!" he said.[69]

Darkness settled as the entire Confederate line struggled forward, crushing pockets of Union resistance. The main body of Porter's corps withdrew deliberately to the south. Federals crossed over the Chickahominy, burning bridges behind them. Beset by confusion and weariness, Lee's soldiers could not make any forceful pursuit.

Jackson had no way of knowing that one of the Union brigades covering Porter's retreat was under the command of Brigadier General William H. French, his commanding officer and nemesis in Florida eleven years earlier.[70]

Gaines' Mill would be the costliest engagement of the Seven Days Campaign. Total losses on both sides exceeded 15,200 men, including 2300 soldiers killed outright. Jackson's three divisions (which were in the battle the shortest period of time) suffered 310 killed and 1519 wounded. Among the fatalities was Colonel Sam Fulkerson, an acting brigadier. Jackson and the judge had quarreled after the Romney Campaign; yet Fulkerson had the fighting qualities and abiding patriotism that impressed Jackson. A month later, Jackson acknowledged a note from Fulkerson's nephew, Captain James Vance of the 37th Virginia. "If your brave uncle was neglected by others, he was highly admired by me you may rest confident. . . . In his death the Army, myself as well as you his kinsman have sustained a great loss."[71]

Early in the evening, Jackson rode in front of his troops with two or three staff officers. He wished to make a personal reconnaissance of the land. Suddenly, the general found himself in the presence of fifteen or twenty Federal soldiers. Recovering before they did, Jackson demanded their immediate surrender. The men laid down their arms. As they were being led to the rear, they passed Arnold Elzey's Confederates. One of the Union prisoners in front shouted as loud as he could: "Gentlemen, we had the honor of being captured by Stonewall Jackson!"[72]

Nighttime shrouded the battlefield. The roar of combat soon gave way to a new sound: the screams, cries, and moans of mangled men sprawled in woods and swamps and fields. Sergeant Thomas Penn of the 42d Virginia sought to write a reassuring note home that evening. "I am seated under a tree right upon the battle ground which is strewn with the dead and dying. Their groans are constantly heard upon every side. Several dead men are in a few feet of me, and many wounded (of the enemy)." Penn commented that he had survived the battle without injury. At the end of the letter, he got back to his surroundings. "The groans of the wounded are truly distressing. I wish the poor fellows could be attended to tonight."[73]

Jackson's commissary wagons were understandably late in overtaking the army. Poor Dabney, who had been without food all day, jumped at a late-night invitation to dine with a compatriot. The cleric gagged after the friend handed him a piece of raw tongue. When the man then offered him whiskey to wash down the meat, Dabney's nausea turned to indignation.[74]

If it was not a happy night at headquarters, it was another long night for Jackson. A lemon seems to have been his major meal that day. Food was incidental to more pressing matters. Near midnight, Jeb Stuart and his Prussian aide, Major Heros von Borcke, were asleep side by side in a tent. Von Borcke felt a hand on his shoulder. He grabbed his sword and demanded to know who was there. A mild voice answered: "General Jackson." Stuart immediately arose. Von Borcke diplomatically walked to a distant campfire while the two generals sat on blankets inside the tent and talked. Referring to the day's battle, Jackson said that it "was the most terrific fire of musketry I ever heard." He then directed Stuart to ride the next morning to Mc-Clellan's old supply base on the Pamunkey River and, if practicable, to occupy the White House site.[75]

Thus did the long day wind down to an end. The Federals had waged an incontestably valiant defense at Boatswain's Swamp. The campaign from the Southern point of view had been a disaster save for the final results. Uncertainty and ineffectiveness continued to mark Confederate efforts. Mistakes were commonplace.

Powell Hill had launched a major attack the first day without authorization. Lee had completely erred on the Union position at Gaines' Mill. Jackson, by following orders, had done nothing on the first day and appeared tardy on the second. Yet the troops who finally broke the Union lines were his.

The absence of a tight chain of command was the root of the June 26–27 Confederate failures. Lee commanded an army, but it was fighting like a group of disconnected divisions. The general's most respected biographer, Douglas Southall Freeman, blamed the division commanders rather than Lee for the disorganization. Each seemed "under no necessity of coordinating his movements with the other."[76] That is somewhat far-fetched. The captain of a ship, not the mates, is responsible for the continuing progress of the vessel on its journey.

Worst of all, the lack of a competent general staff left Lee out of touch with the pieces—and the pieces ignorant of exactly what the commander wanted of them in the strange country where they were supposed to be on the offensive. Basic communication and coordination were sadly missing; and until more control came from the top, the situation was not going to improve.

Dabney noted in later years that at Gaines' Mill, Jackson was thoroughly confused from first to last. "But that was John Harman's fault, and Whiting's, and a result of a wretched, disjointed staff service," the major asserted. "The fact is Jackson died without ever knowing how the battle was won. Providence won it for him, as he devoutly acknowledged."[77]

17

DUTY

SATURDAY CAME WITH AN EERIE silence. The day was an almost unnatural lull in the middle of what would be five days of battle. June 28 resembled the eye of a hurricane as a great storm raged on the Virginia peninsula. Two armies now warily stared at each other and licked their wounds.

Jackson had spent what was left of the night with Jeb Stuart. Shortly after sunrise, he rode to Harvey Hill's headquarters to reassume command of that division as well. Major G. Moxley Sorrel of Longstreet's staff came to Jackson in early morning. Longstreet on the far right of Lee's line was anxious to establish communications with the other end of the Confederate position.

Sorrel found Jackson "brisk enough" as well as "cheerful and pleasant." Jackson told the aide, "Explain, Major, to General Longstreet where I am and how my troops are lying, and say, with my compliments, I am ready to obey any orders he may send me."[1]

Little cooperation would take place that day. McClellan's retirement momentarily paralyzed Lee. Unfamiliar country and dense woods masked all movements. Lee was not sure where McClellan was heading—south to the James, east down the peninsula, a wide swing to the northeast and the old Pamunkey River line, a short distance to a new battleground? Therefore, for most of that Saturday, the Confederates did little but secure better positions. "Cannonading and musketry," a 37th Virginia soldier noted, "were kept up at intervals during the greater part of the day and we were maneuvered in and about our position all day, but no general engagement took place."[2]

By Lee's directive, Ewell's infantry and Stuart's cavalry moved down the Chickahominy to look for Federals and neutralize enemy supply arteries. Confederates slashed telegraph lines and destroyed railroad trackage. Deserted installations gave ample evidence that the Federals had abandoned their Pamunkey River base.

Most Southern soldiers spent the day clearing their front of dead and wounded comrades. Some urgency existed with the former; for in the heat and humidity, corpses began decomposing rapidly. Lieutenant John Hinsdale, a brigade officer in Powell Hill's division, recorded a good account of the day's activities. At first the men rested, "and rest they needed more than anything else."[3] Late in the morning, Hinsdale watched a score of men go onto the battlefield. He wrote: "They buried friend & foe alike in the same trench. They would dig large ditches, wide, and tumble these dead men in without ceremony or decency even. It was shocking to one unaccustomed to the cruelties of war."[4]

Hinsdale got a surprise just as the party completed its portion of the odious task. "I saw 'Stonewall Jackson' to day. He galloped through and turned up the road. . . . What a common, ordinary, looking man is he! There is nothing at all striking in his appearance. He rides an ugly horse, but is a graceful rider. He was evidently in a hurry. All the men cheered him as he passed by. He raised his hat & passed on."[5]

The majority of Jackson's actions that day remain a mystery. While his troops caught their breath, he must have reconnoitered the unfamiliar country in his front and on his flanks. Jackson may have taken one or more naps, but that is unlikely, and no record exists of it.

He was poised for battle. Waiting for Lee's new orders must have made him impatient and ill tempered. Yet he concealed it well. An officer came upon him, seated on a log, and having a casual conversation with General Chase Whiting.[6]

Not until the early morning of June 29 would Lee be sure that McClellan's army was heading for the James on the southern end of the peninsula rather than curling east or northeast. This information would give Lee his best chance to destroy his foe. Meandering streams and land made marshy from excessive rains limited movement on the southern part of the peninsula. The Union army had to move along established, narrow roads, with no room for deviation. McClellan might have a good head start, but his reputation for slowness was widely known.

The Southern commander quickly formulated his plan. He would shift his troops by roads nearer Richmond and, he hoped, strike the enemy between White Oak Swamp and the James. Winding streams and weblike roads might make Confederate marches difficult, but the choices otherwise were extremely limited. A complicated convergence began with Lee's orders.

Jackson was to reconstruct the Grapevine Bridge over the Chickahominy. He would then cross the river and sweep southeastward with his own, Ewell's, Whiting's, and Harvey Hill's divisions. Jackson's destination was White Oak Swamp. As he advanced, he was to clear the country of Federals and close with the Union rear guard in the neighborhood of Savage's Station. This would put Jackson on the left of the division of General John B. Magruder, whose assignment was to push eastward down the Williamsburg road. General Benjamin Huger's troops would advance on Magruder's right. Magruder and Huger could crush the Federal rear before it reached the safety of White Oak Swamp.[7]

At the same time, Longstreet and Powell Hill would swing west and south around the left of McClellan's army and strike it in flank or near its front. As Lee envisioned it, his army would encircle the enemy on three sides and produce the much-desired, smashing victory.

The rising sun was signaling a humid day when Magruder's 11,000 infantrymen and nine batteries shuffled forward toward the rear of McClellan's main column. While Magruder and Huger were familiar with the country, Jackson was not. Lee was unfolding a dangerous strategy.

His army was in four columns, moving by four different roads. Each was miles from the other. A junction was supposed to be made on the field of battle. Cavalry were of no help at the moment. With the exception of a squadron here and there,

Stuart's command was far down on the peninsula. The various elements of the Southern army would have difficulty maintaining even basic communication.[8]

General Porter Alexander repeatedly accused Jackson of doing little on June 29 because he did not want to violate the Sabbath. That is patently false. Jackson may have taken time early in the day for private devotions, but worship did not interfere with his military duties that day. If anything intruded, it was the old culprit, fatigue.[9]

Jackson's first assignment of the day was the rebuilding of the Grapevine Bridge. Federals had barely used the crude and ramshackle span in their withdrawal on the night of June 28 because it was in such rickety condition. One observer called the bridge a "rolling structure of loose logs, half buried in the slushy soil." Federals partially destroyed it after all had crossed to the south bank of the Chickahominy. Southern workmen restored it somewhat by noon on the 29th, and a few companies began gingerly making their way over the bridge.[10]

It did not take Jackson's engineering eye long to see that he was going to need more than one bridge to get all of his forces across the Chickahominy quickly. Someone directed his attention to a bridge 400 yards upstream. It had originally been constructed by Lieutenant Colonel Barton Alexander of the U.S. Engineers and bore his name. This span, although all but demolished, was the answer to Jackson's problem. Contrary to almost all previous accounts about rebuilding Grapevine Bridge, the reconstruction efforts were in reality on Alexander's Bridge.[11]

No engineers were at hand that Sunday morning, so Jackson assigned Major Dabney to oversee construction of a new bridge while Jackson prepared his troops for the advance. Dabney was no bridge builder. He was intellectually blind where engineering was concerned, and the work detail proved so inexperienced that Dabney termed them "shilly-shally" in performance. Most of the morning passed with little progress. Jackson's patience wore thin.

Captain Claiborne R. Mason providentially appeared on the scene. Jackson had met the former contractor during the McDowell Campaign. Mason and a gang of black laborers were then preparing a road to General Edward Johnson's mountaintop position. At Hotchkiss's suggestion, Jackson organized Mason and his little band into a pioneer corps. (Mason was officially an "acting quartermaster.") The Augusta County native was not a trained engineer, but he had a real knack for construction. Jackson gave Mason drawings of what he wanted the new bridge to be and told him to get to work. Soon the pioneers were heavily engaged and making progress.[12]

Around noon, Captain Henry Bryan of Magruder's staff arrived and inquired when Jackson planned to advance. The general replied that the bridge should be repaired within two hours, after which his divisions would begin crossing the Chickahominy. Jackson then detailed a member of his staff, Lieutenant Keith Boswell, to ride back with Bryan—presumably to check out connecting roads between the two Confederate forces. Jackson's statement about a probable advance in two hours convinced a nervous Magruder to wait for his arrival. That would provide protection for Magruder's left flank when he launched his offensive against the Union rear guard.

In early afternoon, confident that his own proclaimed timetable was correct, Jackson ordered his brigades down to the Chickahominy for the crossing. Alexander's

Bridge was not ready when the first units arrived, necessitating more delays. Mason and his men required a little longer to put the structure in workable order—and that was no mean accomplishment.

At 2:50 P.M., Jackson sent a quick note to Stuart, who was guarding the left flank of the army. "This bridge will from appearance be complete in less than two hours," Jackson stated, "when I hope to cross, and I have directed Genl. Ewell to follow me. Magruder is about 2 miles from this point, and has been slightly engaged with the enemy."[13]

Time passed slowly. No message came from Lee or any component of the army. Jackson could stand idly no longer. The bridge was only partially finished, but Jackson silently eased his way over the span and rode three-quarters of a mile to McClellan's old headquarters at the Trent home.[14] He was anxious to learn what Magruder and the rest of the Confederate army was doing. Jackson was ignorant of where everyone was; he was not sure where he was. No Hotchkiss, no maps, no couriers, no news.

Shortly after 3 P.M., while at the Trent mansion, Jackson heard gunfire rumbling from the south. This put him in a real predicament. He could take as many troops as he had across the river toward the sound of battle. This was a move he always preferred. Or Jackson could follow to the letter Lee's directive that he continue east while paralleling the Chickahominy and protecting its bridges and fords.

A courier appeared and handed Jackson a dispatch. It was a message from Lee and was intended for Stuart and Jackson. The communique, unknown to contemporary critics and overlooked by a majority of previous Jackson biographers, was to become the key to Jackson's movements for the next day and a half. Its importance cannot be overemphasized.

Bearing the signature of Lee's assistant adjutant general, Colonel R. H. Chilton, and addressed to Stuart, the message stated: "The Gen'l. Comd'g. requests that you will watch the Chicahominy [sic] as far as Forge Bridge, ascertain if any attempt will be made in that direction by the enemy, advising Genl. Jackson, who will resist their passage until reinforced. If you find that they have passed down below where they cannot cross, leave a force to watch movements which may be made & recross yourself to this side for further operations."[15]

No question remained now of Jackson's immediate course of action. He was clearly under orders to guard the Chickahominy bridges and resist the passage of any enemy troops who attempted to cross the river. Jackson viewed this directive as a change in Lee's basic strategy.

The day had begun with orders for the Confederate army to pursue McClellan's forces and bring at least a large part of them to bay. This latest announcement gave the impression that a Federal move might be underway toward White House on the Pamunkey. By remaining where he was, Jackson would be in position to assail the Federals if they came in his direction.

After rereading the dispatch, Jackson at 3:45 appended an endorsement: "Genl. Ewell will remain near Dispatch Station & myself near my present position." The same courier galloped back to Stuart with the acknowledgement.[16]

Jackson rode rapidly back toward the river and his command. Suddenly, another rider appeared. He was from General David R. Jones, a blunt and outspoken brigadier whose troops formed the left of Magruder's line. Jones wanted to know when Jackson planned to arrive in support of Magruder. Supporting Magruder was no longer an issue, Jackson felt. He sent the messenger back: he could not join Magruder because he had "other important duty to perform."[17]

Now Jackson could relax a bit. He obeyed a superior officer as unquestionably as he expected to be obeyed by subordinates. Lee had issued direct orders. Those orders would be followed without deviation. At the moment, no exigency demanded Jackson's attention. He did not have to press forward. With Lee's order, the tension inside Jackson eased. Weariness took its place. Total fatigue engulfed him by the time he got back to Alexander's Bridge.

There he received encouraging news from his bridge builder. Claiborne Mason was known to be semiliterate at best. When Jackson asked if he had followed the design sent to him, the captain answered: "Gineral Jackson, I ain't seen no sketch, and don't know nothin' about no pictures, nor plans for that bridge, but that bridge is done, sir, and is ready, sir, and you can right now send your folks across in to it."[18]

Jackson placed troops on both sides of Alexander's and Grapevine Bridges, then ordered his men to bivouac for the night. Although Surgeon McGuire and Major Dabney wrote separately after the war that Jackson met with Lee in late afternoon and discussed the next day's movement, neither general made reference to any such conference.[19] It would have been well for the present and the future had such a meeting occurred because misunderstanding had developed about June 29 responsibilities.

Lee had intended for Jackson to cross the Chickahominy, join Magruder, and "push the pursuit vigorously."[20] The poorly drafted letter from Colonel Chilton, apparently offered as a contingency move, gave the opposite impression of a change of plan. Never known for aggressiveness, General Benjamin Huger discovered that day a number of reasons to be late in his parallel advance on Magruder's right. That left Magruder alone to wage an offensive.

He was simply not up to it. Jackson's old artillery captain in the Mexican War always put on a good show. Of commanding form and ostentatious display, Magruder had such a childish love of military pageantry that men called him "El Capitan Colorado" behind his back. He could talk twenty-four hours without interruption, and he had a known fondness for the bottle—especially when too idle or too pressured. Magruder always took his responsibilities seriously. Yet on June 29, he seemed to fall to pieces step by step.[21]

Early in the morning, Lee sent two engineers to survey the abandoned Union works in Magruder's front. Suddenly, a message arrived at army headquarters from Magruder: he was about to launch an assault. Lee replied with a little heavy-handed humor by warning Magruder not to do harm to the two Confederate officers inside McClellan's deserted works.

Magruder became more overwrought as the hours passed. Finally, the harried officer concluded to wait no longer for support. He simultaneously set his advance in motion and lost control of himself. No more than 13,000 Confederates moved forward.

The confrontation came at Savage's Station, an advanced Federal base on the York River Railroad. There a Union rear guard consisting of two corps with full artillery support were in strong redoubts across Magruder's line of advance on the Williamsburg road. Realizing quickly the disparity in numbers, the distraught and befuddled Magruder sent orders desperately down the line for "each commander to attack the enemy in whatever force or works he might be found."[22]

A disorganized assault lasted two hours and gained nothing of consequence. With darkness, Federals resumed their withdrawal toward the James. Lee made little effort to conceal his irritation. In a barbed note to Magruder, the commander stated, "I regret much that you have made so little progress today in the pursuit of the enemy."[23]

Nightfall signaled another day of Confederate frustrations. Lee had accomplished nothing other than Magruder's halfhearted stabs at the Union rear. Huger, who was supposed to support Magruder, "turned aside from the road which had been assigned to him, and when he was recalled by an urgent message from Lee, advanced with the timidity which almost invariably beset the commander of an isolated force in the neighbourhood of a large army."[24]

Jackson's conduct that day has come under unwarranted attack from both contemporaries and historians. A number of writers criticize him for not attacking in support of Magruder. As one officer later wrote: "Had Jackson crossed the Chickahominy any time before 5 P.M. on the 29th and moved with his usual energy and audacity, what would have become of McClellan's army? Alas! Alas!"[25]

In simple truth, Jackson was never aware of any order to attack because Lee never made such a wish clear. Had the army commander told Jackson to launch an assault, Jackson would have done so, whatever the obstacles. That was his nature and the root of his greatness as a field general. Blame for the might-have-beens of June 29 must rest with the army commander—specifically with his abominable staff work.

Lee made little if any attempt to discover where Jackson was or if he was moving toward Magruder's left. Indeed, members of Lee's staff never ascertained the location and actions of the separated army units. Aides appeared to have followed Lee, who had no established field headquarters, and waited for any messages he might have had for delivery. Knowing little of the situation, Lee had few directions to offer. The primary task of the army's staff was to act as communications officers. On June 29, even basic communications practically ceased.

If Lee had any questions about Jackson's long pause at the Chickahominy crossings, he kept them to himself. Lee's faith in the valley general was unshaken.

That evening Jackson summoned his cavalry chief, Colonel Tom Munford. The horsemen were to be at the crossroads five miles from White Oak Swamp at sunrise. After alerting other elements to be ready to march the next day, Jackson made a bed in the open and went to sleep.

Around midnight, rain began pouring. A drenched general awakened and looked for cover. An ambulance was nearby. Surgeon McGuire and Lieutenant Sandie Pendleton were already in it. McGuire narrated what followed. "There was plenty of room in the ambulance for three of us, but Sandie Pendleton was so stupid from sleep as to make it difficult to rouse him enough to move and make a place for Gen. Jackson, and so we were all three made very uncomfortable by Sandie Pendleton's sleepiness, as it seemed impossible to awake him."[26]

Sleep would not return to the one who needed it most. Around 1 A.M., Jackson arose. His body ached from lack of rest, but thoughts flooded his mind. He roused Dabney and directed him to start the forces from Grapevine and Alexander's Bridges at "earliest dawn."

Then Jackson mounted Little Sorrel. Probably accompanied by Lieutenant Keith Boswell (the only member of the staff who knew the way), he sloshed through the mud to Magruder's headquarters. That officer must be reassured that Jackson was ready to move with his four divisions. Such action on Jackson's part infers that during the night he had received some form of clarification from Lee on what he was supposed to do the following day.

It was near 3:30 A.M. when Jackson arrived at Magruder's command post. His old captain was not in good shape. Magruder was pacing back and forth in nervous agitation. He had made an unsupported attack the previous afternoon and been soundly defeated. No reinforcements were in sight. Federals could be everywhere and likely were everywhere. Doom was in the wet night air.

Jackson quietly reassured Magruder. The valley brigades would be on the march "probably by daylight." They would reach Magruder in quick time. Magruder then retired to get some badly needed sleep. Jackson remained at his headquarters.

At sunrise, Lee himself rode into the yard with a change of plans. Jackson would lead the pursuit of the Union army. He would clear the enemy from the woods on the south bank of the Chickahominy, then turn south when he was opposite the rear of the Federals. It was an eight-and-a-half-mile march and entailed passing over White Oak Swamp. Getting through that morass might be troublesome. Meanwhile, Magruder would take his men in a westward arc to lend support to Longstreet and Powell Hill as they approached McClellan's western flank.

As he always did, Jackson listened silently. He nodded his head when a response was needed. This was another of those important conferences that no one overheard. What is clear is that Jackson (in Lee's words) was "to pursue the enemy on the road he had taken." What is not clear is precisely what Lee wanted Jackson to do when or if the Confederates established contact with the enemy rear guard.[27]

When the conversation ended, Jackson saluted and departed. He rode to the crossroads where he was supposed to meet his cavalry chief at dawn. No one was there. Jackson began drying himself at a campfire. A few minutes later, dashing down the road at a furious gallop, came Colonel Thomas Munford and a handful of his cavalrymen. Munford and his command had spent that rainy night lost in thickly wooded country where, he asserted, "one could not see his horse's ears." The colonel sensed at once that Jackson was in bad humor. Before Munford could dismount, the general blurted: "Colonel my orders to you were to be here at sunrise."

Munford explained the previous night's situation, including a lack of provisions. Jackson was not moved.

"Yes, sir," he replied at the end of Munford's statement, "but Colonel, I ordered you to be here at sunrise. Move on with your regiment. If you meet the enemy, drive in his pickets, and if you want artillery, Colonel Crutchfield will furnish you."

With that, Munford started forward with his small group of riders. Others soon galloped out of the woods to rejoin the 2d Virginia Cavalry. As Jackson watched horsemen singly and in small groups riding after their leader, he sent couriers to tell Munford that his men were straggling horribly. Munford finally rode back and patiently repeated his story of the rainstorm and getting lost in the woods. Jackson remained unconvinced. "Yes, sir, but I ordered you to be here at sunrise, and I have been waiting for you for a quarter of an hour."[28]

The day was cloudless and gave promise of mild temperatures. It was a good Monday for a battle; and after two days of delays, Jackson was ready. Excitement momentarily masked fatigue.

Harvey Hill's division came into sight at the crossroads. Joining the head of the column, Jackson rode southward. The line of march on the Williamsburg road took him through Magruder's position. Soldiers stood along the road in awe of the veterans from the valley. "No wonder they march so," one commented. "The men carry no baggage." A company of the 21st Virginia passed, its captain brandishing a naked sword. "See there!" another soldier shouted. "The officers don't even carry scabbards for their swords!"[29] Jackson's foot cavalry were moving in a shuffle that morning. The men had been on the road since 2:30 A.M. and without food.

No enemy resistance materialized as the morning hours passed. Indeed, at every turn Federal stragglers emerged from thickets and woods to surrender. Soon over 1000 prisoners were following in the wake of Jackson's march. Quartermasters also captured "a vast drove of mules" that had been abandoned or turned loose in the Federal effort to cross the swampy bottom land. The Confederates arrived at Savage's Station to find 2500 wounded and sick Yankees in a tented hospital that was, Jackson observed, "remarkable for the extent and convenience of its accommodations."[30] Yet that was not all awaiting the Confederates at the railroad station.

Savage's Station was a forerunner to what Jackson's men would find two months later at Manassas Junction. Piles of abandoned Federal stores of every description were strewn in the fields and along the tracks. Guns, uniforms, blankets, food, ammunition, knapsacks, and cartridge boxes lay packed in boxes. A North Carolina colonel wrote of chancing upon a huge stack of coffins; a Georgia soldier commented that "you could find anything you wanted from a siege gun to a cigar." Dabney asserted that it took weeks for Confederate quartermasters to gather in the spoils.[31]

The "wagon-hunter" was not about to neglect all of those needed supplies. Time passed while soldiers collected stores. So many small arms lay on the ground, Jackson reported, "that it became necessary to detach two regiments to take charge of them and to see to the security of the prisoners."[32]

When an officer grumbled about how expensive it was going to be for the Confederacy to house all of those prisoners, Jackson quietly answered, "It is cheaper to feed them than to fight them."[33]

With nothing to do while his soldiers cleaned up the area around Savage's Station, Jackson wrote a letter to Anna. His wife was now in her fourth month of pregnancy. Jackson had neglected her of late; so little time and so much to do that even the usual Monday letter did not always materialize. "An ever-kind Providence has greatly blessed our efforts and given us great reason for thankfulness in having defended

Richmond," Jackson wrote. "To-day the enemy is retreating down the Chickahominy towards the James River. Many prisoners are falling into our hands. General D. H. Hill and I are together. I had a wet bed last night, as the rain fell in torrents. I got up about midnight, and haven't seen much rest since. I hope that our God will soon bless us with an honorable peace, & permit us to be together at home again in the enjoyment of domestic happiness."[34]

In midmorning, the march resumed down a narrow, twisting road across rough farmland and through menacing woods. After about four miles, the road began sloping toward White Oak Swamp. Jackson's army was not stripped for action, as was customary. Rather, it was an encumbered host weighted down by stores and prisoners. Now White Oak Swamp became an even greater impediment.

Dense underbrush covered both sides of the waterway. Thick woods, mostly pine, gave the area a dark overtone. In the summertime, the stream was a lazy bog barely fifteen feet wide and rarely over six inches deep. Now, swollen by rains, the heavily shaded stream had become a vast quagmire of waterlogged underbrush and slime that slowly worked its way to the Chickahominy, seven miles away.[35]

A single bridge crossed White Oak Swamp. Jackson reached that point around noon. There he found the span burned and its blackened timbers pointing disjointedly out of the water. No crossing existed for artillery or wagons.

Colonel Stapleton Crutchfield and the advance of Jackson's batteries had arrived at the north edge of the swamp at 9:30 that morning. Crutchfield saw Federal wagons making their way southward beyond the stream. The road across the swamp ran straight ahead for a short distance and then disappeared over a rise. On high ground along the east side of the road, some 300 yards distant, there appeared to be several Union batteries in line. Trees and brush hid so much of White Oak Swamp that it was all but impossible to see other fords unless one literally stood in front of them.

On Crutchfield's immediate right was an open ridge parallel to the swamp. It afforded a good locale for a diagonal line of fire at the Federal guns across the way. Yet it was also exposed ground and subject to return fire. Crutchfield decided to take a chance. The young artillery chief began cutting an opening through the woods to enable him to bring up his batteries. Work was well advanced when Jackson arrived. He nodded approval at Crutchfield's plan. Within a couple of hours, seven batteries of twenty-three guns were in position. Around 1:45 P.M., all opened fire with a sudden, deafening roar.[36]

The bombardment caught the Federals completely by surprise. A group of mules watering at the swamp promptly stampeded. Startled Union gunners near the water abandoned three cannon and bolted to the rear seemingly in pursuit of the mules. Widespread confusion was clearly visible from the north side of the swamp. At this point, a smiling Jackson summoned Colonel Thomas Munford. He and his 2d Virginia Cavalry were to cross White Oak Swamp near the destroyed bridge, capture the deserted Union guns, and then reconnoiter around the bridge site. Jackson and Harvey Hill would accompany the horsemen.

Munford had doubts about the enterprise and expressed them. His men and mounts probably could not traverse the apparently bottomless mud pool. Impatience replaced Jackson's smile. "Yes, Colonel, but you haven't tried it! Try it, Colonel!"[37]

As Captain George W. Wooding's Danville Artillery drove off the Federal sharpshooters, Jackson ordered a crew to begin repairing the bridge. Then, just as at Front Royal, he rode to battle with his cavalry. Munford's horsemen eased into the muddy flow, which quickly swirled up to the bellies of the horses. Debris from the bridge further hampered passage. Cavalrymen in columns of two slowly made their way across the stream—"under great difficulties," one officer exclaimed.[38]

Most of the mounted force reached the south side and picked up some prisoners. Then a squadron veered off to seize one or more of the unmanned cannon. Suddenly, heavy musket fire came from their front and an enfilading fire from masked artillery concealed in woods to the west endangered the horsemen. Jackson and Harvey Hill had just splashed through the water and reached land when an artillery shell exploded a few feet from where the generals sat on their horses.

Federal batteries could now be seen unlimbering in the distance; long lines of blueclad infantry were taking battle position. Jackson now realized the impracticality of trying to effect a crossing of White Oak Swamp at that point. The disappointed general made his way back across the bog. By then, enemy sharpshooters and an occasional shell were likewise blocking all attempts at rebuilding the bridge. Jackson simply could not pass over White Oak Swamp by a direct route. He ordered his brigades to stay where they were in line up the road.[39]

"Incessant fire" compelled Munford and his troopers to proceed rapidly downstream in search of an unobstructed ford. They found one after a quarter-mile ride. It was little more than a cow path, but it was usable. Munford sent word to Jackson of the unguarded crossing. There was no response.

Around 2:30, General A. R. "Rans" Wright and his brigade arrived from upstream and reported to Jackson. The general showed little interest in these reinforcements. Instead, he told the darkly bearded Wright to retrace his steps and scout for a suitable upstream crossing. Wright backtracked for a mile and located such a spot at Fisher's Ford. Confederates established a solid beachhead on the enemy side of the swamp. Mysteriously, Wright did not alert Jackson to his find, and Jackson seemed all at once to have become curiously dispassionate.[40]

While Munford was downstream, waiting to take advantage of the ford there, General Wade Hampton (temporarily commanding Fulkerson's old brigade in Winder's division) had found a second possible crossing. It was hidden just to the east of the White Oak bridge. The ford was at a narrow point in the swamp; its bottom was sandy and the water shallow.

Hampton delivered this information personally to Jackson. Could the crossing be bridged? Jackson asked. Yes, Hampton replied, but only for infantry. Cutting a road through the woods for rolling equipment would make too much noise and take too much time. That was not what Jackson wanted to hear, but he instructed Hampton to build the bridge.

The South Carolinian gathered a work crew of some fifty soldiers. They cut down several dozen trees and fashioned a crude but usable footbridge. As soon as it was in place, Hampton galloped back to inform Jackson. Summer heat and humidity were by then oppressively high.

On arriving at the headquarters area, Hampton found Jackson seated on a log. The dingy kepi was pulled down to his nose. Jackson was motionless. Hampton gave his report, then eagerly volunteered to lead the advance over the new bridge with his brigade.

Jackson was not acquainted with Hampton, nor was he ready to launch an unsupported infantry assault to gain nothing more than the south bank of White Oak Swamp. To Hampton's shock, Jackson "sat in silence for some time, then rose and walked off in silence." The mystified brigade commander could do nothing but mount his horse and ride slowly back to his troops.[41]

The artillery duel at White Oak Swamp had developed into a forty-gun contest that increased and ebbed in intensity for over three hours. It was, in Porter Alexander's opinion, "an absurd farce of war." Occasionally, the rumble of battle could be heard three miles to the southwest at a plantation called Glendale. Longstreet and Powell Hill had attacked McClellan's flank.[42]

Confederates overwhelmed the Union skirmish line at Glendale and momentarily pierced the main enemy position. Cannon were captured and recaptured; combat became hand to hand in some sectors. The superiority of Federal numbers, especially on defense, ultimately made the difference. Longstreet and Powell Hill, their divisions already mauled by previous engagements in the Seven Days Campaign, beat themselves out fruitlessly with their assaults. A quarter-century after the war, Longstreet would point a finger of blame elsewhere. "Jackson should have done more for me than he did."[43]

Back at White Oak Swamp, and after Hampton's departure, Jackson walked to a large oak. He sat down under the tree and within seconds was asleep. A full hour passed before he awakened. Then he propped up quietly, disoriented and confused, staring with unseeing eyes, drained of all ability except the power to breathe. When Lieutenant McHenry Howard of Winder's staff rode over in late afternoon, he found nothing taking place but the staff and the lead elements of the army weathering an occasional shell from Union cannon. "It looked to me," Howard stated, "as if on our side we were waiting for Jackson to wake up."[44]

After dark, Jackson joined the staff for supper. The meal was proceeding silently when Jackson's head slowly rolled forward on his chest. The general had fallen asleep again, this time with a biscuit clenched between his teeth. After awhile, he lurched awake. Jackson rose stiffly. "Now, gentlemen," he announced, "let us at once to bed, and rise with the dawn, and see if tomorrow we cannot do *something*."[45]

Whether Jackson was speaking out of a sense of failure or expressing a feeling of frustration is a question students ever since have pondered. The general went from the supper table straight to his tent and to bed. He ended the day unaware that part of the Federal force that had blocked his advance at White Oak Swamp was a brigade under General William H. French. His old antagonist had gained a measure of revenge.[46]

Jackson was never one to hide setbacks or to seek scapegoats. His own explanation for what did not happen at White Oak Swamp came two weeks later. He entered a room in time to overhear staff officers McGuire, Pendleton, and Crutchfield discussing the Seven Days Campaign. One of the officers had just raised the question of why, on June 30, Jackson did not go to the aid of Longstreet and Powell Hill. Jackson's eyes flashed for a moment; he then said brusquely: "If General Lee had wanted me, he could have sent for me." That ended the conversation. As far as Jackson was concerned, that ended the whole question of what happened at White Oak Swamp.[47]

His so-called strange behavior on an uncomfortably hot Monday provoked immediate criticism that continues to this day in some quarters. Dabney's false assumption that Jackson was supposed to attack somewhere in the White Oak Swamp-Glendale area led a number of postwar writers—including some of Jackson's champions—to levy censure on the general. " 'Old Jack' certainly did not come up to the Valley," former aide James Mercer Garnett stated, while Colonel William Allan termed Jackson's conduct at White Oak Swamp "one of the few great mistakes of his marvelous career." General Porter Alexander was even more accusatory. "When one thinks of the great chances in General Lee's grasp that one summer afternoon, it is enough to make one cry . . . to think that our *Stonewall Jackson* lost them."[48]

Never in his life had Jackson been accused of neglect of duty. Nor would he ever be charged again. Yet skepticism prevailed over his behavior at White Oak Swamp. Some of the accusations of reprehensible conduct levied against Jackson after White Oak Swamp are so at variance with his nature and character as to approach the absurd.

General Harvey Hill, who appears repeatedly to have suffered a postwar softening of memory, came forward with an incredible hypothesis—one supported to a degree by Alexander. Jackson deliberately withheld his soldiers from action on the peninsula, Hill declared, under his belief that the valley troops had done more than their share of fighting up to that time.[49] If that were the case, Lee would have been derelict in not removing Jackson from command.

Jackson's military activities are not strange when viewed in the full light of all known facts that day. The brief reconnaissance across White Oak Swamp in early afternoon revealed nothing positive. The enemy was in a strong defensive position. At least three batteries with infantry support became visible. Jackson had every reason to fear that he might be facing an enemy force at least as large as his own. Jackson was daring but not reckless. Kernstown and Port Republic had taught him not to send his forces into action unless the objectives were clear and clearly defined.

Jackson's apprehensions about the enemy host in his front were well founded. Generally forgotten in the June 30 controversy is the Union strength on the south side of the swamp. It consisted of General William B. Franklin's corps: six infantry brigades, six cavalry regiments, seven batteries, and an engineer brigade, all fully equipped, all solidly in a defensive posture, and totaling more than 22,000 soldiers.

The Union corps commander was well known and highly respected. Franklin had graduated first in the West Point class that contained Grant. When civil war began, Franklin was supervising part of the construction of the dome of the U.S. Capitol in Washington. This gifted engineer was likewise skilled in the art of fortifications and defensive works.[50]

Henry Alexander White knew Lee in the postwar years at Washington College and later produced a biography of the commander. White declared of White Oak Swamp that Jackson "saw the odds against him and wisely held back his wearied veterans from a costly charge against the intrenched foe." This statement provoked an outburst from Colonel Munford, who said of White, "I fear this gentleman, with so many letters of distinction to the tail of his kite, has used the lamp at the end of it to poor advantage in studying the facts."[51]

Even if enemy resistance had been weaker, Jackson was unable to launch a successful attack at the waterway. All that he could have sent forward were infantry; and as soon as they advanced beyond the covering fire of their own artillery, they would have been helpless. Guns and supply wagons had no way of getting across the swamp. Jackson himself stated in his report that the heavy cannonading from the Longstreet-Powell Hill sector "made me eager to press forward; but the marshy character of the soil, the destruction of the bridge over the marsh and creek, and the strong position of the enemy for defending the passage prevented my advancing until the following morning."[52]

Perhaps Jackson might have utilized one of the discovered fords and attempted a flanking movement. To assume the Longstreet rationale that such an advance would have succeeded is to ignore the presence of a full Union corps in battle formation blocking the way. All the roads in the area were clogged. Further, such a turning movement by Jackson would have necessitated not only a large and long march up or down White Oak Swamp; the march would have been in essence a careful search across the enemy's front rather than a quick thrust across the morass.

Critics have asked why Jackson ordered "Rans" Wright to reconnoiter upstream and Hampton to build a bridge downstream when the general paid little heed to the results of both undertakings. Assuming that Wright alerted Jackson to what he found—even though no confirmation of that exists—Jackson's "apathy" has explanation. He had a longstanding penchant for anticipating orders and movements. (Charles Faulkner had earlier joined the staff after checking telegraph lines fifty miles west in the Piedmont in the unlikely event that Jackson might shortly be moving in that direction.) Jackson was always formulating contingencies. White Oak Swamp was no exception. If the time came when Lee directed him to move up or down the line of the swamp, Jackson would be ready.

Above these impediments or halfhearted efforts, as some writers have labeled them, is another and overriding factor: Jackson had no orders to execute any flanking move if his advance down the Williamsburg road stalled.

Obedience to orders is the crux of Jackson's June 30 behavior. On the previous afternoon, he and Stuart had received explicit instructions to guard the Chickahominy bridges and to resist any enemy moves in that direction. There were no subsequent written orders. Lee's verbal directives early on the 30th had been simply to pursue the Federals. Lee said nothing to Jackson about making any attack—on his own or in support of other Confederate units.[53] Neither did the army commander ever mention the White Oak Swamp artillery fire and musketry, which he surely must have heard sometime in the afternoon.

Jackson indisputably never had orders to go to the aid of Longstreet and Powell Hill at Glendale. Had such instructions been given, Jackson would still have had to pass White Oak Swamp to get to the Glendale area. The Confederates lost 3300 men in a vain effort to trap part of McClellan's army at Glendale. Jackson's casualties that day were three killed and twelve wounded, all from cannon fire. Those unrelated losses have been unjustly made to appear as dereliction on Jackson's part.

What happened at White Oak Swamp is fundamentally what happened throughout the Seven Days Campaign: an all but complete breakdown in communications between the Confederate generals. June 30 was a day of groping marches, of individual decisions, of one delay after another. The majority of Lee's division commanders bore some degree of culpability. The army commander was not above criticism either.

On that Monday, Lee and Jackson were within forty minutes of each other. Lee never asked Jackson what difficulties, if any, he might be encountering at White Oak Swamp. Jackson did not inform the army commander that his advance was blocked. Once again, there stands—above all factors—Jackson's total obedience to commands. He did what he was ordered to do.

Lee had instructed him expressly on June 29 to march along the south bank of the Chickahominy and to keep himself between the enemy and the river. As a soldier, Jackson did not need to know anything else because he was not ordered to do anything else. That is neither neglect nor disobedience; in military parlance, it is called duty.[54]

Jackson's peculiarities in behavior that day lead to another, obvious conclusion. With striking suddenness on June 30, Jackson reached the breaking point of his physical endurance. The exertions and marches, the battles and cares, the anxieties and contemplations, logistics and logjams—all caught up with him at last. His cavalry chief, Colonel Tom Munford, later summarized it well: "Jackson was mortal, he had been in a whirl incessantly for six weeks . . . his endurance simply gave out . . . he was not at his best. His ambition was too great to flag, but neither man nor beast can go beyond certain limits."[55]

The general was benumbed, incapable for the moment of deep thought or strenuous movement. As frustrations mounted that day, Jackson showed decreasing interest in reports, suggestions, and alternatives. Bone-deep exhaustion had finally triumphed over external efforts. Sleep became imperative. Only with rest could there be a resumption of activity.

One other ingredient must be inserted into this subject. Some time later, probably on Monday, July 7 (the letter is undated), Jackson wrote at length to his beloved Anna. He spoke of recent engagements, the gifts of God, and other matters. One sentence stands forth boldly: "During the past week I have not been well, have suffered from fever and debility, but through the blessing of an ever-kind Providence I am much better today."[56]

This confession is the first time in the Civil War that Jackson admitted being ill. It would be the only time he would ever admit to a physical debilitation. He was sick and he was exhausted. Nothing but a sense of duty on June 30 kept him in command.

July 1 marked the sixth day of Lee's counteroffensive. The Confederate army had suffered 10,000 casualties, including the loss of nine of its thirty-eight brigadiers. Yet Lee still searched for one great thrust that might cripple or destroy the Army of the Potomac.

Jackson was awake early that first day of the month. He must have gotten a solid night's sleep, for he seemed alert and eager for action. Shortly after dawn, Whiting's division felt out the Union position along the south bank of White Oak Swamp. The Federals were gone. Jackson led his column across the stream and through country that his artillery had ripped with fire a day earlier. Soon part of the Glendale battlefield passed in view.

The march continued south on a wagon trail known variously as the Quaker Road and the Willis Church Road. After another mile, Jackson came upon a mass of

Confederate troops on both sides of the lane. They were Magruder's troops, in the process of relieving Longstreet's men at Glendale. Many of them got their first glimpse of the fabled conqueror from the valley.

"Such cheering I had never heard before," Georgia volunteer William Andrews declared. "The soldiers went wild as they tossed their caps in the air." Jackson removed his kepi, spurred his horse, and rode quickly from view. However, the sight of the general left a deep imprint on Andrews. "From what I saw of Jackson, he is a very ordinary looking man of medium size, his uniform badly soiled as though it had seen hard service. He wore a cap pulled down nearly to his nose and was riding a rawboned horse that did not look much like a charger, unless it would be on hay or clover. He certainly made a poor figure on a horseback, with his stirrup leather six inches too short, putting his knees nearly level with his horse's back, and his heels turned out with his toes sticking behind his horse's foreshoulder. A sorry description of our most famous general, but a correct one."[57]

A few hundred yards farther, Jackson spied a cluster of horsemen in the yard of Willis Church. The small, white Methodist church had become temporary headquarters for Lee's army. The commander, Longstreet, the two Hills, and Magruder were all in the saddle and apparently waiting for Jackson. He joined the group, saluted casually, and said nothing. Lee seemed irritated, or perhaps he was impatient. The army must push south, Lee said, and seek to bring McClellan to bay. In all likelihood, he added, the Federals were in position on a broad plateau known as Malvern Hill.

At that, Harvey Hill expressed concern. On Magruder's staff was a resident of the area, and he had told Jackson's brother-in-law of the natural strength of that particular piece of high ground. "If General McClellan is there in force," Hill offered, "we had better leave him alone." Longstreet laughed contemptuously; then displaying the blunt self-assurance that would always plague his career, Longstreet told Hill, "Don't get scared, now that we have him whipped!"[58]

An angry Hill was about to respond when Lee ended the exchange by announcing that Jackson, Magruder, and Huger—none of whom had been engaged the previous day—would do the fighting in the final stab at McClellan. The battle orders were memorable for their vagueness. Confederate units would move toward the James River in a play-it-by-ear fashion. Some nineteen brigades (about 30,000 men) were to advance in columns of four accompanied by guns and ambulances on a single, narrow road. The destination would be the enemy.

Jackson for one had apprehension about such an offensive. Artillery would be an important key in the operations, yet Colonel Crutchfield, Jackson's artillery chief, had taken ill and could not command. Hence, Jackson assumed the additional duty of placing his guns. When he asked permission to take the lead in the resumption of the march, Lee nodded assent.[59]

Confederates eased forward for a mile and a half. Fire between skirmishers increased. Jackson's column came around a curve in the Willis Church Road; a quarter-mile away loomed Malvern Hill. Union cannon fire quickly began exploding in front of the Confederates. Jackson dismounted, sat on a stump, and scribbled a note to Stuart: "I am engaged with the enemy. I trust that God will give our army a glorious victory." While Jackson was writing, a large shell exploded nearby. It killed several soldiers and rained dirt on Jackson. The general flicked the debris from the paper and continued writing as if only a minor nuisance had interrupted him.[60]

Deployment of the Southern troops proceeded rapidly. Jackson's force would form the left of the Confederate battle line. He sent Whiting to man the east side of the Willis Church Road. Those troops crossed fields and entered a shallow woodland on the Poindexter farm. Harvey Hill led his division to the west side of the road. Richard Taylor's brigade of Ewell's division filled the gap between Hill and Whiting.

The remainder of Jackson's force went into reserve, standing at ready to go where needed. These dispositions were complete by 11 A.M. Jackson then had time to examine the enemy position from afar.

Malvern Hill rose only fifty yards above the countryside at its highest point. (As the Confederates were to learn, that is a well-nigh ideal elevation for a defender: high enough to be an impediment, low enough to provide an open and concentrated range of fire.) The hill was actually a long plateau, three-quarters of a mile across the northern face, and a mile and a quarter deep.

Two tributaries protected the flanks; its convex front, jutting to the north, contained enough swells to provide more protection for the troops manning the high ground. Turkey Run on the Federal left sliced due south toward the James. Western Run, meandering more to the southeast, created a swampy obstacle across the front of Malvern Hill before slanting down the east side. On approaching the hill from the Confederate lines, an attacking force would have to proceed across open ground that included a gradual ascent of about a half-mile to the crest of the plateau.

Jackson could not identify all of the elevation's strengths. Yet the massed guns and lines of infantry convinced him that an assault from his sector was out of the question. Longstreet had conducted a similar reconnaissance on the Confederate right. He told Lee that if he and Jackson could put sixty guns in place—half on a rise in Longstreet's area and the remainder in an open field on the Poindexter farm in Jackson's line, the Southerners could open with a crisscross fire with potentially good results. Lee was willing to see what happened.

The Confederate bombardment never materialized. Batteries unlimbered and opened fire in piecemeal fashion. As quickly as one set of Confederate cannon fired its first salvo, dozens of Union pieces blanketed the position with a destructive fire that knocked one gun after another out of commission. Confusion reigned among the few Southern gun crews that came into position. General William N. Pendleton, once the colorful captain of the Rockbridge Artillery but now the rather bewildered commander of Lee's reserve artillery, evidently spent July 1 searching for Lee while Lee searched for him.

Jackson did everything he could to get his guns into firing position, but they accomplished little. Two batteries managed to unlimber—one just in time to be blown to pieces and the other ineffective because of its limited range of fire. Federal General William F. Barry informed Colonel Tom Munford after the war that he "had fifty pieces massed at Malvern Hill which he could concentrate upon any battery that came out in the open and that they melted like wax under his rain of projectiles."[61]

With both Pendleton and Crutchfield useless at Malvern Hill, Jackson tried to do it all himself. Harvey Hill's batteries had exhausted their ammunition the previous day and were in the rear replenishing their supply. Jackson's other guns were subdivided among three commands. No one was available to take charge of the emplacements.

So Jackson spent much time placing field pieces to contest the Union might across the way. More than once, he dismounted and helped roll cannon into place. Some of the soldiers marveled at "Old Jack's" demeanor that afternoon. John G. Gittings, a volunteer aide, was steering a line of infantry forward when he saw Jackson "giving orders to a battery which was being actually destroyed by the concentrated fire of McClellan's artillery. He sat erect on his horse, in this hurricane of canister and grape; his face was aflame with passion, his eyes flashed, his under jaw protruded, and his voice rang out sharp and clear. Before he was entirely obscured from our view, the soldiers would turn, at brief intervals, to look back on him."[62]

At one point, Harvey Hill was sitting with his leg over the pommel of his saddle and chatting with Chase Whiting. Both generals were smoking cigars when an agitated Jackson galloped up and shattered the leisurely atmosphere by telling Whiting to move his guns forward to assist in the action. Whiting balked: his fifty guns were supposed to be at hand, but only sixteen had arrived. Those gunners could not stand such a lopsided duel. Now angry, Whiting shouted: "They won't live in there five minutes!" Jackson was unmoved. "Obey your orders, General Whiting, promptly and willingly." Whiting, barely in control, snapped, "I have always obeyed my orders promptly, but not willingly under such circumstances."[63]

Instructing his staff to bear witness to what he had said, Whiting then directed the battery commanders to move into an open field of grain. Jackson took the lead. "Forward, sir," he shouted to the captain of the first battery, at the same time pointing to a rise in the wheatfield barely a half-mile from the Union lines. The gunners unlimbered their pieces; a moment later, a Confederate artillerist recalled, "all the Yankee batteries on a hill beyond stopped firing into the woods and poured into us the most deadly fire that I ever witnessed during the war."[64]

Whiting could barely watch as his sixteen pieces one by one were blown asunder. "Great God!" he finally exclaimed to everyone around him. "Won't some ranking officer come, and save us from this fool!"[65]

No more than twenty Confederate cannon went into action at a time when more than 100 were needed. Some of Virginia's finest young artillerymen perished in a duel more akin to a bloody farce.[66]

Lee's final battle plan at Malvern Hill, reflective more of the army commander's fatigue and frustration than of any strategic soundness, called for a major assault based on a lone brigadier's opinion. General Lewis Armistead's brigade occupied the center of the Confederate line. When Armistead was convinced that the Federal position had been sufficiently weakened in the exchange of artillery fire, he was to charge with a yell. The bulk of the Army of Northern Virginia would follow.

Roaring cannon, explosions almost every second, clods of dirt and fragments of trees spinning through the air created an aura of hell for two hours. Sometime during this period, Jackson and Harvey Hill dismounted, climbed atop a fence rail, then calmly shared biscuits and syrup as if they were on a picnic in some pastoral setting.[67]

By 2:30 P.M., Lee realized that the uneven artillery exchange did not bode well for his battle strategy. With Longstreet, he rode to the left to see if a turning movement by the soldiers of Longstreet and Powell Hill were possible. This was about the time Whiting's men, in Jackson's front, noticed what they took to be Federal units retreating from the eastern end of Malvern Hill. Lee was pondering the situation when a message arrived: Armistead had started forward. Two other brigades in Magruder's division were taking part in the attack.

It was an almost suicidal attempt. The full strength of the Army of the Potomac concentrated on three small Confederate brigades moving slowly across open ground. Sustained fire tore through the lines and left gaping holes. Southerners bravely continued to move forward into even hotter fire. Soldiers who could stand many things soon found that they could not endure everything. The fragmented gray lines wavered, then broke some 300 yards from the crest of Malvern Hill.

Meanwhile, Jackson followed Lee's directive. While Armistead's troops moved to the attack, Jackson ordered Harvey Hill's division to do likewise. The same horror occurred again, but on a larger scale. Federal guns shifted from the 3500 Confederates in the first attack and opened with equal deadliness on Hill's 10,000 unprotected soldiers.

Confederates lunged forward toward the hilltop, recoiled under murderous fire, and rushed forward again. Enemy cannon raked the attackers unmercifully. Two years after the battle, Harvey Hill would state: "My recollections of Malvern Hill are so unpleasant that I do not like to write about it. Twas a mistake to fight."[68]

Jackson carefully observed Hill's division move forward. When the Federal guns turned on Hill's men, Jackson saw instantly that the advance was doomed. In a few minutes, Hill asked for help. Jackson quickly ordered Ewell and Winder to double-time to the front with their divisions. It was too late. The clogged roads, underbrush, swampy ground, and heavy Federal cannon fire slowed the supporting units. They reached the front in time to see Hill's broken and bleeding command falling back in retreat.

Colonel Bradley T. Johnson with his regimental-size Maryland Line moved forward through wounded men streaming to the rear. Johnson spied a small body of Federals some 100 yards away. He rode swiftly to Jackson and requested permission to attack the party. "No," was all that Jackson said. Darkness was too close; the enemy position was too formidable to test further.[69]

The veil of nightfall mercifully closed the one-sided battle at Malvern Hill. Rain began falling. The cries of hundreds of wounded men on the field, mixed with the lightning and thunder, along with the noise from still-firing cannon, turned the evening into a nightmare. It was 10 P.M. when the shelling finally ceased.

As Jackson rode back up the Willis Church Road to his headquarters, he met General Isaac Trimble. The aged brigadier was urging his men through the darkness toward the front. Jackson asked Trimble what he was doing. "I am going to charge those batteries, sir," came the emphatic answer. "I guess you had better not try it," Jackson responded wearily. "General D. H. Hill has just tried it with his whole division and been repulsed. I guess you had better not try it, sir."[70]

The futility of attacking Malvern Hill was painfully evident in the casualties that day. Confederate losses were 5650 men, while Union casualties were slightly over half as great.[71] Only Gaines' Mill had been more costly for Lee in the Seven Days

Campaign. Malvern Hill was one of the few major battles of the Civil War in which artillery produced more casualties than small arms. For Lee, it was also another battle marked by ignorance of the enemy position and mismanagement of the troops at hand.

Jackson felt fatigue anew. It had been another long day of high expectations and few accomplishments. The rain stopped around midnight, but a confused tangle of wagons and stragglers choked the muddy roads. A loud din filled the area. Jackson was oblivious to it as he yearned for sleep.

Headquarters was in the front yard of the C. W. Smith farm. Jackson's servant, Jim Lewis, made a pallet on a fairly dry patch of ground. The general accepted a small amount of food, then lay down and fell at once into deep slumber.

Around 1 A.M. a group of worried officers rode into the bivouac.[72] The Confederate lines had not been reunited; little resistance could be made if McClellan attacked in daylight. None of the generals was anxious to awaken the commander. So they squatted in a circle around Jackson's form—resembling, Dabney noted, a group of frogs carrying on a conversation.

Surgeon McGuire arrived and watched what happened next. "Some one got [Jackson] up in a sitting posture and held him there, and another one yelled into his ear something about the condition of our army, its inability to resist attack, etc. He answered: 'Please let me sleep. There will be no enemy there in the morning.'" The generals, convinced that Jackson was either drugged by sleep or momentarily mad, eased him back to the ground. Jackson's prediction proved true.[73]

Malvern Hill ended the Seven Days Campaign. Lee had pounded McClellan almost from one end of the peninsula to the other. Still, he had been unable to deliver the crushing blow that might have crippled the Army of the Potomac and produced overtures for peace from the North. Malvern Hill, like the other engagements in the campaign, sparked a host of criticisms by rationalizing Confederate officers. Since Jackson's conduct throughout the campaign seemed enigmatic, it was easy to place some of the Malvern Hill disaster as well on his shoulders.

This is strange, for Jackson's role at Malvern Hill was so minor as to appear detached. What orders—if any—Lee gave him on July 1 are difficult to pinpoint. Jackson was never directed to attack with all of his men. He took more than a personal interest in the placement of artillery; in a couple of instances, he physically helped move guns into position. He did not hesitate when asked for aid: Jackson promptly sent reinforcements to Harvey Hill's hard-pressed ranks.

Despite the fact that Lee and Jackson were together or in close contact for most of the day, Jackson appeared to be almost a bystander at Malvern Hill. He exercised little influence over the action and did only what was asked of him. He and Lee were in the slow process of getting to know one another on a battlefield. The intimacy that would make each man react instinctively to the thinking of the other would come later.

In the inevitable search for scapegoats after the Seven Days Campaign, almost everyone in the army except Lee and Jackson seemed to be pointing fingers of blame at everyone else. Longstreet and the man who became his artillery chief, E. Porter Alexander, repeatedly saved their sharpest barbs for Jackson. For example, Alexander thought that Jackson could and should have turned the Union right flank at Malvern

Hill—presumably on his own volition—in order to avoid the Confederate repulse that followed.[74]

The ever-judgmental Longstreet faulted Jackson at every step of the campaign. Had Jackson been "on time" just once, Longstreet asserted, McClellan's army might have been trapped. Jealousy ultimately began appearing in Longstreet's postwar statements. "Jackson was a very skillful man when pitted against men as Shields, Banks, and Fremont," he wrote, "but when pitted against the best of the Federal commanders, he did not appear so well."[75]

Alexander charged (after Lee's death) that the army chief was "deeply, bitterly disappointed" at Jackson's conduct throughout the fighting on the peninsula. Jackson must have been "under a spell," Alexander solemnly concluded.[76]

One prominent Confederate politician loosed a broadside of disgust. "Stonewall Jackson and his troops did little or nothing in these battles of the Chickahominy," Robert Toombs alleged, "and Lee was far below the occasion." Even Lee's most thorough biographer concluded that "by every test, Jackson had failed throughout the Seven Days."[77] A progression of writers has passed the same judgment.

Some reason existed for such conclusions. To many people—then and now—Jackson appeared an enigma. He had entered the war from the role of a reserved college professor. After the Valley Campaign, Jackson emerged suddenly as the only Confederate genius in the war's first year. Then, in the Seven Days, he became a puzzlement again, with renewed doubts raised about his ability.

Therein lies a misleading deduction. Critics writing after the fact charge that in view of striking successes in the valley, Jackson's was the most spectacular failure on the peninsula. That is akin to comparing apples and oranges.

In the Shenandoah, Jackson operated independently; he knew the country; his daring was as broad as he wished to make it. From Mechanicsville to Malvern Hill, on the other hand, he was under direct orders (few though they were) and in totally unfamiliar surroundings (twice his columns took wrong roads). Jackson then did what he was ordered to do because he was a soldier with an absolute devotion to the chain-of-command system. He was less aggressive on the peninsula than he had been in the valley for one compelling reason: he was not directed to be otherwise. Still, Jackson can hardly be termed lethargic in his first association with the Army of Northern Virginia. His combined casualties at Gaines' Mill and Malvern Hill were more than 5400 men.[78]

Since advance publicity caused so much to be expected of Jackson, his "failings" appeared more glaring; but there were failings throughout the command structure. Few generals at division level or higher performed well in the Seven Days. After the campaign, Lee rid himself of Magruder, Huger, and Theophilus H. Holmes. Several other generals were shunted to one side. Yet Lee not only retained Jackson in high command; he began the next major campaign with Jackson taking the lead.

The Seven Days was a shakedown offensive for the Army of Northern Virginia. As such, the counteroffensive presented the most problems to its commander. Lee was at the head of an army for the first time. He was launching the first Confederate offensive of the war in the east, and he was doing so in flat, swampy country that restricted maneuverability.

Operations extended for at least twenty miles in an area for which no accurate maps were available. Army communication rested on couriers delivering messages and status reports that sometimes were not correct and were rarely up to date. Moreover, while McClellan left something to be desired in leadership, some of his generals fought brilliantly in the campaign.

Finally, Jackson was a human being with human limitations. Exhaustion, lack of sleep, and an unspecified illness all struck simultaneously in the arenas outside Richmond. The issue is not what Jackson failed to do; it is what he accomplished in the face of a host of vexations.[79]

Often overlooked as well is that mistakes notwithstanding, Lee had knocked the Union army from the gates of the Southern capital. The second major enemy advance into Virginia had been repulsed. Harvey Hill was at his sarcastic best after the campaign when he wrote his wife: "We have driven McClellan out of his fortifications & pursued him twenty miles, taking fifty pieces of artillery & ten thousand prisoners. Still he claims that he has gained a great victory. The art of lying can go no farther."[80]

A thick mist hung over the land when July 2 dawned. Jackson was up early riding the lines. By midmorning the mist had become a drizzly rain that turned Malvern Hill into a ghastly sight. Oblivious to the human horror, Jackson ordered details onto the killing ground for nasty duty.

First the men collected the dead, placed them in rows, and covered the bodies with whatever blankets and oilcloths were at hand. Because most of the Confederates had been killed by artillery fire, some corpses were headless. Fragments of bodies and limbs were strewn everywhere. It took hours in the rain to collect all of the pieces under Jackson's close supervision.

Soldiers then dug ditches in the mud. The dead were buried as decently as conditions permitted. The details then moved once more across the field, this time collecting discarded weapons and ammunition. According to one participant, Jackson "trotted incessantly about in every direction among the working parties [and] so hurried them that the men omitted even to rifle the pockets of the slain." Asked later why he ordered the field cleaned in the midst of a steady downpour, Jackson replied with what for him was simple logic: "Why, I am going to attack here presently, as soon as the fog rises, and it won't do to march the troops over their own dead, you know."[81]

It was true to character that when he learned of the Federal withdrawal from Malvern Hill, Jackson wanted to press forward immediately. Yet heavy rain was falling, McClellan's precise whereabouts was unknown, and the few available roads on which the Confederate army could move had once again become mud lanes. Only the surgeons at the field hospitals were busy that Wednesday. At one point in the morning, Dr. McGuire reported having more incapacitated men than he could handle and not knowing what to do with them or where to send them.

Jackson rode to the bullet-riddled Poindexter house, where Lee had his headquarters. He must somehow try to convince the army commander to pursue the enemy quickly and furiously. A fire blazed in the fireplace to ward off the dampness. Only one or two of the army's staff officers were present.

McGuire joined the group around noon, with the wet and muddy Longstreet coming to Poindexter's a few minutes later. Lee and Jackson discussed the situation as they pored over maps on the dining room table, but Lee was hesitant to strike until he knew McClellan's exact location in the five miles between Malvern Hill and the James River.

Early in the rainy afternoon, President Davis and his brother, Colonel Joseph Davis, arrived unannounced at headquarters. A surprised Lee greeted his visitors, exclaiming: "President, I am delighted to see you." The two shook hands; then Davis greeted Major Walter Taylor of Lee's staff while the army commander spoke warmly to Colonel Davis. Jackson, sitting by the fire, had bristled at the sight of the president. He still felt that Davis had treated him unfairly in the past, especially at the end of the Romney Campaign. In a moment, Davis turned and looked inquisitively across the room at the now-standing Jackson. McGuire noted that Jackson "stood as if a corporal on guard, his head erect, his little fingers touching the seams of his pants, and looked at Davis." Lee saw the two men staring silently at one another. "Why, President," he exclaimed, "don't you know General Jackson? This is our Stonewall Jackson." Davis saw instantly that any exchange with Jackson was going to be lukewarm at best. He bowed to the general. Jackson saluted stiffly—"the salute of an inferior to a superior officer," McGuire stated.[82]

No words passed between the two men. Davis and Lee then walked to the table and began studying maps. The army chief explained what had transpired and where the Union army was now judged to be. He outlined possible courses of action as Davis interjected with an occasional suggestion. The polite way in which Lee passed over each of the president's ideas was clear evidence that Lee was fully in control of his army.

While the two leaders talked, Jackson sat back in his corner, "absolutely silent, face showing great anxiety, and in the end great trouble." Lee, Davis, and Longstreet did not seem to comprehend (as Jackson did) that McClellan was defeated. He ought to be pursued hotly and destroyed. Instead, the Union army was being allowed to retire to safety. Davis finally turned politely to Jackson and asked him how he felt about the military picture. Alone in his opinion, Jackson answered in quiet but firm fashion: "They have not all got away if we go immediately after them." Such a move was impracticable. Jackson's face clearly reflected his disappointment. Davis shortly departed for his return to Richmond. Other than ease his divisions slowly toward the new Union base at Harrison's Landing, Jackson did nothing else that day.[83]

Rain stopped early the following day, and the weather turned sunny and warm. Stuart's cavalry found the Union army, as anticipated, on high ground along the north bank of the James River. Lee directed his division commanders to resume the pursuit as quickly as possible. Jackson's men got the lead, followed by the troops of Longstreet. However, since Longstreet had consistently maintained a better march schedule during the campaign, Lee ordered Jackson to give way and let his senior division commander have the lead.

Muddy ground and badly chewed roads were the major reasons for the snail-like pace of the march. By sundown, the Confederates had advanced barely three miles. McClellan and the James River were still five miles distant.

Jackson's temper had grown volatile during the day; his patience was strained to the limit. He found quarters in a farmhouse not far from Willis Church. Staff members gave him a wide berth. Sometime around noon Jackson summoned a private supposedly familiar with the country and asked him about various roads and approaches. The soldier's empty, rather childish replies snapped Jackson's temper. He gave the private a verbal lashing and ordered him from the room with threats of severe punishment.

That night he summoned the staff. "Jim will have breakfast for you punctually at dawn," he told the hushed group. "I expect you to be up, to eat immediately, and be in the saddle with me. We must burn no more daylight." With that, Jackson turned away and sought his pallet.[84]

On July 4, Jackson arose before first light. Jim Lewis, who knew the general well, had gotten up an hour earlier and prepared breakfast. In a few minutes, the sleepy and disheveled Dabney appeared. No other staff member arrived. Light soon appeared in the eastern sky. An infuriated Jackson yelled to his servant: "Jim, put the food in the chest, lock it, have the chest in the wagon and the wagon moving in two minutes! Do you hear?" Dabney, who had barely begun eating, tried to calm the situation by suggesting that Jackson himself take the time to eat. The general was too angry to consider it. He mounted quickly, gave Sandie Pendleton a glare when the aide rushed to a now-empty mess table, and galloped away. The usually reticent Jim Lewis observed, "My stars, but the General is just mad this time—most like lightning struck him!"[85]

July 4 got off to a horrible start for Jackson, and little improvement came during the day. Jackson pressed his men close upon the heels of Longstreet's columns. Confederates reached the Federal front near midday. The fire of battle still smoldered in Jackson. Yet after sending forward a probe, he asked Longstreet (in command of the advance) to delay any attack.

McClellan had been given two unmolested days to select and fortify a new position. Further, the climate and the strain of war on the peninsula now bore heavily on the valley soldiers. The humidity was crushing; typhoid fever and dysentery were sweeping through the ranks; a continuous battle was in progress with mosquitoes and other vermin. "No being lives in this neighborhood," a soldier in the 2d Virginia commented. "Every house is a hospital."[86]

When Lee reached the field, he and Jackson rode forward for a close inspection of the Union position at Harrison's Landing. Even Jackson saw the impropriety of making an attack, and he said so. Lee agreed. The Confederate hope of destroying the Army of the Potomac on the peninsula had disappeared.[87]

Early the following day, July 5, Jackson asked for status reports from all of his brigades. What he learned was discouraging. According to Dabney, "half his men appeared to be out of their ranks, from death or wounds, from the necessary labors of the care of the wounded, from straggling and from the inefficiency of their inferior officers." Jackson at once instructed the men to encamp and rest. Orders went out for Quartermaster Harman to hustle forward with food and supplies. Campfires appeared, as did tents; the aroma of food cooking over campfires drifted through quiet woods. Naturally, Harman complained. "I am the greatest slave in the army and have the hardest master to serve." Yet the "foot cavalry" displayed an elevated spirit not previously seen on the peninsula.[88]

Outside the army, Jackson remained the hero of the hour to Southerners. Baskets of food arrived regularly at his headquarters. The staff intercepted most of it; the aides knew that Jackson's spartan diet might otherwise result in the delectables being returned to the donors. Among gifts to the general were several outlandish hats that no man of Jackson's unpretentious ways would have worn even as a joke.[89]

July 6 was the Sabbath, and Jackson tried his best to observe it in a reverential spirit. Yet there was at least one interruption. Captain Adolph Elhart, a paymaster from Rockbridge County, was on the staff of General G. W. Smith. Earlier, Jackson had sought in vain to have Elhart transferred to his command. Elhart arrived at headquarters on Sunday morning. He and Jackson had a cordial conversation about Lexington, VMI, and associated matters. Then Elhart got to the reason behind his visit. "General," he began, "we are near Richmond. If you would ride with me and see the Secretary of War, one word from you would get me transferred to you."

Jackson quickly grew serious. "Captain, this is no Sunday talk. Come and see me tomorrow."

Elhart apologized but added, "General, I came here today because I didn't know whether I would find you here tomorrow."

The secretive Jackson tensed. "Who told you so?" he asked.

"No one," the captain replied, "and I must quote Scripture to you: 'By their fruits ye shall know them.'"

Jackson smiled and answered warmly, "Come and see me tomorrow."[90]

The next day the two men rode together into Richmond. Within minutes, Jackson secured Elhart's transfer. The captain never forgot that the famous Stonewall Jackson made a long horseback ride on behalf of an insignificant paymaster.[91]

Two nights' sleep restored Jackson to his old aggressive self. He returned to the *idée fixe* of a Northern invasion. To Jackson, the success in the valley and the stalemate on the peninsula were useless if the quest for victory was not pushed continuously and forcefully. Jackson felt so strongly on the matter that he was willing to ignore chain-of-command protocol, skirt insubordination, and take his case directly to the commander in chief.

One evening (probably July 8), Jackson summoned Congressman Boteler to his tent. With unusual agitation, Jackson began the conversation by asking his friend, "Do you know that we are losing valuable time here?"

"How so?" Boteler answered curiously.

"Why, by repeating the blunder we made after the battle of Manassas, in allowing the enemy leisure to recover from his defeat and ourselves to suffer by inaction." Jackson paused a moment, then resumed with increased animation. "Yes! We are wasting precious time and energies in the malarious region that can be much better employed elsewhere, and I want to talk with you about it."[92]

McClellan's army was beaten, Jackson declared. The enemy would need considerable reinforcements and reorganization before it would be operational again. Richmond was safe for the foreseeable future. Therefore, a movement northward should be made without delay. Jackson wanted Boteler to take this proposal straight to President Davis, lay out the plan for the chief executive, and seek his approval.

Jackson desired nothing for himself, he emphasized; he would willingly follow under any officer designated to lead such an offensive.

Boteler was reluctant to go to the top on behalf of Jackson this time. "What is the use of my going to Mr. Davis? He will probably refer me again to General Lee. So why don't you yourself speak to General Lee upon the subject?"

"I have already done so," Jackson told the surprised Boteler.

"Well, what does he say?"

"He says nothing," Jackson snapped. Then he added quickly in more even tones: "Do not think I complain of his silence. He doubtless has good reasons for it."

Boteler asked: "Then you don't think that General Lee is slow in making up his mind?"

"Slow!" Jackson exclaimed in a near shout. "By no means, Colonel. On the contrary, his perceptions are as quick and unerring as his judgment is infallible. But with the vast responsibilities now resting on him, he is perfectly right in withholding a hasty expression of his opinions and purposes."[93]

Jackson paused again, this time for a longer period. He resumed in a low tone as if talking to himself. "So great is my confidence in General Lee that I am willing to follow him blindfolded. But I fear he is unable to give me a definite answer now because of influences at Richmond." With that, Jackson urged Boteler to see the president and plead the case for a Northern invasion.[94]

The congressman rode into Richmond the next day. This was the third time he had served as Jackson's personal emissary to urge a major offensive in the North. He gained an audience with Davis. While the idea might have had promise, the president was not prepared to sanction another counteroffensive while the Confederates licked their wounds from the Seven Days Campaign. More men and material than the South had at hand were needed for so bold an action. Yet Jackson's proposal would be a seed that partially took root a few days later.

Since the end of April, Jackson's soldiers had not been in the same camp for over four days at a time. That ten-week record ended on July 8, when Lee ordered Jackson and Longstreet to proceed "by easy marches" to the vicinity of Richmond. This was welcome news to the valley troops, even though the march toward the capital proved long and offensive to the nostrils. "The smell was almost unendurable," a private in the 31st Virginia observed, "and the sun so extremely hot that men fell in the ranks, exhausted or from sunstroke." Major Harman spoke for many when he declared: "I hope now that we will soon be back in the mountains. If we are not the hospitals will be full."[95]

Weary soldiers marched all day and into the night. Jackson and his staff were far in the lead. All were drowsing in the saddle—especially Jackson, whose head kept dropping onto his breast while his body swung lazily to and fro. The horsemen met several groups of soldiers in bivouac by the roadside.

As Jackson rode slowly past a small party, it mistook the mounted men for a drunken cavalry detail. One of the infantrymen broke the silence by shouting at the leader, "I say, old fellow, where the devil did you get your liquor?" The loud voice startled Jackson.

His head jerked up as he asked: "Doctor McGuire, did you speak to me? Captain Pendleton, did you? Somebody did."

It was then that the foot soldier got a good look at the officer in front. "Great God!" he screamed. "It's Old Jack!" With that, the man bolted into the darkness.[96]

The new camps for Jackson's portion of the army were along the Richmond-Mechanicsville road two miles northeast of the capital. Jackson's headquarters were in the front yard of a stately home. The general moved with his usual dispatch to have his men supplied and kept occupied. Orders were published within hours of arrival at the campsites. Each division commander was to ensure that clothing and tents were properly distributed; sinks were to be dug under the supervision of medical officers; drill would take place three times daily; no soldier was to enter Richmond without a duly authorized pass. Jackson himself set an example for the last-named restriction. He went to the capital only once in four days.

Some of the troops scoffed at Jackson's heavy hand. An Alabama soldier repeated a familiar observation first stated by some of the "foot cavalry" when he told a friend: "some of the boys says that they wish all the yankees ware in hell but I dont for if they ware to go there Old Jackson would follow them there to."[97]

A more serious dissatisfaction affected one of Ewell's officers. Without permission, the brigadier went to the War Department. He announced that members of Ewell's division were unhappy and requested that they be transferred from Jackson's command. Ewell heard of this action and rushed to General Samuel Cooper's office. He angrily denied any major unrest in his command and urged that his division remain under Jackson. Adjutant General Cooper assured Ewell that no change would be made.[98]

Meanwhile, the North was gearing for a long war. On July 1, President Lincoln had issued a call for 300,000 new volunteers. A Federal force under General Ambrose E. Burnside had left the North Carolina coast by boat and was proceeding with at least 10,000 men toward Fort Monroe on the eastern tip of the Virginia peninsula. A second Union column stood poised at Fredericksburg. McClellan's massive army still remained at Harrison's Landing.

Perhaps most ominous of all for the Confederates, the scattered divisions of Banks, McDowell, and Fremont that had pressured Jackson in the valley had been organized into an Army of Virginia under Major General John Pope. That strong force was moving slowly through north-central Virginia. Pope quickly established a reputation as a braggart. He reportedly dated one of his early proclamations "Headquarters in the Saddle." That was not true, but Confederate wags had a field day deriding a big-mouthed enemy general who put his headquarters where his hindquarters ought to be.

On July 12, Lee learned that part of Pope's command had occupied Culpeper on the Orange and Alexandria Railroad, thirty-five miles northwest of Fredericksburg. Twenty-seven miles due south of Culpeper was Gordonsville and an exposed bend in the Virginia Central Railroad. That line was the only direct rail link between Richmond and the fertile, strategic Shenandoah Valley. The area around Gordonsville also had to be defended at all costs from the new Union army because the boastful Yankee commander was threatening to wage war on all helpless citizens in his path.

Lee knew that he had to dispatch part of his army at once to the Piedmont. Who to send was the question. The army chief probably had limited enthusiasm about selecting Jackson. In his report of the Seven Days, Lee never censured Jackson for anything—but neither did he praise him. On the other hand, Jackson was experienced in semi-independent command. Lee knew how eager Jackson was to take the war to the North. The convincing factor for Lee may have been his knowledge that Jackson would not hesitate to fight if there was a real threat.

In a quick reorganization of the Southern army, Lee informally divided his command between Jackson and Longstreet. The latter was to maintain a strong front between McClellan and Richmond, so his wing increased from six to twenty-eight brigades. Jackson, who was going west to delay Pope as much as possible, would do so with only his and Ewell's divisions. This was a reduction in Jackson's peninsula command from fourteen to seven brigades.

Contrary to the conclusion drawn by at least two recent writers, this shuffle was not any punishment of Jackson.[99] His peninsula command had been inflated by the addition of Harvey Hill's division. Lee's reduction of Jackson's command made good sense. He was keeping the bulk of his army at Richmond against the greater threat and sending what amounted to an expeditionary force west to confront the lesser enemy.

After breakfast on Sunday morning, July 13, Jackson rode unobtrusively into Richmond. Major Dabney, too ill to remain in the field, had received an extended leave of absence. The youthful Sandie Pendleton accompanied Jackson as the new adjutant general.

Inside the governor's mansion adjacent to the capitol, Jackson met Lee and Governor John Letcher. They conferred for a short time before Lee and Jackson rode the four blocks to the presidential mansion and an even longer meeting with Davis. There Jackson's role in the days ahead was fully developed.

He was to proceed to Louisa Court House or, if practicable, to Gordonsville. Once in central Virginia, Jackson's tasks were "to observe the enemy's movements closely, to avail himself of any opportunity to attack that might arise," and to carry out both assignments with the understanding that Lee would provide additional help from the Richmond line only if feasible. Both Lee and Jackson were aware that 11,000 Confederates would be facing some 49,500 Federals under Pope.[100]

When the conference ended, the two generals tarried for a few moments on the steps of the Davis home. Captain Charles Blackford of the 2d Virginia Cavalry had just been attached to Jackson's staff. Seeing Lee and Jackson side by side for the first time, Blackford was struck by the contrast in appearance. "Lee was elegantly dressed in full uniform, sword and sash, spotless boots, beautiful spurs, and by far the most magnificent man I ever saw. The highest type of the Cavalier class to which by blood and rearing he belongs. Jackson, on the other hand, was a typical Roundhead. He was poorly dressed, that is, he looked so though his clothes were made of good material. His cap was very indifferent and pulled down over one eye, much stained by weather and without insignia. His coat was closely buttoned up to his chin and had upon the collar the stars and wreath of a general. His shoulders were stooped. . . . He had a plain swordbelt without sash and a sword in no respect different from that of other infantry officers that I could see. His face, in repose, is not handsome or agreeable and he would be passed by anyone without a second look."[101]

Jackson did not return immediately to camp.[102] It was the Sabbath, and the highly esteemed Reverend Dr. Moses D. Hoge was preaching at his Second Presbyterian Church. The congregation was singing a hymn when Jackson arrived. He slipped into the church and took a seat near the door. McGuire, Pendleton, and Douglas were with him. The general "went to sleep soon after the service began and slept through the greater part of it," McGuire noted, and the surgeon added, "A man who can go to sleep under Dr. Hoge's preaching can go to sleep anywhere on the face of this earth." By the time of the benediction, glances and whispers were being made in Jackson's direction and an air of excitement was radiating through the audience. One worshiper noted that "the General seemed uneasy, really appeared confused, pushed for the door, and vanished almost in an instant. I could but smile to see him fairly conquered and made to run."[103]

Jackson returned to his headquarters outside town and busily packed his belongings. Yet the effect of the church service—in spite of his dozing—lingered. He told Anna the next day of the "great comfort to have the privilege of spending a quiet Sabbath, within the walls of a house dedicated to the service of God." Then, overcome by humility, Jackson wrote: "People are very kind to me. How God, our God, does shower blessings upon me, an unworthy servant."[104]

Late that day, Jackson led his column from the camps. The troops expected the march to veer right and head back down the peninsula. Jackson turned left—"toward the mountains and the valley, where pure air and good water could be had," one soldier exclaimed. With that move, "a shout arose that was deafening in its volume," and the cheer rolled down the line from one end to the other. At about that same moment, a War Department clerk in Richmond put an entry in his diary. Federal General John Pope "is simply a braggart, and will meet a braggart's fate," the civilian wrote. "He says his headquarters will be on his horse. . . . Well, we shall see how he will face a Stonewall."[105]

18

RECOVERY AT CEDAR MOUNTAIN

IF THE EASTWARD MARCH of Jackson's army from the valley had been
marked by confusion, the westward march back toward the mountains was pure
chaos. The Virginia Central Railroad was unprepared to move Jackson's 11,000
Confederates. In the spring, enemy cavalry had destroyed sections of track; a replacement trestle over the South Anna River had not yet been completed. Most of the
rolling stock was twenty miles from Richmond on the other side of the South Anna.

Part of Jackson's army took the few available trains at the capital and rode north as
far as possible, then crossed the river on foot before boarding trains. The remaining
portion of the valley force marched from Richmond to beyond the break in the
railroad and then boarded trains. Meanwhile, Virginia Central officials were laying
new track, finishing the bridge, and rounding up all of their rolling equipment plus
what they could borrow from nearby lines.

Seventeen freight trains, averaging fifteen cars each, transported Jackson's men.
They operated day and night at ten-minute intervals over fifty-one miles of track from
Richmond to Fredericks Hall. The wonder is that with the railroad devoid of signals
and up-to-date telegraph facilities, no accidents occurred. However, there were many
close calls.[1]

A weary Jackson reached Fredericks Hall on the 18th. Jeb Stuart and his staff
briefly joined the main column in midafternoon. Jackson was delighted to see the
good-humored young cavalryman, with whom he had little in common but whose
military skills he admired because they were so akin to his own. Jackson invited the
group to share his table at supper.

Stuart's huge Prussian aide, Heros von Borcke, recalled: "The great Stonewall gave
but little thought to the comforts of life, but he was so much the pet of the people that
all the planters and farmers in whose neighbourhood he erected his simple tent, vied
with each other in supplying him abundantly with the delicacies of the table; and
accordingly we found an excellent dinner set out, to which we did full justice."[2]

On learning that the Federals had vacillated in moving toward Gordonsville, Jackson took part of his command there the following day. Union officials continued to
trade rumors of Jackson's whereabouts while he secured the most important point in
his new area of responsibility.[3] "Please direct your next letter to Gordonsville," he
told Anna, "and continue to address me there until you hear otherwise." Then, in a
light vein he displayed only to his wife, he added, "Everybody doesn't know the
meaning and location of 'Headquarters, Valley District!'"[4]

Not all of the men in the army shared Jackson's pleasure at leaving the capital for an unknown destination in the Piedmont. "I feel as if I was the wandering Jew," General William Taliaferro wrote his wife. "Jackson is never satisfied unless he is marching or fighting so that I have no hope of seeing you until the war is over." Corporal Thomas Godwin of the 4th Virginia was equally unhappy about the trip. "It seems that we will never get to a stopping place," he wrote his sister, "for here we are again on our way to—where? If you want to know you will have to ask Genl. Jackson. . . . Our ride on the cars was anything but a pleasant one, it being very hot & the cinders filling our eyes & mouths. I had a seat between the cars where some one was continually climbing over me all the time."[5]

Preliminary reports convinced Jackson that the enemy was opening a second major front in central Virginia. Federal General John Pope seemed ready to push for control of the Virginia Central Railroad, while at Fredericksburg stood 11,000 Union infantry, 500 cavalry, and thirty guns poised to move in any direction. If the two forces united, Jackson could be overwhelmed.

Equally as bad, either might drive south and sever the railroad. Jackson's twofold mission therefore underwent a slight alteration. He now had to guard the Virginia Central from Hanover Junction to Gordonsville; but if he found an opening, he could attack and cripple Federal designs.

Pope's failure to push expeditiously and seize the vital Gordonsville railroad junction was a mistake indicative of the man's speak-loud-act-little generalship. While he impressed some soldiers, Pope irritated most people. A pettiness was always present. Earlier in the war, after a New York captain deserted his command, Pope expressed how he felt about the officer by posting a reward of five cents for the man's apprehension.

Headstrong and blustery, Pope had come east to merge several scattered commands into a smoothly functioning army. He never succeeded, and the failure was largely of his own doing. To raise spirits, Pope issued a jingoistic proclamation that he was accustomed in the West to seeing the backs of his enemies. Eastern soldiers instantly took offense. Pope then published a series of harsh rules for governing the conduct of Virginia civilians in his path—rules that threatened wholesale imprisonments as well as executions. Nothing like this had appeared in the war, and nothing much came of the warnings. Nevertheless, Pope overnight aroused the hatred of the military and civilian population in the Old Dominion.[6]

Jackson knew exactly how to deal with Pope, just as his mind was set on how the Confederacy could and should win this great national test decreed by God. One night during the trip from Richmond, Jackson had dinner and a long talk with a brother-in-law, Rufus Barringer. The North Carolina cavalry officer was not an intimate friend of Jackson's. Yet Presbyterian canons dictated that in the eyes of the church, they were brothers. Therefore, Jackson spoke freely to Barringer, who unfortunately penned the only account of the conversation.

"I myself see in this war, if the North triumph, a dissolution of the bonds of all society," Barringer remembered Jackson saying. "It is not alone the destruction of our property, but the prelude to anarchy, infidelity, and the ultimate loss of free responsible government on this continent." That being the case, Jackson had earlier believed strongly in a black-flag policy: "no quarter to the violators of our homes and fire-sides!"[7]

He had changed his mind in this second year of the war. "I now see clearly enough that the people of the South were not prepared for such a policy. I have myself cordially accepted the policy of our leaders."[8]

All of this had suddenly changed because of the "cruel and utterly barbarous orders" of Pope.[9] Although Jackson had formulated a plan of retribution and laid it before Lee, he had no hope that it would be accepted. Jackson then outlined for Barringer what he would like to see done.

The entire Confederate line cannot be held, Jackson declared. Southern resources were too limited, Union strength too great. A black-flag policy will not work. The alternative was to organize small bands of hard-hitting troops and initiate a veritable series of counterinvasions. A half-dozen such "light movable columns" would strike any Union force that entered Virginia, maintain momentum, and make penetrations into the North. Cities would be held for ransom, prisoners paroled, attack-and-retreat operations conducted everywhere. "I would make it hot for our friends at *their* homes and firesides, all the way to Kansas," Jackson asserted.[10]

His plan would not have the risk of committing an entire army to one offensive. Strike forces could do as much damage with far fewer casualties. Jackson was animated as he built to the climax of his presentation to Barringer. "We have just gained great victories here at Richmond, and our troops would now rejoice at the hope of an aggressive movement. That mode of war best suits the temper of our people and the dash and daring of the Southern soldier, and I would right now seize the golden moment to show the North what they may expect."[11]

Once again Jackson was advocating ruthless, uncompromising war with the enemy. His precedent was the Old Testament; his justification was the freedom of the God-loving people of the South. Jackson biographers have always been uneasy about mentioning this aspect of the general's character, and many of the leading Jackson studies simply ignore it.

The general's feelings were never unusual in this matter. A number of Southern publications and newspaper editors expressed similar sentiments throughout the Civil War. Jackson in essence was trying to point out that a weaker revolutionary government could not triumph against a stronger opponent by waging conventional warfare. That premise was current but unacceptable to Confederate authorities.

Jackson arrived at Gordonsville on July 19 minus his adjutant general, Sandie Pendleton. The young Lexingtonian had fallen ill after the Peninsula Campaign and would not return full-time to the army until mid-September. However, Jackson was delighted to find Jed Hotchkiss waiting for him at the railroad junction.

The mapmaker noticed at once that his general looked "the worse for his Chickahominy trip."[12] Little time existed for an extended visit between the two men. Jackson put Hotchkiss to work preparing maps of the northern Virginia area, just in case his thoughts of a Northern strike materialized.

Headquarters for the next few days was the old Globe Tavern at the north end of Gordonsville's main street. It was then the home of Mrs. Mary Barbour and her three adult daughters. The ladies doted on Jackson whenever possible. He had his tent in the front yard. It "opens upon the Blue Ridge in the distance," he told Anna with a tinge of nostalgia.[13]

Between Globe Tavern and the railroad was the residence of Mary Barbour's son-in-law, the Reverend Daniel B. Ewing. Jackson called at once on his old clerical friend. Ewing too was struck by how "very much broken down" Jackson appeared to be as a result of the recent campaign. Jackson confessed to him that he felt worse than he had since his days in Mexico.

His association with the Ewings in Gordonsville was akin to that which Jackson enjoyed with the Grahams in Winchester. He took meals on occasion, chatted at length with the minister on theological matters, and became so enamored with the Ewing children that when one asked for a button from his coat, she got one.

Jackson participated eagerly in family devotionals. "You that have seen Jackson fight ought to have heard Jackson pray," Ewing said thereafter. "He did not pray to men but to God. His tones were deep, solemn, tremulous. He seemed to realize that he was talking to heaven's King."[14]

People throughout the neighborhood came to get a glimpse of the famous commander. It was the same with the army. "Whenever he is recognized by the soldiers, he is cheered," new staff member Charles Blackford noted. "He seems to have no social life. He divides his time between military duties, prayer, sleep and solitary thought. He holds converse with few."[15]

Jackson often took refuge in the Ewing parsonage. There he catnapped when not attending to a flow of paperwork. A host of military and personnel matters confronted him in the last week of July. Foremost was Pope's menacing army twenty-six miles to the north. Next was the security of Gordonsville. "The place itself is uninteresting, being nothing more than a small village built mostly of frame houses," a physician commented.[16] Yet it was the spot where two of Virginia's primary rail lines crossed. As such, Gordonsville was the most vital locale in central Virginia.

The Piedmont region also contained problems. It was rolling country, dominated by grass and crop lands. Here and there were rises locally known as mountains. Forests were scattered; streams were clear-cut with sharp banks. Roads were fewer and straighter in this open region. All of this meant that military potentials around Gordonsville were limited for both sides.

Jackson insisted at the outset that his strength, if not his presence at Gordonsville, be kept as secret as possible. (Shortly after his arrival, he heard a rumor of Federals crossing the Rapidan River not too far away at Raccoon Ford, whereupon he imposed on the Rev. Ewing, familiar with the area, to make a personal reconnaissance to prove the report unfounded.) Jackson placed strong guard posts along the Virginia Central. Cavalry detachments patrolled far afield. Therein was a perceived weakness that occupied much of Jackson's attention.

The cavalry brigade in Jackson's army was under the command of General Beverly H. Robertson. Jackson—like Stuart—would never have great confidence in the brigadier. Neither did most of the men who served under him. Robertson was then thirty-six, a West Pointer with cavalry experience in the West against the Indians. Somewhat bald, with unsmiling eyes and long-flowing mustache, he was a strict disciplinarian to whom President Davis had assigned Ashby's cavalry with the hope that Robertson could instill improved responsibility in the horsemen.

A few weeks earlier, Ashby's men held an unofficial election and picked their own field officers. The War Department disregarded all such appointments. So morale in Jackson's mounted wing was not high at the moment.

On the day after his arrival at Gordonsville, Jackson met one horseman whom he came to respect. A small, thin, smooth-faced officer appeared at headquarters with a letter from Stuart. "General," the communique stated, "the bearer, Jno. S. Mosby, late 1st Lt. Va. Cavalry, is en route to scout beyond the enemy's lines towards Manassas & Fairfax. He is bold, daring, intelligent and discreet; the information he may obtain & transmit to you may be relied upon, and I have no doubt that he will soon give additional proof of his value." Stuart then added a postscript: "Did you receive the volume of Napoleon & His Maxims I sent you through Gen. Ch. S. Winder's orderly?"[17]

Mosby would develop into a first-rate partisan ranger as well as a valuable source of information on movements in northern Virginia. As for the copy of Napoleon's maxims, Jackson carried it thenceforth in his haversack along with a Webster's dictionary and a Bible given him by the Reverend Ewing.[18]

After three days at Gordonsville, Jackson needed more privacy. He shifted headquarters and a segment of his army four miles north of the village. The new camp was on the slope of a prominent hill, with the Blue Ridge in full view to the west. "That reminds us of our homes," Jackson told the staff.[19]

Captain Blackford was finding staff work under Jackson an oftentimes disappointing experience. Returning one day from a scout toward Fredericksburg, Blackford found Jackson's new headquarters to be "nothing but a roll of blankets strapped up and two camp-stools and a table." Jackson received the aide at once. The two officers sat on the stools facing each other, and Blackford eagerly began an account of his dangerous ride. What occurred next was deflating to the captain.

"After I had been talking a few minutes I perceived that he was fast asleep. I stopped and waited several minutes. He woke up and said: 'Proceed.' I did so for a few minutes when I noted he was asleep again so I stopped. He slept longer this time and when he awoke he said without explanation, apology or further questioning: 'you may proceed to your quarters.' I did so although I felt somewhat put out."[20]

Jackson never dozed when the subject of stragglers or skulkers entered a conversation. Once in a conversation with Mrs. Barbour, mention was made of a skulker. Jackson struck his hand angrily on the table and exclaimed: "Madam, if your son were to come home and try to shirk duty, you ought to shut your door in his face and treat him as a renegade unworthy of your name or regard." A day or so earlier, Jackson emphasized his feelings by approving quickly the death sentences of three soldiers convicted of desertion.[21]

During this time, Jackson also maintained his belief that duty took precedence over all other human feeling. William Lacy, a kinsman of the man who had married Jackson and Anna, was a divinity student then serving in the Rockbridge Artillery. The twenty-year-old received word that his father was seriously ill. Lacy went straight to Jackson and requested an emergency furlough. Jackson was sympathetic but he said no to the plea. "This is a sore trial for you," he told Lacy. "I am under orders; I cannot let you go. You are a soldier, a Christian, a minister of the gospel. Now is the time to test your faith and character. Be patient and do your duty."[22]

More than any other undertaking, Jackson made it repeatedly clear that he wanted to fight for the glory of God and to make his army an instrument of the almighty's will. Discipline sometimes interfered. The Stonewall Brigade straggled badly on the march to Gordonsville. Sidney Winder resolved to prevent a recurrence. He ordered some thirty lazy soldiers taken into the woods and subjected to the painful indignity of being bucked and gagged. Half of the men deserted after nightfall. An officer complained of the harsh treatment to Jackson, who ordered an end to such punishment. By then, however, the damage had been done. At the time when Jackson was attempting to elevate morale, Winder lost the hard-earned respect of the men in Jackson's old brigade. The 33d Virginia's John Casler reported ominously that Winder "was a good general [but] very tyrannical, so much so that he was 'spotted' by some of the brigade; and we could hear it remarked by some nearly every day that the next fight we got into would be the last for Winder."[23]

While the army drilled and rested, Jackson enlarged his staff. The well-educated Captain Richard E. Wilbourn, whose Virginia parents had moved to Mississippi, came on duty as Jackson's signal officer. Also appointed to the staff as an aide was Jackson's brother-in-law, Joseph G. Morrison. The teenager had been granted leave of absence as a cadet at VMI. His appointment came with the understanding that Morrison would display "early rising, boldness, industry and enterprise."[24]

Jackson at the same time bade farewell to his former chief of staff, Robert Dabney. The Presbyterian cleric had suffered such disability from field service that he had requested and received permission to return to civilian life. Jackson sent his friend a kind letter of thanks. He closed the message by repeating a deep desire: "In God's own time I hope that he will send an army North and crown it with victory, and make its fruits peace, but let us pray that He send it not, except He goes with it."[25]

Command matters occupied a good deal of Jackson's attention. Improvement in discipline was an ongoing pursuit. Jackson informed Lee that every general officer he had was on at least one court-martial then in session. He closed a long directive to one of the regimental commanders with the admonition: "I wish that you would have your weekly inspection on Saturday evening instead of Sunday, and give your command every practicable opportunity of observing the Sabbath."[26]

On a Monday, Jackson paused to send a letter to North Carolina. "My darling wife, I am just overburdened with work, and I hope you will not think hard at receiving only very short letters from your loving husband. A number of officers are with me, but people keep coming to my tent—though let me say no more. A Christian should never complain. The apostle Paul said, 'I glory in tribulations!' What a bright example for others."[27]

Jackson unfortunately did not see a glowing example in church. He attended the Reverend Ewing's Sunday services for as long as he was in the Gordonsville area. Yet he slept through every sermon. At one point, Dick Ewell blurted: "What is the use of General Jackson going to church? He sleeps all the time!"[28]

As he was prone to do, the general continually asked the War Department for reinforcements. He also attempted to obtain a replacement for Beverly Robertson. Jackson liked the man's disciplinary spirit but not his unreliability as a scout. Lee thought Jackson was expecting too much of the cavalryman. Besides, there was no one to send. Jackson quickly nominated his old academy friend and fellow Virginian, William E. "Grumble" Jones.

Who was to lead the cavalry was still under discussion when Jackson on July 29 marched his 11,000-man force south through Gordonsville into Louisa County. Jackson made his headquarters in the grove of an old church and then explained that food and fodder were more plentiful in the new surroundings. Naturally, he had told no one in advance why the army was shifting position. Captain Blackford wrote in amazement: "It seems strange to see a large body of men moving in one direction and only one man in all the thousands knowing where they are going. . . . They will go until ordered to stop." That was not totally true. General Taliaferro wrote petulantly of the march to Louisa County: "None of his Division commanders were informed of his intentions, and it was a source of much annoyance to them to be ordered blindly to move without knowing whither, or to what purpose."29

Jackson reached the new encampment just as a long letter from Lee arrived. The army commander had to do something now. Merely to sit in front of the enemy left both Jackson and him vulnerable to attack from two different hosts. Pope's advance was becoming increasingly ominous. It was only a matter of time before Jackson came face to face with the new Union threat. Lee was anxious to strengthen Jackson "without hazard to Richmond, and thus enable [Jackson] to drive, if not destroy, the miscreant Pope."30

Two Confederate brigades were en route to Richmond from South Carolina, increasing Lee's numbers by 4000 men. He now felt in a position to send perhaps as many as 18,000 reinforcements to Jackson. That would leave Lee 56,000 soldiers as a buffer between the inactive McClellan and the Confederate capital.

But who would command the large contingent being sent to Jackson? Longstreet was needed in the Richmond defenses. None of the current brigadiers seemed ready for elevation to division command and transfer to Jackson. The obvious choice therefore was General A. P. Hill, who had demonstrated throughout the Peninsula Campaign a propensity for fighting that Lee appreciated. Yet assigning Hill to Jackson was even more of a gamble than Lee realized.

"Little Powell," nurtured in Virginia Piedmont aristocracy, was high spirited, impetuous, and proud. Jackson, an orphan from the mountains, was a loner, sensitive, and stern. Lee had no way of knowing that an enmity, bred between Jackson and Hill at West Point, had burst into flames on the peninsula. Hill thought Jackson criminally derelict for his tardiness at Mechanicsville, Gaines' Mill, and Glendale.31

Lee was concentrating on another personality when he wrote Jackson. "I want Pope to be suppressed," he stated, as if he were talking about mashing an insect. The rest of the July 27 letter was positive and diplomatic. After informing Jackson that Hill and his six brigades were heading to Jackson's assistance, Lee made a statement as much a veiled rebuke as it was a genuine hope. "A. P. Hill you will find I think a good officer with whom you can consult and by advising with your division commanders as to your movements much trouble will be saved you in arranging details as they can act more intelligently." When Kyd Douglas later read Lee's communique, he declared: "How adroitly put! Lee knew of Jackson's reticence with his subordinate Generals—of which complaint had been made to him—and this was a hint to Jackson to consult with them more, but it had no effect."[32]

The general was waiting for Hill's heavy division when he received a letter from one of his Presbyterian friends, the Reverend Francis McFarland. The cleric "expressed to him how thankful I felt to God for preserving him through many bloody conflicts & crowning his efforts with so much success. And assuring him that I knew many of his friends were praying for him, &c." Jackson responded at length. He closed the letter by writing: "It cheers my heart to think that many of God's people are praying to our ever kind Heavenly father for the success of the army to which I belong. Without his helping hand I look for no success and for every success my prayer is, that all the Glory may be given unto *Him* to whom it is properly due. . . . I trust that you will under God's direction do what you can in securing the progress of His people for the success of our armies especially for the success of those which are entrusted to me, an unworthy servant, but who desires to glorify his name even in my present military calling. My trust is in God for success."[33]

Powell Hill's division was at hand by the first week of August. One of his gunners wrote shortly thereafter: "This is the gayest army I have yet seen. The men seem to have more life and spirit than any troops in service. They swear by Father Jackson, as they call him, and believe him to be the greatest general in the field."[34]

August 3 was the Sabbath. All military activity was suspended. Captain Blackford accompanied a group of generals to church in the Green Springs neighborhood. Despite "a very trashy sermon" by the Episcopal rector, the Reverend Kelsey Stewart, Blackford was impressed. Generals Jackson, Hill, Winder, Dorsey Pender, and several other officers sat side by side. During communion, Blackford noted, "the clanking swords sounded strangely as each man arranged his so as to enable him to kneel at the chancel rail."[35]

While Jackson sought grace through the church, Anna Jackson sought help from Dr. McGuire. She had learned from a cousin that the general was unusually thin and fatigued. In a heartfelt plea to McGuire for help, Anna, now midway through her pregnancy, wrote of her husband: "I have made the strongest appeal in my power to him . . . to treat himself to a *rest* & cessation from labor for a few weeks. Sixteen months of uninterrupted mental & physical labor is enough to break down the strongest constitution, but he is *self sacrificing*, & such a *martyr to duty*, that if he thinks he cannot be spared from the Service, I'm afraid he would sacrifice his life before he would give up. . . . I appeal to you, Dr., to assist me in persuading him to rest for a short time." Apparently, McGuire thought better than to bring the letter to Jackson's attention. Besides, it would have been a waste of effort in view of the developing military situation.[36]

Reports of atrocities committed by Pope's orders were increasing in number. Few of them were factual, but the Union general's presence in northern Virginia gave them credence. "We are all very much incensed at Pope's atrocious orders," Hotchkiss wrote home that Sunday, "and hope the day of retribution may soon come to him &

his vile crew." A member of the Rockbridge Artillery agreed. "Of all the things in the world I hate, it is fighting," he told his father, "but it would afford me the greatest pleasure to thrash that contemptible scoundrel, but we will pay him up for it yet."[37]

In spite of McClellan's belief that Jackson had upwards of 35,000 troops (and some of Pope's officers exaggerated the figure to 60,000 men), the three Confederate divisions at Gordonsville were less than half the size of Pope's army. Nevertheless, Jackson was poised for any opportunity to deliver a quick and heavy strike at a segment of his opponent's force. On August 2, Colonel "Grumble" Jones and his 7th Virginia Cavalry fought a brief action with Union horsemen in the streets of Orange. Ten Confederates were wounded, another fifty captured. Union losses were eight men. Jackson blamed Beverly Robertson for the setback.

A day or so later, Jackson was in rare good humor when Robertson came to headquarters. The commanding general was laughing at McGuire's attempt to eat a raw Bermuda onion when he turned and asked Robertson where the enemy was. "I really do not know," came the response. Jackson's expression instantly became "black as a thunder cloud." He turned abruptly, went to his tent, and sent Lee a telegram asking again that William E. Jones be put in Robertson's place. Lee replied that Jackson was being too hasty: such a change in command was not easy to make, especially when Jones had yet to demonstrate competency for brigade command. There, for the time being, the matter rested in an uncertain state.[38]

Other personnel matters further irritated Jackson's already-prickly disposition. He wanted to convene two courts-martial that had been pending—one for weeks, the other for months. The first involved Colonel Z. T. Conner, who had ingloriously abandoned Front Royal following Jackson's seizure of the lower valley in late May. Jackson completed the paperwork, organized a court, and was preparing to press the case when Conner resigned from the army.

Next was the court-martial of General Richard B. Garnett for dereliction of duty at the March 23 battle of Kernstown. This case would proceed. Garnett had sought for about five months to fight Jackson's charges in an open hearing, and now at last he had the opportunity.

On a sultry August 5, Jackson left his new headquarters at the Jonathan B. Magruder estate north of Gordonsville and rode four miles to Liberty Mills. The hamlet, on the south bank of the Rapidan River, was Ewell's headquarters and site of Garnett's trial. Jackson's personal involvement made it one of the most famous courts-martial of the Civil War. Yet the proceedings almost from the first put Jackson in a bad light.

His seven specifications against Garnett ranged from inaccurate to niggling. Regimental colonels in the Stonewall Brigade were solidly behind Garnett. Colonels Andrew J. Grigsby, John Echols, and Arthur C. Cummings filed letters of support on behalf of the brigadier. Undeterred, Jackson pushed his charges firmly. Icy courtesy marked the entire proceedings.

Garnett got his chance for rebuttal on August 6, when Jackson took the stand. Speaking forcefully, Jackson recited the facts of Kernstown as he recalled them. Garnett then cross-examined, concentrating initially on Jackson's own mistakes in the battle. Jackson next denied making a number of statements alleged by Garnett at the time of the contest. The remembrances of the two men were so far apart that at three points in his copy of the testimony, Garnett wrote in the margin, "*Lie.*"

The next day, Captain Sandie Pendleton took the witness chair. He gave strong testimony in Jackson's behalf, but the young aide was convinced by then that Jackson was losing the case. Suddenly, around noon, Jackson suspended the court-martial. Scouts had arrived with news that a portion of Pope's army had reached Culpeper and was advancing south.[39]

Cashiering Garnett was now of secondary importance to Jackson. Pope had made the mistake for which Old Jack had been waiting. His army was divided; a portion of it was alone and exposed in an advanced position. If the Confederates moved quickly, they could attack the van of the enemy before the rest of Pope's army arrived.

A telegram from Lee at about the same moment told Jackson again not to expect reinforcements anytime soon. "I must now leave the matter to your reflection and good judgment," Lee wrote. "Make up your mind what is best to be done under all the circumstances which surround us, and let me hear the result at which you arrive."[40] The Lee-Jackson partnership was resuming.

That afternoon Jackson's army marched northward in search of battle. The three divisions of Ewell, Hill, and Winder numbered no more than 22,500 men. Most regiments were down to about 20 percent of their ideal size. Yet those marching in the dust were the hard core—the reliable element of Jackson's force. Their general was confident that they would perform well in the forthcoming campaign that would demand the most against two enemies: Federals and the weather. For five days beginning on August 7, the afternoon temperatures soared into the nineties.[41]

Sidney Winder had been so ill for the previous two days that a surgeon advised him not to make the August 7 march. The division commander sent his aide, Lieutenant McHenry Howard, to explain Winder's "enfeebled condition" to Jackson and to ascertain where the army was heading so that Winder could catch up with it as soon as possible. Howard found Jackson at the home of Dr. John T. Jones. He was on his knees stuffing some items into a well-worn carpetbag.

After reporting on Winder's illness, Howard gingerly asked where the army was going. He did so quickly in order to brace for an expected sharp reply. Instead, a hint of a smile crossed Jackson's face. "Say to General Winder that I am truly sorry he is sick," Jackson said evenly. "There will be a battle, but not tomorrow, and I hope he will be up. Tell him the army will march to Barnett's Ford [northwest of Orange on the Rapidan], and he can learn its further direction there."[42]

Jackson, still concerned about the leadership of his cavalry, then sent a personal appeal to Stuart. "I wish you would bring up your command and cooperate with me. If such is impracticable come up and make the inspection that has been assigned to you. I desire you to make it during active operations." With that, Jackson galloped toward the head of his column.[43]

He was unsure what lay in front of him—or, more important, what was on his flank. The Confederate advance might be a signal for a Union drive south from Fredericksburg toward the railroad that Jackson had the responsibility of defending. Actually, the plan that Pope completed on August 5 called for a Union advance to the

Rapidan, the major river in the Orange-Culpeper region. From there, Pope would launch a strong demonstration to the southwest against Charlottesville on the Virginia Central line.

The Union general had concluded that such an offensive gave Jackson three choices, all bad. His Confederate adversary could fall back from Gordonsville to protect Charlottesville; he could weaken his command by sending troops to Charlottesville; or he could start northward to do battle on Pope's own terms.

Pope's deployment of troops was as faulty as his miscalculation of what Jackson might do. Federal divisions were widely scattered: Pope's left wing was at Fredericksburg and his right at Sperryville, fifty-five miles to the west. When Pope directed General Nathaniel Banks to move forward from Culpeper, Jackson determined to hit that exposed segment. If, "through the blessing of Providence," he could defeat Banks before the rest of the Union army could converge, Pope's lines would be hopelessly fractured. Jackson therefore moved by a secret route worked out by Hotchkiss. Throughout the afternoon the long column wound uninformed along country roads. When a staff officer asked Powell Hill where they were heading, the division commander replied sneeringly, "I suppose we will go to the hill in front of us, but that is all I know."[44]

A merciless sun wilted men in both armies as they moved toward one another. Back in the Light Division, a South Carolinian stated, "The straggling was deplorable, although hardly anything else was to be expected in such heat as we had." Federal General George H. Gordon (who had already fought in the valley against Jackson, his West Point classmate) was more opinionated. "Clouds of dust hung over us, there was not a breath of air, and the road was like a furnace. . . . The men ate every miserable, crabbed green apple they came across. . . . If we were not conforming to Pope's order to live on the country, we were doing the next best thing to it—we were dying on it."[45]

Confederates marched eight miles before bivouacking in and around the county seat of Orange. At first, Jackson bedded down on a stile in the street. He soon attracted so much attention that he rode three-quarters of a mile from town to the home of a Mr. Willis to spend the night. There Jackson issued written orders for his three divisions to move out at dawn. Ewell would take the lead; Powell Hill would follow Ewell; Jackson's old division would bring up the rear.

The directive was simple enough; but after the orders were distributed, and in a move out of character, Jackson changed his mind. An aide rode off with verbal directives for Ewell. The lead division was to march by the left of the main line and go to Liberty Mills. There the Madison road crossed the Rapidan. Ewell would then march some six miles northeast along both sides of the river and reunite with the other two divisions at Barnett's Ford.

What prompted Jackson to make this late-night deviation in the plan of march, and to alert only the division commander directly involved, is unknown. Three possibilities exist. He could have wanted to throw the Federals off balance by making it appear that Ewell was moving toward Madison, a weak point in Pope's line. Or Ewell's new route might have been intended as nothing more than to protect the long wagon trains from possible attack. The more logical conclusion is that Jackson spread out his advance so as not to crowd the three divisions and all their equipment along one single-lane road.

On August 8, Jackson's advance fell apart almost as quickly as it began. A combination of confusing orders and sluggishness by some officers were at the root of the trouble. So was the near unbearable heat, with the temperature reaching ninety-six that afternoon.

Neither Powell Hill nor Winder knew of Jackson's revised order of march. At 4 A.M. (earlier than the originally scheduled departure time), Ewell's troops were marching to the west. Dawn came, and Powell Hill leisurely formed his brigades near the Orange street up which Ewell was supposed to march.

Troops began passing shortly after daybreak. Hill watched them with the natural assumption that they were Ewell's. Over half of the division had cleared the town before Hill learned that the soldiers were part of Jackson's division in the rear of the army. Then Hill received the unexpected news of Ewell's departure hours earlier for Liberty Mills.

The aggressive Hill, now in his home country, faced a difficult decision. He could stop Jackson's division and place his own men in the middle of the column. This action would create both disorganization and Jackson's wrath. An alternative for Hill was to start his division double-timing by some alternate parallel route that his scouts might find. Such a move in the extreme heat would sap the strength of his troops. As a final option, Hill could wait and then take up the line of march in the rear of Jackson's division. That was the least confusing move, but it went counter to the instructions he had received from Jackson. Hill chose the last option as the most sensible.

While Jackson later conceded that Hill was unaware of the new marching schedule, Hill took his time in learning about the change of marching order.[46] That morning, however, Jackson's mind was set on getting to the exposed part of Pope's army as rapidly as he could. Yet his column was slow and disjointed.

An angry Jackson rode back to Orange. Spying Hill and giving him a dark look, Jackson demanded to know why Hill's brigades were not moving. Hill snapped back as few words as his own seething anger would allow. Jackson galloped away in obvious fury. The previous two days, he had contended with the insubordinate Garnett. Now it was the foot-dragging Hill. Jackson would never forgive the commander of the Light Division for such dereliction on the eve of battle.[47]

Soldiers straggled badly through the day; animals suffered cruelly. One of Hill's brigade commanders vented his frustrations in a journal. "On this trip to Culpeper we were accompanied by 1,200 baggage wagons, but they make a column so long that we can make no use of their contents, and they had just as well be left behind entirely. It is generally supposed that General Jackson travels without baggage, but it is a great mistake. I think he carries too much. The secret of the celerity with which he moves is that he spends very little time in camps."[48]

That Friday produced the poorest one-day march in the history of Jackson's forces. Culpeper, the destination, was far in the distance. Ewell had marched eight miles to avoid a traffic jam he found at Barnett's Ford. Hill's division advanced a mile, then retraced its steps to Orange. Winder was ill again. Ewell was cursing in exasperation, and Hill was irate over Jackson's attitude. Men were dropping everywhere from the heat. Opposing cavalry had been bumping into each other all day. The element of secrecy was gone. Pope knew of the Confederate advance.[49]

Jackson could barely curb his wrath. That he might be in great part responsible for the mess never occurred to him. The decision he had to make at sundown was whether to continue toward Culpeper with secrecy gone. He decided to push forward. If he could seize Culpeper, he would have a firm anchor on the Orange and Alexandria Railroad as well as the middle of Pope's line.

Nightfall found the Confederate army sprawled over parts of three counties. Jackson rode northwest to Rapidan Station and bivouacked at the home of James Garnett. He spent the night on the front porch while the staff slept on the grass.

Uncertainties and frustrations kept Jackson awake. He prayed unusually long and hard that night, prompting servant Jim Lewis to note: "The General is a great man for praying at all times. But when I see him get up a great many times in the night to pray, then I know there is going to be something to pay, and I go straight and pack his haversack. because I know he will call for it in the morning."[50]

Inside the ranks, men sensed that combat was near. "Jackson must be going to attack," a soldier in Hill's division wrote his sister. "He is so quiet and quick no one can tell what he is going to do. He is the man for me. He has so much energy he seems almost to overcome insurmountable obstacles." The soldier then voiced an ominous thought: "His men rely too much on him and I fear if he were lost his army might lose spirit."[51]

A communique reached Jackson around dawn. It was Lee's approval of the move on Culpeper. The chieftain wanted Jackson to strike Pope or at least maneuver him from his position. Lee added, "Relying upon your judgement, courage, and discretion, and trusting to the continued blessing of an ever-kind Providence, I hope for victory."[52]

Jackson had been up most of the night. That, coupled with the previous day's activities, left him in a sour mood. His reply to Lee was pessimistic from start to end. Yesterday had been "oppressively hot"; several soldiers had fallen victim to sunstroke; Hill had covered only two miles the entire day; the six-brigade Light Division that Hill led was too large and unwieldy. Then Jackson reached the depth of his moodiness. "To-day I do not expect much more than to close up and clear the country around the train of the enemy's cavalry. I fear that [my] expedition will, in consequence of my tardy movements, be productive of but little good."[53]

That did not stop Jackson from preparing his army to march before dawn. Ewell's division again was to take the lead, followed by Winder's men, with the Light Division of the untrustworthy Hill (in Jackson's eyes) bringing up the rear. No one knew the destination. When a chaplain asked Ewell about the day's schedule, "Old Bald Head" screeched with exasperation: "I pledge you my word that I do not know whether we will march north, south, east or west, or whether we will march at all!"[54]

Saturday, August 9, proved to be swelteringly hot, the temperature registering in the low eighties at 7 A.M. Jackson rode northward at the head of 22,500 men, forty-seven guns, and 1200 wagons. Fanned out in front was the cavalry under Beverly

Robertson. That screen gave Jackson no assurance—especially since whenever he urged Robertson to establish contact with the enemy, the cavalry leader responded with grumbles about the straggling in his command.[55]

Believing that only the advanced units of Pope's army had reached Culpeper, Jackson resolved to press forward toward that county seat. However, uncertain about Robertson's effectiveness, Jackson parked his wagons off the road at Crooked Run and detached two infantry brigades to stand guard. Culpeper was still eight miles away.

Jackson stopped at the widow Garnett's farm to have breakfast while he waited for his troops to pass. Soon, Winder arrived to report on the progress of his division. The brigadier who had been ill for several days was barely able to sit on his horse. Surgeon McGuire thought that Winder should relinquish command at least for the day. Winder refused. He was officially leading a division for the first time; he was not withdrawing when battle loomed. This kind of spirit impressed Jackson. He shook Winder's hand warmly and watched the Marylander rejoin his men.[56]

The sun in a cloudless sky baked the marching column from the start. To the west, the Blue Ridge was barely visible in the hot haze. Private William E. Jones in Crenshaw's battery asserted that "we travelled as fast as we could under a sun that must have been one hundred degrees in the shade." A captain in Ewell's division noted: "Oh how hot the weather was. [A] great many fell on the road with exhaustion, some died with sun stroke."[57]

Near midmorning, a large Virginia brigade in Ewell's division arrived at a point about three-quarters of a mile from a "Y" in the road. The left fork went to Madison; Culpeper was to the right. A half-mile beyond the intersection, Union cavalry were visible on a long, open ridge. The brigade commander, General Jubal A. Early, had just returned to duty after a battle wound suffered in May at Williamsburg. He was ready for another fight.

In a Confederate officer corps noted for its genteel and aristocratic flavors, "Old Jube" Early was conspicuous for contrast. Heavy-bearded, hard-eyed, bent from painful arthritis, Early was in his forties but appeared to be at least ten years older. He chewed tobacco as incessantly as he cursed, and he carried a canteen that everyone was convinced was kept full of "Old Crow." A racy and pungent conversation was laced with bitter opinions about everything. Jackson admired Early's fighting qualities; he found little else to like in the man.

Early summoned a battery, which speedily opened fire. The horsemen momentarily disappeared, but an answering salvo of cannon fire came from the ridge. Federal artillery! That could only mean the presence of a portion of Pope's army.

Jackson responded to this development by ordering Early to keep close to the road and to advance beyond the fork. Ewell's other two brigades—Isaac Trimble's and Henry Forno's—were to hasten forward on the right. A tactical mistake was now in progress. Jackson was deploying for battle with fully half of his army strung out for seven miles. At the same time, a parked wagon train had created a major traffic jam for cannon, caissons, ammunition wagons, and ambulances trying to keep pace with the army. The situation was a breeding ground for some of Major Harman's most colorful profanity.

None of this gave Jackson concern. McGuire rode beside him for awhile. The surgeon asked Jackson if he expected battle that day. By then Jackson knew that his opponent was General Nathaniel Banks, his old and ineffectual nemesis in the Shenandoah Valley. Jackson flashed a hint of a smile and replied: "Banks is in our front, and he is generally willing to fight." Riding in silence for a few seconds, Jackson added almost to himself, "And he generally gets whipped."[58]

Four miles from Culpeper, Jackson's men reached what was to be a battleground. It was typical Piedmont rolling ground, with grain fields and pasture land situated between patches of woods. The Confederate march was basically to the right of the Culpeper road and through the Crittenden and Slaughter farms. Farther to the right, a mile and a half from the road, and dominating the immediate area, was a rectangular hill. Most locals knew it as Slaughter Mountain; the fact that a two-forked stream, Cedar Creek, flowed around the height gave it the more widely known name of Cedar Mountain.

Early's position was on high ground behind the south fork of Cedar Creek. A large cornfield almost ready for harvest stood in his front and extended several hundred yards to the elevation on which Federal troops were massing. Jackson dispatched some artillery toward a shoulder of Cedar Mountain. Getting the weapons up the steep slope was a difficult but necessary task. Artillery there would protect the Confederate right and command the Union left. Soon the Confederate cannon opened what Jackson termed "a rapid and well-directed fire" at Federal guns probing Early's position.

This first action, beginning around 1 P.M., occurred while Winder's brigades were arriving in column. Hill's division was miles down the road, parts of it snagged in the traffic foul-up at Crooked Run. The battle at Cedar Mountain was starting with a ring of familiarity. Port Republic had opened the same way with units inserted into action as they arrived on the scene.

Having deployed no more than half of his army, Jackson incredibly turned away from the battle for a short period. Temporary headquarters was the Petty home on the field. After issuing orders to Ewell and Winder, Jackson played with some children in the yard and then stretched out on the porch for a rest. Two division commanders were the only persons who knew what Old Jack had in mind. William B. Taliaferro, leading one of Winder's brigades, reported later of being "ignorant of the plans of the general, except so far as I could form an opinion from my observation of the dispositions made."[59]

Desultory firing slowly magnified into a steady roar. The brigades of Trimble and Harry Hays moved onto the field and took a position at the base of Cedar Mountain. Winder's men were securing positions on the far left. The two-mile Confederate front was not solid; a considerable gap existed between Early and Ewell's two other brigades.

Jackson had twenty-six guns in position, seventeen massed in the center of the line. The general's strategy was to unleash a double envelopment. Early would advance along the Culpeper road to hold the enemy's attention. Trimble and Forno would pass over the shoulder of Cedar Mountain and turn the Federal left. Winder's division, most of which was on the left of the road, would support Early but at the same time extend Jackson's flank until it overlapped the Federal right.

The Confederate line was concave. Artillery on each end would lay down a converging fire at the main Union position. These dispositions were predicated on Jackson's belief that Banks's full force was on the right (east) side of the Culpeper road. If Jackson ordered a reconnaissance of the wooded region to the left of the road, no record of that fact survives.

As the battle began in earnest, Jackson and his staff watched from high ground near Cedar Mountain and behind Ewell's line. There the general expected the contest to be fought and won. A furious, two-hour artillery exchange was in progress. Union infantry were poised for an attack on Early's line in the center. Gunsmoke and flying earth kicked up by exploding shells filled the air. Every man was perspiring heavily as the temperature passed ninety-five degrees.

Lieutenant John Blue, a Virginia cavalryman assigned to perform errands for Jackson, reported to the general. He found Jackson on Little Sorrel, "right leg thrown across the pommel of his saddle as immovable apparently as a statue, with his field glass watching, seemingly with great interest, the artillery duel then going on, apparently ignorant" of danger as Federal shells dropped closer and closer to the mounted party. "General," a member of the staff said haltingly, "had we not better change our position? We are being made a target." Jackson seemed not to hear. A minute or two passed; then he lowered his glass, straightened in the saddle, and smiled. "Our men are making it pretty warm for those people down there."[60]

A shell exploded in front of the group. It killed one horse and crippled another. Jackson finally suggested that he and the staff move a little farther back. He did so, halted, and ordered his staff to continue riding. "They will hardly aim at a single horseman," the general declared.[61]

As cannon fire began to slacken, a line of Federal infantry emerged from the distant woods and started toward the Confederate center. Musketry cracked above the noise of cannon. Jackson watched the infantry assault develop. For a few moments, he "sat like a statue, apparently unconscious that anything unusual was taking place, or about to take place within forty miles."[62]

The Federals drew nearer. Early's men were firing rapidly. Jackson put his glass in his case and stretched in the saddle. Lieutenant Blue noted: "It seemed to be with the greatest exertion that he restrained himself from charging headlong down the hill into the midst of the fray."[63]

Combat now swelled along two-thirds of Jackson's line. The general penned a quick note and handed it to a messenger. Pointing to the rear, he said in a loud voice: "Carry this to General Hill. You will find him in that direction. Be as expeditious as possible!"[64]

Federals were pressing harder on Early's position. The lines were only yards apart. The dozen artillery pieces in Early's immediate rear were in serious peril. Confederates fell back a few paces, then pressed forward and restored the line.

As Jackson observed the action, he occasionally glanced to the rear. Suddenly his countenance brightened. A long dust trail was visible in the distance. He turned quickly to one of his staff. "Ride over to General Early. Say to him: stand firm. General Hill will be with him in a few minutes."[65]

Over on the left side of the Culpeper road, the action in early afternoon appeared to one of Jackson's aides as "only a skirmish line, amusing themselves." The volume of musket fire rapidly increased until it became "a constant roar." Jackson withdrew his field glasses and resumed studying Ewell's front. Occasionally, he lowered the instrument, looked to the left, and listened intently. His hearing impairment made it difficult for him to judge the direction and the volume of the firing in Winder's sector. At length, he concluded out loud, "There is some hard work being done over there."[66] Before long, a courier dashed up with alarming news. The left had become hard pressed and could not hold much longer without reinforcements. Equally as calamitous, the Confederates there were without a commander. Sidney Winder had been mortally wounded.

The sickness besetting the serious-minded brigadier had not improved during the day. By midafternoon, the temperature stood at ninety-eight degrees, the hottest of any major Civil War engagement in Virginia. Winder was struggling, but he went about his duties as faithfully as possible. It was 3 P.M. before he got his whole division on the field.

Winder expected the major enemy activity to be from artillery east of the Culpeper road. He sent his second brigade, under Lieutenant Colonel Thomas S. Garnett, northwest through woods to the edge of a wheatfield. Garnett (no relation to the hapless brigadier Jackson had dismissed following Kernstown) was a New Kent County physician who had served as an officer in the Mexican War. From his advanced position, Garnett could move by flank against the nearest Union battery. On Garnett's right, Taliaferro placed his brigade virtually at right angles to Early's line. These deployments were intended to enable Winder to attack across Early's front at the opportune moment.

It was to be Winchester all over again. Yet the plan quickly went awry. Garnett discovered Federal infantry and artillery blocking the move he wanted to make. He informed Winder, who told Garnett to stay where he was for the time being.

Winder's concern was more with his artillery and what might occur on his front. He brought up three batteries; but at their first fire, the guns took a heavy response from Union cannon across the way. A sharp duel ensued. Captain Joseph Carpenter was adjusting the fire of his battery when a shell fragment struck him in the head, leading to his death six months later. His brother John, a lieutenant in the battery, took command.

A message arrived for Winder from Early, who believed that the Union guns could be taken in flank by moving infantry around the wheatfield north of the Culpeper road. However, Confederate artillery fire was beginning to have effect. Federal cannoneers were shifting positions. Winder was now standing amid the Rockbridge Artillery in shirt sleeves and perspiring heavily.

Edward Moore of the Rockbridge battery observed that the Maryland brigadier "was at my gun (which was between the other two) with an opera glass directing our fire. He called out and asked me a question, but I was so deafened by the firing that I could not hear, though not ten steps from him. I drew nearer; he put his hands to his mouth to repeat it, and had uttered two or three words, when a shell passed through him, tearing his arm nearly off at the elbow. He fell straight back at full length" and lay quivering on the ground.[67]

It has been traditional to deduce that the loss of Winder left his sector leaderless and in disarray. Sandie Pendleton was one who came to such a conclusion. He wrote that "owing to bad management of some of the officers, incident upon the loss of Winder, some confusion resulted."[68] A recent and thorough study of the campaign drew a different conclusion. Winder was not in full control of the Confederate left. He was so intent on the artillery fight that he gave little heed to his infantry line—and therefore would have had as much difficulty as any other officer in stabilizing the line when Federals delivered a surprise attack.

Ironically, command of the division fell to the senior brigadier, William Taliaferro. Although he complained of being left in the dark by Jackson's plans, Taliaferro was more knowledgeable about troop dispositions at the moment than was Winder. Nevertheless, Taliaferro's was an unsteady new hand at a particularly bad time.[69]

Jackson responded to the news about Winder by raising his arm and bowing his head in a moment of silent prayer. Then, without a word, he slipped his leg into the stirrup and wheeled his horse to the left as he tucked the strap of his kepi under his chin. Little Sorrel raced across the 400 yards to the Culpeper road. The staff followed, with a half-dozen couriers bringing up the rear.

Cavalry officer-turned-messenger John Blue recalled that when the party got to the road, Jackson leaped his horse through a partial gap in a fence. "Here he halted a second and ordered some artillery to the rear . . . which was now in great danger of being captured. Jackson then leaped his horse over the fence on the opposite side of the road into the woods" and made for Garnett's command post.[70]

In terse phrases, Jackson told the colonel to watch his left flank and to get reinforcements from Taliaferro. Meanwhile, Taliaferro was still trying to ascertain the position of the rest of Winder's division and what he was expected to do with it. Other weaknesses existed in the command structure. Major Snowden Andrews, one of Jackson's most promising artillery officers, was supervising gun crews when a shell burst overhead. The explosion tore Andrews's clothes to shreds and left him severely wounded.[71]

Command of the Stonewall Brigade was now in the hands of the senior colonel, Charles A. Ronald of the 4th Virginia. The thirty-five-year-old Blacksburg attorney had some Mexican War experience but nothing to prepare him for the battle responsibilities suddenly thrust upon him. Ronald appeared dazed through most of the action.

Early had managed to tighten his line and keep it intact during the Union assault. At 5:45 P.M., Banks intensified the battle by dispatching three regiments and part of a fourth to assail Jackson's left. In retrospect, the Union commander should have sent more than 1500 men into this action, especially in view of the fact that he had no knowledge of Jackson's strength anywhere on the field.

Still, the charging Federals surged into a seam in the Confederate line. This unexpected assault, Jackson wrote, "fell with great vigor upon our extreme left, and by the force of superior numbers, bearing down all opposition, turned it and poured a destructive fire into its rear."[72]

Jackson's left crumbled. Men in Garnett's brigade began streaming to the rear. It was not the fault of Tom Garnett, who had been shot early in the afternoon but had led his troops for hours while oblivious to the life-threatening wound. Confederate organization began to disintegrate as Union soldiers plowed through the lines and began taking Taliaferro in the rear. Artillery shells were exploding in and above Jackson's crouched soldiers. Taliaferro had to withdraw.

In doing so, he exposed Early's left to attack. Jackson, ever the artillerist, ordered his guns to withdraw so as to prevent their capture. Colonel Ronald started the Stonewall Brigade through the woods to provide support. The brigade promptly became scattered amid the trees, undergrowth, noise, and confusion. Jackson's faithful regiments wandered and thrashed about in a rare combination of bewilderment and uselessness. The battle had reached a critical stage for both sides. Banks had initiated a turning movement. Jackson was about to be outflanked!

He was unperturbed initially, trusting as always in the Lord. The deterioration of his left, a courier stated, "seemed to have no other effect upon him than to cause the muscles of his face to become hardened, and his thin lips to be more tightly compressed. He made no remark though, not even to the asking of a question" of the messenger who told him about the collapse of his regiments at the wheatfield.[73]

That resolve evaporated as Jackson saw his entire left disintegrating regiment by regiment. Winder's original line had been turned and doubled back. Federals were assailing it on three sides. Red darts of musketry blinked through gray gunsmoke that limited visibility to little more than 200 yards. "I never felt the protecting goodness of God more forcibly," Hotchkiss confessed.[74]

Lieutenant Blue was convinced that "we had struck a full-grown tornado, loaded with thunder and lightning. This was the most hair-rising fire I had ever struck. . . . The confusion and noise at this time was terrible." Indeed it was. Gunfire at Cedar Mountain was audible in Richmond, seventy-five miles away.[75]

The specter of total defeat now loomed large. Unless something happened at once for the Confederates, this would be another Kernstown—only costlier in every respect. Not merely Cedar Mountain but all of Virginia was suddenly at stake.

Stern reserve, so much a part of Jackson's nature, vanished. He spurred his horse and galloped into the shattered left. A tree knocked off his cap and created the odd sight of the general on a field bareheaded. For the first time in the war, Jackson reached for his saber. Yet it was so rusted from nonuse that it would not slide from the scabbard.

Jackson unsnapped sword and scabbard from his belt and waved the two above his head. He then grabbed another symbol: a Confederate battle flag. With the reins of the horse hanging loose, he waved the banner as well at the fleeing soldiers. Swinging two items frantically in the midst of combat and atop a by-then unsteady horse was no small accomplishment.

The general was also shouting at the top of his voice. Precisely what he was saying cannot be pinpointed. Soldiers recalled him yelling a number of things: "Jackson is with you!" "Rally, brave men, and press forward! Your general will lead you! Jackson will lead you! Follow me!" "Rally, men, remember Winder!" "Forward, men forward!" Other Confederate officers on the field were also laboring furiously to stem the flight.[76]

Bullets were flying in profusion when Taliaferro urged Jackson to take cover. "He looked perplexed, a little surprised," Taliaferro wrote, "but the logic of the situation forced itself upon his mind, and with his invariable ejaculation of 'Good, good,' he rode to the rear." A hatless Jackson, waving a battle flag and shouting for the men to rally on him, was an electrifying spectacle to those in the immediate area. His inspiration took effect. Captain Charles Blackford was deeply moved. "Jackson usually is an indifferent and slouchy looking man but then, with the 'Light of Battle' shedding its radiance over him his whole person had changed. . . . The men would have followed him into the jaws of death itself. . . . Even the old sorrel horse seemed endowed with the style and form of an Arabian."[77]

The 13th Virginia was commanded by expelled VMI cadet James A. Walker. He was the first regimental commander to stabilize his broken unit, and he quickly massed it for a counterattack. The 21st Virginia halted under fire and solidified, although its colonel was killed in the process. Other units, including the Stonewall Brigade, rallied and came back to resume battle. Fighting in many parts of the woods and wheatfield had become hand-to-hand combat. As one soldier explained, "There were few loaded guns on either side and very little chance to load them."[78]

Perspiring, weary, but still caught in the excitement of battle, Jackson rode to the rear in search of help for his thinning lines. He had reached the southern edge of the woods when a red-shirted horseman came riding up the road with a long column of soldiers. It was Powell Hill and the advance elements of his fresh division. Their arrival could not have been more fortuitous. Jackson greeted the division commander courteously and urged Hill to get his men quickly into the contest.[79]

Hill sent his lead element—General Edward Thomas's Georgia brigade—to Early, who needed it to anchor his right and steady that half of his line. As this unit broke off in an irregular but massed battle line, Jackson rode toward them with his recovered cap in hand. The Georgians recognized him "and yelled as only Johnnies could yell at the sight of their beloved leader." Jackson rode at their head for a short distance, then reined Little Sorrel to one side and remained bareheaded as the troops passed.[80]

The second of Hill's brigades to reach the field were the North Carolinians of General Lawrence Branch, the same brigade that had failed to provide a link between Lee and Jackson on June 26 near Mechanicsville. Jackson was not thinking of past mistakes; he needed Branch's men now to help shore Winder's position in the woods to the left of the road. The fighting there had shifted again. Unknown to Jackson, his Stonewall Brigade had charged back into the action with such élan that both flanks were open. The 27th Virginia on the right had been knocked reeling.

Branch was a Princeton graduate and former congressman who enjoyed both oratory and notoriety. He led his regiments into the woods where, Branch reported with obvious satisfaction, "we met the celebrated Stonewall Brigade, utterly routed and fleeing as fast as they could run." What Branch actually saw was one broken regiment, yet he and other Carolinians later delighted in castigating the whole Virginia unit.[81]

Another 100 yards brought Branch's men to the wheatfield. The politician-general concluded that a patriotic speech was in order. He halted his regiments in the midst of the action and began a shouted address. Branch had not gone far into his subject when Jackson galloped on the scene. Without a word, the commander rode rapidly down the brigade line, stopped beside the colors, and lifted his cap in silent salute. The men wildly cheered, Colonel James H. Lane of the 28th North Carolina wrote with pride. (He had been a VMI cadet in Jackson's classes.) The general's presence had instantaneous effect. Branch's whole line—including its now-speechless brigadier—surged ahead.[82]

Hill's artillery was now arriving on the field. Lieutenant Colonel Lindsay Walker, a battalion commander, was trying to get the various sections forward into firing position, but it was an exasperating process. As soon as Walker placed one squad where he wanted it, he would turn his attention to another group of gunners and then discover that the first group had fled. A huge man with a booming voice, Walker drew his sword and, "swearing outrageously," strode back and forth along his cannon line. That was when Jackson appeared. Walker promptly ceased his profanity. Jackson saw what Walker was trying to do but obviously did not understand his words amid the noise of battle. Jackson shouted, "That's right, Colonel, give it to them!" Walker did so as soon as Jackson raced away.[83]

Federals were still advancing through the cornfield in Early's sector when Walker's guns raked their lines. Suddenly, the battery of youthful and bespectacled William J. Pegram lost its supports. Pegram ordered double charges of canister, then seized a flag, went from gun to gun, and impelled his wavering troops by shouting: "Don't let the enemy have these guns or this flag! Jackson is looking at you! Go in, men! Give it to them!" Members of the Percell Artillery responded valiantly.[84]

One more dramatic moment remained in the battle. Down the road from the north galloped 164 horsemen of the 1st Pennsylvania Cavalry, determined to punch another hole in the Confederate line. The Federals came at a rapid gait until they were within fifty yards of the Southern position. A shout rang out, "Charge!" Then, as in days of old, cavalrymen spurred their mounts and thundered forward at full speed. Two Confederate infantry brigades were waiting. The collision lasted only minutes before the Pennsylvanians broke in retreat. Seventy-one riders galloped back to their lines; ninety-three did not.

Jackson's left and center were holding and in places regaining lost ground. On his right, Ewell had been stymied because of Confederate artillery fire across his field of advance. Now the sector was clear. Ewell launched an assault upon the Union left with Forno's and Trimble's brigades.

Banks realized that his right was broken and his left seriously threatened. The sun was setting when, as Jackson reported, "the Federal force fell back at every point of their line and commenced retreating, leaving their dead and wounded on the field of battle." Confederate cheers spread the length of the line as Jackson's men swept across the rolling country at twilight.[85]

Every yard of the battleground bore witness to the severity of the fight. In places the slaughter had been frightful. Some 3000 soldiers had fallen in a ninety-minute span. The woods were in shambles, and among the rows of corn the dead lay thick. Scores of Federals had surrendered. Hundreds of discarded muskets reflected the demoralization at the end of the contest.

This had been teenager "Willie" Preston's first battle. A son of Jackson's close friend in Lexington, John T. L. Preston, and stepson of Margaret Junkin Preston,

William C. Preston had appeared at Jackson's headquarters with the intention of joining the "Liberty Hall Volunteers" of the 4th Virginia. Jackson invited Preston to remain at headquarters awhile before joining his company. Within a day or so, the general and his whole staff had become extremely fond of the gentle lad.

The end of the fight at Cedar Mountain was not enough for young Preston. He and a compatriot rounded up a group of stragglers in the wood and led them in the wake of the Federal withdrawal. They captured enemy soldiers at every turn. Preston then saw Jackson approaching on horseback. The excited eighteen-year-old, by his own admission, ran up to the general, "slapped him on the leg, and . . . slapped his horse so hard that he came near jumping from under the rider." Jackson listened quietly as Preston explained loudly the need to round up stragglers. The general then rode forward to encourage Preston's small group. The boy could not contain himself. "General Jackson is coming! General Jackson is coming!" he shouted. Hundreds of soldiers in the area turned to look, Preston stated. Then "I thought the heavens would have been rent with the cheers!"[86]

Victory was not enough. Jackson was not finished. He wanted to reach Culpeper before dawn and perhaps launch another Winchester-style attack. Occupying Culpeper would puncture the center of Pope's lines and sever the Orange and Alexandria Railroad, the chief artery for Union supplies. Then he could drive Banks's forces beyond Culpeper and possibly to destruction.

First, however, Jackson had to get his army into reasonable fighting form. As darkness was settling, an officer saw the general in the middle of the road and earnestly trying to sort out units and commanders. The men were tired, and the temperature was still a blistering eighty-six degrees. Jackson ignored such incidentals.

Hill's troops, fresher than any others, took the lead in the pursuit. The Confederate column had proceeded a half-mile by nightfall. Jackson halted the men to bombard a wood where Federals had been sighted, after which the advance resumed.

Darkness, dust, heat, and fatigue accompanied the soldiers. At the far end of the trees, Jackson again brought the command to a stop. He ordered Pegram's battery and a brigade of infantry to move forward cautiously and reconnoiter in force. Pegram reached a small knoll and opened a searching fire. Three Union batteries in the distance replied with an explosion of gunfire and a frightful pounding of Pegram's position. The unequal contest lasted an hour before Pegram reluctantly withdrew. It was 11 P.M..

Colonel "Grumble" Jones rode in from the front to report to Jackson. Robertson's cavalry had done little during the day; but Jones, acting on his own, had taken part of his 7th Virginia Cavalry and made a wide nighttime swing around the Union army. From prisoners, Jones learned that General Franz Sigel's divisions were reinforcing Banks.

Jackson halted the pursuit. Two army corps blocked his path, Union guns were laying down a vigorous fire, and the Confederates—as well as Jackson himself—were exhausted. Orders went forth: fall back and consolidate the line.[87]

Stars twinkled in a sky somewhat dimmed by the lingering smoke of combat. Jackson could do nothing else that day. He rode through the bloody battleground, silent now save for the groans of the wounded. The general and his staff stopped at several farmhouses in search of a place to sleep. Each one was filled with soldiers suffering from wounds of every description.

Eventually, the riders came to the encampment of the Stonewall Brigade. Jackson dismounted and asked his friend, Colonel Lawson Botts of the 2d Virginia, where he might find some buttermilk to calm a troubled stomach. Several soldiers volunteered to conduct a hunt. Soon Jackson had as much buttermilk as he could drink. Loud cheers followed "Old Jack" as he rode from the camp.

A short distance down the road, a grassy plot came into view. Colonel Boteler spread a cloak on the ground for Jackson and asked if he wished something to eat. "No," came the reply, "I want *rest*, nothing but *rest*." He then lay face down on the cloak and was asleep in a moment.[88]

Cedar Mountain was a clear victory for the Confederates, but a costly one. Federal losses were 314 killed, 1445 wounded, and a whopping 622 men captured. Jackson's casualties were little more than half those of the enemy: 223 killed, 1060 wounded, and thirty-one missing.

General Jubal Early gained hero status from his role in the engagement. Jackson, always frugal with compliments, praised Early's troops for standing "with great firmness" when it counted. Powell Hill and his division could well be said to have saved the day for Jackson. Nevertheless, they got small mention in Jackson's report because of personal animosity. Jackson was irritated with Hill at the time of Cedar Mountain. Months later, when the general was dictating his official report, relations between the two had deteriorated into formal charges and countercharges.[89]

Two Confederate officers who fell in the battle were especially close to Jackson. One was Lieutenant Colonel Alfred H. Jackson of the 31st Virginia. A kinsman of the general and former member of his staff, Alfred Jackson received a bullet wound that never healed. He died eleven months later. Even harder for the general to bear was the loss of General Sidney Winder. His death was a serious blow to Jackson, Dr. McGuire stated. Winder "was a good soldier, and if he had lived, he would one day have been made Lieut. General. Gen. Jackson felt his loss keenly." When Jackson completed his account of Cedar Mountain the following spring, his esteem for Winder had increased. "It is difficult within the proper reserve of an official report to do justice to the merits of the accomplished officer. . . . Richly endowed with those qualities of mind and person which fit an officer for high command and which attract the admiration and excite the enthusiasm of troops, he was rapidly rising to the front rank of his profession."[90]

If Jackson looked only at the end result of a battle—as he tended to do, he was pleased over Cedar Mountain. So were Southern spokesmen. Neither officials nor the press had anything but praise for the general. The *Richmond Enquirer* announced that the victory had "diffused a lively pleasure throughout our city," and it added, "All honor to the laurel-crowned hero, and his glorious army."[91]

In the perfect vision of hindsight, and underscored by several writers in this century, Jackson's management of the engagement was poor. Douglas Southall Freeman went so far as to conclude that Cedar Mountain "raised doubts concerning Jackson's leadership." The battle was a near disaster for the Confederates, critics have charged, because of a litany of factors. Jackson's secretiveness stands at the top of the list. Then come his lack of communications with subordinates, the evident belief that promptness and impetuosity alone would win the day, the failure to employ his full strength at the outset, overlooking the wooded ground to the left that was clearly a danger point, leaving most of his commanders to fight for themselves, and exhibiting a general lack of control over elements of his army throughout the day.

Banks had done surprisingly well at Cedar Mountain. He stopped Jackson's attack with only half Jackson's numbers. The Union commander launched an assault that rolled up Jackson's left, and he eventually watched from a safe distance as the Confederates retired to their original starting point. Jackson with his superior numbers should have taken better advantage of the Federal general's recklessness.

The Confederate left was not only disjointed; it also was left hanging in the air. Total blame for these errors cannot be placed on Winder. After his fall, Jackson moved quickly to the danger on the left. However, his instructions to brigade commanders were inadequate if not confusing.

Jackson had manipulated his units at Winchester like a skilled puppeteer. At Cedar Mountain, he could not seem to untangle the strings. Further, Jackson customarily dominated a field of battle. This was one time when he did not.

His contemporary defenders asserted that at the critical moment Jackson "restored the battle" and "snatched victory from threatened defeat." The authority on Cedar Mountain thinks otherwise. "There was more of symbolism than substance to the general's heroic five minutes" in rallying his men. Still, Jackson deserved high praise for what he had achieved.[92]

The general himself considered Cedar Mountain "the most successful of his exploits" because he—and God, of course—had been the instruments for saving the battle when it disintegrated. The victory answered a number of questions raised by previous critics. Jackson had confronted a veteran force of the enemy and sent it into retreat. He had done it at the head of the largest command he had known. His personal bravery revealed Jackson anew as a leader of men and a natural field commander. "To the extent that Cedar Mountain restored Jackson's confidence in himself," one historian deduced, "it stands as perhaps his most important battle."[93]

It also proved to be a huge transfusion for Southern morale. With but few exceptions, Jackson's men were thrilled at their accomplishment. A lieutenant in Forno's Louisiana brigade wrote his father and compared service under Jackson at Cedar Mountain with his experiences under other leaders on the peninsula. "The good sense and soldierly mind of Genl. T. J. Jackson accomplished this result with a comparatively small loss on our side which shows to us between him and the *fools* in uniform who commanded us at Richmond. . . . There we lost one half of our Reg. in one battle, here we killed more of the enemy and made him *skedaddle* quicker and lost one man killed and five wounded. . . . Our experience in this battle will give you some idea of what a General Jackson is." To a North Carolina soldier, Jackson was "the greatest man now living."[94]

The victor slept well that night and arose the next morning in good spirits. The weather promised to be as hot as the previous day. Pope's whole army (which outnumbered him two to one) was now in the process of consolidating in Jackson's front. Yet it was the Sabbath. Jackson felt comfortable. He began the day at 6:30 with a telegram to the War Department: "On the evening of the 9th instant God blessed our arms with another victory."[95]

Grumble Jones's late-night report was still on Jackson's mind. An advance on Culpeper now was impracticable. Jackson must wait. Details went forth to bury the dead and remove the wounded to field hospitals, where surgeons did what they could for men whose injuries had gone unattended for twelve hours or more. Jackson, ever the military scavenger, ordered soldiers to collect arms and accoutrements from the battlefield. All told, some 5000 usable muskets were put in wagons for transport back to Gordonsville.[96]

Troops who returned to the battle area viewed the sight with horror mixed with thanksgiving for being alive. Equipment ranging from ammunition to shoes was strewn over a one-mile expanse; many trees with trunks up to a foot thick had been chopped down by gunfire. Worst of all, the dead lay everywhere. "It appeared to me," John Blue noted, "that there was a Yankee on every ten feet square of that field." Only eighteen men were in James Binford's company of the 21st Virginia when the battle opened. Twelve were killed or wounded. "Thanks to a merciful Providence, I breathe & have all my limbs," Binford told the homefolk. "I have had enough of the glory of war. I am sick of seeing dead men, & men's limbs torn from their bodies." A member of the 23d Virginia could not find the right words to convey his revulsion. "The Lords will must be done," he concluded.[97]

Early in these cleanup operations, a jingle of spurs and a loud voice announced the arrival of Jeb Stuart "on a tour of inspection." Jackson greeted the cavalryman warmly. Not only was he glad to see a good friend, but Beverly Robertson had been of no use in the campaign. Stuart would become the eyes of the Confederate force in the Piedmont.

Jackson, Ewell, Hill, and Stuart met later in the morning. The four generals sat on logs beside the Culpeper road a half-mile from the battlefield as Jackson discussed what to do next. All but ignoring Robertson, Jackson asked Stuart to embark on a reconnaissance of Federal positions and strength. Stuart eagerly moved out with a detachment of cavalry and soon returned with information that the enemy was at Culpeper in full force.

Throughout the day, Confederates waited in line for a counterattack that never came. Even though Pope was assuring authorities that he would "do the best I can," attacking Jackson was not in his list of priorities. The opposing forces held their ground three miles apart. By 2 P.M., it was ninety-four degrees. A severe thunderstorm struck in late afternoon and sent men scurrying for cover. Many of Jackson's soldiers, thirsty and wilted by days of heat, stood with upraised faces to enjoy the rain to the fullest.[98]

The storm brought only overnight relief. On August 11, a burning sun returned and sent the temperature climbing again to the mid-nineties. Jackson wrote at least two letters in the morning. The first, a formal request to Adjutant General Cooper, asked that "a good Brig. Gen. of Cavalry be sent to him & if none such, that Col. W. E. Jones be promoted & ordered to report to him." The inept Beverly Robertson must be removed as head of Jackson's cavalry. Next on the general's agenda was an overdue letter to his wife. "On last Saturday God again crowned our arms with victory," he informed Anna. "All glory be to God for his unnumbered blessings." Then Jackson allowed his inner feelings to surface. "I can hardly think of the fall of Brig. Genl. C. S. Winder without tearful eyes. Let us all unite more earnestly in imploring God's aid in fighting our battle for us. . . . Whilst we attach so much importance to being free from temporal bondage, we must attach far more to being free from the bondage of sin."[99]

Federals asked for a two-hour flag of truce beginning at noon to gather the dead and wounded whom Confederates had not already removed. Jackson agreed to the appeal and placed Early in command of the field. By then, Union corpses were "hideously blackened and swelled, already putrefying," a Federal stated nauseously. While burials were hastily done, soldiers on both sides "engaged in friendly converse, trading papers, tobacco, etc." Unknown to Jackson, Northern and Southern officers "sat down and talked the matter away." Captain Blackford thought it amusing that "Old Jack is standing here in line of battle, defiantly holding the enemy at bay while they are burying their dead."[100]

A member of Crenshaw's battery got his first look at Jackson during the armistice. "I should never have taken him for the great Valley hero. He wore a faded uniform coat, pants and cape, somewhat round-shouldered and looks on the ground when he walks as if he had lost something; altogether he presents more the appearance of a well-to-do farmer than a military chieftain. . . . You would pass him in a crowd without his attracting your attention in the least and never know him to be the pride of our people and the terror of the foe."[101]

When Banks requested an extension of the truce to 5 P.M., Jackson quickly granted it. Federal preoccupation with the dead and injured worked to Jackson's advantage as he began to retire from the Cedar Mountain area. He had achieved his major goals: stopping Pope's advance through north-central Virginia, defeating a portion of the Union army, and buying time for Lee at Richmond. Jackson hoped that "by thus falling back General Pope would be induced to follow me until I should be reenforced."[102]

Now the tail of Jackson's army became its head as a slow and deliberate withdrawal southward got underway. The heat was stifling, the dust thick, the orders strict against any straggling. By 5 P.M. and the end of the truce, the Confederate retirement was well advanced. Jackson resorted to the old ruse of having campfires lit at sundown as if the troops were preparing the evening meal. After dark, an artilleryman commented, "a thousand bright beacons blazed over the plains and along the hillsides."[103]

The army bivouacked in and around Orange Court House. Jackson pitched his tent in the front yard of one of the Garnett homes a mile north of town. Colonel S. Bassett French of President Davis's staff had just joined him for a month's duty. A "horribly cooked" meal led French to volunteer to become headquarters chef.

Following supper, the aide and Jackson began a long conversation about the service French was to perform and the recent action at Cedar Mountain. French waxed eloquently on the "noble dead" at the battle. His self-styled "rhapsody" was moving to higher levels when he glanced at Jackson. The general was sound asleep.[104]

August 12 brought a warm message from Lee. "I congratulate you most heartily on the victory which God has granted you over our enemies at Cedar Run. The country owes you and your brave officers and soldiers a deep debt of gratitude. I hope your victory is the precursor of others over our foe in that quarter, which will entirely break up and scatter his army."[105]

In the minds of Confederate officials, Jackson's retirement to Gordonsville made the danger on the Rappahannock line seem more imminent than that on the James. Pope was too strong for Jackson. Rumor persisted that McClellan was preparing to evacuate the peninsula, return to Washington, and reinforce Pope. The wisest course, in Lee's judgment, was to consolidate his army against Pope and seek to dispose of him before McClellan's legions arrived and formed an unbeatable merger.

Reports were already circulating in Richmond that 10,000 Federals under General Ambrose Burnside were on their way from Fort Monroe either to strengthen Pope or to destroy the Virginia Central Railroad. Confirmation that the first elements of McClellan's army were abandoning the peninsula sent Lee into action. He would race McClellan to see who got to Pope first. Lee quickly dispatched Longstreet with ten brigades to Jackson in the Piedmont. Lee would join them as soon as he tidied the defenses of Richmond.[106]

Jackson was not merely marking time at Gordonsville. He sent Hotchkiss to make maps of the northern Piedmont all the way to the Potomac. A strike into enemy territory north of the river was still very much alive in his mind. He would be ready if such a move came to pass.

Meanwhile, Pope was informing superiors that he had planned to pounce upon Jackson on August 12 but that the rebel commander had retired to safety, "leaving many of his dead and wounded on the field and along the road from Cedar Mountain to Orange Court-House." In reality, Pope was seeking—and he received—words of caution from Union authorities. Army chief of staff Henry W. Halleck forwarded a warning from McClellan: "I don't like Jackson's movements—he will suddenly appear when least expected." Halleck then made an admonishment of his own: "Beware of a snare. Feigned retreats are a secesh tactic."[107]

Jackson designated August 14 as a day of thanksgiving for the recent victory. Drill and other military duties were suspended, with the troops expected to devote that Thursday to prayer and religious services. Jackson attended one such gathering in the 5th Virginia. His route back to headquarters took him past Taliaferro's brigade, where Jackson's friend, Presbyterian cleric Daniel Ewing of Gordonsville, was delivering an exhortation. The sound of approaching horsemen caused some of the soldiers to look in that direction. "At the sight of the old grey cap coming down the road," Hotchkiss wrote, "the men all broke and marched to the road-side to cheer the Gen. as he passed, leaving Mr. Ewing in amazement at the height of his eloquence." Taliaferro jokingly said afterwards that he intended to have Jackson arrested "for disturbing a religious meeting, and a Presbyterian one at that!"[108]

Longstreet's troops began streaming into Gordonsville that day. Although he was the senior general, Longstreet refused to take command. Jackson knew the situation better, and Lee would arrive shortly. Everything seemed cordial as the two segments reunited, but this was not the case.

Most of Jackson's troops were from the Shenandoah Valley and the mountains. Their accomplishments in the war were a matter of record, just as devotion to their general was universal and unbridled. Longstreet's divisions were not so localized. They were veterans of Seven Pines and Glendale—engagements not in the same class with Confederate successes in the Shenandoah Valley. Longstreet's soldiers resented Jackson "coming to their rescue" on the peninsula; Jackson's troops looked down on Longstreet and his "still unproven" units.

Friction existed as well at the high command level. As postwar writings revealed bluntly, Longstreet was fighting jealousy and envy where Jackson was concerned. Lee's senior general felt that Jackson was a skilled field commander only against second-rate Union leaders. "When pitted against the best of the Federal commanders," Longstreet asserted, "he did not appear so well." Officers under the two generals felt the resentment and began bickering as soon as Longstreet reached Gordonsville.[109]

Late on the afternoon of the 14th, Lee arrived by train. Jackson met him at the station but made no mention of the current discord as they rode to headquarters. At dinner that night, young Joe Morrison, a recent addition to Jackson's staff, mentioned being with the general at Lee's arrival. A stern rebuke immediately came from the head of the table. Staff officers should keep what they know to themselves, the always-secretive Jackson told his brother-in-law.[110]

As soon as Lee got settled, he called a council of war at the Barbour home. Undoubtedly, Lee, Longstreet, and, to a lesser degree, Stuart viewed Jackson at the time as at least an unknown quantity. The mention of his name brought cheers throughout the Confederacy, but he was still an enigma in the main army.

Neither Jefferson Davis nor Lee knew him well. When Davis met Jackson after Malvern Hill, only a salute passed between them. Lee's acquaintance with Jackson was in the early stage of development. They had corresponded throughout the Valley Campaign, but formally rather than personally. When Lee finally conferred with Jackson on June 23, the latter had ridden fourteen hours to the meeting, was exhausted, and said little. That was hardly an assurance to the new army commander.

Lee, Longstreet, Ewell, Hill, and Stuart were all Regular Army. They had served together, and they cast their lots with the Confederacy simultaneously. Jackson had been out of the army for a decade and was living at the remote southern end of the Shenandoah Valley when civil war came. His successes, other than at Manassas, had been far to the west of Richmond and against enemies of unknown quality. The Seven Days had done nothing to paint Jackson in a more positive light.

Stuart later told Hotchkiss that Lee came to Gordonsville "with rather a low estimate of Jackson's ability."[111] Yet Lee was willing to listen and watch before making any final judgment on the obedient but reticent subaltern.

At that August 15 council, Lee learned from Jackson of a tactical blunder Pope had committed. The Union general and most of his 70,000 troops were encamped twenty miles away on a peninsula formed by the confluence of the Rapidan and Rappahannock rivers. A bridge at Rappahannock Station was the major escape route. If Stuart's cavalry could destroy that span, Pope would be largely cut off from an easy withdrawal.

It took Lee but seconds to realize that Pope might recognize his self-imposed predicament and retreat. The Confederates could gain a smashing victory over the unsupported Pope if they employed secrecy and speed—two basic attributes of

Jackson's strategy. As a result, Jackson asked to cross the Rapidan on August 16 and initiate battle the following day. Longstreet objected: his commissary wagons had not arrived with food for his men. Jackson unhesitatingly offered rations from his own stores and promised more from unguarded Federal provisions at Brandy Station.

Longstreet was likewise skeptical about so hasty a march. Lee listened quietly, realizing that all his cavalry was not at hand. He concluded to cross the Rapidan on the 17th, with battle to commence the following day. At the conclusion of the meeting, a frustrated Jackson "laid down on the ground, under an adjoining tree, and groaned most audibly." Longstreet gave Jackson a stern look and said to Lee that such behavior was disrespectful to the entire council. Thus did Jackson and Longstreet get off to a poor start at Gordonsville.[112]

On August 15, Jackson's three divisions left Gordonsville. The route of march was along the southern side of Clark's Mountain, an eminence rising from the Piedmont in solitary, breath-taking fashion. By nightfall, Jackson was five miles northeast of Orange at Mt. Pisgah Church on the road leading to Somerville Ford at the Rapidan. Jackson issued strict orders for the command to remain quietly in bivouac. Speed and secrecy were at work as Pope's army continued to do nothing but battle the August heat.

Confederate strategy then began unfolding. Stuart's seizure of Rappahannock Station was the first necessary objective. Delays—notably General Fitzhugh Lee's announcement that his horses would not be serviceable until the 19th, plus a near-disastrous ambush of Stuart at the hamlet of Verdiersville—brought that mission to naught. Longstreet's unreadiness, and the tardy arrival of General Richard H. Anderson's division from Richmond, further undermined the schedule. Incomplete preparations, inefficient staff work, misunderstandings, plus other instances of faulty logistics, all worked against Lee. At the last minute, he postponed the assault on Pope to the 19th and later to the 20th.

For men accustomed to rapid marches after battle plans had been formulated, Jackson's "foot cavalry" reacted negatively to Lee's deferments. "Lee is a slow general," one soldier remarked, "and I think Jackson will do better without him." Cannoneer William Jones remarked that with Lee in command, "some of the boys commenced saying . . . we had better go about building winter quarters, for we wouldn't move until next fall."[113]

Jackson was still impatiently marking time on August 17, the Sabbath. Two personnel matters occupied his attention early in the morning. A request went to the War Department that E. Franklin Paxton, a Lexington friend and former officer in the 27th Virginia, be promoted to major and assigned to the staff. Jackson's unhappiness at Beverly Robertson's leadership prompted another plea that the brigadier be sent elsewhere. Lee effected a compromise by assigning all cavalry (Robertson's included) to Stuart. Jackson confirmed the consolidation with Stuart later in the day.

Worshiping the Lord occupied most of Jackson's afternoon. He and the staff rode from headquarters at the Crenshaw farm to Taliaferro's brigade for a religious service. En route, the general became unusually talkative. He spoke of what he considered "the right sort of man" and then defined him as "one always striving to do his duty and never satisfied if anything can be done better."[114]

Jackson was describing himself. Duty is a collective and cooperative action. One cannot be devoted to duty and be an egotist at the same time. Jackson's sober commitment to life, and his almost complete lack of personal ambition, became reflections in his constant search to do his duty in the sight of God.

Word spread through the encampment that Old Jack was attending prayer meeting with Taliaferro's men. As the general returned to headquarters, he again had to weather cheers from soldiers lining the roadside. As usual, Jackson removed his cap and appeared uncomfortable. To a South Carolina officer, Jackson could "scarcely be called intellectual in appearance; but his restless eye gave evidence of the indefatigable activity of his brain, and his thin, compressed lips and fixed features were expressive of that earnestness and resolution which have so pre-eminently characterized him."[115]

By now, Pope's boastfulness was proving brittle. Washington gossip relayed to the Union commander had Jackson preparing to attack with 125,000 men.[116] On the night of August 18, just hours before Lee's advance was to begin, a group of fugitive slaves told Pope of Lee's planned offensive.

The next morning, Lee and Longstreet rode to the top of Clark's Mountain. They watched helplessly through field glasses as Pope's army abandoned the river peninsula and faded into the distance. With that, the hope of trapping Pope between the Rappahannock and the Rapidan ended. It was imperative for Lee to organize a pursuit at once.

August 19 passed with the Army of Northern Virginia cooking three days' rations, cleaning weapons, and preparing to give chase to Pope. At Jackson's Mt. Pisgah camp, another task had to be performed in the afternoon. For the second instance in his Confederate career, Jackson oversaw the carrying out of military executions. This time three soldiers were involved.

Desertion had increased dangerously as one campaign followed another with peace nowhere in sight. Around the time of Cedar Mountain, military tribunals convicted four soldiers of desertion and sentenced them to death. The four had marched under guard with the army to Mt. Pisgah Church. Orders for the troops to get ready for a pursuit of Pope probably led to the executions being scheduled for August 19 at 5 P.M. The condemned men were John H. Layman, John Roadcap, and John Rogers of the 10th Virginia, plus James A. Riddel of the 5th Virginia. Roadcap somehow escaped a few hours before he was to die.

Jackson had no patience with deserters. Anyone who ran away from his "army of the living God" was not only in violation of duty but also in sin against the Almighty. The general responded to all petitions for mercy with the same expression: "Is the accused a soldier? Did he desert? If so, *he must die!*"[117]

In the early afternoon of the 19th, two men infuriated Jackson. The first was Lieutenant Colonel Samuel T. Walker of the 10th Virginia. This former state legislator and newspaper editor thought that mitigating circumstances in two of the cases merited review. He told Jackson so. The general listened silently but with eyes that blazed in anger.

When Walker finished, Jackson astonished him by uttering words as if they were whip lashes. "Sir! Men who desert their comrades in war deserve to be shot! And officers who intrude for them deserve to be hung!" Jackson then snapped: "Mr. Walker, I advise you to resign!"[118]

Not too long afterward, a chaplain noted more for zeal than for tact came to the general and begged that the soldiers be spared. Jackson was in anguish, pacing back and forth, occasionally looking at his watch but making no comment. Then the chaplain made the mistake of saying: "General, consider your responsibilities to the Lord. You are sending these men's souls to hell!" Disgust swept across Jackson's face. He grabbed the cleric by the shoulders and snarled between clenched teeth: "That, sir is my business! Do you do yours!" Jackson then all but shoved the man from the tent. Promptly at 5 P.M., firing squads fulfilled the court-martial sentences.[119]

Whether impatient over the army's delay, still tormented by the executions, or both, Jackson that night summoned Sandie Pendleton and a squad of cavalry. He announced a moonlight reconnaissance of the countryside. Throughout the hours of darkness, seemingly without aim or purpose, Jackson led the group along what one cavalrymen termed "by-paths and unused roads in places where neither friend nor foe would ever pass." That same soldier considered Jackson's all-night expedition "one of those freaks which sometimes seize him and which make many people think he is somewhat deranged."[120]

Even though the chances of catching Pope were slim, Jackson still fidgeted to make a try of it. He became even more kindled when he received Lee's orders for the march. Jackson would lead the "left wing" of the army, Longstreet the right. This was historic because it marked the end of the Army of the Valley. Jackson would continue in charge of the Valley District; on occasion he would date a communication "Headquarters, Valley District." Yet beginning on August 20, he and his "foot cavalry" were a permanent part of the Army of Northern Virginia.

Jackson issued orders for his command to be underway "at moonrise" on the 20th. He himself was ready to go at 3 A.M. After a quick breakfast with his staff, the general mounted Little Sorrel in the predawn light and trotted through camps he expected to be deserted. Instead, he found Hill's Light Division (which was supposed to be the van of Jackson's column) still packing in preparation for the march.

Fuming with anger, Jackson ordered one of Hill's brigadiers whose unit was ready to move to start forward at once. In an obvious lack of confidence in Hill, Jackson directed that henceforth a staff officer would ride with each division to ensure that marching orders were fully obeyed. Execution of deserters the previous day, dereliction of duty on this day, plus official designation as commander of half of Lee's army placed Jackson in a no-nonsense frame of mind. His men, who may have sensed his intensity, crossed the Rapidan at Somerville Ford and covered twenty miles before halting.

Originally, Lee had hoped to strike Pope's left in order to get between him and any reinforcements from Washington or Fredericksburg. Yet with McClellan somewhere on the return journey to northern Virginia, an attack on Pope's eastern flank would leave Lee's own right open to assault from the north or east. Lee now began to think of an advance to the Rappahannock and a swing around Pope's right flank. Time was of the essence, and terrain was also important because it controlled what the opposing armies could and could not do.

The Rappahannock River flows southeast from the Bull Run Mountains, slowly turns east, receives the waters of the Rapidan River, and continues past Fredericksburg to the Chesapeake Bay. What made any turning movement of Pope difficult was the north bank of the Rappahannock. It was higher and more commanding than the south bank. Diligence on Pope's part would enable the Union forces to dispute Lee's attempts to cross at any point. The advantage here lay clearly with the defense; and the longer Pope held off Lee, the better the odds of McClellan's Army of the Potomac arriving to reinforce Pope.

On August 21, with Taliaferro's brigade in front, Jackson's troops moved toward Beverly Ford on the Rappahannock. Confederates spent the day trying first one ford and then another as Federals contested every approach. Soldiers maneuvered, firing and being fired at; riders galloped to and fro; cannon barked. Rain fell most of the afternoon. As Southerners made their way upriver searching for an open ford, Billy Yanks made a parallel march.

Jackson had halted his column just before noon near Cunningham's Ford. Federal artillery across the river opened a brisk fire. Taliaferro positioned four batteries and began a lively duel. Jackson appeared and gave the gun emplacements a nod of approval. Soon the artillerist in Jackson rose to the surface. He became totally absorbed in the contest. To Taliaferro's amazement, the general rode in among the cannon with no thought of personal safety. He leaned forward in the saddle to watch the discharges. Now and then, when a shot had a telling effect, Jackson would exclaim in his quick, sharp way: "Good! Good!"

Men were dropping around him; a courier just behind Jackson was killed by a shell explosion. The general was oblivious to everything but the artillery fire. Taliaferro, who had accompanied Jackson against his better judgment, was very uncomfortable. At one point in the fusillade, Jackson asked the brigade commander quietly: "General, are you a man of family?" "Yes," Taliaferro answered. "I have a wife and five children at home." Taliaferro was convinced that they were soon to be a widow and five orphans. "Good, good," Jackson stated. Then he resumed his concentration on the artillery fire that died away at sundown.[121]

Bivouac that night was the home of a Mr. Thompson near St. James Church. Jackson had only a glass of milk for supper, then went to bed amid another thunderstorm.[122]

Action increased on August 22 as Lee continued probing upriver for an open ford. Ewell's men were leading Jackson's march when the column crossed shallow Hazel Run at Wellford's Ford. Jackson ordered his wagon train to park there, with Trimble's brigade as a guard. The main column then resumed its advance.

Near noon, Federal General Henry Bohlen led three regiments across the Rappahannock and made a dash for the Confederate wagons. Jackson had anticipated such a move. When he received the report, he dismissed it with the observation: "General Trimble will attend to them." The Marylander did just that. Trimble saw the Federals coming, launched an attack, and drove Bohlen's men back "in great disorder." The brigadier added that he "pursued them closely and slaughtered great numbers as they waded the river or climbed up the opposite bank." Among the slain was Bohlen, a bespectacled German immigrant.[123]

With heat and humidity in the nineties, Jackson continued poking along the river. His forces were strung out about nine miles on the roads near the Rappahannock when the van reached the Culpeper-Warrenton road. Situated on the north bank of the river was Warrenton Sulphur Springs, once a fashionable resort but now in shambles, largely the result of being used as a Union field hospital. The bridge there was down, but no Federals were in the area. If the bridge could be reconstructed, Lee's army might cross the river at that point.

Jackson sent the 13th Georgia across the ford to hold the ground on the opposite side. Then he started Ewell's division over the river. Early's brigade went first. When rain began to fall, Ewell asked Jackson what should be done if rising waters made it impossible to ford the Rappahannock. "Oh, it won't get up," Jackson answered. "If it does, I'll take care of that." Lugging eight guns and using a half-demolished dam for footing, Early got his men up on the northern bank. The downpour lasted about two hours and was, in the words of one drenched Confederate, "the heaviest rain I ever witnessed." By the time it stopped, the Rappahannock had risen six feet and washed over its southern bank. Early had eight small regiments and two batteries. All were isolated on the enemy's side of the river.[124]

Jackson made headquarters that night in a small yellow farmhouse overlooking the bridge. A neat paling fence fronted the home. As usual, the general issued orders that soldiers were to respect the property. However, General Maxcy Gregg's brigade of Hill's division bivouacked nearby. After nightfall, the South Carolinians removed the fence for firewood. Jackson discovered the misdemeanor in a heavy mist the next morning and immediately placed all of Gregg's regimental commanders under arrest.

This incident was but one link in a chain of irritants for the general. Things were not going well. His supply lines were unstable, with the result that the men were ill fed. Discipline had momentarily broken down past the level Jackson tolerated. Three firing squads had done so little to shock the men back to a proper sense of duty that Jackson was weighing the propriety of having stragglers shot on sight. Now rain and a swollen, rapidly flowing river had imperiled part of his command. In the meantime, the pursuit of the enemy had ground to a halt.

It grew even worse for Jackson through the first half of Saturday the 23d. Alone and wet at early dawn, he sat on his horse and stared at the river. Blackford joined him with a dispatch from Lee. Apparently, the army commander gave Jackson a mild reprimand for leaving his wagon train open to attack.

Jackson read the message and then angrily ripped up the paper. He continued to watch the Rappahannock until the sun began burning through the mist. Then Jackson spurred his horse, galloped toward the river bank, and rode into the swirling water to the first bridge abutment. There he stopped.

When Taliaferro and his brigade arrived, Jackson rudely demanded the reason why the brigadier had not reached the area the previous night as Jackson expected. As things continued to work against the general, his sour disposition steadily worsened. At one point, he told an unoffending colonel that "field officers were intended to be useful as well as ornamental."[125]

Meanwhile, Jackson sat on his horse and glared at the river. He said nothing, and no one ventured to speak to him. Finally, General Powell Hill rode out into the water, saluted, and tried to initiate a conversation. Yet Jackson was "so abstracted and so rude" that Hill angrily turned around and moved back with his troops.[126]

In the afternoon, the Rappahannock began to recede as fast as it had risen. Jackson organized a work force to begin construction of a bridge. He supervised much of the labor and quickly became mud-covered from head to foot. A makeshift structure resting on driftwood and trash was in place by 4 P.M., whereupon Early led his men back to the south bank. Jackson exceeded his usually reserved praise by stating that Early's "skill & presence of mind" had been "favorably displayed." In reality, as Jackson probably deduced, his prayers and Pope's ineptitude were the greater factors in preventing bloodshed.[127]

Jackson retired early that night. Interestingly, he made no mention of the day's activities in his official report—although every other day was meticulously chronicled.

By sunrise on August 24, the last of Early's men had recrossed the river. Hill's batteries waged a fierce cannonade with Union guns for much of the cool day. Jackson led his men a couple of miles out of range of the Federal batteries to the village of Jeffersonton. Longstreet assumed the task of keeping Pope occupied at the various Rappahannock fords. A young aide in Longstreet's command wrote his wife: "It is said that Pope's army is utterly demoralized & that there was no other alternative but for him to retreat. I hope our forces will catch up with the panic stricken hirelings & destroy them."[128]

That was wishful thinking, for the Army of Northern Virginia was stalled. Four days of starts and jerks, maneuvering and skirmishing, had produced nothing for Lee. On August 22, Stuart and two cavalry brigades had staged a daring raid on Catlett's Station far in Pope's rear. The horsemen returned with $350,000 in Northern currency, several captured members of Pope's staff, that general's coat and hat, plus valuable up-to-date information on Union troop dispositions.[129]

Acquisition of Pope's recent dispatches alerted Lee to the strength of his adversary and to the nearness of McClellan's forces. The two Union armies could merge within five days. Time was running short. Lee must act, or fall back and admit defeat in the face of a stalemate. Open battle with Pope seemed out of the question, yet a daring maneuver had great potential. The key to any undertaking by the Confederates was the 143-mile Orange and Alexandria Railroad, which was Pope's umbilical cord with Washington and his supplies.

Early that Sunday afternoon, Lee summoned Jackson to his field quarters not far from Jeffersonton. Cannon argued in the distance. Confederate infantry were poised in roads and pastures. Jackson was still in a foul mood when he arrived at army headquarters, which had been moved to a table placed in an open field. Lee sat down, maps spread before him. Longstreet was on his right, Stuart on his left. Jackson stood facing the army chief.

Conversation was earnest from the start. Suddenly, Jackson forgot all of the recent annoyances. Lee was proposing an extremely bold plan, and Jackson's eyes blazed in anticipation.

Stuart had discovered that at least two of McClellan's corps were on the way to join Pope. That linkup would increase the Federal strength from 50,000 to 130,000 Federals. McClellan's troops would disembark from boats at Aquia Creek, move through Fredericksburg, and proceed up the Rappahannock toward Pope. This route compelled Pope to keep his left flank in contact with the Federal base at Fredericksburg. It also tightly restricted Pope's movements and left his right flank open and helpless against a turning movement.

Pope had two choices. He could remain where he was for the expected arrival of McClellan's divisions, which already were woefully tardy. Or Pope could retreat toward Washington, in which event he would be moving away from the Army of the Potomac supposedly arriving at Fredericksburg. Either way, Pope was momentarily vulnerable to attack.

Sidling up the Rappahannock in search of an unguarded crossing would cease, Lee declared. He was now going to begin a movement fraught with unparalleled risks. Jackson and his three divisions were to march upriver beyond Pope's right flank, cross the stream where it was opportune, and proceed on a wide sweep to strike the Orange and Alexandria Railroad far behind Pope. Lee, with Longstreet, would hold Pope's attention as long as possible. Once the Union commander backtracked to confront Jackson, Lee would move across the Rappahannock and advance toward Jackson— with Pope caught in the middle.[130]

Contrary to statements by a number of writers over the years, Jackson's target was not Manassas Junction but the Orange and Alexandria Railroad itself. When Jackson asked his engineering officer, Lieutenant Keith Boswell, for "the most direct and covered route to Manassas," he meant that the march might ultimately end at the railroad junction. First, however, Jackson wanted to strike for Bristoe Station. Destruction of the railroad bridge there was essential because it would cut Federal communications. What Jackson did thereafter would depend on circumstances.[131]

The success of Lee's plan rested again on secrecy and speed. Should Pope learn early of Jackson's departure, he could assail Lee, then turn on Jackson, and destroy the Confederate army in pieces. For Jackson, it was an enormous gamble. He would be advancing deep into enemy territory, which was highly dangerous in itself. Jackson might encounter McClellan somewhere along the way; Pope might intercept him at any moment; or Jackson might reach a point and suddenly find himself caught between two huge Federal armies.

If such possibilities entered Jackson's mind, they were dismissed quickly. A general worked toward victory; he did not worry about defeat. Lee was asking him to embark on a daring, independent march. Details would be left open: where Jackson went, and what he did, would evolve from developments along the way. Jackson had every confidence that in doing the Lord's work, the Lord would provide.[132]

At one point during the war council, Jackson excitedly drew a map in the dirt with the toe of his boot. He then began "gesticulating in a much more earnest way than was his habit," McGuire noticed from a distance. Lee listened as his lieutenant verbalized thoughts and outlined a plan. When Jackson finished, the commander bowed his head as if nodding approval. Lee apparently ended the meeting by asking Jackson when he planned to start. "I will be moving within an hour," he replied. A quick salute, and Jackson hastened back to his waiting command.[133]

19

STONEWALL AT MANASSAS, PART 2

A
S FIRED AS JACKSON WAS by the mission suddenly assigned to him, it was impossible to complete all preparations and get three full divisions in motion within a single hour. He nevertheless became a bundle of excitement and impatience that Sunday afternoon. The usual order went out for the men to cook three days' rations—the signal of a hard march ahead for the foot cavalry.

Other directives followed in staccato fashion. Supply wagons and all baggage, including knapsacks, were to be left behind. Food would be carried in haversacks and pockets. The only rolling stock to accompany the troops would be an ordnance train and a few ambulances. A herd of cattle, together with what could be garnered along the way, would make up the food supply. The march was to start at early dawn, "with the utmost promptitude," Jackson stated.[1]

Ewell would be in the lead, followed by Hill and Jackson's old division, now under Taliaferro. Jackson thought carefully over that alignment. Ewell was sure and swift; he would set a good pace. Hill would have to maintain the march, which would prevent another instance of tardiness. If he did lag, the Stonewall Division in the rear would nudge him forward.

Late in the afternoon, Jackson summoned his topographical engineer, Lieutenant Keith Boswell. The genial Boswell, "a handsome little fellow" who was "an excellent, good-natured, honest Presbyterian" as well as a fine engineer, had a sweetheart in Fauquier County. He thus was well acquainted with the area through which the army would move. Jackson's orders to Boswell were to ride ahead and ascertain the best, most concealed route for getting around Pope and reaching the Orange and Alexandria Railroad. Boswell was to keep in mind that 23,500 men organized in fourteen brigades, two cavalry brigades, and eighteen artillery batteries would be using the route.

After dark, bickering cannon along the Rappahannock grew silent. Most of Jackson's men cooked or sat in loud conversation around campfires as they pondered the unknowns of the forthcoming movement. Jackson sought to get some sleep, but camp noise, last-minute details, and the exuberance of a general about to do what he did best kept interfering. A nap was at most Jackson's rest that night.

Sometime in the predawn hours, Jackson said his morning prayers. Then he sent a hurried note to Anna. "The enemy has taken a position, or rather several positions, on the Fauquier side of the Rappahannock. I have only time to tell you how much I love my little pet dove."[2]

The march began around 3 A.M. on August 25. Each soldier had received sixty rounds of ammunition along with the orders: "No straggling; every man must keep his place in ranks; in crossing streams officers are to see that no delay is occasioned by removing shoes and clothing."[3]

Boswell and a detachment from the 6th Virginia Cavalry, many of whose members were from the neighborhood to which they were advancing, took the point. The predawn hours were cool and the troops marched "in the best of humor," one wrote. Daylight brought temperatures into the high seventies. A soldier in the 55th Virginia noted: "The hot August sun rose, clouds of choking dust enveloped the hurrying column, but on and on the march was pushed without relenting. . . . Haversacks were empty by noon; for the unsalted beef spoiled and was thrown away, and the column subsisted itself . . . upon green corn and apples from the fields and orchards along the route."[4]

Jackson's long line moved about five miles due north, passed the hamlet of Amissville, then turned northeast two miles to Hedgeman's River. Beyond the stream, there were no additional water obstacles. Boswell proved to be an excellent guide, especially when it came to shortcuts. "We did not always follow roads, but went through corn fields and bypaths," a soldier wrote. "Occasionally we marched right through someone's yard."[5]

Only Jackson and Boswell knew where the 23,000 men were going. To James Hendricks of the 2d Virginia, "it looked like madness to march away from our supplies and support, but we had learned to obey and to blindly follow."[6]

The hours passed. Cavalry fanned out in front to protect the advance. Guides stood at every road intersection to point the way for the marchers. (Each guide knew only to show the column a particular road.) Conversation in the ranks dwindled as troops concentrated on maintaining the brisk pace.

Because of the urgency of the movement, Jackson abandoned his usual march rate of fifty minutes per hour. The column remained constantly in motion, men eating whatever they had as they lumbered forward. Officers sometimes rode up and down the column with the same order from Jackson: "Close up, men, close up."[7]

The going became difficult. Bad shoes began to irritate feet already sore from tramping. Many of the men walked barefooted. Hunger, thirst, pain all had debilitating effects on the column.

By 9 A.M., Pope was aware of Jackson's advance. Reports from Union scouts confirmed the movement throughout the day. However, Pope again drew a false conclusion. He believed—and so informed authorities in Washington—that the long Confederate line was moving toward the Shenandoah Valley and hence posed no threat.

In midafternoon, Jackson's division passed the village of Orleans and continued through more broken country toward Salem, a tiny village eleven miles farther north. More important, Salem was on the Manassas Gap Railroad. Jackson's longtime friend, Judge G. D. Camden, had received permission from the general to accompany the army. The jurist was impressed that residents all along the way "would fall in and form groups and march with the forces, some dropping off & others falling in so as to keep up little groups most of the time, and from their jokes and conversation it was evident that Genl. Jackson was regarded as the 'man of the war' as well by the soldiers as the people."[8]

The day was growing late as the column neared Salem. Jackson reined Little Sorrel and climbed a large boulder by the side of the road. He removed his sweaty cap and gazed at the setting sun. Its colors illuminated his face as he stood, a weary commander taking his men where nobody knew, but confident in himself and them. The troops saw Jackson, forgot their weariness, and began to cheer loudly. Jackson made a swift but friendly sign for them to be quiet. He did not want any sound to reveal his location to the enemy. Quickly the word went through the ranks: "No cheering."

Soldiers obediently passed in silence. Yet looks, smiles, raised caps, salutes, uplifted arms all told mutely how they felt about their general. Jackson watched, at first sternly; then an unusual display of affection broke the seemingly unbreakable will. Smiling, he turned to a member of his staff and said: "Who could not conquer with such troops as these?"[9]

Ewell's division reached Salem at nightfall and stopped. The troops of Hill and Taliaferro arrived before midnight, completing a twenty-six-mile hike that even the general conceded was a "severe day's march."[10] No rations were available, so most of the men simply lay down alongside the road where they halted and went to sleep.

Meanwhile, Lee had amended the overall plan by a single but valuable addition. Confederate cavalry was rushing to join Jackson. When Stuart reported to Lee earlier that day, the army commander ordered him to ride to Jackson's support. Such a move would leave Lee without his "eyes," but Jackson needed the help of cavalry more than did the Army of Northern Virginia.

Stars were still twinkling when the march resumed. Half-awake, with only the food they could hastily snatch from anywhere, the men tramped down the road in silence. Jackson would push them hard that August 26 because this was the most important day in the entire campaign against Pope. The encirclement must be completed. Victory depended on it.[11]

Confederates noticed at sunrise on Thursday that they were moving east—at right angles to the previous day's march. Ahead of them was the Bull Run Mountain range, with Thoroughfare Gap looming as a potential enemy trap. It was a shallow gap, never more than 200 yards wide. If Pope had any troops stationed there, Jackson would have to fight his way through. The sound of such a battle would immediately alert the rest of the Union army.

To ascertain the situation, Jackson dispatched elements of the 2d Virginia Cavalry at the first light of dawn. The horsemen galloped up the mountain. At the top they discovered nothing, not one Federal soldier. The word went back to Jackson, and a calmness settled over both the commander and his men. Confederates wound slowly but steadily through the pass and descended back into the rolling Piedmont country.

Jackson allowed the men to march at will. He knew how far they had to travel that day. Some straggling resulted, but all of the troops kept moving behind the general. The pace was about three miles per hour. By now, the men sensed something of major importance unfolding. Few realized that they were making history.

Hour after hour, the men trudged on in a cloud of dust. "Our march filled the inhabitants with wonder," a Carolinian noted. "They crowded into the roads as we passed along, asking whence we came, how we came, whither we were going, and many other things which evinced their utter bewilderment at Jackson's great flank movement." Many residents brought parcels of food to distribute; one family sent a wagon load of goods for "glorious old 'Stone Wall.'"[12]

The order of march remained Ewell, Hill, and Taliaferro. Colonel Tom Munford's 2d Virginia Cavalry rode cautiously in front, examining intersections and probing spots of possible Union pressure. At Haymarket, the troopers rounded up a dozen Federals; a like number fell into Confederate hands when Jackson arrived at the Warrenton-Washington Turnpike. Munford was convinced that the prisoners were stragglers rather than scouts because they seemed "entirely ignorant of any movement of our Army."

Everything was going perfectly. Jackson remained dust-covered, alert, and quiet. Around 3 P.M., he received a pleasant surprise. Stuart with the mounted brigades of Fitzhugh Lee and Beverly Robertson overtook the head of the infantry column. In the effort to reach Jackson, the cavalry had been in the saddle for over twelve hours. Stuart himself had missed a night's sleep, but he greeted Jackson in his usual loud and engaging way.

According to one source, Stuart was still so ebullient at the results of his Catlett's Station raid that he carried part of Pope's uniform with him. The cavalryman reined in front of Jackson and shouted: "Hello, General! I've got Pope's coat! If you don't believe it, there's his name!" he said, pointing to the coat in his other hand. Any joyful answer Stuart may have expected never came. Jackson saluted and replied dryly: "General Stuart, I would much rather you had brought General Pope instead of the coat."[13]

At Gainesville, the main road forked. The left route went to Manassas, the other to Bristoe Station. Jackson opted for Bristoe. His objective from the start had been the Orange and Alexandria Railroad. From the fork, the route to Bristoe was two miles shorter to the railroad. It was also a good road and less likely to be under surveillance than the Warrenton Turnpike. Bristoe Station was probably more lightly defended. Destroying the railroad bridge over Broad Run there would neutralize the line for a good while; and with the tracks severed, Jackson could march to Manassas Junction without immediate fear of heavy interference from Pope.

The march continued. On either flank, Stuart's cavalry protected the infantry and guns. Bristoe was four miles away. Jackson halted at a farmhouse a half-mile from his destination to allow all the components of his army to close ranks before advancing on the railroad. He directed each of his brigadiers to post a man at a certain road junction to show the brigades coming behind him where to go.

Jackson then entered the front room of the home, slumped into a cane-bottomed armchair that he tilted back against the wall, and fell instantly to sleep. The staff stretched out on the floor around him.

A dispatch arrived. One of the generals had failed to leave a guide; several brigades in the rear had taken the wrong road. Sandie Pendleton laid a hand on Jackson's shoulder and relayed the news about the delinquent brigadier. The general opened his eyes and snapped: "Put him under arrest and prefer charges." In a moment, Jackson "was gently snoring again."[14]

Only an hour of daylight remained when Jackson started forward for the final advance on Bristoe Station. Munford had been instructed beforehand to prepare his cavalry for the strike into the village. Colonel Henry Forno's Louisiana brigade would supply infantry support. As the Confederates neared the railroad station, the sound of a puffing locomotive and squeaking of freight cars heading north signaled the passing of a train.

Munford's men were within 100 yards of the tracks before a company of Federals spotted them. The alarm went out; Billy Yanks scurried in every direction. Some took cover in town buildings and opened a disorganized fire. It quickly ended when the Louisianians and the 21st North Carolina of Trimble's brigade swarmed into the half-dozen streets of the village. Just as they did, a train whistle sounded. Another northbound freight was approaching Bristoe.

Southerners quickly threw wooden sills across the tracks. A few soldiers tried in vain to disconnect a rail. The train rushed through the village, cars rattling loudly. Sills flew wildly as small-arms fire spattered the cars. The train sped on toward Manassas Junction, where an alarm of Jackson's presence would be flashed everywhere.

Confident that another train would pass shortly, Jackson's men prepared more carefully. This time they opened a derailing switch; and to ensure that the next attempt would be successful, a large detachment from the 21st North Carolina took position along the right of way to deliver a concentrated volley. Barely were these preparations completed when the scream of a whistle to the south echoed across the fields. Within minutes, a train rumbled smoothly into Bristoe. The Carolinians opened fire. Then the locomotive hit the switch and lurched sickeningly to the right. The engine and half of the cars plunged down a shallow embankment.

Jubilant Confederates crowded around the wreck. The locomotive was named "President" and carried a picture of Mr. Lincoln above the cowcatcher. Jackson's men were rummaging among the wreckage when still another train burst into view on the long straight stretch. It consisted of twenty empty boxcars, and it plowed into the cars of the first train that were still on the track. Now the whole line was snarled by twisted metal and splintered wood.

Ewell's men had gone back to plundering when still another whistle shrilled in the distance. This time the Confederates were not as lucky. The engineer spotted the mess in his front, brought his train to a screeching halt, put the train in reverse, and backed quickly toward Warrenton. This meant that word of Jackson's whereabouts would soon be spreading south of Bristoe, just as it already was to the north of the station. With the Orange and Alexandria out of operation, serious work for Jackson's army would now begin.[15]

Darkness shrouded the land as Jackson brought his forces together at the railroad. The troops had made an astounding march of fifty-six miles in two days. They had cut the Orange and Alexandria and now stood where Lee wanted them to be: in Pope's rear and between the Federal army and Washington. Most of Jackson's men, however, were too tired to care about their good fortune. Allen C. Redwood, a member of Hill's division, had made his first long march under Jackson's command. Redwood spoke for many with his summation. "The two days' march . . . must remain a life-time memory to those who were participants in it, and yet it is almost impossible to recall its incidents with any degree of distinctiveness. No systematic halts broke its weary monotony; . . . when the column stopped, far in the night, the weary, foot-sore men, accoutred as they were, dropped beside their stacked muskets, and without so much as spreading a blanket were instantly asleep. . . . Long before the crack of day they were shaken up, to limp in the darkness, still more than half asleep. . . . Men dropped exhausted out of the ranks by the wayside, or got hopelessly in arrears in stopping to gather a few ears of corn or an apple, or to dip a cupful of water from a spring; but the column still pressed on."[16]

A member of the 40th Virginia assessed his weariness with scientific perception. "I had read that walking was an excellent form of exercise because it brought into play every muscle of the body, and having walked nearly sixty miles in two days I was convinced that the reason assigned was valid, for the muscles of my arms and neck were almost as sore as those of my legs."[17]

Not all of Jackson's men viewed their marching feat in a positive light. General Dorsey Pender, one of Hill's best brigadiers, wrote his wife that Jackson "forgets that one ever gets tired, hungry, or sleepy." Pender also asserted: "Jackson would kill up any army the way he marches and the bad management in the subsistence Dept.— Genl. Lee is my man."[18]

That was a minority opinion among Jackson's veterans. Captain Hugh White of the 4th Virginia was the son of Jackson's Presbyterian minister in Lexington and a former member of Jackson's Sunday school class. White wrote home: "I do not think that any man can take General Jackson's place in the confidence and love of his troops. . . . I have learned to look up to him with implicit confidence, and to approach him with perfect freedom, being always assured of a kind and attentive bearing."[19]

Soldiers began seeking rest around Bristoe Station, but Jackson was energized for more action. Ever the "wagon hunter," he ordered Boswell to move all of the railroad cars across Broad Run before destroying the bridge. Boswell reported the rolling stock damaged beyond use. As Jackson weighed the disappointment, local citizens called attention to the even greater prize seven miles down the railroad. Pope had converted the old Confederate base at Manassas Junction into a major supply stockpile of immeasurable proportions. The depot contained what Jackson mildly called "stores of great value."[20]

Jackson was aware of the condition of his troops. "Notwithstanding the darkness of the night and the fatiguing march," he "deemed it important that no time should be lost in securing" Manassas Junction before Federals could reinforce it or set it ablaze.[21] If Jackson could seize the station, it would reduce Pope's army somewhat to the same penury as tattered Confederates.

Who to send was a question Jackson could not answer. His entire command was exhausted after the activity of the past two days. At that moment, Isaac Trimble came to headquarters. The venerable brigadier was always looking for a good fight, and he was growing impatient. "Old Trimble" had confided to a staff officer earlier that at the next battle he expected to be "either a Major General or a corpse." Now he volunteered to lead troops through the night and seize the junction. A grateful Jackson accepted the offer.[22]

Some 600 men were in the 21st North Carolina and 21st Georgia of Trimble's command. Following the 9 P.M. departure of this force, Jackson had an afterthought quite akin to that of Lee. Old Jack concluded that Trimble's chances for success would improve if he had cavalry support. He therefore sent Stuart galloping after the column with orders to take charge of the expedition.

Trimble was not informed of the change in command. He and Stuart both gave total attention to securing control of Manassas Junction. However, they quarreled bitterly in their official reports about who did what and who deserved credit. Again, Jackson's reticence did not serve the army well.

Confederates under Trimble stumbled through the darkness until midnight, when they reached the edge of Manassas Junction. Then began a rare night attack in the Civil War. It proved to be an even rarer one that succeeded. Federal pickets saw the Confederates, fired scattered shots, and fled to the rear. Trimble improvised a battle line and sent it forward. Union artillery opened fire. That revealed the location in the dark of the enemy lines. Trimble bellowed: "Charge!" His men did so and within minutes were in control of the station. Some 500 Confederates captured 300 Federals, including the post commander, Captain Samuel Craig. In addition, the Confederates seized eight cannon, 175 horses, and the full stock of the depot. The junction had also been a refuge for some 200 runaway slaves, who were recovered. Trimble's losses in the action were a dozen men.[23]

Jackson was almost ecstatic at Trimble's success. He not only sent the brigadier a congratulatory message at 5 A.M.; several weeks later, in nominating the Marylander for promotion to major general, Jackson elevated the capture of Manassas Junction to "the most brilliant [achievement] that has come under my observation during the present War."[24]

August 27 began oppressively hot and humid. The temperature would reach ninety degrees by afternoon. Jackson had most of his command marching by sunrise. The divisions of Taliaferro and Hill started to Manassas. In front was the Stonewall Brigade. Other than brushing aside a small party of Federal cavalry east of Broad Run, the men encountered no opposition. Ewell remained at Bristoe Station to dispute the inevitable Federal pursuit. When hard pressed, Boswell was to burn the bridge as Ewell retired northward.

It was 7 A.M. and Jackson's two divisions had barely reached the junction. Riding with William T. Poague's Rockbridge Artillery, Jackson was following the road alongside the railroad tracks. Suddenly, a mile ahead, the general detected the glint of massed bayonets. He conferred with his staff as he gazed long through his field glass. It was a Federal brigade, moving straight for them.

The Confederate presence at Bristoe Station, and the disruption of the Orange and Alexandria line, had spurred officials in Washington to action. The belief among the Union high command was that this whole affair was but another of Stuart's hit-and-run cavalry raids. So the War Department dispatched a brigade of four New Jersey regiments under mustached and gruff-looking General George W. Taylor to proceed along the railroad and secure the vital Bull Run bridge. Other Federal troops—14,000 in all—would shortly be converging on Manassas Junction.

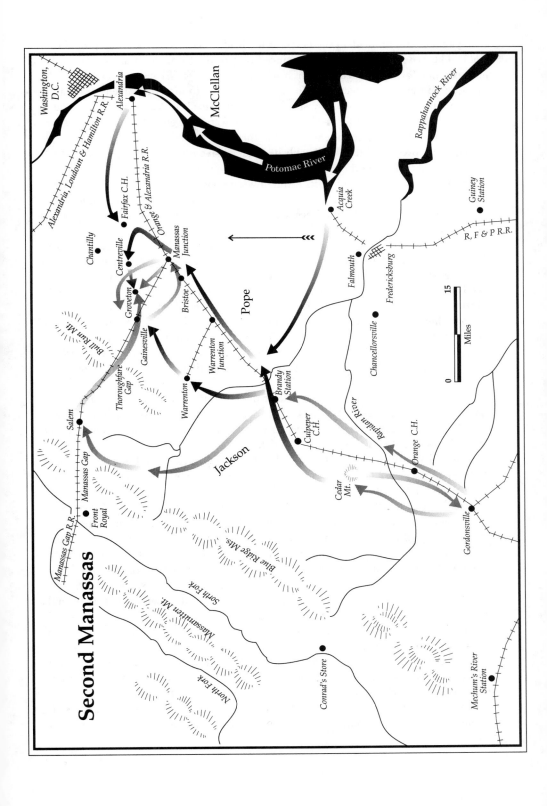

Second Manassas

Washington, D.C.

Alexandria, Loudoun & Hamilton R.R.

Alexandria

McClellan

Potomac River

Rappahannock River

Guiney Station

Acquia Creek

R, F & P R.R.

Fairfax C.H.

Orange & Alexandria R.R.

Chantilly

Centreville

Manassas Junction

Falmouth

Fredericksburg

Chancellorsville

Groveton

Bristoe

Pope

Bull Run Mt.

Gainesville

Warrenton Junction

Thoroughfare Gap

Warrenton

Brandy Station

Rapidan River

Orange C.H.

Salem

Jackson

Culpeper C.H.

Cedar Mt.

Gordonsville

Manassas Gap

Front Royal

Blue Ridge Mts.

Manassas Gap R.R.

South Fork

Massanutten Mt.

Conrad's Store

North Fork

Mechum's River Station

15

Miles

0

Taylor's men detrained a mile north of the bridge because of a wreck up the O&A track. The Federal brigadier was convinced that all the Confederates had fled. In his enthusiasm, Taylor decided to march a couple of miles beyond the bridge to the junction and ensure its security. He ordered his men to discard blankets and haversacks; then, without any artillery support, Taylor placed his 1200 troops in a rough line of battle and started forward. The Federals were unaware of Jackson's presence and advanced with the confidence of ignorance.

With cool precision, Jackson established a defensive line in a wide arc. He put the Rockbridge Artillery on the end of the line to deliver an enfilading fire. The Confederates waited as Taylor's regiments came to within 600 yards, then 500 yards . . . 400 . . . 300 . . . still moving. Jackson gave the order, and the Rockbridge gunners sent canister ripping into the Union lines. Carpenter's battery, in Jackson's center, opened fire as well.

Large gaps appeared in Taylor's ranks; his men reeled and then stumbled to a halt. The Union commander reorganized enough troops to attempt a bayonet charge, but Confederate musketry shredded the ranks before they moved fifty yards. Jackson's two batteries kept shifting to better positions as they blasted the Union lines horribly. Meantime, Hill's division was moving to overwhelm the Federal left.

Something strange then occurred. The general who always wanted to "shoot the brave men" suddenly became compassionate in the thoroughly lopsided contest. Jackson halted the artillery fire. He rode out into the field, drew a white handkerchief from his pocket, and waved it up and down while shouting: "Surrender! Throw down your arms and surrender!"[25]

When a Union soldier sent a musket ball whizzing by the general, Confederate cannon responded angrily. Federals lurched forward a short distance in a renewed attack, only to break under the heavy fire. The New Jersey regiments suffered 200 casualties before Taylor finally ordered them to retreat.[26]

Defeated and disorganized, the New Jersey soldiers abandoned the field at 11 A.M. "The enemy seemed to run, every man for himself," an Alabama soldier observed, "and we ran right after them, shooting as we ran."[27]

The flight of the Federals carried them over the Bull Run railroad bridge (which Confederates destroyed) and past their waiting train (which Confederates burned). In the panicky confusion of crossing Bull Run, large groups of Union soldiers laid down their arms. Taylor fell mortally wounded in the final action. As he was being carried to the rear, he exclaimed: "For God's sake, prevent another Bull Run!"[28]

Jackson reported that Taylor's advance "was made with great spirit & determination & under a leader worthy of a better cause." The futile assault cost the Federals 135 killed and wounded, plus 300 captured.[29]

Officers then directed the weary but still-excited Confederates to march to Manassas Junction. Never in their wildest imagination had famished, ragged, Southern soldiers ever dreamed of the sight they beheld. More than 100 bulging freight cars stood on two tracks waiting to be plundered. There also were streets of sheds loaded with everything necessary or desirable to equip an army. Thousands of food barrels were scattered over acres, as were still-fired field ovens and bakeries of gigantic sizes, pyramids of artillery ammunition, and new ambulance wagons. Here was a collection of foodstuffs and equipment the Southern Confederacy could not have produced in a year.

Jackson placed a guard over badly needed stores such as medicines. At the same time, he directed prisoners to man the bakeries and produce bread, and he ordered all confiscated whiskey poured on the ground.[30] Every bit of the captured supplies, of course, belonged to the Confederate government; but Jackson had no way to transport the mountains of property to Richmond, and he was painfully aware of the destitute condition of his soldiers. For once, he turned his head away from the conduct of his men.

They took instant and maximum advantage of the moment. As was the case around large Federal depots, scores of sutlers had set up booths and displays in the area. Manassas Junction was not merely a military storehouse; it was also a retail shopping center offering the widest variety of goods for soldiers with funds. Confederates sent the sutlers scurrying and confiscated their commodities as well.

Taliaferro's division, then Hill's, helped themselves to anything and everything. Some soldiers danced around campfires, alternately eating lobster salad with one hand and drinking rhine wine with the other. Men strutted in new shoes and "store-clothes." A few dirty Confederates wore women's hats with large ribbons and trimmings as they plundered cars and crates. Individuals wandered off carrying a box of candles, a barrel of coffee, cases of pickled oysters, huge molds of cheese, packages of candy. John Worsham of the 21st Virginia saw one man take nothing but French mustard. "He filled his haversack with it and was so greedy that he put one more bottle in his pocket."[31]

Jackson's order to destroy all whiskey was not executed fully. Many of Stuart's cavalry filled canteens with liquor and, said one, "were just as happy as a lamb with two mammies."[32]

In the afternoon came a report from Ewell: Federals were pressing hard at Bristoe Station. Pope had awakened to the fact that Jackson was not in the Shenandoah Valley but at the Union supply depot and astride the main communications line. The Federal general now ignored the continued presence of Longstreet in his front as well as what Pope thought to be the worn-out condition of his own troops. He abandoned the Rappahannock line, ordered his widely scattered forces to head for Manassas, and informed the army that he would "crush" Jackson. To one of his generals, Pope declared, "If you are prompt and expeditious, we shall bag the whole crowd."[33]

Around 3 P.M. that August 27, Ewell withdrew from Bristoe Station. His artillery had held off the Federals, but now some 5500 infantry were threatening his flanks. Ewell dutifully obeyed orders to start north and rejoin Jackson.

Manassas Junction must be abandoned. Jackson had seized 50,000 pounds of bacon, 1000 barrels of corned beef, 2000 barrels of salt pork, 2000 barrels of flour, plus quartermaster, ordnance, and commissary stores too voluminous to inventory. Old Jack gave quick orders to his troops: do not confiscate any Federal uniforms, put four days' rations of their choice in haversacks, and march north. "Having appropriated all that we could," Jackson wrote, "& unwilling that they should again fall into the hands of the enemy, . . . orders were given to destroy all that remained after supplying the immediate wants of the army."[34]

It was close to midnight when Jackson departed from Manassas Junction. Confederates heard deep explosions as they marched into the darkness. Looking back, they saw the sky reddened by flames from tons of burning stores. Kyd Douglas found the appearance of the marching column intriguing and humorous. "Here one fellow bending beneath the weight of a score of boxes of cigars, smoking and joking as he went, another with as many boxes of canned fruit, another with coffee enough for a winter's encampment, or a long string of shoes hung around his neck like beads."[35]

The destroyer of Pope's supply base knew that Lee and Longstreet were on the way. A natural move would have been for Jackson to march for Thoroughfare Gap and accelerate the reunion of Confederate forces. Yet Jackson's strategy had not been merely to cut the Orange and Alexandria Railroad, or to seize the Union army's major supply depot. They were but first steps in forcing Pope from his strong position along the Rappahannock.

Nor was Jackson content to preserve his forces until the other half of Lee's army arrived. A full retreat would relinquish much of his gain. Jackson now felt it necessary to go for the kill: to bring Pope's more than 51,000 men to battle while uncertainty still marked Union thinking.

Confusion on the night of August 27–28 was not confined only to Pope. Jackson's taciturnity—particularly his ingrained secrecy about movements—produced an all but total mixup in orders.

On leaving Manassas Junction, he sent Taliaferro's division northwest on the road to Sudley Springs Ford at Bull Run. Jackson apparently sent a guide to lead Hill's brigades toward the same destination. Ewell received word that another man would point the way for him. All of this was to occur at night. With such skimpy directions—and skimpy they were because neither division commander had any idea where he was supposed to be going—things promptly went wrong.

The guide leading Hill took the division due north to Centreville, ten miles from where it should have been. The man who was to lead Ewell arrived on schedule, but Trimble's brigade was nowhere in sight. A search proved fruitless. It so happened that Trimble, having no orders and with every intention to stay with the army and the action, formed his regiments behind Hill's division.

Ewell's men soon started north. Yet the guide became hopelessly lost, as did the division he was piloting. Ewell's men zigzagged around Bull Run until they met Trimble's brigade at the tail end of Hill's column. Only Taliaferro had gone where Jackson wanted him. Over 20,000 Confederates, deep in enemy territory, were spread out in a disarray reminiscent of the march to Cedar Mountain.[36]

No doubt Ewell shook his head again in exasperation. Trimble must have resorted to profanity to ease his anger. Hill might have smiled in satisfaction that Jackson's vague orders had resulted in another messy march. The rest of the night passed with exhausted soldiers in two-thirds of Jackson's command backtracking to the southwest on the Warrenton Turnpike.

Mercer Otey of the Rockbridge Artillery called the night's movement "about the weariest I can remember, and it seemed interminable. Ten hours to cover seven miles—what in the world was the matter? We could hear no firing." Many men dropped out of ranks and fell asleep in fence corners, "only to be aroused by a prod from the bayonets of the rear guard."[37]

Taliaferro's division, accompanied by Jackson, naturally had no difficulties in its movements that night. Taliaferro reported the advance "without serious impediment or difficulty." At one point, Jackson halted and dismounted. He left instructions for a staff officer to awaken him in thirty minutes, then curled up inside a fence and went to sleep. Precisely a half-hour later, he rejoined Taliaferro.[38]

The dispersement of the units, marching, and countermarching was not all bad, however. Such confusion attendant to Jackson's abandonment of Manassas Junction, especially Hill's sixteen-mile circuitous trek to Centreville, absolutely befuddled Pope. Real irony now came into play. Pope was hunting for Jackson, and Jackson was hunting for Pope, and neither general knew with any certainty where to look.

Groveton was the rendezvous point for Jackson's force. The hamlet was but a cluster of houses at the foot of a long descent in the Warrenton-Washington Turnpike, but the place was the intersection of the turnpike and the Sudley Springs road. There Jackson determined to make a stand. Groveton was close to the route Lee would take through Thoroughfare Gap, ten miles away.

Jackson also knew from four months in the area the previous year that a low ridge lay north of, and generally parallel to, the turnpike. The high and wooded position would give Jackson a long sweep of the highway without being seen by anyone on the road. In addition, the high ground would be on the flank of any Federal force advancing on the turnpike.

Thursday, August 28, dawned cloudy but warm. Jackson sent cavalry in every direction. Reports around 8 A.M. showed a Federal muddle in which Pope was trying to get his units together. The Union general, wrong again in his deductions, believed that Jackson had taken refuge in the Manassas defenses and would do battle there. Thus, in an order that may well have cost Pope the entire campaign, the Union general changed the direction of march from north toward Gainesville to east toward Manassas.

The Union army began falling back to Manassas Junction by various routes. The whereabouts of McClellan's force was still unclear to both sides. When Jackson learned of the approach of Pope on the turnpike, he sent hasty orders for Hill to move to the Bull Run fords and intercept the enemy. Hill got the message around 10 A.M. between Centreville and the Bull Run bridge.

"Little Powell" had to think carefully about a decision. From dispatches captured near Centreville, Hill knew that Pope was not retreating. He was in fact concentrating at Manassas for a showdown with Jackson. Hill could have blindly followed Jackson's directive, giving the strict obedience that Jackson did not think he always displayed. Instead, Hill ignored the order to attack at the fords and kept moving toward Jackson's position three miles farther at Groveton.

By midmorning, Jackson was receiving regular updates on the Union army's locations. The general still harbored doubts about Pope's destination. Perhaps the Union commander was moving toward Alexandria to unite with McClellan; or Manassas, seven miles from Groveton, might be the rendezvous point for all of Pope's elements. Jackson decided not to advance. He would wait and watch.

Confederate soldiers welcomed the inactivity. Jackson's position was between the turnpike in his front and Bull Run to the rear. Fitzhugh Lee's cavalry guarded his left in the direction of Alexandria, while the horsemen of Colonels Tom Munford and

Thomas L. Rosser were on the other flank near Bristoe. At Jackson's disposal remained fourteen infantry brigades, two cavalry brigades, and eighteen light artillery batteries. Late in the morning, Ewell's division—men dirty, shuffling, and solemn looking from fatigue—moved slowly into position alongside the troops of Taliaferro and Hill.

Some of Jackson's units were physically weak. For example, the 55th Virginia had numbered 620 men when it left Richmond a month earlier to join Jackson. Owing largely to hard marching, the regiment had only eighty-two soldiers at Groveton. The weariness even showed with Jackson. For a good part of a morning full of unknowns and apprehensions, he lay in a fence corner with his head propped on a saddle and napped.[39]

Around noon, a messenger arrived with a captured order. Jackson, Taliaferro, and Ewell were still dozing in spite of the day's heat. The dispatch "aroused Jackson like an electric shock," Taliaferro noted. A large and separate part of Pope's army was advancing on the turnpike in the direction of Centreville. Jackson conferred with no one, made no announcement. He looked at Taliaferro and said, "Move your division and attack the enemy." Then Jackson turned to Ewell. "Support the attack." Both divisions were soon heading through the woods to get into position.[40]

The units had advanced about two and a half miles when Jackson rode up and ordered a halt. Taliaferro and Ewell were near the Brawner farm, just under a mile from the Warrenton Turnpike. Eighteen months earlier, the Brawner acreage and adjacent properties had been well-cultivated and prosperous examples of Virginia agriculture. Now weeds and briers covered fields abandoned by farmers caught in the earthquake of war.

Jackson had stopped the preparations for battle because outposts reported no Federals advancing northeast toward Bull Run. That force originally spotted had turned off the turnpike in the direction of Manassas Junction. In short, the enemy was doing precisely what the captured dispatch said: moving away from Jackson toward the southeast and the smoldering, desolated Federal supply base.

Nothing remained but for Jackson's army to resume waiting. Two divisions were drawn up on the wooded ridge overlooking a broad expanse of open ground that fell in gentle undulations to the turnpike. Men stretched out on the ground in eighty-degree heat. Although "packed like herring in a barrel," they talked, laughed quietly, played cards, or napped with the carelessness of the veteran soldiers that they were.[41]

Jackson passed the early afternoon riding alone and restlessly through the area. An aide thought him "cross as a bear" and added, "The expression of his face was one of suppressed energy and reminded you of an explosive missile, an unlucky spark applied to which would blow you sky high."[42]

Around 3 o'clock a jaded courier arrived at headquarters with a message from Lee. The other half of the Confederate army was approaching the west face of Thoroughfare Gap and would file into the Piedmont the next morning. Jackson "beamed with pleasure," and he went so far as to shake the courier's hand for the good news. Then he downed a quantity of buttermilk and relaxed noticeably. The reunion of the Army of Northern Virginia was imminent; the dangers inherent in Jackson's isolated position were lessening steadily.[43]

Another two hours passed. The sun began slipping toward the horizon. A blue column came into view moving on the turnpike toward Bull Run and the Stone Bridge. The ranks were compact, with flankers fleshed out impressively. However, no cavalry support was visible.

The force was General Rufus King's division of roughly 10,000 troops. They were strung out for a full mile on the turnpike. King himself was absent, sick back at Gainesville. The brigades were totally unaware that the enemy was close at hand. Federals trudged steadily forward through thick dust alone, unprotected, and vulnerable to attack.

Jackson was well aware that if Pope were unmolested, he could concentrate his army behind Bull Run—as he had done at the Rappahannock—and effectively block any movement by Lee. That fact, plus the knowledge that Lee was less than a day's march away, convinced Jackson to strike this portion of the Union army.

When the head of the blue column got to within a half-mile of Jackson's position, a lone, seedy-looking rider emerged from the woods on the left. He moved casually along a hillside and watched the Union force. He rode a decrepit horse awkwardly and bore the appearance of some farmer watching unwanted company pass. The figure was within easy rifle range, but Federals had no interest in a harmless individual.

Inside the woods near the top of the ridge, Jackson's staff sat horrified as the aides watched their general in full exposure to the enemy. Any moment they expected to hear shots and see him reel in the saddle. Jackson soon reined Little Sorrel and galloped back into the woods to a knot of officers. "Here he comes, by God!" several of them exclaimed. Jackson touched his kepi in acknowledgement of their salutes; then, in a voice that was a mixture of calmness and pleasure, he said, "Bring up your men, gentlemen." Almost within seconds, one of Jackson's foot cavalry wrote, "the field was a perfect hubbub—men riding in all directions, infantry rushing to arms, cannoneers running to their guns, and the drivers mounting. We saw the master hand now."[44]

Taliaferro, on the right of Jackson's line, sent his men forward. Ewell, in the center, released two of his brigades to the attack. Isaac Trimble's veteran unit was one of them. An Alabamian in that brigade declared: "Trimble gave the loudest command I ever heard to 'Forward, guide center, march!' I could hear the echo in Bull Run Swamp for miles." Three Confederate batteries were in position to fire over the heads of Jackson's advancing infantry.

Around 6:30 P.M., a shot from Captain George Wooding's Danville Artillery whistled over the Federal column. "We never saw so polite a bow made as a regiment as we made," a Wisconsin soldier acknowledged.[45]

Jackson's assault exploded on the left flank of the Federals. Complete surprise flashed through the Union ranks. The first of the Northern brigades had already passed. Jackson's fury was unleashed against General John Gibbon's brigade in the form of volleys of musketry and a concentrated cannon fire. Southern infantry, Jackson stated, moved "in gallant style until they reached an orchard on the right of our lines & were less than a hundred yards from a large force of the enemy. The conflict here was fierce & sanguinary. Although largely reinforced the Federals did not attempt to advance but maintained their ground with obstinate determination."[46]

Fighting roared unchecked for two and a half hours. Hostile lines fired volley after volley at almost point-blank range. Taliaferro later wrote that "a farm-house, an orchard, a few stacks of hay, and a rotten 'worm' fence were the only cover afforded to the opposing lines of infantry; it was a stand-up combat, clogged and unflinching, in a field almost bare. . . . In the dying daylight . . . they stood, and although they could not advance, they would not retire. There was some discipline in this, but there was much more of true valor."[47]

The Union Iron Brigade grappled with the Confederate Stonewall Brigade, each the pride of its respective side. Neither budged from pressures. Smoke and the confusion attendant to battle engulfed the whole arena. Men were guided in their firing by the flash of opposing guns. As quickly as a soldier fell, a comrade sprang to his place.

Artillery explosions added to the killing. North and South alike kept trying to mount an assault, but resistance was too heavy. Kyd Douglas summarized: "Each attack was weaker, each repulse more difficult—the Federals dispirited, the Confederates worn out. It was a fearfully long day."[48]

Nightfall ended the contest but not the killing. The 28th Georgia rushed to the support of the Stonewall Brigade. In the gunsmoke and gathering gloom, the fresh troops mistook the Virginians for the enemy and opened a low and rapid fire that caused many casualties in Jackson's beloved brigade. With that, Federals withdrew slowly and in good order from the field.[49]

Both sides had displayed heroism and gallantry. Neither had gained anything of note. Worse, the comparatively brief fight had produced stunning losses. On the Union side, 1100 of 2800 engaged had fallen. Jackson's casualties were 1200 of 4500 in the battle.

For the Confederates, the losses were horribly concentrated. The Stonewall Brigade had suffered 200 men killed and wounded, roughly 40 percent of its strength. What was left for duty did not equal a regiment in size. Two Georgia regiments suffered casualties of 70 percent—an astronomical figure for that period in the war.

Equally as bad were the command losses in Jackson's army. Colonel John F. Neff, in spite of a severe cold, insisted on leading his 33d Virginia into action. He was one of the first to die. The 10th Virginia's Colonel Samuel T. Walker, whom Jackson had rebuked a few weeks earlier, fell mortally wounded—as did Colonel Lawson Botts of the 2d Virginia. Colonel Andrew J. Grigsby of the 27th Virginia was slightly wounded.[50]

The Confederate injury list did not stop there. Taliaferro was hit in the neck, foot, and—most seriously—arm. None of the wounds was fatal, but he would be out of action for awhile. Even worse was the fate of "Baldy Dick" Ewell. With his usual impetuosity, Ewell had ridden forward to lead a regiment personally against a line of Federals in a gully. As he knelt to pinpoint the location of the enemy, a few of his troops shouted: "Here's General Ewell, boys!" That was almost a signal to the Federals, who swept their front with musketry. Ewell went down and was not recovered until litter bearers found him after nightfall. One or more bullets had shattered his left knee and tibia. Ewell asked that the leg be amputated there on the battleground. Sounder judgment prevailed; he was taken to a field hospital, where surgeons removed the useless limb. Ewell would be lost to the army for months.[51]

Jackson could not have been pleased with Groveton (or Brawner's Farm, as the battle is sometimes called). It had even more limited results than Cedar Mountain. The planning was ill conceived, the execution ill managed. The specter of Kernstown reappeared at Groveton. Jackson thought that he could rout the Federals with a headlong attack. When it stalled, he should have explored the enemy flanks—as he had demonstrated so craftily in the Shenandoah Valley. Instead, he became content to let bravery contest with bravery while awaiting the outcome of a stand-up fight whose potential for victory faded with the passing moments.

Further, Jackson appeared to ignore his own chain of command by sending brigades into the struggle on his own orders. Taliaferro and Ewell displayed only limited leadership—in part, one suspects, because they were not summoned to do more than attack the Federals on the turnpike. Now Jackson was without two of his three division commanders from an engagement that was a halfway success at best.

High-command gaps had to be filled quickly. To replace Taliaferro, Jackson selected Brigadier General William E. Starke. A native Virginian, the forty-eight-year-old Starke had spent most of his adult life as a cotton broker in New Orleans and Mobile. He led the 60th Virginia before promotion to general and command of one of the Louisiana brigades in Lee's army. Starke had a reputation as a strict disciplinarian and hard fighter, traits that Jackson especially liked. Yet Starke had been a brigadier only since August 6 and had never handled a brigade until Groveton. Now he was to lead a division.

Jubal Early was the logical successor to Ewell. Yet army seniority could not be circumvented. Division command went to General Alexander R. Lawton, a heavy-set, bearded Marylander who had added a Harvard law degree to his West Point training. Lawton was also the brother-in-law of Longstreet's able artillerist, Colonel E. Porter Alexander. While Lawton had been an accomplished field administrator, his talent in field command was considerably less.

By this time, Pope knew precisely where Jackson was. The Union Army of Virginia was rushing to confront Jackson's 20,000 troops. In a 10 P.M. dispatch to Washington, Pope reassured all that he would shortly come to grips with Jackson's army. "I do not see how it is to escape without heavy loss," the Union general concluded.[52]

At about the same time that night, Jackson and Dr. McGuire rode a mile or so west toward Bull Run Mountains. Jackson dismounted wearily and put his ear to the ground to listen for Longstreet's approach. He heard nothing. McGuire wrote: "I shall never forget the sad look of the man that night as he gazed towards Thoroughfare Gap, wishing for Longstreet to come."[53]

Apprehension also existed in the Confederate ranks as the men settled down for the night. A South Carolinian confessed: "Before us was Pope, with at least the bulk of the Federal army, which, of course, we magnified by many thousands; behind us was no base, no subsistence, no reinforcement. . . . God, Jackson and our own hearts were our dependence."[54]

Riding back to his army, Jackson made his way to a house near Sudley Springs. It was his headquarters in addition to being a field hospital. He spent the night sleeping little but praying a lot.

When daylight came on August 29, Jackson found the enemy in force to the east. He assumed that they were between "my command & the Federal Capitol." Actually,

Jackson knew about as much as Pope that morning. The Union general was thoroughly confused from start to end of the whole campaign. Contrary to Pope's thinking, Jackson was not retreating and Longstreet was not encamped quietly south of the Rappahannock. Pope was unaware even of the location of his own brigades, which were scattered all over the region and out of contact with army headquarters. Generals did not know where Pope was or where they were supposed to be. At the same time, Pope was striving to concentrate 25,000 men east of Jackson and a like number to Jackson's west in order "to crush Jackson before Longstreet could by any possibility reach the scene of action."[55]

To counteract Pope's new position, and to take better advantage of the terrain, Jackson methodically drew back his lines. A mile north of Groveton was the roadbed of an unfinished rail line that ran near the top of a ridge in a southwest-northeast direction. Part of the right of way was a deep cut through the high ground. Behind the cut, parcels of open fields occasionally broke the woodland. Farther north, where the Sudley Springs Road met Bull Run, a woody knoll rose above the surrounding country. The most portentous aspect of the area was the land to the east of the railroad cut. It fell away gradually for a full half-mile, and most of the long hillside was cleared land with a few small clumps of trees here and there.

Jackson planted his left on the Sudley Springs knoll. His line stretched one and three-quarter miles to the southwest and ended where the railroad was to cross the Warrenton Turnpike. Hill's division manned the left. It was the most critical part of the field because it lay at the crossings of Bull Run and Catharpin Run, which Jackson would have to use if it became necessary to retire to the north. Ewell's troops (now under Alexander Lawton) held the center, and Starke, with the Stonewall division, took the right. Behind the railroad bed, the ground rose still more and was wooded— an ideal place for artillery emplacement.

The Confederate position had both strengths and weaknesses. Jackson brought up forty guns to support his infantry. The compact battle line gave him about five soldiers per yard of front. Deep cuttings and high embankments were formidable in places. The railroad cut itself was a natural defense. In other sectors of the roadbed, however, some fills were too steep while stretches of excavation were merely a smoothing of the ground.

Jackson's position did not follow the exact line of the railroad. The extreme left was refused on the high rocky spur behind the railroad path. At the other end, Starke had his first infantry line in a cut, but his main line was 200 yards to the rear in woods. Two of Lawton's brigades in the center were the only ones precisely on and along the railroad. (Lawton's other two brigades were posted on the far right alongside the highway from Thoroughfare Gap.) Stuart's cavalry guarded the extreme flanks.

The final weakness for Jackson was the number of troops present for duty. He had three divisions at hand, but casualties, sickness, and furloughs had reduced the effectives to about 18,000 men. Some regiments were skeletons. The 27th Virginia numbered twenty-five men; other regiments had officers no higher in rank than captain. Not a brigade in Jackson's old division was under a brigadier general.

"Perilous in the extreme" was how Kyd Douglas described Jackson's position. "His corps was strongly posted . . . fronting the main position of the enemy, with its back toward its anxiously expected friends. The position was independent but not defiant, not inviting but not avoiding an engagement." One of Ewell's cannoneers thought it "a very melancholy day." Confederates took their positions "with long faces, not with the usual smile when old Lee & Longstreet was near but where [sic] now cut off from there help and had to hold our ground."[56]

Early morning passed with an ominous hush over the land. A few probes on Jackson's right and center triggered brief firefights before the Federals withdrew. Jackson, as he preferred to do, was with his guns. He dismounted where the Rockbridge Artillery had unlimbered on the right of the line. For a time, the general napped while lying against a haystack.

Around 10 A.M., Federal artillery opened "with spirit & animation upon our right," Jackson wrote.[57] Quickly, five Confederate batteries responded, producing a continuous roar over the countryside. Meanwhile, Jackson's infantry were looking less to the front than to the west, from where the rest of Lee's army would be coming that day.

A bit earlier, Major Heros von Borcke of Stuart's staff had received orders to lead two regiments into line and report the same to Jackson. "Where shall I find General Jackson?" von Borcke asked.

Stuart replied with a smile: "Where the fighting is hottest."

The Prussian located Jackson in the middle of the artillery fusillade. The general was seated on a caisson immediately behind the guns and quietly writing dispatches. If he was aware of the noise and exploding shells, Jackson did not show it. Von Borcke felt compelled to tell Jackson of the dangerous position he had selected for doing paperwork.

"My dear Major," came the reply, "I am very much obliged to you for the orders you have given. General Hill will take care of the enemy. . . . And for my position here, I believe we have been together in hotter places before." With that, Jackson turned back to his dispatches, "cannon-shot ploughing up the ground all around him and covering his manuscript with dust, so that, like one of Napoleon's generals under similar circumstances, he was in no need of sand to dry up his ink."[58]

Federal infantry in force soon appeared to be using the artillery cover to shift toward Jackson's left. The general could not dispatch troops from the south end of his line without uncovering the Warrenton Turnpike and leaving his right flank vulnerable. At that precise moment, a brigade-sized unit came into view up the Thoroughfare Gap road just as courier John Cussons reined his horse at Jackson's headquarters.

Cussons noticed that Jackson's sunburnt features "were working," and that he seemed agitated. The courier quietly reported that General John B. Hood's division, with the Texas Brigade in the lead, had cleared Thoroughfare Gap and was moving rapidly to join Jackson. Suddenly, a long cheer swept up from the right. The Texans were filing into position. Longstreet's half of the army was arriving.

Jackson's response to Cusson's message had been an abrupt directive for the courier to get ready to ride back and assist in making troop dispersement. This flash of rudeness by an ungrateful general angered Cussons. Suddenly, the mounted Jackson crossed his hands on the pommel of his saddle, laid his face on the back of his hands, and appeared to fall asleep. After what seemed like "an interminable time" to Cussons, Jackson raised his head. "As I looked into his eyes," the courier remembered, "all my resentment died away. . . . His gaze was steadfast but no longer stern. There was something of authority in his mien—there was always that—but there was pathos, too. . . . His eyes were moist, his voice low and musical."[59] Whether Jackson was napping, or praying, is speculative.

With his right secure, Jackson turned his attention—albeit tardily—to his left. It had been open to attack from the moment it was established. Nothing had been done to clear the front where it passed through a wooded area. A portion of Powell Hill's line stood amid trees and bushes; some of it faced thick undergrowth. Not only was visibility poor, but the timbered region made artillery all but useless.

General Maxcy Gregg and his veteran South Carolina brigade were on the far left: the wooded knoll that overlooked the Sudley Springs Road and the ford. The northern flank of the Carolinians was refused until the front became an obtuse angle. To its right, down the line, was the Georgia brigade of General Edward L. Thomas. Yet for reasons never explained adequately, a huge gap existed between those two northernmost brigades.

In short, Hill had not done a very good job of preparing to receive an attack. Jackson had not bothered to check the dispositions. Given Old Jack's distrust of Hill, this omission is even more strange.

By early afternoon, the temperature was in the high eighties. Union stabs at Jackson's left increased in severity, then gave way to full-scale assaults. Pope was making a determined effort to crumple the Confederate line near Sudley Springs Ford. At first, Hill's men managed to hold their positions. Around 2 P.M., Jackson reported, a heavy Federal attack "pressed forward in defiance of our fatal & destructive fire with great determination, a portion of it crossing a deep cut in the railroad track & penetrating in heavy force an interval of near 175 yards, which separated the right of Gregg from the left of Thomas' Brigade."[60]

One of Gregg's officers noted of this Union assault: "The woods swarmed with them. They closed in upon us from front and right and left, pressing up with an energy never before witnessed by us. . . . Line after line of theirs was hurled upon our single one, which was already fearfully thinned by nearly a whole day's fighting and almost ready to faint from heat and fatigue. And, in addition to all this, they had a cross-fire upon our salient angle. The firing was incessant. They seemed determined not to abandon the undertaking; we were resolved never to yield."[61]

Gray-bearded Maxcy Gregg looked older than his forty-nine years. He was a prominent Columbia attorney with the instinctive talents of a soldier. The Federal breakthrough between his South Carolinians and Thomas's Georgians did not catch the brigadier totally off balance. Gregg brought up the 14th South Carolina, which was in reserve. With the 49th Georgia of Thomas's brigade, the Confederates staged a counterattack. Jackson wrote with satisfaction that the two fresh regiments "attacked the exultant enemy with rigor and drove them back across the Rail Road track with great slaughter, the opposing forces at one time delivering their vollies into each other at the distance of ten paces." Hand-to-hand fighting was commonplace throughout this period in the battle.[62]

At least four massive Union attacks on Jackson's left had failed. Bodies piled in front of the railroad cut and sprawled over the descending ground to the east attested to the severity of the fighting. Yet there was no indication that Pope was finished. The lull that settled over the field was a breath-catching intermission only.

Longstreet's divisions were basically deployed by early afternoon. The Confederate line now extended for almost three miles. Jackson's half faced southeast, Longstreet's position was due east. Lee's army, in other words, was like a giant vise, waiting either for its prey to enter the jaws or for the Confederates to lunge forward and strike Pope on two fronts.

Neither occurred that day. Lee wanted Longstreet to attack at once. Longstreet balked: he preferred to maneuver his units into a position that would force the Federals to attack him disadvantageously. He asked for time to examine the ground fully. Lee concurred. After awhile, Longstreet expressed concern that the Union line in his front might extend far enough south of Groveton to cover a significant part of Longstreet's flank if the Confederates attacked. In truth, Federal General Fitz John Porter's corps was where Longstreet feared. The senior lieutenant urged caution; he asked Lee to defer any assault by his troops until the location of all Federal units could be ascertained. Lee agreed, but with disappointment.[63]

On Jackson's left, meanwhile, the situation had grown critical. Hill's men had repulsed every Federal charge. Yet exhausted and low on ammunition, the Southerners had fallen back 300–400 yards. Part of their line had been broken and then momentarily patched; Gregg's brigade was still somewhat isolated from Jackson's main position. Gregg himself was prancing up and down his line, waving an old Revolutionary War scimitar above his head and shouting: "Let us die here, my men! Let us die here!"[64]

Jackson sent Douglas to get an update on Hill's predicament. The aide found groups of soldiers from various regiments using the lull (and risking the fire of Union sharpshooters) by scampering over the battlefield to collect cartridges from friend and foe. Hill told Douglas of the heavy losses he had already suffered. The position was desperate, Hill shouted. He was not sure he could withstand another enemy attack.

Douglas rode furiously back to Jackson and repeated Hill's assessment. Jackson "was pale, serious and calm," Douglas noted. "His eyes were cast longingly to the rear" in Longstreet's direction. The staff, aware of Jackson's anguish, stood silently around him. "The message from General Hill seemed to deepen the shadow on the general's face, but he answered promptly and sternly: 'Tell him if they attack him again, he can and must beat them!'"[65]

Hill and Jackson had their ongoing differences. Jackson was not personally fond of Hill, and he heartily disliked Hill's relaxed style of command. Yet Jackson knew the fellow Virginian to be an excellent fighter. Hill would not express doubts in battle if his dilemma was not perilous. Jackson thought the situation now so serious that he decided to inspect it himself.

Douglas was galloping back to Hill's sector when Jackson caught up with him. They soon met Hill, who was on his way to report personally to Jackson. Hill repeated the critical nature of his lines. Both generals glanced up at the sun. Jackson then said: "General, your men have done nobly. I hope you will not be attacked again; but if you are, you will beat the enemy back."[66]

All at once, the sharp explosion of musketry broke the afternoon stillness. "Here it comes!" Hill yelled as he spurred his horse and started back to his command. Jackson shouted after him, "I will expect their repulse!"[67]

This latest Union attack (whether it was the sixth or seventh no one could say with accuracy) was more desperate than the others. Thick lines of Federals slammed into Hill's position. One Confederate observed: "The battle, now more furious than before, swayed to and fro; and for sometime doubtful conclusions hung in the balance. The enemy continued to pour in his fresh relays. . . . The contest constantly grew fiercer and more bloody. Often the combatants delivered their fire against each other within ten or a dozen paces. . . . The slaughter was too horrible and sickening."[68]

Waves of Federals charged up the hill, broke, fell back, and charged again. The attacks seemed to have no end. Hill's line bent more with each onslaught. Defeat was near, when six regiments under General Jubal Early reached Hill's sector. These 2500 fresh troops tore into the already bleeding Federal ranks. Pope's battle line wilted almost at once. Union soldiers attempted to conduct a fighting retreat from the field, but the slow withdrawal enabled the Confederates to inflict even more casualties.

Early and his men, excited with success, pursued the Federals for 200 yards or more before Hill relayed Jackson's orders for the Confederates not to advance beyond the railroad. Early broke off the fight and retired to the line the Confederates had held when the day began.

Then the well-known Rebel Yell echoed southward from Hill's lines. Jackson knew what it signaled. Confirmation came a few moments later. A staff officer reined his horse in front of Jackson. "General Hill presents his compliments," the man declared proudly, "and says the attack of the enemy was repulsed." For the first time that day, Jackson smiled. "Tell him I knew he would do it," he replied.[69]

Jackson did not learn until later that Gregg's troops had maintained the extreme left by fighting with clubbed muskets and bayonets, while others who ran out of ammunition desperately hurled stones in an effort to stop the enemy attack. One Carolinian spoke for many: "Our feet were worn and weary and our arms were nerveless. Our ears were deadened with the continuous roar of battle, and our eyes were dimmed with the smoke."[70]

Night ended the fighting. All of Jackson's divisions had seen sharp action. On the right, Starke's lines were weakened but steadfast; Lawton in the center had held; Hill's Light Division had endured some six hours of combat and naturally incurred the highest losses.

Perhaps as many as 30,000 Federals had been beaten in one attack after another. Jackson's skilled use of inner lines of defense, plus Pope's unimaginative and piece-meal assaults, were the keys to Confederate victory. Pope, still ignorant of Longstreet's presence a few hundred yards away, came to another erroneous conclusion that night: Jackson would use the hours of darkness to beat a hasty retreat.

Ever so slowly, the gunfire died away. Then began a new noise: wounded men screaming, hollering, and moaning for help. "The ground was literally covered with their dead and wounded," a Louisiana soldier stated of the Federals. To go onto the field between the lines in order to offer help was suicidal. Troops on both sides had to spend the night listening to the agonies of the maimed and dying.[71]

At Stonewall Brigade headquarters, Colonel Will Baylor invited some of his friends to join him for a short prayer service. Baylor, a graduate of Washington College and the University of Virginia, had been commonwealth attorney of Staunton at war's outset. He had served Jackson well since the spring days of 1861 at Harpers Ferry. He was commanding the 5th Virginia when Winder fell mortally wounded at Cedar Mountain; and for the ensuing weeks, Baylor had been commanding Jackson's old brigade while awaiting promotion to brigadier general.

Chaplain Abner Hopkins opened the August 29 nighttime religious service. Baylor and Captain Hugh White of Lexington led the small group in prayer. Everyone in attendance knew that the already-thin ranks would be thinner if battle resumed on the morrow.[72]

Jackson's headquarters throughout the Second Manassas battle was alongside a large haystack behind the Rockbridge Artillery. He returned there after Hill's final repulse of the Federals. Jackson was standing by a campfire, finishing the supper that Jim Lewis had prepared, when Surgeon McGuire arrived with the casualty lists. It had been a bloody day, he reported. Hill had suffered 1500 losses; Gregg had 620 casualties. The 13th South Carolina had lost half of its strength. General Trimble was wounded and lost for an indefinite period. Generals Charles Fields, Dorsey Pender, and James J. Archer plus Colonel Henry Forno had been injured.[73]

McGuire continued the customary rundown of casualties. Jackson listened expressionless until McGuire revealed that among the mortally wounded now dead was Private William C. Preston of the 4th Virginia, the headquarters guest a couple of days before. Jim Lewis howled in agony and began rolling on the ground. Jackson's face stiffened, McGuire noticed. "The muscles were twitching convulsively and his eyes were all aglow. He gripped me by the shoulder till it hurt me, and in a savage, threatening manner asked why I left the boy. In a few seconds he recovered himself, and turned and walked off into the woods alone."[74]

Grief, death—lifelong companions—now visited Jackson anew. He thought of beloved family and friends in Lexington. John Lyle, Mrs. Junkin, Ellie, the stillborn son, his daughter whose life had been so short, now sweet little Willie—all gone. The loss of young ones hurt the most. It took Jackson awhile to regain his composure.

He returned to headquarters, where he joined McGuire and others seated around a campfire. Jackson accepted a rare cup of coffee. The young surgeon knew that no words of consolation would help the general, so he arose and dutifully continued the report of casualties. McGuire finally completed the list. A moment's silence ensued; then McGuire commented, "General, we have won this battle by the hardest kind of fighting." Jackson looked up with a childlike expression and said gently but with a firm undertone, "No, no, we have won it by the blessing of Almighty God."[75]

Later, in a note to his friends John and Maggie Preston, the general confessed: "I deeply sympathize with you all in the death of dear Willy. He was in my first Sabbath school class, where I became attached to him when he was a little boy. I had expected to have him one of my aides-de-camp, but God in His providence has ordered otherwise."[76]

When the day's fighting was nearing its end, Lee had asked Jackson to come to army headquarters at his convenience to discuss the situation. It was around 9 P.M. when Jackson arrived. Lee was not there. Captain Charles Venable of Lee's staff thought Jackson looked so weak and overcome by the need for sleep that the aide put Jackson in Venable's tent on a couch. Jackson was soon in a deep sleep. Lee returned shortly, learned of Jackson slumbering heavily, and ordered that he not be disturbed. Thus did Jackson, by order of his chief, get a rare night of uninterrupted and needed rest.

The next morning—Saturday, August 30—Jackson began with prayers. He ate a quick breakfast before starting a lengthy conversation with Lee. Then he returned to his lines to await developments.[77] The first hours of daylight were hot, dry, and still. Around 8 A.M., Federal artillery began an hour of desultory firing.

It became quiet again. Jackson had ordered his men during the night to pull back into the woods for better concealment. When Federal skirmishers on Saturday morning found the Confederate line of the previous day deserted, Pope became more convinced than ever that the Southern force had retreated.

Jackson rode to the right sector of his line because enemy artillery seemed concentrated on Starke's position. When Jackson arrived there, massed Federals were visible in woods to the east and apparently poised for battle. Yet Jackson was not convinced that an attack would occur. He conferred quickly with Colonel Baylor, commanding the Stonewall Brigade. As Jackson and his staff were departing, the general said, "Well, Colonel Baylor, it looks as if there will be no fight today, but keep your men in line and ready for action." Baylor smiled and gave his usual friendly salute.[78]

The continued silence on the field, plus simple curiosity on Jackson's part, prompted him to return to Lee's headquarters. Longstreet and Stuart were already there. A Louisiana artillerist nearby watched the four generals engage in earnest conversation. Jackson caught his eye above the others. He "was dressed in a sort of grey homespun suit, with a broken-brimmed hat, and looked like a good driving overseer or manager, with plenty of hard, horse sense, but no accomplishments or other talent—nothing but plain, direct sense. It was because his manners had so little of the air of a man of the world, or because he repressed all expression that he had the appearance of being a man of not above average ability. The remark was then made by one of us, after staring at him for a long time, that there must be some mistake about him—if he was an able man he showed it less than any man any of us had ever seen."[79]

On the previous day, Lee had been anxious to press the attack to its final issue. Now an offensive was secondary in his thinking. Lee was apprehensive that McClellan or other reinforcements might have strengthened Pope's hand during the night. The Confederates would wait and watch for Union developments.

Lee hoped for a resumption of Union assaults, confident that Jackson would maintain his battered line. Lee could then close the jaws of his two wings. Should Pope fail to initiate action, Lee would repeat the Rappahannock plan: have Longstreet rivet Pope's attention while Jackson swung around the Union right flank.

Few changes were made early on the 30th in the Southern dispositions. Jackson asked for no reinforcements in spite of his losses. The one support he got was a battalion of twenty-two guns under Colonel Stephen D. Lee. They unlimbered on high ground beyond Starke's flank and at right angles to the line of battle. With the cannon pointing northeast, Lee commanded an enfilade field of fire over a mile in length.

Morning hours passed. The silence continued. Jackson's men, supplied with rations and ammunition, lounged in the woods. Laughter coursed up and down the ranks as Johnny Rebs swapped jokes—mostly about Pope. The only noise came from occasional picket shots, artillery and caissons creaking in the distance, the constant movement of Federal infantry.

Not even the Union soldiers knew what they were supposed to be doing. A Massachusetts officer declared, "We spent the first half of the day in marching back and forth in an aimless sort of way, occasionally halting as if waiting for some one to put us on the right road."[80]

Noon came and went. Preparations were audible from the Union side, but no gunfire erupted. Federals seemed to be massing in three heavy lines in front of Starke. Around 2 P.M., Jackson made another inspection of his right. He ordered the Rock-bridge Artillery to open on some Union guns pointing menacingly at Starke's lines. The valley gunners sent shells squarely on target, and the Union pieces rapidly withdrew. Jackson nodded. Instead of the usual "Good, good," Jackson practically made a speech. "That was handsomely done, very handsomely done," he told the young artillerymen.[81]

When Lee asked Jackson what the enemy was doing in his front, Jackson responded dryly, "So far, the enemy appear to be trying to get possession of a piece of woods to withdraw out of sight."

That was logical, but it was not John Pope's reasoning. Jackson ought to be withdrawing, he thought; therefore, Jackson was withdrawing. So Pope lit a cigar and, with General Irvin McDowell, "spent the morning under a tree waiting for the enemy to retreat," an aide said.[82]

Seeing no need to make a reconnaissance for verification, Pope at noon ordered his army to move forward "in pursuit of the enemy and press him vigorously during the whole day." Fitz John Porter's corps would sweep around Jackson's right flank and try to cut off the retreat route while the rest of the Union army would advance straight forward in triumph. Two impediments blocked Pope's intentions: Jackson was not falling back, and Longstreet's half of the Confederate army stood in Porter's way.

Jackson returned to the vicinity of the Rockbridge Artillery, dismounted, and sat on a fence rail near the Lexington battery. In the two hours it took Pope to put his army in position for the grand advance, Jackson dozed, chatted with his staff, and stared silently in the distance.

It was almost 3 P.M. when a single Federal cannon broke the stillness. "That's the signal for a general attack!" Jackson shouted as he bolted for his horse.

Almost by reply, loud explosions of Union musket fire came toward the right of the Confederate line. Staff members followed as Jackson galloped toward Starke's position. The roar of cannon fire and musketry gained battle intensity before Jackson reached the sector.

His arrival was somewhat delayed because he was riding a small bay that had been captured the day before. The animal balked as Jackson neared the action, apparently frightened by the noise. Jackson dismounted and told Douglas to swap horses with him. The aide was then directed to find Longstreet and apprise him of the situation on the right.

Jackson leaped onto Douglas's saddle. The stirrups were too long, so he rode away with his legs hugging the horse. Douglas, meanwhile, had to stop in his ride and adjust Jackson's saddle to prevent his knees from hitting his face.[83]

At Starke's position, Jackson beheld some 12,000 Federals—thirty-seven regiments in all—in assault formation that extended a mile and a quarter from Groveton to near Bull Run. It was an awesome sight: battle lines in full array, flags rolling lazily above gleaming bayonets, soldiers maintaining a determined pace. The whole panorama was a picture of how men dream of war. Behind the attack lines, thousands of other Federals stood en masse on the ascending ground in the rear. Numerous Union batteries had eased into position to cover the advance. Yet the Federal attack columns faced intimidations.

The ground in front was open, with no cover except slight swells here and there. As Pope would learn, Stephen Lee's twenty-two guns dominated every square foot of the Union left and center. Further, the unfinished railroad angled away from Porter's planned advance. Union soldiers there would have to advance 600 yards, the last 150 uphill. Moreover, as soon became painfully evident, Union artillery support for the attack would be so weak and uncoordinated as to be all but nonexistent.

All of Stephen Lee's guns sent shells ripping into the advancing blue ranks. Starke's infantry division was in two battle lines. The first occupied the railroad path; the second and heavier line contained the Stonewall Brigade and was 200 yards to the rear along the edge of a woodland.

Ezra Stickley of the 5th Virginia never forgot the first attack. "The Federals came up in front of us suddenly as man rising up out of the ground, showing themselves at the old railroad line opposite our line in double battle phalanx and coming forward in slow time, pouring their shot into our ranks in unmerciful volume. . . . In our front the enemy numbered about five to one of us as the lines confronted each other."[84]

Smoke and gunfire quickly obliterated the dramatic pageantry of the Union assault. The 33d Virginia's John Casler noted: "It was one continuous roar from right to left. My brigade was in a small cut, with a field in front sloping down about four hundred yards to a piece of woods. The enemy would form in the woods and come up the slope . . . as regular as if on drill, and we would pour volley after volley into them as they came; but they would still advance until within a few yards of us, when they would break and fall back to the woods, where they would rally and come again."[85]

Federals surged ahead, endured gaps blown in their ranks by concentrated musketry, and continued pressing forward. In spite of mounting losses, Pope's soldiers bravely rolled toward Jackson's position like a massive blue wave. An Alabama soldier expressed amazement that "we dotted the ground with them, but others were sent to take their places. . . . No amount of killing and wounded we could do would check them."[86]

All the while, Stephen Lee's cannon were sending shells crashing through the thickets and into the Union ranks. Pope's lines, one by one, were shattering like glass, but the fragments kept surging forward. In some places, Federal battle flags stood alone, planted in the ground sometimes as close as ten feet from the Confederate positions. Many Southern soldiers, out of ammunition, had again thrown rocks in an effort to stall the Union assault. Jackson's whole line was now fighting desperately. The battle was gallantry versus heroism.[87]

Starke's front line began to crumple. The Stonewall Brigade moved up into the action and promptly began taking casualties. Colonel Will Baylor saw that Jackson's old unit was faltering. On foot, he took the colors from a fallen bearer and dashed to the head of the brigade. "Boys! Follow me!" he yelled as loud as he could. Baylor then rushed forward a short distance before collapsing to the ground, riddled with bullets.

The Virginians began retiring in some confusion. Captain Hugh White dashed ahead. Like Baylor, he too grabbed a regimental flag and called on the men to rally around him. Only a handful did so. White disappeared into the battle smoke. A few moments later, his body could be seen face down on the ground. The flag covered him like a shroud.

Senior Colonel Andrew Grigsby of the 27th Virginia now took command of the Stonewall Brigade. He ordered it forward across 200 yards of open ground to the railroad cut. The men made it, though they left dozens of bodies on the field. Survivors patched a breach in Starke's line. Now Grigsby needed help to hold the position. He sent Captain Ezra Stickley to appeal personally to Jackson.

Stickley found the commander and had to shout above the din of battle in an effort to be heard. He told Jackson that Baylor was dead, the old brigade battered and in need of reinforcements. Jackson, with his hearing impairment, did not absorb everything that was said. "What brigade, sir?" he shouted. "The Stonewall Brigade!" came the response. Jackson then exclaimed: "Go back, give my compliments to them and tell the Stonewall Brigade to maintain her reputation!" Stickley saluted and turned dejectedly to leave minus any assurance of help. Jackson stopped him. Perhaps the general realized that inspiration alone would not carry this day. "Go tell Grigsby to hold his position for a short time," he told Stickley, "and I will send Pender's brigade to his assistance in ten minutes."[88]

The men in Jackson's old brigade cheered lustily when told of their general's concern. Pender soon came into view at the head of his brigade. Yet the fire his men received as they approached the area was so heavy that the regiments withdrew. Jackson's division would have to hold its own. That was tenuous. Starke's lines had taken a pounding, Lawton's men in the center were maintaining their sector but doing little else, while Hill on the left was furiously trying to close a momentary break in his works made by heavy assaults.

Lines of Federals had been assailing Jackson's position for almost two hours. Confederate resistance was stretched to the utmost. "Our entire line was engaged in a fierce & sanguinary struggle with the enemy," Jackson acknowledged. "As one line was repulsed, another took its place & pressed forward as if determined by force of number & fury of assault to drive us from our positions. So impetuous and well sustained were these onsets as to induce me to send to the Commanding General for reinforcements."[89]

For almost thirty-six hours, Jackson alone had withstood a bloody hammering from the Army of Virginia. Unlike the previous day's combat, Jackson on August 30 had no uncommitted reserves. He needed help. His call for reinforcements was an urgent appeal made when no alternative existed.[90]

Lee started a full division to Jackson's aid and ordered Longstreet to unleash his half of the army. However, Longstreet reasoned that it would take time to dispatch infantry support to Jackson. Yet from his position Longstreet's artillery—pointing silently and directly into the left flank of Pope's assaulting forces—could do a more efficient job quicker. Longstreet sent three batteries to S. D. Lee with orders to open fire at once.

The blasts from these guns literally fragmented the second and third waves of Union attackers. Federals began fleeing the field in near panic. The first Union line, finding itself suddenly without support, broke off the attack and started back across the open field amid intense gunfire and loud yells from the Confederates.

One of Lee's gunners was awestruck as he watched the scene. "As shell after shell burst into the wavering ranks, and round shot ploughed broad gaps among them, you could distinctly see, through the rifts of smoke, the Federal soldiers falling and flying on every side. With the dispersion of the enemy's reserve, the whole mass broke and ran like a flock of wild sheep."[91]

Ten minutes later, Longstreet gave the long-anticipated signal. Almost 25,000 Southern infantry swept down the high ground and across the open expanse. Jackson was caught in the excitement. "Eagerly & fiercely did each Brigade press forward, exhibiting in parts of the field scenes of close encounter and murderous strife not witnessed often in the turmoil of battle. The Federals gave way before our troops— fell back in disorder & fled precipitately, leaving their dead & wounded on the field. During the retreat the Artillery opened with destructive power upon the fugitive masses."[92]

Some Federals halted and tried to make a stand. However, a Pennsylvanian wrote, Confederate fire "came from so many directions that our men were at a loss how to return it effectively."[93]

A Northern correspondent wrote that the ragged and smoke-blackened Confederates "came on, like demons emerging from the earth." Victorious pandemonium exploded on the Southern side, one soldier exclaimed. Longstreet's battle line was moving forward; so was Jackson's; and as the two advanced in converging directions, the Confederates gained both strength and position. "The armies of Jackson and Longstreet dashed forward in the charge with yells and shouts, shooting as they ran, and the very heavens were rent with the shouts . . . The Federals gave way in both fronts, were routed and discomfited, and we pursued them for many miles, firing as long as it was necessary to make the victory complete."[94]

Because Jackson's men had done all of the Confederate fighting so far that day, it took awhile to unravel snarled alignments, reform units, and move forward. The whole line soon swept eastward in wheel-like fashion, Hill's troops moving out first.

Men in Lawton's division to the right heard loud yelling. Their initial reaction was one of anxiety. Then, an Alabama soldier wrote, "around the curve of the old R. R. a man on a horse was seen coming in a slow gallop, with head bare and a cap in his hand in acknowledgement of the cheers that were being given, and as he approached some one recognized him and shouted that's 'Stonewall' Jackson and we went wild with enthusiasm, throwing our hats into the air and giving the 'Rebel Yell' at the top of our voices. He came on top of the railroad embankment . . . followed by one courier. He was dressed in an old dusty, dingy, faded gray uniform with the legs of his pants stuffed in the legs of a coarse pair of boots. Three faded stars and a wreath that he wore upon the collar of his coat was the only mark that distinguished his greatness. He did not go far before he halted, and with raised cap in hand, he hollowed out at the top of his voice 'Attention.' All was ready in a moment, when he in a shrill voice commanded 'forward' and at the word we dashed over the embankment and moved on slowly and cautiously."[95]

In advance of most of the men, Jackson by chance came upon several Union stretcher bearers who had been captured while trying to get to the rear with some dead officers. Jackson stopped to question the men. As he did so, his eyes fell on one of the bodies. It was an old friend, Andrew Jackson Barney, the son of Dr. Lowry Barney, who had invited Jackson in 1851 to be his house guest during treatments for dyspepsia. Andrew Barney was serving as a major in the 24th New York when he was killed in one of the final assaults against Jackson's line.

The general felt a deep pang of sorrow. He ordered Barney's remains treated with all respect, and he directed that the body be returned to Union authorities. Later, Jackson sent a letter through the lines to Dr. Barney, who ultimately came to Virginia and took his son home.[96]

Racing sundown, the Confederates sought to gain the high ground at Henry House Hill (where Jackson had gained his nickname thirteen months earlier). Yet the effort failed. It took Jackson too long to get his broken units together and moving forward. Hence, he and Longstreet did not deliver a coordinated, two-pronged counterstroke on the withdrawing Federals.[97]

In truth, the overriding failure of Lee's army to rout the Federals late in the day was a problem that would always dog Lee: he could gain a victory, but he lacked the manpower to deliver a crushing blow that would destroy rather than merely defeat the enemy.

Rain came with the darkness, and the fighting died away more quickly than usual. Pope's Army of Virginia had suffered one of the worst Union beatings of the war. Ten thousand casualties had accomplished nothing. "Great God how humiliating," a Federal surgeon passionately told his wife. "I would resign today—if not for pure shame when we are so badly beaten. . . . Pope is sunk lower than Hell—where he belongs. . . . We look tomorrow to hear of Jackson's force destroying the Ohio and Baltimore RR—& perhaps taking Baltimore—& going in to Pennsylvania."[98]

A lieutenant in the 12th U.S. Infantry sought to be a bit upbeat when he confided in his journal: "It made things look rather blue and hazy ahead that we had not yet 'bagged Jackson.' Indeed it was reported more than once that we had him bagged; that all we had to do was pull the string. If that were so, either the string was never drawn, or there was a large hole in the bottom of the bag, and instead of bagging him he thrashed and nearly bagged us."[99]

Lee and the Army of Northern Virginia had come closer to destroying a Federal army than they ever would again. The Confederate commander had driven a second major Union force from Virginia in the short space of two months. Near the end of June, Richmond was on the verge of surrender; at the end of August, Washington was on the verge of a possible attack. The Civil War in the Old Dominion had turned completely around, and he who had wrought so startling a change—Lee—now was in control.

On the other hand, never in the war had there been a battle so protracted and so bloody. More than 3000 dead and 15,000 wounded lay on an eight-square-mile area. Jackson's command had taken frightful losses: 805 killed, 3547 wounded, and thirty-five missing. Ten of his regimental colonels had been killed or maimed. The regiments of the Stonewall Brigade were under captains and lieutenants. The only general officer in Jackson's division was its leader, General William Starke, and he appeared to one colonel as so brave and daring as to be "a marked man."[100]

Such was the cost of war, and Jackson had no control over what had to be spent in the quest for victory. Jackson the artillerist was pleased to report the capture of eight guns and caissons, along with 6520 small arms. Where the credit for success was concerned, he left no doubts in his official report: "For these great and signal victories our sincere and humble thanks are due to Almighty God. . . . In view of the arduous labors and great privations the troops were called to endure and the isolated and perilous position which the command occupied while engaged with greatly superior numbers of the enemy we can but express the grateful conviction of our mind that God was with us and gave us the victory, and unto His holy name be the praise."[101]

Second Manassas boosted Jackson to a level of respect equaled only by that for Lee in the Army of Northern Virginia. It had taken Old Jack three months to dissipate the doubts regarding his ability to perform well as a subordinate. The suspicions following the Seven Days Campaign were gone. Jackson had demonstrated unquestionably that he could cooperate as a trustworthy lieutenant as well as he could win spectacular successes as an independent commander.

Pope had competence beneath all that pomposity. Some of his corps commanders had first-rate talent. Yet Jackson's movements had initially dazzled them and then made them look foolish. Old Jack had deceived the Federals, outmaneuvered them, let them come close but never make contact until Jackson himself was ready to fight. Throughout late August, the hunter was unknowingly the prey. That is the stuff of which military genius is made.

At the same time, cooperation with Lee was solidifying into a single mind at work. Communications lacking in the Seven Days were now constant and unrestricted; relations between the two remarkably different personalities were smooth and harmonious. No further lack of understanding would develop between them. Among all of Lee's compatriots, Jackson was now the most understanding and the most reliable.

In their union was also a seedbed of success that gave inspiration to the Confederate cause. A Richmond socialite wrote succinctly, "The two great Virginians seemed to be riding on a wave of popular glory."[102]

To the Federals, Jackson had become mystical—a ghostlike, shadowy figure who popped up anywhere and created terror. To a New Yorker, Jackson had become "our national bugaboo." A Union soldier wrote after talking to some Maryland citizens, "The greatest horror is entertained of Jackson whom they seem to regard as a species of demon." Fears now existed of Jackson suddenly striking for Harrisburg or Philadelphia. Union General John W. Geary told his wife in Pennsylvania, "Escape if you can, for he is a cold blooded rascal."[103]

A Richmond editor observed that in the Southern victories of summer 1862, "there is one name which, in a few months, had mounted to the zenith of fame; which in dramatic associations, in rapid incidents, and in swift and sudden renown, challenged comparison with the most extraordinary phenomena in the annals of military genius." That individual was "the most remarkable man in the history of the war." His name was Jackson.[104]

Rain was still falling when daylight came on August 31. The all-night downpour increased weariness in the ranks. All roads save the Little River Turnpike were mudstreams. Bull Run was rising fast. Retreating Federals had destroyed the major bridges over the stream. Though Pope still outnumbered Lee, his army was retreating. An opportunity might arise for Lee to strike again. However, care would have to be exercised in any new offensive—particularly since McClellan's whereabouts were still unknown.

The odor of death hung in the Manassas air like a fog. Battlefield sights startled even the most hardened of Jackson's soldiers. Rain pelted the bodies of dead and wounded men. Debris—weapons, knapsacks, blankets, pieces of uniform, discarded equipment—covered a wide expanse. "I never saw so many dead Yankees before in my life," North Carolina private Nathan Snead wrote. "Ned" Moore of the Rockbridge Artillery asserted that three-fourths of the Federals who made the final charge the previous day were lying neatly in line where they had fallen. "I could have walked a quarter of a mile in almost a straight line on their dead bodies without putting a foot on the ground," Moore declared.[105]

Assistant Surgeon Harvey Black of the Stonewall Brigade wrote his wife that Sunday. "It makes my heart sad to think how this Brigade has struggled to maintain its fair reputation—how its brave men have been mowed down and that today it paraded under but one [regimental] flag instead of 5." Black stated that he and a helper had 225 men in their care. He openly conceded, "This is more than we can attend to, to do them justice."[106]

With Pope's rear guard alert and waiting on the north side of Bull Run, Lee paused on the morning of August 31 to weigh his options. Jackson put part of that time to personal use. Early on his agenda were letters of condolence to friends for whom Second Manassas had left an empty place on the hearthstone. Doubtless Jackson began with a message to his pastor, Dr. William S. White, over the loss of his son Hugh. He also wrote Dabney about the loss of young White. "His Christian labors were not confined to times of peace. In the army he adorned the doctrine of Christ his Savior. When Testaments or other religious works were to be distributed, I found him ready for the work. Though his loss must be mourned, yet it is gratifying to know that he has left us a bright example, and that he fell, sword in hand, gallantly cheering on his men."[107]

Another letter went to the 33d Virginia's Colonel Frederick Holliday, who was recuperating at his Winchester home after losing an arm at Cedar Mountain. "Baylor & Neff both fell at Manassas within a few hundred yards of each other though on different days," Jackson noted. "Their deaths comported well with their patriotic devotion to our cause. Their names should be held in gratified remembrance by us who have been privileged survivors, and by all who admire patriotic devotion to civil & religious liberty. I have reason to believe that both of them have entered into that rest which remaineth for the people of God."[108]

Douglas alleged that Jackson in the course of the day visited several hospitals for captured Federal soldiers. If he did, it was the only known instance in the war when this occurred. Jackson would have been more apt to call on wounded Confederates, but such activity on the morning of August 31—in the lull between movements and possible fighting—was out of character for Jackson.[109]

Sometime in midmorning, Lee and Jackson rode across Bull Run to reconnoiter. They drew enemy fire by doing so. Yet they were able to learn that with the Stone Bridge destroyed, the only way to pursue Pope was to use a roundabout route. That was not promising of success. However, some such attempt had to be made if Pope were to be trapped before reaching the Washington fortifications.

Jackson must make another circuitous march, Lee concluded. He was nearest Pope's flank and moved faster than Longstreet. The route would be across Bull Run at Sudley Springs, due north to the Little River Turnpike, then southeast on that road to the Federal line of retreat near Fairfax Court House. At the least, Jackson's march would force the evacuation of Centreville. While Jackson was engaged in his turning movement, Longstreet would clean up the battlefield—bury the dead, send the wounded to hospitals, collect equipment—and then follow Jackson.

Lee outlined the plan to his silent lieutenant. It was the Sabbath, following for Jackson three days of combat. The Lord deserved a day of thanksgiving. Such thoughts Jackson kept to himself. When Lee finished his instructions, Jackson mumbled "Good," left the tent without even a smile, and rode back to his troops.

The men were in no condition to make another forced march. It was still raining, and the roads were quagmires. "We needed rest," an Alabama officer remarked, "but the tide of victory if taken at the flood it was hoped would lead on to fortune. So Jackson set his corps in motion."[110]

The foot cavalry drew rations for the first time in three days before taking the road in pouring rain. Just as Jackson's march was getting underway, Pope at Centreville sent a message to his war department: "We shall fight to the last. . . . The plan of the enemy will undoubtedly be to turn my flank. If he does so he will have his hands full." Pope was full of bluster again because he had heard that Ewell was dead, Jackson badly wounded, and "other generals of lesser note" knocked out of action.[111]

In early afternoon, the head of Jackson's column waded across Bull Run at Sudley Springs Ford and headed north on a "road" that was actually a river of mud. The men were bushed, but they plodded ahead. One observer wrote ruefully, "Truly Jackson was the most restless leader the world ever saw, and he seemed to have very little consideration for the bones and sinews of his men."[112]

That was not so. Jackson cared deeply about the well-being of his army. Its performance depended on its condition. Such thinking brought Jackson into another clash with Powell Hill. The division commander had done much at Manassas to redeem himself in Jackson's eyes. On this wet Sunday, Hill's division was in the lead. Its commander, perhaps still smarting from being accused of dragging his feet en route to Cedar Mountain, set a rapid pace through the afternoon. On one occasion, Jackson ordered Hill to slow down. A couple of hours later, Hill was proceeding so swiftly through the mud that he was leaving stragglers in his wake. Jackson made a mental note of these new instances of neglect of duty by the commander of his largest division.

On into the night the column moved. When it reached the Little River Turnpike near Pleasant Valley Church, Jackson called a halt. The troops had covered ten miles in eight hours under the worst of circumstances. That was enough. Getting in Pope's rear would have to wait until another day.[113]

The night was miserable. Rain continued to fall. Supply wagons were trapped in mud several miles behind the infantry. No food was available; most spring water was contaminated by the rain. By then, bodies were numb from fatigue. Jackson took refuge in a small farmhouse near the church and managed to get a few hours' sleep amid the unknowns of this attempt to flank a superior army.

September 1 dawned with still more rain. The downpour stopped around 8 A.M., but the clouds remained heavy. Before resuming the march, Jackson sent a brief letter to Anna."We were engaged with the enemy at and near Manassas Junction Tuesday and Wednesday, and again near the battle-field of Manassas on Thursday, Friday, and Saturday; in all of which God gave us the victory. May He ever be with us, and we ever be His devoted people, is my earnest prayer. It greatly encourages me to feel that so many of God's people are praying for that part of our force under my command."[114]

Just as Jackson was preparing to start the day's march, Stuart arrived at headquarters. He reported a heavy line of Federals astride the turnpike at Germantown, two miles northwest of Fairfax. Jackson had expected some kind of obstacle and was not unduly concerned. He ordered his men to proceed down the turnpike.

The troops were in no condition to display Christian attributes that day. Hotchkiss (who had just returned to duty with Jackson and who was preparing maps as fast as he could draw) noted that the soldiers "were very bad, stealing everything eatable they could lay their hands on, after trying to buy it. They were nearly famished."[115]

Slowly, the troops wound through mud toward Fairfax, struggling too much with gnawing hunger and heavy weariness to realize—or care—that they were barely a day's march from the Northern capital. Of more immediate concern were small parties of Federal cavalry sniping at Jackson's right flank. They did no damage, but their presence told Jackson that his march was no longer a secret.

It also increased the odds against his making a dent in Pope's retreating army. The Union commander was now aware of Jackson's approach from the northwest. Lee had directed that Jackson avoid battle until the two halves of the army could reunite. Longstreet was ten miles behind. So Jackson halted his long column. The general dismounted and found a tree where the ground was not too wet. He sat with his back to the trunk, folded his hands over his chest, and went instantly to sleep.[116]

By noon, Longstreet was within two or three miles of Jackson. The foot cavalry resumed their advance. A march of about three miles took the head of the column past the beautiful mansion, Chantilly, and on to where the turnpike crossed Ox Road. Stuart's horsemen met Jackson at the intersection and reported Federals immediately in front.

Jackson unloosed a heavy skirmish line to test the enemy position. Gunfire exploded; the Confederates returned it. Federals were in battle line, and they were waiting for Jackson.

At this point, Jackson had gained much at little cost. The element of surprise was gone, but his position at Ox Hill would force Pope to abandon Centreville and fall back at least to Fairfax. No advantage existed in starting combat. Jackson would wait for Lee and Longstreet before proceeding farther.

Federals were not going to oblige. Around 4 P.M., General Isaac Stevens's division of the IX Corps advanced on Jackson. Other Federal units moved into a line of battle. Jackson had not expected an attack, but he would not run away from it.

He quickly deployed his divisions on the south side of the turnpike, facing more to the south than perpendicular to the road. Hill was on the right, Lawton in the center, Starke on the left. Jackson arranged his artillery north of the turnpike. The guns were useless as support for an assault in the heavily wooded area, but they would provide cover in the event of a Confederate withdrawal. Little time was lost in making these dispositions, for the enemy seemed intent on making a big fight of it.

Union numbers appeared heaviest in Hill's front, so Jackson ordered the brigades of Lawrence Branch and John M. Brockenbrough to probe the enemy's position. Just as the two units moved forward, a driving rain swept over the field into the faces of the Confederates.

For the next two hours, some of the most bizarre fighting of the war took place. Branch's North Carolinians broke the Federal line and sent enemy soldiers scurrying through woods and out into a field. At the edge of the woods, Branch halted. His men could barely see through the rainstorm, Federal fire was coming from two directions, and Branch's soldiers were running low on ammunition.

The brigadier alerted Hill to his predicament. Hill told Branch to maintain his position even if he had to do it with the bayonet. That was not mere bravado on Hill's part. Rain had drenched everything, including gunpowder. Muskets were momentarily useless. Hill sent an aide to Jackson informing the commander that the ammunition was wet.

Surgeon McGuire was with Jackson when the courier arrived. The general was doubled up on his horse so that his rubber poncho would shed the water over the top of his boots. Jackson's kepi was drawn down even more than usual. In that position, he received Hill's message.

McGuire asserted that "there was always danger and blood" when Jackson began a terse sentence with "Give my compliments . . . " Now such a sentence came forth from beneath the dripping kepi. "Give my compliments to General Hill," Jackson said, "and tell him that the Yankee ammunition is as wet as his and to stay where he is."[117]

Brockenbrough's brigade, meanwhile, had been driven back. That left Branch isolated. Pieces of his brigade began to break off around the edges, but the bulk of the Carolinians fought desperately along the tree line. Hill sent three more brigades into the action, including a portion of Lawton's command. "The conflict now raged with great fury," Jackson stated, "the enemy obstinately & desperately contesting the ground."[118]

Confederates refused to give way. The battle line twisted into an arc as men struggled in rain and mud, bullets slapping against wet leaves and ricocheting off drenched tree trunks with strange noises. Both sides were experiencing confusion in the unnatural environment.[119]

Early in the battle, Federal General Stevens fell dead while leading his former New York regiment in a charge. Toward the end of the contest, New Jersey's most distinguished soldier also met his end. General Philip Kearny became enraged with the passion of battle and inadvertently rode into Jackson's lines. He was killed instantly. The deaths of Stevens and Kearny caused the Federals to break off the engagement. Withdrawal continued after nightfall. Rain was pouring so hard that the Confederates did not know of the retirement.

Each side lost about 500 men in the brief but savage struggle near Chantilly. Jackson especially regretted his losses because they resulted from a contest he never wanted to wage, a contest that offered little if any rewards. If his advance had not been stopped earlier in the day, Jackson would not have opened battle until Longstreet arrived as per Lee's orders.

Chantilly cost the Union superb field commanders. Two days of hard fighting at Manassas had produced no general officer fatalities on the Union side. At Chantilly, two general officers were lost in two hours. For both sides, the engagement was a bloody, totally unnecessary collision.

By the morning of September 2, the great second campaign of Manassas had ended. Most of Virginia was clear of major Federal threat. Pope's battered army had passed Fairfax and was heading to the safety of Washington. Jackson surveyed the situation and supposedly cried, "Behold what God hath wrought!"[120]

Lee's army rested that Tuesday. Soldiers were too jaded to rejoice over their achievements. "We had been marching and fighting ever since we gave battle on August 9," Mercer Otey of the Rockbridge Artillery declared, "so that we had nothing but what remained on our backs. We were hungry and dirty and lousy, and the skin was visible through our flannel or jean shirts." John Shealy of the 47th Alabama was in shock from his brief service under Jackson. "My dear," he wrote his wife, "I tell you a soldier in Jacksons army has got no time to write. . . . If he can only address his wife he is Satisfied to close and retire to bed immediately."[121]

Jackson went to army headquarters that day and received what even for his stoic nature was a shock. Lee had been seriously injured and was in obvious, intense pain. On the previous day, the commander had tripped while reaching for the reins of his horse. Lee instinctively extended both hands to cushion the fall to the ground, breaking a bone in his left hand and severely spraining the right wrist. Both extremities were placed in splints and treated with liniment. For the next several days, Lee would be forced to ride in an ambulance.[122]

That became more of a handicap because Lee was about to undertake the most daring gamble of his military career. Although some historians criticize Lee for the fact that his subsequent campaign led to the bloodiest single day in American history, that was not an inevitability at the outset. Actually, as Lee explained to Jackson, he reached his decision by narrowing his choices.

Attacking the fixed defenses of Washington, where not one but two Union armies were concentrating, was out of the question. Nor could Lee sit back and wait for either Pope or McClellan to reorganize and, at some future date, come out against him. Such a wait was impracticable, for war had stripped northern Virginia of all foodstuffs. Any Confederate march to the west, east, or south would give up much of what had been gained. It would also permit a renewal of Union pressure first in central Virginia and ultimately against Richmond.

Therefore, and by elimination, Lee determined to take the Civil War into the enemy's country. By striking deep into the North, Lee desired first to occupy Hagerstown, Maryland, the southern terminus of the Cumberland Valley Railroad. From there, he next hoped to march all the way to Harrisburg, Pennsylvania. At that place, Lee could destroy two more railroads, level bridges across the mighty Susquehanna River, and sever the main east-west connections for the Union.

Everyone in the Confederate high command knew that the Army of Northern Virginia was not in good shape. It was limping noticeably from the Seven Days, Cedar Mountain, and Second Manassas Campaigns. Losses over the previous three months had exceeded 9000 men, and replacements were slow in arriving. Ammunition reserves were low, the commissary department was undependable at best, wagons were few and rickety. Soldiers resembled scarecrows; almost half of the men were without shoes. Yet morale seemed boundless.

Other factors gave Lee optimism about an invasion. Maryland was a sister state rather than enemy territory. There Lee might obtain supplies from districts untouched by war, as well as additional Maryland sons for the Confederate army. Certainly, the invasion would draw Federals away from Virginia and permit the Old Dominion to catch its breath while farmers gathered in the late-summer crops unmolested. The Federal army would have to pursue Lee, who could choose his battle site if or when the time came.

An overriding consideration, far above the military possibilities, also existed. Lee's two campaigns that summer had won for the Confederacy the admiration of the world. England and France were leaning toward granting recognition—and hence aid—to the Southern nation. Lord Russell, after reviewing Lee's successes in Virginia through the summer, remarked that it "really looks as if he might end the war."[123] Another victorious campaign, this time fought in the North, might bring the foreign assistance that many Southern leaders felt was the best assurance that the "Second American Revolution," like the first, would be triumphant. Moreover, a major victory on Union soil might provoke such a clamor in the North for peace as to bring an end to the war and independence to the South.

Longstreet opposed any invasion. If the army stayed together and waited, he argued (both then and later), "the Federals would not have dared attack."[124] Jackson approved Lee's strategy with unusual enthusiasm. He rushed to his headquarters at a farmhouse a mile west of Chantilly. Orders went forth for the men to march at early dawn. They would be informed later of their destination.

As Jackson sat down for supper late in the day, Stuart and Major von Borcke arrived. They shared Jackson's simple fare of cornbread and coffee. Jackson invited the cavalrymen to sleep for a few hours in his small fly-tent. Both were sleeping soundly when Von Borcke felt a hand on his shoulder. "Major, it is time to rise and start," a voice in the darkness said gently. The figure than placed a basin of water and a towel on a stool near von Borcke's head. "Now, Major," the man said, "wash quickly. A cup of coffee is waiting for you, your horse is saddled, and you must be off at once." The Prussian then realized that his "servant" was Jackson. "The light touch had been given by the iron hand, and the soft voice was that which had been heard . . . amid the tumult of battle." Von Borcke added: "I shall never forget the smile that broke over his kindly face at my amazement in recognizing him."[125]

An hour or so later, at dawn on Wednesday, September 3, the Army of Northern Virginia started northwest toward Leesburg and a crossing of the Potomac. Jackson's divisions were in the lead. What the general had wanted for seventeen months—invasion of the North—was at last about to unfold.

Virginia residents had no inkling of what was getting underway, but the editor of the Lexington newspaper developed an appropriate theory.

While Gen. Lee is undoubtedly the greatest strategist of the age, Gen. Jackson certainly deserves the first rank in one most important respect. He was the first of our commanders who discarded the use of spade and pick. He was the first to discover that breast-works were useless to our army, and he therefore inaugurated a new system of warfare—the active, aggressive system. His plan has always been to attack the enemy whenever and wherever he could find him. The consequence has been that his army has become a terror to the foe wherever its advancing tread is heard.

Another important result is, that other generals have imitated his example, and consequently, our whole army has become an army of veterans who are not afraid to measure swords with the enemy upon his own soil.[126]

☀ 20 ☀
DEATH AROUND A DUNKER CHURCH

O N SEPTEMBER 3, 1862, Anna Jackson wrote a close friend, Elizabeth Smith Brown, in Richmond. Anna did not know her husband's whereabouts, but she considered herself a good judge of his thoughts. "I trust & pray the war may soon be over," she declared. "I think my husband has strong hopes that it will end before the close of the year, but he has always been one of the sanguine, hopeful spirits."[1]

Those spirits were high as Jackson led Lee's army northwestward that day. The men at first had no idea where they were going. Surgeon James Boulware noted: "We were surprised when we took back over the road we came. Conjectures were made all along until we had gone I suppose 1 or 2 miles when we filed to the right. We then thought our destination was Maryland."[2]

The van of the long column passed through Dranesville before halting for the night near the farm of Mrs. Kate Carper. The widow offered Jackson the use of her home, but the general courteously declined. Adalbert Volck of Baltimore, a volunteer messenger whose Confederate errands often included blockade running, was delivering some papers in the area when he came upon Jackson's portion of the army. Volck saw Jackson chatting among a group of officers. The Marylander quickly pulled out a sketchbook and started to draw Jackson's likeness. "I was almost done with it," Volck noted, "when one of the officers pointed me out and Genl. Jackson looked around at me with a pleasant smile and turned away."[3]

That was the last recorded instance of Jackson smiling for the next couple of days. In fact, by sundown on the 3d the general was irritated. His faithful Little Sorrel had been lost or stolen. The cream-colored horse he was riding was a poor substitute. At the same time, straggling had become rampant throughout the day's march. Jackson always viewed a straggler and a sick soldier as one and the same: useless.

In a sour mood, he summoned his three division commanders to headquarters that night. Jackson directed Hill, Lawton, and Starke to set their watches by his timepiece. The commander then spelled out meticulously the details for the next day's movements. Because the day would likely be hot and dusty, the march would be tedious. Nevertheless, it was necessary to make as good a speed as possible in order to put distance between the Confederates and the Federals at Washington. The men were therefore to march at a specific hour; they were to walk fifty minutes and rest ten minutes each hour through the day. No excuses would be tolerated for breach of those orders.

Such directions, issued so pointedly, should have been implemented to the letter. Yet things went awry from the beginning. Jackson started up the road in the predawn hours of September 4 to accompany the lead elements of Hill's division. He found half of the Light Division still in camp. The men were making preparations without any coordination and seemingly oblivious to the fact that they were at least thirty minutes late starting the march. Hill was nowhere in sight.

Jackson galloped hotly in search of a brigadier. The first one he encountered was Maxcy Gregg, who had clashed with Jackson a month earlier not only over hungry soldiers taking apples from an orchard without authorization but also over men using fence rails for firewood in direct disobedience of orders. Gregg's men were not completely guilty; but Jackson thought so, and Gregg felt insulted. Now the general angrily demanded to know why Gregg's men were not marching. The South Carolina aristocrat haughtily replied that they were filling their canteens from nearby Sugarland Run. Jackson raised his voice for the benefit of the partially deaf Gregg—as well as all others within hearing—and snarled, "There are but few commanders who properly appreciate the value of celerity!"[4]

Gregg was fuming when his superior rode away. Jackson then went in search of Hill, who should have been riding along his column to ensure that it was well closed. Instead, Jackson learned that Hill had taken the point and advanced some 200 yards out of sight ahead of his column. Jackson rode to the front and found General Edward Thomas's Georgians setting the pace. Thomas was walking and leading his horse. Jackson dismounted and did the same, which raised less dust.

The time soon came for the ten-minute rest stop. When Thomas continued leading his men, Jackson ordered him to halt as instructed. The rest period expired, and Jackson directed that the march resume. Thomas's regiments had barely started when Hill and his staff came thundering down the road. Hill reined his horse in front of Thomas. Paying no heed to Jackson, Hill ordered Thomas to explain why he had halted. Thomas replied that he had been ordered to do so. Seething with rage, Hill rode up beside Jackson. The division commander whipped his sword from the scabbard and, turning the hilt toward Jackson, exclaimed: "I submit my resignation, sir!"

Jackson stymied his own anger, ignored the extended blade, and answered quietly: "General Hill, consider yourself under arrest for disobedience of orders." At that, Hill sheathed his sword and rode quickly toward the rear. Jackson summoned General Lawrence Branch and placed the senior brigadier in command of the Light Division. Jackson later reported with obvious satisfaction: "I found that under [Hill's] successor, Genl. Branch, my orders were much better carried out."[5]

It was afternoon when Jackson entered Leesburg from the east. He acknowledged cheers from townspeople and, at the county courthouse, turned right and led his men north a mile or so to Big Spring. It was one of the largest sources of fresh water in the area.

Jackson established his headquarters at the nearby home of George W. Ball. With the northward turn of the column, the soldiers now realized that they were going beyond the Potomac. Excitement coursed through the ranks.

Hill was already demanding a copy of the charges against him, but Jackson had no time to attend to such incidentals. He summoned the 1st Maryland's Colonel Bradley

T. Johnson (whom Jackson that day would recommend for promotion to brigadier general). Johnson was a native of western Maryland. In response to Jackson's query, Johnson presented a detailed description of the region and its people. "I impressed upon him emphatically," Johnson stated, that the citizens were equally divided in their sentiments between Union and Confederacy. The area would yield little material aid to Lee's army unless a Confederate occupation "promising at least some permanence" was forthcoming.[6]

After an early supper, Jackson asked Johnson to accompany him to Lee's headquarters and repeat the statement. The two officers rode into Leesburg to the Henry Harrison home, a three-story stately mansion just up North King Street from the courthouse. Johnson repeated to Lee what he had told Jackson. Lee asked several questions about population centers, topography, where resistance might be encountered. The conversation ended; both men looked at Jackson. To their amusement, the general was sitting bolt upright, sound asleep.[7]

Jackson met again with Lee on the morning of the 5th. Local legend has it that the two men also participated in a religious service in the front parlor of the Harrison home. Then Old Jack led his soldiers down a winding country lane toward the Potomac River. Hotchkiss observed that "all the officers and men of our command were joyous at the prospect and marched with a light step—fewer straggling than I almost ever saw."[8]

Hotchkiss was mistaken. Hundreds of Johnny Rebs balked at the idea of entering Maryland. They had enlisted to repel invaders, not to be invaders themselves. Many believed that not even war justified an intrusion on Northern property. In addition, lack of food, lack of shoes, plus new regimental and brigade commanders unfamiliar with how to keep a column solid on the march produced a steady shrinkage of the army.

Large numbers who walked away at Leesburg would return to duty after Lee entered Virginia. Yet their absence, along with that of thousands suffering from wounds, sickness, and exhaustion, reduced Lee's army to the weakest level it would be at any time in the war save in the final weeks. Barely 40,000 Confederates were heading for Maryland.[9]

White's Ford was the first destination. It was the best available crossing and not generally known to the Federals. D. H. Hill's division, momentarily attached to Jackson, led the march down a hill in columns of four and out into an open valley some 400 yards wide. The Potomac River was clearly visible at the far end. More important, the ford was unguarded. While the river was wide at that point, it was shallow. The ford traversed the Potomac somewhat obliquely, the path going over the tip of Mason's Island some two-thirds of the way across.

Soldiers who had shoes removed them, tied them together with the laces, and hung them around their necks. Men rolled trousers up to their knees. With muskets and equipment raised above their heads, they entered the Potomac. "The water did not part for us on either side, to enable us to cross on dry land," a soldier noted, "but we hit it up to our waist and we had to be careful to keep from falling down." Laughter and jokes filled the ranks. Each unit emitted "hearty cheers" as it stepped onto Maryland soil.[10]

A few Confederates were sobered by the grandeur of it all. Captain Thomas Pollock of Starke's staff confessed: "I never expect as long as I live to witness so imposing a spectacle. . . . As I . . . came up on the other bank & turned my horse & looked back at the long dark line stretching across the broad shallow river I felt I was beholding what must be the turning point of our struggle."[11]

Contrary to popular tradition, Jackson did not ride to midstream, remove his cap, and, while a band played "Maryland, My Maryland," cheer his men as they passed. Trouble developed too quickly at White's Ford for such lightheartedness—even if Jackson had been of that temperament. At the Maryland end of the ford, high bluffs stared down at the river. The trail therefore turned left for about 100 yards, crossed the Chesapeake and Ohio Canal, then curled up a defile to the high ground. Infantry had no problems, but in rapid order Jackson's wagon train became snarled at the base of the bluff. The traffic jam extended into the river, where mules and horses were enjoying cool water on a hot summer day.

Jackson summoned Major Harman to untangle the snarl. The Staunton quartermaster splashed into the water among the wagons, kicked stubborn mules, and poured out a volume of profanity "that would have excited the admiration of the most scientific mule-driver."[12] Frightened wagoners yelled at now-frightened mules, and the tie-up disappeared in amazingly short time.

Harman rode slowly up to Jackson, who had silently watched—and heard—everything. The major expected a stern lecture on his profanity. He sought to ease the reproof from Jackson by speaking first. "The ford is clear, General! There's only one language that will make mules understand on a hot day that they must get out of the water!" Jackson's lips twitched slightly. He said: "Thank you, Major," and rode into the river with his staff.[13]

It took most of the day for Jackson's three divisions to cross the Potomac. His objective was Buckeystown alongside the Monocacy River and the Baltimore and Ohio Railroad. He reached that point, but not without interruptions.

First there was a stop on the canal to enjoy a boat load of watermelons "which our men bought," Hotchkiss stated. The melons were fruit, and fruit was the one food that Jackson ate in abundance. Along the way north, citizens swarmed to greet Jackson—"most of them professing friendship and gratification at our coming," Hotchkiss reported.[14]

A field of ripe corn caught Jackson's eye. He ordered it purchased, with the ears issued to the men and the husks and stalks distributed to the animals. One unusually grateful Marylander told Jackson that he had the finest horse in the state and would feel deeply blessed if the general would accept the mount as a gift. The animal was a gigantic gray mare, heavy and awkward in comparison with the still-lost Little Sorrel. Jackson somewhat embarrassingly accepted the horse and tested her that evening. The animal shortly turned out to be a "trojan horse."[15]

Bivouac that night was at Three Springs, eleven miles south of Frederick. Jackson refused several invitations to stay in nearby homes and slept instead on the ground.

Saturday morning, September 6, broke pleasant and bright but quickly took a near-disastrous turn. Jackson mounted the new horse for the ride to Frederick. The animal did not want to move. Jackson touched her with a spur; at that, the mare reared straight up before losing her balance. Horse and rider fell heavily to the ground. Jackson admitted that he was injured "considerably." He lay on the ground a half-hour while surgeons made examinations. The general was stunned and bruised. He had acute pain but nothing seemed to be broken. For a few hours, he rode ingloriously in an ambulance.[16]

Thus did the Army of Northern Virginia enter Maryland with its three ranking generals injured: Lee in an ambulance with both hands in splints, Jackson nursing contusions, and Longstreet hobbling in a "wobbly carpet slipper" from a large heel blister.

Frederick was the principal city of western Maryland. Twenty-three miles north of White's Ford, and situated to the east of the mountains, this commercial center of 8000 residents had a number of attractions both civil and military. The famous National Road passed through it; the B&O was three miles to the south; all around it were farms reflective of the prosperity of a country heretofore untouched by war.

By the time the vanguard of the army reached the outskirts of Frederick, Jackson was mounted again. He could ride, but it was painful. As the long Confederate column started into town, some young girls hissed. Jackson turned to one of his staff. "We do not appear to have many friends here," he said with a slight smile. Soon, however, a class of twenty schoolchildren ran down the street beside him and waved handkerchiefs. Jackson removed his hat. The smile this time was broader.[17]

The general never passed the small home of Barbara Frietschie. This bit of folklore first introduced by poet John Greenleaf Whittier has since been thoroughly disproved.[18] Jackson's first directives were for the divisions of Lawton and Hill to make camps south of town in order to guard the railroad, the Monocacy River, and the major road approaches from Washington. The Stonewall Division was to pitch tents in the suburbs of Frederick. Jackson selected Colonel Bradley T. Johnson's Virginia brigade to be provost guard in town. It had strict instructions to maintain order.[19]

Frederick residents made the most of the military occupation. One soldier noted that he "was kindly greeted by the fair ladies and the majority of the people although some wore long faces." A member of Crenshaw's battery received no greetings from pretty damsels. After visiting Frederick, he declared, "I don't think I ever saw so many ugly women in all my life; the young ones were kept out of view for fear of fascinating some of the 'rebels,' I reckon." Staff officer Pollock commented: "The people receive us kindly & take our money & our army yesterday literally bought out the town. . . . I think we have many devoted friends to our cause here, but there is enough of the opposite element to make us feel something like invaders." As for the Confederate money that the soldiers used, a merchant concluded ruefully that the "notes depreciated the paper on which they were printed."[20]

Lee, Longstreet, and Jackson took quarters close to one another in Best's Grove, a grassy field on a hillside a mile southeast of Frederick. The army commander occupied the Trundle home. Jackson made his headquarters in a small tenant house nearby.

Dust covered and generally seedy, Jackson was not impressive at the time. A Louisiana gunner in Longstreet's command wrote, "Jackson looks as if wading the Potomac and other streams has in no wise improved his appearance." A popular joke outside Jackson's command alleged that the general had not changed his shirt since departing Lexington sixteen months ago.[21]

Another of Jackson's early acts at Frederick was an addition to his staff. James Power Smith, born in Ohio, was the son of a Presbyterian minister. Smith received degrees from Jefferson College and Union Theological Seminary prior to enlisting in 1861 in the Rockbridge Artillery. His close friendship with Professor Robert L. Dabney, plus the fact that his sister was married to a prominent Virginia clergyman, William Brown, helped sway his sentiments to the Confederacy. Smith's pursuit of a career as a Presbyterian minister no doubt attracted Jackson's attention and led to the appointment of the twenty-five-year-old as a lieutenant and aide.

Smith did not get off to a good start with Jackson. At Frederick, the young aide purchased a black mare that was not well broken. Smith conceded: "The first time I rode her beside General Jackson, she started and kicked at him, striking his foot. To the end of our life together, he thought I rode a kicking horse and invariably pulled away from me when I rode up to him."[22]

The sober-faced Smith described himself at the time as "slight and pale, with no experience of outdoor life." Yet in quick time he was one of Jackson's most trusted staff officers. James Graham, Jackson's minister friend in Winchester, observed that "there was something uncommonly beautiful in the attachment and confidence existing between these two men" in spite of their age difference. Jackson "regarded Smith as a brother and son, and Smith viewed Jackson almost as a father."[23]

To his discomfort, and from the moment he reached Frederick, Jackson found himself the center of attraction. Any officer who wore a plumed hat was mistaken for Jackson—particularly the Prussian giant, Major von Borcke. A Virginia soldier told his wife that "Jackson is next to Lee the favorite here and I think Jackson inspires more enthusiasm in the men than Lee."[24]

Neither general ventured forth too often from his headquarters. Lee's hands were still giving him much pain; Jackson, in addition to his usual shyness, remained sore from the fall. Those things did not stop Marylanders from flocking to Best's Grove to get a glance at the two famous generals, especially the man esteemed as "Stonewall." An English observer wrote: "Crowds were continually hanging around his headquarters, and peeping through the windows, as if anxious to catch him at his 'incantations,' for many believed he was in league with the Old Boy and had constant intercourse with him. Others actually thought that he was continually praying, and imagined that angelic spirits were his companions and councillors."[25]

Douglas enjoyed repeating the story of Jackson walking to Lee's headquarters one afternoon. "Two bright Baltimore girls" jumped from their carriage and waylaid the general. One grabbed his hand; the other threw her arms around him; both talked shrilly and without interruption. The ladies' ardor soon passed, whereupon they rode away. Jackson "stood for a moment cap in hand, bowing, speechless, paralyzed." He was so embarrassed by the incident that he remained in his quarters the rest of the day.[26]

September 7 was a hot and breezy Sunday. Jackson broke his rule about going to church in the morning. Too many details needed his attention. He instructed Hotchkiss to prepare several maps of western Maryland. For three days, Powell Hill, still under arrest, had requested a copy of Jackson's charges against him. The diplomatic Sandie Pendleton had been absent sick since Second Manassas; Major Frank Paxton of Lexington was serving as Jackson's assistant adjutant general (chief of staff). Paxton was an able and hard-working officer but one who could be heavy-handed in conversation and communication.

His response to Hill, on behalf of Jackson, was blunt. "Should the interests of the service require your case to be brought before a court martial a copy of the charges and specifications will be furnished in accordance with army regulation. In the meantime you will remain with your division."[27] That only increased Hill's anger.

Another personal confrontation broke the spirit of the Sabbath. This time it was with William E. Starke, the forty-eight-year-old brigadier who had won his general's rank solely on gallantry. He was a Virginian completely devoted to his Louisiana command. Some Frederick merchants complained that "foreign" Confederate soldiers had slipped into town, made purchases, and departed without paying for them. Jackson concluded that Starke's Louisianians were "bringing odium upon the army." He ordered Starke to march the Louisiana brigade into Frederick so that the guilty ones could be identified. Starke protested: this was an unfounded presumption of guilt. Jackson dismissed the objection, Starke refused to obey the order, and Jackson placed him under arrest.

Within a short period, Jackson learned that the soldier-thieves were members of his old Stonewall Brigade. He released Starke from arrest without apology. The brigadier returned to his command with smoldering resentment.[28]

That evening Jackson decided to venture into town and attend a church service. He ordered a bemused Douglas to secure a pass from Major Paxton for a party to go to Frederick. (Rules applied to everyone, Jackson insisted, even commanding officers.) Jackson took Douglas and Anna's brother, Lieutenant Joseph G. Morrison, with him. The Presbyterians were not meeting that night, so Jackson made his way to the brick, twin-turreted Evangelical Reformed Church in the center of town.

He took a seat near the back of the sanctuary. The Reverend Daniel Zacharias was a staunch Unionist and not awed in the least by the distinguished visitor in the congregation. Zacharias preached and then offered a prayer for the President of the United States. His brave act of defiance fell on deaf ears, Douglas wrote. Jackson "went to sleep as soon as the Dr. began, [and] I do not think he heard much of the sermon. His cap fell to the floor out of his hand & he did not awake until the commotion" at the end of the service.[29]

Inability to hear at the rear of the church was the excuse Jackson gave for falling asleep. He praised the minister, the building, and Frederick citizens. "Oh!" he exclaimed to Anna, "if such scenes could only surround me in Lexington, how my heart, under a smiling Providence, I trust would rejoice."[30]

The next day, Lee issued a proclamation to the people of Maryland. His army was in their midst, Lee said, primarily to free them from Federal control. Yet it was becoming increasingly obvious that the Confederate forces were not welcome in western Maryland. Food supplies, notably flour, were beginning to run low.[31] The volume of Maryland recruits for the army could not even be termed a dribble. Few civilians seemed disposed to aid Lee's army in any voluntary way.

Another concern was Harpers Ferry. As Lee advanced into Maryland, he expected Union authorities to order the 14,000 soldiers in garrisons at Harpers Ferry and nearby Martinsburg to withdraw rather than face isolation. In fact, Lee depended on that retirement. Confederate wagon trains would take the safer route northward down the Shenandoah Valley rather than through the Piedmont where cavalry on both sides ranged. Until the wagons arrived, Lee's army would have to forage for itself. Furthermore, Lee intended to use the valley as his main line for communication. When Union Chief of Staff Henry W. Halleck directed instead that the two garrisons remain where they were, Lee found himself in a military predicament.

He had three choices. He could ignore the Union garrisons and hope that the enemy would not cut his major supply line or disturb his wagons. This conclusion was unreasonable. Second, Lee could send forces to clear away the threats. Doing so, however, would sap Lee's already weakened army and make it more vulnerable to attack. The third and safest course would be to retire to the Old Dominion, a regression that would admit defeat before the invasion had proceeded much past the opening stage.

Early on September 8, Lee conversed with Brigadier General John G. Walker. A heavy-set career soldier without formal military education, the forty-year-old Missourian had seen little action thus far in the Civil War. Walker brought with him a reputation as a caring and courageous leader. Equally as important, Walker had brought as needed reinforcements a division of two brigades. Lee informed the brigadier that the Confederate drive into Maryland had produced great agitation in Washington. McClellan had been returned to command of all Union armies in the East and was in guarded pursuit thirty-five miles away.

Lee was not overly concerned about McClellan, he told Walker. The Northern commander "is an able general but a very cautious one," Lee said. "His enemies among his own people think him too much so. His army is in a very demoralized and chaotic condition, and will not be prepared for offensive operations—or he will not think it so—for three or four weeks."[32]

Still, the Union army was approaching; and nudged by an apprehensive War Department, McClellan might accelerate his movement. A few more days would certainly see the Army of the Potomac in the vicinity of Frederick. Lee had to take action, but he had time. McClellan was in command of the pursuing army.

Jackson, summoned by Lee, arrived at the headquarters tent. Lee quickly got to the point. Harpers Ferry must be neutralized. At that, Walker noticed, "Jackson seemed in high spirits, and even indulged in a little mild pleasantry about his long neglect of his friends in the Valley." Lee joined in the momentary levity. "You have 'some friends' in that region who will not, I fear, be delighted to see you." The three-way conversation continued for a few minutes. When it became plain that Lee wished to speak alone with Jackson, Walker found a reason to leave.[33]

Harpers Ferry must be taken quickly, Lee said, to keep his main southward route open. A force large enough to do the job should be sent, and sent quickly. That detachment ought to approach the ferry from different directions both to prevent the garrison from escaping and to block reinforcements coming to its aid. Three columns, moving independently, would approach the ferry from west, north, and east. Jackson would take command when the columns were within cooperating distance of each other. He would also have charge of final operations against the Federal garrison.

Lee then asked Jackson for his opinions. Very familiar with the area, Jackson replied that the surrounding heights had to be secured. Once that was done, artillery on the high ground could blast the Harpers Ferry defenders into submission. The two generals then turned to working out the details.

Jackson would take his three divisions and seal off the ferry from the western side. General Lafayette McLaws, commanding Richard H. Anderson's division, would move south along Elk Ridge to the southern end of Maryland Heights overlooking the ferry. Walker's small division would secure the top of Loudoun Heights on the south side of the Shenandoah River and south of the ferry. Further, General Fitzhugh Lee observed, "daring, skill, celerity, and confidence were the qualifications of an officer to execute the movement. In Jackson they were all combined."[34] Everyone involved knew but did not say that Jackson would also be in charge of a semi-independent expedition—where he seemed to perform best.

At that stage of the talks between Lee and Jackson, Longstreet arrived at headquarters. The tent flaps were closed when Longstreet inquired for the army commander. Lee, hearing Longstreet's voice, quickly invited him to enter. Longstreet was startled to learn that the two officers were planning a heavy, dangerous strike at Harpers Ferry and "both heartily approving it." The burly major general opposed the idea. Sending six full divisions on a sidetrack operation that had little to do with the grand offensive was risky if not foolhardy. At the least, it was dividing an already smaller army. Yet Longstreet discerned immediately that the plans were too advanced for him to be taken seriously. A day or so later, he would exclaim to Lee, "General, I wish we could stand still and let the damned Yankees come to us!" At the moment, however, Longstreet kept his counsel.[35]

What Longstreet would not admit was that the Harpers Ferry offensive was giving Jackson the kind of independent command that Longstreet craved. The jealousy in Longstreet did not show, but it was there. It was also in the ranks of his command. One of Longstreet's privates told the homefolk that Jackson "is the rudest and most arrogant pious man alive. . . . His army they say is a rabble."[36]

September 9 was warm and cloudy. With McClellan and the van of his army now twenty-five miles from Frederick, Lee drafted the directives for the segments of his army. Special Orders No. 191 carefully laid out the schedule for the components that would begin moving separately the following day. The directive included the troops not only of Jackson, McLaws, and Walker but also those of Longstreet, Hood, Harvey Hill, and Stuart.

Jackson's assignment was embodied in the third paragraph. "The army will resume its march tomorrow taking the Hagerstown road. Genl Jackson's command will form the advance and after passing Middletown, with such portion as he may select take the route toward Sharpsburg cross the Potomac at the most convenient point and by Friday morning [September 12] take possession of the Baltimore & Ohio Railroad, capture such of the enemy as may be at Martinsburg and intercept such as may attempt to escape from Harper's Ferry." Jackson was then to reunite with the main army at Boonsboro.[37]

Part of Longstreet's men would accompany Lee to Hagerstown. The rear guard would be Harvey Hill's division. It would screen Lee's movements to the west of the 1300-foot South Mountain. The National Road and two adjacent passes on either side of it were Hill's primary responsibilities.

Two aspects of the Confederate strategy were shaky from the outset. Lee was dividing his army into four components, with three of them heading independently for Harpers Ferry. Each of the three columns would be eight to ten miles from the other until the end. Jackson and Lee would be twenty miles apart, with the Potomac River between them. The fourth component of the Southern army would stand at Boonsboro.

Lee was placing a tight three-day timetable on Jackson for effecting the evacuation of Harpers Ferry. While the movement looked simple on paper, it was anything but simple. Three separate attack forces, two by circuitous routes, would converge on a single target. Three mountaintops had to be taken and secured at Harpers Ferry. The crests also had to be occupied simultaneously to prevent the Harpers Ferry garrison from escaping. Two rivers stood in the way of the Confederate advance. On arrival at the ferry, artillery had to be dragged up steep mountains. The separation of the Confederate wings even after the investment of the ferry would reduce communications between them to a minimum. No time existed for a siege. A fight was likely with a heavily armed garrison. All of this explains why Lee was sending twenty-six of the army's forty brigades to clear the avenue into the Shenandoah Valley.

One other factor at work was the condition of the Confederate soldiers. No great quantity of food, shoes, and clothing had been gathered in Maryland. Jackson's men were still as ragged and destitute as they were footsore. The itinerary for their assignment was all but impossible to fulfill.[38]

Neither Lee nor Jackson thought so. Jackson was not concerned that part of his command had to make a 270-degree forced march of seventy-three miles in two days—including the suppression of whatever Federal resistance appeared. Lee was confident that Jackson could carry out his assignment. He had chosen Jackson for the operation because he was an excellent marcher and, in addition, knew the area and its people.

What should have been a fatal mistake for the Southern Confederacy then occurred. Copies of Lee's Special Orders No. 191 went to all of the division commanders. Harvey Hill had been attached to Jackson's force until the new marching orders were issued. He and his men were now to return to Longstreet. After Jackson received his copy of No. 191, he courteously wanted to advise Hill of the orders and new command structure. So Jackson himself wrote out a copy of the orders and sent it by courier to his brother-in-law.

Hill received the orders in Jackson's handwriting. It was the copy from army headquarters that went astray. It soon resurfaced in the hands of Federal General George B. McClellan, who became the beneficiary of the greatest security leak in American military history.[39]

At sundown on the 9th, Jackson directed the men to cook three days' rations and be ready to march "at early dawn" (3:30 A.M.). General John R. Jones, commanding the Stonewall Division with Starke in arrest, claimed that "never has the army been so dirty, ragged, and ill-provided for as on this march."[40]

For Jackson, these were minor problems that hopefully would be solved by captures along the way. In the predawn hours of September 10, the Stonewall Division marched from Frederick. Behind it came the troops of Lawton and Branch. Powell Hill rode at the rear of the infantry column.

Jackson delayed leaving Frederick for both military and personal reasons. He was hopeful of paying his respects to the Reverend John B. Ross, the local Presbyterian minister whom Jackson had known in Lexington. The general had not had a chance to visit with him during the brief stay in Frederick. In addition, Jackson wanted to mask his movement with as much rumor as he could.

It was 5 A.M. when Jackson rode with aides and a small cavalry detachment into town. He stopped at the intersection of Main and Patrick Streets and inquired of some early risers the direction to Chambersburg, Pennsylvania, and the distance to several other locales to the north. Then Jackson rode to the Presbyterian manse.

The household was still in bed, a servant told him. The general would not let the family be awakened. He quickly wrote and handed to the servant a simple note: "September 10, '62, 5:15 A.M. Regret not being permitted to see Dr. and Mrs. Ross, but could not expect to have the pleasure at so unseasonable an hour." With that, Jackson galloped to overtake the head of his westward moving column.[41]

Jackson's portion of the three wings en route to Harpers Ferry consisted of 14,000 of the 23,000 troops in the undertaking. That segment also had the toughest march: an orbital tramp of seventy-plus miles, double that of McLaws and Walker. At the first rest stop, regimental commanders informed the men where they were going and how they were to get there. Jackson's directive also prescribed the rate of walking. A Carolina officer recalled: "We were to march three miles an hour and no more, except in great emergencies; we were to rest ten minutes in every hour; the sick and those otherwise unable to march were to be transported in the ambulances. . . . No good Samaritans could be expected along this new war-path."[42]

The other units had the pleasure of receiving expressions of kindness from Frederick citizens. South Carolina Surgeon James Boulware wrote: "Saw a number of pretty ladies and amid waving of Secession flags by the ladies and cheering of the soldiers had a lively time. The ladies bowed gracefully to us and once more I was caught lifting my cap, and not a few times either. After passing the town the march was dull and wearisome."[43]

The men made their way up Catoctin Mountain as the sun rose behind them. General Alexander Lawton had apprehensions that day. The cause was Jackson, not the enemy. Lawton was aware that he was the only one among three division commanders not then under arrest. His brother-in-law, Colonel E. Porter Alexander, wrote that Lawton "was in hourly fear lest Jackson might perhaps catch one of his men somewhere in the rear up an apple tree & send an aid ahead & tell Lawton to consider himself under arrest."[44]

That was anything but far-fetched. Lawton's friend, General Maxcy Gregg, kept reminding him that Jackson was "tyrannical & unjust." As if to substantiate the charge, Jackson that day arrested two of Gregg's regimental colonels for allowing the men to break ranks—in order to pick apples from trees along the road.[45]

Dense woods on either side of the twisting route seemed to squeeze the Confederate column. Reaching the crest of the Catoctin, the soldiers marched down into the broad and picturesque Middletown Valley. The road undulated through the heavily German settlement of Middletown before rising up and through Turner's Gap.

This was the second mountain range the men had encountered. At the western base of South Mountain, a mile from Boonsboro and near good water, Jackson bivouacked his force after a fifteen-mile march. Troops camped in fields adjacent to the National Road. Jackson established headquarters at the home of John Murdock.

Late in the afternoon, Jackson hesitantly gave permission for Colonel French and Lieutenant Douglas to ride into Boonsboro. After awhile, Jackson grew restless and started toward town, walking his horse. The day had been so warm that he removed his hat and gloves, swinging them in his hand as he strolled up the road. All of a sudden, Jackson heard a commotion. A few seconds later (according to Douglas and disputed by Hotchkiss), over a rise galloped Douglas and a courier. Each gripped smoking revolvers. Not far behind them were over a dozen hard-riding Federal cavalrymen. Jackson swung quickly into the saddle and rode toward his camp. The Federals soon abandoned the chase. Jackson chided Douglas on the slowness of his horse but said no more of the incident after his smiling aide gave the general his gloves, which he had dropped in the haste to escape capture.[46]

That night Powell Hill requested—and received—permission to return to the head of his division. Jackson did not drop the charges pending against Hill. He simply needed an experienced division commander as the column faced the imponderables of this campaign.[47]

On Thursday morning, September 11, Jackson's force passed through Boonsboro. Townspeople lined the street to see the famous general. Anxious to capture the Union garrison at Martinsburg rather than merely force its withdrawal, Jackson uncharacteristically departed from his orders. He would not strike for the Potomac via Sharpsburg; he would move due west to Williamsport and cross the river that afternoon.

A few hours later, soldiers waded gingerly through the Potomac in waist-deep water at Light's Ford near Williamsport. Another seven miles took Jackson past the Falling Waters area, where he had his Civil War baptism in battle long ago. Then it was on to the North Mountain depot of the B&O. There the troops halted for the day after a march of more than twenty miles.

An advance of a couple of hours the next day would bring them to Martinsburg. The Union commander there, inexperienced General Julius White, knew of Jackson's presence. That night White and his 2500-man brigade evacuated Martinsburg, abandoned their supplies, and moved with all dispatch to Harpers Ferry.[48]

Rain settled the dust and made marching easier the next day. By midmorning of the 12th, the lead elements of Jackson's column were entering Martinsburg. Anticipating resistance, Jackson sent Powell Hill due south on the main Williamsport-Martinsburg road. Lawton and John R. Jones swung west to approach the town from a different direction, while Confederate cavalry approached from the southwest. Not a hostile shot was fired as Jackson's men entered Martinsburg. The general was back in his beloved Shenandoah Valley.

Residents rejoiced collectively—a startling change of heart from the Unionist reputation that Martinsburg had in the first months of the war. Jackson removed his

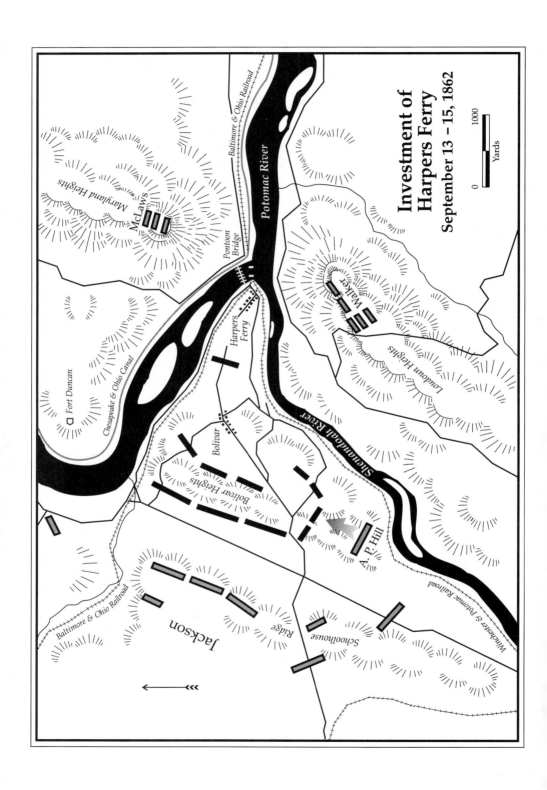

**Investment of
Harpers Ferry
September 13 – 15, 1862**

0   1000
Yards

McLaws

Maryland Heights

Baltimore & Ohio Railroad

Potomac River

Pontoon Bridge

Walker

Loudoun Heights

Fort Duncan

Chesapeake & Ohio Canal

Harpers Ferry

Shenandoah River

Bolivar

Bolivar Heights

A. P. Hill

Winchester & Potomac Railroad

Baltimore & Ohio Railroad

Jackson

Ridge

Schoolhouse

cap as he rode down Martinsburg's main street and acknowledged the cheers. Southern troops found, and devoured, an unbelievable amount of food. One soldier estimated that Jackson's men "ate a ton of bread alone."[49]

Jackson could not escape a huge crowd of well-wishers and souvenir hunters. Women screamed for locks of his hair and buttons from his uniform. Men wanted to talk and grasp his hand; children by the scores pressed close to gawk and be part of the spectacle. At one point, Jackson told a large assemblage of women bent on getting strands of hair, "Really, ladies, this is the first time I was ever surrounded by the enemy!"

Finally, he retreated to the Everett Hotel and tried to attend to some paperwork. It was no use. People rattled doors and swarmed around windows to get a look at him. Poor Little Sorrel was being painfully stripped, hair by hair, as relic hunters sought any memento of the general. Jackson finally led his staff swiftly from town and established secret headquarters in a field five miles southeast of Martinsburg. Hotchkiss managed to purchase at least two hats before departing town. One, of black felt, he gave to Jackson as a replacement for the disheveled and now-shapeless kepi that he wore. The general donned it at once, but wore it only a day or so before reverting to his VMI kepi.[50]

Jackson was now running a day late in Lee's timetable. Even though Jackson dispatched Hill's division toward Harpers Ferry, twenty miles distant, the commander appeared in hindsight to be tardy. A few writers have taken Jackson to task for dawdling. The weakness to such criticism is that Jackson—per Lee's written instructions—was on schedule. Special Orders No. 191 directed that by September 12 Jackson should break the B&O Railroad and seize Martinsburg. That is precisely what he had done. If he and Lee worked out an additional move to Harpers Ferry, they did it by oral arrangement; and apparently Jackson thought that he was proceeding as expected. His lack of concern for time may be attributed to a lack of pressure from Lee to seize Harpers Ferry at a prescribed date. That Lee would later report Jackson having "marched very rapidly" on the ferry would seem to be corroboration.[51]

Confederates were moving before dawn the next morning. About 11 A.M., Jackson came in sight of Bolivar Heights, the eminence west of Harpers Ferry. How familiar the surroundings were! Yet where Jackson was once in the ferry watching for external dangers, now he was the danger for the garrison within the town.

The general moved to Halltown, two miles from the enemy lines, and halted. His troops dispersed into battle position to counter any move in that direction by the Federals, whose numbers made them a threat. With White's "refugees" from Martinsburg, the Union garrison had swelled to 14,000 men. That slightly increased the Federal numbers against Jackson but not enough to give him additional concern. Jackson next sought a vantage point from which he could observe the crests of Loudoun and Maryland Heights. The sound of battle on the latter had echoed through much of the day.

Unable to tell by telescope who held the mountaintops, Jackson resolved to use a semaphore system to maintain contact between his three wings. His signal officer, Captain Joseph L. Bartlett, began around noon to try to make flag contact with McLaws and Walker. There was no response from either sector then or in the early afternoon.

Meanwhile, Union forces elsewhere in western Maryland were active. McClellan was now in possession of Special Orders No. 191. His flood of telegrams to Washington, and his comments to fellow generals, bubbled with optimism. "Now I know what to do! . . . I have the whole rebel force in front of me. . . . I think Lee has made a gross mistake, and that he will be severely punished for it. . . . Here is a paper with which if I cannot whip 'Bobbie Lee,' I will be willing to go home."[52]

Inside the Harpers Ferry garrison, an atmosphere of gloom persisted. General White was the senior officer. Yet a few months earlier, he had been collector of customs in Chicago. His military experience was minor, so he had relinquished command of the ferry to Colonel Dixon S. Miles. That proved to be a poor decision.

Miles looked and acted older than his fifty-eight years. He was then the oldest colonel in the Union army, having graduated near the bottom of his West Point class in 1824, the year Jackson was born. During thirty-eight years in service, Miles won three brevets in the Mexican War and, by 1861, was one of only twenty-one colonels in the U.S. Army. (He outranked R. E. Lee at the outbreak of civil war.) Yet Miles's thinking too often was as dull as his conduct was erratic. He had been drunk at First Manassas but somehow escaped being cashiered from the army. Now he was trying to defend one of the most indefensible sites in the Civil War, and over half of the men at his disposal were Northern recruits who had just enlisted.

Jackson's concerns on the afternoon of September 13 for the high ground to the north of Harpers Ferry were well founded. The ultimate success of Special Orders No. 191 lay with Lafayette McLaws securing Maryland Heights and making the ferry untenable. A Confederate officer explained the terrain in simple terms. "So long as Maryland Heights was occupied by the enemy, Harpers Ferry could never be occupied by us. If we gained possession of the heights, the town was no longer tenable to them."[53]

It is somewhat strange that Lee—presumably with Jackson's approval—entrusted so important a mission to a man whose fighting prowess was still awaiting fulfillment. Born in 1821, Lafayette McLaws had graduated low in his West Point class and performed routine army duties until the coming of civil war. The burly and congenial officer entered the war as colonel of the 10th Georgia. He impressed Confederate authorities enough to gain a major general's rank by the spring of 1862, although his only real action in the field had been at the battle of Williamsburg.

On that record, McLaws became one of the ranking major generals in the Confederate army. Some thought that his appearance had much to do with his promotions. Short but square-built, with a large head and full curling beard, he wore an aura of confidence with aplomb. McLaws was generally well liked and dependable. He was also careful and unhurried—traits that are not always assets.

On September 10, McLaws had left Frederick with 8000 men that included his own four brigades plus six brigades in General Richard H. Anderson's division. Of the three columns converging on Harpers Ferry, McLaws had the shortest distance to travel (twenty miles) but the most demanding task. Maryland Heights was the southernmost promontory of Elk Ridge, an imposing elevation to the west of South Mountain. The heights commanded every block of Harpers Ferry, but it would be difficult to capture if vigorously defended.

McLaws led his troops over South Mountain and into Pleasant Valley. With Elk Ridge looming in front of him, the Georgian stopped to ponder how to get from the valley to the distant height. He decided to split his force. Four miles north of Maryland Heights, Elk Ridge dropped into a saddlelike depression known as Solomon's Gap. McLaws ordered two of his best brigades, Joseph B. Kershaw's South Carolinians and William Barksdale's Mississippians, to scale the mountain via Solomon's Gap.

Once on the crest, the troops would advance southward on abandoned charcoal roads that extended from the gap to the brow of Maryland Heights. McLaws's remaining brigades would trail the Confederates on the mountain and move down Pleasant Valley to the Potomac, thereby sealing off all eastern escape routes from Harpers Ferry.

On the morning of September 12, the brigades of Kershaw and Barksdale climbed slowly into Solomon's Gap. One of the Mississippians reported that "we wrestled with rugged rocks and boulders, dragging our artillery up on the back-bone of the ridge, which seemed so high and dry among the ancient stones that one of the boys . . . thought that it must be Mount Ararat, and began to inquire if the descendants of old man Noah didn't 'live fur about here.' He was answered by a wag in turn: 'No, it is so dry of water and so barren with the rocks that I don't believe there is 'ary rat here.' So we laughed and jested and marched on the ridge, about wide enough to hold the line of one brigade."[54]

By 6 P.M., the units were safely on the summit. In the gathering gloom of nightfall, 2000 Confederates moved southward on the crest. Thick underbrush and rough terrain slowed the march. Apprehension at bumping into some of the 2000 Federals reported to be on the mountaintop added caution to the advance. Soon downed trees and abatis came into view. A concentrated volley from that direction convinced Kershaw that Federals were there in strength. The two opposing forces spent the night almost within speaking distance of one another.

At 6:30 the next morning, battle exploded. Defending the summit were portions of three Union regiments. Only two (the 39th New York and 32d Ohio) could boast of any combat experience. The fight lasted four hours and was spirited. In the middle of the Federal line was the 126th New York. It had been in the army exactly three weeks, and no one had bothered to tell the enlistees how chaotic and damaging war could be. When the colonel of the regiment fell seriously wounded, panic sliced through the ranks. Near 10:30 A.M., Federals who had been holding their own suddenly withdrew to a new position.

The two Confederate brigades eased forward. A quarter-mile to the south, they encountered a second Union position. Kershaw and Barksdale advanced slowly and then spread out in battle formation. It was about 3:30 P.M. when the fight seemed about to begin anew. Colonel Thomas H. Ford ignored Miles's orders; he directed his men to abandon Maryland Heights and retire to Harpers Ferry.

McLaws secured the eminence before sundown. He appeared to have done as well as Jackson and to have outdone John G. Walker in his part of the operation. Yet McLaws was in a precarious spot. While having a commanding position above Harpers Ferry, he also had to watch his rear for a possible Union assault.

Walker, with the third segment of the encircling movement on the ferry, had the easiest time of it. In fact, his was considered such an unobstructed march that Walker performed other duty before departing Frederick with his two brigades. His first assignment was to destroy the aqueduct carrying the C&O Canal over the mouth of the Monocacy River at the Potomac. Yet the thick limestone bridge withstood the best efforts of Walker's engineers. Soon time and approaching Federals forced Walker to abandon the project.

With Lee's orders in hand, he marched his 2400 troops south and west to seal off the ferry from Washington. His men crossed the Potomac but apparently not by the desired ford. A member of the 46th North Carolina observed that "the chill of the water, the multitude of the boulders which literally covered the bottom of the river, coupled with the depth of the stream (which came to the shoulders of the shortest men) all served to impress this bit of experience indelibly upon the memories of those who took that early morning dip."[55]

Then and thereafter, Walker appears to have generated mixed opinion. Some troops regarded him "with highest esteem, for his care of the force under his command, as well as for his courage and coolness under the most trying conditions." Yet a North Carolina colonel thought that Walker was "a timid cautious man & lacks energy, vigor & sagasity." Whatever his faults, Walker by the morning of Saturday the 13th was approaching his objective: Loudoun Heights. (Jackson at the time was departing Martinsburg.) Walker dispatched two regiments to make a dash up the mountain. At 2 P.M., Loudoun Heights was in Confederate hands.[56]

That afternoon, Jackson on School House Ridge could clearly hear the sound of McLaws's advance along the crest of Elk Mountain. It was near sundown when Jackson learned of McLaws's success in placing guns on Maryland Heights. An hour or so later came word from Walker: his batteries were also in position atop Loudoun Heights.

Now Jackson was ready. Rivers separated him from the other two wings of his command. Any attack on the ferry garrison would have to come from his portion of the strike force. Yet the old artillery professor was not thinking of any infantry assault.

Familiar enough with Harpers Ferry, Jackson knew that it was defenseless against firepower from the three surrounding mountains—if that firepower had the necessary range. Many of his guns were not of sufficient caliber, but Jackson could initiate a bombardment from north, south, and west that would surely shatter Union morale first and then Union resistance. So he would take his time and concentrate on artillery fire.

Sandie Pendleton had just returned to staff duties, relieving Jackson of those administrative details that hamper the field performance of any commander. However, the general worked far into the night to get the School House Ridge wing in battle readiness. Jackson considered gun and troop emplacements in this case too important to be detailed to aides.

Sunday morning, September 14, was so quiet that one almost expected to hear church bells summoning the faithful to worship. Jackson now commanded six divisions, the largest force he had ever led. He began the morning by reviewing Lee's orders. McLaws was supposed to blast the ferry into submission from his position atop Maryland Heights. However, Jackson made dispositions as if he planned to storm the town without McLaws's help. This was because Jackson had still not established contact with the stout Georgian.

The morning hours passed without word from McLaws. Jackson marked time impatiently. He did not hear the sound of battle to the north, where McClellan was trying to force his way through the passes of South Mountain. Harvey Hill and 5000 Confederates were disputing the passage in what would become an all-day, Thermopylae-type contest. Jackson dismissed the first noise of combat as merely a cavalry demonstration. He would not believe that his old West Point classmate was moving the Union army with alacrity.

Around 10 o'clock, Walker signaled that he had six rifled guns on the crest of Loudoun Heights. He was anxious to open fire on so tempting a target as Harpers Ferry. Jackson flagged back: "Wait." The general was eager to have McLaws's guns involved in any artillery barrage, but he could not make flag contact with Maryland Heights. Finally, he rode to the signal station and watched as a message went to both McLaws and Walker: "I do not desire any of the batteries to open until all are ready on both sides of the river, except you should find it necessary, of which you must judge for yourself. I will let you know when to open all the batteries."[57]

By noon, Jackson was openly worried about McLaws. He had heard nothing from the Georgian since arriving at the ferry. "I have never seen Jackson exhibit the least impatience before," Colonel French remarked, "but it was unmistakable to me that he was greatly worried at the delay, then inexplicable, in occupying the Maryland Heights."[58]

Jackson then flagged another message to Walker and—Jackson hoped—McLaws: if the enemy did not surrender Harpers Ferry on their accord, the two generals were to open fire on the town. "Let the work be done thoroughly; fire on the houses when necessary." With Federal attention thus occupied, Jackson would launch a full-scale attack at Bolivar Heights and try to seize the strategic elevation with a minimum of loss.[59]

On the morning of the 14th, McLaws had established communication with Walker's flag station but not with Jackson's position at Halltown. His claim that he was building roads to get artillery atop Elk Mountain is not entirely true. He was in fact clearing abandoned roads.[60]

Charcoal trails had been there for twenty years to enable carts to haul timber to the Harpers Ferry armory. McLaws's men probably had to widen and improve the trails for moving cannon and caissons uphill. The steep and difficult terrain made it a hard morning's job for hundreds of troops.

By early afternoon, McLaws had three ten-pounder Parrotts and a three-inch ordnance rifle on the crest of Maryland Heights. Walker's cannon were in place on Loudoun Heights. Over on School House Ridge, west of Bolivar Heights, Confederate gunners had planted batteries within easy range of the Federal lines. Jackson was seeking to coordinate everything from a command post at nearby Halltown. He still wished to wait until all components were ready before opening a systematic and concentrated fire on the ferry.

Walker foiled that. Federals spotted Walker's guns on the Virginia slope and began an ineffectual fire. The Union artillery could not reach Loudoun Heights, a disgusted Federal officer noted, and batteries "seemed to hope to frighten the [Confederates] off with a big noise."[61] Nevertheless, Walker immediately ordered his artillerists to return the fire.

McLaws, as if to announce his arrival at the most strategic site, also began lobbing shells toward Harpers Ferry. The sound of McLaws's guns evoked a noticeable change in Jackson's countenance. "I never saw his eye more brilliant than when the signal of occupation [of Maryland Heights] was made," French stated.[62] Jackson's own batteries on School House Ridge joined the bombardment.

This was the first time most of the Federals under Miles had been under fire. Their cannon quickly ceased firing because the elevation and concentration of Southern artillery rendered the exposed Union guns virtually useless. A shell or two reached the top of Loudoun Heights, but McLaws's cannon were completely out of range.

Inside the ferry, Federal soldiers scurried for cover. New York sergeant James Clark wrote: "At first, their missiles of death fell far short of our camp; but each succeeding shell came nearer and nearer, until the earth was plowed up at our feet, and our tents torn to tatters. . . . They made it too hot for any troops to stand; so we were obliged to change our line very frequently, to save the men from slaughter."[63]

The cannonade roared through the afternoon. Men likened it to a gigantic fireworks display. While it did comparatively little damage to the ferry's defenders (most of whom had taken cover in ravines), the demoralizing effect was significant. Jackson had sought to get a full-scale assault underway, but it was too late in the day to be executed.

Jackson also extended his infantry lines in the form of a semi-circle, the left resting on the Potomac and the right on the Shenandoah. By sundown, September 14, he was becoming master again at his old military post. Jackson was now methodical, no longer impatient. If the general thought of being behind in any schedule, he did not show it. Old Jack stood ready to achieve one of his most smashing victories.

Under cover of darkness, he directed Powell Hill's division along the bank of the Shenandoah River. It bivouacked close enough to the left of the Union line to make a quick assault at first light. John R. Jones and the Stonewall Division took position against Miles's right, with Lawton's men poised in the center of the line. Besieged Federals controlled only a little tongue of land between the two rivers.

Everything was in Old Jack's favor. He outnumbered his opponent, 23,000 to 14,000 men. At no time in the Civil War was Confederate artillery at such a commanding elevation. Jackson would assault the enemy through a typical Jacksonian flanking movement if artillery failed to carry the day. Yet fifty guns were in place to pound the Union garrison from every direction.[64]

Jackson was fortunate in one respect. That day the Federal seizure of the passes at South Mountain almost trapped McLaws. The Union VI Corps might have assailed McLaws on Elk Ridge and in Pleasant Valley. Yet Major General William B. Franklin halted the advance to survey the terrain. He saw two lines of Confederates and concluded—in McClellan fashion—that the Union forces were heavily outnumbered. Federals merely probed McLaws's position, which left the latter free to complete the envelopment of Harpers Ferry.[65]

Meanwhile, Lee's spirits had plunged to a defeatist level. The events of September 14 were all negative: Jackson's investment of Harpers Ferry seemed stalled; McClellan was in possession of the Confederate marching orders; the Union army had fought its way to control of South Mountain, whose gaps were now an avenue toward both Lee and Jackson; the Army of Northern Virginia was still fragmented and retiring slowly in the face of Federal advances.

That evening, Lee concluded that his highly promising invasion of the North had ended in failure. He must retire and concede the Maryland Campaign. In the strongest language by Lee to that date, he told McLaws, "The day has gone against us and this army will go by Sharpsburg and cross the river." Retreat must begin.[66]

A few hours later, a message from Jackson arrived at headquarters. "Through God's blessings the advance [on Harpers Ferry] which commenced this evening, has been successful thus far, and I look to Him for complete success to-morrow. The advance has been directed to be resumed at dawn to-morrow morning."[67]

Lee decided to await word from Jackson on the success of the Harpers Ferry envelopment before making a final decision whether to stay in or withdraw from Maryland. Perhaps Jackson could salvage something from the campaign. If Harpers Ferry collapsed the next day, the route to Virginia would be clear and an opportunity still exist to push the invasion to positive results. Jackson's two-sentence communique had restored hope at a moment when there was no hope inside Lee's army.

That night McLaws either ignored several warnings from Stuart about an unguarded road leading north from the ferry or else became too concerned over 12,000 Federals somewhere in his rear. As a result, all of the Union cavalry at the ferry—some 1300 horsemen—escaped by that route. In the process, the Federal cavalry captured between forty-five and seventy-five of Longstreet's ammunition and supply wagons and several hundred guards.[68]

Confederates huddling in the darkness around Harpers Ferry spent an uneasy night. "We infantry fellows were not allowed to build fires," the 15th Alabama's William McClendon wrote. "We lay in rear of our guns, to sleep if we could, or lie there and imagine the results of the events of the morning. I have no doubt but that there were many prayers offered to the Almighty." Henry L. P. King, a captain on McLaws's staff, confided in his journal: "Tomorrow will doubtless bring a heavy & perhaps decisive battle. . . . Anxious feeling in all our bosoms. . . . All feel that tomorrow will be a bloody day."[69]

During that sleepless night, Jackson directed ten guns to a new position across the Shenandoah River at the base of Loudoun Heights. They would be in position to shatter the Union flank and rear if A. P. Hill had to make an assault. Heavy fog shrouded the area at dawn as McLaws and Walker peered down toward the ferry. They could see nothing.

Jackson had taken a position at daybreak in the center of his line on School House Ridge. Infantrymen waiting to move to a possible attack watched him closely. Lieutenant Lewis E. Powers of the 21st North Carolina was as nervous as his men. "Presently," he stated, "we saw Jackson turn to his couriers and speak a few words to them and immediately they were galloping off to the different divisions. Our hearts trembled. We knew the orders those couriers were carrying. It was the order for a general and simultaneous charge all along the line. The bristling line of bayonets behind strong fortifications was a dangerous thing to approach."[70]

Confederate infantry had no cause for concern that September 15 morning. Artilleryman Jackson was at work. The ten guns near the base of Loudoun Heights opened fire as the fog began rising like a theater curtain. Walker's artillery on the top of the mountain began a bombardment, followed by McLaws's pieces across the Potomac on Maryland Heights. Batteries on School House Ridge in front of Bolivar Heights added their roar to the cannonade.

A gunner in the Rockbridge Artillery noted that "the great circle of artillery" fired "to a common center, while the clouds of smoke, rolling up from the tops of the various mountains, and the thunder of the guns reverberating among them, gave the idea of so many volcanoes."[71]

Inside Harpers Ferry, a New York private observed: "The flash, the whistling shriek and the explosion" of the Southern cannon "came all at once." Colonel William H. Trimble of the 60th Ohio thought that Jackson's bombardment "commanded every foot of [the ground] around the batteries on the left and along the lines . . . producing a terrible cross-fire . . . there was not a place you could lay the palm of your hand and say it was safe."[72]

An immobile Jackson watched with cold enjoyment. His guns were where he wanted them, delivering salvos as he desired, and the enemy pieces were helpless in trying to match his firepower. Converging fire from three directions set a pattern that wreaked destruction everywhere in the artillery grid. So proud was Jackson of the fusillade that in his official report, written months later, he went to pains to describe the exact location of his batteries.

After an hour of the cannonade, the Federal fire slackened and soon stopped. Jackson ordered Hill's guns to cease firing. This was the signal for the infantry attack. Hill's division started forward through the Chambers farm toward the menacing abatis in their front. Two of Hill's batteries moved to within 400 yards of the Federal defenses and opened a point-blank bombardment.

A Federal horseman came into view bearing a large piece of slightly used tent-cloth, the closest thing to a white flag the Union garrison could find in the confusion of the moment. Because of the distance, fog, and gunsmoke, some of the batteries on School House Ridge and Loudoun Heights were not aware of the flag of truce. They continued firing until they realized that they were shooting at Federals trying to surrender.[73]

One of the last shells that morning exploded near Colonel Miles and tore both of his legs to shreds. General Julius White succeeded the mortally wounded commander and promptly asked for a meeting to discuss surrender terms. Near 8 A.M., he met Powell Hill, who escorted him to Jackson.

By then, the general had moved to the schoolhouse along the Bolivar-Halltown road. White was immaculately uniformed and mounted on a handsome black horse. A large contingent of nattily dressed aides rode behind him. Although begrimed and dust covered, Jackson was as neatly attired as possible for the occasion. He was even wearing the new hat given to him two days earlier by Hotchkiss.[74]

To White's question about terms, Jackson answered politely but sternly that only unconditional surrender was acceptable. White had no choice but to acquiesce. Jackson delegated Powell Hill to handle the particulars of extremely generous concessions by the Confederate commander. Federal officers would retain sidearms and baggage; all captured soldiers would be paroled, not imprisoned; enlisted men would be able to keep overcoats and blankets; two days' rations would be distributed to every soldier. Two wagons would be lent to each regiment for carrying baggage. (Later, when the Federal government was slow in returning the wagons, Jackson grumbled that his "liberal terms" were not "properly appreciated by their Government.")

As White and Hill left to work out details, Jackson sent a letter by Stuart to an anxious Lee at Sharpsburg. "Through God's blessing," Jackson announced, "Harper's Ferry and its garrison are to be surrendered. As Hill's troops have borne the heaviest part in the engagement, he will be left in command until the prisoners and public property shall be disposed of, unless you direct otherwise. The other forces can move off this evening so soon as they get their rations. To what place shall they move?"[75]

Lee was vastly relieved by the message. "This victory of the indomitable Jackson and his troops," he informed President Davis, "gives us renewed occasion for gratitude to Almighty God for His guidance and protection." The army commander then ordered Jackson's message read to the army. Soldiers breathed easier at the news. The campaign was still proceeding; most of the army would be reunited soon.[76]

Following his dispatch to Lee, Jackson sent a quick note to Anna. "It is my grateful privilege to write that our God has given us a brilliant victory at Harper's Ferry today. . . . Our Heavenly Father blesses us exceedingly. I am thankful to say that our loss was small, and Joseph [Morrison] and myself were mercifully protected from harm."[77]

At 9 A.M., the Harpers Ferry garrison formally began the surrender procedure. A hot and dusty day made the activities uncomfortable for both sides. Roll calls, paperwork, and similar routine had been transpiring for an hour when Jackson rode down from Bolivar Heights with McGuire.

Lines of Federal soldiers stood waiting to be paroled. Jackson became the instant center of attention. One Billy Yank thought the general resembled "a dirty old Virginia farmer" who wore shoddy clothes "to avoid recognition by our sharpshooters." Another dismissed Jackson as "in no respect to be distinguished from the mongrel barefooted crew who followed his fortunes."[78]

Large numbers of Union prisoners, however, were eager to see Jackson, and they responded to his presence with enthusiasm. A South Carolina soldier whose regiment was guarding captives declared: "Almost the whole mass of prisoners broke over us, rushed to the road, threw up their hats, cheered, roared, bellowed, as even Jackson's own troops had scarcely ever done. . . . The general gave a stiff acknowledgement of the compliment, pulled down his hat, drove spurs into his horse, and went clattering down the hill, away from the noise."[79]

Not having seen the ferry for fourteen months, Jackson must have been surprised and saddened by its deterioration. The place resembled a ghost town. Few of the 3000 residents were still there. The armory had been "fixed," then converted into a quartermaster depot; once-attractive homes had become barracks and stables; charred walls marked where stately buildings had once stood; piers in the rivers were the only reminders of bridges. An observer described Harpers Ferry that September as a place of "filthy desolation" where dogs, hogs, and buzzards were "disputing over the offal of recent camps."[80]

Of most concern to Jackson were the spoils of war crowded into the ferry. He had bagged 435 officers and 12,085 men—the largest surrender of Federal troops in the Civil War and greater than that of Burgoyne or Cornwallis in the American Revolution. The garrison was also well armed and enormously supplied. Seventy-three usable cannon fell into Confederate hands, as did 12,000 weapons (enough to equip a full army corps).

The 200 wagons Jackson seized were in better condition than any comparable number in Lee's army. Over 1200 well-fed mules were badly needed. Other stores were so voluminous that Major Harman and his assistants would require a couple of days just to compile an inventory. All of this booty came at a cost of thirty-nine Confederates killed and 247 wounded. In many respects, Jackson's achievement at Harpers Ferry was the most complete victory in the history of the Southern Confederacy.

Longstreet sought years later to shift the credit for the accomplishment away from its architect. "Jackson was quite satisfied with the campaign," Longstreet wrote, "as the Virginia papers made him the hero of Harper's Ferry, although the greater danger was with McLaws, whose service was the severer and more important."[81]

Before noon on the 15th, Jackson issued swift but complete orders. Everything that could be saved would be sent to the Confederate interior. He did not have enough men to escort captured Federals to prisons, even if he had made the Federals prisoners of war. Hence, the first large-scale implementation of an 1862 cartel would go into effect. Every Federal would be paroled.

A march north and reunion with Lee's army were the next main items on Jackson's agenda. First, however, his men must eat and replenish their supplies. As he had done at Manassas two weeks earlier, Jackson gave the troops the run of the ferry's stores. Some of Hill's brigades had been attending to the New Jersey "intruders" when Jackson's force ransacked Manassas Junction. Now the Light Division got an opportunity to feast. It did so—to negative reactions from the troops of McLaws and Walker on the distant mountaintops.

"We fared sumptuously," one of Hill's men boasted. "In addition to meat, crackers, sugar, coffee, shoes, blankets, underclothing, &c., many of us captured horses roaming at large, on whom to transport our plunder. . . . The ragged, forlorn appearance of our men excited the combined merriment and admiration of our prisoners. It really looked like Pharoah's lean kine devouring the fat."[82]

Jeb Stuart sent his large Prussian aide to congratulate Jackson on the swift capture of the ferry. Von Borcke found the general "quite satisfied with his success." Nevertheless, Jackson interrupted the aide's glowing praises. "Ah, this is all very well, Major, but we have yet much hard work before us."[83]

It was now afternoon, and much remained to be done. A directive just received from Lee put Sharpsburg as the new point of concentration. Reunion would occur a half-day sooner. At 3 P.M., Jackson directed that all troops save Hill's division cook two days' rations and prepare to march. Hill would remain at Harpers Ferry to secure what was left of the post, parole prisoners, and start the transfer of captured stores. Jackson was unaware of the intense battle the previous day at South Mountain. All he sensed from Lee's communique was a call for the army to unite at Sharpsburg.

Just before midnight, Jackson with two of his divisions marched away from Bolivar Heights. The seventeen-mile journey took all night and was "severe" even by Jackson's standards. Confederates four abreast wound upriver to Shepherdstown, crossed the Potomac at Boteler's Ford to the higher ground of Maryland, and proceeded another four miles to Sharpsburg.

A member of the 18th North Carolina never forgot that nighttime tramp. "Our march from Harper's Ferry, wading the Potomac in fours, our clothing saturated with water from the hips down, the efforts to close up the head of the column, making it an up-hill foot-race from the river to the battlefield, caused none but those of unquestioned endurance to be there to go into action."[84]

It was late morning on September 16 when the head of Jackson's command filed into Sharpsburg. Hard marching had produced heavy straggling. The Stonewall Brigade arrived with barely 300 troops. The rest of Jackson's column—the divisions of Lawton and Jones—numbered no more than 5500 troops and sixteen guns. Most of the men were so fatigued on reaching Sharpsburg that when the command to halt came, they dropped down along the road without a word.[85]

Rest was out of the question for Jackson. Covered head to foot in dust, he rode ahead of his men into Sharpsburg to report to Lee. Some of the Confederate soldiers in town caught sight of Old Jack. "A smile played over the dirty faces of Longstreet's men at [the] sight of Stonewall," a Georgia veteran commented, "for they knew that his foot cavalry was not far in his rear."[86]

Jackson spied Lee astride Traveler waiting in the main street. The army commander greeted his lieutenant warmly and without anxiety. A calm had now settled over Lee. Most of his army was coming back together, which enabled him to unfold a new war plan. He led Jackson to headquarters at the Grove House in the center of town. While Jackson shook the dust from his uniform, Lee carefully outlined his strategy.

The army would fight at Sharpsburg, a farming community whose cluster of homes contained no more than 1500 residents, mostly of German extraction. Sharpsburg itself was of no military consequence. However, four roads intersected there. The town also stood on a series of ridges between swift-moving Antietam Creek to the east and the winding Potomac River to the west.

Antietam Creek was fairly shallow, but its banks tended to be steep and rocky. It was passable for an army only at fords and a few bridges. Four miles south of Sharpsburg, the southward-flowing Potomac bent to the east. Antietam Creek flowed into the Potomac a short distance into the bend.

On an average, three miles separated the creek and the river as they moved past Sharpsburg. Lee was basically in a V-shaped neck of land, much like Pope had been a month earlier between the Rapidan and the Rappahannock. Yet Lee possessed several advantages in western Maryland. He had open country in his front. The area around Sharpsburg is elevated and rolling. (Some of the ridges were steeper than those McClellan had enjoyed at Malvern Hill.) Woods, fields, and orchards were interspersed, scarred here and there by limestone outcroppings.

The major road between Sharpsburg and Hagerstown was inside Lee's proposed line. His men would be on the reverse side of the high ground and largely invisible to the Union army. The curve of the ridge on which the Confederates would make their stand was convex, with the flanks curving to the rear. Lee would be able to make maximum use of inner lines of defense and communication.

It was important, Lee told Jackson, that he make a stand on Maryland soil. The commander had announced after entering the state that he was there to protect the rights and liberties of the Maryland people. Politically, therefore, Lee had to fight. He had to wage a contest even though the divisions of Powell Hill, McLaws, and Richard Anderson were not present. By taking a defensive position at Sharpsburg, Lee was forcing McClellan to launch a major attack. The Union general might fumble badly in his first effort at initiating a major battle.

Robert L. Dabney would state in his manuscript biography that Jackson was lukewarm about fighting at Sharpsburg. When Lee read this statement, he replied sharply that when Jackson arrived at the village "& learned my reasons for offering battle, he emphatically concurred with me." Since no record exists of Jackson ever voicing a contrary view, Lee's statement must stand as true.[87]

Sharpsburg was not ideal for battle, as Lee knew. For the most part, the ground was sufficiently open for McClellan to get his 233 cannon in firing position. The Union artillery, with its preponderance of rifled guns such as ten-pounder and twenty-pounder Parrotts, were more powerful than the smoothbores of the Confederates. Further, the Army of Northern Virginia was weaker in numbers and command structure than it had ever been under Lee. Water barriers were on Lee's flanks and in his rear, while the enemy stood in his front. A successful Union flank attack, or a major breakthrough by McClellan, could threaten not merely defeat but ruin.

"An army of liberation was an army of desperation," one authority concluded of Lee's host.[88] Another, even more remarkable situation now existed at Sharpsburg. Two commanders had now switched roles: McClellan became the attacker, Lee the defender.

Temperature and humidity were in the seventies when Jackson left army headquarters with his orders. The village by then was a beehive of activity. Wagon trains jammed the narrow streets; teamsters cursed and mules brayed restlessly; artillery rattled through nearby fields; soldiers slowly zigzagged past stalled conveyances while orderlies sought impatiently to circumvent the whole mass.

Longstreet and Stuart were having a late breakfast at the Philip Grove home in town. They invited Jackson to join them. He declined because he had to oversee the positioning of his troops. Thereupon young Julia Grove packed a meal and sent it to Jackson by one of Longstreet's couriers. Jackson asked the soldier the name of the thoughtful donor. The man replied, "I dunno, General, but it was the fair one."[89]

Jackson's hearing impairment came into play, along with his courtesy. He immediately took pencil and scribbled a note. "Miss Fairfield, I have received the nice breakfast, for which I am indebted to your kindness. Please accept my grateful appreciation of your hospitality. Very sincerely yours, T. J. Jackson."[90]

His men were bushed, ragged, and barefooted. An excess of rations in stomachs unaccustomed to such rich food as the soldiers enjoyed at Harpers Ferry had contributed to an outbreak of diarrhea. Another problem for Jackson was the inexperienced officers in his command. Five of the eight brigades were under colonels. One division commander (Lawton) had been an administrator only; another (Jones) was unproven in the field; the third (Powell Hill) was still at Harpers Ferry.

Arousing his soldiers from a two-hour rest, Jackson led the tired column about a mile north of Sharpsburg.[91] His command would form Lee's left astride the Hagerstown road. The principal landmark was a small, whitewashed brick building that resembled a school but actually was a church of the German Baptist Brethren. They were a kindly, pacifist sect whose most violent action was their belief in baptism by total immersion. That rite had earned them the name "Dunkers."

It was imperative that Jackson place the troops carefully. His defensive position was only a half-mile wide, but he had no more than 6000 men at hand. Something else caught the general's eye. Terrain would force him to position his men almost at right angles to the rest of the army. His men would face north; Harvey Hill's soldiers were in the center of Lee's line and looking northeast; Longstreet on the right was in a southeast configuration.

Back in Jackson's sector, and extending 300 yards in front of the Dunker church, was a large tract of timber. The "West Woods," as it came to be called, stretched from north of the church, around its west side, and a couple of hundred yards farther to the south. A quarter-mile north of the Dunker building, on the east side of the Hagerstown road, was a large field of ripe field corn so tall that it obscured even the outbuildings of the David R. Miller farm behind it. The "East Wood" hugged the far side of the cornfield.

As the ground ran south past the Miller farm and toward the church, it dipped in front of the structure, then rose and leveled off as it continued to the southern edge of the West Wood. Across the road and slightly behind the church was a ridge that overlooked the whole area. The woods and the high ground, Jackson saw at once, must be held. They were the keys to his sector, because he was going to receive the first onslaught from the enemy. With Antietam Creek in front of the Confederate center and right, it seemed logical that McClellan's initial effort would be on Lee's left.

John B. Hood's division was manning the quiet front when Jackson got there. The corps system had not become official in the Southern army, so Hood's command, nominally under Longstreet, was independent at the time and serving directly under Lee's orders. Lee attached Hood temporarily to Jackson.

Mutual respect existed between Lee and Hood because both were aggressive commanders who fought to destroy rather than merely to defeat. Hood was seven years younger than Jackson, son of a Kentucky physician, and an 1853 graduate of the U.S. Military Academy. He stood well over six feet, with sad eyes, heavy beard, and melodious voice.

Because his native state was neutral, Hood had taken command of a Texas brigade. He and his troops had become devoted to one another; and although Hood had moved up in command, his brigade referred to itself until the death of the last man as "Hood's Texans." Jackson was always complimentary of the Kentuckian's battlefield behavior. On one occasion, when a staff member mentioned Hood's name, Jackson responded, "Oh! he is a soldier!"[92]

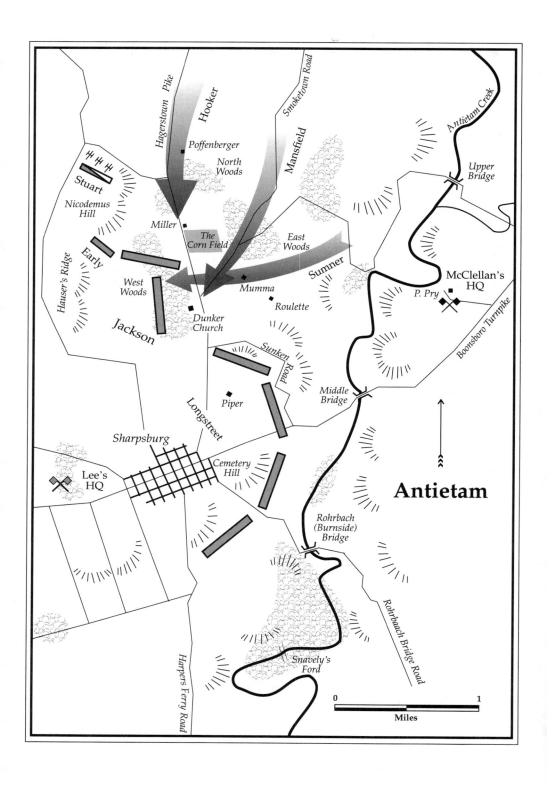

An hour or so before sundown on the 16th, Union cannon began raking the Confederate left. An enemy skirmish line advanced southward toward the Dunker church. Hood's troops opened fire, the Federals replied in kind, and the sound of battle reverberated until darkness brought the action to an uneasy end. Artillery barked at one another for a time, then grew quiet.

This was the first of several mistakes McClellan and the Union army committed at Antietam. The Federal demonstration against Lee's left was by General Joseph Hooker's I Corps. It had made a seven-mile flank march unknown to the Confederates and filed into battle position. Whether or not Confederate cavalry patrols should have uncovered the movement is debatable. In any event, had Hooker kept silent on the late afternoon of the 16th, he might well have caught the Southern army off guard the next morning with a heavy attack. Instead, Hooker gave his presence away by probing too far south. Lee, thus alerted, began shifting troops to his left.

Sometime after nightfall, Jackson sought rest. He had had no sleep for two days. A tree with roots running along the top of the ground caught his eye. He used one of the roots as a pillow and quickly fell asleep. Before long, Hood awakened him. His men were in need of food and ammunition, Hood stated. Could he withdraw from the line for the time being?

Jackson always liked his men as fresh as possible for battle. He agreed to the request, provided Hood would return promptly to the front if needed. The heavy-set Kentuckian was more than willing to comply. At 10 P.M. his troops left the line.

The battle front that Jackson created was the best he could devise with the men he had. Lawton's division was on the right side of the road: two brigades in front and one in reserve slightly to the rear. Colonels Marcellus Douglass and James A. Walker (the latter the same Cadet Walker whom Jackson had expelled from VMI a few days before his graduation) commanded the two front units. Hays's Louisianians were in support. Part of Lawton's line faced the East Wood and connected with Harvey Hill's position in the Confederate center.

John R. Jones and the Stonewall Division were on the left or west side of the Hagerstown road and well in advance of the Dunker church. The all-Virginia brigades of Jones and Andrew J. Grigsby composed the front line, with the brigades of Taliaferro and Starke behind them at the edge of the woods. On the high ground to the west was Early's brigade, supported by Stuart's cavalry. They formed the extreme left of Lee's position.

Colonel Stephen D. Lee had four batteries from his battalion aligned on the plateau near the Dunker church. These guns had a clear field of fire on the turnpike and the land on either side of it. Jackson had another fourteen cannon on the left with Early and Stuart. Kyd Douglas of the general's staff was assigned to move the artillery to prearranged alternates, if necessary, and to ensure that the cannon were sufficiently armed.

That night, Jackson reported, his soldiers slept "upon their arms disturbed by the occasional fire of the pickets of the two armies, who were in close proximity to each other." Drizzling rain added to the heaviness of the night. Douglas confessed, "It was so dark & dismal in that fearful woods which I was rapidly traveling with messages from Jackson that at times I could not tell thunder from artillery & was semi-bewildered as to the locality of our cannon; an experience I have never forgotten."[93]

Until that point in the war, the Confederate army in the east had been on the offensive. Now, for the first time under Lee, it would face an attack. Some 25,000 men were braced to confront three times their number. "Nothing can be more solemn than a period of silent waiting for the summons to battle," one man commented on the long wet hours of darkness.

At 3 A.M. on Wednesday, September 17, the two armies were astir. "With Hooker, there was bustle and cooking," Bradley Johnson declared. "With Jackson there was only a munching of cold rations and water from the spring."[94]

Skirmish lines began firing in the dark. With the first hint of daylight, scattered musketry became drowned by deep explosions of artillery. Cannon belched flame and recoiled on both sides of Jackson's line. The most damaging fire came from beyond the Antietam as Union long-range pieces raked the length of Jackson's position.

The general seemed to be everywhere on Lee's left that day. In reality, he would spend much of the battle on Hauser's Ridge, open ground west of the Dunker church. As always, he would keep in close touch with every phase of the action. He interfered little with his subalterns; he had confidence in them, and they staked their lives on that trust.

The Union attack came at daylight as the sun poked through dissipating clouds. Three Union divisions, backed by ten batteries, moved toward Jackson's position from three-quarters of a mile to the north. General George G. Meade's troops were in the middle; Abner Doubleday's division straddled the road on Meade's right; James B. Ricketts was on the left at the East Wood.

Nearly 10,000 Federals were coming at Jackson. Yet then, as in the entire course of this bloodiest day in the Civil War, the Union assaults were uncoordinated, piecemeal, giant groups of men moving in various directions and with little or no support.

Hooker's opening attack was impressive to behold, however. "The spectacle now presented was one of splendor and magnificence," a staff officer in the Stonewall Brigade noted. "The Federals in apparent double battle line were moving toward us at charge bayonets, common time, and the sunbeams falling on their well-polished guns and bayonets gave a glamour and a show at once fearful and entrancing."[95]

While Jackson's guns played on the Federal lines, Union artillery pounded the Confederate position. The brigades of Douglass and Walker (mostly Georgians) waited. Federals advanced steadily in a wide and massed formation. Valor was about to become a common denominator. A Billy Yank described the first collision: "As we appeared at the edge of the corn[field], a long line of men in butternut and gray rose up from the ground. Simultaneously, the hostile battle lines opened a tremendous fire upon each other. Men, I can not say fell; they were knocked out of the ranks by dozens."[96]

Within minutes, the brigades of Douglass and Walker were in shreds. A soldier in the 12th Massachusetts wrote graphically: "Rifles are shot to pieces in the hands of the soldiers, canteens and haversacks are riddled with bullets, the dead and wounded go down in scores. The smoke and fog lift; and almost at our feet, concealed in a hollow behind a demolished fence, lies a rebel brigade pouring into our ranks the most deadly fire of the war. What there are left of us open on them with a cheer; and the next day the burial parties put up a board immediately in front of the position held by the Twelfth with the following inscription: 'In this trench lie buried the colonel, the major, six line officers, and one hundred and forty men of the [13th] Georgia Regiment.'"97

The 12th Massachusetts had few to cheer the repulse. It suffered the greatest loss of any Federal regiment that day: 224 of 334 men, roughly 67 percent losses.98

Colonel Douglass was killed; Colonel Walker fell badly wounded. The Louisianians tried to move up in support, but Union artillery riddled the column before it collided with waves of Federals. "Never did I see more rebs to fire at than at that moment presented themselves," a Union soldier declared.

In the space of an hour, Douglass's brigade lost 554 of 1150 engaged and five of its six regimental commanders. Walker's brigade suffered 228 casualties of fewer than 700 men and three of four regimental leaders. Hays's Louisianians had 323 losses among 550 men and lost every man leading a regiment.

Even a veteran soldier like Hooker was shocked at the carnage. Prior to being wounded himself, Hooker wrote: "Every stalk of corn in the northern and greater part of the field was cut as closely as could have been done with a knife, and the slain lay in rows precisely as they had stood in their ranks only a few moments before. It was never my fortune to witness a more bloody, dismal battle-field."99

The same living hell existed on the west side of the Hagerstown road. Doubleday's Union division slammed into Jones's 1600-man front. The brigades of Starke and Taliaferro had moved forward through the West Wood and taken a position facing east at a fence alongside the turnpike. Two Federal regiments advanced south, took the brigades in flank, and left dead Southerners at the base of the fence for a full 300 yards.

Federals tore apart the Stonewall Division almost effortlessly. Jones himself was so stunned by concussion from an exploding shell that he was forced to relinquish command to William Starke. That Virginia brigadier frantically tried to shore up his line. After a few minutes, he grabbed a battle flag and galloped forward to rally some troops. In the middle of the action, Starke fell from his horse, mortally wounded by three bullets. The Confederate left was dissolving. Never had so many high-ranking officers been put out of commission so quickly.

Jackson rushed a staff officer to bring up Hood.100 His men had not finished cooking rations, but Hood got them underway at once. At 7:20 A.M., the two brigades rushed to the front, only to find that there was no front. Jackson's line was fractured on either side of the road, bits and pieces fighting as desperately as men had ever struggled. Hood deployed his 2300 troops. Knowing that they would be no dam against the Union tidal wave, Hood saw only one recourse: to lead his men in a charge.

Some of Starke's men on the left were still holding firm with what little they had left. The 27th Virginia's Colonel Grigsby, who had been temporarily leading the Stonewall Brigade at dawn, was now commanding the remains of a division.101 Hood's troops now moved forward amid what Jackson called a "terrific storm of shell, canister, and musketry."

Residents four miles away in Shepherdstown could hear "the incessant explosions of artillery, the shrieking whistles of the shells, and the sharper, deadlier more thrilling roll of musketry; while every now and then the echo of some charging cheer . . . and as the human voice pierced that demonical clangor, we would catch our breath and listen."[102] Inside Sharpsburg, shells set on fire a number of houses, many of which were being used as makeshift hospitals.

Unless reinforcements came from somewhere, Jackson was not sure that his lines could hold. Stephen Lee, with fewer than twenty guns on the plateau, had done a magnificent job of contesting with Union artillery and advancing enemy troops. Yet the heavier Federal fire had also been effective. Lee had lost eighty-five men and sixty horses so far in the action. Around 8:45 A.M., he removed his guns to a ridge farther south.[103]

Jackson was concerned but not panicky. Nor did he have any fears of personal safety. He later told Harvey Hill that he never felt safer in battle than at Antietam. He was convinced that "God would protect him & that no harm would befall him. This security he said extended to him throughout the day."[104]

Hence, he galloped through gunfire to Jubal Early's position on the left. He placed Early in charge of the remnant of Lawton's division. Early was to move east immediately with most of his fresh brigade. Many remaining units in Jackson's old division had withdrawn from the line because of heavy losses and exhausted ammunition. However, about 200 men under Grigsby and Leroy Stafford were still standing fast.

Hood's troops were in action by now. They had rushed from the woods, across the turnpike, and onto the killing ground straight into lines of massed Federals. Hood was doing what Jackson would have done: attack with all his might.

For most soldiers, the battlefield was twenty yards long and ten yards wide, with men shouting, bleeding, and dying in indescribable fashion. "It was here," Hood reported, "that I witnessed the most terrible clash of arms, by far, that has occurred during the war. The two little giant brigades of this division wrestled with this mighty force, losing hundreds of their gallant officers and men but driving the enemy . . . from 400 to 500 yards."[105]

Major Dawes of the 6th Wisconsin likened Hood's attack to "a scythe running through our line. . . . It is a race for life that each man runs for the cornfield." One of Hood's Texans called the action "the hottest place I ever saw on this earth or want to see hereafter. . . . The dogs of war were loose, and 'havoc' was their cry."[106]

This heroic assault by Hood brought Doubleday's division to a stunned halt. For Jackson, the moment was critical. Every Confederate brigade from Early's right to Harvey Hill's left had seen combat and been smashed. The Federals were a huge wedge now extending on either side of the Hagerstown road. Jackson had no force of size to stop them. The enemy was within yards of the Dunker church and the vital high ground.

Part of Harvey Hill's division—the brigades of Roswell Ripley, Samuel Garland, and Alfred H. Colquitt—had rushed north to the East Woods. These units waged a determined contest. Bent but not broken, they poured a flank fire into the Union left. Early came up on the other side, bringing with him the 200 troops from the Stonewall Division, and they likewise were firing at the Union flank. With Hood's men driving straight ahead, Hooker's advance seemed to be caught in a dangerous pocket.

Jackson could not see through the heavy battle smoke that lay low over fields and woods. He dispatched Sandie Pendleton to determine how Hood was progressing. The aide rode through a hail of musketry and reached Hood. Could the general maintain his position? Pendleton asked on behalf of the commander. Hood, without taking his eyes from the action, shouted, "Tell General Jackson unless I get reinforcements, I must be forced back, but I am going on while I can!" Pendleton ran a gauntlet of fire a second time and relayed the message to Jackson. "Good, good," came the reply. Then Pendleton was off again: Jackson was making a direct appeal to Lee for men.[107]

The commands of Hooker and Jackson were now in shambles. At this point, the Union XII Corps, under General Joseph K. F. Mansfield, entered the battle to shore up Hooker's battered ranks. Mansfield was a senior officer but one who had never previously commanded troops in the field. Most of his corps were from Banks's old force in the Shenandoah Valley.

Jackson was looking in every direction for fresh troops. Soon McLaws's division came in sight, with Walker's men not too far behind. Jackson quickly sent McLaws to the aid of Hood. As the head of McLaws's column passed the Dunker church, it met the remains of Hood's once-strong command. Over 1000 of the 2300 men had fallen; some of the troops were down to their last bullet; yet the survivors had withdrawn in orderly fashion and, with battle flags still waving defiantly, had taken a position behind the church. All of Hood's regiments had retired except the 1st Texas. In a twenty-minute fight, it had lost four of every five members—the highest Confederate regimental loss of the entire war.

A veteran of the regiment reported only three members of his company unhurt. Of the regimental flag, he stated: "Just as fast as one man would pick it up, he would be shot down. Eight men were killed or wounded trying to bring it off the field. I can't say we were whipped, but we were overwhelmed."[108]

Walker's men disappeared into positions in the West Wood. The first elements of McLaws's division also entered the timber that Jackson regarded as crucial to maintaining the Confederate left.[109] Their arrival could not have been more timely. Four Union divisions had assailed Jackson's lines. Each had been repulsed. Yet the Confederates had literally fought themselves to the brink of defeat.

That was when General George S. Greene's mixed division of Ohio, New York, Maryland, and Pennsylvania soldiers emerged from the East Woods. The white-bearded Greene was a tough old warhorse, and he moved his brigades south in an effort to flank Jackson's sector. Federals forced their way past Harvey Hill's left-front with minimum loss and got almost to the Dunker church. Suddenly the Confederate line was in jeopardy. Who was going to stop Greene? And how?

Greene himself solved the problem. He halted for lack of support and kept looking north and east for reinforcements that never came. One reason for the confusion was that corps commander Mansfield, who had waited for years to get a field command, had fallen mortally wounded.

The presence of a Union division near the church was not Jackson's only danger. Sometime around 9 A.M., General Edwin Sumner's II Corps arrived on the field, ostensibly to finish off Jackson. This was the largest of McClellan's corps, but it contained many recruits in their first action. Fortunately for Jackson, the venerable Sumner was both shortsighted in strategy and impetuous in action. He directed General John Sedgwick to lead a division from the East Wood to the West Wood. Sumner chose not to wait for his whole corps to arrive and provide support for Sedgwick advancing across the front of the Confederate line.

A number of writers believe that Jackson organized an ambush for Sedgwick's men. To set an ambush requires time, something that Jackson did not have. What occurred was a spontaneous alignment of men in the stone outcroppings and ridges at the western edge of the West Wood. The resultant Confederate line was a giant semicircle whose extremities were outside the flanks of Sedgwick's approaching ranks. This situation for the Federals worsened when another Union division inexplicably drifted south away from the action and was an hour late in arriving where assigned. That unit was under Jackson's old Florida nemesis, the stout and choleric General William H. French.

Sumner believed that two divisions were attacking in strength. He thought too that the exhausted Confederates would make this attack a mere mop-up operation. In the haste to get the movement underway, Sumner was unaware of French's errant advance. As a result, Sedgwick's division entered the West Wood in a 600-yard front, three sets of two lines each, fifty yards apart, and completely unsupported. Union soldiers walked straight into concentrated musketry from thousands of Southerners who happened to be converging there at the same time.

The blaze of bullets tore into the Federal ranks, which naturally constricted instantly into a compact mass. Sedgwick's men were too jammed together to initiate volleys of their own. The division stood in helpless disorder as Confederate gunfire ripped into them from three sides.

After a twenty-minute fight, Union troops sought an escape avenue to the north and east. By then, Sedgwick's brigades had suffered 2200 casualties. Sedgwick, wounded three times, was carried unconscious from the field. Many of his troops were victims of friendly fire.[110] The "West Wood Massacre" was the most one-sided contest in the battle.

A few minutes later, Jackson rode to the top of a plateau behind the Dunker church and began directing the fire of some batteries. Stuart and a scout, John S. Mosby, passed through the area. Mosby was immediately impressed by how Jackson seemed "transfigured with the joy of battle" as he issued orders "in a quiet way."[111]

Exuberant Confederates in the West Wood now sought to take advantage of the turnaround. Segments of Jackson's lines swept across fields and through debris in an attack on Federals in the East Wood. At least fifty Union guns blasted the men with canister. Then the Confederates encountered improvised lines of Federal infantry. "At that point," a soldier under McLaws declared, "our loss was terrible. The ranks were so scattered, and the dead and wounded so thick, it seemed as if we could go no further. . . . Our flag was shot through seventeen times, and the staff cut in two."[112]

Fragmented Confederate units bolted back to the cover of the West Woods. Greene's Federals were immobilized, but they continued to hold the Dunker Church sector until early afternoon before withdrawing.

It was approaching midmorning. The battle had been raging for four hours. For the first time since daybreak, Jackson's front was free of pressure. The general mended his lines as much as available manpower permitted and had his wounded removed to the rear. His soldiers had blocked assaults from two Union corps and the division of another.

Never had Jackson been assailed so violently and for so long. Yet he had not only regained all of the ground lost earlier in the day; he now had a position more favorable for defense. His line was straighter and void of any weak angles.

While Jackson and McLaws conferred on their horses, a Federal shell struck the ground at their feet. It failed to explode, thereby sparing the two officers from almost certain death.[113]

Jackson had now placed every available man into battle line. One more Union assault in force might be too much. Yet the fighting in Jackson's sector had providentially ended. "God has been very kind to us today," a relieved Jackson said. Federal attention had shifted to the center of Lee's line. For the next eight hours, the battle of Antietam roared with equal fury along the high ground east and south of Sharpsburg.

Around noon, Surgeon McGuire came to see Jackson about the disposition of the wounded. He found the general behind the battle line at the Dunker church. In his saddle pockets, McGuire had some peaches that a local woman had sent to the field hospital. He was eating one when he met Jackson. The general's face beamed at the sight of his favorite fruit. "Do you have any more?" was his first question.

The physician handed him several peaches, which Jackson devoured ravenously. He then apologized to the surgeon for being so gluttonous. That was the first food he had eaten all day. McGuire looked across the broken land, bodies lying everywhere, and enemy troops still massed in the distance. "Can our line hold against another attack?" he asked apprehensively. Jackson was perfectly calm. "I think they have done their worst," he replied. "There is now no danger of the line being broken."[114]

Deafening noise of battle continued a mile to the east as Harvey Hill's thin forces fought desperately against seemingly endless lines of the enemy. Jackson was not content with having maintained his position in the first stage of the battle. That was not success in his audacious thinking. Success came through offense. Hence, from the moment McClellan ceased his pounding of the left, and despite the heavy Confederate losses, Jackson sought a chance to make a counterattack.

Early in the afternoon he and Stuart rode to Walker's part of the line. Jackson, in well-worn uniform and mounted on the redoubtable Little Sorrel, was a familiar figure in spite of the kepi that hid his face. He stopped in front of Colonel Matt Ransom of the 35th North Carolina and asked if his regiment could seize a Federal battery that was still firing. Ransom thought it too dangerous; massed Federal infantry, he added, were behind the knoll on which the Union guns were posted. Jackson looked around, then unexpectedly asked: "Have you a good climber in your command?" Ransom called for volunteers. Private William S. Hood leaped forward and said he had experience in climbing. Jackson meanwhile had selected a tall hickory tree that somehow had survived the battle. He directed Hood to scale it. The thin soldier removed his shoes and went up the hickory "like a squirrel." At the top, Hood propped himself against the limbs and peered northward. "How many troops are over there?" Jackson called from below. The young soldier answered excitedly: "Oceans of them!" "Count the flags, sir," Jackson said sternly, "count the flags." Hood began tallying the number of regimental standards: "One, two, five, eight, fourteen . . . " Jackson carefully repeated each number. "Thirty-seven, thirty-eight, thirty-nine," Hood called out. "That will do," Jackson said in disappointment. "Come down, sir." The Federals were too strong for a battery to be silenced.[115]

According to his official report, Jackson received instructions from Lee to turn the Federal right flank if possible. Jackson sought to get McLaws to undertake the move, but the Georgian was occupied with heavy skirmishing in his front. Jackson next summoned Walker. The brigadier found Jackson, a leg thrown over the pommel of his saddle, and enjoying one of several apples someone had given him. Jackson asked Walker for a regiment and a battery to attempt a turning movement. Those elements, with Stuart's command, would form a 5000-man strike force. "We'll drive McClellan into the Potomac!" Walker had Jackson exclaim. That is not correct, for a successful attack on the Union right flank would have driven McClellan *away* from the river, not into it.[116]

Jackson's assault never came to pass. The "numerous artillery" of the enemy, he reported, were "so judiciously established in their front and extending so near the Potomac . . . as to render it inexpedient to hazard the attempt." What Jackson failed to mention was a larger factor: his losses. He simply was unable to pull together enough able-bodied men to launch any kind of surprise attack on the Union flank.

About 40 percent of his command was dead or wounded. Casualty figures for Jackson's sector range from 2220 to 3700 of the approximately 5500 men he took into battle. One foot cavalryman asserted accurately that "the loss in Jackson's command, in proportion to the men he had engaged, was larger than in any battle he fought during the war."[117]

The 38th Georgia lost forty killed and fifty-five wounded. Only three officers and thirty-eight men remained in the unit at nightfall. Parker's battery was in action for forty minutes. At least twenty-one men and twelve horses fell, "and every rammer of the battery [was] shot away by minie-balls while in the hands of the cannoneers." The Stonewall Brigade was down to the size of two companies rather than fifty. Jackson's old division barely numbered 1000 troops. Such skeletal remains existed for every component of the force on Lee's left.[118]

In the middle of the afternoon, far on Lee's other flank, Federals under General Ambrose Burnside broke the Confederate line and seized the high ground. Once again, stark defeat seemed in prospect. Yet once more Confederate reinforcements arrived at the last second. This time it was Powell Hill's division, which reached the field after a forced march from Harpers Ferry that left fully half of the troops gasping for air by the roadside; but those still with Hill slammed into Burnside's exposed flank and sent Federals scampering back to high ground overlooking the Antietam. A division commander against whom Jackson intended to file court-martial charges had saved Lee's army—and possibly the Southern Confederacy.[119]

Sundown brought a merciful end to the fighting and the killing. Over 23,000 dead and injured soldiers were strewn over the fields and woods around Sharpsburg. Never before, and probably never again, would American soldiers incur so many casualties in a one-day battle. Antietam had been a traumatic shock for both sides.

It was the hardest battle in which Jackson ever fought. From first to last, his was a defensive struggle—a contest of endurance surrounded by sacrifice. Jackson's deployment of artillery, the calm and firm manner in which he kept patching his lines and scouring for reinforcements, were remarkable accomplishments in the face of overwhelming numbers. With self-assurance that God was with his troops, Jackson fought with unbroken confidence and with faith always firm. He kept the Confederate left intact. For the third time in the war, he earned the sobriquet "Stonewall."

Jackson's greatness showed twice in the campaign. On the afternoon of September 17, in spite of the beating his ranks had taken, Jackson was still thinking of offense. Assailing McClellan's flank might bring victory, not merely stave off defeat. The following day, Jackson again wanted to smite the Amalekites. Both of those instances demonstrate the indomitable will of the man—the burning desire to drive ahead even in the face of unprecedented losses. Jackson never contemplated defeat. Victory was ever at hand, and all glory be to God when it came.

Such determination is not always infectious. A few officers mistook Jackson's self-confidence for callousness. General Alexander Lawton was among that group. A month after Antietam, General George Pickett (one of Jackson's West Point classmates) relayed to his wife Lawton's opinions about Jackson. "Old Jack holds himself as the god of war, giving short, sharp commands distinctly, rapidly and decisively, without consultation or explanation, and disregarding suggestions and remonstrances. Being himself absolutely fearless . . . he goes ahead on his own hook, asking no advice and resenting interference. He places no value on human life, caring for nothing so much as fighting, unless it be praying. Illness, wounds and all disabilities he defines as inefficiency and indications of a lack of patriotism. Suffering from insomnia, he often uses his men as a sedative, and when he can't sleep calls them up, marches them out a few miles; then marches them back. He never praises his men for gallantry, because it is their duty to be gallant and they do not deserve credit for doing their duty."[120]

Early that night, while "half of Lee's army was hunting the other half," Confederate commanders gathered at army headquarters in an open field west of town. Only two-thirds of Lee's force remained to fight. He could not attack the next day with so small a force, but Lee was unwilling to run. He considered his army strong enough to maintain its position should McClellan wish to renew the struggle.

Jackson made his headquarters in the grassy yard of Captain David Smith on the southern edge of Sharpsburg. No tents were pitched; the general and his staff slept on the soft earth under the stars.[121] Occasional cracks of musketry arose from the battlefield. So did the screams and loud moans of the wounded. Campfires dotted the landscape, winking like giant Southern lightning bugs patrolling the darkness.

Before dawn on September 18, John Hood rode to the front. He was sitting on his horse and staring silently through blood-smeared darkness toward the Union lines when Jackson reined his horse beside him.

"General Hood, have they gone?"

"No, sir," Hood answered.

"I hoped they had," Jackson mumbled as he turned Little Sorrel and started down his line.[122]

The sun rose to a sickening sight. Hundreds of corpses lay on the field and, in places, were piled in rows where soldiers had been cut down as they advanced in formation. Untold numbers of injured troops were still crying for help. Only a few hundred yards separated the two armies. If a soldier ventured onto the no-man's land, a fusillade of musket fire greeted his appearance. The dead and wounded must go unattended.

Stuart had sent Major von Borcke to find Jackson and get instructions for the morning. The Prussian found Jackson "along a fence, and enjoying the luxury of a cup of coffee, quite hot, which his trusty servant had prepared from the contents of a Yankee haversack, and of which we were kindly invited to partake."[123]

Jackson remained convinced that a Confederate assault was feasible. "He seemed ready to fight at the drop of a hat," Douglas noted without enthusiasm.[124] Yet even Jackson came to agree with Lee by early afternoon that the Federals were too strong in numbers and position.

An announcement soon came from headquarters: the army was to withdraw across the Potomac. Jackson concurred. "In view of all the circumstances," he told Lee, "it was better to have fought the battle in Maryland than to have left it without a struggle."[125]

After sundown, with a thunderstorm drenching everything, the Army of Northern Virginia slowly moved south. The dead and seriously wounded, plus a few disabled guns and caissons, had to be left behind. Jackson's command brought up the rear of what a staff officer termed "an immense mass of troops and wagons of all descriptions." One of the surgeons commented that "no one can imagine the crowd and pressure on such occasions unless he has been present in such a time."[126]

That mass became a colossal traffic jam when it reached Shepherdstown and the single ford across the Potomac. The rain by then had stopped, but the mud was real and the night was dark. Torches illuminated Boteler's Ford. The river was 300 yards wide and knee deep. Jackson rode through the clogged line of men and rolling equipment and halted Little Sorrel in the middle of the Potomac. Water concealed the legs of horse and rider as Jackson silently watched the confusion. He knew of no way to untangle the mess. Yet there was someone who did.

Quartermaster John A. Harman appeared on the scene, and his profanity that night rose to new levels of spontaneity, color, and accomplishment. The traffic jam miraculously vanished. Hotchkiss declared strongly that it was Harman alone who got all of Lee's rolling stock safely back to Virginia's shore. "But for his dogged persistence," the mapmaker added, "we would have lost our military trains as well as our artillery."[127]

At 10 A.M. on the 19th, John G. Walker's division crossed the river. Walker saluted Lee, who returned the greeting and asked Walker who was behind him. Only some ambulances and a single battery, Walker replied. "Thank God," Lee said softly.[128]

The commander and Jackson were to discover quickly that the Maryland Campaign had not yet ended. While Jackson led his men to an encampment four miles from Shepherdstown on the Martinsburg road, Lee oversaw the establishment of a defensive line along the Potomac. His hope was to restrain McClellan's army on the north bank of the stream.

For that reason, Lee summoned General William N. Pendleton, who commanded the reserve artillery. Pendleton's orders were to place his batteries along the bluffs overlooking the fords and stop any Union attempt at pursuit. An infantry force would provide cover for the guns.

Pendleton, the father of Sandie Pendleton, was an 1830 graduate of West Point. He had spent most of his mature life as an Episcopal minister. Jackson knew him in Lexington; Pendleton was first captain of the Rockbridge Artillery, the battery with which Jackson had his closest ties. In the first year of the Civil War, Pendleton had risen in rank to a level far beyond his ability. An artillery lieutenant likened him to an elephant. "We have him & we don't know what on earth to do with him, and it costs a devil of a sight to feed him."[129]

On September 19, the white-haired cleric-soldier made his dispositions. Pendleton found positions for thirty cannon; he placed twelve others out of range nearby. The artillery were barely in place before Federals appeared menacingly on the other side of the Potomac. Long-range guns opened fire on Pendleton's sector. He replied carefully, not wishing to waste ammunition.

What was left of the brigades of Alexander Lawton and Lewis A. Armistead—in all about 650 men—moved to Pendleton's support. Lee had instructed the artillery commander to hold the crossings through the night, unless pressure became too great. Such discretionary orders should not have been given to a man who had never led infantry and who had no experience with heavy emplacement of artillery. Moreover, in the two infantry brigades assigned to Pendleton, there was not a single veteran field officer. Perhaps more care should have been taken in assigning the river defenses, but the Confederate army was tired and Lee expected no immediate threat.

Shortly after midnight, the commander was conferring with Jackson when a wild-eyed, all but incoherent Pendleton galloped to headquarters. Federals, he sputtered, had crossed the river somewhere, brushed aside his infantry support (which Pendleton had failed to deploy properly), and captured every one of the reserve guns![130] To Jackson, the professor of artillery, this was a major calamity. For Lee, it was worse: if McClellan advanced rapidly, he could corner the Southern army and blast it to pieces with the guns Lee did not have.

Jackson momentarily forgot his innate courtesy. His reaction was either high anxiety or cold disgust.[131] He demanded to know the size of the enemy force. Pendleton could not say, though he did not think it was sizable. Without waiting for a discussion with Lee, Jackson sent a courier rushing to Powell Hill. The Light Division, at the rear of the army, was to double back to Boteler's Ford and confront the Federals. Try to retake the guns, Jackson ordered, but at least drive the enemy back across the river.

Shortly after these orders went forth, Jackson decided to reconnoiter personally. He galloped toward the Potomac. By the time Hill arrived with his lead brigade, Jackson not only knew the situation but had developed his strategy. "With the blessing of Providence," he told one of Lee's couriers, "they will soon be driven back."[132]

Jackson dispatched two lines of battle against some seventy Union guns staring at him in the early-morning light. Hill's men surged forward. As Jackson guessed after viewing the locale, the Federal attack force was a brigade. One of its four regiments— the 118th Pennsylvania—had been in service less than three weeks. The Federal units were not prepared for the onslaught from Powell Hill's veterans.

Southern troops ignored the cannon fire and crashed through the Union position. Billy Yanks scurried frantically for the river and safety. Many jumped into the Potomac and tried to wade to the north bank. Hill's soldiers, positioned on the bluffs, began picking them off one by one as if at a carnival shooting gallery.

Jackson wrote of "an appalling scene of the destruction of human life." A giddy Hill was convinced that he inflicted 3000 casualties in the hour-long fight. Actual Union losses were seventy-one killed, 161 wounded, and 131 missing. At least 269 of those casualties were from the new Pennsylvania regiment.[133]

After stabilizing the south bank defense line, Jackson learned that Pendleton in fact had not lost all forty of the reserve artillery's guns. Only four had been captured. Battery commanders had hauled the others through the woods to safety in advance of the Federal strike. Still, the promptness of Jackson and Powell Hill had saved forty cannon. The cost was 261 men killed or wounded.

This action (which goes by the name of both Boteler's Ford and Shepherdstown Ford) was a small rear guard collision, relatively speaking. Surgeon McGuire declared, "We had the Yankees driven off into the river, killed and drowned a great many, and the whole affair was disposed of before General Lee ever came over or before Gen. Jackson ever heard from him."[134] Nevertheless, the brief fight sparked a spirited controversy.

McGuire and others felt that Jackson's prompt reaction prevented McClellan from gaining a toehold on the Virginia side of the Potomac. Harvey Hill was too quick to state, in his usual blunt way, that Jackson's swiftness averted a major disaster for Lee's whole army. Hill went further: Lee was so rattled by Pendleton's initial report, Hill told Jackson's early biographer, that his only thought was to throw up an improvised defense line and await attack. When Robert L. Dabney incorporated those statements in his Jackson book, Lee objected strongly to their untruths.[135]

The fact that the Boteler's Ford action occurred on Virginia soil and marked the return of Lee from Maryland brought it far more attention than might otherwise have been the case. Jackson's quick counterattack, and the complete victory, added even more luster to the small affair. Private James Thompson of the 11th Georgia proudly wrote his parents: "When we fell back out of Md. across the river, 'Uncle Stone Wall' lay s[t]ill until the Yankees all got over on this side then he picked into them and just slaughterd them . . . so the river was completely damed up and so thick with blood that the river looked like blood for miles below." A Richmond newspaper put the action in succinct perspective: "Another chastisement, swift and sudden and severe, has fallen upon the enemy from the hand of Jackson."[136]

Meanwhile, the general had already turned his thoughts to other matters. He must rebuild his shattered command, replace fallen officers, instill new morale in the ranks. The northern invasion had failed; Jackson's hope of carrying the war to the enemy had succeeded only briefly. The Lord's will be done.

Now, however, if the North persisted in continuing the struggle, Jackson and his refurbished legions would be ready and eager to meet them again. Thanks to the Almighty, smashing victories had become the Confederate way of life on Virginia's sacred soil. Jackson was optimistic because he had faith.

It was also good to be home again in his beloved Shenandoah Valley.

≹ 21 ≸
LEADING A CORPS

B UNKER HILL, VIRGINIA, bore no resemblance to the American Revolution battle site for which it was named. It was a rural intersection five miles north of Winchester on the Martinsburg road. "There was no town, nothing but a large spring surrounded by a beautiful level, fertile land," an Alabama soldier observed. Fields were fresh, transportation unclogged.[1]

It was an ideal place for a campground. In that general area, Jackson would spend much of the next two months—the most protracted "rest" period in the field he would know during 1862. The general moved the brigade camps every few days because he believed new areas were healthier. Jackson shifted headquarters eleven times in the two months he was in the lower valley. His first command post was at the John E. Boyd estate just south of the Bunker Hill crossroads. The three weeks there represented the longest time Jackson spent at any one place.[2]

The soldiers were in need of practically everything: rest, food, baths, equipment, and reorganization of shattered units. Two ingredients remained strongly in evidence among the men: pride in what they had done in the recent Maryland Campaign and a continuing, high morale. Lee praised his soldiers in a congratulatory message read to every regiment. "Achievements such as these demanded much valor and patriotism. History records few examples of greater fortitude and endurance than this army has exhibited; and I am commissioned by the President to thank you, in the name of the Confederate States, for the undying fame you have won for their arms." Nevertheless, the commander felt compelled to add, "much as you have done, much more remains to be accomplished."[3]

They were stirring words, especially to an army that was physically beaten. Troops present for duty were hungry, ragged, and footsore; droves of sick and wounded men needed to be in hospitals; stragglers by the thousands must be collected and returned to duty; dozens of officers had to be found for command vacancies ranging from lieutenant to brigadier general.

So the latter days of September began a period not of marches and battle preparations but of much internal activity. (McClellan posed no threat. In a single communique to Washington at this time, the Union commander offered at least twelve reasons for not pursuing Lee's army.)

Northward-flowing Opequon Creek, east of both Winchester and Martinsburg, thus became a huge communal bath for the Confederates. Soldiers frolicked and soaked off the dust of long campaigning. Almost everyone washed clothes. "The vermin have become very numerous in camp," the fastidious Hotchkiss admitted.[4]

Recuperation of Jackson's forces was "rapid, successful, and confident," aide James Smith boasted. With the issuance of food and clothing, the 37th Virginia's Captain Wood, discovered, "the arduous and perilous duties of the Maryland campaign were forgotten and the army was itself again." Some troops even revelled "in the best of fresh beef, vegetables, fruits, not forgetting the honey, needing nothing for the stomach's sake, save salt."[5]

The resilience of youth is amazing, and the army's restoration in the lower Shenandoah Valley was impressive. However, full recovery from the campaign took time and care. When Jackson reached Bunker Hill, he had 10,772 troops present for duty. A week later, the ranks had grown to 18,839 soldiers as convalescents, stragglers, conscripts, and men who had taken "French furloughs" (rather than be termed invaders of the North) all began reporting for duty. After two weeks, Jackson's command had swelled to 25,512 men. Yet the overall state of the Southern army was pitiful.

"It is difficult to describe the condition of the troops at this time," an officer in Gregg's brigade commented. "They were sun-burnt, gaunt, ragged, scarcely at all shod, spectres and caricatures of their former selves." The brigade as a whole was "an emaciated, limping ragged, filthy mass, whom no stranger to their valiant exploits could have believed capable of anything the least worthy." With the countryside suffering from drought and all but stripped of subsistence or forage, regaining strength was going to be a slow process.[6]

Meantime, Winchester had again become a vast refuge for the human debris of war. Young Julia Chase wrote in her diary: "Every heart must groan to think of the suffering that is in our midst. Some 3000 wounded soldiers are being brought in today, and our town is thronged with them. Poor fellows." Mrs. Hugh Lee was serving as a volunteer nurse. The demands were overpowering. "I saw such fearful sights in town today that I turned sick," she stated. "Long rows of wounded men sitting on the curbstones, waiting for some shelter to be offered them, the wagons still unloading more. Oh! their pitiful faces, so haggard with suffering."[7]

With reorganization came a strengthening of discipline. Both Lee and Jackson were active in that regard during the first days of autumn. Lee directed Longstreet and Jackson to reinstate roll calls and arms inspections, to punish men who discarded weapons, to secure camps against unauthorized departures, and to arrest anyone who violated private property. In stern, uncharacteristic language, Lee ordered General William Pendleton to dispatch "armed detachments to rid the country of this annoyance of stragglers, using the most stringent measures, punishing them as severely as you choose, handing them over to your men to do your pleasure on them."[8]

Jackson was equally as forceful within his command. He repeated his belief that all deserters should be shot without delay for the good of the service (although Jackson was later known to grant mercy to first-time deserters whose prior record had been exemplary). Courts-martial resumed with a vigor. Within a month, over 100 were pending. Death sentences were not decreed, but severe punishments were. A soldier in the 27th Virginia was ordered to receive twenty-seven lashes, have his head shaved, and be drummed from the service.[9]

When Colonel Daniel Hamilton of the 1st South Carolina failed to have his men fire muskets as promptly as the general wished, Jackson placed him under arrest.

General Maxcy Gregg came immediately to Hamilton's defense. A heated argument erupted between Gregg and Jackson that left both men speaking to the other only when necessary. In similar vein, Jackson sent a curt note to Early and advised the usually dependable general, "If your Division return is not ready this evening you arrest whatever officer is at fault in the matter."[10]

Personnel issues—specifically recommendations for promotion—occupied much of Jackson's time. On September 22, he urged that Isaac R. Trimble be elevated to major general. "I do not regard him as a good disciplinarian," Jackson wrote, "but his success in battle" was an overriding consideration. John B. Hood had performed splendidly as a division commander and likewise merited Jackson's recommendation for promotion to major general. James Power Smith had demonstrated such high ability as a volunteer aide that Jackson asked for his assignment to become official. The general endorsed Hotchkiss's application for a commission as a topographical engineer—but privately informed the mapmaker that his "great fault was talking too much."[11]

Once again Jackson asked that Colonel William E. Jones receive a brigadier's rank. Though "Grumble" Jones and Stuart did not get along well, Jackson admired him greatly. "I have found him prompt and efficient. . . . I am not acquainted with any other field officer of cavalry whom I regard as so well qualified for commanding a Brigade."[12]

The stormiest of Jackson's recommendations was for command of his beloved Stonewall Brigade. To the shock of everyone, he nominated his friend, thirty-four-year-old Frank Paxton, an attorney and bank president in Lexington prior to the war. Paxton was industrious and devout, qualities that Jackson liked. Yet the man's military record reflected a quick peak and steady decline.

"Bull" Paxton (whose loud voice complemented his large size) had entered service as a lieutenant in the 27th Virginia. Gallantry at First Manassas brought him promotion to major. Heavy-handedness and a lack of tact cost him his position in the April 1862 regimental elections. Jackson thereupon named Paxton to his personal staff. While Paxton had conducted administrative duties well, his field service remained limited and his personality unimproved.[13]

Added to those drawbacks was Jackson's action in urging that Paxton be raised three grades from major to brigadier general. The general rarely if ever had disregarded protocol. Jackson explained his action to Lee. "My rule has been to recommend such as were, in my opinion, best qualified for filling vacancies. The application of this rule has prevented me from even recommending for the command of my old brigade one of its own officers because I did not regard any of them as competent as another."[14]

This was an obvious and direct rebuff of Colonel Andrew Jackson Grigsby. Born in 1819 in Rockbridge County, a West Point dropout but Mexican War veteran, "Andy" Grigsby had endured wounds and exhibited bravery as he advanced to command of the 27th Virginia. On the morning of Antietam, he temporarily commanded the Stonewall Brigade; by afternoon he was at the head of Jackson's division. Dauntless and fearless, Grigsby seemed to be the type of leader Jackson most preferred.

Coupled with a fighting prowess, however, were negative qualities. Grigsby's conversation had a tendency to become sulphurous; he often carried whiskey in his canteen; bravery sometimes became impulsiveness; his stern demands of discipline applied to everyone but himself. Jackson therefore bypassed Grigsby for command of the Stonewall Brigade.

The colonel became "as mad as thunder," a member of the 33d Virginia remarked. Several officers in the brigade made pleas on his behalf. Many men openly said that Jackson was a poor judge of officers because he preferred good Presbyterians to good soldiers.

It was all to no avail. An embittered Grigsby resigned his commission and went home, thus depriving the army of a proven soldier. Frank Paxton became the fourth official commander of Jackson's old brigade. He did so under as dark a cloud as Winder had encountered in the spring.[15]

An even thornier issue for Jackson involved his second in command, the senior division commander on duty, A. P. Hill. The Confederate army had barely established camps north and east of Winchester when Hill started a letter through channels to Lee. Hill wanted an immediate resolution of the arrest and the charges levied by Jackson at the outset of the Maryland Campaign. Being removed from command, even briefly, was not consistent with Hill's proud and sensitive nature. The general whom Bradley T. Johnson described as "the lithe and active form of the most graceful man in the army" was now on the warpath.

On September 24, Jackson outlined to Lee all of the circumstances that led to Hill's arrest. What Hill failed to see now, but which Lee discerned at once, was an amelioration on Jackson's part. Old Jack was not anxious—as he had been in the case of Richard Garnett—to push for a court-martial. Hill's conduct at Harpers Ferry, Antietam, and Boteler's Ford had been impeccable. It was proof to Jackson that Hill had learned his lesson.

Perhaps his arrest could serve as a momentary censure and a reminder. Jackson was willing to let the matter drop. He told Lee, "As the object in arresting Genl. Hill, which was to secure his stricter compliance with orders, has been effected, I do not consider further action on my part necessary."[16]

Lee agreed. In an endorsement to Hill's request for a court of inquiry, the army commander replied: "Respectfully returned to Genl. A. P. Hill who will see from the remarks of Genl. Jackson the cause of his arrest. His attention being now called to what appeared to be neglect of duty by his commander, but which from an officer of his character could not be intentional and I feel assured will never be repeated, I see no advantage to the service in further investigating the matter nor could it without detriment being done at this time."[17]

To Lee's disappointment and Jackson's bewilderment, none of this was satisfactory to Hill. His reputation had been challenged, his honor impugned. The wrong must be righted at whatever the cost.

Barely a week later, the lean division commander submitted an official demand for a court of inquiry. Jackson had no choice but to activate the charges he had compiled against Hill. Hotchkiss noted in his diary: "Gen. Hill is a brave officer but perhaps too quick to resent seeming over-steping [sic] of authority. General Jackson intends to do his whole duty. May good and not evil come out of this trouble."[18]

Thereafter, communications between Jackson and his most reliable subaltern were minimal, stiff, and scrupulously formal. Lee's initial efforts to resolve the matter having been unsuccessful, the commander adopted the alternative of letting time have a chance. Lee filed the papers at headquarters and hoped that the dispute would evaporate.

Meanwhile, rumors circulated in the Light Division that Powell Hill and his men were to be transferred elsewhere. Hill "does not work well with Stonewall," Major Andrew Wardlaw of the 14th South Carolina told his wife. The major then observed: "I must admit that it is much pleasanter to read about Stonewall & his exploits than to serve under him & perform those exploits."[19]

Jackson found some moments of pleasure in those first days of autumn. Presbyterian cleric James Graham in Winchester remembered that the general "came to see us once & made a good many hurried calls in town, but gladdened our hearts in those few moments, for he was the idol of the people." That sentiment extended beyond Virginia's borders. A young student from South Carolina wrote his sister that the recent campaign "is another star in Stonewall's crown of victories. Nine cheers & tiger for Jackson!" A Baltimore matron went even further in her praise. Convinced of Jackson's powers to right every wrong, she told a Richmond newspaper that Confederate prisoners at Fort McHenry were being mistreated. Her letter closed with the statement: "Please let Jackson know of the fate of these young men."[20]

Inside the Southern army was pure adulation for Jackson. A Georgia sergeant in one of Longstreet's regiments noted of the post-Antietam period: "One day while [near Winchester], I heard cheering down the road in our front. Some of the boys thought it was Stonewall Jackson or a rabbit. . . . Everyone made for the road, and sure enough, it was Gen. Jackson galloping along the road with his escort. He passed us with his cap off and the cheering continued down the line as far as we could hear. The boys claim that he is getting tired of the army because Longstreet's men keep him bareheaded so much. . . . He certainly creates more excitement than all of the rest of the officers put together."[21]

One Alabama private in Rodes's division ventured so far as to compare Jackson with Jesus of Nazareth. "If Jesus Christ were to ride along the ranks on the foal of an ass," he declared, "there would not be half the cheering and huzzaing that there is when General Jupiter Stonewall Jackson rides along our ranks. The soldiers cheer him as if they think him to possess some supernatural power, and indeed I expect he is a great man. There is one thing about it, he seems to be a great deal keener to get into a fight than I am."[22]

By that stage of the war, Little Sorrel had learned its master's embarrassment at the cheers from the soldiers. Whenever Confederates raised loud and friendly noise, the horse would break into a gallop and carry its rider speedily away.

While Jackson may not have shown it often, his affection for his soldiers matched their feelings for him. Late one night the Rebel yell began in a sector of an encampment. Other units picked it up. As it was swelling to full volume, Jackson emerged from his tent. He walked to a fence, leaned his elbow on the top rail, and cupped his chin in his hand as he listened intently. When the yell finally ran its course, the general turned toward his tent and said partially to himself: "That was the sweetest music I ever heard."[23]

Gifts poured into his headquarters: a sword, gilded spurs, imported field glasses, socks, gloves, and trinkets. Jackson accepted such daily displays of affection in trust only. When he acknowledged receipt of an item, Jackson was careful to emphasize that the credit for his success belonged elsewhere. He expressed this anew in a thank-you letter.

> My dear Mrs. Osburn, Your very kind note and beautiful and useful presents from your daughter have been received. Please give my thanks to her, and accept them for yourself. I know of none who rejoices more than myself at your release from that thraldom [of Federal occupation] to which you refer, but you must not overestimate me in the work. I have been but the unworthy instrument whom it has pleased *God* to use in accomplishing His purpose. My prayer is that God will soon bless our country with an honorable peace and that we may be that "*People Whose God is the Lord.*"[24]

During this same period, Jackson received a special gift—one that aroused curiosity throughout the army. It came as a result of one of the most unusual friendships in the Civil War.

Jackson and Jeb Stuart seemed on the surface to have nothing in common. Although the two were products of Virginia hill country, they were seven years apart in age and grew up at opposite ends of the state. Jackson was a stern Calvinist, humorless and introspective. Stuart was a buoyant cavalier, fun loving and outgoing. While Jackson was an artilleryman now leading infantry, Stuart was the embodiment of a cavalryman.

What bound them together were the twin ties of aggressive leadership and profound faith. Neither hesitated to do battle; both fought for the glory of God. Those similarities pulled the two generals together to an amazing degree. Stuart was the only one who dared to kid Jackson. Most of Jackson's feeble attempts at humor were delivered to Stuart. These two beau ideals of the South were proof of the adage that opposites attract; and during the October-November days in the lower Shenandoah, their friendship deepened.

Stuart's encampment was near Bunker Hill. One visit to Jackson came late at night. Stuart and his young artillerist, Major John Pelham, arrived at headquarters to find Jackson already asleep. That did not bother Stuart. He removed his saber, crawled into Jackson's bed with him, and apparently spent the night unconsciously wrestling with Old Jack for a major share of the one blanket. The next morning, Stuart emerged from the tent to find Jackson and some of his staff standing around a campfire.

"Good morning, General Jackson!" Stuart boomed. "How are you?" Jackson looked at him sternly but could not completely hide a smile.

"General Stuart," he responded, "I'm always glad to see you here. You might select better hours sometimes, but I'm always glad to see you." Then Jackson bent over and tenderly rubbed his legs. "But, General," he added, "you must not get into my bed with your boots and spurs on and ride me around like a cavalry horse all night!"[25]

On another occasion, Stuart was chatting with his aide, Heros von Borcke. The Prussian began praising Jackson and tried to say that "it warms my heart when he talks to me." Yet von Borcke's command of the English language was somewhat shaky. The words that tumbled forth were: "It makes my heart burn when he talks to me." Stuart leaped happily at the misstatement. When he related the story to his headquarters group, the cavalry chief had von Borcke say: "It gives me heartburn to hear Jackson talk." The staff roared with laughter. A day or so later, Stuart repeated the story to Jackson with von Borcke present. Jackson missed the humor completely. He reached over, shook the Prussian officer's hand, and (according to von Borcke) praised him as a good soldier and daring cavalier.[26]

Weary of seeing Jackson in his old uniform coat, buttons long removed by admiring ladies, the garment threadbare and almost colorless as a result of exposure to the elements, Stuart took action. He ordered Jackson a new coat from one of Richmond's best tailors. It arrived, and the cavalry chief sent Major von Borcke with the present and some dispatches to Jackson's headquarters.

The aide delivered the messages first. Then he handed over a package without explanation. Jackson opened it matter-of-factly. Von Borcke could hardly stifle laughter as Jackson looked quizzically at the coat. The general refolded it carefully and laid it on a table. "Give General Stuart my best thanks, Major," he said in obvious embarrassment. "The coat is much too handsome for me, but I shall take the best care of it, and shall prize it highly as a souvenir. And now let us have some dinner."[27]

Von Borcke was not going to let the gift be placed aside so easily. You must try it on, he told Jackson. General Stuart is anxious to know whether it fits. Jackson gave a disconcerted smile; he removed his tattered coat and donned the new one. It fit perfectly. Jackson clearly liked the present. He wore it to dinner. Jim Lewis was bringing food to the table when he saw his general. The servant almost dropped the plate. Jackson's staff sat in shocked silence. Word quickly spread through the encampment. Soon soldiers by the scores "came running to the spot, desirous of seeing their beloved Stonewall in his new attire."[28]

Jackson sent a grateful note by von Borcke. "I am much obliged to you for the beautiful coat you have presented me," he wrote Stuart. "Your injunction will be heeded. My lost buttons have been replaced. We learn by experience. When you come near don't forget to call & see me. Your much attached friend."[29] Yet ten weeks would pass before Jackson wore the coat again in public.

A large and positive result from the long encampment in the lower valley was a reorganization of the Army of Northern Virginia. The Civil War had grown far beyond the expectations of leaders on both sides. Armies had expanded, and battles had reached dimensions unseen previously in the Western Hemisphere. The old system of an army organized by divisions was unwieldy. Division commanders too often were autonomous in thinking if not in action. Military problems had grown larger and more complex than the old chain of command could handle.

The Union army had already shifted into a corps arrangement. On September 18, the Confederate Congress authorized the same new level for the Southern forces. President Davis asked Lee to suggest officers who should be given corps command.

Lee responded promptly. He proposed to reconstitute his army into two corps. Longstreet was the ranking major general and a dependable leader who fought solidly. He was the first candidate.

To the surprise of no one in the army, Jackson was the other nominee for corps command and lieutenant general. None of Lee's officers had performed more brilliantly in recent weeks; no one obeyed Lee's orders more quickly or completely. A bond had already developed between Lee and Jackson. They thought and acted with one mind. For Lee not to have proposed Jackson would have sent shock waves through the ranks.

Historians have wasted too much time on the text of Lee's letter of recommendations to the president. Lee designated Longstreet with a simple statement. "Old Pete's" long service in the Piedmont and Tidewater regions had made him a familiar figure to officials in Richmond. In Jackson's case, Lee appeared to give a two-sentence explanation. "My opinion of the merits of General Jackson has been greatly enhanced during this expedition. He is true, honest and brave; has a single eye to the good of the service and spares no exertion to accomplish his object."

Some writers have felt the need to lift the phrases "been greatly enhanced" and "the good of the service" for special dissection. An inference about the first is that Lee was disappointed in Jackson's performance all the way through Second Manassas, while the second can be twisted as to convey the impression of Jackson being a "loose cannon" but not as badly as before. Such interpretations are nonsense at the least.[30]

Granted, Jackson might have had a shaky moment or two during the Maryland Campaign: a perceived tardiness in investing Harpers Ferry, for example. Yet Lee had no other general who accomplished what Jackson did both at Harpers Ferry and on the left at Antietam. Lee felt a need to elaborate on Jackson's merits in order to convince a possibly hesitant president. An open coolness had existed between Davis and Jackson stretching back to the January operations at Romney, if not to the first battle at Manassas. Davis actively wielded veto power over military appointments. Lee was therefore willing to stake his own reputation on Jackson's advancement.

It was unnecessary for Lee to make the extra effort. By then, the quiet general from the valley enjoyed a fame matched only by that of Lee himself. Whatever Davis's faults, the success of the Southern cause was paramount in his thinking. Promotion of Jackson was a means to that end. In all likelihood as well, any lingering reservations Davis might have possessed about Jackson had slowly vanished in the summer campaigns (and would turn to unadulterated praise in the postwar years).[31]

The promotions were made, and Lieutenant General Jackson officially assumed command of almost half of Lee's army. The Second Corps contained four divisions. At the head of Ewell's old division was the redoubtable Jubal Early: a proven fighter but racked by rheumatism and so profane in conversation that Lee branded him "my bad old man." Early's division consisted of the brigades of General Harry T. Hays and Colonels Edmund N. Atkinson, Robert F. Hoke, and James A. Walker—7716 men, with six batteries of twenty-six guns under Captain Joseph W. Latimer.

A. P. Hill's unusually large six-brigade division also had the most veteran commanders: Generals James J. Archer, Maxcy Gregg, James H. Lane, W. Dorsey Pender, Edward L. Thomas, and Colonel John M. Brockenbrough—11,554 men, with seven batteries of twenty-eight guns under Lieutenant Colonel R. Lindsay Walker.

The Stonewall Division, under the recovered William B. Taliaferro, was predominantly Virginian in makeup. Commanding its brigades were Generals Franklin Paxton and John R. Jones plus Colonels E. H. T. Warren and Edmund Pendleton—in all, 5478 troops, with five batteries of twenty-two guns led by Captain John B. Brockenbrough.

D. H. Hill's division contained the brigades of Generals Alfred H. Colquitt, George Doles, Alfred Iverson, Robert E. Rodes, and Colonel Bryan Grimes—6944 soldiers, with five batteries of twenty-two guns under Major Hilary P. Jones.

Jackson now headed an impressive command: almost 32,000 troops in ninety-two regiments, along with twenty-three batteries of just under 100 cannon. Yet weaknesses were there. A brigade normally averaged about 3500 men, but Jackson's eighteen brigades had a mean strength of less than half that figure.

On the command level, Ewell and Lawton were recovering from battle wounds and would be lost for indefinite periods. Early was handling that division for the time being. Isaac Trimble was battling erysipelas and likewise indisposed for weeks to come. Taliaferro would have to cover for him.

That left Jackson with but a pair of seasoned major generals: the two Hills. Jackson's relations with Powell Hill were exceedingly strained. The same situation may have been developing with Jackson and Harvey Hill. Early charged after the war that Jackson and his brother-in-law were in a very fragile relationship. Perhaps Harvey Hill's caustic nature and fault-finding habits were becoming more than Jackson would tolerate.[32]

Despite this shakiness in the new corps, Jackson's force remained as the more independent segment of Lee's army. It was the portion that Lee dispatched on wide-ranging activities. Members of Jackson's staff had a ready explanation why this was so. "It is well known that General Lee himself invariably remained with [Longstreet's] First Corps because he never expected Longstreet to do what Jackson did."[33]

One of Jackson's new brigadiers was anxious to call on the general, but he hesitated to do so. Then came orders for him to report to Jackson for detached service. James H. Lane had graduated from VMI in 1854 and returned to the institute in 1857 to serve on the faculty. He was well acquainted with Jackson but had not had direct contact with him since the war began. "I reported to my old professor," he wrote,

expecting to be received in the stiff, formal manner of old which I so well remembered, be given my orders, and immediately dismissed with the old familiar military salute.

But I was agreeably surprised; on entering the General's tent, he at once rose with a smile on his face, took my hand in both of his in the warmest manner, expressing his pleasure at seeing me, and asking why I had not been to see him before, at the same time handing me a camp stool and pressing me to a seat beside him. His kind words, the tones of his voice, his familiarly calling me Lane—whereas it had always been Mr. Lane at the Institute—put me completely at my ease. I felt I was in the presence of a warm hearted friend, and then, for the first time, I began to feel that magnetism, which . . . has so endeared him to his troops.

Jackson gained a disciple from that moment.[34]

The new lieutenant general shied away from visitors even more than was customary. A stream of military matters required his attention; small talk was alien to his nature; other conversation he regarded as confidential. Jackson had a tendency to distrust people who wished to discuss the war. For such reasons, he refused to see

Belle Boyd when the female scout came to Bunker Hill specifically to see the general she had helped in the May attack on Front Royal.[35]

Foreign visitors were an exception to Jackson's antisocial rule. In the second week of October, Colonel Bradley Johnson brought three Englishmen to see Jackson. They had visited Lee and were now eager to meet the famous "Stonewall." Colonel Garnet Wolseley was a rising star in the British army (he later became commander in chief of English military forces). Frank Vizitelly was a correspondent for the *Illustrated London Times,* and Francis C. Lawley was a well-known writer with the *Times.*

The Englishmen had been led to believe that they would meet a reincarnated Oliver Cromwell: impersonal, abrupt, dedicated totally to the war effort. They were pleasantly surprised to be greeted by a general who made them feel instantly at ease. The four men took seats in front of Jackson's tent. Before the visitors could open conversation, Jackson began recalling his 1856 trip to England and the Continent. He quizzed the guests so deeply on British subjects that not one of them could ask a question.

As the trio rode away from Jackson's headquarters, Colonel Johnson laughed heartily. He told the foreigners that they had been unknowing victims of finesse. Jackson had maintained a steady conversation to block anyone from asking him leading questions about the military situation in northern Virginia.

Of the three, Wolseley was the most impressed by Jackson. "He looks the hero that he is," the British soldier declared,

and his thin compressed lips and calm glance, which meets you unflinchingly, give evidence of that firmness and decision of character for which he is so famous. . . . The religious element seems strongly developed in him; and though his conversation is perfectly free from all puritanical cant, it is evident that he is a person who never loses sight of the fact that there is an omnipresent Deity ever presiding over the minutest occurrences of life, as well as over the most important. . . .

With such a leader men would go anywhere, and face any amount of difficulties; and for myself, I believe that, inspired by the presence of such a man, I should be perfectly insensible to fatigue, and reckon upon success as a moral certainty. . . . Jackson, like Napoleon, is idolised with that intense fervour which, consisting of mingled personal attachment and devoted loyalty, causes them to meet death for his sake, and bless him when dying.[36]

Lawley found the general "morose, reserved, distant," but at the same time genial and courteous. He concluded his account of the interview with a foreboding statement: "General Jackson has acquired such a fame in that entire neighborhood [of Virginia] that it is sad to think what would happen if the one life round which such prestige clings should yield to a stray bullet or to the chance of disease."[37]

General George E. Pickett, Jackson's West Point classmate, wrote basically the same thing at the same time. "I only pray that God may spare him to see us through," Pickett told his betrothed. Then, referring to the Union general gaining successes in the western theater, Pickett added, "If General Lee had Grant's resources he would soon end the war; but Old Jack can do it without resources."[38]

All such attention had little if any effect on Jackson. In a letter to Anna only two days after his promotion, he did not mention the subject. Instead, Jackson concentrated on things spiritual. "I heard an excellent sermon from the Rev. Dr. Stiles of the

New School. . . . It was a powerful exposition of the word of God. He is a great revival minister, & when he came to the word '*Himself*,' he placed an emphasis on it, & gave to it, thru God's blessing, a power that I had never felt before. . . . Oh! it is a glorious privilege to be a minister of the Gospel of the Prince of Peace. There is no equal position in this world."[39]

In addition to considering the ministry the highest calling of man, Jackson had developed in absentia a deeper love for his adopted area. He told Anna several times in this period that at war's end he wanted to purchase a home in the lower Shenandoah Valley. There he hoped to pursue his rural tastes and live in quiet happiness with his family.

Meanwhile, Jackson told Anna, she must not be offended when a publication was not as laudatory of her soldier-husband as she might wish. "Don't trouble yourself about representations that are made of me. These things are earthly & transitory. There are real & glorious blessings, I trust, in reserve for us beyond this life. It is best for us to keep our eyes fixed upon the throne of God, & the realities of a more glorious existence beyond the verge of time. It is gratifying to be beloved, & to have our conduct approved by our fellow men, but this is not worthy to be compared with the glory that is in reservation for us in the presence of our glorified Redeemer."[40]

The excerpts from the general's letters in Mrs. Jackson's memoir contain no references to her pregnancy. Yet she was approaching her eighth month—a fact of which Jackson would have been very aware. Undoubtedly, he made several tender comments in his letters about her condition and the child she was carrying.

Weather in all of its variations continued to affect the encampments adversely. A major drought prevailed into the second week of October. "It is as hot as midsummer here," Sandie Pendleton wrote from Bunker Hill. "Our camp is out in the middle of a field, with no shade around it. . . . I see regiments drilling in the field two hundred yards from me, enveloped in a cloud of dust which they stir up as they go." The first rain in two months was falling in torrents by the end of the week. Camps became swamps of mud. A week later, snow was falling and the temperature did not rise above the freezing mark. "The worst part of it," Colonel Edward Warren stated, "is that we have in the brigade under my command not less than 175 men in their bare feet, a large number are without overcoats and many are deficient in blankets." Warren then declared: "My heart used to bleed as I would read the account of the sufferings of the patriot army at Valley Forge, and little did I then think that the time would come when I would command men in like destitute condition."[41]

Before the weather turned cold, Lee dispatched Stuart and 1800 horsemen across the Potomac to ascertain McClellan's position and designs. The flamboyant Stuart repeated his peninsula feat of swinging completely around the Union army. His ride took him as far north as Chambersburg, Pennsylvania. He saw no signs of any advance by McClellan, destroyed supplies along the way, and headed back to Virginia with 1200 fresh horses. The Confederates had one narrow escape while on the raid. Stuart's presence sent hundreds of Federal cavalry scurrying in every direction in a vain effort to trap the Southerners.

On the day of his return, Stuart rode to Jackson's headquarters. The general rushed from his tent and, with Stuart still some forty yards away, shouted amusingly: "How do you do, Pennsylvania?" The two men exchanged their usual cordial welcome. Stuart then showed Jackson a picture he had obtained in Pennsylvania. The caption read: "Where is Stonewall Jackson?" Both men laughed, Jackson but briefly.[42]

Harvey Hill reported early in October of seeing Jackson and Lieutenant Joseph Morrison at a religious service in camp. "Very few soldiers attend," Hill complained, "& seem very indifferent about their souls." Again Hill was exhibiting negativism. The facts tell quite a different story.

A religious revival exploded in the Confederate camps that autumn. Motivated by everything from a new awakening to despair over the continuation of the war, soldiers in large numbers flocked to camp meetings. Chaplains redoubled their efforts in preaching and distributing tracts. A number of eminent ministers—such as the Reverend Joseph Stiles, whom Jackson liked—took advantage of the lull in the fighting to visit camps and preach as missionaries.

Jackson cordially welcomed them all and eagerly took part in as many services as possible. James Nisbet, a Georgia captain, wrote of his "good fortune" in seeing the general almost daily. "He would come through the woods from his headquarters, walking and take a seat in our midst on a log or stump" to participate in the prayer meeting or preaching. (Old Jack never became aware that not all of his soldiers were as fervent as he believed. Many of the men followed a set routine. As the general approached a camp for a service, a private would recognize him and run ahead to spread the word. Troops engaged in card games, dice shooting, and other such activities would drop what they were doing and bolt toward the place of prayer. By the time Jackson arrived, a crowd sat bareheaded and reverently.)[43]

Recounting the joy of these services to his friend, Dr. Dabney, Jackson exclaimed: "It pleased our ever Merciful Father to visit my command with the rich outpouring of His Spirit. There was probably more than 100 inquiring the way of life in my old brigade. It appears to me that we may look for growing piety and many conversions in the army, for it is the subject of prayer. If so many prayers were offered for the blessing of God upon any other organization, would we not expect the answer of prayer to hear the petitions, and send a blessing?"[44]

One cold night during the destruction of the Harpers Ferry-Winchester Railroad, Jackson and Dr. McGuire engaged in a long conversation about religion. The surgeon mentioned that in a recent discussion with Dr. Stiles, the missionary had termed repentance the result of love rather than fear. McGuire disagreed; repentance, he told Jackson, began with fear and, after adoption, came to full reality through love.

Jackson concurred, although he denied that fear had any place in his faith. "I have no fears whatever that I shall ever fall under the wrath of God. I am as certain of my acceptance, and heavenly reward, as that I am sitting here." He reflected for a few moments before adding that he would not "exchange one shade" of heavenly hope for all the reputation he had or might yet acquire.[45]

A faithful tither to the Lexington Presbyterian Church, Jackson increased his pledge with his raise in salary as lieutenant general. The general learned that because of galloping inflation, it was necessary for the church to double pew rents. He promptly sent the required sum. A member of the congregation then told the pastor, Dr. White, "The General pays you a very equivocal compliment by paying double as much for your support when he does not hear you, as when he does."[46]

In mid-October, Lee directed Jackson to shift his corps to the area between Berryville and Charles Town, northeast of Winchester. From there, Jackson could oppose any Union advance from Harpers Ferry (which the Federals had reoccupied) or a movement into the valley from east of the Blue Ridge. At the same time, Jackson would be in a good position to threaten McClellan's flank if the enemy should march too far south into the Piedmont.

Jackson sent a warning to D. H. Hill in that sector and then started forward with his other divisions. On October 16, his lead elements plus some of Stuart's cavalry struck a Federal column six miles from Shepherdstown in an indecisive skirmish.[47] Yet it brought Jackson astride the B&O.

The old "Railroad Wrecker" resumed work. In the next three days, Jackson's men systematically destroyed all of the railroad property in Martinsburg as well as over twenty miles of line between Harpers Ferry and North Mountain. Rails were removed, heated, and twisted out of shape; every cross-tie was burned. In the end, an observer wrote, "nothing remained to be done but to cart off the bare ballast."[48]

Confederates were completing the demolition of the railroad facilities at Martinsburg when a tender scene occurred that no witness ever forgot. The young wife of a railroad section foreman had become enraptured with stories told of Jackson. Hearing that the general was in the neighborhood and preparing to depart, she took her eighteen-month-old son and rushed out into the road as Jackson and his entourage were passing. The mother raised the child and implored Jackson to give it his blessing.

If the request seemed out of order to some members of the staff, it was not so with Jackson. While still seated on Little Sorrel, "the warrior-saint of another era, with the child in his arms, head bowed until his greying beard touched the fresh young hair of the child, pressed close to the shabby coat that had been so well acquainted with death . . . closed his eyes, and seemed to be . . . occupied for a minute or two with prayer, during which we took off our hats and the young mother leaned her head over the horse's shoulder as if uniting in the prayer." Jackson finished and gently returned the baby to the mother. She "thanked him with streaming eyes while he rode off back down the road."[49]

Three days of rest followed at Bunker Hill before Jackson led a detachment to the Charles Town area to neutralize what was left of the Harpers Ferry-Winchester railroad. Sandie Pendleton observed, "General J, wishing to see it done well, moved over to superintend the work."[50] The line no longer existed when Confederates finished their labor.

On October 26, the Federal army began crossing the Potomac River into Loudoun County. McClellan's broad advance extended from the eastern base of the Blue Ridge to the Orange and Alexandria Railroad in the middle of the Piedmont. As Union forces eased southward, they sealed off mountain passes and secured railroad stations.

Lee went with Longstreet's corps toward Culpeper to monitor the enemy movements. Jackson was ordered to remain on the road between Berryville and Charles

Town. He would in essence be in a semi-independent command, to act on his own when he could not readily communicate with army headquarters.[51]

The general made an unusual social call late that month. One afternoon, prominent Winchester matron Mrs. Hugh Lee was standing on the porch of her Cameron Street home when she saw Hunter McGuire approach "with a plain looking officer."[52] To her delight, Mrs. Lee found herself being introduced to Jackson. The two officers accepted her invitation to dinner.

Later that night, Mrs. Lee sought to record the conversations in her diary. She led Jackson into the parlor, where

I commenced by telling him how happy I was to make his acquaintance but I think he did not hear me; Hunter told me he was deaf, I must speak louder. He looked around (the room was quite nice) & said 'you do not appear to have been annoyed by the Yankees;' . . . We talked of the mails & papers while the Yankees were here & I told him of how we outwitted them; then he talked of the flag which was hanging over his head & I gave him its history; when he was leaving I begged him not to leave us to the Yankees again & he said I must talk to Genl. Lee about that; I assured him that we looked to him & him alone, whereupon he said, had he his choice Winchester would be his Head Quarters.—That, from him, was a great deal.

Early the next morning, part of the Southern army marched through Winchester en route to its new position. A regimental band played "Old Folks at Home." Townspeople stood along the streets with "universal expressions of sadness." Many, especially women, wept openly. An army chaplain studied the scene and declared: "Could we have spoken to these sorrowing ones, we would have said, 'Be not alarmed, Stonewall Jackson is *somewhere*.'"[53]

The Second Corps moved eastward from the Winchester-Bunker Hill area toward the Shenandoah River. One division advanced to the other side of the Blue Ridge. Jackson established temporary headquarters at the Clarke County home of Mann R. Page. A civilian watching Jackson's men pass thought the army "in fine condition—well fed, and generally well clad and shod. Many of them are still in want of over coats, but they are coming in rapidly. The men are in high spirits—not a gloomy face to be seen—except perhaps here and there some poor fellow, who is not quite in his usual health."[54]

Several times in this period, Jackson rode back to Winchester on military business and an occasional social engagement. One such visit, around November 1, resulted in the first of only two wartime photographs taken of the general.

He and McGuire, along with the Reverend and Mrs. Graham, were having lunch at the McGuire family home on the corner of Braddock and Amherst Streets. The meal was ending when Hunter McGuire's twenty-four-year-old sister Marguerita ("Gettie" to her family and friends) worked up sufficient courage to address the honored guest. "General Jackson," she said, "I want to ask a favor of you."

"Certainly, Miss Gettie," came the reply. "I shall be glad to do anything for you in my power."

"Well, I want you to have your photograph taken for me." At that, Rev. Graham studied Jackson closely. He knew the general's aversion to such things. The minister was shocked when Jackson answered: "Why, yes, I shall be glad to do so, but in that event I shall have to ask you to excuse me now as I have a busy afternoon ahead."[55]

Accompanied by Graham, Jackson left the McGuire home and walked the two and a half blocks to the Loudoun Street photographic studio of Nathaniel Routzahn. This Maryland-born "artist" was in his mid-thirties, short and somewhat paunchy, with an established reputation as the best photographer in the lower valley. Jackson explained to the astonished Routzahn what he wanted. As the general took a seat in front of the camera, Routzahn called attention to a button missing on Jackson's coat. "Yes, yes," came a somewhat impatient reply. "I know it. I have it here in my pocket. If you can find a needle and thread, I will sew it on."[56]

Routzahn got the darning materials. Jackson laid the coat across his knees and studiously began sewing. Graham commented: "He who could find Banks and smash him at will was worsted by a brass button, for he sewed it well out of line—3 buttons from the top of the soldier's side." In spite of the misplaced button, the photograph (almost full length) would become the best-known likeness of Jackson. It was also Anna Jackson's favorite image of her husband.[57]

Jackson's corps spent the first three weeks in November between Winchester and Manassas Gap. Divisions continually darted back and forth through four adjoining counties to keep the Federals off balance; and whenever it became too quiet, Jackson engaged in a favorite pastime of destroying the Baltimore and Ohio Railroad. "He seems to think he has a special mission on earth," a weary South Carolina captain wrote of Jackson, "and that mission dooms him to an everlasting pilgrimage after Yankees."[58]

His movements confused and frustrated the enemy. Two Union soldiers were discussing Jackson's marches. "Ah," said one, "I think we've got him now sure. We have him caught in a band box at last." The companion replied: "Yes, but I have a great fear after all: they'll forget to put the top on!"[59]

Jackson's reputation continued to climb rapidly—and oftentimes to ridiculous levels. A camp rumor of his death in early November sent pangs of anxiety through the ranks. Then an enterprising poet composed a work entitled "My Wife and Child," attributed authorship to Jackson, and did a brisk business selling copies.[60]

Meanwhile, Old Jack pursued his usual ways. On November 2, he attended morning prayer at the Episcopal church in Berryville. The rector, the Reverend Henderson Suter, "preached a very good sermon," Sandie Pendleton thought. Yet Jackson, sitting upright in a conspicuous pew, slept soundly through the exhortation. Two weeks later, he worshiped at the Reverend Graham's church in Winchester. Mrs. Cornelia McDonald observed: "He sat quite near where I was. He had on a splendid new uniform, and looked like a soldier. He looked, too, quiet and modest, and so concerned that every eye was fixed on him." However, the matron added, "his manner was very devout, and attended closely to every word said."[61]

The next day, a freezing Monday, Jackson shifted headquarters to a famous mansion. Eleven miles east of Winchester lay the unincorporated village of Millwood. Founder of the community was Colonel Nathaniel Burwell; his imposing home, "Carter Hall," stood above all other residences in the area. The owner tendered Jackson the use of the entire house. Jackson refused: couriers coming and going at all hours would disturb the family, and soldiers tramping in and out with muddy shoes could only abuse the beauty of the home. The general pitched his tents under large trees in the front yard.

Lee sent him updated instructions on November 6, the day that Jackson's promotion to lieutenant general became official. "The progress of the enemy so far seems to be steadily forward," Lee wrote.

> It would seem to be his desire either to detain you in the valley or to get above you, so as to cut you off from a junction with Longstreet, neither of which must you permit. . . .
>
> You must keep me advised of your position and of the movements of the enemy against you. I request that you will have your divisions as much united as possible, so that you may fall upon any one of the enemy's columns which may expose itself should the opportunity occur to crush it, and that you will endeavor to lead the enemy forward for that purpose.[62]

Jackson reacted at once. The two wings of the Confederate army were divided, but communications had to be maintained. Jackson sent a personal letter to Longstreet:

> My signal officer says that it would not require more than three or four signal stations between Culpeper C. H. & Front Royal. Can you establish them from yr. corps or send me the men & let me establish them? As I fear that I have not enough to connect the different parts of my corps as the country here is too level for giving good signal posts, I am having more men instructed, and in a few days will be able to relieve your men as far as the top of the Blue ridge & will include that post. . . . Please let me know by return courier yr. wishes.[63]

Three days later, Lee repeated his desires for Jackson's corps and gave him the greatest latitude in action. "As my object is to retard & baffle [the enemy's] designs, if it can only be accomplished by maneuvering your corps as you propose, it will serve my purpose as well as if effected in any other way. With this understanding, you can use your discretion, which I know I can rely on, in remaining or advancing up the valley."[64]

Snow began falling on November 7. Yet it did nothing to cool the heated relationships between Jackson and some of his generals. One brigadier still seething was Maxcy Gregg. The South Carolinian had preferred charges against Jackson for arresting two of his colonels on the march to Harpers Ferry. Gregg pushed the case by sending an aide with paperwork to Lee. The army commander informed Gregg that he did not wish the matter pressed further. No good could come of two excellent officers being in a court-martial. Gregg dutifully dropped the charges but not the animosity he felt toward Jackson.[65]

Nor had Powell Hill's anger subsided in the quiet days of autumn. In a mid-November letter to his friend Jeb Stuart, Hill unleashed his most withering blast against Jackson. "I suppose I am to vegetate here all the winter under that crazy old Presbyterian fool—I am like the porcupine all bristles, and all sticking out too, so I know we shall have a smash up before long. . . . The Almighty will get tired, helping Jackson after a while, and then he'll get the d—ndest thrashing—and the shoe pinches, for I should get my share and probably all the blame, for the people will never blame Stonewall for any disaster." Stuart understandably kept this letter to himself.[66]

The positive side of Jackson shown forth as well at the time. When a portion of Powell Hill's command routed a Federal probe at a river crossing, Jackson easily forgot the strained relations and praised his senior division commander. "Your report of the handsome manner in which through the blessings of Providence you repulsed the enemy at Snicker's Ferry was forwarded to the Commanding General of the Army and he desires me to express his appreciation for your conduct. Hoping that whenever you meet the enemy it may be with like success, I remain, General, Yr. Obt. Sert."[67]

One day Jackson and his staff were riding at the head of a column when a farm wife with a child in each hand stopped him. She was earnestly seeking a soldier-son who was serving in "Captain Jackson's company." Jackson introduced himself as the boy's commanding officer and asked for more information on the soldier's unit. All he could learn was that "Johnnie" was in "Captain Jackson's company." The staff began snickering. Jackson whipped around in anger; seconds later, his aides were galloping in every direction to find the man in question. Mother and son were briefly reunited.[68]

By now, the Second Corps had grown to 31,800 officers and men plus twenty-five batteries of 112 guns. In numbers, it was a formidable host; in reality, it was a pitiful mass. "There has been much suffering in my command for want of blankets and shoes, especially the latter," Jackson informed Anna.[69]

His comment was a sad understatement. Sandie Pendleton was writing home at the same time: "There [are at] this moment subjected to the pelting of the storm, half snow, half rainy sleet, no less than six thousand men—not in want of shoes only—but absolutely barefooted, and insufficiently supplied with blankets and other necessary clothing." A South Carolina captain stated of his company: "I tremble every time I look at some of our boys." Young George Greer of the 58th Virginia confided in his diary one icy Saturday: "I fear I will freeze today."[70]

Kyd Douglas left Jackson's staff on November 13 to take command of his old company in the 2d Virginia. He viewed the new assignment with skepticism. "I hardly hope to succeed as the material is far from being what it was when [the company] first went into service."[71]

Confederate soldiers would persevere. They had little choice as soldiers. By that time, General George McClellan was gone as commander of the Army of the Potomac. His procrastination became more than Abraham Lincoln, incredibly patient as he was, could bear. McClellan's successor was General Ambrose E. Burnside, a contemporary of Jackson at West Point.

Lee expected speedy action resulting from the change of commanders. He put Jackson on alert to move at a moment's notice to link with Longstreet in the Culpeper area. Insofar as Jackson's movements in the valley were concerned, Lee gave him wide leeway "to embarrass and produce hesitation in a forward movement of the enemy."[72]

As always, Jackson maintained the strictest secrecy about his intentions. The gathering of the Second Corps at Millwood convinced the staff that an advance eastward across the Blue Ridge would occur the following day. New aide James Power Smith wanted to make a quick visit to Winchester before departing the valley. He went to Jackson's tent, saluted, and said, "General, as we are going over the mountains, I wish to go to Winchester today."

Jackson stared at his aide for a moment. A tiny smile creased the general's face as he replied, "Are you going over the mountains, Lieutenant?"

Smith, somewhat stunned, answered, "Well, I do not know whether we are or not, but we of the staff have concluded from the disposition of the troops that we are to march over the Blue Ridge tomorrow."

Again Jackson paused; another hint of a smile appeared. "Very well, Lieutenant, you may go to Winchester if you wish." As Smith turned to leave, the general called after him: "Don't tell anyone, if you please, that we are going over the mountains."

Smith spent the night in Winchester. Riding swiftly back to headquarters early the next morning, he rounded a curve in the road and almost collided with Jackson and his staff. They were headed toward Winchester. The general smiled broadly and greeted him: "Lieutenant, are you going over the mountains?" The whole party laughed loudly.[73]

A serious matter that Jackson could not continue to overlook in this relatively quiet period was the nonexistence of his official battle reports. He had not written one since Kernstown, eight months earlier. Both army headquarters and the Confederate Congress were pressing him for summaries. Jackson needed someone articulate, possessed of a gifted pen, and reasonably familiar with military terminology. He sent an appeal to Charles J. Faulkner.

Born in Martinsburg of Irish parents, Faulkner had been a prosperous attorney, member of the U.S. Congress for eight years, and American ambassador to France until civil war began. Briefly imprisoned in the North in 1861, Faulkner had become one of the first civilian heroes in the Confederacy. This man of letters and diplomacy was currently unengaged.

Faulkner visited Jackson at Millwood, where the general tendered him appointment as lieutenant colonel and "senior Adjutant General." His primary task would be to compose drafts of official reports. Faulkner recalled that Jackson "spoke of the efforts he had made to have them prepared—of his own disappointment and of the pain and concern which these disappointments gave him—he said I would render him personally an important service in this matter, and he hoped I would not decline to do so." The former ambassador tentatively accepted the offer but needed time to get his affairs in order before entering field service.[74]

Still another embarrassment for Jackson was what Pendleton called the "willing tributes" sent to the general by "the good people of the Valley." Gifts ranged from handkerchiefs and a steady stream of food to gold braid and a captured dress sword. Jackson revealed his deepest thanks in a letter to Anna. "Our gracious Heavenly Father is exceedingly kind to me, & strikingly manifests it by the kindness with which He disposes people to treat me." After describing some of the presents he had received, Jackson commented, "And so God, my exceedingly great joy, is continually showing His blessings upon me an unworthy creature."[75]

By November 19, the cold fogs along the stream where Jackson had been camping became too much to bear. "Our *hero* of many battles has succumbed and declares he must have a cessation of hostilities with the elements," Sandie Pendleton announced.[76] Jackson shifted his headquarters to the vacant Smith home on North Washington Street in Winchester. Rain fell throughout the transfer back into town, stripping the last leaves from trees and heralding the approach of winter.

Meanwhile, Burnside had begun a long sweep away from Lee's front and toward Fredericksburg. The Union general's objective was to cross the Rappahannock River quickly, get around Lee's eastern flank, and make for Richmond. This strategy would compel Lee to fight at a disadvantage. The key to Burnside's shift was pontoon bridges waiting for an uninterrupted crossing of the Rappahannock. The pontoons were not there when the Federals arrived, forcing Burnside to lose a full ten days awaiting the equipment.

Lee moved Longstreet's wing between Burnside and Richmond. The chieftain had no desire to fight at Fredericksburg. He knew that high ground on the other side of the river dominated the field and that Union communication lines by land with Washington were shorter than Lee's connections with Richmond. Lee had wanted to use the North Anna River thirty miles farther south as his line of defense. Yet the massing of the Union army at Fredericksburg convinced Lee that he did not want to cede the broad expanse of land between the Rappahannock and the North Anna. Half of the Confederate army therefore filed onto a long ridge behind Fredericksburg. Burnside continued to wait for his pontoons.

Jackson realized that his remaining time in the valley was short. On the day after establishing headquarters in Winchester, he opened his heart in a letter to Anna. "Our headquarters are about a hundred yards from Mr. Graham's, in a large white house back of his, and in full view of last winter's quarters, where my *esposa* used to come and talk to me." Gravitating to his favorite subject, Jackson wrote: "Peace should not be the chief object of prayer in our Country—It should aim more specially in imploring God's forgiveness of our sins, & praying that He will make our people a holy people. If we are but His, all things shall work together for the good of our Country, & no good thing will He withhold from it."[77]

Later that day, Jackson paid a courtesy call on the Grahams. The Presbyterian minister and his family were delighted to share supper and some private time with their dear friend. Mrs. Graham wrote Anna: "He is looking in such perfect health— far *handsomer* than I ever saw him—and is in such fine spirits, seems so unreserved and unrestrained in his intercourse with us, that we did enjoy him to the full."[78]

Reverend Graham recalled that the children "were permitted to sit up & see him and it was indeed a beautiful sight to see that wonderful man, the idol of the nation, 'the observed of all observers,' & the admiration of the world, playing with the little things, seizing them in his arms, hugging & kissing them with all the tenderness of a father. He was perfectly joyous at returning to the only home which he had known during the war & looking around the room & recognizing every familiar object."[79]

Jackson seemed that evening to be reliving the previous winter. He talked a great deal about the hope of spending another winter in his old room. "Before we parted," Graham stated, "he led us once more to the throne of grace in our family worship." As Jackson said goodbye, his last words to the Grahams were a request: "I would ask an interest in the prayers of you both."[80]

Lee did not have to order Jackson from the valley. Jackson's letters to his commander during this period have been lost. However, Lee's communiques make it clear that Jackson was biding time in hopes that the Union army would make a mistake— thereby enabling him to strike a blow at some weak point. Jackson now felt that the next major battle would be along the Rappahannock, not the Potomac. At least 175 miles separated Jackson and Longstreet's wing of the army. Never before had the Army of Northern Virginia been so widely divided. Jackson, as well as Lee, felt that it was time to consolidate.

Snow lay on the ground on November 22 as Confederate divisions marched through Winchester. Jackson's corps now numbered 38,532 soldiers. Powell Hill's was the largest of the four divisions, with 20,331 troops; Jackson's old division, with barely 6800 men, was the smallest. Attached to the Second Corps were twenty-three batteries of artillery. This was the biggest command Jackson had ever had.

It was also the most pathetic looking. Cornelia McDonald watched Powell Hill's men pass through Winchester. "They were very destitute, many without shoes, and all without overcoats or gloves, although the weather is freezing. Their poor hands looked so red and cold holding their muskets in the biting winds. . . . They did not, however, look dejected, but went their way right joyfully."[81] General "Grumble" Jones and a skeletal force were left to guard the lower valley.

The corps moved south along the familiar valley pike. Memories abounded throughout the march. The route led past the hills from which Taylor's Louisianians had led a breakthrough of Banks's line in the May 25 battle for Winchester. Jackson paused at Kernstown long enough to explain the March 23 battle to his staff. Then there was Middletown, where the chase after Banks had begun in earnest . . . Strasburg and the certain Federal trap that Jackson eluded . . . and on to Mount Jackson. The Massanutten loomed high in the autumn sun as the column followed the valley southward.

At New Market on November 25, Jackson turned left and led the men up the winding road that provoked still more recollections of victory. However, there were snags in the march. Jackson paused in New Market while the soldiers continued in file up the mountain. By the time the general resumed his ride, a sizable portion of the Second Corps was in front of him. Getting to the head of the column brought unexpected revelations to the commander.

The first occurred as Jackson tried to get through the 21st Georgia. A traffic jam of troops existed, and the general "had to listen to some very *risque* couplets." Yet according to a captain in the regiment, Jackson took it in good stride. "The austere Presbyterian elder could not hide his amusement. . . . He did not seem to be worried that his twenty thousand veterans felt happy and light hearted."[82]

The captain was mistaken. Ahead of the Georgians, as Jackson discovered, was the Louisiana brigade. Its soldiers had stripped a New Market tavern of its contents. By the time that portion of Jackson's column began the climb toward Luray Pass, brigade commissary David Boyd noted that "the road was lined with drunken men who had fallen out of ranks. Nearly everybody in the Louisiana brigade, and many in other brigades, had taken a drink too many; and old Jubal [Early] was merry and a-grinning."[83]

Jackson was horrified at what he saw. When the army bivouacked that afternoon, he sent a note asking Early why he had so many stragglers at the rear of his command. Early reportedly answered that the corps commander saw so many stragglers in the rear because he was riding in the rear.

According to Major Boyd, Jackson ordered Sandie Pendleton to place Early under arrest. Pendleton appealed to Jackson: owing to the lateness of the hour, could he wait until daylight? Jackson agreed. The next morning, when Pendleton asked if he still was to deliver the arrest order, Jackson replied no; he himself would discuss the matter with Early. What resolution came of the incident is unknown.[84]

The regular correspondence between Lee and Jackson slowed temporarily with the movement of the Second Corps to the Piedmont. Lee did not know that Jackson was on the way when he sent him a November 23 letter that clearly illustrates the trusting relationship between the two generals. "If you see no way of making an impression on the enemy from where you are," Lee wrote, "and concur with me in the views I have expressed, I wish you would move east of the Blue Ridge and take such a position as you may find best."[85]

Two things are remarkable about that statement. First, Lee had reviewed the military situation on an almost daily basis with Jackson, and he had stressed repeatedly the probable necessity of Jackson bringing his command to Fredericksburg. Yet even though Lee felt strongly that his two corps should be together, his confidence in his lieutenant's judgment caused him to leave the decision for the movement to Jackson. Second, Lee even gave Jackson the option en route of taking any "position" he desired—even if it involved an offensive action.

Monday morning, November 24, was clear and cold. At breakfast atop the Massanutten Mountains, the staff was admiring the view: the great valley to the west, the Luray Valley with the imposing Piedmont stretching to the east. Jackson emerged from his tent. Aides gaped in wonder. The general was wearing the new coat given him by Stuart, the tall hat that Hotchkiss had purchased for him in Martinsburg, plus the captured sword donated by cavalrymen. Jackson ignored the stares save for a trace of a smile. Then he looked at the staff and announced: "Young gentlemen, this is no longer the headquarters of the Army of the Valley, but of the Second Corps of the Army of Northern Virginia."[86]

The long Confederate column passed into the Luray Valley, crossed the Shenandoah River, and climbed the Blue Ridge to Thornton's Gap. Bivouac on November 24 was the village of Hawksbill. Jackson tried to establish a series of signal stations for a communications linkup with Lee, but the plan failed. He then lingered around Madison Court House with a final hope that an opportunity might arise for an attack on the Federal army's right flank or rear. It was soon apparent that Burnside's entire army had concentrated at Fredericksburg. No sweeping flank movement was in order this time.

Exciting and successful days when the foot cavalry, acting independently, had won fame in the valley were at an end. Hereafter, Jackson and his men were to be part of Lee's army. If this was to be a permanent arrangement, no one knew at the time.

Because of the weather, Jackson eased up on his normal marching schedule. Reveille was 4:30 A.M., with the day's march to begin punctually two hours later. An artilleryman commented that "the mornings were generally very cold and marching as we did before sun rise, we suffered no little."[87]

That was the least of the discomforts. Practically every one of Jackson's men who wrote a memoir about the war had something to say about that November tramp from Winchester to Fredericksburg. The Second Corps spilled happily onto the relatively flat Piedmont, only to have the weather become a critical factor. Sleet or snow, whipped by icy winds, pelted the weary line day after day.

An Augusta County soldier declared: "Many of the men are yet without shoes in some of the regiments, and it is almost piteous to see them painfully picking their way along through frost and ice. Men are without blankets. . . . Flour, beef and salt constitute the daily diet of the troops—provided it 'gets up in time,' but in practice it generally arrives after dark, so that the men spend the night in cooking, and therefore don't need blankets to sleep in."[88]

Many soldiers described bare feet "cracked and bleeding on the ice." Throughout the army, desperate men sought to alleviate misery by wrapping fresh cowhide strips around their feet. The results were rarely satisfactory. A North Carolina captain observed that "the regiment appeared like a lot of cripples, the raw hide having curled and shrunk in the most uncomfortable way."[89]

Jackson could not ignore the misery, but his thoughts kept drifting to Anna. Her delivery time was at hand. As one who had already lost his first two children, Jackson was anxious. That meant an increase in daily prayers.

"My heart is with his little darling," he reassured Anna early in the march. "Write to me at Gordonsville." He also gave his wife strict instructions not to telegraph the news of any birth. Childbirth was a personal gift of God, to be announced by private letter. Jackson's secrecy and modesty did not lessen even where an addition to the family was involved.[90]

For the better part of three days, Jackson kept his headquarters in the Orange-Gordonsville area. Sometime around November 28, a quick note came from Anna's sister, Harriet Irwin: Anna had given birth to a daughter at the Irwin home in Charlotte, North Carolina. Mother and child were both fine. The news sent Jackson to his knees in tearful thanksgiving.

A day or so later, a longer letter arrived at headquarters. It was in Mrs. Irwin's handwriting; the contents were the sentiments of someone else.

My own dear Father,—As my mother's letter has been cut short by my arrival, I think it but justice that I should continue it. I know that you are rejoiced to hear of my coming, and I hope that God has sent me to radiate your pathway through life. I am a very tiny little thing. I weigh only eight and a half pounds, and Aunt Harriet says I am the express image of my darling papa, and so does our kind friend, Mrs. Osborne, and this greatly delights my mother. My aunts both say I am a little beauty. My hair is dark and long, my eyes are blue, my nose straight just like papa's, and my complexion not all red like most young ladies of my age, but a beautiful blending of the lily and the rose. . . . My mother is very comfortable this morning. She is anxious to have my name decided upon, and hopes you will write and give me a name, with your blessing. . . . I was born on Sunday [November 23], just after the morning services at church. . . . My friends, who are about me like guardian angels, hope for me a long life of happiness and holiness and a futurity of endless bliss.

Jackson shared the God-given blessing with no one. It was "a joy with which a stranger could not intermeddle," he stated. Some members of the staff did not learn of the birth until a month later. Jackson had initially hoped for a son because, as he told Anna, "men had a larger sphere of usefulness than women." When God gave him a daughter, Jackson accepted the heavenly gift and immediately expressed his preference for a girl.[91]

The next day, still filled with happiness over his daughter, Jackson sat ramrod straight in the saddle at the head of his column. Sometime before midmorning, accompanied by Smith and four couriers, the general spurred Little Sorrel and rode forty miles that Saturday to meet with Lee. At noon, the party received food for themselves and forage for their horses at the home of the Reverend Melzi Chancellor.

Daylight was fading in overcast skies when Jackson moved through a deep tangled woodland known as the Wilderness. Soon he passed an intersection where stood a large brick tavern named "Chancellorsville." Nothing but thick forest could be seen in any direction.

Icy rain was falling when Jackson reached Salem Church. Refugees from Fredericksburg clogged the road. It was dark when Jackson dismounted at the cluster of tents forming Lee's headquarters. The snow-covered site was along the Mine Road near the estate of Muscoe Garnett.

"The arrival of Jackson created quite a stir," Smith noted.[92] In a few moments, Lee strode forth to greet his lieutenant. The two had supper in Lee's tent. Soon Jackson and his party were enjoying pleasant company and warm beds at the Garnett home.

After breakfast the next morning, Jackson rode some five miles down Telegraph Road into Fredericksburg. It was Sunday, but no church bells broke the silence. Homes and streets were deserted.

Founded before the end of the seventeenth century at the fall line of the Rappahannock, Fredericksburg had been a thriving river port and social center. James Monroe had practiced law there; George Washington had spent his boyhood not far away and later purchased a home there for his mother. It was a town of history and pride—a town now about to become a battleground. Jackson sat on his horse at a downtown intersection for awhile and quietly surveyed the scene.

The general and his small entourage then retraced their path on Telegraph Road. Following a brief conference with Lee, Jackson established headquarters at "Sunnyside," the home of the French family. Jackson chose the residence because it was close to Lee's command center. When the Frenches invited Jackson and Smith to dinner, both accepted. First came devotionals, however. In the parlor of the French home, Jackson took the family Bible and led the group in a Sunday evening worship service.

By Monday, December 1, all of the Second Corps had arrived after what a weary soldier called "one of the longest and hardest marches on record." The men had slogged through rain, sleet, mud, snow, freezing temperatures, and on unusually "wretched farm roads" for almost two weeks. Wills Lee of the Richmond Howitzers gave a short but vivid picture of the hardships. On the last day's march, the axle on one of the guns broke. The men found an abandoned blacksmith shop, made necessary repairs, then burned the establishment in order to get warm.[93]

Despite their tattered condition, the spirits of the men were good—better than Jackson's own frame of mind. The general was displeased with Lee's decision to make a stand at Fredericksburg. To Harvey Hill, his brother-in-law, Jackson reportedly voiced an unusually strong opinion: "I am opposed to fighting here. We will whip the enemy but gain no fruits of victory. I have advised the line of the North Anna, but have been overruled."[94]

Whom Jackson "advised" on the subject of the North Anna River was undoubtedly Lee. There was no one else to whom the lieutenant general could have given advice. The army commander had already studied the topography of that central Virginia sector and decided that the Rappahannock defense line was as good a position as any other. Jackson thereafter obeyed orders with customary reticence.

Like any successful general, Lee read the mind of his opponent. Ambrose Burnside was in command because his predecessor vacillated. The new Union army chief must take the offensive. The North expected as much; Lee knew as much. If Lee could merely stop Burnside's advance, that would be a Union defeat. Approaching winter would then block this latest "On to Richmond" drive. So Lee opted to make the stand at Fredericksburg.

He directed Jackson's corps to form the right half of his line. Jackson moved south of Fredericksburg to Guiney Station on the Richmond, Fredericksburg, and Potomac Railroad. He pitched his headquarters tent at "Fairfield," the 2500-acre farm of Thomas Coleman Chandler. The large brick main house had three terraces at the back that sloped down to the single-track railroad 100 yards away. Jackson's tents were a short distance to the south.

Mr. Chandler offered the general the hospitality of his home. Jackson declined it as well as the use of a white outbuilding near the home. He wished to be with his staff and at the nerve center of his tented headquarters. A day later, Chandler and his ten-year-old-daughter Lucy called on Jackson to offer hospitality. Jackson removed his cap when they entered his tent; and while the planter talked, the general stood erect with his hands behind him. At the end of the proffered kindness, Jackson replied: "I thank you, Mr. Chandler, for your gracious invitation, but I never wish to fare better than my men." No amount of pleading could change his mind. Even Mrs. Chandler grew weary of sending to his tent meals that were not eaten. On one occasion, servants carried a turkey dinner that was accepted with profound thanks. The staff rather than Jackson enjoyed the meal.[95]

Because of Lee's uncertainty over where Burnside might cross the Rappahannock, the Confederate defense line was extremely long. On both sides of the river were hills running parallel to it. The usually west-to-east flow of the Rappahannock changed to an almost north-to-south current as the stream passed Fredericksburg. The Federal-held Stafford Heights on the east side dominated the area. On the west side of the river, the town hugged the riverbank. A broad open plain some 600–1000 yards wide stretched from town to Marye's Heights. That range extended about two miles in each direction from the heart of the city.

In addition, Longstreet observed, "the hills occupied by the Confederate forces, although over-crowned by heights of Stafford, were so distant as to be outside the range of effective fire by the Federal guns, and, with the lower receding grounds between them, formed a defensive series that may be likened to natural bastions."[96] The Southerners also had the better part of three weeks to prepare for the confrontation.

The little town of Fredericksburg was under Confederate occupation. Yet it was a no-man's land, caught between two hostile armies massing for battle on opposite sides of the Rappahannock. Recent rain and snow had left the region looking dirty and unwanted.

Jackson initially scattered his corps all along the Rappahannock, including Harvey Hill's division twenty miles downriver at Port Royal. The Second Corps was fatigued; men were still wearing cowhides for shoes. Yet they marched hither and yon to positions on the high ground. "Old Jackson is poking his nose around here," one of Longstreet's gunners wrote home, "so you can look out for squalls soon."[97]

Brigadier General Thomas R. R. Cobb met Jackson shortly after the latter's arrival at Fredericksburg. The quick-tempered Georgian was much taken by the famous Stonewall. Cobb informed his wife: "Jackson is a very plain and simple man having little conversational power, and only two elements of greatness—implicit self-reliance giving great imperturbability of temper and feeling and never-yielding Faith. I like him very much."98

For a week, Jackson made the Chandler estate his headquarters. He enjoyed the family and was much impressed by the home and surrounding farmland. With but one negative interlude, the Fairfield stay for Jackson was pleasant. The exception came when Lee sought a closer balance between the 127 artillery pieces Jackson had and the 117 guns in Longstreet's command. Jackson, the artillerist at heart, fought relinquishing any of his cannon. A brisk exchange of letters ensued, with Jackson being ultimately successful.

This matter was a symptom of Jackson's new position in the Army of Northern Virginia. Most of his cannon were pieces from the old valley army. It is not stretching matters to say that Jackson was familiar with practically every gun. Releasing any to another command was out of the question, in his mind. That Lee acquiesced in his favor shows the extent to which the army chief was treating Jackson as a cooperating equal rather than as a subordinate.

Harvey Hill would later assert that the controversy over the cannon deepened an existing rift between Lee and Jackson. While at Fredericksburg, Hill wrote, "Genl. J's feelings were not kind toward Genl. Lee. He thought that the latter had shown partiality to Longstreet in the distribution of Guns, clothing, camp & garrison equipage, &c. He had felt this keenly after the battle of Sharpsburg & once said that he feared he would be compelled to resign."99

At the time Hill wrote this letter, he was estranged from Lee and apparently not on the best terms with Jackson either. One suspects that Hill was venting frustrations rather than recording truth.

Jackson's happiest moments in the first week of December came when writing Anna and expressing heartfelt love for his daughter. The child would be called Julia, after his mother. He explained why to Anna in simple terms: "My mother was mindful of me, when I was a helpless, fatherless child, and I wish to commemorate her now."100 The lonely childhood—the absence of maternal love—were with Jackson always. Now he would honor the mother whom he remembered only in dreams.

The fullest display of Jackson's love for his daughter came in his first post-birth letter to the wife he had not seen for eight months. On December 4, he wrote: "Oh! how thankful I am to our kind Heavenly Father for having spared my precious wife and given us a little daughter! I cannot tell you how gratified I am, nor how much I wish I could be with you and see my two little darlings. . . . How I would love to see the darling little thing! Give her many kisses for her father."101

Unable to build winter quarters while battle was imminent, Confederates manned their lines exposed to weather that switched from rain to sleet to snow to winds to teasingly brief periods of moderate temperatures. General Frank Paxton praised the fortitude of the men in his Stonewall Brigade. "It seems strange," he wrote home, "but, thanks to God for changing their natures, they bear in patience now what they once would have regarded as beyond human endurance." Randolph Fairfax of the Rockbridge Artillery did not know he had but a week to live when he told his parents: "The weather now is intensely cold. . . . I think when peace is declared I shall be like a man just released from prison."102

The incredible depth of Jackson's allegiance to God appeared on December 10 in two forms. Early that day, he sent a lengthy letter to his congressional "liaison," Colonel Alexander Boteler. Jackson had heard that the Confederate Congress might repeal a law requiring the mails to be carried on Sundays. "I hope that you will feel it a duty, as well as a pleasure, to urge its repeal," Jackson told his friend. He then explained why.

I do not see how a nation that thus arrays itself by such a law against God's holy day can expect to escape His wrath. The punishment of national sins must be confined to this world, as there are no nationalities beyond the grave. For fifteen years I have refused to mail letters on Sunday, or to take them out of the office on that day except since I came into the field. . . . My rule is to let the Sabbath mails remain unopened unless they contain a despatch; but despataches are generally sent by courier, or telegraph, or by some other special messenger.

Jackson closed, as he was wont to do, with a homily. "God has greatly blessed us, and I trust He will make us that people to whom God is the Lord. Let us look to God for an illustration in our history, that 'righteousness exalteth a nation, but sin is a reproach to any people.'"[103]

Later that day, he wrote Anna. Little Julia was the center of attention, of course. Jackson acknowledged the love that Anna was pouring upon the child. Nevertheless, the earthly happiness he felt, and the sad remembrances of his own earlier years, led Jackson to add almost pathetically: "Do not set your affections upon her, except as a gift of God. If she absorbs too much of our hearts, God may remove her from us."[104]

On that Wednesday, Jackson also bade farewell to a "friend." When Hotchkiss bought the soft felt hat for the general back in September at Martinsburg, he asked to be custodian of Jackson's old VMI forage hat that was faded by weather and shapeless from wear. Hotchkiss now learned that Jackson had been asking about the cap but had forgotten where it was. The mapmaker quickly returned it. Jackson put on the hat, remarked about how well it fit, but conceded that it was too unkempt for further use. If you plan to cut it to pieces, Hotchkiss remarked, he would like to have one of the buttons as a souvenir. The two men discussed other matters for awhile. As Hotchkiss rose to leave the general's tent, Jackson said, "I reckon you may have the cap." It became one of Hotchkiss's most prized possessions.[105]

Military events moved to showdown stage the following day. The Rappahannock River changed appearances dramatically in the area. Upriver from Fredericksburg, the stream was narrower but filled with boulders that impeded mass crossings. In front of town, the river was 400 feet wide and smooth bottomed. The banks of the Rappahannock became 1000 feet apart a few miles downstream. Fredericksburg was the logical crossing for Burnside's forces, even though most of Lee's army was concentrated there.

At midmorning on December 11, some 150 Union guns opened a point-blank bombardment of the city. Fog lay heavy on ground that trembled from the cannonade. Smoke and flames curled up through the mist as downtown Fredericksburg succumbed to a hammering "appalling and indescribable," a Confederate soldier wrote. Federals were fighting their way over the river to establish a beachhead at what was left of the town's riverfront.[106]

Lee could count on fully 78,000 men for battle; but in the case of Jackson's sector, they were scattered over the countryside in large part to protect other possible river crossings. Jubal Early, in command of Ewell's old division, was at Skinker's Neck, a horseshoe bend in the Rappahannock twelve miles below Fredericksburg. Harvey Hill's troops were eight miles farther to the east at Port Royal. Powell Hill's Light Division was near the Thomas Yerby farm, about two miles from the right of Longstreet's wing. Taliaferro guarded Guiney Station ten miles to the southeast of A. P. Hill.

The forced crossing by the enemy required Lee's army to consolidate at Fredericksburg. Jackson left the Chandler farm and established a new headquarters only two miles south of Hamilton's Crossing on the John Ewing property. From there he issued directives for the next day.

Powell Hill would relieve John B. Hood's division of Longstreet's corps in the Hamilton's Crossing area and take position on Longstreet's immediate right. Taliaferro would move up as support 400 yards behind Hill. Early and Harvey Hill would hold their positions downriver but be ready to start toward Fredericksburg at a moment's notice.

Jackson was up at 4 A.M. on Friday the 12th. Temperatures were fluctuating from the mid-twenties at night to the mid-fifties in afternoon, producing heavy fog at daybreak. A typically thick murkiness blanketed the countryside as Jackson left his tent that morning.

He had given orders that the staff rise early for a long day's work. When Jackson arrived in the dark at the mess tent, only Jim Lewis was there. Jackson directed that the food be taken outside, where he ate his breakfast in freezing temperature. As he mounted his horse, the general left instructions for the staff to catch up with him as soon as possible. Jackson planned to confer with Lee and then spend the day positioning his men for battle.

Topography seemed to be overwhelmingly in his favor. From the Rappahannock, a broad open plain extended a mile and a half to the wooded ridge that would be Jackson's front line. Bisecting the plain in a north-south axis was the Richmond Stage Road (sometimes called the Old Richmond Road). Ditches existed on either side of the highway. Between it and the ridge, running through a slight depression several hundred yards wide, was the Richmond, Fredericksburg, and Potomac Railroad.

If an enemy gained the tracks, it then had to ascend a slope 100–200 yards into woods at the crest. The high ground faded away as the RF&P turned due south at Hamilton's Crossing. Swampy land to the south and east would hamper movements by both sides but provide a good anchor for Jackson's right.

Powell Hill's men began arriving at the Crossing around 8 A.M. after a march that began at dawn. They would form Jackson's front line: 3300 yards in length and extending from Hood's position on Longstreet's right to Prospect Hill, where the railroad made its ninety-degree turn. The brigades of James J. Archer and John M. Brockenbrough filed to the right at Hamilton's Crossing. Lane's North Carolinians manned the center. Dorsey Pender's men were on the left. Powell Hill placed his pickets on the railroad embankment, with the main defensive line 300 yards to the rear up in the woods.

Jackson would control only two miles of Lee's seven-mile front. Yet that southern end of the line had less natural strength than the longer, higher position assigned to

Longstreet. Jackson compensated for less formidable terrain with a stacked defense. The better part of 35,000 soldiers manned his two-mile-wide front. All were concealed in woods.

Stuart's cavalry plus eighteen cannon were in an oblique position on Jackson's right between Hamilton's Crossing and Massaponax Creek. Powell Hill's artillery chief, Lieutenant Colonel Lindsay Walker, had fourteen guns on Prospect Hill. Another twenty-one cannon were on the left between the brigades of Pender and Lane. Fully two-thirds of Jackson's artillery could not be employed because of the broken ground.[107]

On paper, Jackson's line appeared impenetrable. In reality, a glaring gap existed in the center of the line between the brigades of Archer and Lane. Everyone saw it; everyone seemed to ignore it.

The fog was lifting just before noon when Stuart and von Borcke rode along the line. "On the left wing of A. P. Hill's division," von Borcke noted, "we had to pass a small piece of wood, extending in a triangular shape about six or eight hundred yards outside of our lines, with a base of about half a mile, offering, in my opinion, a great advantage to the enemy, and I remarked to Stuart that I thought it ought to be cut down."[108]

Stuart considered such precaution unnecessary. With the sweeping cross fire that Jackson's artillery would deliver from the flanks, Stuart doubted that any Federals could advance as far as the triangular mass of scrubby woods and dense underbrush. Hill unquestionably saw the projection but discounted it because the marshy wetland would naturally deter any enemy approach. Besides, Gregg's brigade was behind Lane and Archer; it would provide immediate support if needed. Hill left the sector undefended—despite the fact that the gap accounted for just under 20 percent of his battle line.

South Carolina Captain David G. McIntosh commanded half of Powell Hill's batteries. He disputed Stuart's claim from the start. McIntosh wrote of the battle line: "This disposition of the artillery left a considerable space [1,000 yards] . . . unoccupied by any guns, and which could not be reached by front fire from the guns mentioned, and only partially reached by an oblique fire from the right and left."[109]

Colonel Crutchfield, Jackson's artillery chief, told McIntosh that such battery dispositions had been made because the ground at the gap "was unfavorable for the use of artillery, was swampy, and intersected by a deep ravine, and the undergrowth so thick there was no time to clear it away before the action began."[110]

Former chief of staff Robert L. Dabney (who was not with the army at Fredericksburg) claimed that Jackson saw the gap on December 12 and remarked, "The enemy will attack here." Dabney received that quotation a year and a half after the battle from Harvey Hill, who by then was making a veritable series of preposterous assertions. If Jackson had in fact seen the gap, he would have closed it promptly. On the other hand, while Jackson's inspection of the lines might have been sloppy on one occasion, he rode the length of his sector enough times to have become aware of the breach.[111]

Certainly, the strained relations between Jackson and Powell Hill had nothing to do with any oversight. Jackson never let personal feelings interfere with military responsibilities. Artillerist Jackson may have sincerely believed that his fire would be so effective as to block any threat to the Confederate position. Perhaps the general—and Powell Hill as well—concluded that the area of the gap was impassable to any organized assault. Their mistake was in not considering the possibility of a disorganized attack by a thronging mob ignorant of the lay of the land.[112]

The Federal army that morning massed on both sides of the Rappahannock. Lee and Stuart joined Jackson to obtain a better look at the enemy. Accompanied by several aides, the generals rode ahead of the Southern line, then dismounted, left their horses with aides, and walked to the remnants of an old fence. There they had a clear view of the enemy only 400 yards away.

Major von Borcke of Stuart's staff fretted over the prospect of Union sharpshooters discovering their presence. Lee and Jackson concentrated on the Federal movements. This was no feint, both generals concluded; Burnside was preparing to attack.

Jackson immediately sent orders to Early and Harvey Hill to leave their downriver positions and join the army at Hamilton's Crossing. Both division commanders got their columns in motion at sundown. Early had fifteen miles to cover, Harvey Hill nearly twenty miles, and both had to advance through a wintry night over roads half-mud and half-ice.

Early's men reached their assigned places two miles from Hamilton's Crossing around midnight. They huddled the remainder of the night in the darkness. Harvey Hill's troops arrived on the scene at 3 A.M. and got little sleep during what was left of the night.

Notwithstanding the gap in Powell Hill's front, Jackson attended to other items with meticulous detail. He gave stern attention to the subject of straggling. Any soldier who was found unlawfully behind the lines and who refused to return to duty was to be shot on the spot. Likewise, a soldier verified by two other men as straggling for the second time in the battle was to be executed promptly.[113]

Late in the afternoon, Jackson took Hotchkiss and made another check of the area below Hamilton's Crossing. Stuart had alleviated Jackson's concern about an unsupported Confederate right flank by posting several guns with an enfilade view of the open plain across which the Federals would attack. After riding more than a mile parallel to the river, Jackson was satisfied. He started back to his main position, so pleased with his defenses, and so optimistic over the coming engagement, that he began whistling—an act that Hotchkiss found startling.[114]

Artillery exchanges throughout that Friday ended with nightfall. Smoke from guns, a still-burning town, and hundreds of campfires formed a thick and acrid blanket over the whole area. Jackson pitched his tents for the night at a site Hotchkiss called "Darnabud's pond," not far behind Powell Hill's headquarters. No record exists of any contact between the two generals after dark.[115]

Jackson was up before dawn on Saturday. Heavy fog covered the land. Temperatures were still unseasonably balmy. It was two degrees above freezing at 7 A.M.; the afternoon high was almost sixty. Jackson's spirits were similarly elevated. Pride in fatherhood, confidence in victory, and a renewed love of God combined to put the general "in his most serene and cheerful mood."[116]

His outward appearance reflected his inward joy. Jackson donned a new, full uniform. The coat (a gift from Stuart) was trimmed in gold lace; new trousers and shiny boots had come from grateful citizens in the valley; a bluish-gray cap, with the top falling in front and an inch-wide gold band around the base, had been sent by Anna. New saber and spurs completed the outfit.

Little Sorrel was behind the lines, so Jackson called for his newest mount, a large stallion named "Superior." He began riding slowly along his lines in the first inspection of the day. Fog restricted visibility, but troops who saw their general displayed the full run of reactions. Some laughed and hooted. To others, the 21st Virginia's John Worsham declared, "he looked so unlike our 'Old Jack' that very few noticed him and none recognized him until he had passed. Then the old accustomed cheer to him went up with unusual vigor!"[117]

Several Confederates looked at Jackson and shook their heads in disapproval. One man expressed fear that being so well dressed the general "wouldn't get down to work." It did not look natural, another said, "for Old Jack to be dressed up fine as a Lieutenant."[118]

Jackson made his way to Lee's headquarters for a final briefing. "I trust our God will give us a great victory today, Lieutenant," he said to aide James Power Smith. Lee's command post was atop a knoll in the center of the line. Longstreet and Stuart were already there when Jackson dismounted. A beaming Stuart made good-natured remarks about Jackson's new uniform. When a staff member complimented him on his fine appearance, the blushing general mumbled, "I believe it was some of my friend Stuart's doing."[119]

Lee's demeanor was more serious, but he greeted Jackson warmly. The army chief was clad in his plain, well-worn uniform with felt hat and short cape. Lee wore neither sword nor pistol.

As soon as amenities had been exchanged, an enthusiastic Jackson proposed that the Confederates attack first. The thick fog would be a concealing ally as Southern brigades slammed into the unsuspecting Burnside. Stuart eagerly endorsed the suggestion.

Lee said no. The disparity in numbers between the two armies was such that it was better to let the Federals assault and beat themselves against the seemingly impregnable Southern lines. Once that had been accomplished, the time would be propitious for launching a heavy counterattack. Defense must be the first order of the day.

The fog slowly lifted. Massed Federals could be seen a quarter-mile in the distance. Longstreet, who sought to be humorous but never quite succeeded, turned to his fellow corps commander. "Are you not scared by that file of Yankees you have before you down there?" he asked. Jackson never saw levity in military matters. He replied earnestly, "Wait until they come a little nearer, and they shall either scare me or I shall scare them!" The war council ended. Jackson mounted his horse and was saluting Lee when Longstreet made another attempt to be funny. "Jackson, what are you going to do with all those people over there?" Old Jack sat motionless in concentration, then replied, "Sir, we will give them the bayonet!" With that, he started back to his lines.[120]

From the beginning, Jackson expected to win the battle with artillery fire. He made a quick survey of his gun emplacements in company at times with Powell Hill and

Colonels Lindsay Walker and Stapleton Crutchfield. Artilleryman David McIntosh recalled, "We were cautioned to keep ourselves concealed as much as possible, and ordered on no account to reply to artillery fire, or engage in artillery duels: that our fire must be reserved to use upon infantry and then not until the enemy had reached a given point." In the distance, McIntosh heard "the heavy rumble of artillery and ordnance wagons, the bugle calls, and the noise of many bands of music filled the air, and we knew full well what it meant."[121]

A member of James H. Lane's 33d North Carolina saw Jackson returning to his lines after 9 A.M. "He suddenly appeared in our front with his cap pulled down over his forehead, almost hiding his eyes. The troops cheered him wildly. He gave us a sharp, searching, but not unkindly look, raised his cap, and rode rapidly on. His eyes seemed to be on fire, so eager was he for the fray."[122]

Fog still obscured much of the lines, but Jackson was quite satisfied with his preparations. His units were stacked a mile deep, with about eleven men to every yard of the front line. Three-fourths of his infantry and seventy-six of his 123 guns were poised in reserve to go where needed.

All was in readiness for the Federal attack. J. P. Smith declared that "everywhere there was confidence, impatient expectations, and the best of spirits." What Jackson did not like about the openness in front of him was that it offered no advantage for the counterattack he wanted to make once the repulse of the enemy was complete.[123]

When Jackson reached his field headquarters a hundred or so yards from Hamilton's Crossing, Union cannon were firing steadily. The heavy guns found the range of the woods where Jackson's men were posted and began "making it uncomfortable," McIntosh reported. "Some of the shells were of enormous size, and tearing through the tree tops above us brought down huge limbs which was trying to the men and which frightened the horses greatly until they were taken out of reach."[124]

Von Borcke joined Jackson during the bombardment. Stuart on the right, the Prussian reported, had seen Federals about to advance. Three long battle lines were forming. Von Borcke's anxiety was evident. Could Jackson hold against such numbers? Jackson, lips compressed, looked at his foreign friend. "Major," he answered slowly, "my men sometimes fail *to take* a position, but *to defend* one, never! I am glad the Yankees are coming!" The general then sent von Borcke back with instructions for Stuart's horse artillery to open fire.[125]

Around 10 A.M., the fog lifted as some giant curtain rising on a grand drama. One Confederate battery commander thought that "a gorgeous panorama was spread out before us. . . . As far as the eye could see, back towards the river, and stretching up towards Fredericksburg, the vast plain was filled with moving masses of men, rapidly deploying and forming alignments into what appeared to be three lines of battle, and here and there huge gaps in the lines being filled with artillery." The officer concluded: "No grander military spectacle was ever presented to human view."[126]

A signal, then three Union battle lines—stretched to a width of one and a half miles—eased forward. One eyewitness exclaimed: "On they came in beautiful order, as if on parade, their bayonets glistening in the bright sunlight; on they came, waving their hundreds of regimental flags, which relieved with warm bits of colouring the dull blue of the columns and the russet tinge of the wintry landscape, while their artillery beyond the river continued the cannonade with unabated fury over their heads, and gave a background of white fleecy smoke, like midsummer clouds, to the animated picture."[127]

In command of the 60,000-man force in Jackson's front was Major General William B. Franklin, the top graduate in his 1843 West Point class. He was an outstanding engineer; but like his close friend George McClellan, Franklin was a careful, cautious field commander. He should have delivered the heaviest blow possible at Jackson. Instead, misconstruing Burnside's orders (which was easy to do because the directives were late in arriving and rambling in content), Franklin unloosed only two divisions to the attack on Jackson's position.

The Federal advance across the plain did not remain steady for long. Unexpected and withering artillery fire began tearing to shambles the left of the lines. A young Alabamian, Major John Pelham, commanded Stuart's horse artillery. Pelham had left West Point only a few months before graduation to defend his native South. From the beginning of the war, he had demonstrated unusual talents as an artillery officer.

With incredible boldness, Pelham took a single twelve-pounder Napoleon to a road intersection a half-mile in front of Jackson's position and at an angle to the Federal line of advance. He opened fire and continued sending shot from the single gun into the enemy ranks. Minutes later, a Blakely rifled piece unlimbered between Pelham's position and Hamilton's Crossing. It now formed a two-gun bombardment of the Union left flank. The two cannon wreaked havoc on Union infantry. Franklin's advance halted.

(Had Pelham withheld his fire until the assaulting lines had passed his position, then blasted the columns from the rear, the results would have been even more successful. However, a battle progresses as much from instinct as from careful planning. The open target was too tempting for Pelham to display patience.)

Return salvos from Federal artillery knocked out the Blakely. An undeterred Pelham kept shifting the Napoleon and firing it so rapidly that five Union batteries were soon responding to what Federal observers thought was a full battery on the vulnerable end of the lines. Three times Stuart ordered Pelham to withdraw. Not until he was out of ammunition did the youthful officer limber his gun and gallop back to Hamilton's Crossing. Lee had watched Pelham single-handedly and gallantly stop the Federal advance. "It is glorious to see courage in one so young," Lee said admiringly.[128]

With Pelham's withdrawal, Federal batteries blasted Jackson's line for an hour and did considerable damage to the Confederate gun emplacements. The bombardment was fearful. Nevertheless, a Tennessee officer observed, Jackson sat in the saddle "undisturbed, calm, deliberate . . . seemingly unconscious of danger." The general apparently had transferred to Little Sorrel at that point because the same soldier referred to the general's horse as "Old Yellow" and marveled at its nonchalance in battle. It "had the appearance of dozing, under the music of the guns."[129]

When Federal batteries slowly ceased fire, Union infantry columns started forward anew. Incredibly, the enemy attackers consisted of the smallest division in Franklin's command: 5000 Pennsylvanians under crabby but solid General George G. Meade. General Abner Doubleday's division was supposed to support Meade. Yet after

Pelham's enfilade fire, Doubleday remained at the Richmond Stage Road to guard against another threat on the flank. That left Meade alone on a narrow front with an undersized division as well as brigade commanders who were virtual nonentities. Gibbon soon started forward, as much behind Meade as on his right flank.

Franklin ordered several batteries to advance to the Richmond road and open close-range fire. As Union guns pounded Jackson's position, Old Jack walked out on the plain with an aide to get a better view of the situation. A Federal sharpshooter some 300 yards away fired. The bullet whistled between the heads of the two Confederates. The aide winced. Jackson turned with a smile and said: "Lieutenant Smith, had you not better go to the rear? They may shoot you!" With that, the general turned and moved back behind his lines.[130]

Not long afterwards, a courier arrived through the smoke with a message from Lee. The rider was moving back and forth in search of Jackson when a voice behind him shouted: "Dismount, sir, dismount! You will certainly be killed there!" The messenger turned and saw Jackson lying flat on his back. Balls were whistling through the area. The courier dismounted and handed Jackson a note. The general ordered the man to lie beside him while he read the communique. He rolled over, wrote a quick reply, and handed it to the aide. Then, the soldier noted, Jackson "resumed his original position in the coolest and most unconcerned manner imaginable."[131]

Obeying the strict order of their general, Confederate gunners withheld their fire throughout the Federal cannonade. An hour passed, and Union officers became convinced that all of Jackson's guns had been destroyed. Meade received orders to resume his attack.

The Union advance that had started 1200 yards from Jackson's lines had stopped during Pelham's destructive fire. Now it continued. Jackson's whole corps remained silent as the Federals came to within 1000 yards. Faces of the Federal soldiers could be seen now at 900 yards. Tensions were strong on both sides. It was around noon when Meade's first line came to within 800 yards of the Confederate position.

At that point, Jackson gave a signal. Suddenly over fifty Confederate cannon fired in unison. The blue columns reeled in pain and confusion. As Meade reset his lines to renew the advance, a second salvo ripped great holes in the once-impressive formation. Federals heroically regrouped under fire and inched forward through the gunfire and smoke.

With some support from Gibbon now materializing, Meade's units began drifting toward the right because Billy Yanks saw a tongue of woodland jutting in their direction. It offered the closest cover from the furious fire of Confederate artillery. For a time, it appeared that Jackson's guns might stop the assault. The Union advance slowed; then it built momentum anew and resumed. Now the two sides were within musket range, and the small arms fire added to the noise and intensity of battle.

Federals were dropping steadily when, near 1 P.M., the lead elements of Meade's division plunged through the swampy bottom into the apex of the woodland. Suddenly, the Federals were no longer exposed to concentrated fire. Best of all, the coppice was unoccupied. Rushing desperately uphill, Meade's men slammed through the gap between the brigades of Lane and Archer. The enemy had pierced Jackson's line as cleanly as a surgeon with a scalpel.

Never slowing, Meade's soldiers brushed aside the flanks of the two Confederate brigades, expanded the 600-yard interval even more, and drove straight ahead to the top of the hill. There they came upon Maxcy Gregg's South Carolinians in reserve. Gregg's men were resting quietly with their arms stacked!

Acoustical shadows in the Civil War were not unusual, but for a Union attack to have caught Gregg's brigade totally unprepared is astonishing. Obviously, the aged and somewhat deaf Gregg neither saw nor heard the Union onslaught until it smashed into his sector. At first, Gregg mistook the approaching enemy for Confederates. When they fired a point-blank volley, pandemonium exploded. Carolinians bolted toward the rear. The mounted Gregg was frantically trying to stop his men from returning fire when a bullet struck his left side and drove into the spine. Gregg fell to the ground mortally wounded.[132]

Jackson was not aware of any crisis in his center until an officer galloped up and reported breathlessly: "General! The enemy have broken through Archer's left, and General Gregg says he must have help or he and General Archer will both lose their position!"[133]

That Jackson showed no concern is understandable. Although his position was behind Stuart's guns and near Harvey Hill's division, he knew how thickly his troops were packed along the two-mile front. (An entire division was behind Gregg's shattered ranks.) Turning to one of his staff, Jackson calmly directed that Early's division be brought up to reinforce Jackson's right along Prospect Hill. He himself would take charge of extending that flank with Harvey Hill's troops.

Early started forward as told, then learned of the breakthrough farther to the left. "This caused me to hesitate," he later confessed. Early was caught between the explicit instructions of Jackson and the crisis on Archer's front.

After a few moments of contemplation, Early chose military expediency: he would risk Jackson's wrath by disobeying orders to reinforce Hill and going where he thought he was most needed. He pointed his division toward the gap in the center. If Jackson ever disapproved the violation of orders, he kept it to himself.[134]

Meade's breakthrough had lasted an hour and fifteen minutes. Gibbon's division was locked in combat with Lane's North Carolinians when the better part of four fresh Confederate brigades came crashing through the woods with that eerie Rebel yell echoing around them. It was Early's division, plus the brigades of Thomas, Pender, and Paxton.

Confederates struck with full momentum. Archer's regrouped brigade pounded Meade's exposed left flank. No troops could stand a prolonged hammering from two sides.

Federals began falling back through the woods and down the slope. At first the withdrawal was slow. Once the Federals were driven from the woods into the open flatland, the retirement became a wild dash for safety. Southern artillery and musketry inflicted heavy casualties on Meade's brigades as they scampered for Franklin's main line. "The whole field seemed teeming with them in their flight," a Georgia soldier commented.[135]

During the first stage of the Union fallback, Jackson was personally leading Harvey Hill's division into position on the right of the line. A possibility existed that Doubleday's Union division was moving to turn Jackson's right. That required more attention at the moment than Meade's shattered assault. After that threat was discounted, Jackson turned left with the troops and made for the action on Prospect Hill. Harvey Hill's brigades fanned out as a strong and new battle line.

The moment of victory was at hand. Staff officer William Williamson watched Jackson ride to the edge of the woods and peer at the plain. Shells were still flying overhead; noise was deafening.

Then, Williamson observed, "I saw him raise his hand & the expression on his face & the gesture so impressed me that I rode on behind him saying to myself, 'I will get the benefit of that prayer.'" Other troops who caught sight of their praying general likewise bowed their heads in the midst of the still-raging contest.[136]

Now Jackson played again the accomplished artilleryman. His guns not damaged by Union batteries prior to Meade's attack were playing on the retreating Federal infantry. In doing so, they revealed their position. Federal cannon, with the range firmly set, began blasting the Confederate gun emplacements. Several weapons had to be pulled back.

In spite of the rather lopsided artillery exchange, Jackson reined his horse in front of the lines and intently watched the duel. Shells exploded here and there; smoke and death filled the air. What Jackson did next was illogical, to say the least.

To replace the small-caliber guns that had been withdrawn, he ordered Captain William T. Poague of the Rockbridge Artillery to advance two long-range twenty-pounder Parrott rifles and open fire. Poague was to maintain a duel with his two guns against at least a third of the enemy batteries. When the return fire became too heavy, Poague was to shift his salvos into whatever ranks of Union infantry remained in view.

The result was as one might expect. Years later, Poague exclaimed: "Such a tempest of shot and shell I never have witnessed any where during the war. It was as if 'Old Jack' had said to the Yankee Devil, 'seest thou my faithful old Stonewall Battery! Do your worst and see if thou canst terrify it!" Federal artillery exacted a small measure of revenge for defeat by concentrating on Poague's section and knocking out sixteen gunners. Among the slain was youthful Randolph Fairfax, who had aspired to the ministry.[137]

By 2 P.M., the battle of Fredericksburg had moved to Longstreet's front. There Burnside made a veritable series of mistakes. Launching separate offensives against Lee's two corps neutralized much of the Union superiority in numbers. Burnside's major attacks were aimed at the strongest points in Lee's lines. Never did the Union general seriously consider Lee's center, the most vulnerable point in his defenses.

For the rest of that bloody day, Federals continued what became more than a dozen frontal attacks against Longstreet's position. It was one of the strongest defensive works Lee ever created. The battle took on all the characteristics of a massacre. Not one Union soldier got to within fifty yards of Marye's Heights and the Sunken Road, where Longstreet's men stood in line to fire muskets.

At one point, Lee peered through his binoculars toward Jackson's line. He turned to Longstreet and, with a combination of satisfaction and sadness, said: "It is well that war is so terrible! We should grow too fond of it!"[138]

Only intermittent cannonading broke the comparative quiet of the afternoon at

Hamilton's Crossing. Jackson's men congratulated themselves on a clear-cut victory. Two enemy divisions had been whipped and sent scurrying back to the Rappahannock.

It appeared to be a repeat of Antietam. Hundreds of dead and wounded men lay in grotesque positions all over the plain. Soldiers in both armies could only watch helplessly as incalculable numbers struggled in agony. Nobody could go to anyone's aid because artillery fire continued sweeping the field.

Jackson wanted the Federals to attack again. The breakthrough had given him no cause to worry. "I waited some time to receive it," Jackson reported, "but [the Federals] making no formal movement, I determined, if prudent, to do so myself."[139]

The situation invited attack, Jackson determined. He had planned on a counter-blow before the battle began. Now, in late afternoon, the opportunity seemed favorable. "Those who saw him at that hour," one writer declared, "will never forget the expression of intense but suppressed excitement which his face displayed." The "genius of battle" had replaced the introspective commander; "his countenance glowed as from the glare of a great conflagration."[140]

How to overcome the heavy firepower of the Union batteries, especially those atop Stafford Heights, was Jackson's principal concern. The unusual counterattack he wanted to make became even more unorthodox with the planning. He would attack with his artillery in the lead. It would unleash a blanket fire and measure the enemy's response. Then Jackson would hurl his entire Second Corps—now about 26,000 strong—against the unstable Federal positions.

The divisions of Harvey Hill and Taliaferro would form the principal assault force. Neither had been severely engaged in the day's fighting. Powell Hill and Early would follow in close support. The advance would come at sunset so that, if perchance unsuccessful, the Confederates could retire under cover of darkness. That was the only thought Jackson gave to failure. He was convinced that what he advocated would result in the surrender of the Union army or, if it attempted to escape, the loss of thousands of additional men driven into the icy river.

Perhaps Jackson's optimism, or his killer's instinct, was at full power that afternoon. He did not bother to seek or secure Lee's approval for the countermovement. Even odder is the fact that neither Jackson nor Lee made any official reference to such a bold and autonomous movement.

With the basic plan formulated, Jackson summoned Dr. McGuire. "How many yards of bandaging do you have?" he asked the surgeon. "I do not exactly know," McGuire replied. "Certainly enough for another fight." After a moment, the physician's curiosity got the best of him. "What do you want to know how much bandaging I have for?" Jackson looked at him with an earnest expression. "I want a yard of bandaging to put on the arm of every soldier in this night's attack, so that the men may know each other from the enemy." McGuire told him that not enough white cloth existed for such a purpose. The men could not even rip off the tails of their shirts because half of them did not have white shirts. The idea of improvised insignia vanished.[141]

The whole battle strategy then began to unravel. Jackson's erratic orders were the major culprit. Sandie Pendleton was wounded while carrying instructions for Taliaferro, who never received any word of what to do. Powell Hill did not learn of the proposed offensive until sundown, when he was told in the simplest terms to advance his men. The first hint Early got of Jackson's plan came when Harvey Hill's division began marching past him. To get his own division to the front and ready to lead, Early had to give orders to a superior officer, the highly sensitive Powell Hill.

Reminiscent of Cedar Mountain, Jackson moved to battle while pieces of his command were still moving forward. In spite of the infantry turmoil to the rear, Jackson got his guns forward. The first of the batteries unlimbered and fired. Federal cannon across the way replied with heavy salvos. The whole countryside seemed to erupt as Union shells literally rained on the Confederates. Everything was now going wrong for the Southerners. In the confusion, some of Jackson's men actually fired into each other.

"Owing to unexpected delays," Jackson admitted, "the movement could not be gotten ready until late in the evening. The first gun had hardly moved forward from the wood a hundred yards, when the enemy's artillery reopened, & so completely swept our front, as to satisfy me that the proposed movement should be abandoned." Lee apparently knew nothing of Jackson's assault until it had been canceled. The army chieftain made no mention of it in his reports.[142]

Naturally, Jackson was disappointed. Days earlier, he had predicted that the Confederates would win a victory at Fredericksburg but gain no fruits from it. That had come to pass. The one-sided success notwithstanding, long-range dividends were few. Jackson would have preferred to convert defense into offense and finish the day with destruction—rather than defeat—of the enemy. An all-wise Providence ruled otherwise.

Compared with the well-publicized fighting on Longstreet's front, Jackson's losses were surprisingly heavy. The explanation lies in the less formidable topography of the country around Prospect Hill. Jackson reported 344 of his men killed, 2545 wounded, and 526 missing for total casualties of 3415 soldiers. (These figures exclude the casualties of Stuart and John B. Hood, both serving under Jackson during the battle.) Franklin put his losses at 401 dead, 2761 injured, and 625 captured, in all 3787 men.[143]

As at Second Manassas and Antietam, Jackson had waged a defensive battle. He had created a thickly manned position, stationed his reserves properly, and concealed his artillery for the maximum effects of a first fire. Still, if a selection for best performance had to be made between Longstreet and Jackson at Fredericksburg, the former would take the honors. Longstreet established impregnable lines and ensured that they were intact. He made no faulty moves during the battle—in large part because Burnside's unimaginative and blind assaults turned the Marye's Heights into a Union killing ground.

Jackson managed his part of the contest skillfully. Yet there would always remain the nagging question of the oversight of that jutting woodland. Further, the gap in Powell Hill's line was too large to be overlooked. Jackson had to be aware of the interval; and even though his line was the most heavily defended of any he ever had, the general should have corrected that one weak point the first time he saw it.

Unnecessary casualties resulted from it. The gap may have been partly the result of limited communication between Jackson and Hill. If that was the case, Jackson committed a tactical error in assigning the front line to Hill, and the latter was guilty of gross oversight in permitting the gap to exist. Neither Jackson nor anyone else around Prospect Hill seems to have known where Hill was for most of the battle. Both Hill and Jackson must share blame for this void. Thus did victory end on a lingering controversy.

Lee was obviously pleased with the performance of his two corps commanders. In his official report, he declared: "To Generals Longstreet and Jackson great praise is due for the disposition and management of their respective corps. Their quick perception enabled them to discover the projected assaults . . . and their ready skill to devise the best means to resist them." Lee wished to add publicly that his choice of corps commanders had been correct. "I am also indebted to them for valuable counsel, both as regards the general operations of the army and the execution of the particular measures adopted."[144]

The battle of Fredericksburg had been two completely separate engagements fought three miles apart. Both sides came to see this. Captain Abner Small of Maine conceded, "There had been two battles, and we knew that both had been lost."[145]

Jackson had just established his headquarters for the night behind Hamilton's Crossing when unexpected company arrived from Richmond. The general warmly greeted his confidante, Colonel Boteler, and well-known sculptor Adalbert Volcke. Boteler had brought a large quantity of oysters, on which the party feasted. After supper, Boteler requested that Jackson allow Volcke to draw several sketches of him. The group adjourned to Jackson's tent and Volcke began drawing. In a few minutes, the whole party was smiling. Jackson, sitting erect on a camp stool, was sound asleep.

The usually reliable Hunter McGuire created a widely quoted but erroneous story about events of that Saturday night. According to the surgeon, Lee called a council of war to discuss what the army should do next. Much conversation ensued between the generals. Lee turned to Jackson and asked for his advice. Jackson, who had been asleep during most of the conference, raised his head and snarled: "Drive them into the river! Drive them into the river!"[146]

Lee did hold a council of war late that night, but the primary subject was defense. No one in attendance mentioned anything as dramatic as Jackson, aroused from sleep in Lee's presence, arguing for attack. In fact, shortly after sundown Jackson had ordered his artillery and infantry to strengthen their earthworks in anticipation of a new Union offensive the next day.

Boteler was asleep in Jackson's tent when the general returned from the brief meeting with Lee. The congressman awoke as Jackson entered the tent and watched his friend through almost-closed eyes. Jackson lit a candle and laid aside coat, sword, and other accoutrements. He opened the door of the little stove that warmed his Sibley tent to get more light. After taking a seat at his table, Jackson brought out a well-worn Bible and read for awhile. He followed this by kneeling in prayer. Then he removed his boots, lay down beside Boteler, and fell instantly to sleep.

Around 2 A.M., Jackson awakened as if by signal. He arose carefully, trying not to disturb his guest. The light-sleeping Boteler was now aroused but said nothing. Lighting a candle, Jackson began reading at his table. He looked up at one point and saw that the candlelight was shining in Boteler's face. Quietly Jackson secured a book and adjusted it so that it would shield the light in his friend's direction. "It was a little thing for him to do," Boteler stated, but "it was sufficient to indicate to me the thoughtful goodness of that great heart of his, which was as bold as a lion's and as gentle as a lamb's."[147]

The condition of General Maxcy Gregg began to weigh on Jackson's mind in the middle of the night. Near 4:00 that morning, he sent an inquiry to Dr. McGuire about the brigadier's condition. The response: Gregg's case was hopeless. Jackson asked his surgeon to go to Gregg and ensure that he had everything he needed. A few minutes later, Jackson decided to visit the general himself.

McGuire was dismounting at "Belvoir," the Thomas Yerby home where Gregg lay, when Jackson and Lieutenant Smith rode through the darkness into the yard. Jackson quickly stepped into the house. Gregg, conscious but in great pain, was on a couch in the middle of a dimly lit room. At this point, the stern Jackson—he who had gruffly ordered and argued with Gregg in the past—disappeared. Now a husky-voiced corps commander sat down on Gregg's bed and displayed every solicitude to a friend.

Gregg sought to apologize for a discourteous endorsement he had written several days previously. Jackson had no recollection of the communique. His voice shaking with emotion, he took Gregg's hand and said: "The doctor tells me that you have not long to live. Let me ask you to dismiss this matter from your mind and turn your thoughts to God and to the world to which you go." The Carolinian's eyes filled with tears. "I thank you, I thank you very much," he mumbled. Gregg would die twenty-four hours later. Jackson, McGuire, and Smith left the room and started back through the night to corps headquarters. The aides rode silently, waiting for the general to speak. Not until camp was in sight did Jackson utter a word. He suddenly looked up at the sky and exclaimed: "How horrible is war!"

"Horrible, yes," McGuire replied, "but we have been invaded. What can we do?"

"Kill them, sir!" Jackson shouted in savage tones. "Kill every man!"[148]

It was near dawn when Jackson walked into his tent. Boteler was awake. The two began one of their earnest conversations. Jackson expected an attack that Sunday.

"Burnside has doubtless discovered by this time that it's useless for him to make any further attempts on the left and left center of our line. His only chance of effecting something will be to concentrate his force upon our right." Jackson paused, then declared, "But, Colonel, we'll be ready for him, and, with God's help, we'll gain another victory."[149]

The Second Corps waited expectantly in the morning fog. "If we are quiet," Jackson cautioned, "maybe they will renew the attack."[150] Burnside did not. The previous day had convinced him of Lee's invulnerability on the high ground west of Fredericksburg. Every hour or so, Union guns played on the Confederate lines. Jackson's lighter guns, short of ammunition, replied occasionally.

Confederate officer John G. Gittings came upon his old VMI professor early that morning. Gittings was walking along the ridge of Hamilton's Crossing, "and about thirty yards from one of the batteries, I passed within a few feet of General Jackson, who had taken up his position alone on this vantage-ground for the purpose of reconnoitering. But he was not doing very much of it just at that time, for he was seated on the ground, leaning against a hickory sapling, and fast asleep. He held his bridle-rein in one hand and his field glass in the other . . . [and] seemed to be sleeping as calmly as I had seen him sleep years before in the church at Lexington."[151]

Later in the day, Jackson rode with Taliaferro to make another inspection of the position of his old division. The route of generals, staffs, and couriers took them into no-man's land. It was obvious that at least one general officer was in the party, and that was tempting to Federal sharpshooters. "A scattering fire was kept up upon us," Taliaferro commented, "the balls passing uncomfortably near our heads." No one was injured.[152]

In midafternoon, a party of Federal horsemen came to the front of the lines under a white flag. A captain on General Franklin's staff asked for a cessation of hostilities to collect the wounded and bury the dead. Jackson snapped that any such request should be made in writing. The officer quickly scribbled a note; Jackson read it and granted a truce of precisely one hour.

Another member of the Federal group was Surgeon John Junkin, Jackson's brother-in-law by his first marriage. He had ridden through the lines to present Jackson with a package from his father, Dr. George Junkin. The strongly Unionist clergyman had written a polemic on what he considered the many crimes against God committed by the South in leaving the Union. James Power Smith (who had rapidly become one of Jackson's closest aides because he was well versed in Presbyterian theology) opened the package. He informed Jackson that the gift was a copy of Junkin's book, entitled *Political Heresies*. "I expect it is well-named, Lieutenant," Jackson replied with a frown. "That's just what the book contains: political heresies."[153]

That night, as wind-blown rain pounded the countryside, Burnside deftly pulled the Army of the Potomac back across the Rappahannock. By dawn of December 16, with the downpour continuing, the Union works on the Fredericksburg side were empty. Here and there a Federal deserter waited to be captured; dead bodies still dotted the open country; arms and equipment were strewn everywhere; wagons stood or lay in the roads—all of this representing the debris of a retiring army. Even Burnside's pontoon bridges were gone.

Lee regretted the loss of another opportunity to hammer his adversary from Marye's Heights and Prospect Hill. Jackson looked at the battlefield with its torn ground and fresh graves. With a tinge of bitterness, he said: "I did not think that a little red earth would have frightened them. I am sorry that they are gone. I am sorry I fortified."[154]

Shortly after noon, Jackson heard from an outpost that large numbers of Federals were moving across the Rappahannock downriver at Port Royal. Lee dispatched Stuart's cavalry for verification, then concluded that the threat could be critical to his position. At 1 P.M., Jackson started eastward with his entire corps. The general remained in the van as men trudged in mud during a cold and blustery afternoon. A message arrived from Stuart: the report of the enemy being at Port Royal was false. All was quiet there.

The Second Corps was strung out for four miles or more along a single road bordered by thick woods and entanglements. A bivouac there was out of the question. Jackson ordered Early's division south of Port Royal and Powell Hill's brigades in the same direction to Moss Neck. The remainder of the corps must turn around and retrace its steps until it reached an open area. Jackson would supervise all of this; but to do so, he would have to turn Little Sorrel and ride the entire length of his column. No alternate course was available.

So with reluctance, Jackson started back. The narrow road forced general and staff to proceed in single file, their horses sometimes touching the infantrymen. A bemused Hotchkiss wrote: "The General, who was in front, tried to get back to the rear unobserved by his men. He gave his horse to a courier and attempted to get through the woods and 'flank' his line, but could not succeed, and had to come back and remount his horse and ride along the line of march. The soldiers at once 'caught on' to the situation and cheered him, vociferously, as we galloped, in single file through the opening they made for us along the middle of the road."[155]

The stillness of that wintry afternoon vanished as regiment after regiment, battery after battery, squadron after squadron, exploded spontaneously into whoops and shouts. Each unit took up the loud cheering and continued as long as the general was in sight. Before long, and from courtesy, Jackson removed his cap as Little Sorrel pranced and snorted while making its way through the long column. Men suffering from cold, hunger, and weariness forgot their miseries at the sight of Old Jack and added their voices to the acclamation.

It was a grand moment never to be forgotten. Jackson was at the zenith of his career. He had bedazzled his compatriots and bewildered the enemy. Behind that unpretentious, weather-beaten uniform he continued to wear, and beneath a forage cap resting as much on the bridge of his nose as on the top of his head, was a humorless, introspective commander around whom swirled rumors, anecdotes, and legends. He ignored it all as he drove his men hard on a march and hurled them unhesitatingly into battle. In the process, he had made them "foot cavalry"—the pride of the army—and he had led them from one victory to another.

His insistence on the impossible was their challenge; his faith in God was their refuge. Never mind that his ways were strange and his discipline stern. The soldiers in the ranks knew that those who were blessed to survive the war would harbor memories that would impart warmth to old age and inspiration to their children. So they lined the road for miles that icy afternoon and they voiced their love for Old Jack. Thousands of soldiers made him uncomfortable with their open displays of affection. That too was part of the mystique.

Eventually, the general and his staff passed the line of soldiers and reached a clearing that offered a reasonable bivouac area. A sheltered hollow with an abundance of fallen leaves appeared adequate to Jackson. Staff members suggested that they seek instead the hospitality of one of the nearby homes. "No," said Jackson. That ended the conversation.

A large campfire was soon blazing, sparks rising to the limbs of a poplar tree spreading over the party. Jackson asked for food. There was none. The wind was blowing hard, sending a bone-deep chill through everyone. The group went to bed hungry. Awhile later, Jackson sat up. "I am cold and hungry," he declared. At that moment, a large section of the poplar tree, burnt by sparks, fell with a crash across the campfire. Sparks and burning wood sprayed in every direction.

Jackson's endurance was near an end. He sent Pendleton and McGuire to the nearby Corbin home to see if any extra food might be available. They returned with a basket of biscuits, "a half-used ham," and an invitation to make the home their headquarters. The general devoured the food but refused the shelter. He again tried to go to sleep in the subfreezing weather. Jackson soon stood up. "Let's go to the Moss Neck house," he said in resigned fashion.

The long brick home with its imposing frontage beckoned in the darkness as a sanctuary. A staff member knocked on the door; as light after light appeared in the rooms, spirits raised. Here at last was a refuge! The family welcomed the party and quickly prepared rooms for Jackson and his aides. Expressing quick appreciation, the general led the procession to beds and much-needed rest.[156]

Officers awakened the next morning to a sumptuous breakfast. On long tables were plates of sausage, ham, waffles, and muffins. The Corbins were gracious hosts; breakfast conversation was "jolly and bright." Richard Corbin, owner of Moss Neck, was away on duty with the 9th Virginia Cavalry. His wife Roberta begged the general to make a wing of the mansion his headquarters. Jackson politely declined. The home was "too luxurious for a soldier, who should sleep in a tent." He would pitch his tents in the woods 500 yards away, if that was agreeable. The family reluctantly assented.[157]

Watching for enemy movements and waiting for orders to go into winter quarters occupied the next few days. Jackson had hoped to spend the winter in Winchester. That obviously could not occur as long as the Federal army stood in front of Fredericksburg. Jackson at first masked his disappointment with compassion. To the Second Corps, he issued a circular asking for donations for the relief of the destitute citizens of Fredericksburg. Happiness over the new addition to his family remained sublime. He longed for a glimpse of Julia. "I tell you," he wrote Anna, "I would love to caress her and see her smile. Kiss the little darling for her father."[158]

In the same letter, Jackson expressed trust "that our Heavenly Father will continue to bless" the fortunes of the Confederacy. God's will must be acknowledged. Winter quarters would offer such an opportunity. Jackson had told Major Dabney a few weeks earlier that as soon as practicable "unusual efforts should be made for the spiritual improvement of the army." Jackson planned personally to superintend such a new awakening. His own devotion would be the catalyst. In a note of condolence to the brother of an officer who died with Jackson's name on his lips, the general announced, "I look beyond this life to an existence where I hope to know him better."[159]

22

PROBLEMS AND PLEASURES OF WINTER

JACKSON INITIALLY CALLED THE PLACE "Corbyn's Farm"; but in the three months that he spent there, he came to know it correctly as one of the most imposing estates in Virginia. The 1600-acre plantation of the Corbin family was eleven miles downriver from Fredericksburg. "Moss Neck Manor," the home was called; 250 feet long from wing to wing, patterned after an English country residence, it stood on high ground two miles from the Rappahannock.

Corbins had been in the area for more than two centuries. They had intermarried with Lees, Carters, Byrds, Taylors, and other prominent families. A local saying was that a well-to-do man was "as rich as a Corbin." Yet by late 1862, the family was enduring the hard times of war. Federal soldiers and vandals had absconded with much of the furniture. Many of the once-productive fields had deteriorated into weed beds because of a lack of available labor.

Richard Corbin, the owner of Moss Neck, was a trooper in the 9th Virginia Cavalry. His young wife, Roberta, was mistress of the estate. With her in the mansion were a five-year-old daughter, Jane Wellford Corbin, and an unmarried sister-in-law, Catherine Carter Corbin, who had just turned twenty-three.[1]

The headquarters tents were near the stables several hundred yards from the home. With the major fighting apparently over for the winter, Jackson could afford the luxury of thinking of loved ones and personal matters. "Should I remain here," he wrote Anna,

I do hope that you and baby can come to see me before spring, as you can come on the railroad. Wherever I go, God gives me kind friends. The people here show me great kindness. I receive invitation after invitation to dine out, and spend the night, and a great many provisions are sent me, including nice cakes, tea, loaf-sugar, &c., and the socks and gloves and handkerchiefs still come!

I am so thankful to our ever-kind Heavenly Father for having improved my eyes as to enable me to write at night. He continually showers blessings upon me; and that *you* should have been spared, and our darling little daughter given us, fills my heart with overflowing gratitude. If I know my unworthy self, my desire is to live *entirely and unreservedly to God's glory.*[2]

Winter descended in frigid fashion; and after a week in the open, Jackson developed both a cold and a painful earache. (Other than exhaustion and associated ills of the Seven Days Campaign, this is the only recorded instance in the war when Jackson admitted suffering from a physical disability.) Surgeon McGuire insisted that he move indoors. Jackson compromised between Moss Neck Manor and a tent: he consented to use a small wooden office building fifty yards in front of the main house.

Such outbuildings were common on Virginia plantations. There the owner conducted business, kept his books, and sometimes provided a bedroom for an overflow of visitors. The Moss Neck office had three rooms. The entrance opened into a small lobby or vestibule. On the right were stairs leading to a half-story bedroom on the second floor. A wood closet was on the left of the lobby.

Directly inside the entrance and across the lobby was the door to the office. That room contained a fireplace and windows in two walls. Bookcases on either side of the door were filled with a set of Virginia statutes, horse and cattle registers, agricultural reports, and a miscellaneous lot of old books. Adorning the walls were pictures of thoroughbred horses, prize bulls, a cockfight, a terrier famous for the number of rats it could kill within a minute. Such scenes appeared contrary to Jackson's tastes.

He refused to disturb any of the furnishings in the room that became his headquarters. In fact, the farm owner from Lexington could enjoy back issues of *Farmer's Register*, just as the former child jockey at Jackson's Mill certainly appreciated the lines of a prized race horse. The general installed a writing table on one side of the fireplace and a cot on the other. Two or three stools completed the furnishings.

Jackson's overcoat and sword hung on the wall; before retiring at night, he meticulously placed his high boots in a corner. Lieutenant Smith and other members of the staff took turns occupying the upstairs room. Irish soldiers from the 1st Virginia Battalion (the provost guard of the Second Corps) marched to and fro in front of the little building.[3]

Bitterly cold weather marked Jackson's first weekend at Moss Neck. Before confronting a mountain of administrative details, the general attended to some personal matters. He asked his Lexington friend, John L. Campbell, to hire out his two slave boys for another year. Jackson also expressed the hope that, "if practicable," the boys could "have an opportunity of attending the colored Sabbath school in Lexington, if it is still in operation."[4]

On Sunday night, December 21, Jackson had one of his long chats with Hotchkiss. He lamented the needy condition of Fredericksburg citizens. "War is the greatest of evils," he told Hotchkiss. Jackson was prayerful that his appeal to the soldiers for contributions would bring positive results. (A week later he was able to present over $30,000 in aid to the mayor of the town.) In the conversation with his mapmaker, Jackson exulted over "how Providence has blessed us, and our strength has increased during the whole continuance of the war up to this time."[5]

He continued that theme the next day in a letter to close friend John Preston. "I greatly desire to see *peace, blessed peace,* and I am persuaded that if God's people throughout our Confederacy will earnestly and perseveringly unite in imploring His interposition for peace, that we may expect it. . . . We call ourselves a Christian people. . . . Let the framework of our government show that we are not ungrateful to Him."[6]

An end to the war was still on Jackson's mind early on Christmas Day. He wrote Anna: "Yesterday I received the baby's letter with its precious lock of hair. How I do want to see that precious baby! and I do earnestly pray for peace. Oh! that our Country was such a Christian, *God* fearing people as it should be! Then might we very speedily look for peace."[7]

Anna's paramount hope was that Jackson might take leave that winter and come to North Carolina to see his family. He declined to do so with all the reasoning of the Christian soldier. "It appears to me that it is better for me to remain with my command so long as the war continues, if the ever gracious Heavenly Father permits. The Army suffers immensely from absentees. If all our troops, officers & men were at their posts, we might through God's blessing, expect a more speedy termination of the war. . . . *Our God* has greatly blest me & mine during my absence, & whilst it would be a great comfort to see you, & my darling little daughter, & others in whom I take special interest, yet duty appears to require me to remain with my command. It is important that those at Hd. Qrs. set an example by remaining at the post of duty."[8]

Doing so brought some embarrassment to Jackson later that day. He had received so much food from grateful citizens that he invited Generals Lee, Stuart, and Pendleton, along with selected members of their staffs, to Christmas dinner at Moss Neck. Jim Lewis and another servant wore white aprons; the lavish table contained three turkeys, oysters, a ham, fresh biscuits, a variety of vegetables and pickles, plus a large bottle of wine.

Twelve officers arrived for dinner. Both Lee and Stuart pretended shock and outrage at the commodious accommodations enjoyed by Jackson. It was so uncharacteristic of the Second Corps commander. Lee declared that Jackson and his staff were only playing soldiers. He invited Jackson to dine with him and "see how a soldier ought to live." That would have turned Jackson's face even redder than it was if Stuart, with "great glee," had not been teasing Jackson from the time of his arrival. The cavalry chief began when he saw the sporty paintings on the wall. Stuart read aloud the description of each racehorse and splendid bull. At the hearth he paused with affected horror to study the terrier that could kill so many rats in a minute. Stuart pretended to believe that Jackson had selected each painting for his headquarters. He expressed astonishment at Jackson's low tastes in art. All of this caused Old Jack to blush like a girl and respond in a halting and apologetic manner—to the merriment of everyone in attendance. Stuart was not through, however. He commented on waiters in white aprons. The appearance of wine on Jackson's table evoked a playful burst of feigned disgrace. Finally, Stuart looked at the large mold of butter bearing the imprint of a rooster. That must be Jackson's coat of arms, he announced solemnly. Even Lee laughed boisterously. Jackson's slight smile hardly masked his discomfort.[9]

That night Mrs. Corbin gave a Christmas party at the mansion. Jackson did not attend; but Sandie Pendleton did and immediately began losing his heart to vivacious Catherine ("Kate") Corbin.[10]

As the last days of 1862 passed, and the cold weather showed no sign of abating, Confederate soldiers began constructing winter quarters. One of Jackson's veterans declared that "huts were made of any material that could be gotten, and in any way the architect of the party thought best. The greater number were of logs. A few men had tents." A member of the Corbin family later recalled: "What a transformation of our quiet country home! Thousands of soldiers around—the hills echoing with the sounds of army life. . . . In less than six weeks great forests were literally mowed down. Almost Phoenix like sprung into life settlements of little log huts dotted here and there with white tents. The smoke curled from hundreds of camp fires! It was a busy moving panorama."[11]

The Second Corps, with over 36,600 men present for duty, was twice as large as Jackson's valley army at its peak strength. Moreover, corps leaders were part of a tight army chain of command. Jackson had to learn and perform a rash of administrative duties with which he was never comfortable.

To improve his part of the system, he tightened his staff and his regimen. Sandie Pendleton now had a major's commission and served in essence as chief of staff. He ran the staff with a mature judgment far beyond his twenty-three years. So close a relationship existed between the general and his Lexington adjutant that when the name of an obscure officer or record were mentioned, Jackson instinctively replied: "Ask Sandie Pendleton. If he does not know, no one does."[12]

Reports, applications, and minutiae of corps administration filled the mornings and sometimes part of the afternoons. Jackson began the workday by meeting individually with staff members to discuss conditions and needs in medical, quartermaster, commissary, ordnance, and engineering departments. Next came hours with Pendleton over incoming and outgoing correspondence from every level of the army. Notes were made of important matters; orders for the day were dispatched; requests for information and requisitions for supplies were a daily chore. Subjects ranging from gathering evidence for courts-martial to surveying roads for military use all demanded Jackson's attention.

He had never liked paperwork; but good soldier that he was, he did his duty. Young Lieutenant Smith was struck by Jackson's dedication. "The General was never absent for a night, was quite amiable and accessible, though quiet and reserved. He listened pleasantly to our table talk, though he easily grew abstracted, enjoyed our stories, then showed how little impression they made by going away in the midst of the very best, and betaking himself to his work, in which there was little interruption. . . . Of all the multitude of affairs in that large army corps, there was nothing of which he did not know, and there was no part which did not feel the pressure of his will and energy."[13]

Smith became convinced that "every bureau of the War Department in Richmond was kept awake by Jackson's demands. If the stores were not forthcoming, he would know the reason why. In the field it was pleasant to know that the best of bureau officers were disturbed by nightmares, in which Stonewall Jackson rode into the chamber with drawn sabre."[14]

Occasionally in late afternoon, he would lay aside the work long enough to go for a ride or a walk by himself. After supper, he would attack the paperwork anew. Bent over his desk, eyeshade blocking the light's glare, he would sign "T. J. Jackson" to one document after another. Smith once found the general asleep in the middle of his signature.[15]

Visitors wanting to see the famous soldier came in a steady stream. All could not be ignored. Lee and his staff sometimes arrived unannounced. The four division commanders frequently dismounted at headquarters. Every brigadier and regimental colonel came with some special request. Members of Congress were regular callers as they came to see and be seen. Lee was always welcome. So was Stuart, who not only could break Jackson's somber mood in a flash but occasionally elicit a chuckle from the usually humorless corps commander.

As for others whom circumstances forced him to meet, Jackson always greeted them courteously and entertained them to the extent of minimum conversation. One Jackson mannerism continually amused the staff. When a guest entered Jackson's office, the general would say solicitously, "Let me take your hat, sir." After receiving it, he would look around for a moment in search of a place to put it. None ever seemed obvious, whereupon Jackson would drop the hat on the floor.[16]

On December 30, Major von Borcke escorted three Englishmen from Lee's headquarters to Moss Neck. The Marquis of Hartington and Colonel William Leslie of the British army were most anxious to meet the famous Jackson. Accompanying them was correspondent Frank Vizetelly, who had met Jackson a few weeks earlier. The party arrived in midday. Von Borcke noted with amusement: "Old Stonewall so fascinated his English visitors by his kind and pleasant manners and the resources of his conversation, that, quite against their previous intentions, they accepted his invitation to [lunch], and instead of a visit of twenty minutes, many hours were spent under the General's roof." Indeed, the Englishmen were late for dinner with Lee because of their attraction to Lee's lieutenant.[17]

A steady flow of gifts likewise became somewhat worrisome to Jackson. In one short period, the wife of a Georgia soldier sent a basted suit, to be finished after precise measurements had been made. An Englishman shipped a new saddle. One of the North Carolina chaplains forwarded a package containing a cap, gauntlets, buttons, soap, toothbrush, and offer of gold lace. Socks and handkerchiefs arrived with a regularity second only to letters of affection. Two horses, along with full equipment, came from citizens of Staunton and Augusta County.

The general could not personally acknowledge all of the expressions of esteem, but he always sought to write when the donor was a resident of the Shenandoah Valley. To the five men who sent him one of the horses, Jackson voiced sincere gratitude. "This evidence of regard will continue to be appreciated not only for its intrinsic worth but as the kind testimonial of the patriotic people of Augusta."[18]

Jackson then suggested that credit for feelings of security be given where credit was due. "In reply to the complimentary manner in which you speak of my services, permit me to say that they have fallen far short of my desires. I trust that God who has thus far protected your homes may continue to do so & soon bless our country with an honorable & lasting peace."[19]

His concern for his beloved valley was constant. On the last day of the year, he urged Congressman Boteler to exert his influence with the president and War Department in having the region designated a military department. Jackson humbly added: "You must not think from what I have said at any time that I desire to be sent to the Valley, even if it should be made a Department. I would rather remain in a subordinate position as long as the war lasts; provided that my command is kept near my Commanding General."[20]

As a statement from Jackson, this was high praise of Lee. Yet the two men were becoming increasingly dependent upon one another as their joint efforts carried the Army of Northern Virginia from one success to another. Jackson never bestowed compliments lavishly, but he made no effort to hide his admiration for Lee.

Fortunately, distressing news was concealed from Jackson at the time. Little Julia had contracted whooping cough. The disease reached a dangerous level, but a relieved mother would soon tell a friend that the child had "passed the crisis with the coming of the new year."[21]

Jackson did not learn of the illness until Julia was out of danger. Then he wrote Anna: "I am very thankful to our kind Heavenly Father for good tidings from you and baby—specially that she is restored again to health, and I trust that we all three may so live as most to glorify His holy name." The general then reassured his wife of his own well-being. "My ears are still troubling me, but I am very thankful that my hearing is as good as usual. . . . Indeed, my health is essentially good, but I do not think I shall be able in [the] future to stand what I have already stood, although with the exception of the increased sensitiveness of my ears, my health has improved."[22]

A major neglect by Jackson and other generals during 1862 was the preparation of official battle reports. Jackson had done only one: that for the March engagement at Kernstown. Toward the end of December, Lee repeated his call for all outstanding reports to be written and submitted to army headquarters.

Remembering the intricacies of each battle fought during the previous nine months was difficult in itself. Jackson had been involved in fourteen engagements in that time. As an added complication to the huge task, Hotchkiss commented, "most of the men who should have written these reports were killed during the year and the duty of writing them devolved upon subordinates, many of whom were only Majors or Captains in the commands."[23]

Just before Christmas, the staff began collecting information and composing drafts. Jackson tried to be an editor in chief; yet he wrote slowly, painfully, and with exactness as he continually deleted phrases and added others. He was never happy with the finished product. Jackson badly needed literary assistance.

Before leaving the valley for Fredericksburg, Jackson had written Charles J. Faulkner and invited him to join his staff primarily as a writer. Alexander Boteler began urging his Berkeley County friend, neighbor, and fellow politician to enter the field and assist Jackson. Faulkner was recovering from smallpox when Jackson sent a second appeal. On January 2, 1863, after urgings by the general, Faulkner arrived at Moss Neck.

His appointment generated a strong mixture of efficiency as well as hard feelings. Faulkner was a distinguished lawyer, four-time member of the U.S. Congress, and ambassador to France for two years. More important for Jackson's needs, he was literate and articulate, dignified and tactful—"eminently fitted to collect and harmonize conflicting testimony," Hotchkiss declared. The statesman would also demonstrate a propensity to transform Jackson's bland thoughts into readable (and sometimes exciting) prose.

Several negative factors, few of Faulkner's manufacture, marred his presence at headquarters. Jackson apparently thought that Faulkner's age and accomplishments entitled him to first place among his aides. Hence, he appointed the Martinsburg attorney as lieutenant colonel and chief of staff, to be "obeyed and respected accordingly." All of Sandie Pendleton's friends resented this slight to the young adjutant.

Faulkner, at fifty-five, was old enough to be the father of many of Jackson's headquarters personnel. He knew nothing of battles; and not being a military man,

Faulkner was unfamiliar with much of the terminology regularly used. His job was to take notes furnished by Jackson, his staff, as well as subordinate commanders and weave the various summaries into a single flowing narrative.

Perhaps aware of the animosity his presence created, or else uncomfortable in the presence of veteran officers, Faulkner kept to himself and preferred to be left alone when working. He began his work with the official report for Fredericksburg because it was the most recent of the engagements for which statements were needed. Reports thereafter were written in no particular sequence.[24]

Jackson established five ground rules for the compilation of his official reports. They were to be simple, containing only material that could be verified, void of controversial matters, sparing in praise of both the living and the dead, and subject to the general's careful reading and revisions. For example, Jackson deleted a reference to the deep sense of loss following the death of General Sidney Winder lest it be construed as a negative reflection on Winder's successor at the head of the Stonewall Brigade. Jackson was stingy with compliments, even—as in the case of General William Taliaferro—when officers performed more ably than was expected. He would close his lengthy report of the action culminating in the capture of Winchester by observing that "the conduct of officers and men was worthy of the great cause for which they were contending."[25]

Kyd Douglas, formerly of the staff, was critical of the finished reports. He asserted that many officers who had performed gallantly did not receive deserved praise, including staff officers. Yet Jackson refused to be laudatory to individuals, not even to men killed in action. Praise of the dead was unfair to the living.

The general pattern was for Jackson first to dictate his recollections to Smith or another aide. Faulkner would collect other reports on the battle in question as well as interview relevant officers to substantiate points of discrepancy. Sometimes the colonel would read sections to members of the staff before preparing a full draft for Jackson's inspection.

All things considered, Faulkner did a highly competent job. "I know the deep sense of gratitude which Gen. Jackson felt and expressed for the service which Mr. Faulkner . . . rendered in writing his reports," McGuire declared. "These sentiments I have heard the Gen'l. express in strong language."[26] However, Faulkner had to weather sharp editing in the process.

The chief of staff had a penchant for extravagant and boastful language, Jackson soon concluded. Frequently, the general deleted sentences to reduce a report to what he considered "a fair and simple representation of the battle." To Faulkner, it was "severe Roman simplicity."[27] Jackson eliminated certain words from his reports because he thought they might be too revealing to the enemy. Yet Faulkner's prose prevailed in numerous instances. In the Antietam report, phrases such as "the appalling scenes of the destruction of human life" and "the carnage on both sides being terrific" were obviously not Jackson's composition.

Faulkner was an industrious man with a difficult job. Writing battle reports months after the facts was a natural problem. Memories were not always precise; some of the major participants were dead, at home wounded, or captured; what one officer thought might be at variance with the observations of another. And when all of those hurdles had been mastered, editor Jackson stood poised to delete most of the drama, color, and praise from the suggested text.[28]

Preparing official reports continued steadily over the next three months, and they were not completed until the latter part of April. Before then, Jackson reached the saturation point with official reports. At the end of one long evening of writing and rewriting, he turned to his chief of staff and said earnestly, "Now, Colonel Faulkner, when a battle happens, and I hope we may never have another, I want you to get where you can see all that is going on, and, with paper and pencil in hand, write it down, so we may not have so much labor and so many conflicting statements, and then write up the report at once after the battle."[29]

By early January, the Confederate army was in winter quarters well back from the Rappahannock. Units took turns on picket duty and patrolled the south bank of the river. Other military duties were minimal. Hardships were many.

Mid-month found destitution widespread in Jackson's corps. Harvey Hill's division needed 1200 pairs of shoes and at least 400 blankets. One of the brigade adjutants reported: "The Fifth Regiment is unable to drill for want of shoes. The Eighth Regiment will soon be unfit for duty from the same cause; and, indeed, when shoes are supplied, the men will be unable to wear them for a long while, such is the horrible condition of their feet from long exposure."[30]

Lack of sufficient food was continual that winter. Thomas Caffey of the 3d Alabama wrote his wife: "I am leaner than I have been in a long time; and if you ever read Cervante's description of Don Quixote, you have my photograph."[31]

Weather and living conditions were also uncooperative. With the passage of each week, men had to range farther afield in search of firewood. Water was adequate—too much so, most soldiers felt, for mud and camp life became one. A member of Jackson's old brigade solemnly informed the homefolk: "I never saw the like of mud before. I thought it was bad at Romney last winter, there was some bottom in the mountains but there don't appear to be any here."[32]

Jackson was painfully aware of the lack of tents, scarcity of shoes, poor rations, and other hardships. He strove daily to alleviate suffering wherever he could. At one point, in an effort to combat dreaded scurvy, Jackson sent men into the fields to hunt for sassafras roots, wild onions, garlic, and poke sprouts.

Near the end of the winter, the general directed quartermasters and artillery officers "to browse their horses, as much as possible, on the twigs of the poplar, maple, sweet gum, etc. . . . and also that the animals be allowed to graze in the bottoms of the small streams instead of being tied up all day." By the end of February, most of Jackson's horses were being taken twenty miles south to Beaver Dam Depot for forage.[33]

General welfare of the troops was a continual concern, and Jackson's compassion was sincere. However, it was not unlimited. Discipline must prevail if his command was to remain strong and in fighting trim. Such discipline began with being present for duty.

Hard marching and much fighting over the past year had diminished the ranks considerably. The dead and crippled were part of war. Jackson accepted that truism. What he would not tolerate was the large number of soldiers absent without leave.

Some had gone home for food and rest, with every intention of returning; others had staggered away sick in search of better aid than field medicine offered. Jackson viewed such actions as evil.

When he learned that one of his brigades had 1200 absentees on its rolls, Jackson reacted angrily. A January 6 circular announced a prohibition of furloughs for all officers above the rank of lieutenant "unless under extraordinary circumstances." Only those men in the ranks who had reenlisted and thus shown their patriotism would be considered for leaves of absence. Whenever commanding officers granted a furlough, they were to inform Jackson in writing of how many of their troops were absent from duty.

By the latter part of January, one of Jackson's veterans sought to mask disappointment with humor when he wrote: "An order was issued sometime ago granting furloughs to two men at a time until all had gone home who had not been. To-day Stone W. Jackson, Esq., revoked said order. I presume because he anticipated that his ancient friends, the Yanks, would make a movement of some kind soon."[34]

If all absentees could be brought back to the army, Jackson told Congressman Boteler in Richmond, the army would be so strengthened that (with God's help, of course) one more campaign would rid Virginia of the enemy and quite possibly bring peace. The general moved toward that goal by ordering his division commanders to send details to each home area, collect conscripts as well as volunteers, bypass the basic training camps and all stops where exemptions might be granted, and escort them straight to the army.

Clearly, Jackson dismissed as a failure the government's attempts to obtain men for military service. "The country is being ruined by political demagogues," he complained; and he was correct. A War Department clerk wrote at the time: "Conscription drags its slow length along. It is not yet adding men to the army. The Assistant Secretary of War, and several others . . . are granting a fearful number of exemptions daily."[35]

While sharply curtailing furloughs, Jackson himself set a rigid standard by refusing to consider taking a leave even to see his infant daughter. He was just as unbending in applications by others. General Alfred Iverson of Harvey Hill's division filed a routine furlough request. Jackson denied it with such bluntness that Iverson threatened to resign from the army. Jackson was not in the least intimidated. "No one can tell what day a battle may be fought," he wrote to Harvey Hill. "Whilst I would regret to see General Iverson resign yet I would rather see him do so than to approve of his furlough under present circumstances."[36]

Captain Keith Boswell, Jackson's capable engineering officer, requested leave to see his sweetheart. Jackson said no. Boswell, resorting to cunning rather than anger, went to see his friend, General Jeb Stuart. There he found a more sympathetic ear. Stuart requested Boswell's service for a week or so; then he dispatched the captain "on duty" in the area where his sweetheart lived.

Another officer made the double mistake of coming into Jackson's office unannounced and asking for a furlough. James Power Smith was an eyewitness to the event. "Never had I seen General Jackson so surprised and angry. His face flushed, his form grew erect, his hands were clenched behind his back. He quivered with the tremendous effort at self-control. And no word was permitted to pass his lips until his passion was entirely mastered, when he quietly explained wherein the unfortunate colonel was violating all rules and all propriety, and sent him to his quarters, the most thoroughly whipped man I ever saw."[37]

When Kyd Douglas mentioned to Jackson that he had not been out of the army since the day he entered it, the general snapped: "Very good. I hope you will be able to say so after the war is over."[38]

Soldiers guilty of breach of discipline could expect no mercy from Jackson. He regarded their crime as a sin against "the army of the Lord." Punishment was swift and, with Jackson, total. On January 21, he forwarded to Lee the proceedings of the first desertion case tried in his corps. The accused had been found guilty and was to be executed on the last day of the month. "As desertions are still going on in the army," Jackson wrote, "I deem it important that the sentence should be executed at the time named in the order."[39]

The idea of sentencing a dishonorably discharged soldier to remain with his company for a certain period was anathema to Jackson. He returned such a sentence to a court-martial with a demand for reconsideration. The punishment, he declared, was "objectionable in placing the continuance of the accused in the army (which should be regarded as an honorary service) on the footing of the punishment."[40]

In another case, he ordered a man arrested "on charge of disloyalty in aiding the enemy to demoralize our army." The extremely serious offense involved was "selling liquor to the troops after he had been notified not to do so."[41]

A number of personnel matters claimed much of Jackson's attention that winter. Filling gaps at high-command level was among the most pressing matter. Who was to lead Jackson's old division produced the first strained feelings. Brigadier General William B. Taliaferro had been at the head of it since Cedar Mountain. In January, however, Isaac Trimble at last received his major general's commission and command of the division. The volatile Taliaferro did not take that action calmly, its correctness notwithstanding. He openly sulked; and when bypassed for promotion, he asked for a transfer. He soon was on his way to join General P. G. T. Beauregard in South Carolina.

Amid that heated atmosphere, while Taliaferro was still leading the division, he came into conflict with one of his subordinates, Stonewall Brigade commander Frank Paxton. What triggered the disagreement was a minor matter involving chain-of-command procedure: should court-martial papers be forwarded through channels unsealed or did the division commander have the right to inspect the contents?

Taliaferro said most assuredly; Paxton thought not. When the latter voiced his opinion in language that partly explained his nickname "Bull," Taliaferro angrily filed charges against the Lexington brigadier.

Jackson had no choice but to forward the charges to Lee. The army chieftain dismissed the matter, although he did so with statements that seemed to support Taliaferro. On that note, Taliaferro permanently left the Second Corps. Jackson made no comment at his departure. That the general did not recommend Taliaferro for promotion was evidence enough of how he felt. In later years, nevertheless, Taliaferro regularly spread the news that he and Jackson had maintained a most cordial relationship in the field.[42]

For filling other vacant slots, Jackson had always followed a single line of thought. "Whilst I highly prize military education, yet something more is required to make a general," he stated. That something was merit. It "should be the only basis of promotion," Jackson insisted, and the criterion for such merit ought to be "judgment, nerve, and force of character." Hard-fighting Jubal Early fit those standards and was easily advanced to major general. In Jackson's estimation, the devoted, pipe-smoking Bradley T. Johnson was equally worthy. He liked the Marylander and tried repeatedly to get him a brigadier's commission. Not until 1864 did the appointment come to pass.[43]

Edward Johnson deserved elevation to major general, Jackson was convinced, based on his good conduct at McDowell back in May. The War Department was not as impressed by the record of the rough-hewn, profane brigadier, but Jackson's recommendation carried weight. Ed Johnson got his promotion.

To command Taliaferro's old brigade, Jackson made a poor choice. Raleigh E. Colston was a longtime friend, a professor of French and associated subjects at VMI, as well as a trustworthy soldier. Yet like Ed Johnson, Colston had extremely limited field experience. Worse, his appointment made him senior brigadier in the division. If anything happened to his superior, Isaac Trimble, Colston would automatically move up in command. Jackson appeared to be violating his own rules in pushing for the advancements of the comparatively untested Ed Johnson and Colston.[44]

One of Jackson's appointments turned sour that winter. Several members of the Virginia General Assembly became unhappy with General "Grumble" Jones's administration of the Shenandoah Valley. That Jones was doing the best he could with a small force and highly limited means made no difference. Not even Lee's praise of Jones as "active, energetic, and bold" could save the southwest Virginian.[45] On February 26, the War Department removed him from command.

Jackson also became involved in a lengthy and strong exchange of correspondence with Lee over artillery appointments. At the Bunker Hill encampment in the autumn, Lee had approved organization of his artillery on a divisional basis. Four batteries were assigned to each division, with fifteen to twenty batteries held in reserve for use when needed. This system did not work because it made massed artillery at any point all but impossible. Lee then conferred with his artillery commander, William N. Pendleton, and proposed a new arrangement. The artillery would operate in battalions of four batteries (sixteen guns), each battalion to have two field officers and be under the command of a major. Lee forwarded the plan to Longstreet and Jackson, along with suggested assignments of officers.

Longstreet agreed to the change. Jackson was outspokenly opposed. He specifically did not like many of the men recommended for advancement. They were not members of his command and would be elevated over Second Corps captains whom Jackson regarded as more deserving. Unit pride may have been involved in Jackson's reaction; more likely, he knew the good qualities of artillery officers being bypassed and deemed this proposed action to be military injustice.

Lee dropped the matter after Jackson responded to one communique with startlingly blunt words: "I have had much trouble resulting from incompetent officers having been assigned to duty with me regardless of my wishes. Those who assigned them have never taken the responsibility of incurring the odium which results from such incompetency."[46]

The reorganization ultimately took place. Jackson accepted it "for the good of the service." However, his efforts to get his artillery chief, Colonel Crutchfield, elevated to general's rank were unsuccessful.[47]

Corps rivalries, as well as men ambitious for advancement and disappointed when it did not occur, created a sometimes negative atmosphere in the army. A hint of suspicion exists that Jackson and Longstreet were not on the most amiable terms. Longstreet's voluminous and highly opinionated postwar writings give that impression. If such friction was real, Jackson kept completely silent on the matter.

Other criticisms developed. One general complained at length about the excessive attention given in the press to Virginia officers. When General Dorsey Pender did not receive a Jackson recommendation for promotion, he commented, "I never will vote for his being President." Three months later, Pender was referring to Jackson as "the old humbug."[48]

A more delicate case was Jackson's brother-in-law, Harvey Hill. The North Carolinian was a senior division commander and proven fighter. Yet Hill was also opinionated, abrasive, and demanding. His troops called him "Old Rawhide," and the term was not always meant to be complimentary. Beset by illnesses throughout his life, Hill was feeling the effects of twenty uninterrupted months in the field.

More equally damaging factors also existed. Hill was disappointed because no further promotion seemed likely. His wife, Isabella Morrison Hill, was also unwell and urging her husband to come home. Hill's relations with superiors had deteriorated sharply. Although Hill's biographer insisted that the Carolinian and Jackson remained on cordial terms, evidence points otherwise.

For some time, Hill's carping had tried Jackson's patience as well as Lee's. Early in January 1863, Jackson dispatched Boswell to assist Hill in strengthening his Rappahannock defenses. After a week with Hill, Boswell was irate. "He thinks every point where he visits last the most important to be finished without delay," Boswell confided in his journal. At each stop, Hill "interferes as usual and insists on acting as engineer. I am disgusted and will let him take his own way." No doubt Boswell's feelings reached the corps commander.

Jackson endeavored to be as tactful as he could in the Hill situation. He was not pleased with Hill as a subordinate, but the man was a close member of the family. After Hill asked to be transferred from Lee's command, Jackson sent him the friendliest of letters. "If it should be convenient to call and see me at any time before Genl. Lee or the War Dept. is heard from, I hope you will do so as I would like to have a talk with you upon the subject as to leaving at *this time*."[49]

Irrespective of the conversation between the two men, Harvey Hill bade farewell to the Army of Northern Virginia. Jackson then sent an unusually long letter to Mrs. Hill—"My dear Sister Isabella"—in answer to her inquiry about what precisely had occurred in the matter of her husband. He gave a running but somewhat shallow narrative of events. It was clear from what he did not say that another and major reason was behind Hill's reassignment.

My first step was to try and arrange things so that he would remain with this army; but after several interviews with him and also with Genl. Lee, I became satisfied that it would be impolitic to insist on his remaining. . . . We both thought it best that he should be ordered to Richmond where he could be ordered to duty else where, & to some position where he could have more comforts than with this command. . . .

Genl. Hill has probably explained to you before this, the cause which induced him to leave here. I tried to remove what I could influence, but was not successful. For his services the Country owes him a lasting debt of gratitude. My prayer is that he will continue in the service until the war terminates, and that our Heavenly Father will give him success. And that his health and strength will not be so overtaxed in the future as it has been in the past.

On that note, Jackson's long association with his brother-in-law ended. Hill would declare in the postwar years that "Gen. Jackson never spoke an unkind word to me, publically or privately, at any time or any place." Regrettably, Hill could not claim never to have spoken an unkind word about Jackson. As for reaction in the ranks to his departure, Major Eugene Blackford informed his family: "Gen. D. H. Hill has been assigned to duty in N. Carolina, leaving his division behind much to our delight."[50]

January also brought a resumption of A. P. Hill's feud with Jackson. On the 8th, Powell Hill sent a reminder to Lee of the charges still pending against him. The Culpeper soldier wanted a full and public hearing on the matter. Two of his key witnesses (Lawrence Branch and Maxcy Gregg) were dead, and some of the other officers who would testify in Hill's defense were away from the army for various reasons. "Little Powell" was so anxious for a court-martial that he offered to waive having "officers my peers in rank" on the tribunal.

Lee tried to defuse the issue in a January 12 reply. "I do not think that in every case where an officer is arrested," Lee declared in almost paternalistic fashion,

there is a necessity for a trial by Court Martial, and I consider yours one in which such a proceeding is unnecessary. A Commanding Officer has the right to make an arrest, and to release the officer arrested without prosecuting the matter further, when in his judgment, the exigencies of the service require such a course. . . . The exercise of this power may sometimes appear harsh . . . but the power itself is one too important, and essential to the maintenance of discipline, to be denied because it may be abused.

In the present instance, Genl. Jackson exerted the authority for what he thought at the time, good and sufficient reasons. He exercised a discretion which you, or any other commanding officer must use. . . . Upon examining the charges in question, I am of [the] opinion that the interests of the service do not require they should be tried, and have therefore returned them to Genl. Jackson with an endorsement to that effect. I hope you will concur with me that their further prosecution is unnecessary so far as you are concerned, and will be of no advantage to the service.[51]

Powell Hill did not concur at all. Later in January, he pressed the matter further with a second letter to Lee. Jackson's strict adherence to duty and orders, Hill asserted, were such as "to cause me to preserve every scrap of paper received from Corps Hd. Qrs. to guard myself against any new eruption from this slumbering volcano."[52]

Lee chose to ignore the insubordinate statement as well as the whole Hill-Jackson controversy. That did not stop accusations and counteraccusations from swirling back and forth for the remainder of the winter. Each general gathered testimony from uneasy officers who would have preferred not being drawn into the quarrel. On occasion, members of the two staffs exchanged verbal shots.

Jed Hotchkiss, understandably opinionated, reserved his volley until after the war. Powell Hill, he charged, "found in every order that was issued to him something to complain of. . . . Only a surly obedience was rendered by Hill and his subordinates to orders from corps headquarters." Hotchkiss noted further that Powell Hill "was very careless in his manner of obeying orders, and was by no means the vigilant soldier he should have been. . . . Hill did not seem to have the proper appreciation of the element of time in military affairs, and then he had a very hot-headed and badly disciplined temper." This vendetta between two of the Confederacy's most gifted offensive leaders would intensify until the spring campaign began.[53]

The plight of friends under the yoke of Federal occupation also continued to bother Jackson. This feeling began at war's outset with his home area of Lewis and Harrison Counties. By the end of the conflict's second year, Jackson's sympathy was concentrated on the residents of Winchester.

In January, he learned from Colonel Boteler not only that the town was again under Union control; alleged atrocities were being committed against the citizens. Jackson reacted with views both emphatic and compassionate. "Though I have been relieved from command there, and may never again be assigned to that important trust, yet I feel deeply when I see the patriotic people of that region again under the heel of a hateful military despotism. There are the homes of those who have been with me from the commencement of the war in Virginia. . . . There are those who have so devotedly labored for the relief of our suffering, sick and wounded soldiers."[54]

Rain was falling the next day when Jackson wrote Anna. The situation in the lower Shenandoah Valley was still on his mind. He regarded stronger faith as the only solution. "I regret to see our Winchester friends again in the hands of the enemy. I trust that in answer to prayer, our country will soon be blest with peace. If we were only the obedient people that we should be, I should with increased confidence look for a speedy termination of hostilities. Let us pray more, & live more to the glory of God."[55]

Jackson made no mention in any of his writings that month of the passage on January 20 of his thirty-ninth birthday. Celebrations of earthly events held only limited appeal for him.

What was far more meaningful to him were the good health of his wife and child. When Jackson learned that Julia had fallen ill with chicken pox, his parental anxiety ran high. He summoned Dr. McGuire, detailed all the symptoms as he knew them, and asked for the surgeon's opinion as to the seriousness of the illness. At one point, Jackson's voice broke. "Doctor," he mumbled, "I do want the dear baby to live, if it is the will of my Heavenly Father."[56]

McGuire's assurances that all would be well proved true. Once the scare was over, Jackson returned to the father figure who advocated a mixture of orderly conduct with genuine love. "I am gratified at hearing that you have commenced disciplining the baby," he told Anna. "Now be careful, and don't let her conquer *you*. She must not be permitted to have that will of her own, of which you speak. How I would love to see the little darling, whom I love so tenderly, though I have not seen her; and if the war were over, I tell you, I would hurry down to North Carolina to see my wife and baby."[57]

Because that was not practicable, and in light of his deep fondness for children, Jackson formed a loving attachment to the small daughter of his host at Moss Neck. Jane Corbin, as described by Lieutenant Smith of the staff, was "a sweet little child of six years, with a sweet and happy face and fair, flaxen curls. She was very pretty and bright, and as happy and sunny a child as I ever saw. She was a pleasure to us all. She was the General's delight."[58]

The small child quickly captured Jackson's heart. Her mother recalled that the general sent for her every afternoon to come to the office to see him. "She would play there for hours, sitting on the floor with a pair of scissors cutting paper and entertaining him with her childish prattle. One favorite amusement was folding a piece of paper and cutting a long string of dolls—which she called her 'Stonewall Brigade.' I do not know whether she or the Gen. *christened them such.* I can imagine a smile and a merry twinkle of his eyes as he scanned them. They were funny little bow-legged fellows."[59]

Smith noted how little Janie completely "won the faithful man of war to the hearth rug and to relief from care. . . . Somewhere in the drawer there was something reserved for her—an apple, or a cake, or a picture."[60]

Janie especially came to admire a new cap that Anna had sent Jackson. Its broad gilt band was a constant attraction to the impressionable child. Seeing this, and disliking the showy braid anyway, the general one day took his pen knife and removed the band. Jackson then placed it on her head like a crown. "Janie," he said of the braid, "it suits a little girl like you better than it does an old soldier."[61]

Thereafter, young Miss Corbin wore the band as an ornament at every function. Her love for the general matched his affection for her. Staff members were amazed at the sight of the two. One moment their stern, humorless leader was saying of the Federals: "We must do more than defeat their armies; we must destroy them." The next moment he was a tender companion frolicking with a small child. Many people came to the Moss Neck headquarters with the thought that Jackson was incapable of open displays of love. Then they witnessed his uninhibited behavior with a little girl who adored every moment of it, and visitors went away either perplexed or with a more positive opinion of the field commander.[62]

In spite of military matters constantly pressing for attention, winter quarters on the Corbin estate was enjoyable and productive. Engineering officer Keith Boswell found Jackson "one of the most pleasant men as a commander who could be found in the Confederate army." With officers, Boswell added, Jackson was "very reserved, not particularly companionable, but always extremely affable and polite."[63]

His soldiers thought him a demigod whose only rival for adoration was Lee. A correspondent visiting winter quarters wrote in the *Southern Literary Messenger* that Jackson might seem rustic and unassuming, but "let the cannon begin to thunder, the small arms to rattle, and the sabres to flash in the sunlight—and . . . the awkward, calculating pedagogue becomes a thunderbolt. . . . He is the idol of the people, and is the object of greater enthusiasm than any other military chieftain of our day . . . notwithstanding the fact that he marches his troops faster and longer, fights them harder, and takes less care of them than any other officer in the service. . . . This indifference to the comfort of his men is only apparent, however—not real. No man possesses a kinder heart or larger humanity; but when he has something to do, he is so earnest, so ardent and energetic that he loses sight of everything but the work before him."[64]

The general demonstrated a sense of humor during those inactive months. When General Jubal Early protested the number of ladies visiting loved ones in the army and asked Jackson to declare the camps off limits to females, the commander replied: "I will do no such thing. I wish my wife would come to see me."[65]

Early soon did an about-face, and complaints from the medical department arrived at headquarters that the division commander was using ambulances to escort lady friends through the country. The staff persuaded Jackson to play a prank on the gruff bachelor. Over Jackson's signature, a note to Early demanded an explanation why division ambulances were being used for frivolous duty. Smith observed: "Great and hilarious was the merriment when the long report came. [You] may be sure old Jubal did not put in an appearance at our camp for some weeks."[66]

One day Jackson directed his commissary officer, Major Hawks, to send some chickens to headquarters for the main meal. The major replied through McGuire: "Tell him we have no chickens. The Hawks have eaten them." A "greatly amused" Jackson did not pursue the matter.[67]

Lee, like Stuart and Longstreet, enjoyed an opportunity to tease Jackson. In the third week of January, the army chief asked Jackson to accompany him on a visit to "Hayfield," the estate of Lee's kinswoman, Mrs. William Penn Taylor. A small entourage of staff officers rode with the generals to the mansion. Two young ladies were guests there and wanted to meet the famous corps commander.

Lee facetiously introduced the smiling Jackson as "the most cruel and inhuman man you have ever seen." Mrs. Taylor objected; she had always heard of General Jackson as a good Christian soldier. Lee shook his head and looked at her gravely. "Why, when we had the battle up at Fredericksburg, do you know, Mrs. Taylor, it was as much as we could do to prevent him from taking his men, with bayonets on their guns, and driving the enemy into the river?" Laughter coursing through the room eased the situation for the obviously embarrassed Jackson.[68]

These light moments notwithstanding, Jackson never compromised his abiding sense of duty. One afternoon he received word from Lee to come to army headquarters at his convenience. At dawn the following day, with snow blanketing the country, and subfreezing winds blowing wildly, Jackson left with J. P. Smith for Lee's quarters some thirteen miles away.

The journey took most of the day. At the army's command post, Lee expressed both surprise and anger at Jackson's arrival. "General," he told his corps chief, "you know I did not wish you to come in such a storm. It was a matter of little importance. I am sorry that you had that ride." Jackson blushed at the mild reproof. A hint of a smile appeared as he replied: "I received your note, General Lee."[69]

On January 28, Jackson finished his official account of Fredericksburg. Three days later, that first of the required reports went to Lee.

During his early weeks at Moss Neck, Jackson regularly attended services at nearby Old Grace Church. Yet he was not happy going there. For one thing, a neighbor wrote, the congregation stood whenever he entered and left the church. Jackson abhorred such pomp.

A major endeavor by Jackson that winter was the improvement of the religious character of his corps. The unholy attributes of war merely challenged his identification with the biblical forces of righteousness. "He was greatly interested," Anna Jackson recalled, "in providing his army with chaplains, and in trying to infuse more zeal into those who were already in this service." Jackson often quoted the maxim: "Duty is ours; the consequences are God's." He frequently confessed that his greatest military desire would be to lead a "converted army." Yet fewer than half of his regiments had chaplains on duty.[70]

Shortly after the beginning of the new year, the Reverend B. Tucker Lacy, an old friend from Lexington, made an opportune visit to Jackson's headquarters. Lacy was born in 1819 in Prince Edward County, Virginia, and was the son of a respected clergyman. Following graduation from Washington College and Union Theological Seminary, Lacy held pastorates in Winchester and Salem. At one time, he was one of two outside members of the semiannual examination committee at the Virginia Military Institute.

He served as pastor of the Presbyterian church in Frankfort, Kentucky, for the four years before civil war. Lacy spent part of 1862 in Fredericksburg and then shifted to military hospital service at Orange Courthouse. Now he came to Moss Neck to volunteer as a regimental chaplain.[71]

The two men talked far into the night. As they did, Jackson developed a more comprehensive idea for the visitor's talents. Lacy remembered that the general "was extremely anxious to secure hardworking chaplains who would endure hardness and stick it out. He said often that a good chaplain should not resign for any less cause than a brave officer. . . . Otherwise, the troops would be practically taught to feel that their performance was perfunctory and non-essential." Jackson told the cleric: "The only thing which gives me any apprehension about my country's cause is the sin of the army and people." He expressed regret at not having time to look fully into the labors of chaplains, colporteurs, and similar messengers of God. However, he regarded Lacy as the ideal person to assume such duties—for the entire Second Corps.[72]

Lacy was speechless. He had come to see Jackson about lending his services to a regiment; now he was being offered the position of religious overseer for no less than ninety-two regiments of infantry, twenty-three batteries of artillery, and assorted detachments of cavalry. The minister and the field commander discussed the matter; they prayed over it. Lacy asked permission to return to Orange and think further about the offer before giving a final answer.

A couple of weeks later, he returned to Moss Neck. "Was received most kindly," Lacy stated; and when he informed Jackson of his willingness to serve as his religious emissary, the general replied with his customary, "Good, good."[73]

The new religious awakening would unfold in stages. Lacy was announced as an unofficial corps chaplain. He was to live at headquarters, attend to religious correspondence, organize the regimental chaplains, and preach as a missionary at brigade and other high-level services. The Presbyterian Church would hopefully provide him with a stipend.

As "seed money," Jackson gave $200 from his personal funds and promised $500 more if needed. Jackson even donated "Big Sorrel," one of his horses, for Lacy to use. The new army missionary acknowledged that "Jackson's interest, all along, was deep, constant, excessive; it cannot be exaggerated."[74]

An outbreak of religious revivals began in the army when the Stonewall Brigade constructed the first of several log chapels. The building was L-shaped, with a pulpit at the angle. Soldiers met there regularly for prayer, praise, Bible instruction, or simple meditation.

The log structure was a half-mile from corps headquarters. Jackson walked there often for services, attended Sunday worship faithfully, and came to consider the chapel his field church. At the Sunday afternoon services in particular, the general liked to have hymns sung. He was tone-deaf, but he did have favorite hymns that he could recognize.

A member of the Rockbridge Artillery wrote that he saw Jackson many times "come quietly in among the soldiers and occupy a camp stool or modest seat and listen reverently to the singing and the sermons." Troops were "often demonstrative in their exuberant young manhood." Yet silence would descend immediately over a service if someone raised a hand and said: 'Sh-h! Keep quiet! Old Stonewall is praying for you."[75]

Smith normally attended chapel services with Jackson. The young aide was touched by what he saw. "The crowded house, the flickering lights, the smoke that dimmed the light, the earnest preaching, the breathless attention, broken only by sobs of prayers . . . made an occasion never to be forgotten."[76]

Lacy proved indefatigable as an organizer and supervisor. His position gave him special influence and a wide range of usefulness. One of his first accomplishments was formation of a tight-knit Second Corps chaplains association that met regularly at Round Oak Baptist Church in Caroline County. Jackson did not attend the first meeting. Lacy explained that the general "wished the chaplains to move in this matter spontaneously, and not as though pushed on by official machinery." Further, Jackson "did not wish to provoke any criticism by being personally prominent."[77]

Once organization had begun, Lacy reported to Jackson almost daily on chaplains' services and prayer gatherings. The general would always start a conversation with his chaplain by saying, "I hope you had a good meeting today." He would respond to positive statements from Lacy with an observation such as: "Let us give God the glory. We cannot be too thankful." At other times, when Lacy was reporting progress in statistical fashion, Jackson would inject his usual "Good, good."[78]

Letters and other calls went out to prospective chaplains. Prominent clergy received invitations to visit the army as short-term missionaries. In all but name, Lacy became Jackson's chaplain-general. He had what amounted to a roving ecclesiastical commission; thus armed, Lacy toured the circuit of command posts, directed other chaplains, and imparted a wide and deep religious influence to the army.

In addition to being a hard worker, Lacy was also a highly effective preacher. A German officer visiting the corps attended one of Lacy's religious observances and listened to "the truly spiritual and consoling words of the fine pastor, who conducted services in a simple coat and high riding boots, exhorting the people to perseverance, bravery, and manliness. . . . I can not forget the fervor and power of his sermons." A private in the 10th Virginia thought Lacy a superb "Mishionary" and hoped "that we could have him preach every Sabbath."[79]

Jackson considered Lacy's work so vital that he had the cleric live with him at his office. They prayed daily, Lacy stated, Jackson often leading the meditation. However, the cleric noted, "his private devotions were never neglected after these prayers. More than once, when sitting at his business table, when looking perplexed, he moved his chair back and engaged in silent prayer, and then resumed his pen."[80]

Armed with Jackson's full cooperation, Lacy's labors were highly successful. Second Corps chaplains found new inspiration; their redoubled efforts brought rich spiritual dividends. Still, Jackson insisted on more. He expressed pleasure at "an increase of religious interest in my corps," yet he continued to bemoan the lack of chaplains. "You may think that I am despondent," he told John Preston, "but thanks to an Ever Kind Providence, such is not the case. I do not know where so many men brought together without any religious test exhibit so much religious feeling. The striking feature is that so much that is hopeful should exist where so little human instrumentality has been employed for its accomplishment."[81]

No field commander thought chaplains more important than Jackson. "Some ministers ask for leaves of absence for such trivial objects in comparison with the salvation of the soul," he asserted. They needed to be on duty around the clock. "It is the special province of chaplains to look after the spiritual interest of the army, and I greatly desire to see them evincing a national zeal proportional to the importance of their mission."[82]

He frowned at ministers who sought to make denominational distinctions. The only real question to be asked of a potential chaplain, Jackson declared, was, "Does he preach the Gospel?"[83]

Late one wet evening, Jackson and Lacy had a private worship service with the Reverend William Hoge. The Richmond visitor exclaimed afterward: "How anxious he was for his army! . . . In our whole intercourse I could not detect the slightest trace of self-importance, ostentation, or seeking after vainglory. To glorify God possessed all his thoughts."[84]

That was true, but Jackson's high reputation as a military leader was now nation-wide. Congressman Daniel W. Voorhees of Indiana supposedly acknowledged at the time that Jackson was the only man in America who could defeat him in a Hoosier district election.[85]

The general had no interest in such matters. In fact, and at the time, Jackson was lonely and homesick—a state of mind he admitted in a rare confession to Anna. "I trust that in answer to the prayers of *God's people,* He will soon give us peace. I haven't seen my Wife for nearly a year. & my home for nearly two years, & I have never seen my sweet little Daughter." As always, Jackson found solace in faith. "I am thankful to say that my Sabbaths are passed more in meditation than formerly. Time thus spent is genuine enjoyment."[86]

A week later, he explained why those musings were pleasant. "God does not always answer prayer according to our erring feelings. I think that if when we see ourselves in a glass, we would consider that all of us that is visible, must turn to corruption & dust, that we would learn to appreciate more justly, the relative importance of the body that perishes, & the soul that is immortal."[87]

Jackson may have found it easy to overlook earthly things, but his troops were not so capable. February offered some of the most severe weather of the war. At one point, almost a foot of snow lay on the ground. Northwest winds seemed constant. When roads were not icy, they were ribbons of interminable mud. Captain Reuben Pierson wrote home, "It has been a very difficult matter to procure supplies for the army, and at times the Quarter Masters have been compelled to carry provisions on pack horses on account of the impassibility of traveling the roads."[88]

Charles D. Sides, a North Carolina soldier who would not survive the war, wrote his wife in the second week of February: "I pity our case in coming days for times are getting wors and wors. . . . We get our Rashion of flower like we usually did but we only got one quarter of a tiny Bacon a day and that Just as rotten as old ———— himself. It haint fit for a dog to eat and a dog at home would not nigh eat it." Nine days later, Sides added: "The snow was about 4 inches Deep but it rained all night last night and the snow is melting and of all the mud great Jerusalem you never saw the like but go right through you. Poor Devils that is all that is cared for us by the Big Boys."[89]

With field operations at a halt, personnel at headquarters gave full attention to battle reports. The Seven Days Campaign summary took longer than expected to produce. Faulkner knew little of the movements and engagements. Yet he grasped facts so easily that engineer Keith Boswell praised him as "certainly one of the clearest minds that I have ever come in contact with." Boswell also talked at length with Jackson about the Richmond battles. Following an in-depth discussion of Gaines' Mill, Jackson admitted that "he never before had a clear idea of that fight."[90]

On February 20, Jackson approved and forwarded the official report of the Seven Days Campaign. It is an intriguing statement for what it does not say. No explanations, excuses, or rationales are included for such incidents as the tardiness at Ashland and the halt at White Oak Swamp. That Jackson had obeyed orders from first to last in the campaign is implicit throughout the synopsis. He recounted what happened, what he did as a result of instructions, and the losses his command incurred. Then he submitted the report and turned quickly to the statement other members of the staff were preparing on the action at McDowell.

The general may have known of the blossoming romance that winter between his chief aide Sandie Pendleton and Catherine Corbin, the young sister of the owner of Moss Neck. The general said nothing until Pendleton announced his engagement at headquarters. A nod of approval greeted the news. Speaking of Pendleton, Jackson observed: "If he makes as good a husband as he has a soldier, Miss Corbin will do well."[91]

Enforcing discipline and meting out punishments required much of Jackson's last weeks at Moss Neck. A brigade commander had been accused of cowardice and must face a court-martial. This was a humiliating incident for Jackson. He had selected John R. Jones for promotion to brigadier; no general officer in the Stonewall Brigade had ever been accused of so severe a crime. The case gave Jackson considerable pain.

"I have almost lost confidence in man," he told Lacy. "When I thought I had found just such a man as I needed, and was about to rest satisfied with him, I found something lacking in him." Jackson paused before adding: "But I suppose it is to teach me to put my trust only in God."[92]

The trial underwent a number of delays. Jones's behavior in the forthcoming Chancellorsville campaign was suspicious to many. Thereafter, he retired from service and saved everyone involved from further embarrassment.[93]

Jackson took special pride in his old brigade. He had no tolerance for any un-soldierly conduct by members of that unit. An early low moment in the Stonewall Brigade's history came on February 28, when a deserter from one of the valley regiments went before a firing squad. The condemned man "wept bitterly, wishing to see his family," Hotchkiss observed, but "he fell dead, pierced by five bullets. Poor fellow."[94]

While that case was being carried to a conclusion, Jackson was displaying harsh judgment in a group situation. Increased efforts to round up deserters resulted in a number of courts-martial. Six soldiers were arraigned at one time; all were found guilty. One received six months' imprisonment at hard labor and two were ordered flogged (that form of punishment having been reinstated as a deterrent against deser-tion). The remaining three men—all belonging to the Stonewall Brigade—were sentenced to death.

Brigade commander Paxton objected in a carefully worded appeal to Lee. Only one man needed to be an extreme example, he wrote. Let the three choose lots to determine which would die. Jackson forwarded the appeal through channels, but his handwritten endorsement showed clearly how he felt.

With the exception of this application, General Paxton's management of his brigade has given me great satisfaction. One great difficulty in the army results from over lenient Courts and it appears to me that when a Court Martial faithfully discharges its duty that its decisions should be sustained. If this is not done, lax administration of justice and corresponding disregard for law must be the consequence. The Army regulations define the duty of all who are in service and departures from its provisions lead to disorganization and inefficiency.[95]

Lee approved the three death sentences. On the morning of the scheduled execu-tions, a telegram arrived from Richmond. President Davis had granted clemency to the trio. Jackson doubtless reacted with cold disdain. On the other hand, other deserters were not so fortunate. More than a half-dozen executions took place in the Second Corps during the remainder of the winter.[96]

Meanwhile, work on official reports progressed. Jackson approved the battle sum-mary for McDowell on March 6, although the published version bears the date of the following day.[97] A week later, with much help from Hotchkiss and Boswell, Faulkner completed the after-action brief for Winchester. Next, the staff began putting together summaries of the fighting at Cross Keys and Port Republic.

"Making out reports is both slow and troublesome work," Jackson wrote a cousin. Yet a subtle change was growing in the general during those months: he was becoming demonstrably more outgoing. "Socially his character was mellowing," Lacy noticed. The chaplain thought he knew why. "He was more affable and congenial" because of "the growing religious interest in the army."[98]

One afternoon Jackson grew weary of the constant paperwork and lay down on his cot. Suddenly, he bolted upright and asked J. P. Smith to fetch a bottle of wine from one of the nearby supply wagons. The shocked aide got the bottle, at the same time following orders to invite the full staff to headquarters. Jackson then asked the officers to taste the wine and tell him from what section of Europe it came. Much-traveled men like Faulkner and McGuire suggested several locations in France and Italy. The conversation became more earnest. Finally, Jackson smothered his face in a pillow to contain his laughter. He knew that the wine had been made in Virginia.

Another incident that gave Jackson delight involved hot-tempered and profane General Jubal Early. He was inspecting artillery emplacements along the Rappahannock when he came upon a cannon whose muzzle was elevated somewhere between forty-five and sixty degrees. A gunner was sighting the piece at the top of a distant tree. The soldier turned, saw Early, and asked "if there was ary squirrel up that tree." Early replied with a string of oaths. All of the story was relayed to an amused Jackson. Obviously, Dr. McGuire concluded, anecdotes had to be "very plain ones for him to see through."[99]

In the last week of March, staff members completed the final draft of the Port Republic report. Boswell made a few minor corrections and sent it to Jackson, who, on the 28th, approved it. Work then began on the summary for Cedar Mountain.

The passing of March heralded the arrival of spring. In Richmond, a War Department clerk conjectured that "the season of slaughter is approaching." Only the Rappahannock River continued to separate the two opposing hosts. Each knew the other was there. In midmonth a North Carolina soldier wrote his brother: "the blue coats rides up & down the river at night. some has swame over. they say their infantry [are] in camp 15 miles back of the river expecting Jackson to cross. i want them to keep thinking so."[100]

Jackson had begun to prepare mentally for battle. One evening, "with intense fire and energy," he remarked to Lacy: "We must make the coming campaign an exceedingly active one. Only thus can a weaker country cope with a stronger one. Our country must make up in activity what it lacks in strength. A defensive campaign can only be made successfully by taking the aggressive. Napoleon never waited for his army to become fully prepared."[101]

He was eager to become a field commander again. The office at Moss Neck was now too commodious, the activity too routine and burdensome. When Lee expressed a desire to have Jackson's headquarters closer to his own, no further prod was necessary. Jackson informed Anna that "the time has come for campaigning, & I hope . . . to go into a tent near Hamilton's Crossing. . . . It is rather a relief to get where there will be less comfort than in a room, as I hope thereby persons will be prevented from encroaching so much upon my time. I am greatly behind in my reports, and am very desirous to get through with them before another campaign commences."[102]

On the evening of March 16, Jackson went to the Moss Neck mansion and thanked Mrs. Corbin for her many kindnesses. Little Janie had fallen ill with scarlet fever, but she was showing signs of improvement. She sent her love to the general and expressed the hope that he would come back and see her.

The general then rode seven and a half miles northwest to the John Pratt Yerby farm, "Hunter's Lodge." It was a simple frame house located in a broad ravine opening into the Massaponax Valley and about a mile from Lee's command post. Jackson was now a half-mile from the Hamilton's Crossing line and ten miles closer to Fredericksburg.

En route to the new headquarters site, he and Smith made a quick courtesy call at the William P. Taylor home. The two young women visitors were still there. They felt familiar enough in Jackson's presence to beg for locks of his hair. The general tried to sidestep the requests by noting that the ladies had far more hair than he. Moreover, much of his hair was turning gray. Nonsense, the young women giggled, you have no gray hair. Jackson responded with a slight smile: "Why, don't you know the soldiers call me 'Old Jack?'"[103]

The next morning, Smith brought Jackson unexpected and tragic news: Janie Corbin had died of scarlet fever, along with two of her cousins. He who had watched impassively the carnage of many battles now wept like a child, his frame convulsing in uncontrollable grief. Soon Jackson fell to his knees and began praying earnestly. He dispatched Smith back to Moss Neck to express his deep sympathy and to extend any assistance possible to the family. Another outburst of tears came when Jackson learned that members of the Stonewall Brigade had made three coffins from part of a fence enclosing the Moss Neck estate.[104]

Once again, Jackson sought comfort by faith in God. The dead are blessed; earthly life must continue. Placing the loss of Janie into a revered memory, the general kindled a blazing appeal to the Almighty for protection in the military uncertainties that lay ahead.

Hotchkiss described a prayer service he attended at Chaplain Lacy's tent. After a song and a biblical reading, "Gen. Jackson devoutly prayed for all classes, orders, & conditions of the Confederate States, for success to our arms at all times, for confusion & defeat to our enemies, but for blessings to them in all right & proper things, especially that they might have the blessing of peace. He very earnestly prayed that this 'unnatural war' might speedily be brought to a close, and that blessing might come upon our absent dear ones."[105]

Jackson and Lacy continued to share daily morning devotionals. Prayer meetings were held on Sunday and Wednesday evenings. If for some reason Lacy were not available, Jackson unhesitatingly led the service. The main religious gathering of the week was on Sunday afternoon. A makeshift pulpit and rustic seats stood in an open field. Quoting reports she received, Anna Jackson commented: "The constant attendance of General Jackson and frequent appearance of General Lee and other distinguished officers soon drew vast crowds of soldiers to the scene, and many became

changed men. General Jackson often . . . [set] them an example by his devout attention and delight in the services, and, by his personal interest, leading them to follow
the great Captain of their salvation."[106]

The general was "delighted at the immense congregations" that attended the
Sunday services, Lacy proudly remarked. He greeted the faithful "with a face of
beaming commendation," Anna heard. On at least one occasion, an estimated 2000
soldiers jammed the open expanse to join their hearts in a common worship. Spiritually speaking, it was one of the most satisfying periods in Jackson's life.[107]

With the winter restricting all movements, life in camp and at headquarters re-
volved around conversation. Soldiers from general to private relaxed in idleness; and
in that mode they relived past events while speaking wistfully of peace and the future.
Jackson was not averse to such pastime. When his VMI colleague, General Raleigh
Colston, reported for duty in April, the two men sat before a campfire far into the
night and discussed a variety of subjects.

Colston turned the dialogue to Jackson's capture of Harpers Ferry the previous
September. He talked about the immense quantities of Federal men and stores arrayed in line when the garrison surrendered. "General," Colston said, "you must have
felt intensely exulted when you beheld the results of that splendid success." Jackson's
whole countenance suddenly filled with "reverential humility." In a subdued tone, he
answered simply: "It was a great mercy that God granted us." That response touched
Colston. "I was hushed, for I knew the perfect sincerity of Jackson's heart, and what
on the lips of another might have been considered as cant or affectation, was in him
the spontaneous utterance of a deeply religious soul."[108]

One subject never introduced in Jackson's presence was his sister. Laura Jackson
Arnold still lived in the northwestern Virginia town of Beverly. Federal troops had
occupied the area for most of the war. Laura's husband Jonathan and most of the
townspeople were Confederate sympathizers. In fact, Mr. Arnold would be arrested in
the summer of 1863 on disloyalty charges. He was never brought to trial.

Laura was a Jackson: a woman of strong independence and convictions. From the
outset of hostilities, she was a Unionist. As the struggle increased, so did her pro-
Northern sentiments. She became more than an adherent; she developed into a
defiant activist.

Her activities came to the attention of Jackson's staff. On March 23, Hotchkiss
recorded a visit from an old friend. Dudley Long was a lieutenant in the 31st Virginia,
a unit from the northwestern sector of the state. Long told the mapmaker that Laura
Jackson was "a Union woman" who boasted that she "could take care of the wounded
Feds. as fast as brother Thomas could wound them." Although that statement is
suspect, Laura's pro-Union activities were open. She welcomed Federal soldiers in
Beverly and nursed their sick and wounded in her own home. A surgeon reported that
on many occasions he found Mrs. Arnold "the sole watcher at the bedside of a
disabled soldier," and "many were her regrets that she was unable to do greater
good."[109]

Perhaps she did. Rumors were rife among Beverly residents and Federal soldiers
that Laura was sharing her bed with several officers.

The divided loyalties created by the Civil War contained no more pronounced cleavage than that between Jackson and his sister. Since childhood, the two orphans had clung to one another, at times in near desperation. For each, the other was all that remained of the family. Laura helped Thomas fight loneliness at West Point; he helped her battle loss of faith a decade later. A steady flow of correspondence had bridged the eleven months each year when they were apart.

On April 6, 1861, a week before the bombardment of Fort Sumter announced the start of war, Jackson had sought again to buttress Laura's shaky religious beliefs. Yet the words he wrote then seemed later to have a deeper and more personal meaning. "When a cloud comes between you and the sun, do you fear that the sun will never appear again? I am well satisfied that you are a child of God, and that you will be saved in heaven, there forever to dwell with the ransomed of the Lord."[110]

That was Jackson's last communique with Laura. He was much aware thereafter of her activities in Beverly. Travelers who had recently come from that part of the state got queries from Jackson for news about her. Possibly, the general learned that Laura on more than one occasion publicly accused him of cheating on his entrance examination to West Point. Further, she would not tolerate having his name mentioned in her presence.

Jackson commented only once about Laura. A lifelong friend from the northwestern area recalled the general voicing regrets "that his sister Mrs. Arnold entertained union sentiments, but his expressions about her were kind but brief."[111]

The Civil War had seized two strong-willed individuals and destroyed the lifetime of love they had known. It was tragedy a step before death. Jackson, with his customary reticence, kept the hurt to himself. No one at headquarters or elsewhere ventured to broach the subject.[112]

Years later, some men would remember things that they thought Jackson did say in the wintry hush before spring's violence erupted. One of Stuart's aides told how Jackson "looked forward to the coming campaign with the deepest interest"—so much so that at one point the red-faced general leaped to his feet and, with eyes flashing, exclaimed, "I wish they would come!" At another time, a calm Jackson observed, "Certainly no man has more that should make life dear to him than I have, in the affection of my home; but I do not desire to survive the independence of my country."[113]

Jackson may not have spoken those exact words, but his feelings coincided with the thoughts. He still maintained an iron obedience to the will of God. When Hotchkiss informed him that a report of the Federal forces advancing up the Shenandoah Valley was untrue, Jackson replied, "We have been Providentially protected so far and I hope we will still be favored by the same kind Hand." His attention nevertheless was turning increasingly toward family and peace. A minister who preached at corps headquarters early in April felt that the general "is longing to be out of the field, and at home once more."[114]

Those aspirations must have become paramount as labor on more battle reports became drudgery. The staff was toiling on the Cedar Mountain synopsis. Everyone had difficulty. Where various brigades were at specific times could not be easily pinpointed. Hotchkiss, hard at work on a battle map, saw his unfinished chart go awry. "The Gen. was out of humor in the morning about the position of the fences on the field of the map. Boswell took him the map against my wishes, and he gave vent to considerable displeasure." Hotchkiss made the changes and submitted the map the following day. The general was satisfied. "Strange man!" the topographer concluded. "Everything must conform to standards of simplicity and accuracy, severe in all its outlines." Faulkner would have seconded such an assessment.[115]

Some staff members labored on the finishing touches of the Cedar Mountain report while others still toiled on the summaries for Cross Keys and Port Republic. Apparently, Jackson's patience was running thin by those first days of April. He was unquestionably reaching the status of a heavy-handed editor. Faulkner's first draft of the June 8–9, 1862, action ran sixteen legal-size pages. Not one paragraph escaped Jackson's mark. He deleted here and there until the report was barely two-thirds of its original size.

The May 31–June 9 presentation offers the best example of Jackson as a battle reporter. For example, Faulkner wrote at the start: "Leaving Winchester on the 31st of May, past Strasburg before the Federal generals Shields & Fremont effected the contemplated junction in my rear . . . " Jackson changed the statement to read: "Having through the blessing of an ever-kind Providence passed Strasburg before the Federal armies under Generals Shields and Fremont effected the contemplated junction in my rear . . . " Jackson deleted from the draft report this passage praising Federals and criticizing Ashby's cavalry: "Checked for a time at the Little North Mountain the Federal Cavalry . . . pushed on the pursuit with rigor and boldness. Between Strasburg and Woodstock they opened their batteries upon the rear guard, stampeding [our] Cavalry in a manner not very creditable to their discipline & courage."[116] Always the artillerist who counted guns, the general inserted this sentence into the June 8 action at Port Republic: "Another piece of arty. which the Federal Cavalry had advanced was abandoned and subsequently fell into our [hands] about this time."[117]

Whenever Faulkner displayed a tendency toward flowery language, Jackson applied his pen strongly. The chief of staff described the last firing at Port Republic by writing: "Fremont appeared on the opposite bank of the South Fork of the Shenandoah and with his army ranged in order of battle. He satisfied his ambition with interrupting by an incessant discharge of shells the humane labors then in course of execution of attending to our dead & wounded & the dead & wounded left on the ground by Genl. Shields." After Jackson finished with this section, it read: "Fremont appeared on the opposite bank of the South Fork of the Shenandoah with his army and opened his arty. upon our ambulances & parties engaged in the humane labors of attending to our dead & wounded & to the dead & wounded of the enemy."[118]

The final report for Cross Keys and Port Republic went forward on April 14; and while rain poured, additional drafts of Cedar Mountain were written.[119] Late on the 17th, Faulkner and Jackson reached final agreement on the text. Faulkner's work was now done. The former ambassador had completed three months of heavy labor, and he was anything but pleased with efforts that had been constantly modified by Jackson. Faulkner left the army a bruised but wiser man.

A persistent administrative problem still dogged Jackson. Early in the spring the matter exploded into a major confrontation in which the future careers of Jackson, Powell Hill, and, indeed, the army seemed in jeopardy.

The ongoing feud between the two generals had smoldered since late January. It began to spark anew when Hill on March 8 filed his report of Cedar Mountain. Naturally, he explained away delinquencies regarding his "slow marches" prior to battle. In doing so, Hill all but accused Jackson of giving conflicting and confusing orders.

Jackson reacted sharply. He dispatched Paxton, Pendleton, and Douglas (all of whom were his aides in August 1862) to collect every available piece of information on the advance of the army to Cedar Mountain. Armed with much evidence, Jackson wrote an appendix to Hill's report that was a point-by-point rebuttal of Hill's statements. Hill was irate at the length of Jackson's official "endorsement." Anger turned to pettiness on Hill's part: he began questioning practically every chain-of-command directive while bombarding army headquarters with minor complaints.

In April, after Hill blatantly instructed a signal officer not to obey an order from Jackson unless Hill approved it, Jackson reached the end of his tolerance. He forwarded to Lee specifications and charges for a court-martial of Powell Hill. With that mass of paperwork, Jackson included a new request. "When an officer orders in his command such disregard for the orders of his superiors I am of the opinion that he should be relieved from duty with his command, and I respectfully request that Genl. Hill be relieved from duty in my Corps."[120]

Lee must have groaned at reading the statement. His best corps commander wanted his best division leader banished on the eve of a critical campaign. The army chief took no immediate action, preferring to pursue a waiting period with the hope that time might have some healing effect. Jackson gave the matter no additional thought. He had pressed charges against Hill and submitted the necessary paperwork. Discipline and duty would run their respective courses, he was convinced. Besides, something of greater importance was on Jackson's mind.

Throughout the military tribulations of the winter, his thoughts drifted constantly to his family. "Just to think our baby is nearly three months old," he had written Anna in late February. "Does she notice and laugh much? You have never told me how much she looks like her mother. I tell you, I want to know how she looks. If you could hear me talking to my *esposa* in the mornings and evenings, it would make you laugh, I'm sure. It is funny the way I talk to her when she is hundreds of miles away."[121]

By the middle of the month, the press of official reports and military correspondence had decreased. Winter mud had disappeared. Warm weather was an omen of military operations sometime soon. Yet the Union army was currently quiet—even though it was under a new and dynamic commander familiar to Jackson.

A slight prewar acquaintance had existed between Jackson and Joseph Hooker. The Massachusetts native had finished at West Point five years before Jackson entered the academy. They had probably met in the Mexican War, and both emerged from that conflict as heroes. Civil war placed them on opposing sides. In recent months, they had come to know each other painfully. It was Hooker's corps that launched the first heavy assaults against Jackson in the August 29 fighting at Second Manassas; it was also Hooker's corps that made the initial massive attacks on Jackson's line in the bloodbath at Antietam.

Now "Fighting Joe" Hooker commanded the Army of the Potomac. In the winter months, he had displayed commendable organizational skills. The army received new supplies, new units, and new morale; and while it came back to life again, Hooker assured the Lincoln administration that the isolation and destruction of Lee's army was merely a matter of time. Northern leaders as well as Billy Yanks felt a newborn optimism about the approaching campaign.

Jackson no doubt respected the fighting qualities of the new Union army chief. Yet his admiration for Hooker the soldier was more than offset by his contempt for Hooker the man. The Union general was an arrogant and ambitious braggart, given to hard drinking and hard living. Hooker, as handsome as a Greek god, was notorious for a lack of morality. A member of a prominent New England family snorted that "the headquarters of the Army of the Potomac was a place to which no self-respecting man liked to go, and no decent woman could go. It was a combination of bar-room and brothel."[122] Be that as it may, Hooker carefully planned his spring offensive.

The April lull seemed to Jackson to be the time for Anna and the baby to make the long-desired visit. Jackson had found suitable quarters, he informed his wife. Please come quickly. She left Charlotte with the child and a black nurse, Hetty. Because it was impossible to provide Jackson with a precise timetable for the journey, the general was unaware even of the date of their departure. Around April 17, he wrote Anna: "I am beginning to look for my darling and my baby. I shouldn't be surprised to hear at any time that they were coming, and I tell you there would be one delighted man."[123]

The next day, Jackson was more anxious. "There is no time for hesitation if you have not started," he said in another letter. "There is increasing probability that I may be elsewhere as the season advances."[124]

Late in the evening, an ecstatic Jackson received a message from his Lexington friend, Governor John Letcher. Anna and the baby had arrived in Richmond from North Carolina and were spending the night at the governor's mansion. Could the general join them? Jackson declined the invitation. He must remain at the front and await his wife there.

Filled with impatience and love, Jackson the following day attended Sunday church service with Lee. That evening, a newspaperman reported, Jackson "led in prayer meeting at his own camp, offering up one of the most eloquent and thrilling prayers. The man and the general who saved the Confederacy in her hour of peril never fails to thank God for His mercies and blessings and superintending Providence."[125]

Early on Monday, April 20, Jackson wired Letcher and asked that he send his family by train to Guiney Station. An overcast sky did nothing to dampen the "expectant father's" spirits. He worked at headquarters until late morning, then rode through a steady downpour to the railhead. As Guiney Station came into view, so did Fairfield, the Chandler home just to the northeast of the depot.

A northbound train soon wheezed to a halt. In a wet raincoat, Jackson leaped aboard the passenger car with that long and familiar stride. He pushed his way through the detraining crowd, eyes searching expectantly. Then he saw them!

Anna described the first moments: "His face was all sunshine and gladness; and, after greeting his wife, it was a picture, indeed, to see his look of perfect delight and admiration as his eyes fell upon that baby! . . . He was afraid to take her in his arms, with his wet overcoat; but as we drove in a carriage to Mr. Yerby's, his face reflected all the happiness and delight that were in his heart."[126]

Soldiers cheered loudly as Jackson and his family descended from the coach and rode away in a carriage. Jackson had secured accommodations for them at Belvoir, the Georgian-style brick home of Thomas Yerby. The imposing residence was on a high hill and gave a commanding view of the countryside. Of great importance to Jackson, the house was only a mile from his headquarters at J. P. Yerby farm. A large room with three beds became home for the Jackson family.

The moment they reached the room, Anna noted, her husband "speedily divested himself of his overcoat, and, taking the baby in his arms, he caressed her with the tenderest affection, and held her long and lovingly."[127]

Frequently told in the days ahead that the baby resembled him, Jackson always responded: "No, she is too pretty to look like me." Anna disagreed. She later declared: "I never saw him look *so well*. He seemed to be in excellent health & looked *handsomer* than I had ever seen him, & then he was so full of happiness at having us with him & seeing & caressing his sweet babe, that I thought we had never been so blest & so happy in our lives."[128]

Jackson was blissful over his family's presence, but he did not forsake his military duties on their behalf. Each morning before dawn, he was at corps headquarters for breakfast, prayers, and business. Somewhere in the afternoon, he would mount his horse and gallop west to join his wife and daughter. Their time together was further limited by officers, Lexington friends, and prominent citizens in the neighborhood calling to see the child.

Raleigh Colston was one such visitor. His view of the family was decidedly masculine. "The General looked very happy. His wife was sitting by his side, and at my request his little daughter Julia . . . was brought into the room. The General took her in his arms and began playing with her—which I confess he did rather awkwardly and as if quite unused to the occupation." Kyd Douglas observed that "Mrs. Jackson's attractive looks, manners, and good sense did much to make these visits popular and pleasant, and the General was the model of a quiet, well-behaved first father."[129]

That was so to a point. Anna noted that her husband rarely let Julia out of his arms. "When she slept in the day, he would often kneel over her cradle, and gaze upon her little face with the most rapt admiration, and he said he felt almost as if she were an angel, in her innocence and purity."[130]

Nevertheless, and despite the general's adoration, he would not spoil the child. Orderly conduct was the staff of a good life. On those occasions when Julia began screaming for no discernible reason, Jackson would put her in the crib and stand over it (according to Anna) "with as much coolness and determination as if he were directing a battle; and he was true to the name *Stonewall* even in disciplining a baby!"[131]

When Julia became quiet, Jackson again took her in his arms. If she resumed crying, he placed her back in her bed. The child seemed to learn quickly not to make an unnecessary fuss in his presence.

Thursday, April 23, was one of the happiest days of Jackson's life. His daughter was five months old, an ideal time for her baptism. Cold rain whipped by strong winds made no impact on the joy of the occasion. Members of the Yerby family, as well as a cavalcade of staff officers, gathered in the parlor. Often in the past, these soldiers had seen Jackson in many modes. Yet this was the first time they beheld the general tenderly holding a child in his arms "in the presence of God" and for the anointing with holy water.

A momentary snag marred the start of the ceremony. Everyone was waiting for the child to appear. Jackson became impatient. "The decided way with which he went out and brought in the child in his arms" was unneeded proof of the general's insistence on punctuality. Chaplain Lacy conducted the baptismal service. The child was christened Julia Laura in honor of Jackson's mother and sister. From the child's birth, Jackson had wished to name her after his mother. When he decided to remember his estranged sister with the middle name is not known.[132]

That afternoon, Jackson submitted to Lee his official report for the Maryland Campaign. Omitted from the published version was a closing paragraph that was an exhortation to the Almighty. At the same time, Captain Keith Boswell was writing what became his last letter home. "Strange as it may seem," the able engineer said, "not one of Genl. Jackson's staff has ever been killed. . . . I suppose his prayers have shielded us; for if there is a man in the world whose prayers are those of the righteous, that man is Genl. Jackson."[133]

On the slope of a ridge behind the headquarters tents was the outdoor worship site that Jackson frequented regularly. Sunday, April 26, found him unusually anxious to attend church. Anna was with him. It had been so long since they had worshiped together in public. The couple rode in an ambulance from Yerby's and passed a steady stream of soldiers wending their way to the "chapel." Generals Lee, Early, and Joseph B. Kershaw were among the 1000 in attendance. Lacy preached "a solemn and powerful sermon" on Lazarus and the rich man.[134]

Jackson and Anna spent the afternoon alone. "His conversation was more spiritual than I had ever observed before," she remarked.[135]

It was during Anna's visit that Jackson sat for the second of two wartime photographs. A photographer from the Richmond firm of Minnis and Crowell came to camp. Officers warned Mr. Minnis that he could not hope to get Jackson to sit for a picture, so the cameraman resorted to trickery. He called upon Jackson, told him that he had been sent from Richmond to get Lee's photograph, but that the army commander had declined unless General Jackson had his picture taken first.

Jackson hesitated; he did not want to go through such posing, but General Lee ought to have a photograph made for the Southern people. Meanwhile, Anna was urging him to sit for a picture. He looked better than he had since the war began, she said. Under that pressure, Jackson relented.

Anna insisted that he wear "the handsome suit," as she called the uniform coat that was a gift from Stuart. Although one source had the photograph taken "in a tent at Hamilton's Crossing," Mrs. Jackson gave a different and more authoritative account. "After arranging his hair myself, which was unusually long for him, and curled in large ringlets, he sat in the hall of the [Yerby] house." A strong breeze blowing in Jackson's face gave "a sternness to his countenance that was not natural."[136]

Anna always preferred the "Winchester photograph" made in November to the profile portrait taken five months later because it gave her husband "more of the beaming sunlight of his *home-look*." The soldiers preferred the Yerby house portrait, as have subsequent generations.[137]

On April 28, Jackson forwarded his official report of Second Manassas operations. Faulkner had prepared the initial versions, but the final draft again reflected Jackson's interjections. Cumbersome statements had been reduced to simple sentences. The general eliminated pointed praise of individuals, with one exception. Motivated in part by the death of Major John Pelham the previous month at Kelly's Ford, Jackson inserted a statement of the artillerist's August 1862 conduct at Groveton. "Owing to the difficulty of getting artillery through the woods I did not have as much of that arm as I desired at the opening of the engagement; but this want was met by Major Pelham, with the Stuart Horse Artillery, who dashed forward on my right and opened upon the enemy at a moment when his services were much needed."[138]

The religious fervor then permeating the Fredericksburg encampments likewise influenced Jackson's editorial work. Appropriately, he closed this last of his official reports with an exultation: "For these great and signal victories our sincere and humble thanks are due unto Almighty God. We should in all things acknowledge the hand of Him who reigns in heaven and rules among the armies of men. . . . We can but express the grateful conviction of our mind that God was with us and gave us the victory, and unto His holy name be the praise."[139]

It was still dark the next morning when a rider galloped into the yard of the Yerby home. The Jacksons were asleep in the large upstairs bedroom. Heavy footsteps sounded on the stairs, then a knock at the door. A servant announced that an officer needed to see the general at once. As Jackson dressed rapidly, he told Anna, "That sounds as though something stirring were on foot."[140]

The messenger was Jubal Early's adjutant, Major Samuel Hale, Jr. Early's division formed Jackson's left flank and manned a line that the Second Corps had held at the battle of Fredericksburg. Jackson's intuition was correct: Hooker's army was on the move. Despite heavy fog, Federals had been spotted fording the Rappahannock at Deep Run, two miles below town.

Jackson returned to the bedroom. The spring campaign was underway. Yerby's was no place for mother and child. Anna must pack at once and hurry southward to Richmond. Jackson was needed at headquarters. He would hopefully return and assist in her departure. If unable to do so, he would send an aide, Anna's brother Joseph, to escort her and the baby to safety. They had best say goodbye at that moment.

Nine wonderful, unforgettable days they had enjoyed. Nine days of bliss with his wife, boundless joy with his daughter. Now the impersonal pressure of war summoned. "He took an affectionate leave," Anna said, quickly mounted Little Sorrel, and disappeared into the woods. The roar of artillery in the distance seemed to be getting louder.

Anna was finishing breakfast when her brother Joseph arrived. The general needed all of his staff members, young Morrison told her. Therefore, he had asked the Reverend Lacy to take her to the capital. The chaplain soon arrived, with a cheerful note from Jackson. The letter invoked God's protection on mother and child. With a sad heart, Anna made her way aboard a passenger car and held Julia closely as the train carried her away from her beloved.[141]

That Wednesday was cloudy and mild, but spring was in full bloom. Jackson reached Hamilton's Crossing to find that Early had spread his divisions into battle array and positioned three regiments downriver as a picket line. Signs were unmistakable that part of Federal General John Sedgwick's VI Corps was on the south side of the Rappahannock. What the enemy had in mind could not be determined.

Jackson confirmed by personal inspection that Federals had advanced over the river at Deep Run. James Smith must inform Lee of the threat. The aide rode a mile across the field to army headquarters. He awakened Lee, who good-naturedly said: "Well, I thought I heard firing, and was beginning to think it was time some of you young fellows were coming to tell me what it was all about. Tell your good general that I am sure he knows what to do. I will meet him at the front very soon."[142]

The corps commander did not wait. Sedgwick's troops were spreading out along the Rappahannock's south bank and showing no inclination to advance to battle. This could all be an enemy feint. Jackson raced to Lee's camp. There he found rumor after rumor filtering into headquarters. Federals were reported moving in a number of different directions. Estimates of their strength varied widely.

Lee wished the Second Corps to reinforce Hamilton's Crossing while awaiting further developments. He and Jackson alone would be making decisions in the days ahead. Lee had taken advantage of the lull after Fredericksburg to send Longstreet with two of his divisions to secure and forage in the southeastern portion of the state. Longstreet became involved in a siege for the town of Suffolk; and when Hooker went into action sooner than anticipated, Lee was left without his First Corps commander and half of his troops.

Confederate soldiers were in high spirits when Jackson began the ride back to his own command post. Countless numbers cheered him heartily. As always, he removed his hat in appreciation, but his thoughts at the moment were on more critical matters. He had to make quick command decisions about two of his four divisions. Neither Edward Johnson, assigned to lead Harvey Hill's division, nor Isaac Trimble, at the head of Jackson's division, were on duty. Replacements were needed at once. Jackson resorted to the seniority system.

Johnson's place would be taken by Harvey Hill's senior brigadier, Robert Rodes. That was a pleasurable appointment for Jackson to make. Rodes, a native of Lynchburg, Virginia, had graduated in 1848 from VMI. After success as a civil engineer for several railroads, he had returned to his alma mater as a professor of applied mathematics. War cut short his professorial tenure.

Rodes had earned army seniority by hard-hitting tactics and gallant behavior. He was then thirty-four, tall, with long blond mustache and piercing blue eyes. To many, Jackson included, Rodes epitomized the second wave of outstanding Confederate generals.

Frank Paxton of the Stonewall Brigade was Jackson's choice for the other division command. However, Raleigh Colston outranked the Lexington attorney and possessed more military experience. Even though he had been with the Stonewall Division less than a month, Colston got the command.

By 10 A.M., Jackson's camps in the Moss Neck area were a beehive of activity. Orders went out to each division: pack wagons at once and, unless contradicted by subsequent directives, all units were to advance immediately toward Fredericksburg. Wagon trains were to keep abreast of the marching soldiers "so that cooking can be done tonight without fatiguing the men to march."[143] The divisions of Early and Rodes would be in front; those of Powell Hill and Colston would make up a supporting line.

A captain in James H. Lane's brigade described the morning's bustle: "As we listened to [the distant] cannonade great commotion could be seen in our neighboring camps—couriers riding rapidly in every direction. One soon pays his respects to us with orders to be ready to move at a moment's warning. Blankets are soon rolled, swords buckled on, haversacks filled with uncooked rations, rifles in hand we take our position to await the inevitable order which is quickly received to 'march.'"[144]

Officers at corps headquarters noticed "a wondrous change" in the general. To Chaplain Lacy, "his bearing became quicker, energetic, more lofty. The whole man energized and inspired all else."[145]

Sometime that morning, as clouds thickened overhead, Stuart sent an alarming report to Lee. A large force of the enemy was crossing the Rappahannock at Kelly's Ford, twenty-seven miles upriver from Fredericksburg. Either Hooker was attempting to swing around Lee's western flank, or he was making for the Virginia Central Railroad at Gordonsville. So broad a turning movement by at least 14,000 Federals caught Lee by surprise.

With the afternoon came rain and a revised report from the Confederate cavalry chief. Three full Federal corps were involved in the upriver movement. Proceeding on separate roads, they had crossed the Rappahannock in a southwest direction, then swung back to the southeast. Now the enemy columns were heading toward Germanna and Ely's fords on the rain-swollen Rapidan River.

The line of march would take them into the Wilderness, where the roads converged at a large brick home a mile inside the woods. The building was two and a half stories, with columned front porch. Once an inn, it had become a refuge for some of Fredericksburg's dispossessed. Ten members of the Chancellor family, all but two of them women, lived there. With the slaves having fled at the approach of the Union army, these family members performed all of the household duties.

Home and road intersection were called Chancellorsville. A massive Union host was bearing down on the place as it advanced straight toward Lee's left flank.

Now the Southern commander had to ponder how to counteract 134,000 Federal soldiers and 404 guns on two fronts with but 62,000 men and 228 guns. Before nightfall, the Confederate chieftain had reached a partial decision. General Richard H. Anderson, commanding the division on the far left, would move west toward the Chancellorsville crossroads and contest any Federal advance he met. Lee with the rest of the army would continue to monitor enemy movements on Stafford Heights and around Fredericksburg.

Under a steady downpour, the men of the Second Corps bivouacked in fields and woods southeast of town. Jackson spent the night at his old Hamilton's Crossing site. He issued warnings to his division leaders to be especially alert for any Federal activity along the riverbank. A major battle was to begin nearby and soon. Yet only the drumming of the rain marked the hours of darkness.

At some point that night, Jackson read a short letter Anna had managed to compose while on the train. "My precious husband," she wrote, "I do trust that I may be permitted to come back to you again in a few days. I am much disappointed in not seeing you again. But I commend you, my precious darling, to the merciful Keeping of the God of battles & do pray most earnestly for the success of our army this day. Oh! that our Heavenly Father may *preserve & guide & bless you*, is my most earnest prayer."[146]

23

THE GREATEST MARCH

FEW UNION GENERALS ever devised a more promising plan of attack. At the outset, it would appear that nothing could stop General Joseph Hooker, the Army of the Potomac, and the North from complete victory in Virginia that spring.

Hooker had spent the winter months reconstructing the Federal army physically and mentally into one of the finest fighting machines the Western world had ever seen. Discipline in the ranks of the 134,000-man force was finely tuned; morale was unboundedly high. Hooker then devised a strategy that seemed infallible.

He would not repeat Burnside's blunder of butting heads against Lee's strong works at Fredericksburg. Instead, 12,000 Union cavalry under General George Stoneman (who had been the quietest roommate Jackson ever had at West Point) would gallop around Lee's western flank and get in the rear of the Confederate army. The horsemen would disrupt railroad and communication lines in order to cut Lee adrift from Richmond and his main supply bases.

The next stage of Hooker's plan called for 50,000 soldiers under General John Sedgwick to remain in front of Lee and attack when prudent. Meanwhile, Hooker would march five corps far upriver, turn south across the Rappahannock as well as the Rapidan, then curl back against Lee's unprotected left and rear. The Union II Corps would occupy a position between Hooker and Sedgwick, to assist either as needed.

That, Hooker proclaimed, would leave Lee with but two choices. He could abandon Fredericksburg and retreat southward—in which event Hooker's main force would assail Lee's flank and force the Confederate commander to confront Hooker on grounds of the Federal general's choosing; or Lee could stand and fight it out at Fredericksburg—in which event the Army of Northern Virginia would be caught between Hooker advancing east and Sedgwick pushing south.

Never known for modesty, Hooker boasted of having "the finest army the sun ever shone on." The question, he informed Lincoln, was not whether he would take Richmond, but when. "My plans are perfect, and when I start to carry them out, may God have mercy on General Lee, for I will have none."[1]

After three days of steady marching, and through remarkable skill on the part of Hooker, the massive Federal turning movement was precisely where he wished it. Four corps had reached the road junction at Chancellorsville, with the fifth not far away. Hooker should have paid more attention to the surrounding country than to the rendezvous point. The Wilderness, twelve miles long and six miles deep, lay dark and foreboding along the southern bank of the Rappahannock.

The virgin timber had been removed years earlier, most of it to provide fuel for several small iron-smelting furnaces. A tangled second growth had resulted: a thick confusion of stunted pines, along with hardwood saplings so small that the sun swept the ground and caused dense underbrush such as honeysuckle to thicken and spread in every direction. Visibility rarely exceeded twenty yards. Clearings were small and widely scattered. A few streams appeared from nowhere and meandered toward somewhere. The handful of winding roads through the Wilderness resembled trails in a jungle.

In short, the whole area was no place for an army. It was precisely where Hooker ordered his men to halt on the last day of April.

Jackson was up before dawn that foggy Thursday. His four divisions were in a loose battle line extending a mile to the left of Hamilton's Crossing and on the right as far as the point where Massaponax Creek emptied into the Rappahannock. Forsaking the old uniform covered with the dust and mud of weeks in the field, Jackson donned the new coat and trousers that Anna liked. Portents of the day were highly favorable.

First, he had to attend to a host of details relative to putting his corps in motion if such orders came. Equipment was packed, wagons loaded, rations cooked, tents dismantled, ammunition distributed, weapons inspected. All was close to readiness when Jackson walked to his tent. "Hold my horse," he told servant Jim Lewis. The general went inside and closed the flap. Staff and field officers were clustered around the headquarters area and engaged in a buzz of conversation. Lewis called out: "Hush! The General is praying!" Silence fell over the scene. No man spoke. Inside the canvas shelter, alone with his God, Jackson may have read scripture before he prayed. If so, he likely went to his favorite biblical verse: "And we know that all things work together for good to them that love God, to them who are called according to his purpose." A few moments later, Jackson emerged from the tent "with an elevated and serene countenance." He gave a few final instructions, then rode off to join Lee. The soldier was now ready to do the Lord's work.[2]

Lee was busy at his headquarters when Jackson arrived. He entrusted the remaining paperwork to his staff and asked Jackson to ride with him to a ridge overlooking Fredericksburg and Stafford Heights beyond. Any thought the two generals had of keeping their reconnaissance reasonably secret vanished as they passed along the Confederate lines. A South Carolina lieutenant told his mother (in what was to be the last letter he wrote before his death): "The men are in splendid spirits, ready to yell on the least provocation. 'Old Jack' and Lee caught it mercilessly this morning while making the rounds."[3]

The two watched enemy dispositions and discussed possible counterstrategy. Union artillery was visible on the high ground; so were lines of infantry below the guns. That did not impress Jackson. As always, he urged attack. If Lee cleared that front, he would be able to give full attention to the larger threat from the west. Jackson said that his corps would make an assault before noon. It was an enticing thought, but Lee demurred. "I fear it is impracticable as it was at the first battle of Fredericksburg. It will be hard to get at the enemy and harder to get away if we drive him into the river." Jackson persisted. He pointed out the comparative weakness of the Union force at hand, and he repeated the gains that a successful attack would bring. The audacity in Lee rose to the surface. After reflecting for a moment, the commander relented. "If you think it can be done," he told Jackson, "I will give orders for it."[4]

That was what the lieutenant wanted to hear, but he did not react rashly. Jackson asked for time to study the land more carefully before committing troops to battle. When Lee nodded assent, Jackson galloped off to begin preparations.

One of his first acts was to summon Jed Hotchkiss. Jackson wanted eight maps of the country lying between the Rappahannock and the Rapidan and extending to the Virginia Central Railroad. He did not explain why he desired such charts. Surely, Jackson knew that regardless of what success he had in front of Fredericksburg, the army sooner or later would have to march west and do battle with Hooker. If the Confederates moved quickly, they possibly could trap Hooker in the same "V" formed by the two rivers where Jackson almost bagged Pope the previous August.

Jackson turned to the issue at hand. Throughout a rainy afternoon, he meticulously studied everything: topography, reports of enemy strength, Federal gun emplacements, the distances to be covered by assaulting troops. His artillerist's eye kept telling him that a potentially devastating fire from enemy guns could not be overcome. Rain stopped as Jackson finished his inspection. The quick dissipation of the clouds removed all hope of using inclement weather as a mask for his assault.

He rode back to Lee's headquarters. "It would be inexpedient to attack here," he said in disappointing tones. What is the alternative? Lee was ready with an answer. Sedgwick's force along the Rappahannock was but a diversion; the real blow was coming from the Wilderness against the Confederate left. Lafayette McLaws, minus a brigade, would march at midnight to join Richard H. Anderson's division to the west. "Move in the morning up to Anderson," Lee instructed Jackson, and "make arrangements to repulse the enemy." Leave one division behind to confront Sedgwick at Fredericksburg. Jackson immediately selected the 10,000 veterans of Jubal Early to man a five-mile line and face a force at least four times their number.[5]

It was near sundown when Jackson returned to his headquarters. He was "smiling and elated," according to Lacy. For a few minutes, he chatted with a group of officers. The chaplain commented that much talk existed in the ranks about the army falling back.

"Who said that?" Jackson asked roughly. "No, sir, we have not a thought of retreat. We will attack them."[6]

He beckoned to Lacy and walked briskly into his tent. He asked the minister, who had lived two years in the area, if he knew the roads to Chancellorsville. There are three, Lacy replied. Could the chaplain guide the corps in daylight, or did he know anyone who could lead the men into the Wilderness by night? Lacy remembered one of the Yerby boys being knowledgeable about the country west of Fredericksburg. "Let us go to Mr. Yerby's," Jackson said. "I have not called on them for some days." By the time the two reached the Yerby home, the family had gone to bed. Jackson refused to have them awakened.[7]

Earnest conversation marked the return ride of Jackson and Lacy. The general was convinced that an attack on Anderson's division east of Chancellorsville was imminent. Lacy asked why Jackson did not move his corps that night to Anderson's assistance. The moon was bright, and the march of less than ten miles could be easily made. Jackson, partly in thought, answered, "As a general thing I make it a rule not to march troops at night, but the reason you suggest is weighty." With that, he dispatched Lacy to hunt for reliable guides while he conferred with his artillery chief, Colonel Crutchfield.[8]

The decision was a compromise between his two options. He could have made a forced march, which would have left his troops too weary to perform at maximum level should fighting erupt in the Chancellorsville area; or he could have obeyed Lee's orders precisely and departed at dawn. That ran the risk of making Jackson too late to help Anderson if the Federals attacked. At the moment, the line was on high and open ground between Zion and Tabernacle churches. It extended across the two major roads leading east to Fredericksburg. (The Old Turnpike and the Plank Road were the two principal highways through the Wilderness. They came together at Chancellorsville, then branched out again before reuniting midway between Chancellorsville and Fredericksburg.)

Knowing that Anderson's troops were furiously digging breastworks in the night and would welcome any help they could get, Jackson alerted the divisions of Powell Hill, Rodes, and Colston to depart at 3 A.M. The route would be a short distance southwest toward Spotsylvania Courthouse (to deceive the enemy, naturally) and then west by country roads to the front.

On schedule, the three divisions pulled back silently from the Hamilton's Crossing line. Guides proved trustworthy. Jackson rode at the head of his command. Rodes was in the lead. Since Colston's division had marched all day on the 29th, it brought up the rear.[9]

Nighttime and fog shrouded Jackson's advance. The approach of the Second Corps to Anderson's front went undetected. In fact, Hooker's force at Chancellorsville seemed to have gotten itself into the dangerous frame of mind that nothing was going to happen until it went into action. Federal General Darius N. Couch observed: "All of the army lying there that night were in exuberant spirits at the success of their general in getting 'on the other side' [of the Rappahannock] without fighting for a position. As I rode into Chancellorsville that night the general hilarity pervading the camps was particularly noticeable; the soldiers, while chopping wood and lighting fires, were singing merry songs and indulging in peppery camp jokes."[10]

Even Hooker got into the act with a bombastic proclamation: "It is with heartfelt satisfaction the commanding general announces to the army that the operations of the last three days have determined that our enemy must either ingloriously fly, or come out from his defenses and give us battle on our own ground, where certain destruction awaits him."[11]

Dawn on May 1 was bright and breezy, with a promise of heat later in the day. Jackson rode up and down his column, half crouched as usual on Little Sorrel. The general had waited for months for such an advance. A defensive stand was neither on his mind nor to his liking. Lee had told him to "prepare for action." Jackson naturally took this to mean to go on the offensive.

In the middle of that long, westward-moving column was the 14th North Carolina. Its colonel, R. Tyler Bennett, recalled the approach of a lone figure who came riding

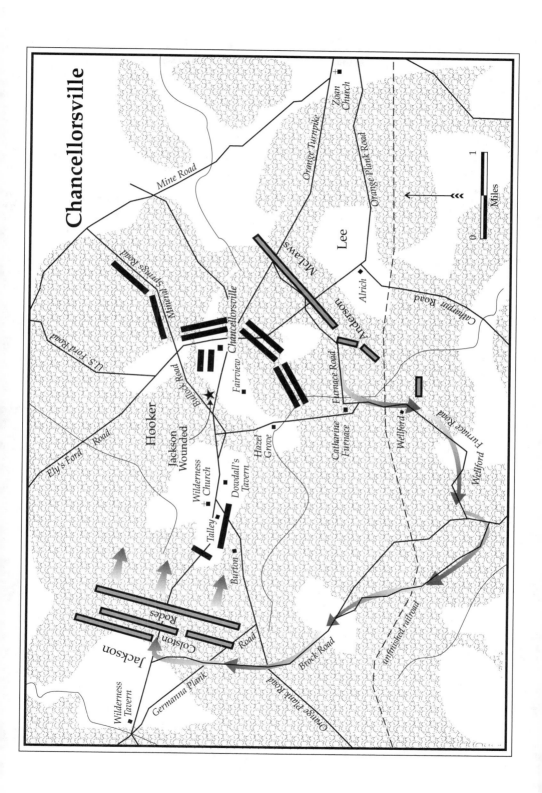

Chancellorsville

Miles

Chancellorsville

Mine Road

Orange Turnpike

Zoan Church

Orange Plank Road

Lee

Catharpin Road

Alrich

Anderson

McLaws

Furnace Road

Fairview

U.S. Ford Road

Mineral Springs Road

Bullock Road

Wellford

Catharine Furnace

Hazel Grove

Wellford Furnace Road

Hooker

Ely's Ford Road

Jackson Wounded

Wilderness Church

Dowdall's Tavern

Talley

Burton

unfinished railroad

Brock Road

Rodes

Colston

Jackson

Road

Germanna Plank Road

Orange Plank Road

Wilderness Tavern

toward the front. "Suddenly the sound of a great multitude. . . . The very air of heaven seemed agitated. . . . The horse and rider cross our vision. The simple Presbyterian Elder, anointed of God, with clenched teeth, a very statue, passes to his transfiguration. . . . He was God's hermit."[12]

Near 8:30 A.M., after a ride of five and a half miles, Jackson reached Anderson's position.[13] Gunfire could be heard to the west. Anderson had done an excellent job of preparing a line of entrenchments facing west and northwest on a one-mile front. The defensive position protected the two roads from Chancellorsville, only four miles away. McLaws's arrival doubled Anderson's strength, but work was still continuing on the defenses.

Jackson liked such devotion to duty in an officer. "Dick" Anderson was a professional soldier in every sense. He was a West Point classmate of James Longstreet, under whom he served for the first half of the war. Anderson never quite emerged from Longstreet's shadow, a situation that was a plus to some and a negative to others. With a prematurely graying beard, blue eyes that stared expectantly, and a becoming modesty, Anderson was well liked at all levels of the army.

He responded quickly to Jackson's request for a briefing on the situation. On April 29, Anderson's three brigades had advanced deep into the Wilderness. Feeling exposed and vulnerable, the South Carolinian had ordered his men to retire toward Fredericksburg and take the best available position. While the Confederates were falling back on the morning of the 30th, a band of Union horsemen struck the rear of the line. They received such rough treatment from Anderson's men that no Federals had since threatened them. Anderson had established a line on a timbered ridge near Tabernacle Church. His men were working frantically on the position in anticipation of a momentary attack.

When Anderson finished his report, Jackson made no criticism. The division commander had exercised normal procedures. Yet civil wars did not follow patterns taught at military academies. Whether Jackson knew that Hooker had more corps than he had divisions made no difference. Old Jack was familiar with the path one traveled to victory.

He told Anderson to drop the picks and shovels, pick up muskets, and prepare for an immediate and general advance against the enemy. McLaws's men would move forward on the turnpike. Anderson's troops, with the Second Corps banked up behind them, would march on the looping Plank Road and strike the Federal left flank if possible. At 11 A.M., with all of his troops at hand, Jackson ordered the two-pronged attack to begin.

Within fifteen minutes, McLaws encountered Federals half-concealed along the turnpike in the Wilderness. "Quite a brisk little engagement" began, a Confederate brigadier observed as soldiers dashed from tree to tree and took cover in ravines and behind logs.[14] When McLaws soon reported an increase in enemy resistance, Jackson ordered him to halt. He summoned Colonel Porter Alexander to move some artillery forward and try to blast the Federals back through the timber. If that did not clear the front, Jackson told McLaws, he would try for the enemy's rear.

The general made his first display of reckless disregard in the campaign by advancing along the Plank Road with the skirmishers. He was anxious to get a firsthand view of enemy dispositions. The heavy skirmish line moved so quickly and with such determination that Federal commanders mistook them for an attacking wave. Jackson's probing line brushed aside a thin line of cavalry, sent Federal outposts reeling, and drove the front elements of Hooker's army back on the main body.

The unexpected and severe onslaught caught Hooker by surprise and knocked asunder his final resolve. Jackson was facing five to one odds, but he had launched a major offensive that not only was successful; it wrenched the initiative completely away from the Union army. Hooker ordered his forces to fall back to Chancellorsville and dig earthworks. This May 1 action by Jackson altered the entire face of the campaign.

As separate Confederate columns diverged farther from one another on the main roads and engaged the enemy, Jackson became concerned about his flanks. The advance slowed because of the danger involved in pressing an opponent whose strength and position were unknown. Federal cannon were visible along the narrow forest lanes. Hooker might be trying to draw the Confederates into an entrapment.

A courier arrived with a message from Stuart. His horsemen had ridden far out on Hooker's right flank. Jackson's left was safe: the Union line now curled in a semicircle with Chancellorsville as the nucleus. There was no threat to Jackson from the south and southwest. Stuart's dispatch ended on a jaunty note: "I will close in on the flank and help all I can when the ball opens." At 12:30 P.M., Jackson scribbled on the back of the note with a stub pencil: "I trust that God will grant us a great victory. Keep closed on Chancellorsville."[15]

Moments later, Lee rode up the Plank Road and joined Jackson. The army commander was ready to concentrate on Hooker's force in the Wilderness. All was going reasonably well, Jackson reported, though the enemy was in strength to the east of Chancellorsville.

The two Confederate leaders rode past lines of soldiers who forgot weariness and anxiety. They filled the woods with cheers. "How splendidly the pair of them looked to us," Colonel Alexander wrote, "& how the happy confidence of the men in them shone in everyone's face, & ran in the cheers which everywhere greeted them."[16]

It was difficult amid the acclamation for Jackson to apprise Lee of the situation. Lee agreed with the actions that Jackson had taken. He left his lieutenant in charge of the Plank Road column while he rode north to inspect enemy positions nearer the Rappahannock.

Confederate skirmishers somehow got the impression that Hooker was abandoning Chancellorsville. That led Jackson to try to split the main Union line. He ordered Brigadier General Henry Heth of Hill's division to take three brigades and angle from the Plank Road to the turnpike in an effort to reach the Chancellorsville intersection more quickly. Heth actually got on the turnpike in advance of McLaws; but like the other Southern stabs, he found enemy resistance too intense.

At 2:30, Jackson notified McLaws that he was "pressing on up the Plank Road; also that you will press on up the Turnpike, as the enemy is falling back. Keep your skirmishers and flank parties well out, to guard against ambuscade."[17]

Jackson resumed his advance. Stephen D. Ramseur's North Carolina brigade was in the lead, with Ambrose R. Wright's Georgians from Anderson's division in close support. The action soon became repetitious and, for Jackson, perplexing. Federals concealed in the woods would fire a volley; Confederates would stop, return the fire, then move forward cautiously to find the enemy position abandoned. The advance resumed, only to be stopped by another burst of gunfire. Jackson's men halted, then moved slowly forward. These stiff firefights occurred along both roads and represented stages in a slow and orderly Union withdrawal. Throughout the afternoon, Jackson was in the forefront, repeatedly urging the troops to "press on, press on."

Soon, the Confederates reached the intersection of the Plank Road and a narrow lane that snaked westward down to the abandoned Catharine Furnace. Jackson detached Wright's brigade to advance on the furnace road in a probe of Hooker's flank. At the furnace, Wright met Stuart. The cavalryman informed him that massed Federals were in entrenchments a mile to the north on high ground known as "Fairview."

Wright brought up a battery and began pounding the position. Enemy soldiers fled the area—only to be replaced by Union artillery atop the height. Shell and canister swept the woods below and made "warm work" indeed for the struggling Georgians.[18]

As Jackson's interest in this turning movement grew, he beckoned to aide Joseph Morrison and started on a long and rapid ride. From Heth's sector, the two galloped across to the Plank Road and followed it to the head of the Catharine Furnace route. Jackson proceeded down the lane to the old ironworks owned by Colonel Charles C. Wellford. This point was about a mile and a half southwest of the Chancellorsville road junction.

It was near 5:30 when Stuart rode up. The two generals exchanged cordial greetings before taking a small bridle path toward a knoll a half-mile away. From there, they hoped to get a better view of the heavily timbered country. Several staff members accompanied them. Enemy movements were clearly visible from the high ground, but woods obscured exactly what the enemy was doing. Several officers in the party thought of how well the dense undergrowth concealed Union activity. Jackson saw the same thick forest as possibly masking a Confederate movement.

The reconnaissance was of necessity brief. Major Robert F. Beckham's battery of horse artillery had sought to clear a path for Wright's infantry. The location was so thickly wooded that only one gun at a time could be pulled into firing position. With the first shot, masked Union batteries let loose a barrage that splintered trees and sent dirt flying. "I do not think that men have been often under a hotter fire than that to which we were here exposed," Beckham noted.[19]

Shells began exploding near the knoll. "General Jackson," Stuart shouted above the din, "we must move from here!" The group of horsemen proceeded gingerly down the muddy slope. A shell exploded nearby. No one was injured except Stuart's young adjutant, Major R. Channing Price. He refused aid by declaring that the wound was not serious, then rode ahead a short distance and fell from the saddle. The injury was mortal. This "sad event" affected Jackson, Morrison noted, "and detained him a short time." With darkness approaching, Jackson rode back to check on progress along the Plank Road.[20]

Two little incidents in late afternoon added to the mystique of Jackson. Colonel

Alexander reported on some Federal movements his gunners had seen in the direction of Chancellorsville. Jackson was listening intently when his eyes slowly fell on one of Alexander's sergeants wearing a Federal rubber poncho. The general interrupted Alexander. "Where did that man get that coat?" Alexander replied, "From a row of knapsacks left by a regiment down the road there." Now angry, Jackson retorted, "Put him immediately under close arrest for stopping to plunder on the battlefield." The colonel did as he was told but released the soldier the following afternoon.[21]

Robert T. Hubard, Jr., adjutant of the 3d Virginia Cavalry, likewise had an unusual experience with Jackson. "The General was standing a little the right of the road, without side arms, in a gray frock coat . . . gray pants, glazed cap, pulled down over his eyes, and with paper and pencil in hand, tracing directions to Lieutenant [Charles R.] Palmore. . . . Receiving his instructions, [Palmore] turned, mounted, and without looking, pulled his horse to the left. The horse's head came in contact with General Jackson's right shoulder, causing him to 'right face' very suddenly. Never taking his eyes from the paper, the General continued his reflections, without being in the least disturbed."[22]

As the sun began to set, Lee and Jackson had as many questions as they had answers. Hooker's large force had suddenly concentrated in a curving perimeter a mile to the west, south, and east of the Chancellorsville crossroads. What were they doing? Why had the Union advance ceased in late morning? What did Hooker plan to do from a defensive posture? What had caused a general, with 70,000 troops at his disposal and moving easily on his opponent's flank, to abandon the offensive at the approach of 25,000 Confederates?

Lack of adequate cavalry reconnaissance was part of the answer. Hooker had assumed that when Stoneman's horsemen struck in the direction of Richmond, Jeb Stuart's troopers would give pursuit. Stuart did nothing of the kind. He remained with Lee's army and provided valuable information. In contrast, Hooker was militarily blind without cavalry of his own to range far afield. Almost as bad, "Stoneman's Raid" proved to be more annoying than destructive.

Another part of the answer lay in sudden and sharp attacks by Jackson's brigades. Confederates had pounded the Federal center and flanks so aggressively as to put at least three of the enemy corps on the defensive. Twilight came that Friday with Hooker thinking not how to gain victory but how to avoid defeat.

Near 7 P.M., Jackson returned to the intersection of the Plank and furnace roads. The Southern line ran west-east at that point. Lee was there because it was a central and important location. The two generals stood in the road and began exchanging reports. Bullets from a Federal sharpshooter flew uncomfortably close, so they retired a short distance into the cover of pine woods on the northwestern side of the intersection. Lee sat down on a fallen log and beckoned for Jackson to join him. What was the position and strength of the enemy on the left? Lee inquired. Jackson responded that Stuart's horse artillery had been engaged in a one-sided contest with Union guns over there. General Wright, providing infantry support, had also met stubborn resistance.

Jackson regarded the heavy enemy fire in the Catharine Furnace area to be either a feint or a strong defensive action. He explained how easily he had advanced on large numbers of Federals through the afternoon. The fight has gone out of Hooker. He will retire across the Rappahannock. "By tomorrow morning," Jackson was convinced, "there will not be any of them this side of the river."[23]

Lee gravely shook his head. He hoped Jackson was correct; he thought otherwise. Hooker would make a major assault from Chancellorsville; he had to do so. He could not abandon his grand strategy so easily, even though his offensive spirit might be momentarily paralyzed.

Powell Hill now joined Lee and Jackson to discuss possible guides for leading the army through the unknowns of the Wilderness.[24] A couple of names were mentioned. After Hill departed, Jackson repeated his belief in a Federal retreat. One thing on which both he and Lee were in agreement, however, was that if the Federals were still in line the next day, they must be attacked.

Hooker's force was in unexplored and difficult country. The Confederates, more familiar with the Wilderness, had a distinct advantage. Of equal urgency, Sedgwick's part of the Union army back at Fredericksburg would soon discover Early's thin division in front. Once the Federals beat it aside, Lee's right flank and rear would be vulnerable to attack from Sedgwick's large contingent.

From Lee's own reconnaissance, he knew that a strike on Hooker's left near the river was unfeasible. The woods in that region were too thick, the opportunities for defense too many. A Confederate assault against the Federal center would be expected and therefore strongly met. It was time for someone else to reconnoiter the Union positions and give a fresh opinion.

Both generals summoned their respective engineering officers, Major T. M. R. Talcott and Captain Keith Boswell. The aides were instructed to make a close inspection and determine what offensive possibilities existed in the middle of the Union line. The moon was high and bright; it offered good potential for a scout.

After Talcott and Boswell left, Lee continued discussing options with his lieutenant. Should the report of the engineers show heavy Federal numbers in front, the remaining alternative was Hooker's right. Jackson was unsure what lay in that direction or how far the enemy line extended westward beyond Chancellorsville.

This was the topic of conversation when Stuart reined to a halt and hastily dismounted. A grim smile was on his face. The army commander's nephew, General Fitz Lee, had been scouting unhindered along the western reaches of the Orange Turnpike, Stuart said. Fitz Lee had made a startling discovery: Hooker's right flank was dangling—it was anchored on no geographical feature—it simply stretched as far as there were Union soldiers and then stopped.

Stuart's announcement instantly changed the whole tone of the conversation. Lee's mind rapidly developed the seed of a plan. If available roads permitted a wide-sweeping march that would bring part of his army opposite Hooker's right flank without being detected . . . If a heavy attack could get underway quickly on the unsuspecting Federal wing . . .

Lee looked up at Stuart. Are there sufficient roads for a turning movement? The cavalryman did not know, but he promised to find out at once. Stuart bounded into the saddle and disappeared down the furnace road.

Jackson continued to believe that a Federal withdrawal was imminent. Still, the thought of another circuitous march on the enemy flank or rear stirred his eagerness. Now the Union right became the focal point of the Lee-Jackson discussion. Sometime before midnight, Talcott and Boswell returned from their two-man reconnaissance. Hooker's left was firmly planted on the river; the center contained heavy entrenchments, protected by dense woods and massed guns. Neither Union left nor center could be carried successfully, in their combined estimation.

That settled the basic question as far as Lee was concerned. "How can we get at those people?" he asked almost to himself. According to Major Talcott, who overheard part of the conversation, Jackson replied that it was the commander's decision; he would undertake whatever Lee ordered him to do. The spirit of such an answer was unlike Jackson, who was always ready to voice his opinion to Lee—preferably for offensive action.

Lee bent over his map and studied it silently. By a flickering candle he began tracing his finger along marked roads that led around Hooker's right flank. Such an assault would turn the enemy position at Chancellorsville and enable Lee to unleash a separate blow from the south. A two-pronged attack against an already somewhat demoralized enemy gave the first genuine picture of victory. Jackson expressed agreement.

Within minutes, Lee had cultivated the framework of a plan that duplicated the Second Manassas strategy. Jackson would make a great sweeping march to the west. The route, and the execution of the attack itself, would be left to his discretion. Stuart's cavalry would screen the movement from start to end.

The strategy brought a smile to Jackson's face. The offensive would be his; he was expected to attack on the morrow. A rapid, secret march, then an onslaught against inferior numbers—this was his favorite tactic. The infidel would feel the wrath of God through his chosen warriors! Jackson rose from the log. "My troops will move at four o'clock," he said eagerly, and walked off into the woods.[25]

At that moment, a silly controversy began and festered for years over the question of who devised the strategy for the flank march at Chancellorsville. Jackson's most loyal defenders—Dabney, Hotchkiss, Morrison, and Henderson—asserted that their general had created the battle plan.[26]

The evidence as a whole points to a different conclusion. It starts with statements by Lee. In January 1866, after reading Dabney's manuscript of the Jackson biography, Lee complained to Anna Jackson: "I am misrepresented at the battle of Chancellorsville in proposing an attack in front, the first evening of our arrival. On the contrary I decided against it and stated to General Jackson, we must attack on our left as soon as practicable."[27]

The following year, Lee gave Albert T. Bledsoe an overview of the battle of Chancellorsville. "There is no question," Lee said, "as to who was responsible for the operations of the Confederates, or to whom any failures would have been charged."

Colonel Charles Marshall, a Lee aide and careful historian, insisted that the idea of a flank movement "was wholly Genl. Lee's conception." Major Talcott compiled a heavily researched paper to reinforce his remembrances that Lee suggested the move.[28]

Why this disagreement arose at all is difficult to comprehend. Eyewitness accounts all agree: Lee originated the idea of a flanking movement; Jackson developed the fine points and put it into motion.

Of much greater importance is what occurred late that night of May 1 in the darkness of the Wilderness. At the intersection of two country roads, Lee and Jackson resolved to risk the future of the Southern nation with an incredible gamble. Lee had already divided his army when he left Fredericksburg. Now he proposed to divide it again—in the very face of the enemy.

A little reflection, however, will show that Lee was not imperiling the cause. It was already in jeopardy. He was badly outnumbered; but precisely because he was, Lee was free to take preposterous chances. The odds against him at the outset were so long that it would not have hurt much, if at all, to lengthen them further. Moreover, any opponent who believed that Robert E. Lee or Stonewall Jackson would do the obvious under any circumstances was drawing a fatal conclusion.

Suddenly, a little grove of pine trees deep inside the Wilderness became Lee's new command post. There, in the middle of a spring night, the flanked determined to become the flanker.

Jackson was moving away from Lee when the commander added a final note: secrecy and speed must be the principal elements of Jackson's march. Such advice was unnecessary. Lee was addressing the general who carried out those designs to a higher degree than anyone else in the field.

Lee knew that. His parting comment was perfunctory—probably nothing more than an expression of his own thinking. A weary Lee then lay down on a saddle blanket and covered himself with his overcoat. He found sleep in spite of what lay just a few hours ahead.[29]

Meanwhile, Jackson's assertion that he would be advancing at 4 A.M. never materialized. It could not. Jackson had first to ascertain what routes Stuart and Hotchkiss might uncover; he needed more information on the unfamiliar lay of the land through which the move would be made. Jackson must therefore wait for further developments.

He made his way a few feet to a small clearing. The headquarters wagon was off somewhere. Jackson had no bedroll and made no request for one. He simply propped his sword upright against a tree and stretched out on the bare ground for badly needed rest. Sandie Pendleton offered Jackson his overcoat. The general politely but firmly declined. Pendleton persisted: would Jackson at least use the long cape of the overcoat as a cover? Yes, came a grateful reply.

The woods grew silent, despite the presence of two warring hosts sharing the Wilderness. No sound was audible. The night was cold and damp. After less than two hours' sleep, Jackson stirred. He was chilled, and he felt the first signs of a head cold. Struggling to his feet, he placed the cape over the sleeping form of his adjutant.[30]

Then he made his way to a nearby campfire that couriers had made. A still-weary general sat down on a discarded Federal cracker box, wrapped his rubber raincoat around his shoulders, and stared silently at the flames. In a few minutes, Chaplain Lacy joined him. The general pulled over another box for his minister friend. When Lacy hesitated, Jackson said: "Sit down. I want to talk to you." Religious topics were not the theme this time. "The enemy are in great force at Chancellorsville, in a commanding position," Jackson began. "To dislodge them by frontal attack would cost a fearful loss." Aware that the Lacy family had holdings in the neighborhood and that the chaplain had preached there on occasion, Jackson asked: "Do you know of any way by which we could flank either their right or left?"

"Yes," Lacy replied. "There is a blind road leading from the furnace, nearly parallel to the Plank Road, which falls into a road running northward, which again would lead into the Plank Road three and a half to four miles above Chancellorsville."[31]

Jackson took one of Hotchkiss's maps from his pocket and said: "Take this map and mark it down." Lacy did so. The general studied the route for a moment. That proposed route, he said, is too close to Hooker's position. "It will go within the line of the enemy's pickets. Do you know no other?" No, Lacy answered. He presumed that the furnace road would intersect again with the Plank Road somewhere to the west, but he had not ridden it himself. However, he knew someone who could help: Colonel Charles C. Wellford, the proprietor of Catharine Furnace. Moreover, his son Charles might be able to serve as a guide.[32]

Jackson awakened Hotchkiss, who was lying on the ground nearby. Hotchkiss and Lacy were ordered to ride to the Wellford residence a mile and a half away. "Ascertain whether those roads meet and are practicable for artillery," Jackson told Lacy. "Send Hotchkiss back with the information. You get me a guide." Even at that preliminary point in the planning, Professor Jackson intended to take his guns with him. They would blast a way for the soldiers to go.[33]

After the departure of the two aides, the general resumed his seat in front of the fire. Dawn was still a couple of hours away. Something then aroused Colonel A. L. Long of Lee's staff. He joined Jackson in front of the fire. The general was shivering. Long saw army cooks at work a short distance away and procured a cup of hot coffee. Jackson expressed thanks, and the two men began chatting idly.

Suddenly, a metallic clang broke the stillness. Jackson's sword, leaning against a tree all night, had fallen to the ground. Long secured it and handed it to Jackson. The general buckled it on without comment. Yet Long saw an omen in the incident. Knights of old viewed a falling sword as a sign of bad luck.[34]

Hotchkiss and Lacy rapidly made their way to the Wellford residence and roused the occupants from bed. While the minister exchanged pleasantries with family members, the mapmaker queried Colonel Wellford. Were there roads whereby a force could secretly pass around Chancellorsville and get to the vicinity of Wilderness Tavern, five miles to the west? By all means, Wellford said. "He himself had recently opened a road through the woods in the direction for the purpose of hauling cordwood and iron ore to his furnace."[35]

He bent over the map with Hotchkiss and traced the route. The colonel offered to act as a guide, if necessary. Hotchkiss and Lacy apologized for awakening the family and rushed back to the Plank Road intersection. There, around 3:30 A.M., the two aides found Lee and Jackson sitting on cracker boxes in earnest conversation. Some impatience was evident. Both generals were alert and energetic. If a flanking movement was to be made, it needed to get underway soon to maximize secrecy and to utilize all the daylight hours.[36]

Hotchkiss grabbed another cracker box and took a seat between the two commanders. He reviewed the wagon trails that Wellford had suggested. The route would begin down the Catharine Furnace road from the Plank Road. At the furnace, Jackson's men would turn left to the southwest for a mile or more before intersecting with the more established Brock Road. Another left on it would carry the Confederates about a third of a mile south and well out of view of the Federals. At that point, a hidden, little-known dirt trail branched off the Brock Road to the west. It soon turned north and continued until it again reached the Brock Road. That artery led northward to the Orange Plank Road, a full two miles west of Hooker's reported flank.

In all, it would be a twelve-mile, roundabout tramp for Jackson's men. Yet the desired end could make the means more than worthwhile.

With that, Hotchkiss concluded his report. The three men sat for a moment in silence. Then Lee politely opened the next stage of the conversation. He stared across the fire. "General Jackson, what do you propose to do?" The two men had already discussed the point.

Jackson traced Hotchkiss's route on the map. "Go around here," he said.

Instead of assigning him the troops to make the march, Lee asked: "What do you propose to make this movement with?"

"With my whole corps," came the abrupt reply.[37]

As audacious as Lee was, the response startled him. Jackson's flanking movement would be the largest of the three pieces of his army. Perhaps Lee should have known that Jackson would be thinking along those lines. His lieutenant never fought merely to repel or defeat an enemy. Jackson was out in quest of one of the smashing victories of the war by destroying the bulk of the Army of the Potomac. He would advance secretly, move quickly, and then strike with the heaviest blow possible.

To make sure that he understood Jackson's answer, Lee asked somewhat tenuously: "What will you leave me?"

"The divisions of Anderson and McLaws."[38]

What Jackson was proposing was a three-two split. He would take three divisions on the march and leave Lee with two. In other words, Jackson would march away with 28,000 men while Lee confronted Hooker's 70,000 Federals with a total of 14,000 troops. Most ominously, two Confederate divisions would be all that stood between Hooker's army and the seat of government at Richmond.

Lee stared at the campfire while he twirled the pencil in his hand. Neither Jackson nor Hotchkiss interrupted his train of thought. Finally, the army commander looked up at Jackson. "Well," he said, "go on."[39]

The army commander then took his pencil and sketched routes a final time on the map. Jackson had what Hotchkiss characterized as an "eager smile upon his face." He nodded assent now and then as Lee summarized the strategy. Around 5 A.M., Lee ended by saying: "General Stuart will cover your movements with his cavalry."[40]

Jackson rose quickly and saluted. "My troops will move at once, sir!" he exclaimed. He and Hotchkiss mounted their horses. A long march and heavy battle were on the day's agenda.[41]

While Jackson was getting his units ready, Lee alerted Anderson and McLaws of the plan. Their divisions must strengthen earthworks made more vulnerable by Jackson's departure—and the men must be noisy about it to distract Federals from the circuitous march about to take place. The two division commanders would use constant skirmishing and frequent demonstrations to perform their assignments well.

Jackson was now fully energized. His every thought was on the coming offensive. With lips shut tightly and eyes set, he rode past Gregg's old brigade of South Carolinians. The men rose to cheer; but when they perceived "battle in his haste and stern looks," they stood silently as he galloped past.[42]

Troops were awakening with a start as officers called for them to grab what food they had and prepare to march. Rodes's division was to take the lead, with Alfred H. Colquitt's Georgia brigade on the point. Colston and the Stonewall Division would follow. Powell Hill's soldiers would bring up the rear. Cavalry would screen the front and right of the column. Ammunition wagons, ambulances, and artillery were assigned places behind the infantry in their respective divisions.

The men were expected to maintain Jackson's brisk pace even though the usual ten-minute rest period each hour was forsaken. (Most Confederates got three rest stops during the twelve-hour march, each pause lasting roughly twenty minutes.) Ranks must be kept closed, Jackson insisted. No dawdling or delays would be tolerated. A North Carolina captain noted, "Regimental commanders were ordered to march in rear of their regiments, with a guard of strong men with fixed bayonets, to prevent straggling."[43]

Sunrise came a little after 5:00; the day broke cloudless, fresh, and invigorating. A chill was in the air. Jackson donned his black India rubber raincoat: a double-breasted, loose-fitting garment with flap pockets. Getting three widely dispersed divisions ready for a concerted march in deep woods took time. It was just before 7:30 when the head of the Second Corps crossed the Plank Road and started down to Catharine Furnace.[44]

Charles Beverly Wellford, the colonel's son, and Jack Hayden, a well-known local hunter, were the guides. Stuart's troopers rode immediately behind them, followed by Colquitt's Georgians and the rest of Rodes's division. In all, seventy regiments of infantry, four regiments of cavalry, plus twenty-one batteries with a total of eighty guns composed Jackson's strike force. The first elements were proceeding down the road when Jackson and his entourage rode toward the front. Lee had emerged from the thicket and was standing by the road.

When Jackson saw the commander, he drew rein. The two held a very brief conversation. Jackson's face seemed flushed; his eyes blazed. While looking at Lee, he pointed emphatically toward the west. Lee nodded. Two men so unalike and yet so similar: professional soldiers nurtured in Virginia's soil—the mountain orphan and the tidewater well-born—one whose audacity matched the other's aggressiveness. Now, early on a cool morning, they exchange words before embarking on a move that could easily win, or lose, this war. Their military partnership was unmatched. To their soldiers, it was unbeatable. Jackson turned Little Sorrel and resumed trotting down the road.[45]

Before leaving that morning, Jackson dispatched Smith with orders for the wagon trains. The aide returned to where he had received the directives, only to find Jackson gone. As the young lieutenant rode past a long segment of the column to reach Jackson, he received a barrage of good-natured shouts from the ranks: "Have a good breakfast this morning, sonny?" "Tell Old Jack we're all a-comin'!" "Don't let him begin the fuss till we get thar!"[46]

The road down to the furnace passed through a clearing caused by Lewis's Creek. There Confederates could look north to the high ground a mile away at Hazel Grove. At the same time, on the other end of the clearing, Union soldiers saw Rodes's division moving west. A Federal battery opened fire.

Fortunately, Confederate officers found a partial detour. An old wagon trail turned left off the furnace road before it reached the open expanse. It would link with the route leading south a mile and a half on the other side of the furnace. Jackson directed the wagon trains to use it. Even though it was a longer route, it would be out of range from Union guns. Jackson also ordered his infantry to double-time through the clearing.

These precautions did nothing to ease Jackson's anxiety. A secret march, underway for less than an hour, was a secret no longer. The issue for Jackson became how the enemy would react to his movement. Federals in General Daniel E. Sickles's III Corps spotted the heavy column with its guns, wagons, and infantry trudging through the woods apparently heading south. Something big was underway.

A message went up through channels to headquarters. There Hooker fell victim to faulty deduction. Still convinced that Lee would ultimately retreat, Hooker saw confirmation of that belief in Jackson's march. The Confederate column was moving west away from the Union line at Chancellorsville.

Hooker still felt the need, however, to be somewhat cautious. He advised General Oliver O. Howard, whose XI Corps manned the far right of the line, to consider the possibility of being flanked. Hooker had already made one miscalculation. He shortly would make another.

The Federal commander had the mistaken notion that Howard's right rested securely on the Rappahannock. Then sometime in midmorning, Hooker's mind did another turn. He convinced himself that Lee was retreating. There was no need to initiate heavy action. Let the Confederates go. Yet Hooker did give Sickles permission to advance a division downhill to the furnace area to get a better idea of what was taking place.

By then, Jackson had reached the substantial open country at the furnace. He declined an offer of breakfast in order to push on. The trail that led northward from the furnace to the Union line bothered him. He ordered one of his lead regiments, the 23d Georgia, to guard the approach and the wagon trains moving back onto the main route while the rest of the column turned left and advanced south.

Contact between the two sides came in late morning. Federals struck the 23d Georgia in heavy numbers. Jackson was not aware of the enemy buildup in the action. When Lee learned of it, the army commander rushed a brigade from Anderson's division to the sector. It joined two brigades from Hill's division that acted on their own and moved toward the fighting. The contest was short but spirited. It had ended by the time Confederate reinforcements arrived. The Georgians had lost 300 men in a gallant defense.

Actually, the Federals who caught sight of Jackson worked ultimately to his advantage. Sickles's probe soon came under heavy fire from the troops sent to the scene by Jackson. Sickles called for help. It came from Howard, who sent most of his reserve to the Union center.

Federals thereby concentrated in an area away from where Jackson was moving.

This produced a sizable gap between Howard on the Federal right and Sickles in the center. If Howard's wing should be broken, those Federals had no immediate fallback point on which to rally. More incredibly, Howard had responded to Hooker's warning about a possible flank attack by posting no more than two regiments and two pieces of artillery in a position facing west.[47]

While Sickles was poking at the tail of Jackson's column near Catharine Furnace, the Confederate commander was miles away angling northward toward Hooker's flank. Confident that his men could hold back any Union "interference" along the way, the general gave his attention to the advance of his corps. He needed to do so, for this was a march unlike any he or his soldiers had ever made.

A North Carolina private marching near the front of the column provided the first overview. The long line of soldiers, he wrote, "went swiftly forward through the Wilderness, striking now and then a dim path or road. Strict silence was enforced, the men being allowed to speak only in whispers. Occasionally a courier would spur his tired horse past us as we twisted through the bush. For hours at the time we neither saw nor heard anything."[48]

Thirst began to overtake the Confederates. More trying, even to the veterans, was the route that Wellford, Hotchkiss, and Jackson had developed. Roads, for the most part, were winding footpaths barely wide enough to accommodate a wagon. The usual practice of rolling stock taking the middle of a road while soldiers marched along the edges could not apply here. Wagons and guns followed the crowded lines of soldiers. Thick spring underbrush constricted the trails even more. Recent rain held down the dust, but mud holes were in the low spots.

Four soldiers marched abreast, with so little space in the ranks that the men had difficulty shifting weapons from one shoulder to the other without hitting someone in front or rear. Some of the route was so primitive that troops had to clear brush and remove stumps in order for artillery to pass.

Close to 700 companies were weaving through what one infantryman called "the broken, brushy wilderness of that section, almost devoid of roads."[49] Troops marched in route step to conserve energy. The head of Jackson's line was making about two and a half miles per hour, the rear about one and a half.

It was simply impossible for the column, which stretched in a semicircle a full ten miles, to remain intact. That so long a line executed so long a march under such conditions is truly remarkable. The accomplishment was greater than many of Jackson's more famous marches in the Shenandoah Valley.[50]

Troops suffered as the temperature climbed into the eighties, but few complained openly. Lieutenant Octavius Wiggins of the 37th North Carolina spoke for the majority: "It was my fortune or misfortune to belong to 'Jackson's foot cavalry' and had participated in most of the hard marches made by his command, but this differed from all others I had ever known in severity. The day was very warm, the route poor. . . . On we rushed, jumping bushes, branches, up and down hill. We did not know and did not care where we were going . . . but there is one thing we did know and knew for a certainty and that was, that Old Jack was going round the bulls horn but unless the bull kept his tail twitching very fast the old hero would have a grip on it before the sun went down."[51]

Jackson rode back and forth along his line throughout the morning. He kept urging the men in a low tone to "press forward, press forward," or "see that the column is kept closed," or the simpler "press on, press on." Surgeon McGuire noted: "Never can I forget the eagerness and intensity of Jackson on that march. . . . His face was pale, his eyes flashing. . . . In his eagerness, as he rode, he leaned over the neck of his horse, as if in that way the march might be hurried. . . . Every man in the ranks knew that we were engaged in some great flank movements, and they eagerly responded and pressed on at a rapid gait."[52]

Colonel Porter Alexander, one of Longstreet's artillery officers, accompanied Jackson's staff. He observed that Jackson "was grave & silent, & there was not much conversation in the party." As the hours passed without further enemy obstruction, Jackson began to relax. Somewhere beyond the midway point, he returned from a prodding ride to the head of the line. He reined Little Sorrel to a walk and began chatting with Robert Rodes, "Polly" Colston, and Colonel Tom Munford of the 2d Virginia Cavalry. All were former VMI men.

According to Munford (whose postwar writings were voluminous and too often exaggerated), Jackson reminisced for awhile about the old days at the institute. He then changed the subject to what he regarded as a basic weakness of the Confederacy. "I hear it said," Jackson supposedly declared, "that General Hooker has more men than he can handle. I should like to have half as many more as I have today, and I should hurl him in the river! The trouble with us has always been to have a reserve to throw in at the critical moment to reap the benefit of advantages gained. We have always had to put in all our troops and never had enough at the time most needed."[53]

Into the afternoon the march continued. The Confederates were proceeding unmolested. One of the Tarheels recalled of this time: "While marching along a narrow road winding through a dense wilderness not seeing a house or clearing or other sign that the section was inhabited by human beings except the narrow road we were traveling, we saw a lone horseman coming with all the speed his horse was capable of, holding aloft a large yellow envelope. We stepped to the side of the road to let him pass. In a short time another courier came riding from the rear, saying General Jackson is coming, but no cheering. We stepped to the side of the road again and along came Gen. Jackson on his long, gaunt sorrel horse in a long gallop with his hat raised but not a word spoken."[54]

The first rider was likely carrying a dispatch from Lee. At 10:30 that morning, Jackson had informed Lee of his progress. The army chief now replied: "I have given directions to all the commanders to keep a watch for any engagement which may take place in rear of Chancellorsville and to make as strong a demonstration as possible with infantry & Artillery & prevent any troops from being withdrawn in their front." After informing Jackson that Federal cavalry had struck the Virginia Central Railroad at Trevilian Station, Lee added: "Everything is quiet in front at present."[55]

Near 2 P.M., Jackson reached the Orange Plank Road. The front of his lines was three miles west of Chancellorsville; the rear elements were just clearing Catharine Furnace. As he paused to survey the lay of the land, an officer on a large gray mount raced down the Brock Road and halted in front of Jackson. It was gregarious General Fitzhugh Lee. He was breathless and obviously agitated. "General," he gasped, "if you will ride with me, halting your columns here, out of sight, I will show you the enemy's right, and you will perceive the great advantage of attacking [farther north] down the old turnpike, instead of the plank road, the enemy's line being taken in reverse. Bring only one courier, as you will be in view from the top of the hill."[56]

Perhaps Fitz Lee was presumptuous in telling Jackson what he ought to do at the moment. Yet Jackson disregarded the bearded cavalryman's excitement to get a look at what he had been marching all day to see. He ordered the long column to halt in the roads. Securing a courier, he rode with Fitz Lee along an obscure trail and through dense woods. They crossed the Germanna Plank Road and moved stealthily to the top of a cleared crest on the Burton farm. Jackson stared silently.

A half-mile away, stretched along the old Orange Turnpike, were entrenchments and lines of encamped Federals. The soldiers were chatting, smoking, playing cards— scattered about in no particular order. Arms were stacked; cannon stood unattended. Campfire smoke swirled lazily skyward. The Union XI Corps was unaware of any danger.

Jackson had expected to get in the enemy's rear via the Plank Road. Now he saw that such an approach would bring him across the Federal front. To achieve his original design, he needed to take his men another mile and a half farther north and launch his attack from the west-northwest along the turnpike. That move would consume more precious time—perhaps as much as two hours—but no workable alternative existed.

The added gamble would be worth it. "Stonewall's face bore an expression of intense interest during the five minutes he was on the hill," Fitz Lee noted. "The paint of approaching battle was coloring his cheeks, and he was radiant to find no preparation had been made to guard against a flank attack."[57]

Jackson said nothing to the cavalryman. Yet his lips were moving. "He was engaged in an appeal to the God of Battles," Fitz Lee was certain. Then Jackson looked to his left toward the turnpike. The well-known Talley farmhouse was visible amid the partially cleared tract. Half a mile to the east was more open ground. That was Melzi Chancellor's place (not the Chancellorsville intersection two miles to the east). The Chancellor farm was then called Dowdall's Tavern.

It was the end of the Union line as well as Federal General Howard's headquarters at the moment. Like the rest of the Wilderness, this was undulating country and covered for the most part with timber and thickets. Only here and there did a small farm provide an opening in the wooded darkness.

With a jerk, Jackson wheeled his horse and said to Fitz Lee in snapping syllables: "Tell General Rodes to move across the plank road and halt when he gets to the old turnpike. I will join him there." He took a final look at the enemy lines. Then, Lee commented, "he rode rapidly down the hill, his arms flapping to the motion of his horse, over whose head it seemed, good rider as he was, he would certainly go."[58]

Many dispositions needed to be made. The troops were not merely trudging another mile and a half; Jackson was taking them deeper into a region where the enemy should be in greater numbers. He was putting the Second Corps in a more vulnerable situation, to be sure, but the Confederates would be in a position to attack the Federal right-rear rather than the right-front.

Jackson, covered with dust, reached the Brock Road and began issuing orders in rapid-fire succession. Paxton and the Stonewall Brigade, along with Fitz Lee's cavalry, would remain on the Plank Road and guard Jackson's right flank. Munford and his cavalry would dash north to a position protecting the left. The main force would strike for the Luckett farm along the turnpike.

It was a sultry Saturday. A beating sun had dried the ground. Dust drifted upward as Rodes's division marched rapidly through the woods. Other units followed in his wake. Always conscious of chain-of-command procedures, Jackson dismounted from Little Sorrel and sat on a stump. He took a small piece of paper and a stub of a pencil to compose a hasty note to his superior:

Near 3 P.M.
May 2d 1863

General,

The enemy has made a stand at Chancellors's which is about 2 miles from Chancellorsville. I hope as soon as practicable to attack.

I trust that an Ever Kind Providence will bless us with great success.

Respectfully,
T. J. Jackson
Lt. Genl.

Genl. R. E. Lee

The leading division is up & the next two appear to be well closed.

T. J. J.

It was the last dispatch Jackson ever wrote.

Jack Hayden, one of the guides who had led the Confederate column throughout the day, had completed his task. Jackson thanked Hayden as he gave him permission to leave. The guide started toward his horse, stopped, and turned back to Jackson. "I desire you to do me one favor," he said.

"What is it, sir?"

Hayden looked Jackson squarely in the eye and said with sincerity: "Take care of yourself."[59]

Midafternoon passed as Rodes's men covered the remaining distance between the Germanna Plank Road and the turnpike. The rest of the Second Corps was moving up steadily. Jackson had accomplished the greatest flank march of his career. Practically his entire force was approaching the wing of an unsuspecting enemy. His assault, if sudden and strong, might result in the climactic victory for the Southern cause. Yet was there enough daylight left for the attack? The sun would set a little before 7 P.M.; and when it did, darkness would descend rapidly on the Wilderness.

Naturally, it would have been better had Jackson gotten an earlier start that day, but the delay was not of his doing. His men had not marched as swiftly as some of them did in the valley. However, nothing like the Wilderness existed west of the Blue Ridge. The wisdom of the plan, the secrecy of the march, the vigor of the advance, all would cause Lee to speak later of Jackson's "matchless energy and skill."[60]

Rodes's division reached the old turnpike, turned east, and moved about a mile to a long, low ridge. From there, Rodes dispatched elements of the 5th Alabama under Major Eugene Blackford to proceed 400 yards farther as a skirmish line. The division commander then deployed his Alabama, Georgia, and North Carolina brigades. Two were north of the turnpike and the other two south of it.

Jackson's instructions to his generals were explicit. Bugles would give the signal for the attack. Then, using the turnpike as a direction beacon, the whole line would sweep forward. Rodes's first objective was the Talley farm, since it was on high ground that commanded the immediate area. Once the Talley area was secure, Rodes was to press forward to Dowdall's Tavern on the crest of a lower ridge. Jackson expected the assault to bog down there, so he directed artillery batteries to wheel into action at that point to help maintain the momentum. Rodes was to continue his advance as far as possible.

Colston's division, 200 yards behind Rodes, would follow in support. His four brigades were also divided in half by the turnpike. Should a brigade commander in Rodes's line need assistance, the officer immediately behind him in the Colston line would move up without waiting for orders. Two hundred yards behind Colston were the brigades of Generals Dorsey Pender and James H. Lane. The Confederate assault would be heavily weighted on the north side of the turnpike, with only four brigades to the south of the narrow road. "Under no circumstances," Jackson repeatedly emphasized, "was there to be any pause in the advance."[61]

Some 21,000 men were stacked in a battle line a mile and a half long. It would have been an awesome sight to anyone who could have seen it all. Yet only a few yards of the line were visible before it vanished in the Wilderness.

Owing to the density of the woods and the long battle front, much time was required for Jackson's assault line to get into position. Knowing this, Jackson had to curb his impatience in the face of a sun descending toward the horizon. The line must be solid and irresistible. A piecemeal attack would be a failure.

Major von Borcke arrived with a report. He found Stuart, Jackson, and their staffs "stretched out along the grass beneath a gigantic oak, and tranquilly discussing their plans for the impending battle." Both generals were confident.

Shortly before 5 P.M., Major Sandie Pendleton dismounted. The line of battle was formed, he announced. Jackson quickly rode to high ground at the Luckett farm. A cluster of officers joined him. Jackson looked around. Familiar faces from VMI stared back. In yesteryear they had been cadets and fellow professors. Now they were division commanders, brigadiers, regimental colonels—seventeen in all—and they were still seeking to please their sometimes strange but always inspiring leader. Emotion overtook Jackson. "The Institute will be heard from today," he said.[62]

One of the line officers kept his eyes on the general in the last moments of waiting. "There sat Gen. Jackson on Little Sorrel as calm as if sitting upon the seashore a thousand miles from a battle field. Not a muscle quivered in his face. . . . As much as I admire the fair sex, I do not believe the most beautiful woman in the whole Southern Confederacy could have diverted them from him. It was as still as a village grave yard; the soldiers moved with great caution."[63]

The attack was to begin at 5:15. Two and a half hours of daylight would remain. General Robert Rodes, tense and excited, made his way to Jackson. He was a militia general's son from Lynchburg; an early disappointment had been the VMI professorship that went to Jackson. Yet Rodes had long forgotten any ill will. He had later become a fellow faculty member, and he was now a distinguished member of a new wave of Confederate generals.

Mounted on Rodes's right was Major Blackford, commanding the skirmishers.

Jackson sat on his horse, watch in hand. As he looked right and left at his line, everyone around Jackson looked at him. The general glanced down again at the watch. It was 5:15. "Are you ready, General Rodes?" he asked.

"Yes, sir," came an emphatic answer.

Jackson replied simply and quietly: "You can go forward, then."[64]

Rodes nodded at Blackford, who relayed a signal. A single bugle echoed through the woods, picked up by buglers all along the attack line. Skirmishers dashed forward.

An acoustical shadow covered the west side of the Wilderness that afternoon. The forest smothered the bugle calls. Not a Union soldier made mention of them. Billy Yanks were cooking supper or taking naps; the strains of a regimental band could be heard in the woods to the rear. The first hint the Federals had of anything unusual came when deer, wild turkeys, and rabbits—all startled by the onrushing Confederates—raced through the Union camps. Northern soldiers gave no thought to the cause behind the stampede; some men gaily chased the critters past tents and campfires.

Suddenly, the unearthly, chilling Rebel yell seemed to come from everywhere. Georgia soldier Sidney Lanier had characterized this high-pitched, screeching yell as "a howl, a hoarse battle-cry, a cheer, and a congratulation, all in one." To Jackson, it remained "the sweetest music I ever heard."[65]

Confederates who had marched all day and who for the past hour had waited nervously in the thickets now sprang forward. Major McIntosh of Jackson's artillery exclaimed: "The surprise was complete. A bolt from the sky would not have startled [the Federals] half as much as the musket shots in the thickets . . . and then a solid wall of gray, forcing their way through the timber and bearing down upon them like an irresistible avalanche. There was no stemming such a tide. . . . The shock was too great; the sense of utter helplessness was too apparent. The resistance offered was speedily beaten down. There was nothing left but to lay down their arms and surrender, or flee. They threw them away, and fled. Arms, knapsacks, clothing, equipage, everything, was thrown aside and left behind. . . . Men lost their heads in terror, and the roads and woods on both sides [of the turnpike] were filled with men, horses and cattle, in one mad flight."[66]

In the first stage of the assault, Jackson remained close to the front. Calmness then disappeared as he too gave way to excitement. The general galloped to whatever vantage point he could find to watch the progress. Over and over Jackson encouraged the men. "Press on! Press on!" he shouted. Around him seemed to be an aura of sheer joy. Several soldiers wrote of seeing Jackson from time to time raise an arm upward while he looked heavenward in obvious supplication.[67]

As for the initial panic that swept over the Federals, a North Carolina officer adjudged: "They did run and make no mistake about it—but I will never blame them. I would have done the same thing and so would you and I reckon the Devil himself would have run with Jackson in his rear."[68]

Meanwhile, a second acoustical shadow had occurred. General Daniel Sickles, whose corps was roughly adjacent to Howard's on the eastern side and near the point of attack, heard nothing until he received word that Howard's corps on his flank was under assault. Sickles refused to believe it until informed of the collapse of Hooker's right. By then, the Confederate attack had the shock of a thunderbolt, and the ends of the battle line overlapped both flanks of Howard's XI Corps.

Jackson's assaulting line might have made maximum use of such position, and of such lack of reaction by the Federals, had not a breakdown begun within the Confederate ranks. The attacking line had moved forward smoothly until the far right began to lag. There General Alfred Colquitt concluded that Federal cavalry were advancing on him from Catharine Furnace.

A thirty-nine-year-old Georgian with a Princeton degree, Colquitt had made his prewar mark as a lawmaker. He later would become a teetotaler, minister, and governor. A Virginia matron who had met Colquitt during the winter encampment thought the general "a very delicate man [who] did not mingle with the people."[69]

On this May evening in the Virginia Wilderness, indecision overcame Colquitt. He disobeyed Jackson's strongest order and halted his brigade to meet the "threat" on his front and flank. Colquitt's standstill removed Jackson's right from the attack. The Georgian not only neutralized his own brigade; when Colquitt stopped, his troops blocked Ramseur's brigade behind him and isolated the Stonewall Brigade back on the Plank Road.

Ramseur, thirteen years Colquitt's junior, raced to the trouble spot. Finding no Union troops, he made his way angrily to Colquitt. Continue the advance, he shouted; he would guard the flank. Yet it was too late to correct the line. Colquitt's unauthorized halt removed a fourth of Jackson's front from the action. Now only 15,000 men in six brigades composed Jackson's attack. Worse, Jackson's right was incapable of overlapping the Federal flank.[70]

Waves of Confederates north of the turnpike had routed the first Union division in their path. The second Federal line, commanded by General Carl Schurz, waged a spirited fight for awhile and retired only when Confederates turned both flanks. By 6 P.M., Jackson's forces had control of the Talley plateau. Another half-hour, another half-mile, and the Southern line swept past Dowdall's Tavern. Then the offensive began to go awry.

Advancing Confederates on either side of the Plank Road (as the old turnpike was called in that sector) left open ground and entered thick woods. No skirmishers led the way. So eager were Johnny Rebs to press forward that alignment vanished. Units became a single mass of humanity. Everyone surged eastward, trying to get in front and be the first to strike the retreating enemy.

The main section of Jackson's battle line was becoming mired in the center, while the less restricted flanks were curling aimlessly in the general direction of the Federal position. "We were all mixed up," a Georgian confessed. "So bad that we could hardly tell which Reg. or Brig. we were in. that however made no difference, as we never stoped to learn who did this or that. but our watchword was onward. Onward we went."[71]

Soon the once-steady advance faltered. Some troops became entangled in abatis or breastworks; others veered off course in the confusion; weary soldiers sat down to discuss the action; officers sought desperately to untangle the mess. All the while the sun was setting and the woods were growing darker.

Jackson moved down the Plank Road with the artillery. He was urging the gunners forward with both gesture and voice. A report came from Rodes: his line and that of Colston were hopelessly mixed. He must halt; but if Jackson could bring Powell Hill's division to the front, the first line would reform and join the advance.

Too much was at stake to stop, Jackson felt. He rode rapidly into the disorganized ranks. "Men, get into line!" he yelled. "Get into line! Whose regiment is this? Colonel, get your men instantly into line!"[72]

They were less than two miles from the center of the Union line. Not far ahead was the road to United States Ford, Hooker's line of retreat across the Rappahannock. "Press on! Press on!" Jackson urged. The road must be secured!

Rodes and Colston reasoned with Jackson. No Federals were visible. Confederates had marched about fourteen miles without food and but little water. They had tramped through heavy woods and dense undergrowth. For almost two hours Jackson's men had been fighting in thickets that had torn away clothing. Darkness was compounding weariness.

The line was foundering but Rodes was openly proud of what his troops had done. Almost impetuously he said, "General Jackson, my division behaved splendidly this evening and you must give them a big name in your report." Jackson smiled. "I shall take great pleasure in doing so and congratulate you and your command for it."[73]

Congratulations were in order. The Union XI Corps had lost a fourth of its strength; yet in two hours of combat Oliver Howard's soldiers had delayed Jackson's advance, inflicted 1000 casualties, and knocked Jackson's assaulting line into disarray. The conduct of the XI Corps was hardly the wild-eyed rout that writers have traditionally portrayed it.

With great reluctance, Jackson halted the attack. Yet his eagerness to resume the advance only increased. This was especially the case when Major Norvell Cobb of Colston's division sent word that he and part of the 44th Virginia had occupied Federal earthworks less than a mile from Chancellorsville. As battle noise began abating, orders went to Hill to push his division to the front and prepare for a night attack. The sun was setting, but a full moon was taking its place. It could be a heavenly lantern to illuminate the path to total victory.

Jackson rode forward to try to bring a semblance of order among the intermingled regiments. Captain Rowland Williams of the 13th North Carolina was advancing his company "as rapidly as we possibly could." Presently, "General Jackson and staff came thundering down the road by us, and as he passed the head of Pender's brigade . . . he called out to halt and throw out a strong skirmish line to protect the column and to 'press the enemy until night-fall.'"[74]

Privates were looking for comrades, officers were looking for commands, and Jackson was looking for a courier. He turned to Major Cobb. "Find General Rodes and tell him to occupy the barricade at once!" Jackson calmed down briefly. "I need your help for a time," Jackson told Cobb. "This order must be corrected. As you go along the right, tell the troops from me to get into line and preserve their order."[75]

Around 8 P.M., for reasons never explained, Captain Marcellus Moorman took two Napoleon guns and a Parrott rifled piece a half-mile east of Dowdall's Tavern. There he opened a ranging fire on Union batteries presumed to be some 1200 yards distant at Fairview. Moorman's salvos were but a signal. Before the smoke cleared from his cannon barrels, at least ten Union cannon replied with deadly accuracy. Jim Lane's brigade of North Carolinians was moving down the Plank Road in rear of Moorman's guns. The rapid fire of enemy guns sent infantry scurrying into woods on the left of the road.

Lieutenant Wiggins of Lane's brigade termed the barrage "the most unmerciful artillery fire I was ever under during the entire war." When the men were ordered into the cover of the woods, Wiggins remembered, we "buried our faces as close to the ground as possible and I expect some of us rubbed the skins off our noses trying to get under it."[76]

Even Jackson hurried from the road to avoid the artillery fire. A few moments later, Hill arrived in the area and asked Lane why his advance had halted. An angry brigadier replied that the Confederate cannon had drawn a heavy and accurate enemy fire. If Southern guns would stop shooting, he believed that the Federal batteries would do likewise. Hill at once gave the order. Cannon noise ceased.

Lane's brigade moved beyond abandoned log works. It was in advance of Jackson's entire force, and it was alone. On the north side of the road, Lane recalled, "there was a dense growth of 'scrubby oaks,' through which it was very difficult for troops to move. . . . I cautioned all of my field officers to watch closely the front, as we were occupying the front line and were expected to make a night attack."[77]

The 7th and 37th North Carolina took position on the right (south) side of the Plank Road; the 18th and 28th North Carolina were on the left, with the 18th's right anchored on the road. The 400 men in the largest of Lane's regiments, the 37th North Carolina, were thrown forward as a heavy skirmish line. They occupied a slight north-south rise of ground. All of the soldiers were painfully aware of their advanced position. In a sense, they were in the no-man's-land between two opposing armies.

Satisfied with the dispositions of his troops to the north of the Plank Road, Lane proceeded toward his right to get those units in better alignment. The brigadier was then in his thirtieth year. A native of the Middle Neck of Virginia, Lane had graduated from VMI in 1854 and returned three years later to teach. His first Confederate service was with a Tarheel unit. Capable and disciplined in battle, affable and sociable in camp, the heavily bearded Lane was the epitome of what a brigadier general should be. He also regarded Jackson with near hero worship. Yet what was about to happen may explain why Lane never received promotion to major general, despite a sterling record to the end of the war.

It was dark when Lane reached the Plank Road. He called out in the woods for his division commander, Powell Hill. Jackson answered. He had been conferring with officers before easing Little Sorrel along the road past Henry Heth's brigade to a position alongside Lane's line. In spite of troops stumbling into each other, battle lines disorganized and uncharted, general officers unsure what lay in their front, Jackson remained convinced that a night attack would be successful.

For a half-hour he had kept staff officers busy putting brigades and batteries in proper positions. With complete victory seemingly a half-mile away, Jackson was tireless, his commands sharp and confident. Soon he had ridden ahead of the skirmishers. Sandie Pendleton remonstrated with the commander. "General, don't you think this is the wrong place for you?"

Jackson was oblivious to any personal risks. "The danger is over!" he shouted. "The enemy is routed! Go back and tell A. P. Hill to press right on!"

Pendleton departed on an errand that may well have saved his life. A moment or two later, the general recognized Lane's voice in the dark. Jackson asked what he wanted with Hill. "My Carolinians are in line," replied Lane. "I am looking for General Hill to ascertain if I should begin the advance."

Jackson pumped his right arm in the direction of the Union lines. With an earnest tone, he exclaimed, "Push right ahead, Lane." Then he touched spurs to Little Sorrel and moved slowly along the road. It was nearing 8:45 P.M.[78]

The general had ridden only a few yards when shirt-sleeved Powell Hill galloped down the Plank Road with his staff. Jackson returned Hill's salute. Anxiety and impatience marked his countenance. Among other things, Jackson's next attack would be in a different direction. Lane would continue east along the Plank Road, but the bulk of Hill's Light Division would strike northeast toward the main Rappahannock ford.

"How long before you will be ready to advance?" Jackson asked.

"In a few minutes," Hill answered, "as soon as I can finish relieving General Rodes."

Jackson was ready with the next question. "Do you know the road from Chancellorsville to the United States Ford?"

Hill thought for a few seconds. "I have not travelled over it for many years."

At that, Jackson turned in the saddle to his engineering officer. "Captain Boswell, report to General Hill." Jackson swung back to Hill and said intently: "General Hill, when you reach Chancellorsville, allow nothing to stop you! Press on to the United States Ford!"[79]

Jackson rode a short distance down the Plank Road and stopped, as if waiting for Hill's brigades to advance. Hill sat on his horse in the middle of the road on a line with Lane's North Carolinians. The full moon, unencumbered by clouds, bathed the Wilderness in a silvery light.

Battle noise had abated considerably; but for Confederates and Federals alike, it was a bad night. Major David McIntosh, commanding an artillery battalion, wrote that "commands were groping in the dark to find the positions assigned them, and struggling groups were wandering around in search of their commands. Alarms were frequent. Intermittent flashes of musketry burst out and threw a glare over the forest, and the guns from Fairview opened at intervals." Federal General Alpheus S. Williams was more profoundly affected. "Human language can give no idea of such a scene; such an infernal and yet sublime combination of sound and flames and smoke, and dreadful yells of rage, of pain, of triumph, or of defiance."[80]

Strangely, no such atmosphere existed in front of Lane's brigade along the north side of the Orange Plank Road. Captain Richard E. Wilbourn, Jackson's chief signal officer, remarked that "the firing had ceased, and all was quiet—the enemy having in the darkness . . . disappeared entirely from our sight."[81]

At that point, eight staff officers had rejoined Jackson after completing various errands. They included Captain Wilbourn, signal officer; Captain William F. Randolph of the 39th Virginia Cavalry, chief of couriers; Lieutenant Joseph G. Morrison, aide; Privates William E. Cunliffe and William T. Wynn of the signal corps; Private David Joseph Kyle of the 9th Virginia Cavalry, guide; and Privates Joshua O. Johns and Lloyd T. Smith, 39th Virginia Cavalry, couriers.

One of the most obscure members of the group was the most important at the moment. Nineteen-year-old David Kyle had been in service for two years; for a period the preceding autumn, he had served as a courier for General W. H. F. "Rooney" Lee. Kyle had begun May 2 as a messenger for Stuart. When he brought a dispatch to Jackson around 6:30, the general learned that the youth had grown up near Chancellorsville and knew the country well. Jackson immediately "impressed" him as a guide.[82]

It was close to 9 o'clock, and Jackson was growing more restless. So much needed to be done while momentum was still with the Confederates. Jackson was too galvanized to sit idly any longer. He himself would ride out beyond the skirmish line and seek to determine both the location and the strength of the makeshift Union line. Placing Wilbourn on his left, the two couriers immediately behind, and the rest of the staff in the same column of two, Jackson proceeded slowly down the Plank Road.

The group passed quietly through the right end of the 18th North Carolina. No officers of that regiment were informed of the Jackson scout. The adjutant of the 18th asserted after the war, "We were never more on the alert, and wide awake that night, and I don't remember to have ever heard of a member of the brigade saying that he knew [Jackson and his staff] had gone to our front."[83]

Powell Hill saw the general start forward and felt a duty to accompany him. The division commander and nine members of his staff trotted several yards behind the Jackson party. At no time would the two mounted groups come together. They were separate clusters of horsemen making their way warily through unfamiliar country. Only Kyle knew exactly where they were going.

A mile west of Chancellorsville, Bullock Road crossed the Plank Road and continued in a northeast direction toward the Rappahannock. Another trail, Mountain Road, made a junction with Bullock Road less than 100 yards north of the main thoroughfare on which Jackson was moving. Mountain Road ran parallel to the Plank Road, which was now too obvious, too dangerous, and too cluttered with battle debris to be an avenue for a reconnoitering party.

Jackson summoned young Kyle. Where do those two roads on the left of the Plank Road go? Kyle replied that one led to the Bullock farm a mile north of the Chancellorsville intersection and the other "ran sorter parallel with the plank road and came out on it about half a mile below towards Chancellorsville."[84]

The Mountain Road seemed to offer the best path to get close to the enemy position. Yet Jackson had doubts about the safety of the rarely used lane, so he ordered Kyle to lead the way. The general remained behind his guide for about 200 yards; then, satisfied that the route was safe, he rode abreast of Kyle and inched forward.

General and staff got almost to the skirmish line of the 33d North Carolina. Sounds became audible some 200–300 yards in the pitch blackness ahead. Officers were giving frantic orders and axes were ringing against trees while pioneers worked loudly to erect barricades in anticipation of Jackson's fury.

For two to four minutes, Jackson sat quietly on Little Sorrel and listened. Then he started back up the Mountain Road. It was almost 9:30. "I followed on pretty close with him," David Kyle stated, "but just before we got in some fifty or seventy-five yards of where Gen. Jackson started to turn out of the road we were in, some four or five of the party rode in between my horse and the generals and I sorter reined my horse in a little which made a little space between my self and Gen. Jackson. I should say ten yards."[85]

General James Lane was having problems at this time. Following the conversation with Jackson on the Plank Road, the brigadier had ridden to the south end of his line and straight into turmoil. A large contingent of Federals, most of them members of the 128th Pennsylvania, had somehow coiled into a position between the 33d North Carolina skirmish line and in front of the 7th North Carolina on Lane's far right.

Fighting erupted in the darkness; and just as Lane was stabilizing his line and the gunfire began to diminish, other Federals approached the area. Musketry became sharper.[86] The sound of the weapons echoed northward to the rest of the Carolina brigade crouched nervously and alone in the woods. In domino fashion, gunfire rolled up the line. Tarheels on the far right shot at something; those farther to the left shot at nothing save potential threats to their front.

It was still relatively quiet north of the Plank Road. Jackson was riding back slowly through the woods, lost in thought. He said nothing. The mounted group came opposite the Van Wert house, a shell-pocked weatherboard structure along the Plank Road (directly opposite the present-day visitors' center). The general turned Little Sorrel from west to southwest as he prepared to leave the Mountain Road for the roomier Plank Road. Kyle observed: "Just as his horses front feet had cleared the edge of the road whilste his hind feet was still on the edge of the bank," a single shot rang out to the right of the Van Wert house.[87]

Hill and his staff were seated on their horses along the Plank Road some sixty yards in front of the 18th North Carolina. This regiment, organized in July 1861 in the coastal region near Wilmington, had been with Lee's army since the Seven Days' Campaign of the previous year. Its service had been gallant, its battle conduct unimpeachable. Jackson was riding some sixty yards to the northeast of Hill's group and a little under 100 yards from the same Tarheel unit.[88] Of the nineteen Confederate horsemen in the woods north of the main road, Jackson ironically was the one farthest from Lane's brigade.

The lone crack of a musket from just across the Plank Road did more than break the silence. It triggered five or six more shots. "Suddenly," wrote Kyle, "a large volley as if from a Regiment was fired."[89] This was the 7th North Carolina on the south side of the Plank Road.

Little Sorrel became skittish and wheeled away from the gunfire. His path took Jackson toward the left of the 18th North Carolina. The general was holding his reins with his left hand while raising his right to protect his face from low-hanging limbs. Shots were ringing in all directions as nervous Confederates reacted to any sound.

Joe Morrison's horse was hit and pitched forward dead. The aide struck his head against a tree and was momentarily stunned. Then he raced toward the line of the 18th North Carolina. "Cease firing!" he yelled. "You are firing into your own men!" What the Carolinians saw were horsemen approaching menacingly from the direction of the Union lines.

"Who gave that order?" Major John D. Barry shouted to his Tarheels. "It's a lie! Pour it to them, boys!" The riders were twenty-five yards away when a blaze of fire exploded from the infantry line. The two parties disintegrated "as if stricken by lightning."[90]

Jackson barely saw the white flash of musketry when searing pain shot through both arms. Three .69-caliber bullets struck him at the same time. One splintered bone and tendons three inches below the left shoulder before passing out the arm. Another entered the left forearm an inch below the elbow and exited on the other side just above the wrist. A third ball passed through his right palm, broke two fingers, and lodged against the skin on the back of the hand.

For the first and only time, Little Sorrel bolted from the sound of gunfire. The horse dashed obliquely toward the northwest as Jackson reeled in the saddle. An oak limb struck him in the face, knocked off his cap, and all but unseated him. This impact sent Jackson almost flat on the back of his horse. It also inflicted facial lacerations that looked more serious than they were—especially in light of the other wounds.

The general somehow recovered, caught the reins in his right hand, and, with what little strength remained, tried to bring his horse under control. Jackson was too blinded by pain to know fully what was happening. Captain Wilbourn and Private Wynn had started after the general when Little Sorrel panicked. Now the two aides succeeded in getting on either side of Jackson and halting the animal momentarily.

The sudden and unexpected explosion of musketry had caused a stampede among the horsemen riding with Jackson and Hill. Mounts not struck by gunfire were racing wildly through the woods. Some were riderless, for the volleys had taken a terrible toll. Captain Keith Boswell and three couriers were dead. Hill's chief of staff, Major William H. Palmer, was wounded along with two others. Three riders were captured when their horses bore them into enemy lines. Ten of nineteen men, plus twelve of the horses, were casualties from friendly fire.[91]

Wilbourn tried to assist Jackson while Wynn held the reins of Little Sorrel. "All my wounds are by my own men," the general said in bewilderment. Jackson stared in astonishment toward Lane's brigade. "He was at a loss to understand why he was fired upon from that direction," Wilbourn noted, "and whether he would be fired at again if he approached them."[92]

Both captain and private asked Jackson if he was badly hurt. "I fear my arm is broken," he responded through clenched teeth.

"See if you can move your fingers," Wilbourn said. "If you can work your fingers, it is not broken."

Jackson looked down at his left hand. "Yes, it is broken. I cannot move my fingers."

A helpless Wilbourn then asked: "General, what can I do for you?"

"I wish you would see if it is bleeding much," Jackson said as much in perplexity as with concern.

Wilbourn dismounted and reached for Jackson's arm. "Where were you struck?" he asked.

"About halfway between the elbow and the shoulder," Jackson replied in obvious pain.[93]

The captain took the limb in both hands. "Is it very painful? Are you hurt anywhere else?"

"Yes," Jackson mumbled, "a slight wound in the right hand."

Now Wilbourn could feel the blood coursing down the left wrist into Jackson's gauntlet. Running his other hand up Jackson's rubber poncho, Wilbourn felt the unnatural lump of a broken bone. The raincoat prevented him from determining how severely the limb was bleeding. "General," he said, "I will have to cut off your sleeve before I can do anything for you."

Jackson's left arm felt as if it were on fire. His right hand throbbed from the hammer blow to the nerves of an imbedded bullet. He managed to reply: "Well, you had better take me down too." With that, he leaned toward the signal officer.[94]

Wilbourn put his arm around the general. His own left arm was still impaired from a battle wound the previous summer; Jackson's injured limb became caught between their bodies. The situation was clumsy and painful. "Hold on, Captain," Jackson cried, "you had better take me on the other side."

The staff officer gently eased Jackson into an upright position in the saddle. Then he raced around Little Sorrel to get on the right-hand side. Wynn had also dismounted and was holding Little Sorrel's reins. Jackson began leaning toward Wilbourn. "He was so helpless and weak," Wilbourn believed, "that he could not even take his feet out of the stirrups." Wilbourn held him in his arms while Wynn released the general's feet from the stirrups. The two signalmen finally got Jackson to the ground, but it required both of them to support the extremely wobbly general. Little Sorrel, meanwhile, could comprehend nothing but fear. When Wynn released the reins, the horse galloped wildly toward the enemy lines.[95]

Slowly, Wilbourn and Wynn carried Jackson away from the road. While they were walking, Wilbourn feared that the silent Jackson had fainted. Partly to determine if he was conscious, the captain said, "General, it is most remarkable that any of us escaped."

"Yes," came a quiet reply. "It is providential."[96]

The two men placed Jackson under a small tree. Wilbourn cradled his head in his lap and dispatched Wynn to find Surgeon McGuire as well as an ambulance. Do not tell any of the troops that the general is wounded, Wilbourn cautioned his assistant. After Wynn hastened away, Wilbourn sought to make Jackson as comfortable as possible.

He moved the general close to the tree trunk to give his head some elevation. Wilbourn began cutting one of the coat sleeves "so as to bandage his arm, which required great caution in the dark to avoid cutting his arm, as I had nothing but a small pen knife. . . . I took off his field glasses and haversack, containing some papers, envelopes and two religious tracts, which were in the way and put them on myself in order to preserve them."[97]

The gunfire had died down when Morrison came racing to the front. He found Jackson on the ground, Wilbourn bending over him. "Are you much hurt?" the young aide inquired in a choking voice.

Jackson was too stunned to answer coherently. "No, but I think my arm is broken." Up dashed A. P. Hill, Captain Benjamin Leigh of his staff, and several couriers. Hill jumped from the saddle. The long and bitter animosity between the two had been subsiding in recent weeks. When Hill saw the Confederate hero lying helpless on the ground, he was genuinely solicitous.

Little Powell knelt beside Jackson and said in a defenseless tone to anyone listening, "I have been trying to make the men cease firing." Then he spoke directly to the commander. "General Jackson, I am sorry to see you wounded and hope you are not hurt much."

Jackson could only reply: "My arm is broken."

"Is it painful?" Hill asked.

"Very painful."

"Are you hurt anywhere else?"

"Yes," Jackson said between clenched teeth, "a slight wound in the right hand." Hill slowly removed Jackson's blood-soaked gloves. He held one of Jackson's arms, supporting his elbow in one hand, while Wilbourn cut away the rest of the sleeve. The captain declared that he would have to rip off all of the sleeves.

Jackson answered: "That is right, cut away everything."[98]

Once all of the left sleeves were removed, Wilbourn and Hill found the limb "very much swollen" but not bleeding. The captain tied a handkerchief around the upper wound and tried to fashion a sling to support the arm. All this time, Wilbourn recalled, "Jackson laid perfectly still, did not complain at all or say anything except when spoken to."[99]

Hill rested Jackson's head on his left leg as he knelt on his right knee. Three men were trying to get bandages of sorts on Jackson. All at once, two Federal soldiers emerged from a cluster of bushes no more than five yards away. Their muskets were cocked, and they stopped menacingly to stare at the strange sight of officers kneeling over a form on the ground. A calm Hill turned to his couriers holding the horses and said quietly, "Take charge of those men." Two or three Confederates sprang forward. The enemy soldiers surrendered without a word.[100]

Jackson needed medical attention badly. Hill directed Captain Leigh to go to the rear in search of a surgeon and an ambulance. The aide had proceeded no more than 100 yards when he met General Dorsey Pender advancing down the Plank Road with his brigade. Leigh informed the brigadier of his mission. Pender replied that Assistant Surgeon Richard R. Barr was nearby. A call went forth and Barr "speedily appeared."[101]

He told Leigh that to his knowledge no ambulance was within a mile of their position. However, he did have a litter at hand and freely offered it. Leigh, Barr, two litter bearers, and James P. Smith (returning from an assignment) hastened to where Jackson lay. Barr made a quick examination, then left to secure some medical materials.

Jackson whispered to Hill: "Is that a skillful surgeon?"

Hill replied earnestly, "I don't know much about him, but he stands very high with his brigade." Then realizing the apprehension behind Jackson's question, Hill added, "He does not propose to do anything and is only here to be in readiness, in case anything should be required before Doctor McGuire arrives."[102]

That seemed to give Jackson a measure of relief. Barr soon returned with a medical tourniquet; yet when he saw that the wrappings on the arm were working satisfactorily, the surgeon did not disturb the injured limb. In the meantime, the appearance of Federal soldiers made it imperative that Confederates secure the area as quickly as possible. Hill was now in temporary command of the Second Corps by reason of seniority, and he was needed elsewhere.

Slowly, Little Powell eased his leg from beneath Jackson's head. As he rose, he told Jackson with compassion: "I will try to keep your accident from the knowledge of the troops."

"Thank you," Jackson replied. It was the last communication between the two.[103]

Morrison by then had become emotional and uneasy. Seeing his famous brother-in-law seriously wounded at the moment of great victory made it difficult for the aide to hold back tears. Morrison was also worried about the appearance of the two enemy soldiers. They might be the front of an advancing Union line.

Leaving Jackson, Morrison walked to the Plank Road some eight to ten paces away. The first thing that caught his eye was a Federal cannon being unlimbered down the road. The lieutenant rushed back to Jackson. "We must get away from here!" he exclaimed. "The Yankees are placing a battery in the road not a hundred yards from us!"[104]

In that tense atmosphere, the officers decided not to wait for an ambulance. Getting the general to safety and to proper medical treatment were the vital issues now. Someone suggested carrying Jackson in their arms. "No," he said, "I think I can walk." Slowly, painfully, with help on either side, Jackson got to his feet just as Union shells exploded in the road and among nearby woods.[105] Leigh's horse took a large wound from the shelling, forcing the captain, close to Jackson, to dismount in order to bring the mount under control. The firing stopped. Leigh moved to support Jackson, whose legs were rubbery, his thinking foggy.

Jackson put his right arm over Leigh's shoulder as the group made its way to the Plank Road. Morrison was on the other side of the general. Wilbourn was holding three horses, which he sought to keep between Jackson and a line of Hill's troops marching toward them. The concealment was not perfect. "Who is that?" men began to ask of the wounded officer being treated so carefully. "Who have you there?"

"Oh," Wilbourn answered, "it is only a friend of ours who is wounded."[106]

That did not suffice. The number of men aiding a wounded comrade, the special attention being extended, the presence of several horses with the group—all aroused suspicion and questions from passing soldiers. Jackson finally told Wilbourn: "When asked, just say it is a Confederate officer."[107]

One private managed to get close enough for a good look at the injured officer in plain dress with heavy beard and large feet. "Great God!" he shouted in an agonized wail. "That is General Jackson!" He took one more look, then turned away in silence.[108]

Jackson continued to make his way step by step up the road. "He was calm," Leigh noted, "and did not utter a groan." So far, the bleeding was minimal.[109]

Ten yards up the Plank Road, Surgeon Barr's litter team caught up with the party. Soldiers gingerly laid Jackson on the canvas stretcher. Four men then raised the litter and started obliquely across the road. Before they advanced forty yards, Federal artillery opened again with a more intense bombardment.

The first shots passed over the heads of the party; the next round was more accurate. A piece of shell struck Private James J. Johnson, 22d Virginia Battalion. He was at the left front corner of the stretcher. The bearers were carrying Jackson at shoulder height. When Johnson pitched to the ground, the litter tilted sharply downward. Jackson tumbled five feet and struck the ground heavily—in all probability on the left shoulder.

Excruciating pain shot through Jackson's body. While Morrison declared that Jackson made no sound after the fall, others heard the general groan "frequently and piteously."[110]

Federal artillery fire increased. (Powell Hill and Colonel Stapleton Crutchfield were among those wounded by the cannonade.) Smith, Morrison, and Leigh lay down as shields beside Jackson, whose head was toward the Federal lines. Once, when the general sought to rise, Smith immediately threw his body over Jackson and urged him to lie quiet or he would certainly be killed.

Morrison noted of the moment that they "could see in every side sparks flashing from the stones of the pike, and caused by the canister shot. . . . The whole atmosphere seemed filled with whistling canister and shrieking shell, tearing the trees on every side." Leigh added: "The road was perfectly swept by grape and canister. A few minutes before, it had been crowded with men and horses, and now I could see no man or beast or thing upon it but ourselves." If Hill's aide was exaggerating, it is understandable why.[111]

Soon the Union fire became elevated. The group then lifted Jackson and bore him in their arms. They left the road and entered woods. Not only was that an easier and safer route, but it would avoid soldiers catching sight of their general. Jackson became faint again. Leigh, who was carrying the litter in case it was needed, unfolded it. He called on several passing troops to serve as bearers, but all refused. Finally, in desperation, Leigh told one group the identity of the wounded officer. Every soldier jumped forward to help.

Three enlisted men and an officer placed Jackson on the litter and resumed the slow journey to the rear. The party was struggling through thick woods a few feet south of the Plank Road when, Leigh reported, one of the bearers "got his foot entangled in a grape vine and fell." Jackson again hit the ground, this time directly on the broken arm. "He must have suffered excruciating agonies" at this second fall, Leigh thought. Whatever the pain, one or both of these accidents tore the artery in the left arm and triggered heavy bleeding.[112]

As the men replaced Jackson on the litter, he uttered one long groan. Smith bent over. "General, are you hurt?" he asked. Jackson, fighting mentally to overcome physical agony, responded, "Never mind me, Lieutenant, never mind me." A moment later, Jackson mumbled something about winning the battle first and attending to the wounded later.[113]

The party was preparing to resume its torturous trek when General Dorsey Pender rode up and dismounted. "Oh, General," he said with feeling, "I hope you are not seriously wounded." Quickly turning to the urgency of the moment, Pender declared, "I will have to retire my troops to re-form them, they are so much broken by this fire."

Jackson stirred; he looked sternly at the North Carolina brigadier and exclaimed in a strong voice: "You must hold your ground, General Pender! You must hold your ground, sir!" It was Jackson's last field command.[114]

As the small group inched westward in darkness and amid the confusion of artillery fire, Jackson grew weaker. Hemorrhaging was steady; pain was almost unbearable and steadily sapping his strength as well. Several times he asked for spirits—the only known instance when Jackson requested liquor. None was available.

Litter bearers carried their patient about 400 yards to the Stony Fork Road, which snaked southward from the Plank Road. There they met Surgeon William R. Whitehead, one of several physicians who had been summoned in the first moments after Jackson's wounding.[115] Whitehead was cordially welcomed; he had with him a bottle of whiskey and a rickety ambulance. The physician administered a little whiskey mixed with water. That would help for the next stage of the journey.

The ambulance of that day had little to provide comfort. It was a crude wagon with metal-rimmed wheels and inadequate (if any) springs. A canvas top gave some protection from the weather for two soldiers stretched out on the wooden floor.

Two wounded officers were already in the ambulance when Jackson reached it. One was Colonel Crutchfield, Jackson's artillery chief, who had suffered a broken leg. The other was Major Arthur L. Rogers of the Loudoun Artillery. Rogers was serving as a volunteer aide to Crutchfield while awaiting orders to a new command. Like Jackson, he was suffering from a gunshot wound of the left arm. It was not a life-threatening injury; and on hearing of Jackson's condition, the major insisted that he take his place in the wagon.[116]

Weary soldiers carefully lifted the litter bearing Jackson and slid it into the ambulance. Morrison climbed into the vehicle to cushion the general's fractured arm. The wagon lurched forward on the Stony Fork Road. It turned northwest up the rutted Hazel Grove Road and bounced onto the Plank Road at the eastern edge of the Melzi Chancellor farm. The wagon now proceeded west—in reverse to the great assault that had swept along the road some five hours earlier.

The driver stopped the wagon at Dowdall's Tavern as passengers sought "some stimulant." There Dr. McGuire caught up with the general.[117] He had been riding behind the lines when a courier reached him with word that the general had been wounded and wanted him at once.

McGuire was on his way when he met Hotchkiss and Pendleton. They too had learned of Jackson's injuries. As the three officers were about to start forward, Wilbourn met them. The general was badly wounded, he said; Confederates were retiring from the area, and Jackson might well become a prisoner.

At the news, Pendleton fainted and fell from his horse. McGuire made a quick examination and found him unharmed. After leaving some whiskey for Hotchkiss to administer when Pendleton awakened, McGuire raced forward in search of his chief.[118] More than professional concern was involved. The surgeon wanted to help a close friend.

When McGuire reached Dowdall's Tavern, Jackson was lying on the litter by the side of the road. One or two soldiers held torches to mark the location. McGuire knelt beside him. "I hope you are not much hurt, General," he began.

Jackson answered evenly but feebly: "I am badly injured, Doctor. I fear I am dying." Jackson paused. "I am glad you have come. I think the wound in my shoulder is still bleeding."

McGuire at once discovered fresh blood. In fact, nothing about the examination was positive. "I found his clothes saturated with blood, and blood still oozing from the wound. I put my finger upon the artery above the wound & held it till lights were procured by candles . . . and then I readjusted the handkerchief which had been applied as a tourniquet, but which had slipped a little. Without this [having] been done, he would probably have died in ten minutes."

By then, Jackson was suffering fearfully. McGuire termed his condition extremely critical. His skin was clammy, his face pale, "and the thin lips so tightly compressed that the impression of his teeth could be seen through them." Still, what impressed McGuire most were Jackson's calmness, his uniform politeness, and the way "he controlled, by his iron will, all evidence of emotion."

The surgeon obtained whiskey and morphine from Surgeon in Charge John A. Straith at the Chancellor field hospital. Jackson drank the items without a word. Soldiers placed him back into the ambulance. McGuire got in front to sit near the general's head. With all in readiness, the wagon resumed its trip to the Second Corps field hospital McGuire had established. It lay almost four more miles to the west, but at least it was beyond the range of enemy artillery. Drivers used torches to light the way and avoid the worst of the ruts and mudholes. Nevertheless, the road was sufficiently chewed from troop movements to make for a rough ride. McGuire continued to keep a finger pressed above the tourniquet to prevent more bleeding.

Crutchfield was extremely sensitive to pain and cried out loudly whenever the ambulance bounced heavily or rolled suddenly to one side. McGuire had his finger on the artery in Jackson's arm to arrest hemorrhaging if it should erupt again. The whiskey and morphine had dulled Jackson's senses, but nothing of note escaped his attention. When an acquaintance saw the physician and asked who was wounded, Jackson would say, "Do not tell them it is me."[119]

Slowly, the wagon pitched and bumped past the Talley farm. At the fork of the Plank Road with the turnpike, the ambulance turned right onto the latter. At one point, Jackson reached up with his wounded hand to McGuire's head and pulled the surgeon down toward him. He asked in a low voice if Colonel Crutchfield was dangerously wounded. No, replied McGuire, the injury is more painful than dangerous. Jackson replied: "Thank you."

Presently, Crutchfield beckoned to McGuire and asked the same thing about the general. When the surgeon answered that Jackson was seriously injured, Crutchfield groaned and then screamed, "Oh my God!" Jackson had been so concerned about the colonel's condition that he interpreted the shout as one of great physical pain. The general ordered the ambulance to stop for Dr. McGuire to do something to relieve the artillerist's suffering.

Sometime after 11 P.M., the wagon reached the Wilderness Tavern, then the home of W. M. Sims. The driver turned north into a field on the edge of the Wilderness, the site of the corps hospital. Dr. Harvey Black, the surgeon in charge there, had received advance word that Jackson was on his way. Black had converted his own tent into a hospital room. A soft bed and stove with fire awaited the general.[120]

Tenderly, Jackson was wrapped in blankets and given another drink of whiskey. This seemed to rally the general, who had been undergoing a bout with chills when he reached Black's tent. McGuire and James Smith watched him closely. Midnight passed. So did 1 A.M. McGuire took the general's pulse regularly in hopes of getting a stronger beat.

Near 2 in the morning, the physician returned to the tent after a brief absence. With him were Surgeons Black, J. William Walls, and Robert T. Coleman. Black was a native of Blacksburg (the village was named for his family) and three years younger than Jackson. He officially was surgeon of the 4th Virginia, but Black served as unofficial second in command to McGuire in a number of medical responsibilities. Walls was only twenty-five, but the extremely tall physician had a year's army experience as surgeon of the 5th Virginia. During part of the recent winter encampment, he was in charge of the Guiney Station field hospital. Richard T. Coleman, a prominent Richmond physician, had been surgeon of the 21st Virginia since its organization.

At the sound of McGuire's voice, Jackson became alert. This in itself was remarkable. He had been awake for a full twenty-four hours, had directed one of the major attacks of the Civil War, had incurred three severe wounds simultaneously, and then had been transported by litter and wagon for two hours. Jackson was approaching total exhaustion. McGuire nevertheless informed him that his pulse was now hearty enough for an examination of the wounds. Chloroform would be administered to make the examination painless. Then the surgeon reached the critical part of his statement. If we find the condition such as to warrant amputation, may we proceed at once? The answer came promptly: "Yes, certainly, Doctor McGuire. Do for me whatever you think right."

Surgeon Coleman then fashioned a piece of cloth into the shape of a cup. Into it he poured less than a half-ounce of chloroform. The physician told Jackson to breathe heavily; then he held the cloth two inches from the general's nose and mouth. Jackson inhaled once, twice, a third time. A sweet, fruity odor went quickly past the general's nostrils and engulfed his senses. Consuming pain began to ease. Relaxation descended over him. Jackson tried to give thanks: "What an infinite blessing . . . blessing . . . blessing . . . "[121]

24

CROSSING THE RIVER

HUNTER HOLMES MCGUIRE was only twenty-seven years old at the time. Yet he had received a degree seven years earlier from the University of Pennsylvania, whose medical school was ranked among the top two or three in the country. Postgraduate studies and a natural flair for medicine had made McGuire one of the most promising physicians in Virginia by the outbreak of civil war. His reputation as a surgeon eclipsed his comparative youthfulness.

On Jackson's staff, he had no enemies. Hotchkiss thought McGuire possessed of "blunt humor & full of honest life." To Kyd Douglas, the Winchester physician was a man "always pleasant, ever faithful."[1]

What was most important in those first hours of May 3, 1863, was the fact that in McGuire's hands lay the fate of the critically injured, premier hero of the Southern Confederacy. Added to that heavy responsibility was the close two-year friendship between surgeon and general. Such personal issues had to be forgotten for the good of both the physician and his patient. A little past 2 A.M., with Jackson fully anaesthetized, McGuire began his examination.[2]

He first looked at the right hand. A round ball from an old smoothbore musket no longer used by Federals had entered the palm, fractured two fingers, and lodged just under the skin at the back of the hand. The surgeon extracted the bullet easily and gave it to Lieutenant Smith, who presented it later to Mrs. Jackson.

Then came a close inspection of the more seriously injured left arm. Two bullets had passed through the limb. The most serious wound, three inches below the shoulder, consisted of a broken bone and severed artery. The second bullet had pierced the outside of the forearm below the elbow, ripped through the lower arm, and passed out the opposite side above the wrist.

Each ball had done irreparable damage. There was no way to save the limb. Immediate amputation was necessary to avoid possible gangrene. The four physicians in attendance had vast experience with such surgery. That made the operation fairly routine.

Coleman administered chloroform and Black monitored the pulse; Walls stood by to control the bleeding while McGuire performed the surgery; Smith held the light above the table and did any other little chore requested of him. Working rapidly, McGuire sliced through the tendons with a scalpel and sawed the bone cleanly. He lifted the limb away as Walls sealed the blood vessels.

The operation was completed by 3 A.M. Little loss of blood had occurred because so many skilled hands were at work. McGuire finished his work by applying isinglass plaster to the two or three lacerations on Jackson's face. The general remained in deep sleep throughout the procedure.

McGuire instructed Smith to watch the patient for the remainder of the night. He was to keep him warmly wrapped; in a half-hour, he should arouse Jackson and give him coffee. Smith watched the time closely. At the thirty-minute mark, he called to the general. Jackson had been sleeping quietly, but he awoke promptly and seemed clearheaded. Smith handed him a cup of coffee, which Jackson termed good and refreshing. It was his first food in over twenty-four hours.[3]

While Jackson was drinking coffee, Lee got the first news of his wounding. Sandie Pendleton had dispatched Captain Wilbourn to army headquarters to inform the commander of the situation at the front. Lee was getting needed sleep when Wilbourn arrived, but the sound of the signal officer's voice awakened the general. He ushered Wilbourn into the tent and toward his cot. "Sit down here by me," Lee said, "and tell me all about the fight last evening." The captain gave him the general facts of the battle. At the end of his report, he said: "I am sorry to inform you that General Jackson was wounded and also General Hill." The injury to Hill was slight, but those of Jackson serious. After Wilbourn finished, Lee was silent for several moments. Then he exclaimed: "Ah, Captain, any victory is dearly bought that deprives us of the services of General Jackson even for a short time." When Wilbourn began describing the nature of the accidental wounds, Lee interrupted. "Oh, don't talk about it. Thank God, it is no worse."[4]

By then, Jackson was back asleep—but not for long. A little before 4:00 that morning, Pendleton arrived at the field hospital. He awakened McGuire. It is imperative that he see the general, Pendleton said. Hill had been wounded and had turned over command of the Second Corps to Jeb Stuart. The cavalry leader was unsure of what he should do.

McGuire at first refused to disturb Jackson. His life may depend on how quiet he remains for the next few hours, he told Pendleton. The blond adjutant remained silent for a time in deep thought. Then he looked at his comrade and close friend. "Mac, you are as well able to decide as I am about it, but the safety of the army and the success of our cause depends upon my seeing him."

The surgeon went to Jackson's tent. As he was making a quick examination, the general awoke. McGuire beckoned to Pendleton. When the faithful aide entered, Jackson said in a clear voice: "Well, Major, I am glad to see you, very glad. I thought you were killed."

Pendleton explained minutely the condition of affairs at the front, relayed Stuart's message, and asked what should be done. McGuire watched Jackson closely. "He tried to think. He contracted his brow, set his mouth, and for some moments appeared to exert every effort to concentrate his thoughts. For a moment we thought he had succeeded, for his nostril dilated, his eye flashed its old fire, and his thin lip quivered again, but it was just for a moment. Presently he relaxed again, and very feebly, and oh so sadly, he answered, 'I don't know. I can't tell. Say to General Stuart that he must do what he thinks best.'"

Jackson lapsed into silence. Pendleton saluted and hastened from the tent so that his idol could not see the tears. Outside, the adjutant wept heavily. When McGuire sought to console him, Pendleton replied, "We didn't know what he was worth, Mac, till we lost him."

It was about 9 A.M. and the sun was high when Jackson awakened again. Pain had subsided. His health and spirits were good for a man who had undergone amputation six hours earlier. He felt strong enough to take a little food. To the east, the roar of battle was quite audible as two armies resumed the struggle for control of the Wilderness. This Sunday—May 3—would be the second bloodiest day of the Civil War, ranking only behind Antietam, as North and South fought desperately in a thirteen-mile zone extending from Hazel Grove and Chancellorsville to Salem Church and Fredericksburg.

Confederates assaulted Hooker's lines with newfound inspiration. Many charged with shouts of "Remember Stonewall Jackson!" Others chanted "Revenge Jackson!" as they advanced through the thick woods.

Lee's reunited wings broke the Union position and seized the Chancellorsville crossroads. Lee was on the verge of one of the most spectacular victories of the war. Jim Lane's North Carolina brigade was especially conspicuous for gallantry that day. It lost a third of its strength in the fighting.[5]

Sometime the preceding night, Jackson had dictated a message to Lee. In typically brief phrases, Jackson congratulated Lee on the May 2 success, mentioned his wounds, and announced that command of the Second Corps had devolved on A. P. Hill. Jackson had been awake only a few minutes on the morning of the 3d when a courier appeared. He bore a short but emotional dispatch from Lee: "General: I have just received your note informing me that you were wounded. I cannot express my regret at the occurrence. Could I have directed events, I should have chosen for the good of the country to have been disabled in your stead. . . . I congratulate you upon the victory which is due to your skill and energy." When James Power Smith finished reading the message, Jackson turned his face away and murmured, "General Lee is very kind, but he should give the praise to God."[6]

The best news that morning at the corps hospital was Jackson's condition. He took nourishment with relish and was sanguine of recovery. Neither chills nor fever was present. It appeared that he was rapidly regaining some strength. This pleased the team of physicians concerned about dangers attendant to amputation.

In the middle of the morning, Jackson complained of pain in his side—presumably a result of falling from the litter. McGuire inspected the area. "I could not discover by examination any evidence of injury," he wrote. "The skin was not bruised or broken, and the lung performed, as far as I could tell, its proper function. I recommended some simple application & rub, telling him it would probably pass off soon." The pain soon abated.

When it did, the general became a field commander from a hospital bed. A rash of orders went forth. One was to Lieutenant Joseph Morrison. The aide was to go to Richmond, find Mrs. Jackson (Morrison's sister), and accompany her to camp. Other staff members were sent to assist Stuart with the Second Corps.

With battle now raging fearfully, Jackson suggested to McGuire that he return to the field and superintend the removal of the wounded. McGuire agreed as long as Smith remained at the general's side. Dr. Harvey Black was operating not more than 100 yards away, McGuire added, and would be available at once if needed.

Chaplain Lacy arrived for a visit. When he saw the stump where Jackson's arm had been, he wailed, "Oh, General, what a calamity!" and began weeping. Jackson quickly consoled the cleric. "You find me severely wounded, but not unhappy or depressed. I believe that it has been done according to the will of God, and I acquiesce entirely in His holy will. It may seem strange, but you never saw me more perfectly contented than I am today, for I am sure that my Heavenly Father designs this affliction for my good." Jackson told Lacy of one of his falls from the litter. "I thought . . . that I would die upon the field, and I gave myself up into the hands of my heavenly father without a fear. I was in the possession of perfect peace." He also expressed strong feelings about the previous day's contest. "Our movement on yesterday was a great success. I think it was the most successful movement of my life, but I expected to receive far more credit for it than I deserve." He then explained, "I simply took advantage of circumstances, as they were presented to me in the providence of God."[7]

The general dozed intermittently after Lacy's departure. When awake, he chatted with the attentive Smith about a variety of subjects. Jackson at one point looked up at the youthful aide, smiled, and asked, "Can you tell me where the Bible gives generals a model for their official reports of battles?" Smith laughed; he admitted to never having thought of Holy Scriptures as such a source. "Nevertheless," Jackson said in professorial tones, "there are such, and excellent models too. Look, for instance, at the narrative of Joshua's battles with the Amalekites. There you have one. It has clearness, brevity, modesty; and it traces the victory to the right source, the blessing of God."[8]

Kyd Douglas claimed to have spent an hour with Jackson that evening. The statement is untrue. Douglas came to the field hospital late in the morning and gave Smith an update on the action at Chancellorsville. Smith then relayed the news to the general. Jackson's attendant stressed the bravery of the Stonewall Brigade—how it charged with shouts of "Remember Jackson!" and of the role it played in helping to break the Union line. Jackson listened intently, his eyes brimming with tears. When Smith paused, the general said: "It was just like them to do so, just like them. They are a noble body of men." Smith felt duty bound to convey the news that the brigade commander and Jackson's longtime friend, General Frank Paxton, had been killed early in the action. "Paxton? Paxton?" Jackson asked in disbelief. Smith nodded. The general turned his face to the tent wall, closed his eyes, and remained in that position for several minutes.[9]

Late that Sunday afternoon, Lee sent another message to Jackson. The situation along the front was unstable; Federal troops might swing around Lee's flank and threaten the Wilderness Tavern area. Jackson must be moved to a safer place as quickly as possible. McGuire could not be spared, but an adequate medical team would go with Jackson. Lee suggested Guiney Station. It was the current railhead of the Richmond, Fredericksburg, and Potomac Railroad. From there, Jackson could be moved with maximum speed if necessary.

At first, Jackson resisted. He did not wish to be moved if, in Dr. McGuire's opinion, it would endanger his condition. He had no objection to remaining hospitalized in a tent; in fact, he would prefer it so long as Mrs. Jackson could find quarters in a nearby home. "If the enemy does come," Jackson concluded, "I am not afraid of them. I have always been kind to their wounded, and I am sure they will be kind to me."[10]

McGuire did not think a transfer would harm the general. Jackson, who had understood the intent behind Lee's directive, thereupon accepted it. He was familiar with Fairfield, the estate of Mr. and Mrs. Thomas Coleman Chandler. They had treated him hospitably back in December by offering him their home as a headquarters. Jackson regarded Mr. Chandler as "a Christian gentleman."[11] The mansion was only a short distance north of Guiney Station along the RF&P Railroad.

Jackson's initial hope was to rest at Fairfield for a day or two, take a train southward to Ashland near the junction of the RF&P with the Virginia Central line, and then proceed to his beloved Lexington. He did not want the bustle of Richmond hospitals. In the quietness of his valley home, he believed, "the pure mountain air would soon heal his wounds" and reinvigorate his body.[12]

Around 8 P.M., McGuire returned from the front, weary but anxious to see his principal patient. The pain in Jackson's side was gone, and McGuire thought he was doing remarkably well. Jackson quizzed the surgeon minutely about the day's battle. McGuire noted: "His face would light up with enthusiasm and interest when I told him how this brigade acted, and that officer displayed conspicuous courage, and his head gave a peculiar shake from side to side, as he uttered his usual 'good, good' with unwonted energy when I spoke of the Stonewall Brigade."

Jackson expressed confidence that "the men of that command will be proud one day to say to their children: 'I was one of the Stonewall Brigade.' I have no right to the name 'Stonewall.' It belongs to the brigade and not at all to me."

Plans were made for Jackson's trip. The general stated that he did not want McGuire to accompany him because it was unfair for a wounded general to take his best surgeon away from the army. Secretly, Jackson badly desired McGuire's calm hand with him yet in good conscience could not ask for it. Lee resolved the matter late that night. Sedgwick's wing of the Union army was advancing west from Fredericksburg. Jackson was in danger. Lee ordered McGuire to go with the general and guard him. "General Lee has always been very kind to me, very kind," Jackson said humbly, "and I thank him."[13] That night Jackson slept comfortably and soundly.

Monday, May 4, was a hot day, the sun baking down from a cloudless sky until late afternoon. Jackson awoke refreshed and in "admirable condition." He asked McGuire how long it would be before he could return to command. He received no definite answer: McGuire was too busy with final arrangements for the trip to engage in speculations.

A twenty-seven-mile journey lay ahead. It would take all day. The core of the staff would go. McGuire was in overall charge of the trip and would sit alongside the ambulance driver. Hotchkiss, who had selected the route, would lead the party. Smith and Lacy were to ride in the ambulance with the general. Jim Lewis had the assignment of bringing up the rear with horses, headquarters supplies, and Jackson's personal belongings.

McGuire had mattresses placed in the ambulance bed. The wounded Stapleton

Crutchfield would ride with Jackson. By 6 A.M., all was in readiness. With well wishes from a crowd of hospital personnel and soldiers, the two-horse wagon moved onto the Orange Turnpike for what would be a fourteen-hour journey. Hotchkiss had carefully selected the shortest and safest route. The party would travel south and east—via Todd's Tavern to Spotsylvania Court House, thence along the south bank of the Po River to Guiney Station.

Progress was slow in deference to the patients. Hotchkiss led the way while a small detail of pioneers cleared boulders and logs from the roads. The ambulance soon began encountering army teamsters carrying supplies to the battle front. The wagon drivers, "usually a rude and uncouth race" to Dabney, were at first reluctant to give way to a lone vehicle heading in the opposite direction. Yet when told who was in the ambulance, the drivers quickly pulled out of the way—and removed their hats as the wagon passed. Many shouted such thoughts as: "I wish it was me, sir!"[14]

That was not all McGuire saw. "At Spotsylvania and along the whole route, men and women rushed to the ambulance, bringing all the food delicacies they had, and with tearful eyes blessed him & prayed for his recovery."

Jackson was bright and talkative for much of the journey. Lacy noted that "he made no complaints and maintained his unfailing courtesy in answer to all inquiries, saying he felt far more comfortable than he had a right to expect." Throughout the morning, Jackson appeared to McGuire to be "cheerful, and disposed to converse on common subjects. All this promised well for his case."[15]

In a lengthy conversation with McGuire, Jackson said that his objective in the recent battle was to isolate the enemy from United States Ford. He planned to take a position between Hooker and the river, thus forcing the Federals to attack him. Jackson then smiled slightly before commenting: "My men sometimes fail to drive the enemy from a position. They always fail to drive us away."

Praise of General Robert Rodes came next. Jackson paid the VMI alumnus the highest compliment: "He is a soldier." The general also had kind words for Colonel Edward Willis, who had led the 12th Georgia in Rodes's assault line. (Jackson had never forgotten that particular regiment since its officers fled from Front Royal in the Valley Campaign.) Bravery by such executives led Jackson to declare: "Our government should promote men on the field, and at once for gallantry, and not delay it so long. Promotions made at such time would be the greatest incentives to gallantry in others." He also remembered with affection and sadness two friends who had given their lives in the battle: General Frank Paxton and Captain Keith Boswell.

Mile after mile the ambulance bumped and pitched. The temperature climbed uncomfortably during the day; so did the humidity. A brief but noisy thunderstorm broke late in the afternoon. By then, the jolting ride had begun to tell on Jackson. The stump was not bothering him. It was the pain in his side plus a developing nausea.

Ever a believer in hydrotherapy, Jackson asked that a wet towel be placed on his stomach. McGuire saw nothing wrong in employing an old remedy. The wagon stopped at a spring, where cloths were dipped in water. For the remainder of the journey, Jackson "expressed great relief" from the wet-towel treatment.

Around 4:00 that afternoon, a courier galloped to a halt at the front porch of Fairfield. The Chandler home, like other residences in the area, had become a hospital for wounded and sick officers from the Chancellorsville Campaign. Soldiers occupied the entire second floor. Mrs. Mary Chandler was sitting wearily on the porch with her eleven-year-old daughter Lucy when the rider appeared. General Jackson has been badly wounded, the man announced. He is a few miles away in an ambulance and is being brought to their home. The forty-six-year-old mistress of the house bounded from her chair. The family would do everything it could for the general, she promised.

With two black servants, Mammy Phyllis and Aunt Judy, Mary Chandler swiftly converted the first-floor parlor into a bedroom. The women were just completing arrangements when Chaplain Lacy arrived. He confirmed that the general was seriously injured. The ambulance was now two miles away. Lacy had to raise his voice to be heard above the thumping and clamor of upstairs. The house is too noisy, he declared. Surgeon McGuire insisted that Jackson be kept quiet.[16]

Mary Chandler reassured the minister that she personally would see to it that the home remained silent. Lacy knew the impossibility of that. Then, as he looked out the parlor window, he saw in the side yard a little frame house that served as an office. He asked if it was occupied. Told that it was not, Lacy accompanied Mrs. Chandler on an inspection of the newly whitewashed cottage and pronounced it as the place where the general would go.

Lacy departed to rejoin the ambulance. Mary Chandler and the two servants scurried to turn the white house into a hospital. Not enough time existed to find a better bed, so what was already there—"a bedstead of the old-fashioned kind that you wind up with a rope," Lucy Chandler called it—was tidied for use. Unneeded furnishings gave way to extra tables and lanterns.[17]

Rain was falling again, and more seemed on the way. A slight chill was in the air. Mrs. Chandler built a fire in the small fireplace. She returned to the mansion and went upstairs. It was 8 P.M. Peering out the window in the gathering darkness, Mary Chandler saw an ambulance crossing the railroad and approaching the house through the rain. A cavalry escort left no doubt who was inside the vehicle.

Separating the office building from the yard of the home was a wooden pale fence. Thomas Chandler, a courtly and dignified planter in his mid-sixties, was waiting at the gate to the fence when the ambulance stopped. He welcomed Jackson but expressed regrets at the circumstances. Jackson thanked him and said in a fatigued voice: "I am sorry I cannot shake hands with you, but one arm is gone and my right hand is wounded."

Bearers carried the general on a litter into the house and placed him in the double rope-trellis bed with headboard, acorn posts at the corners, and pine runners. Beyond the foot of the bed, on the mantlepiece above the fireplace, a Gothic-arched Ingraham clock ticked loudly. Jackson was unconcerned about furnishings. He eagerly ate some bread, drank a little tea, and soon drifted into a sound sleep.

McGuire's first orders after arrival were clear and precise: no one except himself, Smith, Morrison, Lacy, and Jim Lewis was to enter the room without express permission. The surgeon's anxiety remained so real that he sat up the whole night to monitor Jackson's condition.[18]

The general's new residence was strikingly similar to the Moss Neck office where he had spent the winter. It was a cozy, masculine-looking place that faced the side of the Chandler home. Two large oak trees stood in front of the porch on the low-frame structure. The single doorway led into an anteroom. Behind it were two larger rooms. On the second floor, a half-story above, were two small rooms with very low ceilings.

McGuire, Smith, and Morrison occupied the upper level. Jim Lewis took the little downstairs room adjacent to the general's. Jackson was in the most comfortable quarters in the office. It was on the west side of the house, with a window looking out on the railroad 100 yards away. In prewar days, ninety slaves had worked the 1200 acres of the Chandler plantation. By the spring of 1863, war had disrupted agricultural production and reduced the estate to a memory of past glory.

On a Tuesday morning cool from the previous night's rain, Jackson awakened in good condition. He was doing "remarkably well," McGuire continued to think. The stump was closing and "covered with healthy granulation." The wound in the hand was draining and giving Jackson some pain. McGuire applied a splint to stabilize the member. "Simple lint and water dressings" were used on the wounds.

Jackson was pleased at his improvement. He ate a hearty breakfast and was so cheerful that he asked to see his staff and other friends. McGuire refused to admit so much company. Jackson's spirits remained high. That morning he began a conversation with Smith about his injuries. "Many would regard them as a great misfortune," the general said. "I regard them as one of the blessings of my life."

Smith, who aspired to the Presbyterian ministry, replied by quoting Jackson's favorite verse of scripture: "All things work together for good to them that love God."

"Yes!" Jackson responded. "That's it! That's it!"[19]

Chaplain Lacy visited the general around 10 A.M. to conduct a brief prayer service. Jackson so welcomed this bedside worship that he asked the cleric to come every morning at the same hour for Psalms, portions of scripture, and prayers. However, Jackson warned, Lacy would not be able to accompany him to his next resting place. "It would be setting an example of self-gratification to the troops. You had better stay at your post of duty. I have always tried to set the troops a good example."[20]

Before departing, Lacy told Jackson of reports that Hooker's force was entrenching between Chancellorsville and the Rappahannock River. "That is bad, very bad," Jackson answered. He had planned to do the same thing. The Confederate army had failed to drive the enemy as strongly as it should have.

Jackson then took a nap. Dreams carried him momentarily to the battlefield. Suddenly he shouted, "Major Pendleton, send in and see if there is higher ground back of Chancellorsville!"[21]

Late that Tuesday, Joseph Morrison finally reached his sister in Richmond. The young aide and Colonel "Chester" French of Governor Letcher's staff had left Chancellorsville together for the capital. Morrison was to bring Anna Jackson to her husband while French made arrangements for transferring the general to Richmond if the situation warranted it. General George Stoneman's Union cavalry had struck the RF&P Railroad and were still roaming between Guiney Station and Richmond.

After reaching Ashland by train, the two Confederate officers hid in woods for a time. Morrison barely escaped capture at one point. Eventually, they made their way on horseback to the capital. It was past sundown on May 5 when an extremely fearful Anna Jackson suddenly saw her brother appear.[22]

Following her departure from Jackson in late April, Anna had journeyed as far as Richmond. She took quarters in the governor's mansion with Mrs. Letcher for a day or so. Then she accepted an invitation of hospitality from her good friends, Mrs. Susan Hoge and Mrs. Elizabeth Brown. The Reverend William Brown was the uncle of Robert L. Dabney; his wife, Elizabeth, was the sister of James Power Smith. They were living in the Moses D. Hoge home adjacent to the Second Presbyterian Church on Fifth Street.

A decade earlier, Brown and Hoge had founded the religious newspaper *The Central Presbyterian*. In the spring of 1863, Dr. Hoge was in Europe searching for Bibles to distribute to Confederate soldiers. The Browns had no children; the Hoges had many. Hence, Elizabeth Brown was helping Susan Hoge with housekeeping chores while her husband performed clerical duties for Dr. Hoge. Anna felt right at home in a manse crowded with people.

On Sunday morning, after the family had completed private worship service in the Hoge parlor, Dr. Brown entered the room with an expression that portended bad news. He informed Anna that Jackson had been wounded slightly. The next morning the report was that the general had been severely injured. No details were available. Anna wished to go at once to her husband. It was too dangerous: Federal raiding parties were still north of Richmond.

Her apprehension mounted. Finally, on Tuesday night, her brother Joseph arrived at the Hoge residence. From him Anna learned of the amputation. Thereafter, she fidgeted with impatience while waiting for the RF&P line to reopen. She was hardly alone in her concern. The head of the Bureau of War wrote in his diary: "The country is deeply anxious for Jackson's fate."23

A cold drenching rain dripped from the office building at Fairfield on Wednesday. Jackson seemed improved. He spent this day as he had the previous one: discussing theology with Smith and Lacy. Weariness came over him at noon. He napped through most of the afternoon. Other than sending Jim Lewis to the Chandler home for an occasional glass of milk, Jackson displayed no appetite. That was not deemed important at the moment.

Vital signs looked good into Wednesday night. McGuire felt safe in leaving Jackson in the affectionate care of Jim Lewis. The surgeon had been without rest for the better part of two days. Lewis sat quietly and watched Jackson fall asleep. Lacy joined the servant in the evening and spent the night. McGuire stretched out on the sofa in the adjoining room.

Around 1 A.M. on Thursday, May 7, Jackson awakened in discomfort. He was feverish and nauseated; intense pain coursed through his left side. Moans brought Lewis and Lacy to the bedside. Get a wet towel, Jackson said, and bathe my side. That will surely help.

Both servant and chaplain hesitated. Shouldn't Dr. McGuire be summoned? Let him sleep, Jackson replied. He needs rest. Water treatment will make everything better.

Lewis got some towels, soaked one in spring water, and applied it to Jackson's left side. This time the old cure did not work. Paroxysms in the side grew worse. Jackson battled nausea and stabs of pain for three more hours. By dawn, every breath was a piercing sensation in his side. Awaken Dr. McGuire, he told Jim Lewis. The servant went next door and nudged the surgeon. McGuire came from a deep sleep to hear Lewis saying, "The General wants you."

McGuire bounded into Jackson's room, brushing away the dullness of sleep. "Upon turning down the [bed]clothes, to examine his side," McGuire commented, "I found the bed beneath him wet." He then learned of the unauthorized use of water-soaked towels. "I reproved Mr. Lacy harshly for doing any thing of the sort without first consulting me."[24]

He turned to the more important matter of examining Jackson. McGuire found the general breathing heavily and occasionally gasping. In addition to the discomfort in his side, Jackson also had a quickened pulse. The tall, young surgeon stood up and stared for a moment out the window. He was convinced that dreaded pneumonia had developed.

There would be no transfer of Jackson to Ashland or to Lexington. No return to duty with the Second Corps lay in the immediate future. Inside a small frame house beside the railroad track in Caroline County, a battle for life had begun.

McGuire did all that medical knowledge of that age prescribed for pneumonia. He drew blood from Jackson's chest, applied mustard plasters, wrapped Jackson in blankets, and began regular doses of laudanum (a mixture of opium and whiskey). The drug made Jackson insensitive to pain, but repeated doses also put him in a stupor from which he never fully recovered. On that Thursday, the strong-willed, self-assured leader of men ceased to exist. Jackson wandered in and out of consciousness thereafter. Often he seemed to be giving orders at the head of his corps. An occasional muttering, a piece of a sentence, sounds either barely coherent or undecipherable, marked much of his speech.

Surgeon McGuire needed help. He dispatched Lacy to Lee's headquarters to summon one of Jackson's prewar physicians to Guiney Station. Samuel B. Morrison was a native of Rockbridge County, a kinsman of Anna's, graduate of Washington College, and classmate in medical school of Hunter McGuire. Morrison had entered Confederate service as surgeon of the 58th Virginia. He had amputated the leg of General Richard Ewell following Jackson's 1862 attacks at Groveton. When McGuire summoned him to Guiney Station, the thirty-four-year-old Morrison was chief surgeon of Early's division.[25]

While in the act of securing Morrison, Lacy stopped by Lee's tent to inform him that Jackson's condition had worsened. Lee had just won the most spectacular victory of his military career, and he freely acknowledged that the smashing success at Chancellorsville had been achieved in the main by Jackson's sudden and overwhelming flank attack. The commander expressed hope that God would effect Jackson's recovery.

As Lacy prepared to leave, an obviously concerned Lee said: "Give General Jackson my affectionate regards, and say to him: he has lost his left arm but I my right arm. Tell him to get well and come back to me as soon as he can."[26]

Headquarters was not too far from Guiney Station. Hooker and the Union army no longer posed a danger. Lee could have visited Jackson, but he did not. His most frequently quoted biographer claimed that Lee never went to Fairfield "both because he could not trust his emotions and because there was no one in whose hands he would feel safe in leaving the army."[27]

The second reason sounds padded. The first has validity. Lee always sought to avoid personal confrontations. Seeing the critically ill Jackson would have been an emotional challenge. Lee did not want to be seen giving way to his feelings, so he did the only thing he could do: pray for his great lieutenant.[28]

Anna reached Jackson at noon. When the RF&P Railroad was reopened that morning, she was on the first northbound train. Joseph Morrison was with her, along with the baby and a nurse, Aunt Hetty. Smith met the train at Guiney Station. In answer to Anna's first inquiry, he replied that the general was doing "pretty well." Anna was momentarily faint. "From his tone and manners," she wrote of Smith, "I knew something was wrong, and my heart sank like lead."[29]

The little group proceeded quickly to Fairfield. Yet Anna had to sit on the porch while surgeons dressed Jackson's wounds. As she waited, Anna watched horrified as nearby soldiers who appeared at first to be digging a grave actually were exhuming a corpse. The shock was almost overwhelming when Anna learned that the body was that of their old Lexington friend, Frank Paxton.

A little earlier, Jackson had requested a glass of lemonade. Someone asked Anna to make it—largely to keep her occupied while she waited to see her husband. In the trauma of those first moments at Fairfield, she could hardly be blamed for putting too much sugar in the glass. Smith carried the beverage to Jackson. The general took a sip, then said: "You did not mix this. This is too sweet. Take it back."[30]

In a moment, he sensed that another person was in the room. Jackson opened his eyes. There, white-faced but composed, stood his beloved Anna. He stirred to greet her, but strength was not there. When she leaned over and kissed him, Jackson smiled and managed to say: "I am very glad to see you looking so bright." Then he slipped back into unconsciousness.[31]

Anna had maintained a brave front, though the first sight of her husband had broken her heart. Eight days earlier, he had been so healthy and handsome. Now she saw him with an arm missing, hand bandaged, eyes half-closed and sunken, with pneumonia flushing his cheeks and impairing his breathing. The sight "wrung my soul with such grief and anguish as it had never before experienced," she declared. "He looked like a dying man."[32]

Just as she was viewing him with deep sadness, Jackson reawakened. He looked at Anna and said tenderly: "My darling, you must cheer up and not wear a long face. I love cheerfulness and brightness in a sickroom." For the most part, she thenceforth displayed a happy countenance in his presence. The tears came when she left the room.[33]

Mary Chandler quietly prepared the downstairs parlor as living quarters for Anna, Julia, and Aunt Hetty. The rest of the day, Anna wrote, "I never left him except to go to my baby." Jackson emerged from a stupor at one point in the evening. He looked at Anna with joy momentarily covering the pain-lined face. "You are one of the most precious little wives in the world," he murmured.[34]

Lacy returned with Surgeon Morrison late in the afternoon. As the Rockbridge County physician approached the bed, Jackson raised his right arm and remarked to Anna, "There is an old familiar face." Morrison smiled at the word "old," for he was actually five years younger than the general. He exchanged brief pleasantries with Anna, then began studying Jackson with a professional eye. The heavy breathing and the persistent pain in the side gave him the most apprehension. Morrison's initial impression was that Jackson was suffering from extreme prostration rather than pneumonia.[35]

The Rockbridge physician then conferred with McGuire over the situation. They were doing everything medically possible for the patient. They agreed that Anna needed a companion for herself and Julia. When they raised the question, Anna thought for a moment and suggested Susan Hoge. The two surgeons also wanted an expert opinion in the case. Dr. David Tucker of Richmond was the leading authority in Virginia on pneumonia. The decision was made to summon Tucker; he could accompany Mrs. Hoge to Guiney Station. Lieutenant Smith departed at once to make the arrangements.

Rain was still falling at the end of the day. McGuire and Morrison felt that Jackson seemed to be holding his own against the pulmonary disease. (Actually, the "stable" condition was probably the result of mind-dulling opiates Jackson was receiving on a regular basis rather than any newfound resistance.) The general slept little that night. When he was unconscious, spells of delirium broke the rest. "A. P. Hill, prepare for action!" he shouted on one occasion. "Pass the infantry to the front!" he commanded at another time. Twice he said in a calmer voice, "Tell Major Hawks to send forward provisions for the troops." Muttering and disjointed orders continued spasmodically through the night.[36]

Dawn on Friday found Jackson appearing more comfortable and more rational. He "felt better" and believed he "would get well." McGuire knew otherwise. Some restlessness was present, and the painful breathing had not improved. Delirium had passed only for the moment. Jackson said little. When Anna sought to draw him into a conversation, he stopped her. The doctor had advised him not to talk. Then he added, "My darling, you are very much loved."[37]

At McGuire's request, Surgeons Robert J. Breckinridge and J. Philip Smith joined the medical team that morning.[38] All four examined Jackson carefully. The wounds were suppurating, but not heavily. Healing seemed natural. The pain in the side had abated somewhat. Yet the labored breathing told of waning strength.

Jackson was not alarmed. Faith was his shield. "These wounds were given to me for some wise and good purpose," he told McGuire, "and I would not part with them if I could. Some would consider them a misfortune, but I do not."

When Anna visited him later in the morning, she asked if he would like to see his daughter. Jackson declined: he would prefer to wait until he felt better. Anna then expressed fear that his illness was terminal. Jackson responded in matter-of-fact tones: "I do not believe I shall die at this time. I am persuaded the Almighty has yet a work for me to perform. I am not afraid to die. I am willing to abide [by] the will of my Heavenly Father."[39]

He noticed a downcast and helpless look on Anna's face. Jackson said: "I know you would gladly give your life for me, but I am perfectly resigned. Do not be sad. I hope I may yet recover. Pray for me, but always remember in your prayers to use the petition, 'Thy will be done.'"[40]

Jackson had no idea how many thousands of people were in fact praying for him. With the conclusion of the fighting at Chancellorsville, all attention in the eastern portion of the Confederacy turned to the man lying in an outbuilding at Guiney Station. A Richmond newspaper carried a front-page story of Jackson's wounding. The editor expressed optimism that Jackson would soon return to the head of his Second Corps. "General Jackson has done the duty of a great soldier in the field. There is no honor which his countrymen can confer too high to attest their gratitude and attachment." A young Richmond girl later recalled that daily "we anxiously inquired after the condition of his wounds. Anon we would hear, 'He is better—his wounds, though serious, are not necessarily fatal,' and buoyed up with the thought 'he cannot die; he is an immortal reality,' we prayed for his recovery. . . . We hoped on until hope was against hope."[41]

That night delirious spells resumed. When awake, Jackson seemed to recognize anyone who entered the room; he understood everything spoken to him. However, all conversation required exertion. He wanted rest that seemed to elude him. Dr. Morrison pulled a chair to the bedside to watch his patient through the night. At one point, the surgeon roused Jackson for a dose of medicine. "Will you take this, General?" he gently asked. Jackson opened his eyes, looked steadily at Morrison, and replied, "Do your duty." He was silent for a moment, then repeated, "Do your duty."[42]

Little sleep came to Jackson the remainder of the night. A bright sunrise on May 9 found him restless and uncomfortable. Dr. Tucker arrived that morning from Richmond and confirmed the diagnosis. Eight physicians were or had been involved with the case. "All that human skill could devise was done to stay the hand of death," McGuire declared.

Fever and labored breathing marked the morning hours. While Anna was giving him a sponge bath, Jackson opened his eyes. He saw tears on her cheeks. The surgeons had informed her that Jackson could not recover. Jackson shook his head and, in a weak but reproving voice, said: "Anna, none of that, none of that." She proposed to read him some Psalms. Jackson answered that he was suffering too much to absorb the messages. Then he caught himself. "Yes, we must never refuse that. Get the Bible and read them." Young Jimmie Smith was convinced that the Word of God was therapy to Jackson. At noon, Smith wrote his sister: "He had been sinking during the morning but is doing better now, the doctors think."[43]

Anna felt obliged to inform Jackson of the hopelessness of his case. McGuire heard her message as he was leaving the room. Jackson did not want to believe it. "Let us ask Doctor McGuire what he says about it," Jackson commented weakly. The young surgeon replied that he was compelled to conclude that recovery seemed out of the question. Jackson declared: "If it is the will of my Heavenly Father, I am perfectly satisfied."[44]

Early in the afternoon, he awakened to find several surgeons standing by the bed. Jackson looked at McGuire. "I see from the number of physicians that you think my condition dangerous, but I thank God, if it is His will, that I am ready to go. I am not afraid to die."[45]

He then asked to see Chaplain Lacy. The doctors and Anna tried to dissuade him so as to conserve his breath. Jackson insisted. He needed to see the chaplain; it was important. Lacy appeared shortly. Jackson began an earnest conversation on the need to promote better observance of the Sabbath in the army. With assurances from the minister that he was doing everything he could, Jackson seemed relieved. The chaplain then read a chapter from the Bible and offered prayer. As he rose to leave, Lacy offered to come to the room for worship service the next day. No, said Jackson emphatically. The minister was needed with the Second Corps for his usual preaching to the soldiers.[46]

That night the general's sufferings increased. He asked Anna to sing to him. Spying Lieutenant Joseph Morrison also in the room, Jackson invited him to join his sister. Sing the most spiritual pieces you can find, he said. Both Anna and Joseph were under tremendous emotional oppression. Somehow the human spirit was firm. The wife and brother-in-law began with one of Jackson's favorite tunes, "Harwell":

> King of glory! reign forever—
> Thine an everlasting crown;
> Nothing, from thy love, shall sever
> Those whom thou hast made thine own;
> Happy objects of thy grace,
> Destined to behold thy face.
> Hallelujah, Hallelujah, Hallelujah!

The brother-sister duet sang two or three more hymns dear to Jackson. Then they concluded with Isaac Watts's fervent plea, based on Psalm 51:

> Show pity, Lord; O Lord, forgive;
> Let a repenting rebel live;
> Are not thy mercies large and free?
> May not a sinner trust in thee?

Jackson was too uncomfortable to enjoy the music fully. Before seeking sleep, he told Dr. Morrison: "I think I shall be better before morning."[47]

It was a futile wish. Jackson spent the night in feverish tossing, losing ground by the hour. Morrison and other attendants sponged his brow with water. Whenever one would pause, Jackson looked up with glassy eyes and, "by some gesture or sign, begged them to continue." Once during the night, a physician sought to get him to drink a little brandy. Jackson took a sip and turned his head. "It tastes like fire, and cannot do me any good."[48]

By daylight on Sunday, May 10, the worst possible symptom was visible: exhaustion. The great warrior simply had no strength left.

It was a bright, still morning. Doctors McGuire and Morrison examined Jackson early and saw that the end was near. One of them informed Anna.[49] She replied that the general must be told. Several times in the past, he had said that if it was God's will, he hoped to have a few hours' notice of impending death. Mustering all her courage, Anna entered the room as the morning sun grew brighter.

She sat down beside the bed and gently called to Jackson. His eyes opened; he looked at her but seemed incapable of speech. He did not hear Anna as she said in an even voice, "Do you know the doctors say you must very soon be in Heaven?" Jackson was in a mental fog. There was so much he felt he needed to do at the time . . . so many details to address . . . so many things he must remember. . . . He stared blankly at his wife until she repeated the statement. Then he began to understand as she added, "Do you not feel willing to acquiesce in God's allotment, if He wills you to go today?"

Finally, and with difficulty, Jackson replied, "I prefer it." Then, as if fearing that he had not been heard, he said in a louder voice, "I prefer it."[50]

Anna, fighting tears, smiled. "Well, before this day closes, you will be with the blessed Saviour in His glory." Jackson promptly answered: "I will be an infinite gainer to be translated." Asked whether God's presence was with him, Jackson said: "Yes."[51]

While Anna continued talking to him, he slipped off again into sleep. She sought to get his last wishes about several matters. The general's muttering told her that he was somewhere with his troops. She left the room when McGuire and Morrison returned to examine him again. The physicians did not dress the wounds. No reason existed to do so.

Around 11:00 that morning, Anna returned. She knelt beside the bed. Her voice brought Jackson to consciousness. Anna was telling him again that before the sun set, he would be in paradise. The general was not yet willing to surrender. "Oh, no! You are frightened, my child. Death is not so near. I may yet get well." With that, Anna's fortitude collapsed. She buried her head in the bed coverings and, with heavy sobs, told her husband there was no hope for recovery. Jackson lay still, as if trying to comprehend the meaning of Anna's words. Then he called for Dr. McGuire, who had been standing in the anteroom. He was beside the bed within seconds. "Doctor," Jackson said in a surprisingly strong voice, "Anna informs me that you have told her I am to die today. Is it so?" McGuire replied as gently as he could that the surgeons could do nothing more for him. Jackson stared blankly at the doctor for a moment; then his eyes wandered toward the ceiling. Another period of silence followed before he said: "Very good, very good. It is all right."[52]

He turned to his sobbing wife half-lying on the bed. Jackson wanted to console her; there was much to say. Yet his mind seemed to malfunction, and he was too weak to talk at any length.

After awhile, Anna regained her composure. What did he desire for the baby and herself? Should she return to her father's home near Charlotte? Jackson was slipping back into unconsciousness. He managed to say, "You have a kind and good father, but there is no one so kind and good as your Heavenly Father."[53]

More matters had to be settled. Anna forced the conversation. Where did he wish to be buried? Jackson mumbled: "Charlotte . . . Charlottesville . . . " He was becoming delirious again. Anna tried to prompt him. Would he like to be buried in Lexington? "Yes," he answered, "in Lexington, in my own plot."

It was the custom of that day to bring a dying person's children to him near the end. Mrs. Hoge, carrying Julia, and Aunt Hetty came into the room. A bright smile illuminated Jackson's face at the sight of the child. "Little darling! Sweet one!" he exclaimed. The baby cooed in response. Jackson lifted his splinted hand and gently caressed Julia's head while purring: "Little comforter, little comforter." Then, Anna noted, he "closed his eyes as if committing her to God."[54]

Deep but brief sleep ensued. When Jackson awakened, Major Sandie Pendleton stood by his bed. The youthful adjutant could barely control his emotions. Jackson greeted him "with his unfailing courtesy." Having forgotten his earlier orders to Lacy, Jackson asked who was preaching that morning at army headquarters. Mr. Lacy, the aide replied. Then, in a trembling voice, Pendleton added, "The whole army is praying for you, General."

Jackson responded: "Thank God. They are very kind." Silence filled the room save for the ticking of the clock on the mantlepiece. Then Jackson spoke again. "It is the Lord's day. My wish is fulfilled. I have always desired to die on Sunday."[55]

Pendleton walked outside. His body shook with sobs. Everyone in the room was now in tears. Jim Lewis was inconsolable. Anna cried softly.

Jackson would have been pleased to know what was taking place at army headquarters that hour. Some 1800 soldiers had gathered to participate in Lacy's worship service. Lee arrived early to inquire about his lieutenant. The chaplain told him that the case appeared hopeless. "Surely General Jackson must recover," an agonized Lee told Lacy. "God will not take him from us, now that we need him so much."[56]

Lacy preached that morning from the text, "All things work together for good to them that love God." One Confederate soldier was heard to say, "Well, boys, I hardly know that I ever really prayed before, but I did pray today for God to spare the life of our beloved commander, for our good and the good of the country."[57]

The service ended on a solemn note. Afterwards, Lee expressed his belief that his prayers for Jackson would be answered. "When you return," he told Lacy, "I trust you will find him better. When a suitable occasion offers, tell him that I prayed for him last night as I never prayed, I believe, for myself." Lee could say no more. The army commander, Lacy noted, "turned away in overpowering emotion."[58]

By noon, a large crowd of soldiers and civilians had gravitated to the Chandler yard.[59] They stood silently—some prayerful, some disbelieving, all whispering when talk was necessary. Inside the small white building, McGuire tried to ease Jackson's final hours. He roused him to drink some brandy mixed with water. Jackson shook his head. "It will only delay my departure, and do me no good. I want to preserve my mind, if possible, to the end."

With that, he slipped into a deep coma. The ticking of the clock in the bedroom seemed to grow louder; and as it did, its cadence for Jackson assumed the roar of a cannon, the high-pitched crack of a musket. He could hear the distant sound of battle. In his imagination, the general left the room and rejoined his soldiers. They were at Chancellorsville. "Push up the columns!" he ordered. "Hasten the columns! Pendleton, you take charge of that! Where's Pendleton? Tell him to push up the column!"[60]

Visions of combat passed away. Others took their place in his thoughts. Now he was leading his "army of the living God" in a great crusade for good. Men were marching toward the next victory, for which all credit belonged not to him or to them but to the Creator.

Then, scenes in reverse order of time began flashing through Jackson's mind: Antietam . . . Second Manassas . . . campaigns in the Valley . . . fame along Bull Run . . . ten happy years at VMI . . . friends in Lexington . . . Anna . . . and Ellie . . . his spiritual advisors Dr. White and Captain Taylor . . . the excitement of war in Mexico . . . the trying days at West Point . . . the lonely years of youth. All of it had a meaning. It must be a pilgrimage. A forlorn childhood was surely a prelude to eternal happiness. The earthly tabernacle could only be the gateway to the throne of God. After the struggles of life came the peace of death.

Suddenly, the rapidly changing series of visions stopped. The mists lifted as if from a gentle breeze. There, clearly in view, was Jackson's Mill! The West Fork River was still curling like a moat around the boundaries of the family home place. A long, hot workday was ending.

Look! He could see the little boy: tired, withdrawn, alone. He knew where the lad was going. It was where he wanted to go. On the other side of the West Fork was the little grove of white poplars that was his solitude—and his refuge—from the cares of the world. The sanctuary beckoned to him now with an intensity he had never felt before.

"Let us cross over the river," he exclaimed, "and rest under the shade of the trees." Tom Jackson had come home.[61]

25

EPILOGUE

J ACKSON DIED AT 3:15 P.M. The first indication of his passing for the crowd standing in the Chandler yard came when a weeping Anna, supported on either side by Lieutenants Joseph Morrison and James Smith, emerged from the little house. Scores of men instantly removed their hats, the silence broken only by a sob here and there from soldiers who could not contain their grief.

While the Chandler family consoled Anna, staff members began putting the body in order. Jackson's uniform coat had been torn to shreds when Wilbourn and others sought to treat his wounds. Pendleton, McGuire, and Smith clad Jackson in a dark suit. The general's blue military overcoat covered the civilian clothing and became the final shroud.[1]

A crude pine box was Jackson's first coffin. The remains were put in the parlor of the Chandler home. Anna struggled into the room to see her husband. "All traces of suffering had disappeared from the noble face," she wrote, "and, although somewhat emaciated, the expression was serene and elevated, and he looked far more natural than I had dared to hope."[2]

Meanwhile, the news was flashing across Virginia and into the South: the general who at the time had most caught the popularity and the enthusiasm of the Southern people was suddenly no more. The Army of Northern Virginia had come to a turning point in its history.

Lee sent a formal announcement to the secretary of war: "It becomes my melancholy duty to announce to you the death of General Jackson. He expired at 3:15 P.M. to-day. His body will be conveyed to Richmond in the train to-morrow, under charge of Major Pendleton, assistant adjutant-general. Please direct an escort of honor to meet it at the depot, and that suitable arrangements are made for its disposition."[3]

That dispatch concealed Lee's deep hurt. The following day, the grief-stricken commander told his son Custis: "It is a terrible loss. I do not know how to replace him. Any victory would be dear at such a cost." To his brother Charles, Lee exclaimed, "I am grateful to Almighty God for having given us such a man." When Lee tried to talk to General-Reverend William N. Pendleton about his lieutenant, he wept openly.[4]

Inside the ranks of the Confederate army, reaction to Jackson's end was traumatic. General Raleigh Colston, Jackson's colleague and friend on the VMI faculty, watched the first shock hit. When the "dread announcement" came into the camps, Colston noted, "the sounds of merriment died away as if the Angel of Death himself had flapped his muffled wings over the troops. A silence profound, mournful, stifling and

754

oppressive as a funeral pall succeeded to the voices of cheerfulness, and many were the veterans . . . whose bronzed cheeks were now wet with burning tears, and whose dauntless breasts were heaving with uncontrollable sobs." Another soldier who thought Jackson "one of the world's greatest warriors and one of Christ's greatest soldiers" asserted, "It is not extravagant to say that . . . more sorrow was expressed in tears than was ever known in the history of the world at the loss of one man." Major Benjamin W. Leigh had risked his life to get the wounded Jackson to safety. He spoke for thousands when he told his wife: "The Army & the Country mourn for our hero. But we mourn our loss, not his. He had achieved a glorious Fame, & he fell in the arms of Victory. He was a faithful soldier of the Cross; & I feel assured that the Captain of our Salvation will secure him as one who had fought the Good Fight, & for whom there is henceforth laid up a Crown of Glory."[5]

Some soldiers found bitter humor in sorrow. The Lord sent his angels down to escort Jackson to heaven, a story went. They searched and searched but could not find him. Embarrassed, they returned to heaven to make their report and were astonished to learn that Old Jack had outflanked them and reached heaven before they did!

Far larger numbers of Johnny Rebs, however, declared then and later that with the death of Jackson began the defeat of the Confederacy. A young Lexington girl stated somberly that Jackson's passing "was the first time it had dawned on us that God would let us be defeated."[6]

In those dark days of May 1863, the Southern nation had to weather the greatest personal loss it would ever know. Jackson's passing was tragedy in its purest form. The effect on the civilian population could only be called paralyzing. A future commandant at VMI noted that the announcement "came as a shock to the Institute, and to the people of Lexington, where no one had thought seriously of the possibility of losing him. . . . The rich perfumed spring air of Lexington seemed darkened by the oppressive sorrow everywhere to be seen." In Winchester, which Jackson had come to regard as a second home, young Kate Sperry wrote in her diary: "I . . . feel so miserable—nearly cried my eyes out—poor Jackson—so noble—so brave—so loved by all the people—Oh, how we shall miss him." As residents in Richmond passed the three-word message, "Jackson is dead," men of all ages "gazed at each other in dumb amazement. Women were seen in the streets . . . wringing their hands and weeping as bitterly as if one near and dear to their hearts had been taken." A Richmond newspaper did not exaggerate when it proclaimed: "The affections of every household in the nation were twined about this great and unselfish warrior. . . . He has fallen, and a nation weeps."[7]

On the Union side, a Massachusetts private summed up general feeling best with a simple observation, "We shall fear him no more."[8]

Anna went downstairs to the Chandler parlor early on Monday morning (May 11) to look again at her husband. Spring flowers covered the coffin. "His dear face was wreathed with the lovely lily of the valley—the emblem of humility," she commented. Sandie Pendleton walked up beside her, tears streaming down his face. All the adjutant could say was: "God knows I would have died for him!" Sixteen months later, Pendleton would fall in action.[9]

The Stonewall Brigade requested permission to serve as official escort. Lee could not spare troops of any number, for he expected Hooker to renew his offensive at any moment. Only Jackson's staff was allowed to accompany the body to Richmond. Pendleton, Smith, and Lacy would attend Mrs. Jackson. Mrs. Hoge and the Chandlers would also go with the widow.

In midmorning, Jackson's remains were taken down the terrace of Fairfield toward the train station. A locomotive and one car were waiting. The singing of birds was the only sound as the train started southward slowly on a forty-five-mile trip. Throngs of people lined the railroad to watch the passing of a hero.

In Richmond, all businesses closed at 10 A.M. Flags flew at half-staff; not even a bird's chirping interrupted the deep silence that hung over the capital. People forgot the heat of the day as they stood along the streets in sad anticipation. The train stopped in the Richmond suburbs to spare the widow the ordeal of facing a multitude of mourners and sightseers. Mrs. John Letcher and several other ladies met Anna and escorted her by carriage through quiet back streets to the governor's mansion.

"The saddest train that ever came into Richmond" started down the middle of Broad Street a little after 4 P.M. Its bell was ringing in a single dirge; but as the locomotive came into view, church bells throughout Richmond began to peal. A bystander noted: "At the head of Broad Street the speed of the train was slackened and it moved slowly down the street through the lines of citizens who stood in wonderful silence and with uncovered heads, to the depot at the corner of Broad and Eighth streets. The sad tolling of the bells . . . and the dull thud of the minute guns alone broke the stillness." For two miles, the engine and single car moved slowly through the largest crowd ever assembled in the city.[10]

Pallbearers placed the coffin in a hearse. The Confederate Congress had recently authorized a new national flag. The first ever made, intended for the roof of the Capitol, was draped over Jackson's casket. A long procession then wound through the streets to the governor's mansion on Capitol Square. There the body was carried into the large reception room. Bells tolled until sundown while hundreds of people stood in the square in hopes of being able to see the general.

A newspaper stated that never in the history of Richmond had there been such an outpouring "of heartfelt and general sorrow." A young woman visiting in Richmond observed, "I never saw human faces show such grief—almost despair."[11]

Early in the evening, Richmond undertakers embalmed Jackson's body. Sculptor Frederick Volck and an assistant made a death mask of the general. The remains were transferred to a metallic coffin; the new snow-white flag and banks of flowers were placed on and around the bier. The body was then declared ready for viewing.

Anna Jackson, now clad in full mourning clothes, was the first to see her husband lying in state. She was not pleased. "No change had taken place, but, the coffin having been sealed, the beloved face could only be seen through the glass plate, which was disappointing and unsatisfactory."[12]

Long lines of distinguished visitors filed into Governor Letcher's reception room until the lateness of the hour forced a halt. Near midnight, Pendleton and Douglas were standing alone at the coffin. In walked General Richard Garnett. He proceeded straight to the casket and looked silently at the dead warrior. Tears filled Garnett's eyes. He turned to the two aides and said: "You know of the unfortunate breach between General Jackson and myself. I can never forget it, nor cease to regret it. But I wish here to assure you that no one can lament his death more sincerely than I do. I believe that he did me a great injustice, but I believe also that he acted from the purest motives. He is dead. Who can fill his place!" Pendleton invited Garnett to be one of the pallbearers. The brigadier accepted gratefully. Less than two months later, Dick Garnett would be killed in battle.[13]

The day ended on a bizarre note. Governor Letcher received a wire: "Please telegh if Gen. Jackson is dead. If so save me a lock of his hair. Yours truly, Belle Boyd."[14]

May 12 was an uncomfortably warm Tuesday. Disappointment prevailed among Richmond officials that Jackson would not be buried in Hollywood Cemetery at the capital. Yet the 11 A.M. funeral procession from the governor's mansion to the Capitol (where Jackson would lie in state for the general public) was elaborate and impressive. Hours beforehand, dense crowds lined the route.

Promptly at the appointed hour, General Arnold Elzey rode to the head of the line. This Maryland native had led a brigade on Jackson's left at First Manassas. Now, as commander of the Department of Richmond, Elzey was in charge of the funeral arrangements in the capital. He gave the signal; a cannon fired from near the equestrian statue of Washington in Capitol Square. The long procession began moving slowly on a half-mile journey down Governor Street, up Main Street to Second, up Second to Grace, then down Grace to the west entrance of Capitol Square. Behind Elzey came the band of the 30th Virginia. The musicians were trying to play the "Psalm of David," but so many of them were weeping that the music was full of sour notes.[15]

Next came the hearse, drawn by eight horses with sable plumes. On either side of the casket walked an array of generals, most of them from the First Corps stationed nearby. James Longstreet, Richard S. Ewell, George E. Pickett, John H. Winder, Montgomery D. Corse, Richard B. Garnett, James L. Kemper, George H. Steuart, plus Rear Admiral French Forrest of the Confederate Navy, all appeared genuinely bereaved.

Immediately behind the hearse, Jim Lewis led "Superior," one of the last horses Jackson acquired.[16] Fastened in the stirrups were reversed boots. Next came a carriage bearing Anna, Julia, and an equally disconsolate Jefferson Davis.

Perhaps the president realized by then his several mistakes with respect to Jackson. Davis had been painfully slow to recognize his abilities. He wanted no part of Jackson after First Manassas, had sided with Secretary of War Benjamin after Romney, and had ignored Jackson in the Seven Days' Campaign. Yet Jackson's achievements in the valley, his brilliance at Second Manassas, steadfastness at Antietam and Fredericksburg, and his slashing attack at Chancellorsville had made Davis see the error of his thinking.

Now the most brilliant offensive star in the Confederacy rode lifeless just in front of the president; and later that day, when a friend found Davis in the White House staring blankly into the distance, the president bestirred himself and said: "You must forgive me. I am still staggering from a dreadful blow. I cannot think."[17]

A handful of Stonewall Brigade soldiers who had somehow made it to Richmond was next in line. (Two weeks later, the War Department would officially designate Jackson's first regiments as the Stonewall Brigade—the only Confederate unit to have a sanctioned nickname.)[18] Then came heads of government departments, two by two on foot, followed by state and municipal authorities, plus thousands of soldiers and civilians. Other than the band, one bystander observed, "no noisy demonstration of any kind greeted the ear. The people had had time to realize their loss. . . . No one seemed to be talking; there was all the hush and serenity of the Sabbath about the day."[19]

The funeral parade took an hour to make its way to the Capitol. At noon, pall-bearers lifted the casket onto a bier in front of the speaker's chair in the Confederate House of Representatives (the old Virginia Senate chamber). This was the same hall where the Virginia Convention in 1861 had approved the appointment of an obscure VMI faculty member named Jackson as a colonel. White linen covered the coffin stand. Black bunting adorned the walls. Flowers bedecked the bier. On the side of the coffin was a silver plate with the inscription: "Lieutenant General T. J. Jackson. Born January 21st 1824; died May 10th 1863."

During the remainder of the day, while Anna sat in a darkened room in the governor's mansion, an estimated 20,000 people filed by the casket for a final look. Finally, Governor Letcher ordered the doors closed. A few minutes later, a loud voice demanded admittance. When soldiers opened the door, a one-armed veteran pointed to his stump and, with tears spilling from his eyes, shouted: "By this arm which I lost for my country, I demand the privilege of seeing the General once more!" Governor Letcher put his arm around the man's shoulder and ushered him to the coffin.[20]

One of the first people west of the Blue Ridge to learn of Jackson's death was Colonel Francis H. Smith at VMI. The superintendent promptly issued General Orders No. 30, which announced the passing of a well-known faculty member. The directive then called on all cadets to "reverence the memory of such a man" and "imitate his virtues." Plans got underway to receive the remains on Thursday the 14th.[21]

Soon after dawn on Wednesday, Jackson's remains were returned to the governor's mansion. A private memorial rite followed. It is popularly assumed that Jackson's friend, Dr. Moses Hoge, conducted the worship service. However, that Presbyterian cleric was still in Europe at the time. The Reverend Thomas V. Moore of Richmond's First Presbyterian Church gave the eulogy, which was based on Isaiah 2:22: "Cease ye from man, whose breath is in his nostrils: for wherein is he to be accounted of?"[22]

A military guard escorted the casket, family, and such friends as Governor and Mrs. Letcher to the Virginia Central Railroad depot. The train was underway by 8 A.M. and bound for Gordonsville. The route was one that Jackson had used in military movements. "All along the way, at every station at which a stop was made," Anna recalled, "were assembled crowds of people, and many were the floral offerings handed in for the bier. His child was often called for, and, on several occasions, was handed in and out of the car windows to be kissed."[23]

Dr. William J. Hoge was at Gordonsville when the train arrived. "How strange it seemed that a crowd so eager should be so still, and that Jackson should be received with silent tears instead of loud-ringing huzzas." As the train stopped, Hoge added, "I caught sight of the coffin, wrapped in the flag he had borne so high. . . . Many wreaths of exquisite flowers, too, covered it from head to foot. Sitting near the body were young Morrison, his brother-in-law, our dear friend Jimmy Smith, and Major Pendleton." Hoge asked permission to pay his respects to Mrs. Jackson. He found her seated in a car almost alone. "She was patient amid all the pageantry. She was so evidently bearing all and doing all as she felt that her husband could have wished her to do, that she seemed to me just what he would have been in her place—the tender, helpless, stricken, brave little wife of such a saint, such a hero."[24]

Railroad cars were shifted onto the Orange and Alexandria line at the Gordonsville junction, and the second leg of the trip to Lynchburg got underway. There a town's population waited in grief. Stores closed at 5:00 in the afternoon at the request of Mayor William D. Branch. An immense throng met the train when it pulled to a stop downtown at 6:30. Again, church bells tolled and cannon fired each minute.

That evening a service was held in the Lynchburg First Presbyterian Church. Dr. James B. Ramsey officiated. A soloist, Miss Massey, began singing "Come, Ye Desolate." According to a worshiper, "the audience was in tears and Miss Massey wept while singing" but regained her composure and finished the dirge.[25]

Early Thursday morning, May 14, the final stage of the journey began. The body and funeral party boarded the canal boat *Marshall* on the James River.[26] Some 1500 convalescent Confederate soldiers left Lynchburg hospitals and joined local citizens to bid farewell to the general.

It was a slow and uncertain trip to Lexington by water. The *Marshall* was called the "Queen of the James River and Kanawha Fleet." Yet like other sizable vessels going upriver, the boat had to have assistance. Two mules connected to a line from the *Marshall* pulled along the bank. Under the best of circumstances, the barge made about three miles per hour.[27]

The route—along the James to the confluence of the North (now Maury) River at Glasgow, then fifteen miles up the North—took all day. As Anna sat on the boat and watched the banks pass slowly by, she must have pondered her future. All she knew was that with her husband gone, she would return to Cottage Home in North Carolina and, at the age of thirty-one, attempt to reassemble the fragments of her shattered life. Jackson's estate of some $22,000 would be wiped out by the death of the Confederacy.[28] However, the remaining years for Anna were long and respected.

She became the "Widow of the Confederacy" and one of the most popular women in the country. Desiring to stay busy, Anna devoted her energies to a variety of activities ranging from devoted mother to patriotic inspiration. She urged her friend, Robert L. Dabney, to write a suitable biography of her husband, and she supplied much material for the 1866 book. Twenty-five years later, with obvious help from several people, Anna produced her own memoirs of Jackson.

By then, she was extremely active in the United Daughters of the Confederacy. She became an honorary life president of that organization. Her travels and her contacts brought her introductions to a host of Americans, including five presidents. At the age of eighty, Anna demonstrated her still-present strength by having twelve teeth extracted at one sitting and without an opiate. She died March 24, 1915, in Charlotte at the age of eighty-three. The cause of death was pneumonia, the same illness that had claimed her husband. Anna Jackson's remains were taken to Lexington to rest beside those of the general.

Julia Jackson, an infant when her father died, would have a tragically short life. A number of illnesses in youth left her frail as an adult. At the age of twenty-two, she married William E. Christian in Richmond. The union produced two children: Julia Jackson Christian (1887–1991), who married Edmund R. Preston of Lexington, and Thomas Jonathan Jackson Christian (1888–1952).

Sometime in the 1870s, Julia changed her middle name from Laura to Thomas—perhaps to perpetuate her father's name, or else to divorce herself from an aunt whose wartime behavior was a family scandal. In 1889, Julia died of typhoid fever at the age of twenty-six.[29]

Laura Jackson Arnold at the time had no thoughts about the future; and if she ever had any remorse over her estrangement from her brother, she never expressed it publicly. The general's sister maintained her unionism to the end of the war and her distance from the Jackson family to the end of her life. She was one of two women given honorary membership in a Federal veterans' association, the Grand Army of the Republic. In 1870, she emerged the winner in a divorce from Jonathan Arnold. However, and because of poor health, Laura spent the 1881–1910 period in a private sanitorium near Columbus, Ohio. On September 24, 1911, she died at eighty-five at the home of a daughter-in-law in Buckhannon, West Virginia.[30]

The sun was setting that Thursday when the packet boat approached Lexington. Three miles from the landing, Colonel Francis Smith came on board to review the planned ceremonies. Since Jackson was the first VMI faculty member to die in the Civil War, Smith was a bit unsure of all that needed to be done. He had scheduled the burial service for Saturday, May 16; yet Anna had reached the limit of endurance at the outpouring of public sorrow. Another day, especially in beloved Lexington, was more than she could stand. The funeral must be the following day, Friday the 15th, she insisted.[31]

An hour later, the boat eased to a halt at the canal terminus below the bluff on which VMI was located. The entire corps of cadets was waiting at the pier. One of the youths declared, "It was a bitter, bitter day of mourning for all of us." The remains were placed on a caisson. Then, the same cadet noted, "with reversed arms and muffled drums we bore him back to the Institute."[32] Jackson was to lie in state that night in his old classroom. The stairwell leading to the second-floor Section Room 39 was circular and too tight to maneuver the coffin. Hence, the body was taken to the lecture room by way of the straight and wider steps on the inside of the U-shaped building.

"The room was just as he left it two years before," one man wrote, "save that it was heavily draped in mourning, not having been occupied during his absence. . . . It was a touching scene and brought tears to many eyes. When the body was deposited just in front of the favourite chair from which the lectures were delivered, professors, students, visitors, all, were deeply moved by the sad, solemn occasion, and gazed in mute sorrow. . . . Guns were fired every half-hour during the day in honour of the departed chieftain and an air of gloom was visible on every face."[33]

An honor guard of two cadets—one at the head of the coffin and one at the foot— stood hour shifts through the night. Those young men proudly carried memories of their duty through their lives.

Until far into the evening, one remembered, "people of the town and country thronged to the Barracks to view the remains. Men, women, and children wept over Jackson's bier as if his death was a personal affliction. . . . Flowers were piled high upon the casket until it was hidden from view."[34]

At 10 A.M. on Friday, the final ceremony began. It was a military funeral of far grander pageantry than the one a few days earlier for a native son, General Frank Paxton. Jackson's coffin was closed for the last time and placed on a caisson draped in black. The long procession started from the institute downhill into town and to the Presbyterian church.

Major Scott Shipp, commandant of cadets and a former student under Jackson, was in charge. Long before the cavalcade reached the temple, a crowd estimated at 4000 people packed the church to overflowing. Pallbearers bore the coffin to the communion rail in front of the pulpit.

Dr. Ramsey first offered prayers with the "most melting tenderness." The Reverend William F. Junkin, Jackson's kinsman by marriage, gave a brief eulogy and "beautiful prayers." Jackson's pastor, Dr. William S. White, read 1 Corinthians 15 and dwelt on the 26th verse: "The last enemy that shall be destroyed is death." White's sermon was in large part excerpts from letters he had received from Jackson and which "showed plainly what sort of man he was."[35]

Emmett McCorkle was a small boy at the time, but he never forgot the sentiment around the church. "A whole community in tears with every breast bursting with grief. . . . When the old soldiers emerged from the church bearing his body, men whose cheeks had never blanched in battle were wet with weeping." One of John Preston's daughters explained why the sorrow was so intense. "We were not in any sense spectators, we were heart-broken mourners, a clan bereft of its chieftain; a country in peril, from whom its defender had been snatched."[36]

The procession re-formed near noon and slowly made its way up South Main Street toward the cemetery. It was a huge, almost endless line: eight companies of VMI cadets, veterans of the Stonewall Brigade who happened to be in the area, two cavalry companies that by chance were passing through Lexington and joined the procession, dozens of honorary pallbearers, officials from every level of government, Confederate officers, family, and friends.

Conspicuous in the parade was Jim Lewis. Jackson's personal servant still led the riderless horse; and to one and all he exclaimed of Jackson, "I never knew a piouser gentleman."[37]

Graveside rites were brief. Sadness seemed to have fatigued everyone. Jackson was buried beside his first daughter and not far from Ellie and his stillborn son. A stately pine tree shaded his grave.[38]

Wreaths and flowers covered the entire family plot. The large crowd dispersed quickly, as if trying to flee from shock and sorrow. That evening Margaret Junkin Preston, one of the closest friends Jackson ever had, confided in her journal: "Now it is all over, and the hero is left 'alone in his glory.' Not many better men have lived and died."[39]

Writing from camp four days later, Jed Hotchkiss told his wife: "He is gone and sleeps in the Valley he loved so much. We miss him all the time & a void is made here which time can hardly fill."[40]

BIBLIOGRAPHY

ABBREVIATIONS

Since a number of sources appear with great frequency in this work, the following abbreviations have been used:

Arnold
: Thomas J. Arnold, *Early Life and Letters of General Thomas J. Jackson* (New York, 1916)

B&L
: Robert U. Johnson and C. C. Buel, eds., *Battles and Leaders of the Civil War.* 4 vols. (New York, 1887–88)

BV
: Bound Volume, Fredericksburg and Spotsylvania National Military Park

Chambers
: Lenoir Chambers, *Stonewall Jackson*, 2 vols. (New York, 1959)

Cook—WVU
: Roy Bird Cook Collection, West Virginia University

CV
: *Confederate Veteran*, 40 vols. (Nashville, 1892–1932)

CWTI
: *Civil War Times Illustrated* Collection, U.S. Military History Institute

Dabney
: Robert L. Dabney, *Life and Campaigns of Lieut.-Gen. Thomas J. Jackson (Stonewall Jackson)* (Richmond, 1866)

Dabney—LVA
: Dabney-Jackson Collection, Library of Virginia

Dabney—SHC
: Charles W. Dabney Papers, Southern Historical Collection, University of North Carolina

Dabney—UTS
: Robert Lewis Dabney Papers, Union Theological Seminary

Dabney—UVA
: Dabney Papers, University of Virginia

Davis—Tulane
: George and Catherine Davis Collection, Tulane University

FSNMP
: Fredericksburg and Spotsylvania National Military Park

Handley
: Handley Library, Winchester, Va.

Henderson
: G. F. R. Henderson, *Stonewall Jackson and the American Civil War*, 2 vols. (London and New York, 1898)

Hotchkiss—LC
: Jedediah Hotchkiss Papers, Library of Congress

Jackson—Duke
: Thomas Jonathan Jackson Papers, Duke University

Jackson—Holt
: Thomas J. Jackson Collection, Mary K. Holt, Weston, W.Va.

Jackson—Huntington
: Thomas Jonathan Jackson Papers, Henry E. Huntington Library

Jackson—LC
: Thomas J. Jackson Papers, Library of Congress

Jackson—LVA	Thomas J. Jackson Papers, Library of Virginia
Jackson—MC	Thomas J. Jackson Papers, Eleanor S. Brockenbrough Library, Museum of the Confederacy
Jackson—NYHS	Miscellaneous Manuscripts: Jackson, Thomas J., New York Historical Society
Jackson—SHC	Thomas Jonathan Jackson Papers, Southern Historical Collection, University of North Carolina
Jackson—Valentine	Thomas J. Jackson File, Valentine Museum
Jackson—VHS	Thomas Jonathan Jackson Papers, Virginia Historical Society
Jackson—VMI	Thomas J. Jackson Papers, Virginia Military Institute
Jackson—W&L	Thomas J. Jackson Papers, Washington and Lee University
Jackson—WVU	Thomas J. Jackson Papers, West Virginia University
LHAC	Louisiana Historical Association Collection, Tulane University
LSU	Louisiana State University
LVA	Library of Virginia (formerly Virginia State Library)
MC	Museum of the Confederacy, Eleanor S. Brockenbrough Library
MHS	Maryland Historical Society
Mrs. Jackson	Mary Anna Jackson, *Memoirs of Stonewall Jackson, by His Widow* (Louisville, 1895)
NA	National Archives and Records Administration
NBP	National Battlefield Park
NCDAH	North Carolina Department of Archives and History
NMP	National Military Park
NYHS	New York Historical Society
OHS	Ohio Historical Society
OR	U.S. War Dept., comp., *War of the Rebellion: A Compilation of the Official Records of the Union and Confederate Armies.* 128 vols. (Washington, D.C., 1880–1901)
PAHS	Historical Society of Pennsylvania
SHC	Southern Historical Collection, University of North Carolina
SHSP	*Southern Historical Society Papers*, 52 vols. (Richmond, 1876–1959)
SJH	The Stonewall Jackson House, Lexington, Va.
TJJ	Thomas Jonathan Jackson
TSLA	Tennessee State Library and Archives
USMA	U.S. Military Academy
USMHI	U.S. Military History Institute
UVA	University of Virginia

Vandiver	Frank E. Vandiver, *Mighty Stonewall* (New York, 1957)
VHS	Virginia Historical Society
Virginia Tech	Virginia Polytechnic Institute and State University
VMHB	*Virginia Magazine of History and Biography*
VMI	Virginia Military Institute
W&L	Washington and Lee University
W&M	College of William and Mary
WVU	West Virginia University

MANUSCRIPTS

Alabama Department of Archives and History
    James McDowell Campbell Papers
    Hopkins Family Papers
    James G. Hudson Diary
Antietam National Battlefield
    Henry Kyd Douglas Library
    Vertical Regimental Files
Auburn University
    James H. Lane Papers
    Benjamin F. Porter Papers
Stephen F. Austin State University
    Orlando T. Hanks Reminiscences
James Ballengee, Columbus, Ga.
    DePriest Letters
Baylor University
    John Waddill Reminiscences
Hunter Bennett, Weston, W.Va.
    Thomas J. Jackson Manuscripts
University of California, Berkeley
    Thomas J. Jackson Letter
Chicago Historical Society
    Turner Ashby Collection
    Autobiographical File
    William Butler Collection
    Robert Lewis Dabney Collection
    Gunther Collection
Cincinnati and Hamilton County Public Library
    Thomas J. Jackson Hymnal
Clarksburg, W.Va., Public Library
    S. Joseph Bershtein Collection
Cornell University
    Hannah Wright Gould Papers
Lewis C. Crawford, Jr., Collection, Rupert, W.Va.
    Andrew N. Cook Letters
Mrs. E. B. Dakan, Jr., Bridgeport, W.Va.
    Miscellaneous Papers
Davidson College
    Thomas J. Jackson Papers

John E. Divine, Leesburg, Va.
  Civil War Collection
Duke University
  Nathaniel Prentice Banks Letters
  Bedinger-Dandridge Family Correspondence
  Granville W. Belcher Papers
  Alexander Robinson Boteler Papers
  Brown Family Papers
  Rachel Susan Cheves Papers
  Jacob B. Click Papers
  William Samuel Compton Papers
  Francis Warrington Dawson Papers
  Henry Kyd Douglas Letters
  William Dunlop Letters
  Lucy Muse Fletcher Diary
  Robert Newman Gourdin Papers
  Caleb Hampton Papers
  William F. Harrison Papers
  John Cheve Haskell Memoir
  James H. Hewlett Papers
  Hinsdale Family Papers
  Frederick W. M. Holliday Papers
  Robert W. Hooke Papers
  Thomas Jonathan Jackson Papers
  William H. Jones Papers
  Williamson Kelly Papers
  Hector H. McNeill Papers
  Alexander M. McPheeters Papers
  Elizabeth A. Mills Papers
  Munford-Ellis Family Papers
  William Nelson Pendleton Papers
  Green W. Penn Papers
  William Thomas Poague Papers
  Thomas Lee Settle Papers
  Joseph Belknap Smith Papers
  Thomas D. Snead Papers
  Darius Starr Papers
  C. W. Trueheart Papers
  Samuel Hooey Walkup Journal
  Shadrach Ward Papers
  Williamson Weaver Papers
  W. H. Wheeler Reminiscences
  Bryant Wright Papers
  Franklin S. Wright Papers
Emory University
  Confederate Miscellany
Florida Atlantic University
  Thomas J. Jackson Papers
Fredericksburg and Spotsylvania National Military Park
  Bound volumes of manuscripts and printed source material
  "Reminiscences of Aunt Carrie Morton of the Battles around 'Belvoir' and Chestnut Valley, 1862," typescript
  Lucy Pierson Welsh, "The Merging of the Dickenson's/Dickinson's of Chestnut Valley,"

1988 typescript
"The Yerby Houses," typescript
University of Georgia
Shepherd Green Pryor Collection
Handley Library, Winchester, Va.
David Bard Correspondence
James W. Beeler Diary
Benjamin F. Brooke Journal
Julia Chase Diary
John Peyton Clark Journal
Metzer Dutton Letters
Samuel Angus Firebaugh Diary
John Randolph Graham Interview
Harriet Hollingworth Griffith Diary
John P. Hite Diary
Frank Buck Jones Diary
Mrs. Hugh Lee Diary
Abram Schultz Miller Letters
William Franklyn Pearse Diary
Francis Neff Papers
Tradwell Smith Diary
Kate S. Sperry, Jr., Diary
John H. Stone Diary
Historic New Orleans Collection
Thomas J. Jackson and Little Sorrel File
Mary K. Holt, Weston, W.Va.
Thomas J. Jackson Collection
Henry E. Huntington Library
Robert A. Brock Collection
Civil War Collection
Eldridge Collection
Huntington Miscellaneous
Thomas Jonathan Jackson Papers
Joseph Eggleston Johnston Papers
James E. B. Stuart Papers
State Historical Society of Iowa
Thomas J. Jackson Letter
Lafayette College
Earl A. Pope, "George Junkin and His Eschatalogical Vision," Feb. 10, 1970, Jones Faculty Lecture, typescript
Library of Congress
Richard Stoddert Ewell Papers
Jedediah Hotchkiss Papers
Thomas J. Jackson Papers
John Letcher Papers
William Cabell Rives Papers
Charles W. Squires, "Autobiography," typescript
John Ward, Jr., Papers
Louisiana State University
Ezekiel Armstrong Diary
E. A. Burke Collection
Civil War Letters—Miscellaneous
James Foster and Family Papers

George M. Heroman and Family Papers
John N. Shealy Papers
Maine Historical Papers
John Samuel Hill Fogg Autograph Collection
Manassas National Battlefield Park
Earl C. Andis, "The War Correspondence of Earl Carson Andis, 1861–1865," typescript
Philip Bradley Letter
Georgetown Meteorological Observations
John P. Hite Diary
"Jackson's 'Stonewall:' Fact or Fiction?" typescript
Robert E. Lee Krick, "Ewell Wounding," typescript
L. VanLoan Naisawald, "The Location and Frontage of Jackson's Brigade at First Manassas," typescript
Randolph Tucker Shields, Jr., "Recollections of a Liberty Hall Volunteer," article in unidentified publication
Samuel S. Seig Letter
Unknown Confederate artilleryman's letter
Maryland Historical Society
Julia M. Abbott Letters
John F. O'Brien Letter
Isaac Ridgeway Trimble Papers
Charles Sidney Winder Papers
Massachusetts Historical Society
Cutts-Madison Papers
Richmond Autograph Collection
Whitewell Collection
University of Michigan
William Dickson Papers
William Ellis Jones Diary
Schoff Civil War Letters and Documents
Minnesota Historical Society
George Burdick Wright Papers
Mississippi Department of Archives and History
James Hardeman Stuart Papers
Mississippi State Historical Museum
Stonewall Jackson Letter
Mississippi State University
R. E. Wilbourn Collection
Museum of the Confederacy, Eleanor S. Brockenbrough Library
Douglas S. Freeman, "Jackson's Charges against A. P. Hill," typescript
Richard B. Garnett Papers
Thomas J. Jackson Papers
J. Tucker Randolph Diary
National Archives and Records Administration
M474. Letters Received by the Confederate Adjutant and Inspector General
M661. Historical Information Relating to Military Posts and Other Installations, ca. 1700–1900
M727. Returns from Regular Army Artillery Regiments: First Regiment, Jan. 1841–Dec. 1860
RG92. Letters Sent by the Office of the Quartermaster General, Main Series, 1818–1870
RG92. Records of the Office of the Quartermaster General: Letters Received, 1818–1870
RG94. Adjutant General's Office. Records Relating to the U.S. Military Academy. Merit Rolls, 1841–1846
RG94. Engineering Department Records Relating to the U.S. Military Academy, 1812–1867
RG94. Letters Received by the Office of the Adjutant General (Main Series), 1822–1860
RG94. Records of the Adjutant General's Office, 1780–1914

RG94. Records Relating to the U.S. Military Academy. Application Papers of Cadets, 1805–1866

RG94. Records Relating to the U.S. Military Academy. Correspondence, 1841–1846

RG94. Regular Army Muster Rolls and Inspection Returns, 1821–1860

RG94. War with Mexico Records

RG98. Army Commands. Monthly Returns, First U.S. Artillery, 1843–1880

RG109. Compiled Service Records of Confederate Generals and Staff Officers, and Nonregimental Enlisted Men

RG109. Letters and Telegrams Sent by the Confederate Adjutant and Inspector General, 1861–1865

RG109. Office of the Adjutant & Inspector General and of the Quartermaster General, 1861–1865: Letters Received

RG109. Office of the Confederate Secretary of War, 1861–1865: Letters Received

RG391. First U.S. Artillery: Regimental Order Book, Sept. 14, 1849–Dec. 30, 1858

RG391. General, Special, and Other Orders Received from Superior Commands, First U.S. Artillery

RG391. Returns from U.S. Military Posts, 1800–1916: Fort Meade, Fla., December 1849–August 1857

RG391. "Orders Miscellaneous, 1844–1852," Headquarters, First U.S. Artillery

RG391. Regimental Orders Issued, First U.S. Artillery, 1840–1851

RG391. Roster of Officers and Enlisted Men, First U.S. Artillery, 1813–1855

RG393. Army Continental Commands. Western Division. Letters Received, 1851

RG393. Fort Meade, Fla.: Letters Received, June 1850–Aug. 1853

RG393. Fort Meade, Fla.: Letters Sent and Orders, July 8, 1850–Oct. 17, 1853

RG393. Letters Sent, Register of Letters Received . . . Department of Florida

RG393. Orders and Special Orders, 1847–1848, Department of Vera Cruz

RG393. Records of the U.S. Army Continental Commands, 1821–1920, Proceedings of Courts-Martial, Jan. 1850–Oct. 1852

RG407. Biographical File on Thomas J. Jackson, Newberry Library, Chicago, Ill.

Harrison Collection

New York Historical Society

Miscellaneous Manuscripts: Jackson, Thomas J.

North Carolina Department of Archives and History

    A. C. Atkin Paper

    Paul B. Barringer Paper

    L. O'B. Branch Papers

    Henry A. Chambers Diary

    D. H. Hill Papers

    Daniel Harvey Hill, Jr., Papers

    Thomas J. Jackson Letter

    Mary Kelly Smith Papers

    O. A. Wiggins Reminiscences

R. W. Norton Art Gallery, Shreveport, La.

    Henry Woodhouse Collection

Ohio Historical Society

    Robert Bromley Diary

    Albert Durkee Diary

    Thomas Evans Diary

    "Samuel Sexton Civil War Memoirs," typescript

    Augustus B. Tanner Letters

    Wildman Family Papers

    George L. Wood Papers

Historical Society of Pennsylvania

    Turner Ashby Papers

    Thomas J. Jackson Papers

Presbyterian Church (USA) Archives
  Thomas J. Jackson File
  Henry Thompson Sloan Papers
  George William White Collection
Princeton University
  Thomas J. Jackson Manuscripts
Lowell Reidenbaugh, St. Louis, Mo.
  Thomas J. Jackson Collection
James I. Robertson, Jr., Blacksburg, Va.
  Thomas J. Arnold Reminiscences
  Thomas W. Baldwin Reminiscences
  Thomas J. Godwin Letters
  Elijah M. Ingles Letter
  Langhorne Family Papers
  David R. McCauley Letter
  Lewis Tilghman Moore Papers
  John C. Wade Letter
Rosenberg Library, Galveston, Tex.
  Trueheart Papers
Roger D. Rudd, Fairbury, Neb.
  Thomas J. Jackson Letter
  William E. Jones Letters
University of South Carolina
  David Ballenger Papers
  John Charles McClenaghan Collection
  James Rion McKissick Papers
  Means-English-Doby Papers
  John Eldred Swearingen Papers
Southern Historical Collection, University of North Carolina
  Edward Porter Alexander Papers
  William Allan Papers
  Alexander Robinson Boteler Papers
  Campbell Family Papers
  Raleigh Edward Colston Papers
  Moses Ashley Curtis Papers
  Charles W. Dabney Papers and Books
  Edward O. Guerrant Diary
  Thomas Jonathan Jackson Papers
  Henry Lord Page King Diary
  William Nelson Pendleton Papers
  Polk, Brown, and Ewell Family Papers
  Margaret Junkin Preston Papers
  James Jones White Papers
Southern Illinois University
  Civil War Manuscripts
Stonewall Jackson House, Lexington, Va.
  Katharine L. Brown, "Compilation of Chronology of the Life and Work of Thomas J. Jackson of Lexington," typescript
  Canal Boat Register
  J. Compton & Son Ledger
  Vivian E. Dreves, "'Your Devoted Anna': Women in Lexington, 1850–1861," typescript
  Thomas J. Jackson Papers
  Milton H. Key Ledger
  Lexington Tannery Records

Joanna Metzgar, "The Stonewall Jackson House: Interpreter Training Manual," typescript
E. Lynn Pearson, "Thy Kingdom Come: The Evangelical Stewards of Antebellum Lexington, 1851–1861," typescript
Shaffner Collection
Mark E. Snell, "Bankers, Businessmen, and Benevolence: An Analysis of the Antebellum Finances of Thomas J. Jackson," typescript
Tennessee State Library and Archives
Campbell Brown and Richard S. Ewell Papers
University of Texas
John M. Brown Recollections
Tulane University
George and Catherine Davis Collection
Rosemonde and Emile Kuntz Collection
Louisiana Historical Association Collection
Union Theological Seminary
Robert Lewis Dabney Papers
McFarland Papers
Records of the Presbytery of Lexington
U.S. Military Academy
Edward C. Boynton Papers
Albert E. Church File
George Horatio Derby Letters
William Dutton Letters
William M. Gardner, "The Memoirs of William Montgomery Gardner," typescript
Thomas Jonathan Jackson File
Official Register, 1831–1848
Post Orders, 1842–1846
Samuel H. Raymond Letters
Register of Delinquencies Book, Classes of 1845–1846
Register of Merit Book, 1836–1853
Register of Punishments, 1843–1847
Staff Records, 1842–1845
John Caldwell Tidball Papers
West Point Newspaper Files
Working Committee, "Superintendent's Curriculum Study," typescript, 195
U.S. Military History Institute
Charles Bednar Collection
Civil War Miscellaneous Collection
Civil War Times Illustrated Collection
Rod Gragg Collection
Harrisburg Civil War Round Table Collection
Daniel Harvey Hill Papers
Thomas Jonathan Jackson Manuscript
Lewis Leigh Collection
Valentine Museum
Thomas J. Jackson File
Virginia Historical Society
Carrington Family Papers
Robert G. Carter Papers
Beverly Mosby Coleman Papers
Holmes Conrad Papers
Early Family Papers
Thomas Claybrook Elder Papers
Eppes Family Muniments

Faulkner Family Papers
Theodore Stafford Garnett Letter
Grinnan Family Papers
Charles B. Gwathmey Papers
Harlow Family Papers
"Inventory of the Books of Thomas Jonathan Jackson at the Virginia Historical Society, Richmond; Compiled by the Staff of the Society, 1961," typescript
Mary Anna Morrison Jackson Letters
Thomas Jonathan Jackson Library
Thomas Jonathan Jackson Papers
Watkins Kearns Diary
Lee Family Papers
Henry Brainerd McClellan Papers
Hunter Holmes McGuire Papers
David Gregg McIntosh Papers
Samuel J. C. Moore Papers
Joseph Graham Morrison Letter
Old Catalog Collection
Patton Family Papers
Pegram-Johnson-McIntosh Family Papers
James L. Power Letters
Francis Henney Smith Letters
Sara Henderson Smith Papers
James Ewell Brown Stuart Papers
Murray Forbes Taylor Essay
Robert Lee Traylor Papers
Virginia Military Institute Papers
Georgia Callis West Papers
Frederika Mackey White Diary
Wight Family Papers
Library of Virginia (formerly Virginia State Library)
Ted Barclay Letters
Dabney-Jackson Collection
Executive Papers, 1861–1862
Daniel Harvey Hill Papers
Thomas J. Jackson Papers
Virginia Military Institute
Board of Visitors Minutes
Joseph Hart Chenoweth Collection
William Couper Papers
Edward Sixtus Hutter Collection
Thomas J. Jackson Papers
Ross Papers
Thomas Andrew Stevenson Collection
Superintendent's Records: Incoming Correspondence
Superintendent's Records: Outgoing Correspondence
VMI Court Martial Book
VMI Faculty/Staff Records
VMI Order Book
Virginia Polytechnic Institute and State University
John Samuel Apperson Diary
Harvey Black Letters
University of Virginia
Barringer Family Papers
Bowman Family Papers

Buford Family Papers
William H. Burnley Civil War Papers
Dabney Papers
John W. Daniel Papers
Dinwiddie Family Papers
Clement Fishburn Memoirs
Graham and Tate Family Papers
Stonewall Jackson Letters
Kathleen Kincaide (Griebe) Papers
Hunter Holmes McGuire Papers
Thomas H. Pollock Papers
Rives Family Papers
Charles S. Venable, "Personal Reminiscences of the Confederate War"
Virginia. County Court. Lewis County Ledgers, 1840–1843
University of Virginia: School of Mathematics
E. T. H. Warren Letters
Washington and Jefferson College
James Power Smith Reminiscences
Washington and Lee University
Julia Junkin Fishburn Letters
Franklin Society Papers
Thomas J. Jackson Papers
John Newton Lyle, "Sketches Found in a Confederate Veteran's Desk," typescript
Minutes of the Lexington Presbytery
Reid Family Papers
J. D. H. Ross Papers
Withrow Scrapbooks
West Virginia Department of Archives and History
J. H. Diss Debar, "Two Men: Old John Brown and Stonewall Jackson of World-wide Fame," typescript
West Virginia University
Civil War Letters, 1862–1867
Roy Bird Cook Collection
Thomas J. Jackson Papers
Western Historical Manuscript Collection, Columbia, Mo.
William Fitzhugh Lee Letters
Thomas J. Jackson Letter
Curtiss W. Schantz, ed., "The Lost Order Book of the Virginia Military Institute, 1862–64," typescript
Works Project Administration: Historical Records Survey Western Kentucky University
Thomas J. Jackson Letter
Western Reserve Historical Society
William P. Palmer Collection
College of William and Mary
Civil War Collection: Box 2
William B. Taliaferro Papers
Yale University
Samuel G. Flagg Collection

NEWSPAPERS

Bristol Herald-Courier [Va.], 1949
Charleston Mercury [S.C.], 1861
Charleston Sentinel [W.Va.], 1931
Clarksburg Exponent [W.Va.], 1930, 1952, 1985

Clarksburg Exponent-Telegram [W.Va.], 1985
Clarksburg News [W.Va.], 1900
Danville Appeal [Va.], 1863
Fayette Tribune [Fayette County, W.Va.], 1923
Fredericksburg Star, 1889
Harrison County News [W.Va.], 1902
Harrisonburg Daily News Record [Va.], 1992
Lexington Gazette, 1851–1863, 1876, 1891, 1928, 1931
Lexington Gazette and Banner, 1875
London Index, 1863
Lynchburg Daily Virginian, 1863
Macon Daily Telegraph [Ga.], 1865
Maryland Gazette, 1749
New York Times, 1862, 1927
North Carolina Standard, 1862
Northern Virginia Daily, 1961
Philadelphia Weekly Times, 1877–78, 1881–83
Richmond Daily Dispatch, 1859, 1861–63
Richmond Enquirer, 1861–63
Richmond Examiner, 1861–63
Richmond News-Leader, 1937, 1939, 1977
Richmond Record, 1863
Richmond Times, 1898
Richmond Times-Dispatch, 1904–5, 1910, 1979
Richmond Whig. 1862, 1873, 1876–77
Roanoke Times, 1935
Rockbridge County News, 1888, 1935, 1938
Staunton Spectator, 1861–1862
Staunton Vindicator, 1861, 1863
Washington Daily National Intelligencer, 1845
Washington Post, 1881
West Virginia Hillbilly, 1959–1962
Winchester Evening Star, 1901, 1912–13
Winchester Virginian, 1861

OTHER PERIODICALS

Century Magazine, 1869–81
Christian Observer, 1935
Confederate Veteran, 1892–1932
Cottage Hearth, 1872, 1869
The Land We Love, 1866–69
New Eclectic Magazine, 1869
Southern Bivouac, 1882–87
Southern Historical Society Papers, 1876–1952
United Daughters of the Confederacy Magazine, 1961

PERSONAL LETTERS AND RECOLLECTIONS

Adams, Charles F. *Charles Francis Adams, 1835–1916: An Autobiography.* Boston: Houghton Mifflin, 1916.
Alexander, E. Porter. *Fighting for the Confederacy: The Personal Recollections of General Edward Porter Alexander.* Chapel Hill: University of North Carolina Press, 1989.
———. *Military Memoirs of a Confederate.* New York: Charles Scribner's Sons, 1907.
Alfriend, Edward Morrison. "Recollections of Stonewall Jackson." *Lippincott's Magazine,* 69 (1902).

Allan, Elizabeth Preston. *The Life and Letters of Margaret Junkin Preston.* Boston and New York: Houghton Mifflin, 1903.

———. *A March Past.* Richmond: Dietz Press, 1938.

Anderson, Carter S. "Train Running for the Confederacy," typescript of reminiscences written in 1892–93.

Anderson, William Alexander. *Address of William A. Anderson, . . . upon the Laying of the Corner-Stone of the Equestrian Statue to Stonewall Jackson in Richmond, Virginia, on June 3, 1915 . . .* [Richmond, 1915].

Andrews, Marietta Minnegerode. *Scraps of Paper.* New York: E. P. Dutton & Co., 1929.

Andrews, William Hill. *Footprints of a Regiment: A Recollection of the First Georgia Regulars, 1861–1865.* Atlanta: Longstreet Press, 1992.

Annals of the War, Written by Leading Participants North and South. Philadelphia: Times, 1879.

Archer, James Jay. "The James J. Archer Letters: A Marylander in the Civil War." *Maryland Historical Magazine,* 61 (1961)

Arnold, Thomas Jackson. "Beverly in the Sixties." *United Daughters of the Confederacy Magazine,* 29 (1967).

Avirett, James Battle. *The Memoirs of Turner Ashby and His Compeers.* Baltimore: Selby & Dulany, 1867.

Barringer, Paul Brandon. *The Natural Bent: The Memoirs of Dr. B. Barringer.* Chapel Hill: University of North Carolina Press, 1949.

Barton, Randolph. *Recollections, 1861–1865.* Baltimore: Thomas & Evans Printing Co., 1913.

Baylor, George. *Bull Run to Bull Run; or Four Years in the Army of Northern Virginia.* Richmond: B. F. Johnson, 1900.

Beck, Elias W. H. "Letters of a Civil War Surgeon." *Indiana Magazine of History,* 27 (1931).

Benson, Berry. *Berry Benson's Civil War Book: Memoirs of a Confederate Scout and Sharpshooter.* Athens: University of Georgia Press, 1962.

Blackford, Launcelot Minor. *Mine Eyes Have Seen the Glory.* Cambridge, Mass.: Harvard University Press, 1954.

Blackford, Susan Leigh, comp. *Letters from Lee's Army.* New York: Charles Scribner's Sons, 1947.

Blackford, William Willis. *War Years with Jeb Stuart.* New York: Charles Scribner's Sons, 1945.

Borcke, Heros von. *Memoirs of the Confederate War for Independence.* 2 vols. Edinburgh and London: W. Blackwood and Sons, 1866.

Bosang, James N. *Memoirs of a Pulaski Veteran of the Stonewall Brigade.* Pulaski, Va.: privately printed, 1930.

Boyd, Belle. *Belle Boyd in Camp and Prison.* New York: Thomas Yoseloff, 1968.

Boyd, David French. *Reminiscences of the War in Virginia.* Austin, Tex.: Jenkins, 1989.

Boyd, Thomas Massie. "General Stonewall Jackson." *Southern Bivouac,* 2 (1886–87).

Bridges, Hal, ed. "A Lee Letter on the 'Lost Dispatch' and the Maryland Campaign of 1862." *Virginia Magazine of History and Biography,* 66 (1958).

Buck, Lucy R. *Sad Earth, Sweet Heaven: The Diary of Lucy Rebecca Buck.* Birmingham, Ala.: The Cornerstone, 1973.

Buck, Samuel Dawson. *With the Old Confeds: Actual Experiences of a Captain in the Line.* Baltimore: H. E. Houck & Co., 1925.

Caffey, Thomas E. *Battle-fields of the South, from Bull Run to Fredericksburg,* "by an English Combatant." 2 vols. London: Smith, Elder & Co., 1864.

Cammack, John Henry. *Personal Recollections of Private John Henry Cammack.* Huntington, W.Va.: Paragon, [1921].

Casler, John Overton. *Four Years in the Stonewall Brigade.* Dayton, Ohio: Morningside Bookshop, 1971.

Chamberlayne, John Hampden. *Ham Chamberlayne—Virginian: Letters and Papers of an Artillery Officer in the War for Southern Independence, 1861–1865.* Richmond: Dietz Press, 1932.

Chesnut, Mary Boykin. *Mary Chesnut's Civil War.* New Haven and London: Yale University Press, 1981.

Clark, Walter. *The Papers of Walter Clark.* Vol. 1. Chapel Hill: University of North Carolina Press, 1948.

Cooke, John Esten. *Outlines from the Outpost.* Chicago: R. R. Donnelley and Sons, 1961.

———. "The War Diary of John Esten Cooke." *Journal of Southern History,* 7 (1941).

Coombes, Charles E. *The Prairie Dog Lawyer.* Dallas: Texas Folklore Society and University Press in Dallas, 1945.

Cusson, John. *The Passage of Thoroughfare Gap and the Assembling of Lee's Army for the Second Battle of Manassas, by a Confederate Scout.* New York: Penn Gazette Print., 1906.

Dabney, Robert Lewis. "Dabney's Last Lecture on Stonewall Jackson." *Davidson College Magazine*, 16 (Oct. 1899).

Davidson, Greenlee. *Captain Greenlee Davidson, C.S.A.: Diary and Letters, 1851–1863.* Verona, Va.: McClure Press, 1975.

Davis, Jefferson. *The Papers of Jefferson Davis.* Baton Rouge: Louisiana State University Press, 1961.

———. *The Rise and Fall of the Confederate Government.* 2 vols. New York: D. Appleton, 1881.

Davis, Varina Howell. *Jefferson Davis, Ex-President of the Confederate States of America: A Memoir by His Wife.* 2 vols. New York: Bedford, 1890.

Dawes, Rufus Robinson. *Service with the Sixth Wisconsin Volunteers.* Marietta, Ohio: E. R. Alderman and Sons, 1890.

Dunaway, Wayland Fuller. *Reminiscences of a Rebel.* New York: Neale, 1913.

Dwight, Wilder. *Life and Letters of Wilder Dwight.* Boston: Ticknor and Fields, 1868.

Early, Jubal Anderson. *Autobiographical Sketch and Narrative of the War between the States.* Philadelphia: J. B. Lippincott, 1912.

———. "Stonewall Jackson at Fredericksburg." *Historical Magazine*, 3 (1870).

Edmonds, Amanda V. *Journals of Amanda Virginia Edmonds.* Stephens City, Va.: Commercial Press, 1984.

Edmondson, James Kerr. *My Dear Emma (War Letters of Col. James K. Edmondson, 1861–1865).* Verona, Va.: McClure Press, 1978.

Eggleston, George Cary. *A Rebel's Recollections.* New York: Hurd and Houghton, 1875.

Ellison, Joseph M. "Joseph M. Ellison: War Letters (1862)." *Georgia Historical Quarterly*, 48 (1964).

Evans, Thomas. "As a Federal Regular Saw Second Bull Run." *Civil War Times Illustrated*, 6 (Jan. 1968)

Ewell, Richard Stoddert. *The Making of a Soldier: Letters of General R. S. Ewell.* Richmond: Whittet and Shepperson, 1935.

Fisk, Wilbur. *Anti-rebel: The Civil War Letters of Wilbur Fisk.* Croton-on-Hudson, N.Y.: Emil Rosenblatt, 1983.

Fitzpatrick, Marion Hill. *Letters to Amanda.* Culloden, Ga.: Mansel Hammock, 1976.

French, Samuel Bassett. *Centennial Tales: The Memoirs of Colonel "Chester" S. Bassett French.* New York: Carlton Press, 1962.

Frost, Daniel Marsh. "The Memoirs of Daniel M. Frost." *Missouri Historical Society Bulletin*, 26 (Oct. 1969–Apr. 1970).

Fulton, William F. *The War Reminiscences of William Frierson Fulton II, Fifth Alabama Battalion, Archier's Brigade, A. P. Hill's Light Division, A.N.V.* Gaithersburg, Md.: Butternut Press, 1986.

Gibbon, John. *Personal Recollections of the Civil War.* New York: G. P. Putnam's Sons, 1928.

Gill, John. *Reminiscences of Four Years as a Private Soldier in the Confederate Army, 1861–1865.* Baltimore: Sun Printing Co., 1904.

Gittings, John George Jackson. *Personal Recollections of Stonewall Jackson and Other Sketches.* Cincinnati: Editor, 1899.

Gordon, George Henry. *Brook Farm to Cedar Mountain in the War of the Great Rebellion, 1861–62.* Boston: James R. Osgood, 1883.

Goree, Thomas Jewett. *Longstreet's Aide: The Civil War Letters of Thomas J. Goree.* Charlottesville: University Press of Virginia, 1995.

Gorgas, Josiah. *The Civil War Diary of Josiah Gorgas.* University: University of Alabama Press, 1947.

Graham, James Robert. "Some Reminiscences of Stonewall Jackson." *Things and Thoughts*, 1 (1901).

Grant, Ulysses Simpson. *Personal Memoirs of U. S. Grant.* 2 vols. New York: C. L. Webster, 1885–86.

Grimes, Bryan. *Extracts of Letters of Major-General Bryan Grimes to His Wife.* Raleigh: Edwards, Broughton, 1883.

Hall, James Edmond. *The Diary of a Confederate Soldier: James E. Hall.* [Lewisburg, W.Va.: privately printed, 1961].

Harrison, Constance Cary. *Recollections Grave and Gay.* New York: Charles Scribner's Sons, 1911.

Heth, Henry. *The Memoirs of Henry Heth.* Westport, Conn.: Greenwood Press, 1974.

Hill, Daniel Harvey. "The Real Stonewall Jackson." *Century Magazine,* 47 (1893–94).

Hood, John Bell. *Advance and Retreat: Personal Experiences in the United States and Confederate States Armies.* New Orleans: Hood Orphan Memorial Fund, 1880.

Hopkins, Luther Wesley. *From Bull Run to Appomattox: A Boy's View.* Baltimore: Fleet-McGinley Co., 1908.

Hotchkiss, Jedediah. *Make Me a Map of the Valley: The Civil War Journals of Stonewall Jackson's Topographer.* Dallas: Southern Methodist University Press, 1973.

Howard, James McHenry. *Recollections and Opinions.* Baltimore: Sun Book and Job Printing Office, 1922.

Howard, McHenry. *Recollections of a Maryland Confederate Soldier and Staff Officer under Johnston, Jackson, and Lee.* Dayton, Ohio: Morningside Bookshop, 1975.

Huffman, James. *Ups and Downs of a Confederate Soldier.* New York: William E. Rudge's Sons, 1940.

Hunter, Alexander. *Johnny Reb and Billy Yank.* New York: Neale, 1905.

Jackson, Mary Anna. *Life and Letters of General Thomas J. Jackson (Stonewall Jackson).* New York: Harper and Brothers, 1892.

———. *Memoirs of Stonewall Jackson, by His Widow.* Louisville: Prentice Press, 1895.

Johnson, Bradley Tyler. *The First Maryland Campaign: An Address.* Baltimore: Andrew J. Conlon, 1886.

Johnson, Robert Underwood, and Clarence Clough Buel, eds.. *Battles and Leaders of the Civil War.* 4 vols. New York: Century Co., 1887–88.

Johnston, Joseph Eggleston. *Narrative of Military Operations during the Late War between the States.* New York: D. Appleton, 1874.

Jones, John Beauchamp. *A Rebel War Clerk's Diary at the Confederate States Capital.* 2 vols. Philadelphia: J. B. Lippincott, 1866.

Kean, Robert G. H. *Inside the Confederate Government: The Diary of Robert Garlick Hill Kean.* New York: Oxford University Press, 1957.

Kilgore, Gabriel M. "Vicksburg Diary." *Civil War History,* 10 (1964).

Lane, Mills, ed. *"Dear Mother: Don't Grieve about Me. If I Get Killed, I'll Only Be Dead": Letters from Georgia Soldiers in the Civil War.* Savannah: Beehive Press, 1977.

"The Last Battle of 'Stonewall' Jackson, By a Member of His Staff." *The Old Guard,* 6 (1868).

Lee, Robert Edward. *The Wartime Papers of R. E. Lee.* Boston: Little, Brown, 1961.

Lee, Robert Edward, Jr. *Recollections and Letters of General Robert E. Lee.* New York: Doubleday, Page, 1904.

Lincoln, Abraham. *The Collected Works of Abraham Lincoln.* Vol. 5. New Brunswick, N.J.: Rutgers University Press, 1955.

Long, Andrew Davidson. *Stonewall's "Foot Cavalryman."* Austin, Tex.: Walter E. Long, 1965.

Longstreet, James. *From Manassas to Appomattox.* Philadelphia: J. B. Lippincott, 1895.

McClellan, George Brinton. *The Civil War Papers of George B. McClellan: Selected Correspondence, 1860–1865.* New York: Ticknor and Fields, 1989.

———. *McClellan's Own Story.* New York: Charles L. Webster, 1887.

McClendon, William Augustus. *Recollections of War Times.* Montgomery, Ala.: Paragon Press, 1909.

McDonald, Cornelia. *A Diary with Reminiscences of the War and Refugee Life in the Shenandoah Valley, 1860–1865.* Nashville: Hunter McDonald, 1934.

McGuire, Hunter Holmes. *The Memory of 'Stonewall' Jackson: An Address.* New York: Andrew H. Kellogg, 1898.

———, and George L. Christian. *The Confederate Cause and Conduct in the War between the States.* Richmond: L. H. Jenkins, 1907.

McGuire, Judith Brockenbrough. *Diary of a Southern Refugee during the War.* New York: E. J. Hale and Son, 1867.

McIlwaine, Richard. *Memories of Three Score Years and Ten.* New York: Neale, 1908.

McKim, Randolph Harrison. *A Soldier's Recollections.* New York: Longmans, Green, 1910.

Macon, Emma Cassandra Riely, and Reuben Conway Macon. *Reminiscences of the Civil War.* [Cedar Rapids, Ia.: Torch Press], 1911.

Marshall, Charles. *An Aide-de-Camp of Lee.* Boston: Little, Brown, 1927.

Maury, Dabney Herndon. *Recollections of a Virginian in the Mexican, Indian, and Civil Wars.* New York: Charles Scribner's Sons, 1894.

Miller, Robert Henry. "Letters of Lieutenant Robert H. Miller to His Family, 1861–1862." *Virginia Magazine of History and Biography,* 70 (1962).

Moore, Cleon. "The Civil War Recollections of Cleon Moore." *Magazine of the Jefferson County Historical Society,* 54 (Dec. 1988).

Moore, Edward Alexander. *The Story of a Cannoneer under Stonewall Jackson.* New York: Neale, 1907.

Morgan, William Henry. *Personal Reminiscences of the War of 1861–5.* Lynchburg, Va.: J. P. Bell, 1911.

Mosby, John Singleton. *The Letters of John S. Mosby.* [Richmond]: Stuart-Mosby Historical Society, 1986.

———. *The Memoirs of Colonel John S. Mosby.* Boston: Little, Brown, 1917.

Neese, George Michael. *Three Years in the Confederate Horse Artillery.* Dayton, Ohio: Morningside, 1988.

Nichols, George Washington. *A Soldier's Story of His Regiment (Sixty-first Georgia).* Kennesaw, Ga.: Continental, 1961.

Nisbet, James Cooper. *Four Years on the Firing Line.* Jackson, Tenn.: McCowat-Mercer Press, 1963.

Oates, William C. *The War between the Union and the Confederacy and Its Lost Opportunities.* New York: Neale, 1905.

O'Ferrall, Charles Triplett. *Forty Years of Active Service.* New York: Neale, 1904.

Opie, John Newton. *A Rebel Cavalryman with Lee, Stuart, and Jackson.* Chicago: W. B. Conkey, 1899.

Packard, Joseph. *Recollections of a Long Life.* Washington: B. S. Adams, 1902.

Paxton, E. Franklin. *Memoir and Memorials: Elisha Franklin Paxton, Brigadier-General, C.S.A.* [New York: De Vinne Press], 1905.

Pender, W. Dorsey. *The General to His Lady: The Civil War Letters of William Dorsey Pender to Fanny Pender.* Chapel Hill: University of North Carolina Press, 1962.

Pendleton, Alexander Swift. "The Valley Campaign of 1862 as Revealed in Letters of Sandie Pendleton." *Virginia Magazine of History and Biography,* 78 (1970).

Pickett, George Edward. *Soldier of the South: General Pickett's Letters to His Wife.* Boston: Houghton Mifflin, 1928.

Poague, William Thomas. *Gunner with Stonewall.* Jackson, Tenn.: McCowat-Mercer Press, 1957.

Preston, Margaret Junkin. "Personal Reminiscences of Stonewall Jackson." *Century Magazine,* 32 (1886).

[Putnam, Sallie Brock]. *Richmond during the War: Four Years of Personal Observation.* New York: G. W. Carleton, 1867.

Quint, Alonzo Hall. *The Potomac and the Rapidan.* Boston: Crosby and Nichols, 1864.

Quintard, Charles Todd. *Doctor Quintard, Chaplain, C.S.A, and Second Bishop of Tennessee: Being His Story of the War (1861–1865).* Sewanee, Tenn.: University Press of Sewanee, 1905.

Redwood, Allen Christian. "With Stonewall Jackson." *Scribner's Magazine,* 18 (1879).

Ross John De Hart. "Harpers Ferry to the Fall of Richmond: Letters of Colonel John De Hart Ross, C.S.A., 1861–1865." *West Virginia History,* 45 (1984).

Scheibert, Justus. *Seven Months in the Rebel States during the North American War, 1863.* Tuscaloosa, Ala.: Confederate, 1958.

Small, Abner Ralph. *The Road to Richmond: The Civil War Memoirs of Major Abner R. Small of the Sixteenth Maine Volunteers.* Berkeley: University of California Press, 1939.

Smith, Francis Henney. *The Virginia Military Institute: Its Building and Rebuilding.* Lexington: Virginia Military Institute, 1912.

Smith, Gustavus Woodson. *Confederate War Papers.* New York: Atlantic, 1884.

Smith, James Power. *Stonewall Jackson and Chancellorsville.* Richmond: R. E. Lee Camp No. 1, United Confederate Veterans, 1905.

Smith, William Farrar. *Autobiography of Major General William F. Smith, 1861–1864.* Dayton, Ohio: Morningside, 1990.

Sorrel, Gilbert Moxley. *Recollections of a Confederate Staff Officer.* New York: Neale, 1905.

Stiles, Robert. *Four Years under Marse Robert.* New York: Neale, 1903.

Strong, George Templeton. *Diary of the Civil War, 1860–1865.* New York: Macmillan, 1962.

Strother, David Hunter. *A Virginia Yankee in the Civil War: The Diaries of David Hunter Strother.* Chapel Hill: University of North Carolina Press, 1961.

Swank, Walbrook Davis. *Confederate Letters and Diaries, 1861–1865.* Charlottesville, Va.: Papercraft Printing and Design Co., 1988.

Taylor, Richard. *Destruction and Reconstruction: Personal Experiences of the Late War.* New York: D. Appleton, 1879.

Taylor, Walter Herron. *General Lee: His Campaigns in Virginia, . . . 1861–1865, with Personal Reminiscences.* Norfolk, Va.: Nusbaum Book and News, 1906.

Thompson, James Thomas. "A Georgia Boy with 'Stonewall' Jackson." *Virginia Magazine of History and Biography,* 70 (1962).

Toombs, Robert. *The Correspondence of Robert Toombs, Alexander H. Stephens, and Howell Cobb.* Washington, D.C.: Government Printing Office, 1913.

Townsend, George Alfred. *Campaigns of a Non-combatant, and His Romaunt Abroad during the War.* New York: Blelock, 1866.

Tracy, Albert. "Fremont's Pursuit of Jackson in the Shenandoah Valley: The Journal of Colonel Albert Tracy, March–July, 1862." *Virginia Magazine of History and Biography,* 70 (1962).

Trimble, Isaac R. "The Civil War Diary of General Isaac Ridgeway Trimble." *Maryland Historical Magazine,* 17 (1922).

Vickers, George Morley, ed. *Under Both Flags.* St. Louis: People's, 1896.

Watkins, Samuel Rush. *"Co. Aytch": Maury Grays, First Tennessee Regiment, or A Side Show of the Big Show.* Jackson, Tenn.: McCowat-Mercer Press, 1952.

Welton, J. Michael, ed. *"My Heart Is So Rebellious": The Caldwell Letters, 1861–1865.* Warrenton, Va.: Fauquier National Bank, [1991].

White, William Spottswood. *Rev. William S. White, D.D., and His Times: An Autobiography.* Richmond: Presbyterian Committee of Publication, 1891.

Williams, Alpheus Starkey. *From the Cannon's Mouth: The Civil War Letters of General Alpheus S. Williams.* Detroit: Wayne State University Press, 1959.

Wise, John Sergeant. *The End of an Era.* Boston: Houghton Mifflin, 1899.

Withers, Robert Enoch. *Autobiography of an Octogenarian.* Roanoke, Va.: Stone Printing and Mfg. Co. Press, 1907.

Wolseley, Viscount Garnet. *The American Civil War: An English View.* Charlottesville: University Press of Virginia, 1964.

———. "A Month's Visit to the Confederate Headquarters." *Blackwood's Edinburgh Magazine,* 93 (1863).

Wood, James Harvey. *The War: "Stonewall" Jackson, His Campaigns and Battles, the Regiment as I Saw Them.* Gaithersburg, Md.: Butternut Press, 1984.

Worsham, John Henry. *One of Jackson's Foot Cavalry.* Jackson, Tenn.: McCowat-Mercer Press, 1964.

OTHER PRIMARY SOURCES

Arnold, Thomas Jackson. *Early Life and Letters of General Thomas J. Jackson.* New York: Fleming H. Revell, 1916.

Bain, William E. *B&O in the Civil War: From the Papers of Wm. Prescott Smith.* Denver: Sage Books, 1966.

Bartlett, Napier. *Military Record of Louisiana, Including Biographical and Historical Papers Relating to the Military Organizations of the State.* New Orleans: L. Graham, 1875.

Bennett, William Wallace. *A Narrative of the Great Revival Which Prevailed in the Southern Armies.* Philadelphia: Claxton, Remsen and Haffelfinger, 1877.

Bosbyshell, Oliver Christian, ed. *Pennsylvania at Antietam.* Harrisburg: Antietam Battlefield Memorial Commission, 1906.

Brady, James P., comp. *Hurrah for the Artillery! Knap's Independent Battery "E," Pennsylvania Light Artillery.* Gettysburg: Thomas Publications, 1992.

Caldwell, James Fitz James. *The History of a Brigade of South Carolinians, Known First as "Gregg's," and Subsequently as "McGowan's Brigade."* Philadelphia: King and Baird, 1866.

Chew, Roger Preston. *Stonewall Jackson: Address of Colonel R. P. Chew.* Lexington: Rockbridge County News Print., 1912.

Clark, James H. *The Iron Hearted Regiment: Being an Account of the Battles, Marches, and Gallant Deeds Performed by the 115th Regiment, N. Y. Volunteers.* Albany: J. Munsell, 1865.

Clark, Walter, comp. *Histories of the Several Regiments and Battalions from North Carolina in the Great War, 1861–65.* 5 vols. Raleigh: E. M. Uzzell, 1901.

Colt, Margaret Barton. *Defend the Valley: A Shenandoah Family in the Civil War.* New York: Orion Books, 1994.

Conrad, Daniel Burr. "History of the First Fight and Organization of the Stonewall Brigade—How It Was Named." *The United Service,* 7 (1892).

Cook, Benjamin F. *History of the Twelfth Massachusetts Volunteers (Webster Regiment).* Boston: Twelfth Regiment Association, 1882.

Daly, Louise Haskell, *Alexander Cheves Haskell: The Portrait of a Man.* Wilmington, N.C.: Broadfoot, 1989.

Davis, Charles E., Jr. *Three Years in the Army: The Story of the Thirteenth Massachusetts Volunteers.* Boston: Estes and Lauriat, 1894.

Dedication of Tomb of Army of Northern Virginia, Louisiana Division, and Unveiling of Statue of Stonewall Jackson at Metairie Cemetery. New Orleans: M. F. Dunn and Bro., 1881.

Eggleston, George Cary. *The History of the Confederate War: Its Causes and Its Conduct.* 2 vols. New York: Sturgis and Walton, 1910.

Fleet, Benjamin Robert. *Green Mount: A Virginia Plantation Family during the Civil War.* Lexington: University of Kentucky Press, 1962.

Fonerden, Clarence Albert. *A Brief History of the Military Career of Carpenter's Battery.* New Market, Va.: Henkel, 1911.

Ford, Andrew Elmer. *The Story of the Fifteenth Regiment Massachusetts Volunteer Infantry, in the Civil War, 1861–1864.* Clinton, Mass.: Press of W. J. Coulter, 1898.

Gold, Thomas Daniel. *History of Clarke County, Virginia, and Its Connection with the War between the States.* Berryville, Va.: C. R. Hughes, 1914.

Goldsborough, William Worthington. *The Maryland Line in the Confederate States Army.* Baltimore: Kelly, Piet, 1869.

Gordon, Armistead Churchill. *Memories and Memorials of William Gordon McCabe.* 2 vols. Richmond: Old Dominion Press, 1925.

Graham, Henry Tucker. *Stonewall Jackson: The Man, the Soldier, . . . the Christian.* Florence, S.C.: n.d.

Harrison, Walter. *Pickett's Men: A Fragment of War History.* New York: D. Van Nostrand, 1870.

Hoole, William Stanley. *Lawley Covers the Confederacy.* Tuscaloosa, Ala.: Confederate, 1964.

Hornbeck, Betty. *Upshur Brothers of the Blue and the Gray.* Parsons, W.Va.: McClain Printing, 1967.

Hotchkiss, Jedediah. *Virginia,* vol. 3 of Clement A. Evans, ed. *Confederate Military History.* Atlanta: Confederate, 1899.

———, and Allan, William. *The Battle-fields of Virginia: Chancellorsville.* New York: D. Van Nostrand, 1867.

Inauguration of the Jackson Statue . . . on Tuesday, October 26, . . . 1875. Richmond: R. F. Walker, 1875.

Jones, John William. *Christ in the Camp, or Religion in Lee's Army.* Richmond: B. F. Johnson, 1887.

Jordan, Weymouth T., Jr., comp. *North Carolina Troops, 1861–1865: A Roster.* Raleigh: North Carolina Department of Archives and History, 1966.

Lacy, William S. *William Sterling Lacy: Memorial, Addresses, . . . Sermons.* Richmond: Presbyterian Committee of Publication, 1900.

Lee, Susan Pendleton. *Memoirs of William Nelson Pendleton, D.D.* Philadelphia: J. B. Lippincott, 1893.

Long, Armistead Lindsay. *Memoirs of Robert E. Lee: His Military and Personal History.* New York: J. M. Stoddart, 1886.

McClellan, Henry Brainerd. *The Life and Campaigns of Major-General J. E. B. Stuart, Commander of the Cavalry of the Army of Northern Virginia.* Boston: Houghton Mifflin, 1885.

McDonald, William Naylor. *A History of the Laurel Brigade.* Baltimore: Sun Job Printing Office, 1907.

McLaughlin, William. *Ceremonies Connected with the Unveiling of the Bronze Statue of Gen. Thomas J. (Stonewall) Jackson at Lexington, Virginia, July 21, 1891.* Baltimore: John Murphy, 1891.

Marvin, Edwin E. *The Fifth Regiment Connecticut Volunteers: A History.* Hartford: Wiley, Waterman and Eaton, 1889.

Military Historical Society of Massachusetts. *Civil and Mexican Wars, 1861, 1846.* Boston: The Society, 1913.

Moore, Frank, ed. *The Rebellion Record: A Diary of American Events*. 11 vols. New York: D. Van Nostrand, 1864–68.

Murray, Alton Jerome. *South Georgia Rebels*. St. Marys, Ga.: Alton J. Murray, 1976.

Myers, Franklin McIntosh. *The Comanches: A History of White's Battalion, Virginia Cavalry*. Baltimore: Kelly, Piet, 1871.

Owen, William Miller. *In Camp and Battle with the Washington Artillery of New Orleans*. Boston: Ticknor, 1885.

Polley, Joseph Benjamin. *Hood's Texas Brigade: Its Marches, Its Battles, Its Achievements*. New York: Neale, 1910.

Presbyterian Church, C.S.A. *Minutes of the General Assembly of the Presbyterian Church in the Confederate States of America*. Columbia, S.C.: Southern Guardian Steam-Power Press, 1863.

Proceedings on the King's Commissions of the Peace, Oyer and Terminer, and Gaol Delivery for the City of London; and Also the Gaol Delivery for the County of Middlesex, Held at the Justice-Hall in the Old Bailey . . . Second and Fourth Sessions. London: M. Cooper, 1749.

Prowell, George Reeser. *History of the Eighty-seventh Regiment, . . . Pennsylvania Volunteers*. York: Press of the York Daily, 1901.

Quarles, Garland R., et al., eds. *Diaries, Letters, and Recollections of the War between the States*. Winchester, Va.: Winchester-Frederick County Historical Society, 1955.

Skinker, Thomas Keith. *Samuel Skinker and His Descendants*. St. Louis: author, 1923.

Slaughter, Philip. *A Sketch of the Life of Randolph Fairfax*. Baltimore: Innes, 1878.

Solomon, Eric, ed. *The Faded Banners*. New York: Sagamore Press, 1960.

Survivors Association. *History of the Corn Exchange Regiment: 118th Pennsylvania Volunteers*. Philadelphia: J. L. Smith, 1888.

U.S. War Dept., comp. *War of the Rebellion: A Compilation of the Official Records of the Union and Confederate Armies*. 128 vols. Washington, D.C.: Government Printing Office, 1880–1901.

Vautier, John D. *History of the Eighty-eighth Pennsylvania Volunteers in the War for the Union, 1861–1865*. Philadelphia: J. B. Lippincott Co., 1894.

Waddell, Joseph A. *Annals of Augusta County, Virginia, from 1726 to 1871*. Harrisonburg, Va.: C. J. Carrier, 1972.

Waitt, Ernest Linden, comp. *History of the Nineteenth Regiment, . . . Massachusetts Volunteer Infantry, 1861–1865*. Salem, Mass.: Salem Press, 1906.

White, William Spottwood. *Sketches of the Life of Captain Hugh A. White, of the Stonewall Brigade*. Columbia: South Carolinian Steam Press, 1864.

Willson, Arabella M. *Disaster, Struggle, Triumph: The Adventures of 1000 "Boys in Blue."* Albany, N.Y.: Argus, 1870.

Wintz, William D., ed. *Civil War Memoirs of Two Rebel Sisters*. Charleston, W.Va.: Pictorial Histories, 1989.

GENERAL STUDIES

Addey, Markinfield. *"Stonewall Jackson": The Life and Military Career of Thomas Jonathan Jackson, Lieutenant-General in the Confederate Army*. New York: Charles T. Evans, 1863.

Agnew, James B. "General Barnard Bee." *Civil War Times Illustrated*, 14 (Dec. 1975).

Allan, William. *The Army of Northern Virginia in 1862*. Boston: Houghton Mifflin, 1892.

———. *History of the Campaign of Gen. T. J. (Stonewall) Jackson in the Shenandoah Valley of Virginia, from November 4, 1861, . . . to June 17, 1862*. Philadelphia: J. B. Lippincott, 1880.

Andrews, J. Cutler. *The South Reports the Civil War*. Princeton, N.J.: Princeton University Press, 1970.

Andrus, Michael J. *The Brooke, Fauquier, Loudoun and Alexandria Artillery*. Lynchburg, Va.: H. E. Howard, 1990.

Armstrong, Richard L. *The Battle of McDowell, March 11–May 18, 1862*. Lynchburg, Va.: H. E. Howard, 1990.

Barry, Joseph. *The Strange Story of Harper's Ferry*. Martinsburg, W.Va.: Thompson Brothers, 1903.

Bauer, Karl Jack. *The Mexican War, 1846–1848*. New York: Macmillan, 1974.

Bean, William Gleason. "John A. Harman: Jackson's Logistical Genius," *The Iron Worker*, 35 (Summer 1971).

———. *The Liberty Hall Volunteers: Stonewall's College Boys*. Charlottesville: University Press of Virginia, 1964.

———. "Stonewall Jackson's Jolly Chaplain, Beverly Tucker Lacy." *West Virginia History*, 29 (1969).

———. *Stonewall's Man: Sandie Pendleton*. Chapel Hill: University of North Carolina Press, 1959.

———. "The Unusual War Experience of Lieutenant George G. Junkin, C.S.A." *Virginia Magazine of History and Biography*, 76 (1968).

Beck, Brandon H., and Charles S. Grunder. *The First Battle of Winchester, May 25, 1862*. Lynchburg, Va.: H. E. Howard, 1992.

Bigelow, John. *The Campaign of Chancellorsville: A Strategic and Tactical Study*. New Haven: Yale University Press, 1910.

Bisset, Johnson. *The Mysteries of Chancellorsville: Who Killed Stonewall Jackson*. New York: Hobson Book Press, 1945.

Blanton, Wyndham Bolling. *Medicine in Virginia in the Nineteenth Century*. Richmond: Garrett and Massie, 1933.

Boley, Henry. *Lexington in Old Virginia*. Richmond: Garrett and Massie, 1974.

Boney, Francis Nash. *John Letcher of Virginia: The Story of Virginia's Civil War Governor*. University: University of Alabama Press, 1966.

Brice, Marshall Moore. *The Stonewall Brigade Band*. Verona, Va.: McClure Printing, 1967.

Bridges, Hal. *Lee's Maverick General: Daniel Harvey Hill*. New York: McGraw-Hill, 1961.

Brown, Canter, Jr. "Fort Meade: On the South Florida Frontier in the Nineteenth Century." Typescript presented to the author.

Brown, Katherine L. "Stonewall Jackson in Lexington." *Proceedings of the Rockbridge Historical Society*, 9 (1982).

Brown, Stephen Wayne. *Voice of the New West: John G. Jackson, . . . His Life and Times*. Macon, Ga.: Mercer University Press, 1985.

Brown, Tom Watson. "The Military Career of Thomas R. R. Cobb." *Georgia Historical Quarterly*, 45 (1961).

Bushong, Millard Kessler. *Historic Jefferson County*. Boyce, Va.: Carr, 1972.

Caldwell, Willie Walker. *Stonewall Jim: A Biography of General James A. Walker, C.S.A.* Elliston, Va.: Northcross House, 1990.

Camerer, C. B. "The Last Days of 'Stonewall' Jackson." *The Military Surgeon*, 78 (1936).

Casdorph, Paul Douglas. *Lee and Jackson: Confederate Chieftains*. New York: Paragon House, 1992.

Castel, Albert. "Arnold vs. Arnold: The Strange and Hitherto Untold Story of the Divorce of Stonewall Jackson's Sister." *Blue and Gray Magazine*, 12 (Oct. 1994).

Chambers, Lenoir. *Stonewall Jackson*. 2 vols. New York: William Morrow, 1959.

Chapla, John D. *Forty-second Virginia Infantry*. Lynchburg, Va.: H. E. Howard, 1984.

Chase, William C. *Story of Stonewall Jackson*. Atlanta: D. E. Luther, 1901.

Clopton, John Jones. *The True Stonewall Jackson*. [Baltimore]: Ruths' Sons, Printers, 1913.

Cohen, Stan. *Historic Springs of the Virginias*. Charleston, W.Va.: Pictorial Histories, 1981.

Cole, James Reid. *Miscellany*. Dallas: Ewing B. Bedford, 1897.

Confederate States War Department. *Army Regulations Adopted for the Use of the Army of the Confederate States*. New Orleans: Bloomfield and Steel, 1861.

Cook, Roy Bird. *The Family and Early Life of Stonewall Jackson*. Richmond: Old Dominion Press, 1924.

———. *Lewis County in the Civil War, 1861–1865*. Charleston, W.Va.: Jarrett Printing Co., 1924.

Cooke, John Esten. *A Life of Gen. Robert E. Lee*. New York: D. Appleton, 1871.

———. *The Life of Stonewall Jackson*. New York: C. B. Richardson, 1863.

———. *Stonewall Jackson and the Old Stonewall Brigade*. Charlottesville: University of Virginia Press, 1954.

Coulling, Mary Price. *Margaret Junkin Preston: A Biography*. Winston-Salem, N.C.: John F. Blair, 1993.

———. "The Tie That Binds." Address presented at the 1992 Jackson Symposium, Lexington, Va.

Couper, William. *One Hundred Years at VMI*. 4 vols. Richmond: Garrett and Massie, 1939.

Crenshaw, Olinger. *General Lee's College: The Rise and Growth of Washington and Lee University*. New York: Random House, 1969.

Crute, Joseph H., Jr. *Confederate Staff Officers, 1861–1865*. Powhatan, Va.: Dewent Books, 1982.

Cullen, Joseph Patrick. *The Peninsula Campaign.* Harrisburg, Pa.: Stackpole, 1973.

Cullum, George Washington. *Biographical Register of the Officers and Graduates of the U.S. Military Academy at West Point, . . . New York.* 2 vols. Boston: Houghton Mifflin, 1891.

Current, Richard Nelson, ed. *Encyclopedia of the Confederacy.* 4 vols. New York: Simon and Schuster, 1993.

Dabney, Robert Lewis. *Life and Campaigns of Lieut.-Gen. Thomas J. Jackson (Stonewall Jackson).* Richmond: Blelock, 1866.

Dailey, Daphne L. *Memorial Service, May 10, 1970, Documenting a Funeral Service Held at This Church on May 11, 1863, for General Thomas Jonathan "Stonewall" Jackson.* Caroline County, Va.: Bethel Baptist Church, 1971.

Daniel, John Warwick. *The Life of Stonewall Jackson, from Official Papers, Contemporary Narratives, and Personal Acquaintance, By a Virginian.* New York: Charles B. Richardson, 1863.

Davis, Brad. *The Nature of Jackson's Mill.* Wilmington, Del.: Bradford W. Davis, 1982.

Davis, Burke. *They Called Him Stonewall.* New York: Rinehart, 1954.

Davis, Dorothy. *History of Harrison County, West Virginia.* Clarksburg, W.Va.: American Association of University Women, 1970.

———. *John George Jackson.* Parsons, W.Va.: McClain Printing, 1976.

Davis, Thomas Webster, ed. *A Crowd of Honorable Youths: Historical Essays on the First 150 Years of the Virginia Military Institute.* Lexington: VMI Sesquicentennial Committee, 1988.

Davis, William Charles. *Battle at Bull Run.* Garden City, N.Y.: Doubleday, 1977.

Delautier, Roger U., Jr. *Winchester in the Civil War.* Lynchburg, Va.: H. E. Howard, 1992.

Dooley, Edwin L., Jr. "Gilt Buttons and the Collegiate Way: Francis H. Smith as Antebellum Schoolmaster." *Virginia Cavalcade,* 36 (1986–87).

———. "Lexington in the 1860 Census." *Proceedings of the Rockbridge Historical Society,* 9 (1982).

Dowdey, Clifford. *The Land They Fought For.* Garden City, N.Y.: Doubleday, 1955.

———. *The Seven Days: The Emergence of Lee.* Boston: Little, Brown, 1964.

Driver, Robert J. *Fifty-eighth Virginia Infantry.* Lynchburg, Va.: H. E. Howard, 1990.

———. *The First and Second Rockbridge Artillery.* Lynchburg, Va.: H. E. Howard, 1987.

———. *Lexington and Rockbridge County in the Civil War.* Lynchburg, Va.: H. E. Howard, 1989.

Ekirch, A. Roger. *Bound for America: The Transportation of British Convicts to the Colonies, 1718–1775.* New York: Clarendon Press, 1990.

Farwell, Byron. *Stonewall: A Biography of General Thomas J. Jackson.* New York: W. W. Norton, 1992.

Faust, Drew Gilpin. *The Creation of Confederate Nationalism: Ideology and Identity in the Civil War South.* Baton Rouge: Louisiana State University Press, 1988.

Fishel, Edwin C. "The Mythology of Civil War Intelligence." *Civil War History,* 10 (1964).

Freeman, Douglas Southall. *Lee's Lieutenants: A Study in Command.* 3 vols. New York: Charles Scribner's Sons, 1942–44.

———. *R. E. Lee: A Biography.* 4 vols. New York: Charles Scribner's Sons, 1934–35.

Frye, Dennis E. "Henry Kyd Douglas Challenged by His Peers." *Civil War Magazine,* 9 (Sept.–Oct. 1991).

———. *Second Virginia Infantry.* Lynchburg, Va.: H. E. Howard, 1984.

———. "Stonewall Attacks!: The Siege of Harpers Ferry." *Blue and Gray Magazine,* 5 (Aug.–Sept. 1987).

Furgurson, Ernest B. *Chancellorsville, 1863: The Souls of the Brave.* New York: Alfred A. Knopf, 1992.

Gallagher, Gary W., ed. *Chancellorsville: The 1863 Virginia Campaign.* Chapel Hill: University of North Carolina Press, 1996.

———. "The Fall of Prince John Magruder." *Civil War History,* 19 (1989).

———, ed. *The Fredericksburg Campaign: Decision on the Rappahannock.* Chapel Hill: University of North Carolina Press, 1995.

———. "Scapegoat in Victory: James Longstreet and the Battle of Second Manassas." *Civil War History,* 34 (1988).

Gorham, L. Whittington. "What Was the Cause of Stonewall Jackson's Death?" *Archives of Internal Medicine,* 111 (1963).

Graebner, Norman Arthur. "European Intervention and the Crisis of 1862." *Journal of the Illinois State Historical Society,* 69 (1976).

Greene, A. Wilson. "Opportunity to the South: Meade versus Jackson at Fredericksburg." *Civil War History,* 32 (1987).

————. *Whatever You Resolve to Be: Essays on Stonewall Jackson.* Baltimore: Butternut and Blue, 1992.

Grimsley, Mark. "A Legend of the South: 'Stonewall' Jackson." *Civil War Times Illustrated,* 27 (1988).

Hale, Laura Virginia. *Four Valiant Years: The Lower Shenandoah Valley, 1861–1865.* Strasburg, Va.: Shenandoah, 1968.

Hamlin, Augustus Choate. *The Battle of Chancellorsville.* Bangor, Me.: Author, 1896.

Hamlin, Percy Gatling. *"Old Bald Head" (General R. S. Ewell).* Strasburg, Va.: Shenandoah, 1940.

Hanson, Joseph Mills. *Bull Run Remembers . . .* Manassas: National Capitol, 1953.

————. "A Report on the Employment of the Artillery at the Battle of Antietam, Md." Typescript: National Park Service, 1940.

Happel, Ralph. *Jackson.* Richmond: Eastern National Park and Monument Association, 1971.

Harrison, Noel G. *Chancellorsville Battlefield Sites.* Lynchburg, Va.: H. E. Howard, 1990.

Hassler, Warren W., Jr. *Commanders of the Army of the Potomac.* Baton Rouge: Louisiana State University Press, 1962.

Hebert, Walter H. *Fighting Joe Hooker.* Indianapolis: Bobbs-Merrill, 1944.

Heitman, Francis Bernard. *Historical Register and Directory of the United States Army.* 2 vols. Washington, D.C.: Government Printing Office, 1903.

Henderson, George Francis Robert. *Stonewall Jackson and the American Civil War.* 2 vols. London: Longmans, Green, 1898.

Hennessy, John. *The First Battle of Manassas: An End to Innocence, July 18–21, 1861.* Lynchburg, Va.: H. E. Howard, 1989.

————. *Return to Bull Run: The Campaign and Battle of Second Manassas.* New York: Simon and Schuster, 1993.

Hervey, George Winfield. *The Principles of Courtesy.* New York: Harper and Brothers, 1852.

Hewitt, Lawrence L. "A Confederate Foreign Legion: Louisiana 'Wildcats' in the Army of Northern Virginia." *Journal of Confederate History,* 6 (1990).

Holman, Andrew C. "Thomas J. Jackson and the Idea of Health: A New Approach to the Social History of Medicine." *Civil War History,* 38 (1992).

[Hopley, Catherine Cooper]. *"Stonewall Jackson," Late General of the Confederate States Army.* London: Chapman and Hall, 1863.

Horst, Samuel. *Mennonites in the Confederacy: A Study in Civil War Pacifism.* Scottsdale, Pa.: Herald Press, 1967.

Hull, Forrest. "The Mother of 'Stonewall' Jackson." *West Virginia Review,* 23 (1945).

Hungerford, Edward. *The Story of the Baltimore and Ohio Railroad, 1827–1927.* 2 vols. New York: G. P. Putnam's Sons, 1928.

Hunter, Robert F. *Lexington Presbyterian Church, 1789–1989.* Lexington: Lexington Presbyterian Church, 1991.

Johnson, John Lipscomb. *The University Memorial.* Baltimore: Turnbull Brothers, 1871.

Johnson, Thomas Cary. *The Life and Letters of Robert Lewis Dabney.* Richmond: Presbyterian Committee of Publication, 1903.

Johnston, Angus James, III. *Virginia Railroads in the Civil War.* Chapel Hill: University of North Carolina Press, 1961.

Jones, John William, comp. *Army of Northern Virginia Memorial Volume.* Dayton, Ohio: Morningside Bookshop, 1976.

————. *Life and Letters of Robert Edward Lee, Soldier and Man.* New York: Neale, 1906.

Jones, Ray. *Harpers Ferry.* Gretna, La.: Pelican, 1992.

Junkin, David Xavier. *The Reverend George Junkin, D.D., LL.D.: A Historical Biography.* Philadelphia: J. B. Lippincott, 1871.

Kellogg, Sanford Cobb. *The Shenandoah Valley and Virginia, 1861–1865.* New York: Neale, 1903.

Kercheval, Samuel. *A History of the Valley of Virginia.* Strasburg, Va.: Shenandoah, 1925.

Kleese, Richard B. *Shenandoah County in the Civil War: The Turbulent Years.* Lynchburg, Va.: H. E. Howard, 1992.

Krick, Robert Kenneth. "The Army of Northern Virginia in September, 1862," in Gary W. Gallagher, ed. *Antietam: Essays on the 1862 Maryland Campaign.* Kent, Ohio: Kent State University Press, 1989.

————. *Lee's Colonels: A Biographical Register of the Field Officers of the Army of Northern Virginia.* Dayton, Ohio: Morningside Bookshop, 1979.

————. "Maxcy Gregg: Political Extremist and Confederate General." *Civil War History,* 19 (1973).

————. *Stonewall Jackson at Cedar Mountain.* Chapel Hill: University of North Carolina Press, 1990.

Lee, Fitzhugh. *General Lee.* New York: D. Appleton, 1894.

Lee-Jackson Foundation. *Lee and Jackson: Six Appraisals.* Charlottesville: Lee-Jackson Foundation, 1980.

Levin, Alexandra Lee. *"This Awful Drama": General Edwin Gray Lee, C.S.A., and His Family.* New York: Vantage Press, 1987.

Lewis, Lloyd. *Captain Sam Grant.* Boston: Little, Brown, 1960.

Lyle, Roster, Jr. "John Blair Lyle of Lexington and His 'Automatic Bookstore.'" *Virginia Cavalcade,* 21 (Autumn 1971).

[McCabe, James Dabney], *The Life of Thomas J. Jackson, by an Ex-cadet.* Richmond: James E. Goode, 1864.

McCrea, Henry Vaughan. *Red Dirt and Isinglass: A Wartime Biography of a Confederate Soldier.* Privately printed, 1992.

McDaniel, John M., et al. *An Archaeological and Historical Assessment of the Liberty Hall Academy Complex, 1782–1803.* Lexington, Va.: Liberty Hall Press, 1994.

McDonald, Archie Philip. "The Illusive Commission of 'Major' Jedediah Hotchkiss." *Virginia Magazine of History and Biography,* 75 (1967).

McMillen, Sally G. *Motherhood in the Old South: Pregnancy, . . . Childbirth, and Infant Rearing.* Baton Rouge: Louisiana University Press, 1990.

MacRae, David. *The Americans at Home.* New York: E. P. Dutton, 1952.

McWhorter, Lucullus Virgil. *The Border Settlers of Northwestern Virginia from 1768 to 1795.* Hamilton, Ohio: Republican, 1915.

Matheny, Herman E. *Wood County, West Virginia, in Civil War Times.* Parkersburg, W.Va.: Trans-Allegheny Books, 1987.

Meier, Paul Neal. *Guide to Maj. Gen. T. J. "Stonewall" Jackson's Shenandoah Valley Campaign.* Quantico, Va.: USMC Amphibious Warfare School, 1982.

Miller, William J. *Mapping for Stonewall: The Civil War Service of Jed Hotchkiss.* Washington, D.C.: Elliott and Clark, 1993.

Montague, Ludwell Lee. "Subsistence of the Army of the Valley." *Military Affairs,* 12 (1948).

Moore, Robert H., II. *The Charlottesville, Lee, Lynchburg, and Johnson's Bedford Artillery.* Lynchburg, Va.: H. E. Howard, 1990.

Morrison, James L., Jr. *"The Best School in the World": West Point in the Pre-Civil War Years, 1833–1866.* Kent, Ohio: Kent State University Press, 1986.

Morrison, Robert Hall. *Biography of Joseph Graham Morrison, . . . Captain, Confederate States of America.* Charlotte, N.C.: Author, [1955].

Morton, Frederic. *The Story of Winchester in Virginia.* Strasburg, Va.: Shenandoah, 1925.

Murfin, James Vernon. *The Gleam of Bayonets: The Battle of Antietam and the Maryland Campaign.* New York: Thomas Yoseloff, 1965.

Murphy, Terrence V. *Tenth Virginia Infantry.* Lynchburg, Va.: H. E. Howard, 1989.

Musick, Michael P. *Sixth Virginia Cavalry.* Lynchburg, Va.: H. E. Howard, 1990.

Neff, Ray A. *Valley of the Shadow.* Terre Haute, Ind.: Rana Publications, 1989.

Nichols, James Lynn. *General Fitzhugh Lee: A Biography.* Lynchburg, Va.: H. E. Howard, 1989.

Northington, O. F., Jr. "The Revival of the Iron Industry in Eastern Virginia as Exemplified by the History of the Catherine Furnace in Spotsylvania County, Virginia." *William and Mary College Historical Magazine,* 16 (1936).

Offill, Paul Miller, Jr. "Stonewall Jackson: A Case Study in Religious Motivation and Its Effect on Confederate Leadership and Morale." M.A. thesis, University of Pittsburgh, 1962.

O'Reilly, Frank A. *"Stonewall" Jackson at Fredericksburg.* Lynchburg, Va.: H. E. Howard, 1993.

Osborne, Charles C. *Jubal: The Life and Times of General Jubal A. Early, CSA.* Chapel Hill: Algonquin Books, 1992.

O'Sullivan, Richard. *Fifty-fifth Virginia Infantry.* Lynchburg, Va.: H. E. Howard, 1989.

Pennington, Estill Curtis. *The Last Meeting's Lost Cause.* Spartanburg, S.C.: Robert H. Hicklin, Jr., 1988.

Phillips, Edward Hamilton. "The Lower Shenandoah Valley during the Civil War: The Impact of War upon the Civilian Population and upon Civil Institutions." Ph.D. diss., University of North Carolina, 1958.

Pierce, John E. "The Civil War Career of Richard Brooke Garnett: A Quest for Vindication." M.A. thesis, Virginia Tech, 1969.

Pollard, Edward Alfred. *Lee and His Lieutenants.* New York: E. B. Treat, 1867.

———. *The Second Year of the War.* New York: Charles B. Richardson, 1864.

Preston, Julia Jackson Christian. *Stonewall's Widow.* Winston-Salem, N.C.: Hunter, 1961.

Pusateri, Cosmo Joseph. "An Unusual Friendship: Jeb Stuart and Stonewall Jackson." M.A. thesis, St. Louis University, 1962.

Quarles, Garland R. *Occupied Winchester, 1861–1865.* Winchester, Va.: Farmers and Merchants National Bank, 1976.

Randolph, Sarah Nicholas. *The Life of Gen. Thomas J. Jackson (Stonewall Jackson).* Philadelphia: J. B. Lippincott, 1876.

Rankin, Thomas M. *Stonewall Jackson's Romney Campaign.* Lynchburg, Va.: H. E. Howard, 1994.

Reidenbaugh, Lowell. "Mary Anna Morrison Jackson." *Lincoln Herald,* 85 (1983).

———. *Thirty-third Virginia Infantry.* Lynchburg, Va.: H. E. Howard, 1987.

———. *Twenty-seventh Virginia Infantry.* Lynchburg, Va.: H. E. Howard, 1993.

Richards, Warren J. *God Blessed Our Arms with Victory: The Religious Life of Stonewall Jackson.* New York: Vantage Press, 1986.

Riggs, David Foster. "Stonewall Jackson's Raincoat." *Civil War Times Illustrated,* 16 (July 1977).

———. *Thirteenth Virginia Infantry.* Lynchburg, Va.: H. E. Howard, 1988.

Riggs, Susan A. *Twenty-first Virginia Infantry.* Lynchburg, Va.: H. E. Howard, 1991.

Riley, Elihu Samuel. *"Stonewall Jackson."* Annapolis, Md.: Riley's Historic Series, 1920.

Ripley, Edward H. *Vermont General: The Unusual War Experiences of Edward Hastings Ripley, 1862–1865.* New York: Devin-Adair, 1960.

Ritter, Ben. "Jackson's First War-time Portrait: The Widow's Favorite." *Civil War Times Illustrated,* 17 (Feb. 1979).

Roberts, Robert B. *Encyclopedia of Historic Forts.* New York: Macmillan, 1986.

Robertson, James Irvin, Jr. *Fourth Virginia Infantry.* Lynchburg, Va.: H. E. Howard, 1982.

———. *General A. P. Hill: The Story of a Confederate Warrior.* New York: Random House, 1987.

———, ed. *Proceedings of the Advisory Council of the State of Virginia, April 21–June 19, 1861.* Richmond: Virginia State Library, 1977.

———. *The Stonewall Brigade.* Baton Rouge: Louisiana State University Press, 1963.

Robinson, Richard D., and Elisabeth C. Robinson. *Repassing at My Side: . . . A Story of the Junkins.* Blacksburg, Va.: Southern Printing Co., 1975.

Roper, Peter W. *Jedediah Hotchkiss: Rebel Mapmaker and Virginia Businessman.* Shippensburg, Pa.: White Mane, 1992.

Royster, Charles. *The Destructive War: William Tecumseh Sherman, Stonewall Jackson, and the Americans.* New York: Alfred A. Knopf, 1991.

Rozear, Marvin P., and Joseph C. Greenfield "'Let Us Cross over the River': The Final Illness of Stonewall Jackson." *Virginia Magazine of History and Biography,* 103 (1995).

Ruffner, Kevin C. *Forty-fourth Virginia Infantry.* Lynchburg, Va.: H. E. Howard, 1987.

Schildt, John William. *Hunter Holmes McGuire: Doctor in Gray.* Chewsville, Md.: Author, 1986.

———. *Jackson and the Preachers.* Parsons, W.Va.: McClain Printing Co., 1982.

Scott, Eugene Crampton, comp. *Ministerial Directory of the Presbyterian Church, U.S., 1861–1941.* Austin, Tex.: Boeckmann-Jones Co., 1942.

Sears, Stephen W. *Landscape Turned Red: The Battle of Antietam.* New York: Ticknor and Fields, 1983.

———. *To the Gates of Richmond: The Peninsula Campaign.* New York: Ticknor and Fields, 1992.

Selby, John. *Stonewall Jackson as Military Commander.* Princeton, N.J.: D. Van Nostrand, 1968.

Shanks, Henry Thomas. *The Secession Movement in Virginia, 1847–1861.* Richmond: Garrett and Massie, 1934.

Shaw, Maurice F. *Stonewall Jackson's Surgeon, Hunter Holmes McGuire: A Biography.* Lynchburg, Va.: H. E. Howard, 1993.

Smith, Alan DeForest. "Stonewall Jackson and His Surgeon, Hunter McGuire." *Bulletin of the New York Academy of Medicine,* 49 (1973).

Smith, Edward Conrad. *A History of Lewis County, West Virginia.* Weston, W.Va.: Author, 1920.

———. *Thomas Jonathan Jackson: A Sketch.* Weston, W.Va.: Society of Historical Engravings, 1920.

Smith, Hampton Harrison. *Stonewall Jackson: A Character Sketch.* Blackstone, Va.: n.d.

Snowden, Robert Bayard. *Sermon: Half-Century Commemoration at St. John's Church, Fort Hamilton, New York, of the Foundation of the Parish.* Fort Hamilton: St. John's Parish, 1884.

Stark, Richard Boies. "Surgeons and Surgical Care in the Confederate States Army." *Virginia Medical Quarterly,* 87 (1960).

Stiles, Kenneth L. *Fourth Virginia Cavalry.* Lynchburg, Va.: H. E. Howard, 1985.

Stinson, Dwight E., Jr. "Analytical Study of the Action of Greene's Division." Typescript, Antietam National Battlefield, 1961.

Strider, Robert Edward Lee. *The Life and Work of George William Peterkin.* Philadelphia: George W. Jacobs, 1929.

Stutler, Boyd Blynn. "Harpers Ferry Bridge: Nine-Time Loser," *Civil War Times,* 3 (Feb. 1962).

Symonds, Craig Lee. *Joseph E. Johnston: A Civil War Biography.* New York: W. W. Norton, 1992.

Tanner, Robert Gaither. *Stonewall in the Valley.* Garden City, N.Y.: Doubleday, 1976.

Tate, Allen. *Stonewall Jackson, the Good Soldier: A Narrative.* New York: Minton, Balch, 1928.

Thom, DeCourcy W. "Something More of the Great Confederate General, 'Stonewall' Jackson and One of His Humblest Followers in the South of Yesteryear." *Maryland Historical Magazine,* 25 (1930).

Thomas, Clayton Malcolm. "The Military Career of John D. Imboden." M.A. thesis, University of Virginia, 1965.

Thomas, Emory Morton. *Bold Dragoon: The Life of J. E. B. Stuart.* New York: Harper and Row, 1986.

———. *Robert E. Lee, A Biography.* New York: W. W. Norton, 1995.

Thomas, William Henry Baldwin. *Gordonsville, Virginia: Historic Crossroads Town.* Verona, Va.: McClure Printing Co., 1971.

Turner, Charles B. "The Franklin Society, 1800–1891." *Virginia Magazine of History and Biography,* 66 (1958).

U.S. Military Academy. *Regulations Established for the Organization and Government of the Military Academy at West Point, New York . . .* New York: Wiley and Putnam, 1839.

Vandiver, Frank Everson. *Mighty Stonewall.* New York: McGraw-Hill, 1957.

Virginia Military Institute Alumni Association, comp. *The 1989 Register of Former Cadets of the Virginia Military Institute.* Lexington: Alumni Association, 1989.

Walker, Cornelius Irvine. *The Life of Lieutenant General Richard Heron Anderson of the Confederate States Army.* Charleston, S.C.: Art, 1917.

Walker, Charles Duy. *Memorial, Virginia Military Institute.* Philadelphia: J. B. Lippincott, 1875.

Wallace, Lee Alphonso, Jr. *Fifth Virginia Infantry.* Lynchburg, Va.: H. E. Howard, 1988.

———. *A Guide to Virginia Military Organizations, 1861–1865.* Lynchburg, Va.: H. E. Howard, 1986.

Wayland, John Walter. *Stonewall Jackson's Way.* Verona, Va.: McClure Prining Co., 1956.

———. *Twenty-five Chapters on the Shenandoah Valley.* Strasburg: Shenandoah, 1957.

Weber, Thomas. *The Northern Railroads in the Civil War.* New York: King's Crown Press, 1952.

Wert, Jeffrey D. *General James Longstreet, The Confederacy's Most Controversial Soldier: A Biography.* New York: Simon and Schuster, 1993.

Wessels, William L. *Born to Be a Soldier: The Military Career of William Wing Loring.* Fort Worth: Texas Christian University Press, 1971.

White, Henry Alexander. *Robert E. Lee and the Southern Confederacy, 1807–1870.* New York: G. P. Putnam's Sons, 1897.

Wise, Jennings Cropper. *The Long Arm of Lee.* 2 vols. Lynchburg, Va.: J. P. Bell, 1915.

———. *The Military History of the Virginia Military Institute from 1839 to 1865.* Lynchburg, Va.: J. P. Bell, 1915.

NOTES

PREFACE

1. Jubal A. Early praised Jackson as "one of the most illustrious men and grandest characters that have figured in the annals of history." The former Confederate general believed too that Jackson's "loss to the cause of the Confederate States was an irreparable one." Jubal A. Early statement, Mar. 4, 1892, Eldridge Collection, Henry E. Huntington Library.

2. Lord Frederick Roberts, quoted in Arnold, 344, who was quoting a 1914 issue of the *Saturday Evening Post;* Douglas MacArthur to James M. Thomson, Nov. 3, 1955, Jackson—VMI.

3. William McLaughlin, ed., *Ceremonies Connected with the Unveiling of the Bronze Statue of Gen. Thomas J. (Stonewall) Jackson at Lexington, Virginia, July 21, 1891* (Baltimore, 1891), 10; *CV,* 20 (1912): 220.

4. Anna Jackson wrote that her husband "had requested & insisted on my adopting *his* custom of mailing letters on Monday, so as to avoid [their] traveling on the Sabbath." Mary Anna Jackson Manuscript, Dabney—LVA. See also Margaret Junkin Preston discussion in *Century Magazine,* 32 (1886): 930.

5. William Couper, *One Hundred Years at VMI* (Richmond, 1939), 3:179; *CV,* 9 (1901): 379.

6. "John Cheves Haskell Memoir," Duke University; James R. Graham, "Some Reminiscences of Stonewall Jackson," *Things and Thoughts,* 1 (1901): 124.

7. John Esten Cooke, *Stonewall Jackson: A Military Biography* (New York, 1866), 220, and *Outlines from the Outpost* (Chicago, 1961), 51; Richard Taylor, *Destruction and Reconstruction* (New York, 1879), 50.

8. Raleigh E. Colston Reminiscences, SHC. For other examples of writers perpetuating the lemon myth, see Fitzhugh Lee, *General Lee* (New York, 1894), 142; James Cooper Nisbet, *Four Years on the Firing Line* (Jackson, Tenn., 1963), 41, 49. In interviewing Mrs. Jackson for his biography of the general, Robert L. Dabney made the following note: "Jackson's habits of diet queer. Ate at one time *nothing saccahrine.* No tea, coffee, spices. But a great eater of things simple, & of fruit." Dabney Note, Box 20, Dabney—SHC.

9. Randolph H. McKim, *A Soldier's Recollections* (New York, 1910), 92; David French Boyd, *Reminiscences of the War in Virginia* (Austin, Tex., 1989), 7.

10. Preston Narrative, Box 20, Dabney—SHC; Douglas Southall Freeman, *Lee's Lieutenants: A Study in Command* (New York, 1942–44), 2:xvii.

11. Withrow Scrapbooks, W&L, XVIII, 82.

12. Drew Gilpin Faust, *The Creation of Confederate Nationalism* (Baton Rouge, 1988), 28.

13. Walter Clark, *The Papers of Walter Clark* (Chapel Hill, 1948), 1:65; Charles Royster, *The Destructive War* (New York, 1991), 43.

14. Joseph C. Tidball, "Getting through West Point," handwritten memoir, John Caldwell Tidball Papers, USMA, 28.

15. C. S. War Dept., *Army Regulations, Adopted for the Use of the Army of the Confederate States* (New Orleans, 1861), 73–74; Kyd Douglas marginal note in his copy of Mrs. Jackson, 58, Henry Kyd Douglas Library, Antietam NBP. Apparently, Jackson paid little heed to the couriers attached to headquarters. Years after the war, the usually kind Maj. (Rev.) Dabney went out of character by asserting: "What did I have for orderlies and couriers? A detail from some cavalry company which happened to bivouac nearby. Perfect stupes. . . . They were sent to me without reference to their local knowledge of the roads, intelligence or bravery; most probably they were selected for me by their Captain for their lack of. Occasionally I got hold of a very good man, but could not keep him." Robert L. Dabney to Jedediah Hotchkiss, Mar. 31, 1896, Reel 12, Hotchkiss—LC.

16. F. R. Rives to unknown addressee, Jan. 9, 1864, William Cabell Rives Papers, Library of Congress. See also D. Harvey Hill statement in *The Land We Love*, 1 (1866): 116.

17. *CV,* 30 (1922): 61; William B. Taliaferro, "Reminiscences of Stonewall Jackson," William B. Taliaferro Papers, W&M, 8. For more on Jackson's "utter disregard of danger," see W. W. Blackford, *War Years with Jeb Stuart* (New York, 1945), 79.

18. Robert L. Dabney to Goupil & Co., Dec. 20, 1867, Henry Woodhouse Collection, R. W. Norton Art Gallery, Shreveport, La.

19. James Power Smith, *Stonewall Jackson and Chancellorsville* (Richmond, 1905), 12–15; *SHSP,* 35 (1907): 83. See also *SHSP,* 9 (1881): 366. For other comments on "Stonewall" versus "Old Jack," the name the soldiers preferred to call him, see W. H. C. Whiting to Robert L. Dabney, Nov. 30, 1863, Box 19, Dabney—SHC; *CV,* 5 (1897): 287.

20. *Century Magazine,* 47 (1893–94): 627; D. H. Hill to son, June 16, 1882, Daniel Harvey Hill Papers, USMHI.

21. *SHSP,* 25 (1897): 104; Jedediah Hotchkiss to William L. Chase, Mar. 28, 1892, Reel 9, Hotchkiss—LC. See also William C. Oates, *The War between the Union and the Confederacy and Its Lost Opportunities* (New York, 1905), 187.

22. TJJ to William E. Jones, late December 1862, E. A. Burk Collection, LSU.

23. James H. Lane Reminiscences, James H. Lane Papers, Auburn University; Catherine C. Hopley, *"Stonewall" Jackson, Late General of the Confederate States Army* (London, 1863), 174–75.

24. *Century Magazine,* 32 (1886): 935.

25. Cornelia McDonald, *A Diary with Reminiscences of the War and Refugee Life in the Shenandoah Valley, 1860–1865* (Nashville, 1934), 105.

26. *Staunton Spectator,* Dec. 23, 1862; Martin W. Brett Reminiscences, BV 26, FSNMP; Willy Lee Memories, BV 138, FSNMP.

27. *SHSP,* 31 (1903): 251.

28. [James D. McCabe], *The Life of Lieut. Gen. T. J. Jackson, by an Ex-cadet* (Richmond, 1863), 124.

29. Thomas M. Boyd Reminiscences, Cook—WVU.

CHAPTER I   *Struggles of an Orphan*

1. Roy Bird Cook, *The Family and Early Life of Stonewall Jackson* (Richmond, 1924), 18; Daughters of the American Revolution files, copies supplied by Mrs. Vivian Motsinger, Bethesda, Md. John Jackson's gravestone states that he was born in 1719, yet other sources assert that he was eighty-six at his 1801 death. To add to the confusion of John Jackson's origins, a plaque stands at the Birches, near Belfast in County Armagh, Northern Ireland, presumably marking the spot where Jackson was born. DAR files. Another typical example of garbled facts is in William C. Chase, *Story of Stonewall Jackson* (Atlanta, 1901), 50.

2. *Proceedings on the King's Commissions of the Peace, Oyer and Terminer, and Gaol Delivery for the City of London; and also the Gaol Delivery for the County of Middlesex, Held at the Justice-Hall in the Old Bailey . . . Second and Fourth Session* (London, 1749), 22–23, 44.

3. Ibid., 81, 84; James R. Sewell, London City Archivist, to John M. Jackson, Little Rock, Ark., Mar. 7, 1991, copy in possession of the author. John M. Jackson's assistance in supplying the first information on the transportation of John Jackson and Elizabeth Cummins was both unselfish and invaluable. Previous biographers of the general have used romantic legend in place of fact by having Jackson and Cummins migrating voluntarily to America in 1748 to seek a new life. For example, see Mrs. Jackson, 3; Chambers, 2:467. No John Jackson or Elizabeth Cummins appears on passenger lists anytime in the late 1740s, except in the case of the two felons under sentence to the colonies.

4. *The Maryland Gazette,* July 26 and Aug. 30, 1749. Arnold, 39, and Chambers, 2:467–68, both contain an implausible story of a wealthy Elizabeth Cummins traveling to America to join her sister. The sibling died before the planned reunion. Subsequently, the story continued,

Cummins journeyed to Maryland to live with acquaintances and presumably met John Jackson in that colony. See also Chase, *Jackson*, 50–51.

5. A. Roger Ekirch, *Bound for America: The Transportation of British Convicts to the Colonies, 1718–1775* (New York, 1990), 115–16, 142. Professor Ekirch was also of the opinion that the total number of convicts and indentures, while at least 9,400, could well have been in excess of 12,000 men and women.

6. Gideon D. Camden to Robert L. Dabney, Nov. 25, 1863, Box 19, Dabney—SHC; Elizabeth P. Allan to Gideon D. Camden, Sept. 12, 1863, Dabney—LVA.

7. *CV,* 38 (1930): 184; Camden to Dabney, Nov. 25, 1863.

8. George Jackson later served in the Virginia convention that adopted the U.S. Constitution. He was three times elected to Congress. This eldest son helped organize Harrison County and was instrumental in having Clarksburg named the county seat. George Jackson was hardheaded and bold; it was said that he was easy to deal with as a businessman so long as he got his way. Late in life he moved to Zanesville, Ohio, and became prominent in that state's politics. Conversation with Dorothy Davis, Salem, W.Va., Nov. 27, 1990. References to John Jackson's military service are in Lucullus Virgil McWhorter, *The Border Settlers of Northwestern Virginia from 1768 to 1795* (Hamilton, Ohio, 1915), 358, 360, 497; Stephen W. Brown, *Voice of the New West: John G. Jackson, His Life and Times* (Macon, Ga., 1985), 3–4.

John G. Jackson, the firstborn son of George, was "the business genius of the early northwest." A successful lawyer with a variety of investment holdings, he performed long service in the Virginia legislature, served six terms in Congress, received a brigadier generalcy in the state militia, and for six years was a federal district judge for western Virginia. In the first White House ceremony of its kind, John G. Jackson married the sister of Dolley Payne Madison. Edward Conrad Smith, *A History of Lewis County, West Virginia* (Weston, W.Va., 1920), 217; Gideon D. Camden to Robert L. Dabney, Nov. 21, 1863, Box 19, Dabney—SHC; Brown, *Voice of the New West, passim.*

9. Anna Jackson noted that her husband "always said his Jackson relations were very clannish, and he himself was warm in his family attachments, taking an interest in every worthy person who had a drop of blood in his veins." Mrs. Jackson, 6.

10. Allan to Camden, Sept. 12, 1863. See also Cook, *Family and Early Life,* 178. Arnold, 39, wrote that Elizabeth Jackson lived "only" to 101, but this was a mistake in arithmetic. It is quite unlikely that the strong-willed Mrs. Jackson left "thousands of friends to mourn her loss," as is stated in Chase, *Jackson,* 53. John and Elizabeth Cummins Jackson spent their last years at the home of their grandson, John G. Jackson.

11. Camden to Dabney, Nov. 21, 1863.

12. Arnold, 42–43, 45; Edward Jackson Bible, Cook—WVU. For more firsthand material on Edward Jackson and his family, see George W. Jackson to Jonathan Arnold, May 20, 1871, Jackson—VMI.

13. Some writers have concluded that Jonathan Jackson ought to have been born at Jackson's Mill and thus have placed his birth there. See [James Dabney McCabe], *The Life of Lieut. Gen. T. J. Jackson* (Richmond, 1863), 10; Byron Farwell, *Stonewall: A Biography of General Thomas J. Jackson* (New York, 1992), 7. However, Jonathan was eleven years old by the time the family relocated in Lewis County.

14. H. H. Smith, *Stonewall Jackson: A Character Sketch* (Blackstone, Va., n.d.), 2. Margaret Junkin Preston was of the erroneous opinion that Jonathan Jackson pursued a career as an engineer. *Century Magazine,* 32 (1886): 927.

15. Dorothy Davis, *John George Jackson* (Parsons, W.Va., 1978), 182.

16. Ibid., 257, 270.

17. Brown, *Voice of the New West,* 124, 230–31; Jonathan Jackson memo, Feb. 13, 1815, Box 19, Dabney—SHC. Local tradition has it that Jonathan Jackson was also loose with the funds of the Masonic lodge that he helped to establish. Gary Weiner to author, Aug. 5, 1993.

18. Camden to Dabney, Nov. 21, 1863; statement of Weston's Dr. William J. Bland, Box 20, Dabney—SHC (hereafter cited as Bland statement).

19. H. H. Smith, *Jackson,* 2; Dabney, 9; Camden to Dabney, Nov. 21, 1863.

20. Jonathan M. Bennett, Jr., Weston, W.Va., to author, Jan. 20, 1991; Bland statement.

21. Davis, *John George Jackson*, 379.

22. Chase, *Jackson*, 55; Elizabeth P. Allan to G. D. Camden, Sept. 12, 1863, Box 19, Dabney— SHC; Dabney, *Jackson*, 10; Mrs. Jackson, 10–11.

23. Memo in Cook—WVU. Vandiver, 2, asserted that the couple met while Jackson was attending a male academy in Parkersburg. No other source confirms Jackson going to school there. The Wood County marriage records listed Jonathan Jackson marrying "Judith B. Neal." This clerical mistake involving both of Julia's names has created some confusion under the guise of revelation. Farwell, *Stonewall*, 3, 5.

24. *Harrison County News*, Nov. 7, 1902; Chase, *Jackson*, 55. Local legend has long maintained that the tree came from the handiwork of Johnny Appleseed. Cook, *Family and Early Life*, 42.

25. Mrs. Jackson, 11–12; Farwell, *Stonewall*, 5. Because the latter work is not documented, the source of the author's material is unknown.

26. Memo in Cook—WVU; William Couper, *One Hundred Years at VMI* (Richmond, 1939), 3:174; Arnold, 25. Several years ago, the Parkersburg chapter of the United Daughters of the Confederacy erected a plaque claiming that Jackson was born in Parkersburg while Julia Jackson was visiting her father. No factual evidence corroborates this assertion. Members of the family, and a host of writers, have argued convincingly that Jackson was born in Clarksburg. An educated woman in an advanced state of pregnancy would hardly have made a wintertime journey of eighty miles for a family visit. Refutations of the Parkersburg claim are in the Cook—WVU; Charleston *Sentinel*, Mar. 27, 1931; H. E. Matheny, *Wood County, West Virginia, in Civil War Times* (Parkersburg, W.Va., 1987), 22.

27. Camden to Dabney, Nov. 21, 1863; *SHSP*, 22 (1894): 158. Cook, *Family and Early Life*, 43, described the borrowed home as a three-room structure. That the place was only twelve feet square and unrentable is stronger evidence that the family of four endured in one room.

28. Mrs. Jackson, 15; Chase, *Jackson*, 57–58; unsigned biographical sketch of Julia Neale Jackson in Brock Collection, Huntington.

29. R. E. Lee to D. Creel, Mar. 5, 1866, R. E. Lee Letterbook, Lee Family Papers, VHS. See also statement of the Rev. Moses D. Hoge in *Inauguration of the Jackson Statue . . . on Tuesday, October 26, 1875* (Richmond, 1875), 6.

30. Testimony of Luther Haymond of Clarksburg, in *Harrison County News*, Nov. 7, 1902. See also Cook, *Family and Early Life*, 75.

31. Mrs. Jackson, 15; Dabney, 10–11; Camden to Dabney, Nov. 21, 1863; Cook, *Family and Early Life*, 21, 43–44. Three members of Jackson's military staff made comments on Julia Jackson Woodson's religion. Two of them thought she was Methodist. See Dabney, 10, and Henry Kyd Douglas, in *Annals of the War: Written by Leading Participants North and South* (Philadelphia, 1879), 650. Colonel Thomas Preston told Dabney that Julia Neale was reared a Presbyterian but attended Methodist services because no other church was in the region where she lived. John T. L. Preston Narrative, Box 20, Dabney—SHC. Actually, in May 1831, the Rev. Asa Brooks accepted Julia Jackson Woodson into the Presbyterian church. Anna Jackson, "Memory's Mirror," unfinished manuscript, Thomas J. Jackson Papers, Davidson College.

32. Cook, *Family and Early Life*, 21; Bland statement. Robert L. Dabney refused to believe this allegation of abuse against Woodson and did not incorporate it in his biography. Jackson's widow likewise ignored the charge and declared that Woodson "was always kind to the children." Mrs. Jackson, 16. The best evidence in support of the abuse charge is that Jackson himself made no recorded comment in adulthood about his stepfather.

33. J. W. Hamilton, Fayette, W.Va., to Roy Bird Cook, undated letter, Cook—WVU.

34. Woodson file, Cook—WVU; Arnold, 27–28; Chase, *Jackson*, 58–59; Mrs. Jackson, 16. A disarray of facts mysteriously exists with regard to the children being sent to members of the two families. Roy Bird Cook, the longtime authority on Jackson's early life, at first declared that the youngsters went to relatives prior to Mrs. Jackson's marriage to Woodson. Cook later stated that the children accompanied their parents to Fayette County. See *CV*, 32 (1924): 268; Cook, *Family and Early Life*, 47. Arnold, 27, was of the opinion that the three children spent a short time in Ansted before being sent back to Lewis County. Mrs. Jackson, 16, had Warren and Tom going to live with Jackson relations while Laura accompanied her mother to the frontier. Another source discounted the family breakup and put Tom Jackson in Fayette County with his parents for "a part of a year." Forrest Hull, "The Mother of 'Stonewall' Jackson," *West Virginia Review*, (Dec. 1945): 26–27. Dabney, 11, seemed to infer that Warren, Tom, and Laura went to live with relatives prior to the Woodsons' departure from Clarksburg.

35. Mrs. Jackson, 16–17; Arnold, 28. Various sources placed Julia Woodson's death in September, October, and early December 1831; her tombstone bears a September date. Yet extensive research clearly pinpoints December 4 as the date of her passing in Ansted.

36. Woodson file; Hull, "Mother of 'Stonewall' Jackson," 26–27. One of Jackson's proudest soldiers was Capt. Thomas Davis Ranson. A native of Charles Town and member of the 2d and 52d Virginia, Ranson became a postwar resident of Staunton. Several years after the Civil War, and at his own expense, Ranson erected a metallic circular marker for Jackson's mother in what by then was called Westlake Cemetery near Ansted. The inscription stated: "Here lies Julia Beckwith Neale, born Feb. 28, 1798, in Loudoun Co., Va. Married first Jonathan Jackson, second Blake B. Woodson. Died Sept., 1831. To the mother of Stonewall Jackson this tribute from one of his old Brigade." *CV*, 16 (1908): 106–7; 19 (1911): 537. Today a granite, surface-level stone—a gift of Noble Wyatt—stands where the grave is presumed to be.

37. Copy of letter in possession of Gary S. Weiner, Clarksburg, W.Va. A summary of the letter is in Cook, *Family and Early Life*, 47.

38. Cook, *Family and Early Life*, 28, 33, 36–38. The residence depicted on most Jackson's Mill illustrations is not the one in which the future general lived. The more well-known home was constructed in 1843, a year after Jackson entered West Point. The porch was an addition made in the late 1860s.

39. Ibid., 79.

40. Arnold, 54, 60; Bland statement. Typical father-image portrayals of Cummins Jackson are in Dabney, 14–15; Mrs. Jackson, 22; Chase, *Jackson*, 71; *SHSP*, 22 (1894): 158.

41. Newspaper clipping, Aug. 20, 1939, Cook—WVU.

42. Unsigned manuscript on Cummins Jackson, Cook—WVU.

43. Camden to Dabney, Nov. 25, 1863; Smith, *Lewis County*, 147.

44. Charles H. Washburne to Roy Bird Cook, Oct. 3, 1927, Cook—WVU; Bland statement; William Adler, Weston, W.Va., to author, Nov. 28, 1990. One of the ingredients in the counterfeit fifty-cent pieces was glass "to make it ring like silver." William E. Arnold Recollections, George M. Heroman and Family Papers, LSU.

45. TJJ to Laura Jackson, Aug. 8, 1844, in Arnold, 71; Margaret Junkin Preston, in Elizabeth R. P. Allan, *A March Past: Reminiscences of Elizabeth Randolph Preston Allan* (Richmond, 1938), 122. Charles Royster, *The Destructive War: William Tecumseh Sherman, Stonewall Jackson, and the Americans* (New York, 1991), 49, presented a contrasting summary of the years at Jackson's Mill.

46. Arnold Recollections.

47. J. H. Diss Debar, "Two Men: Old John Brown and Stonewall Jackson of World-wide Fame," typescript, West Virginia Department of Archives and History, 6.

48. Mrs. Jackson, 21; Cook, *Family and Early Life*, 50. Chambers, 1:33, called Jackson's raft "a burnt-out canoe."

49. Judge C. H. McWhorter, Conrad Kester's nephew, first narrated for publication the story of the fish. *Clarksburg News*, July 6, 1900. Other versions of the story are in Cook, *Family and Early Life*, 52–53, and *CV*, 8 (1900): 58–59.

50. Markinfield Addey, *"Stonewall Jackson": The Life and Military Career of Thomas Jonathan Jackson* (New York, 1863), 17. Among those who touted Jackson's musical ability were Mrs. Jackson, 21–22; Roy Bird Cook, *Lewis County in the Civil War, 1861–1865* (Charleston, 1924), 147; Couper, *One Hundred Years at VMI*, 3:179, and Chambers, 1:34. Henry Kyd Douglas of Jackson's Civil War staff insisted that the general's "ignorance of music" included everything but the Rebel yell. *Annals of the War*, 646. The story of Jackson's request for "Dixie" is in a marginal note by Douglas in his copy of Mrs. Jackson, 184, Douglas Library, Antietam NBP.

51. Mrs. Jackson, 19–20, erroneously concluded that Warren, not his brother Tom, went to live with the Brakes. For a more positive picture of Tom Jackson's life with the Brakes, see Isaac Newton Brake's reminiscences in the Clarksburg *Sunday Exponent-Telegram,* Apr. 20, 1930.

52. Bland statement; Cook, *Family and Early Life,* 48, Arnold, 29−31, 162.

53. Some previous accounts had Warren living at Jackson's Mill and leaving there on a "wild and impulsive streak" in search of excitement. For example, see Jackson sketch, Robert A. Brock Collection, Huntington; Mrs. Jackson, 22−23; Chase, *Jackson,* 76. Warren Jackson has been variously described as a self-reliant person with a wandering nature, wild and impulsive, a bright youth with good study habits, and one constantly rebelling against authority. Dabney, 15−16; Chase, *Jackson,* 76; Arnold, 31; Mrs. Jackson, 22. Warren was surely more self-confident and outgoing than his younger brother.

54. Handwritten biographical sketch of Jackson, Brock Collection; Arnold, 32−34; Dabney, 16.

55. Cook, *Family and Early Life,* 66; TJJ to Grace Arnold, Feb. 25, 1860.

56. Arnold, 306; Arnold Recollections; TJJ to Grace Arnold, Feb. 25, 1860. See also Raleigh E. Colston Reminiscences, SHC.

57. Cook, *Family and Early Life,* 56.

58. Smith, *Lewis County,* 185, 191.

59. Memoranda, Jackson—Holt; Cook, *Family and Early Life,* 56−58; Cook, *Lewis County,* 147.

60. Bland statement; handwritten biographical sketch, Brock Collection, Huntington. William E. Arnold, who claimed to be Jackson's first schoolmaster, added a dramatic story of young Jackson thrashing a bully after the latter insulted some young girls. *SHSP,* 22 (1894): 158.

61. Dorothy Davis article in *Clarksburg Exponent-Telegram,* May 5, 1985; statement of Mary K. Holt, Weston, W.Va., Nov. 29, 1990.

62. Cook, *Family and Early Life,* 61−62, 79. Religious opportunities were available in Lewis County, and Jackson took advantage of them. The long-held charge that the Jackson uncles stifled religion in every form is an overkill whose seeds are in Dabney, *Jackson,* 23−24.

63. Memorandum, Cook—WVU; Cook, *Family and Early Life,* 61−62.

64. Cook, *Family and Early Life,* 64−65.

65. Charles H. Washburne recollections in Feb. 3, 1925, newspaper, Cook—WVU.

66. Ibid.

67. Cook, *Family and Early Life,* 59−61. The original voucher for Jackson's payment is in Jackson—Holt.

68. Preston Narrative; D. H. Hill, in *Century Magazine,* 47 (1893−94): 626.

69. Handwritten biographical sketch, Brock Collection, Huntington; Margaret Junkin Preston, in *Century Magazine,* 32 (1886): 927; Bland statement; McCabe, *Jackson,* 11.

70. The appointment as constable is part of Jackson—Holt. A copy of the bond is in Cook—WVU. Prominent landowner Gideon D. Camden always believed that Cummins Jackson and others purposefully concealed from the court Tom Jackson's status as a minor. See Camden to Dabney, Nov. 25, 1863, Box 19, Dabney—SHC.

71. Bland statement. A full summary of the allegations is in *Clarksburg Exponent,* Apr. 27, 1952. Robert L. Dabney refused to believe Bland's charge that Jackson fathered an illegitimate child, and Dabney made no reference to the matter in his 1865 Jackson biography. The unidentified handwritten biographical sketch in the Brock Collection, Huntington, contains the passing reference that "the moral influences" to which Constable Jackson "was subject were very unfavorable." No corroborating evidence of any kind has ever surfaced in support of Bland's assertion.

72. Cook, *Family and Early Life,* 69−70. In Dr. Bland's version of the story, Jackson and Holt engaged in a fistfight before the matter was settled. Bland statement. A third version of the encounter had Holt using a whip in an effort to ward off Jackson. Henry Tucker Graham, *Stonewall Jackson: The Man, the Soldier, the Christian* (Florence, S.C., n.d.), 4−5.

73. Debt voucher, Jackson—Holt; leaf from Jackson's constable book, File 55-B, LHAC; Virginia County Court (Lewis County), Ledgers, 1840−43, UVA; John Strange Hall Reminiscences, Jackson—Holt.

74. Moore's remarkable travel narrative, quoted repeatedly here, is printed in toto in Cook,

Family and Early Life, 74–80. A popular Quillan theme in his sermons of the 1840s was: "Wickedness is on the increase in Clarksburg!" Dorothy Davis, *History of Harrison County, West Virginia* (Clarksburg, W.Va., 1970), 580.

75. No evidence survives that Jackson and Moore had any close association thereafter.

76. Mrs. Jackson, 24; memorandum in Cook—WVU. Warren Jackson was buried in the Post Cemetery on the road between Buckhannon and Clarksburg. In later years, Tom and Laura paid to have a suitable marker placed over the grave. Cook, *Family and Early Life*, 180.

77. Bland statement; Virginia Hall, "Why Stonewall Jackson Was Grateful to Cong. Samuel L. Hays," typescript, Cook—WVU; Robert C. Davis, U.S. Adjutant General's Office, to Roy Bird Cook, Apr. 10, 1922, Cook—WVU. First Cook, *Family and Early Life*, 83–84, and then Chambers, 1:50, stated that Butcher got the appointment because of his high exam grades in mathematics. In light of Jackson's known excellence in that one subject, such a conclusion is illogical. The account presented here was based on the meticulous reminiscences of John S. Hall in Jackson—Holt. Local rumor at the time was that Butcher, "of good character and ambition," received the appointment as a result of his "close friendship" with the chief examiner's daughter. Cook, *Family and Early Life*, 82–83.

78. Interview with Dr. Laurie Shea, May 24, 1993; Mrs. Jackson, 27.

CHAPTER 2   *Coming of Age at West Point*

1. Bland statement, Box 20, Dabney, SHC; G. D. Camden to Robert L. Dabney, Nov. 25, 1863, Box 19, Dabney—SHC.

2. Virginia Hall typescript, Cook—WVU; Hall Reminiscences. Bland statement is at variance with this account in a few minor details.

3. *SHSP*, 22 (1894): 159.

4. [Catherine C. Hopley], *"Stonewall" Jackson, Late General of the Confederate States Army* (London, 1863), 3–4; Dabney, 30–31. Slightly different versions of the meeting with Bennett are in Mrs. Jackson, 31, and Cook, *Family and Early Life*, 84–85.

5. Virginia Hall typescript; Hall Reminiscences; Bland statement.

6. Some of the more ludicrous accounts are in Allie Moore statement, Cook—WVU; Hall Reminiscences; John G. Gittings, *Personal Recollections of Stonewall Jackson and Other Sketches* (Cincinnati, 1899), 11–12.

7. Richmond *Daily Dispatch*, May 31, 1862; Dabney, 31; Cook, *Family and Early Life*, 85.

8. All of the endorsements were written in the June 12–14 period. The full correspondence is in Records Relating to the U.S. Military Academy, Application Papers of Cadets, 1805–1866, RG94, NA. Most of the letters are printed in Cook, *Family and Early Life*, 85–89.

9. Records Relating to USMA, Application Papers. Contrary to Farwell, *Stonewall*, 17, only two of the documents of recommendation give a middle initial to Jackson's name. Why the youth had decided to adopt an initial at this time is unknown. Jackson's feelings about his father Jonathan—assuming that the initial stood for him—had undergone no recorded change at this point.

10. Samuel Hays to John C. Spencer, June 17, 1842, Records Relating to USMA, Application Papers. Cook, *Family and Early Life*, 89, printed this letter under the erroneous date of June 19. One early biographer thought that the freshman congressman tried to dissuade Jackson from entering West Point. McCabe, *Jackson*, 11. While a number of writers have stated that Hays escorted Jackson to a personal interview with the secretary of war, and that the lad received both the appointment and a fatherly lecture from the official, such an occurrence is implausible on several counts. See Dabney, 31–32; Mrs. Jackson, 32; Arnold Recollections, George M. Heroman and Family Papers, LSU.

11. Records Relating to USMA, Application Papers.

12. "Academic Record of Thomas Jonathan Jackson," typescript, Thomas J. Jackson File, USMA.

13. USMA Working Committee, "Superintendent's Curriculum Study," typescript (West

Point, 1958), 14; Tidball, "Getting through West Point," 18, USMA; George H. Derby to mother, July 2, 1842, George Horatio Derby Letters, USMA.

14. This account is a composite of Dabney H. Maury, *Recollections of a Virginian in the Mexican, Indian, and Civil Wars* (New York, 1894), 22–23, and his revised manuscript in *SHSP*, 25 (1897): 309–10.

15. James L. Morrison, Jr., *"The Best School in the World": West Point in the Pre-Civil War Years, 1833–1866* (Kent, Ohio, 1986), 64–65.

16. *CV*, 6 (1898): 53.

17. See n. 14.

18. *CV*, 6 (1898): *xx*.

19. Tidball, "Getting through West Point," 27.

20. Lloyd Lewis, *Captain Sam Grant* (Boston, 1960), 89. See also Joseph G. Totten to Secretary of War, July 12, 1842, Engineering Department Records Relating to the U.S. Military Academy, 1812–1867, RG94, NA.

21. Staff Records, 1842–1845, III, 51–53, USMA; Post Orders, 1842–1846, USMA; *SHSP*, 22 (1894): 160. William Gardner, a fellow plebe, later asserted that Jackson failed his June entrance exams, "was permitted to occupy a room in the barracks while the cadet corps was in camp," and then passed a second examination in September. William M. Gardner, "The Memoirs of William Montgomery Gardner," typescript, USMA, 5. Official cadet records refute this story.

22. Records Relating to the U.S. Military Academy, Correspondence, 1841–1846, RG94, NA; Derby to mother, July 2, 1842.

23. Adjutant Thurston Hughes, USMA, to Roy Bird Cook, Nov. 15, 1935, Cook—WVU; *Daily National Intelligencer* [Washington, D.C.], June 21, 1845, newspaper files, USMA; Records Relating to USMA, Correspondence.

24. Morrison, *West Point*, 69; Tidball, "Getting through West Point," 36; William E. Jones Narrative, Cook—WVU.

25. Jones Narrative; Dabney, 33. Childhood friend William E. Arnold went from eulogistic to incredible in relating one West Point story. When the hazing of Jackson by a certain upperclassman became unbearable, Jackson "was forced out of self-respect to give the officer . . . a fearful *bruising*. The result was, he was brought to trial, and only saved himself from expulsion by pleading the order of the Secretary of War." Arnold Recollections.

26. William Dutton to uncle, July 31, 1842, William Dutton Letters, USMA.

27. Register of Delinquencies Book, Classes of 1845–1846, USMA.

28. Daniel M. Frost, "The Memoirs of Daniel M. Frost," *Missouri Historical Society Bulletin*, 26 (1969–70): 10; George H. Derby to mother, Oct. 3, 1842, Derby Letters; Morrison, *West Point*, 71–72. Until 1837, cadets slept in bedding on the floors of their rooms—a situation quite pleasing to a barrack's heavy population of vermin. Superintendent Delafield was responsible for the purchase of metal bedsteads. Richard Delafield to Joseph G. Totten, Dec. 12, 1842, Records Relating to USMA, Correspondence.

29. USMA, *Regulations Established for the Organization and Government for the Military Academy at West Point, New York . . .* (New York, 1839), 66.

30. Samuel H. Raymond to David Raymond, Oct. 16, 1842, Samuel H. Raymond Letters, USMA.

31. George H. Derby to mother, Feb. 26, 1845, Derby Letters; Morrison, *West Point*, 78; Jones Narrative.

32. Albert E. Church File, USMA.

33. USMA, *Regulations*, 10–11.

34. Lewis, *Captain Sam Grant*, 70; Morrison, *West Point*, 40–41.

35. Morrison, *West Point*, 25, 47–52, 56; D. H. Hill to R. L. Dabney, July 1, 1864, Dabney—UTS.

36. Jones Narrative.

37. W. H. C. Whiting to Robert L. Dabney, Nov. 30, 1863, Dabney—UTS.

38. John Gibbon to Jedediah Hotchkiss, Nov. 10, 1893, Reel 9, Hotchkiss—LC.

39. Dabney, 33.

40. Quoted in Edward M. Alfriend, "Recollections of Stonewall Jackson," *Lippincott's Magazine*, 69 (1902): 583. Grant claimed a closer association with Jackson than actually existed. Several years after the Civil War the Union chieftain wrote: "I knew him at West Point and in Mexico. He was very religious. . . . Personally we were always good friends; his character had rare points of merit." *Philadelphia Weekly Times*, Aug. 3, 1878.

41. Arnold Recollections; Turnley quotation in Henderson, 1:20–21; Jones Narrative; Maury, *Recollections*, 23. Maury embellished his earlier account for an article in *SHSP*, 25 (1897): 311.

42. Post Orders; Mrs. Jackson, 34; Arnold Recollections.

43. Adjutant General's Office: Records Relating to the U.S. Military Academy, Merit Rolls, 1841–1846, RG94, NA; Samuel H. Raymond to mother, Jan. 12, 1843, Raymond Letters. Dabney Maury's assertion that Jackson was last on the list of those who passed is untrue. Fourteen other cadets ranked below Jackson after surviving the midterm examinations. *SHSP*, 25 (1897): 311.

44. Jackson's book of maxims is part of Davis—Tulane.

45. Jones Narrative.

46. USMA, "Superintendent's Curriculum Study," 13; Joseph G. Totten to James A. Black, Feb. 26, 1844, Engineering Department Records, USMA.

47. Records Relating to USMA, Merit Rolls; Whiting to Dabney, Nov. 30, 1863. Some discrepancies exist between the merit rolls in the National Archives, the Official Register, 1831–1848, USMA, and the Register of Merit Book, 1836–1853, USMA. The demerits that plebe Jackson received for offense other than tardiness included "trigger rusty at company inspection," "name not printed properly on bulletin board," "coat out of order at inspection," and "shoes not properly blackened at inspection." Register of Delinquencies Book. That Jackson's name does not appear in the Register of Punishments, 1837–1847, USMA, is evidence that as a cadet he was never cited for misbehavior.

48. Register of Punishments.

49. Jones Narrative.

50. Ibid.; Mrs. Jackson, 34–35; Chase, *Jackson*, 99; Margaret J. Preston, in *Century Magazine*, 32 (1886): 927.

51. Morrison, *West Point*, 97; Post Orders.

52. Register of Merit Book. Records Relating to USMA, Merit Rolls, show eighty cadets in the third class.

53. Arnold, 63–64. The superintendent of West Point had the authority to grant leave to a cadet in lieu of the forthcoming summer furlough, if the cadet's guardian so requested it. In this same letter, Jackson urged Laura to ask Uncle Cummins to make such a request. Whether or not the uncle complied (he was then heavily in debt and loser in a recent, costly lawsuit), Jackson did not receive an early leave. Cook, *Family and Early Life*, 94, showed confusion on this matter. A memorandum describing the above lawsuit is in the Cook Collection.

54. Jones Narrative. This incident appears in more general form in Dabney, *Jackson*, 38–39, and Mrs. Jackson, 35.

55. Alan C. Aimone, USMA Special Collections Division, to author, June 11, 1993.

56. Official Register; Register of Merit Book; Records Relating to USMA, Merit Rolls; Register of Delinquencies Book. Arnold, 62, had Jackson taking "engineering studies" rather than English grammar while a third classman.

57. Thomas J. Arnold, "Beverly in the Sixties," *United Daughters of the Confederacy Magazine*, Nov. 1967, 7; Mrs. Jackson, 22; Arnold, 13.

58. Arnold Recollections.

59. *CV*, 32 (1924): 269.

60. Arnold, 66.

61. Post Orders; Arnold, 67. Dabney and Henderson are among several biographers who claimed that Jackson never attained a cadet rank at West Point.

62. Tidball, "Getting through West Point," 33–34.

63. Gardner, "Memoirs," 9.

64. Register of Merit Book. Records Relating to USMA, Merit Rolls, state that sixty-four cadets were then in Jackson's class.

65. TJJ to Laura Arnold, Feb. 10, 1845, Jackson—VMI.

66. *CV,* 6 (1899): 54; Chase, *Jackson,* 99.

67. TJJ to Laura Arnold, May 17, 1845, Jackson Letters—LC; Register of Merit Book. Again, small discrepancies exist in the numbers given in Records Relating to USMA, Merit Rolls, and Official Register.

68. Morrison, *West Point,* 100.

69. Frost, "Memoirs," 18–19.

70. Morrison, *West Point,* 49, 94. TJJ to Laura Arnold, Nov. 25, 1845, Jackson—VMI.

71. Gibbon to Hotchkiss, Nov. 10, 1893.

72. TJJ to Laura Arnold, Nov. 25, 1845.

73. Quoted in Henderson, 1:20; TJJ to Laura Arnold, Jan. 1, 1846, Cook—WVU. Turnley graduated fortieth in the class of 1846. His relatively brief military career was with the quartermaster department. In 1863, he resigned from the army and spent almost thiry years thereafter as a prominent Illinois businessman.

74. Jones Narrative.

75. TJJ to Laura Arnold, Nov. 25, 1845; Jones Narrative; *SHSP,* 25 (1897): 316.

76. Jones Narrative. For other comments on Jackson's poor health, see Addey, *"Stonewall Jackson,"* 17–18; Dabney, 36–37.

77. Register of Merit Book; Register of Delinquencies Book.

78. TJJ to Laura Arnold, Apr. 23, 1846, in Arnold, 74.

79. Couper, *One Hundred Years at VMI,* 3:176; Official Register; Register of Merit Book; Colston Reminiscences; *Century Magazine,* 47 (1893–94): 624; Maury, *Recollections,* 23.

80. Records Relating to USMA, Merit Rolls; Mark A. Snell, "Bankers, Businessmen, and Benevolence: An Analysis of the Antebellum Finances of Thomas J. Jackson," typescript, SJH, 20.

81. The other nineteen generals from Jackson's class were, in order of academic ranking: George B. McClellan, John G. Foster, Jesse L. Reno, Darius N. Couch, Truman Seymour, Charles C. Gilbert, John Adams, Samuel D. Sturgis, George Stoneman, William D. Smith, Dabney H. Maury, Isaac N. Palmer, David R. Jones, Alfred Gibbs, George H. Gordon, Cadmus M. Wilcox, William M. Gardner, Samuel B. Maxey, and George E. Pickett.

82. Maury provided the best account of the hotel party in *SHSP,* 25 (1897): 311–12. The most garbled version is Farwell, *Stonewall,* 39. Cook, *Family and Early Life,* 97, chose to overlook the hotel stopover turning into a wild celebration.

83. Hall Reminiscences.

84. Arnold, 78; Cook, *Family and Early Life,* 97–98.

85. Testimony of Margaret J. Preston, in *Century Magazine,* 32 (1886): 929.

86. Returns from Regular Army Artillery Regiments: First Regiment, Jan. 1841–Dec. 1860, M727, Roll 3, NA. The orders were dated July 17. Jackson's own description of receiving and obeying the order is in TJJ to Laura Arnold, Sept. 25, 1846, Jackson Papers—WVU.

CHAPTER 3   *Mexico and a Hero's Mantle*

1. War with Mexico Records, RG94, NA.

2. Letters Received by the Office of the Adjutant General (Main Series), 1822–1860, RG94, NA; Margaret J. Preston, in *Century Magazine,* 32 (1886): 929.

3. W. P. Martin, "Memoirs of Mexico," 1879 letter to the editor of the *Army and Navy Journal,* in Edward C. Boynton Papers, USMA; Roster of Officers and Enlisted Men, First U.S. Artillery, 1813–1855, RG391, NA; Letters Received by Adjutant General.

4. Francis Taylor to Adjt. Gen. Roger Jones, Aug. 19 and Sept. 7, 1846, Letters Received by Adjutant General.

5. Ulysses S. Grant, *Personal Memoirs of U. S. Grant* (New York, 1885–86), 1:53.

6. TJJ to Alfred Neale, Sept. 22, 1846, Jackson—VMI. The new lieutenant described his long trip in a Sept. 25, 1846, letter to his sister. It is in Jackson—WVU. A strongly edited version of the same letter appears in Arnold, 80.

7. Francis Taylor to Adjt. Gen. Roger Jones, Oct. 31, 1846, Letters Received by Adjutant General. *SHSP,* 25 (1897): 312; Maury, *Recollections,* 28–29.

8. Lewis, *Captain Sam Grant,* 183; Returns from Regular Army Artillery Regiments: First Regiment, Jan. 1841–Dec. 1860, M727, Roll 3, NA. All of the company officers were West Point graduates. Irons fell mortally wounded in the 1847 battle of Churubusco. Mackall and Martin later became Confederate generals.

9. Quoted in Henderson, 1:25.

10. TJJ to Laura Arnold, Apr. 22, 1847, Jackson—VMI.

11. Regular Army Muster Rolls and Inspection Returns, 1821–1860, RG94, NA; Returns from Regular Army Artillery Regiments, Roll 3.

12. TJJ to Laura Arnold, Apr. 22, 1847. Arnold, 89, chose to delete the last sentence in this passage.

13. TJJ to Laura Arnold, Mar. 30, 1847, Jackson—VMI.

14. D. H. Hill to Robert L. Dabney, July 1, 1864, Dabney—UTS. A quarter-century later, Hill dramatically embellished his story for publication. See *Century Magazine,* 47 (1893–94): 624.

15. Hill to Dabney, July 1, 1864.

16. Army Commands, Monthly Returns, First U.S. Artillery, 1843–1880, RG98, NA; Orders and Special Orders, 1847–1848, Department of Veracruz, RG393, NA.

17. TJJ to Laura Arnold, Mar. 30, 1847; Gardner, "Memoirs," USMA, 14; Jennings C. Wise, *The Military History of the Virginia Military Institute from 1839 to 1865* (Lynchburg, Va., 1915), 69.

18. TJJ to Laura Arnold, Mar. 30, 1847.

19. Margaret J. Preston, in *Century Magazine,* 32 (1886): 930.

20. TJJ to Isaac Brake, Mar. 31, 1847, printed in Clarksburg *Sunday Exponent-Telegram,* Apr. 20, 1930.

21. TJJ to Laura Arnold, Mar. 30, 1847; TJJ to Isaac Brake, Mar. 31, 1847.

22. TJJ to Gen. Thomas S. Jesup, Mar. 30, 1847, Jackson—VMI.

23. Jensen, "Daniel M. Frost," 207, 209.

24. Military Historical Society of Massachusetts, *Civil and Mexican Wars, 1861, 1846* (Boston, 1913), 563; Maury, *Recollections,* 29.

25. TJJ to Laura Arnold, Apr. 22, 1847.

26. Francis Taylor official report, Apr. 30, 1847, Letters Received by Adjutant General. For additional comments on Company K at Cerro Gordo, see John V. White to Jedediah Hotchkiss, Dec. 23, 1895, Reel 39, Hotchkiss—LC.

27. Elizabeth Preston Allan, *The Life and Letters of Margaret Junkin Preston* (Boston, 1903), 83. A slightly different version of Mrs. Preston's quotation is in Allan, *A March Past,* 123.

28. Official report of Col. Thomas Childs, in Letters Received by Adjutant General.

29. Mrs. Jackson, 41.

30. Maury, *Recollections,* 40, 42; Frost, "Memoirs," 217–18.

31. Roster, First Artillery; TJJ to Adjt. Gen. Roger Jones, Apr. 26, 1847, Letters Received by Adjutant General.

32. TJJ to Laura Arnold, May 1, 1847, Jackson—LC.

33. Ibid.

34. Regimental Orders Issued, First U.S. Artillery, 1840–1851, RG391, NA; Roster, First Artillery.

35. TJJ to Laura Arnold, May 1, 1847, Jackson—LC.

36. Special Orders No. 83, May 12, 1847, Orders and Special Orders; Returns from Regular Army Artillery Regiments, Roll 4. In addition to Winder, the other officers in Co. G were First Lts. Israel Vogdes and Henry D. Grafton. The company had no second lieutenant until Jackson reported for duty.

37. TJJ to Laura Arnold, May 25, 1847, Jackson—VMI.

38. Ibid. Chambers, 1:95, changed the last word in this paragraph from "desire" to "heart."

39. TJJ to Laura Arnold, May 25, 1847.

40. Ibid. Arnold, 92, thought it prudent to delete his uncle's reference to "this unholy land."

41. TJJ to Laura Arnold, Oct. 27, 1847, in Arnold, 129–30.

42. Regimental Orders Issued, First Artillery.

43. McCabe, *Jackson,* 13. Jackson's reasons for wanting to join Magruder's command are also in Mrs. Jackson, 40–41; Arnold, 95–96.

44. Regimental Orders Issued, First Artillery; Regular Army Muster Rolls; Army Commands, Monthly Returns, First Artillery.

45. Tidball, "Getting through West Point," 39–40, USMA. "F. F. V." is an aristocratic designation for "First Families of Virginia."

46. Frost, "Memoirs," 219.

47. K. Jack Bauer, *The Mexican War, 1846–1848* (New York, 1974), 291.

48. Francis Taylor to Lt. W. H. C. Brooks, AAAG, Aug. 23, 1847, Letters Received by Adjutant General.

49. Magruder's official report, in Letters Received by Adjutant General.

50. D. H. Hill quotation, in Stephen W. Sears, *George B. McClellan: The Young Napoleon* (New York, 1988), 22.

51. Tidball, "Getting through West Point," 44.

52. Regular Army Muster Rolls; Letters Received by Adjutant General.

53. Ibid.

54. The statements of Twiggs and Pillow, as well as a similar accolade from Col. Persifor Smith, are in Letters Received by Adjutant General.

55. On Aug. 20, Jackson received both regular promotion to first lieutenant and brevet elevation to captain. Roster, First Artillery. Jackson's quotation is from Hunter McGuire and George L. Christian, *The Confederate Cause and Conduct in the War between the States* (Richmond, 1907), 207.

56. Regular Army Muster Rolls; Magruder's report, in Letters Received by Adjutant General.

57. Dabney, 52. For praise of Pillow at Chapultepec, see *CV,* 26 (1918): 399–400.

58. Arnold, 130.

59. Raleigh E. Colston Reminiscences, SHC.

60. Military Historical Society of Massachusetts, *Civil and Mexican Wars,* 631–32.

61. Most sources agree on the words Jackson used in an effort to rally his troops. For example, see Mrs. Jackson, 42, and Lewis, *Captain Sam Grant,* 245. More dramatic quotations are in Addey, *"Stonewall Jackson",* 21, and Margaret J. Preston, in *Century Magazine,* 32 (1886): 929–30. An account, supposedly originating with Magruder and passed down by word of mouth into the Civil War period, is without challenge the most distorted. See Alfriend, "Recollections," 583. The statement about the only falsehood intentionally uttered is in *Century Magazine,* 32 (1886): 930, and Mrs. Jackson, 45.

62. Mrs. Jackson, 43; Arnold, 130, 176–77; Dabney, 52.

63. Chambers, 1:114.

64. Arnold, 177; Hill to Dabney, July 1, 1864.

65. Colston Reminiscences. Magruder's official report tended to downplay much of the elan displayed by the three lieutenants at that point in the battle. See Letters Received by Adjutant General.

66. Magruder's report, in Letters Received by Adjutant General; Regular Army Muster Rolls; Arnold, 311.

67. Mrs. Jackson, 45; Margaret J. Preston, in *Century Magazine,* 32 (1886): 929.

68. Magruder's report is in Letters Received by Adjutant General.

69. Pillow's report is part of Davis—Tulane. Worth's statement is in Adjt. John V. White, First Artillery, to Jedediah Hotchkiss, Dec. 23, 1885, Reel 39, Hotchkiss—LC.

70. Scott's report is part of Davis—Tulane.

71. Dabney, 51, repeated in Mrs. Jackson, 44. See also Henderson, 1:47.

72. Frost, "Memoirs," 8.

73. John Gibbon to Jedediah Hotchkiss, Nov. 10, 1893, Reel 9, Hotchkiss—LC. Gibbon, an 1847 graduate of West Point, had the erroneous opinion that Jackson was unaware of his exploits in Mexico.

74. TJJ to Laura Arnold, Oct. 26, 1847, in Arnold, 128–29.

75. Margaret J. Preston, in *Century Magazine*, 32 (1886): 933; Mrs. Jackson, 46. Jackson's wife mistakenly concluded that he did not begin the study of Spanish until he reached Mexico City.

76. Mrs. Jackson, 47; Margaret J. Preston, in *Century Magazine*, 32 (1886): 933. Anna Jackson added that during their Lexington years together, Jackson would sometimes dance the polka in the privacy of their home—but only in view of his wife.

77. W. H. C. Whiting to Robert L. Dabney, Nov. 30, 1863, Box 19, Dabney—SHC.

78. TJJ to Laura Arnold, Oct. 26, 1847, in Arnold, 128. In 1981, Washington newspaperman Holmes Alexander combined Jackson's statement about possibly marrying a Mexican girl with the earlier, unproven allegation that teenager Jackson fathered an illegitimate child. The result was a book, *The Hidden Years of Stonewall Jackson*, in which Alexander would have the reader believe Jackson's greatest loves to have been "women and war" (presumably in that order). The Alexander book is only one of several recent works that twist facts to validate preconceived judgments.

79. Dabney, 54. Mrs. Jackson, 47, admitted that the "fascinations of at least one dark-eyed senorita" proved "almost too great for his resistance."

80. Mrs. Jackson, 46; TJJ to Laura Arnold, Oct. 26, 1847, in Arnold, 129; *Philadelphia Weekly Times*, Apr. 7, 1877.

81. Dabney, 55.

82. Henry Heth, *The Memoirs of Henry Heth* (Westport, Conn., 1974), 52.

83. D. H. Hill, in *Century Magazine*, 47 (1893–94): 624.

84. Mrs. Jackson, 48; Margaret Preston, in *Century Magazine*, 32 (1886): 930.

85. Preston Narrative, SHC.

86. Mrs. Jackson, 48–49; William S. White Narrative, Box 20, Dabney—SHC; Preston Narrative.

87. TJJ to Alexander R. Boteler, Dec. 10, 1862, Alexander Robinson Boteler Papers, Scrapbook 1, Duke University.

88. *SHSP*, 10 (1882): 190–91.

89. D. H. Hill, in *Century Magazine*, 47 (1893–94): 624–25; Nov. 24, 1847, certificate of Dr. Martinez del Rio, Letters Received by Adjutant General; Addey, *"Stonewall Jackson"*, 20.

90. Returns from Regular Army Artillery Regiments, Roll 3; TJJ to Capt. Henry L. Scott, Nov. 11, 1847, Cook—WVU.

91. Special Orders No. 164, Dec. 4, 1847, and General Orders No. 36, Jan. 19, 1848, Regular Army Muster Rolls.

92. Accounts by those in attendance at the Lee-Hartley duel differ sharply, in large part because most were penned years after the event. In Lt. Fry's version (which Chambers, 1:139–40, chose to accept), the two contestants almost fought a second time with pistols at ten paces. See also *SHSP*, 25 (1897): 312–13. Lieutenant James J. Archer's so-called account is little more than a passing reference in *CV*, 8 (1900): 67. The most complete and reliable narrative of the duel, by Capt. M. M. Clark, is in a clumsily entitled article by DeCourcy W. Thom, "Something More of the Great Confederate General, 'Stonewall' Jackson, and One of His Humblest Followers in the South of Yesteryear," *Maryland Historical Magazine*, 25 (1930): 129–57. See likewise Dabney H. Maury statement in the *Richmond Times*, Jan. 23, 1898.

93. Returns from Regular Army Artillery Regiments; Army Commands, Monthly Returns, First Artillery; Regular Army Muster Rolls; Jackson reports of Feb. 2 and 21, 1848, in Records of the Office of the Quartermaster General: Letters Received, 1818–1870, RG92, NA.

94. TJJ to Laura Arnold, Feb. 28, 1848, Jackson—LC.

95. Ibid. An edited version of this letter is in Arnold, 130–33. Jackson's pay at the time was $104 monthly.

96. For the helplessness of Mexico, see TJJ to Jonathan Arnold, Mar. 21, 1848, Jackson—LC.

97. TJJ to Laura Arnold, Mar. 23, 1848, Jackson—VMI.

98. Ibid.
99. TJJ to Laura Arnold, Apr. 10, 1848, Jackson—WVU.
100. Ibid.
101. Ibid.
102. Letters Received by Adjutant General. The actual letter appointing Jackson as commissary officer is in Davis—Tulane. For an example of Jackson's correspondence in that post, see TJJ to Capt. Marsena R. Patrick, July 10, 1848, Samuel G. Flagg Collection, Yale University. Company K's officers are listed in Returns from Regular Artillery Regiments, Roll 3.
103. Regular Army Muster Rolls; Chambers, 1:147.

CHAPTER 4   *Health, Baptism, and Controversy*

1. Regular Army Muster Rolls and Inspection Returns, 1821–1860, RG94, NA; Col. Ichabod Crane to Adjt. Gen. Roger Jones, Nov. 17, 1848, Records of the Office of the Quartermaster General: Letters Received, 1818–1870, RG92, NA; Returns from Regular Army Artillery Regiments: First Regiment, Jan. 1841–Dec. 1860, M727, NA.
2. TJJ to Laura Arnold, Aug. 26, 1848, Jackson—VMI.
3. TJJ to Laura Arnold, Sept. 5, 1848, Jackson—VMI; Regular Army Muster Rolls; Roster of Officers and Enlisted Men, First U.S. Artillery, 1813–1855, RG393, NA. On Sept. 22, Fry swapped positions with Lt. John H. Dickerson of Company G.
4. Clive West, Weston, W.Va., to author, Jan. 26, 1991.
5. "Writings of Thomas Jackson Arnold," photocopy of manuscript in possession of the author, 1–2.
6. *Clarksburg Sunday Exponent-Telegram*, Apr. 20, 1930. In remembering Jackson's visit, Isaac Brake erroneously placed it at Christmas time. Cook, *Family and Early Life*, 107, made the same misstatement. Arnold, 143, was of the opinion that his mother accompanied Jackson to the Clarksburg-Weston area, then unconsciously contradicted himself in his narrative.
7. Diss Debar, "Two Men," 6–7.
8. The account of Jackson meeting with two Weston attorneys is a composite of Arnold Reminiscences, undated newspaper clipping, Heroman Papers, LSU, and John S. Hall Reminiscences, Jackson—Holt.
9. Arnold, 145–46; TJJ to Laura Arnold, Jan. 1, 1849, Jackson—LC.
10. Returns from Regular Army Artillery Regiments, Roll 4; Regular Army Muster Rolls.
11. Returns from U.S. Military Posts, 1800–1916: Fort Hamilton, N.Y., RG391, NA; Robert B. Roberts, *Encyclopedia of Historic Forts* (New York, 1986), 557–58. Fort Hamilton is the only remaining major U.S. Army installation in the metropolitan New York area.
12. Directive of Col. Ichabod B. Crane, Oct. 19, 1848, Roster, First Artillery.
13. TJJ to Laura Arnold, June 6, 1849, Jackson—LC. For examples of routine military correspondence, see TJJ to Quartermaster General, Dec. 16, 1848, Jan. 27, Feb. 1 and 14, Oct. 18 and 30, 1849, Letters Sent by the Office of the Quartermaster General, Main Series, 1818–1870, RG92, NA; TJJ to Quartermaster Gen. Thomas S. Jesup, Oct. 30, 1849, Charles Bednar Collection, USMHI.
14. TJJ to Laura Arnold, Jan. 7, 1849, Jackson—WVU; TJJ to Laura Arnold, Mar. 1, 1849, Jackson—LC.
15. TJJ to Samuel L. Hays, Feb. 2, 1849, Jackson—LC; Cook, *Family and Early Life*, 33. Jackson specifically mentioned one book he was reading in order to make an impression. The work was Charles Rollin, *The Ancient History of the Egyptians, Carthaginians, Assyrians, Babylonians, Medes and Persians, Grecians, and Macedonians*, 8 vols. (New York, 1843–44).
16. "Orders Miscellaneous, 1844–1852," Headquarters, First U.S. Artillery, NA; Regular Army Muster Rolls; Army Commands, Monthly Returns, First Artillery. The possibility exists that Jackson was not satisfied with two brevet promotions. In the National Archives, under date of December 1849—nine months after his elevation to brevet major—is a document entitled "Claim of First Lt. Thomas J. Jackson, First Artillery, to Additional Brevet." See Letters Received by Adjutant General. The unusual summary is not in Jackson's handwriting; it

contains nothing more than excerpts from four official reports that called attention to Jackson's gallantry in the Mexican War. No covering letter is included, and no action on the claim is listed.

17. TJJ to Laura Arnold, Apr. 7, 1849, Jackson—LC.
18. *Century Magazine,* 32 (1886): 934.
19. Andrew C. Holman, "Thomas J. Jackson and the Idea of Health: A New Approach to the Social History of Medicine," *Civil War History,* 38 (1992): 131–55, is an excellent summary of Jackson's health problems. See also Chambers, 1:156–57.
20. TJJ to Laura Arnold, Jan. 1, 1849.
21. TJJ to Laura Arnold, Feb. 1, 1849, Jackson—VMI.
22. Included among the works he read were Andrew Combe, *The Principles of Physiology Applied to the Preservation of Health and to the Improvement of Physical and Mental Education* (New York, 1847), and Orson Squire Fowler, *Physiology, Animal and Mental: Applied to the Preservation and Restoration of Health of Body and Power of Mind* (New York, 1847).
23. Royster, *Destructive War,* 49–50; TJJ to Laura Arnold, Feb. 1, 1849; TJJ to Laura Arnold, Mar. 1, 1849, Jackson—LC. Some modern-day physicians have added narcolepsy to Jackson's list of afflictions. This is an illness marked by brief attacks of deep sleep. No symptoms of such a malady existed at this time. The theory itself is at best speculative.
24. TJJ to Laura Arnold, Apr. 7, 1849.
25. TJJ to Thomas T. Munford, June 18, 1862, Brock Collection, Huntington.
26. Dabney Maury story, related first in Maury, *Recollections,* 71, then embellished slightly in SHSP, 25 (1897): 316.
27. TJJ to Laura Arnold, July 2, 1849, Jackson—VMI.
28. J. Stephen Hudgins, M.D., to author, Jan. 3, 1994.
29. TJJ to Laura Arnold, July 2, 1849.
30. Mrs. Jackson, 71; Preston Narrative, SHC.
31. TJJ to Laura Arnold, July 2, 1849.
32. Tidball, "Getting through West Point," 46.
33. TJJ to Laura Arnold, Dec. 3, 1849, Jackson—WVU.
34. *CV,* 39 (1931): 258; Mrs. Jackson, 49; George W. Cullum, *Biographical Register of the Officers and Graduates of the U.S. Military Academy at West Point, N.Y.* (Boston, 1891), 1:212; Lewis, *Captain Sam Grant,* 82. On July 21, 1853, the Rev. Parks drowned off the coast of New York City.
35. Robert Bayard Snowden, *Sermon: Half-century Commemoration of St. John's Church, Fort Hamilton, N.Y., of the Foundation of the Parish* (Fort Hamilton, 1884), 13. Dabney, 59–60, erroneously declared that Parks was the minister who baptized Jackson. Several explanatory notes should be added to this church register entry. That the rector gave Jackson the wrong middle name is not unusual in light of the national reverence with which Thomas Jefferson was then held. It was natural to assume that any Virginian with the initials "T. J." had to be a namesake of the principal author of the Declaration of Independence. Captain Justin Dimick of the First Artillery, like Taylor, held the brevet rank of lieutenant colonel following service in the Mexican War. Stationed at Fort Lafayette, Dimick was a devout Episcopalian. Every previous Jackson biographer has spelled the rector's name as "Schofield." Parish records clearly identify him as Scofield.
36. Snowden, *St. John's Church,* 8.
37. Ibid.
38. William S. White Narrative, Dabney—SHC. See also Margaret J. Preston, in *Century Magazine,* 32 (1886): 930; Holman, "Jackson Health," 145–46. Jackson's copy of the Episcopal hymnal is now at the Public Library of Cincinnati and Hamilton County, Ohio.
39. TJJ to Laura Arnold, Mar. 1, 1849, Jackson—LC.
40. "Orders Miscellaneous." The other four defendants at Fort Columbus were found guilty. Three were ordered "to receive fifty lashes on the bare back well laid on with a raw hide."
41. Ibid.; First Artillery: Regimental Order Book; Regimental Orders Issued, First Artillery; letter to Laura, in Arnold, 157.

42. TJJ to Laura Arnold, Dec. 3, 1849, in Arnold, 157; Returns from U.S. Military Posts, RG391, NA; Returns from Regular Army Artillery Regiments, NA.
43. TJJ to Laura Arnold, Jan. 7, 1850, Jackson—WVU.
44. TJJ to Laura Arnold, Mar. 8, 1850, Jackson—WVU; TJJ to Laura Arnold, Apr. 4, 1850, Jackson—LC.
45. TJJ to Laura Arnold, Mar. 8, 1850.
46. Ibid. For understandable reasons, Laura's son deleted from his book much of the quoted passages from this letter. See Arnold, 159-60.
47. Matilda L. White to Ruth White, July 27, 1929, Cook—WVU; Cook, *Family and Early Life*, 33, 110.
48. TJJ to James M. Jackson, Apr. 24, 1850, Jackson—VMI. Mrs. Jackson, 29, painted a kinder picture of Cummins Jackson's migration to California.
49. TJJ to Laura Arnold, July 6, 1850, Jackson—VMI.
50. Margaret J. Preston, in *Century Magazine*, 32 (1886): 933; Chambers, 1:159-60. If in traveling Jackson could not secure the precise food that he wanted, he simply fasted until such time as "proper nourishment" was available.
51. "Miscellaneous Orders"; TJJ to Laura Arnold, May 10, 1850, Jackson—LC.
52. TJJ to "Mrs. Gordon," July 11, 1840, Hopkins Family Papers, Alabama Department of Archives and History; Returns from Military Posts, RG391, NA; TJJ to Laura Arnold, Aug. 10, 1850, Jackson—VMI.
53. Maury, *Recollections*, 61-62, 71; TJJ to Laura Arnold, Sept. 3, 1850, Jackson—LC.
54. First Artillery: Regimental Order Book; Army Commands, Monthly Returns, First Artillery, NA. In mid-October, Jackson's old Company K departed Fort Hamilton for duty at Fort McHenry, Md. In Jackson's place was Lt. Abner Doubleday. Chambers, 1:150, created confusion by having Jackson's transfer to Company E take place a year earlier than it did.
55. Regular Army Muster Rolls; First Artillery: Regimental Order Book.
56. Col. Ichabod B. Crane to Lt. Oscar F. Winship, Oct. 11, 1850, General, Special, and Other Orders Received from Superior Commands, First U.S. Artillery, RG391, NA; Army Commands, Monthly Returns, First Artillery; Arnold, 166-67.
57. "Writings of Thomas Arnold," James I. Robertson, Jr., Blacksburg, Va., 3. Jackson's furlough was much shorter than "one or two months," as his nephew tabulated. Company E departed New York City on Oct. 27, 1850, on board the transport *Kate Hunter*. Upon arrival at Tampa Bay, the unit shifted to the steamer *Planter* and, on Dec. 10, reached Fort Casey.
58. Returns from U.S. Military Posts, 1800-1916: Fort Meade, Fla., Dec. 1849-Aug. 1857, RG391, NA; Regular Army Muster Rolls.
59. Col. Thomas Childs to TJJ, Dec. 14, 1850, Fort Meade, Fla.: Letters Received, June 1850-Aug. 1853, RG393, NA.
60. Col. Thomas Childs to Lt. Thomas S. Everett, Dec. 14, 1850, Fort Meade, Fla.: Letters Received.
61. Hampton Dunn, Tampa, Fla., to author, Feb. 2, 1991.
62. Orders No. 58, Dec. 18, 1850, Fort Meade, Fla.: Letters Sent and Orders, July 8, 1850-Oct. 17, 1853, RG393, NA.
63. Capt. William H. French to Col. Thomas Childs, Dec. 21, 1850, and Childs to French, Dec. 23, 1850, Fort Meade, Fla.: Letters Sent and Orders. The background and appearance of Fort Meade came from Canter Brown, Jr., "Fort Meade: On the South Florida Frontier in the Nineteenth Century" (copy of unpublished manuscript graciously presented by Prof. Brown to the author), 1-5. The site of the garrison is adjacent to the present town of Fort Meade.
64. William H. French to Col. Thomas Childs, Dec. 27, 1850, Letters Sent, Register of Letters Received . . . Department of Florida, RG393, NA.
65. Special Orders No. 59, Fort Meade: Letters Sent and Orders.
66. William H. French to TJJ, Dec. 30, 1850, and TJJ to William H. French, Jan. 1, 1851, Fort Meade: Letters Sent and Orders.

67. William H. French to Col. Thomas Childs, Jan. 2, 1851, Letters Sent, Department of Florida; William H. French to Headquarters, undated, Army Continental Commands, Western Division, Letters Received, 1851, RG393, NA; Col. Thomas Childs to William H. French, Jan. 8, 1851, Fort Meade: Letters Received; William H. French to Lt. T. S. Everett, Jan. 16, 1851, Letters Sent, Department of Florida; Garrison court-martial proceedings, Jan. 8 and Jan. 11, 1851, Fort Meade: Letters Sent and Orders.

68. Hill, "Jackson," 624–25.

69. Ibid.

70. Dabney, 62.

71. Lewis, *Captain Sam Grant,* 321; Jonathan Bennett to Gideon Camden, Feb. 17, 1851, letter in possession of Hunter Bennett, Jr., Weston, W.Va.; William H. French to Capt. John M. Brannan, Apr. 16, 1851, Army Continental Commands, Western Division, Letters Received.

72. Col. Thomas Childs to William H. French, Jan. 23, 1851, Fort Meade: Letters Received. (This collection includes all of the correspondence relating to Jackson's first expedition; some related communiques will also be found in Letters Sent, Department of Florida.)

73. Regular Army Muster Rolls; Monthly Returns, First Artillery; Records of the U.S. Army Continental Commands, 1821–1920, Proceedings of Courts-Martial, Jan. 1850–Oct. 1852, RG393, NA.

74. William H. French to TJJ, Feb. 17, 1851, Letters Sent, Department of Florida.

75. TJJ to William H. French, Feb. 25, 1851, Army Continental Commands, Western Division, Letters Received.

76. William H. French to Lt. T. S. Everett, AAAG, Feb. 26, 1851, Letters Sent, Department of Florida.

77. Orders No. 11, Mar. 7, 1851, Fort Meade: Letters Sent and Orders.

78. Francis H. Smith to TJJ, Feb. 4, 1851, Thomas J. Jackson File, VMI Faculty/Staff Records, VMI; TJJ to Francis H. Smith, Feb. 25, 1851, Superintendent's Records: Incoming Correspondence, VMI. The cleaner version of Smith's letter most often cited in Jackson biographies is in Cook, *Family and Early Life,* 126.

79. TJJ to Laura Arnold, Mar. 1, 1851, Jackson—WVU.

80. Ibid.

81. Ibid.

82. TJJ application for furlough, Mar. 3, 1851, Army Continental Commands, Western Division, Letters Received.

83. Monthly Returns, First Artillery; Vandiver, 61.

84. William H. French to Capt. John M. Brannan, Apr. 14, 1851, Army Continental Commands, Western Division, Letters Received.

85. TJJ to Lt. T. S. Everett, Mar. 23, 1851, Letters Sent, Department of Florida.

86. Ibid.

87. William H. French to Everett, Mar. 26, 1851, Letters Sent, Department of Florida.

88. T. S. Everett, AAG, to TJJ, Mar. 29, 1851, Fort Meade: Letters Received.

89. Fort Meade: Letters Sent and Orders.

90. TJJ to Laura Arnold, Apr. 2, 1851, Jackson—VMI.

91. D. H. Hill to Robert L. Dabney, July 1, 1864, Dabney—UTS; *Century Magazine,* 47 (1893–94): 624; Francis H. Smith, *The Virginia Military Institute: Its Building and Rebuilding* (Lexington, 1912), 132–34, 265. See also Couper, *One Hundred Years at VMI,* 1:247–51. Smith's copy of the army register, which Harvey Hill examined, is in the VMI Museum.

92. Francis H. Smith to TJJ, Mar. 28, 1851, William Couper Papers, VMI; Mark E. Snell, "Bankers, Businessmen, and Benevolence: An Analysis of the Antebellum Finances of Thomas J. Jackson," typescript, SJH, 21.

93. The April 13–22 charges, countercharges, and correspondence between Jackson, French, and division headquarters with respect to the servant are all in Army Continental Commands, Western Division, Letters Received. Unless otherwise stated, quoted material in the time period is from that source.

94. Orders No. 21, Apr. 13, 1851, Fort Meade: Letters Sent and Orders.

95. D. H. Hill, in *Century Magazine,* 47 (1893–94): 624–25.

96. TJJ to Francis H. Smith, Apr. 22, 1851, Superintendent's Records: Incoming Correspondence. In March, Jackson had requested a nine-month furlough that would have taken him to the end of the calendar year. When it began to look favorable that he would get the VMI professorship, Jackson asked Smith to intercede on his behalf for a six-month leave. The end of that period would put Jackson at the beginning of the VMI academic year, he assumed.

97. TJJ to Laura Arnold, Apr. 22, 1851, Jackson—LC.

98. Margaret J. Preston was the first to quote Jackson's response to accepting the VMI post under false pretenses. *Century Magazine,* 32 (1886): 932. Francis H. Smith, in Wise, VMI, 74–75, and Mrs. Jackson, 56–57, presented the same rationale for Jackson leaving the army. In their accounts, Jackson began his statement with the phrase, "Not in the least."

99. Returns from U.S. Military Posts: Fort Meade, May, 1851, RG391, NA; TJJ to Laura Arnold, May 16, 1851, Jackson—WVU.

100. Orders No. 30, May 20, 1851, Fort Meade: Letters Sent and Orders; Returns from Regular Army Artillery Regiments, May 1851; *CV,* 6 (1899): 54.

101. Army Commands, Monthly Returns, First Artillery, May 1851; Orders No. 31, May 21, 1851, Fort Meade: Letters Sent and Orders; William H. French to Adjt. Gen. Roger Jones, May 21, 1851, Army Continental Commands, Western Division, Letters Received.

102. General David Twiggs's endorsement, June 30, 1851, Army Continental Commands, Western Division, Letters Received; Regimental Orders Issued, First Artillery, June 29, 1851.

103. William H. French to Adjt. Gen. Roger Jones, July 22, 1851, Army Continental Commands, Western Division, Letters Received. William H. French to Adjt. Gen. Roger Jones, Aug. 22 and Sept. 29, 1851, Letters Received by Adjutant General.

104. Fort Meade: Letters Sent and Orders, Oct. 1, 1851; Gen. David Twiggs to Sec. of War Charles M. Conrad, Mar. 6, 1852, Army Continental Commands, Western Division, Letters Received.

105. French got a respite with the outbreak of civil war. Appointed a brigadier general in September 1861, he eventually attained command of a corps in the Army of the Potomac. His blunders in the November 1863 Mine Run campaign led to his removal from field service in the spring 1864 reorganization of the army. French spent the remainder of his life in Washington. A newspaper account of his 1881 funeral concluded: "The widow of the deceased General is utterly prostrated by the death of her life-long helpmate." *Washington Post,* May 23, 1881. Caroline French died three years later. For ferreting out information on the French family from tombstones and other obscure sources, genuine thanks go to Vicki K. Heilig of Germantown, Md.

CHAPTER 5　　　*Establishing Roots in Lexington*

1. Arnold, 174–76.

2. John S. Wise, *The End of an Era* (Boston, 1899), 245–46; Edwin L. Dooley, Jr., "Gilt Buttons and the Collegiate Way: Francis H. Smith as Antebellum Schoolmaster," *Virginia Cavalcade,* 36 (1986): 30–39.

3. Arnold, 247.

4. Raleigh E. Colston Reminiscences, SHC. It is strange that widely varying figures have long been given for Jackson's height. Measurements of the VMI uniform he wore revealed a man no taller than 5 feet, 10 inches. When Jackson in 1856 applied for a passport, he listed his height at five feet, nine and three-quarters inches.

5. Snell, "Antebellum Finances," SJH, 22.

6. For example, see Mrs. Jackson, 57; Wise, *VMI,* 75.

7. Holman, "Jackson and Health," SJH, 146; Memorandum on Barney in Cook—WVU; *New York Times,* Jan. 16, 1927.

8. Statement in William Couper Papers, VMI; Cook, *Family and Early Life,* 118; Withrow Scrapbooks, W&L, VII, 175. Not far from Dr. Barney's home lived Dr. Samuel Guthrie, who had recently discovered an anaesthesia he called chloroform.

9. *Century Magazine*, 47 (1893–94): 625.

10. TJJ to Lowry Barney, Aug. 18, 1853, Jackson—WVU. Of course, the fact that Jackson's mind was fully occupied with the enjoyable responsibilities of a new and demanding position was also a boon to his good health.

11. Wise, *Military History*, 24, 30, 32–34; Thomas M. Boyd, in *Southern Bivouac*, 2 (1885–86): 355.

12. For details of the fight over VMI's future location, see Couper, *One Hundred Years at VMI*, 1:201–6, 212–14.

13. *Lexington Gazette*, Mar. 13, 1851; Wise, *End of an Era*, 247.

14. Curtiss W. Schantz, ed., "The Lost Order Book of the Virginia Military Institute, 1862–64," typescript, Western Historical Manuscript Collection, 4.

15. Couper, *One Hundred Years at VMI*, 1:62.

16. James T. Murfee to Thomas T. Munford, July 18, 1903, Munford-Ellis Family Papers, Duke University.

17. VMI Order No. 137, Aug. 13, 1851, announced Jackson's arrival. A copy of that order is in the Couper Papers.

18. Thomas T. Munford, "How I Came to Know Maj. Thomas J. Jackson," handwritten memoir, Charles E. and George W. Munford Papers, Duke.

19. Ibid.

20. Ibid.

21. Ibid.

22. Order Book, Aug. 18, 1851, VMI; Couper, *One Hundred Years at VMI*, 1:244; TJJ to Laura Arnold, Aug. 20, 1851, Jackson—VMI.

23. *Lexington Gazette*, Aug. 14, 1851, and Aug. 19, 1852; Stan Cohen, *Historic Springs of the Virginias* (Charleston, W.Va., 1981), 7–9, 99, 122–23.

24. Wise, *Military History*, 75; Cook, *Family and Early Life*, 128.

25. In addition to the four faculty living in the barracks, the institute staff included nine officers, three musicians, and a small custodial staff. Couper, *One Hundred Years at VMI*, 1:246, 254n.

26. Smith, *VMI*, 111; Thomas T. Munford to William T. Poague, Nov. 6, 1903, William Thomas Poague Papers, Duke.

27. Murfee to Munford, July 18, 1903.

28. Wise, *End of an Era*, 261; *Lexington Gazette*, May 1, 1862. For more praise of Williamson, see *Richmond Daily Dispatch*, July 6, 1862.

29. Classroom assignments, Sept. 26, 1851, Order Book, VMI. Where Jackson's section room stood is now three cadet dormitory rooms.

30. Quoted in Arnold, 178.

31. William B. Taliaferro, "Reminiscences of Jackson," William B. Taliaferro Papers, W&M, 1–2.

32. Addey, *"Stonewall Jackson"*, 18. Another description of Jackson's strange style of walking is in *Lexington Gazette*, Sept. 4, 1928.

33. James H. Lane Reminiscences, Auburn University.

34. Edward Sixtus Hutter Collection, VMI; lecture notes, Jackson—Tulane. In trying to explain the intricacies of Jackson's course, an early biographer became equally confused. See Dabney, 62.

35. *SHSP*, 20 (1892): 308; undated Robert L. Dabney interview with Margaret J. Preston, Box 20, Dabney—SHC.

36. McCabe, *Jackson*, 20.

37. Lane Reminiscences.

38. *Rockbridge County News*, Jan. 24, 1935; John G. Gittings, in George M. Vickers, ed., *Under Both Flags* (St. Louis, 1896), 133. See also *SHSP*, 16 (1888): 44–45.

39. *SHSP*, 20 (1892): 308.

40. Colston Reminiscences.

41. Preston Narrative, Box 19, Dabney—SHC.

42. Colston Reminiscences.

43. Thomas B. Robinson textbook, VMI.

44. Charles M. Barton to Joseph M. Barton, Sept. 28, 1855, Charles Marshall Barton Collection, VMI.

45. Couper, *One Hundred Years at VMI*, 3:187; *SHSP*, 16 (1888): 45; 20 (1892): 309. One cadet honored Jackson somewhat by referring to him as "that dignified fool Tom Jackson." Oates, *War between the Union and the Confederacy*, 186.

46. Giles B. Cooke to Roy Bird Cook, Jan. 12, 1925, Cook—WVU.

47. Lane Reminiscences; *SHSP*, 38 (1910): 271.

48. Thomas M. Boyd Reminiscences, Cook—WVU. Several accounts exist of the brick-dropping incident. Boyd's version, while relatively unknown, is one of the earliest and most temperate. Harvey Hill thought Jackson's escape from death or injury to be "almost miraculous." Yet, he added, Jackson continued walking "with contemptuous indifference." *Century Magazine*, 47 (1893–94): 627.

49. Lane Reminiscences.

50. Ibid.

51. Colston Reminiscences. Cadet James McCabe varied this story by having Jackson attempting to correct the institute clock through astronomical measurements. He arranged several instruments in front of the tower where the clock was, did a number of calculations, and solemnly declared it to be 7:30 A.M. Every cadet—and the school clock—knew that it was 12:30 P.M. McCabe, *Jackson*, 25.

52. Couper, *One Hundred Years at VMI*, 3:183.

53. Ibid., 1:168; Taliaferro, "Reminiscences of Jackson," W&M, 3.

54. McCabe, *Jackson*, 24.

55. *Richmond Times-Dispatch*, Oct. 2, 1910; Lane Reminiscences. Addey, *"Stonewall Jackson"*, 22, corroborated Lane's opinion.

56. *SHSP*, 20 (1892): 309.

57. Wise, *End of an Era*, 268.

58. Vickers, ed., *Under Both Flags*, 131–32.

59. Smith, *VMI*, 138.

60. *Rockbridge County News*, Feb. 24, 1888.

61. *Lexington Gazette*, Sept. 4, 1928. Cadet William A. Obenchain voiced a typically negative opinion of the major. "If asked to name the professor at the Institute most likely to rise to the highest rank and win the greatest fame in the event of war, probably four cadets out of five would have thought of Jackson last." *SHSP*, 16 (1888): 45–46. D. H. Hill's appraisal of Jackson the professor was no more positive. See *Century Magazine*, 47 (1893–94): 627. In an 1863 eulogy of Jackson to the VMI Board of Visitors, Supt. Smith was much more expansive in his praise. See Charles D. Walker, *Memorial, Virginia Military Institute* (Philadelphia, 1875), 552–53.

62. Boyd Reminiscences.

63. Munford Address, Jackson—VMI.

64. Barton Collection, VMI. See also *SHSP*, 19 (1891): 83.

65. Colston Reminiscences. The best biographical sketch of "Old Parlez" is in *SHSP*, 25 (1897): 346–51. One of his postwar addresses is in *SHSP*, 21 (1893): 38–49. Cadet James H. Lane told a slighty different story about Jackson's "weak" side. See Lane Reminiscences. Colston's laudatory opinions stand in marked contrast to negative statements by D. H. Hill in *Century Magazine*, 47 (1893–94): 627. Margaret Preston thought that Jackson's equanimity "was not disturbed in the least" by the jabs made about his odd ways. *Century Magazine*, 32 (1886): 930. Such a conclusion is unrealistic.

66. TJJ to Laura Arnold, Aug. 20, 1851; Arnold, 179; TJJ to Laura Arnold, Sept. 7, 1852, Jackson—LC.

67. John M. McDaniel et al., *An Archaeological and Historical Assessment of the Liberty Hall Academy Complex, 1782–1803* (Lexington, 1994), 145–46.

68. William S. White, *Rev. William S. White, D.D., and His Times: An Autobiography* (Richmond, 1891), 160.

69. *Lexington Gazette*, Feb. 6, 1851; Allan, *Margaret Preston*, 45.

70. Henry Boley, *Lexington in Old Virginia* (Richmond, 1974), 19; Wise, *End of an Era*, 240.

71. *Lexington Gazette*, Nov. 7, 1861.

72. *Lexington Gazette*, Mar. 6 and Apr. 17, 1861. Thirty years after Jackson's death, Hill wrote a long article on the man who became his brother-in-law. The essay (already cited several times previously) was at times surprisingly critical of Jackson. Colonel G. F. R. Henderson was stunned at the tone of some of Hill's remarks. "Is D. H. Hill to be trusted?" he asked a friend. The article, Henderson stated, "does not read to me as if [Hill] appreciated Stonewall Jackson as he should have done. It is dogmatic, but it seems as if he took Jackson to be a man of the same calibre as himself, which he *wasn't*." G. F. R. Henderson to Jedediah Hotchkiss, Mar. 14, 1895, Roll 11, Hotchkiss—LC.

Hill's coolness toward Jackson began sometime in the 1858–61 period. After the Civil War, according to one source, Robert E. Lee became "excited and somewhat indignant with General Hill, particularly with his stricture on General Jackson." Lee then stated that Hill "had such a queer temperament that he could never tell what to expect of him." E. C. Gordon to William Allan, Nov. 18, 1886, William Allan Papers, SHC. Such statements run counter to oft-repeated assertions that Hill was "an ardent admirer" of Jackson. See D. H. Hill to Robert L. Dabney, July 1, 1864, Dabney—UTS; R. L. Dabney to Jedediah Hotchkiss, Mar. 10, 1897, Roll 13, Hotchkiss—LC; Robert Stiles, *Four Years under Marse Robert* (New York, 1903), 72; Hal Bridges, *Lee's Maverick General: Daniel Harvey Hill* (New York, 1961), 162–63.

73. Clement D. Fishburne to Paul B. Barringer, 1903 letter reprinted in *Lexington Gazette*, May 12, 1931.

74. Allan, *A March Past*, 39–40. For more on Lyle, see Royster Lyle, Jr., "John Blair Lyle of Lexington and His 'Automatic Bookstore,'" *Virginia Cavalcade*, 21 (Autumn 1971): 20–27; White, *William S. White*, 140–43.

75. Chase, *Jackson*, 157–58.

76. Vickers, ed., *Under Both Flags*, 131.

77. TJJ to Laura Arnold, Mar. 23, 1848.

78. Mrs. Jackson, 63–64.

79. Colston Reminiscences.

80. Dabney, 76–77; Lane Reminiscences.

81. *SHSP*, 9 (1881): 42. For a similar description, see John Newton Lyle, "Sketches Found in a Confederate Veteran's Desk," typescript, W&L, 252–53.

82. *Rockbridge County News*, Jan. 24, 1935; *Century Magazine*, 22 (1886): 928.

83. Vickers, ed., *Under Both Flags*, 133.

84. Fishburne Memoirs, UVA.

85. Withrow Scrapbooks, W&L, XVII, 119; Mrs. Jackson, 65.

86. Preston Narrative.

87. Colston Reminiscences.

88. Lane Reminiscences; Murfee to Munford, July 18, 1903.

89. James L. Hubard to Robert L. Dabney, Sept. 17, 1863, Box 19, Dabney—SHC.

90. *Century Magazine*, 32 (1886): 927; Preston Narrative.

CHAPTER 6   *God and "Dearest Ellie"*

1. E. Lynn Pearson, "Thy Kingdom Come: The Evangelical Stewards of Antebellum Lexington, 1851–1861," typescript, SJH, 9–10.

2. Couper, *One Hundred Years at VMI*, 1:116; *Lexington Gazette*, Mar. 17, 1853. Chambers, 1:241, referred to "a legend" that Jackson visited each of the Protestant churches to experience the various services. Yet Dr. William S. White asserted that in the autumn of 1851 Jackson

"divided the time allotted to public worship equally among all the churches." William S. White Narrative, Box 20, Dabney—SHC.

3. White, *William S. White*, 137–38.

4. Mrs. Jackson, 57. For additional information on Jackson's pastor, see E. C. Scott, comp., *Ministerial Directory of the Presbyterian Church, U.S., 1861–1941* (Austin, Tex., 1942), 767; Robert F. Hunter, *Lexington Presbyterian Church* (Lexington, 1991), 60–63.

5. Arnold, 17.

6. D. H. Hill to Robert L. Dabney, July 1, 1864, Dabney—UTS.

7. White, *William S. White*, 140; Mrs. Jackson, 58. Because Dabney did not know Jackson at the time, he summarized in slanted form Jackson's struggle with some Presbyterian creeds. See Dabney, 84–85. A more balanced account of Jackson's conversion is in White Narrative.

8. White Narrative.

9. Records of the Presbytery of Lexington, UTS. Chambers's assertion that Jackson was one of seven persons admitted to church membership on Nov. 22, 1851, is in error. Church minutes for that date name only three initiates accepted into the Presbyterian fold. It took Jackson several months to adapt completely to the full Presbyterian creed. During that period, he got into a heated debate with Harvey Hill over predestination. An angry Hill suggested that Jackson might henceforth be more comfortable as a Methodist. "Let us go to see Doctor White and see what he thinks," Jackson replied seriously. They did, and the conference ended with White's observation: "Major, you are so good a Presbyterian in practice that we think you should stay with us." Jackson gave no further thought to joining another denomination. Chambers, 1:243; Preston Narrative, Box 19, Dabney—SHC.

10. D. H. Hill to Robert L. Dabney, June 7, 1863, Dabney—UTS; W. S. White to Jubal A. Early, Mar. 5, 1873, *SHSP*, 6 (1878): 265.

11. Edward A. Pollard, *Lee and His Lieutenants* (New York, 1867), 182–83. More authenticity may exist to this letter than historians have previously been willing to concede. Jackson once told his sister: "I derive much pleasure from morning walks, in which is to be enjoyed the pure sweetness of caroling birds." TJJ to Laura Arnold, Apr. 1, 1853, Jackson—LC.

12. Mrs. Jackson, 61, 73.

13. Arnold, 18–19; Mrs. Jackson, 60–61, 63.

14. George Winfred Hervey, *The Principles of Courtesy* (New York, 1852), 243.

15. B. Tucker Lacy Narrative, Box 20, Dabney—SHC.

16. Mrs. Jackson, 59–60. Jackson "greatly desired to preach the Gospel," and he told Dr. White several times how much he "preferred that sacred calling to all others." White Narrative.

17. White Narrative; Boyd Reminiscences, Cook—WVU.

18. Margaret Preston, in *Century Magazine*, 32 (1886): 935.

19. Dr. White's little-known account is the source for the meeting with Jackson over public prayer. White Narrative. More quoted and elaborate versions of what Jackson supposedly said to White are in Dabney, 91, and Mrs. Jackson, 61.

20. Preston Narrative.

21. Mrs. Jackson, 61–62; White Narrative; Preston Narrative. See also D. H. Hill account in *Century Magazine*, 47 (1893–94): 626, and Washington College student Alexander L. Nelson comments in Withrow Scrapbooks, W&L, XI, 100.

22. *Century Magazine*, 32 (1886): 931, 934; Pearson, "Thy Kingdom Come," 10.

23. Withrow Scrapbooks, W&L, IX, 69; *Century Magazine*, 47 (1893–94): 625.

24. Preston Narrative; Withrow Scrapbooks, W&L, IX, 69; *Century Magazine*, 47 (1893–94): 625; *Century Magazine*, 32 (1886): 936. Cadet James H. Lane once remarked: "Often have I seen him . . . fast asleep, evidently taking on faith what the ministers had to say long before they reached the 'sixteenthlies' in their learned discourses." James H. Lane Reminiscences, Auburn University. In the late 1850s, when pews at the Presbyterian church were numbered and rented, Jackson leased his seat 59 and retained it until he left Lexington for war.

25. D. H. Hill, in *Century Magazine*, 47 (1893–94): 625.

26. TJJ to Laura Arnold, Jan. 10, 1852, Jackson—LC.

27. TJJ to Laura Arnold, Feb. 21, 1852, in Arnold, 182.

28. Pearson, "Thy Kingdom Come," 26.

29. Some confusion has prevailed over the exact date of Jackson's resignation. A copy of his letter in Cook—WVU bears the date Feb. 20 and is in all likelihood correct. Another copy is dated Feb. 22; but since that was a Sunday, Jackson would not have written a letter then on any nonreligious subject. Letters Received by Adjutant General. One source used Feb. 29 as the date of Jackson's termination from service. That may have been when Jackson's resignation was officially accepted. Army Commands, Monthly Returns, First Artillery.

30. TJJ to Laura Arnold, Feb. 7, 1852, Jackson—VMI; TJJ to Laura Arnold, May 14 and June 5, 1852, Arnold, 185–86.

31. Raleigh E. Colston Reminiscences, SHC.

32. VMI Court Martial Book, Jan. 21 and Apr. 14, 1852, VMI; Lane Reminiscences; Couper, *One Hundred Years at VMI*, 3:186.

33. Colston Reminiscences. The description of Jackson in anger came from Arnold, 327.

34. Jackson File, VMI Faculty / Staff Records, VMI; VMI Court Martial Book, May 2, 1852; Withrow Scrapbooks, W&L, XVIII, 38. Cadet Christian, a member of Walker's class of 1852, later became a physician who spent most of his career as a surgeon in the U.S. and Confederate navies.

35. Quoted by D. H. Hill in *Century Magazine*, 47 (1893–94), 627.

36. Hill's version of the post-trial activity is dramatic and usually the account cited by writers. However, its truthfulness is strongly open to question. Colonel William Couper of VMI developed a more believable chain of events. *Century Magazine*, 47 (1893–94): 627; Couper Papers. For Walker's side of the controversy, see Willie Walker Caldwell, *Stonewall Jim: A Biography of General James A. Walker, CSA* (Elliston, Va., 1990), xiv, 1–4.

37. What caused this disagreement has led to much speculation in the past. The little-known recollections of Cadet James H. Lane provide the answer. Lane Reminiscences.

38. Wise, *VMI*, 89. When Col. Smith departed sometime later for a European trip, Jackson reportedly was the only VMI officer who failed to bid him goodbye and wish him a pleasant trip. Wise, *End of an Era*, 268–69.

39. Couper, *One Hundred Years at VMI*, 1:263.

40. Ibid., 3:183–84.

41. *Lexington Gazette*, Aug. 19, 1852; TJJ to Laura Arnold, July 12, 1852, Jackson—VMI; TJJ to Laura Arnold, Sept. 7, 1852, Jackson—LC.

42. White Narrative.

43. Ibid.

44. Mrs. Jackson, 63; White Narrative.

45. Harris served in the Civil War as surgeon of the 18th and 20th Battalions of Virginia Heavy Artillery. Afterwards, he became a prominent physician in Parkersburg, W.Va. (not Petersburg, Va., as Couper stated). Couper, *One Hundred Years at VMI*, 1:267; 3:178.

46. TJJ to Laura Arnold, Sept. 7, 1852.

47. TJJ to Laura Arnold, Oct. 25, 1852, Jackson—WVU; TJJ to Laura Arnold, Nov. 1, 1852, Jackson—WVU; Cook, *Family and Early Life*, 136.

48. TJJ to Laura Arnold, Oct. 25, 1852, Jackson—WVU.

49. Ibid.; TJJ to Laura Arnold, Oct. 9, 1852, Jackson—LC. See also TJJ to Laura Arnold, Feb. 1, 1853, Jackson—LC, for more comments on his diet.

50. *Lexington Gazette*, Nov. 11, 1852; Snell, "Antebellum Finances," 25. The establishment of the local Bible society marked the first time that the Lexington newspaper mentioned Jackson's name.

51. White, *William S. White*, 143. J. William Jones, who always dramatized a good story, had Jackson say of the collections from blacks: "They are poor, but ought not on that account to be denied the sweet privilege of helping so good a cause." *SHSP*, 19 (1891): 158. At this period, Laura again turned away from religion. Poor health was apparently the major factor. Jackson sought valiantly by letter to guide her back. "My continual prayer is that you will return unto the fold of *God*. My Dear Sister, if you will but seek God on the *bible* conditions, he will give you a peace and comfort, which all the powers on Earth can not destroy. And the hopes of a coming immortality will make all the ills of life supportable under every circumstance." TJJ to Laura Arnold, Nov. 1, 1852. Three months later, Jackson was still trying to get Laura to see the error of her disinterest. TJJ to Laura Arnold, Feb. 1, 1853.

52. Mary P. Coulling of Lexington, Va., uncovered the facts surrounding Ellie's tragic accident. Mrs. Coulling's book, *Margaret Junkin Preston: A Biography* (Winston-Salem, N.C., 1993), is the definitive source for relationships between Jackson and the two Junkin girls. The particulars of the accident are on pages 12-13.

53. Allan, *Preston*, 61, maintained that Ellie was Jackson's major religious inspiration. Harvey Hill refuted this belief in *Century Magazine*, 47 (1893-94): 625.

54. Allan, *A March Past*, 120; *Century Magazine*, 32 (1886): 927.

55. D. H. Hill wrote two accounts of the conversation with Jackson. The first, and more reliable, had their get-together taking place at night. Hill to Dabney, July 1, 1864. Hill penned a second version close to thirty years later. It suffered in accuracy from time and imagination. Hill then thought that the two men met in the afternoon, and Hill had Jackson replying to the accusation of being in love: "I have never been in love in my life, but I feel differently toward this lady from what I have ever felt before."*Century Magazine*, 47 (1893-94): 625.

56. Coulling, *Preston*, 68-70.

57. Hill to Dabney, July 1, 1864; *Century Magazine*, 47 (1893-94): 625. The name of Jackson's first wife is variously spelled "Elinor" and "Eleanor." The former is used here because it is the name that appears on her tombstone.

58. Colston Reminiscences. See also Mrs. Jackson, 62; Dabney, 72-73; Withrow Scrapbooks, W&L, XVIII, 37. Although Vandiver, 102-3, 503, was of the opinion that Jackson never officially joined the Franklin Literary Society, the minutes of the organization (deposited at W&L) clearly show the steps leading to his election to and acceptance of membership. See also Charles W. Turner, "The Franklin Society, 1800-1891," *VMHB*, 66 (1958): 436. Some circumstantial evidence points to Jackson, like his father, being in the Masonic order. If so, he was not a regular or active member. See *Civil War History*, 3 (1957): 341-42.

59. This was a common practice at the time. A fellow resident of Rockbridge County corresponded secretly with his sweetheart for two years before he approached her parents to ask for the daughter's hand. All the while, the couple pretended to care little for each other. Vivian E. Dreves, "'Your Devoted Anna': Women in Lexington, 1850-1861," typescript, SJH, 14.

60. Arnold, 204; TJJ to Laura Arnold, Apr. 1, 1853; TJJ to Laura Arnold, Apr. 15, 1853, Jackson—VMI.

61. TJJ to Francis H. Smith, June 11, 1853, Sarah Henderson Smith Papers, VHS.

62. Hill to Dabney, July 1, 1864; Mrs. Jackson, 95-98.

63. Coulling, *Preston*, 66; Margaret Junkin to Elinor Junkin, n.d., Box 19, Dabney—SHC.

64. TJJ to Laura Arnold, Aug. 3, 1853, Jackson—LC.

65. Colston Reminiscences; Lane Reminiscences.

66. "Writings of Thomas Arnold," 7-8; *SHSP*, 21 (1893): 340; Mrs. Jackson, 98-99. Graham Ellzey, an 1860 VMI graduate whose reminiscences are cited often here, observed of Jackson that "the roundabout way he took to ask Dick Catlett to be his groomsman suggest the query how in the name of wonder he went about asking Mrs. Jackson to be his wife." M. G. Ellzy to James H. Lane, Dec. 11, 1888, Lane Papers, Auburn.

67. Unidentified newspaper clipping in Withrow Scrapbooks, W&L, XVIII, 113.

68. Chambers speculated that Maggie joined the couple at some later point in their honeymoon. Maggie's biographer left no doubt that she was with the Jacksons from start to end of the wedding trip. Chambers, 1:251; Coulling, *Preston*, 71.

69. TJJ to Laura Arnold, Oct. 19, 1853, Jackson—VMI.

70. Ibid. See also TJJ to Laura Arnold, Nov. 30, 1853, Jackson—VMI.

71. *Century Magazine*, 32 (1886): 930-31; Allan, *Preston*, 62-63.

72. *Century Magazine*, 32 (1886): 932.

73. TJJ to Barney, Aug. 18, 1853, Jackson—WVU. Barney's Jan. 4, 1854, reply is in Old Catalog Collection, VHS.

74. Mary P. Coulling, "The Tie That Binds," typescript copy of talk in possession of the author, 6.

75. Coulling, *Preston*, 71–72; *Century Magazine*, 32 (1886): 933.

76. At this or another revival, Jackson first met Presbyterian cleric Daniel B. Ewing. Their friendship would grow and extend into the Civil War years. D. B. Ewing to Robert L. Dabney, Sept. 8, 1863, Box 6, Dabney—UVA.

77. TJJ to Laura Arnold, Oct. 19, 1853, Jackson—VMI; TJJ to Laura Arnold, Nov. 30, 1863, in Arnold, 206.

78. TJJ to Laura Arnold, Feb. 14, 1854, Jackson—LC.

79. *Lexington Gazette*, Feb. 19, 1852. At the time of Jackson's interest in the University of Virginia position, the *Gazette* ran a less-than-complimentary story on Lexington. "Counting whites and blacks of every age and size," it stated, the town's population did not exceed 1800 residents. Nor were the citizens well read, in the estimation of the editor. He later commented, "Two weekly newspapers are published here, neither of which is remarkable for the length of its subscription list." Ibid., Jan. 19, 1854.

80. Dabney, 69–70. John Preston recorded a far more condensed conversation with Jackson about the Virginia job. "You are giving up your expectation of a military career," Preston told him. "No," Jackson replied, "it will only prepare me better for it." Preston Narrative.

81. TJJ to Board of Visitors, Jan. 2, 1854, Davis—Tulane; D. H. Hill to Board of Visitors, Jan. 2, 1854, School of Mathematics, UVA. Hill's lukewarm endorsement leads to the conclusion that Hill himself, being a mathematics professor, might have wanted the Virginia professorship but that Jackson applied first. Dissatisfaction with Washington College resulted in Hill taking another job that same year.

82. TJJ to John J. Allen, Dec. 28, 1853, Accession #939, UVA; Cook, *Family and Early Life*, 133–35; R. E. Lee to Board of Visitors, Jan. 26, 1854, Davis—Tulane; R. E. Lee to Board of Visitors, Feb. 15, 1854, William Nelson Pendleton Papers, SHC.

83. TJJ to Laura Arnold, June 12, 1854, Jackson—LC.

84. Snell, "Antebellum Finances," 9–10, 57.

85. Arnold, 324–25.

86. Colston Reminiscences.

87. TJJ to Laura Arnold, Feb. 23, 1854, in Arnold, 209–10. For more details on Mrs. Junkin's death, see Julia Junkin to Lizzie Webster, Mar. 14, 1854, Julia Junkin Fishburne Letters, W&L.

88. *Century Magazine*, 32 (1886): 930. John Preston gave a similar account of Jackson's replies in Preston Narrative. James Power Smith produced a more embellished version in *SHSP*, 43 (1920): 70.

89. Laura's oldest son (and Jackson's namesake) edited his uncle's letters for publication. Out of respect, he chose to delete Preston's repeated insistences that Laura abandon her agnosticism and return to God. Jackson's letters of Mar. 4 and Apr. 7 are examples where Arnold removed passages and inserted ellipses to keep his mother from appearing in such a dark light. See Arnold, 210–11. The original letters are in Jackson—WVU.

90. See TJJ to Laura Arnold, Apr. 11, 1854, and May 11, 1854, court affidavit, both in Jackson—WVU.

91. D. H. Hill to "Phelps," Dec. 18, 1850, D. H. Hill Papers, NCDAH; Olinger Crenshaw, *General Lee's College* (New York, 1969), 87, 102. Jackson sought to facilitate Hill's transfer by writing to Gen. Gideon J. Pillow, Hill's commander in the Mexican War, and requesting that a questionable arrest of Hill during that conflict be stricken from the record in order to clear Hill's military career of a lingering stigma. TJJ to Gideon J. Pillow, May 11, 1854, Box 19, Dabney—SHC.

92. "Ellie's face has not yet entirely recovered," Jackson wrote early in May, "but I am of the opinion that time will effect a perfect restoration." TJJ to Laura Arnold, May 2, 1854, Jackson—LC. Although Ellie's facial affliction cannot be unimpeachably diagnosed, the likelihood is that it was neuralgia. Some theories have the malady being Bell's palsy. Yet the pain associated with that illness is so excruciating that Jackson would have made more than a passing reference to the ailment in his letter.

93. Jackson's book of maxims is in Davis—Tulane.

94. Royster, *Destructive War*, 60, revealed that the phrase "You may be whatever you resolve to be" came from the Rev. Joel Hawes and first appeared in an 1851 work, *Letters to Young Men, on the Formation of Character &c.*

95. TJJ to Laura Arnold, June 12, 1854, Jackson—LC.

96. *Lexington Gazette,* June 22, 1854, announced the arrival at the Natural Bridge Hotel of Elinor Jackson, Julia, David, and William Junkin. One side of the Bible society controversy can be seen in Francis H. Smith to TJJ, Oct. 9, 1854, Superintendent's Records: Outgoing Correspondence, VMI.

97. Coulling, *Preston*, 75.

98. TJJ to Laura Arnold, July 1, 1854, Jackson—LC.

99. "Writings of Thomas Arnold," A6.

100. The best work on the subject is Sally G. McMillen, *Motherhood in the Old South* (Baton Rouge, 1990). See especially pages 80–82.

101. TJJ to William E. Jones, Mar. 24, 1855. Jackson was responding to sentiments of sympathy from Jones, a fellow western Virginian and a friend since West Point days. This hitherto unpublished and extraordinary letter is in the possession of Roger D. Judd, Fairbury, Nebr. Not only does it firmly designate the gender of the child; the letter also painfully conveys the length and depth of Jackson's sorrow. The writer is deeply grateful to Mr. Judd for permission to quote from Jackson's reply to "Grumble" Jones.

Jackson's communication with Jones solves a long-standing mystery. For over 135 years, writers have had no hint as to the sex of Jackson's first child. Family lore had always been unanimous in the belief that the stillborn baby was a girl. A recent history of the Junkin family twice contained the reference that Elinor Jackson gave birth to a daughter. See Coulling, *Preston*, 76n.; Richard D. and Elisabeth C. Robinson, *Repassing at My Side . . . A Story of the Junkins* (Blacksburg, Va., 1975), 21. See also Farwell, *Jackson,* 117.

102. Colston Reminiscences. Short obituaries appeared in the *Lexington Gazette,* Oct. 26, 1854, and the session minutes of Nov. 11, 1854, Records of the Presbytery of Lexington, UTS.

103. TJJ to Laura Arnold, Oct. 23, 1854. This letter, previously unpublished, is in the Thomas Jonathan Jackson File, USMA.

104. David X. Junkin, *The Reverend George Junkin, D.D., LL.D.: A Historical Biography* (Philadelphia, 1871), 503; Orders No. 107, Oct. 24, 1854, Superintendent's Outgoing Correspondence, VMI. The cemetery was once the site of the Presbyterian church before a new building was constructed closer to downtown. Hence, the main burial ground was called the Lexington Presbyterian Cemetery until 1946, when the town assumed responsibility and renamed it the Stonewall Jackson Cemetery.

105. Boyd Reminiscences.

106. White Narrative; Vickers, ed., *Under Both Flags,* 134.

107. Hill to Dabney, July 1, 1864.

108. Robert L. Dabney notes of conversation with Margaret J. Preston; TJJ to Laura Arnold, Nov. 14, 1854, Jackson—VMI. Margaret Preston expanded her recollections of Jackson's grief in *Century Magazine,* 32 (1886): 932.

CHAPTER 7   *The Search for Oneself*

1. Boyd Reminiscences, Cook—WVU.

2. Junkin, *George Junkin,* 502; Allan, *Preston,* 77.

3. Jackson Papers, Old Catalog Collection, VHS.

4. Margaret Junkin to TJJ, Dec. 19, 1854, Jackson—VMI.

5. TJJ to Rev. David X. Junkin, Jan. 3, 1855, Jackson File, USMA.

6. Allan, *Preston,* 72–73; Mrs. Jackson, 84–85. A month later, Jackson informed Laura that his eyesight was improving, "but still I have to be careful with them; the spots continue to float before them." TJJ to Laura Arnold, Feb. 20, 1855, in Arnold, 220.

7. TJJ to Margaret Junkin, Feb. 14, 1855, Margaret Junkin Preston Papers, SHC. In the

following week, Jackson asked Laura if there were some keepsake of Ellie's—such as eyeglasses or pencil—that she would like to have. Arnold, 221.

8. Allan, *Preston*, 71.

9. TJJ to Margaret Junkin, Mar. 1, 1855, Preston Papers.

10. TJJ to Margaret Junkin, Mar. 10, 1855, Preston Papers.

11. TJJ to William E. Jones, Mar. 24, 1855, copy of letter graciously made available to the author by Roger D. Judd, Fairbury, Nebr.

12. Mrs. John H. Moore of Lexington stated that when Jackson lived at the Junkin home, "one of his sisters-in-law was an invalid and he used to carry her in his arms down stairs every morning and carried her up stairs to her bedroom every evening." Withrow Scrapbooks, W&L, XVII, 119. In all likelihood, Maggie was the Junkin girl in question. She had been ill for several months when she returned home. Physicians had diagnosed the problem as akin to prolapses, but it seems more probable that Maggie had a hemorrhoidal problem that made it extremely painful to negotiate stairs. Mary P. Coulling to author, Jan. 26, 1993.

13. *Century Magazine*, 32 (1886): 927.

14. Allan, *Preston*, 77.

15. Ibid.; Allan, *A March Past*, 121–22. One of Maggie's future stepdaughters remarked that the "devoted friendship" between Jackson and his sister-in-law became "welded into permanency" at this time. Allan, *A March Past*, 120.

16. TJJ to Laura Arnold, Apr. 4, 1855, Jackson—VMI.

17. J. Stephen Hudgins, M.D., to author, Jan. 3, 1994.

18. TJJ to Laura Arnold, Dec. 6, 1855, Jackson—WVU. Woodson resided in California for only a few years. He then moved to New Harmony, Indiana, became a farmer, married in 1863, and fathered seven children. He died Nov. 26, 1875; his widow lived for another fifty-four years. Cook, *Family and Early Life*, 21. For other references to Woodson, see Cook, *Family and Early Life*, 139–41; Arnold, 220–22, 235–38; TJJ to Laura Arnold, Oct. 6, 1855, Jackson—VMI.

19. TJJ to Laura Arnold, June 1, 1855, Jackson—VMI. The gravestone was put in place in October of that year.

20. "Writings of Thomas Arnold," Robertson Collection, 5.

21. Ibid.

22. TJJ to Laura Arnold, July 24, 1855, Thomas Jonathan Jackson File, USMA; Arnold, 228, 234–35.

23. Diss Debar, "Two Men," 7.

24. TJJ to Margaret Junkin, Aug. 16, 1855, Preston Papers.

25. TJJ to Clementine Neale, Sept. 4, 1855, Cook—WVU. See also Hull, "Mother of 'Stonewall' Jackson," 27; 1919 newspaper clipping in Withrow Scrapbooks, W&L, XVIII, 86.

26. TJJ to Laura Arnold, Oct. 6, 1855, Jackson—VMI.

27. Records of the Presbytery of Lexington, UTS; William C. Preston to J. Cleveland Cady, November 1898, Reel 34, Hotchkiss—LC.

28. Staff officers' files, Reel 39, Hotchkiss—LC; Boley, *Lexington*, 179; James T. Murfee to Thomas T. Munford, July 18, 1903, Munford-Ellis Family Papers, Duke University; Barton Collection, VMI; Lyle, "John Blair Lyle," 22. The most revealing sketch of Preston is in Thomas W. Davis, ed., *A Crowd of Honorable Youths: Historical Essays on the First 150 Years of the Virginia Military Institute* (Lexington, 1988), 46–60.

29. Pearson, "Thy Kingdom Come," 35–39; December 1851–February 1852, minutes of the sessions, Records of the Presbytery of Lexington. Pearson erroneously had Jackson taking charge of a black Sunday school in 1852, which was the year he began teaching stern theology to students and cadets. Dr. White attributed the failure of the first black class at the Presbyterian church to the fact that the slaves "had become so enamored with a boisterous sort of meeting that they could not relish our calm and quiet method of proceeding." White, *William S. White*, 158.

30. J. William Jones, in *SHSP*, 19 (1891): 158–59; *Lexington Gazette*, Sept. 4, 1928; Mrs. Jackson, 77–78.

31. White, *William S. White*, 158.

32. Jackson's granddaughter mentioned "some local antagonism" when the new school opened. *CV,* 38 (1930): 184. See also unidentified newspaper clipping, Reel 58, Hotchkiss—LC. *Lexington Gazette,* Sept. 4, 1928, is the source for the threat of court action. The November 1898 correspondence over the Cady charge is in Reel 34, Hotchkiss—LC.

33. William S. White Narrative, Box 20, Dabney—SHC.

34. White, *William S. White,* 158–59; *The Cottage Hearth,* 3 (1876): 310.

35. Dabney, 93.

36. White Narrative. The best summary of the Sunday school is in an obscure letter from Jackson himself. See TJJ to J. L. Campbell, June 7, 1859, Jackson—W&L.

37. Allan, *Preston,* 82; White Narrative. See also Vandiver, 110–11; Coulling, *Preston,* 80. The black Sunday school class lasted until the late 1880s and closed "only when the necessity for its continuance passed away." White, *William S. White,* 159.

38. TJJ to Laura Arnold, Mar. 31, 1856, Jackson—LC; *Lexington Gazette,* Apr. 24, 1856.

39. TJJ to Clementine Neale, May 19, 1856, Cook—WVU.

40. TJJ to Margaret Junkin, May 31, 1856, Preston Papers.

41. James T. Murfee to Francis H. Smith, Aug. 7, 1856, Superintendent's Records: Incoming Correspondence, VMI.

42. Board of Visitors Minutes, 1856–1857, VMI.

43. Anna Jackson to William N. Pendleton, Dec. 30, 1872, Pendleton Papers, SHC; Couper, *One Hundred Years at VMI,* 1:263, 313; 3:183. In 1875, when Gov. James L. Kemper of Virginia recalled his days in the 1850s as a member of the VMI Board of Visitors, he became confused. Kemper had this confrontation occurring a year later in 1857, with no fewer than 200 cadets in attendance to protest Maj. Jackson's "intellectual incompetency." Withrow Scrapbooks, W&L, XVIII, 37. For another garbled account of this effort to get Jackson removed from the VMI faculty, see M. Graham Ellzey Reminiscences, Cook—WVU.

44. Board of Visitors Minutes, 1856–1857, VMI.

45. TJJ to Laura Arnold, May 12 and June 6, 1856, Jackson—LC.

46. *Lexington Gazette,* July 10, 1856.

47. TJJ to Laura Arnold, July 18, 1856, Jackson—LC.

48. *Century Magazine,* 32 (1886): 931, 934; Hopley, *"Stonewall" Jackson,* 14–15.

49. Mrs. Jackson, 85–86. Jackson's "Autograph Book" is apparently the only surviving volume of his European notebooks. It is in Davis—Tulane. Once asked for a written account of his journey, Jackson replied with a one-page itinerary of places visited on particular dates. Clement E. Fishburne Letters, Thomas J. Jackson File, Presbyterian Church (USA) Archives. However, Jackson wrote two lengthy travelogs. In April 1859, he sent "notes on travel" to J. Jaquelin Smith. That account is in Jackson—VMI. The best source on the European trip is Jackson's running commentary to Laura in letters of Oct. 25, Oct. 27, Dec. 1 and 6, 1856, and Feb. 26, 1857, plus a Dec. 1, 1856, letter to nephew Thomas J. Arnold, all in Jackson—VMI.

50. Jackson Autograph Journal, Davis—Tulane.

51. *SHSP,* 19 (1891): 310. McGuire expanded the story in a May 19, 1896, letter to Jedediah Hotchkiss. See Reel 34, Hotchkiss—LC.

52. Chase, *Jackson,* 174.

53. TJJ to Clementine Neale, Oct. 27, 1856, in Cook, *Family and Early Life,* 142; Mrs. Jackson, 86. Jackson's sister-in-law reported that the major "was very much hurried" throughout his European trip but that he "enjoyed it very much indeed." Julia J. Fishburn to Lizzie Webster, Oct. 31, 1856, Fishburne Letters, W&L.

54. Margaret Preston, in *Century Magazine,* 32 (1886): 934. Somewhat different versions of Jackson's reply are in Mrs. Jackson, 88; Dabney, 116.

55. Boyd Reminiscences.

56. *CV,* 7 (1899): 120. A similar statement is in undated newspaper clipping, Mrs. E. B. Dakan, Jr., Collection.

57. *The Cottage Hearth,* 3 (1876): 310.

58. Henderson, 1:70, asserted: "The Jacksons were far from affluent. The professor had nothing but his salary, and his wife, one of a large family, brought no increase to their income." The British writer was incorrect on every part of that statement.

59. Snell, "Antebellum Finances," 15. See also miscellaneous financial notes in Jackson—VMI.

60. Snell, "Antebellum Finances," 33–34.

61. Ibid., 1, 57.

62. TJJ to Laura Arnold, Dec. 6, 1856, Jackson—LC; Allan, *Preston*, 91. Coulling, *Preston*, 77–80, 84–87, is the best source for the romantic attractions and church impediments between Maggie and Jackson.

63. *Constitution of the Presbyterian Church* (Philadelphia, 1853), Confession of Faith, chap. 24, sec. 4.

64. Mrs. Jackson, 100. The introductory description of Anna Morrison came from her granddaughter, Julia J. Preston, to Mrs. E. B. Dakan, Jr., July 7, 1951, Dakan Collection.

65. Undated letter, Clement E. Fishburne Letters. Varina Howell Davis, wife of the Confederate president, later made an incorrect observation: Jackson "wrote to Anna in such ardent fashion that everyone, but the object of his affection, suspected his frame of mind." By such accounts, everyone was privy to Jackson's letter. *SHSP*, 21 (1893): 341.

66. Robert Hall Morrison, *Biography of Joseph Graham Morrison, Captain, Confederate States of America* (Charlotte, N.C., 1955), 1; Walter L. Lingle, "Our First President and His Daughters," *Christian Observer*, June 19, 1935, 3–4 (copy in Davidson College Library).

67. Chase, *Jackson*, 168.

68. James R. Graham, "Some Reminiscences of Stonewall Jackson," *Things and Thoughts*, 1 (1901): 198. Ben Ritter of Winchester, Va., called the author's attention to this all-but-forgotten publication. A copy is in Winchester's Handley Library. Anna withdrew from Salem Academy without graduating. In 1914, she received an honorary degree from what by then was called Salem College.

69. Mrs. Jackson, 100.

70. TJJ to Laura Arnold, Feb. 26, 1857, Jackson—VMI.

71. TJJ to Anna Morrison, Apr. 18, 1857, Box 20, Dabney—SHC.

72. TJJ to Anna Morrison, Apr. 25, 1857, Box 20, Dabney—SHC.

73. TJJ to Anna Morrison, May 9, 1857, Dabney—LVA; TJJ to Anna Morrison, May 16, 1857, Box 20, Dabney—SHC.

74. Mrs. Jackson, 77; John T. L. Preston Narrative, Box 20, Dabney—SHC.

75. TJJ to Margaret Junkin, May 25, 1857, Preston Papers. Maggie spent $123 of the money Jackson gave her for the wedding presents. Anna was delighted with the gifts. Coulling, *Preston*, 98; Mrs. Jackson, 104.

76. TJJ to Clement D. Fishburne, May 25 and June 8, 1857, Clement E. Fishburne Letters. Clement Fishburne's great-grandson is the source for the casual friendship between Fishburne and Jackson. Gray Williams, Jr., to author, Aug. 13, 1993.

77. TJJ to Laura Arnold, undated, in Arnold, 254–55.

78. The pre-wedding sequence of events is a composite of an undated letter, Clement E. Fishburne Letters, and the Clement Fishburne Memoirs, UVA. Chambers, 1:278, either thought the wedding day was on Sunday or else sought to combine several days' events into one.

79. Mrs. Jackson, 103–4.

80. *CV*, 30 (1922): 413.

81. TJJ to Laura Arnold, Aug. 11, 1857, Jackson—LC.

82. Holman, "Jackson Health," 151; Mrs. Jackson, 39, 104–5.

83. Chase, *Jackson*, 114; TJJ to Laura Arnold, Aug. 11, 1857, Jackson—LC.

84. Mrs. Jackson, 105.

85. Ibid., 80.

86. Vandiver, 116. See Allan, *A March Past*, 124, for the continuing closeness between Jackson and John Preston.

87. Cook, *Family and Early Life,* 146.

88. TJJ to Laura Arnold, Nov. 1, 1857, Jackson—VMI.

89. TJJ to Laura Arnold, Dec. 19, 1857, Jackson—VMI.

90. TJJ to Laura Arnold, Feb. 8 and Mar. 8, 1858, Jackson—LC.

91. TJJ to Laura Arnold, May 1, 1858, Jackson—VMI.

92. McCabe, *Jackson,* 20.

93. The atlas converted into a biblical directory is in the Old Catalog Collection, VHS.

94. Mrs. Jackson, 74–75, 78; Chase, *Jackson,* 142.

95. Records of the Presbytery of Lexington, Dec. 31, 1857–Jan. 4, 1858, UTS.

96. Ibid.; Hunter, *Lexington Presbyterian Church,* 70.

97. White Narrative.

98. Henry Tucker Graham, *Stonewall Jackson: The Man, the Soldier, the Christian* (Florence, S.C., n. d.), 12.

99. List of church pledges, Jackson Papers, SJH. Dr. White offered a slightly expanded observation of Deacon Jackson in White, *William S. White,* 138–39.

100. Wise, *End of an Era,* 102.

101. Vickers, ed., *Under Both Flags,* 132. Speaking of one of those ceremonies at VMI, Gittings added: "In the gray dawn of the morning [Jackson] would come marching on the parade-ground, with his fine sabre tucked well under his left arm. He had the long stride peculiar to the dismounted cavalryman, and on such occasions his manner would be brisk, if not cheery, for he took special pride in those celebrations and was very punctilious in all their observations." For particulars on the cadets' trip to the capital, see John F. Neff to parents, Mar. 4, 1858, Francis Neff Papers, Handley Library.

102. Colston Reminiscences, SHC.

103. Ibid.

104. McCabe, *Jackson,* 20.

105. Allan, *Preston,* 108; Fishburne Memoirs.

106. Mrs. Jackson, 111.

107. TJJ to Rufus Barringer, May 1, 1858, Paul B. Barringer Paper, NCDAH.

108. TJJ to Laura Arnold, May 1, 1858, Jackson—VMI. Although Cook, in *Family and Early Life,* 22, put Mary Graham's birthdate as Feb. 28, no evidence exists to support that claim.

109. TJJ to Laura Arnold, May 22, 1858, Jackson—VMI; copy of Milton H. Key Ledger, SJH.

110. Shaffner Collection, SJH; Michael Anne Lynn to author, Apr. 13, 1995.

111. Mrs. Jackson, 111; Mrs. Jackson article, in *Philadelphia Weekly Times,* Apr. 7, 1877. One of the Jacksons' closest friends came to the same conclusion. See Graham, "Some Reminiscences," 198.

112. 1876 *Lexington Gazette* clipping, in Winthrow Scrapbooks, W&L, III, 38. A more complete account of the argument over the Sunday school class is in *SHSP,* 9 (1881): 45–46. A year later, another Virginia community wanted to start a black Sunday school and asked the state's attorney general, J. Randolph Tucker, for an interpretation of the law. Tucker replied that he considered such assemblies legal as long as a white man conducted the meeting. The leader could call on blacks to pray, read scripture, and sing hymns. *Lexington Gazette,* July 28, 1859.

113. TJJ to Francis H. Smith, with endorsement, May 28, 1858, Cook—WVU.

114. TJJ to Grace Arnold, June 7, 1858, Jackson—LC.

115. TJJ to Laura Arnold, June 19, 1858, Jackson—VMI.

116. Paul B. Barringer, *The Natural Bent: The Memoirs of Dr. Paul B. Barringer* (Chapel Hill, 1949), 5; Mrs. Jackson, 112.

117. Mrs. Jackson, 112–13; copy of J. H. Clopton's Canal Boat Register, SJH. On July 20, while the Jacksons were in New York, John Lyle died at the age of fifty. His great patron, John Preston, buried Lyle in the Preston family lot. On Lyle's tombstone is the inscription: "He was the truest friend, the bravest man, and the best Christian ever known to him who erects this stone to his memory." Couper, *One Hundred Years at VMI,* 1:337n.; White, *William S. White,* 142–43.

118. TJJ to Laura Arnold, July 21, 1858, Jackson—VMI, and Aug. 18, 1858, in Arnold, 265–66; Cook, *Family and Early Life,* 153. Couper, *One Hundred Years at VMI,* 1:338, was of the opinion that VMI faculty member Maj. Thomas H. Williamson was the man who wrote Col. Smith.

119. "Writings of Thomas Arnold," 4; Arnold, 270–71. For Jackson's reports to Laura on the lad's progress, see Arnold, 266–69. Farwell, *Stonewall,* 132, asserted that in the late autumn of 1858 Eugenia Barringer's "three-year-old son" Paul also came to live with the Jacksons. Barringer himself claimed to have vague recollections of a two-year stay with his aunt and uncle. Both writer and subject are in error. Barringer was only eighteen months old at the time. The Barringer family would hardly have entrusted so young a child to a couple 400 miles away from the homeplace near Charlotte, N.C. Barringer's "recollections" of Lexington life appear to have been based on family hearsay. Barringer, *A Natural Bent,* 6–8. Neither Jackson nor Anna ever mentioned the child's presence in Lexington in any surviving correspondence.

120. Records of the Presbytery of Lexington, Oct. 2–19, 1858; M. L. R. White to Samuel Reid, Oct. 21, 1858, Reid Family Papers, W&L. Druggist John T. McCrum succeeded Jackson as superintendent of the black Sunday school class. Late that year McCrum also became a deacon in the church.

121. R. P. Chew, *Stonewall Jackson: Address of Colonel R. P. Chew* (Lexington, 1912), 8.

122. McCabe, *Jackson,* 25–26.

123. Johanna Metzgar, "The Stonewall Jackson House: Furnishing Plan," typescript, SJH, 8–10; newspaper clipping, Withrow Scrapbooks, W&L, VII, 143. In 1811, John Preston was born in the house. Couper, *One Hundred Years at VMI,* 1:22–23.

124. The description of Jackson's house is based on Metzgar, "Stonewall Jackson House," 34, 42–43, 68.

125. Copy of J. Compton & Sons Ledger, SJH.

126. Mrs. Jackson, 106–7.

CHAPTER 8   *Home Life Gives Way to War*

1. Arnold, 280; Metzgar, "Stonewall Jackson House," 3, 46; Mrs. Jackson, 107. The original deed for the home is in the Shaffner Collection, SJH.

2. Mrs. Jackson, 72.

3. Anna Jackson to Robert L. Dabney, [autumn] 1863, Box 20, Dabney—SHC.

4. Mrs. Jackson, 109–10.

5. Arnold, 272.

6. Mrs. Jackson, 111; Dabney, 119–20. See also Davis MacRae, *The Americans at Home* (New York, 1992), 194.

7. For the contents of Jackson's library, see Anna Jackson to Jedediah Hotchkiss, Aug. 19, 1895, Reel 11, Hotchkiss—LC; "Inventory of the Books of Thomas Jonathan Jackson at the Virginia Historical Society, Richmond, compiled by the staff of the Society, 1961," typescript, VHS; Robert K. Krick, "Summary of Jackson's Library as Preserved at Virginia Historical Society," handout at 1994 Stonewall Jackson Symposium, Lexington, Va.

8. Mrs. Jackson, 47, 108–9, 121–22.

9. Anna Jackson to Robert L. Dabney, [autumn] 1863, Box 20, Dabney—SHC.

10. Ibid.

11. Ibid.

12. Mrs. Jackson, 116; Jackson File, VMI Faculty/Staff Records, VMI.

13. Allan, *A March Past,* 133–34; Mrs. Jackson, 117.

14. Mrs. Jackson, 117.

15. Ibid., 119; Metzgar, "Stonewall Jackson House," 3; Chase, *Jackson,* 193. Anna received five slaves as a wedding present, one source claimed, but Jackson promptly sold two of them. Snell, "Antebellum Finances," 46–48. In the Shaffner Collection is a Jan. 29, 1859, receipt attesting that Jackson had hired out a slave girl named Ann for a $25 annual fee. The identity of the girl remains obscure.

16. Mrs. Jackson, 108–9; Dabney, 118–19; Cook, *Family and Early Life*, 147–48. The farm stood on the north side of present-day US 60 East. A rock quarry now operates on the property.

17. TJJ to *Planter*, undated, Davis—Tulane. Jackson's copy of the Buist guide to gardening, with his penciled notes in the margin, is at VHS.

18. Anna Jackson to Margaret Poor Norcross, Jan. 22, 1901, Mary Anna Morrison Jackson Letters, VHS; Mrs. Jackson, 120–21. Some Jackson students have felt that the facial problem suffered by both Ellie and Anna was actually Bell's palsy. Yet that illness—an interruption of the nerve signals on one side of the face—almost always results in the mouth dropping, difficulty in chewing food, and persistent drooling. Neither wife displayed those symptoms. If Anna had shown signs of palsy, Jackson no doubt would have mentioned one or more of them to Laura and voiced greater concern over her condition.

19. Mrs. Jackson, 121–22.

20. TJJ to Anna Jackson, Apr. 12, 1859, Box 20, Dabney—SHC.

21. TJJ to Anna Jackson, Apr. 13, 1859, Box 20, Dabney—SHC.

22. TJJ to Anna Jackson, Apr. 20, 1859, Dabney—LVA; Mrs. Jackson, 123.

23. TJJ to Laura Arnold, May 9, 1859, Jackson—VMI; TJJ to Anna Jackson, May 12, 1859, Dabney—LVA.

24. *Lexington Gazette*, July 7, 1859; Thomas M. Boyd, "General Stonewall Jackson," *Southern Bivouac*, 2 (1886–87): 359. Following Confederate service as a captain in the 19th Virginia, Boyd became a clergyman and spent his final years in Arkansas.

25. *SHSP*, 43 (1920): 1–2.

26. Mrs. Jackson, 126; TJJ to Laura Arnold, Aug. 15, 1859, Jackson—VMI.

27. Mrs Jackson, 126; TJJ to Anna Jackson, Aug. 27, 1859, Jackson—VMI. See also TJJ to Anna Jackson, Aug. 18, 1859, Dabney—LVA.

28. James L. Hubard to Robert L. Dabney, Sept. 17, 1863, Box 19, Dabney—SHC. Hubard was colonel of the 44th Virginia in the Civil War. He spent the postwar years as an attorney and farmer in Cumberland County.

29. TJJ to Laura Arnold, Sept. 15, 1859, Jackson—WVU.

30. Mrs. Jackson, 128–29.

31. *SHSP*, 9 (1881): 41.

32. McCabe, *Jackson*, 25–26.

33. *SHSP*, 22 (1894): 162–63; Preston Narrative, Box 20, Dabney—SHC.

34. M. Graham Ellzey Reminiscences, Cook—WVU. A native of Leesburg, Ellzey obtained a medical degree and served in the Civil War as a Confederate surgeon. In his postwar years, Ellzey was a chemistry professor and well-known writer. Randolph Barton, who later became a trusted staff officer in Jackson's command, presented a too critical and misleading view of the VMI professor in the late 1850s. See *SHSP*, 38 (1910): 270–71.

35. Hunter, *Lexington Presbyterian Church*, 71–72.

36. Mrs. Jackson, 129.

37. *Lexington Gazette*, Oct. 20 and 27, 1859; Wise, *Military History*, 106; Lyle, "Sketches," W&L, 11.

38. Tidball, "Getting through West Point," 58.

39. *Lexington Gazette*, Nov. 17 and 24, 1859. Samuel H. Letcher was first captain of the Rockbridge Rifles; other officers were E. Franklin Paxton, first lieutenant, and James K. Edmondson, second lieutenant.

40. Joseph H. Chenoweth to mother, Nov. 19, 1859, Joseph Hart Chenoweth Collection, VMI; Couper, *One Hundred Years at VMI*, 2:8. For fears in Lexington at the time of a slave insurrection, see Ellzey Reminiscences.

41. Couper, *One Hundred Years at VMI*, 2:10–11. It was at this time, according to Dabney H. Maury, that Jackson sat all night in Supt. Smith's office because the colonel never specifically dismissed him. The story, more apocryphal than accurate, is in *CV*, 6 (1898): 54, and *SHSP*, 25 (1897): 313.

42. *CV*, 7 (1899): 120; Wise, *Military History*, 106–7; *Richmond Daily Dispatch*, Nov. 30, 1859.

43. Mrs. Jackson, 129–30; *Lexington Gazette*, Dec. 1, 1859; Smith, *VMI*, 170. Although the amount of military protection seems excessive, rumors abounded for weeks that grand-scale attempts would be made to rescue Brown from the gallows. A "friend" warned Gov. Wise in writing of a plot whereby a large balloon would drift eastward from Ohio on the day of execution. Once over the site, occupants would drop a number of explosive shells on the people gathered below, followed by several barrel loads of nitric acid sent raining down to complete the work of annihilation of all connected with taking Brown's life. (How Brown himself was to escape death was never mentioned.) Such reports were so many and so wild that the governor took every possible precaution against violence. Ray Jones, *Harpers Ferry* (Gretna, La., 1992), 128.

44. *Lexington Gazette,* Dec. 8, 1859.

45. *Richmond Daily Dispatch,* Dec. 5, 1859; Wise, *Military History,* 112–13.

46. Richard D. Rutherford, "Recollections," Davis—Tulane.

47. TJJ to Anna Jackson, Dec. 2, 1859, Dabney—LVA.

48. John Preston, also in attendance at the execution, wrote an equally long account that on occasion has been attributed to Jackson. Preston's narrative is in the *Lexington Gazette,* Dec. 15, 1859. Then-cadet W. N. Mercer Otey's version of the hanging is in *CV,* 7 (1899): 120–21. According to another eyewitness, Brown's body swung from the gallows for forty to fifty minutes and no fewer than twenty-five physicians examined Brown before pronouncing him officially dead. *CV,* 16 (1908): 396.

49. Raleigh E. Colston Reminiscences, SHC.

50. Quoted in Wise, *Military History,* 113.

51. Wise, *Military History,* 95. See also p. 114; Couper, *One Hundred Years at VMI,* 2:22–24.

52. TJJ to Laura Arnold, Dec. 12, 1859, Jackson—VMI.

53. *Rockbridge County News,* Feb. 24, 1888; Francis H. Smith to Rt. Rev. Charles P. McIlvaine, Dec. 24, 1859, Superintendent's Records: Outgoing Correspondence, VMI.

54. *Lexington Gazette,* Jan. 5 and 19, 1860; TJJ to Laura Arnold, Jan. 28, 1860, Jackson—VMI.

55. TJJ to Clementine Neale, Jan. 19, 1860, in Mrs. Jackson, 132. Cook, *Family and Early Life,* 153, misdated Jackson's letter to his aunt a year later than was the case.

56. TJJ to Grace Arnold, Feb. 25, 1860, Jackson—LC.

57. *Lexington Gazette,* Mar. 1, 1860; Records of the Presbytery of Lexington, UTS; copy of Lexington Tannery Records, SJH.

58. John Kyd Berkenbaugh Manuscript, Cook—WVU. Berkenbaugh was the nephew of Henry Kyd Douglas, one of the most quoted and most unreliable sources on Jackson. In this instance, Douglas took Berkenbaugh's account and published it first in the late 1870s with himself, not the nephew, being the one who questioned Terrill. That version, which does not quote Terrill accurately, is in *Annals of the War,* 644–45. Douglas was more faithful to the Berkenbaugh reminiscence in his own "memoirs," *I Rode with Stonewall* (Chapel Hill, 1940), 233–34, even though Douglas again told the story as if he were the one who questioned Terrill about Jackson.

59. See Wise, *Military History,* 117–19; Jennings Cropper Wise, *The Long Arm of Lee* (Lynchburg, Va., 1915), 1:63–64. The other two members of the state commission were Col. Philip St. George Cocke and Capt. George W. Randolph. In the West Point class of 1824, Dennis Hart Mahan ranked number one and Parrott number three. Parrott was the best-known developer of cannon and projectiles at the time of the Civil War.

60. TJJ to Laura Arnold, June 4, 1860, Jackson—WVU; TJJ to Laura Arnold, June 30, 1860, Jackson—LC; *Lexington Gazette,* July 12, 1860.

61. *Lexington Gazette,* July 8, 1860; TJJ to Laura Arnold, July 21, 1860, Jackson—VMI. A "Capt. Woodbury of Cheshire, Conn." asserted in the postwar years that Jackson left the Brattleboro spa because the management sought to charge him more than the listed price for accommodations. *Winchester Evening Star,* Sept. 17, 1913. According to two contemporary sources, another attempt was made at the end of the 1859–60 to have Jackson discharged from the VMI faculty. No official or substantive evidence survives to support this allegation. See James H. Lane Reminiscences, James H. Lane Papers, Auburn University; *SHSP,* 19 (1891): 146.

62. TJJ to Laura Arnold, July 21, 1860, Jackson—VMI; Mrs. Jackson, 134. Anna Jackson inferred in her memoirs that the northern trip was her first encounter with hydropathy. She apparently forgot spending two weeks the previous summer at Rockbridge Alum Springs.

63. *Winchester Evening Star,* Sept. 17, 1913.

64. Mrs. Jackson, 134-35.

65. TJJ to Laura Arnold, Aug. 4, 1860, Jackson—VMI; TJJ to Laura Arnold, Sept. 3, 1860, Jackson—LC.

66. *Lexington Gazette,* Sept. 6 and 13, 1860.

67. TJJ to Laura Arnold, Sept. 24, 1860, Jackson—VMI; TJJ to Anna Jackson, Sept. 25, 1860, in Mrs. Jackson, 136.

68. Joseph H. Chenoweth to father, Nov. 2, 1860, Chenoweth Collection, VMI.

69. William S. White Narrative, Box 20, Dabney—SHC; Mrs. Jackson, 139. Anna Jackson's statement about her husband's feelings on secession is somewhat open to question. Matthew W. Paxton was a member of one of Lexington's most prominent families. In a postwar letter, Paxton avowed that in the autumn of 1860 Jackson "firmly expressed himself in conversation as favoring secession and declared that he was ready to fight for it. He so stated in conversation with Prof. C. J. Harris and Judge William McLaughlin. Both have so told me." W. M. Paxton to Jedediah Hotchkiss, Nov. 6, 1897, Reel 14, Hotchkiss—LC. Margaret Junkin Preston was just as emphatic that Jackson was never a secessionist. See *Century Magazine,* 32 (1886): 936.

70. Undated *Pittsburgh Dispatch* clipping, Reel 58, Hotchkiss—LC. A more embossed account of the Breckinridge rally is in *SHSP,* 9 (1881): 42-43. Both narratives were the work of George H. Moffett, who attended Washington College and in later years served first in the 11th Virginia Cavalry and subsequently as speaker of the West Virginia House of Delegates.

71. *Lexington Gazette,* Nov. 8, 1860. Bell carried Virginia by only 358 votes. He received 74,681 votes; Breckinridge, 74,323; and Douglas, 16,290. Lincoln's 1,929 votes came almost entirely from the mountainous region of western Virginia. The best analysis of the 1860 vote in the Old Dominion is in Henry T. Shanks, *The Secession Movement in Virginia, 1847-1861* (Richmond, 1934), 115-19.

72. White Narrative; *Lexington Gazette,* Nov. 29, 1860.

73. Mrs. Jackson, 141-42; Dabney, 153-54. While Jackson relied on God to settle the national dispute in time, he made at least one preparation of his own. At some point in this period, he asked a friend in Washington to send him a new study on heavy artillery. "If Virginia should become involved in a war," the acquaintance quoted Jackson as saying, "I wish to be ready for the issue and to fly to her rescue." John T. Harris to TJJ, Feb. 6, 1862, Davis—Tulane. Wise, *Military History,* 126, gave a highly improbable story of Jackson telling a junior faculty member that he opposed war as a Christian but welcomed it as a soldier.

74. White Narrative. The version presented by Mrs. Jackson, 141, contained several differences in wording. White's account is preferred because Jackson expressed his feelings to him.

75. TJJ to Laura Arnold, Dec. 19, 1860, Jackson—VMI.

76. M. W. Paxton to Jedediah Hotchkiss, Nov. 6, 1897, Reel 14, Hotchkiss—LC.

77. M. W. Paxton to Jedediah Hotchkiss, Oct. 16, 1897, Reel 14, Hotchkiss—LC. Paxton was one of the first volunteers to leave Lexington for war, and he would enjoy a close association with Jackson until his death at Chancellorsville.

78. Paxton to Hotchkiss, Nov. 6, 1897.

79. Robert Morrison to Henry R. Morrison, Jan. 7, 1861, Henry Ruffner Morrison Letters, *CWTI.* For examples of divided sentiment in the Lexington area, see William T. Poague, *Gunner with Stonewall* (Jackson, Tenn., 1957), 2; Edward A. Moore, *The Story of a Cannoneer under Stonewall Jackson* (New York, 1907), 20; James H. Wood, *The War* (Gaithersburg, Md., 1984), 4-5.

80. TJJ to Thomas J. Arnold, Jan. 26, 1861, Jackson—WVU. This letter is the first known instance when Jackson advocated a "black flag" policy of taking no prisoners should war erupt between North and South. Arnold was so shocked by the statement that he eliminated it when printing Jackson's letter in Arnold, 293-94.

As will be shown in detail later, Jackson's conviction was neither singular nor stern among

Southern leaders. In fact, the Confederacy's first "Hero of the Hour," Gen. P. G. T. Beauregard, stated early in the contest: "We are not fighting for glory or political purpose, but for our homes, firesides & liberties. Should we fail in our undertaking, the sufferings & miseries of the Poles and Hungarians would not be comparable to our own—hence 'victory or death' should be our motto—& cursed be he who shrinks from the task." P. G. T. Beauregard to Robert L. Dabney, Aug. 6, 1861, Dabney—UTS. For other stated endorsements of a black-flag policy, see *Richmond Daily Dispatch*, May 10, Nov. 1, and Dec. 9, 1861; Adjt. James H. Langhorne to father, Dec. 15, 1861, Langhorne Papers, Robertson Collection; *Richmond Enquirer*, Apr. 8, 1862; *Lexington Gazette*, Aug. 28, 1862.

81. TJJ to Laura Arnold, Feb. 2, 1861, Cook—WVU.

82. Undated *Louisville Courier-Journal* clipping, Jackson—Valentine.

83. Mrs. Jackson, 137. For the details of Anna's well-chaperoned journey, see William W. Morrison to Samuel M. Reid, Feb. 15, 1861, and M. L. R. White to Samuel R. Reid, Feb. 20, 1861, Reid Family Papers, W&L; TJJ to Laura Arnold, Feb. 23, 1861, Jackson—VMI.

84. Charles Copland Wight Recollections, Wight Family Papers, VHS.

85. Wise, *Military History*, 127; Couper, *One Hundred Years at VMI*, 2:78–79. The *Lexington Gazette* never learned of this disturbance. Its Feb. 24, 1861, issue praised the artillery salute and the snappy manner in which the cadets fired the weapons. Both of the cadets who raised the secession flag were fourth classmen. James W. Thomson became a major of horse artillery and died in the Apr. 6, 1865, action at Sailor's Creek. D. Murray Lee, son of a well-known naval officer, later performed staff duties in the Confederate army.

86. *Richmond Daily Dispatch*, Mar. 11 and 14, 1861.

87. Lyle, "Sketches," W&L, 5–7; William S. White to Robert L. Dabney, Aug. 25, 1862, Dabney—UTS. For Junkin's outbursts, see *Lexington Gazette*, Nov. 22, 1860–Feb. 21, 1861 *passim*.

88. Hundley's account is in *SHSP*, 23 (1895): 295–96.

89. Arnold, 296–97.

90. Sara Henderson Smith Papers, VHS. Lieutenant William H. Bray of the 53d Virginia was killed at Gettysburg; James E. Heath had no war record and became a judge; Branson E. Coltrane served as a captain in the 24th Virginia; Sgt. Maj. Thomas G. Hart died of wounds received at Drewry's Bluff in 1864; Campbell G. Lawson was a captain in the 15th Virginia.

91. Wood, *The War*, 6–7; Wight Recollections, VHS. So many versions of the downtown affair and Jackson's "sword-and-scabbard" speech developed in the years thereafter that no single telling is faithful to the facts. Only the last phrase of Jackson's remarks appears intact in each rendition. Since both Wood and Wight were participants in the whole affair that day, their accounts have far more authenticity than reports based on hearsay. Couper, *One Hundred Years at VMI*, 2:79–98, is also highly reliable because the VMI historian did more research into the Apr. 13 events than any other writer.

92. Wood, *The War*, 7.

93. Ibid., 10; Wight Recollections.

94. Couper, *One Hundred Years at VMI*, 2:86.

95. Wood, *The War*, 11.

96. *SHSP*, 38 (1910): 273. For illustrations of the widest variations of what transpired on Apr. 13, see Murray Forbes Taylor Notes, BV 18, FSNMP; Wise, *Military History*, 128–31; Boyd Reminiscences, Cook—WVU; *Rockbridge County News*, Feb. 24, 1888; *SHSP*, 16 (1888): 36–47; *CV*, 22 (1914): 261–62. Insights into the activities that day of John Preston and E. Franklin Paxton are in Paxton to Hotchkiss, Nov. 6, 1897.

97. Records of the Presbytery of Lexington; Schantz, "Lost Order Book," Western Historical Collection, 7; *Lexington Gazette*, Apr. 11 and 25, 1861. Dr. White was convinced that but for Jackson's intervention, "blood would have been shed" in downtown Lexington. White, *William S. White*, 173.

98. *OR*, Ser. 3, 1:67–78; *Staunton Spectator*, Apr. 23, 1861.

99. *Richmond Daily Dispatch*, Apr. 19, 1861.

100. Paxton to Hotchkiss, Nov. 6, 1897; *Lexington Gazette*, May 30, 1861.

101. *SHSP,* 9 (1881): 44; Moore, *Cannoneer,* 22-23.

102. Thomas A. Stevenson to sister, Apr. 19, 1861, Thomas Andrew Stevenson Collection, VMI; Couper, *One Hundred Years at VMI,* 2:88.

103. Couper, *One Hundred Years at VMI,* 2:90-91. The other members of the Advisory Council were Judge John J. Allen of the Virginia Court of Appeals and Matthew Fontaine Maury, the recently resigned superintendent of the United States Naval Observatory in Washington. For a summary of Virginia's military unpreparedness at the time and its haste to improve the situation, see Dabney, 179; James I. Robertson, Jr., ed., *Proceedings of the Advisory Council of the State of Virginia, April 21-June 19, 1861* (Richmond, 1977), *passim.*

104. Order No. 61, Apr. 18, 1861, VMI Order Book, VMI; Thomas A. Stevenson to sister, Apr. 19, 1861. Stevenson graduated from VMI in 1864 and was a sergeant of subsistence in Virginia forces for the last year of the Civil War. He spent most of his postwar life as a St. Louis attorney.

105. Couper, *One Hundred Years at VMI,* 2:90-92; *Richmond Daily Dispatch,* Apr. 20, 1861.

106. *Philadelphia Weekly Times,* Apr. 7, 1877. Anna Jackson made a more emphatic statement about Jackson's support of state sovereignty in *CV,* 19 (1911): 591. See also *Century Magazine,* 32 (1886): 936; Royster, *Destructive War,* 46.

107. Junkin, *Rev. George Junkin,* 518-26; Early A. Pope, "George Junkin and His Eschatalogical Vision," typescript, Lafayette College Library, 31-35.

108. Coulling, *Preston,* 114-16; Pope, "George Junkin," 21; Julia J. Preston, "The Ebony Cane," *UDC Magazine,* Dec 1955, 39. Junkin spent a night in Winchester with his Presbyterian colleague, Rev. James R. Graham. "I am escaping from a set of lunatics!" Junkin raved to his host. "Lexington is one vast mad-house. There is not a sane man there, nor woman too." The angry cleric added that Maj. Jackson "is the best and bravest man I ever knew, but he is as crazy as the rest." Graham, "Some Reminiscences," 122. Within a year, Junkin produced a book, *Political Falacies,* which lambasted the South for misassumptions and belligerence. He sent a copy through the lines to Jackson. George Junkin to "Brother," Apr. 19, 1862, copy of letter in possession of Mary P. Coulling, Lexington, Va.

109. Mrs. Jackson, 144; copy of J. Compton and Sons Ledger, SJH.

110. *Richmond Enquirer,* Apr. 20, 1861.

111. *Lexington Gazette,* Aug. 13, 1891.

112. Mrs. Jackson, 144; *Lexington Gazette,* Aug. 13, 1891. In later years, hotel proprietor J. Fulton Tompkins claimed to have delivered to Jackson the order for him to lead the cadets to Richmond. On arriving at the Jackson home, Tompkins further alleged, he found Jackson standing in the parlor and buckling on his sword. See unidentified newspaper clipping, Withrow Scrapbooks, W&L, III, 35.

113. Mrs. Jackson, 145.

114. Order No. 63, Apr. 21, 1861, VMI Order Book.

115. Colston Reminiscences.

116. *SHSP,* 9 (1881): 44-45; unidentified newspaper clipping, Reel 58, Hotchkiss—LC. The *Richmond Enquirer,* Apr. 27, 1861, reported 175 cadets in the group ordered to the capital. Other sources have the total running as high as 200 cadets. See Wise, *Military History,* 142; Couper, *One Hundred Years at VMI,* 2:98.

117. Colston Reminiscences; Wise, *Military History,* 140-41. Chambers, 1:311, presented a somewhat different wording of the exchange between Jackson and "an officer" but did not give the source of his version. Dispute prevails over the exact time of departure for Jackson and the cadets. Three usually reliable sources thought that the column moved out at 1 P.M. Mrs. Jackson, 144-45; Wight Recollections; Couper, *One Hundred Years at VMI,* 3:190. Other authorities were certain that the march began at noon. Colston Reminiscences; Allan, *A March Past,* 119. Chambers, 1:310, gave two different departure times on the same page. The weight of evidence points to 12:30 P.M. See Order No. 63, Apr. 21, 1861, VMI Order Book; *Lexington Gazette,* Aug. 13, 1891; *SHSP,* 19 (1891): 159-60; Wise, *Military History,* 139-40. The sound of the tower clock is not a factor in the debate, because it tolled every half-hour. William Couper to John W. Wayland, Nov. 9, 1939, Couper Papers.

118. Murray Forbes Taylor to Carl H. Schultz III, undated letter, BV 18, FSNMP.

119. 1911 newspaper clipping, Withrow Scrapbooks, W&L, IX, 47. Sincere thanks go to Lt. Col. Keith Gibson, Director of Museums, VMI, for escorting the author through every phase of the Apr. 21 departure. Confusion has long prevailed over Jackson's command because of the assumption that the cadets marched away four abreast. VMI companies formed in two lines, not four. Jackson's reference to "file left" was for the far left component, Company A, to begin the march. The route was down a narrow dirt road that would have made four-abreast marching all but impossible.

120. George H. Moffatt account in *Pittsburgh Dispatch,* undated clipping, Jackson File, Reel 58, Hotchkiss—LC.

121. Colston Reminiscences. That no one at the time expected much of Jackson in the field is evident from the testimony in Colston Reminiscences and Lane Reminiscences.

CHAPTER 9   *Virginia Drillmaster*

1. For example, see Wood, *The War,* 15–16; Wise, *Military History,* 142; Couper, *One Hundred Years at VMI,* 3:190.

2. Colston Reminiscences, SHC. On the afternoon of Apr. 20, M. G. Harman had informed Maj. Preston that stage transportation for the cadets would be provided as far as Staunton. Couper, *One Hundred Years at VMI,* 2:95.

3. Couper, *One Hundred Years at VMI,* 2:98–99; John W. Wayland, *Stonewall Jackson's Way* (Verona, Va., 1956), 12; *Staunton Spectator,* Apr. 23, 1861. The William Couper Papers, VMI, provided the time of departure from Staunton.

4. Wood, *The War,* 17–18; TJJ to Anna Jackson, Apr. 22, 1861, Box 20, Dabney—SHC. The *Richmond Daily Dispatch,* Apr. 23, 1861, contains an ambiguous story that includes Jackson's troop train picking up companies all along its route.

5. Some sources have maintained that Jackson's group arrived at Richmond in late afternoon of the 22d. See Wood, *The War,* 18, and Wise, *Military History,* 144, as examples. Such an arrival time was impossible. The train left Staunton at 10:15 A.M. and lost at least two hours in the tunnel derailment. Assuming that "late afternoon" implied 5 P.M. or thereabouts, the troops train had five hours to cover the 110 miles between Staunton and Richmond. Yet more time was lost in the two or more stops necessary to load water and wood into the small locomotive tenders. Furthermore, and under the most ideal circumstances, the 4-4-0 "American" class engines of the Virginia Central could average but fifteen miles per hour. It therefore was at least 8 P.M. when Jackson's train wheezed to a stop at the Richmond station.

6. *Richmond Daily Dispatch,* Apr. 24, 1861; Wood, *The War,* 19. Another Richmond newspaper exulted over the mobilization then taking place: "We are prouder than ever of the land of our birth. Virginia gives today satisfactory assurance to the world that she has not 'lost the breed of noble blood.' . . . Her sons, from the sea-shore to the mountains, come forth with unexampled enthusiasm. . . . God bless the old Commonwealth!" *Richmond Enquirer,* Apr. 23, 1861.

7. TJJ to Anna Jackson, Apr. 23, 1861, Dabney—LVA; Colston Reminiscences. Chambers, 1:315, mistakenly confused Camp Lee with the Heritage Fairgrounds on the north side of the capital. The latter did not come into its own as a major camp of instruction until the autumn of 1861. See *SHSP,* 26 (1898): 241–46.

8. J. B. Jones, *A Rebel War Clerk's Diary at the Confederate States Capital* (Philadelphia, 1866), 1:27; Joseph E. Johnston, *Narrative of Military Operations Directed during the Late War between the States* (New York, 1874), 12. Since Jones lavishly reworked his diary prior to publication, the praise of Jackson may have been hindsight.

9. Wood, *The War,* 19–20.

10. Wise, *Military History,* 145; Robert Enoch Withers, *Autobiography of an Octogenarian* (Roanoke, Va., 1907), 132.

11. Julia Jackson Christian Preston, *Stonewall's Widow* (Winston-Salem, N.C., 1961), 28.

12. Mrs. Jackson, 149.

13. Robert L. Dabney memorandum, Box 19, Dabney—SHC; Robertson, *Advisory Council,*

21–22; W. A. Anderson, *Address of William A. Anderson, Upon the Laying of the Corner-Stone of the Equestrian Statue to Stonewall Jackson* . . . [Richmond, 1915], 6. Slightly different versions of Moore's reply are in Mrs. Jackson, 150; *SHSP*, 9 (1881): 92; Henderson, 1:86. Jackson's commission as colonel is in Davis—Tulane. Mrs. Jackson, 151, showed Jackson sending her a letter on "Apr. 27" from Winchester. That typographical error (it should have read "Apr. 29") has triggered confusion among several Jackson biographers. See Henderson, 1:114; Chambers, 1:317.

14. Jonathan M. Bennett to John J. Allen, Apr. 27, 1861, Cook—WVU.

15. Undated *Baltimore American* clipping, Antietam NBP; Order Book of T. J. Jackson, as Colonel, C.S.A., and Post Commandant at Harper's Ferry, Va., MC. A printed version, with slight alterations, of Lee's first communique to Jackson is in *OR*, 2: 784–85. For Letcher's instructions to Lee on Jackson's jurisdiction, see *Richmond Whig*, Apr. 26, 1873.

16. Preston quotation is in Wise, *Military History*, 158.

17. D. B. Ewing to Robert L. Dabney, Sept. 8, 1863, Dabney—UVA.

18. TJJ to Anna Jackson, Apr. 29, 1861, Box 20, Dabney—SHC. Governor Letcher never used the phrase "independent command," but Jackson was quick to assume that he was on his own and with unrestricted authority. This proved to be a sore misassumption on his part.

19. Couper, *One Hundred Years at VMI*, 2:112.

20. *Philadelphia Weekly Times*, Dec. 22, 1883.

21. James K. Edmondson, *My Dear Emma: War Letters of Col. James K. Edmondson, 1861–1865* (Verona, 1978), 5; Andrew N. Cook to wife, May 31, 1861, Lewis C. Crawford, Jr., Collection, Rupert, W.Va. For varying comments on the Apr. 18 destruction at Harpers Ferry, see *Richmond Enquirer*, Apr. 23, 1861; *Staunton Spectator*, Apr. 30, 1861. As might be expected, different figures exist for the size of the Union garrison as well as for the number of muskets destroyed at the evacuation. A local source put the Federal contingent at forty-four men and the number of arms rendered useless at 15,000 pieces. Joseph Barry, *The Strange Story of Harper's Ferry* (Martinsburg, W.Va., 1903), 97–99.

22. Order Book of T.J. Jackson, MC; A. R. H. Ranson to Henry Ranson, Apr. 21, 1861, A. R. H. Ranson Letters, Lewis Leigh Collection, USMHI. See also *OR*, 51: Pt. 2, 57. The figure of 2500 troops at Harpers Ferry when Jackson arrived came from his brother-in-law, writing in the *Philadelphia Weekly Times*, Dec. 22, 1883.

23. Charles Grattan Reminiscences, CWTI. Captain John D. Imboden of the artillery expressed similar contempt for the militia commanders. *B&L*, 1:118. Each company had its own distinctive uniform, a recruit observed, and as a result "all the colors of the rainbow were represented." N. H. R. Dawson to Elodie Todd, May 18, 1861, N. H. R. Dawson Papers, SHC.

24. Emma C. R. Macon and Reuben C. Macon, *Reminiscences of the Civil War* (n.p., 1911), 140; Grattan Reminiscences. See also N. H. R. Dawson to Elodie Todd, June 27, 1861, Dawson Papers; Willian N. Pendleton to wife, June 5, 1861, Pendleton Papers.

25. Charles Copland Wight Recollections, Wight Family Papers, VHS.

26. Robert C. Tanner, *Stonewall in the Valley* (Garden City, N.Y., 1976), 31; *OR*, 2:809. Cadet Murray Forbes Taylor gave a different version of Jackson greeting his former students. According to Taylor, the new colonel responded to their warm greetings by looking at each one and saying: "Remember, Virginia expects much of her cadets." Taylor Notes, BV 18, FSNMP.

27. Quoted in Chase, *Jackson*, 222.

28. David L. Hopkins to Louisa Hopkins, Apr. 28, 1861, Lewis Leigh Collection, USMHI.

29. *B&L*, 1:121; Edward L. Phillips, "The Lower Shenandoah Valley during the Civil War" (Ph.D. diss., University of North Carolina, 1958), 115. One source had Jackson's headquarters being at the Barbour House for most of the Harpers Ferry stay. Chase, *Jackson*, 219.

30. Charles R. Norris to mother, May 1861, Mrs. Brantz M. Roszel, "An Informal Talk on Chew's Battery and Its Captain" (typescript), and other papers in the possession of John E. Divine, Leesburg, Va. Chew in time became lieutenant colonel and chief of horse artillery for the Army of Northern Virginia. Rouss served as a lieutenant in the 12th Virginia Cavalry but spent most of the last half of the struggle as a prisoner of war.

31. See A. W. Garber notes on Harman in Reel 39, Hotchkiss—LC; Grattan Reminiscences; W. G. Bean, "John A. Harman: Jackson's Logistical Genius," *Iron Worker*, 35, No. 3 (Summer

1971): 2–13. In mid-May 1861, Harman got into a violent argument with Lt. Col. Blanton Duncan of the Kentucky volunteers. Bloodshed and a duel were barely avoided. See *Richmond Enquirer*, June 4, 1861.

32. *Staunton Spectator*, Apr. 30, 1861; TJJ to "Dear Sir," Aug. 5, 1861, Jackson—LVA; Lottie Baylor Landrum biographical sketch, Reel 9, Hotchkiss—LC. Lewis T. Moore was another officer retained by Jackson. Former colonel of the 6th Virginia Militia, Moore served ten days under Jackson and received appointment as lieutenant colonel of the 4th Virginia Volunteers. He would later repay Jackson's trust by giving him his Winchester home to use as a headquarters.

33. Vickers, ed., *Under Both Flags*, 134–35; Daniel B. Conrad, "History of the First Fight and Organization of the Stonewall Brigade—How It Was Named," *United Service*, 8 (1892): 466–67.

34. Daniel B. Ewing to Robert L. Dabney, Sept. 8, 1863, Box 19, Dabney—SHC.

35. Order Book of T. J. Jackson, MC.

36. *OR*, 2:815; Bean, "Harman," 4. One reason for the middle-of-the-night call to duty was to cool the high ardor of the recruits. A newspaper correspondent informed his readers at this time of the volunteers "becoming impatient" for any kind of action against the enemy. *Richmond Enquirer*, May 10, 1861.

37. *Richmond Daily Dispatch*, May 4, 1861; Lyle, "Sketches," W&L, 110. Meanwhile, ladies in Winchester and elsewhere in the lower valley were sending to the camps handmade items such as socks, havelocks, mattresses, and even bandages. *Winchester Virginian*, May 8, 1861.

38. Order Book of T. J. Jackson; Cleon Moore, "The Civil War Recollections of Cleon Moore," *Magazine of the Jefferson County Historical Society*, 54 (Dec. 1988): 92; *Staunton Spectator*, May 24, 1861. The false alarms at Harpers Ferry appear to have continued for another month. See James G. Hudson Diary, May 28–31, 1861, Alabama Department of Archives and History.

39. *Staunton Vindicator*, May 24, 1861.

40. Wells J. Hawks to Robert L. Dabney, Sept. 7, 1863, Box 19, Dabney—SHC; Muster Roll, "Frederick Mounted Rifles," Frederick W. M. Holliday Papers, Duke University.

41. *Staunton Spectator*, May 24, 1861; *B&L*, 1:121. Imboden claimed to have been responsible for mustering the first contingent of volunteers at Harpers Ferry into Virginia service. This may have been true, but Imboden's postwar writings must be ignored in most instances or handled with extreme caution in the other cases. The impeccable Jed Hotchkiss in later years wrote of Imboden (whom he had known in prewar Staunton): "I do not like to say that my friend is unreliable; and yet the truth of the matter is that his statements will not bear the tests of criticism. . . . He writes from a confused memory and never takes the trouble of verifying his statements by a reference to documents." Jedediah Hotchkiss to G. F. R. Henderson, Apr. 26, 1895, Reel 11, Hotchkiss—LC.

42. *Richmond Enquirer*, May 17, 1861; *OR*, 2:809–10; Terrence V. Murphy, *Tenth Virginia Infantry* (Lynchburg, Va., 1989), 1–2.

43. John DeHart Ross, "Harpers Ferry to the Fall of Richmond: Letters of Colonel John DeHart Ross, C.S.A., 1861–1865," *West Virginia History*, 45 (1984): 160; Wight Recollections.

44. Henderson, 1:116–17. For an Imboden story about one of Jackson's inspections, see *B&L*, 1:122.

45. Mrs. Jackson, 156. Colston Reminiscences had Jackson using the figure 20,000 men. A strange twisting of this story is in Chase, *Jackson*, 220.

46. Robert E. Lee, *The Wartime Papers of R. E. Lee* (Boston, 1961), 32. Imboden told the fable of the B&O dismantlement first in *B&L*, 1:122–23. Henderson, 1:121–22, repeated it with an air of authority. Railroad historians followed suit. See Hungerford, *Baltimore & Ohio Railroad*, 2:6–7; Thomas Weber, *The Northern Railroads in the Civil War, 1861–1865* (New York, 1952), 76–77; Angus James Jonnston III, *Virginia Railroads in the Civil War* (Chapel Hill, 1961), 23, 25. Next came historical writers such as Allen Tate, *Stonewall Jackson: The Good Soldier* (New York, 1928), 70; Burke Davis, *They Called Him Stonewall* (New York, 1954), 139–40; Clifford Dowdey, *The Land They Fought For* (Garden City, N.Y., 1955), 110; Chambers, 1:338–39; and others.

Not even a hint exists in official records of Jackson manipulating the B&O schedule for a massive capture of rolling stock. The B&O's master of transportation, W. P. Smith, kept personal memoranda on the railroad during the war. On May 14, 1861, he recorded a "seizure of a train of cars at Harper's Ferry." Such a loss would have been at most a locomotive and eighteen cars. William E. Bain, ed., *B&O in the Civil War: From the Papers of Wm. Prescott Smith* (Denver, 1966), 29, 34.

47. Jackson's petitions for additional guns are in *OR*, 2:809-10, 814, 822, 823-25, 833, 836, 863.

48. *CV,* 12 (1904): 447; *Richmond News-Leader*, Mar. 23, 1939; *SHSP,* 43 (1920): 96; marginal comment by Kyd Douglas on page 173 of his copy of Mrs. Jackson's book, Henry Kyd Douglas Library, Antietam NBP; Lyle, "Sketches," 371. For more on Little Sorrel, see Withrow Scrapbooks, W&L, II, 37; XVIII, 100-2.

49. James I. Robertson, Jr., *The Stonewall Brigade* (Baton Rouge, 1963), 26; Order Book of T. J. Jackson; Andrew N. Cook, 27th Virginia, to wife, May 31, 1861, Crawford Collection. Cook believed that "some abolitionists put Strychnia" in the whiskey to murder the Confederates. Mention of the whiskey ban is also in *Lexington Gazette*, May 23, 1861.

50. R. Henry Campbell to mother, May 4, 1861, BV201, FSNMP.

51. *OR*, 2:832-33; Grattan Reminiscences. Exaggerated estimates of Jackson's strength ranged as high as 12,000 troops. See Earl C. Andis, 4th Virginia, to homefolk, May 12, 1861, "The War Correspondence of Earl Carson Andis," Manassas NBP.

52. "Dr. McGuire's Narrative," handwritten manuscript, Box 19, Dabney—SHC; *SHSP,* 19 (1891): 301. Chambers, 1:337, erred in putting A. S. Pendleton and Wells J. Hawks on Jackson's staff at this time. These two officers became part of Jackson's inner family a month later.

53. R. E. Lee to TJJ, May 6, 1861, Davis—Tulane.

54. Wallbrook D. Swank, *Confederate Letters and Diaries, 1861-1865* (Charlottesville, Va., 1988), 88.

55. *OR*, 2:809-10.

56. Ibid., 814.

57. Ibid. See also Ross, "Letters of Colonel Ross," 161. Joseph G. Morrison, Jackson's brother-in-law and later a member of his staff, wrote after the war that Jackson considered Harpers Ferry a "man-trap" and wanted to abandon the place after all of the arsenal machinery had been removed. *Philadelphia Weekly Times*, Dec. 22, 1883. In light of Jackson's abhorrence of any military movement resembling a withdrawal, Morrison's statement has no weight of authority. On the other hand, Jackson is often quoted as asserting that "I'd rather take that place fifty times than undertake to defend it once." Ray Jones, *Harpers Ferry* (Gretna, La., 1992), 148.

58. *OR*, 2:860, 863.

59. G. C. Camden to Robert L. Dabney, Nov. 25, 1863, Cook—WVU.

60. Ibid. It should be remembered that the state of West Virginia had come into existence by the time of Camden's letter.

61. W. G. Bean, "The Unusual War Experience of Lieutenant George G. Junkin, C.S.A.," *VMHB,* 76 (1968): 182-83.

62. Ibid.

63. Ibid., 183. Both Chambers, 2:211, and Vandiver, 388-89, had this conference taking place in September 1862. The key reason it occurred sixteen months earlier lies in Jackson's statement: "if Virginia adheres to the Union." Obviously, voters in the Old Dominion had not yet approved the ordinance of secession.

64. TJJ to Anna Jackson, May 8, 1861, Jackson—LVA. On the same day, Confederates seized a B&O train carrying 1000 hogs and fifteen horses in retaliation for a Federal raid on Jackson's outpost near Relay House. *Richmond Enquirer*, May 14, 1861.

65. R. E. Lee to TJJ, May 9, 1861, Dabney—LVA; *OR*, 2:824; R. E. Lee to TJJ, May 10, 1861, Jackson Papers. A newspaperman described the undersized Kentucky regiment as being armed only with bowie knives and pistols but "in high spirits and disposed to grumble at nothing except inactivity." *Staunton Spectator*, May 14, 1861. Jackson put the Kentuckians on Maryland Heights in part because they had arrived at Harpers Ferry without any orders and were thus acting in a semiofficial capacity.

66. Mrs. Jackson, 310.

67. Dabney, 192–93. John Ross to Agnes Reid, May 10, 1861, J. D. H. Ross Papers, W&L. Ross added in the same letter: "It has been raining all day and I have been wet as a drowned rat—don't expect to get dry til tomorrow—don't drink any whisky, however."

68. *Richmond Enquirer,* May 21, 1861. For veiled criticism of Jackson as a post commander, see William N. Pendleton to John Letcher, May 20, 1861, Pendleton Papers.

69. *Staunton Vindicator,* May 24, 1861.

70. *Richmond Daily Dispatch,* May 17, 1861; John Cheves Haskell Memoir, Duke; Douglas, *I Rode with Stonewall,* 192–93. The most thorough study of Stuart is Emory M. Thomas, *Bold Dragoon* (New York, 1986).

71. Charles T. O'Ferrall, *Forty Years of Active Service* (New York, 1904), 29–30; Moore, "Civil War Recollections," 105; Douglas, *I Rode with Stonewall,* 41.

72. James B. Avirett, *The Memoirs of General Turner Ashby and His Compeers* (Baltimore, 1867), 91. John Imboden took credit for talking a disgruntled Ashby out of "resigning" from service over Stuart's appointment. Whether Imboden even interceded in this dispute is problematical. Further, Ashby did not threaten to leave the Confederate army until a year later. *B&L,* 1:123–24.

73. *OR,* 2:832; R. E. Lee to TJJ, May 12, 1861, Dabney—LVA. Lee's reply, with minor grammatical changes, is also printed in *OR,* 2:836.

74. James H. Langhorne, 4th Virginia, to father, May 21, 1861, Langhorne Family Papers, Robertson Collection; *OR,* 2:867–70.

75. Joseph A. Waddell, *Annals of Augusta County, Virginia, from 1726 to 1871* (Harrisonburg, Va., 1972), 458; *Staunton Vindicator,* May 31, 1861; Francis McFarland Diary, May 23, 1861, UTS.

76. *OR,* 2:844–45, 856; William N. Pendleton to "Philip," May 25, 1861, Pendleton Papers.

77. *OR,* 2:871–72; W. H. C. Whiting to Robert L. Dabney, Nov. 30, 1863, Box 19, Dabney—SHC. Johnston and some of his biographers maintained that Whiting talked Jackson into relinquishing command. That is not true. See Johnston, *Narrative,* 14; Craig L. Symonds, *Joseph E. Johnston: A Civil War Biography* (New York, 1992), 103. Johnston's version of the episode has an overtone of bitterness. This arose from Dabney, 196–97, whose earlier account portrayed Johnston in a less-than-favorable light.

78. Symonds, *Joseph E. Johnston,* is the best study to date of Johnston. For other praise, see A. S. Pendleton to father, Mar. 6, 1862, Pendleton Papers; Benjamin S. Ewell postwar address, in Richard Stoddert Ewell Papers, LC.

79. *OR,* 2:877. On the same day (May 24) that Johnston searched for proof of command, Lee advised the commander of the Manassas defenses to keep Johnston at Harpers Ferry apprised of any Federal movements in his front. Ibid., 2:872. A partially whitewashed statement of the subsequent Jackson-Johnston relationship is in Mrs. Jackson, 157. The usually reliable Dr. McGuire, who did not like Johnston personally, gave two different and questionable accounts of what Jackson supposedly said about turning over command to Johnston. In the first, members of the staff asked Jackson one evening what he would have done had Johnston forcibly sought to take command. McGuire had Jackson replying: "I'd have whipped him." Repeating the story years later, McGuire portrayed Jackson answering the same question with a smile and the observation: "I would have put him in the guard-house." Hunter H. McGuire to Robert L. Dabney, June 20, 1867, Dabney—UTS; *SHSP,* 19 (1891): 301–2.

80. *Richmond Enquirer,* June 4, 1861; *OR,* 2:849.

81. Andis, "War Correspondence," Manassas NMP. At the end of that same letter, Andis declared: "You told me to take Old Lincoln's scalp and come home. I need no encouragement for if I get a chance he is a goner."

82. TJJ to Francis H. Smith, May 30, 1861, Sara Henderson Smith Papers, VHS.

83. Mrs. Jackson, 157–58.

84. Ibid., 146, 152–53. Mary Pendleton to daughter, May 23, 1861, Pendleton Papers. Anna was so imprecise in her memoirs over the date she left Lexington that Jackson biographers have traditionally placed her departure a week or more earlier than was the case. See Chambers,

1:341, as an example. A young Lexington soldier was of the opinion that Mrs. Jackson lived with the Rev. and Mrs. White until late July. Randolph Tucker Shields, Jr., "Recollections of a Liberty Hall Volunteer," article in unidentified publication, Manassas NMP, 20. White made no mention in his autobiography of Anna being a houseguest.

85. *OR*, 2:883; Order Book of T. J. Jackson.

86. Tippie Boteler to Lizzie Boteler, May 1861, Alexander Robinson Boteler Papers, Duke; Moore, *Cannoneer*, 36; Walker, *Memorial, VMI*, 21–25.

87. For a more detailed discussion of the composition of Jackson's command, see Robertson, *Stonewall Brigade*, 10–22. The 33d Virginia was the fifth regiment in the brigade, but it did not reach full strength and report for duty until mid-July. Ibid., 27, 33.

88. William N. Pendleton Memorandum, May 16, 1861, Pendleton Papers; H. Kyd Douglas to Tippie Boteler, Oct. 14, 1861, Henry Kyd Douglas Letters, Duke; *SHSP*, 23 (1895): 99.

89. Lyle, "Sketches," 113.

90. W. G. Bean, *The Liberty Hall Volunteers: Stonewall's College Boys* (Charlottesville, Va., 1964), 21–23.

91. Wells J. Hawks to Jedediah Hotchkiss, Jan. 17, 1866, New York Historical Society.

92. George Baylor, *Bull Run to Bull Run; Or, Four Years in the Army of Northern Virginia* (Richmond, 1900), 18–19.

93. Mrs. Jackson, 159.

94. *SHSP*, 25 (1897): 103. McGuire slightly increased the drama of the story in *Confederate Cause and Conduct*, 207. For Johnston's written feelings about volunteers, see his *Narrative*, 16.

95. *Richmond Daily Dispatch*, June 1 and 8, 1861.

96. Robert Hooke to father, June 3, 1861, Robert W. Hooke Papers, Duke; Phillips, "Lower Shenandoah Valley," 262. One of the few positive views at this time of life at the Ferry is in *Richmond Daily Dispatch*, June 10, 1861.

97. *OR*, 2:471, 881.

98. Johnston's requests to abandon Harpers Ferry are in *OR*, 2:471, 881, 889–90, 895–96, 899. See also Johnston, *Narrative*, 17–20, for hindsight judgments. Lee's rejections are in *OR*, 2:894, 897, 901, 910. Some of the Confederates in the ranks at the time agreed with Johnston's negative assessment. See James H. Langhorne to father, June 5, 1861, Langhorne Papers.

99. *SHSP*, 19 (1891): 84.

100. Randolph H. McKim, *A Soldier's Recollections* (New York, 1910), 99; McCabe, *Jackson*, 30.

101. TJJ to Jonathan M. Bennett, June 4, 1861, Cook—WVU. This letter appears in more polished form in Arnold, 332.

102. *Richmond Daily Dispatch*, June 13, 1861; *OR*, 2:471–72, 924. Confederates had declared Thursday, June 13, as a fast day. In Winchester, the Methodist minister delivered a sermon based appropriately on a verse in Isaiah 26: "Come, my people, enter thou into thy chambers, and shut thy doors about thee: hide thyself as it were for a little moment, until the indignation be overpast." Benjamin F. Brooke Journal, June 13, 1861, Handley Library.

103. See Boyd B. Stutler, "Harpers Ferry Bridge: Nine-Time Loser," *Civil War History*, 3 (1962): 9–10.

104. TJJ to Anna Jackson, June 14, 1861, Dabney—LVA; Capt. Porter King Diary, Civil War Miscellaneous Collection, USMHI; Hudson Diary, June 13–14, 1861. Two soldiers in the 4th Virginia destroyed the railroad bridge. James H. Langhorne to father, June 18, 1861, Langhorne Papers. A VMI drillmaster looked back from the top of Bolivar Heights and commented: "We saw volums of smoke rising from some of the public buildings. . . . I was horrifed at seeing all these valuable houses burned & it struck me that war was a cruel thing, tho sometimes necessary." Wight Recollections.

105. *Richmond Daily Dispatch*, June 25, 1861; Andrew N. Cook to wife, June 18, 1861, Crawford Collection; A. W. Hawks to Jedediah Hotchkiss, Nov. 11 and 16, 1897, Reel 14, Hotchkiss—LC.

106. TJJ to Anna Jackson, June 19, 1861, Dabney—LVA.

107. Ibid. *OR*, 2:937. For descriptions of the march toward Winchester, see Lt. James H.

Langhorne to father, June 18, 1861, Langhorne Papers; Capt. J. J. White to Mary White, June 21, 1861, James Jones White Papers, SHC. Patterson's entire Union force at the time numbered 10,600 men. *OR*, 2:730.

108. TJJ to Anna Jackson, June 19, 1861, Dabney—LVA.

109. *OR*, 2:471–72; 5:858–59; Edward Hungerford, *The Story of the Baltimore & Ohio Railroad, 1827–1927* (New York, 1928), 2:9–14; Alexander T. Barclay to mother, June 22, 1861, Barclay Letters, LVA. Drillmaster Charles Wight of the 27th Virginia thought that Martinsburg residents differed strongly in their sentiments toward Jackson's men. "Some were moved to tears at the thought that they were about to be left to the enemy, and begged us to return soon, but the greater part of the population was evidently pleased at our departure and made taunting remarks as 'Won't you stay longer with us? What's your hurry?' &c. &c." Wight Recollections.

110. W. H. C. Whiting to TJJ, June 19, 1861, Dabney—LVA; Lyle, "Sketches," 98.

111. *Lexington Gazette*, July 4, 1861.

112. For strong criticism of Johnston's temerity by another member of the 4th Virginia, see Thomas W. Reed to unknown addressee, June 21, 1861, Morrison Letters, CWTI.

113. W. H. C. Whiting to TJJ, June 23, 1861, Old Catalog Collection, VHS. Jackson's surgeon reacted bitterly to these decisions. See Hunter McGuire to Robert L. Dabney, June 20, 1867, Dabney—UTS.

114. James H. Langhorne to mother, June 23, 1861, Langhorne Papers; [Thomas E. Caffey], *Battle-fields of the South, from Bull Run to Fredericksburg*, by an English Combatant (London, 1863), 1:202–3. As Jackson dejectedly led the column back to Martinsburg, one soldier standing on the roadside sought to be witty. He snapped to attention and saluted as the apparently sleeping colonel passed. To the man's surprise, Jackson promptly returned the salute. Lyle, "Sketches," 100.

115. TJJ to Anna Jackson, June 24, 1861, Box 20, Dabney—SHC.

116. TJJ to Jonathan M. Bennett, June 24, 1861, Cook—WVU; Anna Jackson to John Letcher, Mar. 17, 1877, Jackson—VMI.

117. Dennis E. Frye, *Second Virginia Infantry* (Lynchburg, Va., 1984), 9; James J. White to Mary White, June 30, 1861, White Papers.

118. Ted Barclay to sister, June 25, 1861, Ted Barclay Letters, LVA; James J. White to wife, June 30, 1861, White Papers; James H. Langhorne to mother, June 26, 1861, Langhorne Papers; *OR*, 2:187, 730. The 4th Virginia's Lt. Lyle believed that one of Jackson's characteristics as a great commander was the care he exhibited toward his men. When a Martinsburg baker supplying the troops with bread began delivering half-baked loaves to camp, "Jackson hailed him to headquarters and gave him such a roasting that his bread thereafter proved to be of superior quality." Lyle, "Sketches," 112.

119. The basic facts of the skirmish at Falling Waters as presented here came from Jackson's official report, in *OR*, 2:185–86; TJJ to Anna Jackson (letter beginning "My precious darling"), July 4, 1861, Dabney—LVA; *Lexington Gazette*, July 11, 1861; Col. Kenton Harper's unpublished official report, in William Nelson Pendleton Papers, Duke. Why Jackson chose Staunton's 5th Virginia for this action is unknown. Logic pointed more to the 2d Virginia, many of whose members were from the Falling Waters area. That regiment was also under the command of Col. James W. Allen, a graduate of and former professor at VMI.

120. *OR*, 2:185; Harper report.

121. *OR*, 2:185. For years thereafter, Confederates exaggerated the number of Federals who went down from the first shot fired by Pendleton's little gun. Yet everyone who was near the weapon or who later wrote an account agreed on what the captain essentially said in his order to fire. For variations, see *Richmond Enquirer*, July 9 and 16, 1861; *Lexington Gazette*, July 18, 1861; *SHSP*, 23 (1895): 106; Kyd Douglas marginal note in Mrs. Jackson, 165, Douglas Library; *Philadelphia Weekly Times*, Apr. 14, 1883. Pendleton himself made no reference to his words in his narrative of the skirmish. Susan P. Lee, *Memoirs of William Nelson Pendleton, D.D.* (Philadelphia, 1893), 145–46.

122. *OR*, 2:185–86.

123. Conrad, "History of the First Fight," 468.

124. Joseph E. Johnston to TJJ, July 2, 1861, Davis—Tulane; Brown statement in Lyle, "Sketches," 135–36. A different telling of this incident is in Thomas W. Baldwin Reminiscences, Robertson Collection, 7. One soldier correspondent asserted that Jackson "was as cool as a cucumber, writing orders on his horse while the balls flew round him like hail." *Richmond Daily Dispatch,* July 12, 1861.

125. As would be expected after the first contest, both sides exaggerated the losses each inflicted on the other. A member of Pendleton's battery was certain that 200–300 Federals were killed in the brief engagement. George R. Bedinger to sister, July 4, 1861, Bedinger-Dandridge Family Correspondence, Duke. See also F. T. Griffin to "Col.," July 17, 1861, Joseph Belknap Smith Papers, Duke; *Lexington Gazette,* July 18, 1861; *OR,* 2:157, 160; *Richmond Daily Dispatch,* July 4, 1861. A recent VMI graduate proclaimed the skirmish "one of the most brilliant exploits of the war." McCabe, *Jackson,* 29.

126. TJJ to Anna Jackson, July 4, 1861, Box 20, Dabney—SHC.

127. Porter King Diary, Civil War Miscellaneous Collection, USMHI.

128. *SHSP,* 23 (1895): 107; *Richmond Daily Dispatch,* July 12, 1861.

129. Lyle, "Sketches," 145.

130. W. H. C. Whiting to Robert L. Dabney, Nov. 30, 1863, Box 19, Dabney—SHC; *OR,* 2:185, 473, 963; Mrs. Jackson, 166. The official certificate of promotion, which was made retroactive to June 17, is in Jackson—LVA. Always-opinionated Col. William C. Oates of Alabama stated that when President Davis approved Jackson's promotion, "it provided laughter among those who thought they knew him well." Oates, *War between the Union and the Confederacy,* 186–87.

131. Quoted in Henderson, 1:130.

132. TJJ to Anna Jackson, July 8, 1861, Box 20, Dabney—SHC.

133. Anna Jackson to Mrs. Templeman Brown, Sept. 28, 1863, Jackson—VMI. Jackson was not by himself in his displeasure with Johnston's leadership. Mrs. William N. Pendleton informed her husband from Lexington: "There is a general disposition to censure Gen. Johnston for his management of affairs. This I find from remarks on the street, and from letters from camp." Anzolette Pendleton to W. N. Pendleton, July 13, 1861, Pendleton Papers.

134. James J. White to Mary White, July 7, 1861, White Papers; Andrew N. Cook to wife, July 9, 1861, Crawford Collection; Mrs. Jackson, 168.

135. John O. Casler, *Four Years in the Stonewall Brigade* (Dayton, Ohio, 1971), 21; Lyle, "Sketches," 166.

136. Johnston, *Narrative,* 33; Mrs. Jackson, 168.

137. TJJ to Anna Jackson, July 16, 1861, Dabney—LVA.

CHAPTER 10   *Emergence of "Stonewall"*

1. Samuel S. Seig to Carrie Davis, July 25, 1861, Manassas NBP; *B&L,* 1:196. See also [Caffey], *Battle-fields of the South,* 1:46–47.

2. *OR,* 2:473, 972; Johnston, *Narrative,* 33–34; Phillips, "Lower Shenandoah Valley," 178–79. Sergeant Cook of the 27th Virginia was one of the ill soldiers left behind in Winchester. He estimated 2500 incapacitated men being in the hospitals there, with an average of six men dying each day. Andrew N. Cook to wife, July 19, 1861, Lewis C. Crawford, Jr., Collection, Rupert, W.Va.

3. Hunter McGuire to Jedediah Hotchkiss, May 28, 1896, Reel 12, Hotchkiss—LC.

4. Cornelia P. McDonald, *A Diary with Reminiscences of the War and Refugee Life in the Shenandoah Valley, 1860–1865* (Nashville, 1934), 28.

5. McGuire to Hotchkiss, May 28, 1896. Johnston and Jackson both thought that the march began "around noon." Chaplain James G. Hudson was in the 4th Alabama of Bee's brigade, the last in the line of march. He noted carefully that Jackson's troops began passing through downtown Winchester at 1 P.M. A soldier in Jackson's brigade (obviously near the rear of the column) put 3 P.M. as the time of departure. Johnston, *Narrative,* 36; Mrs. Jackson, 175; James

G. Hudson Diary, July 18, 1861, Alabama Department of Archives and History; Conrad, "History of the First Fight," 469.

6. *Richmond Daily Dispatch*, Aug. 6, 1861; Elijah M. Ingles, 4th Virginia, to mother, July 24, 1861, copy of letter in author's possession.

7. Johnston's order, William Nelson Pendleton Papers, SHC; Mrs. Jackson, 175; Lyle, "Sketches," typescript, W&L, 190. See also Conrad, "History of the First Fight," 470; Thomas W. Baldwin Reminiscences, Robertson Collection.

8. Johnston, *Narrative*, 36–37, 58. By Johnston's computation of his army's pace, the forty-four-mile march from the Shenandoah River to Manassas would require three days. In contrast, one of the Confederacy's premier artillerymen tracked Johnston's movement at one and three-quarters mile per hour and "an excellent march under the circumstances." E. P. Alexander, *Military Memoirs of a Confederate* (New York, 1907), 19.

9. Lyle, "Sketches," 190, 192; Mrs. Jackson, 175; Conrad, "History of the First Fight," 470. Jackson's brigade forded the Shenandoah and continued east. The other brigades in Johnston's force bivouacked at the river and crossed the next day.

10. Mrs. Jackson, 175–77; Dabney, 212; Henderson, 1:134; "Memorial Tribute to Stonewall Jackson," Dickson Papers, University of Michigan. Johnston mistakenly had Jackson arriving at Paris "two hours after dark." Johnston, *Narrative*, 37. Paris is now the community of Delaplane.

11. "Dr. McGuire's Narrative," Box 19, Dabney—SHC; Hill statement in *Century Magazine*, 47 (1893–94), 624.

12. McGuire later wrote a second, more dramatic account of the late-night activities. See Reel 8, Hotchkiss—LC. The strangest aspect of the "lone sentry" story is Jedediah Hotchkiss's silence. Unwavering in his pursuit of the truth about Jackson, Hotchkiss read most of G. F. R. Henderson's chapters in manuscript. He caught a number of errors in the Englishman's incomparably detailed biography because in the postwar years Hotchkiss became the most knowledgeable authority on Jackson's life. Yet he made no mention about Jackson acting as a sentry. Indeed, Hotchkiss's only comment in his postwar journal about the night of July 17–18 was that rain fell in the predawn hours. Hotchkiss Journal, Reel 1, Hotchkiss—LC.

13. Conrad, "History of the First Fight," 471. Jackson put the time of arrival at Piedmont Station at 6 A.M. That was probably the hour when the march resumed at Paris. Mrs. Jackson, 176–77. Rumors of a July 18 engagement at Manassas are in Watkins Kearns Diary, July 19, 1861, VHS. Edmondson, *My Dear Emma*, 34, is the source for the troops going twenty-four hours without food.

14. Mrs. Jackson, 177. The pleasantries of the train ride came from Moore, "Civil War Recollections," 94; Charles Copland Wight Recollections, Wight Family Papers, VHS; *SHSP*, 19 (1891): 87. John Lyle recalled a moving scene on the trip. "In one group of refugees, clustered near the track, I saw an old woman in a calico dress and sunbonnet kneeling as if in prayer. Her eyes and hands were raised to heaven, and her moving lips and reverent attitude told plainly that she was asking God to bless us and give us the victory." Lyle, "Sketches," 196.

15. Jubal A. Early, *Autobiographical Sketch and Narrative of the War between the States* (Philadelphia, 1912), 10–11; *SHSP*, 19 (1891): 307. Hotchkiss Journal, Reel 1, Hotchkiss—LC, had Jackson's men stopping for the night at Blackburn's Ford. Dabney, 213, thought that the brigade went to "the pine-coppices near Mitchell's Ford." Jackson actually bivouacked his regiments between and to the south of the two fords.

16. Lowell Reidenbaugh, *Twenty-seventh Virginia Infantry* (Lynchburg, Va., 1993), 13.

17. Lyle, "Sketches," 199; Randolph Tucker Shields, Jr., "Recollections of a Liberty Hall Volunteer," article in unidentified publication, Manassas NMP, 13.

18. Wight Recollections.

19. *OR*, 2:486–87.

20. John N. Opie, *A Rebel Cavalryman with Lee, Stuart and Jackson* (Chicago, 1899), 28.

21. The basis of the First Manassas narrative here are two accounts that Jackson wrote. One is his official report, submitted two days after the engagement. It is deposited in the Joseph E. Johnston Collection, Henry E. Huntington Library, and printed with editorial changes in *OR*,

2:481–82. Jackson's other battle summary was a July 28, 1861, letter to Jonathan M. Bennett, in Cook, *Family and Early Life*, 160–62. Unless otherwise stated, all Jackson quotations are from those two sources. The general's official report of First Manassas was unusually brief because of the pain in his wounded left hand. TJJ to "My dear Colonel," Mar. 7, 1862, Jackson—VMI. The regiments that Jackson lent briefly to Longstreet were the 2d and 5th Virginia.

22. Chisholm's unpublished official report is in A. R. Chisholm File, Compiled Service Records of Confederate Generals and Staff Officers, and Nonregimental Enlisted Men, RG109, NA. For verification of the confused movements of the morning, see *OR*, 2:488–89; *B&L*, 1:205; Edwin G. Lee to Aunt Mary, Nov. 18, 1861, William Fitzhugh Lee Letters, Western Historical Manuscript Collection.

23. L. VanLoan Naisawald, "The Location and Frontage of Jackson's Brigade at First Manassas," typescript, Manassas NBP, 1; *Lexington Gazette*, Aug. 1, 1861; C. A. Fonerden, *A Brief History of the Military Career of Carpenter's Battery* (New Market, Va., 1911), 7.

24. Had McDowell exploited momentum and pressed his advantage, his men would likely have seized Henry Hill. That in turn would have enabled them to take Beauregard's army in flank and win the battle. Yet from Matthews Hill the Confederate height across the way appeared lightly defended and there for the taking. McDowell allowed his infantry to rest, which it did for two-and-a-half hours. It was during this interim that Jackson established his brigade on Henry Hill. John Hennessy, *The First Battle of Manassas* (Lynchburg, Va., 1989), 126.

25. Captain Edwin Lee, one of Jackson's aides at this battle, stated that Bee requested Jackson's support. This is highly improbable. Bee had little if any idea what troops were available in his rear. Edwin G. Lee to Aunt Mary, Nov. 18, 1861, Lee Letters. Jackson reached the base of Henry Hill around 11:30 that morning. Ibid.; Naisawald, "Location and Frontage of Jackson's Brigade," 1–2.

26. Elijah M. Ingles, 4th Virginia, to mother, July 24, 1861, Robertson Collection; Lyle, "Sketches," 202.

27. *B&L*, 1:234–35.

28. Hennessy, *First Manassas*, 70–71.

29. Georgetown Meteorological Observations, July 21, 1861, Manassas NBP. The precise location and position of the cannon attached to Jackson's command remain in dispute. See Hennessy, *First Manassas*, 150. In a rare oversight, Stanard's name was not included in the index to *OR*, volume 2, or in the general index for the work as a whole.

30. Naisawald, "Location and Frontage of Jackson's Brigade," 5; *SHSP*, 34 (1906): 368.

31. *OR*, 2:491–92; *Richmond Daily Dispatch*, Aug. 6, 1861; Wise, *Long Arm of Lee*, 1:132. Pendleton claimed that because of the "telling" fire of the Southern cannon, "the batteries of the enemy were greatly crippled and their advance effectively checked." This is one of the more flagrant exaggerations in official reports of the battle of First Manassas. *OR*, 51: Pt. 1, 34–35. Some early accounts of the engagement had Pendleton repeating his Falling Waters benediction by shouting: "Fire, boys! and may God have mercy on their guilty souls!" Jones, *War Clerk's Diary*, 1:70; Hopley, *Jackson*, 133.

32. Baldwin Reminiscences; Lyle, "Sketches," 204; *SHSP*, 38 (1910): 280.

33. Cooke, *Outlines from the Outpost*, 52; Lyle, "Sketches," 206–7.

34. Although both Jackson and Surg. McGuire stated that the wound came in the climactic Confederate assault in late afternoon, too many eyewitnesses have the injury occurring hours earlier during the fierce artillery exchange. One soldier stated that Jackson got the wound while directing the fire of one of his batteries. In the heat of battle, Jackson paid so little attention to the laceration that he can be excused for mistaking the exact time he was shot. See *B&L*, 1:236; *Richmond Enquirer*, Aug. 3, 1861; *SHSP*, 19 (1891): 91, 303; 23 (1895): 112; 43 (1920): 10.

35. Conrad, "History of the First Fight," 471; *Charleston Mercury*, July 25, 1861.

36. Maury, *Recollections*, 24. Two years later, for unknown reasons other than a desire to be more a part of the scenario, Maj. W. H. Chase Whiting of Johnston's staff sought to plant the story that Jackson uttered those words during a brief noon meeting with Johnston and his staff. W. H. C. Whiting to Robert L. Dabney, Nov. 30, 1863, Box 19, Dabney—SHC. For Bee's background, see James B. Agnew, "General Barnard Bee," *CWTI*, 14 (Dec. 1975): 4–8, 44–47.

37. Precisely what Bee said will never be known with absolute certainty. A correspondent's story in the *Charleston Mercury*, July 25, 1861, republished verbatim in the *Richmond Daily Dispatch*, July 29, 1861, and the *Lexington Gazette*, Aug. 15, 1861, was the first account of Bee's statement to appear in print. The same expression, with but minor deviations, is in McCabe, *Jackson*, 32; [Caffey], *Battle-fields of the South*, 1:66; Dabney, 222; Sallie A. Putnam, *Richmond during the War* (New York, 1867), 61; Fitzhugh Lee, in *Dedication of Tomb of Army of Northern Virginia, Louisiana Division, and Unveiling of Statue of Stonewall Jackson at Metairie Cemetery* (New Orleans, 1881), 27; *SHSP*, 13 (1885): 325; 19 (1891): 166; 25 (1897): 313; A. R. Chisholm to Isaac Markens, June 23, 1891, Joseph Eggleston Johnston Papers, Huntington; *CV*, 30 (1922): 262.

The second most quoted rendition has the phrase "stone wall" directed at Jackson's men rather than to their commander. In this case, Bee is thought to have said: "Look at Jackson's brigade standing like a stone wall! Rally on the Virginians!" One could argue that this is the most realistic interpretation, since a line of men bears more resemblance to a wall than would an individual—even Jackson. This reference to the Virginia brigade also originated immediately after the battle. It remained popular for a quarter-century following the war. Among the first men to present this version was Brig. Gen. (later Episcopal bishop) Ellison Capers, a fellow South Carolinian and good friend of Bee's. See Margaretta Barton Colt, *Defend the Valley: A Shenandoah Family in the Civil War* (New York, 1994), 83; Tippie Boteler to Lizzie Boteler, Aug. 4, 1861, Alexander Robinson Boteler Papers, Duke University; Baldwin Reminiscences; Douglas, *I Rode with Stonewall*, 10; Mary B. Chesnut, *Mary Chesnut's Civil War* (New Haven, 1981), 108; Heth, *Memoirs*, 137; Shields, "Liberty Hall Volunteers," 18; *CWTI*, 1 (July 1962): 39–40.

Surgeon McGuire led a host of Virginians by combining the two versions and having Bee shout: "There stands Jackson like a stone wall! Rally behind the Virginians!" *SHSP*, 13 (1885): 323; 19 (1891): 307–8.

At least three reports of the incident have twisted the facts totally out of context. The most preposterous account came from Jackson's first biographer, who stated that Jackson himself coined the phrase "stone wall" while assuring Beauregard that his men would hold Henry Hill. Addey, *Jackson*, 32–33. General Johnston is reported to have turned to Capt. E. P. Alexander that afternoon and praised the 4th Virginia alone for standing "like a stone wall." Alexander, *Military Memoirs*, 36; E. Porter Alexander, *Fighting for the Confederacy* (Chapel Hill, 1989), 51. The always theatrical Kyd Douglas, who regarded veteran soldier Barnard Bee as having "the excitement and mortification of an untried but heroic soldier," presented a version too sophisticated to have credence. *Annals of the War*, 642–43.

Exactly what Bee meant in his war cry has created negative interpretation among a few writers. The origin of this viewpoint began with two staff officers: Maj. Chase Whiting, whose resentment of Jackson at Winchester in the spring escalated in time to open dislike, and Maj. Thomas G. Rhett, who graduated sixth in the West Point class of 1845 but never progressed beyond staff assignments. These two men, with Whiting by far the more outspoken, told another South Carolina officer that Jackson refused to advance to Bee's relief. "In a passionate expression of anger [Bee] denounced him for standing like a stone wall and allowing them to be sacrificed." John Cheve Haskell Memoir, Duke. No established facts support any part of that statement. One of Bee's own aides, William P. Shingler, wrote a little-known account that refutes all negative overtones placed on the origin of the nickname. See *New Eclectic Magazine*, 4 (1869): 745–46.

D. Harvey Hill dismissed the "stone wall" story with praise. "The name was least suited to Jackson, who was ever in motion, sweeping like an eagle on his prey." *Century Magazine*, 47 (1893–94): 623. For a current negative view, see John Hennessy, "Jackson's 'Stonewall': Fact or Fiction?," typescript, Manassas NBP, and Hennessy, *First Manassas*, 83, 152.

More than fifty years ago, Douglas Southall Freeman discussed the pros and cons relative to the nickname in *Lee's Lieutenants: A Study in Command* (New York, 1944), 1:733–34. His conclusions remain sound. The story of "Stonewall" Jackson's exploits were circulating joyfully in Richmond three days after the battle. A South Carolina newspaperman, who was the first to report what Bee shouted, would not have mentioned the story—or been as laudatory—if the incident had not had positive overtones. The enthusiasm attendant to those early days of the war gives the action the appearance of probability. Freeman concluded that it was up to anyone not believing the traditional origins of the nickname to offer convincing evidence to the contrary.

Another discussion of the "stone wall" story is in Couper, *One Hundred Years at VMI*, 2:161-62. See also *Richmond Whig*, Jan. 27, 1877.

38. *OR*, 2:394; *Lexington Gazette*, Aug. 1, 1861.

39. W. W. Blackford, *War Years with Jeb Stuart* (New York, 1945), 26-27.

40. *OR*, 2:384-85; *SHSP*, 34 (1906): 368-69; Casler, *Stonewall Brigade*, 36. Adjutant Randolph Barton of the 33d Virginia was obviously wrong in asserting that Jackson gave no official praise to the regiment for its gallant assault because it took place without his knowledge and approval. On the other hand, Barton raised a valid question by asking why Jackson did not take strong disciplinary action against Cummings when he later court-martialed officers for lesser disobedience of orders. *SHSP*, 38 (1910): 276-77.

41. Casler, *Stonewall Brigade*, 29.

42. Walker, *Memorial*, VMI, 22; Henderson, 1:150. The conduct of the 14th New York in the battle varied from courageous to erratic. See *OR*, 2:347, 387, 403, 410.

43. Unidentified newspaper clipping, Withrow Scrapbooks, W&L, IX, 45. Jackson repeated essentially the same language in his post-battle letter to Jonathan Bennett, although he made no reference to telling the men to "yell like furies." Two other members of the 4th Virginia claimed to have heard Jackson add to his orders: "This day we will drive them across the Potomac!" Lyle, "Sketches," 209; Shields, "Liberty Hall Volunteers," 17. See also *CV*, 39 (1931): 345.

44. Jackson manuscript report, Johnston Collection, Huntington.

45. *Lexington Gazette*, Aug. 1, 1861.

46. *CV*, 31 (1923): 275. See also *Richmond Times-Dispatch*, Nov. 27, 1904; W. H. Andrews, *Footprints of a Regiment* (Atlanta, 1992), 53.

47. *OR*, 2:386, 394, 494.

48. Ibid., 2:494-95; William T. Poague to Jedediah Hotchkiss, Mar. 25, 1895, Reel 11, Hotchkiss—LC. Poague condensed the story for publication in his *Gunner with Stonewall*, 9-10.

49. Clement Fishburne Memoirs, UVA; *SHSP*, 23 (1895): 112. Surgeon Hunter McGuire also tended to scoff at the notion that when Jackson lifted his arm into the air, he was making an appeal to heaven. Hunter McGuire to Jedediah Hotchkiss, Nov. 8, 1897, Reel 14, Hotchkiss—LC. Yet the majority of Jackson's men became convinced that he kept in direct "communication" with God during battle.

50. McGuire wrote four different accounts of treating Jackson's finger. The version most used here is the earliest and least known. Jedediah Hotchkiss memorandum of conversation with McGuire, Aug. 22, 1863, Reel 8, Hotchkiss—LC. McGuire's other three recollections, in descending order of reliability, are "Dr. McGuire's Narrative," Box 19, Dabney—SHC; *SHSP*, 19 (1891): 303-4; McGuire, *Confederate Cause and Conduct*, 196-97. The surgeon concluded by stating, "The motion of the joint improved for several months after the wound had healed, and in the end the deformity was trifling." That medical overview ignored the pain and impairment through which Jackson went for several weeks after First Manassas.

51. All four of the McGuire narratives contain this story. The first two editions had Jackson asking for three cheers for Davis. In the earliest version, Jackson declared that he could seize the Northern capital that night rather than the next day.

52. Contrary to popular belief, McGuire was not the sole source for the incident. Robert L. Dabney, later Jackson's chief of staff, gave a long account of these events at the field hospital. Captain Porter Alexander presented essentially the same facts, except that he had the Federals running like sheep and Jackson needing only 5000 troops to seize Washington. Cavalryman John S. Mosby added further corroboration. See Farwell, *Jackson*, 194; Dabney, 226-27; Alexander, *Military Memoirs*, 42; John S. Mosby, *The Memoirs of Colonel John S. Mosby* (Boston, 1917), 81.

53. Hunter McGuire to Robert L. Dabney, June 20, 1867, Dabney—UTS. Months after the battle, Jackson reportedly said in the hearing of another staff officer, "The victory at Bull Run was a great misfortune for the Confederacy—a very great disaster." H. Kyd Douglas to John C. Ropes, Mar. 22, 1884, copy of letter in possession of the author. See also Graham, "Some Reminiscences," 126.

54. *Philadelphia Weekly Times,* Apr. 7, 1877.

55. *OR,* 2:482; TJJ to Maj. Thomas G. Rhett, July 24, 1861, Johnston Collection; Casler, *Stonewall Brigade,* 30; Lyle, "Sketches," 207.

56. *OR,* 2:500.

57. Alexandra Lee Lavin, *"This Awful Drama": General Edwin Gray Lee, C.S.A., and His Family* (New York, 1987), 29; E. Franklin Paxton, *Memoir and Memorials: Elisha Franklin Paxton, Brigadier-General, C.S.A.* ([New York], 1905), 12. Johnston's praise of Jackson was far more controlled. *OR,* 2:475, 477–78.

58. Cook, *Family and Early Life,* 162; TJJ to Anna Jackson, July 22, 1861, Box 20, Dabney—SHC. A decade later, Kyd Douglas wrote patronizingly that Jackson should be forgiven for the statement about his brigade being the "Imperial Guard" of the Confederate army. It was the arrival of Kirby Smith and Jubal Early that actually saved the day at Manassas, Douglas felt. *Annals of the War,* 643. Major Frank Jones, serving temporarily on Jackson's staff, wrote his wife a few days after the battle: "Thus has the Lord of Host's fought on our side, and given us a glorious victory . . . gained too not behind entrenchments, but in the open field. . . . Gen. Jackson tells me no battle in Mexicao equalled it." Colt, *Defend the Valley,* 89.

59. *Richmond Daily Dispatch,* July 29, 1861; *Richmond Whig,* quoted in *Lexington Gazette,* Aug. 15, 1861. The only mention of Jackson by the *Richmond Enquirer* was as a slightly wounded brigade commander. More than one Virginia soldier reacted angrily to state newspapers over-looking heroism by Old Dominion troops. See John S. Mosby, *The Letters of John S. Mosby* (Richmond, 1986), 11.

60. Andrew N. Cook to brother, Aug. 1, 1861, Crawford Collection.

61. Lyle, "Sketches," 222–23; Watkin Kearns Diary, July 22, 1861. John Imboden erroneously had Anna Jackson arriving at Manassas on July 22 to visit her husband, and the Staunton artilleryman also gave a highly improbable conversation he claimed to have had with Jackson. *B&L,* 1:238.

62. Mrs. Jackson, 181–82. Although Dr. White never told this story himself, his friend and colleague, the Rev. Moses D. Hoge, related it publicly. *SHSP,* 13 (1885): 323.

63. War Memoranda, Reel 1, Hotchkiss—LC; Casler, *Stonewall Brigade,* 47; James T. Thompson, "A Georgia Boy with 'Stonewall' Jackson," *VMHB,* 70 (1961): 315; John P. Hite Diary, July 26, 1861, Handley Library.

64. TJJ to Thomas G. Rhett, July 30, 1861, Johnston Collection. Dabney, 234, asserted that Johnston's poor planning in selecting campsites resulted in "camp fevers tenfold more fatal than the bullets of the enemy." Johnston, *Narrative,* 65–66, retorted that the valley soldiers were sickly before they reached the Manassas area.

65. *SHSP,* 19 (1891): 304; Lyle, "Sketches," 252; Mrs. Jackson, 179; Colt, *Defend the Valley,* 92.

66. Lyle, "Sketches," 257–58; Hite Diary, July 28, 1861.

67. Hotchkiss Journal, Reel 1, Hotchkiss—LC; J. J. White to Mary White, July 28, 1861, White Papers, SHC; Baldwin Reminiscences.

68. Fishburne Letter, Presbyterian Church (USA) Archives; Alexander S. Pendleton to Mary Pendleton, Aug. 10, 1861, Pendleton Papers. A number of writers, beginning with Clem Fishburne of the Rockbridge Artillery, mentioned the brigade's encampment at the "Utterback farm." The 1860 Fairfax County census returns give a different spelling and picture of the place where Jackson had his headquarters for six weeks. The "farm" was more akin to a manorial estate. In 1860, the land value was $100,000—equivalent to at least $1 million by modern-day standards. Living there in the summer of 1861 were Philip Utterback, who was thirty-five, and his wife Rose, twenty-three. Both were natives of Washington, D.C. The Utterbacks had listed their personal property in 1860 at $10,000, an enormous sum for that day.

69. Moore, "Civil War Recollections," 96; Lyle, "Sketches," 261.

70. TJJ to Anna Jackson, July 29, 1861, Box 20, Dabney—SHC.

71. TJJ to Anna Jackson, Aug. 5, 1861, Box 20, Dabney—SHC.

72. *Richmond Daily Dispatch*, Aug. 9, 1861; *Richmond Enquirer*, Aug. 10, 1861. Jackson had little involvement with the August 8–9 visit to the Confederate army by the French dignitary, Prince Napoleon. For Jackson's participation, see G. Moxley Sorrel, *Recollections of a Confederate Staff Officer* (New York, 1905), 28–29; A. S. Pendleton to Mary Pendleton, Aug. 10, 1861, Pendleton Papers.

73. James J. White to Mary White, Aug. 10, 1861, White Papers; Lyle, "Sketches," 264.

74. Andrew N. Cook to wife, Aug. 13, 1861, Crawford Collection.

75. Jacob B. Click to Evaline G. Haney, Aug. 12, 1861, Jacob B. Click Letters, Duke University; Ted Barclay to sister, Aug. 12, 1861, Ted Barclay Letters, LVA.

76. *Lexington Gazette*, Sept. 5, 1861; W. B. Switzer to cousin, Aug. 18, 1861, Switzer Letters, Robertson Collection; J. B. Evans to cousin, Aug. 25, 1861, Robertson Collection.

77. Major Frank Jones identified the aggrieved officer as Col. Kenton Harper. Colt, *Defend the Valley*, 95. Douglas, *I Rode with Stonewall*, 13, 236–37, is the source for the words that passed between Jackson and Harper. Since Douglas was not on the staff at the time, his testimony is the result of hearsay. Mrs. Jackson, 183, contains Jackson's statement of his devotion to the Southern cause. A soldier in the 27th Virginia bitterly resented Jackson's "capricious will" in denying him a furlough. Andrew N. Cook to wife, Sept. 15, 1862, Crawford Collection.

78. Joseph Packard, *Recollections of a Long Life* (Washington, 1902), 268. On Sept. 24, Packard made a second visit to Jackson's headquarters. He found the general "standing by a fire out of doors reading his Bible." Ibid., 268–69.

79. Thomas Cary Johnson, *The Life and Letters of Robert Lewis Dabney* (Richmond, 1903), 243.

80. William S. White Narrative, Box 20, Dabney—SHC.

81. Ibid.

82. J. William Jones, *Christ in the Camp; or, Religion in Lee's Army* (Richmond, 1887), 89. Clem Fishburne reported Jackson at every religious meeting held in the brigade. The general sat attentively in a camp chair. Yet at one service, Fishburne declared, "the chair upset with him, which gave rise to the conjecture . . . that he had slept and lost his balance while asleep." Fishburne Letter, Presbyterian Church (USA) Archives.

83. Haskell Memoir.

84. A. M. Garber notes, Reel 39, Hotchkiss—LC.

85. Mrs. Jackson, 182.

86. TJJ to Anna Jackson, Aug. 15, 1861, Box 20, Dabney—SHC.

87. Mrs. Jackson, 183.

88. TJJ to Anna Jackson, Aug. 22, 1861, Box 20, Dabney—SHC.

89. Mrs. Jackson, 185.

90. Ibid. Although Jackson had no contact during the war with his sister, Anna apparently sought to maintain at least a loose tie. The best account of her first trip to Jackson's encampment is Anna to Laura Arnold, Sept. 9, 1861, Jackson—VMI. Ironically, Laura at the time was going out of her way to befriend Federal soldiers occupying Beverly. See William Samuel Compton Papers, Notebooks 12 and 14, Duke.

91. James J. White to Mary White, Sept. 1861, White Papers.

92. Edmondson, *My Dear Emma*, 50.

93. Mrs. Jackson, 191. Anna Jackson also noted that Jackson at the time had three servants: a hired man, a cook named George, and a "very black negro." Ibid.

94. Daniel J. Hileman, 27th Virginia, to Philip Hileman, Sept. 22, 1861, Daniel J. and Philip C. Hileman Letters, Lewis Leigh Collection, USMHI; Hotchkiss Memoranda, Reel 1, Hotchkiss—LC; Betsy Nelson to Thomas F. Nelson, Sept. 19, 1861, Kathleen Kincaide (Griebe) Papers, UVA.

95. Henderson, 1:162–63.

96. Mrs. Jackson, 192.

97. Ibid., 194–95. That Confederate officials then regarded Jackson as a somewhat unstable commander of limited ability is reflected in the writings of several contemporaries. For example, see Mrs. Jackson in *Philadelphia Weekly Times*, Apr. 7, 1877; Cooke, *Outlines from the*

Outpost, 76–77; Douglas, *I Rode with Stonewall*, 14. Jackson was not alone in his feelings of pessimism and frustration. Major Frank Jones of the 2d Virginia wrote at this time to a friend in Winchester: "Our policy is clearly to act on the defensive, and I never knew so well before that we are *obliged* to do it *because we are weak*. I have given up all hope of peace. A gloomy war, a long war, and a bloody one, you may depend upon it, is before us, and we may as well make up our minds to it." Colt, *Defend the Valley*, 102.

98. Edmondson, *My Dear Emma*, 52.

99. TJJ File, Compiled Service Records of Confederate Generals and Staff Officers, RG109, NA; *OR*, 5:892; TJJ to Judah P. Benjamin, Oct. 10, 1861, Davis—Tulane; October 31 appointment, Davis—Tulane.

100. Mrs. Jackson, 195–96.

101. Johnston, *Narrative*, 77–78.

102. Henderson, 1:175.

103. Ibid.

104. Ibid., 176. See also Gustavus W. Smith, *Confederate War Papers* (New York, 1884), 30–31. The following spring, Jackson would voice to his friend Cong. Alexander Boteler the same reasons for a Northern invasion. See *SHSP*, 40 (1915): 172–73. Many of Jackson's men then felt as he did about the virtues of an offense. Captain Ruffner Morrison of the 4th Virginia wrote home at this time: "I am tired of the constant anxiety and suspense to which we have long been subjected. I have no desire to go upon another field of battle, but if it must come, I prefer to have it now. . . . A battle could not destroy more lives than are lost by disease and inaction." Henry R. Morrison to unknown addressee, Oct. 21, 1861, Morrison Letters, *CWTI* Collection, USMHI.

105. TJJ to William H. Richardson and Thomas S. Haymond, Oct. 22, 1861, Jackson—LVA.

106. *OR*, 5:889–90.

107. Ibid., 919.

108. Judah P. Benjamin to TJJ, Oct. 21, 1861, Dabney—LVA.

109. Ibid. See also *OR*, 5:913.

110. McFarland Diary, Oct. 23, 1861, in McFarland Papers, UTS; White Narrative. Jackson's official acceptance of the assignment is in *OR*, 5:921.

111. Captain Langhorne of the 4th Virginia wrote that the valley defenses Jackson was to command were "a few hundred militia and some companies of Cavalry, all of which does not constitute a force equal to his old Brigade." Yet "this in one sense is a compliment to him, as it shows that they think he can achieve more with a few raw men than any other Genl. they have." James H. Langhorne to mother, Nov. 4, 1861, Langhorne Family Papers, Robertson Collection.

112. Robert G. H. Kean, *Inside the Confederate Government* (New York, 1957), 60. Kean, an official in the War Department, later wrote of Jackson's statement: "The hero knew the country, the people, and himself. The last was not known to any other in the country."

113. Special Orders No. 192, Oct. 28, 1861, Old Catalog Collection, VHS; *OR*, 5:934, 936; 51: Pt. 2, 361. Jackson did not allow promotions or higher assignments to obliterate the little things that were right and proper. On Nov. 1, he informed the adjutant general's office that while he had been paid at the rank of colonel through June, his commission as a brigadier general dated from June 17; hence the Confederacy owed him $49.46 in extra pay. Whether the sum was ever forwarded is unknown. Jackson File, Compiled Service Records of Confederate Generals and Staff Officers, RG109, NA.

114. James H. Langhorne to mother, Nov. 4, 1861, Langhorne Papers.

115. Edmondson, *My Dear Emma*, 65.

116. This previously unpublished version of Jackson's farewell speech is from Langhorne to mother, Nov. 4, 1861. Langhorne recorded the presentation immediately after Jackson gave it; his account is short and to the point in typical Jackson style. This rendition alone among all others closes with an appeal to God, which is characteristic of every formal message Jackson ever sent. Douglas, *I Rode with Stonewall*, 16–17, provided a widely quoted speech so worthy of an orator that Jackson could not have given it. Equally exaggerated are the quoted remarks in Henderson, 1:166–67. The British biographer went as far as Douglas in adding statements of his own. For other versions of Jackson's farewell remarks, see Frederika Mackey White Diary, November 1861, VHS; *Richmond Daily Dispatch*, Nov. 8, 1861; McCabe, *Jackson*, 35-36; Dabney, 248-49; Mrs. Jackson, 200-2; John W. Daniels, *The Life of Stonewall Jackson . . . by a Virginian* (New York, 1863), 34-35; Casler, *Stonewall Brigade*, 57-58; George Baylor, *Bull Run to Bull Run* (Richmond, 1900), 27-28. Several soldiers commented on the sight of the stern Jackson with tears in his eyes. For example, see Andrew N. Cook to A. H. McClung, Nov. 14, 1861, Crawford Collection. Jackson's mention of the "Army of the Potomac" was a reference to the first name attached to the Beauregard-Johnston forces in the Manassas area.

117. Packard, *Recollections*, 270; undated *Lexington Gazette* article, Barringer Family Papers, UVA; *SHSP*, 23 (1895): 122. A member of the 27th Virginia wrote of Jackson that day, "he bid us farewell, he didnt want to leave us, he shed tears." Daniel J. Hileman to Philip Hileman, Nov. 10 [?], 1861, Hileman Letters.

118. This letter is an amalgamation of two printed renditions in Mrs. Jackson, 200, and Alexander R. Boteler in *Philadelphia Weekly Times*, June 2, 1877.

CHAPTER 11   *Stormy Road to a Resignation*

1. Kean, *Inside the Confederate Government*, 60; *Richmond Daily Dispatch*, Nov. 7, 1981, reprinted in *Staunton Spectator*, Nov. 12, 1861.

2. *OR*, 5:389, 937; Garland R. Quarles, *Occupied Winchester, 1861-1865* (Winchester, 1976), 56. Some writers have Jackson not reaching Winchester until November 5, but in his own dispatches to Richmond he told of arriving late on the previous night. Commissary Wells J. Hawks related a delightful story of Jackson encountering an intoxicated admirer during the brief stopover in Strasburg. Since Hawks was not with Jackson at the time, the incident must be discounted. Wells J. Hawks to Jedediah Hotchkiss, Jan. 17, 1866, Jackson—NYHS.

3. *Lexington Gazette*, May 15, 1861.

4. John W. Wayland, *Twenty-five Chapters on the Shenandoah Valley* (Strasburg, 1957), 333, 336, 344. A Union soldier observed of the turnpike: "This surface after a rain is almost as smooth, clean and solid as a slate, and when dry a thin white coating, perhaps a quarter of an inch deep . . . rises in clouds when disturbed by travelers and settles upon their clothing, making all look like millers." Edwin E. Marvin, *The Fifth Connecticut Volunteers: A History* (Hartford, 1889), 69.

5. Jedediah Hotchkiss to William L. Chase, Mar. 28, 1892, Reel 9, Hotchkiss—LC.

6. Quarles, *Occupied Winchester*, 2. The town was captured and recaptured at least seventy-two times during the Civil War. In one twenty-four-hour period, it changed hands four times! Frederic Morton, *The Story of Winchester in Virginia* (Strasburg, 1925), 193.

7. William Allan, *History of the Campaign of Gen. T. J. (Stonewall) Jackson in the Shenandoah Valley of Virginia* (Philadelphia, 1880), 12; Dabney, 256; Edmondson, *My Dear Emma*, 67.

8. Julia Chase Diary, Sept. 16, 1861, Handley Library.

9. *OR*, 5:936, 974; Baylor, *Bull Run to Bull Run*, 48; Turner Ashby to Gen. Samuel Cooper, Nov. 7, 1861, Turner Ashby Collection, Chicago Historical Society; Avirett, *Memoirs of Ashby*, 131.

10. *OR*, 5:389, 937, 942-43.

11. Mrs. Jackson, 203; Daniel J. Hileman to Philip C. Hileman, November 1861, Hileman Letters, Lewis Leigh Collection, USMHI.

12. *OR*, 5:938-40, 944, 947.

13. Poague, *Gunner with Stonewall*, 12; Andrew N. Cook to A. H. McClung, Nov. 14, 1862, Lewis J. Crawford, Jr., Collection; James H. Langhorne to father, Nov. 8, 1861, Langhorne Family Papers, James I. Robertson, Jr., Blacksburg, Va.

14. Opie, *Rebel Cavalryman*, 48-49. See also H. Kyd Douglas to Tippie Boteler, Nov. 16, 1861, Henry Kyd Douglas Letters, Duke University. John P. Hite wrote of the departure of his 33d Virginia from Manassas Junction: "The whole of the Irish company gets drunk save a few; they get to fighting, in which swords, bayonets and knives are used; have a hard time tying them and

putting them in the guardhouse. Several of both parties got seriously wounded." John P. Hite Diary, Nov. 9, 1861, Handley Library.

15. Biographical sketch in Alexander Robinson Boteler Papers, Duke; *Richmond Daily Dispatch*, May 11, 1861, contains the text of Boteler's resignation speech. For some reason, Surg. Hunter McGuire did not have a high opinion of the legislator. Referring to Boteler as "a refugee from near Shepherdstown," McGuire added that the congressman served "as a sort of volunteer Aide for short periods and at irregular times." Hunter McGuire to Jedediah Hotchkiss, Sept. 22, 1897, Reel 14, Hotchkiss—LC.

16. Boteler Memorandum, Dabney—LVA; *OR*, 5:651. In his first strength-report, apparently submitted late in November, Jackson listed 4000 infantry and artillery, twenty guns, 1000 militia, and 540 cavalry. *OR*, 5:974. However, a Union officer assured his headquarters, "there is great discontent & disaffection" among Jackson's units. David H. Strother to Gen. Nathaniel P. Banks, Nov. 16, 1861, Nathaniel Prentice Banks Letters, Duke.

17. TJJ to Margaret Preston, Nov. 16, 1861, Thomas J. Jackson Manuscripts, Princeton University; TJJ to Easter J. Campbell, Dec. 3, 1861, Reel 58, Hotchkiss—LC.

18. For examples of writers who referred to Lewis as Jackson's servant, see Allan, *A March Past*, 152; Mrs. Jackson, 288, 299, 370, 418, 440; Preston, *Stonewall's Widow*, 29. For examples of writers who considered him a freedman, see Bean, *Pendleton*, 69; Farwell, *Stonewall*, 338.

19. The small book is item 295 at WVU. Colonel Preston's statement is in Allan, *Preston*, 122.

20. Couper, *One Hundred Years at VMI*, 4:79; Douglas, *I Rode with Stonewall*, 154–55; Lucy C. Pendleton Reminiscences, BV 188, FSNMP; *Philadelphia Weekly Times*, Aug. 6, 1881. The author is indebted to graduate intern Megan Haley at SJH for assisting in the effort to unravel the mysteries of Jim Lewis.

21. General Orders No. 9, Nov. 14, 1861, MC; Graham, "Some Reminiscences," 122, 203.

22. Graham, "Some Reminiscences," 203.

23. Ibid.

24. *Northern Virginia Daily*, Dec. 16, 1961; Mrs. Jackson, 209–10.

25. Lyle, "Sketches," W&L, 327–28; Allan, *A March Past*, 123; Allan, *Preston*, 135. Other information supplied by Ben Ritter, who combines an unrivaled knowledge of wartime Winchester with an unselfish willingness to share it with friends.

26. Paxton, *Memoir*, 28.

27. Untitled memorandum, Reel 5, Hotchkiss—LC; Allan, *Valley Campaign*, 16.

28. TJJ to Maj. T. G. Rhett, Dec. 2, 1861, MC. For a contrasting view of camp life at the time, see 4th Virginia soldier's letter in *Lexington Gazette*, Nov. 17, 1861.

29. Incidents in this case varied with the narrator. One source had Capt. Henderson part of the drunken party when the argument began. See Brooke Journal, Nov. 26, 1861, Handley Library; Chase Diary, Nov. 26, 1861; *Staunton Spectator*, Dec. 3, 1861.

30. Graham, "Some Reminiscences," 127–28; H. Kyd Douglas to Tippie Boteler, Nov. 26, 1861, Douglas Letters. Benjamin Brooke, the Methodist minister in Winchester, stated that a local citizen went to Richmond with a petition asking Jefferson Davis for clemency. The sympathetic president signed a commutation order. Yet the messenger got intoxicated on the return trip and got to Winchester too late to save Miller. Brooke Journal, Nov. 26, 1861.

31. Federal barbarities in the Romney area had been flagrant since August. See *Richmond Enquirer*, Aug. 16, 1861.

32. TJJ to Judah P. Benjamin, Nov. 20, 1861, Old Catalog Collection, VHS. A highly edited version of this letter is in *OR*, 5:965–66.

33. *OR*, 5:966, 969.

34. Ibid., 983–84. In a confidential and unpublished letter to Jackson, Johnston expressed concern about the valley commander overextending his forces. Jackson should let Loring seize Romney while his own troops continued destroying the B&O Railroad. Johnston's apprehensions included his own front as well. In a final statement that clearly revealed his fears as well as his limited vision of the war in Virginia, Johnston declared, "The troops you prepare to employ farther west, might render better & more immediate service elsewhere—especially on the lower Potomac—or in this district." J. E. Johnston to TJJ, Nov. 23, 1861, Old Catalog Collection.

35. TJJ to Gov. John Letcher, Nov. 30, 1861, Executive Papers—1861, Box 505, LVA.

36. Jackson official report of Romney campaign, Old Catalog Collection (also printed in *OR*, 5:389–90).

37. Judah P. Benjamin to TJJ, Dec. 6, 1861, Jackson—LVA; *OR*, 5:988–89. Meanwhile, Johnston remained unreconciled to Jackson being away from the Centreville line. On hearing that Loring was en route to Winchester, Johnston quickly suggested that Jackson ought to be sent back to Centreville while Loring guarded the lower valley. Confederate authorities ignored the request. *OR*, 5:986.

38. TJJ to Alexander R. Boteler, Dec. 7, 1861, Office of the Confederate Secretary of War, 1861–1865: Letters Received, RG109, NA; Lyle, "Sketches," 323–24; Allan, *Preston*, 122.

39. Garnett was appointed to command on Dec. 4 and arrived in Winchester three days later. *OR*, 5:981; Hite Diary, Dec. 7, 1861. Jackson's chief of staff was openly unhappy over Garnett's assignment. "The brigade ought to be commanded by one of its own colonels," John Preston declared. "They have made their own glory, and a stranger should not have been made to share it." Allan, *Preston*, 125.

40. James H. Langhorne, 4th Virginia, to father, Dec. 7, 1861, Langhorne Papers; George E. Pickett, *Soldier of the South: General Pickett's War Letters to His Wife* (Boston, 1928), 27.

41. James G. Updike, 4th Virginia, to Williamson Weaver, Dec. 9, 1861, Williamson Weaver Papers, Duke; Tanner, *Stonewall in the Valley*, 55. No likeness of Garnett exists. Two photographs long supposed to be of Richard Garnett and his cousin, Gen. Robert S. Garnett, are in fact different images of the latter. See Robert K. Krick, "Armistead and Garnett," in Gary W. Gallagher, ed., *The Third Day at Gettysburg and Beyond* (Chapel Hill, 1994), 95–96, 124–25.

42. Paxton, *Memoir*, 32; *OR*, 5:390; Allan, *Preston*, 63; *Century Magazine*, 32 (1886): 931.

43. Lyle, "Sketches," 319–20. Douglas asserted that the persimmon tree incident occurred during one of the expeditions to Dam 5. *I Rode with Stonewall*, 19. Lyle was more specific in saying that it happened in the course of Jackson's advance to Martinsburg.

44. For hardships that Loring's men endured on the long march to Winchester, see George K. Harlow to father, Dec. 6, 1861, Harlow Family Papers, VHS.

45. Charles J. Faulkner Memorandum, Reel 1, Hotchkiss—LC; *OR*, 5:389; *Richmond Daily Dispatch*, Dec. 11, 1861; *Richmond Enquirer*, Dec. 13, 1861.

46. Allan, *Preston*, 64.

47. Jackson manuscript report, Old Catalog Collection. John Imboden erroneously stated that Jackson took four infantry brigades on the expedition. *B&L*, 2:282.

48. Watkins Kearns Diary, Dec. 17, 1861, VHS; *SHSP*, 19 (1891): 315. According to Kyd Douglas, Jackson "said he could nip [whiskey] like coffee or tea & did not believe any man in the army liked it as well." Marginal note in Henderson, 1:74, Henry Kyd Douglas Library, Antietam NBP. William S. White, Jackson's pastor, related that the general once declined a drink by exclaiming: "No, thank you. I am more afraid of that than I am of Yankee bullets." White Narrative, Box 20, Dabney—SHC.

49. James H. Langhorne, 4th Va., to mother, Dec. 23, 1861, Langhorne Papers; *Richmond Enquirer*, Dec. 27, 1861; Faulkner Memorandum, Reel 1. Other accounts of the Dam No. 5 operation are in Hite Diary, Dec. 17–23, 1861, Handley; Andis, "War Correspondence," Dec. 25, 1861, Manassas NBP; Marvin, *5th Connecticut*, 45–48. At precisely the time Jackson was ripping a hole in Dam No. 5, Federal Gen. Nathaniel Banks was reassuring Washington that all of Jackson's attempts at destroying C&O Canal dams had failed. *OR*, 5:398–99.

50. Mrs. Jackson, 205, 210–14; Lyle, "Sketches," 335.

51. *Staunton Spectator*, Jan. 14, 1862; John C. Wade to wife, Dec. 25, 1861, Robertson Collection; H. Kyd Douglas to Tippie Boteler, Dec. 22, 1861, Douglas Letters.

52. Sam R. Watkins, *"Co. Aytch": Maury Grays, First Tennessee Regiment, or a Side Show of the Big Show* (Jackson, Tenn., 1952), 56.

53. TJJ to Joseph E. Johnston, Dec. 24, 1861, MC. Jackson placed his potential strength at 7500 volunteers, 2234 militia, and 664 cavalry. See also TJJ to J. E. Johnston, Dec. 24, 1861, Johnston Collection, Henry E. Huntington Library. Johnston's excuses for not sending the desired reinforcements are in J. E. Johnston to TJJ, Dec. 29, 1861, Davis—Tulane.

54. Faulkner Memorandum, Reel 1; Jedediah Hotchkiss to Fitzhugh Lee, Oct. 22, 1891, Reel 49, Hotchkiss—LC. Loring's habit of looking contemptuously at all volunteers led one to retort, "The men were very indignant and put Loring down at once as an officer who knew nothing." John H. Worsham, *One of Jackson's Foot Cavalry* (Jackson, Tenn., 1964), 14.

55. *Richmond Daily Dispatch*, Dec. 31, 1861; *Fredericksburg Star*, Jan. 5, 1889.

56. Broadside, Faulkner Family Papers, VHS; Faulkner Memorandum, Reel 1.

57. Worsham, *Jackson's Foot Cavalry*, 23.

58. John M. Patton, "Reminiscences of Jackson," Patton Family Papers, VHS.

59. For Jackson and the Indian regiment, see Jackson Letterbook, Dec. 26, 1861, Reel 49, Hotchkiss—LC; R. H. Chilton to TJJ, Dec. 30, 1861, Letters and Telegrams Sent by the Confederate Adjutant and Inspector General, 1861–1865, RG109, NA.

60. Worsham, *Jackson's Foot Cavalry*, 23; John Blue, 77th Virginia Militia, "Reminiscences," *CWTI*, 16, 19–20. For the rundown condition of Loring's units, see Harriet Hollingworth Griffith Diary, Jan. 6, 1861, Handley.

61. *Richmond Daily Dispatch*, Jan. 16, 1862; Dabney, 254, 258; Avirett, *Memoirs of Ashby*, 139.

62. Gov. John Letcher to TJJ, Dec. 28, 1861, Davis—Tulane; Jackson Letterbook, Dec. 31, 1861, Reel 49; James H. Langhorne to mother, Dec. 31, 1861, Langhorne Papers.

63. *Philadelphia Weekly Times*, June 2, 1877. Temperatures given for the month of January are from Cumberland, Maryland, weather reports, which Larry James of the Fredericksburg-Spotsylvania National Military Park compiled. Most sources assert that Jackson's march did not get underway until noon, six hours late. Yet Col. Gilham told of starting his brigade of Loring's command at 9:00 and moving fast enough to pass the wagon train of the Stonewall Brigade. William Gilham to Jedediah Hotchkiss, Nov. 25, 1866, Reel 5, Hotchkiss—LC. Staff officer Randolph Barton of the 33d Virginia stated that his regiment was in motion "about eight o'clock." Randolph Barton, *Recollections, 1861–1865* (Baltimore, 1913), 18.

64. Graham, "Some Reminiscences," 123. In a quickly prepared narrative immediately after the war, the minister stated that he went up to Jackson's headquarters to escort Anna to the manse and that the general walked down the street with them. Graham Narrative, Box 20, Dabney—SHC.

65. Alfred D. Kelley, 21st Virginia, to brother, Jan. 19, 1862, Williamson Kelly Papers, Duke; Bean, "Harman," 4.

66. Charles T. Quintard, *Doctor Quintard, Chaplain, C.S.A.* (Sewanee, Tenn., 1905), 37. An example of soldiers' uncertainty about their destination is in Surg. Abram Miller, 30th Virginia Militia, to Julia Miller, Jan. 1, 1862, Abram Schultz Miller Letters, Handley.

67. Douglas, *I Rode with Stonewall*, 21–22; *SHSP*, 23 (1895): 124. For a running account of the severities of the march, see Watkins Kearns Diary, Jan. 5–16, 1862. Kearns was a member of the 27th Virginia.

68. *Fayette Tribune* [Fayette County, W.Va.], Feb. 21, 1923.

69. Ibid. This version of the story had it taking place as Jackson returned to Winchester from Romney. Yet since he made that trip in nonstop fashion during the course of a single day, the chronology is in error. It is more likely that the incident occurred early in the campaign, when the weather was at its severest. Douglas, *I Rode with Stonewall*, 20, is the source for the best-known account of Jackson overimbibing. Douglas was not then a member of the staff and could only have heard of the incident secondhand. Moreover, his penchant toward exaggeration makes the newspaper version more reliable.

70. William Gilham to Jedediah Hotchkiss, Nov. 25, 1866, Reel 5, Hotchkiss—LC.

71. TJJ to J. E. Johnston, Jan. 2, 1862, Johnston Collection; Lyle, "Sketches," 346; TJJ to "Major," Jan. 2, 1862, Jackson—VMI. This is the first documented instance of Jackson eating lemons in the field. Lemon stories rapidly became part of the Jackson myth. See Conrad, "History of the First Fight," 466.

72. Alexander G. Garber Notes, Reel 39, Hotchkiss—LC; Faulkner Memorandum, Reel 1; *OR*, 5:1066, 1070; Watkins, *"Co. Aytch,"* 57.

73. Henderson, 1:190. This exchange between Jackson and the new Stonewall Brigade commander was a major reason why the soldiers "soon learned to love" Garnett. They began to see, a member of the 2d Virginia stated, "that he looked upon them as men and fellow soldiers, not machines or dogs to be ordered and kicked around at his fancy." Thomas D. Gold, *History of Clarke County, Virginia, and Its Connections with the War between the States* (Berryville, Va., 1914), 210.

74. *SHSP,* 16 (1888): 90; Faulkner Memorandum, Reel 1; William Gilham to Jedediah Hotchkiss, Nov. 25, 1866, Reel 5, Hotchkiss—LC; *CV,* 22 (1914): 211.

75. Lyle, "Sketches," 348.

76. Quintard, *Captain Quintard,* 37–38.

77. Jackson manuscript report. In later years, some of Gilham's fellow officers sought to come to his defense but made ineffective arguments. See Scott Shipp to Thomas T. Munford, June 26, 1903, and W. E. Cutshaw to Munford, July 13, 1903, Munford-Ellis Family Papers, Duke. Gilham's own defense was to blame Jackson for not maintaining a more cohesive march and for entrusting militia to storm Bath from the west. William Gilham to Jedediah Hotchkiss, Nov. 25, 1866, Reel 5, Hotchkiss—LC.

78. Jackson manuscript report.

79. Ibid.; Faulkner Memorandum, Reel 1. Henderson, 1:191, asserted that the January 4 action occurred in "a blinding storm." No other source mentioned snow falling that day. The Cumberland, Maryland, weather station termed that Saturday "dull," which can be interpreted as merely overcast. Federal reports of the action at Bath are in *OR,* 5:400–2.

80. Lyle, "Sketches," 349; *Richmond Daily Dispatch,* Jan. 15, 1862; Avirett, *Memoirs of Ashby,* 143.

81. Jackson manuscript report; Faulkner Memorandum, Reel 1; William B. Taliaferro, "Reminiscences of Jackson," William B. Taliaferro Papers, W&M, 4.

82. Jackson manuscript report. The quoted passage was an addition by Jackson to the original draft of his official report. For more on the Jan. 6–7 action, see long soldier letter in *Richmond Daily Dispatch,* Jan. 15, 1862.

83. George M. Neese, *Three Years in the Confederate Horse Artillery* (Dayton, Ohio, 1988), 18; Lyle, "Sketches," 351–52; H. Kyd Douglas to Tippie Boteler, Jan. 12, 1862, Boteler Papers.

84. W. B. Colston, "Wartime Experiences," typescript, BV 168, FSNMP; Moore, "Recollections," 101. John Lyle added: "Getting up grade was somewhat like the frog's climbing out of the well, for every step forward we slipped two back. We never would have made progress but for the fact that when marching down hill we made up by slipping three feet forward for every step we took." Lyle, "Sketches," 353.

85. Jackson manuscript report; *OR,* 5:396, 1018. For accounts of the Hanging Rock action, see Blue, "Reminiscences," *CWTI,* 21–22, 25a; *Richmond Enquirer,* Jan. 10, 13, and 28, 1862.

86. James H. Langhorne to mother, Jan. 12, 1862, Langhorne Papers.

87. Lee A. Wallace, Jr., *Fifth Virginia Infantry* (Lynchburg, Va., 1988), 22; *SHSP,* 23 (1895): 126–27. On Jan. 8, Jackson issued strict orders against using fences for firewood. The next day Col. Gilham permitted his soldiers to burn fence rails—a violation that undoubtedly hastened his departure from Jackson's command. TJJ to William W. Loring, Jan. 9, 1862, Jackson Letterbook, Reel 49.

88. TJJ to Judah P. Benjamin, Jan. 10, 1862, Accession #62.383, Mississippi State Historical Museum. Barton served as acting chief engineer for Jackson during much of the Romney campaign. President Davis delayed official action on the recommendation for Barton's promotion until Mar. 11, 1862, when the Fredericksburg native received elevation to brigadier general and assignment to the Tennessee theater.

89. J. Tucker Randolph Diary, Jan. 10, 1862, MC; Worsham, *Foot Cavalry,* 27; *OR,* 5:676, 696–97. Romney changed hands at least fifty-six times during the Civil War, a record exceeded only by Winchester.

90. Gold, *Clarke County,* 165–66.

91. Colt, *Defend the Valley,* 112; Neese, *Three Years,* 19; Colt, *Defend the Valley,* 112; [Caffey], *Battle-fields of the South,* 1:209.

92. A. S. Pendleton to mother, Jan. 15, 1862, William Nelson Pendleton Papers, SHC.

93. Jackson manuscript report; *OR*, 5:1033.
94. *SHSP*, 23 (1895): 128; George K. Harlow to father, Jan. 17, 1862, Harlow Family Papers. Jackson's initial communique to the War Department stated merely that Taliaferro's brigade "was not in a condition to move." *OR*, 5:1039.
95. TJJ to J. E. Johnston, Jan. 16, 1862, Box 5, Dabney Papers, UVA; TJJ to J. E. Johnston, Jan. 17, 1862, Thomas J. Jackson Papers, PAHS; Jackson manuscript report. The printed versions of the correspondence above are in *OR*, 5:393–94, 1034, 1036.
96. Ted Barclay to Hannah Barclay, Jan. 22 and 25, 1862, Ted Barclay Letters, LVA.
97. Quintard, *Doctor Quintard*, 38; Lyle, "Sketches," 362.
98. See *Richmond Daily Dispatch*, Jan. 21, 1862; Tanner, *Stonewall in the Valley*, 90. Rheumatism, pneumonia, scarlet fever, and frostbite were the most prevalent illnesses among the soldiers. For more on hospital patients in the Winchester area, see Chase Diary, Jan. 17, 1862; Surg. Abram Miller to Julia Miller, Jan. 18, 1862, Abram Schultz Miller Letters; Treadwell Smith Diary, Jan. 22, 1862, Handley. James H. Langhorne of the 4th Virginia exaggerated by stating that not more than a third of every regiment in Jackson's army was on duty. Langhorne to father, Jan. 16, 1862, Langhorne Papers.
99. Mrs. Jackson, 236.
100. Ibid., 237.
101. Graham, "Some Reminiscences," 123.
102. Dabney, 274–76; William F. Harrison to Maria Harrison, Jan. 27, 1862, William F. Harrison Papers, Duke. In April 1862, Harrison was dropped from the rolls of the 23d Virginia.
103. Lyle, "Sketches," 335.
104. *OR*, 5:703.
105. *Staunton Spectator*, Feb. 4, 1862; Quintard, *Doctor Quintard*, 39; Poague, *Gunner with Stonewall*, 18; [Caffey], *Battle-fields of the South*, 1:207.
106. Hunter McGuire to Jedediah Hotchkiss, Nov. 8, 1897, Reel 14, Hotchkiss—LC.
107. *OR*, 5:1040–41.
108. Ibid., 1042.
109. Ibid., 1046–47. See also Jackson Letterbook, Reel 49.
110. William B. Taliaferro to W. W. Loring, Jan. 29, 1862, Cook—WVU.
111. Alexander R. Boteler, in *Philadelphia Weekly Times*, June 2, 1877.
112. *OR*, 5:1054–56; TJJ to Adjt. Gen., Jan. 10, 1862, Office of the Adjutant & Inspector General and of the Quartermaster General, 1861–1865: Letters Received, RG109, NA.
113. *OR*, 5:1051; 51: Pt. 2, 461.
114. Ibid., 5:1053.
115. TJJ to J. P. Benjamin, Jan. 31, 1862, Davis—Tulane (printed with editorial changes in *OR*, 5:1053). For a typical condemnation of the pliant Benjamin, see George Cary Eggleston, *The History of the Confederate War: Its Causes and Its Conduct* (New York, 1910), 1:365, 368.
116. Graham, "Some Reminiscences," 195–96.
117. TJJ to John Letcher, Jan. 31, 1862, Executive Papers, 1862, Box 508, LVA. Jackson also explained his resignation to his brother-in-law, Harvey Hill. His thoughts and phrases were the same. See *The Land We Love*, 1 (1866): 115.
118. Graham, "Some Reminiscences," 196; McGuire, *Confederate Cause*, 209. For a scathing commentary by Capt. Samuel Letcher of Lexington, see Withrow Scrapbooks, W&L, IX, 87–88.
119. *OR*, 5:1053, 1056.
120. J. E. Johnston to TJJ, Feb. 3, 1862, Davis—Tulane. See also Johnston, *Narrative*, 90–91, for his dislike of Benjamin.
121. Boteler account in *Philadelphia Weekly Times*, June 2, 1877.
122. Ibid. H. Kyd Douglas article in *Philadelphia Weekly Times*, July 16, 1881.
123. *Richmond Whig*, Apr. 26, 1873; Judge S. H. Letcher newspaper article in Withrow Scrapbooks, W&L, IX, 88.
124. *Civil War History*, 10 (1964): 174.
125. Jonathan M. Bennett to TJJ, Feb. 7, 1862, Davis—Tulane; John Letcher to TJJ, Feb. 4,

1862, Old Catalog Collection; S. Bassett French to TJJ, Feb. 3, 1862, Jackson—VMI; John T. Harris to TJJ, Feb. 6, 1862, Jackson—LVA; S. Kay to Jefferson Davis, February 1862, Jackson—NYHS.

126. Francis McFarland to TJJ, Feb. 5, 1862, Davis—Tulane; Henry R. Morrison to Luther Morrison, Feb. 6, 1862, Morrison Letters, *CWTI* Collection, USMHI. See also TJJ to Francis McFarland, Feb. 11, 1862, Jackson—VMI. The caustic brother-in-law, Gen. Harvey Hill, observed that Jackson's "loss from the Army at this critical time would be irreparable. He is more feared by the Yankees than any man in our Army." Hill to Isabella Hill, Feb. 3, 1862, Daniel Harvey Hill Papers, USMHI.

127. *Philadelphia Weekly Times*, June 2, 1877.

128. Ibid.

129. Ibid.

130. Ibid. For Robert L. Dabney's notes of a conversation with Boteler over this subject, see Boteler Memorandum, Dabney—LVA.

131. *OR*, 5:1062–63; H. Kyd Douglas to Tippie Boteler, Feb. 7, 1862, Douglas Letters.

132. John A. Harman to Asher W. Harman, Feb. 3, 1862, Reel 39, Hotchkiss—LC; Jackson's original charges against Loring, Jackson—LVA; TJJ to Adjt. Gen., Feb. 7, 1862, Office of Adjt. General: Letters Received, RG109, NA; *OR*, 5:1965. Loring's responses to the Jackson accusations are in *OR*, 5:1070–71. See also *ibid.*, 51: Pt. 2, 468–69. Similar charges brought by Jackson against Col. Gilham were never prosecuted.

133. *OR*, 5:1067, 1076, 1079. Most of Loring's soldiers had no idea why they were being transferred hither and yon. Yet one private in Taliaferro's brigade stated that "the cause of our going to Manassas is on account of General Jackson & General Loring cannot agree." George K. Harlow to friends, Feb. 17, 1862, Harlow Family Papers.

134. OR, 51: Pt. 1, 529. Lieutenant Sandie Pendleton of Jackson's staff expressed open contempt for the Army of the Northwest when it arrived back in Winchester. "Genl. Loring's men heap all sorts of abuse on Genl. J., and the first [Stonewall] brigade returns it with interest and rightly for Genl. Loring has not acted well. In coming back from Romney Genl. Loring has destroyed all his baggage and stores—he says because the roads were so bad, doubtful I think." W. G. Bean, ed., "The Valley Campaign of 1862 as Revealed in Letters of Sandie Pendleton," *VMHB*, 78 (1970): 330.

135. The general was quick to censure Regular Army officers, who, he thought, should know how to perform flawless duty. In the case of a bewildered militia officer, on the other hand, Jackson displayed amazing patience and understanding. A typical case in point was Colonel Jacob M. Sencindiver. The military experience of this "corpulent and good-natured Dutchman" consisted of whatever he learned at the annual militia musters, which themselves were considered primarily as social gatherings rather than military maneuvers.

Sencindiver was in command of the Bloomery Gap garrison, which fled precipitously in the face of an unexpected attack. A week before that disaster, Sencindiver had confessed to Jackson that he could not make the men obey his orders. Jackson dictated a fatherly but firm reply through his aide, Lieutenant George Junkin.

"The General regrets to hear from an officer that it is *impossible* to execute an order. If your cavalry will not obey your orders you must *make them* do it and if necessary go out with them yourself. He desires you to go out and post your cavalry where you want them to stay and arrest any man who leaves his post and prefer charges and specifications against him that he may be Court Martialed. It will not do to say that your men cannot be induced to perform their duty. *They must be made to do it.*"

Events of seventy-two hours later demonstrated that Colonel Sencindiver was not up to the responsibilities entrusted to him. TJJ to Jacob M. Sencindiver, Feb. 11, 1862, Reel 49, Hotchkiss—LC. An oft-quoted but edited version of this letter is in *SHSP*, 43 (1920): 140–41. For Sencindiver's report of the Bloomery Gap action, see *OR*, 5:406–7.

136. Chase Diary, Feb. 4, 1862; Jackson manuscript report.

137. George B. McClellan, *The Civil War Papers of George B. McClellan: Selected Correspondence, 1860–1865* (New York, 1989), 162.

CHAPTER 12   *The Lessons of Kernstown*

1. A. S. Pendleton to mother, Feb. 11, 1862, William Nelson Pendleton Papers, SHC; Algernon S. Wade to Louisa F. Hopkins, Feb. 20, 1862, Lewis Leigh Collection, USMHI.
2. Graham Narrative, Box 20, Dabney—SHC; James R. Graham Interview, Handley Library.
3. E. C. Scott, comp., *Ministerial Directory of the Presbyterian Church, U.S., 1861–1941* (Austin, Tex., 1942), 261; Graham Interview. Alfred Graham subsequently became a Presbyterian minister and married Anna Jackson's niece, Isabel Irwin. Mrs. Jackson, 237.
4. Graham, "Some Reminiscences," 123.
5. Ibid., 125–26.
6. Ibid., 123, 198–99; Graham Narrative, Box 20, Dabney—SHC.
7. Graham, "Some Reminiscences," 126, 197; *SHSP,* 43 (1920): 64.
8. Graham, "Some Reminiscences," 126.
9. L. Osborn and Mary Osborn to TJJ, Feb. 20, 1862, Jackson—VMI.
10. Brooke Journal, Feb. 23, 1862, Handley; Kate S. Sperry, Jr., Diary, Feb. 23, 1862, Handley.
11. Jackson Letterbook, Reel 49, Hotchkiss—LC; Douglas, *I Rode with Stonewall*, 26–27. The original of Jackson's note to Boteler cannot be found, and the tone of the letter is unusual for Jackson. Some suspicion about authenticity must therefore remain. Jackson's friends in the Congress, notably Boteler, sought to air the Romney reports and make the campaign the subject of a congressional debate. Such an open discussion would surely have put Jackson in a favorable light and his detractors, notably Loring and President Davis, at the opposite end of the spectrum. Political maneuvers blocked the proposal. A summary of this matter is in Chambers, 1:442–45.
12. John A. Harman to Asher W. Harman, Feb. 28, 1862, Reel 39, Hotchkiss—LC.
13. *Winchester Evening Star,* Mar. 12, 1901.
14. Chase, *Jackson,* 311; Dabney, 285.
15. TJJ to A. R. Boteler, Feb. 1862, Jackson—NYHS.
16. *OR,* 5:1016, 1086.
17. Ibid., Ser. 4, 1:911–12, 1011–12; Ted Barclay to Hannah Barclay, Feb. 10, 1862, Ted Barclay Letters, LVA.
18. *Lexington Gazette,* Feb. 17, 1862; TJJ to Joseph E. Johnston, Feb. 12, 1862, Jackson—LC; General Orders No. 3, Jan. 4, 1862, Jackson Letterbook, Reel 49. Late in January, the *Rockingham Register* asserted: "We learn that in Brig. Gen. Carson's Brigade of Militia . . . there are only about 250 men and officers, all told, at least one-third of whom are officers! The pay of the privates amounts to $2,000 per month, whilst the pay of the horde of leech like officers amounts to near $14,000! . . . If the Government will not strip the epaulettes from the shoulders of some of these officials, some of whom are utterly unfit to command any body, our Army will soon be as worthless as Lincoln's." Quoted in *Staunton Spectator,* Feb. 11, 1862. For dissatisfaction inside the militia, see Ephraim Bowman, 4th Virginia Militia, to father, Feb. 28, 1862, Bowman Family Papers, UVA.
19. *OR,* Ser. 4, 1:968. Jackson expressed similar feelings in a Mar. 3, 1862, letter to A. R. Boteler, Jackson—NYHS.
20. *OR,* 5:1086; *Richmond Daily Dispatch,* Mar. 7, 1862.
21. TJJ to D. H. Hill, Feb. 16, 1862, Daniel Harvey Hill Papers, LVA.
22. Ibid.; TJJ to Joseph E. Johnston, Feb. 24, 1862, Jackson Letterbook, Reel 49.
23. Jackson circular, Feb. 25, 1862, Reel 49, Hotchkiss—LC; TJJ to A. R. Boteler, Feb. 25, 1862, Cook—WVU. See also Chew, *Address,* 17.
24. Madge S. Robertson to Jedediah Hotchkiss, Sept. 30, 1897, Reel 14, Hotchkiss—LC; Jedediah Hotchkiss to Sara Hotchkiss, Apr. 14, 1862, Reel 4, Hotchkiss—LC. For Boswell's somewhat humorous account of reporting to Jackson for duty, see Thomas Keith Skinker, *Samuel Skinker and His Descendants* (St. Louis, 1923), 268.
25. TJJ to D. H. Hill, Feb. 24, 1862, Davis—Tulane.

26. TJJ to Joseph E. Johnston, Feb. 24, 1862, Jackson Letterbook, Reel 49; TJJ to D. H. Hill, Feb. 26, 1862, Hill Papers, LVA; Charles J. Faulkner Memorandum, Reel 1, Hotchkiss—LC.

27. Johnston, *Narrative*, 106.

28. TJJ to Joseph E. Johnston, Mar. 3 and 8, 1862, Johnston Collection, Henry E. Huntington Library; TJJ to A. R. Boteler, Mar. 3, 1862, Jackson—NYHS.

29. Mrs. Jackson, 239-40. G. F. R. Henderson had Mrs. Jackson taking a train to Staunton. The rail line running south in the valley ended forty-two miles short of that town. Henderson, 1:214.

30. Johnson, *Dabney*, 261. Another reason for Anna visiting the Dabneys may well have been to go under the care of Dr. John Peter Mettauer, a prominent Hampden-Sydney College physician who specialized in obstetrics and gynecology.

31. Worsham, *Foot Cavalry*, 31.

32. Bean, "Harman," 6; Vandiver, 199. Jackson did not leave "a dollar's worth of public property" behind when he departed Winchester. *Staunton Spectator*, Mar. 18, 1862. Similar statements are in Sperry Diary, Mar. 11, 1862; *OR*, 51: Pt. 2, 534.

33. John W. Green to "my dear friend," Mar. 3, 1862, Munford-Ellis Family Papers, Duke University. Sergeant Ham Chamberlayne of the 21st Virginia informed his mother at this time, "Our force is small but of good material & in fine heart & it is now thought that Jackson will defend the town at all hazards." J. Hampden Chamberlayne, *Ham Chamberlayne—Virginian* (Richmond, 1932), 72-73.

34. *OR*, 5:517; George H. Gordon, *Brook Farm to Cedar Mountain in the War of the Great Rebellion* (Boston, 1883), 119; A. S. Pendleton to William N. Pendleton, Mar. 6, 1862, Pendleton Papers. An even more pointed criticism of Jackson's defenses is in David Hunter Strother, *A Virginia Yankee in the Civil War* (Chapel Hill, 1961), 13-14. For commendation of Ashby's conduct at this time, see TJJ to Turner Ashby, Mar. 6, 1862, Jackson Letterbook, Reel 49; TJJ to D. H. Hill, Mar. 8, 1862, Hill Papers, LVA.

35. Mrs. Jackson, 243.

36. *The Land We Love*, 1 (1866): 119.

37. Neese, *Confederate Horse Artillery*, 26.

38. Jackson set no specific hour for his proposed attack. As a result, later writers have fostered confusion in describing the main thrust at the council of war. Most chroniclers asserted that Jackson wanted to make a "night attack." See Boteler Memorandum, Dabney—LVA; Graham, "Some Reminiscences," 199-200; Henderson, 1:299; Mrs. Jackson, 241; McGuire and Christian, *Confederate Cause*, 199. William Allan, in *Valley Campaign*, 41, had Jackson's intention being to "make the attack before dawn." Tanner, *Stonewall in the Valley*, 108, wrote of a "predawn surprise attack." Some elements inside the army apparently knew of the plan. Robert Barton of the Rockbridge Artillery later stated: "It was believed and confidently hoped that we were to return in the night and make a night attack on them. . . . We were fairly wild to try it." Colt, *Defend the Valley*, 116. Jackson's propensity for early movements in the day, plus the time required to get his men in battle position, point to the likelihood that the general thought of an assault in the 3-5 A.M. time period.

39. Graham Reminiscences, Box 20, Dabney—SHC.

40. Ibid. See also Graham, "Some Reminiscences," 199-200.

41. A. R. Boteler Memorandum, Box 20, Dabney—SHC.

42. Brooke Journal, Mar. 11, 1862.

43. *SHSP*, 25 (1897): 97.

44. Lyle, "Sketches," W&L, 371; Faulkner Memorandum, Reel 1. A member of Chew's Battery recalled seeing Jackson around 2 A.M. warming his hands before a campfire, then pulling his hat farther over his brow and riding off toward Newtown. Neese, *Confederate Horse Artillery*, 27.

45. *OR*, 5:59, 746; Lee Diary, Mar. 12, 1862, Handley; "Samuel Sexton Civil War Memoirs," OHS, 83. A New York newspaperman with Banks's force wrote that Winchester "is just about 100 years behind the age—a dirty, slovenly, ill paved, rickety, unpainted, foul smelling town. . . . At the Taylor House, the tip-top hotel, which would have been a hospital before this, but for its excessive inconvenience and dirt, there is great difficulty in getting anything to eat, or room to sleep in; and, if possible, other houses are worse. . . . As a general thing the natives shun the invaders." Quoted in *Richmond Enquirer,* Apr. 11, 1862.

46. Faulkner Memorandum, Reel 1; Moore, "Civil War Recollections," 104; Bean, *Liberty Hall Volunteers,* 100–1; Paxton, *Memoir,* 52.

47. *OR,* 5:1097; 51: Pt. 2, 495; Lyle, "Sketches," 378. Summoning the militia to active duty had its ludicrous moments. Ranks of the Augusta County units that assembled at Staunton were very thin because so many of the able-bodied men were already in service. One observer noted that "when Company A, One Hundred and Sixtieth Regiment, was ordered into line, ———— marched out, solitary and alone. He was afterwards joined by several others." Waddell, *Annals of Augusta County,* 466.

48. Lyle, "Sketches," 379.

49. Although Henderson, 1:230, put Shields's strength at 11,000 men, Shields himself on March 17 listed his division as having 9549 troops present and on duty. *OR,* 12: Pt. 2, 4–5.

50. James R. McCutchan to Kate, Mar. 17, 1862, McCutchan Letters, BV 139, FSNMP.

51. "Ned," in *Richmond Daily Dispatch,* Mar. 16, 1862.

52. Jedediah Hotchkiss to William L. Chase, Mar. 28, 1892, Reel 9, Hotchkiss—LC.

53. Robert E. L. Strider, *The Life and Work of George William Peterkin* (Philadelphia, 1929), 52.

54. *OR,* 11: Pt. 3, 21; Strother, *Virginia Yankee,* 17.

55. Jedediah Hotchkiss to Sara A. Hotchkiss, Mar. 20, 1862, Reel 4, Hotchkiss—LC; Hotchkiss Journal, Mar. 20, 1862, Reel 1, Hotchkiss—LC; Hotchkiss Diary, Mar. 21, 1862, Reel 1, Hotchkiss—LC. Hotchkiss is the largest single source for material on Jackson. He maintained a daily journal of events that included such subjects as weather and Jackson's precise location. Beginning with his association with Jackson and continuing until his death in 1899, Hotchkiss collected everything he could find on his chieftain. In the postwar year, Hotchkiss reworked his daily jottings at least twice. He saved each version. Discrepancies were inevitable. For example, in his "journal" Hotchkiss wrote of going to see Jackson on March 21 in company with Col. William S. Sproul and Lt. Col. John H. Crawford of the militia. In his more-quoted "diary," Hotchkiss stated that on March 20 he reported to Jackson with Lt. William T. Poague of the Rockbridge Artillery. Strangely, Hotchkiss never held a military rank even though he served in the Confederate army for three years. See Archie P. McDonald, "The Illusive Commission of 'Major' Jedediah Hotchkiss," *VMHB,* 75 (1967): 181–85.

56. TJJ to S. Bassett French, Mar. 21, 1862, Box 20, Dabney—SHC (printed in *OR,* 12: Pt. 3, 835). See also Samuel Horst, *Mennonites in the Confederacy: A Study in Civil War Pacifism* (Scottsdale, Pa., 1967), 3, 15, 29.

57. Hotchkiss Diary, Mar. 21, 1862, Reel 1; Hotchkiss Journal, Mar. 21, 1862.

58. *OR,* 12: Pt. 1, 164, 380.

59. Jackson's statements relative to the battle of Kernstown are from his original after-action report, deposited in Jackson—NYHS. An edited version is printed in *OR,* 12: Pt. 1, 380–84.

60. Jedediah Hotchkiss to Henry A. White, Mar. 24, 1898, Reel 1, Hotchkiss—LC.

61. Moore, "Civil War Recollections," 105.

62. Worsham, *Foot Cavalry,* 31. See also Maj. Frank Buck Jones Diary, Mar. 22, 1862, Handley.

63. "Sexton Civil War Memoirs," OHS, 83.

64. *OR,* 12: Pt. 1, 139; Lee Diary, Mar. 22, 1862; John A. Harman to Asher W. Harman, Mar. 26, 1862, Reel 39, Hotchkiss—LC. See also John Peyton Clark Journal, Mar. 22, 1862, Handley, for another account of Federal chaos when Ashby struck the Winchester defenses.

65. Avirett, *Memoirs of Ashby,* 157; William N. McDonald, *A History of the Laurel Brigade* (Baltimore, 1907), 40; *Staunton Spectator,* Apr. 1, 1862; Lucy R. Buck, *Sad Earth, Sweet Heaven: The Diary of Lucy Rebecca Buck* (Birmingham, Ala., 1973), 39; Ashby's after-action report, Jackson—LVA. A captain in the 23d Virginia later told his wife that because of "a Yankee trick" that Jackson and his officers were "credulous enough to believe," the general "was completely taken in" and moved to attack the Federals. William F. Harrison to Maria Harrison, Mar. 28, 1862, William F. Harrison Papers, Duke.

66. TJJ to Joseph E. Johnston, Mar. 23, 1862, Johnston Collection.

67. *OR*, 12: Pt. 1, 383, 385–86.

68. Jackson manuscript report, Jackson—NYHS. Henderson, 1:237, mysteriously accused Jackson's staff of allowing the Southern force to be in a position where it could be seen. Another writer is of the opinion that at Kernstown Jackson "was compelled to improvise a battle plan he did not want." Tanner, *Stonewall in the Valley*, 119.

69. Mrs. Jackson, 249.

70. George McCulloch Mooney Reminiscences, Grinnan Family Papers, VHS. Mooney added that he had no gun in his first two battles. "All I could do was to help 'Rebel Yell' to keep the Yankees on the run."

71. Fonerden, *Carpenter's Battery*, 20; *Century Magazine*, 47 (1893–94): 626.

72. Jackson manuscript report.

73. Walker, *VMI Memorial*, 218; Lyle, "Sketches," 391–92. For excellent accounts of the battle from the Union viewpoint, see Capt. George L. Woods Journal, Mar. 28, 1862, OHS; Sgt. David Bard to "Kind Friend," Mar. 25, 1862, David Bard Correspondence, Handley. Both soldiers were members of the 7th Ohio.

74. Ronald after-action report, Jackson—LVA.

75. A. S. Pendleton to mother, Mar. 29, 1862, Pendleton Papers.

76. George K. Harlow to father, Mar. 26, 1862, Harlow Family Papers, VHS.

77. *OR*, 12: Pt. 1, 374.

78. John M. Brown Reminiscences, University of Texas; Moore, "Civil War Recollections," 106.

79. Worsham, *Foot Cavalry*, 33.

80. Richard B. Garnett to Samuel Cooper, June 2, 1862, Garnett Court-Martial Papers, Richard B. Garnett Papers, MC.

81. *Richmond Daily Dispatch*, May 14, 1862; Hotchkiss Memorandum, Reel 5, Hotchkiss—LC; Jackson testimony, Aug. 6, 1862, Garnett Court-Martial Papers; Moore, *Cannoneer*, 32. One wartime writer who was not at Kernstown had Jackson riding among his fragmented lines and calling out, "One more volley, my brave boys!" No credibility can be attached to such a scenario. Edward A. Pollard, *Lee and His Lieutenants* (New York, 1867), 192.

82. *OR*, 12: Pt. 1, 384, 400–1, 404. The 5th and 42d Virginia each suffered about 20 percent losses. Colonel Harman of the 5th Virginia correctly stated in his report, "I believe that, under the providence of God, my regiment had the honor of contributing materially to the protection of the artillery and the preservation of the gallant men of other regiments, who from overpowering force and want of ammunition, were compelled to retire from the field."

83. "Dr. McGuire's Narrative," Box 20, Dabney—SHC, is the original source for Jackson defiantly remaining at Kernstown to collect everything. This idea of "cleaning a battlefield" received further credence later from two Confederate officers. General Richard Taylor stated: "In advance [Jackson's] wagon trains were left far behind. In retreat, he would fight for a wheelbarrow." Richard Taylor, *Destruction and Reconstruction: Personal Experiences of the Late War* (New York, 1879), 56. Thomas T. Munford wrote at the same time, "If a tire came off a wagon, [Jackson] would stop the whole train and wait for it to be fixed on, and let the 'rear guard' hold its position." *SHSP*, 7 (1879): 528. However, for statements of Union soldiers attending to Jackson's dead and wounded at Kernstown, see Gordon, *Brook Farm*, 122, 128; Strother, *Virginia Yankee*, 19.

84. Casler, *Stonewall Brigade*, 67.

85. The exchange with the young cavalryman first appeared in Henderson, 1:247. A variation of the same story is in Poague, *Gunner with Stonewall*, 20.

86. The narrative of Jackson's activities that night is a composite of two accounts written by his commissary. Wells J. Hawks to Robert L. Dabney, Aug. 31, 1863, Box 19, Dabney—SHC; Wells J. Hawks to Jedediah Hotchkiss, Jan. 17, 1866, Jackson—NYHS.

87. *OR*, 12: Pt. 1, 335.

88. Gold, *Clarke County*, 170.

89. Strider, *Peterkin*, 53; Robert J. Driver, Jr., *The First and Second Rockbridge Artillery* (Lynchburg, Va., 1987), 17.

90. Jackson manuscript report, Jackson—NYHS.

91. *OR*, 12: Pt. 1, 372–73; Lee Diary, Mar. 25, 1862. Federal casualties at Kernstown were 20 percent fewer in number. They included 118 killed, 450 wounded, and only twenty-two missing. *OR*, 12: Pt. 1, 346–47. Confederate losses came from Jackson's official report. Major Dabney amended the casualties to only 717 men. Box 5, Dabney—UVA. For more on Jackson's captured aide, see Bean, "Junkin," 181–90.

92. Jackson manuscript report, Jackson—NYHS. Mrs. Jackson, 248–49. On Apr. 5, Jackson told Gen. James Longstreet, "If Banks is defeated it may greatly retard McClellan's movements." *OR*, 12: Pt. 3, 844. Southern newspaper accounts of Kernstown were laudatory of Jackson but garbled with respect to accuracy. One reporter had Jackson personally leading five different assaults on the Federal position; another account stated that the general had inflicted a bloody repulse on the enemy and withdrawn to await another opportunity to do the same. See *Richmond Daily Dispatch*, Mar. 28, Mar. 31, and Apr. 11, 1862. The strongest case for Jackson winning a victory at Kernstown is in Henderson, 1:247–52.

93. Wells J. Hawks to Jedediah Hotchkiss, Jan. 17, 1866, Jackson—NYHS; Mrs. Jackson, 247. In a quick dispatch at the same time to Johnston to the east, Jackson likewise attributed his defeat to superior numbers. *OR*, 12: Pt. 1, 379.

94. Gordon, *Brook Farm*, 136–37.

95. Metzer Dutton to mother, Mar. 25, 1862, Metzer Dutton Letters, Handley.

96. TJJ to A. W. Harman, Mar. 28, 1862, Jackson—VHS.

97. Mrs. Jackson, 247.

98. Hotchkiss Journal, Mar. 27, 1862, Reel 1.

99. TJJ to Robert L. Dabney, Mar. 29, 1862, Dabney—UTS.

100. Ibid.

101. William S. Lacey, *William Sterling Lacey: Memorial, Addresses, Sermons* (Richmond, 1900), 45–46; Jedediah Hotchkiss to Sara Hotchkiss, Apr. 4, 1862, Reel 4, Hotchkiss—LC; Bean, "Pendleton Letters," 344, 346. Having made it to Rude's Hill without any major fighting, Jackson told his staff, "We have been favored by Providence today." Hotchkiss Diary, Apr. 2, 1862, Reel 1. Similarly, when Maj. Hawks observed that they had been lucky in not having any stores captured, Jackson replied to his commissary, "Yes, Major, we have been very much blessed." Wells J. Hawks to Jedediah Hotchkiss, Jan. 17, 1866, Jackson—NYHS.

102. TJJ to Judah P. Benjamin, Jan. 10, 1862, Accession 62.383, Mississippi State Historical Museum.

103. David G. McIntosh served under Jackson as an artillery colonel for over a year. The South Carolina attorney-soldier later gave an incisive summary of Jackson and discipline.

> General Jackson was absorbed in the cause to which he gave his life. His nature was intense. He felt the great responsibilities which rested on him. This, with his conscientious sense of duty and his deep religious enthusiasm, made him habitually grave.
>
> He did not look upon life lightly. As a good soldier he knew the value of discipline, and he would never tolerate even a seeming breach of it. He formed his opinions quickly and it was difficult to change them, but I do not believe he was ever consciously unjust in dealing with subordinates, and I say this, having once suffered an arrest under his order. [David G. McIntosh, 1911 letter to *Baltimore Sun*, David Gregg McIntosh Papers, VHS.]

104. Sidney Winder Diary, Mar. 28, 1862, Charles Sidney Winder Papers, Maryland Historical Society; Jackson Letterbook, Apr. 1 and 29, 1862, Reel 49. Jackson literally "threw the book" in his specifications of misconduct against Garnett. The brigadier was derelict in positioning his brigade, he failed to stay with his troops, did not support the lines properly, allowed units to become intermingled and disorganized, left his command at a critical moment, ordered a withdrawal not only in the face of the enemy but without authorization, and directed a reserve unit moving into action to halt and form position in the rear. See Garnett Court-Martial Papers.

105. Frank Buck Jones Diary, Apr. 2, 1862; Lyle, "Sketches," 405–6. For praise and defense of Garnett, see *Staunton Spectator*, Jan. 28, 1862; Douglas, *I Rode with Stonewall*, 37; McHenry

Howard, *Recollections of a Maryland Confederate Soldier and Staff Officer under Johnston, Jackson, and Lee* (Dayton, Ohio, 1975), 81; Poague, *Gunner with Stonewall*, 20.

106. W. G. Bean, *Stonewall's Man: Sandie Pendleton* (Chapel Hill, 1959), 59.

107. Colt, *Defend the Valley*, 130.

108. Bean, "Pendleton Letters," 344.

109. *OR*, 5:1058; Howard, *Recollections*, 75; Casler, *Stonewall Brigade*, 73, 102; Winder Diary, Aug. 5 and Sept. 16, 1861.

110. Winder Diary, Apr. 1, 1862; Robertson, *Stonewall Brigade*, 81–82.

111. Jedediah Hotchkiss to Sara Hotchkiss, Apr. 2, 1862, Reel 4, Hotchkiss—LC. The meticulous Jackson would not have been pleased at what the editors of the *Official Records* later did to his Kernstown narrative. Arbitrary paragraphing was a regular policy. Where the general used abbreviations for rank and "P.A.C.S.," the *OR* compilers spelled out the words. Jackson's regular use of "till" became "until" in the printed version, just as one of his favorite words, "whilst" would always be changed to "while." Likewise, "upon the enemy" appears as "on the enemy." Jackson did not know one of his officers well. The editors would change Capt. "R. D. Bridgford" of the 1st Virginia Battalion to read "D. B. Bridgeford."

112. John M. Brown Reminiscences.

113. Edmondson, *My Dear Emma*, 87–88; TJJ to John R. Jones, Apr. 11, 1862, Jackson Letterbook, Reel 49.

114. Alexander M. Garber Notes, Reel 39, Hotchkiss—LC. For Jackson's statements on combining militia with volunteers, see TJJ to Va. Adjt. Gen. William B. Richardson, Apr. 14, 1862, Jackson Letterbook, Reel 49.

115. Years after the war, Gen. James Longstreet claimed to have suggested that he and Jackson unite forces and deliver a swift, heavy attack against Federals in the valley. Longstreet, of course, would lead the assault (his unfamiliarity with the valley notwithstanding). Jackson supposedly opposed the plan. "As the commander of the district did not care to have an officer there of higher rank," Longstreet wrote sneeringly, "the subject was discontinued." James Longstreet, *From Manassas to Appomattox* (Philadelphia, 1895), 65. No corroboration of any kind exists to validate Longstreet's assertions. One of Jackson's letters to Longstreet at this time seems to imply that the latter was urging a defensive stand. Like so many of Longstreet's postwar utterances, the statements are long on imagination and short on truth. For Jackson's correspondence at the time with Longstreet and Johnston, see *OR*, 12: Pt. 3, 842–44. The originals of the three letters are in the Johnston Collection.

116. Strother, *Virginia Yankee*, 26; Augustus B. Tanner to mother, Apr. 4, 1862, Augustus B. Tanner Latters, OHS. For a similar statement from Banks to McClellan, see *OR*, 12: Pt. 3, 51.

117. Mrs. Jackson, 247–48. In Jackson's letter to Anna, he quoted 2 Cor. 4:17.

118. TJJ to Robert L. Dabney, Apr. 9, 1862, Dabney—UTS; Johnson, *Dabney*, 262–63; D. H. Hill to Robert L. Dabney, Mar. 26, 1862, Dabney—UTS.

119. Frank Buck Jones Diary, Apr. 10, 1862.

120. Johnston, *Narrative*, 110; *OR*, 12: Pt. 3, 851–52, 863.

121. TJJ to Richard S. Ewell, Apr. 12, 1862, Sotheby's Books and Manuscripts Catalogue 6424, New York, Spring 1963; TJJ to Richard S. Ewell, Apr. 13, 1862, Whitewell Collection, Massachusetts Historical Society; TJJ to Richard S. Ewell, Apr. 14, 1862, Campbell Brown and Richard S. Ewell Papers, TSLA. For Jackson and the religious tracts, see Jedediah Hotchkiss to Sara Hotchkiss, Apr. 14, 1862, Reel 4, Hotchkiss—LC; *Richmond Enquirer*, May 16, 1862.

122. TJJ to Adjt. Gen. Samuel Cooper, Apr. 14, 1862, Jackson Letterbook, Reel 49.

123. TJJ to John A. Harman, Apr. 14, 1862, Patton Family Papers, VHS. Other renditions of the Jackson letter are in Reel 1, Hotchkiss—LC; Withrow Scrapbooks, W&L, XVI, 40. Because some details of the letter had previously not been uncovered, earlier writers placed its date wherever they thought it appropriate. For example, Mrs. Jackson, 170, implied that Jackson wrote the letter prior to First Manassas. Chambers, 1:449, inserted the letter in his discussion of events in February 1862.

124. Hotchkiss Journal, Apr. 14, 1862, Reel 1.

125. Bean, "Harman," 6.

126. Alexander M. Garber Notes, Reel 39, Hotchkiss—LC.

127. Avirett, *Memoirs of Ashby*, 401–2; *OR*, 12: Pt. 1, 426–27; Jedediah Hotchkiss, "Memoranda—Valley Campaign of 1861," Jackson—NYHS. One description of Ashby at Mt. Jackson has all the characteristics of a Hollywood script. See Douglas, *I Rode with Stonewall*, 41. Eleven months later, Jackson would describe Ashby as "an officer whose judgement, coolness, and courage eminently qualified him for the delicate and important trust" of guarding the rear of the Valley army. In April 1862, Jackson's opinion of his cavalry chief was far from that high level. Jackson manuscript report of McDowell campaign, Georgia Callis West Papers, VHS.

128. Hotchkiss, "Memoranda." Hotchkiss slightly embellished this story in later versions.

129. Ibid.; John W. Wayland, *Stonewall Jackson's Way* (Verona, Va., 1956), 86. For soldier discontent at sending excess baggage to Staunton, see Worsham, *Foot Cavalry*, 37.

130. Hotchkiss Journal, Apr. 19, 1862, Reel 1; Jedediah Hotchkiss to Sara Hotchkiss, Apr. 19, 1862, Reel 4, Hotchkiss—LC.

131. *OR*, 12: Pt. 3, 853–54, 857, 860.

132. Ibid.: Pt. 1, 446–47; Pt. 3, 94, 106, 118–19.

133. Wilder Dwight, *Life and Letters of Wilder Dwight* (Boston, 1868), 236.

134. John A. Harman to Asher W. Harman, Apr. 20, 1862, Reel 39, Hotchkiss—LC; Harvey Black to wife, Apr. 22, 1862, Harvey Black Letters, Virginia Tech.

135. Mrs. Jackson, 248, 254.

CHAPTER 13   *"A Crazy Fool"*

1. Hotchkiss Journal, Apr. 21, 1862, Reel 1, Hotchkiss—LC; Worsham, *Foot Cavalry*, 37; Harvey Black to wife, Apr. 23, 1862, Harvey Black Letters, Virginia Tech; John A. Harman to Asher W. Harman, Apr. 23, 1862, Reel 39, Hotchkiss—LC.

2. Jedediah Hotchkiss to Sara Hotchkiss, Apr. 14, 1862, Reel 4, Hotchkiss—LC; Campbell Brown, "Military Reminiscences," Campbell Brown and Richard S. Ewell Papers, TSLA, 32; *CV*, 11 (1903): 126.

3. *Lexington Gazette*, May 1, 1862; John B. Purcell to Jedediah Hotchkiss, Sept. 28, 1897, Reel 14, Hotchkiss—LC. For other praise of Williamson, see *Richmond Daily Dispatch*, July 6, 1861; James T. Murfee to Thomas T. Munford, July 18, 1903, Munford-Ellis Family Papers, Duke University.

4. Douglas, *I Rode with Stonewall*, 351–58; H. Kyd Douglas to Tippie Boteler, Nov. 16, 1861, Henry Kyd Douglas Letters, Duke; Jedediah Hotchkiss to Sara Hotchkiss, Apr. 14, 1862, Reel 4, Hotchkiss—LC. Regrettably, with the passing years Douglas overestimated his wartime contributions. *I Rode with Stonewall* is an exercise in egocentricity that might more appropriately have been entitled *Stonewall Rode with Me*.

5. *SHSP*, 11 (1883): 129.

6. Ibid.

7. Johnson, *Dabney*, 263, 270. Dabney stated in his letter of resignation from Union Theological Seminary that Jackson's staff was "almost wholly unorganized at a critical time." Yet his main object in entering service again (at the outset of the war he had served a six-month stint as chaplain of the 18th Virginia) was "to exercise a religious influence among my brethren and fellow-citizens now acting as defenders of our country." Dabney to Board of Directors, Apr. 21, 1862, Dabney—UTS. Thirty-five years later, blind and infirm, Dabney still delighted in presenting embellished versions of that first day on staff duty. See "Dabney's Last Lecture on Stonewall Jackson," *Davidson College Magazine*, 16 (Oct. 1899): 3–4.

8. Alpheus S. Williams, *From the Cannon's Mouth* (Detroit, 1959), 70.

9. *OR*, 12: Pt. 3, 880; Avirett, *Memoirs of Ashby*, 169; McDonald, *Laurel Brigade*, 49–50; E. T. H. Warren to wife, Apr. 24, 1862, E. T. H. Warren Letters, UVA. Hotchkiss thought the cavalry "a lawless horde" and added, "When Ashby's men are with him they behave gallantly, but when they are away from him they lack the inspiration of presence and being undisciplined they often fail to do any good." Jedediah Hotchkiss, "Memoranda—Valley Campaign of 1861,"

Jackson—NYHS; Hotchkiss Journal, Apr. 19, 1862, Reel 1, Hotchkiss—LC. For a strong and well-considered defense of Ashby and his men, see Tanner, *Stonewall in the Valley*, 283–85.

10. Judah P. Benjamin to Turner Ashby, Feb. 22, 1862, Letters Received by the Confederate Adjutant and Inspector General, M474, Reel 3, NA. A differently worded version of Benjamin's letter is in Jackson Letterbook, Reel 49, Hotchkiss—LC.

11. R. E. Lee to TJJ, Apr. 16, 1862, Old Catalog Collection, VHS; S. Bassett French to TJJ, Apr. 16, 1862, Davis—Tulane.

12. McDonald, *Laurel Brigade*, 51.

13. John A. Harman to Asher W. Harman, Apr. 25, 1862, Reel 39, Hotchkiss—LC. According to Hotchkiss, Ashby was convinced that he "could easily manage" all of his companies without further need for drill. Hotchkiss Journal, Apr. 24, 1862, Reel 1.

14. Turner Ashby to A. R. Boteler, Apr. 25, 1862, Turner Ashby Papers, PAHS. An early Jackson biographer thought that Ashby only threatened to resign. See Dabney, 327, and a refutation in Avirett, *Memoirs of Ashby*, 177. Major Funsten also submitted a letter of resignation.

15. Howard, *Recollections*, 90; TJJ to Walter H. Taylor, May 5, 1862, Box 20, Dabney—SHC.

16. John A. Harman to Asher W. Harman, Apr. 26, 1862, Reel 39, Hotchkiss—LC.

17. TJJ to Anna Castleman, Apr. 22, 1862, Davis—Tulane.

18. Jedediah Hotchkiss to Sara Hotchkiss, Apr. 24, 1862, Reel 4, Hotchkiss—LC.

19. Johnston was so involved on the peninsula that he had not communicated with Jackson since the first week of April. He had written Ewell only once during the month. Johnston, *Narrative*, 110; *OR*, 12: Pt. 3, 852.

20. Lee, *Wartime Papers*, 151; *OR*, 12: Pt. 3, 863.

21. Lee, *Wartime Papers*, 156–57.

22. Ibid., 160, 163; *OR*, 12: Pt. 3, 863.

23. *OR*, 12: Pt. 3, 106, 868; Wise, *Military History*, 194; Hotchkiss Journal, Apr. 24, 1862, Reel 1. On that same April day, a Massachusetts officer wrote sarcastically to his mother: "Our army is now in Harrisonburg. . . . 'The Valley' is cleared; and General Banks has been enjoying himself with a 'general order' of congratulation, back-patting, and praise, worthy of little Jack Horner, and his thumb and his plum." Dwight, *Life and Letters*, 237.

24. *OR*, 12: Pt. 3, 869–71.

25. Harvey Black to wife, Apr. 28, 1862, Harvey Black Letters; Jones Diary, Apr. 27, 1862, Handley Library. Proverbs 27:1 was the source for Dabney's sermon.

26. TJJ to Francis H. Smith, Apr. 28, 1862, Superintendent's Records: Incoming Correspondence, VMI.

27. TJJ to Richard S. Ewell, Apr. 28, 1862, Autobiographical File, Chicago Historical Society; David French Boyd, *Reminiscences of the War in Virginia* (Austin, Tex., 1989), 7–10.

28. Nisbet, *Four Years*, 97. Although Ewell is usually described as a tall man, an "official" physical description is in his July 19, 1865, parole in the Richard Stoddert Ewell Papers, LC. Another word-picture of Ewell is in *Richmond Daily Dispatch*, Sept. 25, 1861. Surgeon McGuire praised "brave, chivalrous, splendid, eccentric Dick Ewell, whom everybody loved." Hunter H. McGuire to Jedediah Hotchkiss, June 27, 1896, Reel 12, Hotchkiss—LC.

29. W. W. Goldsborough, *The Maryland Line in the Confederate States Army* (Baltimore, 1869), 43–44. Reports circulated then and later that Jackson left the Swift Run Gap encampment without telling Ewell anything and that the latter either cursed in anger or sat on a fence and sobbed in frustration. In truth, on April 29, Ewell spent what Quartermaster Harman estimated as "several hours" in conference with Jackson. Ewell himself told of Jackson informing him of a proposed secret march to join Gen. Edward Johnson in the Staunton area. Samuel D. Buck, *With the Old Confeds: Actual Experiences of a Captain of the Line* (Baltimore, 1925), 27–28; John Gill, *Reminiscences of Four Years as a Private Soldier in the Confederate Army, 1861–1865* (Baltimore, 1904), 50; John A. Harman to Asher Harman, Apr. 30, 1862, Reel 39, Hotchkiss—LC; Richard S. Ewell to Robert L. Dabney, Oct. 1, 1863, Box 19, Dabney—SHC; *OR*, 12: Pt. 3, 876.

30. *OR*, 12: Pt. 3, 111–12, 118. Shenandoah Valley residents were of the same opinion. A

Winchester citizen heard "in despair" that Jackson "was en route to Yorktown. . . . His move-ment to the right, towards the [Blue] Ridge, has caused a panic in Staunton & I suppose in Charlottesville; & the gloomy ones here regard it as evidence that the Valley is to be aban-doned." Mrs. Hugh Lee Diary, early May 1862, Handley.

31. Neese, *Confederate Horse Artillery*, 49–50; Worsham, *Foot Cavalry*, 38.

32. Brandon H. Beck and Charles S. Grunder, *The First Battle of Winchester* (Lynchburg, Va., 1992), 20; Pendleton, "Pendleton Letters," 352–53; Hotchkiss, "Memoranda."

33. Hotchkiss, "Memoranda."

34. *SHSP*, 43 (1920): 182; Wayland, *Twenty-five Chapters*, 188.

35. Worsham, *Foot Cavalry*, 38; Moore, *Cannoneer*, 44. The march that day, George Buswell of the 33d Virginia declared, was on "the worst road I ever saw. Mud and water were knee-deep. . . . Gen. J. that day played the part of General, wagon-master, road master and a 'hand at the wheel.'" Buswell Diary, May 1, 1862, BV 224, FSNMP.

36. James Huffman, *Ups and Downs of a Confederate Soldier* (New York, 1940), 45–46; Harvey Black to wife, May 2, 1862, Harvey Black Letters. The Richmond newspapers gave little attention to Jackson's activities in May for two reasons: it was difficult to obtain accurate and up-to-date information on Jackson's movements in the valley, and McClellan's huge Union army was moving up the peninsula toward the capital, an event of overriding importance to everything else happening in the state.

37. TJJ to Richard S. Ewell, May 3, 1862, Collection 420, Maine Historical Society; TJJ to Francis H. Smith, May 3, 1862, Francis Henny Smith Letters, VHS. Jackson spelled out the reserve duties he had in mind for the cadets in a May 6 letter to Smith, Francis Smith Letters.

38. R. E. Lee to TJJ, May 1, 1862, Davis—Tulane. Jackson was by no means making a stab in the dark with his circuitous movement from Swift Run Gap. Rather, he had put his aides to work in far-ranging ways. Jed Hotchkiss wrote after the war: "Jackson made constant use of his staff officers in the execution of positions to be attacked, and as a rule relied on their re-ports. . . . The roads leading to Staunton were gone over by staff officers prior to his movement towards McDowell and their reports induced Jackson to go the way he did, via Mechums River as the roads were much better in that direction, they having been examined simultaneously. . . . The position of the advance of Fremont's forces west of Staunton were carefully examined and reported on, not only a week prior to the movement, but also on the day preceding his attack." Jedediah Hotchkiss to William L. Chase, Mar. 28, 1892, Reel 9, Hotchkiss—LC.

39. Some sources have the trains reaching Staunton at noon or thereabouts. See *B&L*, 2:286; Tanner, *Stonewall in the Valley*, 164. Given the fact that at least a third of the sixteen-mile journey from Mechum's River Station to Staunton involved scaling the Blue Ridge, it is more likely that the first train did not arrive before 3 P.M. Waddell, *Annals of Augusta County*, 469; Vandiver, 227.

40. *OR*, 12: Pt. 3, 125–26, 133–35, 140.

41. Since there was no senior class at the time, practically all of the cadets were teenagers. At the head of the four companies was VMI's commandant of cadets, twenty-four-year-old Maj. Scott Shipp. It had taken the youngsters three days to march the thirty-eight miles from Lexington to Staunton. Eleven cadets had remained behind, ostensibly to guard the institute. Most of them were down with mumps. Couper, *VMI*, 2:147–48. A VMI official wrote of the quality of the wartime cadets: "They are a fine set of fellows—much better than we had before and I think will turn out [to be] good soldiers to defend our Southern homes from the cowardly minions of the North." William S. Polk to A. M. McPheeters, Jan. 22, 1862, Alexander M. McPheeters Papers, Duke.

42. Hotchkiss Journal, May 5, 1862, Reel 1; *SHSP*, 38 (1910): 283.

43. *CV*, 20 (1912): 280; *Lexington Gazette*, June 26, 1862; McFarland Diary, May 5, 1862, McFarland Papers, UTS. Kyd Douglas verified the delivery of the "Stone W. Jackson" letter. Douglas to Tippie Boteler, July 24, 1862, Douglas Letters.

44. Wight Recollections, Wight Family Papers, VHS.

45. *OR*, 12: Pt. 3, 880; TJJ to Alexander R. Boteler, May 6, 1862, Boteler Papers, Duke. The heavy-set John Echols had commanded the 27th Virginia of the Stonewall Brigade until wounded at Kernstown. He returned to duty with Loring in southwestern Virginia—a fact that no doubt influenced Jackson's negative judgment of the man.

46. TJJ to Alexander R. Boteler, May 6, 1862.

47. Ibid.

48. Hotchkiss Journal, May 7, 1862, Reel 1, Hotchkiss—LC. See also TJJ to Richard S. Ewell, May 7, 1862, Richmond Autograph Collection, Massachusetts Historical Society; Hotchkiss, "Memoranda." By Jackson's order, the VMI cadets brought up the rear of the column. The general did not want to put the youths into battle if it could be avoided.

49. A. S. Pendleton to mother, May 12, 1862, Pendleton Papers.

50. Albert Tracy, "Fremont's Pursuit of Jackson in the Shenandoah Valley," *Virginia Magazine of History and Biography*, 70 (1962): 171.

51. TJJ to Richard S. Ewell, May 8, 1862, Western Historical Manuscript Collection, Columbia, Mo.

52. Ross, "Letters of Colonel Ross," 170.

53. Edward A. Alfriend, "Recollections of Stonewall Jackson," *Lippincott's Magazine*, 69 (1902): 582.

54. Shepherd G. Pryor to wife, Mar. 28, 1862, Shepherd Green Pryor Collection, University of Georgia.

55. Chesnut, *Mary Chesnut's Civil War*, 444.

56. Jackson manuscript report of McDowell campaign, Georgia Callis West Papers, VHS.

57. Brigadier Gen. William B. Taliaferro was openly critical of Jackson after the battle for not employing artillery. The fact that Taliaferro's brigade suffered 101 men killed and wounded in the fight clouded his judgment. "Guns might have been dragged up the heights to good advantage," Taliaferro wrote. Jackson "was urged to send some to the front but declined. Why nobody knows. He rarely gave reasons. He gave orders that were all short, sharp, quick, decisive. The tone and manner stopped inquiry." *OR*, 12: Pt. 1, 476; Taliaferro, "Reminiscences of Jackson," William B. Taliaferro Papers, W&M, 3. See also Casler, *Stonewall Brigade*, 74.

58. Jackson manuscript report.

59. *CV*, 6 (1898): 418.

60. Worsham, *Foot Cavalry*, 40. The 44th Virginia was one of the regiments hard pressed on the right. Colonel William Scott wrote of it: "The front rank, after delivering its fire, would retire some three or four paces to the rear and lie down and load, [and] as they were shielded from danger while loading, I allowed this system to continue. . . . But observing that some men retired farther to the rear than necessary, and were lying on their faces and taking no part in the battle, I attempted to rouse them by words, but finding that neither harsh words nor threats were of any avail, I commenced riding over them, which soon made them join the line of battle." *OR*, 12: Pt. 1, 486.

61. Major Ross of the 52d Virginia, a former VMI student and colleague of Jackson, regarded the Federal discipline at McDowell as "immensely superior to ours. . . . I never saw Cadets at drill march with greater precision and more regularity. . . . Not a man shrunk from his position but they all marched like true soldiers to the attack." John DeHart Ross to Agnes Reid, May 13, 1862, Ross Papers, VMI. For praise of the gallantry of the Confederates, see Taliaferro's after-action report in *OR*, 12: Pt. 1, 480-81.

62. Hotchkiss Journal, May 8, 1862, Reel 1.

63. Ibid.

64. Watkins Kearns Diary, May 8, 1862, BV 186, FSNMP; Hotchkiss, "Memoranda."; Hotchkiss to G. F. R. Henderson, Apr. 18, 1895, Reel 11, Hotchkiss—LC. Jackson's chief of staff was mistaken in stating that the general reached headquarters at 1 A.M. and that he went at once to bed in the inn. Dabney, 346-47.

65. Fremont put Jackson's strength at "upward of 14,000 men and thirty pieces of artillery." *OR*, 12: Pt. 1, 9. Jackson's always disgruntled quartermaster, Maj. John A. Harman, had reason to complain on the day after McDowell. The ever-secretive Jackson refused to tell him where he should take the supply wagons. The result was that Harman had to play "catch up" throughout the day. That evening, in a pique, he wrote of the battle: "We have been worsted by miss-management. I am more than ever satisfied of Jackson's incompetency. . . . We have the battle-field but no victory." John A. Harman to Asher Harman, May 9, 1862, Reel 39, Hotch-kiss—LC.

66. Richard L. Armstrong, *The Battle of McDowell, March 11–May 18, 1862* (Lynchburg, Va., 1990), 100–1. The 12th Georgia, with fifty-two dead and 123 injured, suffered the highest regimental casualties on the field.

67. *B&L*, 2:287–88; Lacy, *William Sterling Lacy*, 47.

68. Judith W. McGuire, *Diary of a Southern Refugee during the War* (New York, 1867), 112.

69. *Lynchburg Virginian*, quoted in *Lexington Gazette*, May 15, 1862.

70. Wells J. Hawks to Jedediah Hotchkiss, Jan. 17, 1866, Jackson—NYHS.

71. Hotchkiss Journal, May 12, 1862, Reel 1.

72. Hotchkiss, "Memoranda."

73. Hotchkiss Journal, May 10, 1862, Reel 1.

74. William Montgomery to "Brother & Friends," [May 1862], BV 24, FSNMP.

75. *OR*, 12: Pt. 1, 11; Hotchkiss to Chase, Mar. 28, 1892.

76. TJJ to Richard S. Ewell, May 10, 1862, PAHS. A cleaned-up version of this dispatch is in *OR*, 12: Pt. 3, 486.

77. Franklin M. Myers, *The Comanches: A History of White's Battalion, Virginia Cavalry* (Baltimore, 1871), 38.

78. Howard, *Recollections*, 98–99.

79. Jackson manuscript report; Jackson Letterbook, Reel 49. In 1897, Dabney gave the last of many postwar lectures on Jackson. By then the cleric was in his late sixties and totally blind. Dabney described a long horseback ride he and Jackson purportedly took on May 12, 1862, and the conversation the two men had. Remembering "substantially" Jackson's comments thirty-five years earlier, Dabney had the general (1) advocating anew a black-flag policy of neither side taking prisoners; (2) predicting that the slaves would be liberated and many would become Union soldiers; (3) not liking to hear criticisms of the Confederate government; and (4) expressing the wish not to live if the Southern nation did not fully achieve its independence. Strong questions of credibility exist with every part of the Dabney presentation. "Dabney's Last Lecture," 6–7.

80. O'Ferrall, *Forty Years of Active Service*, 33; Thomas R. Wade, Jr., to Louisa Hopkins, May 13, 1862, Thomas M. Wade Letters, Lewis Leigh Collection, USMHI.

81. Alfriend, "Recollections," 584.

82. Ibid. In his postwar memoirs, McIlwaine confessed to having only a casual acquaintance with Jackson. He did state that following the service in question, Jackson took refuge from the rain in his tent. Richard McIlwaine, *Memories of Three Score Years and Ten* (New York, 1908), 196.

83. *SHSP*, 9 (1881): 364.

84. Ibid., 364–65. A more constructed account of Ewell's tirade to Walker is in Caldwell, *Stonewall Jim*, 38–39.

85. *SHSP*, 7 (1879): 526–27. For another and similar outburst by Ewell at the time, see Percy Gatling Hamlin, *"Old Bald Head" (General R. S. Ewell)* (Strasburg, Va., 1940), 84. After the war, Gen. Harvey Hill stated of his brother-in-law: "I think it was Jackson's reticence more than anything else that gave offense. His next in command knew no more than the private soldier what he intended to do. I think that this must have had a palsying effect at times on his next in command." *Century Magazine*, 47 (1893–94): 628.

86. See Dabney, 352; Joseph E. Johnston to TJJ, May 12, 1862, Davis—Tulane; *OR*, 12: Pt. 3, 859, 889.

87. Ross, "Letters of Colonel Ross," 172.

88. TJJ to Francis H. Smith, May 15, 1862, Francis H. Smith Letters.

89. Jackson Letterbook, May 13, 1862, Reel 49.

90. James E. Hall, *The Diary of a Confederate Soldier* [Lewisburg, W.Va., 1961], 55–56.

91. Murphy, *10th Virginia*, 26; George K. Harlow to father, May 17, 1862, Harlow Family Papers, VHS.

92. Moore, *Cannoneer*, 51. See also Paxton, *Memoir*, 58.

93. Richard S. Ewell to Elizabeth Brown, May 13, 1862, Ewell Papers, LC.

94. TJJ to Ewell, May 13, 1862, Richmond Autograph Collection, Massachusetts Historical Society (reprinted with heavy editorial changes in *OR*, 12: Pt. 3, 888–89); *OR*, 12: Pt. 3, 890. See also Ewell to TJJ, May 13, 1862, Davis—Tulane. Ostensibly, Branch's brigade was to join Ewell. The movement of the five North Carolina regiments was actually a ruse to make Federals believe that reinforcements were en route to the valley. James H. Lane to Thomas T. Munford, Jan. 4, 1893, Munford-Ellis Family Papers.

95. Howard, *Recollections*, 103–4; John A. Harman to Asher Harman, May 15, 1862, Reel 39, Hotchkiss—LC.

96. Jackson Letterbook, Jan. 27, Mar. 1, and May 16, 1862, Reel 49.

97. Walker, *VMI Memorial*, 145, 148; Wise, *Long Arm of Lee*, 1:170; TJJ to Adjt. Gen. Samuel Cooper, Apr. 13, 1863, Reel 49, Hotchkiss—LC. "Trueheart was with us on the Romney Campaign," Dr. McGuire stated. "He got very drunk while we were in front of Hancock and was sent away. He scarcely deserves to be mentioned as one of the Staff officers." Hunter McGuire to Jedediah Hotchkiss, Sept. 22, 1897, Reel 14, Hotchkiss—LC. Surgeon Graham Ellzey (VMI, 1860) made a provocative statement a quarter-century later: "I always felt that Crutchfield comprehended Jackson better than any man I ever talked with about him. I rather think Crutchfield was himself the ablest man I ever met. If he had lived to write the analysis of Jackson's greatness, we should have a work indeed." M. Graham Ellzey to James H. Lane, Dec. 1, 1888, James H. Lane Papers, Auburn University.

98. *OR*, 12: Pt. 3, 897; McKim, *Recollections*, 40–41; James McHenry Howard, *Recollections and Opinions* (Baltimore, 1922), 33; Jedediah Hotchkiss to G. F. R. Henderson, Apr. 26, 1895, Reel 11, Hotchkiss—LC. Henderson stated in his Jackson biography (1:382) that Steuart had "much to learn." Kyd Douglas wrote in the margin of his copy of Henderson, "He never learned it!" Henry Kyd Douglas Library, Antietam NBP.

99. Dabney, 354.

100. Kearns Diary, May 15, 1862, BV 186, FSNMP. Chambers, 1:483–84, gave the impression that this incident occurred at least a month earlier than it did.

101. *OR*, 12: Pt. 3, 891.

102. Ibid., 893. See also TJJ to Richard S. Ewell, May 15, 1862, Collection 420, Maine Historical Society.

103. Lee, *Wartime Papers*, 174.

104. Ibid., 175.

105. TJJ to Richard S. Ewell, May 17, 1862, Saltby's Auction Sale Catalogue 6618 (New York, 1994), 61. See also *OR*, 12: Pt. 3, 895.

106. *OR*, 12: Pt. 3, 895.

107. Ibid., 896.

108. TJJ to Joseph E. Johnston, May 17, 1862, Joseph Eggleston Johnston Papers, Henry E. Huntington Library.

109. Henderson, 1:303, had the conference between Jackson and Ewell taking place a day earlier. Even worse is Douglas's account. He put the meeting on May 20, and the conversation he quoted the generals as having is out of character with both men. *I Rode with Stonewall*, 93.

110. Dabney, 359.

111. *OR*, 12: Pt. 3, 897; John A. Harman to Asher Harman, May 18, 1862, Reel 39, Hotchkiss—LC.

112. *OR*, 12: Pt. 3, 897. May 16 was the date of Lee's dispatch suggesting an attack on Banks. Ewell's acknowledgement of Jackson's letter is in Jackson—SHC.

113. Hotchkiss Journal, May 19, 1862, Reel 1; Mrs. Jackson, 257–58.

114. James L. Power to Roberta Smith Power, May 19, 1862, James L. Power Letters, VHS. Campbell Brown of Ewell's staff maintained that at the Mount Solon conference it was Ewell who suggested the secret march about to be made down the Luray Valley. This is untrue. Brown confused Ewell's proposal for sidestepping Johnston's orders with Jackson's strategy for getting at Banks. Campbell Brown, "Military Reminiscences," Campbell Brown and Richard S. Ewell Papers, TSLA, 37.

115. Casler, *Stonewall Brigade*, 76; Nisbet, *Four Years*, 40.

116. Hall, *Diary of a Confederate Soldier,* 57.

117. *OR,* 12: Pt. 1, 701.

118. *OR,* 12: Pt. 3, 898. No copy of Lee's response to Jackson exists.

119. *OR,* 12: Pt. 3, 897.

120. Joseph E. Johnston to Richard S. Ewell, May 18 1862, Old Catalog Collection, VHS. See also Freeman, *Lee's Lieutenants,* 1:371. Previous Jackson biographers have placed too much emphasis on Jackson and Ewell acting in extra-legal fashion. For example, see Farwell, *Stonewall,* 273. Johnston's little-known message of the 18th gave the two generals full authority for the movements they undertook. For good measure, Johnston repeated his approval three days later by telling Jackson: "If you & Gen. Ewell united can beat Banks, do it. I cannot judge at this distance. My previous instructions warned you against attacking fortifications." Joseph E. Johnston to TJJ, May 21, 1862, Davis—Tulane.

121. Oates, *The War.* 81; Abram Miller to Julia Miller, Oct. 7, 1862, Abram Schultz Miller Letters, Handley. See also Beck and Grunder, *First Winchester,* 25; Putnam, *Richmond during the War,* 35–36.

122. Moore, *Cannoneer,* 77; Boyd, *Reminiscences,* 13; John Cheve Haskell Memoir, Duke University; *SHSP,* 7 (1879): 345; 20 (1892): 33.

123. Taylor, *Destruction and Reconstruction,* 49.

124. Ibid., 49–50. Several years after publication of the Taylor book, Col. David G. McIntosh blasted the Jackson caricature in a long letter submitted to the *Baltimore Sun.* "I should never have thought of describing General Jackson as uncouth or ungainly in appearance," the artillery commander wrote, and he dismissed out of hand Taylor's statement about Jackson's mania for lemons. McIntosh then asserted: "General Jackson's appearance and manners were not, as I recall them, either harsh or repellant. While they could not be termed courtly, or possibly as polished as those of some others of high rank, they were in no sense lacking in dignity and refinement." David G. McIntosh, 1911 letter to *Baltimore Sun,* David Gregg McIntosh Papers, VHS. Staff officer John C. Haskell openly challenged the accuracy of Taylor's recollections, especially those sections treating of Jackson and Ewell. See Haskell Memoir.

125. Myers, *The Comanches,* 48–49. Jackson was evidently not aware at the time that Ewell would intersect with him west of Luray.

126. Howard, *Recollections,* 105. Taylor, *Destruction and Reconstruction,* 50, made the claim that his Louisiana brigade led Jackson's march that day. This is questionable. Jackson would hardly have put an unknown entity to set the pace for the day's march, unless he wanted the strange collection of soldiers up front where he could keep an eye on them. Given the fact that the advance was passing through two separate areas of the valley, it seems more likely that a brigade native to or familiar with the region would lead the way.

127. Colt, *Defend the Valley,* 140.

128. Taylor, *Destruction and Reconstruction,* 50; Raleigh E. Colston Reminiscences, SHC. As hard as Judge Brockenbrough tried, he could not get Jackson to tell him the destination of the march.

129. *Lexington Gazette,* May 22, 1862.

130. *OR,* 12: Pt. 1, 522–24; Gordon, *Brook Farm,* 172.

131. *SHSP,* 9 (1881): 189; Wayland, *Stonewall Jackson's Way,* 120. An unusually large number of attractive women greeted Ewell's men as they tramped down the Luray Valley. An Alabama officer was led to comment, "I felt that I was marching to a carnival of death, through the portals of Heaven, and that the angels were singing and cheering me on." Oates, *The War,* 95–96.

CHAPTER 14   *Encouraging Hope*

1. Julia Chase, a staunch Unionist in Winchester, noted in her diary at this time: "Some 50 letters & papers have been taken from Miss Bell Boyd, who has been making herself very officious since the Federal troops have been here. She acts as a spy I imagine. I should think there must be some complicity between a Federal officer & the Army, as he was in company

with this Miss Boyd. He ought with her to have been arrested." Julia Chase Diary, May 24, 1862, Handley Library.

2. G. Campbell Brown, "Military Reminiscences," TSLA, 37–38.

3. Among the more magnified accounts of Boyd's Front Royal activities are in Douglas, *I Rode with Stonewall*, 51–51; Lyle, "Sketches," W&L, 123–24; Taylor, *Destruction and Reconstruction*, 53–54. Naturally, Boyd presented the most hair-raising version in her own memoirs, *Belle Boyd in Camp and Prison* (New York, 1968), 161–67. She even included two letters of thanks allegedly from Jackson himself. See pp. 167, 211. A number of writers all but dismiss Boyd's value as a Confederate agent. For example, see Alexander, *Fighting for the Confederacy*, 155; Edwin C. Fishel, "The Mythology of Civil War Intelligence," *Civil War History*, 10 (1964): 352–53.

4. *SHSP*, 10 (1882): 52–53; Goldsborough, *Maryland Line*, 47–48.

5. Gordon, *Brook Farm*, 186.

6. Buck, *Diary*, 77–78; *Lexington Gazette*, June 19, 1862.

7. *OR*, 12: Pt. 1, 702.

8. Ibid., 725. Colonel Bradley Johnson remained bitter for many years over the Front Royal battle. His 1st Maryland and Wheat's battalion together had numbered only 425 men, Johnson stated, while the enemy was close to three times that number. "Not a gun was fired by any other infantry during the fight. It was evidently General Jackson's intention to make us whip the enemy by ourselves, and consequently we were left struggling in the unequal contest for four or five hours before we succeeded in driving them from their position." Jackson would have been surprised at that twisted interpretation of the action. *SHSP*, 10 (1882): 56.

9. *SHSP*, 9 (1881): 189.

10. Dabney, 365–66.

11. Alexander, *Military Memoirs*, 98. Dabney made too much of the courier not reaching Winder. Jackson had overall responsibility for troop displacement at Front Royal. Crutchfield surely should have known what types of artillery pieces he had and where they were located.

12. Joseph M. Ellison, "Joseph M. Ellison: War Letters (1862)," *Georgia Historical Quarterly*, 48 (1964): 230; Michael P. Musick, *Sixth Virginia Cavalry* (Lynchburg, Va., 1990), 11–13.

13. *OR*, 12: Pt. 1, 565–66, 703.

14. Dabney, 368. As events would show, Cedarville was the only engagement in the valley campaign where Confederate cavalry performed well.

15. *OR*, 12: Pt. 1, 559, 703, 962; Hotchkiss Journal, May 23, 1862, Reel 1, Hotchkiss—LC.

16. John Samuel Apperson Diary, May 23, 1862, Virginia Tech; Taylor, *Destruction and Reconstruction*, 58. Taylor's memoirs become chronologically confusing at this point because the Louisianian inadvertently combined events of May 22 and 23 into one twenty-four-hour period. This caused subsequent days to be erroneously dated.

17. *OR*, 12: Pt. 1, 546.

18. Ibid., 626, 703. Farwell's assertion, in *Stonewall*, 284, that Jackson should have marched through the night of May 23–24 to maintain his momentum ignores the physical condition of the Southern army at the time.

19. *OR*, 12: Pt. 1, 703; Jedediah Hotchkiss to William L. Chase, Mar. 28, 1892, Reel 9, Hotchkiss—LC.

20. Gordon, *Brook Farm*, 192–93.

21. *OR*, 12: Pt. 1, 525–27, 536, 595; Strother, *Virginia Yankee*, 40. A Connecticut soldier observed that as the Union army made its way northward on the turnpike, onlookers jeered and dogs ("a half dozen at every house") barked when they were not snapping at the men. Some of the Federals recalled seeing roosters "on the fence posts in front of the farmers' houses, crowing of our departure." Marvin, *Fifth Connecticut*, 93, 97. Union soldiers also complained of marching knee-deep in mud. An Ohioan claimed that he saw two mules drown in the middle of the road. Another Buckeye infantryman confessed, "It was about this time I began to wish for my quiet life at home." Robert Bromley Diary, May 25, 1862, OHS; Thomas Evans Diary, May 26, 1862, OHS.

22. Hotchkiss Journal, May 24, 1862, Reel 1. Henderson, 1:329, was incorrect in stating that

elements of three Federal cavalry units delayed Confederate movements that morning. The enemy units in question saw little if any action that day. *OR,* 12: Pt. 1, 575–77, 587–88, 623.

23. *OR,* 12: Pt. 1, 703. Dabney, 371, asserted that Steuart "found evident signs of a general retreat upon Winchester." That is not quite accurate. Steuart had chanced upon the van of Banks's column, but no one on the Confederate side knew Banks's destination.

24. *SHSP,* 8 (1880): 141.

25. *OR,* 12: Pt. 1, 704. The colonel of the 1st Maine Cavalry reported the bodies of horses and men so piled up in the road that "it was impossible to proceed." *OR,* 12: Pt. 1, 576. See also Neese, *Horse Artillery,* 56.

26. Marginal note by Douglas in Henderson, 1:407, Henry Kyd Douglas Library, Antietam NBP; Jedediah Hotchkiss to Sara Hotchkiss, May 26, 1862, Reel 4, Hotchkiss—LC.

27. *OR,* 12: Pt. 1, 704; 51: Pt. 2, 562–63.

28. Colt, *Defend the Valley,* 143; Watkins Kearns Diary, May 24, 1862, BV 186, FSNMP.

29. *OR,* 12: Pt. 1, 704.

30. Moore, *Cannoneer,* 54.

31. *OR,* 12: Pt. 1, 704.

32. Ibid., 726; Neese, *Firing Line,* 59–60; Dabney, 373. While Lt. Charles O'Ferrall of the 12th Virginia Cavalry described Jackson's cavalry chief as "dealing death in [Federal] ranks, and crippling and capturing men every rod between every mile post," Capt. Poague of the Rock-bridge battery saw Ashby quite differently. "His cavalry were looting wagons and capturing horses, utterly undisciplined. This was Ashby's weak point." O'Ferrall, *Forty Years,* 30; Poague, *Gunner with Stonewall,* 23. For a good description of Union chaos on the turnpike around Newtown, see William D. Wintz, ed., *Civil War Memoirs of Two Rebel Sisters* (Charleston, W.Va., 1989), 48.

33. Douglas, *I Rode with Stonewall,* 55.

34. Writing a quick letter early on the morning of May 25, Algernon Wade of the 27th Virginia told his sister: "We have taken two pieces of rifle canon, a car load of commissary stores &c., and about one hundred wagons very heavily laden with provisions and yankee plunder and also horses & mules attached to the wagons. a great many of the wagons were up set, the horses runing of and tearing things to pieces generally. . . . they have destroyed a number of the wagons by setting them on fire, some of the fires were extinguished before going far. . . . it is a grand victory." Algernon S. Wade to Louisa F. Hopkins, May 25, 1862, Lewis Leigh Collection, USMHI.

35. Wood, *The War,* 52–53.

36. Poague, *Gunner with Stonewall,* 23; Dabney, 375.

37. Taylor, *Destruction and Reconstruction,* 60. The best accounts of the delaying actions from the Union side are in Gordon, *Brook Farm,* 219–24, and Dwight, *Life and Letters,* 253–57.

38. The exchange between Fulkerson and Jackson first appeared in Averitt, *Memoirs,* 196–97. Douglas gave a slightly different version in *I Rode with Stonewall,* 57.

39. Taylor, *Destruction and Reconstruction,* 56.

40. *SHSP,* 9 (1884): 234; Douglas, *I Rode with Stonewall,* 56–57.

41. Dabney, 376.

42. Gordon, *Brook Farm,* 231n.

43. Myers, *The Comanches,* 52.

44. *OR,* 12: Pt. 1, 549–50. Banks sought to put his own strength at only 4000 soldiers. Ibid., 528.

45. *OR,* 12: Pt. 1, 705.

46. Ibid., 758–59, 762; Wise, *Long Arm of Lee,* 1:171–72. A Rockbridge gunner called the hour-long fight "by far the hottest and most destructive fire this battery has ever been under." L. Minor Blackford, *Mine Eyes Have Seen the Glory* (Cambridge, Mass., 1954), 189.

47. Howard, *Recollections,* 110.

48. Worsham, *Foot Cavalry,* 45.

49. Dabney, 378. Neff's own report of the conversation with Jackson is in his after-action report and, hence, abbreviated. *OR,* 12: Pt. 1, 755.

50. Taylor never missed an opportunity to tell a good story, but he reported only that Jackson ordered him to seize the ridge. *Destruction and Reconstruction,* 57. See also Colt, *Defend the Valley,* 148, for confirmation of the brevity of the Taylor-Jackson exchange. As might be expected, Douglas gave a fanciful account, replete with manufactured conversation. *I Rode with Stonewall,* 58. Although several eyewitnesses mentioned the Louisianians arriving on the field in brisk and sprightly fashion, Jackson's chief of artillery made it clear that they were not in the best of shape for action. *OR,* 12: Pt. 1, 726.

51. Taylor, *Destruction and Reconstruction,* 62–63; *OR,* 12: Pt. 1, 705–6. A Louisiana soldier later wrote with pride of the assault: "Closing many gaps made by the fierce fire the brigade continued to advance shoulder to shoulder, preserving its alignment as if it were on dress parade, and soon drove the federals from the crest of the ridge amid the cheers of the whole of Jackson's army." LHAC, 55-B.

52. *OR,* 12: Pt. 1, 705–6.

53. Various authors have attributed many statements to Jackson when the Federal line broke in defeat. Typical examples are in Chase, *Jackson,* 337–38; Dabney, "Dabney's Last Lecture on Stonewall Jackson," *Davidson College Magazine,* 16 (Oct. 1899): 5; Douglas, *I Rode with Stonewall,* 58–59; Mrs. Jackson, 261; Worsham, *Foot Cavalry,* 46. Hotchkiss's unpublished account, in "Memoranda—Valley Campaign of 1861," Jackson—NYHS, is the most credible and hence the one used here. Statements on the "Rebel Yell" are from McKim, *Recollections,* 101; Beck and Grunder, *First Winchester,* 57.

54. Hotchkiss, "Memoranda," Jackson—NYHS.

55. Lacy, *William Sterling Lacy,* 53.

56. Gordon, *Brook Farm,* 248; *OR,* 12: Pt. 1, 617, 706. Some Union sources insist that Banks's withdrawal from Winchester was slow and orderly. Kate McIvar, a teenage resident, saw it as anything but that. "Officers and soldiers alike lost their heads in the same manner that a woman generally does if her clothing takes fire. She could generally put it out with even a slight exercise of reason, but she becomes panic stricken and flies, thus adding to her danger a thousand fold." *Winchester Evening Star,* May 22, 1912.

57. Edmondson, *My Dear Emma,* 95.

58. Unknown soldier to mother, May 26, 1862, Mary Kelly Smith Papers, NCDAH.

59. *Winchester Evening Star,* Mar. 12, 1901; Mrs. Jackson, 265. One Confederate remembered that "even Genl. Jackson smiled, something I never saw him do before." Worsham, *Foot Cavalry,* xix.

60. Hotchkiss, "Memoranda." For a slightly different version of this story, see Hotchkiss to William L. Chase, Mar. 28, 1892, Reel 9, Hotchkiss—LC. See also McDonald, *Diary,* 162–63; *Lexington Gazette,* June 19, 1862.

61. Jedediah Hotchkiss to Sara Hotchkiss, May 26, 1862; *OR,* 12: Pt. 1, 706; *Winchester Evening Star,* May 22, 1912; Dabney, 381. Ashby's nonexistent force on May 25 was the result of the pillaging of the previous day. The night march and battle at sunrise gave Ashby no chance to collect his men. Of course, had he maintained firmer control over his cavalry beginning on May 24, no excuses would have been necessary. For defenses of Ashby during the battle of Winchester, see Avirett, *Memoirs,* 198–205; Chew, *Address,* 27–28; Tanner, *Stonewall in the Valley,* 283.

62. Pendleton undated affidavit, Box 19, Dabney—SHC. A printed version is in *OR,* 12: Pt. 1, 709–10, because Jackson was angry enough to include it as an addendum to his official report. Other indictments of Steuart are in Hotchkiss, "Memoranda"; Brown, "Military Reminiscences," 43–44.

63. Pendleton affidavit.

64. Jedediah Hotchkiss to Sara Hotchkiss, May 26, 1862, Reel 4, Hotchkiss—LC.

65. Lacy, *William Sterling Lacy,* 53; Blackford, *Mine Eyes,* 190–91, additional praise of Jackson is in Ellison, "Letters," 231. For insights on the Union retreat, see Strother, *Virginia Yankee,* 42–44; Gordon, *Brook Farm,* 247–48.

66. *OR,* 12: Pt. 1, 551, 707. General Harvey Hill quoted Jackson as stating, "Had my cavalry done their duty," Banks "would have been destroyed." *Century Magazine,* 47 (1893–94): 626. A number of writers have blamed the breakdown of Jackson's cavalry for the escape of the Union forces from Winchester. A typical example is Gill, *Reminiscences,* 55.

67. Fanny Graham to Anna Jackson, Aug. 9, 1862, Cook—WVU; Graham, "Some Reminiscences," 200.

68. *SHSP,* 9 (1881): 273. Douglas, *I Rode with Stonewall,* 62, put Jackson's headquarters at the local hotel. Dabney stated that Jackson was too weary to eat before going to bed. In all likelihood, the general had refreshment of some kind at the Graham's. The chief of staff was not with Jackson on the visit. Dabney also got confused and had the general with his men at Stephenson's Depot, three miles outside Winchester. Dabney, 383–84. The Winder Diary, MHS, is the source for how long the men had been without food.

69. *OR,* 12: Pt. 1, 551; Alfred D. Kelley to brother, May 25, 1862, Williamson Kelly Papers, Duke University; Beck and Grunder, *First Winchester,* viii.

70. *OR,* 12: Pt. 1, 553–54, 708, 720–21, 723–24, 961; Hotchkiss, "Memoranda.". For other inventories of the captured stores, see *Richmond Daily Dispatch,* June 2 and 10, 1862.

71. A. S. Pendleton to mother, May 28, 1862, William Nelson Pendleton Papers, SHC; Hunter McGuire to Charles J. Faulkner, March 1863, Office of the Adjutant & Inspector General and of the Quartermaster General, 1861–1865: Letters Received, RG109, NA; Hunter McGuire to Marcus J. Wright, Sept. 30, 1898, Reel 14, Hotchkiss—LC. In a Dec. 26, 1898, communique to Dr. Kent Black, former hospital steward John S. Apperson of southwestern Virginia stated: "I remember, and very clearly . . . that General Jackson regarded the medical officers of the opposing army as non-combatants and not answerable to the same restrictions as other prisoners of war. And this is in perfect harmony with the christian character of this great soldier. . . . He never failed to require the utmost care on the part of his medical officers for his own sick and wounded, and a feeling of compassion, akin to sympathy, for a maimed and crippled foe was manifested in all he did." LHAC, 55-B. Such a statement appears somewhat at odds with Jackson's advocacy of a black-flag policy.

72. Beck and Grunder, *First Winchester,* 66; J. E. B. Stuart to Flora Cooke Stuart, May 28, 1862, James Ewell Brown Stuart Papers, VHS.

73. *Richmond Daily Dispatch,* May 27, 1862. See also the issues for May 28, 29, and 31, 1862; *Richmond Enquirer,* May 27, 1862.

74. For criticisms of Jackson in the May 23–25 actions, see Tanner, *Stonewall in the Valley,* 254–55, 258.

75. Abraham Lincoln, *The Collected Works of Abraham Lincoln* (New Brunswick, N.J., 1953–55), 5:235–36.

76. See *OR,* 12: Pt. 3, 232, 242–43; Ser. 3, 2:69–70. Precisely how alarmed Union authorities initially were at Jackson's Front Royal-Winchester victories is controversial. Royster, *Destructive War,* 42, insisted that any "panic" or "fear" was an overstatement. On the other hand, Federal Gen. William F. Smith was in Washington at the time and felt that "lively consternation was the result" of Jackson's movements. William F. Smith, *Autobiography of Major General William F. Smith, 1861–1864* (Dayton, Ohio, 1990), 40.

77. *OR,* 12: Pt. 1, 707; Hotchkiss, "Memoranda."

78. Mrs. Jackson, 265.

79. TJJ to R. J. Sheetz, May 27, 1862, Cook—WVU.

80. Jackson Letterbook, May 25–27, 1862, Reel 49, Hotchkiss—LC. Jackson's general orders pertaining to uniforms and Winchester visits are in *OR,* 12: Pt. 3, 900.

81. Dabney, 386, may have been confused in stating that Jackson "sent a trusty officer" to Richmond with dispatches of the Winchester fighting. No such reports, or proposals from Jackson, survive. Similarly, no directions to Jackson from Confederate authorities at this time exist in print. This leads to the conclusion that Boteler relayed verbal instructions when he arrived from Richmond. The May 30 announcement of Col. Boteler's reassignment to the staff is in the Polk, Brown and Ewell Family Papers, SHC.

82. Dabney, 389; John A. Harman to Asher Harman, May 27, 1862, Reel 39, Hotchkiss—LC.

83. Charles W. Trueheart to Henry Trueheart, July 7, 1862, Trueheart Papers, Rosenberg Library, Galveston, Tex.

84. *OR*, 12: Pt. 1, 707.

85. Ibid., 738–39.

86. Wells J. Hawks to Jedediah Hotchkiss, Jan. 17, 1866, Jackson—NYHS. Winder thought that the "very hospitable" citizens of Charles Town were "rejoiced" over the presence of Jackson's army. Winder Diary, May 28, 1862.

87. *OR*, 10: Pt. 2, 225; 12: Pt. 1, 643; Pt. 3, 221.

88. Who informed Jackson when of the movements of Shields and Fremont is more conjectural than factual. One account had an elderly gentleman endangering his life by rushing to Jackson with news of Shields's advance. See Douglas, *I Rode with Stonewall*, 63. For years, local legend had it that two sisters, Esther and Rebecca Washington, who lived near Romney, brought Jackson word that Fremont was at Keyser and moving toward his flank. The father had dispatched the two girls to find Jackson. They rode for two days across fields and through woods before delivering their message to the general near Charles Town. Undated newspaper clipping, Mary K. Holt, Weston W.Va. See also Tanner, *Stonewall in the Valley*, 265.

89. Richard N. Current et al., eds., *Encyclopedia of the Confederacy* (New York, 1993), 2:529–30.

90. Howard, *Recollections*, 114–15.

91. *Philadelphia Weekly Times*, Feb. 11, 1882. Boteler's recollections appeared anew in *SHSP*, 40 (1915): 164–70.

92. *Philadelphia Weekly Times*, Feb. 11, 1882. Why Jackson chose the figure 40,000 as the number of men he needed is unknown. Yet such manpower was just not there. With every Confederate soldier east of the Blue Ridge moving into line at Richmond against the massive Union army of George McClellan, Jackson's request for any sizable reinforcements was going to fall on deaf ears.

93. Hotchkiss Journal, May 30, 1862, Reel 1.

94. Alonzo H. Quint, *The Potomac and the Rapidan* (Boston, 1864), 134.

95. *Philadelphia Weekly Times*, Feb. 11, 1862.

96. *OR*, 12: Pt. 1, 682. Captain Shepherd Pryor of the 12th Georgia later described the debacle: "Col. Conner got information that there was a large force comeing against him & close by. he commenced a retreat amediately. before wee got two miles they over took us. the Cavalry charge us [and] took 126 of our men prisonors." The captain added that the regimental officers "ought [to] be Cashiered, no doubt in my mind." Shepherd G. Pryor to Penelope Pryor, June 11 and 13, 1862, Shepherd G. Pryor Collection, University of Georgia. Major Harman was "mortified" at the destruction of badly needed stores. "We had to burn all that was left in the town and abandon those wagons on the road that had been loaded." Harman to Asher W. Harman, May 31, 1862, Reel 39, Hotchkiss—LC. See also *CV,* 23 (1915): 437, and William Allen to Asher Harman, May 31, 1862, Eldridge Collection, Henry E. Huntington Library, for more details on the rout of the Georgians.

97. This version of the meeting between Jackson and Conner is an amalgamation of two accounts: Hotchkiss Journal, May 30, 1862, Reel 1, and Wells J. Hawks to Jedediah Hotchkiss, Jan. 17, 1866, Jackson—NYHS. Ewell once observed that Conner "was a brave man, but thrown off his balance by responsibility." *OR*, 12: Pt. 1, 793.

98. *Philadelphia Weekly Times*, Feb. 11, 1882.

99. Hotchkiss Journal, May 31, 1862, Reel 1.

100. Jedediah Hotchkiss to Abner C. Hopkins, Sept. 2, 1896, Reel 13, Hotchkiss—LC. According to Boteler, Jackson subsequently commented that if Fremont and Shields sealed the valley route, "I should have fallen back into Maryland for reinforcements." *Philadelphia Weekly Times*, Feb. 11, 1882. One has to conclude that Boteler's recollections for once were faulty. Jackson had no reason to believe that Maryland would be sympathetic to his presence. The origin of this incident may have been a newspaper report that Jackson had invaded Maryland. *Richmond Daily Dispatch*, May 30, 1862.

101. *OR,* 12: Pt. 1, 535, 636.

102. Henry Kyd Douglas to Tippie Boteler, July 24, 1862, Henry Kyd Douglas Letters, Duke. Benjamin Brooke, a local Methodist minister, recorded in his diary that "Stonewall Jackson went through Winchester this morning on Old Sorrell, his darky at his heels." Brooke Journal, Handley.

103. Douglas, *I Rode with Stonewall,* 66.

104. *OR,* 12: Pt. 3, 295.

105. Ibid., Pt. 1, 10–11, 295, 643–49, 682–83. More on Fremont's beguiling movements is in Tracy, "Fremont's Pursuit," 173–83. No sense of speed or urgency existed in the ranks of either Shields's or Fremont's forces. See Davis, *Thirteenth Massachusetts,* 74–77; Bromley Diary, May 30, 1862, OHS. Hampering the efforts of other elements of McDowell's command marching to the valley was equipment. Each soldier was carrying about sixty pounds, mostly in the knapsack. On a single day's march, 150 members of a single Federal regiment collapsed along the roadside. A Confederate prisoner commented to one of his heavily supplied captors, "You uns is pack mules, we uns is race horses." Rufus R. Dawes, *Service with the Sixth Wisconsin Volunteers* (Marietta, Ohio, 1890), 45–47.

106. Kyd Douglas, in *Annals of the War,* 649.

107. Charles W. Trueheart to Henry Trueheart, July 7, 1862, Trueheart Papers.

108. G. Campbell Brown to mother, May 30, 1862, Polk, Brown and Ewell Family Papers. See also *Richmond Daily Dispatch,* June 11, 1862.

109. *Philadelphia Weekly Times,* Feb. 11, 1882. When Ewell received Jackson's orders to move against Fremont, the irascible division chief sent copies to his brigade commanders with the endorsement: "As we ought to be in front instead of in rear, it is hoped the within order will be carried out, so as to be in motion by the earliest dawn." The general who once wailed "I never saw one of Jackson's couriers approach without expecting an order to assault the North Pole!" was now using such Jackson phrases as "earliest dawn." Henderson, 1:438; *OR,* 12: Pt. 3, 904.

110. Avirett, *Memoirs,* 209.

111. *OR,* 12: Pt. 1, 14, 708.

112. Frye, *Second Virginia,* 27–28; McKim, *Recollections,* 108; Douglas, *I Rode with Stonewall,* 70. Chaplain Abner Hopkins of the 2d Virginia put Winder's departure time on June 1 at 7 A.M., yet Winder himself stated that he arose at 3 A.M. and started his men in motion at 5:30 on a "rainy disagreeable morning." Abner C. Hopkins to Jedediah Hotchkiss, Aug. 26, 1896, Reel 13, Hotchkiss—LC; Winder Diary, June 1, 1862.

113. Lyle, "Sketches," 275

114. McCabe, *Jackson,* 47.

115. Neese, *Horse Artillery,* 64; A. S. Pendleton to mother, June 1, 1862, Pendleton Papers. Tanner, *Stonewall in the Valley,* 275, is correct in concluding that Jackson's "genius" in these movements actually consisted of following a logical route with foresight and determination. General William B. Taliaferro, a master of hindsight, wrote later that "invincible pluck and push" saved Jackson at Strasburg. "It seemed like a miracle—his escape from dangers which other men would have avoided, but which he seemed to delight to push himself into. The result proved that what his officers often thought rashness was close calculation, based upon factors which they did not possess." William B. Taliaferro, "Reminiscences of Stonewall Jackson," William B. Taliaferro Papers, W&M, 10.

116. Captain Samuel B. Coyner of the 7th Virginia Cavalry was in charge of the destruction of the White House and Columbia bridges. His men and mounts were exhausted when they began the fifteen-mile ride through pouring rain to the South Fork of the Shenandoah. Coyner recalled: "While enroute we were obliged to wait the fury of the storm, and for sometime afterward could only see how to go by flashes of lightning. My men clung like children to a parent." *CV,* 3 (1895): 141.

117. Jedediah Hotchkiss to Holmes Conrad, Sept. 8, 1896, Reel 34, Hotchkiss—LC; *OR,* 12: Pt. 1, 651, 711–12, 721. For other details of this action, see pp. 650, 730–31; Taylor, *Destruction and Reconstruction,* 67–68.

118. Strother, *Virginia Yankee*, 55. Jackson reported his casualties as 400 men, while Dabney subsequently computed losses at 613 soldiers. *OR*, 12: Pt. 1, 708; Dabney, 390.

119. Mrs. Jackson, 268–69.

120. Douglas, *I Rode with Stonewall*, 71.

121. Patton, "Reminiscences of Jackson," VHS. This well-known quotation regrettably appears at various times and in slightly altered versions throughout Jackson studies. Dabney, 397, had it being said at the correct time. Surgeon McGuire thought that Jackson's statement came at Port Republic. Colonel Edwin Hobson of the 5th Alabama was certain Jackson uttered a similar remark during the September 1862 investment of Harpers Ferry. McGuire also reported an almost identical quotation on the night of the victory at Fredericksburg. *SHSP*, 9 (1881): 277; 25 (1897): 104–5; Chambers, 1:563.

122. TJJ to Joseph E. Johnston, June 2, 1862, Thomas J. Jackson Manuscripts, Princeton University.

123. Throughout that week, relations between Shields and Fremont remained chilly. The former complained of his own division: "Too many men, no supplies." As for his fellow commander, Shields grumbled, "we would have occupied Strasburg, but dare not interfere with what was designed for Fremont. His failure has saved Jackson." *OR*, 12: Pt. 3, 322. For examples of Shields's frustrations, see *OR*, 12: Pt. 3, 325, 334, 360.

124. James Dinwiddie to mother, June 4, Dinwiddie Family Papers, UVA; Edmondson, *My Dear Emma*, 97. See also Macon, *Reminiscences*, 149–50.

125. *OR*, 12: Pt. 3, 905.

CHAPTER 15   *Victory in the Valley*

1. *OR*, 12: Pt. 1, 718–19; Hotchkiss Journal, June 4, 1862, Reel 1, Hotchkiss—LC.

2. Watkins Kearns Diary, June 5, 1862, BV 186, FSNMP.

3. *OR*, 12: Pt. 3, 906; John A. Harman to Asher W. Harman, June 5, 1862, Reel 39, Hotchkiss—LC.

4. Bean, "Harman," 7.

5. G. D. Camden to Robert L. Dabney, Nov. 25, 1863, Box 19, Dabney—SHC; Henderson, 1:425–27; Winder Diary, June 5, 1862, MHS. Hotchkiss prepared a memo showing that in a three-week period from mid-May through the first week in June, McClellan's Army of the Potomac traveled twenty miles up the Virginia peninsula while Jackson's men tramped 200 miles through the valley. Reel 39, Hotchkiss—LC. See also Blackford, *Mine Eyes*, 192–93.

6. *Annals of the War*, 649. For example, a Richmond newspaper happily speculated: "We know of no man who may be left so entirely to his own devices without apprehension on the part of his friends. . . . The enemy understand him better than his friends, and they will be cautious with him where they should be bold with another." *Richmond Daily Dispatch*, June 6, 1862.

7. John A. Harman to Asher W. Harman, June 6, 1862, Reel 39, Hotchkiss—LC.

8. *OR*, 12: Pt. 3, 906–7.

9. *OR*, 12: Pt. 3, 907.

10. *OR*, 12: Pt. 1, 652, 732; William A. McClendon, *Recollections of War Time* (Montgomery, Ala., 1909), 64; *SHSP*, 10 (1882): 103–4. First Sgt. Holmes Conrad of the 1st Virginia Cavalry took credit for the capture of Wyndham. Conrad to Jedediah Hotchkiss, Sept. 5, 1896, Reel 34, Hotchkiss—LC. Wyndham survived the Civil War, later commanded the army of the King of Burma, and died in Rangooon from the crash of a reconnaissance balloon he had built.

11. H. Kyd Douglas to Tippie Boteler, July 24, 1862, Henry Kyd Douglas Letters, Duke University. For good accounts of the details surrounding Ashby's death, see Thomas T. Munford to Jedediah Hotchkiss, Aug. 19, 1896, Reel 13, Hotchkiss—LC; Avirett, *Memoirs*, 221–23. A strong likelihood exists that in the heat of battle, Ashby was accidentally shot by one of his own men. See Thomas Green Penn, 42d Virginia, to brother, June 8, 1862, Green W. Penn Papers, Duke; Hotchkiss Journal, June 6, 1862, Reel 1; Vandiver, 517. A photograph of the dead Ashby in his coffin is in the Chicago Historical Society.

12. Hotchkiss Journal, June 6, 1862, Reel 1; Dabney, 401. See also Douglas, *I Rode with*

Stonewall, 81. Charles W. Trueheart of the Rockbridge Artillery (and later a Confederate surgeon) wrote a month after Ashby's death that the cavalryman "was strictly moral and temperate; read & revered the Bible which he always carried with him. He seldom, if ever, made use of profane language; was highly polished in his manners, & admired & respected by everyone. . . . No man has killed with his own hand as many of the enemy." Charles W. Trueheart to Henry Trueheart, July 7, 1862, Trueheart Papers, Galevston, Tex. The remains of the cavalryman were first buried in Charlottesville; after the war they were removed to Winchester.

13. Unless otherwise stated, all Jackson quotations on the action at Cross Keys and Port Republic are from his after-action manuscript report, Jackson—NYHS. The printed version of that report is in *OR*, 12: Pt. 1, 711–16. Colonel Charles J. Faulkner composed most of Jackson's battle reports the following winter. He used materials at hand, with Jackson closely scrutinizing every paragraph. That was wise, for Faulkner could be overly eloquent as well as verbose. One passage relative to Ashby and deleted by Jackson in the final draft stated: "As a soldier he was without reproach. As a Field officer his defect was a want of just appreciation & proper enforcement of discipline amongst his men. Looking back to the aid which I derived from his invaluable services I may be allowed to mingle my sorrows with those of the nation at the fall of this noble champion of his Country's Independence." Jackson never voiced criticism of a Confederate officer who fell in battle. His several problems with Ashby vanished from Jackson's mind with Ashby's death.

14. Winder Diary, June 7, 1862; A. S. Pendleton to mother, June 7, 1862, William Nelson Pendleton Papers, SHC.

15. Jackson mentioned none of these oversights in his report. See also Samuel J. C. Moore, "Jackson's Narrow Escape," manuscript, Robert A. Brock Collection, Henry E. Huntington Library.

16. *OR*, 12: Pt. 1, 686–87; Pt. 3, 316–17.

17. Allan, *Shenandoah Valley Campaign*, 147; *SHSP*, 11 (1883): 146.

18. *OR*, 12: Pt. 3, 907–8. In later years, Hotchkiss was emphatic in his belief that the general and his staff were riding down Port Republic's main street when the enemy opened fire and fell on his rear. Jedediah Hotchkiss to G. F. R. Henderson, May 23, 1895, Reel 11, Hotchkiss—LC. However, Hotchkiss earlier—as well as writers subsequently—had Jackson starting toward the village on foot after gunfire began. Hotchkiss Journal, June 8, 1862, Reel 1, *ibid.*; Allan, *Shenandoah Valley Campaign*, 148; Freeman, *Lee's Lieutenants*, 1:439.

19. A number of legends arose with time over this June 8 episode. One myth had Jackson stopping in the middle of his ride through town to admonish Surg. McGuire, who was cursing ambulance drivers trying to flee to safety. Hunter McGuire to Jedediah Hotchkiss, May 28, 1896, Reel 12, Hotchkiss—LC. Another and more quoted bit of romanticism is that Jackson galloped past one of the Union cannon and shouted cease-fire orders to the crew, who obeyed the instructions with alacrity. One "eyewitness" even had Jackson "taking across the fields on foot." See Harvey Black to wife, June 10, 1862, Harvey Black Letters, Virginia Tech; Mooney Reminiscences, Grinnan Family Papers, VHS; Charles W. Trueheart to Henry Trueheart, July 7, 1862, Trueheart Papers; McCabe, *Jackson*, 57.

20. Willis's account of his experiences that day is in *SHSP*, 17 (1889): 172–77.

21. See Robert H. Moore II, *The Charlottesville, Lee, Lynchburg and Johnson's Bedford Artillery* (Lynchburg, Va., 1990), 5–10; L. W. Cox to Jedediah Hotchkiss, Aug. 17, 1896, Reel 13, Hotchkiss—LC.

22. Captain Moore and another member of the 2d Virginia bitterly resented Dabney taking credit in his biography of Jackson for blunting the Union move on the Kemper estate. All accolades, the two soldiers asserted, belonged exclusively to Moore's little band and Carrington's gunners. Dabney, 411; Moore, "Jackson's Narrow Escape"; Gold, *Clarke County*, 175–76.

23. Poague, *Gunner with Stonewall*, 26.

24. *OR*, 12: Pt. 1, 739; Taylor, *Destruction and Reconstruction*, 81.

25. Howard, *Recollections*, 122; Moore, *Cannoneer*, 68–69; *SHSP*, 43 (1920): 271.

26. Diary of an unidentified soldier in the 37th Virginia, William Couper Papers, VMI; Wood, *The War*, 59–60.

27. William B. Taliaferro, "Reminiscences of Stonewall Jackson," William B. Taliaferro Papers, W&M, 13. A typographical error in the printed version of Jackson's report identified Fulkerson's regiment as the 57th Virginia.

28. Sentimental legend cropped up again at this point in the action. Both Dabney, 411, and Mrs. Jackson, 265, claimed that Jackson "placed himself at the head of the leading regiment . . . and rushed at double-quick towards the bridge." In a marginal note in his copy of Anna Jackson's memoirs, Kyd Douglas wrote: "He didn't do any such thing. Jackson sat on his horse on the hill" and watched the action. Henry Kyd Douglas Library, Antietam NBP.

29. Harvey Black to wife, June 10, 1862, Harvey Black Letters. Federal Col. Carroll reported that before his infantry force could arrive in support, his cavalry "broke and ran in every direction by which they could secure a retreat." Carroll put his losses at nine killed and thirty-one wounded, plus two cannon abandoned. *OR*, 12: Pt. 1, 698–99. One disgruntled Federal stated, "We had Jackson in a box with the lid on, but he kicked the bottom out and got away." *CV*, 6 (1898): 419.

30. Samuel Fulkerson File, MC; Recollections of Chaplain Alexander B. Carrington, 37th Virginia, Box 19, Dabney—SHC.

31. *OR*, 12: Pt. 1, 712; Colt, *Defend the Valley*, 158.

32. Generally lost in accounts of Cross Keys is the poor condition of Fremont's army at the time. Thomas Evans of the 25th Ohio wrote in his diary early on June 8: "We had marched 146 miles through mud and weather, wet and cold, oftentimes enduring intolerable suffering and exposure. We had left Franklin with 25 thousand troops, the flower of the U.S. Army. We were now reduced by exposure, fatigue and sickness to half that number. With this weather beaten army we must disperse Jackson's veteran host." Thomas Evans Diary, OHS.

33. A spent rifle ball hit Elzey and incapacitated him for a short period. Steuart was struck in the shoulder by grape shot and knocked out of action for the next six months. *OR*, 12: Pt. 3, 782; Gill, *Reminiscences*, 60.

34. *OR*, 12: Pt. 1, 797–98. See also Howard, *Recollections*, 125.

35. *OR*, 12: Pt. 1, 798.

36. Jedediah Hotchkiss to G. F. R. Henderson, Apr. 26, 1895, Reel 11, Hotchkiss—LC. To his credit, Richard Ewell was void of overriding ambition. He gave praise freely where praise was due. On the day after Cross Keys, Ewell told Thomas Munford that Trimble was "the hero of yesterday's fight. . . . They will call it mine, but Trimble won the fight; and I believe now if I had followed his views we would have destroyed Fremont's army." *SHSP*, 7 (1879): 530.

37. *OR*, 12: Pt. 1, 165, 784, 795–99. One of the more revealing personal accounts of Cross Keys is in G. Campbell Brown, "Military Reminiscences," TSLA, 48–53. In later years on the banquet circuit, Dr. McGuire told of Jackson saying to Ewell early that day: "Let the Yankees get very close before your infantry fires. They won't stand long." *SHSP*, 25 (1897): 95.

38. Winder Diary, June 8, 1862.

39. Mrs. Jackson, 276–77; Howard, *Recollections*, 123–24.

40. *SHSP*, 11 (1883): 153–55; Dabney, 418.

41. Harvey Black to wife, June 10, 1862, Harvey Black Letters; Wood, *The War*, 60; Howard, *Recollections*, 124.

42. Dabney, 415.

43. Douglas, *I Rode with Stonewall*, 89; Jackson manuscript report.

44. Hotchkiss Journal, Apr. 4, 1863, Reel 1.

45. The Ewell-Munford exchange given here is a blend of two accounts. One is in the Thomas T. Munford manuscript, Munford-Ellis Family Papers, Duke. The other version, which Munford thought occurred the following night, is in *SHSP*, 7 (1879): 530. A staple of local folklore in the Port Republic area is that Jackson transferred his headquarters on the night of June 8–9 to the two-story home of Stephen Harnsberger in the village. Wayland, *Stonewall Jackson's Way*, 152–53; *Harrisonburg Daily News-Record*, Feb. 22, 1992. Hotchkiss, who meticulously recorded the location of every bivouac and every headquarters, stated that Jackson returned in the evening to the Kemper home.

46. Taliaferro, "Reminiscences," 15.

47. Dabney, 419; Mrs. Jackson, 279.

48. John M. Patton, "Reminiscences of Jackson," Patton Family Papers, VHS.

49. Ibid. Henderson, 1:377, gave only a partial citation for Jackson's assertion, and it contained a typographical error. The correct reference should have been *SHSP,* 9 (1881): 362. Dabney, 421–22, is the original source of the story that J. William Jones retold in *SHSP.* Captain Edward Alfriend of the 44th Virginia wrote a garbled version of the Jackson-Patton exchange and ended with Jackson putting his time of arrival at 10:30 A.M. Alfriend, "Recollections," 586.

50. See Douglas, *I Rode with Stonewall,* 40, 234; D. H. Hill, in *Century Magazine,* 47 (1893–94): 625. Surgeon McGuire made the charming observation: "Many a night I have kept him on his horse by holding on to his coat-tail. He always promised to do as much for me when he had finished his nap. He meant to do it, I am sure, but my turn never came." *SHSP,* 19 (1891): 313.

51. Most Jackson biographers have him awakened before daybreak on June 9 by Col. John D. Imboden of the Partisan Rangers. Imboden's popular account is so manufactured and inflated that it simply cannot be accepted as approaching truthfulness. See *B&L,* 2:293–94. At one point, Imboden had Jackson referring to "Charley Winder" and "Dick Taylor." This provoked an outburst from Kyd Douglas, who wrote in the margin of his copy of *B&L:* "General Jackson never said Charley Winder; he was always on dignified terms with him, nor did [he] ever say Dick Taylor. The fact is the General was never on familiar terms with any officer of any rank. He often spoke to and of Sandy Pendleton but to no one else in that way; he did not know how to do it." Douglas Library.

52. For more on the bridge and the obstacle it became, see Dabney, 419–21; *SHSP,* 7 (1879): 529–30; Worsham, *Foot Cavalry,* 50. Dabney's attempt to blame Jackson's uncoordinated attacks solely on the makeshift bridge is a rationale that rings hollow.

53. *OR,* 12: Pt. 1, 691, 697. Despite the fact that Jackson surveyed a battle ground with the eye of an artillerist, he apparently assumed that no more than one or two Federal cannon were in place atop the spur overlooking the valley. See Hotchkiss to Henderson, May 23, 1895.

54. *OR,* 12: Pt. 1, 740, 745, 747; Detroit newspaper clipping in LHAC, 55-B.

55. Oates, *The War,* 104.

56. Taylor, *Destruction and Reconstruction,* 74; Oates, *The War,* 104; Capt. Daniel A. Wilson, undated letter, LHAC, 55-B; Hotchkiss to Henderson, May 23, 1895.

57. *OR,* 12: Pt. 1, 728, 760, 785–86. John D. Imboden enjoyed relating the story of Jackson galloping onto the field as his old brigade was being pounded into pieces. The men cheered their general, who responded by shouting: "The Stonewall Brigade never retreats! Follow me!" Jackson then personally led the soldiers back through the gunfire to their original position. *B&L,* 2:295–96. No other source mentions such extraordinary behavior by Jackson in this battle.

58. Winder Diary, June 9, 1862.

59. Captain G. Campbell Brown, one of Ewell's aides, overstated the situation when he wrote his mother five days after the engagement that "each Regiment and each Brigade" in Jackson's division "was hurried into the fight as it came up, without being allowed time to form or to collect a large body & make a strong simultaneous attack. The consequence was that when our Divn. came up, three or four Brigades having been successively sent up against a force of Yankees just strong enough to whip them, our whole force previously engaged was in full retreat from the field, having suffered heavily." Polk, Brown and Ewell Family Papers, SHC.

60. Unidentified July 7, 1897, newspaper clipping, S. Joseph Bershtein Collection, Clarksburg, W.Va., Public Library.

61. Jackson manuscript report. One of the improbable accounts associated with Port Republic had Taylor leaving his brigade in the midst of his fight and riding to Jackson to report on the progress of the battle at the coaling. Jackson asked the Louisianian how the action was going. To the shock of the pious Jackson, Taylor replied, "It is Nip and Tuck, General, but I'll be damned if I don't think Tuck has got it!" Taliaferro, "Reminiscences," 15. When Chief of Staff Dabney later criticized Taylor's vacillating fight at the coaling, Hotchkiss sent an angry response. See Jededish Hotchkiss to Robert L. Dabney, July 27, 1897, Reel 14, Hotchkiss—LC.

62. Wood, *The War*, 63–64. Douglas asserted that Jackson met Ewell at this point and exclaimed, "General, he who does not see the hand of God in this is blind, Sir, blind!" *I Rode with Stonewall*, 94. Actually, Jackson would make that statement on the night after the opening day's fighting at Second Manassas. He uttered the words to Surg. McGuire, a far more reliable source than Douglas.

63. Writing in 1882, a Union soldier who signed his name "M. D." stated that at first he and his compatriots fell back foot by foot. Soon they "faced about for Luray and acknowledged defeat. It was not panic, but Shields was routed. He was punished for a couple of miles and then left to pursue his way towards the Potomac with only cavalry to sting his rear-guards and keep him going." LHAC, 55-B.

64. Jackson's manuscript report, in Jackson—NYHS, is at variance about the length of the pursuit with the printed version of the report in *OR*, 12: Pt. 1, 715. The manuscript summary stated that two infantry brigades followed Tyler for five miles, with Munford's cavalry continuing the chase for another three miles. Winder was of the opinion that his brigade marched four miles before being ordered to halt and turn around. Winder Diary, June 9, 1862.

65. Alexander, Military Memoirs, 107; Hotchkiss Journal, June 9, 1862, Reel 1. Fremont's own admission of the unnecessary artillery fire is in *OR*, 12: Pt. 1, 22–23. A member of Fremont's staff strongly opposed turning the guns on the ambulances. See Tracy, "Fremont's Pursuit," 342.

66. George K. Harlow to Father, June 13, 1862, Harlow Family Papers, VHS; *OR*, 12: Pt. 1, 690, 717–18.

67. TJJ to Gen. Samuel Cooper, June 9, 1862, MC; TJJ to Anna Jackson, June 9, 1862, Davis—Tulane. In his first official report, filed June 11, Jackson continued to give few details but to offer all credit to God. "Early on Monday morning, the 9th, I attacked the Federals on the east side of the river, and after about four and a half hours' hard fighting the same Providence which had so blessed us on Sunday completely routed the enemy." *OR*, 12: Pt. 1, 711.

68. Taliaferro, "Reminiscences," 11–12.

69. *OR*, 12: Pt. 1, 24, 655; Susan A. Riggs, *Twenty-first Virginia Infantry* (Lynchburg, Va., 1991), 15.

70. "Sexton Memoirs," OHS, 135.

71. Gordon, *Brook Farm*, 264.

72. A quarter-century later, Col. Thomas T. Munford sought in vain to convince his compatriots that Lee masterminded the valley campaign and that Jackson merely executed in a spectacular degree plans developed by Lee. See Thomas T. Munford to R. A. Brock, Oct. 6, 1891, and Feb. 11, 1892, Brock Collection, Huntington.

73. William A. Lyman statement, LHAC, 55-B; *New York Times*, June 16, 1862.

74. Kearns Diary, June 15, 1862, BV 186, FSNMP.

75. See Tanner, *Stonewall in the Valley*, 309.

76. *B&L*, 2:297.

77. Alexander, *Fighting for the Confederacy*, 94; Field Marshal Viscount Wolseley, *The American Civil War: An English View* (Charlottesville, Va., 1964), 129.

78. McCabe, *Jackson*, 61.

79. Thomas R. Wade, Jr., to Louisa Hopkins, June 14, 1862, Wade Letters, Lewis Leigh Collection, USMHI; Robert Edward Lee Strider, *The Life and Work of George William Peterkin* (Philadelphia, 1929), 279; Shepherd G. Pryor to Penelope Pryor, June 11, 1862, Shepherd Green Pryor Collection, University of Georgia.

80. John M. Brown Reminiscences, University of Texas.

81. *Macon Daily Telegraph* [Ga.], June 27, 1862; Casler, *Stonewall Brigade*, 92, 94.

82. V. W. Southall to mother, June 14, 1862, Valentine W. Southall Letters, Harrisburg Civil War Round Table Collection, USMHI.

83. Wood, *The War*, 66; D. H. Hill to Isabella M. Hill, June 10, 1862, Daniel Harvey Hill Papers, USMHI. See also George P. King to Virgie King, June 14, 1862, LHAC, 55-C.

84. Slaughter, *Randolph Fairfax,* 34.

85. Statement of unidentified soldier, LHAC, 55–B; Robert H. Miller, "Letters of Lieutenant Robert H. Miller to His Family, 1861–1862," VMHB, 70 (1962): 83.

86. *Richmond Daily Dispatch,* June 11, 1862. For similar newspaper praise, see *Richmond Whig,* June 11, 1862; *Richmond Daily Dispatch,* June 14, 1862; *Richmond Examiner,* June 17, 1862.

87. Addey, *Jackson,* 92–93.

88. Buck, *With the Old Confeds,* 39.

89. Mrs. Jackson, 283.

90. *OR,* 12: Pt. 3, 909; TJJ to Gen. James Shields, June 11, 1862, Box 20, Dabney—SHC.

91. TJJ to Gen. Samuel Cooper, June 10, 1862, Compiled Service Records: Generals, Staff Officers, and Nonregimental Enlisted Men, RG109, NA.

92. Alfriend, "Recollections," 584–85.

93. TJJ to Thomas T. Munford, June 13, 1862, Brock Collection; *OR,* 12: Pt. 1, 716, 732. For a detailed (and highly dramatic) account of the Southern cavalry movements at the time, see Thomas T. Munford to Robert L. Dabney, Dec. 31, 1865, Box 19, Dabney—SHC. Little attention has been given to the Union army in the days after Port Republic. General Carl Schurz made an inspection at President Lincoln's behest. Schurz's report—previously unpublished—stated in part: "The men have had some rest and feel better, but still the spirit of the army is not what it ought to be. . . . The army is weaker than I supposed when I wrote you [earlier]. . . . Fatigue and sickness has decimated our ranks fearfully. Most of the hospitals are said to be in shocking condition. . . . Hunger and want seems to operate as a danger on heroism." Carl Schurz to Abraham Lincoln, June 16, 1862, Civil War Collection, Henry E. Huntington Library. See also *OR,* 12: Pt. 3, 368.

94. Jackson Letterbook, June 13, 1862, Reel 49, Hotchkiss—LC. Jackson delegated his chief of staff, the Rev. Dabney, to compose a congratulatory order to the army. The cleric, as he had done after McDowell, produced a document with soaring prose. "The fortitude of the troops under fatigue and their valour in action have again under the blessing of Divine Providence, placed it in the power of the Commanding General to congratulate them upon the victories of June 8th and 9th inst. Beset on both flanks by two powerful and boastful armies, you have escaped their toils, inflicting successively crushing blows on each of your pursuers. Let a few more such efforts be made, and you may confidently hope that our beautiful valley will be cleaned from the pollution of the Invader's presence." With that, Dabney humbly announced "a season of thanksgiving" and a "divine service" for the following day. Orders No. 58, June 13, 1862, Eldridge Collection, Henry E. Huntington Library.

95. *The Land We Love,* 1 (1866): 311–12.

96. Wells J. Hawks to Jedediah Hotchkiss, Jan. 17, 1866, Jackson—NYHS.

97. Chambers, 1:589–90; TJJ to Anna Jackson, June 14, 1862, Dabney—LVA.

98. Samuel V. Fulkerson to unknown addressee, June 14, 1862, Fulkerson File.

99. Hotchkiss Journal, Apr. 15, 1863, Reel 1; John A. Harman to Asher Harman, June 13, 1862, Reel 39, Hotchkiss—LC.

100. John A. Harman to Asher Harman, June 14, 1862, Reel 39, Hotchkiss—LC.

101. Taylor, *Destruction and Reconstruction,* 78–79. Mysteriously, the chronicler of Winder's staff, McHenry Howard, overlooked the confrontation between Winder and Jackson in his recollections of the war. Winder at times could be as inflexible as his superior. That summer he had a "misunderstanding" with the youthful and usually mild-mannered Dunkard, Col. John F. Neff of the 33d Virginia. Winder promptly placed Neff under arrest. Walker, *VMI Memorial,* 403; *Civil War Times,* 3 (Feb. 1962): 17. Douglas considered Jackson and Winder cut from the same mold. "At first their relations were not very cordial and each certainly underrated the other; in many ways, they were too much alike to fit exactly." *I Rode with Stonewall,* 125.

102. *OR,* 12: Pt. 3, 906; William Allan, "Conversations with Lee," William Allan Papers, SHC; Lee, *Wartime Papers,* 183–84, 187.

103. Lee, *Wartime Papers,* 188.

104. *OR,* 11: Pt. 3, 584, 594; 12: Pt. 3, 910.

105. Henderson, 1:391; Charles Marshall, *An Aide-de-Camp of Lee* (Boston, 1927), 84; *OR,* 11:

Pt. 23, 590. Typically, the *Richmond Daily Dispatch* of June 18, 1862, broadcast the troop movements. "It is no longer a secret that heavy reinforcements have been sent to 'Stonewall' Jackson, in the Valley, and that he now has an army sufficiently large to cope with any force that can be brought against him by the enemy. . . . Jackson now has as many men as he wants."

106. For example, see Allan, "Conversations with Lee"; Marshall, *Aide-de-Camp*, 84.

107. Lee, *Wartime Papers*, 193.

108. *Philadelphia Weekly Times*, Feb. 11, 1882.

109. Boteler Memorandum, Dabney—LVA; *SHSP*, 40 (1915): 173–74.

110. Lee, *Wartime Papers*, 194.

111. *OR*, 12: Pt. 1, 680; Pt. 3, 913. For Munford's activities, see Dabney, 432–34. Contrary to several postwar statements by Munford, the cavalry chief did not know Jackson's plans for the move to Richmond until sometime on June 16. Allan, *Valley Campaign*, 170, stated that Jackson met Munford at Mt. Sidney the following night. That is untrue. Jackson sent Hotchkiss with instructions for the cavalryman. Hotchkiss to Henderson, May 23, 1895.

112. *OR*, 12: Pt. 3, 914; *B&L*, 2:296–97.

113. *B&L*, 2:297. Imboden reported these events happening five days before they actually did. Field Marshal Wolseley reacted sharply when he later read Whiting's remarks. "The vanity of small-minded subordinates," the British army commander declared, "makes them long to be consulted in the plans under consideration." Whiting "allowed his personal vanity" to get the best of him. Wolseley, *American Civil War*, 131. Douglas considered Whiting a "quick-tempered" officer who "expressed his disgust very freely." *I Rode with Stonewall*, 96.

114. L. A. Fesperman to J. J. Fesperman, June 15, 1862, Caleb Hampton Papers, Duke.

115. G. W. Nichols, *A Soldier's Story of His Regiment* (Kennesaw, Ga., 1961), 41.

116. TJJ to Thomas T. Munford, June 17, 1862, Brock Collection.

117. Myers, *The Comanches*, 72–73. The same basic story first appeared in McCabe, *Jackson*, 63–64.

118. Jedediah Hotchkiss to William L. Chase, Mar. 28, 1892, Reel 9, Hotchkiss—LC; Hotchkiss memo of June 17 activities, Reel 39, Hotchkiss—LC.

119. McClendon, *Recollections of War Time*, 69–70.

120. Hotchkiss Journal, June 18, 1862, Reel 1.

121. Ibid.; William S. White Statement, Box 20, Dabney—SHC.

CHAPTER 16   *Fatigue*

1. Hotchkiss Journal, June 19, 1862, Reel 1, Hotchkiss—LC.

2. By the end of the war, Maj. Dabney thought that the hotel meeting was in Charlottesville. Dabney, 434. Douglas asserted that Jackson remained at Mechum's River Station only fifteen minutes, "and shaking hands all around and saying good-by as earnestly as if he was off for Europe, he departed and gave no sign." *I Rode with Stonewall*, 97. This interesting portrayal has only the factual base that Douglas implied.

3. *SHSP*, 40 (1915): 176–77. The memorandum that Jackson dictated is printed verbatim on pp. 177–78.

4. Ibid., 176–77.

5. Henry A. Chambers Diary, June 19, 1862, NCDAH.

6. TJJ to Robert E. Lee, July 25, 1862, Jackson—Duke; Angus J. Johnston III, *Virginia Railroads in the Civil War* (Chapel Hill, 1961), 60.

7. *Philadelphia Weekly Times*, Feb. 11, 1882; Hunter McGuire to Jedediah Hotchkiss, Mar. 30, 1896, Reel 12, Hotchkiss—LC; Buck, *With the Old Confeds*, 40. See also Worsham, *Foot Cavalry*, 54, for secrecy surrounding the march, and *CV*, 32 (1924): 469, for weariness in the ranks. John Casler of the Stonewall Brigade probably stretched the truth when he wrote: "As there were not trains enough for all, our old brigade had to march, as we had gained the name this time of 'Jackson's Foot Cavalry.' We could break down any cavalry brigade on a long march." Casler, *Stonewall Brigade*, 86–87.

8. Some historians have criticized Jackson for not proceeding by train nonstop to Richmond for a conference with Lee. For example, see Alexander, *Military Memoirs*, 115; Farwell, *Stonewall*, 338. Those writers overlook at least three factors: Lee had not requested Jackson to come to Richmond with all haste; the Virginia Central line had been broken west of the capital and was unusable between Louisa Court House and Hanover Junction; June 22 was a Sunday and, unless directed otherwise, Jackson kept the Sabbath holy by suspending military operations.

9. Gill, *Reminiscences*, 63; D. B. Ewing to Robert L. Dabney, Sept. 8, 1863, Dabney—UVA. Ewing claimed that Jackson did not leave Gordonsville until 10 P.M. on Sunday. According to the minister, the general received a telegram, read it by candlelight, and said only, "I must go." However, the weight of evidence points to Jackson departing Gordonsville the previous day. Many Federal officers thought they knew where Jackson was at the time, but no one could pinpoint his exact location. *OR*, 12: Pt. 3, 419–25, 428, 434, 440.

10. See Douglas, *I Rode with Stonewall*, 98.

11. J. William Jones Memorandum, Reel 39, Hotchkiss—LC; *SHSP*, 19 (1891): 150. Jackson's host was the son of Frederick Harris, first president of the Louisa Railroad and the man for whom Fredericks Hall was named.

12. See *B&L*, 2:350; Mrs. Jackson, 291; Henderson, 1:396; Alfred E. Doby to Elizabeth K. Doby, June 23, 1862, Means-English-Doby Papers, University of South Carolina. Two members of Jackson's staff thought that only a single courier went to Richmond with Jackson. Dabney, 435; McGuire to Hotchkiss, Mar. 30, 1896.

13. Letter signed "Calvin" to Hector McNeill, June 1862, Hector H. McNeill Papers, Duke University.

14. Five members of Lee's class also had unscathed behavior records at the academy. Emory M. Thomas, *Robert E. Lee, A Biography* (New York, 1995), 49.

15. William Stanley Hoole, *Lawley Covers the Confederacy* (Tuscaloosa, Ala., 1964), 31.

16. John Wetmore Hinsdale Diary, June 28, 1862, Hinsdale Family Papers, Duke.

17. See James I. Robertson, Jr., *General A. P. Hill* (New York, 1987), 11–12.

18. Hopley, *"Stonewall" Jackson*, 102. A member of Lee's staff observed that Jackson "presented the same tall, gaunt awkward figure and the rusty gray dress and still rustier gray forage-cap by which he was distinguished from the spruce young officers under him." Armistead L. Long, *Memoirs of Robert E. Lee* (New York, 1886), 263.

19. *B&L*, 2:347–48; Longstreet, *From Manassas to Appomattox*, 121–22; Dec. 17, 1868, conversation between R. E. Lee and William Allan, William Allan Papers, SHC; Marshall, *Aide-de-Camp*, 85. Lee drafted the battle orders the next day. The original copy to Jackson is in Old Catalog Collection, VHS; slightly differing printed versions are in *OR*, 11: Pt. 2, 498–99; Lee, *Wartime Papers*, 198–200.

20. Winder Diary, June 24, 1862, MHS; McGuire to Hotchkiss, Mar. 30, 1896.

21. Freeman, *Lee's Lieutenants*, 1:499. E. Porter Alexander, Lee's chief of ordnance, considered Jackson's advance onto the peninsula as "the cream of the whole campaign." The sluggishness of the valley force on June 24, Alexander concluded, shattered all hope for a quick Confederate victory. Alexander, *Military Memoirs*, 116.

22. Dabney never admitted culpability for the breakdown of the march from Fredericks Hall. Thirty years later, in commenting on Jackson's return to the army on June 24, Dabney stated somewhat petulantly: "Being absolutely reticent he did not tell me *one word* of the instructions just received from Lee; and I do not believe he told anyone." Contrary to Lee's battle plan, Dabney was of the opinion that once Jackson got into position on the Union flank, he was supposed to "make his dispositions so as to strike McClellan a side blow while retiring." Robert L. Dabney to Jedediah Hotchkiss, Mar. 10, 1896, Reel 12, Hotchkiss—LC.

23. Howard, *Recollections*, 134; Jedediah Hotchkiss to G. F. R. Henderson, May 1, 1896, Reel 12, Hotchkiss—LC.

24. Dabney to Hotchkiss, Mar. 10, 1896. A member of Winder's staff remembered the Stonewall Brigade coming to a stream with no bridge and out of its banks. Axemen felled two trees on opposite sides of the river so that they fell parallel across it. The men then balanced themselves precariously as they filed in two lines over the rushing water. Howard, *Recollection*, 135.

25. See *OR,* 11: Pt. 1, 49, 51, 116; Pt. 2, 19.

26. Freeman secured a scrap of the letter and surmised that in it Lee proposed some sort of two-pronged advance by Jackson. *Lee's Lieutenants,* 1:504–5.

27. R. E. Lee to TJJ, June 25, 1862, Davis—Tulane. By then, Jackson had become deeply dependent upon maps—a testimonial to Hotchkiss's able charts and excellent tutoring. Not having either on the peninsula essentially blinded Jackson. Hotchkiss later stated: "Jackson made constant use of all maps. He not only studied the general maps of the country, but made a particular study of those of any region where he might make marches or where he expected to have engagements, constantly using sketch maps made upon the ground to inform him as to portions of the field of operations that did not immediately come under his own observations." Jedediah Hotchkiss to William L. Chase, Mar. 28, 1892, Reel 9, Hotchkiss—LC.

28. Robert L. Dabney to Jedediah Hotchkiss, Sept. 12, 1896, Reel 13, Hotchkiss—LC.

29. Ibid. See also Dabney, 439.

30. Winder Diary, June 26, 1862, MHS.

31. Dabney to Hotchkiss, Mar. 10, 1896; Douglas, *I Rode with Stonewall,* 101.

32. *OR,* 11: Pt. 2, 561; Blackford, *War Years with Jeb Stuart,* 71. The adjutant also noted: "Until after the battles around Richmond, General Jackson was careless about his dress and equipments, and though always clean, his clothes looked as if they formed no part of his thoughts." Ibid. Chambers, 2:34, had the meeting between Jackson and Stuart occurring several hours later than it did.

33. James F. Hendricks Recollections, BV 162, FSNMP.

34. Robert B. Giles to author, Dec. 16, 1991. Jackson's original message to Branch is in MC. A printed version can be found in *OR,* 11: Pt. 3, 620. Branch acknowledged receipt of the message an hour later.

35. Alexander R. Boteler to TJJ, May 15, 1862, Cook—WVU. Branch reported that he put his command immediately in motion after receiving Jackson's note and marched to the north bank of the Chickahominy. *OR,* 11: Pt. 2, 882.

36. TJJ to J. E. B. Stuart, June 26, 1862, James E. B. Stuart Papers, Henry E. Huntington Library.

37. Some writers, seeking to show Jackson apathetic at every stage of the Seven Days Campaign, have accused him of listlessness on the June 26 march. Such diverse sources as Surg. McGuire and Lt. Douglas stated otherwise. Hunter McGuire to Jedediah Hotchkiss, Mar. 30 and Apr. 14, 1896, Reels 12 and 34, Hotchkiss—LC; Douglas, *I Rode with Stonewall,* 101.

38. Jackson's official report of the June 26 action is in *OR,* 11: Pt. 2, 552–53. For Federal estimates of his strength, see Pt. 1, 269; Pt. 2, 215, 224.

39. Ibid., Pt. 3, 620. Chambers, 2:33, got Jackson's second message to Branch confused with the first.

40. *Southern Bivouac,* 2 (1886–87): 653. Law, Harvey Hill, and Richard Taylor were among several officers ignorant of the terrain where Lee's counterofensive unfolded.

41. Robert L. Dabney to Jedediah Hotchkiss, Apr. 6, 1896, Reel 12, Hotchkiss—LC; Freeman, *Lee's Lieutenants,* 1:513; *OR,* 11: Pt. 2, 553, 562. Some veterans and historians, using the always revealing instrument of hindsight, have criticized Jackson for failing to go to Powell Hill's assistance. A few examples of Jackson's "inactivity" are in *OR,* 11: Pt. 2, 614; *B&L,* 2:397–98; Long, *Memoirs of Lee,* 171; Alexander, *Military Memoirs,* 119. A general feeling inside Lee's army at the time attributed Jackson's delays on June 26 to "high water & obstructions in the road." Thomas J. Goree, *Longstreet's Aide* (Charlottesville, Va., 1995), 92.

42. Robertson, *General A. P. Hill,* 68–70; Marshall, *Aide-de-Camp,* 95; Jedediah Hotchkiss to G. F. R. Henderson, Apr. 26, 1895, Reel 11, Hotchkiss—LC. Hotchkiss's reference was to Fitzhugh Lee, *General Lee* (New York, 1894), 160.

43. Lee, *Wartime Papers,* 213.

44. *SHSP,* 40 (1915): 179; Jay B. Hubbell, ed., "The War Diary of John Esten Cooke," *Journal of Southern History,* 7 (1941): 531.

45. McClellan, *Civil War Papers,* 352.

46. *OR,* 11: Pt. 2, 223.

47. Robert L. Dabney to Jedediah Hotchkiss, Mar. 3 and 10, 1896, Reel 12, Hotchkiss—LC. Surgeon McGuire also observed the incident with Whiting and Jackson. McGuire to Hotchkiss, Mar. 30, 1896.

48. Lee, *Wartime Papers,* 214.

49. Robert B. Giles and Donald C. Timberlake to author, Dec. 16, 1991; Dabney, 443. Timberlake, who had joined the "Hanover Light Dragoons" on Mar. 3, 1862, was listed as absent with leave for a period in 1863 and then wounded in action in June of the following year. He served as clerk of the Hanover County court in the postwar years. Kenneth L. Stiles, *Fourth Virginia Cavalry* (Lynchburg, Va., 1985), 139.

50. Dabney, 444.

51. *OR,* 11: Pt. 2, 605, 614–15.

52. Ibid., 554; *B&L,* 2:354–55; Henderson, 2:30.

53. Jedediah Hotchkiss to Robert L. Dabney, Mar. 24, 1896, Reel 12, Hotchkiss—LC. See also Hotchkiss to G. F. R. Henderson, Mar. 24, 1896, Hotchkiss—LC.

54. Henderson, 2:33–34; Robert L. Dabney to Jedediah Hotchkiss, Mar. 3, 1896, Reel 34, Hotchkiss—LC. In the same letter, Dabney dismissed Harman as "a finishing wagon maker and horse dealer without education, who had imposed on Jackson by his bustling parade of zeal in the cause."

55. Dabney to Hotchkiss, Mar. 3, 1896; Robert L. Dabney to Jedediah Hotchkiss, Dec. 28, 1896, Reel 13, Hotchkiss—LC; Howard, *Recollections,* 137. See also Dabney, 448–49, for a milder version of the incident, and Dabney to G. F. R. Henderson, Mar. 24, 1896, Reel 12, Hotchkiss—LC, for an exhaustive account. Longstreet would claim later that Whiting's division assisted his men in the Gaines' Mill battle. That was but one of countless errors in Longstreet's postwar thinking. *From Manassas to Appomattox,* 656; Jedediah Hotchkiss to G. F. R. Henderson, Dec. 10, 1896, Reel 13, Hotchkiss—LC.

56. Long, *Memoirs of Lee,* 172. Another Confederate termed the Union works so strong "that the most experienced European soldiers would well might have pronounced them absolutely invincible." Joseph C. Stiles to wife, undated letter, Civil War Collection, Huntington.

57. *OR,* 11: Pt. 2, 595; Alexander Hunter, *Johnny Reb and Billy Yank* (New York, 1905), 170–71. For other excited reactions, see John Waddill Reminiscences, Baylor University; *Richmond Daily Dispatch,* June 30, 1862.

58. Cooke, *Outlines from the Outpost,* 50–51. This is the third and final instance in the war where Jackson reportedly enjoyed a lemon. Douglas developed a moving picture of Jackson devouring the fruit at Gaines' Mill. *I Rode with Stonewall,* 103–4. Colonel Raleigh Colston, Jackson's VMI colleague, also stated that Jackson had a lemon when the climactic assault got underway. Raleigh E. Colston Reminiscences, SHC.

59. Charles S. Venable, "Personal Reminiscences of the Confederate War," handwritten narrative, UVA, 43; John Esten Cooke, *Stonewall Jackson: A Military Biography* (New York, 1876), 200. Although a novelist is the only direct source for the Lee-Jackson meeting, none of the contemporary and more reliable associates of Jackson refuted the story. McGuire, *Diary of a Refugee,* 125, contains a slightly different reply by Jackson.

60. Dabney, 455.

61. Robert L. Dabney to unknown addressee, Dec. 20, 1867, Robert Lewis Dabney Collection, Chicago Historical Society.

62. *SHSP,* 9 (1881): 559; Dabney, 455. Chaplain J. William Jones thought that Jackson sent only Capt. Sandie Pendleton to order the divisions into action. Such a task by a lone officer would have taken hours. *SHSP,* 9 (1881): 559–60. Alexander Boteler became so excited at this point in the engagement that he lost his coat somewhere on the field. Cooke, "Diary," 533–34.

63. Douglas, *I Rode with Stonewall,* 104; *OR,* 11: Pt. 2, 555, 570.

64. Colt, *Defend the Valley,* 170.

65. John F. Neff to parents, Aug. 4, 1862, CWTI Collection, USMHI.

66. Huffman, *Ups and Downs,* 52. For a similar statement on the Union side, see *OR,* 11: Pt. 2, 301.

67. *SHSP*, 10 (1882): 151. Another account of Jackson praying at that climactic moment is in James Reid Cole, *Miscellany* (Dallas, Tex., 1897), 180–81.

68. O. T. Hanks, "Sketch History of Captain B. F. Bentons Company," handwritten memoir, Stephen F. Austin State University; Dabney, 454. Another dramatic version of the action by the Texans is in *CV*, 14 (1906): 183–84.

69. John B. Hood, *Advance and Retreat* (New Orleans, 1880), 28.

70. *OR*, 11: Pt. 2, 75–77.

71. Ibid., 39–41, 558, 973–84; Wood, *The War*, 73–75; Dabney, 452; TJJ to James Vance, July 17, 1862, *The Confederate Philatelist*, Jan.–Feb. 1990, 2–6. See also Dabney, 452, for additional praise of Fulkerson.

72. *B&L*, 2:359. A number of stories regarding Jackson took root that night on the Union side. Rumors circulated that the Confederate general had been killed in the action. At the same time, a Pennsylvania artillerist swore that Jackson had personally led an assault on his guns. *OR*, 11: Pt. 2, 411; Pt. 3, 277.

73. Thomas Green Penn to mother, June 27, 1862, Green W. Penn Papers, Duke.

74. Johnson, *Dabney*, 271.

75. Heros von Borcke, *Memoirs of the Confederate War for Independence* (Edinburgh and London, 1866), 1:60; Cooke, "Diary," 532; Blackford, *War Years*, 74.

76. Douglas Southall Freeman, *R. E. Lee: A Biography* (New York, 1934–1935), 2:171–72.

77. Dabney to Hotchkiss, Dec. 28, 1896.

CHAPTER 17   *Duty*

1. *OR*, 11: Pt. 2, 626; Sorrel, *Staff Officer*, 82.

2. Unnamed soldier's diary, June 28, 1862, William Couper Papers—VMI.

3. Hinsdale Diary, June 28, 1862, Hinsdale Family Papers, Duke University.

4. Ibid.

5. Ibid.

6. Cooke, "Diary," 536.

7. Throughout the Tidewater region, popular terminology for centuries has been to designate a slow-moving, shallow stream as a swamp. Just as Boatswain's Swamp played a significant role in the June 27 fighting, so White Oak Swamp would figure prominently in the June 29–30 actions. Both are actually creeks.

8. Lee, *Wartime Papers*, 217.

9. Alexander, *Military Memoirs*, 145; Alexander, *Fighting for the Confederacy*, 105; E. Porter Alexander to James Longstreet, Sept. 10, 1902, typescript of letter in the author's possession. Lee's chief of ordnance completely misunderstood the June 29 directive from headquarters with respect to what Jackson was supposed to do. Lee's instructions were for Jackson to "operate down the Chickahominy." Alexander interpreted this to mean that Jackson was to cooperate with Magruder in an attack. Alexander, *Military Memoirs*, 135–37.

10. Cooke, *Stonewall Jackson*, 231; *OR*, 11: Pt. 2, 663.

11. See Stephen W. Sears, *To The Gates of Richmond: The Peninsula Campaign* (New York, 1992), 269, 428. Another confirmation of the use of Alexander's Bridge is in Gilbert Thompson to Jedediah Hotchkiss, May 7, 1898, Reel 15, Hotchkiss—LC.

12. Jedediah Hotchkiss to Hunter McGuire, Apr. 17, 1896, Reel 12, Hotchkiss—LC; M. A. Miller to Jedediah Hotchkiss, May 26, 1896, Reel 34, Hotchkiss—LC; *SHSP*, 30 (1902): 149. John Casler of the 33d Virginia told of seeing Jackson carrying logs for the new bridge. Hence, some soldiers must have been assigned to aid Mason and the pioneers in the work. Casler, *Stonewall Brigade*, 92.

13. *OR*, 11: Pt. 2, 663; TJJ to J. E. B. Stuart, June 29, 1862, James E. B. Stuart Papers, Henry E. Huntington Library.

14. Dabney was confused when he wrote that the Stonewall Brigade accompanied Jackson across Alexander's Bridge. The valley regiments had moved to the north bank of the river and gone into bivouac. Dabney, 459; *OR*, 11: Pt. 2, 571; Howard, *Recollections*, 146–47.

15. R. H. Chilton to J. E. B. Stuart, June 29, 1862, Stuart Papers.

16. Ibid.

17. *OR*, 11: Pt. 2, 664, 675.

18. Fonerden, *Carpenter's Battery*, 28. Another account of the bridge-building story is in *SHSP*, 9 (1881): 564. For some reason, Harvey Hill sought to take credit for repairing the bridge. He asserted that the work was done by his pioneers under Capt. William Proctor Smith. *OR*, 11: Pt. 2, 627.

19. Hunter McGuire to Jedediah Hotchkiss, Apr. 20, 1896, Reel 12, Hotchkiss—LC; Robert L. Dabney to Jedediah Hotchkiss, Apr. 22, 1896, Hotchkiss—LC.

20. *OR*, 11: Pt. 2, 664, 680, 687.

21. William B. Taliaferro, "Reminiscences of Stonewall Jackson," William B. Taliaferro Papers, W&M, 2; Benjamin S. Ewell postwar address, Richard Stoddert Ewell Papers, LC. Six months earlier, Harvey Hill had observed: "Poor Magruder, I hear, has taken to opium and has destroyed his mind. The way of the transgressor is hard." Hill to Isabella Hill, Jan. 8, 1862, Daniel Harvey Hill, Jr., Papers, USMHI. For contrasting views of Magruder, see H. E. Young to Robert N. Gourdin, July 20, 1862, Robert Newman Gourdin Papers, Duke; Gary W. Gallagher, "The Fall of 'Prince John' Magruder," *Civil War History*, 19 (1989): 8–15.

22. *OR*, 11: Pt. 2, 664.

23. Ibid., 687. Surgeon McGuire wrote of riding up that afternoon to where Lee and Magruder were talking. The army chief, McGuire reported, was saying "some right bitter things about giving McClellan time to re-organize his troops. You know Gen. Lee in his quiet way could make very cutting remarks. He worked Magruder up into a state of perfect fury." McGuire to Hotchkiss, Apr. 20, 1896.

24. Henderson, 2:47.

25. Asbury Coward to E. Porter Alexander, Jan. 17, 1903, Edward Porter Alexander Papers, Box 6, SHC.

26. McGuire to Hotchkiss, Apr. 20, 1896; Dabney, 461. Jackson's surgeon was of the impression that the general got more sleep that night than was the case. See McGuire to Jedediah Hotchkiss, Apr. 24, 1896, Reel 12, Hotchkiss—LC.

27. *OR*, 11: Pt. 2, 665; Lee, *Wartime Papers*, 218. Thirty years later, Maj. Robert Stiles of the Richmond Howitzers wrote at least two accounts of the Seven Days Campaign. He devoted considerable space to a meeting in the early morning of June 30 between Lee and Jackson. Stiles described in dramatic detail the two generals talking in the middle of the Williamsburg road. Jackson suddenly drew a three-sided diagram in the dirt with his right foot; and when the triangle was complete, he stamped his foot on the ground and shouted emphatically: "We've got him!"

Several writers have accepted the Stiles narratives at face value. As dramatically full as the reported incident is, however, Stiles's picture is a fabrication. In the first place, nothing in Confederate strategy that day involved a triangular movement. Stiles's explanation of why he was absent from his command and lounging alone on the Williamsburg road is unconvincing. Jackson could not have been—as Stiles described him—"all one neutral dust tint" because he had been drenched by the midnight rain. Finally, after a torrential downpour only a few hours earlier, there could not have been any dust in the road for Jackson to use to make tracings with his foot. *SHSP*, 21 (1893): 22–24; Stiles, *Four Years under Marse Robert*, 97–99. See also Farwell, *Stonewall*, 360; Sears, *To the Gates of Richmond*, 277.

28. Henderson, 2:49–50.

29. Worsham, *Foot Cavalry*, 58.

30. *OR*, 11: Pt. 2, 556.

31. Bryan Grimes, *Extracts of Letters of Major-General Bryan Grimes to His Wife* (Raleigh, 1883), 18; Mills Lane, ed., *"Dear Mother: Don't Grieve about Me, If I Get Killed, I'll Only Be Dead"* (Savannah, Ga., 1977), 153; Dabney, 461.

32. *Or,* 11: Pt. 2, 556, 627.

33. Mrs Jackson, 298.

34. TJJ to Mary Anna Jackson, June 30, 1862, Dabney—LVA. Jackson's uncharacteristic admission to Anna of being weary that morning is noteworthy.

35. Hotchkiss, who never saw White Oak Swamp, gave a quite erroneous description of the stream in a May 23, 1895, letter to G. F. R. Henderson, Reel 11, Hotchkiss—LC.

36. *OR*, 11: Pt. 2, 561, 655. "While the roar of the guns was waking the echoes of swamp and forest," Lt. Frank Myers of the cavalry noted, Jackson rode along the artillery line and "held one hand up as high as his shoulder nearly all the time." The tall trooper concluded that Jackson "was praying to the God of battles." Myers, *The Comanches*, 79–80. Confederate observers that day differed widely in their estimate of the number of Federal cannon they faced. General Wade Hampton claimed to have seen only four guns in Jackson's front. Dabney put the number at fifteen to twenty pieces. Major Hilary P. Jones of the Confederate artillery counted twelve guns. Actually, four Union batteries (about sixteen guns) were in position, but one of the batteries was so weakened that it had been limbered up and was behind the other three. Alexander, *Military Memoirs*, 150; Dabney, 464; *OR*, 11: Pt. 2, 465–66, 653.

37. Thomas T. Munford to John C. Ropes, Dec. 7, 1897, Munford-Ellis Family Papers, Duke.

38. James W. Watts to Thomas T. Munford, May 4, 1898, Munford-Ellis Family Papers.

39. *SHSP*, 1 (1876): 62–63; Hunter McGuire to Jedediah Hotchkiss, June 15, 1896, Reel 12, Hotchkiss—LC.

40. *OR*, 11: Pt. 2, 810–11.

41. Alexander, *Military Memoirs*, 150–51; Marshall, *Aide-de-Camp of Lee*, 111–12. When Alexander compiled a longer memoir years later, he had Jackson saying "H m-m" at one point and "um-h-m-m" at another. Alexander, *Fighting for the Confederacy*, 108.

42. Alexander, *Military Memoirs*, 108. See also *OR*, 11: Pt. 2, 55, 58–60. Most modern accounts refer to the June 30 engagement as the battle of Frayser's Farm. Yet twenty years prior to civil war, the Frayser family had sold the estate to the Nelsons. They renamed it "Glendale"—which was what the property was called when combat exploded over its fields and woods.

43. *B&L*, 2:402. Chambers, 2:70, alleged that in the afternoon Longstreet sent an aide, Maj. John W. Faifax, to relay some sort of message to Jackson. Longstreet made no mention of this in either his report or his memoirs.

44. Howard, *Recollections*, 149.

45. Dabney to Hotchkiss, Apr. 22, 1896. Forty years after the Civil War, Maj. Asbury Coward of Gen. David R. Jones's staff asserted that Jackson dined with them on the evening of the 30th. Coward stated to Gen. Porter Alexander: "While waiting a few minutes for dinner (bacon, hominy and greens), he fell asleep. When the dinner was ready, he was roused; he sat at [the] table, ate rapidly and fell asleep again in his chair before the others had dined." Jackson's table manners would have stopped him from eating before everyone else. More to the point, the general had no reason to ride over to Magruder's sector that tense evening in order to have supper with a division commander he barely knew. Coward's account remains unsubstantiated. Asbury Coward to E. P. Alexander, Jan. 17, 1903, Edward Porter Alexander Papers, Box 6.

46. *OR*, 11: Pt. 2, 77–78.

47. McGuire statement, in Henderson, 2:57. Henderson himself wrestled at some length in seeking a suitable interpretation for Jackson's behavior at White Oak Swamp. The English biographer began attributing Jackson's inactivity to "fever"; finally, he concluded that Jackson was correct in not trying to fight his way through Franklin's corps. G. F. R. Henderson to Jedediah Hotchkiss, Jan. 7, 1896, Reel 12, Hotchkiss—LC.

48. Dabney, 466; *SHSP*, 30 (1902): 149; William Allan, *The Army of Northern Virginia in 1862* (Boston, 1892), 121; Alexander, *Fighting for the Confederacy*, 109. See also Long, *Memoirs of Lee*, 175–76; Longstreet, *From Manassas to Appomattox*, 134, 150–51. Even Jackson's foremost military biographer thought that the general was supposed to give flank support to the Longstreet-Hill attack. Henderson, 2:51–53.

49. *B&L*, 2:389; Alexander, *Military Memoirs*, 152. See also Sorrel, *Staff Officer*, 82; *SHSP*, 9 (1881): 564–65.

50. Franklin's force outnumbered Jackson's by at least 5000 men. Thomas T. Munford to Benjamin Blackford, Nov. 30, 1898, Reel 15, Hotchkiss—LC.

51. Henry Alexander White, *Robert E. Lee and the Southern Confederacy, 1807–1870* (New

York, 1897), 163; Thomas T. Munford to Wade Hampton, Feb. 1901, Munford-Ellis Family Papers.

52. *OR*, 11: Pt. 2, 557. For Franklin's accounts of the day's action, see p. 431; *B&L*, 2:378–81. At least one Union general considered Franklin's position impregnable. *OR*, 11: Pt. 2, 390.

53. In Lee's official report, written several months later, the commander stated: "Huger not coming up, and Jackson having been unable to force the passage of White Oak Swamp, Longstreet and Hill were without the expected support." Exactly what Lee meant by "expected support" he never explained. Lee, *Wartime Papers*, 218.

54. Surgeon McGuire, who knew Jackson as well as any man in the Confederate army, declared that the general "demanded of his subordinates implicit blind obedience. He gave orders in his own peculiar, terse, rapid way, and he did not permit them to be discussed or questioned. He obeyed his own superiors with the same blind, unquestioning obedience." At White Oak Swamp, Jackson "was looking anxiously for some message from Gen. Lee, but he received none, and therefore, as a soldier, he had no right to leave that road." McGuire to Hotchkiss, Apr. 20, 1896.

55. Thomas T. Munford to John C. Ropes, Dec. 7, 1897, Munford-Ellis Family Papers. See also statement by Surg. Harvey Black in *SHSP*, 25 (1897): 211.

56. Mrs. Jackson, 302. For other, in-depth discussions of Jackson's health at this time, see Freeman, *Lee*, 2:572–82; Clifford Dowdey, *The Seven Days: The Emergence of Lee* (Boston, 1964), 196–210; Tanner, *Stonewall in the Valley*, 358–60.

57. W. H. Andrews, *Footprints of a Regiment: A Recollection of the First Georgia Regulars, 1861–1865* (Atlanta, 1992), 49. A similar description of Jackson at the time is in Poague, *Gunner with Stonewall*, 30.

58. *B&L*, 2:391.

59. *OR*, 11: Pt. 2, 495, 562, 574, 667. Campbell Brown of Ewell's staff did not know that Crutchfield was ill at Malvern Hill. Brown dismissed Crutchfield as "a competent but lazy officer" who made "very little use of his artillery" at Malvern Hill. Campbell Brown, "Military Reminiscences," Campbell Brown and Richard S. Ewell Papers, TSLA, 74.

60. TJJ to J. E. B. Stuart, July 1, 1862, Stuart Papers, Huntington; Douglas, *I Rode with Stonewall*, 108. It cannot be verified that Jackson was writing specifically to Stuart when the shell exploded at his side. However, the sequence of events points strongly to such a conclusion. Campbell Brown described two other moments that day when cannon fire came dangerously close to Jackson. Brown, "Military Reminiscences," 72–74. McCabe, *Jackson*, 67, contains a third version. See also Leroy W. Cox Statement, Reel 14, Hotchkiss—LC.

61. Thomas T. Munford to William T. Poague, Nov. 6, 1903, William Thomas Poague Papers, Duke.

62. Vickers, ed., *Under Both Flags*, 136. The guns that Jackson did manage to get in position sent such a "severe converging fire" into the Union right that McClellan had to send reinforcements to his flank. *OR*, 11: Pt. 2, 319, 351.

63. William L. Balthis Memoirs, Reel 39, Hotchkiss—LC. See also Poague, *Gunner with Stonewall*, 29,

64. Balthis Memoirs.

65. McKim, *Recollections*, 92. Twenty years after the war, when Whiting was fully aware of the adoration of Jackson by the Southern people, he confessed, "I take back all I said about his being a fool." *B&L*, 2:297. For supporting evidence of the Jackson-Whiting exchange, see Carter Berkeley Recollections, Reel 39, Hotchkiss—LC.

66. One Southern gunner termed the Union bombardment the heaviest cannon fire to which he had ever been subjected. "Shot and shell seemed to pour over in one successive stream and burst in our midst." Slaughter, *Randolph Fairfax*, 35. See also *OR*, 11: Pt. 2, 572, 574.

67. Cooke, *Outlines from the Outpost*, 71–72, repeated by Capt. Robert E. Park in *SHSP*, 33 (1905): 230.

68. D. H. Hill to Robert L. Dabney, July 21, 1864, Dabney—UTS. Twenty years later, Hill was even more succinct. Malvern Hill "was not war," he commented, "it was murder." *B&L*, 2:394.

69. *OR*, 2: Pt. 2, 558, 622.

70. Oates, *The War*, 142–43.

71. *OR*, 11: Pt. 2, 24–37, 973–84.

72. Contemporary sources disagree over the identity of the generals who reported to Jackson late that night. One writer thought that Magruder and Lafayette McLaws were the visitors; another "eyewitness" had Harvey Hill, Ewell, and Jubal A. Early in the party.

73. Robert L. Dabney to Jedediah Hotchkiss, May 7, 1896, Reel 8, Hotchkiss—LC; Alfriend, "Recollections," 587; *SHSP*, 19 (1891): 311; McGuire and Christian, *Confederate Cause*, 197.

74. Alexander, *Military Memoirs*, 167; Alexander, *Fighting for the Confederacy*, 113–14.

75. *B&L*, 2:405.

76. Alexander, *Military Memoirs*, 116; Alexander, *Fighting for the Confederacy*, 96, 144, 569. In later "memoirs" that he did not write, Longstreet fired some final blows at Jackson. See *From Manassas to Appomattox*, 134, 150, 406.

77. Robert A. Toombs, *The Correspondence of Robert Toombs, Alexander H. Stephens, and Howell Cobb* (Washington, 1913), 601; Freeman, *Lee*, 2:247.

78. *OR*, 11: Pt. 2, 559. The largest proportion of losses, of course, came from D. H. Hill's division, then attached to Jackson's command.

79. A recent and excellent defense of Jackson's conduct on the peninsula is A. Wilson Greene, *Whatever You Resolve to Be: Essays on Stonewall Jackson* (Baltimore, 1992), 73–74. See also Dabney, 479–80; Hunter McGuire Statement, Box 6, Dabney—UVA.

80. D. Harvey Hill to Isabella Hill, July 9, 1862, D. H. Hill Papers, NCDAH.

81. Blackford, *War Years*, 80–82.

82. Hunter McGuire to Jedediah Hotchkiss, May 28, 1896, Reel 14, Hotchkiss—LC.

83. Ibid.; Jefferson Davis, *The Rise and the Fall of the Confederate Government* (New York, 1881), 2:150; *OR*, 11: Pt. 2, 558–59.

84. *OR*, 11: Pt. 2, 760; Robert L. Dabney to Jedediah Hotchkiss, May 7, 1896, Reel 8, Hotchkiss—LC.

85. Hunter McGuire to Jedediah Hotchkiss, May 28, 1896, Reel 14, Hotchkiss—LC; Henderson, 2:72. Kyd Douglas genuinely abhorred Dabney. His account of the breakfast, in *I Rode with Stonewall*, 110–12, differs markedly from the Dabney version. Douglas and Dabney each claimed to have been the only person to arrive for the early-morning meal. Henderson, 2:72, accepted the Dabney account. In his copy of the Henderson work, Douglas wrote in the margin: "This is not true. I was with the General before Major Dabney. In fact I got my breakfast. The two staff officers who were late that morning were without exception the two most valuable men on his staff: Crutchfield & Pendleton, compared with whom Dabney was *in battle* a mere cipher." Henry Kyd Douglas Library, Antietam NBP.

86. *OR*, 11: Pt. 2, 761; Moore, *Cannoneer*, 91; Robert H. DePriest to Mary DePriest, July 3, 1862, DePriest Letters, in possession of James Ballengee, Columbus, Ga. A soldier in Taliaferro's brigade declared in his diary that "the big, swamp mosquitoes were very energetic, making good use of every favorable opportunity of taking on a supply." Huffman, *Ups and Downs*, 55.

87. *OR*, 11: Pt. 2, 922; Robert E. Lee to Anna Jackson, Jan. 26, 1866, Davis—Tulane. Porter Alexander was highly unrealistic—and hence highly critical—because Lee "reluctantly yielded to Jackson's persuasion" that day. *Military Memoirs*, 171. Seven months later, when Jackson and an aide completed his official report of the Seven Days, the general took a positive attitude about the fruits of the campaign. "Undying gratitude is due to God for this great victory, by which despondency increased in the North, hope brightened in the South, and the capital of Virginia and of the Confederacy was saved." *OR*, 11: Pt. 2, 559.

88. Dabney, 477; John A. Harman to Asher W. Harman, July 5, 1862, Reel 39, Hotchkiss—LC; Poague, *Gunner with Stonewall*, 32; Casler, *Stonewall Brigade*, 97. McHenry Howard of Winder's staff asserted without foundation that the Maryland brigadier urged Jackson to grant the troops some rest and that Jackson did so reluctantly. Howard, *Recollections*, 157–58.

89. Mrs. Jackson, 302; Douglas, *I Rode with Stonewall*, 117–18.

90. Arnold, 329–30. Elhart later joined Ewell's staff. On that Sunday afternoon, the Rev.

Joseph C. Stiles conducted a religious service to a huge gathering of Jackson's men. Joseph C. Stiles to Clifford Stiles, July 8, 1862, Civil War Collection, Huntington.

91. Arnold, 330.

92. Boteler account in *Philadelphia Weekly Times*, Feb. 11, 1882, reprinted with minor changes in *SHSP*, 40 (1915): 180–81.

93. *Philadelphia Weekly Times*, Feb. 11, 1882.

94. Ibid. Dabney, 486, repeated the Boteler story but with different expressions by Jackson. For example, he had Jackson wanting 60,000 troops for carrying "the horrors of invasion from their own borders" to those of the North. Douglas Southall Freeman was hesitant to accept the Boteler account because in later years the congressman-aide might have confused what Jackson said with events that occurred subsequently. Freeman, *Lee's Lieutenants*, 1:661n. However, no one has ever openly challenged the authenticity of the Boteler narrative. Jackson's proposal apparently became a widespread rumor. Jed Hotchkiss wrote his wife from halfway across the state at Gordonsville that Jackson was preparing to strike for Harrisburg, Penn., with 80,000 soldiers. Hotchkiss to Sara Hotchkiss, July 11, 1862, Reel 4, Hotchkiss—LC.

95. *OR*, 11: Pt. 2, 636; Huffman, *Ups and Downs*, 55; John A. Harman to Asher W. Harman, July 8, 1862, Reel 39, Hotchkiss—LC. The stench came from unburied dead soldiers scattered over the peninsula. McClendon, *Recollections*, 86.

96. Kyd Douglas account, in *Annals of the War*, 646–47, and later embellished considerably for inclusion in *I Rode with Stonewall*, 115–16.

97. General Orders No. 61, July 10, 1862, Reel 1, Hotchkiss—LC; Douglas, *I Rode with Stonewall*, 117; James Banks to Bryant Wright, July 10, 1862, Bryant Wright Papers, Duke.

98. Hamlin, *"Old Bald Head"*, 116.

99. See Farwell, *Stonewall*, 373; Jeffrey D. Wert, *General James Longstreet* (New York, 1993), 151.

100. *OR*, 12: Pt. 2, 176; Pt. 3, 915.

101. Susan Leigh Blackford, comp., *Letters from Lee's Army* (New York, 1947), 86. The Blackford account of Jackson visiting the Confederate White House should be handled with some caution. Both the date and the facts do not easily fit the chronological picture. It was unusual for Davis to preside over a meeting between an army commander and one of his lieutenants. Jackson's relations with Davis were sufficiently cool for neither man to want such a meeting. That no one else on Jackson's staff mentioned the general going to the presidential mansion prior to departure for Gordonsville is also a challenge to Blackford's recollections. However, the cavalry officer's writings to that point were incisive and without signs of events being manufactured.

102. This statement is contrary to a delightful but improbable anecdote on the trip back to camp. It is in ibid., 87–88, and Mrs. Jackson, 302.

103. *SHSP*, 19 (1891): 313; William S. White, *Sketches of the Life of Captain Hugh A. White of the Stonewall Brigade* (Columbia, S.C., 1864), 101–2. Three weeks later, Hoge wrote an account of Jackson's attendance at the service. See *London Index*, June 4, 1863.

104. TJJ to Anna Jackson, July 14, 1862, Dabney—LVA.

105. Wood, *The War*, 85; Jones, *A Rebel War Clerk's Diary*, 1:143.

CHAPTER 18   *Recovery at Cedar Mountain*

1. Carter S. Anderson, "Train Running for the Confederacy," typescript of 1892–1893 memoirs in possession of the author, 20–25; Johnston, *Virginia Railroads*, 69–71.

2. Von Borcke, *Confederate War*, 1:104.

3. For some of the Federal speculations about Jackson's whereabouts over a two-week period, see *OR*, 12: Pt. 3, 463, 476, 486–87, 505–6, 509, 512, 516, 525.

4. Mrs. Jackson, 304.

5. William B. Taliaferro to wife, July 14, 1862, William B. Taliaferro Papers, W&M; Thomas J. Godwin to sister, July 17, 1862, Thomas J. Godwin Letters, James I. Robertson, Jr., Blacksburg,

Va. Indicative of the positive comments about Jackson's movement was that of Georgia Capt. Shepherd Pryor. "If there is sent 10000 of them," he wrote of the Federals, "they had best begin to move now, for Old Jack will be on them before long and then they will have to get out of the way for he makes things happen where he goes." Shepherd G. Pryor to Penelope Pryor, July 17, 1862, Shepherd Green Pryor Collection, University of Georgia.

6. Pope's first bombastic announcement is in *OR*, 12: Pt. 3, 474. For praise of the general, see Strother, *Virginia Yankee*, 65, 74–75. Strongly negative views are in Gordon, *Brook Farm*, 273–75. On July 22, McClellan wrote his wife: "I see that the Pope bubble is likely to be suddenly collapsed—Stonewall Jackson is after him, & the paltry young man who wanted to teach me the art of war will in less than a week either be in full retreat or badly whipped." McClellan, *Civil War Papers*, 368.

7. A chapter containing Rufus Barringer's recollections about Jackson and a black-flag strategy was in the first edition of Mrs. Jackson's biography, *Life and Letters of General Thomas J. Jackson (Stonewall Jackson)*, 307–21. This first quotation by Jackson is in ibid., 310. On the advice of several ex-Confederate officers, the widow omitted the chapter in the later and larger printings of her work, *Memoirs of Stonewall Jackson*. For rejections of the Barringer presentation, see Henderson, 2:202; Jedediah Hotchkiss to Hunter McGuire, June 15, 1898, Reel 14, Hotchkiss—LC.

8. Ann Jackson, *Life and Letters*, 310.

9. Ibid.

10. Ibid., 315.

11. Ibid.

12. A. S. Pendleton to William N. Pendleton, Aug. 25, 1862, William Nelson Pendleton Papers, SHC; Hotchkiss Journal, July 19, 1862, Reel 1, Hotchkiss—LC.

13. Mrs. Jackson, 322–23. Dabney, 489–90, erroneously had Jackson staying in the home of the Rev. Daniel Ewing.

14. Mrs. Jackson, 323; Daniel B. Ewing to Robert L. Dabney, Sept. 8, 1863, Box 6, Dabney—UVA.

15. Blackford, *Letters from Lee's Army*, 89.

16. William H. B. Thomas, *Gordonsville, Virginia: Crossroads Town* (Verona, Va., 1971), 47.

17. J. E. B. Stuart to TJJ, July 19, 1862, Beverly Mosby Coleman Papers, VHS.

18. G. F. R. Henderson to Hunter McGuire, Nov. 2, 1896, Hunter Holmes McGuire Papers, VHS. In 1907, Douglas Southall Freeman examined the copy of Napoleon's maxims and concluded that the book had never been opened. *Lee's Lieutenants*, 2:2.

19. Jedediah Hotchkiss to Sara Hotchkiss, July 22, 1862, Reel 4, Hotchkiss—LC. Several writers have fallen victim to Dabney's misstatement that Jackson moved southward into Louisa County at the time and established a new headquarters. Dabney, 490–91.

20. Blackford, *Letters from Lee's Army*, 95.

21. Daniel B. Ewing to Robert L. Dabney, Sept. 8, 1863, Box 6, Dabney—UVA. The three soldiers were Pvts. James A. Riddel of the 5th Virginia, Isaac T. Kyle of the 25th Virginia, and Warwick W. Green of the 31st Virginia. Office of the Confederate Secretary of War, 1861–1865: Letters Received, July 1862, RG109, NA.

22. Lacy, *William Sterling Lacy*, 59–60. The father recovered from his malady.

23. Casler, *Stonewall Brigade*, 101–2. This extraordinary statement is the only known instance in all of Civil War history where soldiers reportedly vowed to kill one of their own officers in the confusion of the next engagement.

24. Morrison, *Joseph Graham Morrison*, 6; TJJ to Francis H. Smith, Aug. 7, 1862, Superintendent's Records: Incoming Correspondence, VMI.

25. TJJ to Robert L. Dabney, July 24, 1862, Dabney—UTS.

26. TJJ to R. H. Chilton, July 28, 1862, Jackson Letterbook, Reel 49, Hotchkiss—LC; TJJ to "Colonel," July 25, 1862, copy of letter in author's possession.

27. Mrs. Jackson, 324.

28. *SHSP*, 10 (1882): 83–84.

29. Jedediah Hotchkiss to Sara Hotchkiss, Aug. 3, 1862, Reel 4, Hotchkiss—LC; Blackford,

Letters from Lee's Army, 95; William B. Taliaferro, "Reminiscences of Stonewall Jackson," William B. Taliaferro Papers, W&M, 18–19. One earlier biographer considered Jackson's movement a ruse to lure Pope's army farther south. Henderson, 2:83. Jackson made no mention of any such intent, which also would have been an illogical action to take. The first loss for the Confederates in such a move would be Gordonsville.

30. *OR*, 11: Pt. 2, 936. See also *OR*, 12: Pt. 3, 916–17.

31. Robertson, *General A. P. Hill*, 9, 75–76, 83, 99.

32. Lee, *Wartime Papers*, 239; Douglas marginal note in his copy of Henderson, 2:98, Henry Kyd Douglas Library, Antietam NBP.

33. Francis McFarland to Robert L. Dabney, Nov. 26, 1863, Box 20, Dabney—SHC; TJJ to Francis McFarland, July 31, 1862, Jackson—VMI.

34. William Ellis Jones Diary, Aug. 3, 1862, University of Michigan.

35. Blackford, *Letters from Lee's Army*, 97.

36. Anna Jackson to Hunter McGuire, Aug. 4, 1862, McGuire Papers.

37. Jedediah Hotchkiss to Sara Hotchkiss, Aug. 3, 1862, Reel 4, Hotchkiss—LC; Adam S. Dandridge to father, Aug. 5, 1862, Bedinger-Dandridge Family Correspondence, Duke University. See also *Richmond Enquirer*, Aug. 5, 1862.

38. *OR*, 11: Pt. 3, 342; 12: Pt. 2, 112–14, 181–82; Pt. 3, 926, 934; Col. Speed Butler to William Butler, Aug. 6, 1862, William Butler Collection, Chicago Historical Society; Hunter McGuire to Jedediah Hotchkiss, June 27, 1896, Reel 12, Hotchkiss—LC.

39. All of the major paperwork relative to the court-martial is in the Richard B. Garnett file, MC. Members of the court were Gens. Ewell, Early, Trimble, and James J. Archer, Cols. Daniel H. Hamilton (1st South Carolina), John M. Brockenbrough (40th Virginia), and Alexander G. Taliaferro (23d Virginia), plus Capt. John Lyon (12th Virginia). General Orders No. 89, July 28, 1862, copy in Eldridge Collection, Henry E. Huntington Library.

40. *OR*, 12: Pt. 3, 925–26.

41. Georgetown Meteorological Observations, Manassas NBP. All temperatures given for Aug. 1862 are from that source.

42. Winder Diary, Aug. 5–7, 1862, Charles Sidney Winder Papers, MHS; Howard, *Recollections*, 162–63.

43. TJJ to J. E. B. Stuart, Aug. 7, 1862, James E. B. Stuart Papers, Huntington.

44. *OR*, 12: Pt. 2, 182; Pt. 3, 536; Blackford, *Letters from Lee's Army*, 99.

45. J. F. J. Caldwell, *The History of a Brigade of South Carolinians Known First as "Gregg's," and Subsequently as "McGowan's Brigade"* (Philadelphia, 1866), 26; Gordon, *Brook Farm*, 277.

46. *OR*, 12: Pt. 2, 216–17.

47. For the Jackson-Hill confrontation on Aug. 8, see Robert K. Krick, *Stonewall Jackson at Cedar Mountain* (Chapel Hill, 1990), 25–30; Robertson, *General A. P. Hill*, 100–2; Jackson endorsement of Hill after-action report, Dabney—LVA. Hunter McGuire to Jedediah Hotchkiss, June 27, 1896, Reel 12, Hotchkiss-LC, is the source for Jackson's permanent animosity toward Hill.

48. Lawrence O. Branch, in *OR*, 12: Pt. 2, 223; Casler, *Stonewall Brigade*, 103.

49. Pope did know of Jackson's movement but considered it nothing more than a heavy reconnaissance. *OR*, 12: Pt. 2, 25; Pt. 3, 548, 550.

50. Hotchkiss Journal, Aug. 8, 1862, Reel 1; Mrs. Jackson, 288; *SHSP*, 10 (1882): 84. The earliest account of Lewis's observation is in *North Carolina Standard*, Aug. 13, 1862. Other variations of the statement are in Dabney, 492, and Henderson, 1:442. Douglas insisted that Lewis said, "There is going to be *hell* to pay." Marginal annotation in Douglas's copy of Mrs. Jackson, Douglas Library.

51. John S. Foster to Sarah Foster, Aug. 9, 1862, James Foster and Family Papers, LSU.

52. *OR*, 12: Pt. 2, 181; Pt. 3, 926.

53. *OR*, 12: Pt. 2, 181.

54. Hamlin, *"Old Bald Head"*, 117.

55. Hotchkiss Journal, Aug. 9, 1862, Reel 1.

56. *OR*, 12: Pt. 2, 188, 215; Blackford, *Letters from Lee's Army*, 99–100; Hunter McGuire to

Jedediah Hotchkiss, June 27, 1896, Reel 12, Hotchkiss—LC. In the predawn hours of Aug. 9, Winder scribbled in his pocket journal: "Enemy's cavalry attacked on flank at 2 A.M. Up, formed & moved out. . . . Enemy repulsed. Went back and tried to sleep. No use. Another alarm." Winder Diary, Aug. 9, 1862.

57. William Ellis Jones Diary, Aug. 9, 1862; S. G. Pryor to wife, Aug. 9, 1862, Shepherd Green Pryor Collection. See also *CV,* 28 (1920): 24.

58. *Philadelphia Weekly Times,* Jan. 28, 1882; McGuire and Christian, *Confederate Cause,* 197.

59. *OR,* 12: Pt. 2, 182–83, 189; Myers, *The Comanches,* 88. Powell Hill was even more in the dark about Jackson's intentions. When he reached the field at the height of the fighting, Hill assumed that Taliaferro's troops were part of the main battle line (rather than perpendicular to it) and that the Light Division was supposed to reinforce Early on the right rather than Winder on the left. *OR,* 12: Pt. 2, 215.

60. John Blue, "Reminiscences," CWTI, 53. The Blue manuscript, which appears to have been written as a series of articles for a West Virginia newspaper, provides the most personal chronicle of Jackson at Cedar Mountain. Blue was a member of the 11th Virginia Cavalry.

61. Ibid., 54.

62. Ibid.

63. Ibid.

64. Ibid.

65. Ibid.

66. Ibid., 55.

67. *OR,* 12: Pt. 2, 183, 200; *Lexington Gazette,* Aug. 28, 1862. Moore later polished his letter to the newspaper and incorporated it into *Cannoneer,* 95. As Winder fell, his left arm and side ripped open, he shouted, "My God, I'm shot!" Two aides, Capt. John F. O'Brien and Lt. McHenry Howard, accompanied the litter to the rear. Winder was moaning in pain. On learning that his wounds were fatal, the Marylander exclaimed: "My poor darling wife and little pets. What will become of them?" He became quieter, often absorbed in prayer, and died an hour later. John F. O'Brien to Edward Wilder, Dec. 16, 1862, John F. O'Brien Letter, MHS; Howard, *Recollections,* 169–71; Fonerden, *Carpenter's Battery,* 30.

68. Lee, *Pendleton,* 203.

69. Krick, *Cedar Mountain,* 97, 111–12.

70. *Richmond Whig,* May 8, 1876; Blue, "Reminiscences," 55.

71. Moore, *Cannoneer,* 95–96.

72. *OR,* 12: Pt. 2, 183.

73. Ibid., 187, 197, 205, 234; *Richmond Whig,* May 8, 1876.

74. Jedediah Hotchkiss to brother, Aug. 14, 1862, Reel 4, Hotchkiss—LC.

75. Blue, "Reminiscences," 55; *Richmond Enquirer,* Aug. 12, 1862.

76. Dabney, 501; Blackford, *Letters from Lee's Army,* 104–5; *SHSP,* 10 (1882): 87; Jedediah Hotchkiss to G. F. R. Henderson, Sept. 5, 1896, Reel 12, Hotchkiss—LC. Kyd Douglas disputed all utterances attributed to Jackson in the battle of Cedar Mountain, particularly those cited by Dabney. On page 311 of his copy of Mrs. Jackson, Douglas wrote angrily: "He said no such thing or Dr. Dabney would have known if he had been with him as I was. Genl. Jackson never did that sort of thing. As he rode to the front, he saw Genl. ————— harranging his Brigade. He simply cried out 'General, move forward—Forward!' & led the way himself. . . . Genl. Jackson never & I mean *never* indulged in rhetorical heroics on the battlefield." Douglas Library.

77. Taliaferro, "Reminiscences," W&M, 17; Blackford, *Letters from Lee's Army,* 105.

78. *CV,* 24 (1914): 406; Marvin, *Fifth Connecticut,* 162. In rapid succession, two colorbearers of the 21st Virginia were killed and a third shot in three places. *OR,* 12: Pt. 2, 202.

79. Hotchkiss subsequently wrote that Hill's movements "preceding and during" the battle were unsatisfactory to Jackson because "he had failed to promptly comply with orders." Hotchkiss memorandum on A. P. Hill, Reel 49, Hotchkiss—LC. This was one of the few times when Hotchkiss's opinions beclouded his accuracy. He did not like Hill personally. With the passing years, Hotchkiss got the events of Aug. 8 and Aug. 9 confused. (See Hotchkiss to

G. F. R. Henderson, Apr. 26, 1895, Reel 11, Hotchkiss—LC.) Hill quickly obeyed every order issued to him on the 9th, and his arrival on the field at Cedar Mountain was a turning point in the battle.

On the other hand, Taliaferro alleged that when Jackson first met Hill on the Culpeper road, he snarled that the division chief was late and then curtly dismissed him to place his brigades in battle order. Taliaferro, "Reminiscences," 18. Taliaferro went to great efforts in the postwar years to ingratiate himself with Jackson partisans. This was one instance. If his statement of Hill's tardiness were true, Jackson would surely have mentioned it in an official report. Instead, he wrote that Hill's men "met the Federal forces, flushed with their temporary triumphs, and drove them back with terrible slaughter." *OR*, 12: Pt. 2, 184.

80. Blue, "Reminiscences," 54–55; *OR*, 12: Pt. 2, 184.

81. *OR*, 12: Pt. 2, 223; Walter Clark, ed., *Histories of the Several Regiments and Battalions from North Carolina in the Great War, 1861–65* (Goldsboro, N.C., 1901), 2:28.

82. Douglas, *I Rode with Stonewall*, 124; Clark, ed., *Histories of North Carolina Regiments*, 2:68, 472. In one of Douglas's first printed recollections, he asserted that Jackson personally led the North Carolina brigade into the battle. *Philadelphia Weekly Times*, Jan. 28, 1882.

83. *SHSP*, 19 (1891): 314–15.

84. David G. McIntosh Memoir, CWTI.

85. *OR*, 12: Pt. 2, 141, 184.

86. Allan, *A March Past*, 148–49. Jackson made up his mind to appoint Willie Preston to his staff after the next battle. Bean, *Liberty Hall Volunteers*, 131–32.

87. *OR*, 12: Pt. 2, 184, 218. For the fatigued condition of Jackson's soldiers, see Blackford, *Letters from Lee's Army*, 106.

88. Blue, "Reminiscences," 56; *CV*, 27 (1919): 448–49; Boteler Memorandum, Dabney—LVA; Mrs. Jackson, 326.

89. *OR*, 12: Pt. 2, 139, 183–85. For an example of the first, exaggerated casualty reports from the field, see *Richmond Daily Dispatch*, Aug. 14, 1862.

90. Hunter McGuire to Jedediah Hotchkiss, June 27, 1896, Reel 12, Hotchkiss—LC; *OR*, 12: Pt. 2, 183.

91. *Richmond Enquirer*, Aug. 12, 1862. The *Lexington Gazette*, Sept. 4, 1862, reprinted a *Chicago Tribune* story in which the Northern field correspondent was highly laudatory of Jackson's performance at Cedar Mountain.

92. Freeman, *Lee's Lieutenants*, 2:44–46; Henderson, 2:94; Jedediah Hotchkiss to G. F. R. Henderson, Sept. 5, 1896, Reel 11, Hotchkiss—LC; Krick, *Cedar Mountain*, 210. See also Douglas, *I Rode with Stonewall*, 123; Chamberlayne, *Ham Chamberlayne*, 90.

93. D. B. Ewing Reminiscences, Box 6, Dabney—UVA; Vandiver, 345.

94. Miller, "Letters," 89; E. D. Snead to Thomas Snead, Aug. 12, 1862, Thomas D. Snead Papers, Duke.

95. TJJ to Samuel Cooper, Aug. 10, 1862, Jackson—MC.

96. *OR*, 12: Pt. 2, 184; Dabney, 504. Although some Federal soldiers accused Jackson of ignoring his dead on the field, Confederate accounts are specific about burials occurring throughout that Sunday. See T. H. McBee to father, Aug. 10, 1862, Civil War Letters, 1862–1867, WVU; William F. Fuller, *The War Reminiscences of William Frierson Fuller* (Gaithersburg, Md., 1986), 43; Blue, "Reminiscences," 58.

97. Strother, *Virginia Yankee*, 80–81; Ephraim Bowman to sister, Aug. 17, 1862, Bowman Family Papers, UVA; Blue, "Reminiscences," 58; James M. Binford to Annie and Caroline Gwathmey, Aug. 13, 1862, Charles B. Gwathmey Papers, VHS; George K. Harlow to father, Aug. [12], 1862, Harlow Family Papers, VHS.

98. Blue, "Reminiscences," 58; *OR*, 12: Pt. 2, 132; Krick, *Cedar Mountain*, 334.

99. TJJ to Samuel Cooper, Aug. 11, 1862, Office of the Adjutant & Inspector General and of the Quartermaster General, 1861–1865: Letters Received, RG109, NA; TJJ to Anna Jackson, Aug. 11, 1862, Dabney—LVA.

100. Strother, *Virginia Yankee*, 80; Worsham, *Foot Cavalry*, 68; Hotchkiss Journal, Aug. 11, 1862, Reel 1; Blackford, *Letters from Lee's Army*, 100.

101. William Ellis Jones Diary, Aug. 11, 1862. A Louisiana soldier who caught sight of Jackson for the first time at Cedar Mountain likened him to "a Jew peddlar" who rode "a little sorrel horse like a house on fire." Lawrence L. Hewitt, "A Confederate Foreign Legion: Louisiana 'Wildcats' in the Army of Northern Virginia," *Journal of Confederate History*, 6 (1990): 62.

102. *OR*, 12: Pt. 2, 184.

103. Neese, *Horse Artillery*, 90. "Pope should be cashiered for letting Jackson escape him," Charles Blackford told his parents. "Had either Lee or Jackson been in his place we would all be either dead or in a yankee prison." Blackford, *Letters from Lee's Army*, 111.

104. S. Bassett French, *Centennial Tales: The Memoirs of Colonel "Chester" S. Bassett French* (New York, 1962), 12–13.

105. *OR*, 12: Pt. 2, 185.

106. Ibid., Pt. 3, 675; *Richmond Examiner*, Aug. 12, 1862; *Richmond Daily Dispatch*, Aug. 14, 1862.

107. *OR*, 12: Pt. 2, 28; Pt. 3, 564; McClellan, *Civil War Papers*, 393.

108. William Ellis Jones Diary, Aug. 14, 1862; Jedediah Hotchkiss to Sara Hotchkiss, Aug. 16, 1862, Reel 4, Hotchkiss—LC.

109. *B&L*, 2:405; Thomas C. Elder to Anna Elder, Aug. 15, 1862, Thomas Claybrook Elder Papers, VHS.

110. Hotchkiss Journal, Aug. 14, 1862, Reel 1; Douglas, *I Rode with Stonewall*, 129. Jackson had the benefit of several good espionage agents at this time. An undated dispatch from Philip Bradley, an "Operative, Military Secret Service," kept Jackson up to date on Pope's troop dispositions. Philip Bradley Letter, Manassas NBP.

111. Hotchkiss Journal, Mar. 5, 1863, Reel 1; Henderson, 2:115.

112. A. G. Grinnan statement, quoting prominent Louisa County resident Jeremiah Morton, Reel 34, Hotchkiss—LC.

113. Shepherd G. Pryor to Penelope Pryor, Aug. 18, 1862, Pryor Collection; William Ellis Jones Diary, Aug. 19. 1862. Controversy still surrounds what exactly caused the delay in the movement against Pope. Thirty years after the war, Dr. McGuire reminded his friend Jed Hotchkiss: "You know that General Lee wanted to attack Pope while he was encamped on the Rapidan but Fitz Lee failed to get up. My impression is that the reason he did not attack was because he could not get Longstreet to move." A few days later, McGuire talked with Fitzhugh Lee. "He says he has been misrepresented by Longstreet and by others," McGuire told Hotchkiss. Fitzhugh Lee was then recommending Henry B. McClellan's biography of Jeb Stuart as "a fair and honest statement of the whole affair." McGuire to Hotchkiss, Nov. 18 and Dec. 2, 1896, Reel 13, Hotchkiss—LC. Marshall, *Aide-de-Camp*, 125, and Henderson, 2:114–15, blamed Lee for the delay. McGuire's book reference was to Maj. Henry B. McClellan, *The Life and Campaigns of Major-General J. E. B. Stuart* (Boston, 1885).

114. TJJ to Samuel Cooper, Aug. 16, 1862, Office of Adjt. General: Letters Received, RG109, NA; *OR*, 12: Pt. 3, 934; Hotchkiss Journal, Aug. 17, 1862, Reel 1.

115. Caldwell, *South Carolina Brigade*, 28.

116. *OR*, 51: Pt. 1, 742.

117. French, *Centennial Tales*, 15.

118. Ibid., 18–19. See also Wallace, *Fifth Virginia*, 37; Murphy, *Tenth Virginia*, 44–46, 170.

119. Henderson, 2:365–66. Incredibly, John Roadcap reenlisted in December 1863 and deserted a second time within two months. Colonel Walker did not resign; he was wounded in action barely a week later and killed in an 1863 action. Jackson's whole division was mustered out to witness the executions. The most accurate of several accounts of the deaths of the three soldiers is in Moore, *Cannoneer*, 99–100.

120. Blackford, *Letters from Lee's Army*, 112–13.

121. *OR*, 12: Pt. 2, 654; Taliaferro, "Reminiscences," 19–21; Blackford, *Letters from Lee's Army*, 117–18; Hotchkiss Journal, Aug. 21, 1862, Reel 1. For the effect of the Confederate fire, see Von Borcke, *Confederate War*, 1:116–17. Jackson referred to the artillery duel as "animated firing" maintained for most of the day. Jackson's manuscript report, Jackson—NYHS.

122. Hotchkiss Journal, Aug. 21, 1862, Reel 1.

123. Jackson manuscript report, Jackson—NYHS; *SHSP,* 35 (1907): 92; *OR,* 12: Pt. 2, 64, 719.

124. Von Borcke, *Confederate War,* 1:121; *OR,* 12: Pt. 3, 331; Campbell Brown, "Military Reminiscences," Campbell Brown and Richard S. Ewell Papers, TSLA, 89. The spa was also known at the time as Fauquier White Sulphur Springs.

125. Early, *Autobiographical Sketch,* 108; *SHSP,* 14 (1886): 209–10; Blackford, *Letters from Lee's Army,* 124, 127; Hotchkiss Journal, Aug. 24, 1862, Reel 1.

126. Blackford, *Letters from Lee's Army,* 125.

127. Douglas, *I Rode with Stonewall,* 130; Jackson's manuscript report, Jackson—NYHS. Pope claimed during this time that he was containing Lee's army all along the Rappahannock. *OR,* 12: Pt. 2, 13.

128. Alfred E. Doby to Elizabeth K. Doby, Aug. 24, 1862, Means-English-Doby Papers, University of South Carolina.

129. The raid on Catlett's Station lives in both fact and fiction. For personal comments in the former category, see Emory M. Thomas, *Bold Dragoon: The Life of J. E. B. Stuart* (New York, 1986), 145–50; *B&L,* 2:528; Blue, "Reminiscences," 59–60. Kyd Douglas's unique observations of Stuart's return with all of his booty are in *Philadelphia Weekly Times,* Apr. 20, 1878.

130. Some difference of opinion persists over who devised the strategy of Jackson marching behind the Federal army. Jeb Stuart told Hotchkiss that Jackson "was entitled to all the credit" for a plan that Lee "very reluctantly" accepted. Hotchkiss Journal, Mar. 4, 1863, Reel 1. Henderson, 2:124, made a strong case that the campaign was Jackson's idea. However, the weight of evidence points to Lee as the architect of the wide-swinging flank march. In his gentle way, the army chief made it clear in his official report that he proposed the movement. Lee wrote: "In pursuit of the plan of operations determined upon, Jackson *was directed.* . . . " Lee surely would have given credit to Jackson if the latter had come forth with the idea. *OR,* 12: Pt. 2, 553–54. See also p. 642; Marshall, *Aide-de-Camp,* 129; *B&L,* 2:522.

131. *OR,* 12: Pt. 2, 554, 642–43, 650.

132. Lee felt the same way. After the war, discussing criticisms made of the high risks he took, Lee said to Col. William Allan, "Such criticisms were obvious [yet] the disparity of force between the contending armies rendered the risks unavoidable." Allan, *Army of Northern Virginia,* 200.

133. Douglas, *I Rode with Stonewall,* 132–33, has been the traditional but somewhat confused source for the conference at Jeffersonton. Douglas's first version appeared in *Philadelphia Weekly Times,* Apr. 20, 1878. Since the aide was not privy to the generals' conversation (despite his original statement that he was at the table), his narratives might be suspect. However, Dr. McGuire presented essentially the same chronicle of Jackson's actions in a May 19, 1896, letter to Hotchkiss, Reel 34, Hotchkiss—LC.

CHAPTER 19   *Stonewall at Manassas, Part II*

1. *OR,* 12: Pt. 2, 678.

2. Buck, *Lucy Buck,* 152; Hotchkiss Journal, Apr. 14 and Aug. 24, 1862, Reel 1, Hotchkiss—LC; Mrs. Jackson, 317.

3. *CV,* 17 (1909): 549.

4. *CV,* 29 (1921): 297; *B&L,* 2:532. Tennessee soldier H. T. Childs stated that each man carried "six biscuits and one pound of midling meat." When Jackson's column reached high ground, Childs continued, "I looked back in the valley below where General Lee's army was camped, and Jackson's corps looked like a huge worm making its way out." *CV,* 28 (1920): 100.

5. Edwin C. Wilson Reminiscences, William P. Palmer Collection, Western Reserve Historical Society.

6. *CV,* 17 (1909): 549; *B&L,* 2:501.

7. *B&L,* 2:533.

8. *OR,* 12: Pt. 3, 653, 665–66, 675; G. D. Camden to Robert L. Dabney, Nov. 25, 1863, Box 19, Dabney—SHC.

9. Dabney, 516–17; Buck, *With the Old Confeds*, 51. Dabney was not witness to this scene, but his account is creditable and obviously based on eyewitness testimony. The embellished version of this incident in Cooke, *Jackson*, 275, is ample evidence why novelists generally do not make good historians.

10. All Jackson statements in this chapter are from his manuscript report, Jackson—NYHS. The printed version is in *OR*, 12: Pt. 2, 641–48.

11. Jackson maintained far greater secrecy on this march than did the Richmond press. That Thursday morning, the *Enquirer* announced that Jackson's three divisions were en route for Manassas Junction in the rear of Pope's army. Fortunately, the newspaper had its facts garbled: it placed Jackson near Warrenton, far to the east of his actual location. Federal authorities, who knew that Jackson was not in the vicinity of Warrenton, discounted the entire news story.

12. Blackford, *War Years*, 109; Caldwell, *South Carolina Brigade*, 30; Marietta M. Andrews, *Scraps of Paper* (New York, 1929), 57–58.

13. *OR*, 12: Pt. 2, 734, 747; *CV,* 34 (1926): 221.

14. Blackford, *War Years*, 111–12.

15. Ibid., 113–15; *OR*, 12: Pt. 2, 747–48; *B&L*, 2:502–3; McClendon, *Recollections*, 102. Typical among the exaggerated accounts of derailing trains at Bristoe Station is that of Georgia soldier I. Gordon Bradwell in *CV,* 29 (1921): 297.

16. Allen C. Redwood, "With Stonewall Jackson," *Scribner's Magazine*, 18 (1879): 228–29.

17. Wayland F. Dunaway, *Reminiscences of a Rebel* (New York, 1913), 38.

18. W. Dorsey Pender, *The General to His Lady: The Civil War Letters of William Dorsey Pender to Fannie Pender* (Chapel Hill, 1962), 171, 173. Another anti-Jackson sentiment is in C. F. Mills to sister, Aug. 26, 1862, Elizabeth A. Mills Papers, Duke University.

19. White, *Sketches of White*, 61.

20. *OR*, 12: Pt. 2, 643.

21. Ibid.

22. *OR*, 12: Pt. 2, 554, 651, 720; Campbell Brown, "Military Reminiscences," Campbell Brown and Richard S. Ewell Papers, TSLA, 93. For an account containing the supposed conversation between Jackson and Trimble, see Nisbet, *Four Years*, 88.

23. The disputatious reports of Stuart and Trimble are in *OR*, 12: Pt. 2, 720–23, 734, 741–43. See also *CV,* 18 (1910): 231; Clark, ed., *Histories of North Carolina Regiments*, 2:152–53. Conflicting figures in official reports and personal memoirs make it impossible to give Trimble's precise losses. Carpenter's battery, one of Jackson's favorite artillery units, abandoned its four little six-pounders for two new twelve-pounder Napoleons and two ten-pounder Parrott rifles seized by Trimble's men. Fonerden, *Carpenter's Battery*, 34.

24. TJJ to Isaac R. Trimble, Aug. 27, 1862, Jackson—VMI; TJJ to War Department, Sept. 22, 1862, Isaac Ridgeway Trimble Papers, MHS.

25. Hotchkiss Journal, Apr. 15, 1863, Reel 1.

26. *OR*, 12: Pt. 2, 401–2, 408, 536, 540–41; Moore, *Cannoneer*, 103–4, 107.

27. Fulton, *War Reminiscences*, 45.

28. *OR*, 12: Pt. 2, 408.

29. Ibid., 644. See also pp. 543, 670. Colonel Charles Faulkner wrote the first draft of Jackson's report of the Second Manassas Campaign. After Jackson's statement about Gen. Taylor being "a leader worthy of a better cause," Faulkner added: "Yet it was all in vain. Want of force alone would have rendered the conflict too unequal." Jackson deleted those sentences in his revised draft. Other but garbled accounts of the one-sided contest are in *CV,* 7 (1899): 263; 17 (1909): 549; Poague, *Gunner with Stonewall*, 35.

30. Casler, *Stonewall Brigade*, 107; Fulton, *War Reminiscences*, 44; *B&L*, 2:504, 529. In giving the order to dump all alcohol on the ground, Jackson added almost to himself, "I fear the liquor more than General Pope's army." Unidentified newspaper clipping, Reel 34, Hotchkiss—LC.

31. *Lexington Gazette*, Sept. 11, 1862; Oates, *The War*, 135; Worsham, *Foot Cavalry*, 71.

32. John Blue, "Reminiscences," CWTI, 61. See also Redwood, "With Stonewall Jackson," 230; von Borcke, *Confederate War*, 1:137. Colonel French of Jackson's staff wrote that servant Jim Lewis secured "a barrel of ginger cakes" for the general. French, *Centennial Tales*, 37.

33. *OR*, 12: Pt. 2, 34, 70–71; Pt. 3, 704; *B&L*, 2:460–61.

34. Jackson manuscript report.

35. Caldwell, *South Carolina Brigade*, 31; *Philadelphia Weekly Times*, Apr. 20, 1878. For a description of the smoldering depot the following day, see Strother, *Virginia Yankee*, 91.

36. Of the negative comments made of this march by Jackson's subordinates, that of Taliaferro is the most exaggerated. See his "Reminiscences of Stonewall Jackson," William B. Taliaferro Papers, W&M, 25–27.

37. *CV*, 7 (1899): 263.

38. *B&L*, 2:507; William Allan to Jedediah Hotchkiss, Oct. 22, 1886, Reel 22, Hotchkiss—LC.

39. *OR*, 12: Pt. 1, 304; Pt. 2, 664, 670; *B&L*, 2:508–9, 534.

40. *B&L*, 2:507–8; *SHSP*, 25 (1897): 100. Taliaferro's account, in *B&L*, is confusing because he gave the wrong time for the capture of the Federal courier. The man was not seized in early morning but just before noon.

41. Blackford, *War Years*, 116.

42. Ibid., 118.

43. Ibid., 118–19; *B&L*, 2:509.

44. Blackford, *War Years*, 120–21; *OR*, 12: Pt. 2, 645, 656–57; Worsham, *Foot Cavalry*, 74.

45. Oates, *The War*, 138; John J. Hennessy, *Return to Bull Run* (New York, 1993), 170–71.

46. After reviewing the first draft of his official report, Jackson personally added the following to the manuscript: "This obstinate resistance of the enemy appears to have been for the purpose of protecting the flank of his column until it should pass the position occupied by our troops. Owing to the difficulty of getting Art. through the woods I did not have as much of that arm as desired at the opening of the engagement; but this want was met by Maj. [John] Pelham with the Stuart Horse Artillery dashing forward on my right and opening upon the enemy at a moment when his services were much needed." See *OR*, 12: Pt. 2, 644–45.

47. *B&L*, 2:510.

48. Douglas, *I Rode with Stonewall*, 137.

49. Edwin C. Wilson Reminiscences.

50. *OR*, 12: Pt. 2, 372–73, 378, 663–64; Henderson, 2:148; Ray A. Neff, *Valley of the Shadow* (Terre Haute, Ind., 1989), 68; French, *Centennial Tales*, 43.

51. *OR*, 12: Pt. 2, 645, 658; Hamlin, *"Old Bald Head"*, 129; Early, *Autobiographical Sketch*, 121. For a detailed account of Ewell's injury, see Robert E. Lee Krick, "Ewell Wounding," typescript, Manassas NBP.

52. *OR*, 12: Pt. 3, 721.

53. *SHSP*, 19 (1891): 307.

54. Caldwell, *South Carolina Brigade*, 32.

55. *OR*, 12: Pt. 2, 38.

56. Ibid., 659, 711; *Philadelphia Weekly Times*, Apr. 20, 1878; unknown Confederate artillery-man's letter, Manassas NBP.

57. Jackson manuscript report.

58. Von Borcke, *Confederate War*, 1:144, 148.

59. Poague, *Gunner with Stonewall*, 37; Cussons article, in *Richmond Times-Dispatch*, Aug. 20, 1905. Cussons expanded his recollections for publication as a booklet: *The Passage of Thoroughfare Gap . . .* (New York, 1906). For the elation of Jackson's men at the arrival of the first of Longstreet's troops, see Charles J. Lewis undated letter, File 55-B, LHAC.

60. Jackson manuscript report.

61. Caldwell, *South Carolina Brigade*, 35–36; *OR*, 12: Pt. 2, 681.

62. Jackson manuscript report.

63. Longstreet's movements to Manassas on Aug. 26–27, and his insight (or procrastination) on Aug. 29, have long generated controversy among Civil War historians and students. The details are beyond the realm of this study. One of several rationales Longstreet produced is in *B&L*, 2:518–20. Modern writers are giving Longstreet the best defense he has ever had. See Gary Gallagher, "Scapegoat in Victory: James Longstreet and the Battle of Second Manassas,"

Civil War History, 34 (1988): 294–307; Hennessy, *Return to Bull Run*, 226–31, 460–61. A "traditional" attack on Longstreet's behavior on Aug. 29 is in Clifford Dowdey, *Lee* (Boston, 1965), 291–92.

64. *SHSP*, 13 (1885): 32, 34.

65. *Philadelphia Weekly Times*, Apr. 20, 1878.

66. Ibid.

67. Ibid.

68. Wood, *The War*, 93–94.

69. *Philadelphia Weekly Times*, Apr. 20, 1878.

70. Dabney, 528–29. *SHSP*, 13 (1885): 32–33. During the afternoon lull, Col. Edward Mc-Crady of the 1st South Carolina wrote, Jackson calmly walked down Hill's line and examined the position while miraculously escaping fire from the enemy. *SHSP*, 13 (1885): 26. No verification of this incident can be found.

71. Strother, *Virginia Yankee*, 94; R. A. Pierson to James F. Pierson, Sept. 7, 1862, Rosemonde and Emile Kuntz Collection, Tulane University.

72. *SHSP*, 14 (1886): 371; White, *Hugh A. White*, 117; Poague, *Gunner with Stonewall*, 38.

73. Moore, *Cannoneer*, 112; *OR*, 12: Pt. 2, 672, 681, 693. A bullet shattered Trimble's left knee. The venerable general, whom Jackson openly admired, got his major general's commission early the following year just before returning to duty. At Gettysburg, Trimble was shot again in the left leg and underwent amputation of the limb.

74. *SHSP*, 25 (1897): 107; Withrow Scrapbooks, W&L, XVIII, 81–82.

75. Withrow Scrapbooks, W&L, XVIII, 22. Allan quoted McGuire. Dabney, 531, gave a slightly different but more widely cited version of the McGuire-Jackson exchange. Since Dabney was not present at Second Manassas, the McGuire rendition is far more reliable. Some writers have placed Jackson's comment about God and victory on the evening of Aug. 31, when the two-day battle ended. Yet careful study shows the comment to have been made at the end of the first day's fighting. William Couper to Lenoir Chambers, Feb. 28, 1956, William Couper Papers, VMI.

A saddened Lexington editor announced the young recruit's death by exclaiming: "Willie Preston—alas! alas! dear boy, if our cruel foe was seeking a shining mark for their deadly missils, they found it in thee. . . . A bud of fairest promise has been blighted in its opening." *Lexington Gazette*, Sept. 11, 1862.

76. Allan, *Preston*, 147. See also p. 152.

77. Charles S. Venable, "Personal Reminiscences of the Confederate War," UVA, 56.

78. *CV*, 22 (1914): 231.

79. Napier Bartlett, *Military Record of Louisiana* (New Orleans, 1875), 98.

80. Davis, *Three Years in the Army*, 108.

81. Moore, *Cannoneer*, 118.

82. *OR*, 12: Pt. 2, 563; Pt. 3, 741; Strother, *Virginia Yankee*, 95.

83. *Philadelphia Weekly Times*, Apr. 20, 1878. Douglas amended his account a few years later. In his copy of John C. Ropes, *The Army under Pope* (New York 1881), Douglas wrote in the margin that Jackson was writing a note to Lee about 4 P.M. when "the sound of a single gun smote the air. The general rose rapidly to his feet saying 'Bring my horse. That is the signal for a general attack.'" Henry Kyd Douglas Library, Antietam NBP.

84. *CV*, 22 (1914): 231.

85. Casler, *Stonewall Brigade*, 112–13.

86. McClendon, *Recollections*, 116.

87. *B&L*, 2:536; *OR*, 12: Pt. 2, 666, 671, 698. For verification of stone throwing by Confederates on Aug. 31, see Chamberlayne, *Ham Chamberlayne*, 101; *SHSP*, 6 (1878): 66.

88. *CV*, 22 (1914): 231; Thomas G. Pollock to father, Sept. 6, 1862, Thomas H. Pollock Papers, UVA; *OR*, 12: Pt. 2, 660. Captain James Garnett, ordnance officer for the Stonewall Brigade, felt that Baylor and his followers acted bravely but rashly. "Neither the Yankees nor we could cross the railroad cut at that point." *SHSP*, 40 (1915): 227.

89. Jackson manuscript report.

90. Longstreet's postwar statement that "Jackson sent to me and begged for reenforcements"

incurred the wrath of Jackson supporters for generations. *B&L*, 2:521. Such a statement stands in negative contrast to the report of Jackson, who went to pains to underscore the "timely and gallant advance of General Longstreet" later in the battle. In addition, Longstreet followed practice by seeking to take all of the credit for turning the battle in the Confederates' favor. For one of the bitter rejoinders, see Col. S. D. Lee's article in *SHSP*, 6 (1878): 59–70.

91. Cooke, *Jackson*, 297–98.

92. *OR*, 12: Pt. 2, 577; Jackson manuscript report.

93. John D. Vautier, *History of the Eighty-eighth Pennsylvania Volunteers in the War for the Union, 1861–1865* (Philadelphia, 1894), 56. A Wisconsin officer acknowledged that after the Confederates unleashed the Rebel Yell and a concentrated musketry, Union troops "ran back in great disorder." Dawes, *Sixth Wisconsin*, 71.

94. Henderson, 2:179; *CV*, 22 (1914): 231.

95. McClendon, *Recollections*, 119.

96. *New York Times* clipping in Jackson—Valentine. See also *Battle-fields in the South*, 2:316, for another description of Jackson at this time. Douglas, *I Rode with Stonewall*, 142, related a touching story of Jackson riding over the field and encountering a young wounded soldier in the 4th Virginia. The general gave words of encouragement to the lad, who sobbed with gratitude as he was entrusted to the care of Dr. McGuire. Since no other staff member—including McGuire—ever mentioned the incident, its authenticity remains in question.

97. A recent writer faulted Jackson for a two-hour delay in striking back at Pope's forces. His contention is that greater promptness on Jackson's part might have secured Henry House Hill and ended the Second Manassas battle with the destruction of Pope's army. For this argumentative deduction, see Hennessy, *Return to Bull Run*, 427–28.

98. Elias W. Beck, "Letters of a Civil War Surgeon," *Indiana Magazine of History*, 27 (1931): 141.

99. Thomas Evans, "As a Federal Regular Saw Second Bull Run," *Civil War Times Illustrated*, 6 (1968): 35. Major Rufus Dawes's Wisconsin regiment took heavy casualties in the fighting from Groveton through Second Manassas. Pope's entire campaign, he concluded, had been made "against a dark background of blunders, imbecilities, jealousies and disasters." Dawes, *Sixth Wisconsin*, 68.

Naturally, a host of apocryphal stories arose in Confederate circles regarding Pope's ineptitude. A Johnny Reb of somewhat limited education recounted the following: "Gen. Pope has been misplaced, he telegraphed on to Washington that he had encountered J[ackson], had him surrounded withe the loss of 15000, that help must be sent on to take charge of the wounded directly, that J. would be his prisinor in 2 hours. Where upon 20 carrs were loaded with women & men & sent directly on to Manassas; 60 men got off & went directly to the battle field & to their surprise were Jackson's prisonors. The Engeneer was a little suspicious & put back. The men passed here [Jeffersonton] this evening. They are cursing Pope & abusing him dreadfully for lying so." Unidentified soldier to mother, Sept. 6, 1862, William H. Burnley Civil War Papers, UVA.

100. *OR*, 12: Pt. 2, 668.

101. Jackson manuscript report. A Lynchburg newspaper editorialized of Jackson: "It is really marvelous how this extraordinary man escapes [injury], and we may only account for his safety hitherto, upon the assumption that he is under the special protection of that Providence that has selected him to accomplish a great work." Quoted in *Lexington Gazette*, Sept. 18, 1862.

102. Mrs. Burton Harrison, *Recollections Grave and Gay* (New York, 1911), 89.

103. George Templeton Strong, *Diary of the Civil War, 1860–1865* (New York, 1962), 252; Royster, *Destructive War*, 43–44. Writing home about "the ubiquitous Jackson," a Vermont soldier stated disgustingly: "If a tithe of the reports concerning this bold, dashing General had proven true, he would have been thrice killed, 'chawed up' by the Union forces, or annihilated long ago. . . . But notwithstanding all the straits to which this General has been pushed, and all the deaths to which he has been subjected, there was still enough left of him to give zest and spirit to our march on Bull Run." Wilbur Fisk, *Anti-rebel: The Civil War Letters of Wilbur Fisk* (Croton-on-Hudson, N.Y., 1983), 41.

104. Edward A. Pollard, *The Second Year of the War* (New York, 1864), 117–18.

105. Nathan Snead to brother, Sept. 8, 1862, Thomas D. Snead Papers, Duke; Moore, *Cannoneer*, 123. Jed Hotchkiss informed his wife: "Never have I seen such horrors. . . . Their dead were strewn over a space 5 miles long and 3 wide—piled upon one another, sometimes in long lines as they stood in their ranks." Hotchkiss to Sara Hotchkiss, Sept. 1, 1862, Reel 4, Hotchkiss—LC.

106. Harvey Black to wife, Aug. 31, 1862, Harvey Black Letters, Virginia Tech.

107. Jones, *Christ in the Camp*, 141.

108. TJJ to Frederick W. M. Holliday, Aug. 31, 1862, Frederick W. M. Holliday Papers, Duke.

109. Douglas, *I Rode with Stonewall*, 143.

110. Longstreet, *From Manassas to Appomattox*, 191; Oates, *The War*, 149.

111. *OR*, 12: Pt. 2, 81.

112. *Battle-fields of the South*, 453.

113. Robertson, *General A. P. Hill*, 126–27. North of Sudley Springs Ford, Jackson passed within a few miles of his mother's birthplace. He at most had the opportunity to think about the Neale home as he led his troops through the rain.

114. Mrs. Jackson, 341. Jackson's mention of people praying collectively for him in all likelihood referred to the Lexington Presbytery. At this time, it unanimously passed a resolution that all members would pray to the "Lord of Hosts" to protect Jackson and his men "and grant them abundant success in the defence of our country." Minutes of the Lexington Presbytery, W&L, XIV, 344–45.

115. Hotchkiss Journal, Sept. 1, 1862, Reel 1.

116. *OR*, 12: Pt. 2, 744; Cooke, *Outlines from the Outpost*, 69.

117. Hunter McGuire to Jedediah Hotchkiss, May 19, 1896, Reel 34, Hotchkiss—LC; McGuire and Christian, *Confederate Cause*, 202; *SHSP*, 25 (1897): 99. The account in Chambers, 2:174, is confused.

118. Jackson manuscript report.

119. Longstreet subsequently claimed that he arrived on the battlefield just before darkness and found Jackson's men "retiring in a good deal of confusion." When Longstreet observed that the Confederates appeared somewhat disjointed, Jackson reputedly answered, "Yes, but I hope it will prove a victory." Thereupon, according to Longstreet, he sent some of his troops into the action to help stabilize Jackson's dangling lines.

What makes this narrative highly suspicious as truth is another statement by Longstreet. In his official report, he declared that the battle of Chantilly was over by the time his men reached the area. *B&L*, 2:521; *OR*, 12: Pt. 2, 566. For his memoirs, Longstreet embellished some parts of the story and corrected other parts. *From Manassas to Appomattox*, 193–94.

120. Dabney, 542.

121. *CV*, 7 (1899): 366; John N. Shealy to wife, Sept. 2, 1862, John N. Shealy Papers, LSU. One of Longstreet's men wrote home at this time. An officer "very well able to judge," he told a kinsman, had said of Jackson, "A month uncontrolled and he would destroy himself and all under him." H. E. Gourdin to R. N. Gourdin, Sept. 15, 1862, Robert Newman Gourdin Papers, Duke.

122. Longstreet, *From Manassas to Appomattox*, 192; Sorrel, *Staff Officer*, 103; Abram Miller to Julia Miller, Sept. 7, 1862, Abram Schultz Miller Letters, Handley Library, Winchester, Va.

123. Norman A. Graebner, "European Intervention and the Crisis of 1862," *Journal of the Illinois State Historical Society*, 69 (1976): 41.

124. *B&L*, 2:663. Longstreet, or one of his ghost writers, ameliorated his pre-Maryland feelings for the Longstreet memoirs. *From Manassas to Appomattox*, 199–201.

125. Von Borcke, *Confederate War*, 1:176–77.

126. *Lexington Gazette*, Sept. 25, 1862.

CHAPTER 20   *Death Around a Dunker Church*

1. Anna Jackson to Elizabeth S. Brown, Sept. 3, 1862, Jackson—VMI.

2. James R. Boulware Diary, Sept. 3, 1862, BV 27, FSNMP.

3. Howard, *Recollections*, 131–32. A copy of the Volck drawing is in the Howard book. The same sketch, with a mislabeled caption, is in *B&L*, 1:123.

4. Robert K. Krick, "Maxcy Gregg: Political Extremist and Confederate General," *Civil War History*, 19 (1975): 307–8.

5. Details of the Jackson-Hill confrontation, heretofore never reported with complete accuracy, are a composite of several accounts that dovetail together (despite the variations in each source). See Jackson's Sept. 24, 1862, endorsement of Hill's request for a court of inquiry, Davis—Tulane; Berry Benson, *Berry Benson's Civil War Book* (Athens, Ga., 1962), 25; Edward L. Thomas to E. Franklin Paxton, Sept. 24, 1862, Davis—Tulane; Jedediah Hotchkiss to William L. Chase, Mar. 28, 1892, Reel 9, Hotchkiss—LC; Robertson, *General A. P. Hill*, 130–32. The Douglas version, in *I Rode with Stonewall*, 146–47, is dramatized beyond truth. Surgeon M. Graham Ellzey (VMI, 1860) thought that Jackson overreacted. "In military life the incident of arresting A. P. Hill and taking his sword," Ellzey wrote, "was a sort of tragi-comic procedure very characteristic of Jackson and like no body under heaven." Ellzey to James H. Lane, Dec. 1, 1888, James H. Lane Papers, Auburn University. That Hill's arrest "caused a great deal of talk" in the army was an understatement. Alexander, *Personal Recollections*, 142.

6. Leesburg area tour by John E. Divine, Feb. 22, 1994; Mrs. Jackson, 344–45; Bradley T. Johnson, *The First Maryland Campaign: An Address* (Baltimore, 1886), 6. For Jackson's written recommendation of Johnson, see TJJ to Samuel Cooper, Sept. 4, 1862, MC. An insufficient number of Maryland troops in the Confederate army is usually given as the reason Johnson was not elevated to brigadier general until sixteen months later.

7. Johnson, *Maryland Campaign*, 7.

8. Jedediah Hotchkiss to Sara Hotchkiss, Sept. 8, 1862, Reel 4, Hotchkiss—LC.

9. *SHSP*, 12 (1884): 506–7; Clark, ed., *Histories of North Carolina Regiments*, 2:296. More information on Confederates balking at an invasion of Maryland is in Robert K. Krick, "The Army of Northern Virginia in September 1862," in Gary Gallagher, ed., *Antietam: Essays on the 1862 Maryland Campaign* (Kent, Ohio, 1989), 43–44. At one point in the march north, Lee supposedly turned to Lt. Col. E. Porter Alexander and said in a trembling voice, "My army is ruined by straggling." *SHSP*, 13 (1885): 13.

10. McClendon, *Recollections*, 127–28; Fulton, *War Reminiscences*, 48–49; O'Ferrall, *Forty Years*, 51. The river was deeper than stated in Chambers, 2:181. Unknown to Jackson that day, his sister Laura was caring for sick Union soldiers at a Beverly hospital. Federals described her as "a woman of marked intelligence" and possessed "of tender solicitude for their welfare." George R. Prowell, *History of the Eighty-seventh Regiment, Pennsylvania Volunteers* (York, Pa., 1901), 32. Coincidentally on Sept. 5, Gen. Richard Garnett was released from Jackson's arrest and ordered to report to Longstreet for assignment. *OR*, 19: Pt. 2, 595.

11. Thomas G. Pollock to father, Sept. 6, 1862, Thomas H. Pollock Papers, UVA. See also Abram Miller to Julia Miller, Sept. 7, 1862, Abram Schultz Miller Letters, Handley Library, Winchester, Va.; Jedediah Hotchkiss to Sara Hotchkiss, Sept. 8, 1862, Reel 4, Hotchkiss—LC.

12. Early, *Autobiographical Sketch*, 43; *B&L*, 1:238. Cooke, *Jackson*, 308, is the source for Jackson allegedly reviewing his men in the middle of the Potomac.

13. *B&L*, 1:238.

14. TJJ to D. H. Hill, Sept. 5, 1862, Daniel Harvey Hill Papers, LVA; Hotchkiss Journal, Sept. 5, 1862, Reel 1, Hotchkiss—LC.

15. French, *Centennial Tales*, 50; *B&L*, 2:620.

16. Mrs. Jackson, 360; Hotchkiss Journal, Sept. 6, 1862, Reel 1; Jedediah Hotchkiss to Sara Hotchkiss, Sept. 8, 1862, Reel 4, Hotchkiss—LC; *B&L*, 2:620. Douglas asserted that Jackson refused to ride the mare again. Sometime during September 6–8, Little Sorrel was returned to the general. A field correspondent noted near the end of the Frederick encampment that Jackson was on "his old horse." [Caffey], *Battle-fields of the South*, 2:331.

17. Hotchkiss Journal, Sept. 6, 1862, Reel 1; Chase, *Jackson*, 436; Abram Miller to Julia Miller, Sept. 7, 1862, Miller Letters.

18. See John Greenleaf Whittier confession to Wright Gould, Sept. 24, 1886, Hannah Wright Gould Papers, Cornell University; Julia M. Abbott to Samuel Gilson, Aug. 5, 1916, Julia M.

Abbott Letters, MHS; Armistead Churchill Gordon, *Memories and Memorials of William Gordon McCabe* (Richmond, 1925), 2:308–13; Bradley Johnson, *First Maryland Campaign*, 17–18. Johnson was a Frederick native.

19. Unless otherwise stated, all Jackson statements in this chapter are from his manuscript official report of the Harpers Ferry-Antietam campaign in the Gunther Collection, Chicago Historical Society. The edited, printed version is in *OR*, 19: Pt. 1, 952–58. Of all of Jackson's official reports, this one should be handled with the greatest caution. Surgeon McGuire had to assist biographer G. F. R. Henderson through inconsistencies in the document. The reason for the statement's shortcomings lay with Col. Charles J. Faulkner and the "extravagant language" the chief of staff was inclined to use as he prepared most of Jackson's official reports in the winter of 1862–63. Jackson edited his manuscripts carefully. However, the Antietam report appeared after Jackson's death; and in all likelihood, the general never saw it even in semi-completed form.

Dabney, 545, erred twice in his account of Jackson's arrival at Frederick. A citizens' committee did not greet the general and present him with "a costly horse," nor did "a few hundred" young men rush forward to enlist in the Confederate army.

20. Diary of soldier in the 37th Virginia, William Couper Papers, VMI; William Ellis Jones Diary, Sept. 9, 1862, University of Michigan; Thomas G. Pollock to father, Sept. 7, 1862, Pollock Papers; Addey, *Jackson*, 157.

21. Charles W. Squires, "Autobiography," typescript, LC.

22. *SHSP*, 43 (1920): 6, 16–17.

23. Graham, "Some Reminiscences of Stonewall Jackson," 200.

24. Von Borcke, *Confederate War*, 1:190; Thomas C. Elder to Anna Elder, Sept. 4, 1862, Thomas Claybrook Elder Papers, VHS. By late summer 1862, at least one dealer in Richmond was doing a brisk business selling engraved portraits of Jackson. *Richmond Enquirer*, Sept. 12, 1862.

25. [Caffey], *Battle-fields of the South*, 2:230–31.

26. *B&L*, 2:620; Douglas, *I Rode with Stonewall*, 149.

27. Hotchkiss memorandum in Hill court-martial records, Reel 49, Hotchkiss—LC.

28. French, *Centennial Tales*, 59–60. Bartlett, *Military Record of Louisiana*, 31, stated that the soldiers were guilty not of stealing but of discourtesy toward ladies.

29. Douglas annotation in his copy of Mrs. Jackson, 346, Henry Kyd Douglas Library, Antietam NBP. In a postwar speech, Douglas stated that Jackson rode to church in an ambulance. He deleted this inaccuracy from his memoirs. *CV*, 8 (1900): 215; Douglas, *I Rode with Stonewall*, 151. For other particulars on attending the church service in Frederick, see *Annals of the War*, 646; Douglas, *I Rode with Stonewall*, 149–50.

30. TJJ to Anna Jackson, Sept. 8, 1862, Box 6, Dabney—UVA. Mrs. Jackson, 346, changed Jackson's words to a more simple statement.

31. *OR*, 19: Pt. 2, 596, 601–2.

32. *B&L*, 2:605–6.

33. Ibid.

34. Fitzhugh Lee, *General Lee* (New York, 1894), 201.

35. *B&L*, 2:663.

36. H. E. Gourdin to Robert N. Gourdin, Sept. 15, 1862, Robert Newman Gourdin Papers, Duke University; William Allan conversation with R. E. Lee, Feb. 15, 1868, William Allan Papers, SHC. See also Longstreet, *From Manassas to Appomattox*, 201–3. Although a number of writers (for example, see Chambers, 2:188) placed Lee's conference with Jackson and Longstreet on September 9, it occurred the previous day. Harvey Hill, whose postwar statements must be treated with great caution, asserted that in January 1863 Jackson talked to him at length about the decisions made at Frederick. Jackson remained silent throughout most of the discussions because, as he allegedly told Hill, "I opposed the separation of our forces in order to capture Harper's Ferry. I urged that we should all be kept together." D. H. Hill to Robert L. Dabney, July 21, 1864, Dabney—UTS. Every other contemporary source refuted the Hill account. While Dabney, 549, was somewhat influenced by Hill, one of Lee's staff officers in attendance at the conference wrote that Jackson displayed "strong approval" of the plan. Long, *Memoirs of Lee*, 264. In the 1880s, with a quarter-century's perception, Longstreet would proclaim: "The great mistake of the [Maryland] campaign was the division of Lee's army. If General Lee had kept his forces together, he could not have suffered defeat." *B&L*, 2:673.

37. Lee, *Wartime Papers*, 302–3, or *OR*, 19: Pt. 603–4. Another instance of Harvey Hill's strange postwar thinking developed over the contents of Special Orders No. 191. Hill declared that Jackson was supposed to return to the army after seizing Martinsburg. Going to Harpers Ferry was a "violation of Lee's order." When Lee in 1868 heard of Hill's statement, he took sharp exception. Jackson from the beginning had verbal instructions to move to Harpers Ferry, the army commander stated, and Jackson carried out his assignment as ordered. Hal Bridges, ed., "A Lee Letter on the 'Lost Dispatch' and the Maryland Campaign of 1862," *VMHB*, 46 (1958): 164–65.

38. Dennis E. Frye, "Stonewall Attacks! The Siege of Harpers Ferry," *Blue and Gray Magazine*, 5 (Aug.–Sept. 1987): 17. Quartermasters had managed to buy 1000 pairs of shoes in Frederick. That was but a fraction of what was needed. One has to dismiss as poetic musings the comments of Maj. Hazael J. Williams of the 5th Virginia. He wrote on the departure from Frederick: "Our short sojurn in the land of promise wrought a salutary change in the general appearance of the troops. . . . The inner man [was] rejoiced by a number and variety of delicacies to which it had been a stranger for long, long weary months before." *OR*, 19: Pt. 1, 1011.

39. The Jackson copy of Special Orders No. 191 is in the D. H. Hill Papers, NCDAH. So are a number of statements by Hill's defenders that he never received the official directive sent from Lee's headquarters. The "Lost Dispatch" generated years of charges and countercharges. At one point, Lee himself said angrily, "I do not know who lost the dispatch—I knew it was lost and the losing of it, with the fact that it fell into General McClellan's hands, enabled him to discover my whereabouts, revealed to him in part my plans, and caused him to act as to force a battle on me before I was ready for it." Lee to D. H. Hill, Feb. 21, 1868, Lee Letterbook, Lee Family Papers, VHS; Edward C. Gordon to William Allan, Nov. 18, 1866, Allan Papers. For more on the lost dispatch, see Stephen W. Sears, *Landscape Turned Red: The Battle of Antietam* (New York, 1983), 91–92, 112–14, 349–56.

40. *OR*, 19: Pt. 1, 1007.

41. *CV*, 20 (1912): 556; Douglas, *I Rode with Stonewall*, 151.

42. Caldwell, *South Carolina Brigade*, 42.

43. Boulware Diary, Sept. 3, 1862.

44. Alexander, *Personal Recollections*, 141.

45. Ibid., 157. Gregg stewed so much from this latest affront that he subsequently filed charges against Jackson.

46. Douglas, *I Rode with Stonewall*, 152–54. As might be expected, Douglas embellished the story with each rendition. For a version he gave Gen. Bradley T. Johnson, see *Winchester Evening Star*, Feb. 15, 1901. French escaped capture at Boonsboro by hiding in a cellar. Hotchkiss Journal, Sept. 10, 1862, Reel 1. A soldier-correspondent who signed himself "A. T." also reported most of the incident. See *Richmond Daily Dispatch*, Sept. 20, 1862.

47. Following Douglas's lead, most historians have asserted that Hill returned to command on Sept. 13 when Jackson arrived before Harpers Ferry. Douglas, *I Rode with Stonewall*, 158. However, see TJJ to Lawrence O. Branch, Sept. 11, 1862, D. H. Hill Papers, NCDAH; Robertson, *General A. P. Hill*, 134–35. Years later, when Hotchkiss called attention to the error in time, Douglas "became highly indignant." Hotchkiss to G. F. R. Henderson, Apr. 26, 1895, Reel 11, Hotchkiss—LC.

48. *Philadelphia Weekly Times*, Dec. 22, 1883.

49. Alton J. Murray, *South Georgia Rebels* (St. Marys, Ga., 1976), 89.

50. John Newton Lyle, "Sketches Found in a Confederate Veteran's Desk," typescript, W&L, 99; Hotchkiss Journal, Sept. 12, 1862, Reel 1; Caldwell, *South Carolina Brigade*, 42.

51. In the postwar years, Thomas T. Munford (who succeeded Ashby in command of Jackson's cavalry in the valley) became inexplicably anti-Jackson over the Confederate movement to

Harpers Ferry. Munford also became an ardent defender of Gen. Lafayette McLaws in the Maryland Campaign. See Thomas T. Munford to Lafayette McLaws, Apr. 9, 1895, Munford-Ellis Family Papers, Duke; Munford to Robert A. Brock, Nov. 26, 1895, Robert A. Brock Collection, Henry E. Huntington Library. Lee's statement is in his official report. Lee, *Wartime Papers*, 314–15.

52. McClellan, *Civil War Papers*, 453–56; John Gibbon, *Personal Recollections of the Civil War* (New York, 1928), 73. McClellan tempered his bravado somewhat by reminding the War Department that Lee still had "120,000 or more" soldiers in Maryland.

53. *OR*, 19: Pt. 1, 852.

54. *CV,* 5 (1897): 173.

55. *OR*, 19: Pt. 1, 912–13; Clark, *Histories of North Carolina Regiments*, 3:67.

56. Clark, *Histories of North Carolina Regiments*, 3:69; Samuel Hooey Walkup Journal, Sept. 11, 1862, Duke.

57. *B&L*, 2:659; *OR*, 19: Pt. 1, 958; Pt. 2, 607.

58. French, *Centennial Tales*, 120.

59. Jackson manuscript report. See also TJJ to John G. Walker, Sept. 14, 1862, copy of unpublished letter in possession of Dennis E. Frye, Harpers Ferry, W.Va. Jackson's plan was to demand the surrender of the garrison; if it refused, he would establish a twenty-four-hour grace period so that all noncombatants could leave. This was so uncharacteristic of the general that when Walker reported the incident two decades later, Gen. Bradley T. Johnson indignantly challenged Walker's truthfulness. *B&L*, 2:609, 615–16. Jackson was serious about a truce. See *OR*, 19: Pt. 2, 607. Alexander, *Personal Recollections*, 144, made the absurd statement that Jackson did little on Sept. 14, in order to keep the Sabbath holy.

60. *OR*, 19: Pt. 1, 854.

61. Ibid., 913; French, *Centennial Tales*, 120; Edward H. Ripley, *Vermont General* (New York, 1960), 30.

62. French, *Centennial Tales* , 120.

63. James H. Clark, *The Iron Hearted Regiment* (Albany, N.Y., 1865), 15–16.

64. Special Orders No. 267, Sept. 14, 1862, Reel 1, Hotchkiss—LC; *OR*, 19: Pt. 1, 962, 984.

65. McLaws himself was convinced that on Sept. 14 he barely avoided destruction. He presented a hair-raising account of the day's activities in a Sept. 28, 1862, letter to Lizinka C. Brown, Richard Stoddert Ewell Papers, LC.

66. Lee, *Wartime Papers*, 307–8.

67. *OR*, 19: Pt. 1, 951.

68. *OR*, 19: Pt. 1, 142, 583–84, 629–31, 818. In the literary battles of the postwar years, McLaws vigorously defended himself from veterans' charges of neglect of duty. See Lafayette McLaws to Thomas T. Munford, Apr. 20, 1895, Munford-Ellis Family Papers.

69. McClendon, *Recollections*, 137; Henry Lord Page King Diary, Sept. 14, 1862, SHC.

70. Clark, *Histories of North Carolina Regiments*, 2:156.

71. Moore, *Cannoneer*, 139.

72. Arabella M. Willson, *Disaster, Struggle, Triumph: The Adventures of 1000 "Boys in Blue"* (Albany, N.Y., 1870), 83; *OR*, 19: Pt. 1, 528, 743.

73. Fonerden, *Carpenter's Battery*, 37.

74. Sandie Pendleton described White as an erstwhile "Chicago tailor" and added, "You can picture him by imagining Bumpass dressed like a Brigadier." A. S. Pendleton to mother, Sept. 15, 1862, William Nelson Pendleton Papers, SHC. Too much folklore has been interpolated in the White-Jackson meeting. Cooke, *Jackson*, 325, had the general asleep when White reached his headquarters. Douglas, in *B&L*, 2:626, specifically remembered Jackson mounted and "exceedingly wide-awake" at the time. On the other hand, Douglas went to great lengths to portray Jackson that morning as one of the worst-looking figures of note in the war. *I Rode with Stonewall*, 162. McGuire disputed this caricature. Withrow Scrapbooks, W&L, XVIII, 76.

75. *OR*, 19: Pt. 1, 819, 951.

76. Ibid., 141. William M. Miller, *In Camp and Battle with the Washington Artillery of New Orleans* (Boston, 1885), 139.

77. Mrs. Jackson, 352.
78. John Ward, Jr., to Press Ward, Nov. 7, 1862, John Ward, Jr., Papers, LC; Withrow Scrap-books, W&L, XVIII, 76. See also [Caffey], *Battle-fields of the South,* 2:341–42.
79. Caldwell, *South Carolina Brigade,* 44. A New Yorker stated that Jackson raised his hat in return salute as he rode past the Federal prisoners. Willson, *Disaster, Struggle, Triumph,* 86. Several Union soldiers later claimed to have had individual conversations with the general as he entered Harpers Ferry. For example, see *Richmond Daily Dispatch,* Sept. 30, 1862; Ripley, *Vermont General,* 33–34; Pollard, *Lee and His Lieutenants,* 206. McGuire reported scores of Federals snapping to attention and saluting Jackson as he passed. Since Douglas was not with Jackson at the time, his dramatic and oft-quoted account of events is fabrication.
80. Gordon, *Brook Farm,* 26; Frye, "Stonewall Attacks!," 12; Phillips, "Lower Shenandoah Valley," 123.
81. *OR,* 19: Pt. 1, 548–49, 951, 960–61; *B&L,* 2:674.
82. Frye, "Stonewall Attacks!," 52; Caldwell, *South Carolina Brigade,* 43. Many soldiers were happiest at being able to replace antiquated muskets with new Springfield rifle-muskets. Clark, *Histories of North Carolina Regiments,* 2:32.
83. Von Borcke, *Confederate War,* 1:221–22.
84. *OR,* 19: Pt. 1, 1007; *Richmond Daily Dispatch,* Sept. 27, 1862; Clark, *Histories of North Carolina Regiments,* 2:33. Various times have been given for the start and the end of the Sept. 15–16 march. One source had Jackson leaving the Ferry at 2 A.M.; a second writer put Jackson's arrival at Sharpsburg shortly after dawn. *OR,* 19: Pt. 1, 1011; Henderson, 2:234n. Another biographer covered himself well by having Jackson reach his destination first "on the morning" of the 16th and then "at mid-day." Dabney, 556, 560.
    Longstreet's assertion that Jackson should have marched east (rather than north) and swung around McClellan's rear is a flagrant product of hindsight. *From Manassas to Appomattox,* 233. Neither Jackson nor any other Confederate field general at the time had any idea of the location and displacement of the Union army. Further, and of more relevance, Lee had ordered Jackson to join him at Sharpsburg. No mention was made of Jackson staging en route a demonstration against the enemy.
85. Henderson, 2:235.
86. *CV,* 16 (1908): 578.
87. R. E. Lee to Robert L. Dabney, Jan. 25, 1866, Dabney—UTS; R. E. Lee to Anna Jackson, Jan. 26, 1866, Davis—Tulane.
88. Freeman, *Lee's Lieutenants,* 2:204. For artillery at Antietam, see Joseph Mills Hanson, "A Report on the Employment of the Artillery at the Battle of Antietam, Md.," typescript (1940), Antietam NBP, especially 10, 17, 19–20.
89. Douglas, *I Rode with Stonewall,* 167.
90. TJJ to "Miss Fairfield," Sept. 16, 1862, Jackson—WVU.
91. A soldier in Harvey Hill's division asserted that when he saw Jackson's men approaching, "I thought they were Yankees, for they had on lots of the Yankees' clothes." Samuel D. Mashbourne Memoir, BV 2, FSNMP. This statement is in direct contrast to Jackson's always-strict orders against his men wearing Federal uniforms.
92. Hunter McGuire to Jedediah Hotchkiss, Mar. 30, 1896, Reel 12, Hotchkiss—LC. See also [Caffey], *Battle-fields of the South,* 2:148; John Cheve Haskell Memoir, Duke.
93. Marginal annotation made in Henderson, 2:228, Douglas Library.
94. Dawes, *Sixth Wisconsin,* 87; Johnson, *First Maryland Campaign,* 31.
95. *CV,* 22 (1914): 66.
96. Dawes, *Sixth Wisconsin,* 90.
97. *OR,* 19: Pt. 1, 974; Benjamin F. Cook, *History of the Twelfth Massachusetts Volunteers (Webster Regiment)* (Boston, 1882), 73.
98. *OR,* 19: Pt. 1, 190.
99. Ibid., 189; Wilson Reminiscences, William P. Palmer Collection, Western Reserve Historical Society; *OR,* 19: Pt. 1, 218.
100. Longstreet was blatantly incorrect in asserting that he "was obliged to send Hood to

support our center." Hood had been under Jackson's command since the preceding afternoon. Yet Longstreet did provide a good picture of Jackson's predicament at that moment in the battle. "The line swayed forward and back like a rope exposed in rushing currents. A force too heavy to be withstood would strike and drive in a weak point till we could collect a few fragments, and in turn force back the advance till our lost ground was recovered." *B&L*, 2:668.

101. A Virginia soldier later commented: "It was horrible in the extreme to witness the men with mangled limbs and bodies making their way to the rear. . . . The whole face of the country seemed covered with them." *Richmond Daily Dispatch*, Sept. 27, 1862. Grigsby's refusal to move the Stonewall Brigade to a more protected position without orders incurred the permanent resentment of at least one regimental commander. See H. J. Williams to Jedediah Hotchkiss, Nov. 25, 1896, Reel 13, Hotchkiss—LC.

102. *Richmond Enquirer*, Sept. 23, 1862.

103. *B&L*, 2:690–91; Stephen D. Lee to Jedediah Hotchkiss, Aug. 10, 1896, Reel 13, Hotchkiss—LC; Boulware Diary, Sept. 17, 1862. Starke was buried in Richmond's Hollywood Cemetery beside his son, Lt. Edwin Starke, who had died exactly two months earlier—July 17—from wounds received at the battle of Seven Pines.

104. D. H. Hill to Robert L. Dabney, June 7, 1863, Dabney—UTS.

105. *OR*, 19: Pt. 1, 923.

106. Dawes, *Sixth Wisconsin*, 91; *CV*, 22 (1914): 555.

107. Dwight E. Stinson, Jr., "Analytical Study of the Action of Greene's Division," typescript (1961), Antietam NBP, 2–5; Hood, *Advance and Retreat*, 44; Lee, *Pendleton*, 216. Sandie Pendleton added: "Such a storm of balls I never conceived it possible for men to live through. Shot and shell shrieking and crashing, canister and bullets whistling and hissing their most fiend-like through the air until you could almost see them."

108. H. Watters Berryman to mother, Sept. 22, 1862, BV 113, FSNMP.

109. McLaws's march from the Harpers Ferry area left something to be desired in the minds of a few Confederate officers. The troops did not reach Sharpsburg until either 3 A.M. or after the battle was underway. McLaws lost time hunting for Lee and getting instructions. Even though Lee permitted McLaws's men to rest for a short period, the advance from Harpers Ferry had reduced McLaws's command to skeletal strength. The best defenses of McLaws are in *OR*, 19: Pt. 1, 857–58, 883; Thomas T. Munford to Lafayette McLaws, Apr. 9, 1895, Munford-Ellis Family Papers; Sears, *Landscape Turned Red*, 195, 220, 224; Krick, "Army of Northern Virginia," 48.

110. A large number of men were later convinced that in the confusion attendant to the struggle, Union soldiers in the rear files delivered volleys into the backs of their comrades. See Andrew E. Ford, *The Story of the Fifteenth Regiment, Massachusetts Volunteer Infantry, in the Civil War, 1861–1864* (Clinton, Mass., 1898), 195–96; Ernest L. Waitt, comp., *History of the Nineteenth Regiment, Massachusetts Volunteer Infantry, 1861–1865* (Salem, Mass., 1906), 137.

111. Early, *Autobiographical Sketch*, 144; Mosby, *Memoirs*, 144.

112. *SHSP*, 35 (1907): 350.

113. Stinson, "Greene's Division," 11–17; Henry Lord Page King Diary, Sept. 17, 1862.

114. Hunter McGuire to Jedediah Hotchkiss, Mar. 30, 1896, Reel 12, Hotchkiss—LC. Variations of Jackson's words are in *SHSP*, 25 (1897): 95, 101; Hunter McGuire, *The Memory of "Stonewall" Jackson* (New York, 1898), 4; Henderson, 2:256. Jackson's brother-in-law, Rufus Barringer of the 1st North Carolina Cavalry, developed a parallel account. That day he supposedly asked Jackson if the Confederates were not pretty beaten. Barringer had Jackson reply, "Yes, but oh! how I'd like to see the Yankee camp right now!" Mrs. Jackson, 318.

115. Clark, *Histories of North Carolina Regiments*, 2:603–4.

116. McGuire and Christian, *Confederate Cause*, 204–5; *B&L*, 2:679–80.

117. *OR*, 19: Pt. 1, 958; Henderson, 2:235, 255; Worsham, *Foot Cavalry*, 89.

118. Nichols, *A Soldier's Story*, 53; J. Thompson Brown to Jedediah Hotchkiss, Apr. 23, 1895, Reel 11, Hotchkiss—LC; Robertson, *Stonewall Brigade*, 158–60. Inevitable rumors about Jackson developed on the Union side after Antietam. A Philadelphia newspaper reported him captured in the action. In the preposterous category was a story that had Jackson riding through the heavy smoke of battle to a Federal battery. He ordered the guns to be elevated for more effective fire, then disappeared back in the smoke. The artillerists did as they were told, thereafter hurling shells far over the heads of their intended victims. Jones, *War Clerk's Diary*, 1:154; Oliver C. Bosbyshell, ed., *Pennsylvania at Antietam* (Harrisburg, 1906), 162.

119. See Robertson, *General A. P. Hill*, 141–47.

120. George E. Pickett, *Soldier of the South* (Boston, 1928), 27–28. Harvey Hill was also upset over the battle of Antietam, not only at the high losses among his good soldiers but for the limited praise he received for his leadership. At one point he sneered, "Oh History, History, what a tissue of lies thou art!" D. H. Hill to Isabella Hill, Oct. 18, 1862, Daniel Harvey Hill Papers, USMHI.

121. Douglas, *I Rode with Stonewall*, 174.

122. Hood, *Advance and Retreat*, 45.

123. Von Borcke, *Confederate War*, 1:237–38.

124. Douglas, *I Rode with Stonewall*, 179.

125. R. E. Lee to Anna Jackson, Jan. 26, 1866, Davis—Tulane.

126. Henry Lord Page King Diary, Sept. 18, 1862; Boulware Diary, Sept. 19, 1862.

127. Bean, "Harman," 8; Jedediah Hotchkiss to G. F. R. Henderson, Mar. 24, 1896, Reel 12, Hotchkiss—LC. Jackson praised Harman's efforts in his official report. He made no mention of his language, however.

128. *B&L*, 2:682.

129. Chamberlayne, *Ham Chamberlayne*, 134. For other criticism of the brigadier, see David G. McIntosh to Cecil Battine, Apr. 5, 1907, David Gregg McIntosh Papers, USMHI; Thomas T. Munford to N. I. Hoey, Nov. 19, 1890, LHAC, 55-B.

130. *OR*, 19: Pt. 1, 142, 831–32; Lee, *Pendleton*, 214. Pendleton knew at once that he was guilty of flagrant negligence at Boteler's Ford. For his first rationale, see W. N. Pendleton to Anzolette E. Pendleton, Sept. 22, 1862, Pendleton Papers.

131. Mrs. Jackson, 345; Douglas, *I Rode with Stonewall*, 184.

132. Dabney, 579.

133. Robertson, *General A. P. Hill*, 148–50; *Northern Neck News*, Feb. 26, 1897, clipping in BV 186, FSNMP. For obvious reasons, the regimental historian devoted a full chapter to the Pennsylvanians' action at Shepherdstown. Survivors' Association, *History of the Corn Exchange Regiment: 118th Pennsylvania Volunteers* (Philadelphia, 1888), 54–94.

134. Hunter McGuire to Jedediah Hotchkiss, May 28, 1896, Reel 12, Hotchkiss—LC.

135. D. H. Hill to Robert L. Dabney, July 19, 1864, Dabney—UTS; R. E. Lee to Robert L. Dabney, Jan. 25, 1866, Dabney—UTS. For Lee's alleged excited condition after Pendleton's announcement, see J. W. Ratchford to Robert L. Dabney, Apr. 27 1869, Dabney—UTS.

136. Thompson, "Georgia Boy," 329; *Richmond Enquirer*, Sept. 24, 1862.

CHAPTER 21   *Leading a Corps*

1. McClendon, *Recollections*, 155.

2. Built in 1837 by Elisha Boyd for his son John and his family, the Boyd mansion was a local landmark. It was there, on July 15, 1863, that Gen. J. Johnston Pettigrew died of wounds received at Gettysburg.

3. *OR*, 19: Pt. 1, 69–70; Pt. 2, 645.

4. Hotchkiss Journal, Sept. 21, 1862, Reel 1, Hotchkiss—LC.

5. *SHSP*, 43 (1920): 21; Wood, *The War*, 102; Clark, *Histories of North Carolina Regiments*, 3:68.

6. *OR*, 19: Pt. 2, 621, 639; Caldwell, *South Carolina Brigade*, 53; Jedediah Hotchkiss to brother, Sept. 28, 1862, Reel 4, Hotchkiss—LC. Another South Carolina officer felt that the troops were "in good fighting trim, as far as the *spirit* is concerned." He then philosophized: "I am much inclined to the opinion that half-clad, half-shod, half-fed troops fight better than those better taken care of." Andrew B. Wardlaw to wife, Oct. 5, 1862, BV 206, FSNMP.

7. Julia Chase Diary, Sept. 20, 1862, Handley Library, Winchester, Va.; Mrs. Hugh Lee Diary,

Sept. 20, 1862, Handley. Martinsburg did not become a major hospital center for Confederates because war sentiment among its residents was so sharply divided. On Sept. 27, Crenshaw's battery moved down the main street. One of the Virginia gunners declared: "The women as we passed through Martinsburg indulged in some scurrilous remarks to our soldiers, snatching up their clothes and running in the house with the remark, 'Don't touch me, you nasty trash.' We would like to have a chance to shell that place." William Ellis Jones Diary, Sept. 27, 1862, University of Michigan. Surgeon Harvey Black had a similar opinion of Martinsburg citizens. See Black to his wife, Sept. 26, 1862, Harvey Black Letters, Virginia Tech.

8. *OR*, 19: Pt. 2, 618-19, 629-30; R. E. Lee to William N. Pendleton, Sept. 23, 1862, William Nelson Pendleton Papers, SHC. Contempt for stragglers was fairly universal through the army's ranks. Randolph Fairfax of the Rockbridge Artillery exclaimed: "It is shameful. . . . The scoundrels were straggling over the country and eating out the hospitable farmers on their way, while their comrades were beating back McClellan." Slaughter, *Randolph Fairfax*, 40.

9. General Orders No. 93, Sept. 5, 1862, Reel 5, Hotchkiss—LC; TJJ to C. R. Mason, Nov. 18, 1862, Jackson Letterbook, Reel 49, Hotchkiss—LC; Records of the 27th Virginia, MC.

10. Caldwell, *South Carolina Brigade* (already cited in fn. 6), 85n.; TJJ to Jubal A. Early, Sept. 22, 1862, Eldridge Collection, Henry E. Huntington Library.

11. TJJ to Samuel Cooper, Sept. 22, 1862, Isaac Ridgeway Trimble Papers, MHS; TJJ to Samuel Cooper, Sept. 22, 1862, Jackson—VMI; Hotchkiss Journal, Sept. 29, 1862, Reel 1.

12. TJJ to Samuel Cooper, Sept. 24, 1862, Office of the Adjutant & Inspector General and of the Quartermaster General, 1861-1865: Letters Received, RG109, NA. Trimble received his promotion in Jan. 1863 while recuperating from his Second Manassas wound. The assignments of Smith and Hood were all but automatic. The gruff and argumentative Jones also got his promotion solely through Jackson's persistence. For one of Jackson's strongest endorsements, see TJJ to Robert E. Lee, Oct. 23, 1862, Cook—WVU.

13. See W. M. Paxton biographical sketch of his father in Reel 9, Hotchkiss—LC; French, *Centennial Tales*, 51.

14. *OR*, 25: Pt. 2, 645; W. M. Paxton to Jedediah Hotchkiss, Nov. 6, 1897, Reel 14, Hotchkiss—LC. Jackson stated of Paxton's qualifications: "There is no officer under the grade proposed whom I can recommend with such confidence for promotion to a Brigadier-Generalcy." Paxton, *Franklin Paxton*, 65. See also *SHSP*, 38 (1910): 281; Edmondson, *Dear Emma*, 111.

15. French, *Centennial Tales*, 51; Robertson, *Stonewall Brigade*, 163-65; Edwin G. Lee to F. W. M. Holliday, Nov. 15 [?], 1862, Frederick W. M. Holliday Papers, Duke University; Reidenbaugh, *Twenty-seventh Virginia*, 72-73. Response in Lexington to Paxton's promotion was not universally favorable. When Sandie Pendleton heard the news, the aide wrote home: "I am surprised that you should think Paxton so bad an appointment & so unpopular. He is an excellent officer & much liked. No one but Grigsby thought of resigning." Pendleton to sister, Dec. 5, 1862, Pendleton Papers. Lieutenant Howard of the Stonewall Brigade staff spoke for many in assessing the controversy over brigade command: "I think Grigsby ought to have been promoted, but his bluff manner and reckless speech were against him." Howard, *Recollections*, 181.

16. Johnson, *First Maryland Campaign*, 40; TJJ to Robert H. Chilton, Oct. 3, 1862, Reel 49, Hotchkiss—LC.

17. Lee endorsement to Sept. 26, 1862, A. P. Hill letter, Davis—Tulane. ✓

18. A. P. Hill to R. E. Lee, Sept. 22, 1862, Davis—Tulane; Hotchkiss Journal, Oct. 6, 1862, Reel 1. See also Robertson, *General A. P. Hill*, 152-54.

19. Andrew B. Wardlaw to wife, Oct. 5, 1862, BV 206, FSNMP.

20. Graham Reminiscences, Box 20, Dabney—SHC; B. R. Tillman to Anna Tillman, Sept. 28, 1862, John Eldred Swearingen Papers, University of South Carolina; *Richmond Enquirer*, Oct. 31, 1862.

21. Andrews, *Footprints*, 87-88.

22. David Ballenger to Nancy Ballenger, Oct. 24, 1862, David Ballenger Papers, University of

South Carolina. A few soldiers found it difficult to explain the charisma of Jackson. Captain Andrew Wardlaw of the 14th South Carolina told his wife of seeing Jackson cheered by the men. "He presented a fine appearance as he dashed by. . . . The whole army was carried away with excitement. I never was so struck with any man as with him on that occasion. Is it not strange that the man who works his troops harder than any others in the army should be the only one whose presence gives rise to such enthusiasm?" Andrew B. Wardlaw to wife, Oct. 26, 1862, BV 206, FSNMP. See also John W. Carlisle to B. B. Foster, Oct. 26, 1862, James Rion McKissick Papers, University of South Carolina.

23. *SHSP*, 43 (1920): 21–22; Douglas, *I Rode with Stonewall*, 198.

24. TJJ to Mrs. Osburn, Sept. 29, 1862, Cook—WVU.

25. Douglas, *I Rode with Stonewall*, 196.

26. Von Borcke, *Confederate War*, 2:36–37.

27. Ibid., 1:295–96.

28. Ibid., 296–97.

29. TJJ to J. E. B. Stuart, Sept. 30, 1862, James E. B. Stuart Papers, Huntington.

30. *OR*, Ser 4, 2:198; Ser. 1, 19: Pt. 2, 643; Vandiver, 406; Chambers, 2:239–40. On Oct. 11, the president announced the promotion of seven officers to the rank of lieutenant general. Longstreet was the senior at the top of the list, followed in turn by E. Kirby Smith, Leonidas Polk, William J. Hardee, Jackson, Theophilus H. Holmes, and John C. Pemberton. Not until Nov. 6 were the formal announcements made of the promotions of Longstreet and Jackson. By then, the reorganization of the Army of Northern Virginia had been all but completed. Jefferson Davis, *The Papers of Jefferson Davis* (Baton Rouge, 1971–), 8:410; *OR*, 19: Pt. 2, 698–99.

31. For example, see Davis, *Papers*, 8:236, 244.

32. *OR*, 21:541–44; Chambers, 2:237; Freeman, *Lee's Lieutenants*, 2:274. At this time, Harvey Hill was venting his anger and sarcasm at his own people. "The Yankees are drilling their new recruits every day, it is said even at night," he informed his wife, "while our Congressional fools are doing nothing. . . . If we had all our stragglers up & present who ought to be here, the Army would be five times as numerous as it is. The dogs who are hanging about home ought to be forced into the field." D. H. Hill to Isabella Hill, Oct. 9, 1862, Daniel Harvey Hill Papers, USMHI.

33. Jedediah Hotchkiss to William L. Chase, Mar. 28, 1892, Reel 9, Hotchkiss—LC. In mid-October, Capt. Henry L. P. King of McLaws's staff was temporarily assigned to Jackson's headquarters. The aide noticed that the general rose early and attended to paperwork for an hour or so before having a cold breakfast. "I found him more gentle in manner than on the Battle field," King wrote, "in fact quite urbane, and thought him very good looking indeed." Henry Lord Page King Diary, Oct. 20, 1862, SHC.

34. James H. Lane, "Reminiscences," James H. Lane Papers, Auburn University, 1–2.

35. *SHSP*, 43 (1920): 21. Miss Boyd claimed not only to have had a lengthy conference with Jackson but to have received as well a commission as captain and "honorary Aide-de-camp" to the general. Boyd, *Belle Boyd*, 209–10. No verification exists of those assertions.

36. Garnet Wolseley, "A Month's Visit to the Confederate Headquarters," *Blackwood's Edinburgh Magazine*, 93 (1863): 21.

37. Hoole, *Lawley*, 32.

38. Pickett, *Soldier of the South*, 28. Interestingly, a Georgia private at this time was describing Jackson to his parents as "a sorry looking chance . . . a little old drid up looking man." Thompson, "Georgia Boy," 330.

39. TJJ to Anna Jackson, Oct. 13, 1862, Dabney—ULV. After hearing Stiles preach one evening, a refreshed Jackson told Chaplain Asa M. Marshall of being "more convinced than ever that if sinners had justice they would all be damned." Jones, *Christ in the Camp*, 506.

40. Mrs. Jackson, 204; TJJ to Anna Jackson, Oct. 27, 1862, Dabney—ULV. An edited version of the Oct. 27 letter is in Mrs. Jackson, 349, and misdated as Oct. 20.

41. A. S. Pendleton to mother, Oct. 8, 1862, Pendleton Papers; Samuel Angus Firebaugh Diary, Oct. 10–12, 1862, Handley; Murphy, *Tenth Virginia*, 55.

42. Blackford, *Letters from Lee's Army*, 128; *Century Magazine*, 47 (1893–94): 627. Douglas, *I Rode with Stonewall*, 192, gave a much more involved salutation from Jackson. For Stuart's Chambersburg raid and the mixed reactions it produced, see Thomas, *Bold Dragoon*, 173–80.

43. D. H. Hill to Isabella Hill, Oct. 6, 1862, Hill Papers, USMHI; Nisbet, *Four Years*, 113; Douglas, *I Rode with Stonewall*, 197.

44. TJJ to Robert L. Dabney, Dec. 5, 1862, Dabney—UTS.

45. Dr. McGuire's Narrative, Box 19, Dabney—SHC.

46. William S. White Narrative, Box 20, Dabney—SHC.

47. TJJ to D. H. Hill, Oct. 16, 1862, Harrison Collection, Newberry Library; *OR*, 19: Pt. 2, 86; Early, *Autobiographical Sketch*, 163.

48. Worsham, *Foot Cavalry*, 91; A. S. Pendleton to Rose Pendleton, Oct. 24, 1862, Pendleton Papers, SHC; Addey, *Jackson*, 174–75.

49. Blackford, *Letters from Lee's Army*, 130–31. In contrast, engineering officer Duncan G. Campbell of McLaws's staff met Jackson for the first time on this expedition. Campbell was obviously unfamiliar with the general's reticence. "He is a very silent man," the staff officer wrote, "and not at all agreeable." Duncan G. Campbell to Nellie Campbell, Oct. 23, 1862, Campbell Family Papers, SHC.

50. A. S. Pendleton to Nancy Pendleton, Oct. 26, 1862, Pendleton Papers.

51. *OR*, 19: Pt. 2, 685.

52. Mrs. Hugh Lee Diary, Oct. 28, 1862, Handley.

53. Ibid.; William W. Bennett, *A Narrative of the Great Revival Which Prevailed in the Southern Armies* (Philadelphia, 1877), 231–32.

54. Gold, *Clark County*, 111; *Lexington Gazette*, Nov. 6, 1862. Surgeon Abram Miller of the 25th Virginia also mentioned the momentary good condition of the Confederates. Abram Miller to Julia Miller, Oct. 28, 1862, Abram Schultz Miller Letters, Handley. Harvey Hill's division crossed the mountains and took position in the Upperville area. TJJ to D. H. Hill, Oct. 30, 1862, Daniel Harvey Hill Papers, LVA.

55. Ben Ritter, "Jackson's First War-time Photograph: The Widow's Favorite," *Civil War Times Illustrated*, 17 (Feb. 1979): 36–39; Graham, *Jackson*, 9.

56. Graham, *Jackson*, 9.

57. Ibid., 9–10; *CV*, 19 (1911): 183, 430; Douglas, *I Rode with Stonewall*, 199–200.

58. Washington P. Shooter to John C. McCleneghan, Nov. 10, 1862, John Charles McClenaghan Collection, University of South Carolina.

59. *VMHB*, 91 (1983): 502–3.

60. Henry A. Chambers Diary, Nov. 3, 1862, NCDAH; *Richmond Daily Dispatch*, Nov. 19, 1862. For examples of the confusion Jackson's movements created on the Union side, see *OR*, 19: Pt. 2, 540, 550, 562, 572, 577–78, 585–86.

61. A. S. Pendleton to Anzolette Pendleton, Nov. 2, 1862, Pendleton Papers; McDonald, *Diary*, 105; Mrs. Hugh Lee Diary, Nov. 16, 1862. Jackson paid slight heed to his uniform during this time. While he still wore the same faded coat, his friend Judge Camden noted, "he had disposed of the old cap and supplied its place with an old black wool hat, the brim turned down all round and the band about halfway up the crown. Upon the whole I was forced to concede to myself that the General's appearance did not set him off to the best possible advantage." G. D. Camden to Robert L. Dabney, Nov. 25, 1863, Cook—WVU.

62. *OR*, 19: Pt. 2, 696, 698–99.

63. TJJ to James Longstreet, Nov. 6, 1862, Cutts-Madison Papers, Massachusetts Historical Society.

64. Lee, *Wartime Papers*, 330.

65. Alexander, *Personal Recollections*, 157–58.

66. A. P. Hill to J. E. B. Stuart, Nov. 14, 1862, James Ewell Brown Stuart Papers, VHS.

67. *OR*, 19: Pt. 1, 983; TJJ to A. P. Hill, Nov. 10, 1862, Reel 49, Hotchkiss—LC.

68. Henderson, 2:283–84. At this time, Jackson also purchased a $1000 Confederate bond paying 8 percent interest and redeemable in ten years. The bond is in Davis—Tulane.

69. *OR*, 19: Pt. 2, 713, 718; 51: Pt. 2, 640; Mrs. Jackson, 365.

70. A. S. Pendleton to Mary Pendleton, Nov. 7, 1862, Pendleton Papers; Washington P. Shooter to John C. McClenaghan, Nov. 10, 1862, McClenaghan Collection; George H. T. Greer Diary, Nov. 8, 1862, CWTI. Federal Gen. Alfred Pleasonton observed, "The enemy are, I think, somewhat disconcerted just now." *OR*, 19: Pt. 2, 121.

71. H. Kyd Douglas to Tippie Boteler, Nov. 14, 1862, Alexander Robinson Boteler Papers, Duke.

72. Lee, *Wartime Dispatches*, 333–36; *OR*, 19: Pt. 2, 717.

73. *SHSP*, 43 (1920): 23. When Smith narrated this story a half-century after the war, he referred to himself by his final rank of captain. In the autumn of 1862, he had just been commissioned a lieutenant.

74. C. J. Faulkner [Jr.] to Jedediah Hotchkiss, Sept. 14, 1897, Reel 14, Hotchkiss—LC; broadside, Faulkner Family Papers, VHS. Captain Sandie Pendleton thought that he deserved promotion to chief of staff but acknowledged that youthfulness and limited experience were probably against him. Pendleton concluded of Jackson that he was "willing to stay with him, do all the work, & be continually passed over." A. S. Pendleton to Anzolette Pendleton, Nov. 15, 1862, Pendleton Papers. On Nov. 21, Jackson officially recommended Faulkner's appointment to the staff. Office of Adjt. General: Letters Received, RG109, NA.

75. A. S. Pendleton to Anzolette Pendleton, Nov. 15, 1862, Pendleton Papers; Myers, *The Comanches*, 129; TJJ to Anna Jackson, Nov. 11, 1862, Dabney, LVA. Some of the gift-letters are in Old Catalog Collection, VHS.

76. A. S. Pendleton to Anzolette Pendleton, Nov. 19, 1862, Pendleton Papers; *SHSP*, 43 (1920): 23.

77. TJJ to Anna Jackson, Nov. 20, 1862, Dabney—LVA.

78. Mrs. Jackson, 358–59.

79. Graham, "Reminiscences," 200–1.

80. Graham Reminiscences, Box 20, Dabney—SHC;

81. *OR*, 21:1025, 1054; McDonald, *Diary*, 107. See also *Lexington Gazette*, Nov. 20, 1862, for the hardships being borne by the soldiers. In rather startling contrast, the usually reliable Virginia artillerist, "Ham" Chamberlayne, was writing at the time that the troops were "in fine condition" and the army "in the best condition I have ever known it." Chamberlayne, *Ham Chamberlayne*, 140–41.

82. Nisbet, *Four Years*, 118.

83. Boyd, *Reminiscences*, 30–31.

84. *The Land We Love*, 1 (1866): 71–72. One soldier claimed that Early set the pace for the drinking that day. *CV*, 30 (1922): 18. Another wrote amusingly of an intoxicated captain stumbling up the road and proclaiming to no one in particular: "The drunken man falleth by the wayside, but the sober man passeth over the mountains safely and sleepeth in the valley beyond." Oates, *The War*, 165.

85. R. E. Lee to TJJ, Nov. 23, 1862, Davis—Tulane. Subsequent writers have tended to change Lee's wording from "such a position" to "such action." For example, see Chambers, 2:260. Yet the inference is clear in either case. Not until Nov. 25 was Lee aware that Jackson was on the way with the other half of the army. *OR*, 21:1030.

86. Mrs. Jackson, 351; *SHSP*, 43 (1920): 24.

87. Greenlee Davidson, *Captain Greenlee Davidson, C.S.A.: Diary and Letters, 1861–1863* (Verona, Va., 1975), 60.

88. *Staunton Spectator*, Dec. 2, 1862.

89. Clark, *Histories of North Carolina Regiments*, 1:168–69. For other statements of Jackson's men leaving bloody prints in the snow, see Clark, *Histories of North Carolina Regiments*, 1:664; 2:34–35, 438; Early, *Autobiographical Sketch*, 165. Writing with obvious exaggeration, a Georgia soldier informed his wife: "I marched so much that it wore the ends of my toenails down to the quick, blistered my feet, and made them sore generally." McCrea, *Red Dirt and Isinglass*, 377.

90. Mrs. Jackson, 360.

91. Ibid., 361, 363, 366. There are claims that the child was born at the home of Harvey and

Isabella Hill. Anna Jackson is the source for the birth occurring at the residence of James P. and Harriet Irwin. Shortly after giving birth, Anna wrote Laura Arnold to inform her of the event. Laura by then had become so notorious for her Unionist views that her feelings were initially given as the reason for the postwar divorce from Mr. Arnold. Rumors that Laura had "taken up" with a Union officer soon became an issue. Divorce Papers, Cook—WVU.

92. *SHSP*, 43 (1920): 24–25.

93. Davidson, *Captain Davidson*, 60; Wills Lee Memoirs, BV 138, FSNMP.

94. D. H. Hill to Robert L. Dabney, July 21, 1864, Dabney—UTS. Another version of Jackson's statement is in McGuire and Christian, *Confederate Cause*, 205. James Power Smith suggested that the Confederate government, not Lee, vetoed Jackson's idea of a North Anna stand. *SHSP*, 43 (1920): 27. Jackson's principal objection to Fredericksburg was that no room existed for the Confederates to counterattack once Burnside had been repulsed (as Jackson expected him to be). *SHSP*, 25 (1897): 102.

95. Lucy Chandler Pendleton Reminiscences, BV 188, FSNMP; unidentified newspaper clipping, Thomas J. Jackson File, Valentine Museum. The Chandler offer of hospitality at "Fairfield" was to Jackson and not his staff. At no time was the home ever tendered as a headquarters for the Second Corps.

96. *B&L*, 3:73.

97. William H. Morgan, *Personal Reminiscences of the War of 1861–5* (Lynchburg, Va., 1911), 144; William M. Dame to mother, Dec. 2, 1862, Dame Letters, BV 138, FSNMP.

98. Tom Watson Brown, "The Military Career of Thomas R. R. Cobb," *Georgia Historical Quarterly*, 45 (1961): 351.

99. *OR*, 21:1044, 1047–48; D. H. Hill to Robert L. Dabney, July 21, 1864, Dabney—UTS.

100. Mrs. Jackson, 19.

101. Ibid., 361–62.

102. Paxton, *Memoir*, 74; Slaughter, *Fairfax*, 41.

103. TJJ to Alexander R. Boteler, Dec. 10, 1862, Alexander Robinson Boteler Papers.

104. Mrs. Jackson, 377.

105. Hotchkiss Journal, Dec. 10, 1862, Reel 1. Jackson had a number of VMI forage hats. The one he gave Hotchkiss was probably the oldest—and obviously his favorite.

106. For reactions by Confederates to the senseless bombardment of Fredericksburg, see *SHSP*, 36 (1908): 20–21; A. S. Pendleton to Anzolette Pendleton, Dec. 11, 1862, Pendleton Papers; *B&L*, 3:122.

107. *OR*, 21:553; Jackson manuscript report, Georgia Callis West Papers, VHS; David G. McIntosh, "The Battle of Fredericksburg," typescript, CWTI, 35.

108. Von Borcke, *Confederate War*, 2:106.

109. Robertson, *General A. P. Hill*, 160–61; McIntosh, "Battle of Fredericksburg," 36.

110. McIntosh, "Battle of Fredericksburg," 34.

111. D. H. Hill to Robert L. Dabney, July 21, 1864, Dabney—UTS.

112. Frank A. O'Reilly to author, June 6, 1995.

113. *OR*, 21:635, 641, 643, 645. Apparently, the first couriers sent to Early and Harvey Hill failed to reach their destinations. An anxious Jackson, receiving no word of the advance of the two commanders, finally dispatched Lt. Smith to activate their forces. This is the explanation for the late start of the two divisions from below Fredericksburg. *SHSP*, 43 (1920): 28.

114. Hotchkiss Journal, Dec. 12, 1862, Reel 1.

115. *Richmond Enquirer*, Dec. 16, 1862; Jedediah Hotchkiss to G. F. R. Henderson, Apr. 20, 1897, Reel 34, Hotchkiss—LC.

116. Frank A. O'Reilly, *"Stonewall" Jackson at Fredericksburg* (Lynchburg, Va., 1993), 26. Douglas, *I Rode with Stonewall*, 205. See also *CV*, 14 (1906): 66. Hotchkiss stated in his journal that December 13 began cool but later became pleasant under an almost cloudless sky. Yet in two postwar letters written less than a week apart, Hotchkiss's memory played tricks on him. He recalled the day being "exceedingly raw" with a wind that was "stiff and biting." Hotchkiss to James P. Smith, Apr. 16, 1897, and Hotchkiss to G. F. R. Henderson, Apr. 20, 1897, Reel 34, Hotchkiss—LC.

117. Worsham, *Foot Cavalry*, 93.
118. *B&L*, 3:114; Douglas, *I Rode with Stonewall*, 205.
119. *SHSP*, 43 (1920): 70; Sorrel, *Recollections*, 140–41.
120. Frank Moore, ed., *The Rebellion Record* (New York, 1864–68), 6:110.
121. McIntosh, "Battle of Fredericksburg," 35.
122. Clark, *Histories of North Carolina Regiments*, 2:556.
123. *SHSP*, 43 (1920): 29.
124. McIntosh, "Battle of Fredericksburg," 35–36.
125. Von Borcke, *Confederate War*, 2:113. The Prussian officer probably was using his own words in regards to Jackson's statement. The general rarely made heroic pronouncements; and if his declaration was authentic, Jackson had momentarily forgotten the defensive stand he lost at Kernstown.
126. McIntosh, "Battle of Fredericksburg," 35–36. McIntosh also wrote of seeing "squadrons of cavalry" as well in the Union buildup. However, only one brigade of Federal horsemen accompanied the Union force in Jackson's front, and it was patrolling the riverbank out of sight of the Confederate position.
127. Henderson, 2:313.
128. O'Reilly, *Jackson at Fredericksburg*, 31–32, 41. Although Burnside is traditionally criticized for hazy orders on December 13, the most recent biographer of the Union commander shifts the blame for the Federal failure in Jackson's sector on Franklin. Gary W. Gallagher, ed., *The Fredericksburg Campaign* (Chapel Hill, 1995), 10–14.
129. O'Reilly, *Jackson at Fredericksburg*, 63, 205.
130. The Smith incident first appeared in Dabney, 613–14, and received further credence in Mrs. Jackson, 369. Chambers, 2:290, and other writers have placed the two-man reconnaissance near the end of the fighting rather than at the opening stage.
131. McCabe, *Jackson*, 107.
132. Caldwell, *South Carolina Brigade*, 59. For Gregg's culpability in this action, see Krick, "Maxcy Gregg," 310–11; Greene, *Essays*, 130.
133. Mrs. Jackson, 369.
134. *OR*, 21:664; Early, *Autobiographical Sketch*, 172; O'Reilly, *Jackson at Fredericksburg*, 113–15. In Jackson's official report, he stated unemotionally, "Before General A. P. Hill closed the interval which he had left between Archer & Lane, it was penetrated and the enemy [pressed] forward in overwhelming numbers through that interval." Jackson manuscript report, Georgia Callis West Papers.
135. Lane, *"Dear Mother"*, 202.
136. William G. Williamson to Jedediah Hotchkiss, Oct. 6, 1897, Reel 14, Hotchkiss—LC; McCabe, *Jackson*, 107. See also O'Reilly, *Jackson at Fredericksburg*, 125, 135, 157.
137. Poague, *Gunner with Stonewall*, 55–58. Rockbridge artillerist Ned Moore asserted after the war, "This section of the battery was exposed to a fire unsurpassed in fierceness during the war." Moore, *Cannoneer*, 163. The section lost six killed and ten wounded. *OR*, 21:640.
138. It is popularly assumed that Lee was referring to the carnage in front of Marye's Heights rather than the damage done to the enemy in Jackson's sector. Frank A. O'Reilly to author, June 6, 1995. A member of Stuart's staff first cited this most famous of all Lee quotations. See Cooke, *Lee*, 184. Douglas Southall Freeman altered the statement somewhat for drama's sake in his *Lee*, 2:262. The original version is presented here. Gallagher, ed., *Fredericksburg Campaign*, vii, xii.
139. Jackson manuscript report, Georgia Callis West Papers.
140. John Esten Cooke, *A Life of Gen. Robert E. Lee* (New York, 1871), 232.
141. Hunter McGuire to Jedediah Hotchkiss, May 19, 1896, Reel 34, Hotchkiss—LC. Like so many writers, McGuire felt in later years that Jackson planned a nighttime assault rather than one begun in late afternoon. Douglas S. Freeman dismissed Jackson's strategy as a "myth." Freeman, *Lee*, 2:465–66. Yet a host of writers verified the planned offensive. For example, see *OR*, 21:652, 666, 687; Hotchkiss Journal, Dec. 13, 1862, Reel 1. One officer claimed to have seen Jackson, eyes flashing, pointing toward the Rappahannock and shouting, "I want to move

forward to attack them—to drive them into the river yonder!" Caldwell, *South Carolina Brigade*, 61.

142. Allan, "Conversations with Lee," Vol. III, William Allan Papers, SHC; Jackson manuscript report, Georgia Callis West Papers; O'Reilly, *Jackson at Fredericksburg*, 176–80. Two sources make it apparent that Lee did not know of Jackson's offensive intentions until they were already underway. Von Borcke, *Confederate War*, 2:129–30; *SHSP*, 43 (1920): 31. A quarter-century later, Hotchkiss remarked: "Lee was a disciplined soldier. . . . Jackson only differed from him in this, that he would take the responsibility of going beyond permission when the prospect of success was clear to him." Jedediah Hotchkiss to William L. Chase, Mar. 28, 1892, Reel 9, Hotchkiss—LC.

143. Jackson manuscript report, Georgia Callis West Papers; *OR*, 21:142.

144. Lee, *Wartime Papers*, 174.

145. Abner R. Small, *The Road to Richmond* (Berkeley, Calif., 1939), 69.

146. *SHSP*, 25 (1897): 96; 43 (1920): 32. The earliest appearance of Jackson's alleged statement about driving the enemy into the Rappahannock appeared in *Richmond Daily Dispatch*, Jan. 10, 1863. A garbled account of the episode is in Clark, *Histories of North Carolina Regiments*, 2:557–58. General Jubal Early was especially vehement in denying that any such meeting took place at Lee's headquarters. See *The Historical Magazine*, 18 (1870): 34–36. However, Col. Boteler specifically remembered Jackson riding to a conference with Lee late that night. *Philadelphia Weekly Times*, Aug. 6, 1881.

147. *Philadelphia Weekly Times*, Aug. 6, 1881.

148. Several accounts (including two different versions by McGuire) exist of Jackson's visit to the dying Gregg. The events as narrated here seemed to be the most logical composite and are from *SHSP*, 19 (1891): 309; 43 (1920): 32–34, 42; McGuire, *Memory*, 10; G. D. Camden to Robert L. Dabney, Nov. 25, 1863, Dabney—UTS. See also Chaplain J. Monroe Anderson to "Misses Gregg," Jan. 9, 1863, BV 29, FSNMP; *Richmond Daily Dispatch*, Dec. 17, 1862. Jackson's statement about killing all of the enemy came from Henderson, 2:326. The British writer obtained it from McGuire.

149. *Philadelphia Weekly Times*, Aug. 6, 1881.

150. Ibid.; *The Land We Love*, 1 (1866): 116–17.

151. Vickers, ed., *Under Both Flags*, 137.

152. William B. Taliaferro, "Reminiscences of Stonewall Jackson," William B. Taliaferro Papers, W&M, 27.

153. Blackford, *Mine Eyes*, 211; Samuel Angus Firebaugh Diary, Dec. 15, 1862, CWTI; James Power Smith 1898 address, Reel 39, Hotchkiss—LC. While some writers have put the delivery of the Junkin book before the battle, it is more reasonable that the package came through the lines with the Federal flag-of-truce party.

154. *SHSP*, 43 (1920): 73; Henderson, 2:327; *The Land We Love*, 1 (1866): 117.

155. Hotchkiss Journal, Dec. 16, 1862, Reel 1.

156. *SHSP*, 43 (1920): 35–37; James Power Smith, *Stonewall Jackson and Chancellorsville* (Richmond, 1905), 3–4. In a fifteen-year period, Smith published three accounts of the return ride, bivouac, and transfer to the Corbin home. Each differs markedly from the others in content. However, in all three versions, Smith referred to Surg. McGuire as "Captain Hugh McGuire." Several subsequent writers compounded this error.

157. Roberta Cary Corbin Kinsolving Reminiscences, William Couper Papers, VMI; Mrs. Jackson, 387. In December 1895, Hotchkiss obtained a copy of Mrs. Kinsolving's recollections. He noted in the margin a number of clarifications. For example, it was frosty and windy, not raining, on the night of Jackson's arrival; "some of the staff" who knocked at the door and asked for accommodations were Hotchkiss and Smith; Jackson's horse was Little Sorrel, not Old Sorrel. Reel 49, Hotchkiss—LC.

158. TJJ circular, Dec. 17, 1862, Jackson Letterbook, Hotchkiss—LC; Mrs. Jackson, 386.

159. TJJ to Robert L. Dabney, Dec. 5, 1862, Dabney—UTS; Jones, *Christ in the Camp*, 117, 18.

CHAPTER 22   *Problems and Pleasures of Winter*

1. TJJ to J. E. B. Stuart, Dec. 19, 1862, Jackson—Huntington; Bean, *Pendleton,* 93. For firsthand descriptions of Moss Neck, see James Power Smith 1898 address, Reel 39, Hotchkiss—LC; Roberta Cary Corbin Kinsolving Reminiscences, William Couper Papers, VMI; "The Last Battle of 'Stonewall' Jackson, By a Member of His Staff," *The Old Guard,* 6 (1868): 447–48.

2. Mrs. Jackson, 362. Shortly after the battle of Fredericksburg, Anna wanted to take Julia on a visit to the general. Yet "he was so afraid of the babe & myself being injured by hardness in the winter, that he would not consent to our coming until Spring." Anna Jackson to sister, Sept. 12, 1864, Jackson—VMI.

3. Smith, *Stonewall Jackson,* 4–5; J. P. Smith to Jedediah Hotchkiss, July 21, 1897, Reel 14, Hotchkiss—LC. Smith told the story of Jackson returning to headquarters at an unusually late hour. The Irish sentry did not know him and refused to allow him into the building until the officer of the day vouched for Jackson. James Power Smith 1898 address.

4. TJJ to John L. Campbell, Dec. 20, 1862, Jackson—Huntington.

5. Hotchkiss Journal, Dec. 21, 1862, Reel 1, Hotchkiss—LC; *SHSP,* 43 (1920): 60.

6. Allan, *Preston,* 153.

7. TJJ to Anna Jackson, Dec. 25, 1862, Dabney—LVA. An edited version of this letter is in Mrs. Jackson, 387–88.

8. TJJ to Anna Jackson, Dec. 25, 1862, Dabney—LVA.

9. James Power Smith 1898 address.

10. Ibid.; Smith, *Stonewall Jackson,* 6–7.

11. Worsham, *Foot Cavalry,* 95; Roberta Cary Corbin Kinsolving Reminiscences.

12. *OR,* 21:1075; Bean, *Pendleton,* 89.

13. Smith, *Stonewall Jackson,* 5.

14. Ibid.

15. *SHSP,* 43 (1920): 39–40.

16. Blackford, *War Years,* 99; Smith, *Stonewall Jackson,* 5.

17. Von Borcke, *Confederate War,* 2:166; A. S. Pendleton to Mary Pendleton, Dec. 31, 1862, William Nelson Pendleton Papers, SHC.

18. TJJ to "Hon. Alex. H. H. Stuart & Other Gentlemen," Dec. 30, 1862, Davis—Tulane.

19. Ibid. See also *Staunton Spectator,* Jan. 6, 1863. Many of the letters accompanying presents are in Davis—Tulane.

20. Douglas, *I Rode with Stonewall,* 32.

21. Anna Jackson to Mrs. Templeman Brown, Jan. 2, 1863, Jackson—VMI.

22. Mrs. Jackson, 412.

23. General Order No. 1, Jan. 9, 1863, Jackson—Huntington; Jedediah Hotchkiss to G. F. R. Henderson, Nov. 19, 1896, Reel 13, Hotchkiss—LC.

24. Broadside, Faulkner Family Papers, VHS; "Last Battle of 'Stonewall' Jackson," 448. For contrasting opinions of Faulkner, see Douglas, *I Rode with Stonewall,* 210–11; Dabney, 633.

25. Broadside, Faulkner Family Papers; *OR,* 12: Pt. 1, 709.

26. Douglas, *I Rode with Stonewall,* 211; Hunter McGuire to Jedediah Hotchkiss, Nov. 23, 1896, Reel 13, Hotchkiss—LC.

27. McGuire to Hotchkiss, Nov. 23, 1896; Hotchkiss Journal, Mar. 29 1863, Reel 1.

28. J. P. Smith summary, Reel 39, Hotchkiss—LC; Hotchkiss Journal, Apr. 4, 1863, Reel 1. The battle report for Cross Keys posed a problem in the initial stages of composition. At first, the opinion at headquarters was to make it a subordinate part of the summary of Port Republic. Yet when an unusually long draft materialized, Jackson agreed with the staff recommendation that the two engagements be treated separately and then combined. Jackson manuscript report, Jackson—NYHS.

29. Hotchkiss Journal, Mar. 26, 1863, Reel 1.

30. *OR,* 21:1097–98.

31. *CV,* 26 (1918): 157.

32. Wallace, *Fifth Virginia,* 45. See also Wood, *The War,* 112–15.

33. *OR,* 25: Pt. 2, 687; Circular of Mar. 30, 1863, Eldridge Collection, Henry E. Huntington Library; Charles J. Faulkner to Jubal A. Early, Feb. 25, 1863, Huntington.

34. Headquarters Circulars of Jan. 6, 9, 14, and 21, 1863, Eldridge Collection; *CV,* 26 (1918): 157.

35. Jackson Letterbook, Jan. 14, 1863, Reel 49, Hotchkiss—LC; Hotchkiss Journal, Mar. 5, 1863, Reel 1; Jones, *War Clerk's Diary,* 1:243.

36. Jackson Letterbook, Feb. 10, 1863.

37. Skinker, *Samuel Skinker,* 258; *SHSP,* 43 (1920): 72.

38. Douglas, *I Rode with Stonewall,* 217.

39. Jackson Letterbook, Jan. 21, 1863.

40. Ibid.

41. President Davis interceded to spare the condemned man, artillerist John Edwards. Robert H. Chilton to TJJ, Feb. 18, 1863, Letters and Telegrams Sent by the Confederate Adjutant and Inspector General, 1861–1865 RG 109, NA.

42. Hotchkiss Journal, Jan. 23, 1863, Reel 1; Paxton, *Franklin Paxton,* 83–84; William B. Taliaffero Papers, W&M, *passim.* The fact that Paxton was ill at the time and compelled to go home for a period was an influence on his temper in the dispute with Taliaferro. *Lexington Gazette,* Feb. 12, 1863.

43. Chambers, 2:318; TJJ to Bradley T. Johnson, Feb. 4 and 14, 1863, MC. The men in the ranks shared Jackson's confidence in Bradley Johnson. See Worsham, *Foot Cavalry,* 80.

44. Jackson Letterbook, Feb. 10, 1863; *OR,* 25: Pt. 2, 683, 705.

45. *OR,* 25: Pt. 2, 604, 614.

46. Ibid., 614–19, 633, 645–646.

47. Ibid., 644; TJJ to Samuel Cooper, Apr. 14, 1863, Jackson Letterbook, Reel 49, Hotchkiss—LC. See also McIntosh Reminiscences, Civil War Miscellaneous Collection, USMHI. Jackson followed the same line of thinking with respect to infantry officers. He successfuly prevented Gen. Roger A. Pryor being assigned to brigade command in the Second Corps. Jackson explained: "Officers who have served with me, and won reputations and satisfied me of their qualifications for high positions should be recommended by me in preference to filling the vacancies with those who have never been under my command." TJJ to Alexander R. Boteler, Mar. 7, 1863, Jackson—W&L.

48. Chambers, 2:326–27; Lafayette McLaws to Lizinka C. Brown, Feb. 18, 1863, Richard Stoddert Ewell Papers, LC; Pender, *Letters,* 197, 221.

49. Hal Bridges, *Lee's Maverick General: Daniel Harvey Hill* (New York, 1961), 162–63; Skinker, *Samuel Skinker,* 257–58; TJJ to D. H. Hill, Jan. 13, 1863, Daniel Harvey Hill Papers, LVA.

50. TJJ to Isabella M. Hill, Jan. 24, 1863, Jackson—VMI; Bridges, *Lee's Maverick General,* 163; Eugene Blackford to father, January, 1863, Lewis Leigh Collection, USMHI.

51. R. E. Lee to A. P. Hill, Jan. 12, 1863, Davis—Tulane.

52. Robertson, *General A. P. Hill,* 171–72.

53. Hotchkiss Memorandum on Hill, Reel 49, Hotchkiss—LC.

54. TJJ to Alexander R. Boteler, Jan. 21, 1863, Alexander Robinson Boteler Papers, Duke University.

55. TJJ to Anna Jackson, Jan. 22, 1863, Dabney—LVA. See also Dabney, 636.

56. Dr. McGuire's Narrative, Box 19, Dabney—SHC.

57. Mrs. Jackson, 413. Anna's secondhand account of Jackson's statement differs from that given by McGuire. Ibid., 411.

58. James Power Smith 1898 address.

59. Roberta Cary Corbin Kinsolving Reminiscences; Dr. McGuire's Narrative, Box 19, Dabney—SHC.

60. James Power Smith 1898 address.

61. *CV,* 20 (1912): 26.

62. *SHSP*, 43 (1920): 29, 73; "Dr. McGuire's Narrative," Box 19, Dabney—SHC; Douglas, *I Rode with Stonewall*, 214.
63. Skinker, *Samuel Skinker*, 281.
64. J. Cutler Andrews, *The South Reports the Civil War* (Princeton, N.J., 1970), 294–95.
65. James Power Smith 1898 address.
66. Ibid.
67. Ibid.
68. Jedediah Hotchkiss to Sara Hotchkiss, Jan. 23, 1863, Reel 4, Hotchkiss—LC; Mrs. Jackson, 394. James Power Smith gave a different version of the exchange between Mrs. Taylor and Lee. See *SHSP*, 43 (1920): 42–43.
69. James Power Smith 1898 address. Smith altered the original account slightly for later publication in *SHSP*, 43 (1920): 41–42.
70. "Reminiscences of Aunt Carrie Morton of the Battles around 'Beauvoir' and Chestnut Valley, 1862," typescript, FSNMP, 3; Mrs. Jackson, 395, 408.
71. McCabe, *Jackson*, 126; Scott, *Ministerial Directory*, 384; *Lexington Gazette*, Feb. 19, 1857. The best source on Lacy is W. G. Bean, "Stonewall Jackson's Jolly Chaplain, Beverly Tucker Lacy," *West Virginia History*, 29 (1968): 77–96.
72. Beverly Tucker Lacy Narrative, Box 20, Dabney—SHC; TJJ to Robert L. Dabney, Jan. 15, 1863, Dabney—UTS.
73. *Richmond News-Leader*, Mar. 23, 1939. John A. Lacy to Jedediah Hotchkiss, Sept. 23, 1897, Reel 14, Hotchkiss—LC.
74. Lacy Narrative. Lacy initially maintained that the Confederate War Department gave approval for the unauthorized position of corps chaplain. Years later, he admitted that he was not an official member of Jackson's staff. According to Lacy's son, "his position at Headquarters was under a verbal understanding and arrangement with General Jackson by which he was to be accorded quarters, rations, and other accommodations . . . and do general religious work as a Chaplain throughout the Corps." John A. Lacy to Jedediah Hotchkiss, Sept. 23, 1897, Reel 14, Hotchkiss—LC. See also TJJ to John T. L. Preston, Mar. 2, 1863, Margaret Junkin Preston Papers, SHC.
75. John M. Brown Recollections, University of Texas; Jones, *Christ in the Camp*, 260, 468–69.
76. *SHSP*, 38 (1910): 282; *Staunton Spectator*, Feb. 17, 1863.
77. Lacy Narrative.
78. Ibid. See also TJJ to William S. White, Feb. 12, 1863, Withrow Scrapbooks, W&L, XVIII, 54; *Richmond Enquirer*, Mar. 18, 1863. A "call-to-arms" address by Second Corps chaplains is in *SHSP*, 14 (1886): 348–56.
79. Justus Scheibert, *Seven Months in the Rebel States during the North American War, 1863* (Tuscaloosa, Ala., 1958), 40–41; Firebaugh Diary, Mar. 8, 1863, CWTI.
80. Lacy Narrative.
81. TJJ to John T. L. Preston, Feb. 23, 1863, Margaret Junkin Preston Papers.
82. Jones, *Christ in the Camp*, 94.
83. Ibid.
84. Hoge quoted in Hopley, *Jackson*, 140. A more poetic picture of "the old hero" who "impatiently awaits the advance of the perfidious foe" is in *Staunton Spectator*, Feb. 17, 1863.
85. *Richmond Daily Dispatch*, Feb. 10, 1863.
86. TJJ to Anna Jackson, Feb. 4, 1863, Dabney—LVA.
87. TJJ to Anna Jackson, Feb. 14, 1863, Dabney—LVA. Anna too was experiencing the same pangs of separation. She told a friend that "I sometimes feel reconciled" to Jackson not seeing little Julia, "as she will be so much more entertaining & intelligent when he does see her, but then it is a trial for him to miss so much of her babyhood, & not be able to see her development from day to day." Anna Jackson to Mrs. Templeman Brown, Feb. 21, 1863, Jackson—VMI.
88. *Richmond Daily Dispatch*, Feb. 26, 1863; R. A. Pierson to W. H. Pierson, Mar. 8, 1863, Rosemonde and Emile Kuntz Collection, Tulane University.
89. C. D. Sides to wife, Feb. 10 and 19, 1863, Charles Bednar Collection, USMHI.

90. Skinker, *Samuel Skinker*, 266–67; TJJ to Thomas T. Munford, Feb. 12, 1863, Robert A. Brock Collection, Huntington.

91. Hotchkiss Journal, Feb. 20, 1863, Reel 1; Bean, *Pendleton*, 111.

92. Jackson Letterbook, Mar. 2, 1863; Hotchkiss Journal, Mar. 29, 1863, Reel 1.

93. TJJ to S. Bassett French, Mar. 16, 1863, copy in author's possession; *OR*, 25: Pt. 1, 1005.

94. Jedediah Hotchkiss to Sara Hotchkiss, Feb. 28, 1863, Reel 4, Hotchkiss—LC. The *Danville Appeal* [Va.], Mar. 7, 1863, identified the executed soldier as William Pace of the 33d Virginia. However, no soldier by that name was in the Stonewall Brigade. For a dramatic account of the execution, see Mager W. Steele to sister, Mar. 1, 1863, in Garland A. Quarles et al., eds., *Diaries, Letters, and Recollections of the War between the States* (Winchester, 1955), 95.

95. Hotchkiss Memorandum, Reel 5, Hotchkiss—LC; Douglas, *I Rode with Stonewall*, 213.

96. For other Jackson correspondence relative to executions, see TJJ to R. H. Chilton, Jan. 21, 1863, Jackson Letterbook, Reel 49, Hotchkiss—LC; R. H. Chilton to TJJ, Feb. 18, 1863, Letters Received by Adjt. Gen., RG109, NA.

97. The original draft of the McDowell report is in Jackson—NYHS. An interesting comparison exists between what Jackson wrote and what the editors of the *OR* incorporated. Jackson's "8th of May" appears as "May 8"; his "towards" is "toward"; the "half past 4" he wrote became "4:30." The editors also corrected two errors. Jackson's reference to "Campbell of the 42nd" became "Campbell of the 48th." The general's praise of someone "for his cordial and patriotic . . . " was amended to read "for his conduct and patriotic . . . "

98. Hotchkiss Journal, Mar. 15 and 26, 1863, Reel 1; TJJ to William L. Jackson, Mar. 31, 1863, Schoff Civil War Letters and Documents, University of Michigan; Lacy Narrative.

99. *SHSP*, 19 (1891): 312–13; 43 (1920): 64–65.

100. Jones, *War Clerk's Diary*, 1:274; Lemuel B. Ward to J. Q. A. Ward, Mar. 13, 1863, Shadrach Ward Papers, Duke.

101. Lacy Narrative. In recounting Lacy's statement, Robert L. Dabney embellished the language considerably. Dabney, 660. Both Mrs. Jackson and Dr. McGuire claimed to have heard Jackson make the same statement in their respective presence. Mrs. Jackson, 429; *SHSP*, 25 (1897): 108.

102. TJJ to Anna Jackson, Mar. 14, 1863, Dabney—LVA.

103. *SHSP*, 43 (1920): 73. Hotchkiss Journal, Apr. 14, 1863, contains a slightly different version of the hair story as related to Hotchkiss by Smith..

104. Roberta Cary Corbin Kinsolving Reminiscences; *SHSP*, 43 (1920): 73; Douglas, *I Rode with Stonewall*, 214–15; Clement Fishburne Memoirs, UVA.

105. Jedediah Hotchkiss to Sara Hotchkiss, Mar. 27, 1863, Reel 4, Hotchkiss—LC.

106. Jones, *Christ in the Camp*, 299; Mrs. Jackson, 399–400, 419.

107. Lacy Narrative.

108. Raleigh E. Colston Reminiscences, SHC.

109. Hotchkiss Journal, Mar. 23, 1863, Reel 1; Albert Castel, "Arnold vs. Arnold: The Strange and Hitherto Untold Story of the Divorce of Stonewall Jackson's Sister," *Blue and Gray*, 12 (Oct. 1994): 29.

110. Arnold, 296.

111. Royster, *Destructive War*, 46–47; G. D. Camden to Robert L. Dabney, Nov. 25, 1863, Cook—WVU.

112. For other information on Laura Arnold's wartime and postwar activities, see Castel, "Arnold vs. Arnold," 29–36; *Buckhannon Record*, June 4, 1937, Cook—WVU; unidentified clipping, Reel 58, Hotchkiss—LC; newspaper clipping in possession of Mrs. Henry W. Bassel, Jr., Clarksburg, W.Va.

113. Cooke, *Jackson*, 394; Henderson, 2:346.

114. Jedediah Hotchkiss to Sara Hotchkiss, Apr. 6, 1863, Reel 4, Hotchkiss—LC; Allan, *Preston*, 161. Jackson might have been thinking of peace, but his reputation for unexpected flank marches was circulating widely. Early in April, a diarist on the Mississippi River heard that Old Jack was then rapidly approaching the rear of a Union army near Nashville, Tennessee. Gabriel M. Killgore, "Vicksburg Diary," *Civil War History*, 10 (1964): 41.

115. Hotchkiss Journal, Apr. 3, 1863, Reel 1.

116. Jackson manuscript report, Jackson—NYHS. In the printed version of the official report (*OR,* 12: Pt. 1, 708), War Department editors deleted the religious references.

117. Jackson manuscript report, Jackson—NYHS; *OR,* 12: Pt. 1, 713.

118. Jackson manuscript report, Jackson—NYHS; *OR,* 12: Pt. 1, 716.

119. *OR,* 12: Pt. 1, 711; *Richmond Daily Dispatch,* Apr. 16, 1863.

120. A handwritten copy of the indictments levied by Jackson against Hill is in the Henry Brainerd McClellan Papers, VHS. Another copy, with additional letters bearing on the case, is in Davis—Tulane. See also Robertson, *General A. P. Hill,* 172–76.

121. Mrs. Jackson, 402.

122. Warren W. Hassler, Jr., *Commanders of the Army of the Potomac* (Baton Rouge, 1962), 126–34; Charles F. Adams, *Charles Francis Adams, 1835–1916: An Autobiography* (Boston, 1916), 161.

123. Mrs. Jackson, 407.

124. Ibid., 408. Some writers have interpreted Jackson's statement as a warning to Anna that he might be transferred to the western theater or some other distant point. See Henderson, 2:396; Chambers, 2:346. Jackson was merely implying that the Army of Northern Virginia would be going into action soon and likely at some other point than the Rappahannock River line.

125. Boney, *John Letcher,* 191; Mrs. Jackson, 421; *Richmond Enquirer,* Apr. 28, 1863.

126. TJJ to John Letcher, Apr. 20, 1863, John Letcher Papers, LC; Mrs. Jackson, 408–9.

127. Mrs. Jackson, 425–26; James P. Smith to Jedediah Hotchkiss, July 21, 1897, Reel 14, Hotchkiss—LC; Jedediah Hotchkiss to Sara Hotchkiss, Apr. 24, 1863, Reel 4, Hotchkiss—LC.

128. Mrs. Jackson, 423; Anna Jackson to Laura Arnold, Sept. 12, 1864, Jackson—VMI.

129. Mrs. Jackson, 409–11; Colston Reminiscences; Douglas, *I Rode with Stonewall,* 217–18. Two members of Jackson's inner circle mentioned a "Mrs. Neal" at the Yerby home and how close she became to the Jacksons. Several statements are attributed to her, including a near-supreme compliment she paid Jackson: "I pray that God may preserve your life till the war is over and then take you to Himself, for no earthly honors are adequate." Hotchkiss Journal, Apr. 21, 1863, Reel 1; Lacy Narrative.

130. Mrs. Jackson, 423.

131. Ibid., 424.

132. Ibid., 424–25; Jedediah Hotchkiss to Sara Hotchkiss, Apr. 24, 1863, Reel 4, Hotchkiss—LC.

133. Jackson manuscript report, Gunther Collection, Chicago Historical Society; Skinker, *Samuel Skinker,* 280.

134. Jones, *Christ in the Camp,* 488.

135. Mrs. Jackson, 425.

136. *CV,* 19 (1911): 183; Douglas, *I Rode with Stonewall,* 200; Mrs. Jackson, 427–28. The ultimate in transposition of Civil War photographs is Philadelphia engraver William Sartain's 1866 print of Jackson and his family. Jackson's body (with the exception of the face) is an exact copy of Matthew Brady's 1865 photograph of R. E. Lee on the back porch of his Richmond home. Even the chair and the wrinkles in the coat are identical. *VMHB,* 98 (1990): 280–81.

137. Jackson's kinsman and friend, Judge G. D. Camden, wrote shortly after the general's death: "I have not seen a good likeness of him. None that I have seen does him justice. . . . I do not think that the fault was in his face, for it was striking. All that I have seen makes it appear too long for me. Like his father, his face was somewhat square and not long." G. D. Camden to Robert L. Dabney, Nov. 25, 1863, Box 19, Dabney—SHC.

138. Jackson Letterbook, Apr. 28, 1863; Jackson manuscript report, Jackson—NYHS.

139. Jackson manuscript report, Jackson—NYHS. See also *OR,* 12: Pt. 2, 645, 648.

140. Anna Jackson Memorandum, Dabney—LVA.

141. Mrs. Jackson, 429–30.

142. Dabney, 665; *SHSP,* 43 (1920): 44. A more colorful version of Lee's statement to Smith is in R. E. Lee, Jr., *Recollections and Letters of General Robert E. Lee* (New York, 1904), 94–95.

143. Jedediah Hotchkiss to Sara Hotchkiss, Apr. 29, 1863, Reel 4, Hotchkiss—LC; Jackson

Letterbook, Apr. 29, 1863. A Georgia private was among those who saw Jackson riding to join Lee that morning. "He rode along our line," the man wrote, "and long before his arrival we knew of his approach by the loud cheering (he was the only one of our generals whom the troops ever cheered). . . . He sat his horse perfectly erect and showed himself an excellent horseman. I heard it remarked, and I perceived myself, that morning that he was unusually pale." Lane, *"Dear Mother,"* 241.

144. O. A. Wiggins Reminiscences, NCDAH.

145. Mrs. Jackson, 432; Lacy Narrative. See Dabney, 666, for a more dramatic description of the energized Jackson.

146. Anna Jackson to TJJ, Apr. 29, 1863, Jackson—VMI. The letter closed with sentiments designed to gladden Jackson's heart. "Our little darling will miss dearest Papa. She is so good & sweet this morning."

CHAPTER 23   *The Greatest March*

1. Walter H. Hebert, *Fighting Joe Hooker* (Indianapolis, 1944), 183, 196; Hassler, *Commanders of the Army of the Potomac,* 134.

2. Lacy Narrative, Box 20, Dabney—SHC. Dabney, 666–67, embellished Lacy's account for spiritual effect when he incorporated it into his biography.

3. John Lipscomb Johnson, *The University Memorial* (Baltimore, 1871), 358.

4. Allan, "Conversations with Lee," William Allan Papers, SHC.

5. Fitzhugh Lee narrative in J. William Jones, comp., *Army of Northern Virginia Memorial Volume* (Dayton, Ohio, 1976), 310; *OR,* 25: Pt. 2, 762. One of Lee's early biographers had the conference with Jackson occurring on May 1 rather than April 30. Long, *Memoirs of Lee,* 251.

6. Lacy Narrative.

7. Ibid.

8. Ibid.

9. Dabney, 670; Grimes, *Extracts of Letters,* 29; *OR,* 25: Pt. 1, 885, 1004.

10. *B&L,* 3:157.

11. *OR,* 25: Pt. 1, 171.

12. *SHSP,* 34 (1906): 55. Another Tarheel was likewise moved when the cry "Stonewall's coming!" swept down the line. "Soon the old hero came dashing by, his horse at full speed, and hat in hand, followed by a single courier. He cast his eyes from one side of the road to the other, his head working, as if it were on wires." Quoted in Ernest B. Furgurson, *Chancellorsville, 1863* (New York, 1992), 120.

13. Although Anderson and a number of subsequent writers put Jackson arriving at the front at 8 A.M., two of the general's aides were precise in saying that he arrived a half-hour later. *OR,* 25: Pt. 1, 850; Hotchkiss Journal, May 1, 1863, Reel 1, Hotchkiss—LC; J. Keith Boswell Memorandum of May 1, 1863, Reel 36, Hotchkiss—LC.

14. *OR,* 25: Pt. 1, 862.

15. *SHSP,* 11 (1883): 137–38.

16. Alexander, *Personal Recollections,* 196. For other descriptions and praise of Jackson that day, see *CV,* 5 (1897): 287; 7 (1899): 131.

17. *OR,* 25: Pt. 2, 764, 890.

18. Furgurson, *Chancellorsville,* 133; John Bigelow, *The Campaign of Chancellorsville* (New Haven, 1910), 252–53. Captain Alexander C. Haskell later claimed that after Jackson reconnoitered on a hilltop to which Haskell had taken him, the general told the staff officer not only what his next move was to be but also the sign and countersign for use that night. This assertion, which is totally out of keeping with Jackson's known penchant for secrecy, came from one of the two staff officers who alleged that Bee's reference to "Stonewall" at First Manassas was meant in a negative sense. Such statements cast crippling suspicions over the reliability of any part of Louise Haskell Daly, *Alexander Cheves Haskell* (Wilmington, N.C., 1989), 100–1.

19. *OR,* 25: Pt. 1, 1049.

20. Bigelow, *Chancellorsville*, 253; *The Land We Love*, 1 (1866): 180. See also von Borcke, *Confederate War*, 2:218–22. For more on Col. Wellford's ironworks, see O. F. Northington, Jr., "The Revival of the Iron Industry in Eastern Virginia as Exemplified by the History of the Catharine Furnace in Spotsylvania County, Virginia," *William and Mary College Quarterly Historical Magazine*, 16 (1936): 71–80.

21. Alexander, *Personal Recollections*, 199.

22. *SHSP*, 8 (1880): 254.

23. *SHSP*, 34 (1906): 17.

24. See Murray Forbes Taylor Essay, typescript, VHS, 3.

25. *SHSP*, 34 (1906): 16–17.

26. Dabney, 673; Joseph G. Morrison to Robert L. Dabney, Oct. 29, 1863, Box 5, Dabney—UVA; Jedediah Hotchkiss and William Allan, *The Battle-fields of Virginia: Chancellorsville* (New York, 1867), 41–42; Henderson, 2:431–32.

27. R. E. Lee to Anna Jackson, Jan. 26, 1866, Davis—Tulane.

28. See Lee Letterbook, Oct. 28, 1867, Lee Family Papers, VHS; David G. McIntosh Memorandum on Feb. 24, 1887, Dinner Party, David Gregg McIntosh Papers, VHS; *SHSP*, 34 (1906): 1–27. See also Fitzhugh Lee statement in *SHSP*, 7 (1879): 566–68.

29. Joseph G. Morrison to Robert L. Dabney, Oct. 29, 1863, Box 5, Dabney—UVA; D. H. Hill to Robert L. Dabney, July 21, 1864, Dabney—UTS; *SHSP*, 34 (1906): 12–17. James P. Smith had to awaken Lee an hour later with a report. His exchange with the fatherlike Lee is in *SHSP*, 43 (1920): 45–46.

30. Dabney, 675, and Cooke, *Jackson*, 411, are the sources for the romanticized story of Jackson placing Pendleton's coat over another sleeping soldier. Writers thereafter created a veritable series of myths about how the general shared the covering with a fellow officer. For example, McCabe, *Jackson*, 111–12, had the general returning the coat after a few minutes and lying back down on the damp ground. Douglas's version had James Power Smith as the one who lent and received the wrap. *I Rode with Stonewall*, 220. None of these accounts is true. In all likelihood, Jackson simply draped the cape over its sleeping owner.

31. Lacy Narrative.

32. Ibid.

33. Ibid.

34. Long, *Memoirs of Lee*, 258.

35. *CV*, 28 (1920): 94, 246.

36. Hotchkiss Journal, May 2, 1863; Jedediah Hotchkiss to Hunter McGuire, Oct. 8, 1898, Reel 14, Hotchkiss—LC.

37. Henderson, 2:431–32, quoting a letter from Hotchkiss.

38. Ibid.

39. Ibid.

40. Ibid.

41. Ibid. See also Hotchkiss and Allan, *Chancellorsville*, 41–42; James Power Smith Address, Reel 39, Hotchkiss—LC.

42. Caldwell, *South Carolina Brigade*, 74.

43. *OR*, 25: Pt. 2, 719; Clark, *Histories of North Carolina Regiments*, 1:191.

44. A multitude of erroneous times exist for the start of Jackson's march. The earliest of the alleged departures came from Jackson's bodyguard, Capt. William F. Randolph. He had the advance beginning at dawn. Colonel David McIntosh of the artillery believed that Jackson ordered the march to get underway at 4 A.M. but that it was 5:30 when the first brigade of Rodes's division started down the road. *SHSP*, 29 (1901): 330; 40 (1915): 71. See also George Buswell Diary, May 2, 1863, BV 206, FSNMP; *OR*, 25: Pt. 1, 940; Bigelow, *Chancellorsville*, 274.

45. Taylor Essay, 3–4; Wise, *Long Arm of Lee*, 1:467–68; *SHSP*, 7 (1879): 569–70; Alexander, *Military Memoirs*, 329; Henderson, 2:433. James Power Smith, who could not have heard the exchange between Lee and Jackson, nevertheless thought that Jackson's words were clipped and

uttered quickly, "as though all were distinctly formed in his mind and beyond all question."
B&L, 3:205.

46. *SHSP*, 43 (1920): 47; *B&L*, 3:205.

47. *OR*, 25: Pt. 1, 636, 924, 940, 949; Bigelow, *Chancellorsville*, 276−80. Years after the war,
Thomas L. Rosser of Lee's cavalry made a startling analysis of the action that began at
Catharine Furnace. "Jackson is the only man in history who would have continued his march
. . . after his rear was attacked by Sickles. . . . Gen. Lee showed poor generalship in allowing
Sickles to escape from the Furnace after Jackson had cut him off. Jackson had a terrible fight
and a glorious victory in rear of Sickles, on the flank of Hooker and in front of Gen. Lee, and
got little or no help from Gen. Lee." Rosser to Jedediah Hotchkiss, Nov. 9, 1897, Reel 14,
Hotchkiss—LC.

48. Clark, *Histories of North Carolina Regiments*, 2:228.

49. *OR*, 25: Pt. 1, 992; Brett Reminiscences, BV 26, FSNMP.

50. See Alexander, *Military Memoirs*, 330−31.

51. Wiggins Reminiscences, NCDAH.

52. McGuire and Christian, *Confederate Conduct*, 214. Artillery officer David McIntosh voiced
the same sentiments. "The intense energy of General Jackson's nature was never more in
evidence than on this march. He knew well the hazardous character of the undertaking."
SHSP, 40 (1915): 72. Yet Col. Daniel H. Hamilton, commanding Gregg's brigade, termed the
day's march "the most trying ordeal to which any troops could be subjected." *OR*, 25: Pt. 1,
901.

53. Alexander, *Personal Recollections*, 201−2; Munford Memorandum, Munford-Ellis Family
Papers, Duke. See also *Lexington Gazette*, Apr. 24, 1935. In another statement about the
Chancellorsville flank march, Munford said, "My cavalry is all the cavalry Jackson required."
He further alleged that Jackson preferred the 2d Virginia Cavalry because "some twenty or
more officers" in the regiment were VMI men. *Lynchburg Advance* [Va.] clipping, Apr. 20,
1913, in Munford-Ellis Family Papers.

54. Carr Reminiscences, BV 2, FSNMP.

55. Lee to TJJ, May 2, 1863, Robert A. Brock Collection, Henry E. Huntington Library.

56. *SHSP*, 7 (1879): 572−73.

57. *SHSP*, 40 (1915): 75; Lee, *General Lee*, 247−48.

58. Jones, *Army of Northern Virginia*, 320. Fitzhugh Lee's caricature of Jackson riding away
from the hill may have been irritation over the fact that Jackson had expressed neither congratulations nor thanks for Lee's discovery of the Union position. Major Marcellus Moorman of
Stuart's Horse Artilley later gave a word-by-word conversation with Jackson on the latter's
return to the Brock Road. This account does not coincide with other narratives of what
transpired at the time. *SHSP*, 30 (1902): 110−11.

According to one authority, the Burton farm "is one of the most mysterious landmarks on
the Chancellorsville battlefield." No family named Burton lived in Spotsylvania County at the
time. The home's occupants, if any, are unknown. Noel G. Harrison, *Chancellorsville Battlefield
Sites* (Lynchburg, Va., 1990), 66−69.

59. *SHSP*, 38 (1910): 284; Taylor Essay, 4. While a number of depositories lay claim to having
the original of the "last dispatch," that prized copy is at LVA and, understandably, heavily
protected. See *Richmond News-Leader*, Nov. 9, 1977.

60. *OR*, 25: Pt. 1, 803.

61. *OR*, 25: Pt. 1, 940−41, 1004; *SHSP*, 43 (1920): 48.

62. Von Borcke, *Confederate War*, 2:225; Munford statement in *Lynchburg Advance* [Va.], Apr.
20, 1923, in Munford-Ellis Family Papers. For a list of VMI graduates in Second Corps high
positions that day, see Couper, *One Hundred Years at VMI*, 2:171. The institute made itself
heard all through the Civil War. Just under 1800 cadets and former cadets served in the
Confederate army. That figure is 94 perent of the matriculates at the time. Couper, *One
Hundred Years at VMI*, 3:100.

63. Wiggins Reminiscences.

64. *SHSP*, 43 (1920): 48−49; *B&L*, 3:208. J. P. Smith was with Jackson at the time. This makes his two accounts, cited above, reliable. Henderson, 2:442, had Jackson saying: "You may go forward, sir." Another source recalled Jackson silently waving his hand toward the enemy lines as the signal. *SHSP,* 38 (1910): 286. Lee and a number of officers put the starting time of the assault at 6 P.M. Yet Rodes was certain that 5:15 was the actual moment. *OR,* 25: Pt. 1, 798, 941; Raleigh E. Colston Reminiscences, SHC; Alexander, *Military Memoirs,* 334. Precise timing in the Civil War did not exist. Few soldiers carried watches, and synchronization of timepieces rarely occurred. Many officers resorted to looking at the sun in order to "determine" the hour.

65. *CV,* 28 (1920): 94; Eric Solomon, ed., *The Faded Banners* (New York, 1960), 53.
66. *SHSP,* 40 (1915): 76–77. See also Benjamin W. Leigh to wife, May 12, 1863, Chancellorsville File, Reel 39, Hotchkiss—LC; R. A. Pierson to W. H. Pierson, May 8, 1863, Rosemonde and Emile Kuntz Collection, Tulane University; Hoole, *Lawley,* 51. Unlikely anecdotes are in *SHSP,* 29 (1901): 332; Clark, *Histories of North Carolina Regiments,* 2:229.
67. Cooke, *Jackson,* 416; Jedediah Hotchkiss to Hunter McGuire, Oct. 8, 1898, Reel 14, Hotchkiss—LC.
68. Wiggins Reminiscences.
69. "Morton Reminiscences," FSNMP, 4.
70. *OR,* 25: Pt. 1, 975, 995. Hamlin, *Chancellorsville,* 68–69, stated that Colquitt's "singular act of stupidity blocked the movement of seventeen Confederate regiments for the critical hour of the battle." A similar statement is in Clark, *Histories of North Carolina Regiments,* 2:232–33.
71. Unknown Georgia soldier letter, May 18, 1863, BV 129, FSNMP.
72. *OR,* 25: Pt. 1, 941, 1004–5; Mrs. Jackson, 426; R. E. Wilbourn to Robert L. Dabney, Dec. 12, 1863, Box 19, Dabney—SHC. Of the several factors that brought Jackson's assault to a standstill, darkness was paramount. A Tarheel soldier called the late-afternoon action "the second edition of the Bull Run races" and added: "I tell you we carried them two miles and half at 2.40 speed, and would believe, have completely routed the whole army if we had made the attack three hours sooner. Darkness was all that saved them." John C. Ussery to father, May 8, 1863, BV 130, FSNMP. See also Benjamin W. Leigh to wife, May 12, 1863.
73. Wilbourn to Dabney, Dec. 12, 1863.
74. Clark, *Histories of North Carolina Regiments,* 1:667.
75. *OR,* 25: Pt. 1, 916, 1049–50; Henderson, 2:448.
76. Wiggins Reminiscences.
77. Unidentified newspaper clipping, courtesy of William C. Davis, Mechanicsburg, Pa.
78. Lane Reminiscences, James H. Lane Papers, Auburn University; Bean, *Pendleton,* 115.
79. Taylor Essay, 5–6; *CV,* 12 (1905): 232. Other versions of what Jackson said to Hill are in Jedediah Hotchkiss, *Volume III: Virginia,* in Clement A. Evans (ed.), *Confederate Military History* (Atlanta, 1899), 385; *SHSP,* 29 (1901): 332; Dabney, 682; Hamlin, *Chancellorsville,* 107.
80. *SHSP,* 40 (1915): 83; Williams, *From the Cannon's Mouth,* 194.
81. Wilbourn to Dabney, Dec. 12, 1863.
82. The most authoritative account of Jackson's scout and wounding on this night is Robert K. Krick, "The Smoothbore Volley That Doomed the Confederacy," in Gary W. Gallagher, ed., *Chancellorsville: The Spring, 1863, Virginia Campaign* (Chapel Hill, 1996), 107–42. With but minor variances, the narrative here follows the Krick presentation. Another source claimed that a local resident, John Talley, also acted as a guide on the fateful ride. Robert G. Carter, "Memoranda on the Death of 'Stonewall' Jackson," Robert G. Carter Papers, VHS. No verification of this point could be found.
83. Hamlin, *Chancellorsville,* 108; Clark, *Histories of North Carolina Regiments,* 2:38.
84. David J. Kyle 1895 manuscript, BV 207, FSNMP. Kyle's handwritten recollections are far superior to the heavily edited printed version in *CV,* 4 (1896): 308–9. Lieutenant Morrison was not aware that the party had left the Plank Road. See Joseph G. Morrison to Robert L. Dabney, Oct. 29, 1863, Dabney—UVA.
　　The best contemporary accounts of Jackson's wounding are Kyle and Morrison, both cited above; Robert E. Wilbourn to Robert L. Dabney, Dec. 12, 1863, Box 19, Dabney—SHC; and William H. Palmer, in *CV,* 13 (1905): 232–33. These men were all witnesses to at least part of

the events. Other narratives, including those by Kyd Douglas, Fitzhugh Lee, Marcellus Moorman, and James Power Smith, were based on hearsay. Twenty-one different recitals of the shooting of Jackson are in a bound volume at FSNMP. Marcellus Moorman argued the truth of his reminiscences in a strongly worded letter to Jedediah Hotchkiss, Apr. 8, 1898, Reel 15, Hotchkiss—LC. Typical examples of implausible accounts of the wounding are J. S. Saul statement in Jackson—LC; clipping from Nov. 14, 1940, *News-Ronceverate* (W.Va. newspaper), Cook—WVU; von Borcke, *Confederate War*, 2:231. The most unreliable of the one or two untrustworthy statements by Hotchkiss was an error-filled account he gave to Hunter McGuire, Oct. 8, 1898, Reel 15, Hotchkiss-LC. No doubt the aging cartographer was trying to join the crowd of "eyewitnesses" to the wounding.

85. Kyle Memoir, BV 207, FSNMP.

86. The 212 casualties suffered by the Pennsylvania regiment at Chancellorsville included 199 men captured. Most of them (including the regimental colonel, Joseph A. Mathews) became prisoners in the nighttime action against the right of Lane's brigade. *OR*, 25: Pt. 1, 184, 670, 685–87.

87. Kyle Memoir.

88. Jackson was about seventy yards northeast of the spot where the 1888 monument now stands along Virginia Route 3 (the Plank Road). The actual spot where he was shot is approximately the southwest corner of the parking lot to the modern visitors' center.

89. Kyle Memoir.

90. Joseph G. Morrison to Robert L. Dabney, Oct. 29, 1863, Box 5, Dabney—UVA; Morrison to Shier Whitaker, Apr. 27, 1900, Brock Collection; Benjamin W. Leigh to wife, May 12, 1863; Clark, *Histories of North Carolina Regiments*, 5:97–99. Evidence is now unimpeachable as to the unit whose fire mortally wounded Jackson. For example, see Benjamin B. Carr Reminiscences, BV 2, FSNMP; Richard M. V. B. Reeves Memoirs, BV 130, FSNMP; Murray F. Taylor Memoirs, BV 208, FSNMP. Lane, who would deeply bemoan the loss of Jackson, wrote of the wounding: "Col. [sic] John D. Barry . . . informed me that he knew nothing of Generals Jackson & Hill having gone to the front, that he could not distinguish friend from foe in the dark, and through the scrubby undergrowth, that soon after the skirmish line opened and the firing began, he heard the clattering of approaching horsemen . . . and knowing that he was in the front line . . . he not only ordered his men to fire, but made them keep it up, so convinced was he that they were enemies." Lane Reminiscences. Barry died two years after the Civil War at the age of twenty-seven. Family tradition put the cause of death as melancholia over the orders he gave that night at Chancellorsville.

91. For more on Hill staff members wounded by the gunfire, see Taylor Essay, 15–16. A host of soldiers claimed later to have been couriers with the two staffs. One of the better assertions is that of John A. Green of the 3d Virginia Cavalry. See Charles E. Coombes, *The Prairie Dog Lawyer* (Dallas, 1945), 84–87.

92. McCabe, *Jackson*, 113; Wilbourn to Dabney, Dec. 12, 1863.

93. Wilbourn to Dabney, Dec. 12, 1863.

94. Ibid.

95. Ibid. Private Thomas R. Yeatman of Stuart's horse artillery is generally credited with recapturing Little Sorrel a few days later. Ironically, word was sent to Jackson of the recovery of the horse on the day the general died. Unidentified newspaper clipping, Reel 58, Hotchkiss—LC; Marcellus N. Moorman to TJJ, May 10, 1863, Davis—Tulane.

96. Wilbourn to Dabney, Dec. 12, 1863.

97. Ibid. Wilbourn was born in Mississippi, although both parents were Virginians. He was at the University of Virginia when war began. At Second Manassas, while performing staff duties, he received a severe wound in the left arm. Wilbourn's postwar career as a Mississippi merchant ended in 1878 when he died of yellow fever. D. P. Bestor to Jedediah Hotchkiss, Dec. 27, 1898, Reel 14, Hotchkiss—LC.

For the long and strange travels of Jackson's raincoat after the wounding, see R. E. Lee to J. Randolph Bryan, Dec. 13, 1867, Lee Family Papers, VHS; Lee to Bryan, Jan. 10, 1868, and Lee to Anna Jackson, Jan. 18, 1868, Lee Letterbook, Lee Family Papers; Hunter McGuire to

Anna Jackson, Feb. 7, 1899, Mary Anna Jackson Letters, Lee Family Papers; Theodore S. Garnett to Joseph Bryan, Theodore Stanford Garnett Letter, VHS; David F. Riggs, "Stonewall Jackson's Raincoat," *Civil War Times Illustrated,* 16 (July 1977): 36–41.

98. *The Land We Love,* 1 (1866): 181; Robertson, *General A. P. Hill,* 188.

99. Wilbourn to Dabney, Dec. 12, 1863.

100. *SHSP,* 6 (1878): 270. See also Kyle Memoir; Benjamin W. Leigh to wife, May 12, 1863.

101. Barr was an interesting figure in spite of the small role he played in the Jackson drama. He had enlisted the previous year as a private in the 42d North Carolina, but within a month he was named assistant surgeon in the 34th North Carolina. Just before Chancellorsville, Barr apparently moved up to medical service on the brigade or division level. His service record with the 34th North Carolina ends in April 1863. Weymouth T. Jordan, Jr., comp., *North Carolina Troops, 1861–1865: A Roster* (Raleigh, 1966–), 9:253; 10:259.

102. Benjamin W. Leigh to wife, May 12, 1863; Joseph G. Morrison to Shier Whitaker, Apr. 27, 1900; Wilbourn to Dabney, Dec. 12, 1863. Surgeon Benjamin P. Wright of the 55th Virginia later stated that Powell Hill summoned him to make a preliminary examination of Jackson at this time. Wright's service record lists him as the first physician to reach Jackson's side. Yet none of the officers with Jackson mentioned him. Wright Reminiscences, BV 176, FSNMP; Richard O'Sullivan, *Fifty-fifth Virginia Infantry* (Lynchburg, Va., 1989), 160.

103. Wilbourn to Dabney, Dec. 12, 1863.

104. Morrison to Whitaker, Apr. 27, 1900. The guns were part of the 1st New York Light Artillery, under Capt. Thomas W. Osborn. He ordered the salvos when he saw in the moonlight a Confederate column moving toward his position on the Plank Road. *OR,* 25: Pt. 1, 483–84.

105. Joseph G. Morrison to Robert L. Dabney, Oct. 29, 1863, Box 5, Dabney—UVA.

106. Wilbourn to Dabney, Dec. 12, 1863.

107. Ibid.

108. Ibid.

109. Benjamin W. Leigh to wife, May 12, 1863.

110. *SHSP,* 10 (1882): 143; *CV,* 8 (1900): 36. Douglas S. Freeman (whose account Chambers accepted without alteration) was of the opinion that Jackson did not fall from the litter in spite of Johnson's severe injuries. *Lee's Lieutenants,* 2:573; Chambers, 2:418. The wounds to Johnson were so severe that he lost his right arm at the shoulder as well as all use of the left arm. He returned home to Fluvanna County and lived until 1899, though unable to perform such functions as feeding himself.

111. Benjamin W. Leigh to wife, May 12, 1863.

112. Ibid.

113. *SHSP,* 14 (1886): 155. Smith ended the war as a captain, and in his reminiscences he had Jackson addressing him by that rank instead of the lieutenant he was at Chancellorsville. Dabney, 691, quoted Jackson as saying, "Don't trouble yourself about me."

114. *B&L,* 3:212. Wilbourn remembered Pender saying he would have to retire because his troops had become demoralized. Robert E. Wilbourn to Robert L. Dabney, Dec. 12, 1863, Box 19, Dabney—SHC.

115. The Suffolk-born Whitehead is another of those unheralded but unique Civil War field surgeons. He was then thirty-one and an 1851 graduate of VMI. After studying medicine in Philadelphia and Russia, Whitehead was a professor of clinical medicine in New York City until the outbreak of civil war. He would be captured with the wounded at Gettysburg; however, Whitehead escaped from confinement at Fort McHenry, Md., and made his way back to the Confederacy via Canada and Bermuda. In the 1870s, he founded the medical schools at the University of Denver and the University of Colorado. Kevin C. Ruffner, *Forty-fourth Virginia Infantry* (Lynchburg, Va., 1987), 112.

116. Cooke, *Jackson,* 428–29, was the first writer to mention Maj. Rogers by name. Freeman, *Lee's Lieutenants,* 2:576, mistakenly identified him as a North Carolina infantry officer. Rogers is remembered most as the man who designed the Third National Confederate flag. Michael J. Andrus, *The Brooke, Fauquier, Loudoun and Alexandria Artillery* (Lynchburg, Va., 1990), 109; John E. Divine to author, Feb. 23, 1994.

117. Unless otherwise noted, McGuire's activities and statements henceforth are from one of his earliest manuscript accounts in Jackson—NYHS and a subsequently published article in *SHSP*, 14 (1886): 154–63. See also *Richmond Whig*, Oct. 7, 1865.

118. Wilbourn confirmed the fainting of Pendleton in *SHSP*, 6 (1878): 273. So did McGuire in a Nov. 17, 1898, letter to Hotchkiss, Reel 15, Hotchkiss—LC. The adjutant's biographer attributed the swoon to exhaustion from a hard ride. Bean, *Pendleton*, 116.

119. McGuire Narrative, Jackson—NYHS.

120. Of Black's thirty known wartime letters, none recounted his part in the treatment of Jackson. On the afternoon of May 10, the surgeon wrote his wife that Jackson's condition was grave. "How we would all mourn his loss," Black said. "You can scarcely conceive the strong affection which his men have for him. He has outlived every prejudice and is regarded [as] a great Military Chieftain and a faithful Christian." Harvey Black Letters, Virginia Tech. Black's wartime writings were recently published in *A Surgeon with Stonewall Jackson* (Baltimore, 1995).

121. In the several accounts that McGuire wrote of the treatment of Jackson, he always mentioned how the general went under anaesthesia repeating the last word of the sentence.

CHAPTER 24   *Crossing the River*

1. Jedediah Hotchkiss to Sara Hotchkiss, Apr. 6, 1862, Reel 4, Hotchkiss—LC; Douglas, *I Rode with Stonewall*, 98. For obituaries of, and tributes to, McGuire, see *SHSP*, 28 (1900): 276–79; 31 (1903): 253–66. Other and more formal insights of McGuire are in Stuart McGuire to Jedediah Hotchkiss, Mar. 18, 1893, Reel 39, Hotchkiss—LC; Hunter McGuire to Hotchkiss, Sept. 22, 1897, Reel 14, Hotchkiss—LC.

2. As in the previous chapter, McGuire's actions and quotations are from his manuscript account in Jackson—NYHS and a subsequently published article in *SHSP*, 14 (1886): 154–63.

3. Dabney, 695–96. Later in the day, Chaplain Lacy found the amputated arm wrapped in a cloth and lying outside Jackson's tent. The chaplain buried it in the family cemetery of the J. Horace Lacy estate near the field hospital. B. Tucker Lacy Narrative, Box 20, Dabney—SHC. Dabney, 696, reported Jackson and Smith having a lengthy talk on "the blessings of chloroform" and other topics. Smith (*B&L*, 3:214) made no mention of any such conversation.

4. Robert E. Wilbourn to Robert L. Dabney, Dec. 12, 1863, Box 19, Dabney—SHC. An hour after Wilbourn reported to Lee, Hotchkiss arrived at army headquarters with the same news of Jackson's injuries. According to Hotchkiss, Lee "was much distressed and said he would rather a thousand times it had been himself. He did not wish to converse about it." Hotchkiss Journal, May 3, 1863, Reel 1, Hotchkiss—LC.

5. Casler, *Stonewall Brigade*, 149; French, *Centennial Tales*, 104–5; Murray Forbes Taylor Memoirs, BV 208, FSNMP; *OR*, 25: Pt. 1, 917–18. Of course, not all of the Confederate troops knew of Jackson's wounding. Years later, John S. Kimbrough of the 14th Georgia wrote: "Certain it was that his men, inspired with the thought that he was somewhere on the field, fought with the old-time confidence which his presence always inspired. Perhaps 'twas well that the wounded chieftain's condition was kept from the knowledge of the troops until the day's work was done." BV 199, FSNMP.

6. Lee, *Wartime Papers*, 452–53; *B&L*, 3:214. Two members of Jackson's inner family believed that Lee's message arrived before daybreak. Dabney, 702; Hotchkiss, *Virginia*, 387. James P. Smith was with the general at the time and asserted that the note was received around 9:00 that morning. Smith's account is the more believable. An uncreditable narrative relative to this dispatch by Lee is in Henderson, 2:461. The biographer had Lee receiving Jackson's short message while participating in the morning action near the Chancellor house. Biographer Lenoir Chambers repeated this version in his presentation.

7. Lacy Narrative. Lacy doubtless enhanced Jackson's actual words for the sake of spirituality and inspiration, but nowhere to the degree that Dabney altered them for his biography. Dabney, 707–8. A week after this visit, Lacy related his conversation with Jackson to a surgeon. The chaplain quoted the general as saying "that he would not replace his arm if he could, that it was

a blessing to him from God, that he could not understand it, but that he should know how it was, either in this world or the next, that he was *perfectly content.*" Daniel Lyon to Annie Lyon, May 14, 1863, Eppes Family Muniments, VHS.

8. Henderson, 2:380–81. The reference to Joshua and the Amalekites is in Exodus 17:8–16.

9. Dabney, 708–9; Douglas, *I Rode with Stonewall*, 226–27; Paxton, *Memoir*, 105; Robertson, *Stonewall Brigade*, 186–87.

10. McGuire manuscript narrative, Jackson—NYHS; *SHSP*, 14 (1886): 159.

11. Unidentified 1925 newspaper clipping, Jackson—Valentine.

12. Dabney, 711. Douglas Southall Freeman wrote that Lee gave Jackson the choice of places he could be taken behind the lines. That contrasts with Hotchkiss, who ended his May 4 diary entry with the statement, "General Jackson came to Guiney's by Genl. Lee's advice." Hotchkiss Journal, Reel 1.

13. McGuire and Christian, *Confederate Cause*, 224; McGuire manuscript narrative, Jackson—NYHS for last quotation. When the surgeon misdated Lee's order as Monday, May 4, many early biographers followed suit. Years later, J. P. Smith corrected the mistake by giving May 3 as the date of Lee's command to remove Jackson from the battle arena.

14. Dabney, 711, 713; Lee, *Pendleton*, 271–72; Lacy Narrative.

15. Lacy Narrative; McGuire Narrative, Box 19, Dabney—SHC.

16. Lucy Chandler Pendleton Reminiscences, BV 188, FSNMP. For over a century, the story has persisted that McGuire vetoed Jackson being placed in the Chandler home because he learned of several cases of erysipelas among the upstairs occupants. For example, see Alan DeForest Smith, "Stonewall Jackson and His Surgeon, Hunter McGuire," *Bulletin of the New York Academy of Medicine*, 49 (1973): 607. Lacy made the decision not to use the Chandler home; and if any streptococcus infections did exist at Fairfield, McGuire learned about them after he arrived there with Jackson.

17. Lucy Chandler Pendleton Reminiscences.

18. McGuire and Christian, *Confederate Cause*, 225; J. A. Chandler to R. A. Lancaster, Oct. 16, 1894, copy in author's possession.

19. McGuire and Christian, *Confederate Cause*, 226.

20. Lacy Narrative.

21. Lee, *Pendleton*, 271.

22. Morrison, *Morrison*, 12; French, *Centennial Tales*, 106, 139. Morrison had diligently kept a diary after joining Jackson's staff. When he appeared to be in danger of being captured, he burned the journal—a painful loss to history as well as to the aide. Joseph G. Morrison to Robert L. Dabney, Oct. 29, 1863, Box 5, Dabney—UVA.

23. Anna Jackson Memorandum, Dabney—LVA; Mrs. Jackson, 461–63; Kean, *Confederate Government*, 57. In later years, Anna's recollection of events became clouded by emotionalism. More reliance has been placed here on the memorandum she wrote for Dabney during the war.

24. All other accounts of the night of May 6–7 have only Jim Lewis attending Jackson. Yet Lacy admitted being there; and McGuire, in his first narrative of the events, told of criticizing the chaplain for allowing applications of wet towels. Lucy Chandler Pendleton Reminiscences; Lacy Narrative; McGuire manuscript narrative, Jackson—NYHS. McGuire did not blame Lacy or Lewis for the subsequent onset of pneumonia. "The disease came on too soon after this application to admit of the supposition. The Pneumonia was doubtless caused by the fall from the litter." McGuire manuscript narrative, Jackson—NYHS.

25. Robert J. Driver, Jr., *Fifty-eighth Virginia Infantry* (Lynchburg, Va., 1990), 124.

26. Lacy Narrative. Lacy's account was later refined for publication. Dabney, 716.

27. Freeman, *Lee*, 2:561.

28. Thomas, *Robert E. Lee, A Biography*, 287.

29. Anna Jackson Memorandum; Mrs. Jackson, 449–51.

30. Dabney, 716; Mrs. Jackson, 450–51.

31. Cook, *Family and Early Life*, 173.

32. Ibid.; Anna Jackson Memorandum.

33. Mrs. Jackson, 451.

34. Cook, *Family and Early Life*, 173.

35. Samuel B. Morrison to William Brown, May 13, 1863, BV 135, FSNMP; Morrison Memorandum, Dabney—LVA. The surgeon diagnosed the prostration as "resulting from high excitement, fatigue, & lack of nourishment, when relaxation came on." A modern authority disputed this finding by emphasizing that pneumonia leads to the prostration that Morrison described. Charles L. Cooke, M.D., to author, Aug. 31, 1992.

All eight doctors ultimately involved in Jackson's case pronounced his illness as pneumonia. That has not stopped a number of later physicians from suggesting other causes. In the early 1970s, New York City physician and Civil War student Beverly C. Smith contacted ten colleagues across the nation. He provided each with Jackson's symptons and asked each for an opinion on the cause. Ten different diagnoses came forth. Beverly C. Smith to Beverly M. Read, May 19, 1975, BV 4, FSNMP.

At least three other physicians have proposed emboli as the fatal malady. Richard Boies Stark, "Surgeons and Surgical Care in the Confederates States Army," *Virginia Medical Monthly*, 87 (1960): 236; Smith, "Stonewall Jackson," 608–9; L. Whittington Gorham, "What Was the Cause of Stonewall Jackson's Death?" *Archives of Internal Medicine*, 103 (1963): 540–44.

Recently, two medical professors asserted that Jackson died of sepsis as a result of insufficient drainage from the amputation. Another physician queried on the matter gave support to this theory. Marvin P. Rozear and Joseph C. Greenfield, "'Let Us Cross over the River': The Final Illness of Stonewall Jackson," *Virginia Magazine of History and Biography*, 103 (1995): 29–46, 389–91; Edwin J. Harvie, M.D., to author, Apr. 13, 1995.

An equally plausible case can be made that Jackson's death was the result of a combination of toxic shock syndrome and septicemia. Robert F. Bondurant, M.D., to author, May 18, 1995.

These twentieth-century theories all contain possibilities. Yet to McGuire and his associates, Jackson on the night of May 1–2 contracted a cold. Then followed the intense labor and excitement of battle, the debilitating effects of three bullet wounds, two heavy falls from a stretcher, a severed artery, hours of uncomfortable riding in a wagon, and amputation of an arm five hours after the injury. Such trauma drained the general's resistance and triggered what doctors of the day knew as pleuropneumonia (pneumonia with pleurisy). In all likelihood, Jackson suffered fatally from pneumonia complicated by sepsis. For historical purposes, the original diagnosis of pneumonia is followed here.

36. Morrison Memorandum; Dabney, 718–19.

37. Anna Jackson Memorandum; Anna Jackson to Laura Arnold, Sept. 12, 1864, Jackson—VMI.

38. Breckinridge began his Confederate service as surgeon of the 5th Texas. After being commended for gallant service at Antietam, he became medical inspector for the Army of Northern Virginia. John Philip Smith, a Winchester physician, was attached to the 2d Virginia in the first weeks of the war. The remainder of his army service was at general hospitals in Virginia.

39. Morrison to Brown, May 13, 1863; Anna Jackson Memorandum. Dabney, 719, had Dr. Morrison suggesting to Jackson that he might not survive the illness. However, the physician attributed the conversation to Jackson and his wife. Morrison Memorandum. Jackson never expressed a fear of life's end. On Nov. 12, 1855, he had written an aunt, "I look upon death as being that moment which of all earthly ones most to be desired by a child of God." Cook—WVU.

40. *SHSP*, 14 (1886): 161.

41. *Richmond Enquirer*, May 8, 1863; Putnam, *Richmond*, 218. See also *OR*, 18:1055.

42. Morrison to Brown, May 13, 1863.

43. Anna Jackson Memorandum; Dabney, 721; *Richmond Times-Dispatch*, May 17, 1979.

44. McGuire Narrative.

45. Ibid.; McGuire and Christian, *Confederate Cause*, 227. A Richmond newspaper echoed Jackson's lack of concern over death. "We have no fears for Jackson," the editor stated. "He is no accidental manifestation of the powers of faith and courage. He came not by chance in this

day and to this generation. He was born for a purpose, and not until that purpose is fulfilled will his great soul take flight." *Richmond Whig,* May 9, 1863.

46. Mrs. Jackson, 453; Lacy Narrative; Dabney, 721.

47. Morrison to Brown, May 13, 1863. Anna Jackson Memorandum; Dabney, 722.

48. Each physician claimed to have been the one who told Mrs. Jackson of the general's approaching end. McGuire manuscript narrative, Jackson—NYHS; Morrison to Brown, May 13, 1863.

49. Anna Jackson Memorandum; Anna Jackson to Laura Arnold, Sept. 12, 1864, Jackson—VMI; McGuire and Christian, *Confederate Cause,* 227.

50. Dabney, 722.

51. Ibid.; Anna Jackson Memorandum.

52. McGuire manuscript narrative, Jackson—NYHS; Anna Jackson to Laura Arnold, Sept. 12, 1864, Jackson—VMI.

53. McGuire and Christian, *Confederate Cause,* 227–28.

54. Dabney, 723; Mrs. Jackson, 456.

55. McGuire and Christian, *Confederate Cause,* 228.

56. Lacy Narrative.

57. *CV,* 32 (1924): 469. For exaggerated reports of the worship service, see Scheibert, *Seven Months,* 80; Jones, *Christ in the Camp,* 75–76.

58. Lacy Narrative.

59. Unidentified 1925 newspaper clipping, Jackson—Valentine.

60. William N. Pendleton to wife, May 14, 1863, William Nelson Pendleton Papers, SHC.

61. Three people were in the room when Jackson died: McGuire, Anna, and Smith. All attested to his final words. See marginal notation in Kyd Douglas copy of Mrs. Jackson, 471, Antietam NBP. The *Macon Telegraph* [Ga.] on May 25 reported Jackson's words as history remembers them. (A copy of the story is in BV 201, FSNMP.) That Jackson's deathbed statement was widely circulating two weeks after his passing gives it added authenticity and further protection against being termed a later fabrication.

CHAPTER 25   *Epilogue*

1. Dabney, 728; Mrs. Jackson, 458. Cooke, *Jackson,* 447, erred in stating that the desire to preserve the general's overcoat was the reason civilian attire was placed on the body.

2. Mrs. Jackson, 472. Lucy Chandler was only twelve years old when Jackson died. Fifty years later, she sought to recall the events. In doing so, understandably, she occasionally got the events of May 10–11 badly garbled. Her claim that Richmond undertakers arrived at Guiney Station late on Sunday to embalm the body is untrue.

3. *OR,* 25: Pt. 1, 791.

4. Lee, *Wartime Papers,* 484; *CV,* 31 (1923): 287; J. William Jones, *Life and Letters of Robert Edward Lee, Soldier and Man* (New York, 1906), 242. In announcing Jackson's death to the Army of Northern Virginia, Lee stated in part: "The daring, skill and energy of this great and good soldier, by the decree of an all-wise Providence, are now lost to us. But while we mourn his death, we feel that his spirit still lives, and will inspire the whole army with his indomitable courage and unbroken confidence in God as our hope and our strength. Let his name be a watchword to his corps. . . . Let officers and soldiers emulate his invincible determination to be every thing in the defence of our beloved country." General Orders No. 61, Jackson's compiled service file, in Compiled Service Records: Generals, Staff Officers, and Nonregimental Enlisted Men, RG109, NA. For Lee's well-known praise of Jackson in his official report of Chancellorsville, see Lee, *Wartime Papers,* 469.

5. *SHSP,* 21 (1893): 45–46; Luther W. Hopkins, *Bull Run to Appomattox: A Boy's View* (Baltimore, 1908), 85–87; Benjamin W. Leigh to wife, May 12, 1863, Box 19, Dabney—SHC. A South Carolina newspaperman termed Jackson's death "one of the heaviest blows of the war" and added: "No one of our many distinguished leaders occupied a larger space in the public eye. . . . No one was more deeply imbedded in the affection of the nation." Unidentified clipping, Reel 2, Hotchkiss—LC.

6. McKim, *Recollections,* 95; Allan, *A March Past,* 152. See also Dunaway, *Reminiscences,* 69; Josiah Gorgas, *The Civil War Diary of Josiah Gorgas* (University, Ala., 1947), 39, 69; Vickers, ed., *Under Both Flags,* 138; James H. Lane Reminiscences, Auburn University; Opie, *Rebel Cavalryman,* 144; Worsham, *Foot Cavalry,* 102.

7. Wise, *Military History,* 226; Kate S. Sperry, Jr., Diary, May 13, 1863, Handley Library, Winchester, Va.; Hunter, *Johnny Reb and Billy Yank,* 362; *Richmond Daily Dispatch,* May 12, 1863. See also *Richmond Daily Dispatch,* May 15, 1863, for eulogies from other Southern newspapers. A postwar writer who began collecting dirges on Jackson quit after reaching forty-seven.

8. Franklin S. Wright to mother, May 14, 1863, Franklin S. Wright Papers, Duke University. Even the *New York Herald* lauded Jackson in its death notice. "It is agreed on all hands that Jackson was the most brilliant rebel general developed by the war. From his coolness and sagacity, rapid movements and stubbornness in the fight, and his invariable good fortune, he resembled Napoleon in his early career. . . . He was a great general, a brave soldier, a noble christian and a pure man." Yet, the newspaper felt compelled to state, "he is not the first instance of a good man devoting himself to a bad cause." Quoted in *Staunton Vindicator,* May 22, 1863.

9. Mrs. Jackson, 305, 473; Casler, *Stonewall Brigade,* 155; Pendleton Reminiscences, BV 188, FSNMP.

10. Mrs. Jackson, 459; 1929 newspaper clipping, Withrow Scrapbooks, W&L, XVIII, 55; James D. McCabe account in *Philadelphia Weekly Times,* Nov. 16, 1878. At that time, the RF&P Railroad ran down the center of Broad Street, Richmond's main thoroughfare.

11. *Philadelphia Weekly Times,* Nov. 16, 1878; *Richmond Daily Dispatch,* May 12, 1863; *Richmond Whig,* May 12, 1863; Andrews, *Scraps of Paper,* 109. Another eyewitness described the crowd along the streets of Richmond as "a surging mass of humanity." Hunter, *Johnny Reb and Billy Yank,* 363.

12. Mrs. Jackson, 474; Douglas, *I Rode with Stonewall,* 229. New evidence has been uncovered to prove that Jackson's body was not embalmed until after it reached Richmond. On May 11, a North Carolina officer wrote his daughter of trying to make funeral arrangements in the capital for a fallen comrade. He had little success, he noted, because "the Embalmer is so busy with Genl. Jacksons Body he can give me no attention." E. Neil McAuley to daughter, May 11, 1863, Robert G. McAuley Letters, CWTI. For more on the death mask, which is at the Valentine Museum, see Jackson—Valentine. One source (Bean, *Pendleton,* 120) asserted that Fredericksburg citizens donated the coffin for Jackson. At that point in the war, it is highly unlikely that any metal caskets would have been in war-ravaged Fredericksburg.

13. Douglas, *I Rode with Stonewall,* 38; Walter Harrison, *Pickett's Men* (New York, 1870), 21.

14. Belle Boyd to John Letcher, May 11, 1863, LVA.

15. Withrow Scrapbooks, W&L, XVIII, 53; *Richmond News-Leader,* Feb. 8, 1937; statement of bandmaster Andrew B. Bowering in *Baltimore Sun,* June 30, 1923, BV 176, FSNMP.

16. Following Chancellorsville and its recapture, Little Sorrel accompanied Anna Jackson to North Carolina. He eventually was sent to VMI, where the horse became an institutional tradition. In 1880, the cadet corps took Little Sorrel to the state fair in Richmond and posted a special guard to protect him from treasure hunters seeking hair from the mane or tail. The horse died in Richmond at the age of thirty-six, a life span only three years less than that of his famous owner. The stuffed remains of the animal are in the VMI Museum at Lexington. *The Land We Love,* 1 (1866): 312; *CV,* 38 (1930): 5; 40 (1932): 424–25; Withrow Scrapbooks, W&L, II, 37; XVIII, 100–2; *Bristol Herald-Courier* [Va.], Apr. 10, 1949.

17. *Philadelphia Weekly Times,* Nov. 16, 1878; Jones, *War Clerk's Diary,* 1:321; Varina H. Davis, *Jefferson Davis, Ex-President of the Confederate States of America: A Memoir* (New York, 1890), 2:382–83.

18. For the proceedings to have the name Stonewall Brigade made official, see resolution by

Virginia regimental commanders, May 16, 1863, Davis—Tulane; *Staunton Vindicator,* May 29, 1863.

19. Hunter, *Johnny Reb and Billy Yank,* 364.

20. *Richmond Examiner,* May 13, 1863; *Richmond Daily Dispatch,* May 13, 1863.

21. Henderson M. Bell to Francis H. Smith, May 12, 1863, VMI Papers, VHS; Schantz, "Lost Order Book," Western Historical Manuscript Collection, Columbia, Mo., 62–63; *Richmond Enquirer,* May 22, 1863.

22. *SHSP,* 33 (1905): 234; Andrews, *Scraps of Paper,* 109.

23. Mrs. Jackson, 477.

24. Hoge; *Moses Drury Hoge,* 184–85. See also James McClure Scott, "Confederate War Reminiscences," BV 23, FSNMP.

25. *Lynchburg Daily Virginian,* May 13, 1863; *Richmond Daily Dispatch,* May 16, 1863; Withrow Scrapbooks, W&L, XVI, 40; XVIII, 65; D. G. Elzey Memoirs, Cook—WVU. Several writers have asserted that the burial party passed through Lynchburg without pause. For example, see Chambers, 2:455.

26. For more on the canal boat (a fragment of which still survives in a Lynchburg park), see Withrow Scrapbooks, W&L, XVIII, 67–70. A wartime photograph of one of the riverboats at Lexington is in Couper, *One Hundred Years at VMI,* 1:66.

27. Paul B. Barringer Paper, NCDAH; Memorandum, Cook—WVU.

28. In December 1865, a nationwide appeal was made "for the relief of the widow of the brave Jackson." An untrue report circulated that Anna "had been compelled to sell everything" in order to survive. See *New York News* clipping, Eliza Kidd Porter Album, Benjamin F. Porter Papers, Auburn.

29. *CV,* 23 (1915): 226; 30 (1922): 412–14; *SHSP,* 21 (1893): 342–43; Lowell Reidenbaugh introduction to new edition of Mary Anna Jackson, *Memoirs of "Stonewall" Jackson* (Dayton, Ohio, 1976); Anna Jackson to Mrs. Templeman Brown, Sept. 28, 1863, Jackson—VMI.

30. See Anna Jackson to Laura Arnold, Oct. 21, 1864, Jackson—VMI; Laura Arnold to Anna Jackson, Nov. 11, 1865, Jackson—VMI; unidentified newspaper clipping in possession of Mrs. Henry W. Bassel, Jr., Clarksburg, W.Va.; *Wheeling Intelligencer* [W.Va.] story, Reel 58, Hotchkiss—LC.

31. The *Lexington Gazette* of May 14 announced the funeral for Saturday the 16th at 10 A.M. In the May 20 edition of the newspaper, the editor gave no explanation in reporting the May 15 burial service.

32. Wise, *End of an Era,* 270.

33. Addey, *Jackson,* 227.

34. Couper, *One Hundred Years at VMI,* 2:190; Wise, *Military History,* 229.

35. Annie Hilleman to William McCauley, June 17, 1863, *The United Daughters of the Confederacy Magazine,* 24 (Oct. 1961): 22. The most complete account of the funeral procession is in *Lexington Gazette,* May 20, 1863.

36. Withrow Scrapbooks, W&L, XVIII, 71; Allan, *A March Past,* 152. In the army camps two days later, as well as in churches throughout the Confederacy, Sunday services dwelled on the loss of Jackson. Countless ministers preached from 2 Timothy 4:6–8: "I have fought the good fight, I have finished my course, I have kept the faith." Other clergy used as a sermon text 2 Samuel 3:38: "Know ye not that there is a prince and a great man fallen this day?" R. A. Pierson to W. H. Pierson, May 17, 1863, Rosemonde and Emile Kuntz Collection, Tulane University; George W. White sermon, George William White Collection, Presbyterian Church (USA) Archives.

37. Allan, *Preston,* 166. Lewis subsequently became a field servant to Maj. Sandie Pendleton. At the death of the adjutant a year later, the black man returned to Lexington. "De dear old General's gone, and Marse Sandie too," he wailed, "and it's Jim's time next." Shortly thereafter, Lewis died—in part presumably from grief. The location of his grave in Lexington is unknown. *Lexington Gazette and Banner,* Dec. 17, 1875.

38. The tree survived until 1938, when it was so disease-ridden that it had to be removed.

Rockbridge County News, Oct. 20, 1938. In 1891, Jackson's remains were transferred several yards to the east beneath the statue that still stands over his final resting place.

39. Allan, *Preston*, 166.

40. Jedediah Hotchkiss to Sara Hotchkiss, May 19, 1863, Reel 4, Hotchkiss—LC. Another staff member, James Power Smith, paid his tribute twenty-five years later. "Great, the world believes him to have been in many elements of generalship; he was greatest and noblest in that he was good, and, without a selfish thought, gave his talent and his life to a cause that, as before the God he so devoutly served, he deemed right and just." *B&L,* 3:214.

Stonewall Jackson: The Man, the Soldier, the Legend
Winner of the 1997 Douglas Southall Freeman History Award
Sponsored by the Military Order of Stars and Bars

Previous Winners

1984   *Five Tragic Hours* by James McDonough and Thomas L. Connelly, University of Tennessee Press

1985   *The Last Review* by Virginius Dabney, Alquonquin Books

1986   *Rebel Raider: The Life of General John Hunt Morgan* by James A. Ramage, University Press of Kentucky

1987   *The Man Who Tried to Burn New York* by Nat Brandt, Syracuse University Press

1988   *Forts Henry and Donelson: The Key to the Confederate Heartland* by B. F. Cooling, University of Tennessee Press

1989   *The Illustrated Confederate Reader* by Rod Gragg, Harper & Row, Publishers

1990   *Fighting for the Confederacy: The Personal Recollection of General Edward Porter Alexander* edited by Gary W. Gallagher, University of North Carolina Press

1991   *Stonewall Jackson at Cedar Mountain* by Robert K. Krick, University of North Carolina Press

1992   *In Deadly Earnest: The History of the First Missouri Brigade* by Phil Gottschalk, Missouri River Press

1993   *The Confederacy's Fighting Chaplain: Father John B. Bannon* by Philip T. Tucker, University of Alabama Press

1994   *Encyclopedia of the Confederacy* edited by Richard N. Current, Simon & Schuster

1995   *Andersonville: The Last Depot* by William Marvell, University of North Carolina Press

1996   *Seasons of War* by Daniel E. Sutherland, Free Press